United States Naval Aviation

1910–2010

United States Naval Aviation

1910–2010

Volume I
Chronology

Mark L. Evans
Roy A. Grossnick

Naval History and Heritage Command
Department of the Navy
Washington, D.C.

Library of Congress Cataloging-in-Publication Data

Evans, Mark L.
United States naval aviation 1910-2010 / Mark L. Evans, Roy A. Grossnick. -- 5th ed.
pages cm
Includes index.
ISBN 978-0-945274-75-9 (v. 1 : alk. paper) 1. United States.
Navy--Aviation. 2. United States. Navy--Aviation--Chronology. I. Grossnick, Roy A. II. Naval History & Heritage Command (U.S.) III. Title.
VG93.E95 2015
359.9'409730904--dc23

2015002942

For sale by the U.S. Government Publishing Office
Superintendent of Documents, Mail Stop: SSOP, Washington, DC 20402-9328
ISBN 978-0-945274-75-9

Contents

Information on Photographs

The illustrations in this volume are official U.S. Navy, Marine Corps, Coast Guard, or National Aeronautics and Space Administration (NASA) photographs. Negatives for most of these photographs exist at the Still Pictures Branch of the National Archives and Records Administration (NARA).

Photograph numbers for illustrations in the book appear at the end of the captions. The History and Archives Division of the Naval History and Heritage Command holds photographs with an NH or NAH preceding the number and images without photograph numbers. Coast Guard photographs—with a USCG preceding the number—exist at either the Coast Guard Historian's Office or NARA. The NASA images are located at NASA Headquarters, Public Affairs Office (News and Imaging Branch).

Illustrations containing numbers but not letter prefixes are U.S. Navy photographs. When ordering these images from NARA, please add USN in front of these numbers. Prefixes of K or KN indicate that the originals are in color; these, too, are USN photographs. All unnumbered images are official DOD photographs.

Preface

United States naval aviation celebrated more than 100 years of service in 2010. Its story as told in this volume and its companion had its origins in the 1950s. The book was first published as *United States Naval Aviation 1910–1960* and celebrated the first 50 years of naval aviation. Two subsequent editions added the decades of the 60s and 70s. A fourth edition brought the chronology up to 1995. This is the fifth update and, because naval aviation continually transforms and because of the extensive role it has played in its country's history, the book is published in two volumes.

This volume documents the people and events that proved crucial to naval aviation's history. The work expands upon the previous chronological format by providing additional information of campaigns and technical aspects, and it provides the researcher and the Navy a more detailed account of specific subjects pertinent to better understanding its history. This edition, while attempting to maintain the professional standards established by the previous editions, also corrects errors and omissions in the preceding volumes. It does not seek to be the comprehensive source on naval aviation but offers a basic guide to educate readers on the topic.

Compiling statistical information requires the historian to search a very wide range of sources, but over the past 15 years many of those reliable sources have ceased to exist. This loss was the result of the Navy discontinuing publication of specialized documents, as well as the trend toward computerized data that is not being maintained or transferred to the Naval History and Heritage Command archives. I made an exhaustive effort to research all possible sources and, when the records provided conflicting data, selected the most accurate information after reviewing all of the possible sources.

Special recognition is made to the naval aviation historians preceding me who researched and published the previous editions of this book: Roy A. Grossnick, Adrian O. Van Wyen, Lee M. Pearson, Dr. William J. Armstrong, and Clarke Van Vleet. As primary compiler for these chapters, I am fully responsible for any errors of fact or mistakes that may have occurred in this volume.

Mark L. Evans
Naval Aviation Historian

Acknowledgments

This centennial update of United States Naval Aviation would not be possible without the previous editions covering the periods 1910–1960, 1910–1970, 1910–1980, and 1910–1995. The dedication and professionalism of the authors of these original editions—Adrian O. Van Wyen, Lee M. Pearson, Clarke Van Vleet, Dr. William J. Armstrong, Roy A. Grossnick, and Major John M. Elliott, USMC (Ret.)—laid the foundation for this new version.

In addition, the extensive revisions and updates to the previous versions' appendices would not have been possible without the generous support of the Naval Historical Foundation. Updating of this primary reference work on naval aviation was facilitated by a generous donation from former CNO Admiral James L. Holloway III, USN (Ret.). His donation to the Naval Historical Foundation enabled an aviation historian to research, write, and update all the chapters of volume II. The Naval Historical Foundation then gifted the completed text to the Naval History and Heritage Command.

A project of this magnitude requires the work of many people. The authors owe a debt of gratitude to historians Dr. Michael J. Crawford, Dr. Timothy L. Francis, Dr. Jeffrey G. Barlow, Dr. Robert J. Schneller Jr., Dr. John D. Sherwood, and Robert J. Cressman of the Naval History and Heritage Command who reviewed chapter manuscripts. Their subject matter expertise, insight, and exacting verification of salient points ensured the historical accuracy and the development of cogent themes.

Additional people outside the command generously reviewed chapter manuscripts. Vice Adm. Robert F. Dunn, USN (Ret.) of the Naval Historical Foundation; Maj. Elliott; Dr. Sarandis Papadopoulos, Secretariat Historian, Department of the Navy; Capt. Edmund T. Wooldridge, USN (Ret.); and Capt. Rosario M. Rausa, USNR (Ret.) examined the voluminous material and provided critical objectivity and analysis.

Other members of the command played a key role by researching information or by providing their extensive background knowledge in specific areas. The then Head, Archives Branch Curtis A. Utz and archivists Dale J. Gordon and John L. Hodges provided an incalculable wealth of specific knowledge of naval aviation and archival sources.

Historian Dr. Regina T. Akers of the command contributed her unparalleled knowledge of diversity issues to ensure a balanced representation of the people who comprise the rich heritage of naval aviation. Then-Art Director Morgan I. Wilbur cheerfully disregarded the repeated interruptions to help with the accurate and comprehensive selection of images. Librarians Glenn E. Helm, A. Davis Elliott, J. Allen Knechtmann, and Linda J. Edwards provided crucial, enthusiastic, and knowledgeable reference support. Former photographic curator Robert Hanshew offered technical expertise that enabled the timely processing of the numerous photographic images.

The extent of the material involved required the assistance of additional people outside the command. Historian and consultant Harold Andrews was an indispensable technical expert, and his lifetime of experience and attentive character facilitated the compilation of multiple entries. Marine Corps historian Annette D. Amerman and Coast Guard historian Scott Price consistently offered immediate and vital assistance. William C. Booth of Aircraft Inventory N8812A provided indispensable support. Machinist's Mate 1st Class Ray H. Godfrey (Ret.) and Senior Master Sergeant William L. Slupe, USAF (Ret.), of the USS *Enterprise* (CVN 65) Association offered historical information.

A special acknowledgment goes to editors Wendy Sauvageot, James M. Caiella, and Caitlin Conway of the Naval History and Heritage Command. Their keen professionalism, diligent attention to detail, and unique combination of naval aviation knowledge and matchless editorial skills proved invaluable, and every page bears their legacy.

Because an index is the key to making this book a successful reference document, the final thanks go to those who helped with it: Cmdr. Austin W. O'Toole, USNR; Cmdr. Ronald B. Mitchell, USNR (Fleet Historian, Undersea Warfare Operations Det. D); and Byron W. Hurst, Communication and Outreach Division, NHHC.

Glossary

1st MAW	First Marine Aircraft Wing
6th FLT	Sixth Fleet
7th FLT	Seventh Fleet
A&R	Assembly & Repair
A.P.	armor piercing
AAF	United States Army Air Forces
AAM	air-to-air missile
AARGM	Advanced Anti-Radiation Guided Missile
AAS	United States Army Air Service
ABATU	advanced base training unit
ABDA	American-British-Dutch-Australian Command
ACC	Air Combat Command
ACLS	automatic carrier landing system
ACMR	Air Combat Maneuvering Range
ACNO	Assistant Chief of Naval Operations
ACP	aviation continuation pay
ADVCAP	advanced capability
AED	Aeronautical Engineering Duty
AEDO	Aeronautical Engineering Duty Officer
Aéronautique Militaire	Army Air Service (France)
AESR	active electronically scanned radar
AEW	airborne early warning
AEWWINGPAC	Airborne Early Warning Wing, Pacific
AFB	Air Force base
AIM	aircraft intermediate maintenance
AIM	air-launched aerial intercept guided missile
AIMD	Aircraft Intermediate Maintenance Division
AirDet/AIR DET	air detachment
AirLant/AIRLANT	Air Force, Atlantic Fleet or Commander, Air Force, U.S. Atlantic Fleet
AirPac/AIRPAC	Air Force, Pacific Fleet or Commander, Air Force, U.S. Pacific Fleet
ALARS	air-launched acoustical reconnaissance
ALM	Antilliaanse Luchtvaart Maatschappij (airline)
ALNAV	All Navy
ALVRJ	advanced low volume ramjet
AMD	aeronautical maintenance duty
AMO	aviation medical officer
AMRAAM	advanced medium range air-to-air missile
ANA	Association of Naval Aviation
ANG	Air National Guard
AOCP	aviation officer continuation pay
AOCS	aviation officer candidate school
ARAPHAHO	merchant ship portable modular aviation facility
ARG	amphibious ready group
ARM	antiradiation missile
Arowa	Applied Research: Operational Weather Analysis
ARPA	Advanced Research Projects Agency
ARPS	automatic radar processing system
ASM	air-to-surface missile
ASMD	antiship missile defense
ASO	aviation supply office
ASR	antisubmarine rocket
ASROC	Anti-Submarine Rocket
ASTOVL	advanced short takeoff/vertical landing
ASV	surface vessel detection
ASW	antisubmarine warfare
ATARS	Advanced Tactical Airborne Reconnaissance System
ATC	Air Transport Command
ATFLIR	advanced targeting forward looking infrared
ATG	air task group
ATS	Air Transport Service
ATU	advanced training unit
AVG	American Volunteer Group
AWACS	airborne warning and control systems
BAMS	Broad Area Maritime Surveillance
BAMS-D	Broad Area Maritime Surveillance Demonstrator
BRAC	Defense Base Closure and Realignment
BTG	basic training group
BuAer	Bureau of Aeronautics
BuC&R	Bureau of Construction and Repair
BuMed	Bureau of Medicine
BuNav	Bureau of Navigation

BuOrd	Bureau of Ordnance
BuPers	Bureau of Naval Personnel
BuShips	Bureau of Ships
BuWeps	Bureau of Naval Weapons
CAA	Civil Aeronautics Administration
CAA	Civil Aeronautics Authority
CAEWWS	Carrier Airborne Early Warning Weapons School
CAINS	carrier aircraft inertial navigation system
CalTech	California Institute of Technology
CAP	Civil Air Patrol
CAP	combat air patrol
CARDIV	carrier division
CASU	carrier aircraft service unit
CASU(F)	combat aircraft service unit (forward)
CC	Construction Corps
CCR	circulation control rotor
CEC	cooperative engagement capability
CG	commanding general
CGAS	Coast Guard Air Station
CHNAVRSCH	Chief of Naval Research
CIA	Central Intelligence Agency
CIC	combat information center
CincPac/CINCPAC	Commander in Chief, Pacific
CincPacFlt/CINCPACFLT	Commander in Chief, U.S. Pacific Fleet
CINCUS	Commander in Chief, U.S. Fleet
CIWS	Close-In Weapons System (Phalanx)
CJTF	Combined Joint Task Force
CNATRA	Chief of Naval Air Training
CNATT	Center for Naval Aviation Technical Training
CNO	Chief of Naval Operations
CNR	Chief of Naval Research
COD	carrier on-board delivery
COIN	counter insurgency
ComAirLant	Commander, Naval Air Force, U.S. Atlantic Fleet
ComAirPac	Commander, Naval Air Force, U.S. Pacific Fleet
ComFAIR/COMFAIR	Commander, Fleet Air
COMHATWING	Commander, Heavy Attack Wing
COMHSLWINGPAC	Commander, Helicopter Antisubmarine Light Wing, U.S. Pacific Fleet
COMINCH	Commander in Chief, U.S. Fleet
COMINCUS	Commander in Chief, U.S. Fleet
COMLATWING	Commander, Light Attack Wing
COMMATWING	Commander, Medium Attack Wing
COMNAVAIRESFOR	Commander, Naval Air Reserve Force
COMNAVAIRLANT	Commander, Naval Air Force, U.S. Atlantic Fleet
COMNAVAIRPAC	Commander, Naval Air Force, U.S. Pacific Fleet
COMNAVELEX	Naval Electronic Systems Command
COMNAVFOR Somalia	Commander, Naval Forces Somalia
COMNAVSUPFOR	Commander, Naval Support Force
COMOPDEVFOR	Commander, Operational Development Force, U.S. Fleet
COMPATWING	Commander, Patrol Wing
COMSTRKFIGHTWING	Commander, Strike Fighter Wing
CONUS	Continental United States
CTF	Combined Task Force
DARPA	Defense Advanced Research Projects Agency
DASH	Drone Anti-Submarine Helicopter
DCNO	Deputy Chief of Naval Operations
DEW	Distant Early Warning line
DICASS	directional command active sonobuoy system
DIFAR	directional frequency analysis and recording
DMZ	demilitarized zone
DOD	Department of Defense
DODGE	Department of Defense Gravity Experiment satellite
EALS	Electromagnetic Aircraft Launch System
ECM	electronic countermeasures
ECMO	electronic countermeasures operator/officer
ECP	Enlisted Commissioning Program
EDO	engineering duty officer
EFM	enhanced fighter maneuverability
ELEX	Naval Electronic Systems Command
EOD	explosive ordnance disposal
ESG	expeditionary strike group
EW	electronic warfare
EXCAP	expanded (extended) capability
FAA	Federal Aviation Administration
FAA	Fleet Air Arm
FAB	Fleet Air Base
FAC	Federal Aviation Commission
FAC	forward air controller
FAETU	fleet airborne electronics training unit

FARP	forward arming and refueling point
FASOTRAGRULANT	Fleet Airborne Specialized Operational Training Group Atlantic
FAW	fleet air wing
FAWTUPAC	Fleet All Weather Training Unit, Pacific
FBM	fleet ballistic missile
FEMA	Federal Emergency Management Agency
FEWSG	Fleet Electronic Warfare Support Group
FKR	frontoviye krilatiye raketi (frontal rocket)
FLIR	forward looking infrared radar
FMS	foreign military sales
FOB	forward operating base
FORSCOM	Forces Command
FROG	free rocket over ground
FTEG	Flight Test and Engineering Group
FY	fiscal year
G.P.	general purpose
GBU	guided bomb unit
GCA	ground-controlled approach
Glomb	guided glider bomb
GMGRU	guided missile group
GMU	guided missile unit
Halon	fire suppression agent
HARM	High Speed Anti-Radiation Missile
HATWING	heavy attack wing
HIPEG	high-performance external gun
HTA	heavier-than-air
HUD	heads-up display
Huff-Duff	high frequency direction-finder
HVAR	High-Velocity Aircraft Rocket
IBM	International Business Machine Company
ICAP	improved capability
IFF	identification friend or foe
IGY	International Geophysical Year
IO	Indian Ocean
IOC	initial operational capability
IR	imaging infrared
IR	infrared
ITALD	Improved Tactical Air Launched Decoy
JAGM	Joint Air-to-Ground Missile
JASSM	Joint Air-to-Surface Standoff Missile
JATO	jet-assisted takeoff
JCM	joint common missile
JCS	Joint Chiefs of Staff
JDAM	Joint Direct Attack Munition
JPALS	Joint Precision Approach and Landing System
JPATS	Joint Primary Aircraft Training System
JRB	joint reserve base
JRFB	joint reserve force base
JSF	joint strike fighter
JSOW	joint standoff weapon
JSTARS	Joint Surveillance Target Attack Radar System
KIA	killed in action
LAMPS	Light Airborne Multipurpose System
Lant/LANT	Atlantic
LANTIRN	low altitude navigation/targeting infrared for night
Laser-JDAM	Laser-Joint Direct Attack Munition
LCAC	landing craft, air cushion
LCS	littoral combat ship
LDO	limited duty officer
LGB	laser-guided bomb
LIC	low intensity conflict
LJDAM	Laser Joint Direct Attack Munition
Lofti	Low Frequency Transionospheric satellite
LORAN	Long Range Navigation
LRAACA	Long-Range Air Antisubmarine Warfare Capable Aircraft
LSO	landing signal officer
LTA	lighter-than-air
LTV	Ling-Temco-Vought Corp.
MAC	Military Airlift Command
MACV	Military Assistance Command, Vietnam
MAD	magnetic airborne/anomaly detection
MAG	Marine Aircraft Group
MAGTF	Marine Air-Ground Task Force
MATS	Military Air Transport Service
MAU	master augmentation unit
MAW	Marine Aircraft Wing
MAWSPAC	Medium Attack Weapons School, Pacific
MC	Medical Corps
MCAAS	Marine Corps Auxiliary Air Station
MCAF	Marine Corps Air Facility
MCAS	Marine Corps Air Station

MCB	Marine Corps Base
MCM	mine countermeasures
MEB	Marine Expeditionary Brigade
Med	Mediterranean Sea
MEF	Marine Expeditionary Force
MEU	Marine Expeditionary Unit
MIA	missing in action
MiG	Russian aircraft designed by Artem I. Mikoyan and Mikhail I. Gurevich
MIO	maritime interception operations
MIRALC/SLBD	mid-infrared advanced chemical laser/Sea Lite Beam Director
MIT	Massachusetts Institute of Technology
MLS	microwave landing system
MMA	multimission maritime aircraft
MOL	Manned Orbiting Laboratory
MOUT	military operations in urban terrain
MRASM	medium range air-to-surface missile
MRBM	medium range ballistic missile
MRC	major regional conflict
MSC	Military Sealift Command
MSO	maritime security operations
NAA	National Aeronautic Association
NAAF	Naval Air Auxiliary Facility
NAAS	Naval Air Auxiliary Station
NAATSC	Naval Air Advanced Training Subordinate Command
NAB	Naval Air Base
NACA	National Advisory Committee for Aeronautics
NAD	Naval Aviation Depot
NADC	Naval Air Development Center
NADEP	Naval Aviation Depot
NADS	Naval Air Development Station
NAEC	Naval Air Engineering Center
NAESU	Naval Aviation Electronic Service Unit
NAF	Naval Air Facility
NAF	Naval Aircraft Factory
NAFC	Naval Air Ferry Command
NAILS	Naval Aviation Integrated Logistic Support
NALCOLANTUNIT	Naval Air Logistics Control Office, Atlantic Unit
NAMC	Naval Air Material Center
NAMO	Naval Aviation Maintenance Office
NAMTC	Naval Air Missile Test Center
NAO	naval aviation observer
NAOTS	Naval Aviation Ordnance Test Station
NAP	naval aviation pilot/naval air pilot
NAR	Naval Air Reserve
NARF	Naval Air Rework Facility
NARTS	Naval Air Rocket Test Station
NARTU	Naval Air Reserve Training Unit
NARU	Naval Air Reserve Unit
NAS	Naval Aeronautic Station
NAS	Naval Air Station
NASA	National Air and Space Administration
NASM	National Air and Space Museum
NATB	Naval Air Training Base
NATC	Naval Air Training Center
NATC	Naval Air Training Command
NATEC	Naval Airship Training and Experimental Command
NATMSACT	Naval Air Training Maintenance Support Activity
NATO	North Atlantic Treaty Organization
NATOPS	Naval Air Training and Operating Procedures Standardization
NATS	Naval Air Transport Service
NATT	Naval Air Technical Training
NATTC	Naval Air Technical Training Center
NAVAIR	Naval Air Systems Command
NAVAIRSYSCOM	Naval Air Systems Command
NAVCAD	naval aviation cadet
NAVICP	Naval Inventory Control Point
NAVMAT	Naval Material Command
NAVPRO	Naval Plant Representative Office
NAVRES	Naval Reserve
NAVSEA	Naval Sea Systems Command
Navstar	navigation satellite
NAWC	Naval Air Warfare Center
NAWCAD	Naval Air Warfare Center Aircraft Division
NAWCWD	Naval Air Warfare Center Weapons Division
NAWS	Naval Air Weapons Station
NB	Naval Base
NERV	Nuclear Emulsion Recovery Vehicle
NFO	naval flight officer
NMC	Naval Material Command
NME	National Military Establishment
NMF	Naval Missile Facility

NNV	national naval volunteers
NOB	Naval Operating Base
NORAD	North American Air Defense Command
NorLant	Northern Atlantic Ocean
NorPac	Northern Pacific Ocean
NOTS	Naval Aviation Ordnance Test Station
NOTS	Naval Ordnance Test Station
NR	Naval Reserve/Navy Reserve
NRAB	Naval Reserve Aviation Base
NRFC	Naval Reserve Flying Corps
NRL	Naval Research Laboratory
NROTC	Naval Reserve Officer Training Corps
NS	Naval Station
NSA	Naval Support Activity
NSAWC	Naval Strike and Air Warfare Center
NSC	National Security Council
NSRB	National Security Resources Board
NTPS	Naval Test Pilot School
NVG	night vision goggles
NVN	North Vietnam
NWC	Naval Weapons Center
OASU	Oceanographic Air Survey
OCS	Officer Candidate School
ODM	operational development model
ONR	Office of Naval Research
OPNAV	Naval Operations
Ops	operations
OSD	Office of the Secretary of Defense
OSRD	Office of Scientific Research and Development
P/A	pilotless aircraft
Pac/PAC	Pacific
PASU	Patrol Aircraft Service Unit
Patriot	Phased Array Tracking Intercept of Target missile
PatSU/Patsu	Patrol Aircraft Service Unit
PatWing/PATWING	Patrol Wing
PIMA	planned incremental maintenance availability
PLAF	People's Liberation Armed Forces (Viet Cong)
PLAT	Pilot Landing Aid Television system
PMTC	Pacific Missile Test Center
POL	petroleum, oil, lubricants
POW	prisoner of war
PPI	plan position indicator
RAAF	Royal Australian Air Force
radar	radio detection and ranging
RAF	Royal Air Force
RAG	replacement air group
RAM	Rolling Airframe Missile
RAST	recovery assist, securing, and traversing system
RCA	Radio Corporation of America
RDT&E	research, development, test, and evaluation
retrorocket ASR	rearward-firing antisubmarine rocket
REWSON	reconnaissance, electronic warfare, and special operations
RFC	Royal Flying Corps
RimPac	Rim of the Pacific Exercise (Joint)
RIO	radar intercept officer
RN	Royal Navy
RNAS	Royal Naval Air Station
ROK	Republic of Korea
RPG	rocket-propelled grenade
RPV	remotely piloted vehicle
RVN	Republic of Vietnam
SAM	surface-to-air missile
SAR	search-and-rescue
SCS	sea control ship concept
SDB	small diameter bomb
SEAL	Sea-Air-Land team
SEAPAC	sea activated parachute automatic crew release
SecDef/SECDEF	Secretary of Defense
SecNav/SECNAV	Secretary of the Navy
SEVENTHFLT	Seventh Fleet
SIXTHFLT	Sixth Fleet
SLAM	Standoff Land Attack Missile
SLAM-ER	Standoff Land Attack Missile–Expanded Response
SLCM	Sea/Surface Launched Cruise Missile
SLEP	Service Life Extension Program
SoLant/SOLANT	Southern Atlantic Ocean
SolRad	Solar Radiation (satellite)
SoPac/SOPAC	Southern Pacific Ocean
SPASUR	Navy Space Surveillance System
SSM	surface-to-surface missile
STAG	Special Task Air Group
STM	supersonic tactical missile
STOL	short takeoff and landing

STOVL	short takeoff/vertical landing
STRATCOM	Strategic Command
SWIP	System Weapons Integration Program
SWOD	Special Weapons Ordnance Device
T&E	test and evaluation
TACAMO	Take Charge and Move Out
TACAN	tactical air navigation system
TACELWING	Tactical Electronic Warfare Wing
TACGRU	tactical group
TALD	tactical air launch decoy
TARPS	Tactical Aerial Reconnaissance Pod System
TERCOM	terrain contour matching
TF	task force
TG	task group
TINS	Thermal Imaging Navigation Set
TLAM	Tomahawk land-attack missile
TOW	tube-launched, optically tracked, wire-command-link
TRAM	Target Recognition Attack Multisensor
TraWing/TRAWING	Training Air Wing
TRIM	Trail Road Interdiction Mission
TU	task unit
TWA	Trans World Airlines
UAS	unmanned aerial systems
UAV	unmanned aerial vehicle
UCAS	unmanned combat air system
UDT	underwater demolition team
UN	United Nations
USA	United States Army
USAAF	United States Army Air Forces
USAAS	United States Army Air Service
USACOM	United States Atlantic Command
USAF	United States Air Force
USCG	United States Coast Guard
USMC	United States Marine Corps
USN	United States Navy
USNR	United States Naval/Navy Reserve
USNRF	United States Naval/Navy Reserve Force
USNS	United States Naval Ship
V/STOL	vertical and/or short takeoff and landing
VAST	versatile avionics shop test
VCNO	Vice Chief of Naval Operations
VFAX	advanced experimental fighter aircraft
Viet Cong	People's Liberation Armed Forces
VOD	vertical on-board delivery
VOR	very-high frequency omni-range direction finder
VORTAC	very-high frequency omni-range direction finder tactical air navigation system
VSTOL	vertical/short takeoff and landing
VT	variable-time (fuze)
VTOL	vertical takeoff and landing
VTUAV	vertical takeoff and landing tactical unmanned aerial vehicle
VTXTS	fixed-wing experimental training aircraft training system
VWS	ventilated wet suit
WAVES	Women Accepted for Volunteer Emergency Service
WestPac/WESTPAC	Western Pacific Ocean
WNY	Washington Navy Yard
WWI	World War I
WWII	World War II

Note: Acronyms or abbreviations for squadron designations, air groups or air wings, aviation ship designations, and aviation ratings may be found in the Vol. II appendices, as will other more specialized acronym meanings.

CHAPTER 1

A Few Pioneers

1898–1916

The United States Navy's official interest in airplanes emerged as early as 1898. That year the Navy assigned officers to sit on an interservice board to investigate the military possibilities of Samuel P. Langley's flying machine. In subsequent years naval observers attended air meets in the United States and abroad, and public demonstrations staged by Orville and Wilbur Wright in 1908 and 1909. These men became enthusiastic about the potential of airplanes as fleet scouts, and by 1909, many naval officers, including a bureau chief, urged the purchase of aircraft.

The next year the Navy made a place for aviation in its organizational structure when Capt. Washington I. Chambers was designated as the officer to whom all aviation matters were to be referred. Although holding no special title, he pulled together existing threads of aviation interest within the Navy and gave official recognition to the proposals of inventors and builders. Before the Navy had either planes or pilots, he arranged a series of tests in which civilian aircraft designer and entrepreneur Glenn H. Curtiss and Eugene B. Ely, a pilot who worked for Curtiss, dramatized the airplane's capability for shipboard operations and showed the world and a skeptical fleet that aviation could go to sea.

Early in 1911 the first naval officer reported for flight training. By mid-year the Navy appropriated the first money, purchased the first aircraft, qualified the initial pilot, and selected the site of the first aviation camp. The idea of a seagoing aviation force began to take form as plans and enthusiasms transformed into realities. By the end of the year a humble beginning had been made.

Recognizing the need for more science and less rule of thumb, Capt. Chambers collected the writings and scientific papers of leaders in the new field, pushed for a national aerodynamics laboratory, and encouraged naval constructors to work on aerodynamic and hydrodynamic problems. The Navy built a wind tunnel, and the nation established the National Advisory Committee for Aeronautics. A board under Chambers' leadership conducted the first real study of what was needed in aviation and included in its recommendations the establishment of a ground and flight training center at Pensacola, Fla., the expansion of research, and the assignment of an airplane to every major combatant ship of the Navy.

Naval aviation's progress in these early years included setting an endurance record of six hours in the air; the first successful catapult launch of an airplane from a ship; exercises with the fleet during winter maneuvers at Naval Station Guantánamo Bay, Cuba; and combat sorties at Vera Cruz, Mexico. These were but some of the accomplishments of pioneer pilots, whose activities furthered the importance of aviation to the Navy. In 1914 Secretary of the Navy Josephus Daniels announced that the Navy had reached the point "where aircraft must form a large part of our naval forces for offensive and defensive operations."

1898

25 MARCH • Assistant Secretary of the Navy Theodore Roosevelt recommended to Secretary of the Navy John D. Long that he appoint two officers "of scientific attainments and practical ability" who, with representatives from the War Department, would examine Professor Samuel P. Langley's flying machine and report upon its practicability and its potential for use in war.

29 APRIL • The first joint Army-Navy board on aeronautics submitted the report of its investigation of the Langley flying machine. Since the machine was a model with a 12-foot wing span, its value for military purposes was largely theoretical, but the report expressed a general sentiment in favor of supporting Professor Samuel P. Langley in further experimentation.

1908

17 SEPTEMBER • Lt. George C. Sweet and Assistant Naval Constructor William McEntee served as Navy observers at the first Army demonstration trials of the Wright flying machine at Fort Myer, Va.

2 DECEMBER • Rear Adm. William S. Cowles, Chief of the Bureau of Equipment, submitted a report on aviation prepared by Lt. George C. Sweet to Secretary of the Navy Truman H. Newberry. The report outlined the specifications of an airplane capable of operating from naval vessels on scouting and observation missions, discussed the tactical advantages of such capability for naval forces, and recommended that the service purchase a number of aircraft and place them "in the hands of the personnel of the Navy to further develop special features adapted to naval uses."

1909

16 AUGUST • Acting Secretary of the Navy George von L. Meyer disapproved a request by the Bureau of Equipment for authority to advertise for the construction of "two heavier than air flying machines," with the comment: "The Department does not consider that the development of an aeroplane has progressed sufficiently at this time for use in the Navy."

1 SEPTEMBER • Cmdr. Frederick L. Chapin, the Naval Attaché at Paris, reported his observations at the Reims aviation meet. Chapin opined that "the airplane would have a present usefulness in naval warfare, and that the limits of the field will be extended in the near future." He also noted two means by which aircraft were to be operated from naval vessels—the use of the Wright launching device (a catapult) to launch planes from the cleared quarterdeck of battleships, and the construction of a floor (flight deck) over the deck houses of auxiliary ships to provide the clear space required for takeoff runs and landings.

3 NOVEMBER • Lt. Frank P. Lahm, USA, piloted the first Army Wright plane during its initial flight at College Park, Md. Navy Lt. George C. Sweet accompanied Lahm as a passenger and is credited as the first Navy officer to fly in an airplane.

1910

26 SEPTEMBER • The Secretary of the Navy informed the Aeronautical Reserve (an organization of private citizens formed to advance aeronautical science as a means of supplementing the national defense) that Capt. Washington I. Chambers, Assistant to the Aid for Material, had been designated as the officer to whom all correspondence on aviation was to be referred. This is the first recorded reference to a provision for aviation in the Navy Department organization.

1 OCTOBER • The General Board, of which Admiral of the Navy George Dewey was president, recommended to Secretary of the Navy George von L. Meyer that, in recognition of "the great advances which have been made in the science of aviation and the advantages which may accrue from its use in this class of vessel," the problem of providing space for airplanes or dirigibles was to be considered in all new designs for scouting vessels.

7 OCTOBER • Chief of the Bureau of Steam Engineering Capt. Hutch I. Cone wrote a letter to Secretary of the Navy George von L. Meyer that pointed to "the rapid improvement in the design and manipulation of airplanes and the important role they would probably play" and requested authority to requisition an airplane for *Chester* (Cruiser No. 1) and the services of an instructor to teach one or more officers to fly the machine.

13 OCTOBER • Secretary of the Navy George von L. Meyer approved the recommendation of the Chief Constructor that an officer from the Bureau of Construction and Repair and another from the Bureau of Steam Engineering were to be appointed to investigate the subject of aviation and gain technical knowledge of airplanes. Meyer also directed that these officers keep Assistant to the Aid for Material Capt. Washington I. Chambers, previously designated to serve in a similar capacity in the secretary's office, fully informed of the work contemplated and the results of all experiments.

22 OCTOBER • The International Aviation Tournament opened at Belmont Park, N.Y. Assistant to the Aid for Material Capt. Washington I. Chambers, Assistant Naval Constructor William McEntee, and Lt. Nathaniel H. Wright,

42878

Eugene B. Ely flies a Curtiss pusher from *Birmingham* (Cruiser No. 2) at Hampton Roads, Va., in the first takeoff from a ship, 14 November 1910.

the three men recently named to investigate aviation, attended as official Navy observers.

31 OCTOBER • The Chief of the Bureau of Construction and Repair suggested to Secretary of the Navy George von L. Meyer that the Navy take steps to obtain one or more aeroplanes to develop their use for naval purposes, and recommended that in the absence of specific funds for their purchase, the specifications for *Texas* (Battleship No. 35) be modified so as to require contractors to supply one or more aircraft as a part of their obligation.

14 NOVEMBER • Flying a 50 hp Curtiss plane, civilian exhibition stunt pilot Eugene B. Ely made the first takeoff from a ship. Ely flew from an 83-foot slanted wooden platform built onto the bow of *Birmingham* (Cruiser No. 2) at anchor off Old Point Comfort, Hampton Roads, Va. Despite light rain and fog, the pilot elected to continue with the flight. As he left the platform, the plane settled slowly and touched the water, but rose again and landed about 2½ miles away on Willoughby Spit. The aircraft sustained slight splinter damage to the propeller tips.

29 NOVEMBER • Aircraft designer and entrepreneur Glenn H. Curtiss wrote to Secretary of the Navy George von L. Meyer offering flight instruction without charge for one naval officer as a means of assisting "in developing the adaptability of the aeroplane to military purposes."

23 DECEMBER • Lt. Theodore G. Ellyson, the first naval officer to undergo flight training, received orders to report to the Curtiss aviation camp at North Island, San Diego, Calif.

428455

450108

Eugene B. Ely, flying a Curtiss pusher, approaches a platform built over the stern of *Pennsylvania* (Armored Cruiser No. 4) in the first shipboard landing of an aircraft, 18 January 1911 (top). The plane was arrested by hooks attached to the plane's landing gear, which engaged a series of ropes, with sandbags at each end, stretched across the temporary deck and held above it by boards laid along its length (bottom).

1911

18 JANUARY • At 1048 civilian exhibition stunt pilot Eugene B. Ely flew the same Curtiss pusher that he had used during his launch from *Birmingham* (Cruiser No. 2) on 14 November 1910 and took off from Selfridge Field south of San Francisco, Calif., and at 1101 landed on board *Pennsylvania* (Armored Cruiser No. 4) at anchor off Hunters Point in San Francisco Bay. The plane made a smooth landing from astern onto a specially built 130-foot long by 32-foot wide platform. At 1158 Ely took off and returned to Selfridge Field, completing the earliest demonstration of the adaptability of aircraft to shipboard operations.

26 JANUARY • Glenn H. Curtiss piloted a hydroaeroplane during the first successful flight of that type of plane at North Island, San Diego, Calif. Lt. Theodore G. Ellyson, who had assisted in preparing for the test, witnessed this important step in adapting aircraft to naval needs.

1 FEBRUARY • Glenn H. Curtiss made two successful flights from the water in a standard biplane at San Diego, Calif., using a single main float in place of the tandem triple float used in earlier tests. These takeoffs demonstrated the superior efficiency of the sled profile float that the Navy would use on hydroaeroplanes up to WWI.

10 FEBRUARY • Acting Secretary of the Navy Beekman Winthrop directed the Point Loma, Calif., Wireless Station to cooperate with Capt. Harry S. Harkness of the Aeronautical Reserve in experiments with the use of wireless from aeroplanes.

17 FEBRUARY • In another early demonstration of the adaptability of aircraft to naval uses, Glenn H. Curtiss taxied in a hydroaeroplane alongside *Pennsylvania* (Armored Cruiser No. 4) at anchor in San Diego Harbor, Calif. Curtiss arrived alongside the ship at 0845 and sailors manned the cruiser's crane to hoist the machine on board. At 0905 *Pennsylvania* hoisted the aircraft out and Curtiss taxied the plane to his hangar on North Island.

4 MARCH • The first funds appropriated for naval aviation provided $25,000 to the Bureau of Navigation for "experimental work in the development of aviation for naval purposes."

9 MARCH • The Wright Co. made a formal offer to train one pilot for the Navy, contingent on the purchase of one airplane for the sum of $5,000. Naval officials expressed their displeasure at the contingency, and Assistant to the Aid for Material Capt. Washington I. Chambers could not immediately arrange for the order of the aircraft, so the company repeated the offer without the contingency on 13 March.

424786

Capt. Washington I. Chambers.

17 MARCH • Lt. John Rodgers, who became Naval Aviator No. 2, reported to the Wright Co. at Dayton, Ohio, for instruction in flying. Despite rough weather and lack of equipment, he completed training at the encampment by making his first solo flight on 18 April.

1 APRIL • Assistant to the Aid for Material Capt. Washington I. Chambers reported for duty with the General Board, a move suggested by board president Admiral of the Navy George Dewey because of a lack of space for aviation in the office of the Aid for Operations and to enable Chambers to have a stronger voice to impact policy.

14 APRIL • With Congress' allocation of a $25,000 appropriation for aviation within the Bureau of Navigation budget, the fledgling office of naval aviation transferred from the General Board and was established in BUNAV.

8 MAY • Capt. Washington I. Chambers of the Bureau of Navigation prepared requisitions for two Curtiss biplanes. One, the Triad, was to be equipped for arising from or alighting on land or water; with a metal-tipped propeller designed for a speed of at least 45 miles per hour; provisions for carrying a passenger alongside the pilot; and controls that either the pilot or passenger could operate. The machine described became the Navy's first airplane, the Curtiss hydroaeroplane A-1 (later AH-1). Although these requisitions lacked the signature of the Chief of BUNAV—necessary to direct the General Storekeeper to enter into a contract with the Curtiss Co.—they indicated Chambers' decision as to which airplanes the Navy should purchase. The Navy thus considers 8 May 1911 the date upon which the service ordered its first airplane, and the official birthday of naval aviation.

27 JUNE • Lt. j.g. John H. Towers, who was to become Naval Aviator No. 3, reported for duty and instruction in flying at the Curtiss School at Hammondsport, N.Y.

1 JULY • At 1850 Glenn H. Curtiss demonstrated A-1 (later AH-1), the first aircraft built for the Navy. The plane took off from and alighted on Keuka Lake at Hammondsport, N.Y. The five-minute flight reached an altitude of 25 feet. The aircraft completed three other flights the same evening, one by Curtiss with Lt. Theodore G. Ellyson as a passenger, and two by Ellyson alone. In the longest of these flights Ellyson was in the air for 15 minutes and achieved an altitude of 300 feet. However, a special motor that Curtiss had constructed for A-1 encountered mechanical difficulties and a standard Curtiss 50 hp motor was used in these flights.

NHF1061-84

The first Navy plane A-1 taxiing on Keuka Lake, N.Y.

Capt. Washington I. Chambers, seated left, prepares for a flight with Lt. Theodore G. Ellyson in A-1 Triad at Hammondsport, N.Y.

424469

3 JULY • Lt. Theodore G. Ellyson completed the first night flight by a member of the naval service. Ellyson took Capt. Washington I. Chambers of the Bureau of Navigation in A-1 (later AH-1) from Hammondsport, N.Y., to Penn Yan, N.Y. Light winds kept the plane from climbing aloft, and Ellyson and Chambers taxied 22 miles with a brief stop at Keuka. At 2015 Ellyson lifted off to return alone. He stopped for oil at Keuka after dusk, but the distance to the water's surface appeared misleading in the darkness and the aircraft struck the water. The plane rose again and landed successfully on the water on the second attempt, without the aid of lights, at 2045. These were the 12th and 13th flights of A-1.

6 JULY • Capt. Washington I. Chambers of the Bureau of Navigation received orders for temporary duty at the Naval Academy, Annapolis, Md., in connection with the establishment of an aviation experimental station, the site for which had been previously selected on Greenbury Point near Annapolis. Although the aviators did not occupy the site until September, this became the first base for naval aviation.

10 JULY • The 24th flight of the Triad demonstrated the amphibious features of the Navy's first aircraft. Pilot Glenn H. Curtiss took off from land, lifted the plane's wheels while in the air, and landed the Triad in the water.

13 JULY • Glenn H. Curtiss made the first flight of the Navy's second aircraft, A-2 (later AH-2), at Hammondsport, N.Y. Lt. Theodore G. Ellyson accomplished the second flight. Each attempt lasted for several minutes and reached an altitude of 100 feet.

23 AUGUST • The officers on flight duty with the Curtiss Co., Hammondsport, N.Y., and Wright Co., Dayton, Ohio, were ordered to report for duty at the Engineering Experiment Station at the Naval Academy, "in connection with the test of gasoline motors and other experimental work in the development of aviation, including instruction at the aviation school," which was being established on Greenbury Point, Md.

7 SEPTEMBER • A memorable experiment in the Navy's search for a shipboard launching device concluded at Hammondsport, N.Y., when Lt. Theodore G. Ellyson made a successful takeoff in a Curtiss plane from an inclined wire rigged from the beach down to the water. Capt. Charles F. Pond, who commanded *Pennsylvania* (Armored Cruiser No. 4), had suggested the technique, and Capt. Washington I. Chambers of the Bureau of Navigation and Glenn H. Curtiss had developed the method to the point of the test. Ellyson's report described the historic experiment, "The engine was started and run at full speed and then I gave the signal to release the machine. . . . I held the machine on the wire as long as possible as I wanted to be sure that I had enough headway to rise and not run the risk of the machine partly rising and then falling. . . . Everything happened so quickly and went off so smoothly that I hardly knew what happened except that I did have to use the ailerons, and that the machine was sensitive to their action."

1051558

Glenn H. Curtiss, standing atop the wing of his D-III tractor hydroaeroplane, attaches the hook of the ship's crane in preparation to being hoisted on board *Pennsylvania* on 17 February 1911.

16 SEPTEMBER • In a letter to the Navy Department, Lt. Theodore G. Ellyson described plans to purchase flight clothing in the hope of persuading the Navy to pay for them later. The Navy had outlined the requirements as a light helmet with detachable goggles, or a visor, with covering for the ears, yet with holes so the pilot could hear the engine; a leather coat lined with fur or wool; leather trousers; high rubber galoshes and gauntlets; and a life preserver of some description. Ellyson purchased some of this gear from Brooks Brothers clothiers using his own funds.

20 SEPTEMBER • The attempt to equip aircraft with navigational instruments was reflected in a Bureau of Navigation request to the Naval Observatory for temporary use of a boat compass in experimental work connected with the development of aviation.

428450

Preparing A-1 for a launch from an inclined wire rigged from the beach down to the water at Hammondsport, N.Y.

427990

Lt. John H. Towers, left, and Lt. Theodore G. Ellyson.

10 OCTOBER • Assistant Naval Constructor Lt. Holden C. Richardson, CC, reported to the office of aviation at the Washington Navy Yard, D.C. Richardson became the Navy's first engineering and maintenance officer for aviation.

16 OCTOBER • Capt. Washington I. Chambers of the Bureau of Navigation described plans for a scientific test of hydroaeroplane floats at the Washington Navy Yard Model Basin, D.C., in a letter, in which he stated that a model of the pontoons with Forlanini planes (hydrovanes) was nearly ready for testing.

17 OCTOBER • Searching for improved powerplants, Capt. Washington I. Chambers of the Bureau of Navigation, in a letter to Glenn H. Curtiss, discussed heavy oil (or diesel) engines and turbine engines similar in principle to those that, some thirty years later, would make jet propulsion practical. Chambers wrote, "In my opinion, this turbine is the surest step of all, and the aeroplane manufacturer who gets in with it first is going to do wonders."

19 OCTOBER • Civilian exhibition pilot Eugene B. Ely lost control of an aircraft and crashed while landing before spectators during an exhibition at the state fair at Macon, Ga. Ely died from a broken neck when the plane struck the ground, throwing the pilot from the seat. On 16 February 1933 President Herbert C. Hoover presented the Distinguished Flying Cross as a posthumous award to the aviator's son, Col. Nathan D. Ely, USA (Ret.).

25 OCTOBER • Lt. Theodore G. Ellyson and Lt. John H. Towers flew A-1 (later AH-1) during an experiment to test the plane's durability on a cross-country flight from Annapolis, Md., to Fort Monroe, Va. A leaking radiator forced the aircraft down near Milford Haven, Va., after covering 112 miles in 122 minutes. This flight began a ten-day struggle to make the round trip.

8 NOVEMBER • Ens. Victor D. Herbster, later designated Naval Aviator No. 4, reported for flight instruction at the aviation camp at Greenbury Point, near Annapolis, Md.

14 NOVEMBER • The Navy's first major aircraft modification, the conversion of landplane B-1 (later AH-4) into a hydroaeroplane, began with a telegraphic order to the Burgess Co. and Curtis, Inc., Marblehead, Mass., for a suitable float.

20 DECEMBER • Lt. John H. Towers piloted A-1 (later AH-1) during experiments with airborne wireless transmission at Annapolis, Md. The plane made four flights, three with Ens. Charles H. Maddox and one with Assistant Naval Constructor Lt. Holden C. Richardson, CC. The men discovered that the trailing wire antenna reeled out after takeoff was too weak, and failed to obtain definite results.

26 DECEMBER • The search for a shipboard launching device continued when Capt. Washington I. Chambers of the Bureau of Navigation reported on interest by the Bureau of Ordnance concerning experimentation with a catapult for launching aeroplanes, somewhat after the manner of launching torpedoes. Chambers noted that the bureau decided to make a trial "with a device that gathers speed more gradually, something like the Curtiss air cylinder such as we use in ammunition hoists." These observations indicate the genesis of the Navy's compressed air catapult.

29 DECEMBER • The aviators at Greenbury Point, Md., received orders to transfer with their equipment to North Island, San Diego, Calif., to set up an aviation camp on land.

1912

9 MARCH • Assistant Naval Constructor Lt. Holden C. Richardson, CC, defined interest in steel and aluminum as aircraft structural materials in a letter to Capt. Washington I. Chambers of the Bureau of Navigation, stating, "From all I can gather, there is little doubt that much greater confidence would be felt if pontoons were constructed with a metal skin. . . . It would be unwise to make any requisition for such a construction until a practically standard design has been developed."

11 MARCH • Secretary of the Navy George von L. Meyer authorized the expenditure of not more than $50 for developing models of a helicopter design proposed by MMC F. E. Nelson of *West Virginia* (Armored Cruiser No. 5). Meyer did allow for the possibility of an expanded interest in the future, stating, "The Department recognizes the value of the helicopter principle in the design of naval aircraft and is following closely the efforts of others in this direction."

23 MARCH • Chief Electrician Howard E. Morin conducted experiments with wireless communications at Mare Island Navy Yard near San Francisco, Calif., in which he made transmissions from a dummy airplane fuselage hoisted to a height of 85 feet. An operator at a station at Point Richmond, 20 miles distant, received the signals "distinctly."

22 MAY • 1st Lt. Alfred A. Cunningham, USMC, the first Marine Corps officer assigned to flight instruction and afterward designated Naval Aviator No. 5, reported to the Superintendent of the Naval Academy for "duty in connection with aviation." Cunningham subsequently detached to the Burgess Co., at Marblehead, Mass., for flight instruction. This date is recognized as the birthday of Marine Corps aviation.

650871

Lt. Holden C. Richardson, CC.

21 JUNE • Lt. Theodore G. Ellyson ascended to 900 feet in A-1 (later AH-1) over Annapolis, Md., in 3 minutes 30 seconds.

20 JULY • The men of the aviation camp at Greenbury Point, Md., conducted comparative tests of Wright steel wire and Monel wire at Engineering Experiment Station, Annapolis, Md. These, the earliest recorded naval tests of aircraft structural materials, showed the Monel wire to be both free of corrosion and 50 percent stronger than the steel wire.

25 JULY • On the basis of the Navy's experience with its first airplanes, Secretary of the Navy George von L. Meyer published *Requirements for Hydroaeroplanes*, the first general specifications for naval aircraft. The Secretary's expressed purpose was "to assist manufacturers in maintaining the highest degree of efficiency, while improving the factors which govern safety in aviation, without demanding anything that may not be accomplished under the limitations of the present state of the art and without confining purchases to the products of a single factory."

26 JULY • Lt. John Rodgers continued airborne wireless communications tests in hydroaeroplane B-1 at Annapolis, Md. On one flight, Ens. Charles H. Maddox sent messages to *Stringham* (Torpedo Boat No. 19) at a distance of about 1½ miles. Subsequent tests over the following days included transmissions at short intervals and while the plane ran on the water. Maddox later received a letter of commendation noting his "valuable work" in the development of aviation radio equipment, including his personal manufacture and installation of the first radio transmitter used by the Navy in airplane communications.

31 JULY • Lt. Theodore G. Ellyson piloted A-1 (later AH-1) during the Navy's first attempt to launch an airplane by catapult, at the dock of the Naval Academy, Annapolis, Md. The aircraft, which was not secured to the catapult, reared at about mid-stroke; a crosswind caught it and the machine plunged into the water, although the pilot escaped without

466256

Ens. Godfrey deC. Chevalier.

650864

A-1 poised to launch during the Navy's first attempt to launch a plane from a catapult at Annapolis, Md., July 1912.

serious injuries. This catapult, powered by compressed air, was constructed at the Naval Gun Factory at the Washington Navy Yard, D.C., from a plan proposed by Capt. Washington I. Chambers of the Bureau of Navigation.

18 SEPTEMBER • 1st Lt. Bernard L. Smith, USMC, the second Marine officer assigned to flight training and later designated Naval Aviator No. 6, reported for instruction at the aviation camp at the Naval Academy, Annapolis, Md.

3 OCTOBER • The Davis recoilless gun underwent initial tests at Naval Proving Ground, Indian Head, Md. Cmdr. Cleland Davis designed the gun to fire from an aircraft a caliber shell large enough to damage submarines, but with a recoil slight enough to be absorbed by the aircraft. Davis tested the gun again in early December; however, the results of the two series of experiments demonstrated that although the gun was recoilless, the blast from the muzzle would pose problems should they install the weapon on board aircraft.

6 OCTOBER • Lt. John H. Towers took off in A-2 (later AH-2) from the water at Greenbury Point, Md., at 0650 and remained in the air 6 hours 10 minutes 35 seconds, setting a new American endurance record for planes of any type.

8 OCTOBER • Tests of a Gyro 50 hp rotary motor were completed at the Engineering Experiment Station, Annapolis, Md. The motor underwent three brief dynamometer tests, followed by ground runs and flight tests, marking the Navy's first recorded attempt to use laboratory equipment and methods to evaluate an aircraft engine.

8 OCTOBER • The Navy first defined physical requirements for prospective naval aviators in Bureau of Medicine and Surgery Circular Letter 125221. Standards concerned equilibrium, hearing, vision, and organs of the circulatory and respiratory systems.

25 OCTOBER • Ens. Godfrey deC. Chevalier, later designated Naval Aviator No. 7, reported for flight training at the aviation camp at Annapolis, Md.

12 NOVEMBER • Lt. Theodore G. Ellyson accomplished the Navy's first successful launching of an airplane by catapult, in A-3 (later AH-3) at the Washington Navy Yard, D.C. The following month a flying boat successfully launched from this catapult.

26 NOVEMBER • Lt. j.g. Patrick N. L. Bellinger, later Naval Aviator No. 8, reported for flight instruction at the aviation camp at Greenbury Point, Md.

30 NOVEMBER • Lt. Theodore G. Ellyson tested C-1 (later AB-1), the Navy's first flying boat, at Hammondsport, N.Y. The pilot described its performance as "Circular climb, only one complete circle, 1,575 feet in 14 minutes 30 seconds

Lt. Theodore G. Ellyson accomplishes the Navy's first successful catapult launch, flying in A-3 at the Washington Navy Yard, D.C., 12 November 1912.

fully loaded. On glide approximately 5.3 to 1. Speed, eight runs over measured mile, 59.4 miles per hour fully loaded. The endurance test was not made, owing to the fact that the weather has not been favorable, and I did not like to delay any longer."

2 DECEMBER • Ens. William D. Billingsley, later Naval Aviator No. 9, reported for duty at the aviation camp at Greenbury Point, Md. Billingsley subsequently began his assignment with instruction in hydroaeroplane B-2 (later AH-5).

18 DECEMBER • Lt. John H. Towers reported completion of a series of tests begun on 26 October to determine the ability to spot submarines from aircraft. Towers concluded that the best altitude for observation was about 800 feet, and that aircraft could detect submarines running a few feet below the surface. Noting that the waters of Chesapeake Bay were too muddy for a fair test, he suggested that additional trials be held at NS Guantánamo Bay, Cuba.

19 DECEMBER • President William H. Taft, acting on a recommendation made by Secretary of the Navy George von L. Meyer, created a "Commission on Aerodynamical Laboratory" to determine the need for and a method of establishing such a laboratory. Capt. Washington I. Chambers of the Bureau of Navigation and Naval Constructor David W. Taylor represented the Navy on the commission.

1913

6 JANUARY • The Navy's entire aviation element arrived at NS Guantánamo Bay, Cuba, and set up an encampment on Fisherman's Point for initial operations with the fleet. The assignment, which included scouting missions and exercises in spotting mines and submerged submarines as part of the fleet maneuvers, served both to demonstrate operational capabilities of the aircraft and to stimulate interest in aviation among sailors and Marines, more than a hundred of whom were taken up for flights during the aviation element's eight-week stay.

8 FEBRUARY • Lt. John H. Towers reported on experimental aviation work underway at NS Guantánamo Bay, Cuba, including bombing, aerial photography, and wireless radio transmission, stating in part: "We have become fairly accurate at dropping missiles, using a fairly simple device gotten up by one of the men. Have obtained some good photographs from the boats at heights up to 1,000 feet. I believe we will get some results with wireless this winter."

26 FEBRUARY • The Chief Constructor of the Navy formally approved action to provide the service with a wind tunnel, a basic tool in aeronautical research and development. The resulting tunnel was built at the Washington Navy Yard, D.C.

4 MARCH • The Navy Appropriations Act for fiscal year 1914 provided an increase of 35 percent in pay and allowances for officers detailed to duty as flyers of heavier-than-air craft, limited to 30 the number of officers that could be so assigned, and further provided that no naval officer above the rank of lieutenant commander in the Navy or major in the Marine Corps was to be detailed to duty involving flying.

652044

The base for the first aviation detachment to operate with the Fleet at Guantánamo Bay, Cuba, January 1913.

426948

Men of the aviation detachment at Guantánamo Bay, Cuba: 1st Lt. Bernard L. Smith, USMC, Lt. j.g. Patrick N. L. Bellinger, 1st Lt. Alfred A. Cunningham, USMC, Ens. William D. Billingsley (standing), Ens. Victor D. Herbster, and Ens. Godfrey deC. Chevalier (seated).

5 MARCH • Reporting on tests held at NS Guantánamo Bay, Cuba, from 3 to 5 March, Lt. John H. Towers stated that aircraft had spotted submarines from the air at a variety of depths. They discerned a submarine painted slate grey at depths up to 45 feet; a light blue boat at a depth of 40 feet; and a "dark greenish blue" boat at 30 feet.

13 MARCH • Capt. Washington I. Chambers of the Bureau of Navigation received the medal of the Aeronautical Society for 1912, and was cited for "his unusual achievements in being the first to demonstrate the usefulness of the aeroplane in navies, in developing a practical catapult for the launching of aeroplanes from ships, in assisting in the practical solution of the hydroaeroplane by the production in association with others of the flying boat, in having been instrumental in the introduction into our halls of Congress of bills for a National Aerodynamic Laboratory, and a Competitive Test, and through his perseverance and able efforts in advancing the progress of Aeronautics in many other channels."

31 MARCH • A list of aircraft instruments and allied equipment planned for installation in flying boat D-1 (later AB-6) included a compass, altimeter, inclinometer, speed indicator, chart board, radio, and generator. Although mechanics had not installed the radio and generator by this date, the other equipment represents instrumentation installed on naval aircraft of the period.

10 APRIL • The Secretary of the Navy approved performance standards for qualification as a Navy Air Pilot and the issuance of a certificate to all officers meeting the requirements. Capt. Washington I. Chambers of the Bureau of Navigation described these requirements as being different from those of the "land pilot," and more exacting than those of the international accrediting agency, the Federation Aeronautique Internationale.

28 APRIL • Rear Adm. Victor Blue, Chief of the Bureau of Navigation, approved a proposal that the Navy, Glenn H. Curtiss, and the Sperry Co. cooperate in testing the gyroscopic stabilizer on a new naval aeroplane.

9 MAY • President Woodrow Wilson approved the designation of representatives from governmental departments to serve on an advisory committee for the Langley Aerodynamical Laboratory, which the Smithsonian Institution had closed after the death of laboratory director Samuel P. Langley and reopened on 1 May to study questions relating to aerodynamics. Navy members of the advisory committee were Capt. Washington I. Chambers of the Bureau of Navigation and Assistant Naval Constructor Lt. Holden C. Richardson, CC.

12 JUNE • Secretary of the Navy Josephus Daniels approved detailing Lt. Jerome C. Hunsaker, CC, to the Massachusetts Institute of Technology to develop "a course of lectures and experiments on the design of aeroplanes and dirigibles, and to undertake research in that field." After making a tour of aeronautical research facilities in Europe, Hunsaker participated in establishing a course of aeronautical engineering in MIT's Department of Naval Architecture.

13 JUNE • Lt. j.g. Patrick N. L. Bellinger set an American altitude record for seaplanes when he reached 6,200 feet in A-3 (later AH-3) over Annapolis, Md.

20 JUNE • Ens. William D. Billingsley suffered an accident while flying B-2 (later AH-5) at 1,600 feet over the water near Annapolis, Md. Billingsley was thrown from the plane and fell to his death, becoming the first fatality in naval aviation. The mishap also unseated passenger Lt. John H. Towers, who clung to a piece of B-2 but fell with the plane's wreckage into the water and received serious injuries. Destroyer *Billingsley* (DD 293) was later named in honor of the fallen pilot.

23 JUNE • General Order No. 41 fixed the cognizance of various bureaus in aviation in a manner paralleling the division of responsibility for naval vessels.

30 AUGUST • A Sperry gyroscopic stabilizer (automatic pilot) was flight tested in flying boat C-2 (later AB-2) by Lt. j.g. Patrick N. L. Bellinger at Hammondsport, N.Y.

30 AUGUST • In a report to Secretary of the Navy Josephus Daniels, the General Board expressed its opinion that "the organization of an efficient naval air service should be immediately taken in hand and pushed to fulfillment."

5 OCTOBER • The Navy's first amphibian flying boat, the Over-Water-Land type, completed its initial trials at Hammondsport, N.Y., under the supervision of Assistant Naval Constructor Lt. Holden C. Richardson, CC. The aircraft, which was subsequently redesignated E-1, was hydroaeroplane A-2 (later AH-2), in which a flying boat hull containing a three-wheel landing gear replaced the pontoon.

7 OCTOBER • Secretary of the Navy Josephus Daniels appointed a board—dubbed the Chambers Board, after senior member Capt. Washington I. Chambers—to draw up "a comprehensive plan for the organization of a Naval Aeronautic Service." The board's members also included Cmdr. Carlo B. Brittain, Cmdr. Samuel S. Robison, Lt. Manley H. Simons, Lt. John H. Towers, Assistant Naval Constructor Lt. Holden C. Richardson, CC, and 1st Lt. Alfred A. Cunningham, USMC. Following 12 days of deliberation the board submitted a report emphasizing the need for expansion and for the integration of aviation within the fleet. This was the first comprehensive program for an orderly development of naval aviation. The board's recommendations included establishing an aeronautic center at Pensacola, Fla., for flight and ground training and for the study of advanced aeronautical engineering; creating a central aviation office under the secretary to coordinate the aviation work of the bureaus; assigning a ship for training in operations at sea and to make practical tests of equipment necessary for such operations; and assigning one aircraft to every major combatant ship. The board requested $1,297,700 to implement the program.

17 DECEMBER • Capt. Mark L. Bristol reported to the Navy Department for special duty as officer in charge of aviation, and relieved Capt. Washington I. Chambers of that duty.

72-CN-6422

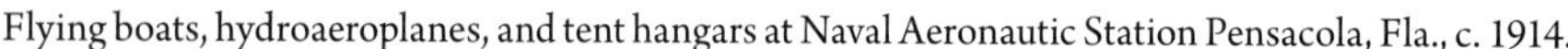

Flying boats, hydroaeroplanes, and tent hangars at Naval Aeronautic Station Pensacola, Fla., c. 1914.

1061482

Lt. Cmdr. Henry C. Mustin.

1914

6 JANUARY • The Marine Corps element of the aviation camp at Greenbury Point, Md., 1st Lt. Bernard L. Smith, USMC, commanding, equipped with a flying boat, an amphibian, spare parts, and hangar tents, received orders to deploy to Culebra Island, Puerto Rico, for exercises with the Advance Base Unit to experiment with aircraft operations during fleet maneuvers.

7 JANUARY • The Office of Aeronautics, with Capt. Mark L. Bristol in charge, transferred from the Bureau of Navigation to the Division of Operations in the Office of the Secretary of the Navy.

10 JANUARY • Secretary of the Navy Josephus Daniels announced that "the science of aerial navigation has reached that point where aircraft must form a large part of our naval force for offensive and defensive operations."

20 JANUARY • The aviation unit from Annapolis, Md., consisting of 9 officers, 23 enlisted men, 7 aircraft, portable hangars, and other gear, under Lt. John H. Towers, arrived at the former Navy yard at Pensacola, Fla., on board the aeronautic training ship *Mississippi* (Battleship No. 23) and *Orion* (Fuel Ship No. 11) to set up a flying school. Lt. Cmdr. Henry C. Mustin, in command of *Mississippi*, also commanded the aeronautic station.

16 FEBRUARY • Lt. j.g. James M. Murray, Naval Aviator No. 10, died when he crashed into the water from 200 feet while on a flight in flying boat D-1 (later AB-6) at Pensacola, Fla.

20 FEBRUARY • The beginnings of aviation medicine were apparent in a letter from the Office of Aeronautics to the commanding officer of the aeronautic station at Pensacola, Fla., on the subject of physical requirements for aviator candidates, which expressed the opinion that useful information was to be obtained by observing pilots during flight and by physical examination before and after flight. The letter further directed that a program should be developed that would permit incorporation of such practice in the work of the flight training school.

9 MARCH • The construction of the wind tunnel at the Washington Navy Yard, D.C., was completed and the tunnel turned over its fan for the first time. Calibration required about three months, and the Navy first used the tunnel in July to test a ship's ventilator cowling. The wind tunnel remained in operation throughout WWII.

27 MARCH • General Order No. 88 changed the designations of aircraft to two letters and a number, with the first letter denoting class, the second letter the type, and the number the order in which aircraft within class were acquired. Four classes were set up: A for all heavier-than-air craft; B for balloons; D for airships or dirigibles; and K for kites. Within the A class, the types of aircraft were B for

An aircraft flies over Vera Cruz, Mexico, as the pilot searches for enemy snipers.

flying boats, C for convertibles, H for hydroaeroplanes, L for land planes, and X for combination land and water machines. For example, the third hydroaeroplane, formerly designated A-3, became AH-3, and the first flying boat, formerly designated C-1, became AB-1.

20 APRIL • The First Section, an aviation detachment from Pensacola, Fla., embarked *Birmingham* (Cruiser No. 2), which sailed to join the ships of the Atlantic Fleet operating off Tampico and Vera Cruz during a crisis in Mexican waters. The detachment comprised three aircraft—hydroaeroplane AH-2, carrying spare parts including most of AX-1, and flying boats AB-4 and AB-5—with pilot Lt. John H. Towers in command, pilots 1st Lt. Bernard L. Smith, USMC, and Ens. Godfrey deC. Chevalier, and 12 enlisted men. This operation signified naval aviation's first call to action.

20 APRIL • Albert B. Lambert, an entrepreneur from St. Louis, Mo., who had organized the "U.S. Aviation Reserve Corps" the year before, informed Secretary of the Navy Josephus Daniels that he would make the corps' services available for use in the Mexican crisis. Lambert listed the names of 44 members—not all of naval origins—20 of whom could furnish their own aircraft; however, the Navy declined his offer.

21 APRIL • The Second Section, an aviation detachment from Pensacola, Fla., embarked the aeronautic training ship *Mississippi* (Battleship No. 23) and sailed for Mexico to assist in operations at Vera Cruz. The detachment consisted of two aircraft—hydroaeroplane AH-3 and flying boat AB-3—with pilot Lt. j.g. Patrick N. L. Bellinger in command and student pilots Lt. j.g. Richard C. Saufley, Ens. Melvin L. Stolz, and Ens. Walter D. LaMont.

22 APRIL • The Bureau of Navigation approved formal courses of instruction for student aviators and student mechanics at the Pensacola, Fla. aeronautic station flying school.

25 APRIL • Lt. j.g. Patrick N. L. Bellinger piloted flying boat AB-3 on the Second Section's first flight at Vera Cruz, Mexico, during a preliminary search for a purported mine in the harbor. The plane nearly failed to take off through the heavy swells but rose to a height of about 3,000 feet for a 28-minute flight around the harbor. Bellinger returned and picked up Ens. Melvin L. Stolz, but the weather forced him to go inside the breakwater to find smooth water, and the crew failed to spot the mine.

28 APRIL • Lt. j.g. Patrick N. L. Bellinger and Ens. Walter D. LaMont took the Navy's first recorded aerial photographs during wartime from flying boat AB-3 at an average altitude of barely 200 feet over Vera Cruz, Mexico. The flight was cut short, however, when the crew reported that the engine "worked poorly."

2 MAY • Lt. j.g. Patrick N. L. Bellinger and Ens. Walter D. LaMont completed naval aviation's first mission in direct support of ground troops while flying hydroaeroplane AH-3. Marines encamped near Tejar, Mexico, had reported receiving fire from Mexican troops during the forenoon watch and requested that the aviation detachment at Vera Cruz locate the attackers.

6 MAY • Orders directed the Second Section to investigate a company of about 100 Mexican soldiers encamped near Punta Gorda, around one mile north of Vera Cruz. Lt. j.g. Patrick N. L. Bellinger, pilot, with Lt. j.g. Richard C. Saufley, observer, responded in hydroaeroplane AH-3. As the plane followed the coast north toward Boca del Rio Antigua at an average altitude of 3,200 feet, it flew low over a group of Mexican stragglers who opened fire with rifles, hitting the frail craft. Bellinger immediately pulled up and although he

On 28 April 1914, Lt. j.g. Patrick N. L. Bellinger and Ens. Walter D. LaMont take the Navy's first documented aerial photographs during wartime from AB-3 over the fortress of San Juan de Ulua and the harbor of Vera Cruz, Mexico.

and Saufley escaped unhurt, AH-3 bore the first marks of battle on a Navy plane.

19 MAY • As the need for scouting services diminished at Vera Cruz, Mexico, the Second Section resumed routine flight instruction at that city while awaiting orders to return to Pensacola, Fla.

24 MAY • The First Section—the aeronautic detachment on board *Birmingham* (Cruiser No. 2)—arrived at Vera Cruz, Mexico, following a brief deployment to Tampico, to join the Second Section in the school routine of flight instruction.

26 MAY • On the basis of flight tests, Assistant Naval Constructor Lt. Holden C. Richardson, CC, recommended that the Navy purchase two swept-wing Burgess-Dunne hydroaeroplanes "so that the advantages and limitations can be thoroughly determined . . . as it appears to be only the beginning of an important development in aeronautical design." The service subsequently designated the aircraft obtained as AH-7 and AH-10.

1 JULY • The Navy formally recognized aviation by establishing the Office of Naval Aeronautics in the Division of Operations under the Secretary of the Navy. Secretary of the Navy Josephus Daniels had recommended the establishment on 26 March, which President Woodrow Wilson approved.

28 JULY • Lt. j.g. Victor D. Herbster reported on bombing tests that he and 1st Lt. Bernard L. Smith, USMC, carried out at Indian Head Proving Grounds, Md. They dropped both dummy and live bombs over the side of the aircraft from about 1,000 feet against land and water targets. Herbster reported his bombing would have been more accurate "if I had been able to disengage my fingers from the wind-wheel sooner."

21 AUGUST • Lt. Cmdr. Henry C. Mustin, Lt.j.g. Patrick N. L. Bellinger, and 1st Lt. Bernard L. Smith, USMC, arrived in Paris, France, from a voyage on board *North Carolina* (Armored Cruiser No. 12) for a two-day tour of aircraft factories and aerodromes in the immediate area. This temporary assignment marked the first use of naval aviators

391984

Lt. j.g. Patrick N. L. Bellinger, far right, and some of the other men of the aviation camp at Vera Cruz, Mexico, stand before hydroaeroplane AH-3, the Navy's first plane struck by enemy gunfire.

as observers in foreign lands, and established a precedent for the assignment of aviation assistants to naval attachés, which began the same month when Lt. John H. Towers was dispatched to London, England, "for special duty in connection with the study of aviation." The following month Lt. j.g. Victor D. Herbster and 1st Lt. Smith reported to Berlin, Germany, and to Paris, respectively.

16 NOVEMBER • An administrative reorganization at Pensacola, Fla., shifted overall command of the flying school from the station ship to headquarters ashore, and the station was officially designated Naval Aeronautic Station, Pensacola.

23 NOVEMBER • The Navy established the title Director of Naval Aeronautics to designate the officer in charge of naval aviation. Capt. Mark L. Bristol, already serving in that capacity, was ordered to report to Secretary of the Navy Josephus Daniels under the new title.

25 NOVEMBER • Director of Naval Aeronautics Capt. Mark L. Bristol established requirements for special meteorological equipment to measure and record velocity and direction of winds, gusts, and squalls, for installation at the two ends of the speed course at Pensacola, Fla.

1915

1 FEBRUARY • The Division of Naval Militia Affairs in the Bureau of Navigation directed that an aeronautic corps was to be organized in each state's Naval Militia.

Lt. Cmdr. Patrick N. L. Bellinger served at Vera Cruz, Mexico, as a lieutenant, junior grade.

The AH-7 flies over Pensacola, Fla.

3 MARCH • A rider to the Naval Appropriations Act of 1915 created the National Advisory Committee for Aeronautics. Navy members in the original organization were Director of Naval Aeronautics Capt. Mark L. Bristol and Assistant Naval Constructor Lt. Holden C. Richardson, CC. Futhermore, the Act added enlisted men and student aviators to those eligible for increased pay and allowances while flying on duty, increased the amount previously provided for qualified aviators, and provided for the payment of one year's pay to the next of kin of officers and men killed in aircraft accidents. The same act also raised the limits on sailors assigned to aviation to a yearly average of not more than 48 officers and 96 enlisted men for the Navy, and 12 officers and 24 enlisted men for the Marine Corps.

22 MARCH • The title Naval Aviator began to replace the former Navy Air Pilot designation for naval officers who had qualified as aviators.

16 APRIL • Lt.j.g. Patrick N. L. Bellinger successfully catapulted from a coal barge in flying boat AB-2 at Pensacola, Fla. Assistant Naval Constructor Lt. Holden C. Richardson, CC, had designed and fabricated the device at the Washington Navy Yard, D.C., in 1913. The success of this and subsequent launches by Lt. Kenneth Whiting, Lt. j.g. Richard C. Saufley, and Ens. Clarence K. Bronson led to the installation of catapults on board ships.

23 APRIL • Lt.j.g. Patrick N. L. Bellinger established a U.S. altitude record for seaplanes by ascending to 10,000 feet in AH-10 on a flight of 1 hour 19 minutes, over Pensacola, Fla.

Lt. Kenneth Whiting, at the controls of a Wright aircraft, later became instrumental in the formation of naval carrier aviation.

8 MAY • Student aviator Lt. j.g. Melvin L. Stolz died when his Curtiss hydroaeroplane crashed at Pensacola, Fla. Although Stolz had not been designated a naval aviator, he had qualified for Aero Club Hydroaeroplane Certification No. 19.

28 MAY • The Naval Militia was informed that refresher flight training at Pensacola, Fla., had become available for a limited number of its aviators.

1 JUNE • The Navy let its first contract for a lighter-than-air craft when it ordered a non-rigid airship from the Connecticut Aircraft Co. of New Haven. The craft, later designated DN-1, arrived at Pensacola, Fla., in December 1916. However, men had to remove one of the engines to lighten the ship enough to lift into the air, so DN-1 did not make its first flight until Lt. Cmdr. Frank R. McCrary piloted the ship aloft on 20 April 1917, the month that the U.S. entered WWI. The airship completed two additional flights but later received severe damage while being towed over water. Because of its poor performance the Navy removed DN-1 from inventory and broke up the airship. The Navy had developed its first and only floating hangar to accommodate DN-1, and afterward used the structure for the operation of B-class airships during WWI.

7 JULY • Secretary of the Navy Josephus Daniels attempted to mobilize scientific achievement to the modernization of the fleet by writing inventor Thomas A. Edison, stating in part: "One of the imperative needs of the Navy, in my judgment, is machinery and facilities for utilizing the natural inventive genius of Americans to meet the new conditions of warfare." This letter led to the establishment of the Naval Consulting Board, a group of civilian advisors that functioned during the WWI period and included in its organization a "Committee on Aeronautics, including Aero Motors."

10 JULY • Secretary of the Navy Josephus Daniels issued the authorization to outfit a building at Washington Navy Yard, D.C., for testing aeronautic machinery. This marked the beginning of the Aeronautical Engine Laboratory.

10 JULY • After a test of a sextant equipped with a pendulum-type artificial horizon, Lt. Cmdr. Henry C. Mustin, the

439969

Lt. Cmdr. Henry C. Mustin makes the first catapult launch from a ship, flying AB-2 from *North Carolina* (Armored Cruiser No. 12) at Pensacola, Fla., 5 November 1915.

commanding officer of Naval Aeronautic Station Pensacola, Fla., reported that while the pendulum principle was basically unsatisfactory for aircraft use, a sextant incorporating a gyroscopically stabilized artificial horizon might be acceptable.

10 JULY • A standard organization prescribed by General Order No. 153 became the first to provide for an aeronautic force within the Naval Militia. Its composition, paralleling that of other forces established at the same time, consisted of sections not to exceed 6 officers and 28 enlisted men, with two sections forming a division. Officers served in the "aeronautics duty only" category, with the highest rank provided as lieutenant commander at the division level. The enlisted structure provided that men taken in under regular rates of machinist mates and electricians were to perform duties as aeronautic machinists; carpenter mates were to perform duties as aeronautic mechanics; and landsmen (equivalent to later strikers) were to perform special duties.

22 JULY • Based on recommendations received from the Naval Aeronautic Station, Pensacola, Fla., the Director of Naval Aeronautics established requirements for 13 instruments to be installed in service aeroplanes: air speed meter, altitude barometer, binoculars, clock, compass, course and distance indicator, fuel gauge, incidence indicator, magazine camera, oil gauge, sextant, skidding and sideslip indicator, and tachometer. All except the binoculars, camera, clock, and navigational instruments were also required for school aeroplanes.

5 AUGUST • Lt.j.g. Patrick N. L. Bellinger flew AH-10 while spotting mortar fire for Army shore batteries at Fort Monroe, Va. Bellinger signaled his spots with Very pistol flares.

11 AUGUST • The Naval Observatory requested the Eastman Kodak Co. to develop an aerial camera with high-speed lens, suitable for photography at 1,000 to 2,000 yards altitude, and so constructed that the pressure of the air during flight would not distort the focus.

Ens. Wadleigh Capehart holds a sample bomb from the cockpit of a Burgess-Dunne plane.

416327

12 OCTOBER • A directive was issued establishing an Officer in Charge of Naval Aeronautics under the Chief of Naval Operations and giving authority for aviation programs in the Navy to CNO and to the bureaus. Although this had the effect of abolishing the Office of the Director of Naval Aeronautics, that office continued to exist until the incumbent director detached on 4 March 1916.

15 OCTOBER • Secretary of the Navy Josephus Daniels referred to the General Board a proposal, made by Director of Naval Aeronautics Capt. Mark L. Bristol, to convert a merchant ship to operate aircraft. Daniels commented that the fleet had a more immediate need to determine how they could operate *North Carolina* (Armored Cruiser No. 12), which had already been fitted to carry aeroplanes.

5 NOVEMBER • Lt. Cmdr. Henry C. Mustin made the first catapult launch from a commissioned warship, launching in flying boat AB-2 from the stern of *North Carolina* (Armored Cruiser No. 12) at 1158 in Pensacola Bay, Fla. Sailors had originally removed the catapult from a coal barge, and on 28 October installed the device onto the cruiser's stern. Assistant Naval Constructor Lt. Holden C. Richardson, CC, and Lt.j.g. Patrick N. L. Bellinger completed an additional takeoff on 6 November, and 1st Lt. Alfred A. Cunningham, USMC, completed the first Marine Corps launch on 8 November.

3 DECEMBER • Lt. j.g. Richard C. Saufley set a U.S. altitude record for hydroaeroplanes in AH-14 at 11,975 feet over Pensacola, Fla., surpassing the pilot's own record of 11,056 feet, which he had set only three days before. The Aero Club of America awarded Saufley its Medal of Merit for "twice breaking the American Hydroaeroplane altitude record in one year."

1916

6 JANUARY • Instruction commenced at Pensacola, Fla., for the first group of enlisted men to receive flight training.

11 JANUARY • The Naval Observatory forwarded two magnetic compasses to Pensacola, Fla., for tests under all conditions. These compasses, modified from the British Creigh-Osborne design on the basis of recommendations by naval aviators, provided a model for the compasses widely used in naval aircraft during WWI.

21 JANUARY • In a step that led to the establishment of an aviation radio laboratory at Pensacola, Fla., the Officer in Charge of Naval Aeronautics requested the Superintendent, Radio Service authorize the radio operators at the Pensacola Radio Station to experiment with aircraft radio. Simultaneously, men at Pensacola received four sets of radio apparatus for aeroplanes. Although initiation of developmental work did not begin immediately, by late July an officer and a civilian radio expert had been detailed to aircraft radio experimentation at Pensacola, and the Bureau of Steam Engineering had ordered approximately 50 aircraft radio sets.

10 FEBRUARY • The Bureau of Construction and Repair implemented a Navy Department decision, directing that designation numbers were to be assigned to all aircraft under construction, and that these numbers were to be used for identification purposes until the aircraft were tested or placed in service, at which time standard designations provided by the order of 27 March 1914 were to be used. The service simultaneously assigned numbers to 33 aircraft, beginning with 51-A, introducing the system of serial numbers hereafter assigned to all aircraft.

4 MARCH • Capt. Mark L. Bristol detached as Director of Naval Aeronautics and both the title and the office ceased to exist. Bristol received orders to command *North Carolina* (Armored Cruiser No. 12) and, under a new title of Commander of the Air Service, assumed operational supervision over all aircraft and aeronautic stations, as well as the further development of aviation in the Navy. Lt. Clarence K. Bronson assumed the remaining aviation duties in the Office of Chief of Naval Operations.

7 MARCH • During an exhibition flight at Mobile, Ala., a wind gust struck the hydroaeroplane AH-10 at an altitude of 75 feet, causing it to crash into the schooner *Melba*, at anchor in the Mobile River. The pilot, Lt. Edward O. McDonnell, survived because the vessel's rigging checked his fall. AH-10 was demolished and *Melba* sustained damage to her rigging and stays, but the plane was subsequently rebuilt.

25 MARCH • General Order No. 198 defined qualifications for officers and enlisted men in the Aeronautic Force of the Naval Militia in addition to those prescribed for the same ranks and ratings of the Naval Militia. These extras were cumulative for ranks in ascending order. Ensigns were required to have knowledge of navigation (except nautical astronomy) and scouting problems, practical and theoretical knowledge of airplanes and motors, and ability to fly at least one type of aircraft. Lieutenants (junior grade) were to have some knowledge of nautical astronomy and principles of airplane design, and to qualify for a Navy pilot certificate. Additional requirements for lieutenants called for a greater knowledge of nautical astronomy and ability to fly at least two types of naval aircraft, while those for lieutenant commanders, the highest rank provided for the force, included knowledge of Navy business methods used in aeronautics. Enlisted aviation mechanics were to have knowledge of aircraft maintenance; aviation machinists, a similar knowledge of motors.

29 MARCH • Lt. Richard C. Saufley bettered his own U.S. altitude record, piloting a Curtiss hydroaeroplane to 16,010 feet at Pensacola, Fla. On 2 April Saufley again extended the record by attaining a mark of 16,072 feet.

30 MARCH • Secretary of the Treasury William G. McAdoo informed Secretary of the Navy Josephus Daniels that Coast Guard officers 2d Lt. Charles E. Sugden and 3rd Lt. Elmer F. Stone had been assigned to flight instruction at Pensacola, Fla., in accordance with an agreement between the two departments.

15 APRIL • A Bureau of Construction and Repair drawing prescribed an anchor and a two-digit numeral, both in dark blue on a white background, as "Distinguishing Marks for Naval Aeroplanes." The anchor and numeral were painted outboard on the upper and lower wing surfaces; the anchor was generally placed on the vertical tail surfaces; and the numeral, fore and aft on both sides of the fuselage.

13 MAY • Chief of Naval Operations Adm. William S. Benson requested appropriate bureaus to undertake development of gyroscopic attachments for instruments and equipment, including base lines, bombsights (forerunners of turn and bank indicators), and compasses.

20 MAY • The Navy initiated development of a gyroscopically operated bomb-dropping sight and allocated $750 to the Bureau of Ordnance, for use in placing an order with the Sperry Gyroscope Co.

22 MAY • The Naval Observatory sent a color camera, made by the Hess-Ives Corp., to Naval Aeronautic Station Pensacola, Fla., to determine if color photography would be of value in aeronautic work.

3 JUNE • Formal instruction in free and captive balloons began at Pensacola, Fla., when Secretary of the Navy Josephus Daniels approved a course proposed by Lt. Cmdr. Frank R. McCrary, and directed that the curriculum was to be added to the Bureau of Navigation Circular "Courses of Instruction and Required Qualifications of Personnel for the Air Service of the Navy."

9 JUNE • During an endurance flight over Santa Rosa Island off Pensacola, Fla., Lt. Richard C. Saufley crashed in AH-9 from a height of about 700 feet, killing him. The aircraft had been in the air for 8 hours 52 minutes. Investigators attributed the loss to a structural defect in the plane's tail surfaces. The destroyer *Saufley* (DD 465) and Saufley Field at NAS Pensacola were named in his honor.

20 JUNE • The issuance of General Order No. 222, superseding that of 23 June 1913, defined the cognizance for aeronautics in the Navy Department. In addition to extending the subject from "Naval Aeroplanes" to "Aeronautics," this order embraced lighter-than-air and certain heavier-than-air components that had not been provided for in the earlier order.

12 JULY • Lt. Godfrey deC. Chevalier was catapulted from *North Carolina* (Armored Cruiser No. 12) in flying boat AB-3 in Pensacola Bay, Fla. The launch completed calibration of the first catapult designed for shipboard use. *North Carolina* became the first U.S. Navy ship equipped to carry and operate aircraft.

The novel Gallaudet 59-A; note the propeller mounted in the fuselage aft of the wings.

17 JULY • Civilian pilot David H. McCulloch made the first flight of the Gallaudet 59-A, a novel airplane with the propeller mounted in the fuselage aft of the wings, at Norwich, Conn. Navy Inspector Lt. j.g. George D. Murray witnessed the event. On 11 September Commander of the Air Service Capt. Mark L. Bristol, in command of *North Carolina* (Armored Cruiser No. 12), requested that 59-A be assigned to the cruiser. Despite substantial tests which showed the aircraft failed to meet contract requirements, a trial board recommended on 29 January 1917 that the Navy accept it into inventory. The service struck the machine on 21 July 1919.

18 JULY • Secretary of the Navy Josephus Daniels established flight clothing allowances. Aviators were to be furnished helmets, goggles, and safety jackets. Enlisted men whose duties involved flying were also to receive wool head covers, suits, gauntlets, and boots.

22 JULY • Serious interest in the development of light metal alloys for aeronautical use led Chief Constructor Rear Adm. David W. Taylor to request that the Aluminum Company of America develop a suitable alloy for use in fabricating Zeppelin-type girders. German successes in operating Zeppelins with a hitherto unknown aluminum alloy (later revealed as duralumin) prompted the Navy's interest.

8 AUGUST • The Secretary of the Navy clarified the place of aviation in the departmental organization by redefining the responsibilities of bureaus and offices for specific elements of the naval aviation program. While the new directive followed the division of cognizance over material established by a general order on 20 June 1916, it went further in that it assigned the General Board responsibility for advising as to the numbers and general characteristics of aircraft, and in effect made the Bureau of Construction and Repair a lead bureau for aircraft development and procurement.

10 AUGUST • Negotiation for the first aircraft production contract began with a telegram to Glenn H. Curtiss requesting him to "call at the Bureau [of Construction and Repair] Monday with a proposition to supply at the earliest date practicable thirty school hydro aeroplanes." Specified characteristics included two seats, loading of about 4 pounds per square foot, and power loading of about 20 pounds per horsepower. The telegram concluded, "Speed, climb and details of construction to be proposed by you. Rate of delivery is important and must be guaranteed." The telegram resulted in a contract for 30 N-9 seaplanes, which the company delivered between November 1916 and February 1917. The N-9 became a popular training aircraft during WWI.

12 AUGUST • Secretary of the Navy Josephus Daniels agreed with Secretary of War Newton D. Baker that the Navy and War departments should adopt the straight Deperdussin system of controlling aircraft in flight as the standard system for use in all of their aircraft. The French aviation firm Societé de Production Armand Deperdussin's system—comprising a central control stick to manipulate aircraft elevators and ailerons, with pedals or a rudder bar to control the vertical rudder—had proven its reliability during testing.

17 AUGUST • The Secretary of the Navy approved a reorganization of the Naval Aeronautic Station, Pensacola, Fla., which reassigned the training of commissioned and enlisted sailors for aeronautic services with the fleet as a primary mission, and ordered the establishment of an aeronautics school and departments for experimental test and inspection, manufacturing, medical, public works, and supply.

29 AUGUST • The Naval Appropriation Act for fiscal year 1917 provided for the establishment of a Naval Flying Corps composed of 150 officers and 350 enlisted men in addition to those provided by law for other branches of the Navy. It also provided for the establishment of a Naval Reserve force of six classes, including a Naval Reserve Flying Corps composed of officers and enlisted men transferring from the Naval Flying Corps, surplus graduates of aeronautics schools, and members of the Naval Reserve Force with experience in aviation.

9 SEPTEMBER • The Secretary of the Navy issued an order initiating formal flight testing as a basis for accepting new aircraft and establishing procedures to determine whether operational aircraft were safe to fly.

12 SEPTEMBER • Lt. Theodore S. Wilkinson of the Bureau of Ordnance witnessed a demonstration of a piloted hydroaeroplane equipped with automatic stabilization and direction gear developed by the Sperry Gyroscope Co. and electrical engineer Peter C. Hewitt at Amityville, Long Island, N.Y. Wilkinson reported: "The automatic control of the aeroplane is adequate and excellent. The machine left the water without difficulty, climbed to its desired height, maintained this altitude until the end of the run, when it dived sharply; and, unless controlled by the aviator, would have dived to the earth." This is one of the first recorded instances of the Navy's development of what became guided missiles.

20 SEPTEMBER • The Navy issued the earliest extant instruction regarding the color of naval aircraft. This instruction canceled the use of slate color and provided that the wings, body, and pontoon of Curtiss N-9 aircraft were to be finished with opaque yellow (or greenish-yellow) varnish.

11 OCTOBER • Secretary of War Newton D. Baker recommended to Secretary of the Navy Josephus Daniels that a joint Army-Navy board be appointed to consider the requirements for developing a lighter-than-air service in the Army or Navy or both. The secretary's concurrence set the stage for the establishment of an agency for interservice cooperation in aeronautics, subsequently named the Aeronautical Board, which served until 1948.

24 OCTOBER • The Bureau of Steam Engineering requested that the Navy Yard in Philadelphia, Pa., was to undertake the development of a radio direction finder for use on aeroplanes, and specified that the apparatus was to be as light as possible and use wavelengths of 600 to 4,000 meters.

27 OCTOBER • Chief of Naval Operations Adm. William S. Benson directed that all aircraft loaned or donated to the Naval Militia by private individuals or organizations were to

Pioneer naval photographer W. L. Richardson, left, and pilot E. F. Johnson.

be designated NMAH and be given numbers in sequence beginning with one.

8 NOVEMBER • During an experimental bomb test flight at Naval Proving Ground, Indian Head, Md., a bomb exploded about three feet below an N-9 seaplane, killing pilot Lt. Clarence K. Bronson (Naval Aviator No. 15) and Lt. Luther Welsh. The explosion tore the tail off, and the seaplane plummeted into the Potomac River.

17 NOVEMBER • Efforts to develop high-speed seaplanes for catapulting from ships led Chief Constructor Rear Adm. David W. Taylor to solicit suitable designs from manufacturers. The requirements included a speed range of 50 to 95 miles per hour, a 2½-hour endurance, and provisions for radio.

18 NOVEMBER • Lighter-than-air tests were completed on board *Nevada* (Battleship No. 36) and *Oklahoma* (Battleship No. 37) that demonstrated that kite balloons potentially provided an added advantage for battleships in gunfire spotting and scouting/reconnaissance. However, additional tests on board *Oklahoma* during succeeding days revealed problems, namely that balloons carrying hydrogen posed an increased hazard; it took time to inflate them, and they leaked; they became easy targets for antiaircraft gunners at ranges under 12,000 yards; and if kept inflated and moored to ships, balloons restricted vessels' maneuverability. *Oklahoma*'s commanding officer, Capt. Roger Welles, reported that if they were to correct these problems balloons would become valuable to battleship operations, but he neglected to note that whenever men raised balloons for scouting or spotting the fall of shot, the craft also revealed the surface ships' positions. Meanwhile, Lt. j.g. Robert R. Paunack (Naval Aviator No. 27) was also assigned to lighter-than-air training on board *Nevada* during this period, and was designated as the first lighter-than-air pilot the following November.

72-CN-6423

A model of 82-A, the first airplane designed and built by the Navy, undergoes a wind tunnel test.

7 DECEMBER • Lt. Cmdr. Henry C. Mustin reported that an Eastman Aero camera, tested at altitudes of 600 to 5,100 feet over Naval Aeronautic Station Pensacola, Fla., was the best camera tested up to that time, and produced photographs satisfactory for military purposes.

12 DECEMBER • Capt. Mark L. Bristol detached as Commander of the Air Service, and the functions of the command but not the title were transferred to Rear Adm. Albert Gleaves, Commander Destroyer Force, Atlantic Fleet.

13 DECEMBER • The Navy modified specifications for a training dirigible—which Chief of Naval Operations Adm. William S. Benson had originally ordered in October 1916—to require a top speed of 45 miles per hour; a 12-hour endurance at 35 miles per hour; a crew of three; a radio range of 150 miles; and the capability of landing at sea and for being towed.

30 DECEMBER • The Commission on Navy Yards and Naval Stations, which had been authorized by the Naval Act of 29 August 1916 to select new sites for the expansion of Navy yards and for submarine and air bases along the coastlines of the United States, submitted its preliminary report to Congress. For aviation the commission reported that "the present development of aeronautical machines . . . and the practical experience so far obtained in the utilization of such machines to meet the tactical and strategical requirements of the Fleet and the defense of the coast, is such as to preclude the determination at this time of any extensive system of aviation bases." The commission—commonly referred to as the Helm Board after senior member Rear Adm. James M. Helm—recommended that a joint Army-Navy board decide upon locations for use by both services.

CHAPTER 2

Test of Strength

1917–1919

A small group of pioneer Navy and Marine Corps aviators nurtured the early growth of naval aviation, but the program emerged from these early trials too poorly equipped to wage war. When the call came on 6 April 1917, the U.S. Fleet counted only one operating air station, 48 available aviators and students, and 54 aircraft on hand. Naval aviation expanded remarkably during the 19 months between the U.S. declaration of war with Germany and the Armistice. Air stations sprang up on both sides of the Atlantic. Officers established training programs at new air stations, on university campuses, and with private industry. The Naval Reserve Flying Corps produced thousands of aviators, ground officers, mechanics, and technical specialists. Aircraft of many types entered production, and Liberty aircraft engines advanced from concept to mass production and operation.

Naval aviation achieved a good wartime record despite the chaos generated by the speed and breadth of its expansion. One detachment became the first from the United States to reach France. Naval aircraft flew more than three million nautical miles and attacked and damaged 12 German submarines. By war's end Navy and Marine Corps squadrons had organized the Northern Bombing Group, which prepared a round-the-clock air campaign that was to have led toward the first strictly American air offensive of the war. When the fighting ended, Navy and Marine Corps aviators were flying from 27 stations in Europe, two in Canada, one in the Panama Canal Zone, one in the Azores islands, and 12 in the United States.

Naval aviation's outstanding technical product of the war arguably became long-distance flying boats. Although the designs progressed through HS-1s and H-16s to British Felixstowe F-5s, which the Americans converted into F-5Ls by installing superb Liberty engines, all of these aircraft types traced their ancestry to the earlier work of the designer and pilot Glenn H. Curtiss. The Curtiss NC-type flying boats secured a place in aviation history in 1919 as the first aircraft to fly across the Atlantic. Flying boats evolved into impressive weapons, and many naval aviators urged the Navy to adopt them as the major means of taking airpower to sea. Other pilots held the opinion that aircraft should fly from warships of the fleet, and enthusiasts of lighter-than-air craft pointed to airship successes in the war and urged development of their specialty. Planners could not ignore the logic of these claims and the usefulness of these aeronautic types, and the 1920s witnessed development in lighter-than-air, flying boat, and shipboard design and operations. The sentiment in favor of aircraft carriers also gained currency, and in 1919 the Navy decided to convert a collier to a carrier. This decision represented a modest beginning for a program that occupied the attention of a host of shipbuilders, aircraft designers, and naval tacticians for years following World War I.

1917

6 JANUARY • A committee of Army and Navy officers recommended to Secretary of the Navy Josephus Daniels and Secretary of War Newton D. Baker the design and construction of an airship of the Zeppelin type under the direction of the Chief Constructor of the Navy, with funds provided equally by the Army and Navy. The committee also recommended the creation of a board of three Army and three Navy officers to ensure effective interservice cooperation in prosecution of the work. The secretaries approved the recommendation, which led to the appointment of the Joint Army and Navy Airship Board.

8 JANUARY • A Benet-Mercie machine gun installed in a flexible mount in the AH-10 hydroaeroplane performed satisfactorily during firing tests at altitudes of 100 and 200 feet above Pensacola, Fla.

1312

A Burgess-built Curtiss N-9H seaplane with a Hispano-Suiza engine used for training.

10 JANUARY • The Navy initiated its first production order for aerial photographic equipment when the Naval Observatory issued requisitions for 20 aero cameras and accessories for manufacture by the Eastman Kodak Co.

15 JANUARY • *Seattle* (Armored Cruiser No. 11) arrived at Culebra, Puerto Rico, with an aviation detachment and aircraft on board for fleet exercises at the Southern Drill Grounds. Her air detachment operated from ship and temporary shore bases, and performed scouting and other missions in conjunction with fleet operations until 23 March.

4 FEBRUARY • Secretary of the Navy Josephus Daniels directed the procurement of 16 B-class nonrigid airships. Two days later the Navy issued specifications to five companies—Connecticut Aircraft Co., Curtiss Aeroplane and Motor Corp., Goodyear Tire & Rubber Co., B. F. Goodrich Co., and U.S. Rubber Co. This quantity proved beyond the capabilities of any one company, and only Connecticut Aircraft had any experience in building airships. On 19 March the Navy awarded contracts for two airships to Connecticut, three to Curtiss, two to Goodrich, and nine to Goodyear. The U.S. Rubber Co. was confined to providing fabric to Connecticut Aircraft.

5 FEBRUARY • Chief of Naval Operations Adm. William S. Benson recommended that eight aeronautic coastal patrol stations be established. The admiral did not mention specific sites but noted that planners were to consider locations "in the vicinity of" Massachusetts Bay; Newport, R.I.; New York Cty; Cape May, N.J.; Hampton Roads, Va.; Key West, Fla.; Galveston, Texas; and the Panama Canal Zone. Seven days later officers began suitability studies in these areas.

10 FEBRUARY • The National Advisory Committee for Aeronautics established a patent subcommittee with Lt. John H. Towers as a member. The necessity for this subcommittee arose from the threat of infringement suits brought by the holders of basic aeronautic patents that caused prohibitive prices for aircraft and general demoralization of the entire industry.

13 FEBRUARY • Capt. Francis T. Evans, USMC, performed the first loop with a seaplane in an N-9 at 3,000 feet over Pensacola, Fla. Evans then forced the craft into a spin and recovered, consequently receiving the Distinguished Flying Cross for this contribution to aviation.

12 MARCH • A committee of Army and Navy officers submitted the first interservice agreement regarding the development of aeronautic resources and aircraft operations. The Secretaries of War and Navy subsequently approved the agreement, which recognized a general division of aeronautical functions along lines traditional to the services but stressed the importance of joint development, organization, and operation.

13 MARCH • The Bureau of Construction and Repair directed that all seaplanes be finished in an opaque yellow color overall.

22 MARCH • A Bureau of Ordnance letter to Chief of Naval Operations Adm. William S. Benson listed machine guns under consideration for naval aviation: Colt, Marlin, and Vickers types for synchronized fire through propellers, and Benet-Mercie, Berther, Colt, Lewis, Marlin, and Vickers for all-round fire for observers.

24 MARCH • The First Yale Unit of 29 men enlisted in the Naval Reserve Flying Force and departed four days later to train at West Palm Beach, Fla. These volunteers became the first of several college groups to join as a unit for war service. Four of the Yale men subsequently attained distinguished positions: F. Trubee Davison became Assistant Secretary for War; Artemus L. Gates, Under Secretary of the Navy and Assistant Secretary of the Navy for Air; David S. Ingalls, Assistant Secretary of the Navy for Air; and Robert A. Lovett, Secretary of Defense. Commander, Naval Forces Operating in European Waters Rear Adm. William S. Sims later paid them tribute, stating, "Whenever the French and English asked us to send a couple of our crack men to reinforce a squadron, I would say, 'Let's get some of the Yale gang.'"

An H-12 twin-engine flying boat, April 1917.

6 APRIL • The United States declared that a state of war existed with the German Empire. The strength of naval aviation (Navy and Marine Corps combined) totaled 54 airplanes, 1 airship, 3 balloons, 1 air station, 48 officers, and 239 enlisted men.

6 APRIL • Following the approval of the recommendation of the Board on Flying Equipment, Secretary of the Navy Josephus Daniels established standard flight clothing for the Naval Flying Service and authorized its issuance as Title B equipage. The clothing consisted of a tan sheepskin long coat, short coat and trousers, moleskin hood, goggles, black leather gloves, soft leather boots, waders, brogans, and life belts.

7 APRIL • President Woodrow Wilson's Executive Order 2587 directed the transfer of the Coast Guard from the Treasury Department to operate as part of the Navy until further orders.

14 APRIL • The Navy's first guided missile effort began when the Naval Consulting Board recommended to the Secretary of the Navy the apportionment of $50,000 to carry on experimental work on aerial torpedoes in the form of automatically controlled aeroplanes or aerial machines carrying high explosives.

19370

The Navy's first airship *DN-1* approaches its floating hangar during flight tests at Pensacola, Fla., April 1917.

20 APRIL • The Navy's first airship *DN-1* made its initial flight at Pensacola, Fla. The airship's performance proved unsatisfactory on several counts, and following two more flights this month the service grounded it and *DN-1* did not return to the air.

26 APRIL • The first dead-load tests on a catapult installed on board *Huntington* (Armored Cruiser No. 5) were performed at Mare Island Navy Yard, Calif. *Huntington* thus prepared for her employment as the Navy's third ship equipped to carry and operate aircraft.

27 APRIL • The Marine Aeronautic Company, Advance Base Force, under Capt. Alfred A. Cunningham, USMC, was established at Marine Barracks, Philadelphia Navy Yard, Pa., with the transfer of men from the Marine Aviation Section at Pensacola, Fla., other Marine Corps commands, and the Marine Corps Reserve Flying Corps to the new organization.

1 MAY • The Bureau of Navigation issued an aviation circular concerning expansion of the training program, calling for assignment of new classes every three months and the establishment of an 18-month-long course to qualify officers as pilots of either seaplanes or airships. The program also provided for training enlisted men as aviation mechanics, and selecting a few men for pilot training and qualification as quartermaster.

4 MAY • The Commandant of the First Naval District received direction to assume control of the Naval Militia station at Squantum, Mass., for use in air training. Also on this day the Navy completed arrangements to take over the Naval Militia station at Bay Shore, N.Y. These were two of several actions taken immediately following the declaration of war to expand the flight training program during the construction of stations of a more permanent nature.

5 MAY • Secretary of War Newton D. Baker agreed to a proposal from the Secretary of the Navy concerning the establishment of a joint board for the purpose of standardizing the design and specifications of aircraft. The board subsequently established was initially called the "Joint Technical Board on Aircraft, Except Zeppelins."

5 MAY • Naval Aeronautic Station Pensacola, Fla., reported on a test firing of a Berthier machine gun made by Hopkins and Allen Arms Co., synchronized to fire through the propeller arc from an R-3 floatplane as it taxied on water and stood on the beach. Draftsman W. M. Fellers designed the synchronizing gear to keep projectiles from striking the propeller.

15 MAY • Secretary of the Navy Josephus Daniels established an order of precedence for work involved in the preparation for war, which placed "aircraft and their equipment" ninth on a list of 20 major fields of material procurement.

16 MAY • A resolution of the Council of National Defense established the Aircraft Production Board as a subsidiary agency to act in an advisory capacity on questions of aircraft production and procurement. Membership included a representative from each service, with Chief Constructor Rear Adm. David W. Taylor representing the Navy.

17 MAY • Secretary of the Navy Josephus Daniels requested the purchase of 50 aircraft machine guns synchronized to fire through the propeller arcs and 50 for all-around fire. The secretary noted that tests had determined that the belt-fed Vickers gun manufactured by the Colt Co. for the Army proved the most suitable for synchronized firing, and the 47-round magazine-fed Lewis gun manufactured by the Savage Arms Co. was best for all-around fire.

17 MAY • Capt. Noble E. Irwin received orders to the Material Branch to relieve Lt. John H. Towers as Officer in Charge of Aviation at the Office of the Chief of Naval Operations. Towers continued to assist Irwin but received additional duty orders to the Bureau of Navigation as Supervisor, Naval Reserve Flying Corps.

17 MAY • To continue experimental work in aerial torpedoes the Navy presented plans to Sperry Co. to furnish six sets of automatic control gear, install five of them in Navy furnished N-9 seaplanes, and provide suitable testing grounds.

17 MAY • The Navy awarded a contract to the Curtiss Exhibition Co. to train 20 men of the Naval Reserve Flying Force as aviators at the company field at Newport News, Va.

18 MAY • Representatives from the Bureau of Standards demonstrated to Army and Navy officers experimental self-sealing fuel tanks consisting of double-walled galvanized iron containing layers of felt, gum rubber, and an Ivory soap-whiting paste.

19 MAY • General Order No. 299 described a distinguishing insignia for all U.S. government aircraft and directed its placement on all naval aircraft. The insignia called for a red disc within a white star on a blue circular field to be displayed on the wings and for red, white, and blue vertical bands on the rudder, with the blue forward.

19 MAY • The Secretary of the Navy directed the placement of the building (bureau) number of each aircraft in figures three inches high at the top of the white vertical band on each side of the rudder. As a result of this order, the practice of assigning numbers to aircraft using the AH prefix was discontinued and the building (bureau) or serial number became the sole means of identifying a particular aircraft.

19 MAY • The Chief of Naval Operations requested that two small seaplanes and one pilot be detailed for duty in connection with radio experimentation at Pensacola, Fla.

19 MAY • The Harvard unit, comprising seven student aviators, with Lt. Henry B. Cecil in charge, reported for flight instruction to the Curtiss Field at Newport News, Va.

23 MAY • The Joint Technical Board on Aircraft, Except Zeppelins, recommended that the initial production program to equip the Navy with the aircraft necessary for war consist of 300 school machines, 200 service seaplanes, 100 speed scouts, and 100 large seaplanes. The board recommended N-9s and R-6s as the most satisfactory for school and service seaplanes, but determined that the scouts and large seaplanes were not sufficiently developed to permit a selection.

28 MAY • *Huntington* (Armored Cruiser No. 5) arrived from Mare Island, Calif., at Pensacola, Fla., where she participated in various aeronautic experiments involving the operation of seaplanes and kite balloons from her deck through 1 August.

29 MAY • The Navy awarded a contract to Goodyear Tire & Rubber Co. of Akron, Ohio, to train 20 men as lighter-than-air pilots.

30 MAY • Airship *B-1* completed an overnight test flight from Chicago, Ill., landing in a meadow ten miles from Akron, Ohio. Goodyear had manufactured *B-1* at Akron and assembled it in Chicago. Goodyear pilot Ralph H. Upson flew the airship on this flight. A crew of three consisting of a pilot, assistant pilot, and engineer manned subsequent B-class airships.

4 JUNE • The Aircraft Production Board and the Joint Technical Board on Aircraft, Except Zeppelins authorized construction of five prototype models of 8- and 12-cylinder Liberty motors. J. G. Vincent of the Packard Motor Car Co. and E. J. Hall of the Hall-Scott Motor Car Co. worked out the design of these engines—based on conservative engineering practices specially adapted to mass production techniques—in a hotel room in Washington, D.C.

5 JUNE • The First Aeronautic Detachment, Lt. Kenneth Whiting commanding, arrived on board the collier *Jupiter* (Fuel Ship No. 3) at Pauillac, France. This marked the deployment of the initial U.S. military command to that country during WWI. When the ship reached a position about 60 miles off the estuary of the Gironde River, lookouts spotted an apparent torpedo pass ahead of the ship and a second wake pass astern, indicating an attack by a German submarine. The detachment comprised 7 officers and 122 enlisted men and included an element on board the collier *Neptune* (Fuel Ship No. 8) that arrived at St. Nazaire three days later. The entire detachment completed offloading by 10 June. The men from *Jupiter* originally billeted on board a French receiving ship at Bordeaux, while those from *Neptune* housed at a French naval air station at Camaret. The French had requested the early deployment of the men to bolster allied morale.

11 JUNE • *Seattle* (Armored Cruiser No. 11) transferred all of her aviation sailors and planes ashore in preparation for convoy duty at the Brooklyn Navy Yard, N.Y. The men left the raised catapult on board but lowered and secured the apparatus to the deck so it would not interfere with normal operations at sea.

13 JUNE • NAS Dunkirk, France, was established as the first U.S. naval air station developed on foreign soil during WWI. The station was disestablished on 1 January 1919.

14 JUNE • The Navy let the first contract for construction of new patrol stations along the Atlantic coast, starting with sites located at Bay Shore, Montauk, and Rockaway on Long Island, N.Y.

17 JUNE • A joint Army-Navy team, called the Bolling Commission after its senior member Maj. Raynal C. Bolling, USA, sailed for Europe to study air developments among the allies and to recommend a policy and program for the American air services. The Navy members were Cmdr. George C. Westervelt and Lt. Warren G. Child. The commission met key allied leaders across England, France, and Italy including Commander-in-Chief, American Expeditionary Forces Gen. John J. Pershing, USA.

20 JUNE • The first R-5 twin-float seaplanes assigned to naval service were received at NAS Pensacola, Fla. R-type aircraft briefly served on cruisers, in flight training, and in a number of early experiments with torpedoes.

22 JUNE • Enlisted men of the First Aeronautic Detachment began preliminary flight training in Caudron landplanes under French instructors at the *Ecole d'Aviation Militaire* (Military Aviation School) at Tours, France. About the same time, 50 men of the detachment began training as mechanics at St. Raphael, France.

22 JUNE • Change No. 11 in uniform regulations became the first to make special provision for aviators. The change provided for a summer service flying uniform of Marine Corps khaki in the same pattern and design as service whites, to be worn when on immediate active duty with aircraft. The order also provided for a working dress uniform made as a coverall from canvas, khaki, or moleskin of the same color as the flying uniform.

28 JUNE • Landsman Thomas W. Barrett of the First Aeronautic Detachment was killed in an airplane crash during training at Tours, France. Barrett thus became the first member of naval aviation to die in that country during WWI.

4 JULY • The first eight-cylinder Liberty motor arrived for testing by the Bureau of Standards in Washington, D.C. The Packard Motor Car Co. had assembled the engine from parts made by manufacturers in various plants from Philadelphia, Pa., to Berkeley, Calif. The design, manufacture, and assembly of the motor required less than six weeks.

7 JULY • Commander First Aeronautic Detachment Lt. Kenneth Whiting cabled Secretary of the Navy Josephus Daniels the results of his negotiations with the French regarding training and establishment of air stations, and requested departmental approval. The French agreed to train the detachment at existing French Army aviation schools (pilots at Tours and mechanics at St. Raphael, both in France). They also agreed to start construction of three patrol stations—Dunkirk, which was established on 13 June; Le Croisic, on an island at the mouth of the Loire River; and St. Trojan, at the mouth of the Gironde River—and a training station at Moutchic near Lake Lancanau, each for U.S. use.

9 JULY • A group of 24 potential naval aviators, Ens. Frederick S. Allen officer in charge, reported to the University of Toronto in Canada for the start of flight training under the British Royal Flying Corps (RFC). The U.S. Army and the RFC arranged for the instruction to include 25 men from the U.S. Navy in a contingent of 100 Americans for which the Canadians agreed to provide flight training.

10 JULY • A plan for training student officers of the Naval Reserve Flying Corps, which circulated for comment within the Navy, proposed a three-part program: a Ground School for indoctrination into the Navy and study of subjects related to aircraft and flight; a Preliminary Flight school for flight training through five to ten hours of solo flights; and a Completing Flight school for advanced flight training and qualification as a naval aviator and a commission as ensign, USNRF. The Navy implemented the plan without a formal directive, establishing the Ground School in late July and later dividing flight training into elementary and advanced courses.

HS flying boats moored at NAS Moutchic, France.

23 JULY • Ground instruction for prospective pilots and for aviation ground officers began at the Massachusetts Institute of Technology, with a class of 43 students comprising the Naval Air Detachment, Lt. Edward H. McKitterick commanding. In this and similar programs later established at the University of Washington, in Seattle and the Dunwoody Institute in Minneapolis, Minn., officers received indoctrination and introduction to the fundamentals of aviation. The Navy subsequently divided this training into elementary and advanced.

26 JULY • The Army and Navy Airship Board endorsed a proposal by the Bureau of Mines for the experimental production of helium and recommended the allotment of $100,000 to construct a small plant for that purpose. Both departments subsequently approved the action, which initiated helium production in the United States.

27 JULY • Public Law 31 of the 65th Congress authorized President Woodrow Wilson to take possession of North Island, San Diego, Calif., for use by the Army and Navy in establishing permanent aviation stations and aviation schools. Lt. Earl W. Spencer arrived on 8 November under orders to establish and command a station for the purpose of training pilots and mechanics and conducting coastal patrols, marking the beginning of what became NAS North Island. Spencer trained these men at Balboa Park on the mainland until they began to move into permanent quarters on the island on 8 June 1918.

27 JULY • Construction of the Naval Aircraft Factory at the Philadelphia Navy Yard, Pa., was authorized for the purposes of constructing aircraft, undertaking aeronautical developments, and providing aircraft construction cost data. Ground was broken for the facility on 10 August.

NH 2493

Women at work at the Naval Aircraft Factory, Philadelphia, Pa.

8 AUGUST • Secretary of the Navy Josephus Daniels approved plans to establish one training and three coastal patrol stations in France. The decision marked the first of several such plans dealing with an overseas base construction program. The plan underwent successive expansion and ultimately provided 27 locations in France, England, Ireland, and Italy, from which naval aviation operated by the close of WWI.

14 AUGUST • An experiment initiated through the efforts of Rear Adm. Bradley A. Fiske and conducted by Lt. Edward O. McDonnell launched a dummy torpedo from beneath a wing of an F-5L flying boat at Huntington Bay, Long Island, N.Y. The weapon struck the water at an unfavorable angle, ricocheted, and nearly struck the plane. The experiment marked the beginning of serious Navy interest in launching torpedoes from aircraft.

15 AUGUST • The Bureau of Construction and Repair authorized the Curtiss Co. to paint the wings of naval aircraft with "English–Khaki–Gray–Enamel," and all aircraft manufacturers to use either opaque yellow or clear varnish on floats and hulls. These variations to the color scheme that had been established the preceding March were followed by so many other exceptions that no standard existed during the next six months. The trend developed to use an opaque yellow finish for school machines and a khaki finish similar to that used on British aircraft for service machines.

16 AUGUST • The initial students of the First Aeronautic Detachment to complete the flight course at Tours, France, transferred to Lake Hourtin, France, for training in Franco–British Aviation flying boats. These students completed training by November when 13 men received orders to Moutchic, France. Some of the other graduates went to St. Raphael, France, 12 of whom also received orders to the Army's training school at Issoudun, France, for instruction in *Chasse* (chase or scout) planes and from there to Scotland for further hours in British machines.

25 AUGUST • Chief Constructor David W. Taylor initiated NC flying boat development in a memo to Naval Constructor Jerome C. Hunsaker that outlined certain general requirements of an airplane needed in war and directed his staff to investigate the subject further. Taylor stated, "The 'United States Liberty Motor' gives good promise of being a success, and if we can push ahead on the airplane end, it seems to me the submarine menace could be abated, even if not destroyed, from the air. The ideal solution would be big flying boats or the equivalent, which would be able to fly across the Atlantic to avoid difficulties of delivery, etc."

25 AUGUST • The 12-cylinder Liberty motor passed a 50-hour test, with a power output of 301 to 320 hp, preliminary to entering mass production.

31 AUGUST • NAS Moutchic, France, was established as a flight and ground training station, Lt. John L. Callan commanding. Meanwhile, NAS Montauk, N.Y., was also established earlier in the month, Lt. Marc A. Mitscher (Naval Aviator No. 33) commanding. The Navy operated Montauk initially as a seaplane patrol station but later expanded the facilities to include lighter-than-air operations. NAS Moutchic was disestablished on 1 January 1919.

4 SEPTEMBER • The technical members of the Bolling Commission submitted a report to the Secretaries of War and Navy following the commission's return from studying air developments in Europe. Their recommendations included assigning air measures precedence over all other air measures against submarines, establishing and operating as many coastal patrol stations in Europe as possible, and obtaining European aircraft for use at those stations until more satisfactory types manufactured in the United States became available.

HS-1L flying boats at NAS Tréguier, France, used to patrol the English Channel for German submarines.

72979

7 SEPTEMBER • An R-6 flying from NAS Pensacola, Fla., sent radio signals to operators at Naval Radio Station New Orleans, La., approximately 140 miles distant. The successful test led to additional orders for 300 Simon radio transmitters.

7 SEPTEMBER • Secretary of the Navy Josephus Daniels approved a change in the uniform regulations which authorized a forestry green winter service flying uniform, of the same design as the summer uniform, for all officers assigned to aviation duty.

7 SEPTEMBER • Secretary of the Navy Josephus Daniels approved a change in the uniform regulations designating a winged foul anchor with the letters "U.S." as the official device to be worn on the left breast by all qualified Navy and Marine Corps aviators. An additional change, approved on 12 October, directed the deletion of the letters "U.S." from the design, establishing the basic form of the device, which is still in use today.

8 SEPTEMBER • NAS Hampton Roads, Va., was established as an air training station and patrol base to conduct experimental work in seaplane operations at Naval Operating Base Hampton Roads, Va. Detachments under training at the Curtiss School at Newport News, Va., and at Squantum, Mass., were transferred to the naval air station the following month.

17 SEPTEMBER • *Huntington* (Armored Cruiser No. 5) passed through European waters during the morning and hoisted observer Lt. j.g. Henry W. Hoyt aloft in a kite balloon. When Hoyt reached about 400 feet, the temperature suddenly dropped, causing the balloon to descend almost 200 feet. As sailors worked to haul the balloon down, a sudden squall slammed the balloon into the water. Hoyt was knocked from the basket and the balloon's rigging entangled him underwater. Shipfitter First Class Patrick McGunigal noted his plight and jumped overboard, clearing the tangle and putting a bowline around Hoyt. Men hauled the observer on deck, and McGunigal subsequently received the Medal of Honor.

17 SEPTEMBER • Secretary of the Navy Josephus Daniels approved the establishment of 15 overseas naval air stations equipped for seaplane missions to be operational by 1 July 1918. Five of these stations were also to support airship and kite balloon operations.

18 SEPTEMBER • The Joint Technical Board on Aircraft, Except Zeppelins, established a production program of 1,700 operational aircraft of the following Curtiss types under consideration: 235 H-16 and 825 HS-1 flying boats and 640 R-6 seaplanes.

26 SEPTEMBER • The Naval Air Detachment at Akron, Ohio, Lt. Louis H. Maxfield commanding, reported the qualification of 11 students, including Maxfield, as lighter-than-air pilots and requested their designation as Naval Aviator (Dirigible). These men became the first to accomplish training specifically as dirigible pilots and subsequently received naval aviator numbers ranging from 94 to 104.

27 SEPTEMBER • Ens. Robert A. Lovett, USNRF, made the first flight in a Franco–British Aviation flying boat, BuNo A-295, at NAS Moutchic, France. Lovett had also directed the assembly of the aircraft and subsequently became the fourth Secretary of Defense.

6 OCTOBER • Secretary of War Newton D. Baker authorized the Navy to use a part of the Army landing field at Anacostia, D.C., to erect and maintain a seaplane hangar. The terms of use were laid out in a revocable license beginning on 1 November and ending within six months of the war's conclusion, and with the understanding that the Army was to have use of the Navy area at any time.

6 OCTOBER • NAS Cape May, N.J., was established as a seaplane and lighter-than-air patrol station. The First Marine Aeronautic Company trained here from 14 October until its departure for the Azores on 9 January 1918.

11 OCTOBER • *North Carolina* (Armored Cruiser No. 12) completed the removal of her catapult, aircraft, and all aeronautics gear at the Brooklyn Navy Yard, N.Y.

13 OCTOBER • *Huntington* (Armored Cruiser No. 5) transferred her aeronautic equipment ashore at New York City, N.Y., marking the end of the operational test of aircraft on board three warships, which had started with *North Carolina* (Armored Cruiser No. 12) in 1916.

14 OCTOBER • The Marine Aeronautic Company at Philadelphia, Pa., was divided into the First Aviation Squadron composed of 24 officers and 237 men, and the First Marine Aeronautic Company composed of 10 officers and 93 men. On the same day the First Marine Aeronautic Company transferred for training in seaplanes and flying boats to NAS Cape May, N.J., and three days later the First Aviation Squadron transferred for training in landplanes to the Army field at Mineola on Long Island, N.Y.

21 OCTOBER • An HS-1 made the first successful Navy flight test of a 12-cylinder Liberty engine at Buffalo, N.Y. The flying boat climbed 4,000 feet in ten minutes and attained a speed of 95 mph at 1,680 rpm using the No. 3 experimental engine. This flight and other successful demonstrations led to the adoption of both the engine and the airplane as standard service types. The engine subsequently received the designation L-12.

22 OCTOBER • The Ground School program at the Massachusetts Institute of Technology expanded to include special courses to train men as inspectors, with 14 students enrolled. The program was eventually established as an inspector school and met the expanding need for qualified inspectors of aeronautical material by producing 58 motor and 114 airplane inspectors before the end of the war.

24 OCTOBER • U.S. Naval Aviation Forces, Foreign Service, which had evolved from the First Aeronautic Detachment, became operational when Capt. Hutch I. Cone relieved Lt. Cmdr. Kenneth Whiting of command over all naval aviation forces abroad.

24 OCTOBER • Routine instruction in flight and ground courses began at NAS Moutchic, France.

2 NOVEMBER • Twelve men organized as the Second Yale Unit who undertook flight training at their own expense at Buffalo, N.Y., received commissions as ensigns, USNRF. The pilots soon thereafter received their designations as naval aviators.

5 NOVEMBER • To coordinate the aviation program Officer in Charge of Aviation Capt. Noble E. Irwin requested that representatives of bureaus having cognizance over some phase of the program meet each week to discuss and expedite all matters pertaining to aviation.

9 NOVEMBER • The Argentinean government granted permission to use as instructors in the ground school at Pensacola, Fla., three Argentine naval officers who had recently qualified as U.S. naval aviators—Lt. Ricardo Fitzsimmon Jr., Lt. Carlos F. Pichon Jr., and Lt. Marco A. Zar.

10 NOVEMBER • A Navy "flying bomb" manufactured by the Curtiss Co. arrived for testing at the Sperry Flying Field at Copiague on Long Island, N.Y. Designers intended the flying bomb (also called an aerial torpedo) for automatic operation carrying 1,000 pounds of explosive, with a range of 50 miles and a top speed of 90 mph. In addition to this specially designed aircraft, N-9s received conversions for automatic operations as flying bombs that closely resembled subsequent guided missiles.

14 NOVEMBER • Secretary of War Newton D. Baker approved a recommendation "that priority be given by the War Department to naval needs for aviation material necessary to equip and arm seaplane bases." This was a major step toward the expansion of the Navy's aircraft production.

15 NOVEMBER • The National Advisory Committee for Aeronautics' Subcommittee on Standardization and Investigation of Material established a committee to intensify efforts to develop light metal alloys for aeronautical use. The members included Naval Constructor Jerome C. Hunsaker.

18 NOVEMBER • Naval aviation began aerial coastal patrols in European waters from Le Croisic, France. Lt. j.g. Reginald C. Coombe and Ens. Henry H. Landon of the First Yale Unit piloted a pair of Tellier flying boats on a two hour familiarization flight. The aircraft were unarmed because they had not received ordnance. A consignment of bombs reached Le Croisic two days later, enabling the station's planes to stand ready to fly combat patrols.

21 NOVEMBER • Chief Signal Officer Maj. Gen. George O. Squier, USA, witnessed a demonstration of the N-9 flying bomb at Amityville, Long Island, N.Y. The Army subsequently established a parallel aerial torpedo project.

22 NOVEMBER • Pilot Ens. Kenneth R. Smith, USNRF (Naval Aviator No. 87), and crewmembers Electrician Homer M. Wilkinson and Machinist's Mate Second Class T. J. Brady flew Seaplane No. 87, a Tellier flying boat, from Le

651988

The Curtiss "flying bomb" is the predecessor of today's guided missiles.

Croisic, France, to investigate reports of up to four German submarines that had been spotted south of Belle-Île. This was the first armed patrol by a U.S. naval aviator in European waters. The aircraft's motor died, forcing Smith to make a "tail to wind" landing in rough water. Two days later, a French destroyer rescued the survivors minutes before the damaged plane sank about 25 miles southeast of Rochebonne.

22 NOVEMBER • Commander, U.S. Naval Aviation Forces, Foreign Service Capt. Hutch I. Cone reported to Commander, U.S. Naval Forces Operating in European Waters Vice Adm. William S. Sims that they had allotted for 16 seaplanes, 20 officers, and 183 men at each of 15 planned stations ashore. Six of these stations were under consideration for development in the United Kingdom and nine in France. Lighter-than-air allotments included four airships and a complement of 15 officers and 198 men each at three stations in France, and 6 kite balloons, 13 officers, and 60 men each at three stations in the United Kingdom (Ireland). The school at NAS Moutchic required 9 officers, 150 men, and a repair and assembly base. The program also needed a further store depot and receiving barracks to be established at NAS Pauillac, France, and 75 officers and men in Paris and at the headquarters in London for a total of 870 officers and 8,454 men.

24 NOVEMBER • Chief of Naval Operations Adm. William S. Benson issued a report regarding the development of aircraft torpedoes and torpedo planes, in which he pointed

The two-seat Curtiss Model F, at Pensacola, Fla., in 1918, was the standard Navy flying boat trainer.

out that available aircraft could carry no more than a 600-pound ordnance load, and were thus incapable of delivering a torpedo with an explosive charge large enough to seriously damage large, modern warships. These concerns hindered torpedo plane development in WWI and beyond.

27 NOVEMBER • NAS Le Croisic, France, was established, Lt. William M. Corry commanding. It was disestablished on 28 January 1919.

1 DECEMBER • NAS Pauillac, France, was established as an assembly and repair station supporting naval air stations in France. It was disestablished on 15 February 1919.

5 DECEMBER • The secretaries of the War and Navy departments established a policy regarding helicopter development on the basis of recommendations made by the Joint Technical Board on Aircraft, Except Zeppelins. The members recognized the need for improvements in power plants and propellers in order to successfully obtain a helicopter, but limited support of development efforts to moral encouragement of potential vendors until they demonstrated a helicopter of military value.

7 DECEMBER • The Navy initiated fighter aircraft development with the Secretary of the Navy's authorization for the Curtiss HA type, subsequently known as the "Dunkirk Fighter." Planners intended the aircraft to function in the escort and air superiority role over the French coast from Calais to Dunkirk. Dual synchronized machine guns forward and dual flexible machine guns in the rear cockpit equipped the two-man, single-pontoon seaplane.

7 DECEMBER • Naval Aeronautic Station Pensacola, Fla., was redesignated Naval Air Station (NAS) Pensacola.

15 DECEMBER • The Marine Aeronautic Detachment, Capt. Roy S. Geiger, USMC, commanding, activated at Marine Barracks, Philadelphia Navy Yard, Pa.

18 DECEMBER • NAS Key West, Fla., was established chiefly as an elementary flight training station and as a base for limited patrol operations.

22 DECEMBER • The start of classes with a single student enrolled marked the addition of an Aerography School in the training program at the Massachusetts Institute of Technology. The school carried out a major portion of the new instruction program at the Blue Hill Observatory at Harvard University, Mass., but held some classes at the Aerographic Laboratory on the MIT campus. Fifty-four men qualified as aerologists by the end of the war.

31 DECEMBER • The First Aviation Squadron of the Marine Corps, Capt. William M. McIlvain, USMC (Naval Aviator No. 12), commanding, transferred from Mineola, N.Y., to Gerstner Field, Lake Charles, La., for advanced training in landplanes.

1918

JANUARY • NAS Chatham, Mass., Lt. Edward H. McKitterick commanding, was established.

JANUARY • During the New Year a detachment of about 12 American volunteer chase pilots from Escadrille (squadron) N124 of the French Aéronautique Militaire (Army Air Service), popularly known as the Escadrille Lafayette, offered their services to naval aviation. Several of the men had seen action over the lines and officers recognized the value of their experience for pursuit operations at Dunkirk. Following their release from French service the men enrolled as ensigns and traveled to NAS Moutchic, France, for training in seaplanes.

1 JANUARY • The Experimental and Test Department at Pensacola, Fla., transferred to NAS Hampton Roads, Va., to overcome difficulties arising from the Florida location's remoteness from the principal manufacturing and industrial areas.

18 JANUARY • During a nighttime raid the Germans bombed the French air station adjacent to NAS Dunkirk, France. Four bombs destroyed seven French HD-2 seaplane fighters and a large wooden hangar. Another four bombs landed between NAS Dunkirk and Chantier de France, the nearest of which knocked out windows and cut several holes in the storehouse and pay office. About 50 men from NAS Dunkirk helped the French fight fires, and the Americans subsequently loaned their allies four HD-2s for temporary use. The Germans struck again on the night of 21 January and a small bomb tore out the end of the mess hall. At about 0100 the Germans fired a 15-inch gun, and during the battle several ships steaming offshore opened fire. At least six large caliber and several smaller rounds impacted within the perimeter of the station but failed to inflict casualties. Enemy aircraft returned three nights later, and a bomb shattered the windows of the commanding officer's office. The Germans frequently bombed the area during the succeeding days but did not inflict significant damage. This was the first instance of enemy aerial bombardment of naval aviation facilities on record.

19 JANUARY • NAS Anacostia, D.C., was established to provide a base for short test flights, as well as housing and repair services for seaplanes on test flights from NAS Hampton Roads, Va., and the Army station at Langley Field, Va., and to display new seaplanes for study.

22 JANUARY • The 12 officers and 133 enlisted men of the First Marine Aeronautic Company, Capt. Francis T. Evans, USMC, commanding, disembarked from the transport *Hancock* escorted by *Beale* (Destroyer No. 40) and *Terry* (Destroyer No. 25) at Naval Base 13 at Ponta Delgada in the Azores. Commander Azores Detachment Rear Adm. Herbert O. Dunn also arrived on board the ship and six days later hoisted his flag aloft. This marked the arrival of the first trained and equipped American aviation command to be deployed overseas during WWI. The Marines subsequently flew antisubmarine patrols over convoy lanes in the Azores area with two N-9s and ten R-6s, later reinforced by six HS-2Ls.

25 JANUARY • Supervisor, Naval Reserve Flying Corps requested that the director of Harvard University's Blue Hill Observatory, Dr. Alexander G. McAdie, be enrolled as a lieutenant commander in the Naval Reserve, and that he be assigned to the Chief of Naval Operations Aviation Office to create a Naval Aerological Organization.

3 FEBRUARY • Aerial gunnery training for prospective naval aviators and enlisted men began under British Royal Flying Corps instructors at the Army's field at Camp Taliaferro near Fort Worth, Texas.

3 FEBRUARY • Work began on a lighter-than-air station for airships at Gujan southwest of Bordeaux, France. The station never became operational because of frequent delays resulting from material transportation difficulties and the necessity of using the men there for other work. The Navy returned the facility to the French on 15 January 1919.

4 FEBRUARY • NAS Fromentine, France, was established. Aircraft began to fly seaplane patrols from the facility the following July. It was disestablished on 28 January 1919.

8 FEBRUARY • General Order No. 364 promulgated a change in national aircraft insignia, which replaced the white star on the outer sections of the wings, above and below, with concentric circles of red and blue around white, and reversed the order of the red, white, and blue vertical bands on the rudder, placing the red nearest the rudder post.

10 FEBRUARY • The Marine Aeronautic Detachment, Capt. Roy S. Geiger, USMC, commanding, transferred to operate water-based aircraft from Marine Barracks, Philadelphia Navy Yard, Pa., to NAS Miami, Fla. The detachment consequently moved to nearby Marine Flying Field, Miami.

13 FEBRUARY • Lt. Grattan C. Dichman took command of the U.S. air station at Brest, France, which served as a base for seaplane and kite balloon operations, and as an assembly plant for aircraft shipped overseas. This began what became NAS Brest, which was disestablished on 15 February 1919.

15 FEBRUARY • Two H-12s—one with pilot Ens. Albert D. Sturtevant, copilot British Flight Lt. C. C. Purdy, and crewmembers S. J. Holeridge and A. H. Stevenson, and the other with a South African pilot named Faux and copilot British Flight Lt. C. W. Bailey—departed the British station at Felixstowe, England, to escort a convoy to Dutch waters. At least five German W.29 fighter floatplanes, Oberleutnant Friedrich Christiansen commanding, attacked the two aircraft. Faux managed to escape, but the Germans shot down Sturtevant. British and German eyewitnesses reported that the Americans continued to fire as they fell. Sturtevant posthumously received the Navy Cross for this action and for previous patrols over the North Sea, and became the first U.S. naval aviator to fall in battle with enemy forces.

16 FEBRUARY • A German submarine appeared off L'Aber Vrach, France, in view of men ashore but departed without incident. French islanders told the Americans that prior to the arrival of the naval aviation detachment, German submarines often shelled sailing craft or power boats at sea just off the coast.

21 FEBRUARY • The Italian and United States flags rose simultaneously over the establishment of NAS Bolsena, Italy, Ens. William B. Atwater commanding. The first of two air stations opened in that country during WWI, Bolsena operated primarily as a flying school. U.S. naval aviation operations in Italy consisted of training American pilots on Italian machines, conducting bombing raids on Austro-Hungarian targets including the naval fortress at Pola, and flying as chase pilots with Italian planes that contended the Habsburg advance in autumn 1918. Plans for the establishment of several additional stations in Italy were cancelled following the Armistice, and NAS Bolsena was disestablished on 2 January 1919.

22 FEBRUARY • Officer in Charge of Aviation Capt. Noble E. Irwin asked the Director of Naval Communications to provide wireless transmitting and receiving equipment to permit pilots on patrol to communicate with the naval air stations at Cape May, N.J.; Chatham, Mass.; Montauk and Rockaway, N.Y.; Key West, Fla.; San Diego, Calif.; and Coco Solo, Panama Canal Zone. The following May officers expanded this request to cover all naval air stations.

22 FEBRUARY • NAS Queenstown, Ireland, was established, Lt. Cmdr. Paul J. Peyton commanding. The facility served as the assembly and repair station for all naval air stations in Ireland. Aircraft began to fly patrols from Queenstown on 30 September. NAS Queenstown was disestablished on 10 April 1919.

26 FEBRUARY • Recognizing the importance of data on weather phenomena in the upper atmosphere to flight operations, and acting largely on the recommendations of Lt. Cmdr. Alexander G. McAdie, formerly of Harvard University's Blue Hill Observatory, Mass., the Chief of Naval Operations established an allowance list of aerographic equipment for air stations abroad.

28 FEBRUARY • President Woodrow Wilson issued Proclamation No. 1432, effective in 30 days but published in General Order No. 407 of 8 July. This order prohibited private flying over the United States, as well as its territorial waters and possessions, without a special license issued by the Joint Army and Navy Board on Aeronautic Cognizance.

1 MARCH • NAS Paimboeuf, France, was established as the Americans assumed control of the airship station there, Lt. Cmdr. Louis H. Maxfield commanding. Several U.S. naval aviators had served with the French at Paimboeuf since November 1917. Prior to the Armistice the U.S. Navy obtained 12 airships from the French, but the station at Paimboeuf was the only airship facility that became operational before war's end. NAS Paimboeuf was disestablished on 26 January 1919.

6 MARCH • The Bureau of Navigation established instrument allowances for naval aircraft, allotting a compass, two altimeters, and a clock for service in seaplanes and flying boats; a compass, altimeter, clock, and statoscope for airships and free balloons; and an altimeter and clock for kite balloons and training planes.

6 MARCH • A falling-weight type catapult launched an unmanned flying-bomb type plane that flew 1,000 yards at the Sperry Flying Field at Copiague on Long Island, N.Y.

7 MARCH • Wartime expansion drove the establishment of the Office of the Director of Naval Aviation in the Office of the Chief of Naval Operations and the expansion of the Aviation Section into a division.

9 MARCH • The Navy initiated a revised training program for naval aviators (seaplanes), which provided that following a period of general training, all student aviators were to specialize in one of three general types of seaplanes—fighting scouts, light fast bombing, and patrol. In addition, the change divided the program into elementary, advanced, and advanced specialization courses and designated the stations at which the respective courses were to be given.

11 MARCH • Work began on an airship station at Guipavas near Brest, France, Lt. J. F. Maloney commanding. Planners originally scheduled the station for establishment on 15 November and it consequently failed to open prior to the Armistice. The Americans returned the facility to the French on 13 January 1919.

14 MARCH • NAS Ile Tudy, France, was established, 1st Lt. Charles E. Sugden, USCG, commanding. NAS Ile Tudy was disestablished on 25 January 1919.

15 MARCH • The Bureau of Construction and Repair directed that all new naval aircraft be painted in low-visibility naval gray enamel.

17 MARCH • Twenty-two kite balloon pilots arrived at Liverpool, England, and received orders to British Royal Naval Air Station Roehampton to commence instruction. Upon graduation the men detached to kite balloon stations in Britain and France. Ten additional kite balloon pilots arrived in May 1918 for duty in France.

19 MARCH • As combat operations underlined the need for aviation intelligence officers Commander, U.S. Naval Aviation Forces, Foreign Service Capt. Hutch I. Cone distributed a circular letter to his subordinate commands defining the duties and functions performed by such officers at British Royal Navy air stations, with the suggestion that provisions for similar services be made at naval air stations "as may seem expedient." Supplementary letters clarified the duties and functions, and on 31 October it was specifically stated that aviation intelligence officers be specially trained for this work.

19 MARCH • A formation of flying boats flew a long-range reconnaissance mission over the Heligoland Bight off the German coast. German seaplanes attacked the planes, and pilot Ens. Stephan Potter, USNRF (Naval Aviator No. 130), shot down one of the attackers to receive credit as the first U.S. naval aviator to shoot down an enemy seaplane, an exploit for which he also received the Navy Cross. Potter had trained with the Second Yale Unit at the Curtiss plant at Buffalo, N.Y.

NAH 2121

The first H-16 flying boat built at the Naval Aircraft Factory, Philadelphia, Pa., leaves the assembly building.

21 MARCH • Thousands of German guns opened fire on the allied lines to begin Operation Michael, the first of a series of German offensives along the Western Front in France, and allied leaders feared an enemy drive on Paris. The French began to move some government offices and industrial facilities from the vicinity of the capital to other areas of the country, including arrangements for sections of the headquarters of U.S. naval aviation in France to relocate to NAS Pauillac.

21 MARCH • Curtiss test pilot Roland Rohlfs and observer Capt. Bernard L. Smith, USMC, made the first flight of the prototype HA seaplane, or "Dunkirk Fighter," BuNo A-2278, at Port Washington on Long Island, N.Y. During the fighter's second flight on 15 April the aircraft capsized and was heavily damaged. A fire destroyed the plane on 7 August.

25 MARCH • Ens. John F. McNamara made the first attack on an enemy submarine by a U.S. naval aviator during a flight from British Royal Naval Air Station Portland, England. Commander, U.S. Naval Forces Operating in European Waters Vice Adm. William S. Sims reported the attack as "apparently successful," and Secretary of the Navy Josephus Daniels commended McNamara for his "valiant and earnest efforts." McNamara received the Navy Cross for his services during the war, though the citation did not specifically mention this battle.

27 MARCH • The first aircraft built at the Naval Aircraft Factory at Philadelphia, Pa., an H-16, BuNo A-1049, made its first flight. Navy H-16s, equipped with two 230-pound bombs and five Lewis machine guns, conducted antisubmarine patrols from U.S. and European stations during WWI.

30 MARCH • Commander, U.S. Naval Forces Operating in European Waters Vice Adm. William S. Sims sent a message to Navy forces in France to prepare to reinforce the allies to "the utmost of our capacity" to contain the German breakthrough on the Western Front. Commander, U.S. Naval Aviation Forces, Foreign Service Capt. Hutch I. Cone cabled air stations in France to determine the availability of men for "transport and other auxiliary work," not including those qualified or in training. Cone directed a temporary halt to construction on these stations, which provided an estimated 2,070 men and several hundred machine guns. After the Germans overextended their supply lines and allied reinforcements stabilized the front, on 3 April the French declined the offer of the men and rescinded their orders, but directed the retention of these reinforcements to stand ready for deployment within a "fortnight."

30 MARCH • The Navy ordered an 18-T (Kirkham) triplane fighter from Curtiss Engineering Corp. The principal armament of this single-engine, two-seater landplane consisted of two synchronized and two flexible machine guns.

31 MARCH • The First Aviation Squadron transferred from Gerstner Field at Lake Charles, La., to Marine Flying Field, Miami, Fla.

APRIL • NAS La Trinité, France, which had been in operation since November 1917, was established, Ens. Charles M. Johnson commanding. Located in the fishing village of La Trinité-sur-Mer about four miles from Carnac on the Bay of Morbihan, the facility had been selected with a view to relay kite balloons for convoys between Brest and La Pallice while ships entered Quiberon Bay. Due to later modifications in the convoy system, however, the base never achieved this function. NAS La Trinité was disestablished on 5 February 1919.

10 APRIL • A training school for female apprentices began at the Naval Aircraft Factory at Philadelphia, Pa.

The first Curtiss-built 18T Kirkham fighter, shown in its 1919 18T-2 guise with extended wings, set records for both speed and altitude.

15 APRIL • The First Marine Aviation Force, Capt. Alfred A. Cunningham, USMC, commanding, was formed with men of the First Aviation Squadron and the Aeronautic Detachment, USMC, at Marine Flying Field, Miami, Fla. The latter two commands had disbanded the day before. A headquarters company and four squadrons, designated A, B, C, and D, were organized within this force on 16 June. These squadrons later deployed to France and operated as the Day Wing of the Northern Bombing Group, where they subsequently received the designations of 7 through 10. These squadrons normally comprised an authorized strength of 18 planes each.

16 APRIL • The first detachment of trained aerologists consisting of 9 officers and 15 enlisted men, Lt. Cmdr. Alexander G. McAdie commanding, departed to naval air stations in Europe.

17 APRIL • Lt. William F. Reed Jr. reported for "aerographical" duty at NAS Pensacola, Fla., marking the first such assignment made to a U.S. naval air station.

17 APRIL • NAS Berehaven, United Kingdom (Ireland) was established. The station was disestablished on 12 February 1919.

22 APRIL • Pilot QM1 R. H. Harrell with observer QM2 H. W. Studer and pilot Ens. Kenneth R. Smith with observer O. E. Williams flew two planes on a patrol from NAS Ile Tudy, France. Both aircraft bombed and damaged a U-boat stalking a convoy of about 20 ships escorted by the Americans off the coast of France. The second plane dropped two bombs and then flew to *Stewart* (Destroyer No. 13) and directed her to attack. The French

426915

Naval planes, including two Curtiss F-boats (foreground), on the beach at Pensacola, Fla., May 1918.

antisubmarine gunboat *Ardente* joined the battle. *Ardente* attempted to ram the boat, but her action compelled *Stewart* to turn away from her depth charge run at the last moment. The destroyer dropped three depth charges, and wreckage, bits of sea growth, and oil floated to the surface. Smith received the Navy Cross for this exploit. The French credited Smith and Williams for probably sinking the boat and awarded Smith their *Croix de Guerre* and also bestowed upon the pilot the Legion of Honor, rank of *Chevalier*.

23 APRIL • The first shipment of Liberty engines to naval aviation commands in France arrived at the assembly and repair station at NAS Pauillac.

25 APRIL • Ens. Stephan Potter, USNRF, and Capt. N. A. Magor, Royal Air Force, flew an Felixstowe F.2A—an improved British variant of an H-12—Side No. 8677, as one of two flying boats on a patrol from Felixstowe, England. German Oberleutnant Friedrich Christiansen led a flight of five single-seat planes and a pair of two-seaters that attacked the patrol about six miles west-southwest of North Hinder Light. Christiansen shot the F.2A's stern gunner, and his gunner fired a burst that ignited a fire on board the flying boat. Potter attempted to climb, but he was too low to turn into the wind and crashed. Potter, Magor, and two crewmen died in Christiansen's fifth (claimed) victory.

25 APRIL • The airship *Capitaine Caussin* suffered an accident during a patrol from NAS Paimboeuf, France. A gas valve, which had failed to close after valving, caused the airship to lose pressure and dive into the sea from several hundred feet. The impact threw two crewmembers into the water; Lt. Cmdr. Louis H. Maxfield and Lt. Frederick P. Culbert jumped from the airship and aided them until rescuers recovered all the swimmers. Ens. Merrill P. Delano and French Commandant Leroy guided *Capitaine Caussin* while it drifted to the beach where the crew then dismantled the airship. Maxfield received a gold life saving medal, and he and Culbert each received French life saving medals.

27 APRIL • The airship *AT-1*, Lt. Frederick P. Culbert commanding, and manned by a crew comprising Ens. Arthur D. Brewer, Ens. Merrill P. Delano, and Ens. Thomas E. McCracken, completed a 25-hour, 43-minute flight from NAS Paimboeuf, France. During the patrol the airship escorted three convoys through a mined zone. This was the longest flight on record for an airship of this type.

29 APRIL • The British transferred the Royal Air Force kite balloon station at Berehaven in the United Kingdom (Ireland) to the Americans, who immediately established NAS Berehaven, Ens. Carl E. Shumway commanding.

30 APRIL • Secretary of the Navy Josephus Daniels approved a plan recommended by the General Board and developed by Naval Forces in Europe for the Northern Bombing Group to undertake air operations in the Dunkirk–Bruges–Ostend–Zeebrugge region against German submarines and their support facilities, and directed that the bureaus and offices expedite the assembly of the necessary men and equipment.

2 MAY • NAS Wexford in the United Kingdom (Ireland) was established. The station was disestablished on 15 February 1919.

6 MAY • NAS Coco Solo, Panama Canal Zone, was established, Lt. Ralph G. Pennoyer commanding, to maintain patrols over the seaward approaches to the Panama Canal.

15 MAY • The Bureau of Steam Engineering reported that a Marconi SE 1100 radio transmitter designed for use on H-16s had demonstrated dependability in voice communications at distances of up to 50 nautical miles, and in code communications at up to 120 nautical miles. This became one of the first radio sets used in, and the first tube set developed for, naval aircraft.

18 MAY • The Chief of Naval Operations set training goals to provide pilots for foreign service and directed that eight elementary training squadrons be operated—two at Bay Shore, N.Y., two at Key West, Fla., and four at Miami, Fla. He also directed that elementary training at Pensacola, Fla., be discontinued as soon as the students on board had graduated, and that six advanced training squadrons be organized there to begin training patrol plane and night bomber pilots as soon as practicable.

20 MAY • Work began on a naval air station at La Pallice, France, Lt. j.g. John H. Dashiell commanding. The station never formally established, and the Americans returned the facility to the French on 5 January 1919.

24 MAY • The first consignment of American-built HS-1 flying boats, consisting of six planes (BuNos A-808 through A-813) on board the transport *Houston* and two planes (BuNos A-1575 and A-1583) on board the cargo ship *Lake Placid* arrived at NAS Pauillac, France.

4 JUNE • NAS L'Aber Vrach, France, was established, Lt. Cmdr. Henry B. Cecil commanding. NAS L'Aber Vrach was disestablished on 22 January 1919.

8 JUNE • NAS Arcachon, located southwest of Bordeaux, France, was established, Ens. Joseph N. Brown, USNRF, acting commanding officer until relieved by Lt. Zeno W. Wicks on 15 June. NAS Arcachon was disestablished on 7 January 1919.

13 JUNE • Pilot Lt. Charles P. Mason and passengers Cmdr. James B. Patton and Lt. William B. Jameson, USNRF, made the first flight of the initial American-built aircraft to be assembled in France, an HS-1, at NAS Pauillac.

19 JUNE • Sailors at NAS Pensacola, Fla., began taking upper atmospheric weather soundings to provide information on wind velocity and direction required for navigational training flights. The station's Meteorological Officer, Lt. William F. Reed Jr., developed a technique to carry recording instruments aloft in a kite balloon, gradually refining his method to take six soundings a day at an altitude of 1,000 feet.

29 JUNE • Two Levy-Le Pen HB-2s became the first aircraft to operate from St. Trojan, France, when they arrived from NAS Le Croisic.

1053765

The last of the six rotary-engine Thomas-Morse S-5s purchased by the Navy.

30 JUNE • The first Navy pilots of the Night Wing, Northern Bombing Group, to take special training with the British marked the completion of their course by participating as observers in a night bombing raid by No. 214 Squadron of the British Royal Air Force.

1 JULY • An act of Congress repealed all laws relating to the National Naval Volunteers and authorized President Woodrow Wilson to transfer as a class all of its members in their confirmed ranks and ratings to the Naval Reserve, Naval Reserve Flying Corps, or Marine Corps Reserve.

1 JULY • NAS Lough Foyle, United Kingdom (Ireland), was established, Cmdr. Henry D. Cooke commanding. NAS Lough Foyle was disestablished on 22 February 1919.

4 JULY • NAS Whiddy Island was established as a small seaplane station on the western end of the Irish island located in Bantry Bay in the United Kingdom. This was to be the westernmost air station established in Europe during the war. Patrol planes from the island met Atlantic convoys as they approached the British Isles. NAS Whiddy Island was disestablished on 29 January 1919.

4 JULY • A detachment of 12 kite balloons and 42 men arrived at NAS Berehaven in the United Kingdom (Ireland). The detachment initially operated from the adjoining French kite balloon station at Lannion, which marked the beginning of extensive lighter-than-air operations in Europe.

7 JULY • The Naval Aircraft Factory, Philadelphia, Pa., completed its first order for 50 H-16s.

14 JULY • NAS St. Trojan, France, was established, Lt. Virgil C. Griffin commanding. NAS St. Trojan was disestablished on 19 January 1919.

19 JULY • During a patrol in an H-12 from Killingholme, England, pilot Ens. John J. Schieffelin and crewmembers Lt. j.g. Roger W. Cutler, USNRF, E3 Taggert, and LMM Bernstein sighted a surfaced U-boat east of Whitby. The plane dropped a bomb that burst 20 feet to port of the submarine's waist, thrusting the boat's bow downward and lifting her stern until the screws almost broke the surface. The plane had encountered turbulence en route, forcing it to jettison a bomb. After signaling the U-boat's position to a trawler, the plane departed the area. British ships including destroyer *Garry*, subsequently depth charged *UB-110* about 15 miles from that position and forced her to surface, and *Garry* rammed and sank the boat. Interviews with the survivors revealed they failed to submerge because of damage sustained during a previous attack, but Schieffelin surmised that *UB-110* was a different boat than the one he had bombed because of the distance between the two positions. For this battle and an action on 9 July Schieffelin later received the Navy Cross.

19 JULY • The German submarine *U-156* sank *San Diego* (Armored Cruiser No. 6) off Fire Island, Long Island. Two planes on patrol from NAS Montauk, N.Y., sighted the stricken cruiser and sent the first reports of her sinking. Two days later *U-156* slipped through fog and attacked the tug *Perth Amboy* of the Lehigh Valley Railroad as she towed the barges *Lansford* and *Nos. 403, 740,* and *766* three miles off Nauset Beach, Cape Cod, Mass. German shooting started fires on board the tug that burned her to the waterline, sank three of the barges, and wounded three men. At 1050 on 21 July two planes took off from NAS Chatham, Mass., to intercept the submarine—an HS-2L, A-1695, with pilot Ens. Eric A. A. Lingard and crewmembers Ens. Edward M. Shields and MMC Edward H. Howard; and R-6, A-991, with pilot 1st Lt. Philip B. Eaton, USCG (Coast Guard Aviator No. 6). They bombed but missed the submarine. German gunfire drove the aircraft to higher altitudes, and then *U-156* submerged and escaped. Eyewitnesses dubbed the action "The Battle of Chatham."

20 JULY • NAS Killingholme, England, Lt. Cmdr. Kenneth Whiting commanding, was established when the British

1053803

HS flying boats at NAS Brest, France.

turned their Royal Air Force station over to the Americans. U.S. Navy aircraft had patrolled from the station since February 1918. NAS Killingholme was disestablished on 6 January 1919.

23 JULY • NAS Eastleigh, England, was established at the British Royal Air Force facility at that location on the English Channel, Lt. Cmdr. Godfrey deC. Chevalier commanding. The facility served as a supply, assembly, and repair station to support the Northern Bombing Group. NAS Eastleigh was disestablished on 10 April 1919.

24 JULY • NAS Porto Corsini, Italy, was placed in operating status, Lt. Wallis B. Haviland commanding. The Austro-Hungarians learned of the event and bombed the station that night but failed to inflict serious damage. NAS Porto Corsini was disestablished on 31 December 1918.

25 JULY • Secretary of War Newton D. Baker approved a recommendation by the Joint Army and Navy Airship Board assigning responsibility for the development of rigid airships to the Navy.

27 JULY • N-l, the first experimental aircraft designed and built at the Naval Aircraft Factory, Philadelphia, Pa., made its fourth successful flight and first test of the Davis gun for which it was designed. Lt. Victor Vernon piloted N-1, and Lt. Sheppard operated the gun, which performed satisfactorily against a target moored in the Delaware River near the factory.

30 JULY • One hundred seven officers and 654 enlisted men of Headquarters Company and Squadrons A, B, and C of the First Marine Aviation Force arrived on board transport *DeKalb* at Brest, France. They proceeded to aerodromes between Calais and Dunkirk for operations as the Day Wing, Northern Bombing Group. Part of their equipment, including some planes, arrived separately at NAS Pauillac. The squadrons were subsequently redesignated Squadron Nos. 7, 8, and 9, respectively.

2 AUGUST • The first Marines of the Northern Bombing Group arrived at the front. The Marines requested permission from the British to operate with the Royal Air Force (RAF) to maintain proficiency, and the British accepted their service and assigned them to missions. The Marines subsequently flew with Nos. 217 and 218 (bombing) Squadrons of the RAF, and with French Aéronautique Militaire (Army Air Service) bombing and observation squadrons.

3 AUGUST • Pilot QM1 C. J. Boylan and observer QM2 L. W. Wintsch flew a Donnet-Denhaut flying boat from NAS Ile Tudy, France, in response to a U-boat sighting. At 1640 the plane spotted an apparent periscope almost immediately disappear and then a large spot of oil. The aircraft detected converging wakes approaching the surface and dropped two bombs, which caused more oil, bubbles, and debris to appear. French trawlers also fired at the (possible) submarine and sighted a long trail of oil. Meanwhile, two seaplanes, one piloted by Ens. Morris H. Bailey, USNRF, with observer E2 G. Wolff, and the other by Boatswain L. T. O'Loughlin, USNRF, with observer MM1 R. Haizlett, arrived several minutes later and each dropped two bombs that caused more oil and bubbles to rise. The planes circled the position, spotted additional wreckage, and departed.

5 AUGUST • Pilot Ens. Ashton W. Hawkins and second pilot Lt. j.g. George F. Lawrence took off in a flying boat from NAS Killingholme, England, in rain and poor visibility at 2230 to patrol a course intercepting a reported German Zeppelin raid. The plane patrolled in good weather above the clouds without sighting the Germans but dropped through heavy weather at South Shields at 0530, having almost consumed its fuel to complete the first U.S. night combat patrol from Killingholme.

10 AUGUST • NAS Pauillac, France, received 300 pigeons from the French. During WWI naval aviation used homing pigeons as an additional means of sending and receiving messages. Observers on board aircraft and airships "liberated" the birds by throwing them upward and clear of the craft, in some cases from altitudes of 1,500 to 2,000 feet. French trainers experienced in handling the birds cared for the creatures until 21 August when trainers from the American Racing Pigeon Union, National Aeronautic Association, and International Federation of American Homing Pigeon Fanciers arrived from the United States. At least one French trainer each then remained at the headquarters in Paris and at Pauillac to facilitate operations. The French officially transferred the pigeons to the U.S. handlers beginning on 12 October 1918.

11 AUGUST • Pilot Ens. James B. Taylor made the initial flight of the M-2 Kitten landplane at Mineola on Long Island, N.Y. This aircraft had originally been intended for use on board ship and did not prove successful, but is of special interest because it was the first monoplane developed under Navy contract. It was also one of the smallest manned aircraft built for the Navy, with an empty weight of less than 300 pounds. Although equipped with a British ABC engine, the aircraft was designed for use with a two-cylinder Lawrance 30 hp air-cooled engine that became the predecessor of the large American air-cooled radial engines.

13 AUGUST • During a patrol from NAS Dunkirk, France, pilot Ens. Julian F. Carson sighted a surfaced U-boat. The Germans challenged the plane and opened fire with their deck gun, hitting the aircraft in several places with fragments. Carson returned fire and bombed the submarine as it attempted to submerge, which drove the boat back to the surface at a sharp angle. The U-boat stayed there briefly and then slid stern first underwater. The French credited Carson with sinking the craft and awarded him the Croix de Guerre.

13 AUGUST • Ens. Frank E. Wade received the designation of Naval Aviator No. 1,000 at NAS Pensacola, Fla. Because of fractional numbers assigned to men who had preceded him, however, he was not the actual 1,000th naval aviator.

15 AUGUST • The independent offensive operations of the Northern Bombing Group began as pilot Ens. Leslie R. Taber, second pilot Ens. Charles Fahy, and rear gunner D. C.

Hale of Squadron 1 participated in a night raid in a Ca-44 on the German submarine repair docks at Ostend, Belgium.

17 AUGUST • The blimp *AT-1* made a brief flight from NAS Paimboeuf, France, carrying Assistant Secretary of the Navy Franklin D. Roosevelt as a passenger during his tour of overseas facilities.

19 AUGUST • NAS Halifax, Nova Scotia, was placed in operating status, Lt. Richard E. Byrd Jr. commanding. The facility was the first of two air stations established in Canada, and located near Eastern Passage at Dartmouth, Nova Scotia, to dispatch patrols over the northern approaches to the Atlantic coast.

19 AUGUST • The 18-T Kirkham experimental triplane fighter achieved speeds of 161, 162, and 158 mph in trial runs over a measured course. Naval Constructors Holden C. Richardson, CC, and Charles N. Liqued observed the trials.

20 AUGUST • While preparing to depart NAS St. Trojan, France, for a patrol, Ens. Edmund B. Barry, USNRF (Naval Aviator No. 421), died when his seaplane exploded on the slipway because of defective bomb-carrying gear. The blast also killed seven other men—QM2 Miles H. Holley and E3 Earl J. Vath died immediately, and CMM Ellsworth W. Stoker, MM1 Jessee C. Richardson, and QM2s Leonard L. Kneeland, John J. McVeigh, and Lewis F. Tucker died during the succeeding days. Sixteen other men received injuries. This was the station's only fatal accident during WWI.

21 AUGUST • At 1120 a flight of five Macchi M-5 single-seat fighters and two M-8 two-seat bombers from NAS Porto Corsini, Italy, dropped leaflets on the Austro-Hungarian fortress of Pola on the Adriatic Sea. Enemy guns fired at the incoming aircraft, and five fighters and two seaplanes rose to intercept the Americans, shooting down pilot Ens. George H. Ludlow (Naval Aviator No. 342) in an M-5 three miles from the harbor entrance and damaging a fighter flown by Ens. Charles H. Hammann, USNRF (Naval Aviator No. 1494). Hammann evaded his pursuers, landed alongside the downed pilot, took him on board, and returned to Porto Corsini. Hammann later received the Medal of Honor. The Navy subsequently named two ships in his honor.

1053768

An HS-2L flying boat powered by a Liberty engine.

27 AUGUST • Following almost a year's operation, NAS Hampton Roads, Va., was established, Lt. Cmdr. Patrick N. L. Bellinger commanding.

31 AUGUST • NAS North Sydney was established as a seaplane station on Cape Breton Island, Nova Scotia, 1st Lt. Robert Donahue, USCG, commanding.

1 SEPTEMBER • Commander, U.S. Naval Aviation Forces, Foreign Service Capt. Hutch I. Cone detached to head the aviation section of the staff of Commander, U.S. Naval Forces Operating in European Waters Adm. William S. Sims in London, England. Cone had supervised the construction and operation of air stations in France. All naval forces deployed in France, with the exception of the Northern Bombing Group, Capt. David C. Hanrahan commanding, were placed under the command of Rear Adm. Henry B. Wilson. Capt. Thomas T. Craven of the admiral's staff relieved Cone. Unit commands were set up for France, England, Ireland, Italy, and the Northern Bombing Group to control and direct the operations of stations in these areas.

3 SEPTEMBER • Aircraft began the first naval air operations from NAS Lough Foyle in the United Kingdom (Ireland) with patrols over the North Channel entrance to the Irish Sea.

1053766

The Davis recoilless antisubmarine gun mounted on a flying boat.

7 SEPTEMBER • The first U.S. day-bombing plane arrived at the front in France—a DH-4 designated D-1, BuNo A-3295.

23 SEPTEMBER • The flywheel catapult, a forerunner of those subsequently installed on board *Lexington* (CV 2) and *Saratoga* (CV 3), launched a flying bomb from Copiague on Long Island, N.Y. The Sperry Co. developed this catapult in connection with the Bureau of Ordnance's flying bomb project.

23 SEPTEMBER • The Aircraft Radio School at Pensacola, Fla., began a course of instruction for aircraft radio electricians that included code work, semaphore and blinker study, gunnery, and laboratory work. In November the school transferred to Harvard University, Mass.

24 SEPTEMBER • While on a test flight in a Sopwith Camel, Lt. j.g. David S. Ingalls, USNRF (Naval Aviator No. 85), sighted a German two-seat Rumpler over Nieuport, Belgium. In company with another Camel, Ingalls attacked and scored his fifth aerial victory in six weeks to become the Navy's first ace. Ingalls also shot down at least one enemy observation balloon while serving with No. 213 Squadron of the British Royal Air Force. For these and other meritorious acts the British awarded Ingalls the Distinguished Flying Cross, and the United States conferred upon him the Distinguished Service Medal. "He is one of the finest men," the British evaluated his service, "No. 213 Squadron ever had."

25 SEPTEMBER • Pilots Ens. John A. Jova and ACMM Francis E. Ormsbee Jr., during a flight in two planes observed a two-seat plane go into a tailspin and crash about three-quarters of a mile away in Pensacola Bay, Fla. Ormsbee landed his plane nearby, dove overboard, and swam for the wreck as the stricken aircraft sank. He pulled out the gunner and held his head above water until other men arrived in a speedboat, then made repeated dives into the tangled wreckage in an unsuccessful attempt to rescue the pilot. Ormsbee later received the Medal of Honor.

25 SEPTEMBER • NAS Whiddy Island in the United Kingdom (Ireland) became operational.

27 SEPTEMBER • Pilot Ens. Edwin S. Pou, USNRF, with observer QM2 H. F. Duffy, and pilot QM2 P. H. Tuttle with observer QM1 Otis Wherley flew two seaplanes during a patrol over a northbound convoy from NAS Ile Tudy, France. Pou and Duffy spotted three trawlers firing on a suspected mine about four miles south of Point de Penmarc'h. As the trawlers departed, the aviators sighted a "dark spot" four miles distant and dropped two bombs and a smoke bomb on the suspected U-boat. Their attack generated a "violent explosion" that brought oil to the surface, the force of which shook the aircraft. The seaplanes dropped a message buoy to the leading trawler and departed.

28 SEPTEMBER • Pilot Lt. Everett R. Brewer, USMC, and observer Sgt. Harry Wershiner, USMC, flying a plane with No. 218 Squadron of the British Royal Air Force, shot down a German Fokker aircraft to score the first Marine Corps victory in aerial combat.

30 SEPTEMBER • The Goodyear twin-engine airship *C-1*, BuNo A-4118, accomplished its maiden flight. The war ended before the Navy introduced all of the C-class lighter-than-air craft originally planned, and only 10 of the 30 airships ordered were built.

1 OCTOBER • NAS La Trinité in France became operational.

1 OCTOBER • The airship *AT-13* (also designated P-4) flew from NAS Paimboeuf, France, and rendezvoused with a convoy sailing from La Pallice to Quiberon. As *AT-13* circled the convoy, the airship approached a suspicious object, which it discovered to be a surfaced U-boat, about ten miles south of the lighthouse of Le Four, France. The Germans opened fire and 13 shrapnel shots rapidly burst near the craft. The airship could not return fire because the firing spring had broken on its solitary 47 mm gun during a second practice shot en route. *AT-13* alerted escort ships to the submarine's presence, came about, and resumed coverage of the convoy.

1 OCTOBER • The French disestablished a naval air station located at Lake Cazaux on the Gironde River about five miles southeast of NAS Arcachon. The Americans at NAS Arcachon agreed to accommodate up to several aircraft from the French station at Bayonne. Two Donnet-Denhaut flying boats arrived that afternoon and later made the first flight operations from NAS Arcachon.

2 OCTOBER • Pilot Capt. Francis P. Mulcahy, USMC, second pilot Capt. Robert S. Lytle, USMC, and crewmembers 2d Lt. Frank Nelms Jr., USMC, Sgt. Archie Paschal, USMC, Sgt. Amil Wiman, USMC, and Cpl. Henry L. Tallman, USMC, flew a plane during the earliest recorded U.S. aerial food-dropping mission. On this day and the next the aircraft made five low-level runs in the face of enemy artillery, machine gun, and rifle fire and delivered 2,600 pounds of food and badly needed supplies to a French regiment surrounded by German troops near Stadenburg, Belgium. Paschal, Wiman, and Tallman threw the food packages overboard. The pilots consequently received the award of the Distinguished Service Medal and the gunners received the Navy Cross. (The precedence of these medals was reversed in 1942.)

4 OCTOBER • Cmdr. Holden C. Richardson, CC, and Lt. David H. McCulloch made the initial flight of the first NC flying boat, NC-1, BuNo A-2291, at NAS Rockaway, N.Y.

5 OCTOBER • Squadron D of the First Marine Aviation Force, comprising 42 officers and 188 enlisted men, arrived at an aerodrome at Le Fresne, France, completing the Day Wing, Northern Bombing Group. Additional planes reinforced the group during the month.

8 OCTOBER • Pilot 2d Lt. Ralph Talbot, USMC, and observer GySgt. Robert G. Robinson, USMC, of Squadron C flew D-1, the first Marine DH-4 received in France, during a raid against German-occupied Westend, Belgium. Nine German scout planes attacked the Marines, but D-1 shot down one of the attackers.

The F-5L was a Naval Aircraft Factory version of the British Felixstowe F.5, which itself was an improved American Curtiss H.12.

10 OCTOBER • German submarine *UB-123* sank the British steamer *Leinster* in the Celtic Sea while the ship sailed from Dublin, Ireland, to Holyhead, Wales. Capt. Hutch I. Cone traveled on board while en route to head the aviation section of the staff of Commander, U.S. Naval Forces Operating in European Waters Adm. William S. Sims in London. Cone was among the casualties but recovered despite his wounds.

14 OCTOBER • Eight DH-4s and DH-9As of Marine Day Squadron 9 made the first day raid-in-force by the Northern Bombing Group, flying against the German-held rail junction at Thielt Rivy, Belgium. Despite mist that obscured their targets the aircraft dropped 17 bombs. At least 11 German aircraft counterattacked. 2d Lt. Ralph Talbot, USMC, with observer GySgt. Robert G. Robinson, USMC, in a DH-4 designated D-1 shot down a German plane, but two other German aircraft attacked and wounded Robinson. Talbot came about and downed a German plane, and landed at a Belgian aerodrome at Hondschoot. For this battle and an earlier raid in which they had engaged enemy aircraft, Talbot and Robinson later received the Medal of Honor.

15 OCTOBER • The Bureau of Steam Engineering reported the construction of five Hart and Eustiss reversible pitch propeller hubs for use on twin-engine airships. The Navy consequently ordered two of these for F-5Ls.

17 OCTOBER • A pilotless N-9 training plane converted to an automatic flying machine launched from Copiague on Long Island, N.Y. The plane flew a prescribed course but failed to land at the preset range of 14,500 yards. Observers last saw the plane over the air station at Bay Shore, flying eastward at an altitude of 4,000 feet.

19 OCTOBER • While flying as part of a convoy escort in the Lough Foyle sector off northern Ireland, Ens. George S. Montgomery Jr. (Naval Aviator No. 300) sighted and bombed a U-boat stalking the convoy. The explosions brought heavy turbulence and oil to the surface. Montgomery received a commendation for "probably damaging" the submarine and preventing the Germans from attacking the convoy.

22 OCTOBER • Maj. Bernard L. Smith, USMC, and crewmembers Lt. Ralph A. D. Preston, USNRF, Lt. j.g. Donald T. Hood, USNRF, Ens. Warner L. Hamlen, USNRF, Ens. Marcus H. Estorly, USNRF, and civilian mechanics M. Roulette and James Royal delivered the airship *C-1* from Akron, Ohio, via Washington, D.C., to NAS Rockaway, N.Y. Smith and Hamlen later received the Aero Club of America's Medal of Merit for this flight.

22 OCTOBER • Pilot Ens. Edwin S. Pou, USNRF, with observer QM2 H. F. Duffy, flew an HS-1 from NAS Ile Tudy, France, to investigate an area in which the Germans had made an attack earlier in the day. The men sighted and exploded a mine by bombing. The French patrol boat *Leger* detected what she believed to be a submarine on listening devices, but the sounds faded following the attack, which led the French to surmise that Pou and Duffy drove off a U-boat.

25 OCTOBER • Pilot 2d Lt. Ralph Talbot, USMC, with observer 2d Lt. Colgate W. Darden Jr., USMC, flew a DH-4

229907

A sea sled used to transport and launch planes, with a Caproni Ca-44 heavy bomber on board, November 1918.

designated D-1 that struck a bank of earth on the edge of an ammunition dump in a field near Le Fresne in France. The aircraft rebounded, crashed into a newly arrived pile of 1,500 bombs, and caught fire. The impact threw Darden clear, but Talbot was trapped in the front cockpit and died. Marines pulled the bombs from the pile and rolled them in the mud until the fire was extinguished. The destroyer *Ralph Talbot* (DD 390) was commissioned in the pilot's honor on 14 October 1937.

26 OCTOBER • Pilot Ens. William C. Sprague, with observer H. A. Ropke, flew a plane on a patrol and sighted an oil wake indicating a possible U-boat about four miles southwest of Point de Penmarc'h, France. Sprague and Ropke dropped two bombs. Four minutes later pilot Ens. Elbert J. Dent and observer Ens. Morris H. Bailey, USNRF, arrived in a second plane and dropped two more bombs on the same position. Pilot Ens. Harold J. Rowen with Bailey again on board as observer, who had returned with Dent and accompanied Rowen, reached the scene in a third aircraft and bombed the same spot. The determined attacks proved ineffective.

1 NOVEMBER • The night flight training program was discontinued at NAS Pensacola, Fla.

1 NOVEMBER • NAS Tréguier, France, was established, Lt. Augustus M. Baldwin commanding. The rise and fall of the tide on the river and the steep incline of the shipway at the former French station necessitated an unusual method of launching flying boats. To prevent planes from immersing nose-first, men put the machines onto a cradle on tracks and then eased the aircraft into the water by a line. NAS Tréguier was disestablished on 19 January 1919.

11 NOVEMBER • The Allied Countries and Central Powers signed an armistice to end WWI. During the 19 months of U.S. participation the total strength of naval aviation comprised 2,107 aircraft, 15 airships, and 215 kite and free balloons on hand, together with 6,716 officers and 30,693 men for the Navy, and 282 officers and 2,180 men for the Marine Corps. About 570 aircraft and 18,000 officers and men had shipped abroad. Naval aircraft had dropped a total of 155,998 pounds of ordnance on the enemy and flown more than three million nautical miles of war patrols. Naval aircraft made at least 39 attacks against U-boats and partially succeeded in driving off submarines during at least ten of these battles. The Marines participated in 43 missions with the British and French, and the Day Wing of the Northern Bombing Group flew 14 independent raids behind the German lines. The naval air arm suffered 208 casualties, including 74 officers. Following the Armistice the Navy cancelled contracts for 1,728 planes. When representatives from the Commission for the Relief of Belgium reported their inability to continue their work without support, sailors and Marines transferred trucks, ambulances, and motorcycles to the charity during early examples of naval aviation humanitarian relief efforts.

12 NOVEMBER • Naval aviation headquarters in France sent a dispatch to all air stations: "Suspend patrol flights. Only flights now authorized are those necessary to look for dangerous mines and harbor flights reduced to strict minimum to test planes and train personnel. Deflate all kite balloons except those judged necessary for mine sweeping. Limit ascensions and trips to mine searching, test of material and training of personnel."

17 NOVEMBER • NAS Hampton Roads, Va., reported that an H-16 equipped with a radio direction finder using the British six-stage amplifier had received signals from a radio station at a distance of 150 miles at Arlington, Va.

22 NOVEMBER • Pilot Lt. Victor Vernon and observer S. T. Williams dropped a 400-pound dummy torpedo from an F-5L from a height of 40 feet during the initial test of a torpedo launching gear at the Naval Aircraft Factory at Philadelphia, Pa. The weapon's development had begun the preceding July.

23 NOVEMBER • Secretary of the Navy Josephus Daniels authorized the use of the titles Aerographic Officer and Navigation Officer in naval air station organization to identify officers trained to perform the special duties involved.

27 NOVEMBER • Flying boat NC-1, BuNo A-2291, established a new world record for people carried in flight by embarking 51 persons during a flight from NAS Rockaway Beach, N.Y.

2 DECEMBER • The Chief of Naval Operations renewed efforts to develop planes to operate from ships by requesting that the Bureau of Construction and Repair provide aircraft of the simplest form, lightly loaded, and with the slowest flying speed possible.

6 DECEMBER • The Marines of the Day Wing of the Northern Bombing Group, minus Squadron 10, embarked on board transport *Mercury* at St. Nazaire, France, for their return to Newport News, Va. Squadron 10 remained behind and sailed separately on 28 December.

8 DECEMBER • Commander, Naval Forces Operating in European Waters Adm. William S. Sims ordered the preparation of two airships with photographers on board to rendezvous with the convoy of ships carrying President Woodrow Wilson and the U.S. delegates to the peace conference at Versailles, France. Planners subsequently added a flight of seaplanes from NAS Brest, France. At dawn on 13 December airships *AT-13* and *Capitaine Caussin* lifted off from Guipavas, France, but severe wind and rain squalls compelled them to steer almost entirely by compass. The airships separately sighted and then escorted the convoy ships despite intermittent fog that afternoon. Sailors began to deflate *Capitaine Caussin* the next day, and it was shipped to the United States in January. On 13 December one H-16, two HS-1s, and four HS-2Ls took off from Brest, but 25 mph winds and a rough sea disrupted their attempts at formation flying. Six of the planes reached and escorted the ships at different times.

12 DECEMBER • Airship Officer Lt. George Crompton Jr. at NAS Rockaway, N.Y., conducted a test to determine the feasibility of carrying fighter aircraft on lighter-than-air craft. Crompton piloted airship *C-1* and lifted 1st Lt. A. W. Redfield, USA, commanding officer of the 52d Aero Squadron at Mineola, in an Army JN-4 Jenny in a wide spiral climb to

2,500 feet over Fort Tilden, N.Y. Crompton then released Redfield from that height, and the Jenny made a free flight back to earth.

24 DECEMBER • Pilot Ens. Thomas E. Maytham completed a flight in a B-class airship from NAS Key West to Tampa, Cape Sable, and Palm Beach, Fla., and back, covering approximately 690 miles. This accomplishment bettered Maytham's endurance mark of 32 hours on 23 November with a continuous flight of 40 hours 26 minutes, ending on 26 December. Although recognized only as a U.S. record, this flight surpassed by more than 25 hours the existing world record.

30 DECEMBER • Pilot Lt. Thomas C. Rodman, USNRF, flew an H-16 to score the Navy's first win in the Curtiss Marine Trophy Race at NAS Pensacola, Fla. Aircraft designer and pilot Glenn H. Curtiss had set up the annual competition in 1915 to encourage seaplane development. The contest standard evaluated the basis of the miles traveled in ten hours of flight, with extra mileage credit for the passenger load. Rodman carried 11 passengers 670 statute miles and received credit for a total of 970 miles.

1919

1 JANUARY • During this period the worldwide influenza epidemic caused more than 50 million deaths. Navy medical facilities treated 121,225 Navy and Marine victims including 4,158 fatalities during 1918. "The morgues were packed almost to the ceiling with bodies stacked one on top of another," Navy Nurse Josie Brown of Naval Hospital, Great Lakes, Ill., recalled. Naval aviation in Europe dispersed following the Armistice, however, and despite proximity to the outbreak and the adverse weather of the northern climate, few men succumbed. Exceptions included an outbreak in September 1918 at NAS St. Trojan, France, that killed one officer and five men and incapacitated 210 men, rendering the station inoperative at times. During the first two months of 1919 a recurrence of the epidemic affected NAS Brest, France, when Marines and sailors of the Northern Bombing Group experienced respiratory exposure during transportation in cold and crowded rail cars en route to that station. Similar outbreaks of lesser concern occurred at other stations. Medical inspectors noted that naval aviation staff predominantly confronted these issues with "skill and good judgment."

24 JANUARY • The Marines at Ponta Delgada, Azores, received orders to abandon their station and return to the United States. On 17 March the men arrived at Marine Flying Field, Miami, Fla.

3 FEBRUARY • Capt. George W. Steele Jr. assumed command of Fleet Air Detachment, Atlantic Fleet, on board *Shawmut* (Minelayer No. 4) at Boston Navy Yard, Mass. The detachment's establishment enabled testing of the capabilities of aviation to operate with fleet forces and marked the beginning of a permanent provision for aviation in fleet organization. All elements of the detachment did not immediately assemble but consisted of *Shawmut* as flagship and aircraft tender (commonly referred to by pilots as the "mother ship"); a squadron of six H-16s, Lt. Cmdr. Bruce G. Leighton commanding; a division of three single-seat scout planes, Lt. Cmdr. Edward O. McDonnell commanding, on board *Texas* (Battleship No. 35); and a division of six kite balloons, Lt. j.g. John G. Paul commanding, assigned to various ships including *Shawmut*.

9 FEBRUARY • The submission of aerological data obtained at various naval air stations to the Weather Bureau for use in coordinated study of weather conditions commenced with a report submitted by NAS Pensacola, Fla.

15 FEBRUARY • The Fleet Air Detachment, Atlantic Fleet, completed assembling at Guantánamo Bay, Cuba. Two days later the detachment began operations by participating in long-range spotting practice. The men gave a practical demonstration of the capabilities of aircraft and the advantages to be gained from their coordinated employment with ships. Secretary of the Navy Josephus Daniels reported the exercise to be a "considerable success."

7 MARCH • Pilot Lt. j.g. Frank M. Johnson launched in an N-9 from a sea sled and attained a speed of approximately 50 knots during a test at NAS Hampton Roads, Va. Cmdr. Henry C. Mustin had recommended that a powerful motor boat be converted into a sea sled to launch a plane at a point within range of a target as a means of attacking German submarine pens. The firm of Murray and Tregurtha of

A Sopwith 1 1/2–Strutter sits on a flying-off platform atop a 14-inch gun turret of most likely *Oklahoma* (BB 37) during operations off Guantanamo Bay, Cuba, c.1920.

South Boston, Mass., manufactured the sled, and civilian industrialist Albert Hickman designed and patented the essential features of the device.

9 MARCH • Lt. Cmdr. Edward O. McDonnell made the first flight of a Sopwith Camel from a turret platform on board a U.S. Navy battleship when he successfully took off from the No. 2 14-inch gun turret of *Texas* (Battleship No. 35) as she lay at anchor at NS Guantánamo Bay, Cuba.

12 MARCH • Lt. j.g. Harry Sadenwater, USNRF, demonstrated the feasibility of using voice radio and telephone relay for air to ground communications when he carried on a conversation from an airborne flying boat with Secretary of the Navy Josephus Daniels, who was seated at his desk in the Navy Department 65 miles away.

13 MARCH • The Chief of Naval Operations issued a preliminary program for postwar naval airplane development. The specialized types desired comprised fighters, torpedo carriers, and bombers for fleet use; single-engine, twin-engine, and long distance patrol and bomber planes for station use; and a combination landplane and seaplane for Marine Corps operations.

21 MARCH • A gyrocompass developed by Sperry Gyroscope Co. for the Navy was tested in an aircraft. The evaluations failed to find this particular instrument acceptable but marked the first recorded tests of this device, which subsequently proved an invaluable navigational instrument for long-range flight.

7 APRIL • The Seaplane Squadron and *Shawmut* (Minelayer No. 4) of Fleet Air Detachment sailed from NS Guantánamo Bay, Cuba, for the United States following almost seven weeks of participation in fleet exercises. The squadron operated entirely afloat and without support from ashore during this period.

8 APRIL • Capt. Thomas T. Craven detached from the Bureau of Navigation for duty in the Office of the Chief of Naval Operations. The following month Craven relieved Capt. Noble E. Irwin as Director of Naval Aviation.

10 APRIL • The roll-up of naval air stations in Europe that began on 31 December 1918 with the disestablishment of NAS Porto Corsini, Italy, completed with the disestablishment of NAS Eastleigh, England.

26 APRIL • Flying an F-5L (BuNo A-3589) equipped with two 400 hp Liberty engines, pilot Lt. Harold B. Grow and crewmembers Ens. Rutledge Irvine, Ens. Hugh S. Souther, and Ens. Delos Thomas completed a record flight of 20 hours 19 minutes covering 1,250 nautical miles from Hampton Roads, Va. Although the record was unofficial because the crew made the flight without National Aeronautic Association supervision and prior to the date on which seaplanes received recognition as a separate class for record purposes, their achievement stood as the longest seaplane flight until 1 May 1925.

28 APRIL • In the process of developing and testing navigational equipment for the forthcoming NC flying boats' transatlantic flight, Lt. Cmdr. Richard E. Byrd Jr. requested from the Naval Observatory a supply of bubble levels, which he adapted for attachment to navigational sextants, thereby providing an artificial horizon that made it possible for men to use these instruments for astronomical observations from aircraft.

1061650

Airship *C-5* makes a record flight but fails to cross the Atlantic.

8 MAY • At 0959 flagship NC-3, the first of three NC flying boats of Seaplane Division One, Cmdr. John H. Towers commanding, took off from NAS Rockaway, N.Y., for Halifax, Nova Scotia, on the first leg of a projected transatlantic flight. Towers commanded NC-3, BuNo A-2293; Lt. Cmdr. Patrick N. L. Bellinger commanded NC-1, A-2291; and Lt. Cmdr. Albert C. Read commanded NC-4, A-2294, along with crewmembers Lt. James L. Breese, Lt. Elmer F. Stone, USCG, Lt. j.g. Walter K. Hinton, Ens. Herbert C. Rodd, and MMC Eugene S. Rhoads. Each plane completed the flight's second leg, from Halifax to Trepassey Bay, Newfoundland, over the next three days.

14 MAY • Lt. Cmdr. Emory W. Coil commanded the airship *C-5* during a record flight for nonrigid airships from Montauk Point, Long Island, N.Y., to Pleasantville, St. Johns, Newfoundland, covering 1,050 nautical miles in 25 hours 50 minutes. Coil and his crew of six made the nonstop voyage to determine whether they were able to cross the Atlantic, and determined that such a flight would be feasible. However, shortly following *C-5*'s arrival a heavy gale sprang up, and despite efforts to deflate the bag, the gale tore the airship from the moorings and swept her to sea. The two sailors on board jumped clear and survived.

16 MAY • A few minutes after 1800 three NC flying boats of Seaplane Division One (NC-1, NC-3, and NC-4) took off from Trepassey Bay, Newfoundland, for the voyage to the Azores with NC-3 in the van. At one point Radioman Ens.

1061649

The crew of NC-4 with Commander Azores Detachment Capt. Richard H. Jackson, left to right: 1st Lt. Elmer F. Stone, USCG, CMM Eugene S. Rhoads, Lt. j.g. Walter K. Hinton, Ens. Herbert C. Rodd, Lt. James L. Breese, Lt. Cmdr. Albert C. Read, and Capt. Jackson.

Herbert C. Rodd of NC-4 intercepted a radio message from steamship *George Washington* 1,325 miles distant. Also on this date a radio station at Bar Harbor, Maine, intercepted a message from one of the planes from about 1,400 miles away.

17 MAY • At 1323 NC-4 descended to Horta in the Azores. NC-4 became the only one of the three NC flying boats that left Trepassey Bay, Newfoundland, the previous day to reach the Azores by air. The other NC boats lost their bearings in the fog, landed at sea to determine their positions, and sustained damage that rendered them unable to resume the flight. Lt. Cmdr. Patrick N. L. Bellinger of NC-1 descended to the water 45 miles on the other side of Flores, but heavy seas disabled the plane. After five hours on the water, Greek steamer *Ionia* took NC-1 in tow but the lines parted. *Gridley* (Destroyer No. 92) attempted to tow NC-1, but NC-1 broke up and sank. The crew clambered on board *Ionia* and arrived at Horta at 1230 the following day. Cmdr. John H. Towers landed NC-3 about 35 miles from the island of Fayal. The plane encountered rough seas, drifted backward toward the Azores, and arrived at Ponta Delgada at 1650 on 19 May.

27 MAY • At 2001, Lt. Cmdr. Albert C. Read of NC-4 completed the first Atlantic Ocean crossing by air when he landed at Lisbon, Portugal after departing from the Azores early on the morning of 26 May. On 31 May, Read lifted off again and arrived at Plymouth, England at 1326.

Lt. Cmdr. Albert C. Read runs flying boat NC-4 into Lisbon, Portugal, following the completion of the first flight across the Atlantic, 27 May 1919.

31 MAY • By this point 669 officers and 7,100 enlisted men remained in naval aviation, and their numbers continued to drop because of the rapid postwar demobilization.

12 JUNE • A contract was issued to construct a revolving platform for use in the experimental development of techniques and equipment for landing aircraft onto ships at Hampton Roads, Va.

14 JUNE • Medal of Honor recipient Ens. Charles H. Hammann, USNRF, died when the flying boat he was piloting during a flying circus at Langley Field, Va., fell into a tailspin and crashed.

21 JUNE • The Bureau of Construction and Repair reported a modification to the aircraft color scheme whereby stretched fabric surfaces were to be finished with aluminum enamel. Thus, wing and tail and in some instances fuselage surfaces were to be aluminum-colored, while the specified color for other exterior surfaces continued as naval gray enamel.

23 JUNE • The General Board submitted the last of a series of reports to Secretary of the Navy Josephus Daniels concerning a policy for developing a naval air service. The board stated that "aircraft have become an essential arm of the fleet," and urged the adoption of a broad program for peacetime development to establish a naval air service "capable of accompanying and operating with the fleet in all

Secretary of the Navy Josephus Daniels with the NC transatlantic fliers, 2 July 1919, left to right: first row, Lt. Cmdr. Albert C. Read, Secretary Daniels, Cmdr. John H. Towers, Assistant Secretary of the Navy Franklin D. Roosevelt, Lt. Cmdr. Patrick N. L. Bellinger; second row, Ens. Herbert C. Rodd, Lt. Harry Sadenwater, USNRF, Lt. Louis T. Barin, USNRF, Cmdr. Holden C. Richardson, CC, Lt. David H. McCulloch, USNRF; third row, Lt. James L. Breese, Lt. Robert A. Lavender; fourth row, CMM Eugene S. Rhoads, MM Rasmus Christensen, Lt. Elmer F. Stone, USCG, and Lt. j.g. Walter K. Hinton.

waters of the globe." On 24 July the secretary approved (with some modification) the report, and this program provided the direction for a number of actions taken during the following months.

25 JUNE • NAS Anacostia, D.C., reported experiments in which planes carried aloft instruments to measure the temperature and humidity of the upper atmosphere.

1 JULY • The Secretary of the Navy authorized installation of launching platforms on two main turrets in each of eight battleships. During WWI *Texas* (Battleship No. 35) received a platform to launch aircraft from one of her 14-inch gun turrets at Newcastle, England. Experience with *Texas* and the battleships subsequently converted disclosed that these platforms interfered with operating the turrets and planes and reduced visibility from the bridge, which eventually led to discarding these plans and increasing the emphasis on catapults. At times a mix of Hanriot HD-2s, Nieuport 28s, Sopwith Camels, and Sopwith 1 ½–Strutters operated from the battleships.

1 JULY • British Maj. George H. Scott commanded the rigid airship *R-34* during a flight across the Atlantic to Mineola,

An uncowled R-6 drops a torpedo.

N.Y. Scott arrived on 6 July and remained until midnight three days later when he lifted off for the United Kingdom. Lt. Cmdr. Zachary Lansdowne (Naval Aviator No. 105) and Lt. j.g. Ralph Kiely had become the first two U.S. naval aviators to report for European duty in airships during WWI, and Lansdowne accompanied *R-34* by Scott's invitation on the return flight. The British achievement spurred American interest in the development of lighter-than-air craft.

2 JULY • The officer in charge of the Navy Detachment under instruction in landplanes at the Army Air Service School at Langley Field, Va., reported that 27 naval aviators had completed their preliminary flight phase in JN-4s, and were approaching the end of the formation flight syllabus in DH aircraft. This training was to prepare the men to operate landplanes from battleship turrets.

2 JULY • Secretary of the Navy Josephus Daniels and Assistant Secretary of the Navy Franklin D. Roosevelt received some of the NC flying boat crewmembers and presented them to the American public from the steps of the Navy Department Building in Washington, D.C. The Navy subsequently dispatched NC-4 on a recruiting tour across the United States that began in Boston, Mass., on 1 October and finished in Charleston, S.C., on 1 January 1920. Upon completion the plane was returned to NAS Rockaway, N.Y.

11 JULY • The Naval Appropriations Act for fiscal year 1920 made several important provisions for the future of

1053767

The crew and gondola of a C-class airship with a bomb on its starboard rack.

naval aviation, including conversion of the collier *Jupiter* (Fuel Ship No. 3) into an aircraft carrier, subsequently named *Langley* (CV 1); conversion of two merchant ships into seaplane tenders, only one of which, later named *Wright* (AZ 1), actually was commissioned as such; construction of a rigid airship, later designated ZR-1 and named *Shenandoah*; and purchase of a rigid airship from abroad, later designated ZR-2 (*R-38*). The act also limited to six the heavier-than-air stations along the coasts of the United States.

1 AUGUST • To merge aviation with other naval activities the Aviation Division of the Office of the Chief of Naval Operations was abolished, and its functions were reassigned to other divisions and to the Bureau of Navigation. The Director of Naval Aviation retained his title as head of the Aviation Section of the Planning Division. The decision included the transfer of the Aircraft Test Board to the Board of Inspection and Survey.

19 AUGUST • The Secretary of the Navy ordered the use of the prewar white star national insignia on all naval aircraft in place of the concentric circle design adopted during WWI. By this order the red, white, and blue vertical bands on the rudder reverted to their prewar position with the blue forward.

23 AUGUST • General Order No. 499 directed that airships were to carry enough parachutes during flights for each person on board. General Order No. 509 of 5 November 1919 amplified this directive to apply also to flights in kite balloons, and added that life preservers were to be carried in all lighter-than-air craft during flights over water.

28 AUGUST • President Woodrow Wilson issued Executive Order 3160 that returned the Coast Guard from the wartime command of the Navy to the Treasury Department.

22 OCTOBER • Secretary of War Newton D. Baker approved the Navy's request for 18 naval aviators and 10 mechanics to attend landplane training at the Air Service Training School at Carlstrom Field, Arcadia, Fla. Two days later Secretary Baker approved a similar program at March Field, Riverside, Calif. Secretary of the Navy Josephus Daniels requested this training as an extension of the program already conducted under the Army at Langley Field, Va., as necessary to the successful operation of scouting planes from battleship turrets.

1 NOVEMBER • The Aerological School opened with a class of one Marine and four Navy officers at NAS Pensacola, Fla.

18 NOVEMBER • Secretary of the Navy Josephus Daniels informed Secretary of War Newton D. Baker that in response to his request arrangements had been made for six Army soldiers to attend the enlisted men's course in meteorology at NAS Pensacola, Fla. Secretary Josephus Daniels suggested their arrival for about 1 December to coordinate with the start of classes.

21 NOVEMBER • Engineering plans for the conversion of the collier *Jupiter* (Fuel Ship No. 3) to an aircraft carrier were modified and the Bureau of Construction and Repair issued a summary specification. In addition to an unobstructed "flying-on and flying-off deck," stowage space for aircraft, and facilities for repair of aircraft, the new plans provided for catapults to be fitted on both forward and aft ends of the flying-off deck. The schedule had originally earmarked her completion for 5 July 1920.

5 DECEMBER • Secretary of the Navy Josephus Daniels approved the basic agreement covering the procurement of the rigid airship *R-38* (ZR-2) from the British Air Ministry.

Chapter 3

The Roaring Twenties

1920–1929

The 1920s stand out in the history of naval aviation as a decade of growth. The air arm steadily increased in size and strength while improving its administrative and operational position within the Navy.

The period began under the leadership of a director without authority to direct but ended with a flourishing Bureau of Aeronautics. In the early 1920s small air detachments in each fleet proved effective during operations at sea. At the end of the decade three carriers sailed in full operation, patrol squadrons performed scouting functions, and commanders regularly assigned planes to battleships and cruisers. Together these elements played important roles in the annual fleet war games.

Impressive technical progress also characterized the decade. Despite slim funds, radial air-cooled engines developed into efficient and reliable sources of propulsion. Better instruments came into use, and an accurate bombsight was developed. Aircraft equipped with oleo struts and folding wings enhanced the operating capabilities of carriers. Each year planes flew faster, higher, and longer, and naval aviation contributed to world records.

Sailors and Marines developed innovative tactics and learned techniques of dive bombing, torpedo attack, scouting, spotting for gunfire, and operating from advanced bases. Naval pilots used their skills to turn airplanes to new uses in polar exploration and photographic surveying, and solved the basic and unique problems of taking aviation to sea.

Controversy also riddled these years, however, as journalists reported angry statements by the proponents of airpower and virulent retorts from its opponents. Critics directed charges of duplication, inefficiency, prejudice, and jealousy toward aviation advocates. Debates over the role of airpower and such issues as the role of the services in coastal defense included questions on the further need for a Navy. Many naval aviators grew frustrated with their career limitations and lack of command responsibilities. People within the aircraft industry became discontented with small peacetime orders, government procurement policies, and federal competition. Most of this controversy was typical of new technology developing at a rapid pace, but some of these questions would persist for decades.

1920

8 JANUARY • The policy of the Army and Navy relating to aircraft was published, defining the functions of Army, Navy, and Marine Corps aircraft as a guide to procurement, training, and expansion of operating facilities. It also set forth the conditions under which commanders coordinated air operations in coast defense, enunciated the means by which to avoid duplication of efforts, and provided for the free exchange of technical information.

19 JANUARY • The commandant at NAS Pensacola, Fla., reported that in the future no students were to be designated naval aviators or given certificates of qualification as Navy Air Pilots unless they could send and receive 20 words per minute on radio telegraph.

20 JANUARY • An allocation of $100,000 to the Bureau of Steam Engineering initiated the development and purchase of 200-hp radial air-cooled engines from the Lawrance Aero Engine Company.

22 JANUARY • CQM Harold H. Karr became the first enlisted man to receive the designation Naval Aviation Pilot under a program enabling enlisted sailors to undergo flight training.

184698

An MBT bomber drops a torpedo in the Potomac River, 12 May 1920.

17 MARCH • The approval of a change in the flight training program to overcome an acute shortage of pilots separated the heavier-than-air (seaplane) and lighter-than-air (dirigible) courses, and reduced the overall training period from nine to six months for the duration of the shortage.

24 MARCH • The first Coast Guard air station opened in Morehead City, N.C. The station began operations with six HS-2L flying boats borrowed from the Navy, but a lack of funds compelled the closure of the facility following 15 months of operation.

27 MARCH • Testers completed examination of a Sperry gyrostabilized automatic pilot system in an F-5L flying boat at NAS Hampton Roads, Va.

2 APRIL • NAS Hampton Roads, Va., reported the success of night weather soundings since January, using candle-lighted free balloons to measure the force and direction of the wind.

1 MAY • A report from the Bureau of Construction and Repair disclosed developmental and experimental work in metal construction for aircraft. Twelve German Fokker D.VIIs, which used welded steel extensively, were to be obtained from the Army, and two sets of metal wings for an HS-3 flying boat procured from contractor Charles Ward Hall.

12 MAY • An MBT bomber dropped a torpedo in the Potomac River off Hains Point, D.C. The event marked renewed Navy interest in aerial torpedoes.

18 JUNE • A reversible pitch propeller designed by Seth Hart and manufactured by the Engineering Division of the Army Air Service was installed onto the airship *C-10* at NAS Rockaway Beach, N.Y. The Navy ordered Hart's reversible pitch propellers for VE-7 biplanes in June.

22 JUNE • The Bureau of Navigation revealed plans to select four officers for a two-year postgraduate course in aeronautical engineering at the Naval Academy and at the Massachusetts Institute of Technology, and asked for volunteers for the fall semester. Part of the requirement was that appointees take flight instruction and qualify as naval aviators after completing their studies.

28 JUNE • Six F-5L flying boats of the Atlantic Fleet Airboat Squadron, Lt. Cmdr. Bruce G. Leighton commanding, returned to Philadelphia, Pa., following a seven-month cruise through the West Indies during which the squadron logged 12,731 nautical miles, including 4,000 flown on maneuvers with the fleet.

6 JULY • In a test of the radio compass as an aid to navigation, an F-5L flying boat flew from NAS Hampton Roads, Va., to *Ohio* (Battleship No. 12) while she sailed in a maneuvering area unknown to the pilot 94 miles at sea. The pilot located the ship and, without landing, made the return trip to Hampton Roads, this time navigating by signals from Norfolk, Va.

12 JULY • A General Order provided for the organization of forces afloat into the Atlantic, Pacific, and Asiatic fleets, and for the formation of seven type forces: Battleship, Cruiser, Destroyer, Submarine, Mine, Air, and Train. Under this order the air detachments in each fleet became air forces.

17 JULY • The Navy prescribed standard nomenclature for types and classes of naval vessels and aircraft, using "Z" for lighter-than-air craft and "V" for heavier-than-air craft. Class letters assigned within the Z type consisted of K, N, and R for kite balloons, nonrigid dirigibles, and rigid dirigibles, respectively. Within the V type, the class letters F, G, O, P, S, and T identified fighter, fleet, observation, patrol, scouting, and torpedo and bombing planes, respectively.

AUGUST • The Navy directed that all Marine Corps aircraft were to carry an insignia that comprised a circle pierced by an anchor and surmounted by a North American bald eagle. The circle's outer ring would be red, the middle circle blue, and the center white.

17 SEPTEMBER • The site of the naval aviation activities on Ford Island, Territory of Hawaii, was designated NAS Pearl Harbor.

2 OCTOBER • Pilot Lt. Arthur C. Wagner and passenger Lt. Cmdr. William M. Corry crashed in a JN-4 near Hartford, Conn. The impact threw Corry clear, and despite the intense flames rising from the stricken Jenny, he valiantly but unsuccessfully attempted to pull Wagner clear of the wreckage. Corry died from his burns four days later and posthumously received the Medal of Honor.

13 OCTOBER • F-5L and H-16 flying boats carried out a series of tests at Tangier Sound in the Chesapeake Bay under controlled conditions to determine the accuracy with which aircraft could drop bombs on stationary targets and the damage caused by near-misses and direct hits. Planes bombed target ship *Indiana* (Battleship No. 1) twice between 13 and 16 October, and completed a third evaluation on 4 November.

1921

20 JANUARY • Secretary of the Navy Josephus Daniels approved a recommendation that the Bureau of Ordnance and the Bureau of Engineering develop radio-controlled aircraft.

20 JANUARY • The Bureau of Construction and Repair approved a Naval Aircraft Factory design of a turntable catapult powered by compressed air for fabrication at the Philadelphia Navy Yard, Pa.

7 MARCH • Capt. William A. Moffett relieved Capt. Thomas T. Craven as Director of Naval Aviation. Moffett would later become instrumental in the development of the naval air arm.

12 MARCH • A Marine air detachment designated Flight L arrived at Guam to reinforce the island's aerial defenses. The detachment was subsequently redesignated VP-3M and in 1933 returned to San Diego, Calif.

466366

William A. Moffett, who later becomes the first chief of the Bureau of Aeronautics.

15 MARCH • The Metallurgical Laboratory at the Naval Aircraft Factory, Philadelphia, Pa., reported that a high strength, chromium-vanadium steel alloy proved satisfactory in laboratory tests and in the manufacture of aircraft fittings. These findings marked an advance in the development of metal as a high-strength aircraft structural material.

16 JUNE • The Navy ordered two CR-1 racers, the first of the series with which Navy and Army fliers captured many world speed records.

161903

A bomb explodes near the German battleship *Ostfriesland* off the Virginia Capes, July 1921.

21 JUNE • The services began a series of controversial bombing tests off the Virginia Capes, designed to provide detailed technical and tactical data on the effectiveness of aerial bombing against ships, and of the value of compartmentation in enabling vessels to survive such damage. The Army participated subject to the Navy's requirement that the bombing be accomplished as a series of controlled tests, and that inspectors board the target vessels following each attack to assess the results. In the first test, three naval F-5L flying boats dropped 12 bombs from 1,100 feet on the German submarine *U-117,* which sank in 12 minutes after the first hit. On 29 June Navy planes located the radio-controlled *Iowa* (Coast Battleship No. 4) 1 hour 57 minutes after being alerted to her approach somewhere within a 25,000-square-mile area, and attacked the ship with dummy bombs. The Navy opposed an Army proposal to attack *Iowa,* because the ship provided an unfair advantage by maneuvering under radio control. The rudimentary aerial navigation equipment available hindered testing, however, and many of the participants could not have found the ship without aids. Army bombers sank the German destroyer *G-102* on 13 July. Five days later the German light cruiser *Frankfurt* sank beneath 74 bombs dropped from Army and Navy aircraft. Bombing runs against the German battleship *Ostfriesland* began on 20 July when Army, Navy, and Marine planes dropped 52 bombs, ending the next day when Army NBS-1 bombers sank the battlewagon with a total of eleven 1,000- and 2,000-pound bombs. The incident escalated the controversy on the effectiveness of aerial bombing against ships when the Army refused to allow investigators to board *Ostfriesland,* and their planes continued their runs until they sank the ship. Additional tests sank (decommissioned) *Alabama* (BB 8) on 27 September 1921, and *New Jersey* (BB 16) and *Virginia* (BB 13) on 5 September 1923. Brig. Gen. William Mitchell, USA, proclaimed the obsolescence of warships and increased his lobbying for an independent air force. Naval officers upheld the effectiveness of ships by noting that the target vessels had not been able to maneuver or defend themselves, but many observers noted the capability of unopposed planes to sink capital ships.

1 JULY • The Aviation Machinist's Mate, Aviation Metalsmith, Aviation Carpenter's Mate, Aviation Rigger, and Photographer basic aviation ratings were established. These five ratings were the first concerned specifically with the air arm and based solely on aviation requirements. Prior to this time the Navy had identified certain general service ratings parenthetically as pertaining to aviation, and their qualifications required meeting the standards of the general rating in addition to those required for the aviation specialty.

12 JULY • An act of Congress created the Bureau of Aeronautics and charged it with matters pertaining to naval aeronautics as prescribed by the Secretary of the Navy.

1 AUGUST • Torpedo Squadron, Atlantic Fleet, tested a WWI high-altitude bombsight mounted on a gyroscopically stabilized base at Yorktown, Va. The occasion marked the successful completion of the first phase of designer Carl L. Norden's development of an effective high-altitude bombsight for the Bureau of Ordnance.

9 AUGUST • Rear Adm. Bradley A. Fiske (Ret.) proposed "a nice soft cushion" as a landing surface for aircraft carriers, so mounted "that it was to take up the forward motion of the airplane and not check its forward velocity at once."

10 AUGUST • A general order established the Bureau of Aeronautics and defined its duties under the Secretary of the Navy as comprising "all that relates to designing, building, fitting out, and repairing Naval and Marine Corps aircraft." The order granted BUAER the authority to make recommendations to the Bureau of Navigation and the Commandant of the Marine Corps on all matters pertaining to aeronautic training and the assignment of men to aviation; described the scope of its relationships with other bureaus having cognizance of aeronautical materials and equipment; and directed that BUAER make special provision in its organization to furnish information "covering all aeronautic planning, operations and administration that may be called for by the Chief of Naval Operations."

11 AUGUST • The practical development of carrier arresting gear began when pilot Lt. Alfred M. Pride taxied an Aeromarine plane onto a dummy deck and engaged arresting wires at NAS Hampton Roads, Va. These tests resulted in the development of arresting gear for *Langley* (CV 1) that consisted essentially of athwartship wires attached to weights along with fore and aft wires.

428435

An N-9 seaplane prepares to launch from a ship-type turntable catapult on a pier at the Naval Aircraft Factory, Philadelphia, Pa.

23 AUGUST • The rigid airship *R-38* (ZR 2), which the Navy had purchased from the British Royal Air Force, lifted off on her fourth trial flight at 0710 from Howden Aerodrome in England. At 1737 on 24 August, an explosion in the forward section broke the airship into two parts, and both of the sections together with men and debris fell into the Humber River near Hull. The crash killed 16 Americans, including prospective skipper Cmdr. Louis H. Maxfield, Lt. Cmdr. Emory W. Coil, and Lt. Henry W. Hoyt, and 28 Britons, including Air Commodore E. M. Maitland, RAF.

1 SEPTEMBER • The Bureau of Aeronautics began functioning as an organizational unit of the Navy Department under Rear Adm. William A. Moffett.

26 OCTOBER • A compressed air, turntable catapult launched an N-9 seaplane piloted by Naval Constructor Cmdr. Holden C. Richardson, CC, during the first successful test of the device from a pier at the Philadelphia Navy Yard, Pa.

3 NOVEMBER • Civilian pilot Bert Acosta in a CR-1 racer, BuNo A-6080, powered by a 400-hp Curtiss engine and on loan to the builder, won the Pulitzer Race with a world record speed of 176.7 mph in Omaha, Neb.

The Navy's first vessel especially fitted as a seaplane tender, *Wright* (AZ 1).

1 DECEMBER • Lt. Cmdr. Ralph F. Wood piloted the *C-7* during the first flight of an airship inflated with helium gas at Norfolk, Va.

16 DECEMBER • The seaplane tender *Wright* (AZ 1), uniquely designed as a heavier-and lighter-than-air tender, was commissioned at New York, N.Y., Capt. Alfred W. Johnson commanding.

20 DECEMBER • To meet requirements of several Pacific Fleet commands, the commanding officer of NAS San Diego, Calif., received authorization to establish a school to train naval aviators in the use of landplanes.

1922

16 JANUARY • The Bureau of Aeronautics directed the shipment of Army-type seat pack parachutes for heavier-than-air use to Marines in Haiti, the Dominican Republic, Guam, and Quantico, Va.

6 FEBRUARY • At a meeting in Washington, D.C., British, French, Italian, Japanese, and U.S. representatives signed the Washington Treaty limiting naval armament. The treaty established a respective tonnage ratio of 5–5–3 for British, American, and Japanese capital ships, and lesser figures for the French and Italians. The same ratio for aircraft carrier tonnage set the overall limits at 135,000–135,000–81,000 tons. The treaty also limited new carriers to 27,000 tons with a provision that, as long as the nations did not exceed total carrier tonnage by doing so, they could build two carriers of not more than 33,000 tons each or obtain them by converting existing or partially constructed ships that the treaty would otherwise require to be scrapped. The

Fighters and torpedo planes pack the deck of the first U.S. aircraft carrier, *Langley* (CV 1).

Americans, British, and Japanese scrapped 66 existing or partially constructed capital ships totaling more than 1.8 million tons.

7 FEBRUARY • The completion of a 50-hour test run of the 200-hp Lawrance J-1 radial air-cooled engine by the Aeronautical Engine Laboratory at the Washington Navy Yard, D.C., foreshadowed the successful use of radial engines in naval aircraft.

11 FEBRUARY • The first cradle of the rigid airship designated ZR-1, subsequently named *Shenandoah,* was completed at NAS Lakehurst, N.J., marking the initial step in the assembly of the Navy's first rigid airship. The Secretary of the Navy had authorized her construction on 9 August 1919. The first materials for ZR-1 arrived at the Naval Aircraft Factory, Philadelphia, Pa., where construction began in 1920. NAS Lakehurst later completed the assembly. During this period, the Navy constructed at Lakehurst the largest hangar built to date in the United States to accommodate the craft, measuring 804-feet-long by 318-feet-wide by 200-feet-high.

2 MARCH • The Navy initiated experimental investigation and development of catapults using gunpowder, which eventually produced a new type of catapult for use in launching aircraft from capital ships.

20 MARCH • The first U.S. aircraft carrier *Langley* (CV 1) was commissioned at Norfolk, Va., under the command of Executive Officer Cmdr. Kenneth Whiting. The Norfolk Navy Yard had converted *Langley* from the collier *Jupiter* (AC 3), replacing her coal-handling derricks with a wooden flight deck and converting holds to hangars and fuel tanks. *Langley* was named in honor of aviation pioneer Samuel P. Langley.

25 MARCH • The Secretary of the Navy established an Experimental and Research Laboratory as provided for in a public law passed in August 1916. Following the construction of buildings at Bellevue, D.C., the Aircraft Radio Laboratory at NAS Anacostia, D.C., the Naval Radio Research Laboratory from the Bureau of Standards, and the Sound Research Section of the Engineering Experiment Station were consolidated at the new organization in Bellevue prior to its establishment in July 1923. People generally called this facility the Naval Research Laboratory, and with the Naval Appropriations Act of 1926 this name became official.

27 MARCH • To comply with a provision of the law establishing the Bureau of Aeronautics that emphasized that its chief and at least 70 percent of the bureau's officers were to consist of either pilots or observers, the bureau defined the functions and qualifications of Naval Aviation Observers and recommended a course of study for their training. Upon approval of the course and its qualifications by the Bureau of Navigation, Rear Adm. William A. Moffett reported for training, qualifying as the first Naval Aviation Observer on 17 June 1922.

29 MARCH • The Navy promulgated a change in the aircraft designation system: adding the identity of the manufacturer to model designations. Symbols consisted of a combination of letters and numbers in which the first letter identified the manufacturer and the second, the class (or mission) of the aircraft. Numbers that appeared between letters indicated the series of designs within classes built by the same manufacturer (the 1 being omitted), and numbers following a dash after the class letter indicated modifications of the basic model. For example, MO would indicate a Martin observation plane; the second modification of MOs were MO-2s; and the second-design observation planes built by Martin were M2Os.

1 APRIL • The Bureau of Aeronautics sent descriptive specifications of arresting gear of the type later installed in *Lexington* (CV 2) and *Saratoga* (CV 3) to various design engineers, including Carl L. Norden and Warren Noble. "The arresting gear will consist of two or more transverse wires stretched across the fore and aft wires . . . [and which] lead around sheaves placed outboard to hydraulic brakes. The plane after engaging the transverse wire is guided down the deck by the fore and aft wires and is brought to rest by the action of the transverse wire working with the hydraulic brakes."

22 APRIL • Secretary of the Navy Edwin Denby approved a recommendation from the General Board to assign a spotting plane to each fleet battleship and cruiser, and test the feasibility of operating more aircraft from these ships.

24 APRIL • Seeking to increase the service life of aircraft engines beyond the 50 hours then required, the Bureau of Aeronautics issued a contract to the Packard Motor Car Co. for a 300-hour test of a Packard 1A-1551 dirigible engine. Such endurance testing—whereby runs to destruction identified the weaker components of an engine, which were then redesigned for longer life—came to be an important step in both increasing the operating life of engines and in the development of new high performance engines.

25 APRIL • Pilot Eddie Stinson made the initial flight of an ST-1 twin-engine torpedo plane built by Stout Engineering Laboratory as the first all-metal airplane designed for the Navy. The aircraft possessed inadequate longitudinal stability, but its completion marked a step forward in the development of all-metal aircraft.

24 MAY • Routine operation of shipboard catapults commenced when pilot Lt. Andrew C. McFall and passenger Lt. DeWitt C. Ramsey launched in a VE-7 biplane via a compressed air catapult from the battleship *Maryland* (BB 46) off Yorktown, Va. The Navy subsequently installed catapults on battleships and then on cruisers, thereby achieving the ability to operate aircraft from existing capital ships. From these platforms, enterprising aviators developed techniques for supporting conventional surface forces by scouting and spotting for ships' guns.

31 MAY • Two free balloons represented the Navy in the National Elimination Balloon Race at Milwaukee, Wis. The first, manned by Lt. Cmdr. Joseph P. Norfleet and Chief Rigger James F. Shade, operated with helium in the first recorded use of the gas in a U.S. free balloon. The second balloon, with Lt. William F. Reed Jr. and Chief Rigger K. Mullenix, finished third in the race with a distance of 441 miles and became the only Navy qualifier for the International Balloon Race held later in the year in Geneva, Switzerland.

17 JUNE • The practice of numbering aircraft squadrons to conform to the number of the ship squadron they served was changed to a system of numbering squadrons serially by class in the order of their initial authorization. The Navy also adopted the use of letter abbreviations to indicate missions.

17 JUNE • In anticipation of a reorganization that was to merge the Atlantic and Pacific fleets into a U.S. Fleet (and further divide it into the Battle Fleet and the Scouting Fleet) on 6 December, the fleet aviation commands whose titles had previously been changed from Air Forces to Air Squadrons were retitled Aircraft Squadrons of the Scouting and Battle fleets.

26 JUNE • The Navy ordered a rigid airship from the Zeppelin Airship Co., Friedrichshafen, Germany. The United States obtained the zeppelin, designated *LZ-126* by the builder, as a nonmilitary aircraft as part of WWI reparations under the terms approved by the Conference of Ambassadors on 16 December 1921. The Navy subsequently christened the ship *Los Angeles* (ZR 3).

1 JULY • The training of nucleus crews for two rigid airships, subsequently named *Los Angeles* (ZR 3) and *Shenandoah* (ZR 1), began at NAS Hampton Roads, Va.

1 JULY • The first eight medical officers to report for flight training began instruction at NAS Pensacola, Fla. Four of these officers had previously completed the flight surgeon course at the Army Technical School of Aviation Medicine.

1 JULY • Congress authorized the conversion of the unfinished battle cruisers *Lexington* (CC 1) and *Saratoga* (CC 3) to carriers as permitted under the terms of the Washington Treaty.

1 JULY • Sailors began training in the care and packing of parachutes as ten chief petty officers arrived for two months of instruction at the Army's Chanute Field at Rantoul, Ill.

3 JULY • Class XVI, the first class of student naval aviators to receive training in landplanes, commenced training at NAS Pensacola, Fla.

17 JULY • The Chief of Naval Operations forwarded a list of bureau and division representatives to the Bureau of Navigation, and requested that they be ordered to meet as a board in order to draw up tactical doctrine governing the employment of spotting aircraft in fleet fire control.

601020

Lt. Adolphus W. Gorton wins the Curtiss Marine Trophy Race for seaplanes in a TR-1, 8 October 1922.

27 SEPTEMBER • Eighteen PT seaplanes of Torpedo and Bombing Plane Squadron One conducted the first mass torpedo practice against a live target when they attacked the battleship *Arkansas* (BB 33) while she sailed in a formation of three battleships maneuvering at full speed off the Virginia Capes. During the 25-minute attack the bombers approached the ships from port and starboard and released 17 Mk VII Model 1 A torpedoes at distances of 500 to 1,000 yards and scored eight "hits" on *Arkansas*. Despite artificialities that prevented the practice from demonstrating the true combat capabilities of either the surface or air servicemembers, the bombing run demonstrated that planes could launch torpedoes, which were capable of running straight.

27 SEPTEMBER • The commanding officer at NAS Anacostia, D.C., proposed the use of radios to detect the passage of ships at night or during heavy fog. The reported "best method of detection" resulted from the unexpected nature of a radio signal observed by Cmdr. A. Hoyt Taylor and civilian L. C. Young of the Aircraft Radio Laboratory at that station, when a passing river steamer interrupted experimental high-frequency radio transmissions between Anacostia and a receiver across the river at Hains Point. The observation and analysis of the phenomenon marks the first step in the chain of events that led to the Navy's introduction of radar.

8 OCTOBER • Lt. Adolphus W. Gorton won the Curtiss Marine Trophy Race for seaplanes, held during the National Air Races at Detroit, Mich. Gorton averaged 112.6 mph in a TR-1, BuNo A-6303, powered by a Lawrance J-1 engine over the 160-mile course. Second place went to Lt. Harold A. Elliott in a VE-7H.

1053781

The 1922 Pulitzer Trophy Air Race third-place finisher Lt. Harold J. Brow poses with his CR-2 racer.

651598

A VE-7 biplane similar to the first plane to take off from *Langley* (CV 1).

14 OCTOBER • Lt. Harold J. Brow and Lt. Alford J. Williams flew CR-2 and CR-1 racers with D-12 engines to finish third and fourth, respectively, in the Pulitzer Trophy Race at Detroit, Mich. The planes attained speeds of 193 and 187 mph.

14 OCTOBER • Pilots Lt. Ben H. Wyatt and Lt. George T. Owen flew two DH-4B-1 biplanes during a round trip transcontinental flight. Wyatt flew BuNo A-6377. The pilots made the trip in short hops along a southern route on the outward leg from San Diego, Calif., through Tucson, Ariz., New Orleans, La., and Pensacola, Fla., and on the homeward leg from Washington, D.C., through Dayton, Ohio, Omaha, Neb., Salt Lake City, Utah, and San Francisco, Calif. They completed the 7,000-mile trip in about 90 hours of flight and returned to San Diego on 29 November. Layovers caused by mechanical difficulties, poor-quality gasoline, inclement

215821

An Aeromarine similar to the one that first landed on board *Langley* (CV 1) practices landings on the ship.

weather, and lack of navigating equipment accounted for most of their elapsed time.

17 OCTOBER • Lt. Virgil C. Griffin (Naval Aviator No. 41) completed the Navy's first carrier takeoff, flying a VE-7SF biplane, BuNo A-5932, from *Langley* (CV 1) at anchor at Berth No. 58 in the York River, Va.

26 OCTOBER • Lt. Cmdr. Godfrey deC. Chevalier (Naval Aviator No. 7), flying an Aeromarine 39-B, made the first landing on board the carrier *Langley* (CV 1) while she steamed off Cape Henry, Va.

12 NOVEMBER • Lt. Cmdr. Godfrey deC. Chevalier (Naval Aviator No. 7) crashed in a VE-7 at Lochaven near Norfolk, Va. He died from his injuries two days later while in the Naval Hospital, Portsmouth, Va.

1053779

An aerial camera fitted to the gun mount of a DH-4 biplane.

18 NOVEMBER • Cmdr. Kenneth Whiting, flying a PT seaplane, made the first catapult launch from *Langley* (CV 1) at anchor in the York River, Va.

1923

6 FEBRUARY • Secretary of the Navy Edwin Denby authorized the transfer of the Aeronautical Engine Laboratory from the Washington Navy Yard, D.C., to the Naval Aircraft Factory, Philadelphia, Pa., thereby clearly establishing the factory as the center of the Navy's aeronautical development and experimental work.

12 FEBRUARY • The Bureau of Navigation informed Commandant Eighth Naval District Rear Adm. Thomas P. Magruder at Pensacola, Fla., that two years' service in an operating unit subsequent to graduation from flight training was no longer required for designation as naval aviator.

18 FEBRUARY • In annual fleet problems, the Navy conducted maneuvers on the largest scale and under the most realistic conditions attainable. Fleet Problem I included a test of the defenses of the Panama Canal against aerial attacks. The "Blue" fleet and Army coast artillery and aircraft defended the canal assisted by 18 patrol planes of Scouting Plane Squadron 1 operating from the tenders *Wright* (AZ 1), *Sandpiper* (AM 51), and *Teal* (AM 23). Planners compensated for the lack of carriers and aircraft for the attacking "Black" fleet by designating two battleships as simulated carriers. On 21 February the battleship *Oklahoma* (BB 37) approached the area and launched a seaplane by catapult to scout ahead of the Black Fleet. Early the following morning a single plane representing an air group took off from Naranyas Cays in the Panama Canal Zone, flew undetected and without encountering aerial opposition or antiaircraft fire, and theoretically destroyed Gatun Spillway with ten miniature bombs. The lessons learned included the need for more planes and antiaircraft guns to defend the canal, to rush completion of carriers, and to fit all battleships with catapults.

21 FEBRUARY • *Langley* (CV 1) tested aircraft handling with Aeromarine planes operating in groups of three. The tests revealed that it took two minutes to prepare the deck following each landing.

21 FEBRUARY • Recognizing that newer aircraft engines offered advantages of longer life and lower cost, the Bureau of Aeronautics issued guidelines that severely restricted the repair and reuse of engines more than two years old. The Navy promptly expended its residual stocks of WWI engines, equipped most new aircraft with newer engines, and freed itself of stocks of obsolescent engines, thereby enabling the service to aggressively sponsor the development of improved aircraft engines to meet requirements.

10 MARCH • The Navy modified its aircraft model designation system by reversing the order of letters, placing the class letter first and manufacturer's letter last. The designation FB thus indicated fighters built by Boeing. This system, which applied only to new aircraft and did not change designations already assigned, remained in use until 18 September 1962.

15 MARCH • Ground school work began during the training of nucleus crews for two rigid airships, subsequently named *Los Angeles* (ZR 3) and *Shenandoah* (ZR 1), at NAS Lakehurst, N.J., under lighter-than-air expert Capt. Anton Heinan, formerly of the Imperial German Navy.

19 MARCH • Fighting Plane Squadron Two was established under Commanding Officer Lt. Cmdr. Robert P. Molten Jr. and Executive Officer Lt. Homer C. Wick. The squadron served with Aircraft Squadrons, Battle Fleet, attached to the tenders *Aroostook* (CM 3) and *Gannet* (AM 41) at NAS San Diego on North Island, Calif.

15 APRIL • The Naval Research Laboratory reported that an evaluation of equipment for radio control of aircraft in an F-5L flying boat proved satisfactory up to a range of ten miles, and announced the feasibility of radio control of airplanes during landings and takeoffs.

17 APRIL • Pilot Lt. Rutledge Irvine established a world altitude record for Class C airplanes, with a useful load of 1,000 kilograms, reaching 11,609 feet in a DT torpedo bomber equipped with a Liberty engine over McCook Field near Dayton, Ohio.

26 APRIL • The General Board completed a study on naval strategy in the Pacific that anticipated Japan as the most likely future enemy. The board recommended that the U.S. develop and fortify bases in the Hawaiian Islands, in the

1053770

Minelayer *Aroostook* (CM 3) serves as an aircraft tender, 1919–1931.

Philippines, and at locations along the supply lines to these points, including Guam, and advocated the creation and maintenance of a fleet capable of sustained operations in the western Pacific.

26 MAY • The chief of the Bureau of Aeronautics agreed with the chief of the Air Service on the advantages to the aviation industry and the military services of working under identical aeronautic specifications whenever possible and further stated the desirability of Army and Navy working together toward that end. In December Lt. Ralph S. Barnaby received orders to McCook Field, Dayton, Ohio, as the bureau's representative at an interservice conference on standardization during a series of annual meetings that continued until 1937, when the Aeronautical Board assigned a full-time staff to carry on the work.

426931

Two versions of the Douglas-designed DT—the first planes designed and built for the Navy as torpedo bombers.

1053769

An F-5L flying boat, left, and a DT torpedo bomber, right, on board aircraft tender *Teal* (AM 23).

6 JUNE • Planes and pilots of Aircraft Squadrons, Battle Fleet established seven world records for Class C seaplanes at San Diego, Calif.:

- Lt. j.g. Mainrad A. Schur set the speed record for 500 km in a DT-2 torpedo bomber at 72 mph.
- Lt. Henry T. Stanley set distance and duration records, with a 250-kg payload, in an F-5L patrol plane at 574.75 miles, and 10 hours 29 minutes 58 seconds.
- Lt. Herman E. Halland set distance and duration records, with a 500-kg payload, in an F-5L at 466 miles, and 7 hours 35 minutes 54 seconds.
- Lt. Robert L. Fuller set distance and duration marks, with a 1,000-kg payload, in a DT-2 at 205.2 miles, and 2 hours 45 minutes 9 seconds.

7 JUNE • Planes and pilots of Aircraft Squadrons, Battle Fleet continued their assault on the record books with eight new world marks for Class C seaplanes:

- Lt. Earl B. Brix set an altitude record of 10,850 feet for planes carrying a 250-kg useful load in a DT-2 torpedo bomber.
- Lt. Robert L. Fuller set an altitude record of 8,438 feet for planes carrying a 500-kg load in an F-5L patrol plane.
- Ens. Edward E. Dolecek set an altitude record of 7,979 feet for planes, with a 1,000-kg load, in an F-5L.
- Lt. Cecil F. Harper set the altitude record of 13,898 feet for planes, with "no useful load," in a DT-2.
- Lt. Henry T. Stanley set an altitude record of 5,682 feet in an F-5L, with a 1,500-kg load and the duration mark at 2 hours 18 minutes.
- Lt. Herman E. Halland set an altitude record of 4,885 feet in an F-5L, with a 2,000-kg load and a duration record of 51 minutes.

12 JUNE • Pilot Lt. j.g. Mainrad A. Schur set three world records for Class C seaplanes in a DT-2 torpedo bomber powered by a Liberty engine at San Diego, Calif.: a duration mark of 11 hours 16 minutes 59 seconds; distance mark of 792.25 miles; and speed of 70.49 mph for 1,000 km.

13 JUNE • Pilot Lt. Ralph A. Ofstie set world speed records for Class C seaplanes for 100 and 200 km in a TS-1 seaplane equipped with a Lawrance J-1 engine with speeds of 121.95 and 121.14 mph, respectively, at San Diego, Calif.

13 JUNE • Following a demonstration at a flying exhibition to civil and military dignitaries near Washington, D.C., *Langley* (CV 1) moored at the Washington Navy Yard where President Warren G. Harding boarded the ship, marking the first presidential visit to a U.S. carrier.

5 JULY • Chief of Naval Operations Adm. Edward W. Eberle directed the selection of a destroyer undergoing overhaul for a trial installation of a catapult and a seaplane. Four days later Commander Scouting Fleet Vice Adm. John D. McDonald assigned the destroyer *Charles Ausburn* (DD 294) while the ship finished an overhaul at the Philadelphia Navy Yard, Pa. The destroyer completed the installation of the catapult before her bridge on 23 August and sailed to Hampton Roads, Va., where between 29 and 31 August she received a TS-1 seaplane, BuNo A-6300. Operational experience revealed that the seaplane impacted the destroyer's visibility during navigation; the guy-wires and support structure for the fly-off rails restricted the arc of the forward 4-inch gun off the bow; and the wings extended beyond the ship and twice received damage during mooring. The seaplane and catapult were removed from *Charles Ausburn* at Philadelphia over 20 to 29 December, and skipper Lt. Cmdr. Frank C. McCord recommended to the fleet that future installations on board destroyers be located between their No. 4 stacks and mainmasts.

21 JULY • The Bureau of Aeronautics established a policy of assigning experimental airplanes to fleet squadrons for operational evaluation before adopting them as service types.

13 AUGUST • The establishment of Naval Aviation Reserve Units at Ft. Hamilton, N.Y., and at Squantum, Mass., marked constructive action toward building an effective aviation branch of the Naval Reserve Force.

23 AUGUST • The light cruiser *Detroit* (CL 8) received the first UO-1 observation biplane, BuNo A-6551, to operate from one of the ten *Omaha* (CL 4)-class scout cruisers. The delivery marked the introduction of routine float plane operations from cruisers.

175426

Lt. David Rittenhouse wins the 1923 Schneider Trophy in a CR-3 seaplane converted from the CR-2 racer.

4 SEPTEMBER • The rigid airship *Shenandoah* (ZR 1) made her first flight, Capt. Frank R. McCrary commanding, at NAS Lakehurst, N.J.

28 SEPTEMBER • Pilots Lt. David Rittenhouse and Lt. Rutledge Irvine won first and second place in the international seaplane race for the Schneider Trophy in two CR-3 seaplanes equipped with D-12 engines at Cowes, England. Their victory established a new world record for seaplanes with a speed of 169.89 mph for 200 km. Rittenhouse placed first at 177.38 mph and Irvine second with 173.46 mph.

6 OCTOBER • Navy planes swept the Pulitzer Trophy Race at St. Louis, Mo., taking the first four places all at faster speeds than the previous year's winning time. Both first and second place bettered the world's speed mark. Pilot Lt. Alford J. Williams set the new records for 100 and 200 km in an R2C-1 racer, BuNo A-6692, at 243.812 and 243.673 mph, respectively.

15 OCTOBER • Aircraft Nos 2-F-7, 2-F-9, and 2-F-11 of VF-2, Lt. Forrest P. Sherman commanding, took off from NAS San Diego, Calif., for San Francisco, Calif., to participate in an American Legion convention. 2-F-7 crashed en route at Mojave but a working party returned the plane in a truck three days later, which enabled sailors to subsequently salvage the aircraft. On 16 October, Aircraft Nos 2-F-2, 2-F-5, and 2-F-12 of VF-2, Lt. E. H. Barkelew commanding, departed for San Francisco via Bakersfield.

458279

1923 Pulitzer Trophy Air Race winner Lt. Alford J. Williams takes off in his R2C-1 racer.

These flights necessitated long journeys over alternating deserts and mountains. All of the planes returned by 23 October 1923.

2 NOVEMBER • Pilot Lt. Harold J. Brow established a world speed record in an R2C-1 racer equipped with a D-12 engine at Mitchel Field on Long Island, N.Y., averaging 259.47 mph in four flights over the 3-km course.

4 NOVEMBER • Pilot Lt. Alford J. Williams raised the world speed record to 266.59 mph in an R2C-1 racer equipped with a D-12 engine at Mitchel Field, N.Y., bettering the record set two days before by Lt. Harold J. Brow.

459589

Lt. Alford J. Williams stands alongside his winning R2C-1 racer at the 1923 Pulitzer Trophy Air Race.

5 NOVEMBER • The submarine *S-1* (SS 105), Lt. Powel M. Rhea commanding, carried out a series of tests designed to show the feasibility of stowing and launching a seaplane on board a submarine at Hampton Roads, Va. Lt. Cmdr. Virgil C. Griffin supervised a crew from *Langley* (CV 1) that cooperated with *S-1* by removing a disassembled MS-1 from a tank on board the submarine, assembling the plane, and launching it by submerging the boat.

6 NOVEMBER • Pilot Lt. Alford J. Williams climbed in an R2C-1 racer to 5,000 feet in a minute, bettering the best previously reported climb of 2,000 feet in the same time.

12 NOVEMBER • The battleship *Mississippi* (BB 41) received the first UO-1 observation biplane to operate routinely from battleships, BuNo A-6605.

16 NOVEMBER • The Bureau of Aeronautics directed that all planes attached to vessels of the fleet were to be overhauled once every six months.

3 DECEMBER • Chief of Naval Operations Adm. Edward W. Eberle approved the establishment of VS-3 as a special service squadron for the purpose of developing long-distance scouting planes, Lt. Cmdr. Charles P. Mason commanding, at NAS Anacostia, D.C.

7 DECEMBER • The Bureau of Aeronautics established a new designation system for catapults whereby a type letter indicated the energy sources—"A" for compressed air, "P" for powder, and "F" for flywheels—while Mark numbers indicated major design modifications. Under this system the compressed air, turntable catapult demonstrated at the Naval Aircraft Factory, Philadelphia, Pa., and installed on board the battleship *Maryland* (BB 46) received the designation type A, Mark I, and the device on board *Langley* (CV 1) of catapult type A, Mark III. The Navy subsequently extended this designation system with modification to include other energy sources, notably the type letter "H" for hydraulic catapults.

1924

JANUARY • During the winter the Battle Fleet, Scouting Fleet, and Control Force carried out tactical exercises for Fleet Problems II, III, and IV en route to Panama and from those waters to the point of mobilization at Culebra Island, P.R. During Fleet Problem III, VF-2 reported to Commanding Officer 6th Composite Group, Army Air Service, screened VO-2, and strafed opposing force Marines who simulated an opposed landing to seize the Panama Canal.

3 JANUARY • VT-20, Lt. Cmdr. George D. Murray commanding, embarked the cargo ship *Vega* (AK 17), which sailed from San Diego, Calif., for the Philippines. Upon arrival VT-20 operated from the tender *Ajax* (AG 15) as the first air detachment of the Asiatic Fleet.

16 JANUARY • A storm ripped the rigid airship *Shenandoah* (ZR 1) away from her mooring mast at NAS Lakehurst, N.J. Only some of the crew were on board and, despite their efforts, the airship drifted over New York City later that evening, where onlookers below reported observing the airship's red and green warning lights dimly through the clouds. Cmdr. M. R. Pierce returned the ship as the storm subsided.

25 JANUARY • VF-2 embarked the collier *Jason* (AC 12) and sailed from Coco Solo in the Panama Canal Zone for Culebra Island, P.R. Disembarking there on 2 February, the squadron operated from an improvised camp at Coontz Field subsequently (informally) designated Camp Robison.

4 FEBRUARY • The Bureau of Aeronautics directed naval aviation squadrons to discontinue the practice of striping or camouflaging aircraft and instructed them to paint all aircraft by 1 July with the prescribed naval gray, except the stretched fabric on the wing and tail and some aluminum fuselage surfaces. In one exception all squadrons of a station, force, or fleet could uniformly paint the upper wing chrome yellow or another color to increase visibility in case of a forced landing.

26 FEBRUARY • VS-3 received authorization to fly one division of Curtiss CS seaplane torpedo bombers from NAS Anacostia, D.C., to NAS Miami, Fla., and NAS Key West, Fla., and back to conduct service tests under actual operating conditions.

19-N-967C

Airship *Shenandoah* (ZR 1) and oiler *Patoka* (AO 9) accomplish the first use of a mooring mast on board a ship, 8 August 1924.

8 MARCH • Pilot Lt. L. V. Grant won the race for the Curtiss Marine Trophy in a VE-7 fighter at an average speed of 116.1 mph in Miami, Fla.

21 MARCH • The Bureau of Aeronautics directed the use of service parachutes by all sailors and Marines on all flights.

21 APRIL • The Bureau of Aeronautics requested that the Bureau of Steam Engineering investigate the development of a single-wave radio sending and receiving set suitable for installation in fighting planes, with a 20-mile sending radius and powered by a small battery- or engine-driven generator.

2 MAY • Pilot Lt. W. M. Dillion and gunnery officer Lt. Stanton H. Wooster launched by catapult in a DT torpedo bomber carrying a dummy torpedo from *Langley* (CV 1) at anchor in the bay off Pensacola, Fla.

19 JUNE • The Bureau of Ordnance issued a contract for the development of an antiaircraft director for shipboard fire control to the Ford Instrument Co.

22 JUNE • Pilot Lt. Frank W. Wead and gunnery officer Lt. John D. Price set five world records for class C seaplanes in a CS-2 with a Wright T-3 Tornado engine over a two-day period at NAS Anacostia, D.C.: one for distance, with 963.123 miles; one for duration, with 13 hours 23 minutes 15 seconds; and three for speed, attaining 73.41 mph for 500 km, 74.27 mph for 1,000 km, and 74.17 mph for 1,500 km.

24 JUNE • The Bureau of Aeronautics issued a technical order prescribing the external color of naval aircraft. The overall color was to be aluminum enamel with clear varnish on wooden spars and struts. Naval yellow enamel was to be used on the top surfaces of upper wings of training planes and yellow or other high visibility color could similarly be applied to all aircraft of any station, force, or fleet.

11 JULY • Pilot Lt. Frank W. Wead and gunnery officer Lt. John D. Price broke world records for Class C seaplanes in a CS-2 equipped with a Tornado engine over two days at NAS Anacostia, D.C., with new marks for a distance of 994.19 miles and a duration of 14 hours 53 minutes 44 seconds.

8 AUGUST • The rigid airship *Shenandoah* (ZR 1) secured to the mooring mast of the oiler *Patoka* (AO 9) while underway in Narragansett Bay, R.I. *Shenandoah* remained moored to *Patoka* during the ship's passage to anchor off Jamestown, R.I., and cast off the following day. This achievement marked the first use of a mooring mast erected on board ships to facilitate airship operations with the fleet.

11 AUGUST • Observation planes from the light cruiser *Raleigh* (CL 7) took off from the water near the Arctic Circle on the first of several reconnaissance flights over the Greenland coast from Angmagsalik to Cape Farewell. The aircraft intended to locate suitable emergency landing areas for Army aircraft crossing the Atlantic via Iceland on the last leg of a round-the-world flight.

15 AUGUST • In the first use of rigid airships with the fleet, *Shenandoah* (ZR 1) lifted off from NAS Lakehurst, N.J., to take part in a Scouting Fleet problem 300 miles at sea. *Shenandoah* discovered the "enemy" fleet, but heavy rains compelled her early retirement to base. The airship returned to Lakehurst on 17 August after 40 hours in the air.

1 SEPTEMBER • The first parachute school in the Navy opened to train enlisted men in the care, operation, maintenance, and testing of parachutes at NAS Lakehurst, N.J.

15 SEPTEMBER • An N-9 training seaplane equipped with radio control and without a human pilot on board conducted a 40-minute flight at the Naval Proving Ground, Dahlgren, Va. Although the aircraft sank from damage sustained while landing, this test demonstrated the practicability of radio control of aircraft.

18 SEPTEMBER • The repair ship *Medusa* (AR 1) was commissioned at the Navy Yard Puget Sound, Bremerton, Wash., Capt. R. T. Menner commanding. A section of VO-2 consisting of 2 officers and 20 enlisted men served as a ship-plane repair detail to support the operations of VO-1—both of which operated ashore.

7 OCTOBER • The rigid airship *Shenandoah* (ZR 1), Lt. Cmdr. Zachary Lansdowne commanding, began a round-trip transcontinental cruise from NAS Lakehurst, N.J. The airship's voyage included stops at Fort Worth, Texas, San Diego, Calif., and a stay of 11 days on the West Coast, including a flight to Camp Lewis at Tacoma, Wash. The airship returned to Lakehurst on 25 October having covered 9,317 miles in 258 hours of flight.

10 OCTOBER • Lt. Andrew Crinkley and Lt. Rossmore D. Lyon landed a CS-2 seaplane at Quantico, Va., following a continuous flight from NAS Anacostia, D.C., of 20 hours 28 minutes and 1,460 miles. The flight exceeded world records for endurance and distance but was not officially timed and therefore not an official record.

12 OCTOBER • The rigid airship designated ZR-3 lifted off from Friedrichshafen, Germany, under the command of Dr. Hugo Eckener, and with prospective skipper Capt. George W. Steele Jr. on board. The airship flew more than 5,000 miles in 81 hours and arrived on 15 October at NAS Lakehurst, N.J. The oiler *Patoka* (AO 9) and the light cruisers *Detroit* (CL 8) and *Milwaukee* (CL 5) sailed into the Atlantic to provide ZR-3 with weather reports and forecasts. The airship was subsequently named *Los Angeles*.

25 OCTOBER • Following the withdrawal of all foreign entrants from the Schneider Cup Race scheduled at Bayshore Park, Md., the United States agreed to cancel the race rather than to attain victory by a flyaway. The Navy instead staged a series of record attempts in which the scheduled contestants and other naval aircraft put 17 world records in the book for Class C seaplanes: Lt. George T. Cuddihy broke a world speed record of almost two years standing in a CR-3 racing seaplane powered by a D-12 engine with 188.078 mph. Lt. Ralph A. Ofstie broke world speed records for 100, 200, and 500 km in a CR-3 with marks of 178.25 mph for both the 100 and 200, and 161.14 mph for the 500. Lt. George R. Henderson set four records for speed over 100 and 200 km, with loads of 250 and 500 kg, in a PN-7 flying boat equipped with two Wright T-2 engines at 78.507 mph; and four records, with a useful load of 1,000 kg, with a speed of 78.507 mph for both 100 and 200 km, a distance record of 248.55 miles, and a duration record of 5 hours 28 minutes 43 seconds. Lt. Osborne B. Hardison set world records for speed over 100 km in a PN-7, and for distance, with a useful load of 1,500 kg, at 68.4 mph and 62.137 miles, and three more, with a useful load of 2,000 kg, in speed over 100 kilometers of 68.4 mph, distance 62.137 miles, and duration 1 hour 49 minutes 11.9 seconds.

11 NOVEMBER • Pilot Lt. Dixie Kiefer completed a successful night catapult launch in a UO-1 observation biplane from the battleship *California* (BB 44) at anchor at San Diego, Calif. Searchlights trained about 1,000 yards ahead aided the launch.

14 NOVEMBER • The chiefs of the Bureau of Aeronautics and the Bureau of Medicine and Surgery agreed on qualifications for flight surgeons that included a three-month course at the Army's school of aviation medicine and three months of satisfactory service with a naval aviation command before receiving the designation. The requirement that qualified medical officers make flights in aircraft was limited to emergencies and the desire of the officers.

17 NOVEMBER • *Langley* (CV 1) ended more than two years in experimental status upon reporting to the Battle Fleet as the first operational aircraft carrier in the U.S. Navy. On 1 December *Langley* became the flagship of Aircraft Squadrons, Battle Fleet.

25 NOVEMBER • First Lady Grace A. Coolidge christened the rigid airship designated ZR-3 as *Los Angeles*, Capt. George W. Steele Jr. commanding, at NAS Anacostia, D.C.

13 DECEMBER • The all-metal NM-1 biplane flew at the Naval Aircraft Factory, Philadelphia, Pa. The Navy designed and built the plane to develop metal construction for naval airplanes, and intended the type for Marine Corps expeditionary use.

14 DECEMBER • Pilot Lt. L. C. Hayden and passenger Lt. William M. Fellers launched in an MO-1 observation plane via a powder catapult from a forward turret of the battleship *Mississippi* (BB 41) at the Navy Yard Puget Sound, Bremerton, Wash. Following this demonstration the Navy began wide-scale use of powder catapults on board battleships and cruisers.

1925

17 JANUARY • A special board headed by Chief of Naval Operations Adm. Edward W. Eberle submitted its report to Secretary of the Navy Curtiss D. Wilbur. The secretary had appointed the board on 23 September 1924 to consider recent developments in aviation, and to recommend a policy for the development of the Navy in its various branches. The members of the board devoted most of their discussion to the importance of battleships, but their recommendations gave prominence to aviation, including construction of carriers up to treaty limits, expeditious completion of *Lexington* (CV 2) and *Saratoga* (CV 3), and laying down of a new 23,000-ton carrier; introduction of a progressive aircraft building program to ensure a complete complement of modern planes for the fleet; expansion of aviation offerings at the Naval Academy and assignment of all qualified academy graduates to aviator or observer training following two years of sea duty; and establishment of a defined policy governing assignment of officers to aviation.

22 JANUARY • VF-2 began landing practice on board *Langley* (CV 1) off San Diego, Calif. This marked the introduction to the fleet of the first command trained to operate as a squadron from a carrier, and the beginning of *Langley*'s operations as a ship of Aircraft Squadrons, Battle Fleet.

2 MARCH • Fleet Problem V off the coast of Southern California became the first problem to incorporate aircraft carriers. The small size of *Langley* (CV 1) and the inexperience of the ship's crew in aircraft handling restricted its operations to sending no more than ten planes aloft simultaneously to scout in advance of the "Black" fleet movement to Guadalupe Island. *Langley* once launched ten planes in 13 minutes but the carrier's limited performance convinced Commander in Chief U.S. Fleet Adm. Robert E. Coontz to recommend the rapid completion of *Lexington* (CV 2) and *Saratoga* (CV 3). The admiral advocated the introduction of steps to develop planes of greater durability, dependability, and radius, and the further improvement of catapult and recovery gear. Coontz also reported that experience now permitted routine catapulting of planes from battleships and cruisers. The problem concluded on 11 March.

11 MARCH • NAS Anacostia, D.C., reported arrangements for routine aerological sounding flights to an altitude of 10,000 feet to obtain weather data and to test upper-air sounding equipment. These flights began in mid-April; the following February the schedule extended to weekend and holiday flights, and the altitude increased to 15,000 feet.

13 MARCH • Rear Adm. William A. Moffett was appointed for a second tour as chief of the Bureau of Aeronautics.

2 APRIL • Pilot Lt. Cmdr. Charles P. Mason and passenger

Lt. Braxton Rhodes demonstrated the feasibility of using flush-deck catapults to launch landplanes when they catapulted in a DT-2 torpedo bomber from *Langley* (CV 1) while the carrier lay moored at NAS San Diego, Calif.

Cmdr. John Rodgers attempts to fly a PN-9 flying boat from San Francisco to Honolulu but completes the voyage 450 miles under sail, 31 August–10 September 1925.

8 APRIL • Lt. John D. Price of VF-1 made the first planned night landing on board a U.S. aircraft carrier when he landed on *Langley* (CV 1) at sea off San Diego, Calif. Lts. Delbert L. Conley, Adolphus W. Gorton, and Rossmore D. Lyon followed shortly thereafter. (An accidental landing occurred on the night of 5 February 1924 when Lt. Harold J. Brow stalled while practicing night approaches.)

8 APRIL • Almost two years following the abolition of a special aviation uniform, the Navy authorized new forestry green uniforms for winter and khaki for summer for naval aviators, observers, and other officers on duty that involved flying. Although the design received minor modifications in later years, the entire service adopted the khaki uniform in 1941.

1 MAY • Lt. Clarence H. Schildhauer and Lt. James R. Kyle broke the world endurance record for Class C seaplanes during a test flight in a PN-9, BuNo A-6878, at Philadelphia, Pa. The Naval Aircraft Factory there manufactured the metal-hulled flying boat equipped with two Packard engines. The plane remained in the air into the next day for a total time of 28 hours 35 minutes 27 seconds.

5 MAY • Secretary of the Navy Curtiss D. Wilbur approved the reorganization of certain departments at the Naval Academy as required to make aviation an integral part of the curriculum. His decision established a program that began with the Class of 1926, in which all midshipmen received three months of special ground and flight instruction, and additional instruction as necessary to qualify graduates as aviators or observers during the first two years after graduation.

29 MAY • The Bureau of Aeronautics issued a directive modifying the standard color of naval aircraft. The hulls and floats of seaplanes were to be painted Navy gray; the wings, fuselages, landing gear, etc., aluminum color; and the top surface of upper wings, stabilizers, and elevators, orange-yellow.

17 JUNE • The MacMillan Expedition departed from Boston, Mass., to accomplish aerial exploration of the area of northern Greenland. The Naval Air Detail, Lt. Cmdr. Richard E. Byrd Jr. commanding, sailed with three Loening amphibians on board the destroyer *Peary* (DD 340). The civilian research ship *Bowdoin* joined *Peary* off Wiscasset, Maine. Following a 3,000-mile voyage the expedition reached Etah in northern Greenland on 1 August, and the aerial explorers covered 30,000 square miles before the end of the month.

1 JULY • When a law enacted on 28 February became effective on this date, the Naval Aviation Reserve began to organize into ten squadrons of four divisions each. Authorized squadron complements for each of three scouting and three bombing squadrons were established at 40 officers and 130 enlisted men, and for each of four fighting squadrons at 18 officers and 20 enlisted men.

31 AUGUST • Pilot Cmdr. John Rodgers, copilot Lt. Byron J. Connell, and a crew of three attempted to fly the metal hulled PN-9 flying boat, BuNo A-6878, equipped with two Packard engines, from San Francisco, Calif., to Honolulu,

184669

Cmdr. John Rodgers and his crew receive a traditional Hawaiian greeting at Kauai after their harrowing crossing.

Territory of Hawaii. Lack of fuel, however, forced the plane down shortly after 1600 on 1 September. Despite an extensive air and sea search, Rodgers and his crew remained lost at sea for ten days, but they rigged sail from the wing fabric and set course for the island of Kauai. The PN-9 covered about 450 miles under sail when the submarine *R-4* (SS 81) sighted the flying boat on 10 September barely ten miles from the goal of the voyage. The Fédération Aéronautique Internationale accepted the 1,841.12 statute miles that had been flown until the landing as a new world airline distance record for Class C seaplanes. The record remained unbeaten for almost five years.

3 SEPTEMBER • A severe squall tore the rigid airship *Shenandoah* (ZR 1) apart as she flew over Byesville, Ohio, en route from NAS Lakehurst, N.J., to Scott Field, Ill. The control car and aft section of the hull fell directly to the ground, but navigation officer Cmdr. Charles E. Rosendahl and six crewmembers manning the forward section free-ballooned for an hour before they landed 12 miles from the scene of the crash. Fourteen men died, including skipper Lt. Cmdr. Zachary Lansdowne, and 29 survived the ordeal.

29 SEPTEMBER • Chief of Naval Operations Adm. Edward W. Eberle directed the training of all heavier-than-air naval aviators in the operation of landplanes if they were not already qualified as such.

3 OCTOBER • In view of the need for an accumulation of upper air data for improved weather forecasting, the Bureau of Aeronautics requested that aircraft squadron flagships take upper air soundings twice a day when at sea.

5 OCTOBER • VJ-1B, Lt. John F. Moloney commanding, was formed from VS-2B at NAS San Diego, Calif. This first of the Navy's utility squadrons received assignment to Aircraft Squadrons, Battle Fleet.

26 OCTOBER • During the Schneider Trophy Race at Bay Shore Park, Md., engine trouble forced the two Navy entries flown by Lt. George T. Cuddihy and Lt. Ralph A. Ofstie from the race during the last lap.

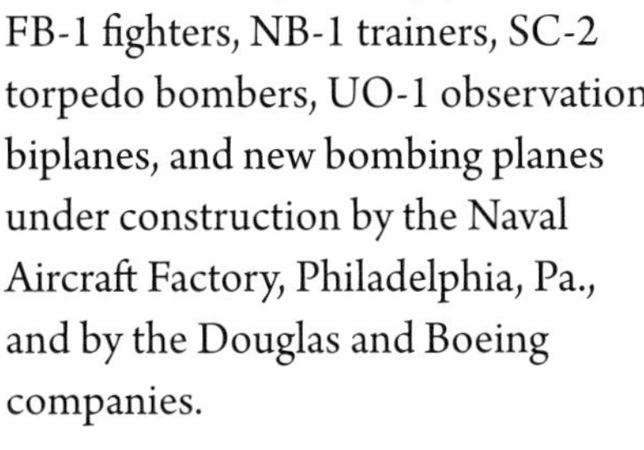

27 OCTOBER • The Bureau of Aeronautics reported the use of oleo shock-absorbing landing gear on FB-1 fighters, NB-1 trainers, SC-2 torpedo bombers, UO-1 observation biplanes, and new bombing planes under construction by the Naval Aircraft Factory, Philadelphia, Pa., and by the Douglas and Boeing companies.

An SC-1 scout bomber and torpedo plane.

30 NOVEMBER • The President's Aircraft Board, known as the Morrow Board after its senior member, submitted its report to President Calvin Coolidge. On the basis of views expressed in extended hearings by prominent civilian and military leaders, the board made recommendations on the aviation industry and military aviation that influenced a number of legislative actions taken during the following months. Its recommendations against a separate air force and in favor of representation for aviation in operational commands and high-level administrative offices, and its recognition of the need for long-range procurement and standard replacement schedules, were among the items of special interest to the Navy.

14 DECEMBER • The Lampert Committee filed its report. The House of Representatives had established this committee as the Select Committee of Inquiry into the Operations of the U.S. Air Services on 24 March 1924. The review favored establishment of a Department of National Defense and an adequate representation of aviation in the high military councils. Expressing particular concern over the state of the aircraft industry, the report recommended the government cease competing to produce aircraft, their engines, and their accessories; abolish the competitive bidding requirement in favor of other restrictions that promote the government's best interests; expend for new flying equipment $10 million annually in both the War and the Navy departments; and implement a five-year construction and procurement program.

18 DECEMBER • The competitive trials of Consolidated, Curtiss, and Huff-Daland aircraft designed as land, sea gunnery, and training planes ended at NAS Anacostia, D.C. These trials led to the procurement of the Consolidated NY series of training planes used into the 1930s.

1926

1 MARCH • The combined U.S. Fleet participated in a joint Army-Navy exercise that included Fleet Problem VI in the Panamanian and Caribbean areas through 15 March.

21 APRIL • Secretary of the Navy Curtiss D. Wilbur directed that beginning with the Class of 1926 all Naval Academy graduates were to complete a 25-hour course on flight instruction during their first year of sea duty. To provide for this instruction, the Navy would establish flight schools at NAS Hampton Roads, Va., and NAS San Diego, Calif.

9 MAY • Pilot Lt. Cmdr. Richard E. Byrd Jr. and Aviation Pilot Floyd E. Bennett made the first flight over the North Pole in Fokker trimotor *Josephine Ford.* After circling the Pole, they returned to base at Kings Bay, Spitzbergen, Norway, completing the round trip in 15.5 hours.

460634

A D-12 engine powers this F6C-1 fighter, which later became the protoype F6C-4.

14 MAY • Lt. Thomas P. Jeter won the Curtiss Marine Trophy Race held over the Potomac River off Hains Point, D.C., in an F6C-1 Hawk, with a speed of 130.94 mph.

6 JUNE • The last elements of the Alaskan Aerial Survey Expedition, Lt. Ben H. Wyatt commanding, departed Seattle, Wash., for Alaska. The mission comprised the tender *Gannet* (AM 41), three OL amphibians, and the barge *YF-88*, which housed a photo lab. The expedition, performed in cooperation with the Department of the Interior to conduct early aerial mapping of Alaska, continued through September.

16 JUNE • The Bureau of Aeronautics reported that the emergency barricade on board *Langley* (CV 1) had successfully prevented landing aircraft from crashing into planes parked on the flight deck during landing operations in Californian waters on 16 June.

24 JUNE • Congress approved an act implementing the recommendations of the President's Aircraft Board, known as the Morrow Board after its senior member. The act authorized the assignment of naval aviators to command aviation stations, schools, and tactical flight units as well as naval aviators or naval aviation observers to command aircraft carriers and tenders; the creation of the office of an assistant secretary of the Navy to foster naval aeronautics; the establishment of a five-year aircraft program to increase the number on hand to 1,000 useful planes; and the requirement that the number of enlisted pilots was to comprise not less than 30 percent of the total number of pilots on active duty in the Navy. The law became effective on 1 July.

2 JULY • Congress authorized the Distinguished Flying Cross as an award for acts of heroism or extraordinary achievement in aerial flight by any member of the armed services, including the National Guard and the Reserves, retroactive to 6 April 1917.

10 JULY • Edward P. Warner took the oath of office as the first Assistant Secretary of the Navy for Aeronautics.

28 JULY • The submarine *S-1*, (SS 105) Lt. Charles B. Momsen commanding, surfaced and launched Lt. Dolph C. Allen in a Cox-Klemin XS-2 seaplane. The submarine also recovered the aircraft, secured the XS-2 in a tank affixed to the deck, and submerged, completing the first cycle of operations in a series of tests investigating the feasibility of basing planes on board submarines.

Edward P. Warner becomes the first Assistant Secretary of the Navy for Aeronautics, 10 July 1926.

9 AUGUST • In a day of tests to determine the speed of handling aircraft at sea, planes of VF-1 completed 127 landings on board *Langley* (CV 1) off southern California. This experience allowed the squadron to land 12 planes in 21 minutes under the emergency conditions encountered when the ship ran into a heavy mist on a later date.

18 AUGUST • The Navy let a contract to the Aircraft Development Corp., of Detroit, Mich., for a metal-clad airship designated ZMC-2. The descriptive term "metal-clad" resulted from the fact that a gas-tight stressed-aluminum skin covered the lightly framed hull. The design also had to be pressure-rigid in that positive internal gas pressure maintained the shape of the hull.

27 AUGUST • While attempting to land at the Philadelphia Navy Yard after a flight from NAS Anacostia, D.C., pilot Cmdr. John Rodgers (Naval Aviator No. 2) and aircrewman AMM1 Samuel J. Schultz crashed in a VE-9 biplane, BuNo A-6470, in the Delaware River near the dock of the Naval Aircraft Factory. Sailors extricated Rodgers from the wreck and took him to a hospital, but he died from his injuries. Schultz survived but sustained serious injuries.

22 OCTOBER • In a display of tactics developed by VF-2, a flight of F6C-2 carrier-based fighters, Lt. Cmdr. Frank D. Wagner commanding, simulated an attack on the heavy ships of the Pacific Fleet as they sortied from San Pedro, Calif. The Hawks conducted almost vertical dives from 12,000 feet at the preappointed time of which the fleet had been forewarned, but nonetheless achieved complete surprise. The general consensus among observers was that the tactic proved operationally effective. This became the first fleet demonstration of dive bombing. Although VF-2 had independently initiated this demonstration, VF-5 on the East Coast was simultaneously developing similar tactics, indicating the obvious nature of the solution to the problem of effective bomb delivery.

13 NOVEMBER • Lt. Christian F. Schilt, USMC, took second place in the Schneider Cup Race in an R3C-2 racing seaplane at Hampton Roads, Va., with an average speed of 231.363 mph. Schilt's achievement marked the final Navy participation in international racing competition.

19 NOVEMBER • The battleship *Maryland* (BB 46) conducted experimental firing of the Mark XIX antiaircraft fire control system. Developed by the Ford Instrument Co., the system incorporated a stabilized line of sight to aid in tracking approaching aircraft.

13 DECEMBER • Commander Aircraft Squadrons, Battle Fleet Rear Adm. Joseph M. Reeves reported on the results of the first dive-bombing exercise, known as "light bombing," conducted in a formal fleet gunnery competition. One Marine Corps and two Navy fighter squadrons, along with three Navy observation squadrons,

1053777

Lt. Dolph C. Allen launches XS-2 seaplane from the submarine *S-1* (SS 105), 28 July 1926.

participated. The Marine and Navy fighters separately made 45-degree dives and dropped 25-pound fragmentation bombs. The observation squadrons simulated attacks from 1,000 feet. A flight of F6C and FB-5 biplanes of VF-2, Lt. Cmdr. Frank D. Wagner commanding, scored 19 hits with 45 bombs on a 100-by-45 foot target. The uses visualized for this tactic included disabling or demolishing flight decks, destroying enemy aircraft in flight, attacking exposed people on ships or ashore, and assailing light surface craft and submarines.

1927

1 JANUARY • A flight test section was established as a separate department at NAS Anacostia, D.C., Lt. George R. Henderson in charge.

1 JANUARY • VF-2 was established at NAS San Diego, Calif., Lt. Cmdr. James M. Shoemaker commanding. Four naval aviators and ten aviation pilots manned the squadron to test the feasibility of using enlisted pilots in fleet squadrons.

18 JANUARY • Lt. Cmdr. John R. Poppen, MC, reported for duty in charge of the Aviation Section of the Naval Medical School in Washington, D.C. For the next three months the school devoted all of its resources to intensive instruction in aviation medicine. This marked the beginning of flight surgeon training in the Navy as well as the end of an interservice agreement, in effect since 1922, by which Navy medical officers trained at the Army's flight surgeon school.

2 MARCH • Just prior to Fleet Problem VII the Army and Navy engaged in a joint exercise to test the U.S. defenses of the Panama Canal. During the simulation ships bombarded the Pacific side of the canal, and aircraft bombed the Miraflores Locks. Evaluators noted that the exercises confirmed their opinion that ships alone could not knock out the canal but could do so in combination with aerial attacks. These findings called for greater defense of the canal from attacks from above. The exercise concluded on 5 March.

9 MARCH • During Fleet Problem VII conducted in the Caribbean through 14 March, sailors and Marines gained further experience in carrier operations. The Bureau of Aeronautics reported that the exercises revealed that ships should be allowed great latitude in maneuvering, that carriers need to provide constant protection against air attack, and that Commander Aircraft Squadrons must be allowed wide freedom of action in employing planes.

9 MARCH • The Navy purchased a JR-1 trimotor from the Ford Motor Co. as its first passenger transport following a demonstration at NAS Anacostia, D.C.

31 MARCH • Pilot Lt. j.g. William T. Rassieur, copilot Cmdr. Robert W. Cabaniss (Naval Aviator No. 36) and the commanding officer of the aircraft tender *Aroostook* (CM 3), with crewmembers Lt. Martin B. Stonestreet, ACMM C. Vincent, RM1 J. R. Roe, and AAM2 E. W. Oliver, crashed in a PN-9 flying boat, BuNo A-6878, at NS Guantánamo Bay, Cuba. The PN-9 took off in a moderate swell during the morning watch but encountered a cross wind and heavy seas while flying off the northwestern tip of Navassa Island. The wind carried away the plane's tail and it crashed nose down, caught fire, and sank. Cabaniss died, and the other men all sustained varying degrees of injuries, including burns. On 9 July 1941 the Navy dedicated Cabaniss Field in his honor at NAS Corpus Christi, Texas.

14 APRIL • Lt. George R. Henderson broke the world altitude record for Class C seaplanes, with a 500-kg useful load, reaching 22,178 feet in an O2U Corsair equipped with a Pratt & Whitney Wasp engine over Washington, D.C.

23 APRIL • Lt. Steven W. Callaway set a new 100-km world speed record for Class C seaplanes, with a 500-kg useful load, in an O2U Corsair at 147.263 mph at NAS Hampton Roads, Va.

30 APRIL • Lt. James D. Barner broke the 500-km world speed record for Class C seaplanes carrying a useful load of 500 kg in an O2U Corsair with a speed of 136.023 mph at NAS Hampton Roads, Va.

5 MAY • Lt. Carleton C. Champion took off in the Wright XF3W Apache equipped with a Pratt & Whitney Wasp engine and National Advisory Committee for Aeronautics supercharger from NAS Hampton Roads, Va., and climbed to an altitude of 33,455 feet, breaking the existing world record for Class C seaplanes by better than 3,000 feet.

426930

O2U-1 Corsairs observe for battleship *Florida* (BB 30).

21 MAY • Lt. Rutledge Irvine established a world record for Class C Seaplanes for 1,000 km in an O2U Corsair with a speed of 130.932 mph above NAS Hampton Roads, Va.

23 MAY • A major advance in the transition from wooden to metal aircraft structures resulted from a report that the Naval Aircraft Factory, Philadelphia, Pa., submitted on this date. Researchers discovered that the application of anodic coatings decreased the corrosion of aluminum by salt water, hitherto a serious obstacle to the use of aluminum alloys on naval aircraft.

27 MAY • Chief of Naval Operations Adm. Edward W. Eberle ordered the Commander in Chief, Battle Fleet, to conduct tests to evaluate effectiveness of dive bombing against moving targets. VF-5S carried out the tests in late summer and early fall, the results of which generated wide discussion of the need for special planes and units and led directly to the development of equipment and adoption of the tactic as a standard method of attack.

1 JULY • A new system of squadron designation became effective providing, in addition to the standard class designation letters and identification number, a suffix letter to indicate the fleet, force, or unit to which the squadron served. Under this system VF-1 of Battle Force became VF-1B.

1 JULY • The practice of sending Naval Reserve aviation officers to one year of training duty with the fleet following graduation from NAS Pensacola, Fla., began with the assignment of the first group of 50 newly commissioned ensigns.

4 JULY • Lt. Carleton C. Champion reached 37,995 feet in the XF3W Apache over NAS Anacostia, D.C., breaking the world altitude record for Class C seaplanes that he had established two months earlier. This achievement exceeded any altitude previously reached by heavier-than-air planes.

5370

An RR-5 trimotor transport assigned to NAS Anacostia, D.C.

8 JULY • Pilot Lt. Byron J. Connell and copilot and naval aviation pilot S. R. Pope set new world duration and distance records for Class C seaplanes, with a useful load of 2,000 kg, and a new world duration record with a 1,000-kg load, on the same flight from NAS San Diego, Calif. in a PN-10 flying boat equipped with two Packard engines. The flight logged 11 hours 7 minutes 18 seconds in the air and a distance of 947.705 miles.

15 JULY • Maj. Ross E. Rowell, USMC, led a flight of five DH-4B-1 biplanes of VO-7M in a strafing and dive-bombing attack against bandits surrounding a garrison of 41 U.S. Marines and 48 Nicaraguan National Guardsmen at Ocotal, Nicaragua. The planes dove in sequence in approximately

1027066

Saratoga (CV 3) launches her planes.

50-degree dives from 1,000 feet, and dropped 17-pound fragmentation bombs from as low as 300 feet. The de Havillands broke up the attackers in less than an hour. The bandits lost 40 to 80 men, while the Marines lost one killed and one wounded, and the Nicaraguan guardsmen suffered three wounded and four captured. Aircraft from other nations had accomplished diving attacks during WWI and the Marines used similar techniques in Haiti in 1919, however, the Navy and Marine Corps recognize these organized dive-bombing and low-altitude attacks at Ocotal as the first made in direct support of ground troops.

25 JULY • Lt. Carleton C. Champion reached 38,419 feet in the Wright Apache rigged as a landplane above NAS Anacostia, D.C., establishing a new world record that stood for two years.

16 AUGUST • Pilot Lt. Byron J. Connell and copilot Lt. Herbert C. Rodd broke three world records for Class C seaplanes during two days of flights in a PN-10 flying boat with two Packard engines over San Diego, Calif.—distance; distance with a 500-kg load; and duration with a 500-kg load. They flew a total of 1,569 miles and spent 20 hours 45 minutes 40 seconds in the air.

18 AUGUST • Pilot Lt. Byron J. Connell and copilot Lt. Herbert C. Rodd took off in a PN-10 flying boat from NAS San Diego, Calif., with a useful load of 7,726 pounds, and climbed to 2,000 meters to break the world record for the greatest payload carried to that altitude to date by a Class C seaplane.

25 AUGUST • A blast of cold air raised raised the stern of *Los Angeles* (ZR 3) on her moorings at NAS Lakehurst, N.J., until the rigid airship stood on her nose. The craft then slowly settled back down 180 degrees from the original position. Twenty-five men rode the craft over the mooring mast during the extraordinary incident, but *Los Angeles* did not suffer appreciable damage.

16 NOVEMBER • *Saratoga* (CV 3) was commissioned at Camden, N.J., Capt. Harry E. Yarnell commanding. The former battlecruiser was the first carrier and fifth ship of the Navy to bear the name. *Saratoga*'s heavy displacement enabled the operation of a large air group of 80 to 90 planes and thus allowed for a mix of fighters, scouts, and bombers as needed for missions. Designers, however, retained four twin 8-inch gun turrets fore and aft of the bridge that limited the space for aircraft, fuel, and stores.

2 DECEMBER • The first F2B-1 fighter to serve in squadron inventory arrived at VF-1B, and the squadron subsequently operated from *Saratoga* (CV 3). The planes contributed to fighter development with their air-cooled radial engines and tubular steel frames.

14 DECEMBER • *Lexington* (CV 2) was commissioned at Quincy, Mass., Capt. Albert W. Marshall commanding, as the first carrier and fourth ship of the Navy to carry the name.

1928

5 JANUARY • Lt. Alfred M. Pride made the first takeoff and landing in a UO-1 observation biplane on board *Lexington* (CV 2), as the ship moved from the Fore River Plant to the Boston Navy Yard, Mass.

6 JANUARY • Nicaraguan rebels drove two separate columns of Marines to the village of Quilahi. Pilot 1st Lt. Christian F. Schilt, USMC, of VO-7M, voluntarily made the first of 11 flights in which he landed an O2U-1 Corsair observation biplane on a crude airstrip the Marines created. Through 8 January, Schilt flew in Marines and supplies while under fire, and evacuated 2 wounded officers and 14 enlisted men one or two casualties at a time. Schilt subsequently received the Medal of Honor.

521201

1st Lt. Christian F. Schilt, USMC, receives the Medal of Honor for his heroism under fire in Nicaragua.

424479

A UO-1 observation biplane similar to the one that first landed on board *Saratoga* lands on the ship.

11 JANUARY • Air Officer Cmdr. Marc A. Mitscher made the first takeoff and landing in a UO-1 observation biplane on board *Saratoga* (CV 3).

27 JANUARY • The rigid airship *Los Angeles* (ZR 3) landed on board *Saratoga* (CV 3) at sea off Newport, R.I. The airship remained on board long enough to transfer passengers and take on fuel, water, and supplies.

1 FEBRUARY • Joint Army-Navy nomenclature for aircraft engines became effective whereby standard type names were assigned to engines based upon the cubic inches of piston displacement to the nearest ten. Under this scheme, the V-type Curtiss D-12 engine received the standard type name Curtiss V-1150, and the air-cooled radial J-5 Whirlwind became the Wright R-790.

27 FEBRUARY • Pilot Cmdr. Theodore G. Ellyson (Naval Aviator No. 1) and crewmembers Lt. Cmdr. Hugo Schmidt and Lt. Roger S. Ransehousen died when their XOL-7 observation amphibian, BuNo A-7335, crashed into the Chesapeake Bay while en route from NAS Hampton Roads, Va., to Annapolis, Md. Portions of the amphibian's tail and wing drifted onto a beach several days later. The aviation pioneer had received the Navy Cross for his service with submarine chasers in WWI, and the destroyer *Ellyson* (DD 454, later DMS 19) was named in his honor.

28 FEBRUARY • The Navy issued an order limiting the application of standard type names for aircraft engines to air-cooled engines of recent design. This order abolished, for example, the standard type name Curtiss V-1150 and reassigned this engine its earlier D-12 designation. On the other hand, the designation Wright R-790 was retained with provisions for use of R-790-A to indicate a major modification; earlier models of this engine kept the old designations, J-2, J-3, and J-4.

28 FEBRUARY • A contract for the XPY-1 flying boat was issued to the Consolidated Aircraft Corp. This aircraft was designed for alternate installation of two or three engines. The initial configurations of this first large monoplane flying boat procured by the Navy evolved into the PBY Catalina.

2 MARCH • During a flight from New York to the Panama Canal, the rigid airship *Los Angeles* (ZR 3) attempted to moor at NAS Lakehurst, N.J., but heavy wind gusts snapped her mooring lines. Commanding Officer Lt. Cmdr. Charles E. Rosendahl attempted to maneuver the airship, but a snow squall buffeted the craft and Rosendahl ordered men to release the landing lines. The ship rose skyward carrying four sailor line handlers to the control car hundreds of feet into the air. Rosendahl called all stop for the engines, and crewmembers pulled the four sailors into the car without injuries.

18 APRIL • Naval aviation gained limited experience in carrier operations and in scouting patrols during Fleet Problem VIII in Pacific waters between San Francisco, Calif., and the Hawaiian Islands. *Langley* (CV 1) took part with a lengthened flight deck and altered arresting gear, and in combination with her crew's improved expertise in aircraft handling operated 42 planes—30 fighter and 12 observation types. The aircraft tenders *Aroostook* (CM 3) and *Gannet* (AM 41) also took part. The Bureau of Aeronautics reported that "little could be expected from a problem in which air operations were so limited and where the air forces available were so small." The problem concluded on 28 April.

3 MAY • Pilot Lt. Arthur Gavin and copilot Lt. Zeus Soucek set the world duration record for Class C seaplanes in a PN-12, BuNo A-7384, equipped with two Wright Cyclone engines in a two-day flight of 36 hours 1 minute that culminated over Philadelphia, Pa.

11 MAY • An Act of Congress provided that duty performed by officers assigned to airships, which required them to make regular and frequent aerial flights, could be certified by the Secretary of the Navy as service equivalent to sea duty.

19 MAY • Maj. Charles A. Lutz, USMC, won the Curtiss Marine Trophy Race in an F6C-3 Hawk at NAS Anacostia, D.C., with a speed of 157.6 mph over the 100-mile course.

25 MAY • Lt. Arthur Gavin and copilot Lt. Zeus Soucek set world marks for Class C seaplanes, with a 1,000-kg useful load, in a PN-12, BuNo A-7384, over two days: speed over 2,000 km at 80.288 mph; distance at 1,243.20 miles; and duration at 17 hours 55 minutes 13.6 seconds.

12 JUNE • *Lexington* (CV 2) anchored in Lahaina Roads, Territory of Hawaii, at the end of a speed run from San Pedro, Calif., to Honolulu that broke all existing records for the distance, with an elapsed time of 72 hours 34 minutes.

26 JUNE • Lt. Arthur Gavin set a world altitude record of 15,426 feet in a PN-12, BuNo A-7384, at Philadelphia, Pa., for Class C seaplanes, with a payload of 2,000 kg.

27 JUNE • Lt. Arthur Gavin made a world record altitude flight for Class C seaplanes in a PN-12, BuNo A-7384, equipped with two 525-hp Pratt & Whitney engines, to 19,593 feet at Philadelphia, Pa., with a useful load of 1,000 kg.

30 JUNE • The Navy issued a contract to the Martin Co. for development of the XT5M-1 "diving bomber," which evolved in later production versions into BM-1s. These

416531

Lexington (CV 2) anchors off Diamond Head, Hawaii.

aircraft and the similar XT2N-1 from the Naval Aircraft Factory, Philadelphia, Pa., became the first dive bombers designed to drop 1,000-pound bombs.

11 JULY • Pilot Lt. Adolphus W. Gorton and copilot BMC Earl E. Reber set five world records for Class C seaplanes in a PN-12, BuNo A-7384, equipped with two 525-hp Pratt & Whitney engines, at Philadelphia, Pa., over two days: distance and speed for 2,000 km, with both 1,000- and 2,000-kg loads, at 1,336 miles and 81.043 mph; and a duration of 16 hours 39 minutes, with a 2,000-kg load.

25 JULY • The Bureau of Aeronautics authorized the removal of bow and stern catapults on *Langley* (CV 1) because the ship had not operated either for three years.

6 OCTOBER • The Navy let contracts for the 6.5 million-cubic-foot rigid airships ZRS-4 and ZRS-5, subsequently christened *Akron* and *Macon*, respectively, to the Goodyear Zeppelin Corp., Akron, Ohio.

14 DECEMBER • The shipment of 14 fighting-plane radio telephone sets, operating on a frequency of 3,000 to 4,000 kilocycles and featuring an engine-driven generator, to VB-2B on board *Saratoga* initiated service tests. This equipment was designed at NAS Anacostia, D.C., and manufactured at the Washington Navy Yard, D.C., to provide early evaluation of radio equipment in single-seat aircraft.

1929

16 JANUARY • Experience in night flying became a requirement for all heavier-than-air naval aviators and naval aviation pilots. Chief of Naval Operations Adm. Charles F. Hughes ordered that, by 1 July 1930, each qualified aviator must pilot a plane for 10 hours at night and make at least 20 landings, and that student aviators meet the same requirement during the first year of their initial assignment.

21 JANUARY • The Naval Proving Ground at Dahlgren, Va., recommended the acceptance of three prototypes of the production version of the Mark XI Norden bombsight, and reported that on the first trial two of the three sights had placed a bomb within 25 feet of the target.

23 JANUARY • The participation of *Lexington* (CV 2) and *Saratoga* (CV 3) in Fleet Problem IX attached to opposing forces introduced new elements into fleet operations, including *Saratoga*'s employment to achieve the theoretical destruction of the Panama Canal. The aircraft tenders *Wright* (AV 1), *Sandpiper* (AM 51), and *Teal* (AM 23) operated near Bahía Honda in Cuba in support of planes that flew from NAS Hampton Roads, Va. The aircraft tender *Aroostook* (CM 3) relieved *Langley* (CV 1), which was delayed by yard work, as part of the train that supported *Saratoga*. On the morning of 26 January, *Saratoga* launched 69 planes that arrived over the Miraflores and Pedro Miguel Locks undetected shortly after dawn and destroyed the locks without opposition. The Bureau of Aeronautics noted that the losses incurred drove home the necessity of providing carriers with "maximum escort protection." The concussion from the gunfire of the battleships and light cruisers repeatedly rendered their planes inoperable. Observers noted the concentration of naval airpower in a handful of ships that confirmed the need for small carriers to supplement larger fleet types. The problem concluded on 27 January.

1 MARCH • Secretary of the Navy Curtiss D. Wilbur directed the designation of 33 officers of the Construction Corps and one officer of the line for engineering duty only. As the exigencies of the Navy permitted and the needs of the Bureau of Aeronautics required, the additional naval constructors and EDO officers were to be assigned to duty in the aeronautical organization.

1 MARCH • The Navy changed the indoctrination courses at NAS Hampton Roads, Va., and NAS San Diego, Calif., to emphasize flight familiarization and determine aptitude, open only to those meeting the physical requirements for aviators. This effort sought to increase the proportion of officers completing the flight training course at NAS Pensacola, Fla., and thereby reduce per capita training expense.

13 MARCH • Rear Adm. William A. Moffett was appointed for a third consecutive tour as chief of the Bureau of Aeronautics.

9 APRIL • Evaluators confirmed the feasibility of abandoning fore-and-aft wire arresting gear during operations on board *Langley* (CV 1). Together with similar operations on board *Saratoga* (CV 3) later in the month, their conclusions culminated a year of experimental development on the landing platform at NAS Hampton Roads, Va., and led Secretary of the Navy Charles F. Adams to authorize the removal of the wires in September.

4 MAY • Lt. Thomas G. W. Settle and Ens. Wilfred Bushnell won the National Elimination Balloon Race during a two-day flight from Pitt Stadium in Pittsburgh, Pa., to Savage Harbor on Prince Edward Island, Canada. The balloon won the Litchfield Trophy, qualified for the International Race held later in the year, and established world distance records for balloons in three categories from 1,601 to 4,000 cubic meters' capacity, with a flight of 952 miles.

8 MAY • The Bureau of Aeronautics announced the policy of providing all carrier planes with brakes and wheel-type tail skids following successful tests of a T4M-1 torpedo plane so equipped on board *Langley* (CV 1).

8 MAY • Pilot Lt. Apollo Soucek set a new world record for Class C landplanes, reaching 39,140 feet in the XF3W Apache equipped with a 425-hp Pratt & Whitney Wasp engine over NAS Anacostia, D.C.

10 MAY • Lt. Alford J. Williams received the Distinguished Flying Cross from Secretary of the Navy Charles F. Adams for extraordinary achievement in aerial flight. Williams had studied the action of aircraft in violent maneuvers and inverted flight, and developed and applied principles of operation, which contributed directly to flight safety and aircraft performance test accuracy.

25 MAY • Pilot Lt. William G. Tomlinson won the race for the Curtiss Marine Trophy held at NAS Anacostia, D.C., in the XF7C-1 Seahawk, BuNo A-7653, with a speed of 162.52 mph.

4 JUNE • Pilot Lt. Apollo Soucek set the new world altitude mark for Class C seaplanes in the XF3W Apache at 38,560 feet.

11 JUNE • A conference at the Bureau of Standards established general standards for shielding aircraft engine ignition, which were essential to long-range radio reception. Navy representatives included Lt. Cmdr. Allen I. Price from the Bureau of Aeronautics, and civilians C. B. Mirick and L. A. Hyland from Naval Research Laboratory. A naval radio group attached to the Bureau of Standards had developed basic techniques for shielding airborne radios from ignition interference at the close of WWI, which permitted some remarkable radio reception. Although limited use of ignition shielding had been made throughout the 1920s, the results appeared generally indifferent in that adequate shielding had brought with it undue cost in terms of aircraft maintenance or degradation of plane performance. At this conference spokesmen for aircraft, engine, and radio fields and for magneto, sparkplug, and cable specialties considered each other's problems in order to develop practical shielding standards. Later, the 1932 edition of the *General Specification for the Design and Construction of Airplanes for the United States Navy* included a requirement for ignition shielding.

9 AUGUST • The metal-clad 200,000-cubic-foot airship ZMC-2 built by Aircraft Development Corp. made its first flight at Grosse Ile Airport in Detroit, Mich. This airship subsequently served for several years for training purposes at NAS Lakehurst, N.J.

20 AUGUST • Pilot Lt. Adolphus W. Gorton in a specially equipped UO-1 observation biplane made several successful hook-ons to the trapeze of the rigid airship *Los Angeles* (ZR 3) over NAS Lakehurst, N.J. Gorton's earlier attempts on 3 July had been foiled when the hook failed to operate after making contact with the trapeze.

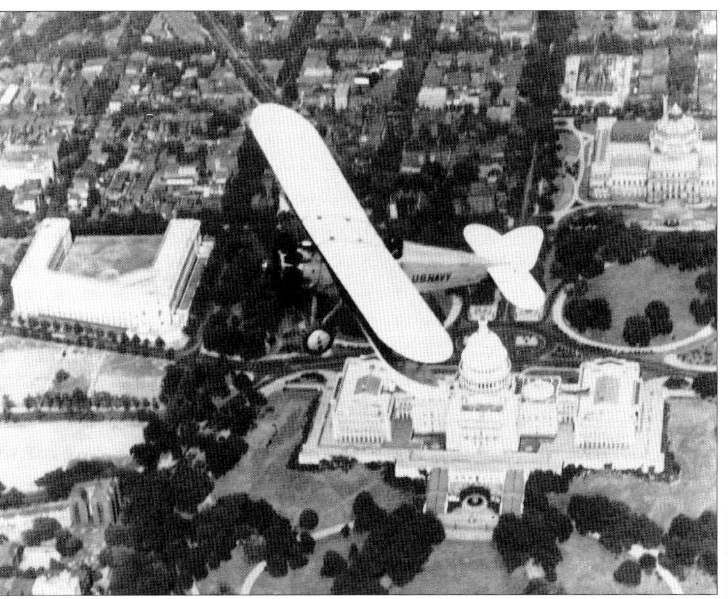

80-G-416204

Lt. Apollo Soucek sets a new world altitude record in the XF3W Apache over Washington, D.C., 8 May 1929.

21724

Metal-clad airship ZMC-2 joins the fleet in 1929.

SEPTEMBER • Secretary of the Navy Charles F. Adams authorized the removal of the fore-and-aft wires and associated equipment from carriers. *Langley* (CV 1) became the first carrier to complete this work, during an overhaul at Puget Sound Navy Yard from 13 November 1929 to 24 January 1930.

29 NOVEMBER • Commander and navigator Cmdr. Richard E. Byrd Jr., civilian pilot Bernt Balchen, civilian copilot and radio operator Harold June, and photographer Capt. Ashley C. McKinley, USA, made the first flight over the South Pole in a Ford 4-AT trimotor named *Floyd Bennett*. The plane took off from Little America on McMurdo Sound at 1529 on 28 November, reached the pole at 0114 on this date, stopped briefly for fuel at Axel Heiberg Glacier, and returned to Little America at 1008.

18 DECEMBER • *Lexington* (CV 2), one of a small number of naval ships equipped with turboelectric power plants, sailed from Bremerton, Wash., to a specially dredged berth at Tacoma, Wash., to alleviate the city's shortage of hydroelectric power following a severe drought. The carrier supplied 4,251,160 kilowatt-hours of energy through 16 January.

27 DECEMBER • Based upon scores obtained with the new Norden gyro-stabilized Mk XI bombsight during fleet exercises, the Bureau of Ordnance reported that the device gave about 40 percent more hits than earlier bombsights.

461642

Lt. Adolphus W. Gorton, flying a UO-1 observation biplane, hooks on to rigid airship *Los Angeles* (ZR 3), 20 August 1929.

184590

PD-1 patrol planes demonstrate high-altitude horizontal bombing.

426932

Sailors release a T4M-1 torpedo plane from arresting gear on board *Langley* (CV 1)—the fiddle bridges in the background support the fore and aft wires.

426947

A trio of F4B carrier-borne fighters of VF-1B.

CHAPTER 4

The Great Depression

1930–1939

The 1930s began quietly with an international treaty that extended previous agreements to reduce naval armaments. As the years passed the peace dissipated, however, and the nations moved inexorably toward global war.

In the United States, the period began with the stock market crash of October 1929, culminating in the Great Depression. Business declined, and unemployment staggered the nation. These circumstances slowed the expansion of naval aviation, aircraft inventory barely sufficed to equip operating commands, and research and development programs suffered. The fleet drastically curtailed operations. When the Republic struggled to recover prosperity through the initiation of public works, money became available for more naval aircraft, new ships, and modernization of naval air stations. Slowly, an upward swing began.

In spite of the hardships the fleet made gains in aviation technology. As engineers and aircraft manufacturers produced more reliable products and aviation equipment, aircraft performance rose. Better and smaller radios, more accurate bombsights, forced induction power plants, controllable-pitch propellers, efficient retractable landing gear, and folding wings all improved aircraft performance, making the airplanes better weapons.

The Navy installed hydraulic arresting gear and catapults on board aircraft carriers and developed better recovery procedures for battleship and cruiser observation planes. Pioneers demonstrated the feasibility of instrument flight ashore and at sea. Dependable radio-controlled planes were put to practical use as targets for antiaircraft guns. Engineers and designers learned more about the value of a streamlined, clean design.

Entire squadrons had begun to turn in the record performances once accomplished by individual pilots. Tactical innovations of the 1920s became fleet doctrine. Three new aircraft carriers enabled the Navy to equip peacetime forces with a respectable seagoing air arm. As it acquired broader respect, naval aviation achieved prominence in both fleet organization and operations and became a truly integrated element of naval power.

Serious setbacks occurred in the field of lighter-than-air, and the crashes of airships *Akron* (ZRS 4) and *Macon* (ZRS 5) sounded the death knell of the Navy's rigid airship program. In spite of favorable reports from investigating committees, continued German successes, and repeated testaments to the value of these airships in specialized operations, the service gradually struck them from its inventory. By association, nonrigid airships almost followed the rigid airships into oblivion.

As the decade drew to a close the ominous rumblings of war echoing across the seas grew louder. The Navy expanded its pilot training program and designed and laid down new ships; aircraft on the drawing boards or rising into the air would soon operate from their decks. The United States proclaimed neutrality as WWII erupted, but the fleet patrolled the seas under conditions that approached war.

1930

29 JANUARY • A Bureau of Aeronautics report revealed that hydraulic arresting gear, a type that eventually proved capable of great refinement to absorb the energy of heavy aircraft landing at high speeds, was under development at NAS Hampton Roads, Va.

31 JANUARY • Lt. Ralph S. Barnaby made a successful air-to-ground flight in a glider from rigid airship *Los Angeles* (ZR 3) at an altitude of 3,000 feet over NAS Lakehurst, N.J.

7 FEBRUARY • The Bureau of Aeronautics initiated action to develop a means of recovering seaplanes by ships

The XF5B-1, the Navy's first monoplane designed for carrier operations.

underway when it requested that the Naval Aircraft Factory, Philadelphia, Pa., study the problem and work up designs for a system able to recover O2U-3 Corsairs.

14 FEBRUARY • The first monoplane designed for carrier operations, a Boeing Model 205 fighter later purchased by the Navy and designated XF5B-1, arrived for testing at NAS Anacostia, D.C. The Board of Inspection and Survey later reported adversely on the XF5B-1's landing, takeoff, and high-altitude characteristics, but recommended developing the aircraft further to facilitate a rational comparison of monoplane and biplane types.

15 FEBRUARY • The design of retractable landing gear, particularly attractive for its promise to improve performance in fighting planes, had progressed to the point that the Naval Aircraft Factory, Philadelphia, Pa., received authorization to construct working models to establish the practicability of various retracting mechanisms.

10 MARCH • Despite adverse weather during Fleet Problem X in the Caribbean, commanders employed light forces and aircraft in search operation exercises and practiced maneuvers to gain tactical superiority over "enemy" forces. Carriers *Lexington* (CV 2), *Saratoga* (CV 3), and *Langley* (CV 1) and aircraft tenders *Aroostook* (CM 3) and *Wright* (AV 1) participated. The exercises underscored how suddenly airpower could reverse engagements by enabling a fleet to achieve long-range gunnery superiority, enhance the strength of light forces, and assure that torpedo planes could attack the enemy. Observers recognized the shortcomings of the scouting planes in the inventory. In addition, failures in differentiating friend and foe led ships to shoot at friendly planes, and cruiser gunfire damaged *Langley*. The problem concluded on 15 March.

21 MARCH • The XT5M-1, the first prototype dive bomber designed to deliver a 1,000-pound bomb, met its strength and performance requirements in diving tests.

14 APRIL • Carriers *Lexington* (CV 2), *Saratoga* (CV 3), and *Langley* (CV 1) and aircraft tenders *Wright* (AV 1) and *Sandpiper* (AM 51) took part in Fleet Problem XI in the Caribbean. The problem focused on scouting and on concentrating dispersed forces, as well as studied how concentrated forces attacked dispersed opponents.

Unfavorable weather and visibility complicated the exercise. Light cruiser *Richmond* (CL 9) briefly fired her 6-inch guns at *Lexington* on 16 April. The umpire ruled that the shots knocked out six planes on the flight deck and evaluated the failure of *Lexington*'s other aircraft to lay smoke as a serious tactical omission. Two nights later "Black" battleships *Tennessee* (BB 43) and *West Virginia* (BB 48) mistakenly identified their carrier *Saratoga* as "Blue" *Lexington* and opened fire at her from a range of 9,000 yards with their respective 14- and 16-inch guns. The umpire subsequently ruled *Saratoga* out of action, but not before her planes dropped eleven 1,000-pound bombs on Blue battleships from an altitude of 10,000 feet before the problem ended on 18 April.

Experience from Fleet Problem X the preceding month and in this exercise led the Bureau of Aeronautics to call for the establishment of several "semi-permanent task groups [each] consisting of carrier, cruisers and destroyers," the equipping of all airplanes with radios, the development of "proper type" scouting planes, the growth of scouting squadrons to 18 aircraft, and an increase in the value of extreme long-range patrol planes.

21 APRIL • The Bureau of Navigation issued a circular letter directing that no more enlisted applicants be recommended for pilot training. When men already in the system or under instruction completed their course in early 1932, this order caused a temporary lull in enlisted pilot training.

22 APRIL • The signatories of the Washington Naval Treaty signed an additional accord at London, England, which carried forward the general limitations of the earlier agreement and provided for further reductions of naval armaments. The signatories broadened the definition of aircraft carriers to include ships of any tonnage designed primarily for aircraft operations; agreed that the installation of landing-on or flying-off platforms on warships designed and used primarily for other purposes were not to make such ships aircraft carriers; and stated no capital ships in existence on 1 April 1930 were to be fitted with such platforms or decks.

31 MAY • Capt. Arthur H. Page Jr., USMC, won the last annual Curtiss Marine Trophy Race for service seaplanes in an F6C-3 Hawk, with a speed of 164.08 mph over the Potomac River at NAS Anacostia, D.C.

4 JUNE • On the first anniversary of the pilot's seaplane altitude record, Lt. Apollo Soucek reached a new height of 43,166 feet in a Wright F3W-1 Apache landplane equipped with a Pratt & Whitney 450-hp engine over NAS Anacostia, D.C., regaining the world altitude record he had held briefly the previous year.

21 JULY • Capt. Arthur H. Page Jr., USMC, from a sealed hooded cockpit of an O2U Corsair completed an instrument flight of about 1,000 miles from Omaha, Neb., to NAS Anacostia, D.C., via Chicago, Ill., and Cleveland, Ohio—the longest blind flight to date. 1st Lt. Vernon M. Guymon, USMC, acted as safety pilot and took over the controls only for the landings after Page brought the plane over the fields at 200 feet.

1 SEPTEMBER • Capt. Arthur H. Page Jr., USMC, comprised the only military entry in the race for the Thompson Trophy in Chicago. The pilot gained and increased an early lead in an XF6C-6 Hawk, but on the 17th of 20 laps Page crashed—in all likelihood from carbon monoxide poisoning—and later died.

5 NOVEMBER • The director of the Naval Research Laboratory reported that researchers Leo C. Young and L. A. Hyland had detected an airplane flying overhead during experiments in the directional effects of radio. Their success led to the formal establishment of a project at the laboratory for "Detection of Enemy Vessels and Aircraft by Radio."

460434

Capt. Arthur H. Page Jr., USMC, left, and 1st Lt. Vernon M. Guymon, USMC, complete the longest blind flight to date, 21 July 1930.

28 NOVEMBER • Chief of Naval Operations Adm. William V. Pratt issued a naval air policy effective on 1 April 1931 that reorganized naval aviation and established it as an integral part of the Navy under Commander in Chief, U.S. Fleet. Adm. Pratt's guidelines stressed fleet mobility and offensive action to protect against invasion from overseas; assigned the development of the offensive power of the fleet, including advanced base forces, as the primary task of naval aviation; and relegated participation in coastal defense to secondary status. The policy also directed fleet operation of air stations in strategic naval operating areas; only stations necessary for training, test, aircraft repairs, and support functions were to be maintained by shore commands.

2 DECEMBER • Seaplane tender *Aroostook* (CM 3), one utility squadron, and two patrol squadrons of the Battle Fleet reported for duty to Commander Base Force, providing that command with its first aviation organization.

1931

8 JANUARY • The completion of tests at the Naval Proving Ground, Dahlgren, Va., ensured the further development of dive-bombing equipment and tactics. The evaluators discovered that displacing gear eliminated the recently encountered danger of bombs colliding with releasing airplanes.

9 JANUARY • Chief of Naval Operations Adm. William V. Pratt and Army Chief of Staff Gen. Douglas A. MacArthur announced an agreement on the division of their respective air forces' responsibilities for coast defense. The terms of the agreement concentrated naval aviation with mobile operations of the fleet while recognizing the primacy of the Army Air Corps, the land-based air arm of the Army, in the defense of coasts and overseas possessions.

22 JANUARY • The Navy ordered its first rotary-wing aircraft, an XOP-1 autogiro, from Pitcairn Aircraft Co.

15 FEBRUARY • Carriers *Langley* (CV 1), *Lexington* (CV 2), and *Saratoga* (CV 3) together with aircraft tenders *Wright* (AV 1), *Patoka* (AO 9), and *Swan* (AM 34) fought across the Eastern Pacific toward Panamanian waters during Fleet Problem XII, practicing strategic scouting, the employment of carriers and light cruisers, the defense of a coastline, and the attack and defense of a convoy.

The problem pitted one fleet strong in aircraft and weak in battleships against another fleet with reverse strengths. Rigid airship *Los Angeles* (ZR 3) took part in her first problem as a scout, but her "extreme vulnerability" generated controversy. Aircraft checked but did not stop the battleship fleet advance, and despite inferior air support, the battleship fleet defeated the carrier fleet. The limitations of carriers became apparent when their aircraft expended half of their fuel and ammunition in just two days. In addition, many heavy cruisers lacked sufficient stability for catapult and recovery operations. The problem concluded on 21 February.

25 FEBRUARY • The Bureau of Aeronautics issued a new pilot training syllabus, which added advanced seaplane training courses and reinstated bombing and torpedo courses and observation and gunnery courses that were dropped in November 1929. These changes expanded the regular flight course to 258.75 hours or, for those also taking advanced combat, to 282.75 hours. The new syllabus also expanded the ground school course to 386.5 hours, with a short course in photography among the additions.

2 MARCH • The Bureau of Aeronautics awarded a contract for two variable-pitch propellers, suitable for use on combat aircraft, to Hamilton Standard Propeller Co., initiating development of a propeller type the Navy would later adopt and which would help aircraft engines realize their full potential during WWII.

3 MARCH • The Bureau of Aeronautics approved a recommendation of two officers from the postgraduate aeronautical engineering group for study at the California Institute of Technology. As a result, the Navy's practice of assigning postgraduate students to civilian institutions broadened to permit greater specialization, and for the next three academic years students received assignments to either Massachusetts Institute of Technology to study aircraft engines or CalTech to study aircraft structures.

31 MARCH • *Lexington* (CV 2) sailed from NS Guantánamo Bay, Cuba, to Nicaraguan waters to help Marines, hospital ship *Relief* (AH 1), and other vessels assist

1053789

Marine expeditionary aircraft at Marine Corps Field Quantico, Va., 1931.

victims of an earthquake that demolished much of Managua, Nicaragua. Early the next afternoon, *Lexington* inaugurated carrier relief operations when she launched five aircraft carrying medical teams, supplies, and provisions to the stricken capital.

1 APRIL • The U.S. Fleet was reorganized into Battle, Scouting, Submarine, and Base Forces. Effective on this date, General Order No. 211 of 10 December 1930 provided for the appointment of dedicated commanders for aircraft and for each type of ship. Aviation type commands in the Battle, Scouting, and Base Forces were designated Commander Aircraft [name of force].

2 APRIL • Grumman received a contract for a protoype XFF-1 two-seat fighter, BuNo A-8878. This plane marked the first naval aircraft to incorporate retractable landing gear for the purpose of reducing aerodynamic drag and thereby increasing performance.

9 APRIL • Glenn L. Martin Co. received a contract for 12 BM-1s. These planes were further developments of the XT5M-1 and the first dive bombers capable of attacking with heavy (1,000-pound) bombs procured in sufficient numbers to equip a naval squadron.

1 JUNE • The Bureau of Aeronautics issued new specifications for aircraft markings that directed use of 20 inch-wide colored bands around the fuselage of section leader planes, assigning royal red, white, true blue, black, willow green, and lemon yellow for sections 1 through 6 respectively. The same order permitted use of distinguishing colors on the empennage whenever two or more squadrons of the same class operated together.

1053772

A BM-1 dive bomber carrying a 1,000-pound bomb.

215856

C. J. Faulkner lands an XOP-1 autogiro at NAS Anacostia, D.C., 1 June 1931.

1 JUNE • After civilian test pilot C. J. Faulkner arrived at NAS Anacostia, D.C., in an XOP-1 autogiro, Assistant Secretary of the Navy for Aeronautics David S. Ingalls and Assistant Chief of the Bureau of Aeronautics Capt. John H. Towers completed a 30-minute evaluation flight in the plane.

1 JULY • NAS Coco Solo, Panama Canal Zone, and NAS Pearl Harbor, Territory of Hawaii, were redesignated Fleet Air Bases (FABs) to conform with their transfer to the U.S. Fleet and their function of providing mobile air units for fleet operations.

19 JULY • Lts. Thomas G. W. Settle and Wilfred Bushnell received the Litchfield Trophy—awarded to the aeronauts who stayed aloft for the greatest number of hours—when they won the National Elimination Balloon Race in Akron, Ohio, with a distance of 195 miles overnight to Marilla, N.Y., qualifying them for the subsequent international race.

8 AUGUST • Lou Hoover, the wife of President Herbert C. Hoover, christened rigid airship *Akron* (ZRS 4) at the Goodyear-Zeppelin Corp., Akron, Ohio.

10 SEPTEMBER • Chief of the Bureau of Aeronautics Rear Adm. William A. Moffett directed the expedition of the variable-pitch propeller test and evaluation program. The admiral noted that in recent tests at NAS Anacostia, D.C., a variable-pitch propeller on an F6C-4 Hawk had provided a 20 percent reduction in takeoff run and a slight increase in maximum speed.

23 SEPTEMBER • Pilot Lt. Alfred M. Pride and passenger Capt. Kenneth Whiting completed three landings and takeoffs in an XOP 1 autogiro on board *Langley* (CV 1) while the carrier was underway, marking the first such onboard autogiro operations at sea.

23 SEPTEMBER • Rigid airship *Akron* (ZRS 4) made her first trial flight around the Cleveland, Ohio area. The 112 passengers included Secretary of the Navy Charles F. Adams and Chief of the Bureau of Aeronautics Rear Adm. William A. Moffett.

26 SEPTEMBER • The keel for *Ranger* (CV 4), the first U.S. Navy ship designed and constructed as a carrier, was laid at the Newport News Shipbuilding and Dry Dock Co., Va.

30 SEPTEMBER • The Bureau of Aeronautics reported that it was conducting studies for catapulting landplanes on wheels. The investigators visualized the installation of powder catapults on hangar decks. The technology was expanded to include the use of compressed air to launch a plane, and by the end of 1932 the Naval Aircraft Factory, Philadelphia, Pa., used this method to successfully launch an O2U-3 Corsair.

7 OCTOBER • Aircraft obtained 50 percent hits with the newly developed Norden Mk XV bombsight in a bombing demonstration conducted from an altitude of 5,000 feet against anchored target ship *Pittsburgh* (CA 4), compared to slightly more than 20 percent hits with the earlier Mk XI model.

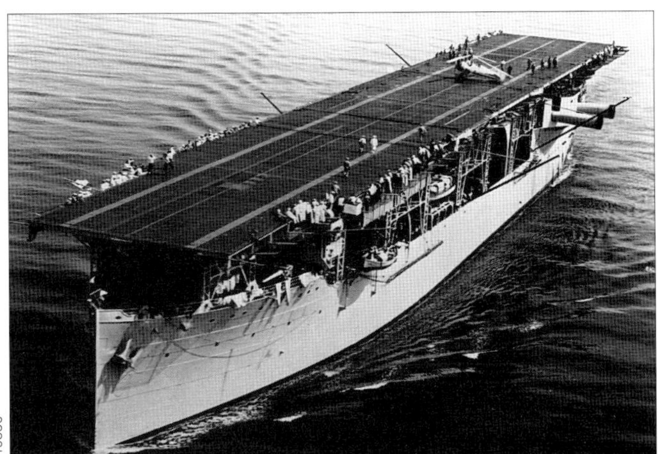
215836

Lt. Alfred M. Pride and Capt. Kenneth Whiting complete the first XOP-1 autogiro operations on board *Langley* (CV 1), 23 September 1931.

7 OCTOBER • Evaluation of experimental K-class airship K-1 began at NAS Lakehurst, N.J. K-1 featured an enclosed all-metal car and a 320,000-cubic-foot envelope that made her the largest nonrigid airship designed especially for the Navy until that time.

27 OCTOBER • Rigid airship *Akron* (ZRS 4) was commissioned at NAS Lakehurst, N.J., Lt. Cmdr. Charles E. Rosendahl commanding.

2 NOVEMBER • VS-14M and VS-15M, embarked on board *Saratoga* (CV 3) and *Lexington* (CV 2), respectively, began operations as an integral part of Aircraft, Battle Force, and as the first Marine aviation squadrons assigned to carriers. They served as such until late 1934. From then until 1941 other Marine squadrons maintained some carrier proficiency through periodic operations afloat and field carrier landing practice ashore.

3 NOVEMBER • Rigid airship *Akron* (ZRS 4) made a ten-hour flight out of NAS Lakehurst, N.J. She set a new record for the largest number of individuals carried into the air by a single craft—207.

9 DECEMBER • *Langley* (CV 1) completed nine days of operations off the New England coast in which sailors tested the cold-weather operating capabilities of carrier deck gear and aircraft as well as the effectiveness of protective flight clothing.

1932

9 JANUARY • Rigid airship *Akron* (ZRS 4) operated with the Scouting Fleet off the Carolinas and northeast of the Bahamas. The airship deployed without her planes because the trapeze had not been installed and the vessel's aircraft storage facilities remained incomplete.

22 FEBRUARY • Rigid airship *Akron* (ZRS 4) incurred damage while being towed from her hangar. The ensuing repairs caused her to miss Fleet Problem XIII.

7 MARCH • Planners envisioned Fleet Problem XIII off the West Coast as the first step in an overseas campaign in which an advanced force moved from a concentration point to a first objective. *Langley* (CV 1), *Lexington* (CV 2), and *Saratoga* (CV 3) took part in the problem, which included scouting and tracking, convoy attack and defense, and attrition attacks by aircraft, light vessels, and submarines. Repairs delayed rigid airship *Akron* (ZRS 4) from participating. Planes from "Blue" carrier *Saratoga* and FAB Pearl Harbor bombed "Black" submarine *Narwhal* (SS 167), rendering her out of action on 10 March, after which *Argonaut* (SM 1) took over command of the Black submarine division. Blue aircraft subsequently sank submarines *Barracuda* (SS 163) and *Bonita* (SS 165). Observers called for increased antiaircraft measures against dive bombers, including .50-caliber shipboard machine guns and six to eight additional carriers to project forces overseas. Evaluators also noted the vulnerability of submarines to aerial attack and the need for better flotation gear on board battleship and cruiser planes. The problem concluded on 18 March.

24 MARCH • The Army Air Corps responded to enthusiastic reports from its observers at the Mk XV Norden bombsight trials against *Pittsburgh* (CA 4) in October 1931. The corps requested that the Navy provide the service with 25 Mk XV sights, marking the Army's first commitment to the Navy-developed sight that became so essential to the high-altitude precision bombing in WWII.

2 APRIL • Torpedo Squadron 5A (ex-VT-20) sailed from the Philippines on board seaplane tender *Jason* (AV 2) for NAS San Diego, Calif. When VS-8A, the single squadron remaining in the area, was disestablished the following June, aviation in the Asiatic Fleet was reduced to the observation aircraft on board cruisers.

441980

Akron (ZRS 4) hoists an F9C-2 Sparrowhawk into the rigid airship's hangar.

2 MAY • The Bureau of Aeronautics directed the installation of hydraulic cylinder-type arresting gear on board *Langley* (CV 1) to replace the weight-type gear. This decision resulted from operational experience with two sets of hydraulic gear installed on board *Langley* in June and September 1931.

8 MAY • Rigid airship *Akron* (ZRS 4) flew across the country from NAS Lakehurst, N.J., arriving on 11 May at Camp Kearny, San Diego, Calif. *Akron* embarked the prototype XF9C-1 Sparrowhawk and an N2Y-1 trainer during the voyage.

18 MAY • With enough qualified students to fill several classes at Pensacola, Fla., the Bureau of Navigation approved a request by the Bureau of Aeronautics to discontinue the practice of waiving the two-year sea duty requirement instituted in 1930. In effect, this marked the beginning of almost a year in which no new prospective aviators enrolled.

1 JUNE • President Herbert C. Hoover accepted the resignation of Assistant Secretary of the Navy for Aeronautics David S. Ingalls. The service announced that it was suspending the appointment of a successor as a cost-saving measure. The office remained vacant until 1941.

1 JUNE • Rigid airship *Akron* (ZRS 4) took part in her second exercise with the Scouting Fleet off the California coast. The airship twice located and tracked the enemy, but seaplanes shot *Akron* down. Commander Scouting Force cited rigid airship vulnerabilities and recommended against further expenditures for the craft.

30 JUNE • *Los Angeles* (ZR 3) was decommissioned for fiscal reasons at NAS Lakehurst, N.J., after eight years of service and more than 5,000 hours in the air.

1 JULY • An amending act became effective that reduced the requirement for the Navy's share of enlisted pilots from 30 percent to 20 percent. The restrictive nature of the requirement was modified to include an exception for when, in the opinion of the Secretary of the Navy, it proved impracticable to obtain the required number of enlisted pilots.

28 JULY • The Bureau of Aeronautics allocated funds to the Bureau of Medicine and Surgery for research into the physiological effects of high acceleration and deceleration that pilots encountered in dive bombing and other violent maneuvers. Lt. Cmdr. John R. Poppen, MC, performed the pioneer research under the direction of Dr. C. K. Drinker at Harvard University School of Public Health, Mass. The results of their studies pointed to the need for anti-G or anti-blackout equipment.

15 AUGUST • NAS Hampton Roads, Va., was redesignated NAS Norfolk, Va.

25 SEPTEMBER • Lts. Thomas G. W. Settle and Wilfred Bushnell won the International Balloon Race at Basel, Switzerland, in a two-day flight that ended on the Polish-Latvian border near Vilna, Poland. Settle and Bushnell established a new world distance record of 963.123 miles for balloons in three categories of volume.

10 NOVEMBER • The Navy issued its first production order for radio equipment suitable for installation in single-seat fighters, with a contract for 125 sets of GF-1 radios to the Aviation Radio Corp.

22 NOVEMBER • Following tests of an XOP-1 with the 2d Marine Brigade in Nicaragua, Maj. Francis P. Mulcahy, USMC, reported the autogiro's chief value in expeditionary duty as inspecting small fields for landing areas, evacuating casualties, and ferrying officers and noncommissioned officers.

1933

4 JANUARY • The Postgraduate School Council approved a new plan for postgraduate work that combined the existing programs for specialists and for the general line and extended the aeronautical engineering program to three years. All of the officers selected for postgraduate work commenced with one year in the School of the Line. Those men who demonstrated ability and interest in an advanced technical specialty studied a second year in that area; in the third year, they detached to civilian institutions for work, leading to master of science degrees in most instances.

25 JANUARY • The Bureau of Navigation announced it would resume assigning naval officers to flight training at NAS Pensacola, Fla., in May or June—almost a year after the last group had received assignments.

10 FEBRUARY • Fleet Problem XIV began off the West Coast to train the fleet for the complex mission of escorting an expeditionary force overseas while enemy forces threatened to raid an outlying possession. The problem consisted of tracking, organizing the coast for defense, repelling a carrier raid, and practicing carrier air group tactics. Both sides achieved surprise attacks. Aircraft from *Saratoga* (CV 3) bombed an oil refinery at Venice, an oil field at El Segundo, and docks at Long Beach, Calif., without encountering antiaircraft fire, but opposing planes surprised and damaged the ship. Overnight on 15–16 February the clouds thickened, precluding flying operations. *Lexington* (CV 2) lost contact with her cruisers and made speed to reach a launching point during the morning watch, but two battleships surprised and sank the carrier from a range of 4,500 yards. The evaluation succinctly summarized the episode: "The LEXINGTON had not launched a plane."

Lessons learned included the "crying" need for planes capable of better performance and the "great handicap" that the slow speeds of patrol, bomber, and torpedo aircraft were causing; the necessity for carriers to attain the treaty strength of three 18,000-ton ships; the superiority of cruisers over destroyers as plane guards; and the need to improve communication procedures and the system of identification.

16 FEBRUARY • President Herbert C. Hoover presented the Distinguished Flying Cross to Col. Nathan D. Ely, USA (Ret.), awarded posthumously to Ely's son Eugene B. Ely for extraordinary achievement as a pioneer aviator and for significant contribution to the development of naval

46266

The XF11C-3, later redesignated the XBF2C-1.

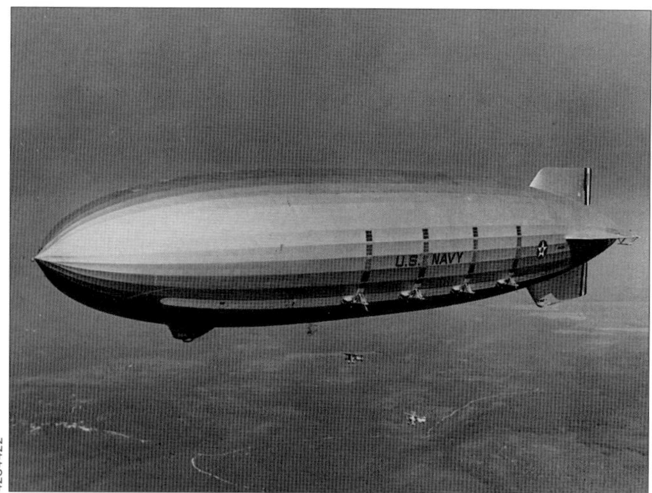

F9C-2 Sparrowhawks return to their mothership, the rigid airship *Macon* (ZRS 5). Her hangar bay could accomodate five of the little fighters.

aviation as a civilian. The younger Ely had demonstrated the feasibility of operating aircraft from ships in 1910 and 1911.

4 MARCH • Rigid airship *Akron* (ZRS 4) flew over the inauguration ceremonies for President Franklin D. Roosevelt in Washington, D.C.

10 MARCH • Navy ships, including *Langley* (CV 1), provided aid to the victims of an earthquake that occurred in Long Beach, Calif. Many buildings without reinforced masonry walls collapsed and at least 120 people perished.

11 MARCH • Mrs. William A. Moffett, the wife of the Chief of the Bureau of Aeronautics, christened the rigid airship *Macon* (ZRS 5) in Akron, Ohio. *Macon* was the last such airship procured for the Navy.

1 APRIL • Fleet aviation was reorganized and divided between two principal commands: carriers and their aircraft were assigned to Battle Force; tender-based aviation squadrons and FABs Pearl Harbor, Territory of Hawaii, and Coco Solo, Panama Canal Zone, to Base Force. Each of the two commanders exercised type functions within his force. Commander Aircraft, Battle Force, served as type commander for all fleet aircraft, and the reorganization abolished Aircraft, Scouting Force.

4 APRIL • Rigid airship *Akron* (ZRS 4), with Chief of the Bureau of Aeronautics Rear Adm. William A. Moffett embarked, lifted from NAS Lakehurst, N.J., at 1830 to assist in calibrating radio direction finders along the Atlantic coast. Skipper Cmdr. Frank C. McCord left the airship's F9C-2 Sparrowhawks behind. *Akron* encountered fog and then thunderstorms as she neared New York. McCord attempted to elude the storms and then brought her about, but a downdraft violently thrust the ship into the sea at about 0300 on 5 April off Barnegat Light, N.J. The survivors attempted to escape through the fabric fuselage, but the airship lost power and lights when she crashed, and the men who straggled from the wreckage in the darkness faced the cold Atlantic without life vests. Passing German tanker *Phoebus* rescued Cmdr. Herbert V. Wiley and two crewmen but Moffett, McCord, and 71 other sailors perished. The Navy struck *Akron* on 30 April.

18 APRIL • Pilot Lt. George A. Ott and passenger Lt. j.g. Bruce A. Van Voorhis in an O2U Corsair made the first operational test of a device later called the Plane Trap, installed on battleship *Maryland* (BB 46). Lt. Lisle J. Maxson had proposed the device, which consisted of a V-shaped float attached to the stern by a system of struts that permitted the float to ride in the water at an even depth. A seaplane taxied toward the float pushing a knobbed probe on the nose of its pontoon into the V-float, which engaged the probe and held the seaplane in position for hoisting on board. The success of the mechanism led to proposals to install the same gear on five additional battleships.

21 APRIL • *Macon* (ZRS 5) made her first flight. The rigid airship executed preliminary turning and climbing trials as well as a speed run in which she reached 70 knots.

29 APRIL • The Bureau of Aeronautics recommended that postgraduate instruction in aerology resume. Classes had been suspended since 1929. By year's end the bureau completed arrangements for a two-year course at the postgraduate school and a third year at a civilian university.

13 JUNE • The Bureau of Aeronautics issued a contract for the development of special radio equipment for making blind landings on board carriers to the Washington Institute of Technology.

16 JUNE • Under the terms of the National Industrial Recovery Act, President Franklin D. Roosevelt allotted $238 million to the Navy for new ship construction, including two aircraft carriers. In less than two months contracts were awarded for the Navy's fifth and sixth carrier, which were commissioned as *Yorktown* (CV 5) and *Enterprise* (CV 6), respectively.

22 JUNE • An underway recovery device proposed by Lt. George A. Ott on board battleship *Maryland* (BB 46) was tested off Point Fermin, Calif. The device resembled a cargo net fitted with a wood spreader at its forward edge and canvas underneath which, when towed by the ship, rode the surface forward and remained slightly submerged aft so that seaplanes taxied on and caught the net with a hook on the bottom of its pontoon. Recovery over the stern succeeded on the first attempt. Sailors then attempted an alongside recovery, which was necessary for ships with cranes amidships. With the net trailing from a boom, a seaplane again caught the net but then swung into the ship and crumpled its wing. In spite of the partial failure, the possibilities of the plane net were apparent and later adjustments corrected deficiencies.

23 JUNE • Rigid airship *Macon* (ZRS 5) was commissioned at Akron, Ohio, Cmdr. Alger H. Dresel commanding.

7 JULY • Rigid airship *Macon* (ZRS 5) received her planes on board for the first time, while underway over Long Island Sound. Lt. D. Ward Harrigan tested the trapeze with an N2Y-1 trainer, and then together with Lt. j.g. Frederick N. Kivette checked the apparatus with heavier F9C-2 Sparrowhawks.

8 AUGUST • Commander Aircraft, Battle Force, requested

441982

A trio of F9C-2 Sparrowhawks fitted with airship hook-on gear.

462618

An F4B-4 fighter.

authority to use variable-pitch propellers on six F4B-4 fighters of VF-3, based on board *Langley* (CV 1), and on one F4B-4 of VF-1, operating from *Saratoga* (CV 3), during forthcoming exercises. This request stemmed from the successful trials VF-3 had conducted on board *Langley* and marked the Navy's initial acceptance of variable-pitch propellers.

9 AUGUST • Commander Battle Force, commenting on tests of the plane net made by battleship *Maryland* (BB 46), pointed out that construction of the net and pontoon hook were well within the capacity of the ship's company and directed that all battleships under his command experiment with, and attempt to develop, techniques for underway recoveries.

2 SEPTEMBER • Lt. Cmdr. Thomas G. W. Settle and Lt. Charles H. Kendall took second place in the Gordon Bennett International Balloon Race at Chicago, Ill., with a distance of 776 miles into 4 September. Their 51 hours in the air set new world records for duration in three categories of volume.

7 SEPTEMBER • A flight of six P2Y-1 flying boats, Lt. Cmdr. Herman E. Halland of VP-5F commanding, flew nonstop from NAS Norfolk, Va., to FAB Coco Solo, Panama Canal Zone, into 8 September, completing a record distance formation flight of 2,059 miles in 25 hours 19 minutes.

12 OCTOBER • Rigid airship *Macon* (ZRS 5) departed NAS Lakehurst, N.J., for her new home on the West Coast at NAS Sunnyvale, Calif. The airship followed the Atlantic coast down to Macon, Ga., and turned westward over the southern route. The craft arrived at Sunnyvale on the afternoon of 15 October, completing the 2,500-mile nonstop flight in approximately 70 hours. *Macon* embarked a single N2Y-1 trainer for the voyage.

17 OCTOBER • In order to prevent a pilot shortage as a result of the curtailment in naval aviator training, the Bureau of Navigation approved a request by the Bureau of Aeronautics to authorize additional instruction for specially recommended students who had failed to qualify on their first attempt or whose training had been interrupted. The next month a requalification course for naval aviators and naval aviation pilots who had been on non-flying duty was also authorized.

24 OCTOBER • Initiating development of its anti-blackout equipment, the Navy authorized the Naval Aircraft Factory, Philadelphia, Pa., to develop and manufacture a special abdominal belt according to the specifications prepared by Lt. Cmdr. John R. Poppen, MC, for use by pilots in dive bombing and other violent maneuvers.

28 OCTOBER • A contract was issued to Consolidated Aircraft for the XP3Y-1, which marked the initiation of Navy-sponsored development of the PBY Catalina series of flying boats.

14 NOVEMBER • Rigid airship *Macon* (ZRS 5) participated in fleet exercises. During Exercise D the following day cruiser antiaircraft guns shot the airship down. Thirty-six fighters subsequently downed *Macon* a second time.

17 NOVEMBER • The sum of $7.5 million was allotted to the Navy from National Industrial Recovery Act funds for the procurement of new aircraft and equipment. The decision permitted the Bureau of Aeronautics to maintain its 1,000-plane program, to equip operating aircraft with modern navigation instruments and radios, and to make other improvements in naval aircraft and accessories not possible under the annual appropriation.

20 NOVEMBER • Lt. Cmdr. Thomas G. W. Settle and Maj. Chester L. Fordney, USMC, set a global altitude record of 61,237 feet in a 600,000-cubic-foot free balloon flying into the stratosphere from Akron, Ohio, and landing near Bridgeton, N.J.

20 DECEMBER • To organize the aviation element of the newly formed Fleet Marine Force, Aircraft Squadrons East Coast Expeditionary Forces was redesignated Aircraft One, Fleet Marine Force and Aircraft Squadrons West Coast Expeditionary Forces became Aircraft Two, Fleet Marine Force.

1934

3 JANUARY • Rigid airship *Macon* (ZRS 5) took part in fleet exercises. The following night she flew over the "enemy" fleet with all her lights lit; antiaircraft guns promptly shot the airship down. On 5 January fighters downed *Macon* a second time.

10 JANUARY • A group of six P2Y-l flying boats, Lt. Cmdr. Knefler McGinnis of VP-10F commanding, made a nonstop formation flight from San Francisco, Calif., to FAB Pearl Harbor, Territory of Hawaii, into the next day, in 24 hours 35 minutes. Their accomplishment bettered the best previous time for the crossing, exceeded the distance of previous mass flights, and broke a nine-day-old Class C seaplane world record for distance in a straight line with a new mark of 2,399 miles.

426937

Six P2Y-l flying boats complete a nonstop formation flight from San Francisco, Calif., to Pearl Harbor, Territory of Hawaii, 11 January 1934.

14 MARCH • Dr. A. Hoyt Taylor, head of the Radio Division, Naval Research Laboratory, authorized the development of pulse radar (as later known) to detect ships and aircraft. Project researcher Leo C. Young had proposed the basic concept involving special sending, receiving, and display equipment—all mounted in close proximity. This equipment was to send out pulses of radio energy of a few microseconds in duration separated by time intervals tens to thousands of times longer than the duration of a pulse. Reception of an echo was to indicate a target; time of travel to the target and back, the distance; and directional sending or receiving antenna, the bearing. Compared to the beat in a continuous radio wave technique under development at NRL for nearly four years, the pulse technique promised much greater utility because it was to provide range and bearing as well as detection, and because the entire apparatus could be installed on board a single ship. Researchers based the feasibility of the pulse technique on new developments by the radio industry, including the cathode ray tube, high-power transmitting tubes, and special receiving tubes.

27 MARCH • An act of Congress, approved by President Franklin D. Roosevelt and popularly known as the Vinson-Trammell Act after the two members of Congress who sponsored the measure, Carl Vinson (D-Ga.) and Park Trammell (D-Fla.), established the composition of the Navy at the limits prescribed by the Washington Naval Treaty of 1922 and the London Naval Treaty of 1930. The act authorized the President to procure naval aircraft for ships and naval purposes in numbers commensurate with a treaty Navy and authorized construction of, among other ships, an aircraft carrier of about 15,000 tons. The fleet comprised 65 percent of its allotted treaty strength at the time of the act's approval; the Japanese, by comparison, had built to 95 percent of their ratios. The treaty designers intended the act to enable U.S. naval strength to expand to these limits within eight years. The bill also provided that not less than 10 percent of the authorized aircraft and engines were to be manufactured in government plants. Under the act, the carrier subsequently named *Wasp* (CV 7) was laid down in 1936.

19 APRIL • Three separate exercises designed to enhance realism comprised Fleet Problem XV in the Caribbean and in Panamanian waters. Aircraft sank *Saratoga* (CV 3) and put *Lexington* (CV 2) out of action. On 6 May six FF-1 fighters from *Lexington* shot down rigid airship *Macon* (ZRS 5)—though she transmitted a sighting report of the carrier. The increased complexity and duration of the fleet problems led umpires to initiate periodic recesses to rest crews. Observers noted the liability of airships in fleet operations and counterbalanced their great cost, slow speed, and vulnerability unfavorably with their value as scouts. The lessons learned included the utility of small carriers in recovering battleship- and cruiser-based planes, the inefficiency of battleship and cruiser plane handling, the necessity of carrier planes capable of carrying 500- and 1,000-pound bombs, and the need for improved aircraft tenders to replace the slow and poorly equipped ships in service. The exercise concluded on 12 May.

20 APRIL • Rigid airship *Macon* (ZRS 5) made a transcontinental flight from Moffett Field, Calif., to Opa-Locka, Fla. The airship encountered severe turbulence en route that caused diagonal and interring girders to buckle, but the crew accomplished temporary repairs and continued. *Macon*'s planes flew cross country independently. *Macon* returned to Moffett Field on 16 May.

1061485

An FF-1 fighter, the first naval aircraft to incorporate retractable landing gear.

28 APRIL • The equipment and techniques of alongside recovery by plane net had developed to the point that Commander Cruisers, Battle Force, issued a directive describing the method that each ship of his command was to use. The success of the method was such that the only plane trap in use, that on board battleship *Maryland* (BB 46), was removed in June, and underway recovery of seaplanes by battleships and cruisers soon became routine.

1 MAY • Lt. Frank Akers made a hooded landing in an OJ-2 observation biplane at College Park, Md., in the first demonstration of the blind landing system intended for carrier use and under development by the Washington Institute of Technology. In subsequent flights Akers took off under a hood from NAS Anacostia, D.C., and landed at College Park without assistance.

428440

Ranger (CV 4), the first Navy ship designed and constructed as a carrier.

22 MAY • The Navy ordered its first single-engine NS-1 biplane trainers from Stearman Aircraft Co., Wichita, Kan.

4 JUNE • *Ranger* (CV 4), the first U.S. ship built from the keel up as a carrier, was commissioned at Pier 7 at NOB Norfolk, Va., Capt. Arthur L. Bristol commanding.

21 JUNE • *Ranger* (CV 4) Air Officer Lt. Cmdr. Arthur C. Davis and MMC H. E. Wallace of the carrier's V-2 division made the first takeoff and landing on board the ship in an O3U-3 Corsair, BuNo 9318. *Ranger* completed normal operations, including the recovery of aircraft over her stern, and then went full speed astern, with aircraft landing using her bow arresting gear. The ship anchored overnight off Virginia Beach, Va., continued flight operations the next day, and hosted a brief visit by Chief of the Bureau of Aeronautics Rear Adm. Ernest J. King. *Ranger* was the first U.S. carrier equipped with bow and stern arresting gear.

30 JUNE • The Navy awarded a contract to Douglas for the XTBD-1 torpedo bomber.

18 JULY • Fourteen Class of 1933 Naval Academy graduates reported to NAS Pensacola, Fla., for special training toward qualification as naval aviators. Their route to designation in January 1935 was circuitous—they received an honorable discharge upon graduation from the academy because of a lack of vacancies in the Navy, enrolled and trained as Flying Cadets in the Army Air Corps, accepted a commission in either the Navy or Marine Corps, and, finally, completed the Pensacola course.

19 JULY • Pilots Lt. Harold B. Miller and Lt. j.g. Frederick N. Kivette launched from the trapeze of rigid airship *Macon* (ZRS 5) in F9C-2 Sparrowhawks without their wheel landing gear and discovered heavy cruisers *Houston* (CA 30) and *New Orleans* (CA 32) when the ships sailed from Panama to the Hawaiian Islands via Clipperton Island. Miller and Kivette dropped bags of newspapers and magazines onto *Houston*'s deck for embarked President Franklin D. Roosevelt. Because of the improved performance of the aircraft on this first flight without landing gear, it became *Macon*'s standard operating procedure to fly planes from the trapeze in this configuration.

1 AUGUST • Lts. j.g. Charles H. Kendall and Howard T. Orville completed a 206.4-mile flight from Birmingham, Ala., to Commerce, Ga., to win the National Elimination Balloon Race and qualify for the international race.

1061904

A TBD-1 Devastator torpedo bomber.

8 AUGUST • During a training flight over the area of San Francisco–Oakland Bay, Calif., rigid airship *Macon* (ZRS 5) streamed her spy-basket in the first attempt since rigid airship *Akron* (ZRS 4) had performed an aborted test in 1932. Crewmembers initially lowered the basket empty; its instability and poor performance validated their caution.

1 NOVEMBER • The Naval Aircraft Factory, Philadelphia, Pa., received authorization to manufacture and test a Type H Mk I flush-deck hydraulic catapult. Planners intended it to launch landplanes from aircraft carriers. This type, the initial step in the Navy's development of hydraulic catapults, proved capable of extensive refinement and eventually attained acceptance as a primary carrier launch system.

7 NOVEMBER • During training with the fleet, rigid airship *Macon* (ZRS 5) sent her planes ahead as scouts, which spotted and shadowed *Saratoga* (CV 3) for several hours. The airship returned to Moffett Field, Calif., two days later.

15 NOVEMBER • Plans to install hydraulic flush-deck catapults on board carriers were formalized in a Bureau of Aeronautics request that *Enterprise* (CV 6) and *Yorktown* (CV 5) reserve space for two bow catapults (each) on their flight decks, and one athwartships on their hangar decks.

The XBT-1 heavy dive bomber, which preceded the SBD Dauntless.

18 NOVEMBER • The Navy issued a contract to Northrop Corp. for the two-seat XBT-1 scout and dive bomber.

5 DECEMBER • Rigid airship *Macon* (ZRS 5) flew from Moffett Field, Calif., to take part in a minor tactical training exercise. Two days later her planes spotted and tracked *Lexington* (CV 2), but dive bombers from the carrier shot the airship down. The exercise suspended on 8 December when a pair of planes failed to return to light cruiser *Cincinnati* (CL 6). *Macon* found the aircraft and hovered over the scene until ships arrived to rescue the pilots.

14 DECEMBER • The reinflation of rigid airship *Los Angeles* (ZR 3) after nearly three years in decommissioned status enabled her to become airborne in the hangar at NAS Lakehurst, N.J. Although *Los Angeles* did not fly again, she continued in use as a test and experimental ship for another five years and was stricken on 29 October 1939. Sailors subsequently dismantled the airship in seven weeks.

The cameraman in an SU-1 Corsair scout takes an oblique photograph, 13 December 1934.

An SOC-1 Seagull observation seaplane launches from the catapult of a heavy cruiser.

15 DECEMBER • Secretary of the Navy Claude A. Swanson approved the acceptance of the XO3C-1 single-engine biplane observation seaplane, which was later redesignated XSOC-1.

21 DECEMBER • The flight tests for NS-1 Kaydet biplane trainers concluded at NAS Anacostia, D.C.

1935

2 JANUARY • Rigid airship *Macon* (ZRS 5) conducted visibility tests with carrier *Lexington* (CV 2) to determine how easily ships could sight the airship and who would discover whom first—airships or ships. Judges considered the test a draw. The airship returned the next day to Moffett Field, Calif.

5 JANUARY • The Bureau of Navigation stated that Lt. Cmdr. John R. Poppen, MC, was to be ordered to the Naval Dispensary at the Philadelphia Navy Yard, Pa., with additional duty at the Naval Aircraft Factory in that city to observe pilots, conduct their annual physical examinations, and work on hygienic and physiological aspects of research and development projects. Poppen's orders marked the first assignment of a flight surgeon to the factory other than as part of a specific mission.

14 JANUARY • While *Ranger* (CV 4) completed post-trial repairs and alterations at the Norfolk Navy Yard, Va., some of her squadrons made the first of a series of cross-country flights from Norfolk to Hartford, Conn., and Buffalo, N.Y., to test carrier aircraft, special equipment, and flight clothing under the exacting conditions they could encounter in cold weather. The squadrons completed the tests on 2 February, and the lessons learned were used to prepare for experiments on board *Ranger* the next winter.

22 JANUARY • The Federal Aviation Commission, appointed by President Franklin D. Roosevelt as provided in the Air Mail Act of 12 June 1934, submitted a report that in essence set forth a broad policy covering all phases of aviation and the relation of the government thereto. A major share of its recommendations referred to commercial and civil aviation, but some had implications for military aviation: expansion and close coordination of experimental and development work by the National Advisory Committee for Aeronautics, larger appropriations to support the Reserve organizations, and assignment of officers with special engineering ability and industrial experience to continuous related duty.

9 FEBRUARY • The XN3N-1 prototype of the Canary primary trainer was ordered from the Naval Aircraft Factory, Philadelphia, Pa.

1061654

An XN3N-2 "Yellow Peril" trainer built at the Naval Aircraft Factory, Philadelphia, Pa.

11 FEBRUARY • Cmdr. Herbert V. Wiley, commanding rigid airship *Macon* (ZRS 5), imaginatively sent four of her planes on a sortie up to 225 miles distant during a fleet exercise off the Santa Barbara Islands, Calif. The following day the airship came about to return to Moffett Field, Calif., but encountered fog off Cape San Martin.

Wiley turned away from the coast to avoid the fog, but the airship passed through a rainstorm. A severe gust of wind struck *Macon* at about 1705 and carried away her unreinforced upper fin, causing a structural failure. The damage worsened and the loss of gas from the after gas cells placed her at an extreme angle of trim, bow up. The helmsman reported that the wheel felt slack in his hands. Crewmembers dropped excessive ballast and *Macon* shot over pressure height where her automatic gas valves opened, which blew away the small margin of lift that remained.

Twenty-four minutes later *Macon* crashed and sank off Point Sur. Two of the 83 men on board died, and the ship took four of her F9C-2 Sparrowhawks to the bottom. *Macon* was the fourth rigid airship lost, and her fall signaled the demise of the type in the Navy. On 26 February Secretary of the Navy Claude A. Swanson informed all bureaus and divisions of the Chief of Naval Operations that *Macon* had been stricken.

19 FEBRUARY • The initial F2F-1 arrived at VF-2B as the first single-seat Navy fighter with an enclosed cockpit to serve in squadron inventory.

12 MARCH • The Navy issued a contract to Pitcairn Aircraft Co. to remove the fixed wings from an XOP-1 autogiro, thereby converting it to an XOP-2 as the service's first heavier-than-air craft without fixed wings.

15 APRIL • Passage of the Aviation Cadet Act created the grade of Aviation Cadet in the Navy and Marine Corps Reserves. The act set up a new program for pilot training in which qualified college graduates between the ages of 18 and 28 were to be eligible for one year of flight instruction, benefits of pay, and uniform gratuities and insurance. Following three additional years on active duty they were to be commissioned as ensigns or second lieutenants, paid a bonus of $1,500, and returned to inactive duty as members of the Reserves. The program provided many of the aviators who manned cockpits during WWII.

29 APRIL • The five phases of Fleet Problem XVI covered a vast area from the Aleutian Islands to Midway, Territory of Hawaii, and the eastern Pacific. Patrol and Marine aircraft took the major aerial role during landing exercises when combined forces launched a strategic offensive against the enemy. Severe weather hampered the operations in Alaskan waters. During her first fleet problem *Ranger* (CV 4) joined *Langley* (CV 1), *Lexington* (CV 2), and *Saratoga* (CV 3) in the main body of the "White" fleet. The slowness of sending patrols on 30 April enabled "Black" submarine *Bonita* (SS 165) to close within 500 yards and fire six torpedoes at *Ranger* as she recovered planes, and for *Barracuda* (SS 163) to fire four torpedoes from 1,900 yards. Planes pursued the submarines, and a dive bomber caught *Bonita* on the surface and made a pass before she submerged, but the ease with which the boats penetrated the screen boded poorly for the ships. Patrol squadrons marred by casualties subsequently made a mass flight from FAB Pearl Harbor via French Frigate Shoals. The exercise concluded on 10 June.

1 MAY • The Bureau of Navigation issued a new pilot training syllabus that required about 300 hours of flight instruction and 465 hours of ground school in a total time of one year. The new course did not differentiate between student naval aviators and student aviation pilots but specified 90 additional hours of indoctrination courses for reservists.

5 JUNE • An act of Congress authorized the designation of specially qualified officers for the performance of

One of three Douglas RD-2 Dolphins built for the Navy as VIP transports painted in Navy Blue.

aeronautical engineering duty only. Secretary of the Navy Claude A. Swanson appointed a board in September to select the first officers for this designation, and his subsequent approval of the board's report brought about the assignment of 11 officers of the line and 33 members of the Construction Corps to this category.

20 JULY • The first class of Aviation Cadets to report for flight training convened at NAS Pensacola, Fla. Elliott M. West became the first of the group to become a naval aviator when he was designated Naval Aviator No. 4,854 on 12 June 1936.

30 JULY • Lt. Frank Akers made the first blind landing on board a carrier in an OJ-2 observation biplane with a hooded cockpit. Akers took off from NAS San Diego, Calif., located *Langley* (CV 1) underway in an unknown position, and landed on board catching the number four arresting wire. Akers subsequently received the Distinguished Flying Cross.

2 SEPTEMBER • A storm known locally as the "Labor Day Hurricane" devastated the middle Florida Keys, killing at least 423 people, including 258 WWI veterans working on the Federal Emergency Relief Administration Overseas Highway. The hurricane caused additional damage along the Florida panhandle and through Georgia and the Carolinas. Lt. Clemmer, USCG, had dropped more than 100 message blocks from a Coast Guard PJ-1 Flying Lifeboat to warn

NAS Anacostia, foreground, and the Army's Bolling Field, D.C., prior to the Navy's acquisition of the airfield.

1053771

The XP3Y-1—the prototype Catalina—sets a 3,443-mile record when, under the command of Lt. Cmdr. Knefler McGinnis, shown here with his crew, it lands in Alameda, Calif., on 15 October 1935 after taking off from the Panama Canal Zone.

people of the approaching tempest. Five additional Coast Guard planes flying from CGASs Miami and St. Petersburg in Florida searched for survivors, directed patrol boats toward victims, and carried the injured and recovered bodies to Miami. During one flight Clemmer flew 16 victims to Miami for treatment—the largest number of people carried in that type of plane to date.

26 SEPTEMBER • President Franklin D. Roosevelt approved an Army-Navy proposal for the transfer of air station properties, culminating several years of study and discussion of the joint use of aviation facilities in certain areas. By this approval and a subsequent executive order, the Army agreed to turn the following over to the Navy: Bolling Field at NAS Anacostia, D.C.; Luke Field on Ford Island, Oahu, Hawaiian Islands; and Rockwell Field on North Island, Calif. The Navy agreed to turn over to the Army NAS Sunnyvale, Calif. In this exchange, both parties understood the Army's intention to construct new fields at Bolling (adjoining its previous location) and on Oahu (Hickam Field).

5 OCTOBER • The first G-class airship G-1 arrived at NAS Lakehurst, N.J. The Navy used it, formerly *Defender* of the Goodyear Corporation's commercial fleet of advertising and passenger airships, for training purposes.

14 OCTOBER • Pilot Lt. Cmdr. Knefler McGinnis, Lt. j.g. James K. Averill, naval aviation pilot Thomas P. Wilkinson, and a crew of three completed a flight in the XP3Y-1 patrol plane, powered with two 825-hp Pratt & Whitney engines, from Cristobal Harbor in the Panama Canal Zone to Alameda, Calif., in 34 hours 45 minutes into 15 October.

A late version of the F2A Buffalo, the type that became the Navy's first production monoplane.

They established new world records for Class C seaplanes of 3,281.383 miles airline distance and 3,443.255 miles broken line distance.

15 NOVEMBER • The chief of the Bureau of Aeronautics approved recommendations from a fighter design competition and thereby initiated development of the XF4F-1 biplane and the XF2A-1 monoplane. Although it included subsequent changes and modifications, this developmental sequence provided prototypes of the Navy's first-line fighters in use when the United States entered WWII.

9 DECEMBER • During a second naval disarmament conference in London, England (the first was held in 1930), the Japanese naval delegation walked out following the Americans' refusal to grant the Imperial Japanese Navy parity with the U.S. Navy. The final agreement on 25 March 1936 between the Americans, British, and French—also rejected by the Italians—proved ineffective and spelled the last attempt at disarmament treaties before WWII.

1936

20 JANUARY • The Bureau of Engineering acted on a request from the Bureau of Aeronautics to initiate naval support to the Bureau of Standards for the development of radio meteorographs. These instruments—later renamed radiosondes—were attached to small free balloons and sent aloft to measure pressure, temperature, and humidity of the upper atmosphere, and to transmit this information to ground stations for weather forecasting and flight planning.

1061653

An SBU-1 dive bomber.

18 MARCH • The XN3N-1 prototype of the "Yellow Peril" primary trainer completed flight testing at NAS Pensacola, Fla.

1 APRIL • The Marine Corps Aviation Section, which had been set up independently under the Commandant of the Marine Corps in the previous year, was established as a division. The officer in charge received the title Director of Aviation, and as such continued to serve in the dual capacity of advisor to the commandant on aviation and head of the Marine Corps organization in the Bureau of Aeronautics, under an arrangement that had been in effect since the establishment of that bureau.

22 JANUARY • The nine *Lapwing* (AM 1)-class minesweepers were redesignated small seaplane tenders (AVP).

22 JANUARY • *Ranger* (CV 4), with the Cold Weather Test Detachment and 16 Army, Marine, and civilian observers embarked, arrived in Cook Inlet, Alaska. The detachment comprised six F2F-1 single-seat fighters, three BF2C-1 Goshawks, six BG-1 dive bombers, three SBU-1 dive bombers, three O3U-3 Corsairs, and two JF-1 Ducks. The expedition studied the effects of cold weather on operating efficiency and determined what materials and improvements were necessary to increase carrier capabilities under extreme weather conditions. The next day a "williwaw"—strong, gusty winds that blow down from the mountains and glaciers through passes leading to the water—swept across *Ranger*'s anchorage in the inner arm of Kachemak Bay. The winds reached gale force and stranded a party ashore. *Ranger* encountered additional foul weather and endured a "local squall of considerable violence" on 27 January; snow and icing hindered operations. On 11 February the ship came about for North Island, Calif.

27 APRIL • Fleet Problem XVII consisted of a five-phase exercise to meet a surprise offensive by an enemy fleet at a time when the U.S. Fleet had divided. The forces involved included two carriers to either side and ranged from the West Coast to Panama, and the western coast of Central America. Participants included carriers *Langley* (CV 1), *Lexington* (CV 2), *Saratoga* (CV 3), and *Ranger* (CV 4). Patrol squadrons played a significant role, supported by seaplane tenders *Wright* (AV 1), *Gannet* (AVP 8), *Lapwing* (AVP 1), *Sandpiper* (AVP 9), *Teal* (AVP 5), and *Thrush* (AVP 3). Lessons learned included the requirement for the installation of automatic pilots in all planes, the improvement of optical equipment for patrol planes, and the ineffectiveness of aircraft tenders. The problem concluded on 6 June.

28 APRIL • Researchers R. C. Guthrie and Robert M. Page of the Naval Research Laboratory began testing a laboratory

465883

Langley (AV 3) following her conversion to a seaplane carrier, including the removal of the forward flight deck.

model of a pulsed radio wave detection device (pulse radar). At one point Guthrie and Page detected planes at distances of up to 25 miles.

6 MAY • Construction of a facility, later named the David W. Taylor Model Basin, was authorized by legislation that provided buildings and appliances for use by the Bureau of Construction and Repair in determining vessel and aircraft shapes and forms.

11 JUNE • In an effort to adapt commercial airplane maintenance techniques to naval use, the Bureau of Aeronautics authorized Commander Aircraft, Base Force, to provide patrol squadrons an extra aircraft as a rotating spare to replace squadron planes undergoing maintenance inspections.

1 JULY • Gunboat *Erie* (PG 50) was commissioned at New York Navy Yard, N.Y., Cmdr. E. W. Hanson commanding. Together with her sister ship *Charleston* (PG 51), commissioned the following week, these gunboats each operated a mix of an average of one to two SOC-1, -2, and -3 Seagulls at times into 1943.

10 JULY • The chief of the Bureau of Aeronautics approved a program of improvements to the XF4F-1 and XF2A-1 fighters under development by Grumman and Brewster, respectively.

21 JULY • Lt. Cmdr. Delmer S. Fahrney received orders to report to the chief of the Bureau of Aeronautics and the director of the Naval Research Laboratory in connection with an experimental project. This marked the implementation of a May recommendation by the Chief of Naval Operations to obtain radio-controlled aircraft for use as aerial targets. In a subsequent report, Fahrney proposed a procedure for developing radio-controlled target planes and also recognized the feasibility of using such aircraft as guided missiles.

23 JULY • The Navy awarded a contract to Consolidated Aircraft for the XPB2Y-1 four-engine flying boat. This aircraft had been selected for development as a result of a design competition held late the previous year.

7 AUGUST • The Bureau of Navigation approved a change in the flight syllabus that emphasized instrument flying. A new instrument flying unit consequently formed at NAS

Pensacola, Fla. The new course, inserted between the service seaplane and fighter courses, included six hours in Link trainers, nine hours of modified acrobatics in NS aircraft, and two hours of radio-range flying under the hood.

19 AUGUST • Pilot Lt. Boynton L. Braun and aircrewman Chief Aviation Ordnanceman W. B. Marvelle completed test bombing in a T4M-1 torpedo bomber scout against submarine ex-*R-8* (SS 85) off the Virginia Capes. Braun and Marvelle flew at an altitude of 2,500 feet and dropped twelve 100-pound bombs over a two-day period, obtaining four near-misses, with a cumulative effect that caused the submarine to sink.

15 SEPTEMBER • Carrier *Langley* (CV 1) detached from Battle Force for duty as a seaplane tender to Commander Aircraft, Base Force. Following a brief period of operation she entered the yard for conversion. The ship emerged early in 1937 with the forward part of her flight deck removed and was redesignated AV 3 on 21 April of that year.

18 SEPTEMBER • Squadron 40-T, Rear Adm. Arthur P. Fairfield commanding, sailed for Spanish waters to evacuate Americans trapped in the fighting during the Spanish Civil War, which had begun in Spanish Morocco on 17 July. At times ships equipped with aircraft, including *Omaha* (CL 4)–class light cruisers, operated with the squadron.

1937

14 JANUARY • Heavy rains generated widespread flooding along the Ohio and Great Miami rivers that devastated the Mississippi River Basin. The flooding killed at least 200 people and rendered more than 230,000 homeless in Louisville, Ky. On 24 January multiple gasoline tanks exploded and spread fires in the area of Cincinnati, Ohio. The Coast Guard reported that 1,848 Coast Guardsmen operating 11 planes and 351 boats rescued 839 people "from imminent peril" and "transported to safety" a total of 67,613 people. The Coast Guardsmen also saved livestock, helped restore communications, carried the mail, and assisted in controlling looting.

27 FEBRUARY • The Secretaries of the War and Navy Departments approved the expansion of the Working Committee of the Aeronautical Board and the extension of its functions to include work in aeronautical standardization. By this decision, interservice efforts in standardization changed from a part-time program of annual conferences to one employing a full-time joint staff of officers and civilians.

15 MARCH • The Bureau of Aeronautics assigned distinguishing colors to aircraft carriers for use as tail markings by all squadrons on board, thereby changing the existing practice of assigning colors to squadrons and eliminating confusion when squadrons transferred between carriers.

4 MAY • During the nine phases of Fleet Problem XVIII an enemy fleet attempted to establish an advance base in the Hawaiian Islands. The problem included a simulated attack on facilities on Oahu. *Lexington* (CV 2) of the Northern Force launched a strike against Wheeler Field (Army Air Corps). *Saratoga* (CV 3) of the Oahu Bombardment Force sent her planes against coastal guns between Pearl Harbor and Diamond Head. *Ranger* (CV 4) of the Hilo Force sent her aircraft against the Pearl Harbor Navy Yard. In addition, "Black" carriers *Lexington* and *Saratoga* and "White" *Ranger* launched strikes against each other. This problem enabled the fleet to assess whether to employ carriers with the main body or as a detached asset and to gain "valuable data" on aircraft-hunting submarines. As a result, the Navy recommended using small carriers to take over scouting and spotting duties. The problem concluded on 9 May.

21 JUNE • Twelve PBY-1 Catalinas of VP-3, Lt. Robert W. Morse commanding, completed a nonstop, 3,292-mile flight overnight in 27 hours 58 minutes from San Diego, Calif., to Coco Solo in the Panama Canal Zone.

30 JUNE • The Navy issued a contract to the Martin Co. for the XPBM-1 two-engine flying boat patrol plane. The aircraft became the prototype in the PBM Mariner series of flying boats used during and after WWII.

1 JULY • The Navy revised its system of aircraft squadron designation numbers. Carrier squadrons were numbered according to the hull numbers of their carriers; battleship and cruiser squadrons, the same numbers as their ship divisions; Marine squadrons, according to their aircraft groups; and patrol squadrons, serially without regard to assignments. The change also abolished the use of suffix letters to indicate organizational assignment, except for Naval

105378

An SB2U-1 Vindicator readies to take off from *Saratoga* (CV 3).

District and Reserve squadrons, and interposed the M for Marine squadrons between the V prefix and mission letters.

2 JULY • The Navy agreed to accept Army airships and lighter-than-air equipment. The transfer included airships TC-13 and TC-14, which flew antisubmarine patrols during the early stages of WWII.

3 JULY • Pilot Amelia Earhart (Putnam) and navigator Fred J. Noonan disappeared in a Lockheed 10E Electra, NR-16020, while attempting to reach Howland Island from Lae, New Guinea. Commander in Chief, U.S. Fleet Adm. Arthur J. Hepburn dispatched *Lexington* (CV 2), Capt. Leigh Noyes commanding, to coordinate the search. An air group from *Lexington*, *Saratoga* (CV 3), and *Ranger* (CV 4) embarked on board *Lexington*: ten BG-1 dive bombers of VB-4 (*Ranger*), eleven SBU-1 dive bombers of VS-2 (*Lexington*), nine SBU-1s of VS-3 (*Saratoga*), fourteen SBU-1s of VS-41 (*Ranger*), nine SU-4 Corsairs of VS-42 (*Ranger*), nine BM-2 biplanes of VT-2 (*Lexington*), and one O3U-3 Corsair of *Lexington* Utility.

4 JULY • *Lexington* (CV 2) sailed from Coronado Roads and initiated the search for Amelia Earhart and Fred J. Noonan from about 100 miles north of Howland Island on the morning of 13 July. The weather worsened to squall conditions when *Lexington* began the search. Despite several days of winds stronger than expected, the planes passed through or around squalls. Men also contended with equatorial heat. The afternoon flight on 14 July (unintentionally) started at 00° and 180°. The hunt covered 151,556 square miles but failed to locate Earhart and Noonan. Noyes concluded, however, that "the search made was efficient and that the areas covered were the most probable ones, based on the facts and information available." *Lexington* came about during the first dog watch on 18 July.

15 JULY • The Ship Experimental Unit, responsible for the development and testing of equipment and techniques for carrier landings, began operating at the Naval Aircraft Factory, Philadelphia, Pa. Officers and men transferred to the unit from NAS Norfolk, Va., where this function had been performed since 1921.

6 AUGUST • The Navy issued a contract to Goodyear Corp. for two new nonrigid airships, L-1 for training purposes and K-2 for coastal patrols.

9 AUGUST • Contractor demonstration flights of the XOZ-1 rotary-wing aircraft, which included a water takeoff, were completed at the Naval Aircraft Factory, Philadelphia, Pa. Pennsylvania Aircraft Corp. had modified the craft from an N2Y-1 trainer into an experimental gyroplane by installing a new engine and a rotary wing with cyclic control.

9 SEPTEMBER • The XPBS-1 four-engine monoplane flying boat made its first flight. Sikorsky constructed this aircraft as a long-range patrol plane and it later served as a transport.

30 SEPTEMBER • *Yorktown* (CV 5) was commissioned at NOB Norfolk, Va., Capt. Ernest D. McWhorter commanding.

1 OCTOBER • Patrol aviation with its associated tenders was transferred from Base Force to Aircraft, Scouting Force, which was reestablished effective on this date. With the change, five patrol wings numbered 1 through 5 were established as separate administrative commands over their assigned squadrons.

17 DECEMBER • The Navy accepted the XPTBH-2 twin-float seaplane designed for patrol and torpedo attack from Hall Aluminum Aircraft Co., Inc. This was the last twin-float torpedo plane developed for the service.

23 DECEMBER • A JH-1 drone successfully made radio-controlled flight at CGAS Cape May, N.J. The drone took off and landed via a land-based radio set, but control shifted for flight maneuvers to an airborne TG-2.

1938

2 FEBRUARY • Two PBY-2 Catalinas collided in the dark: BuNo 0462, manned by Lt. Elmer G. Cooper, Naval Aviation Observer E. J. Koch, AMCM M. J. Fitzmaurice, AMM1 G. G. Griffin, AMM2s J. E. Walton and W. P. Landgreber, and ARM2 J. Rawles; and BuNo 0463, manned by Lt. Carlton B. Hutchins, AMCMs V. O. Hatfield, D. B. McKay, and M. W. Woodruff, AMM1 J. G. Niedzwiecki, ARM1 J. H. Hester, and AMM2 L. S. Carpenter. The collision occurred when a formation of nine planes on a bombing training run from *Langley* (AV 3) entered a cloud bank without warning. Both Catalinas crashed, burned, and sank within two hours. Hutchins remained at the controls of his flying boat to enable McKay, Hatfield, and Carpenter to escape with injuries and posthumously received the Medal of Honor. All the men on board the other Catalina died.

16 MARCH • Severe weather hampered the 12 phases of Fleet Problem XIX in the Northern Pacific between Alaska and the Hawaiian Islands. The problem emphasized air attacks against enemy shores by several carriers approaching at high speed from separate directions, and the development of fast carrier task forces. During Phase One 36 patrol bombers flew more than 1,000 miles from San Diego, Calif., and bombed several ships, including *Lexington* (CV 2), destroying the planes spotted on her flight deck and damaging the deck beyond repair.

In Phase Five the "Blue" fleet attacked the Hawaiian Islands, which were defended by the "Red" fleet, and mined approaches. An epidemic of tonsillitis on board *Lexington* deleted her from flight operations and *Saratoga* fulfilled the role of *Lexington*. *Saratoga* (CV 3) attacked at 0450 on 29 March from a position about 100 miles north of Oahu, having masked her approach by sailing on the easterly side of a weather front. *Saratoga*'s reconnaissance

Enterprise (CV 6) en route to Pearl Harbor with the planes of her air group arrayed on the flight deck, 8 October 1939.

aircraft spotted light cruiser *Richmond* (CL 9) north of Lahaina Roads, and her attack group bombed FAB Pearl Harbor, Wailupe Radio Station, and Hickam and Wheeler Fields (Army Air Corps), recovering on board by 0835. The carrier launched a second strike that morning against the ships and facilities at Lahaina, but the defenders retaliated and lightly damaged *Saratoga*. The problem concluded on 27 April.

21 APRIL • The delivery of the XF2A-1 to the Langley Memorial Aeronautical Laboratory of the National Advisory Committee for Aeronautics initiated full-scale wind tunnel tests on decreasing aerodynamic drag to increase speed. These tests, recommended by Cmdr. Walter S. Diehl, indicated a potential increase in the speed of the XF2A-1 of 31 mph over the 277 mph already achieved. The data led the Army and the Navy to aim to decrease drag when designing other high-performance aircraft.

12 MAY • *Enterprise* (CV 6) was commissioned at Newport News, Va., Capt. Newton H. White commanding.

17 MAY • Congress passed the Naval Expansion Act, which provided for a 20 percent increase in active naval vessels. Among the provisions for naval aviation the act authorized an increase in the total tonnage of underage naval vessels, amounting to 40,000 tons for aircraft carriers, and also authorized the president to increase the number of naval aircraft to "not less than" 3,000. The carriers built as a result were laid down in 1939 and 1941 and named *Hornet* (CV 8) and *Essex* (CV 9), respectively.

1 JUNE • Researchers initiated the routine use of radiosondes (or radio meteorographs) to obtain data on weather conditions in the upper atmosphere at NAS Anacostia, D.C. By year's end, *Lexington* (CV 2) and battleship *California* (BB 44) received modifications to use radiosondes.

8 JUNE • After more than two years of evaluation by fleet squadrons and naval shore activities, the anti-blackout or abdominal belt for use by pilots in dive bombing and other violent maneuvers returned to developmental status, with a finding by Commander Aircraft, Battle Force, that the belt's advantages did not offset its disadvantages.

8 JUNE • Secretary of the Navy Claude A. Swanson established a policy limiting the provisions for maintenance of aircraft on board carriers and aircraft tenders to those required for upkeep and minor repairs.

1 JULY • Chief of Naval Operations Adm. William D. Leahy authorized new command billets entitled Commander Carrier Air Group, and carrier squadrons organized into groups designated by the name of the carriers to which they were assigned.

23 AUGUST • The Navy issued a contract to Martin for the XPB2M-1 four-engine flying boat. Initially intended as a patrol plane, this craft was later converted to the PB2M-1R Mars transport and served as a prototype for the JRM series of flying boats.

24 AUGUST • In the first U.S. use of a drone target aircraft in antiaircraft exercises, *Ranger* (CV 4) fired upon a radio-controlled JH-1 making a simulated horizontal bombing attack. This event heralded a new departure in antiaircraft practice and indicated the usefulness of radio-controlled aircraft as training devices in the fleet.

14 SEPTEMBER • A radio-controlled N2C-2 target drone engaged in a simulated dive-bombing attack against mobile target/gunnery training ship *Utah* (AG 16) during test firing of her antiaircraft batteries. Observers viewed this as the first demonstration of air-to-surface missiles, and proponents of guided missile development subsequently cited the test as an example of the weapons' efficacy.

15 OCTOBER • The Bureau of Aeronautics issued a new specification prescribing color for naval aircraft. Trainers were to be finished in orange-yellow overall with aluminum-colored floats or landing gear. (The color of service aircraft remained essentially as prescribed in 1925, aluminum overall with orange-yellow on wing and tail surfaces visible from above.)

1053773

Nonrigid airship K-2, the prototype for the airships of WWII.

2 NOVEMBER • A revision of the pilot training syllabus instituted minor adjustments in the flight program and changes of greater significance in the ground program. Additions included a special course for flight surgeons, celestial navigation for enlisted students, and game board problems as a practical approach to instruction in scouting and search.

1 DECEMBER • The Hepburn Board, appointed by Secretary of the Navy Claude A. Swanson in accordance with the Naval Expansion Act of 17 May and named after its senior member Rear Adm. Arthur J. Hepburn, reported on its survey of aviation shore establishments. The board recognized the demands that were to be met if the approach of war precipitated a great expansion, and that the existing shore stations "had failed to keep pace with the requirements of the number of planes authorized by the act of 1936."

The principal considerations that determined the locations of shore establishments included the total number of planes to be maintained, the requirements of training, and strategic considerations. The board recommended enlarging 11 stations and building 16 new ones, including Oahu (Kaneohe Bay), Midway Island, Wake Island, Guam, and five other Pacific Islands. The facilities at San Diego, Calif., were to be expanded to accommodate four carrier groups; those at FAB Pearl Harbor, Territory of Hawaii, to support two carrier groups.

Lexington (CV 2) leads, right to left, *Ranger* (CV 4), *Yorktown* (CV 5), and *Enterprise* (CV 6) from Limon Bay, Panama Canal Zone, 19 January 1939.

9 DECEMBER • Battleship *New York* (BB 34) received prototype shipboard radar designed by the Naval Research Laboratory.

16 DECEMBER • Airship K-2 arrived for trials at NAS Lakehurst, N.J. She was the archetype for the WWII K-class patrol airships, of which the Navy was to procure 135.

1939

20 FEBRUARY • Fleet Problem XX ranged the Caribbean and the northeast coast of South America and included *Enterprise* (CV 6) and *Yorktown* (CV 5) for the first time. The problem tested the use of planes and carriers in a convoy escort, the coordination of antisubmarine measures between aircraft and destroyers, and the trial of evasive tactics against attacking planes and submarines. Controversy arose over the efficacy of patrol planes taking part in attacks on carriers and other ships instead of adhering to their principal role as scouts. Evaluators also recommended fast battleships to supplement cruisers in carrier task forces. The problem concluded on 27 February.

27 MARCH • Following the successful experimental refueling of patrol planes by submarine *Nautilus* (SS 168), Commander in Chief, U.S. Fleet, directed that Submarine Division 4 and Patrol Wing 2 were to conduct refueling tests at frequent intervals and carry out an advanced base problem each quarter to develop the possibilities for refueling patrol planes under a variety of conditions.

7 APRIL • The Navy ordered an amphibian version of PBY Catalina flying boats from Consolidated Aircraft. This was the prototype for the Navy's first successful amphibian patrol plane procured by the service, the PBY-5A.

15 MAY • The Navy issued a contract to Curtiss-Wright for the XSB2C-1 dive bomber, thereby completing action on a 1938 design competition. The month before, Brewster received a contract for the XSB2A-1. As part of the mobilization in ensuing years, large production orders were placed for both bombers, but serious managerial and developmental problems eventually contributed to discarding SB2A Buccaneers and prolonged preoperational development of SB2C Helldivers.

27 MAY • The first Marine Aviator, Lt. Col. Alfred A. Cunningham, died at his home in Sarasota, Fla. Cunningham had reported for flight training at Annapolis, Md., on 22 May

16455

A Marine SBC-4 Helldiver dive bomber.

1912, a day subsequently celebrated as the birthday of Marine Corps aviation. During WWI Cunningham organized and commanded the first Marine aviation command, was among the men who proposed operations, and was later assigned to the Northern Bombing Group to lead its Day Wing. During the postwar period he served as the first administrative head of Marine Corps aviation and then commanded the First Air Squadron in Santo Domingo.

13 JUNE • *Saratoga* (CV 3) and oiler *Kanawha* (AO 1) completed a two-day underway refueling evaluation off southern California, confirming the feasibility of refueling carriers at sea.

13 JUNE • The revised Aviation Cadet Act of 1935 provided for the immediate commissioning as ensigns or second lieutenants of all cadets on active service and for the future commissioning of others upon completion of flight training. The law also extended the service limitation to seven years following training, of which the first four were to be required, and provided for promotion to the next higher grade on the basis of examination after three years of service. The bonus payment upon release to inactive duty was reduced, but aviation cadets already serving in the fleet would choose either to remain on the old pay scale with the $1,500 bonus, or accept commissioned pay and the new $500 discharge payment.

1 JULY • The Navy adopted a standard system of numbering patrol squadrons in reference to patrol wings, by which the first digit of a squadron designation number became the same as the wing to which the squadron was attached.

1 JULY • By Executive Order the Aeronautical Board, Joint Board, Joint Economy Board, and Munitions Board commenced functioning under the direction and supervision of the president as commander in chief of the Army and Navy. These boards all previously functioned by understanding between the Secretaries of War and Navy.

13 JULY • The Chief of Naval Operations authorized a Fleet Air Tactical Unit to provide research and advisory activities related to operational use of new aircraft.

4 AUGUST • *Enterprise* (CV 6) and *Yorktown* (CV 5) launched SBC-3 Helldivers and O3U-3 Corsairs from flight deck and hangar deck catapults in the first practical demonstration of launching planes from carriers by means of hydraulic flush-deck catapults. The event also marked the first demonstrations of catapulting aircraft from hangar decks.

24 AUGUST • The acting Secretary of the Navy approved the detailing of a medical officer to the Bureau of Aeronautics to establish an aviation medical research unit.

30 AUGUST • Lt. Cmdr. Thurston B. Clark made 11 landings and takeoffs in a twin-engine XJO-3 equipped with tricycle landing gear while operating with *Lexington* (CV 2) off Coronado Roads, Calif. Clark demonstrated the basic adaptability of twin-engine aircraft and of tricycle landing gear to carrier operations.

5 SEPTEMBER • President Franklin D. Roosevelt proclaimed the neutrality of the United States in WWII and directed the Navy to organize the Neutrality Patrol. In compliance, the Chief of Naval Operations ordered Commander Atlantic Squadron to establish combined air and ship reconnaissance of the sea approaches to the United States and the West Indies to report and track belligerent air, surface, or underwater threats in the area. The first ships sailed to enforce the patrol the following day.

8 SEPTEMBER • President Franklin D. Roosevelt proclaimed a limited national emergency and directed measures to strengthen national defenses within the limits of peacetime authorizations, including an increase in the Navy's enlisted strength from 110,813 to 145,000 and the recall of retired officers, enlisted men, and nurses.

11 SEPTEMBER • In the first redeployment of patrol squadrons for the Neutrality Patrol, PBY-3 Catalinas of VP-33 transferred from the Panama Canal Zone to NS Guantánamo Bay, Cuba, for operations over the Caribbean. Two days later PBY-1s of VP-51 arrived at San Juan, P.R., from Norfolk, Va., to patrol the southern approaches to the Caribbean through the Lesser Antilles.

14 SEPTEMBER • The principal Atlantic Squadron naval aviation commands deployed for the Neutrality Patrol were PBY-2 Catalinas of VP-54 and minesweeper (seaplane tender) *Owl* (AM 2) from Narragansett Bay, R.I.; P2Y-2 flying boats of VP-52 and -53 from Chesapeake Bay; and PBY-3s of VP-33 and PBY-1s of VP-51, together with small seaplane tenders *Gannet* (AVP 8), *Lapwing* (AVP 1), and *Thrush* (AVP 3), in the Caribbean. *Ranger* (CV 4), with VB-4, VF-4, and VS-41 and -42 embarked, formed the core of a reserve striking force at Hampton Roads, Va.

21 SEPTEMBER • Fourteen PBY-4s of VP-21 took off from Pearl Harbor in the Territory of Hawaii for the Philippines via Midway, Wake—where seaplane tender *Childs* (AVD 1) provided support—and Guam. The squadron encountered a typhoon between Guam and the Philippines but arrived in Manila on 25 September as the first patrol unit in the Asiatic Fleet since 1932. Meanwhile, *Langley* (AV 3), the only "carrier" (she had been converted into a seaplane tender) in the Asiatic Fleet, reached Manila the preceding day. The following June VP-26 flew to Sangley Point, also in the Philippines, traded its reconditioned PBY-4s with those of VP-21 and returned to the Hawaiian Islands to overhaul VP-21's Catalinas. The squadron returned the aircraft to the Philippines in December 1940 and joined with VP-21 to form the nucleus of Patrol Wing 10. VP-21 and -26 were redesignated 101 and 102, respectively, before the Japanese attack on Pearl Harbor.

28 SEPTEMBER • The establishment of the Hawaiian Detachment, U.S. Fleet, including *Enterprise* (CV 6), expanded the naval presence at Pearl Harbor, Territory of Hawaii, to counter Japanese aggression during the Second

463784

The airships J-4 and L-1 conduct training exercises at Barnegat Bay, N.J., c.1939.

Sino-Japanese War. The detachment sailed for Pearl Harbor on 5 October.

1 OCTOBER • In order to expand pilot training immediately, Naval Air Training Base Pensacola, Fla., set up a program of concentrated instruction that reduced the training period from 12 to 6 months. The new program provided a primary course in landplanes and a basic phase in service landplanes and instrument flying for all students. It also restricted advanced program students to specialization in observation planes, carrier aircraft, or patrol and utility aircraft. Ground school was similarly compressed from 33 to 18 weeks.

14 OCTOBER • The Naval Aircraft Factory, Philadelphia, Pa., received authorization to develop radio control equipment for use in remote-controlled flight testing so test pilots could perform dives, pullouts, and other maneuvers within the aircraft's designed strength without risking their lives.

16 OCTOBER • The Germans dispatched tanker *Emmy Friedrich* from Tampico, Mexico, to deliver refrigerants for magazine cooling systems to the armored ship *Admiral Graf Spee*, which hunted Allied merchantmen across the Atlantic and Indian oceans during this period. Neutrality Patrol ships sailed to trail the tanker, including *Ranger* (CV 4). British light cruiser *Orion* and Canadian destroyer *Saguenay* located the blockade runner in the Yucatán Channel, and on 24 October

By the end of the decade, the rotund F3F biplane with fabric-covered wings was decidedly obsolete. First delivered to the Navy in 1936, all were phased out of squadron service by the end of 1941. The Marines of VMF-2 flew this F3F-2 variant, February 1938.

British light cruiser *Caradoc* intercepted *Emmy Friedrich*, but the Germans scuttled the ship to avoid her capture.

23 OCTOBER • Chief of Naval Operations Adm. Harold R. Stark directed the modification of decommissioned and Reserve destroyer *Noa* (DD 343) to operate the XSOC-1 or SON-1 Seagull. *Noa* underwent the removal of her aft torpedo tubes and the fitting of a seaplane before her aft deckhouse at the Philadelphia Navy Yard, Pa. She was recommissioned on 1 April 1940 and nine days later the XSOC-1, BuNo 9413, was assigned to the destroyer, and on 10 May an SOC-1 arrived on board. While anchored for seaplane handling trials on 15 May at Harbor of Refuge, Del., *Noa* hoisted Lt. George L. Heap and the XSOC-1 over the side to make an emergency flight to transfer a sick seaman from *Noa* to the Naval Hospital in Philadelphia. Heap accomplished additional underway takeoffs and, on 20 May *Noa* commanding officer Cmdr. Ernest S. L. Goodwin reported to navy yard CO Capt. Rufus W. Mathewson on the success of these operations. Mathewson forwarded Goodwin's conclusions to CNO, and the report influenced Secretary of the Navy Charles Edison to direct, on 27 May 1940, the outfitting of six destroyers of the DD-445 class with planes, catapults, and plane handling gear.

4 NOVEMBER • President Franklin D. Roosevelt signed the Neutrality Act into law. The measure repealed the arms embargo, prohibited U.S. vessels from entering combat zones, and established a National Munitions Control Board. The chief executive also declared the waters surrounding the British Isles a combat zone.

1 DECEMBER • Ens. Albert L. Terwilleger was designated a Master Horizontal Bomber, becoming the first naval aviator in a fleet squadron to so qualify.

8 DECEMBER • To effect a higher degree of coordination in research, the Secretary of the Navy directed the Bureaus of Aeronautics and Ordnance (acting separately) and the Bureaus of Engineering and Construction and Repair (acting as one unit) to designate an officer to head a section in their respective bureaus devoted to science and technology, act as a liaison officer with the Naval Research Laboratory, and serve as a member of the Navy Department Council for Research. The same order transferred the research and invention duties performed in the Office of the Chief of Naval Operations to the secretary's office and placed them under the administration of the director of the laboratory.

20 DECEMBER • The Navy issued a contract to Consolidated Aircraft for 200 PBY Catalina-type aircraft to support an increase in patrol plane squadrons that resulted from Neutrality Patrol requirements. The contract comprised the largest single U.S. order for naval aircraft since the end of WWI.

Chapter 5

World War II

1940–1945

The fleet faced the supreme test of war only 30 years after acquiring its first airplane and just 19 years after commissioning its first aircraft carrier. Naval aviation carried the fight to the enemy and forged ahead to become the backbone of fleet striking power.

In one swift, skillfully executed stroke at Pearl Harbor, Japanese carrier planes temporarily crippled the Navy's battle line. The handful of carriers in the Pacific filled the ensuing void and demonstrated the potency of naval airpower when they struck a retaliatory blow against the Japanese home islands in 1942.

Although the geographic position of the United States provided the strategic advantage of the ability to move ships between the Atlantic and Pacific fleets via the Panama Canal, it also placed the nation squarely between two wars with few commonalities.

Air operations in the Atlantic consisted of a blockade and campaign to protect convoys of ships that delivered raw materials, munitions, and reinforcements to the Allies. The convoys' safe arrivals enabled a series of amphibious operations that liberated the European continent from Axis hegemony.

In the Pacific, Allied strategy focused first on stopping Japan's alarmingly rapid advance, and then on the bitterly contested task of driving the enemy forces back over a broad expanse.

The United States entered World War II unprepared to execute either Allied strategy—Atlantic or Pacific. The Navy and Marine Corps air arms mustered only one small and seven large commissioned aircraft carriers, five patrol wings, and two Marine aircraft wings, about 5,900 pilots and 21,678 enlisted men, 5,233 aircraft of all types, including trainers, and a few advanced air bases.

Distance from the enemy and tremendous industrial power, however, enabled the United States to build the ships, planes, and equipment necessary for victory. American armed forces drove the Axis from strategically located bases, cut off its raw materials, and placed the Allies in position to launch the final air and amphibious offensives. These late efforts would be rendered unnecessary by the destructive power of the atom unleashed upon the Japanese cities of Hiroshima and Nagasaki, but the fleet's liberation of Japanese-held islands in the Central Pacific made the atomic attacks possible.

For the first time in naval history the opponents engaged each other entirely in the air without sighting enemy ships. Radar pierced the night, giving the fleet new eyes, as technological progress improved the defense and added power to the offense. Scientists contributed to the war effort by developing specialized equipment and applying scientific principles to operational tactics. Logistics assumed new importance, and advances in replenishment at sea increased naval mobility.

In the course of the war, Navy and Marine pilots claimed the destruction of more than 15,000 enemy aircraft in the air and on the ground; sank 174 Japanese warships, including 13 submarines totaling 746,000 tons; destroyed 447 Japanese merchant ships totaling 1,600,000 tons; and sank 63 U-boats in the Atlantic. In combination with other agents, Navy and Marine air forces helped sink another 157,000 tons of warships and 200,000 tons of merchant ships, and another 6 Japanese and 20 German submarines.

Although World War II contributed significantly to the development of aviation, experience proved some prewar theories on the role of airpower to naval operations to be misconceived. The bombing tests of the 1920s had persuaded some airpower proponents of the obsolescence of navies, but carrier task force operations in the war gave little credence to such conclusions. Those who questioned the importance of airplanes to navies were equally off the mark. Advocates of independent airpower had also doubted the possibility and usefulness of close air support for troops; battle experience validated such support as indispensable. The disappointment of naval officers who visualized decisive fleet engagements in the tradition of Trafalgar and Jutland matched that of airpower theorists who saw their predictions go awry. By the test of war it became exceedingly clear that neither armies nor navies could achieve objectives in war without first achieving air superiority, and that neither could exert as much force alone as with the aid of air striking power.

1940

4 JANUARY • The establishment of Project Baker in Patrol Wing 1 expanded experiments with blind landing equipment.

15 FEBRUARY • Commander in Chief, U.S. Fleet, noting that reports on air operations in the European war stressed the problem of aircraft vulnerability, recommended equipping naval aircraft with leak-proof or self-sealing fuel tanks, and pilots and observers with armor. The Bureaus of Aeronautics and Ordnance had investigated these forms of protection for two years, but this formal statement of need accelerated procurement and installation of both.

24 FEBRUARY • The Bureau of Aeronautics issued a contract for television equipment, including a camera, transmitter, and receiver capable of airborne operation. Researchers used this equipment to transmit instrument readings obtained from radio-controlled structural flight tests and to provide target and guidance information for the conversion of radio-controlled aircraft to offensive weapons.

27 FEBRUARY • The Navy awarded a contract to Vought-Sikorsky Aircraft for the design of a full-scale flying model (as distinguished from a military prototype) of a "Flying Flapjack" fighter, designated VS-173, with an almost circular wing. This design, which produced a potential high speed of nearly 500 mph combined with a very low takeoff speed, originated in the research of former National Advisory Committee for Aeronautics engineer Charles H. Zimmerman.

29 FEBRUARY • The Bureau of Aeronautics initiated action that led to a contract with University of Iowa professor H. O. Croft to investigate the possibilities of a turbojet propulsion unit for aircraft.

19 MARCH • The Navy authorized fleet activities to apply additional national star insignia on the sides of the fuselages or hulls of Neutrality Patrol aircraft to assist in their identification.

22 MARCH • The Navy initiated guided missile development at the Naval Aircraft Factory, Philadelphia, Pa., with the establishment of a project for adapting radio controls to a torpedo-carrying TG-2 airplane.

APRIL • Fleet Problem XXI, consisting of two phases and lasting into May, involved coordination of commands, protection of a convoy, and seizure of advanced bases around the Hawaiian Islands and eastern Pacific. Observers noted the tendency of commanders to overlook carrier limitations and assign them excessive tasks, the need for reliefs for flight and carrier crews under simulated war conditions, the success of high-altitude tracking by patrol aircraft, and the ineffectiveness of low-level horizontal bombing attacks. The war compelled the cancellation of Fleet Problem XXII in 1941.

23 APRIL • Cmdr. Donald Royce was designated to represent the Navy on an Army Air Corps evaluation board for rotary-wing aircraft. The board was incidental to legislation directing the War Department to undertake rotary-wing aircraft development.

25 APRIL • *Wasp* (CV 7) was commissioned at Boston, Mass., Capt. John W. Reeves Jr. commanding.

7 MAY • President Franklin D. Roosevelt ordered fleet ships to remain in Hawaiian waters indefinitely as a signal of American resolve to deter Japanese aggression. Subsequently, Commander in Chief, U.S. Fleet Adm. James O. Richardson asserted that the facilities at Pearl Harbor were inadequate to support the fleet and protect against attack. Richardson's stance contributed to his relief on 1 February 1941 by Adm. Husband E. Kimmel.

16 MAY • President Franklin D. Roosevelt requested a congressional appropriation of $1.18 billion to strengthen national defense, including $250 million for the Navy and Marine Corps.

27 MAY • Secretary of the Navy Charles Edison directed the equipment of six DD-445–class destroyers with planes, catapults, and plane handling gear. *Halford* (DD 480), *Hutchins* (DD 476), *Leutze* (DD 481), *Pringle* (DD 477), *Stanly* (DD 478), and *Stevens* (DD 479) were subsequently selected. On 23 December 1942 *Pringle* received the first aircraft, an OS2U-3 Kingfisher, BuNo 5870. Just before the new year, BuNo 01505, an OS2N-1, was assigned to *Hutchins*. Before these two ships and *Stanly* joined the fleet in early 1943, however, shortcomings in the plane hoisting gear led to removal of the aviation equipment. *Halford* and *Stevens* performed limited aircraft operations, but in October 1943, the Navy ordered the equipment removed from both ships and cancelled its installation on *Leutze*.

14 JUNE • The Naval Expansion Act of 1940 was signed into law. The measure authorized an 11 percent increase in the size of the fleet, approved a 79,500-ton augmentation of aircraft carrier tonnage over the limits set by the 1938 expansion act, and sought to increase the number of naval aircraft by instituting a cap of 48 airships and 4,500 planes. The next day, President Franklin D. Roosevelt approved an Act of Congress to raise the total number of planes to 10,000, including 850 for the Naval Reserve.

17 JUNE • Chief of Naval Operations Adm. Harold R. Stark requested $4 billion from Congress to increase the authorized strength of the Navy by 70 percent. This measure was subsequently known as "The Two Ocean Navy Act" and signed into law on 19 July.

20 JUNE • The Bureau of Construction and Repair merged with the Bureau of Engineering to form the Bureau of Ships. In addition, the Office of the Undersecretary of the Navy was established, with naval aviator James V. Forrestal of World War I service assuming the position on 22 August.

25 JUNE • The Navy abolished the aeronautical engineering duty only designation, resulting in the designation of all men subsequently appointed to that group as engineering duty only.

25 JUNE • Chief of Naval Operations Adm. Harold R. Stark promulgated plans to expand the flight training program. They called for the assignment of 150 students per month beginning on 1 July, and a regular increase to an entry rate of 300 per month within a year.

27 JUNE • President Franklin D. Roosevelt established a National Defense Research Committee to correlate and support scientific research on the mechanisms and devices of war. Among its members were officers of the War and Navy departments appointed by the respective secretaries. Although the committee's functions specifically excluded research on the problems of flight, the organization made substantial contributions in various fields important to naval aviation, including airborne radar.

14 JULY • Scientists E. L. Bowles, Ralph Bowen, Alfred L. Loomis, and Hugh H. Willis attended the initial meeting of what became the National Defense Research Committee's Division 14, or Radar Division. During this and subsequent meetings with other researchers, the group defined its mission: "to obtain the most effective military application of microwaves in minimum time." In carrying out this mission, Division 14 developed airborne radar the Navy used for aircraft interception, airborne early warning, and other specialized applications.

19 JULY • Another expansion of the Navy authorized an increase of 200,000 tons over the aircraft carrier limits of the Two Ocean Navy Act and a new aircraft ceiling of 15,000 planes. This act also allowed further increases in aircraft strength upon presidential approval.

5 AUGUST • Chief of Naval Operations Adm. Harold R. Stark established ground rules for the exchange of scientific and technical information with the British Tizard Mission, named after its senior member, Sir Henry T. Tizard. In general, the rules provided for the expected free exchange of information on matters concerning aviation, including the field later known as radar. On 12 August, following reports of British progress, the Bureau of Ordnance requested that the National Defense Research Committee sponsor development of the proximity fuze, which had already been under consideration, on a priority basis and with emphasis on its antiaircraft use.

17 AUGUST • A team known as Section T after its chairman, Dr. Merle A. Tuve of Division A of the National Defense Research Committee, was established to examine the feasibility of various approaches to developing the proximity fuze. Eight days later, the Navy issued a contract to the Department of Terrestrial Magnetism at the Carnegie

Institution, Washington, D.C., for research culminating in the radio VT fuze for antiaircraft guns as well as radio and photoelectric VT fuzes for bombs and rockets.

22 AUGUST • Former naval aviator James V. Forrestal assumed his duties as the first Undersecretary of the Navy.

29 AUGUST • The exchange of radar development information with the British Tizard Mission began at a conference attended by Sir Henry T. Tizard, two of his associates, and representatives of the U.S. Army and Navy, including Lt. John A. Moreno of the Bureau of Aeronautics. The conference dealt primarily with British techniques for detecting German bombers, but also touched on means of identifying friendly aircraft. Later meetings focused on British development of shipboard and airborne radar. A British disclosure of particular importance for airborne radar application was the cavity magnetron, a tube capable of generating high-power radio waves of a few centimeters in length.

2 SEPTEMBER • The Americans and the British made an agreement in which the United States exchanged 50 overage World War I Emergency Program destroyers for 99-year leases of sites for naval and air bases in Antigua, the Bahamas, British Guiana (Guyana), Jamaica, St. Lucia, and Trinidad, and similar rights without consideration for bases in Bermuda and Newfoundland. The acquisition of these sites advanced the sea frontiers of the United States and provided bases from which ships and aircraft covered the strategically important sea approaches to the East Coast and Panama Canal. The British received 44 of the destroyers and the Canadians the remaining six. British Prime Minister Winston S. Churchill had appealed to President Franklin D. Roosevelt for the reinforcements as a matter of "life and death" during the Battle of the Atlantic.

3 OCTOBER • Chief of Naval Operations Adm. Harold R. Stark requested that the naval attaché in London obtain samples of British radio echo equipment (radar), including aircraft installations for interception (AI), surface vessel detection (ASV), and aircraft identification (IFF).

5 OCTOBER • Secretary of the Navy William F. Knox placed all organized reserve divisions and aviation squadrons on short notice for call to active duty and granted authority to call fleet reservists as necessary—Naval Reserve sailors had hitherto been ordered to active duty on a voluntary basis. On 24 October, the Bureau of Navigation announced plans for mobilizing aviation squadrons that called for ordering to active duty one-third the number of squadrons by 7 November, and the remainder by 1 January 1941.

9 OCTOBER • Secretary of the Navy William F. Knox approved a recommendation by the General Board to equip 24 submarines authorized for construction with gasoline for delivery to seaplanes on the water. This move followed a demonstration in which submarine *Nautilus* (SS 168) refueled patrol planes and conducted a successful test dive to 300 feet with aviation gasoline on board; it also came after the Navy made plans to prepare *Argonaut* (SS 166) and *Narwhal* (SS 167) to carry 19,000 gallons of aviation gasoline.

11 OCTOBER • Rear Adm. Harold G. Bowen, the technical aide to the Secretary of the Navy, proposed a program for the development of radio ranging equipment (radar). This formed the basis for the Navy's prewar radar development effort, which included an airborne radar for surface search in addition to identification equipment and shipbased radar.

12 OCTOBER • *Wasp* (CV 7) launched 24 Army Curtiss P-40 Warhawks of the 8th Pursuit Group and 9 North American O-47s of the 3rd Observation Squadron off the Virginia Capes, marking the first launches of Army aircraft from a U.S. carrier. The participants gathered data on the comparative takeoff runs of Army and Navy planes.

23 OCTOBER • The Navy set up an administrative command for carrier aviation within the Atlantic Squadron, entitling it Aircraft, Atlantic Squadron.

24 OCTOBER • An administrative command for patrol aviation in the Atlantic Squadron was established under the title Patrol Wings, Atlantic Squadron.

28 OCTOBER • The Chief of Naval Operations reported the entrance into service of planes with armor and fuel protection, and announced the addition of such protection to all fleet aircraft—except those assigned to Patrol Wing 2—within a year.

1 NOVEMBER • A fleet reorganization divided aviation forces administratively between the Atlantic and Pacific oceans and marked the beginning of the independent development of forces according to strategic requirements. In the Atlantic, aviation was transferred from Scouting Force to Patrol Force, which replaced the Atlantic Squadron as a fleet command parallel to Scouting Force. The Pacific patrol wings remained attached to Scouting Force under the combined command Commander Patrol Wings, U.S. Fleet, and Commander Aircraft, Scouting Force.

11 NOVEMBER • The first general meeting of the Radiation Laboratory occurred at the Massachusetts Institute of Technology. The laboratory served as the principal scientific and developmental agency of Division 14 of the National Defense Research Committee and became instrumental in airborne radar development.

15 NOVEMBER • Seaplane tender *Curtiss* (AV 4), Cmdr. Samuel P. Ginder commanding, was commissioned in Philadelphia, Pa., as the first of two ships of her class.

15 NOVEMBER • PBY-2 Catalinas of VP-54 began the first U.S. naval air operations from Bermuda, supported by seaplane tender *George E. Badger* (AVD 3).

16 NOVEMBER • The Bureau of Aeronautics established a catapult procurement program for *Essex* (CV 9)-class carriers, providing for the installation of one flight deck catapult and one athwartships hangar deck catapult on each of the 11 projected ships of the class.

18 NOVEMBER • The Chief of Naval Operations authorized use of the abbreviation "RADAR" in unclassified correspondence and conversation, and directed the use of the phrase "radio detection and ranging equipment" in lieu of various terms used before, including radio ranging equipment, radio detection equipment, radio echo equipment, and pulse radio equipment.

30 DECEMBER • The Bureau of Aeronautics directed the painting of fleet aircraft in nonspecular colors. Ship-based aircraft were to be Light Gray all over. Patrol planes were to be Light Gray except for surfaces seen from above, which were to be Blue Gray.

1941

9 JANUARY • The first group of contractors arrived on Wake Island to construct an air station.

1 FEBRUARY • The establishment of the Atlantic and Pacific Fleets completed the transition that began in November 1940 to divide aviation between the two oceans. The titles of the Atlantic Fleet aviation commands became Aircraft, Atlantic Fleet, and Patrol Wings, Atlantic Fleet. No change was made in the aviation organization of the Pacific Fleet.

10 FEBRUARY • A one-month instruction course began under Project Baker to train patrol plane pilots to make blind landings using radio instrument landing equipment, which the Navy was procuring for all patrol aircraft and their bases. One pilot from each of 13 squadrons, one radioman from each of five patrol wings, and two radiomen from each of five naval air stations attended the course.

26 FEBRUARY • An extensive modification of aircraft markings added the national star insignia to both sides of the fuselage or hull and eliminated those markings on the upper right and lower left wings; discontinued colored tail markings, fuselage bands, and cowl markings; mandated removal of red, white, and blue rudder stripes; and changed the color of all markings except the national star insignia to those of least contrast to the background.

1 MARCH • Support Force, Atlantic Fleet, Rear Adm. Arthur L. Bristol commanding, was established for operations on the convoy routes across the North Atlantic. The directive placed the component patrol squadrons under a patrol wing that was established at the same time.

11 MARCH • An act of Congress empowered President Franklin D. Roosevelt to provide goods and services to those nations whose defense he deemed vital to that of the United States. Isolationists criticized the Lend-Lease program for drawing the country close to war, but the act allowed the United States to provide the Allied belligerents with war material, food, and financial aid without joining in combat. The "cash and carry" provisions of the Neutrality Act of 1939 were also changed to permit the transfer of munitions, and on 17 November, *Archer*

(BAVG 1) became the first of 38 aircraft escort vessels (escort carriers) transferred to the British under the program during World War II.

17 MARCH • The chief of the Bureau of Aeronautics approved a proposal for establishing a special subcommittee of the National Advisory Committee for Aeronautics to promptly review the status of jet propulsion and to recommend plans for its application to flight and assisted takeoff.

27 MARCH • The Americans, British, and Canadians signed the ABC-1 Staff Agreement in Washington, D.C. The accord established a Combined Chiefs of Staff, outlined a framework for strategic cooperation between the Allies, and directed the Atlantic Fleet to reinforce the British in convoying ships to Britain as soon as possible.

28 MARCH • Capt. Elliott Buckmaster, *Yorktown* (CV 5) commanding officer, reported that during five months of operational experience with the CXAM radar the ship had tracked planes at a distance of 100 miles. Buckmaster recommended equipping aircraft with electronic identification devices, and carriers with separate and complete facilities for tracking and plotting all radar targets.

19 APRIL • The development of a guided glider bomb (GLOMB) began at the Naval Aircraft Factory, Philadelphia, Pa. The prototype was designed to be towed long distances by a powered aircraft, released in the vicinity of a target, and guided by radio control in an attack. A television camera enabled the GLOMB to transmit a view of the target to a control plane.

20 APRIL • The first successful test of electronic components of radio-proximity fuzes occurred at a farm in Vienna, Va. A 37mm pack howitzer fired a radio oscillator, or sonde, that made radio transmissions during its flight, demonstrating that radio tubes and batteries could be constructed ruggedly enough to withstand firing from a gun. The presentation led Section T of the National Defense Research Committee to concentrate on the development of radio-proximity fuzes for antiaircraft guns.

26 APRIL • The project officer of the Naval Aircraft Factory, Philadelphia, Pa., reported the successful flight test of an unmanned Vought O3U-6 Corsair under radio control beyond the safe bounds of piloted flight. The information obtained proved valuable in overcoming flutter encountered at various speeds and accelerations.

30 APRIL • The Bureau of Aeronautics directed the preliminary design of a transport glider, an initial step toward a glider development program, at the Naval Aircraft Factory, Philadelphia, Pa. As the program progressed, requirements were clarified, leading to the construction of 12- and 24-place wooden or plastic amphibian gliders by firms not already engaged in building military aircraft.

30 APRIL • The commanding officer of NAS Lakehurst, N.J., ordered the salvage of metal-clad airship ZMC-2 and its assignment, complete with engines, instruments, and appurtenances, to the Lighter-Than-Air Ground School at Lakehurst. ZMC-2 had flown more than 2,250 hours since August 1929.

2 MAY • Fleet Air Photographic Unit, Pacific, was established under Commander Aircraft, Battle Force. The move preceded by one day the establishment of a similar unit in the Atlantic Fleet under Commander Patrol Wings, Atlantic.

3 MAY • Project Roger was established at the Naval Aircraft Factory, Philadelphia, Pa., to install and test airborne radar equipment. Its principal assignment was to support the Radiation Laboratory at the Massachusetts Institute of Technology and the Naval Research Laboratory in various radar applications, including search and blind bombing, and radio control of aircraft.

8 MAY • The Bureau of Aeronautics directed the establishment of Aviation Repair Units 1 and 2 to provide a nucleus of aircraft repair and maintenance people ready for overseas deployment as advanced bases were constructed.

10 MAY • The Naval Aircraft Factory, Philadelphia, Pa., reported to the Bureau of Aeronautics that it was in the midst of negotiations with the Radio Corporation of America for the development of a radio altimeter suitable for use in radio-controlled assault drones.

15 MAY • Seaplane tender *Albemarle* (AV 5) arrived at Argentia, Newfoundland, to establish a base for Patrol Wing,

Support Force operations and to prepare for the imminent arrival of the first squadron, VP-52, to fly patrols over the North Atlantic convoy routes.

A PBM Mariner launches using jet-assisted takeoff (JATO) rockets.

19 MAY • German battleship *Bismarck* sailed from Gotenhafen (Gdynia) in German-occupied Poland for *Rheinübung* (Exercise Rhine)—a sortie into the North Atlantic to raid Allied convoys. The battleship rendezvoused with heavy cruiser *Prinz Eugen,* and the two ships broke into the shipping lanes and then detached to maraud independently. On 24 May, PBY-5 Catalinas from VP-52 battled strong gales during an unsuccessful search for *Bismarck* from Argentia, Newfoundland. On 26 May, British Pilot Officer Dennis A. Briggs, Royal Air Force, of Coastal Command's No. 209 Squadron, and U.S. Navy observer and copilot Ens. Leonard B. Smith in AH545A, an RAF PBY-5 Catalina from Lough Erne in Northern Ireland, spotted *Bismarck* as she made for Brest, France. Briggs transferred the controls to Smith while he sent a sighting report. The Catalina broke through the clouds on the port beam of the battleship and received minor damage from antiaircraft fire. American observer Lt. James E. Johnson served on board the British Catalina from No. 240 Squadron that subsequently relieved AH545A, maintained contact with the quarry, and assisted in directing the pursuers toward *Bismarck*. Ships of the British Home Fleet sank the German battleship on 27 May.

21 MAY • The Bureau of Aeronautics requested the Engineering Experiment Station at Annapolis, Md., to develop a liquid-fueled assisted takeoff unit for patrol planes. This marked the Navy's entry into the field of designated jet-assisted takeoff and its first program, outside of research into jet exhaust from reciprocating engines, directed toward utilizing jet reaction for aircraft propulsion.

27 MAY • President Franklin D. Roosevelt proclaimed an unlimited national emergency and a need to ready military, naval, air, and civilian defenses to repel aggressive acts or threats directed toward any part of the Western Hemisphere.

2 JUNE • *Long Island* (AVG 1), Cmdr. Donald B. Duncan commanding, was commissioned as the first aircraft escort vessel of the U.S. Navy at Newport News, Va. The flush-deck carrier was converted in 67 working days from cargo ship *Mormacmail.*

4 JUNE • The Naval Aircraft Factory, Philadelphia, Pa., reported to the Bureau of Aeronautics that its development of airborne television had progressed to the point that signals thus transmitted could be used to direct the pilot of the transmitting plane to alter its course.

11 JUNE • An aircraft armament unit was formed at NAS Norfolk, Va., with Lt. Cmdr. William V. Davis as the officer-in-charge, to test and evaluate armament installations of increasing complexity.

26567

The first U.S. aircraft escort vessel, *Long Island* (AVG 1), steams at sea with two Brewster F2A fighters parked at the forward end of her flight deck, 8 July 1941.

1 JULY • The test, acceptance, and indoctrination units—which had been established in May in San Diego, Calif., and Norfolk, Va., to fit out new patrol aircraft and to indoctrinate new crews in their use—were expanded and set up as separate commands. The San Diego unit retained its description and was placed under Commander Aircraft, Scouting Force. The Norfolk unit was named the Operational Training Squadron and moved under Commander Patrol Wings, Atlantic.

1 JULY • Patrol Wing, Support Force, was redesignated Patrol Wing 7, Capt. Henry M. Mullinnix commanding.

3 JULY • Seaplane tender *Barnegat* (AVP 10) was commissioned at Puget Sound Navy Yard Bremerton, Wash., Cmdr. Felix L. Baker commanding. *Barnegat* became the first of 26 ships of her class.

28 JUNE • To strengthen the provisions for using science in war, President Franklin D. Roosevelt created the Office of Scientific Research and Development. He included in its organization both the National Defense Research Committee and the newly established Committee on Medical Research.

30 JUNE • Initiating an Army-Navy turboprop engine development project, the Navy awarded a contract to Northrop Aircraft for the design of an aircraft gas turbine developing 2,500 horsepower at a weight of less than 3,215 pounds.

1 JULY • VS-201 commanding officer Lt. Cmdr. William D. Anderson completed the first U.S. Navy landing, takeoff, and catapult launch from an aircraft escort vessel when he flew from *Long Island* (AVG 1).

1 JULY • Commander in Chief, Atlantic Fleet Adm. Ernest J. King organized ten task forces to support the defense of Iceland and to escort convoys between the island nation and the United States. The two countries had agreed for U.S. forces to occupy and defend Iceland.

4 JULY • PBY-5 Catalinas of VP-72 flew protective patrols until 17 July from Reykjavik, Iceland, to cover the arrival of a Marine garrison from the United States. Seaplane tender *Goldsborough* (AVD 5) supported the squadron.

7 JULY • The 1st Marine Aircraft Wing (MAW), consisting of a headquarters squadron and Marine Aircraft Group 1, was organized at Quantico, Va., Lt. Col. Louis E. Woods, USMC, commanding. The wing became the first of its type in the Marine Corps, and the first of five MAWs organized during World War II.

8 JULY • Patrol Wing 8 was established at Norfolk, Va., Cmdr. John D. Price commanding.

12 JULY • The Naval Research Laboratory was transferred to the Bureau of Ships from the Office of the Secretary of the Navy, where the Naval Research and Development Board was established. The board members, led by a civilian scientist with the title Coordinator of Research and Development, represented the Chief of Naval Operations and the Bureaus of Aeronautics, Ordnance, Ships, and Yards and Docks. Dr. Jerome C. Hunsaker served as coordinator until his relief in December by Rear Adm. Julius A. Furer.

17 JULY • The realignment of Section T for proximity fuze development enabled the organization to devote its entire effort to radio-proximity fuzes for antiaircraft projectiles. The responsibility for photoelectric and radio fuzes for bombs and rockets shifted to Section E of the National Defense Research Committee at the National Bureau of Standards.

18 JULY • Senior Support Force staff officer Cmdr. James V. Carney reported the installation of British-type ASV radar in one PBY-5 Catalina each of VP-71, -72, and -73, and in two PBM-1 Mariners of VP-74. Identification equipment was first installed at about the same time in various planes. In mid-September, the Navy issued radar to five additional PBM-1s of VP-74 and one PBY-5 of VP-71, and, shortly thereafter, other aircraft in Patrol Wing 7 squadrons, making that wing the first operational naval command to receive radar-equipped aircraft. Its squadrons operated from Norfolk, Va., Quonset Point, R.I., and advance bases on Greenland, Newfoundland, and Iceland during the final months of the Neutrality Patrol.

18 JULY • *Pocomoke* (AV 9), Cmdr. Lester T. Hundt commanding, was commissioned as the first of two seaplane tenders of her class at Portsmouth, Va.

18 JULY • The Joint Board membership was revised to include the Deputy Chief of Staff for Air and the chief of the Bureau of Aeronautics, giving aviation representation on the highest of the Army and Navy boards.

21 JULY • The Navy abolished the requirement that all students assigned to the carrier phase of flight training were to train in each of the three basic aircraft types, and it began the practice of assigning students to specialized training in either fighters, scout bombers, or torpedo planes.

25 JULY • *Wasp* (CV 7) loaded 30 Army Curtiss P-40C Warhawks and three Stearman PT-13 primary trainers of the 33rd Pursuit Squadron at Norfolk, Va., for transport to Reykjavik, Iceland. The carrier sailed with Task Force 16, Rear Adm. William R. Monroe commanding, for the 6 August delivery of Army reinforcements to Iceland's Allied garrison.

28 JULY • The Chief of Naval Operations directed additional gunnery and tactical training in the pilot training program. He also confirmed the establishment of advanced carrier training groups within both the Atlantic and Pacific Fleets, at Norfolk, Va., and San Diego, Calif., to teach newly designated naval aviators how to operate current-model carrier aircraft. Last, the CNO assigned a number of patrol squadrons in each fleet to provide familiarization, indoctrination, advanced gunnery, and tactical training for new flight crews.

28 JULY • The Navy redesignated the Operational Training Squadron of the Atlantic Fleet and the Test, Acceptance, and Indoctrination Unit of the Pacific Fleet as transition training squadrons.

29 JULY • The Secretary of the Navy approved the installation of a radar plot on board carriers.

1 AUGUST • A microwave radar (AI-10) developed by the Radiation Laboratory at the Massachusetts Institute of Technology, which featured a plan position indicator, underwent its initial test in the Lockheed XJO-3 twin-engine test plane, BuNo 1267, at Boston Airport, Mass. During the test flights, scientists operated the radar and devised modifications while Project Roger sailors (most frequently, Chief Aviation Pilot Cecil L. Kullberg) flew the aircraft. The operators detected ships up to 40 miles away and achieved radar-guided approaches to simulated enemy aircraft at ranges of up to 3.5 miles. Operational radars developed from this equipment, including the ASG for K-class airships and the AN/APS-2 for patrol planes, were capable of searching a circular area—a tactically important feature for search-and-rescue operations and finding submarines. The evaluations continued until 16 October.

1 AUGUST • The Bureau of Aeronautics requested the Naval Research Laboratory to develop radar guidance equipment for assault drones to relay target information to a control operator and to serve as automatic homing equipment, initiating radar application to guided missiles.

5 AUGUST • As President Franklin D. Roosevelt traveled to Placentia Bay, Newfoundland, for a conference with British Prime Minister Winston S. Churchill, the president's flag still flew from presidential yacht *Potomac* (AG 25) to conceal his departure with heavy cruisers *Augusta* (CA 31) and

Tuscaloosa (CA 37) and five destroyers. *Augusta* embarked three SOC-1 Seagulls and one SOC-2 of her aviation unit, while *Tuscaloosa* operated one SOC-3 and three SON-1 Seagulls of VCS-7. On 7 August, the U.S. ships reached Placentia Bay, and on 9 August British battleship *Prince of Wales* arrived at nearby NAS Argentia with Prime Minister Churchill and senior leaders embarked. Also present were Chief of Naval Operations Adm. Harold R. Stark and the president's son, Ens. Franklin D. Roosevelt Jr., USNR, temporarily detached from destroyer *Mayrant* (DD 403). Discussion included a forthcoming joint declaration, subsequently known as the Atlantic Charter, which outlined the Allied obligation to the "final destruction of Nazi tyranny." The chief executive also offered planes and warships to escort British merchant ships between the United States and Iceland (Prime Minister Naval Plan 4). The conference concluded on 12 August. Prime Minister Churchill departed on board *Prince of Wales*, and the president sailed with *Augusta* to *Potomac* at Blue Hill Bay, Maine.

6 AUGUST • VP-73 and VP-74 initiated air patrols over North Atlantic convoy routes from Reykjavik, Iceland.

6 AUGUST • The Chief of Naval Operations issued *Tentative Doctrine for Fighter Direction from Aircraft Carriers*, recognizing the anticipated impact of radar on fighter operations, and directed the immediate organization of fighter direction centers on board radar-equipped carriers and other ships.

7 AUGUST • The Chief of the Bureau of Aeronautics issued a preliminary plan to install long-range search radar (British ASV or American ASA) in patrol planes, as well as short-range search radar (British Mk II ASV modified for Fleet Air Arm or American ASB) in one torpedo plane in each section—starting with TBF-1 Avengers. Space needed for search radar was to be reserved in new scout-dive-bombers and scout-observation planes. The plan also called for British AI Mk IV radar in an SBD Dauntless, with a view to the radar's use as an interim interceptor; interception equipment in some F4U Corsairs as available; appropriate radio altimeters in patrol and torpedo planes; and recognition equipment in all service airplanes.

1 SEPTEMBER • The Navy assumed responsibility for transatlantic merchant convoys from a point off Argentia, Newfoundland, to the Mid-Ocean Meeting Point south of Iceland. Seventeen days later, U.S. destroyers rendezvoused with Canadian-escorted convoy HX-150 south of Newfoundland for the first such voyage.

5 SEPTEMBER • Artemus L. Gates (Naval Aviator No. 65), who was discharged from the Naval Reserve in 1928, took the oath of office as Assistant Secretary of the Navy for Aeronautics, the first person to hold the post since David S. Ingalls resigned on 1 June 1932.

9 SEPTEMBER • The Bureau of Aeronautics requested that the National Defense Research Committee and the Naval Research Laboratory develop an interceptor radar suitable for installation in single-engine, single-seat fighters, such as F4U Corsairs.

1 OCTOBER • Secretary of the Navy William F. Knox approved popular names for 17 projected or in-service naval aircraft: F2A Buffalo, F4F Wildcat, F4U Corsair, J2F Duck, OS2U/OS2N Kingfisher, PBB Sea Ranger, PBM Mariner, PBY Catalina, PB2Y Coronado, SB2A Buccaneer, SB2C Helldiver, SB2U Vindicator, SBD Dauntless, SO3C Seagull (subsequently renamed Seamew), SOC Seagull, TBD Devastator, and TBF Avenger.

1 OCTOBER • The Navy established the Aviation Supply Office in Philadelphia, Pa., under the joint cognizance of the Bureaus of Aeronautics and Supplies and Accounts. The office provided centralized control over the procurement and distribution of all aeronautical materials regularly maintained in the general stock.

8 OCTOBER • The Navy established Special Project Dog within VJ-5 to test radio-controlled offensive weapons and to train people in their use. VJ-5 was also directed to develop a radio-controlled fighter plane as an "aerial ram," or aerial torpedo, to be flown into enemy bomber formations and exploded.

13 OCTOBER • The Bureau of Aeronautics directed the painting of all fleet aircraft nonspecular Light Gray, except for surfaces seen from above, which were to be Blue Gray. Beginning in late December, this color scheme extended to shore-based airplanes, except trainers.

20 OCTOBER • *Hornet* (CV 8) was commissioned at Norfolk, Va., Capt. Marc A. Mitscher commanding.

21 OCTOBER • In tests with magnetic airborne detector (later magnetic anomaly detector) gear carried out in cooperation with the National Defense Research Committee, a PBY Catalina from NAS Quonset Point, R.I., located submarine *S-48* (SS 159).

29 OCTOBER • VP-82 received the first Lockheed PBO-1 of a planned full complement of Hudsons at NAS Norfolk, Va., marking the beginning of patrol squadrons' extensive use of land planes during World War II. These aircraft were painted with British markings because they were originally destined for the Royal Air Force's Coastal Command.

1 NOVEMBER • President Franklin D. Roosevelt placed the Coast Guard under the operational control of the Navy for the duration of the national emergency.

4 NOVEMBER • British oiler *Olwen* reported a German raider in Atlantic equatorial waters. Two days later, SOC-1 and -3 Seagulls of VCS-2 operating from light cruiser *Omaha* (CL 4) en route to Recife, Brazil, screened *Omaha* and destroyer *Somers* (DD 381) during the capture of blockade runner *Odenwald,* disguised as U.S. freighter *Willmoto*. The Germans attempted to scuttle *Odenwald,* but a boarding party from *Omaha* saved the ship.

18 NOVEMBER • Dr. L. A. DuBridge of the Radiation Laboratory reported complete the initial design of a 3cm aircraft intercept radar.

26 NOVEMBER • *Kitty Hawk* (AVP 1) was commissioned at the New York Navy Yard, N.Y., Cmdr. E. C. Rogers commanding. She was converted from merchant ship *Seatrain New York* as the first of two aircraft ferries.

27 NOVEMBER • Chief of Naval Operations Adm. Harold R. Stark—persuaded by intercepted and decrypted Japanese messages; Allied intelligence information, including aerial reconnaissance that identified the movements of key Japanese ships; and the apparent failure of negotiations to find a diplomatic solution to Japanese expansionism—sent a "war warning" message to the commanders of the Atlantic and Pacific Fleets. The previous day, the *Dai-ichi Kidō Butai* (1st Mobile Striking Force) had departed Japanese waters to attack Oahu in the Hawaiian Islands.

28 NOVEMBER • In response to the war warning message the Chief of Naval Operations issued the previous day, Task Force 8, Vice Adm. William F. Halsey Jr. commanding, formed around *Enterprise* (CV 6), sailed from Pearl Harbor, Territory of Hawaii, to deliver 12 F4F-3 Wildcats from VMF-211 to augment Wake Island's defenses. Halsey approved Battle Order No. 1 stating that *Enterprise* steamed "under war conditions." The Wildcats launched during the morning of 4 December, and the carrier returned to Hawaiian waters. The ship's mission and heavy seas that delayed her return ensured *Enterprise* eluded the Japanese attack on 7 December.

1 DECEMBER • Patrol Wing 9 began to form at NAS Quonset Point, R.I., with the appointment of Lt. Cmdr. Thomas U. Sisson as the wing's acting commanding officer.

5 DECEMBER • In a response to the war warning message of 27 November, Task Force 12, Rear Adm. John H. Newton commanding, including *Lexington* (CV 2), sailed from Pearl Harbor in the Territory of Hawaii to deliver 18 SB2U-3 Vindicators from VMSB-231 to reinforce the defenders of Midway Atoll. *Lexington* thereby escaped Japan's 7 December attack.

6 DECEMBER • On the eve of the Japanese attack, the U.S. Navy possessed 790 vessels manned by approximately 380,000 sailors.

7 DECEMBER • The Japanese *Dai-ichi Kidō Butai* (1st Mobile Striking Force), Vice Adm. Nagumo Chūichi commanding, including carriers *Akagi, Kaga, Hiryū, Sōryū, Shōkaku*, and *Zuikaku*, launched a morning attack by 353 aircraft in two waves against military installations on Oahu in the Hawaiian Islands. Destroyer *Ward* (DD 139) sighted and sank—with assistance from pilot Ens. William P. Tanner of VP-14 in a PBY-5 Catalina designated 14-P-1—Japanese midget submarine *I-22tou* when the vessel attempted to infiltrate Pearl Harbor. The Japanese nonetheless attained surprise.

The ships struck included seaplane tenders *Curtiss* (AV 4) and *Tangier* (AV 8). An Aichi D3A1 Type 99 carrier bomber also crashed *Curtiss*. The attackers destroyed

19948

Two sailors, next to the wing and float of a destroyed PBY Catalina flying boat, watch as destroyer *Shaw* (DD 373) explodes in the center background during the Japanese 7 December 1941 attack on Pearl Harbor.

188 planes at NASs Ford Island and Kaneohe Bay, Ewa Mooring Mast Field (USMC), and the Army's Bellows, Hickam, and Wheeler Fields. Many planes were easily lost because they had been parked wingtip to wingtip as a security precaution. Despite his wounds, AOMC John W. Finn of VP-14 mounted a machine gun on an instruction stand and shot down one of the three Japanese planes downed at Kaneohe Bay. Finn subsequently received the Medal of Honor.

The attack killed 2,403 servicemembers, including 2,008 sailors and 109 Marines; it wounded 1,143, including 710 sailors and 69 Marines. In addition, 68 civilians died and 35 were wounded. The Japanese lost 29 planes, 5 midget submarines (U.S. forces recovered one), and fewer than 100 men. Concluding that he had inflicted a devastating victory and suffered minimal casualties, Nagumo turned back to Japan, sparing the fuel tank farms and ship repair facilities that later helped the counterattack of the Pacific Fleet's three carriers, which had been absent.

Task Force 8, Vice Adm. William F. Halsey Jr. commanding, formed around *Enterprise* (CV 6), sailed about 200 miles west of Pearl Harbor. A VS-6 search flight launched in two-plane sections of SBD-3 Dauntlesses and arrived off Oahu during the raid. The Japanese shot down some of them, and others succumbed to friendly fire. The first U.S. naval night recovery during World

War II occurred that evening when *Enterprise* turned on her searchlights to aid returning F4F-3 Wildcats of VF-6, SBD-2s and SBD-3s of VB-6 and VS-6, and TBD-1 Devastators of VT-6, that launched at dusk to locate Japanese ships erroneously reported off Oahu. Friendly fire downed four of the Wildcats that attempted to land at Ford Island. Some Dauntlesses landed at Kaneohe Bay in spite of automobiles and construction equipment parked on the ramp to prevent landings.

Lexington (CV 2), steaming with Task Force 12, 425 miles southeast of Midway Island, launched planes to search for the attackers and changed course with the SB2U-3 Vindicators she had set out to deliver to Midway still on board. Rendezvousing about 120 miles west of Kauai, *Lexington* and *Enterprise* joined Task Force 3, Vice Adm. Wilson Brown Jr. commanding, and searched southwest of Oahu before returning to Pearl Harbor on 13 December. *Saratoga* (CV 3) had completed overhaul and on 7 December reached San Diego, Calif.

7 DECEMBER • Japanese destroyers *Sazanami* and *Ushio* shelled Midway Island. The 6th Marine Defense Battalion returned fire and claimed damage to both ships, which retired. The Japanese carriers that attacked the Hawaiian Islands considered launching a raid against Midway during their return to Japan, but rough weather spared the bastion from an attack.

8 DECEMBER • The national emergency forced the Navy to dispatch reinforcements on board *Saratoga* (CV 3) during her voyage to the Hawaiian Islands, totaling 103 planes—4 additional F4F-3 and -3A Wildcats of VF-3, 14 F2A-3 Buffaloes of VMF-221, and 15 miscellaneous aircraft.

8 DECEMBER • Thirty-four Japanese Mitsubishi G3M2 Type 96 land-attack planes of the Chitose *Kōkūtai* (Air Group) from Roi, Kwajalein, reached Wake Island undetected because the island lacked radar, and a rain squall cloaked their approach. The attackers bombed the airfield and installations, knocked out eight F4F-3 Wildcats of VMF-211, and killed 25 servicemembers and wounded 30. They also killed five Pan American Airways employees and wounded one, and slightly damaged the airline's Martin 130 *Philippine Clipper* with bullets. The plane left the island with the company's 39 surviving Caucasian employees and passengers, abandoning the Chamorro staff. The enemy eluded patrolling Marine Corps Wildcats, but ground fire slightly holed eight bombers and killed one crewman. The Japanese bombed the island almost daily during the ensuing two weeks.

9 DECEMBER • The Secretary of the Navy authorized the Bureau of Ships to contract with RCA Manufacturing Company for 25 sets of ASB airborne search radar. The Naval Research Laboratory had developed this radar (under the designation XAT) for dive bombers and torpedo planes.

10 DECEMBER • An SBD-3 Dauntless of VS-6, embarked on board *Enterprise* (CV 6), sank Japanese fleet submarine *I-70* north of the Hawaiian Islands. *I-70*, the first Japanese warship sunk by U.S. aircraft during World War II, had scouted the Hawaiian area during the attack on Oahu.

10 DECEMBER • Japanese aircraft bombed the Cavite Navy Yard in the Philippines. As American planes raced to escape, three Japanese Mitsubishi A6M Type 0 carrier fighters of the 3rd *Kōkūtai* (Air Group) pounced on a PBY-4, Aircraft No. P-5, piloted by Lt. Harmon T. Utter of VP-101. Bow gunner ABMC Earl D. Payne shot down one of the fighters with his .30-caliber machine gun to claim the Navy's first verifiable air-to-air kill of World War II. Despite extensive damage, the Catalina survived because the Japanese apparently believed that they shot down the flying boat. On 7 April 1945, Utter coordinated carrier air strikes that led to the destruction of Japanese battleship *Yamato*.

10 DECEMBER • PBY-5 Catalinas of VP-52 initiated antisubmarine patrols over the South Atlantic from Natal, Brazil.

11 DECEMBER • The garrison of Wake Island repulsed a Japanese attack. Marine Corps 5-inch coast-defense guns sank or damaged several Japanese ships, and four F4F-3 Wildcats from VMF-211 bombed and strafed the invaders. Capt. Henry T. Elrod, USMC, flew Wildcat 211-F-11, BuNo 4019, and bombed and strafed Japanese destroyer *Kisaragi*, touching off a catastrophic explosion on board, probably attributed to her depth charges. The ship sank with all hands. Elrod returned to Wake, but antiaircraft fire had perforated an oil line so Marines cannibalized his plane. Strafing runs also damaged light cruiser *Tenryu* and armed merchant cruiser *Kongo Maru*. Wildcat pilot 2d Lt. David D. Kliewer, USMCR, spotted Japanese submarine *RO-66* on the surface south of the island. He strafed and bombed the boat three times before she submerged. On 17 December, *RO-66* sank in a collision with *RO-62*.

12 DECEMBER • The Naval Air Transport Service was established under the Chief of Naval Operations to provide rapid air delivery of equipment, spare parts, and specialists to the fleet.

14 DECEMBER • Patrol Wing 10 began its withdrawal from the Philippines when it departed Cavite Island. Before reaching Australia, the wing's two patrol squadrons and four seaplane tenders operated from various bases, including Balikpapan, Soerabaja and Ambon, Netherlands East Indies (Indonesia).

15 DECEMBER • Patrol Wing 8 transferred from Norfolk, Va., to NAS Alameda, Calif.

16 DECEMBER • Task Force 14, Rear Adm. Frank J. Fletcher commanding and formed around *Saratoga* (CV 3), sailed from Pearl Harbor, Hawaiian Islands, to relieve the garrison on Wake Island. Embarked reinforcements included 18 F2A-2 and -3 Buffaloes of VMF-221 on board *Saratoga* and Marines on board seaplane tender *Tangier* (AV 8). Task Force 11, Vice Adm. Wilson Brown Jr. commanding and formed around *Lexington* (CV 2), intended to launch a diversionary raid on Jaluit Island. Revised intelligence, however, persuaded Brown to first attack Makin Island in the Gilberts and then divert to Wake. *Enterprise* (CV 6) supported the other two carriers at a distance. Meanwhile, *Saratoga* and *Tangier* encountered delays owing to the slower speed of oiler *Neches* (AO 5), and doubt concerning the movements and number of Japanese carriers. Also, reports of the enemy landings on Wake Island persuaded Commander Battle Force Vice Adm. William S. Pye, temporarily in command of the Pacific Fleet, to avoid risking his carriers and order the retirement of the Task Force 14 relief expedition. Fletcher, who had been refueling some of his destroyers, continued to do so and returned to Hawaiian waters. The Japanese, despite heavy seas and determined resistance from the garrison, overran Wake Island on 23 December.

16 DECEMBER • The Secretary of the Navy approved an expansion of the pilot training program from 800 students to 2,500 per month. The action led to a production of 20,000 pilots annually by mid-1943.

17 DECEMBER • The Naval Research Laboratory reported satisfactory flight test results in a PBY Catalina of radar using a duplexing antenna switch, which made it possible to use a single antenna for both transmission of the radar pulse and reception of its echo. This development eliminated the cumbersome "yagi" antenna and contributed to the reliability and effectiveness of World War II airborne radar.

17 DECEMBER • A PBY-3 Catalina of VP-21 led the arrival of 17 SB2U-3 Vindicators of VMSB-231 at Midway Island from Oahu, Territory of Hawaii. The planes completed the longest mass flight by single-engine aircraft on record in 9 hours 45 minutes. VMSB-231 had been on board *Lexington* (CV 2) en route to Midway on 7 December when the carrier turned around.

18 DECEMBER • Two-plane detachments from Patrol Wings 1 and 2 based in the Territory of Hawaii began scouting patrols from Johnston Island.

18 DECEMBER • The operational loss of an American Volunteer Group Curtiss P-40B Tomahawk and a confrontation between its flight leader, Eriksen Shilling, and Chinese mountaineers, who mistook him for a Japanese pilot, marked the beginning of "blood chit" use. (Maj. Gen. Claire L. Chennault, USAAF, had formed the American Volunteer Group—nicknamed the Flying Tigers, some of the group had naval aviation experience—to battle the Japanese over the China-Burma-India Theater. He arranged for the diversion of 100 Tomahawk IIBs [P-40Bs] from a British order.) On this date, Chinese intelligence printed on silk the first blood chits to be stitched on the back of the Americans' flight jackets, displaying the Stars and Stripes and offering in several languages a reward for assisting the bearer. Blood chits in various forms continued in use into Operation Desert Storm in 1991.

20 DECEMBER • Ten Japanese Army Kawasaki Ki-48-Is of the 21st *Hikōsentai* (regiment) raided Kunming, China. During the first battle of the American Volunteer Group, Curtiss P-40Bs of the Flying Tigers' 1st Squadron downed three of the bombers and damaged three of the surviving Ki-48-Is—one of which may have fallen—without combat loss. Ens. Edward F. Rector, USNR, who had resigned and transferred from VS-41 on board *Ranger* (CV 4) to the Flying Tigers, crash-landed his Tomahawk because of fuel exhaustion. Through the winter, Japanese aircraft indiscriminately bombed and strafed the British colonial capital of Rangoon. The Flying Tigers at times coordinated their efforts with British Brewster Buffalo Is (F2A-2s exported as B-339Es) of No. 221 Group of the Royal Air Force, shooting down a number of enemy planes. Following the Japanese capture of Rangoon, Allied aircraft desperately strove to stem the enemy advance in repeated aerial battles until May 1942, when the Japanese conquered Burma.

25 DECEMBER • Two-plane detachments from various squadrons at Pearl Harbor and Kaneohe in the Territory of Hawaii began patrols across the Central and South Pacific from Palmyra Island, a principal staging base to the South Pacific.

30 DECEMBER • Naval aviator Adm. Ernest J. King assumed duties as Commander in Chief, U.S. Fleet.

1942

2 JANUARY • The first organized naval lighter-than-air units of World War II, Airship Patrol Group 1, Cmdr. George H. Mills commanding, and ZP-12, Lt. Cmdr. Raymond F. Tyler commanding, were established at NAS Lakehurst, N.J.

3 JANUARY • Twelve PBY-5 Catalinas of VP-22, Lt. Cmdr. Frank O'Beirne commanding, in two groups of six planes joined Patrol Wing 10 as the first aviation reinforcements from the central Pacific to reach Southwest Pacific forces. O'Beirne led the first group from Pearl Harbor on this date and, on 8 January, reached Townsville, Australia. Two days later, the Catalinas landed at Darwin, Australia, and began to load on board seaplane tender *Langley* (AV 3). Squadron executive officer Lt. Doyle G. Donaho led the second group along the same route and, on 11 January, arrived at Darwin. The deteriorating situation, however, precluded VP-22's deployment as a concentrated squadron, and the planes operated in small detachments at Soerabaja, Java and Ambon, Netherlands East Indies (Indonesia).

5 JANUARY • A change in regulations covering the display of the national star insignia on aircraft returned the star to the upper right and lower left wing surfaces and revised rudder striping to thirteen red and white horizontal stripes.

7 JANUARY • President Franklin D. Roosevelt approved the expansion of naval aviation to 27,500 useful planes.

11 JANUARY • Japanese submarine *I-6* fired a deep-running torpedo into the port side amidships of *Saratoga* (CV 3) about 500 miles southwest of Oahu, Territory of Hawaii. Six men died, water poured into three firerooms, and the ship listed to port. *Saratoga* made for Oahu, where her 8-inch guns were removed, and then to Puget Sound Navy Yard at Bremerton, Wash. for repairs and modernization that included improved watertight integrity and antiaircraft armament. The departure of *Saratoga* temporarily reduced U.S. fleet carrier strength in the Pacific to three ships, and led to the distribution of her air group among the other carriers.

13 JANUARY • German submarines *U-66*, *U-123*, and *U-125* commenced Operation *Paukenschlag* (Drumbeat), an attack against Allied shipping off the East Coast of North America and in the West Indies. Through 31 August 1942, U-boats sank a staggering total of 609 ships of 3.1 million tons—one fourth of the Allied merchant ships lost to submarine attacks in the Battle of the Atlantic. The reasons for these casualties included: the delay of the introduction of a network of interlocking coastal and transatlantic convoys, the lack of planes and escorts following the transfer of 50 destroyers and ten *Lake*-class cutters to the British and Canadians, insufficient training and expertise in antisubmarine warfare, resistance to the deployment of planes from hunter-killer operations to convoys, diversion of reinforcements to the Pacific, opposition by the Army for doctrinal and political reasons to naval control of aircraft that operated from ashore, and Allied ULTRA signals intelligence failure to decipher the German Triton (Shark) Enigma naval key in February 1942, which obscured the extent of the enemy offensive. U.S. naval planes shepherded convoys, however, detected U-boats, and searched for survivors of attacks, and during this period, the Allies extended a coastal convoy system across American and Caribbean waters and convoyed about 157,000 U.S. troops to the British Isles.

14 JANUARY • The formation of four carrier aircraft service units from four small service units that had been previously established in the Hawaiian area, was approved.

15 JANUARY • The American-British-Dutch-Australian Command (ABDA) was established at Batavia, Java in the Netherlands East Indies (Indonesia). The command coordinated Allied defense across a huge area with limited forces. Adm. Thomas C. Hart initially commanded the ABDA naval forces in addition to the Asiatic Fleet.

16 JANUARY • To protect the advance of Task Force 8, Vice Adm. William F. Halsey Jr. commanding, including *Enterprise* (CV 6), for its strike against the Marshall and Gilbert Islands, PBY-5 Catalinas of VP-23 began daily searches of the waters between their temporary base at Canton Island and Suva in the Fiji Islands as the first combat patrols by aircraft in the South Pacific.

16 JANUARY • During a routine search from *Enterprise* (CV 6), pilot AMMC F. Dixon of VT-6 crashed at sea in a Douglas TBD-1 Devastator because of fuel starvation. Dixon and his two crewmen subsisted on occasional fish speared with a pocketknife, two birds, and rainwater during a 34-day journey in their raft to the Danger Islands on 19 February. The straight-line distance of their voyage measured 450 miles, but their estimated track was 1,200 miles. Dixon received the Navy Cross for this epic of survival.

23 JANUARY • OS2U-3 Kingfishers of VS-1 Detachment 14 arrived in Samoa with Marine reinforcements from San Diego, Calif., as the first naval aircraft to operate there during the war. *Yorktown* (CV 5) passed through the Panama Canal from the Atlantic Fleet and rendezvoused with and escorted the convoy during part of its voyage. *Enterprise* (CV 6) covered the ships during the final portion of their journey.

23 JANUARY • During the Battle of the Points, the Japanese made amphibious landings on the west coast of the Bataan Peninsula in the Philippines to outflank U.S. and Filipino troops. One assault deployed men of the 2nd Battalion, 20th Regiment to Longoskawayan Point on southwestern Bataan. Through 1 February, U.S. and Filipino soldiers defeated the invaders at Longoskawayan. In addition, a provisional naval battalion, Cmdr. Francis J. Bridget of Patrol Wing 10 commanding, consisting of stranded naval aviation sailors of the wing and ships and of the 4th Marines, advanced from nearby Mariveles. Despite the lack of training in infantry tactics, the battalion sailors cleared the summit of Mt. Pucot of the enemy on the first day of action. The fighting for the observation post raged for days but the sailors and Marines regained the peak.

29 JANUARY • Five-inch projectiles containing radio-proximity fuzes were test fired at the Naval Proving Ground, Dahlgren, Va. Fifty-two percent of the fuzes functioned satisfactorily by proximity to water at the end of a five-mile trajectory. Researchers obtained this performance with samples selected to simulate a production lot and the results led to immediate small-scale production of the devices.

30 JANUARY • The Secretary of the Navy authorized a glider program for the Marine Corps consisting of small and large types in sufficient numbers for the training and transportation of two battalions of 900 men each.

1 FEBRUARY • The Secretary of the Navy announced that all prospective naval aviators were to begin their training with a three-month course emphasizing physical conditioning conducted by pre-flight schools to be established at universities. The training began at the Universities of North Carolina and Iowa in May; the University of Georgia and St. Mary's College, Calif., in June; and at Del Monte, Calif., in January 1943.

1 FEBRUARY • Task Forces 8, Vice Adm. William F. Halsey commanding, and 17, Rear Adm. Frank J. Fletcher commanding, including *Enterprise* (CV 6) and *Yorktown* (CV 5), respectively, launched the first carrier counterattack against the Japanese occupied Gilbert and Marshall Islands. Task Force 8 attacked Kwajalein and Wotje and Task Force 17 struck Jaluit, Makin, and Mili. Task Force 11, Vice Adm. Wilson Brown Jr. commanding, including *Lexington* (CV 2), supported the raid from the vicinity of Christmas Island. The attackers sank three vessels and damaged 11 more including light cruiser *Katori* and submarine *I-23*. A crashing land attack plane from the Japanese Chitose *Kōkūtai* (Air Group) narrowly missed *Enterprise*. A Mitsubishi A5M4 Type 96 carrier fighter damaged heavy cruiser *Chester* (CA 27) and killed eight men and wounded 38. A TBD-1 Devastator from VT-5 disappeared, and a Japanese reconnaissance flying boat of the Yokohama *Kōkūtai* unsuccessfully attacked destroyer *Sims* (DD 409) as she searched for the missing aircrew. Two F4F-3 Wildcats of VF-42 shot down the intruder, but the searchers failed to locate the Devastator crew in the heavy seas.

10 FEBRUARY • Japanese submarine *I-69* shelled Midway Island, but Brewster F2A-3 Buffaloes of VMF-221 bombed and damaged the boat.

12 FEBRUARY • The Chief of Naval Operations promulgated an advanced base program using the code names "Lion" and "Cub" to designate major and minor bases, respectively, and in July added "Oaks" and "Acorns" for aviation facilities. The move marked the beginning of a concept of functional components that provided planners and commanders with a means of ordering standardized units of people, equipment, and material to meet special needs in any area.

16 FEBRUARY • The Germans began Operation *Neuland* (New Land) to cut the Allied flow of oil and bauxite from South America to North America by attacks on Dutch and Venezuelan oil ports. Despite supply problems, submarines *U-67, U-129, U-156, U-161,* and *U-502* wreaked havoc on poorly guarded ships and tankers sailing independently. Additional U-boats and Italian submarines subsequently reinforced these boats. Allied aircraft, including U.S. Navy PBY Catalinas, intelligence breakthroughs in ULTRA decryptions of Axis messages and high frequency direction-finder (Huff-Duff) receivers that detected U-boat radio transmissions, and Axis failure to concentrate their effort contained the menace in Caribbean waters.

16 FEBRUARY • A Navy developed air-track blind landing system reached daily use in Iceland for landing flying boats. Other blind-landing systems were in various phases of development, including work on the ground controlled approach system, and sailors had accomplished talk-down landings at the East Boston (Commonwealth) Airport in Massachusetts.

17 FEBRUARY • Commander in Chief U.S. Fleet authorized the removal of athwartships hangar deck catapults from *Yorktown* (CV 5), *Enterprise* (CV 6), *Wasp* (CV 7), and *Hornet* (CV 8).

An amphibious PBY-5A Catalina of VP-63, based out of Port Lyautey, Morocco, carries antisubmarine retro-rockets while on patrol of the Strait of Gibraltar.

19 FEBRUARY • One hundred eighty-nine aircraft from the Japanese carriers *Akagi, Kaga, Hiryū,* and *Sōryū,* and 54 Mitsubishi G4M1 Type 1 land attack planes from the Kanoya and 1st *Kōkūtais* (groups) attacked Darwin, Australia. The ships in the harbor included USS *William B. Preston* (AVD 7) after the seaplane tender's escape from the Philippines. Despite damage, a temporarily loss of steering control, and 11 dead, two missing, and three wounded, *William B. Preston* defiantly reached the open sea. Nine Mitsubishi A6M Type 0 carrier fighters shot down Lt. Thomas H. Moorer of VP-22 while he piloted a PBY-5 Catalina, BuNo 2306, off northern Australia. Freighter *Florence D* under charter with the Army rescued the survivors, only to be sunk by enemy carrier planes. One of Moorer's crew and three of the 37 men on board *Florence D* died, but Moorer survived to become the 18th Chief of Naval Operations and later Chairman of the Joint Chiefs.

20 FEBRUARY • A Japanese Kawanishi H6K4 Type 97 flying boat of the Yokohama *Kōkūtai* (Air Group) spotted Task Force 11, Vice Adm. Wilson Brown Jr. commanding, en route to attack Japanese forces at Rabaul, New Britain. Brown cancelled the strike and two waves of 17 Japanese Mitsubishi G4M1 Type 1 land attack planes of the 4th *Kōkūtai* attacked the Americans off Bougainville, Solomon Islands. F4F-3 Wildcats from VF-3 and SBD-3 Dauntlesses from VS-2, embarked on board *Lexington* (CV 2), broke up the attackers. The carrier avoided damage from bombs and from two

208-PU-14842

Barely two months after he shot down four Japanese planes and damaged two others on 20 February 1942, Lt. Edward H. O'Hare of VF-3 smiles from the cockpit of his F4F Wildcat for photographers during a publicity break at Kaneohe Naval Air Station on 10 April. He later received the Medal of Honor for his actions.

bombers that attempted *taiatari* (body-crashing) suicide dives. Fifteen Japanese bombers, three flying boats, and an Aichi E13A1 Type 0 floatplane failed to return; most had been shot down. Wildcat pilot Lt. Edward H. O'Hare claimed four of the attackers and damaged two more, an exploit for which he received the Medal of Honor. Lt. Cmdr. John S. Thach shot down a bomber and assisted in downing a second one and a H6K4 Type 97 flying boat. Two Wildcats fell to the enemy with the loss of Ens. John W. Wilson, and seven fighters received damage, some caused by *Lexington*'s guns.

21 FEBRUARY • Seaplane tender *Curtiss* (AV 4) and VP-14 arrived at Nouméa, New Caledonia, to begin operations from what developed into a principal Navy base in the South Pacific.

23 FEBRUARY • BUAER outlined a comprehensive program, which became the basis for the wartime expansion of pilot training. In place of the existing seven-month course, the new program required 11 1/2 months for pilots of single- or twin-engine aircraft, and 12 1/2 months for four-engine pilots. The curriculum consisted of three months at induction centers, three months in primary, three and one-half months in intermediate, and two or three months in operational training, depending on the types of aircraft used.

24 FEBRUARY • Task Force 16, Vice Adm. William F. Halsey Jr. commanding, raided the Japanese garrison at Wake Island. Thirty-six SBD-2 and -3 Dauntlesses from VB-6 and VS-6, respectively, and TBD-1 Devastators from VT-6 launched from *Enterprise* (CV 6) bombed and strafed ships and installations, supported by a bombardment from cruisers and destroyers. The raiders caused minimal damage and sank only two guardboats, but U.S. Marines, sailors, and construction workers captured by the Japanese during the seizure of the island survived the raid unscathed. The enemy shot down one Dauntless.

26 FEBRUARY • The Navy's coordinator of Research and Development requested the development by the National Defense Research Committee of an expendable radio sonobuoy for use by lighter-than-air craft to hunt submarines.

27 FEBRUARY • Allied attempts to reinforce the Netherlands East Indies (Indonesia) included convoy MS-5 among which was seaplane tender *Langley* (AV 3) and four freighters transporting 65 Curtiss P-40Es of the Army's 35th and 51st Pursuit Groups embarked from Melbourne, Australia. *Langley* ferried 32 of the Warhawks. Planners considered rerouting the convoy to India, but the Dutch requested aid and thus *Langley* and several ships made for Tjilatjap, Java. Nine Japanese two-engine naval land attack planes and six fighters irreparably damaged *Langley* 74 miles from Tjilatjap. Destroyer *Whipple* (DD 217) shelled and torpedoed the tender but the possibility of renewed attacks compelled the flight of the survivors and they did not record her sinking. Some survivors were transferred to oiler *Pecos* (AO 6) and, on 1 March, endured the demise of another ship when Japanese Aichi D3A1 Type 99 carrier bombers from carriers *Akagi*, *Kaga*, *Hiryū*, and *Sōryū* sank *Pecos* south of Christmas Island. Sixteen men from *Langley* died. Freighter *Sea Witch* delivered 27 crated Warhawks to Tjilatjap, but on 2 March they were destroyed to prevent their capture, and *Sea Witch* escaped.

1 MARCH • With the impending fall of Java in the Netherlands East Indies (Indonesia), the Allies dissolved the American-British-Dutch-Australian Command.

1 MARCH • Ens. William Tepuni, USNR, of VP-82, piloted a PBO-1 Hudson from Argentia, Newfoundland, and spotted German submarine *U-656* inbound to North

American waters on the surface about 60 miles southeast of Cape Race, Newfoundland. The Hudson sank *U-656* with all hands—the first U-boat confirmed sunk by the United States during World War II. Tepuni received the Distinguished Flying Cross.

1 MARCH • Carrier Replacement Air Group 9 was established at NAS Norfolk, Va., Cmdr. William D. Anderson commanding. The action marked the first numbered air group in the Navy and the end of the practice of naming air groups for the carriers to which they were assigned.

2 MARCH • The Naval Air Transport Service inaugurated regularly scheduled operations with a Douglas R4D Skytrain flight from NAS Norfolk, Va., to Squantum, Mass.

4 MARCH • Task Force 16, Vice Adm. William F. Halsey Jr. commanding, raided Marcus Island. *Enterprise* (CV 6) moved to within 1,000 miles of Japan and just before sunrise launched six F4F-3A Wildcats of VF-6 and 32 SBD-2 and -3 Dauntlesses of VB-6 and VS-6, respectively. The carrier's radar directed the planes to their attack. Japanese antiaircraft fire shot down one of the Dauntlesses but both crewmen survived captivity.

7 MARCH • Patrol Wing 10 completed its withdrawal from the Philippines and the Netherlands East Indies (Indonesia) and patrolled along the west coast of Australia from its newly established headquarters in Perth. The command lost 41 of its 45 planes during the first several months of the war including 14 shot down. More than half of its men captured by the Japanese in the Philippines died in captivity.

7 MARCH • Blimp K-5 and submarine *S-20* (SS 125) demonstrated the practicability of using a radio sonobuoy in aerial antisubmarine warfare during an exercise off New London, Conn. The buoy detected the sound of the submerged submarine's propellers at distances of up to three miles, and radio reception on board the blimp proved satisfactory up to five miles.

8 MARCH • VS-2 Detachment 14 inaugurated air operations from the Society Islands. The squadron arrived at Bora Bora on 17 February.

9 MARCH • Air transport squadron VR-1, Cmdr. Cyril K. Wildman commanding, was established as the first of 13 such squadrons created under the Naval Air Transport Service during World War II at NAS Norfolk, Va.

10 MARCH • Task Force 11, Vice Adm. Wilson Brown Jr. commanding, and elements of Task Force 17, Rear Adm. Frank J. Fletcher commanding, attacked Japanese ships landing troops and supplies at Lae and Salamaua, New Guinea. *Lexington* (CV 2) and *Yorktown* (CV 5) launched F4F-3 Wildcats of VF-3 and -42, SBD-2 Dauntlesses of VB-2, SBD-3s of VB-5 and VS-2 and -5, and TBD-1 Devastators of VT-2 and -5. The planes flew over the Owen Stanley Mountains and sank armed merchant cruiser *Kongō Maru*; auxiliary minelayer *Tenyō Maru*; and transport *Yokohama Maru*; and damaged seaplane carrier *Kiyokama Maru*; light cruiser *Yūbari*; destroyers *Asanagi*, *Asakaze*, *Oite*, *Yakaze*, and *Yūnagi*; minelayer *Tsugaru*; transport *Kokai Maru*; and minesweeper *No. 2 Tama Maru*. One VS-2 Dauntless was shot down. A following raid by USAAF Boeing B-17 Flying Fortresses and Royal Australian Air Force Lockheed Hudsons failed to inflict appreciable damage. The raid helped convince the Japanese of their need for additional carrier support to complete their conquest of the region, and thus indirectly set the stage for the Battle of the Coral Sea.

10 MARCH • The Office of Scientific Research and Development at Johns Hopkins University signed a Navy contract to operate a laboratory. The facility became known as the Applied Physics Laboratory and proved one of several important steps in the transition of the radio-proximity fuze from development to large-scale production. Some of the other steps taken within the following six weeks included the organizational transfer of Section T from the National Defense Research Committee directly to the Office of Scientific Research and Development, and the relocation of most of the Section T staff from the Carnegie Institution of Washington to the Applied Physics Laboratory at Silver Spring, Md.

26 MARCH • Naval aviator Adm. Ernest J. King relieved Adm. Harold R. Stark as Chief of Naval Operations under the provisions of an executive order that combined the duties of Commander in Chief U.S. Fleet and CNO.

26 MARCH • The Navy and Army Air Forces agreed to vest unity of command to the Navy for aircraft operating over the sea to protect shipping and hunt submarines.

26 MARCH • Task Force 39, Rear Adm. John W. Wilcox Jr. commanding, including *Wasp* (CV 7), sailed from Portland, Maine, to reinforce the British Home Fleet at Scapa Flow in the Orkney Islands during the bitterly contested Arctic convoys to aid the Soviets. The next day, Wilcox was lost overboard from battleship *Washington* (BB 56) during heavy seas, and the command of the force devolved upon Rear Adm. Robert C. Giffen. *Wasp* participated in the Arctic convoys during the succeeding months.

29 MARCH • The forward echelon of VMF-212 arrived at Efaté, New Hebrides (Vanuatu), to construct an air strip from which, on 27 May, the squadron initiated operations.

3 APRIL • Commander in Chief Pacific Fleet Adm. Chester W. Nimitz assumed additional duties as Commander in Chief Pacific Ocean Areas—the North, Central, and South Pacific. Gen. Douglas A. MacArthur, USA, was named as Commander, Southwest Pacific Area.

6 APRIL • Aircraft, Atlantic Fleet, was redesignated Carriers, Atlantic Fleet.

7 APRIL • Aircraft Repair Units 1 and 2 merged to form the Advanced Base Aviation Training Unit at NAS Norfolk, Va. The merger provided aviation maintenance sailors with the specialized training required to support air operations at advanced bases.

9 APRIL • Control pilot Lt. Moulton B. Taylor of Project Fox directed a radio controlled Great Lakes TG-2 drone in a torpedo attack on destroyer *Aaron Ward* (DD 483) as she steamed at 15 knots in Narragansett Bay, R.I. Taylor used a view of the target obtained by a television camera mounted in the drone, and guided the attack to release the torpedo about 300 feet directly astern of the target. The weapon passed beneath the destroyer as planned.

10 APRIL • A reorganization of the Pacific Fleet abolished the Battle and Scouting Forces and set up new type commands for ships and aviation. With the change, the titles of the aviation type commands became Aircraft Carriers, Vice Adm. William F. Halsey Jr. commanding, and Patrol Wings, Rear Adm. John S. McCain commanding.

13 APRIL • German and Italian aerial attacks on Malta threatened to overwhelm the British defenders of the embattled island without the arrival of reinforcements. The exigencies of the war temporarily deprived the British of available carriers, and Prime Minister Winston S. Churchill appealed to President Franklin D. Roosevelt to provide *Wasp* (CV 7). On this date, *Wasp* embarked 47 Royal Air Force Supermarine Spitfire Mk Vs at King George Dock at Glasgow, Scotland, during Operation Calendar—the aerial reinforcement of Malta. The next day, *Wasp* sailed to rendezvous with British Force W and make for the Mediterranean. On 20 April the ship launched the Spitfires toward Malta. Axis air raids, however, reduced the operational Spitfires to six in four days, which necessitated a second operation the following month. On 26 April, *Wasp* returned to Scapa Flow in the Orkney Islands.

18 APRIL • The Doolittle Raid struck Japan. Lt. j.g. Henry L. Miller had trained the North American B-25B Mitchell crews of the Army's 17th Bombardment Group, Lt. Col. James H. Doolittle, USAAF, commanding, in carrier procedures at Eglin Field, Fla. On 1 April, *Hornet* (CV 8) embarked 16 Mitchells at NAS Alameda, Calif.

Hornet set out the following day and subsequently rendezvoused with Task Force 16, Vice Adm. William F. Halsey Jr. commanding, including *Enterprise* (CV 6), north of the Hawaiian Islands. On this date, Japanese guardboat *No. 23 Nitto Maru* discovered the approach of the force 668 miles from Tōkyō. The Americans had intended to close the Japanese homeland to shorten the flying range but the discovery compelled Halsey to launch the raid earlier than planned. The attackers bombed military and oil installations and factories at Kōbe, Nagoya, Tōkyō, Yokohama, and Yokosuka. A bomb struck Japanese carrier *Ryūhō* at Yokosuka but the strike inflicted negligible damage. All the Mitchells were lost—15 crashed in China and one was interned at Vladivostok in the Soviet Union. The Japanese retaliated with reprisals against the areas in China where people succored the aviators, captured eight of the fliers, and later executed three of them.

F4F-3A Wildcats of VF-6 with SBD-3 Dauntlesses of VB-3 and SBD-2s of VB-6 flying from *Enterprise* coordinated with surface attacks and damaged armed merchant cruiser

Awata Maru and ten guardboats, four of which sank. The Japanese downed a Dauntless, but the force escaped. Despite the infinitesimal material damage inflicted, the psychological impact of an aerial threat to Japan and to the emperor ended debate within the Japanese high command concerning a decisive thrust against the U.S. Pacific Fleet. Reporters later queried President Franklin D. Roosevelt for the location from which the bombers launched and he replied, "Shangri-La."

Hornet (CV 8) launches Lt. Col. James H. Doolittle, USAAF, and 16 Army B-25B Mitchells against the Japanese homeland, 18 April 1942.

18 APRIL • A night fighter development unit named Project Argus was established at NAS Quonset Point, R.I. It was renamed Project Affirm to avoid confusion with the electronic element (Argus Unit) of an advanced base. Its official purpose was the development and testing of night fighter equipment for naval aircraft, but it also developed tactics and trained officers and men for early night fighter squadrons and as night fighter directors.

19 APRIL • Two tests of the feasibility of using drone aircraft as guided missiles were conducted in Chesapeake Bay. In one evaluation, VJ-5 used visual direction to crash-dive a Great Lakes BG-1 drone into the water beyond the wreck of target ship *San Marcos* (former battleship *Texas*). Project Fox carried out the second successful test from a Civil Aeronautics Administration intermediate field at Lively, Va., using a television camera fitted to the XB2G-1 drone, BuNo 9722, to view the target. Lt. Moulton B. Taylor flew a control plane 11 miles distant to direct the drone's crash dive into a raft under tow at a speed of eight knots.

22 APRIL • *Ranger* (CV 4) sailed from NAS Quonset Point, R.I., to West African waters with 68 embarked Curtiss P-40Es of the USAAF 33rd Pursuit Squadron. On 10 May, she launched the Warhawks 82 miles off Accra, Gold Coast (Ghana). From Accra, the fighters were flown in a series of hops to Karachi, India (Pakistan), to operate in the China-Burma-India Theater. The ship turned for Port of Spain in Trinidad. This event marked the first of four ferry trips that *Ranger* made to deliver Army fighters across the Atlantic, accomplishing the subsequent launches on 19 July 1942, and 19 January and 24 February 1943.

24 APRIL • A new specification for the color of naval aircraft went into effect. Service aircraft remained nonspecular Light Gray with nonspecular Blue Gray on surfaces visible from above. Advanced trainers were to be finished in glossy Aircraft Gray with glossy Orange Yellow on wing and aileron surfaces visible from above, while primary trainers were to be finished glossy Orange Yellow with glossy Aircraft Gray landing gear.

27 APRIL • Operation Gridiron—the evacuation of Americans including radio interception specialists from the Philippines—began. Pilot Lt. Cmdr. Edgar T. Neale, copilot Lt. j.g. Thomas F. Pollack, and aircrewmen AMMCs David W. Bounds and Mario Ferrara, AMM1 W. F. Drexl, ARM1 L. Gassett, and ARM2 H. F. Donahue, and pilot Lt. j.g. Leroy C. Deede, copilot Lt. j.g. William V. Gough Jr., aircrewmen AMMC W. D. Eddy, AMM1s M. H. Crain and M. C. Lohr, ARM1 Edward W. Bedford, and ARM3 W. F. Kelley of Patrol Wing 10, manned two PBY-5s. The Catalinas took off from Perth, Australia, refueled en route and, on 29 April, landed off Caballo Island. They dropped off parts and medical supplies, embarked passengers, and returned to Lake Lanão on Mindanão. While being towed away from shore to attempt takeoff on 30 April, the first Catalina struck a reef and could not take off. The second continued on to Perth. After cursory repairs, the first was able to get airborne, although some of the evacuees including Cmdr. Francis J. Bridget of the wing remained behind and were later captured. By 3 May the Catalinas returned to Perth after the completion of flights of almost 7,000 miles. Gridiron saved 36 evacuees, and all 14 flight crewmembers received the Silver Star.

30 APRIL • The Air Operational Training Command was established with headquarters at NAS Jacksonville, Fla. Four days later the new command assumed authority over the naval air stations and their satellite fields at Banana River, Jacksonville, Key West, and Miami, Fla.

2 MAY • SBD-3 Dauntlesses of VS-5 and TBD-1 Devastators of VT-5, embarked on board *Yorktown* (CV 5), bombed Japanese submarine *I-21* in the Coral Sea. *I-21* escaped and reported the attack but failed to identify the aircraft as carrier-based. The error enabled Task Force 17, Rear Adm. Frank J. Fletcher commanding, to approach the Solomon Islands undetected.

3 MAY • After Axis aerial attacks on Malta nearly annihilated the British fighters on the island, Prime Minister Winston S. Churchill asked President Franklin D. Roosevelt to provide *Wasp* (CV 7) for "another good sting." On this date, *Wasp* embarked 47 British Royal Air Force Supermarine Spitfire Mk Vs and sailed with British Force W for the Mediterranean during Operation Bowery—the aerial reinforcement of Malta. The ships rendezvoused with British carrier *Eagle* (D 94), which embarked 17 Spitfires. On 9 May, *Wasp* and *Eagle* launched their planes to Malta. Two days later the Prime Minister signaled the carrier, "Who said a wasp couldn't sting twice?" On 15 May, *Wasp* arrived at Scapa Flow in the Orkneys.

4 MAY • The Battle of the Coral Sea began, the first naval engagement fought without opposing ships making contact. The Japanese launched Operation MO—the seizure of Port Moresby, New Guinea, and points in the Solomon Islands, Nauru, and the Ocean Islands—preparatory to the neutralization of Australia as an Allied bastion. Task Force 17, Rear Adm. Frank J. Fletcher commanding, attacked the invading Japanese at Gavutu and Tulagi in the Solomons. F4F-3 Wildcats of VF-42, SBD-3 Dauntlesses of VB-5 and VS-5, and TBD-1 Devastators of VT-5 from *Yorktown* (CV 5), sank destroyer *Kikuzuki*, minesweeper *Tama Maru*, and auxiliary minesweepers *Wa 1* and *Wa 2*, and damaged destroyer *Yuzuki*, minelayer *Okinoshima*, transport *Azumasan Maru*, and cargo ship *Kozui Maru*.

Japanese transports sailed from Rabaul for Port Moresby. On 7 May, Task Force 17, which had been joined by Task Force 11, Rear Adm. Aubrey W. Fitch commanding, including *Lexington* (CV 2), turned north to engage the Japanese Carrier Strike Force, Vice Adm. Takagi Takeo commanding, including carriers *Shōkaku* and *Zuikaku*. SBD-2s from VB-2, SBD-3s of VS-2, and TBD-1s from VT-2, embarked on board *Lexington*, and Dauntlesses of VB-5 and VS-5 and Devastators of VT-5, flying from *Yorktown*, sank light carrier *Shōhō* of the Close Support Force, Rear Adm. Goto Aritomo commanding, in the Coral Sea. Japanese planes sank destroyer *Sims* (DD 409) and damaged oiler *Neosho* (AO 23), which was later scuttled.

The battle concluded the following day. Dauntlesses from *Lexington* and *Yorktown* damaged *Shōkaku* and forced her retirement. Pilot Lt. John J. Powers of VB-5 pressed an attack in an SBD-3 on *Shōkaku* but failed to recover from his dive. He received the Medal of Honor posthumously.

Japanese carrier bombers and attack planes struck Task Force 17. The few available U.S. fighters compelled the continuation of the use of Dauntlesses as an anti-torpedo plane patrol. Pilot Lt. William E. Hall, USNR, of VS-2 in an SBD-2 defended *Lexington*. Although wounded, Hall returned in his damaged Dauntless after participating in the destruction of at least three carrier attack planes and later received the Medal of Honor. The Japanese bombed and torpedoed *Lexington* and bombed *Yorktown*. Gasoline vapors flowing through *Lexington* ignited and triggered massive explosions that led to her abandonment, and destroyer *Phelps* (DD 360) scuttled the carrier at 15°12'S, 155°27'E.

The Americans sustained heavy casualties including the loss of at least 69 planes while the Japanese lost approximately 92 aircraft. The damage to *Shōkaku* and the aerial losses temporarily denied the Japanese the availability of *Shōkaku* and *Zuikaku*. The United States achieved a strategic victory by halting the push southward

SBD Dauntlesses from *Yorktown* (CV 5) attack Japanese carrier *Shōkaku* during the Battle of the Coral Sea on the morning of 8 May 1942.

and blunting the seaborne thrust toward Port Moresby. The Japanese deferred and then abandoned their occupation of Port Moresby by sea and shifted their advance overland across the Owen Stanley Mountains.

10 MAY • An experiment at the Naval Aircraft Factory at Philadelphia, Pa. demonstrated the possibility of increasing the range of small aircraft by operating them as towed gliders. Lt. Cdrs. William H. McClure and Robert W. Denbo piloted F4Fs attached to tow lines streamed behind a twin-engine Douglas BD-1 (A-20A Havoc), BuNo 4251, and, with their engines off underwent tows for an hour at 180 knots at 7,000 feet.

10 MAY • A base construction and garrison convoy, with VS-4 Detachment 14 embarked, arrived in the Tonga Islands and set up facilities to conduct antisubmarine patrols from Nukualofa Harbor, Tongatabu.

11 MAY • President Franklin D. Roosevelt ordered the establishment of the Air Medal for award to any persons who, while serving in any capacity in or with the Army, Navy, Marine Corps, or Coast Guard after 8 September 1939, distinguished or had distinguished themselves by meritorious achievement while participating in aerial flight.

15 MAY • The design of the national star insignia was revised by the elimination of the red disc in the center of the star, and the discontinuance of the use of horizontal red and white rudder striping.

15 MAY • The Chief of Naval Operations ordered the establishment of an Assistant Chief of Naval Operations (Air) to deal with aviation matters directly under the VCNO, and for the chief of BUAER to fill the new office as additional duty. The VCNO subsequently concentrated the aviation functions already performed in his office into a new Division of Aviation. The office was abolished in mid-June 1942.

15 MAY • VR-2, with a flight from NAS Alameda, Calif., to Honolulu, Hawaiian Islands, initiated air transport service in the Pacific during the first transoceanic flight by planes of the Naval Air Transport Service.

20 MAY • Rear Adm. John S. McCain reported as Commander Air Force, South Pacific, a new command established to direct the operations of tender and shore-based aviation in the South Pacific area.

26 MAY • Lt. j.g. C. Fink Fischer demonstrated the feasibility of rocket-assisted takeoff during a test flight in a Brewster F2A-3 Buffalo using five British antiaircraft solid propellant rocket motors at NAS Anacostia, D.C. The takeoff distance was reduced by 49 percent.

26 MAY • Aircraft ferry *Kitty Hawk* (AVP 1) disembarked reinforcements for Marine Aircraft Group 22, including seven F4F-3 Wildcats and 19 SBD-2 Dauntlesses, at Midway Island. The ship returned to Pearl Harbor in the Hawaiian Islands on 1 June.

27 MAY • The transfer of Patrol Wing 4 from Seattle, Wash., to the North Pacific began with the arrival of Commander, Kodiak, Alaska.

3 JUNE • The Japanese *Dai-ni Kidō Butai* (2nd Mobile Striking Force), Rear Adm. Kakuta Kikuji commanding, including carriers *Junyō* and *Ryūjō*, attacked Dutch Harbor in the Aleutians, Alaska. PBY-5A Catalinas of VP-41 and -42 of Patrol Wing 4 supported by seaplane tenders *Casco* (AVP 12), *Gillis* (AVD 12), and *Williamson* (AVD 2) patrolled the likely approaches. Harsh weather cloaked the raiders and they eluded discovery and surprised the defenders. The Japanese inflicted light damage and destroyed a Catalina in the harbor. They cancelled a second strike because of the weather, but their fighters shot down three patrolling PBYs.

The next day, the raiders again achieved surprise and shot down a Catalina and began bombing and strafing runs. Fighters downed another Catalina separately and a PBY-5A disappeared. Patrol Wing 4 lost six Catalinas and, the Eleventh Air Force, five planes. The Japanese lost a Mitsubishi A6M Type 0 carrier fighter, five Aichi D3A1 Type 99 carrier bombers, a Nakajima B5N2 Type 97 carrier attack plane, and two Nakajima E8N2 Type 95 floatplanes. Despite this, the Japanese failed to lure strong U.S. forces from Hawaiian waters.

Pilot PO Koga Tadayoshi flew the A6M from *Ryūjō* but ground fire damaged the plane and it nosed over during a forced landing on Akutan Island, killing Koga. On 10 July pilot Lt. William N. Thies of VP-41 in a PBY-5A spotted the wreckage, and afterward led a party to retrieve the aircraft. This provided an example of the foremost Japanese naval fighter to the Allies for study.

3 JUNE • The threat posed by the carriers of the U.S. Pacific Fleet convinced the Japanese to occupy Midway Island to lure the Pacific Fleet into a decisive battle. Japanese Commander in Chief Combined Fleet Adm. Yamamoto Isoroku developed Operation MI—a comprehensive plan that emphasized surprise. U.S. cryptanalysts, however, deciphered some enemy messages through ULTRA, and the Japanese also failed to deploy their submarines in time to discover the movements of the U.S. carriers. On 27 May, *Dai-ichi Kidō Butai* (1st Mobile Striking Force), Vice Adm. Nagumo Chūichi commanding, including carriers *Akagi*, *Kaga*, *Sōryū*, and *Hiryū* sailed from Japanese waters.

Commander in Chief Pacific Fleet Adm. Chester W. Nimitz deployed Task Forces 16, Rear Adm. Raymond A. Spruance commanding, including *Enterprise* (CV 6) and *Hornet* (CV 8); and 17, Rear Adm. Frank J. Fletcher commanding, including *Yorktown* (CV 5). On 3 June, planes from Midway located the Japanese Second Fleet Escort Force about 600 miles west of the island. The next day, 108 Japanese aircraft attacked Midway and F2A-3 Buffaloes and F4F-3 Wildcats of VMF-221 intercepted the raiders. Mitsubishi A6M Type 0 carrier fighters brushed aside the Marines, but the Japanese failed to suppress Midway. Nagumo thus decided upon a second raid.

SBD-2 Dauntlesses and SB2U-3 Vindicators of VMSB-241, TBF-1 Avengers—their introduction to combat—from a detachment of VT-8, and Army Martin B-26 Marauders equipped with torpedoes and Boeing B-17 Flying Fortresses from Midway struck the Japanese ships separately but suffered grim losses. TBD-1 Devastators of VT-3, -6, and -8 gallantly but futilely assailed the enemy carriers as fighters and antiaircraft fire virtually wiped-out all three squadrons. The multiple attacks drew off the Japanese fighters and threw their ships' formation into disarray. The arrival of Dauntlesses from VB-6 and VS-6, embarked on board *Enterprise*, thus caught the Japanese unprepared and resulted in the ensuing loss of *Kaga* and damage to *Akagi*. Dauntlesses of VB-3 from *Yorktown* sank *Sōryū*.

Hiryū launched dive bombers that damaged *Yorktown*. Fletcher transferred his flag to heavy cruiser *Astoria* (CA 34) and turned over tactical command to Spruance, but torpedo bombers from *Hiryū* further damaged *Yorktown* during a second attack. Dauntlesses of VB-3 operating from *Enterprise* in lieu of stricken *Yorktown* and from VS-6 damaged *Hiryū*. The loss of the carriers and the irretrievable failure to control the air compelled Yamamoto to retire.

On 5 June, Japanese destroyers scuttled *Akagi* and *Hiryū*. Heavy cruisers *Mikuma* and *Mogami* collided, and, on the 6th, Dauntlesses from *Enterprise* and *Hornet* sank *Mikuma* and damaged destroyers *Arashio* and *Asashio* by near misses. *Enterprise* and *Hornet* recovered their planes and turned around to refuel. The same day, Japanese submarine *I-168* damaged *Yorktown* and sank destroyer *Hammann* (DD 412). The submarine escaped and *Yorktown* foundered the next day. Planes searched for downed aviators and on 21 June, a PBY-5A Catalina of VP-24 made the final rescue 360 miles north of Midway of a two-man crew from a VT-6 Devastator that ditched on 4 June. In addition to the ships, the Japanese lost 258 aircraft plus experienced aircrew and mechanics. While the Americans lost at least 92 carrier and 40 shore-based planes in addition to *Yorktown* and *Hamman*, their decisive victory accelerated the attrition that led to the demise of Japanese naval offensive power.

6 JUNE • *Saratoga* (CV 3) arrived at Pearl Harbor, Territory of Hawaii, after repairs from torpedo damage that she sustained on 11 January. The ship thus missed participation in the Battles of Coral Sea and Midway.

6 JUNE • The Japanese landed on Kiska in the Aleutians, and the following day on Attu. Lt. Litsey of VP-41 piloted a PBY-5A and spotted the enemy there. On 11 June, Commander in Chief Pacific Adm. Chester W. Nimitz directed Patrol Wing 4 to "bomb the enemy out of Kiska." From 11 to 14 June, about 20 Catalinas from VP-41, -42, -43, and -51, supported by seaplane tender *Gillis* (AVD 12) at Nazan Bay, Atka Island, and USAAF Consolidated B-24 Liberators and Boeing B-17 Flying Fortresses, bombed the Japanese at Kiska in what was dubbed the "Kiska Blitz." The strikes interfered with Japanese efforts to consolidate their gains until *Gillis* expended her supplies of bombs and fuel, and failed to drive the invaders from the island. Lt. William N. Thies of VP-41 and Ens. James T. Hildebrand Jr. of VP-40, each received the Navy Cross for their separate actions in the fighting. In addition, B-17s, B-24s, and an LB-30 of the Eleventh Air Force damaged Japanese destroyer *Hibiki* on 12 June and sank fleet tanker *Nissan Maru*, on 18 June.

TBF-1 Avengers in flight off Ft. Lauderdale, Florida, January 1943.

10 JUNE • Project Sail was established to conduct airborne testing and associated work on magnetic anomaly detection (MAD) gear at NAS Quonset Point, R.I. Researchers intended this device to reveal submarines by the change they induced in the earth's magnetic field. The Naval Ordnance Laboratory and the National Defense Research Committee undertook the principal developmental efforts. The promising results of the early trials made with airships and a USAAF Douglas B-18 Bolo led to the procurement of 200 sets of MAD gear.

13 JUNE • The first airborne test of long-range radio navigation (LORAN for LOng RAnge Navigation equipment) occurred. A receiver mounted in airship K-2 accurately determined its position when the airship flew over various identifiable objects during a flight from NAS Lakehurst, N.J. The test culminated with the first LORAN homing from a distance 50 to 75 miles offshore during which operator Dr. J. A. Pierce issued instructions to the airship's commanding officer that brought them over the shoreline near Lakehurst on a course that caused the skipper to remark, "We weren't [just] headed for the hangar. We were headed for the middle of the hangar." The success of these tests led to immediate action to obtain operational LORAN equipment.

15 JUNE • *Copahee* (AVG 12), Capt. John G. Farrell commanding, was commissioned at Puget Sound Navy Yard, Bremerton, Wash. She was the first of ten escort carriers of the *Bogue* class converted from Maritime Commission hulls.

16 JUNE • Congress authorized an increase in the Navy's airship strength to 200 lighter-than-air craft.

17 JUNE • The National Defense Research Committee began the development of the Pelican antisubmarine guided missile with Bureau of Ordnance sponsorship. The device consisted of a glide bomb capable of automatically homing on a radar beam reflected from the target.

17 JUNE • Following the abolition of the newly created office of the Assistant Chief of Naval Operations (Air), the revision of an earlier order that had established an aviation organization in the Office of CNO made the Director of the Aviation Division responsible directly to VCNO.

17 JUNE • A contract was awarded to Goodyear Aircraft Corporation for the design and construction of a prototype M-class scouting and patrol airship with 50 percent greater range and volume (625,000 cubic feet) than the K class. Four M-class airships were built and served during World War II.

25 JUNE • The preliminary investigation of early warning radar had proceeded to the point that the coordinator for research and development requested the development of airborne early warning radar including automatic airborne relay and associated shipboard processing and display equipment. Interest in early warning radar arose when Adm. Ernest J. King observed to Head, Office of Scientific Research and Development Dr. Vannevar Bush the requirement of Navy ships to "see" beyond the line of sight.

26 JUNE • VR-2 initiated scheduled Naval Air Transport Service operations between the West Coast and Alaska.

26 JUNE • Lt. Cmdr. Frank A. Erickson, USCG, inspected Igor I. Sikorsky's VS-300 helicopter, and three days later, recommended their acquisition for antisubmarine convoy and life-saving duty.

27 JUNE • The Naval Aircraft Factory, Philadelphia, Pa., received directions to participate in the development of high-altitude pressure suits with particular emphasis on testing existing types and obtaining information to facilitate the tailoring and fitting of them for flight use. The Navy thus joined the Army in its sponsorship of work on pressure suits. The factory expanded its use of high-altitude equipment, including the design of a pressure cabin airplane and construction of an altitude test chamber.

1 JULY • *Ranger* (CV 4) sailed from NAS Quonset Point, R.I., to West Africa with 72 embarked Curtiss P-40Fs of the USAAF 57th Fighter Group. On 19 July, she launched the Warhawks to Accra, Gold Coast (Ghana), from where the planes were shipped to the China-Burma-India Theater. The ship turned for Port of Spain, Trinidad.

3 JULY • In the first successful firing of an American rocket from a plane in flight, gunnery officer of Transition Training Squadron, Pacific Fleet Lt. Cmdr. James H. Hean launched a rearward-firing antisubmarine rocket (retrorocket ASR) from a PBY-5A Catalina at Goldstone Lake, Calif. The rocket had been designed at the California Institute of Technology to be fired aft with a velocity equal to the forward velocity of the airplane and thus to fall vertically. After successful tests, the retrorocket became a weapon complementary to magnetic anomaly detection gear. In February 1943, VP-63 received the first service installation.

7 JULY • The Army agreed to deliver to the Navy a specified number of B-24 Liberators, B-25 Mitchells, and Lockheed B-34 Venturas to meet the Navy's requirement for long-range landplanes. The Navy was to relinquish its production cognizance of the Renton, Wash., Boeing plant to the Army for expanded B-29 Superfortress production, and to limit its orders for PBY Catalinas to avoid interference with the production of Liberators.

12 JULY • Patrol wings were reorganized to increase the mobility and flexibility of patrol aviation. The authorization of headquarters squadrons for each wing furnished administrative and maintenance services to the attached squadrons. Each wing was assigned geographic areas of responsibility, and the discontinuance of permanent squadron assignments facilitated requirements.

19 JULY • Seaplane tender *Casco* (AVP 12) established an advanced base in Nazan Bay, Atka Island, in the Aleutian Islands. The station supported seaplane antishipping searches, bombing of Japanese positions, and cover for ship bombardments against Kiska.

24 JULY • BUAER issued a planning directive calling for the procurement of four Sikorsky helicopters for study and development by the Navy and Coast Guard.

30 JULY • The Women Accepted for Volunteer Emergency Service (WAVES) was established and, on 2 August, Lt. Cmdr. Mildred H. McAfee assumed duties as the first commandant. By the end of the year the WAVES reached a strength of 3,879 officers and enlisted, and by 31 July 1945 their numbers grew to 86,291 women.

1 AUGUST • Ens. Henry C. White, USCG, of Coast Guard Squadron 212, piloted a Grumman J4F-1 Widgeon from Houma, La., and scored the first Coast Guard kill of a German submarine with the sinking of surfaced *U-166* off the passes of the Mississippi. White received the Distinguished Flying Cross.

7 AUGUST • Marine Aircraft Wings, Pacific, Maj. Gen. Ross E. Rowell, USMC, commanding, was organized at San Diego, Calif., for administrative control and logistic support of Marine Corps aviation units assigned to the Pacific Fleet. In September 1944, this command was renamed Aircraft, Fleet Marine Force, Pacific.

7 AUGUST • The Americans landed on Japanese-held Guadalcanal, Florida, Gavutu, Tanambogo, and Tulagi in the Solomon Islands during Operation Watchtower—the first U.S. land offensive of World War II. Task Force 61, Vice Adm. Frank J. Fletcher commanding, included Task Group 61.1, Rear Adm. Leigh Noyes commanding, with *Saratoga* (CV 3), *Enterprise* (CV 6), and *Wasp* (CV 7). Task Force 63, Rear Adm. John S. McCain commanding, provided Navy, Marine, and USAAF planes flying from New Caledonia and the New Hebrides (Vanuatu). The Marines wrestled control of the neighboring islands from the Japanese, and simultaneously moved inland on Guadalcanal. The next day, the Marines captured the unfinished Japanese airstrip and redesignated it Henderson Field in honor of Maj. Lofton R. Henderson, USMC, who had been shot down while leading VMSB-241 on an unsuccessful attack on Japanese carrier *Hiryū* at the Battle of Midway.

236837

Vice Adm. John S. McCain.

9 AUGUST • During the Battle of Savo Island, a Japanese force, Vice Adm. Mikawa Gunichi commanding, slipped undetected to the west of the island in the Solomons and inflicted a singularly devastating defeat upon the U.S. Navy. Heavy cruisers *Astoria* (CA 34), *Quincy* (CA 39), *Vincennes*

45345

Marine F4F Wildcats line Henderson Field during the battle for the control of Guadalcanal as a formation of Army Air Forces B-17 Flying Fortresses approaches, August 1942.

(CA 44), and Australian *Canberra* were sunk, and heavy cruiser *Chicago* (CA 29) and destroyers *Patterson* (DD 392) and *Ralph Talbot* (DD 390) sustained damage. The Americans lightly damaged four Japanese ships. Japanese gunfire set some of the SOC Seagulls embarked on board the cruisers alight, and the ensuing conflagrations spread flaming gasoline that further illuminated the ships for enemy spotters. Despite the overwhelming victory, Mikawa sought to escape aerial retaliation by clearing the area before sunrise, and consequently failed to attack the nearby transports. The defeat prompted the withdrawal of the U.S. carriers and the transports before they had unloaded all their cargoes, but the limited amount of supplies, which had been landed combined with those the Marines seized from the Japanese, enabled the Leathernecks to maintain their tenuous hold on Guadalcanal.

10 AUGUST • The headquarters of Patrol Wing 3 was shifted within the Panama Canal Zone from NAS Coco Solo to Albrook Field for closer coordination with the Army.

12 AUGUST • Light cruiser *Cleveland* (CL 55) operating in Chesapeake Bay tested the effectiveness of radio-proximity fuzes against planes during simulated combat conditions by destroying three radio-controlled drones with four proximity bursts from her 5-inch guns. This demonstration led to the mass production of the fuzes.

12 AUGUST • *Wolverine* (IX 64), Cmdr. George R. Fairlamb Jr. commanding, was commissioned at Buffalo, N.Y. This ship and *Sable* (IX 81)—which was commissioned on 8 May 1943—were Great Lakes excursion ships *Seeandbee* and *Greater Buffalo*, respectively, converted for aviation training. *Sable* and *Wolverine* operated for the remainder of World War II on Lake Michigan providing flight decks upon which student naval aviators qualified for carrier landings and flight deck crews received practical experience in handling aircraft on board ships.

13 AUGUST • Commander in Chief U.S. Fleet directed the establishment on about 30 September 1942 of an aircraft experimental and developmental squadron at NAS Anacostia, D.C. This squadron replaced the Fleet Air Tactical Unit to conduct experiments with new aircraft and equipment to determine their practical application and tactical employment.

15 AUGUST • Patrol Wing 11, Cmdr. Stanley J. Michael commanding, was established at Norfolk, Va. Five days later, the wing moved to operate within the Caribbean Sea Frontier from San Juan, P.R.

An SBD Dauntless flies over *Enterprise* (CV 6), foreground, and *Saratoga* (CV 3), near Guadalcanal in December 1942.

16 AUGUST • Blimp L-8 of ZP-32 departed Treasure Island for a routine patrol off the coast of San Francisco, Calif., but crashed several hours later in Dale City. Despite adequate fuel, her engines ceased operation, and crewmembers Lt. j.g. Ernest D. Cody and Ens. Charles E. Adams disappeared. The lighter-than-air craft apparently drifted with the wind toward land, exceeded her pressure height, and deflated and returned to earth. Local residents referred to the mysterious tragedy as the "Ghost Blimp." The Navy salvaged L-8, the former advertising airship *Ranger* of the Goodyear Aircraft Corporation, and after the war returned the blimp to the company.

20 AUGUST • The escort carrier designation was changed from Aircraft Escort Vessel (AVG) to Auxiliary Aircraft Carrier (ACV).

20 AUGUST • *Long Island* (ACV 1) launched the first Marine planes to arrive at Henderson Field on Guadalcanal, Solomon Islands—19 F4F-4 Wildcats of VMF-223 and 12 SBD-1 Dauntlesses of VMSB-232. A Japanese flying boat from the Shortland Islands sighted *Long Island*, but the ship retired beyond the range of enemy land-based aircraft. On 22 August, Bell P-400 Airacobras of the USAAF 67th Fighter Squadron joined the Marines, followed two days later by SBD-3s of VB-6 and VS-5 from *Enterprise* (CV 6). Marine planes carried the major air support burden during the campaign, and also flew 2,117 sorties against Japanese planes, losing 118 aircraft in battle and 30 operationally, while claiming the destruction of 427 enemy aircraft.

24 AUGUST • *Santee* (ACV 29), Capt. William D. Sample commanding, was commissioned at the Norfolk Navy Yard, Va. *Santee* was the first commissioned of four *Sangamon*-class auxiliary aircraft carriers converted from *Cimarron*-class fleet oilers.

24 AUGUST • During the Battle of the Eastern Solomons, Task Force 61, Vice Adm. Frank J. Fletcher commanding, including *Saratoga* (CV 3), *Enterprise* (CV 6), and *Wasp* (CV 7), supported by Marine and USAAF planes from Henderson Field on Guadalcanal, turned back a Japanese attempt to recapture Guadalcanal and Tulagi. The enemy deployed multiple forces including one of carriers *Shōkaku* and *Zuikaku* to cover a group of four transports, and a diversionary force formed around light carrier *Ryūjō*.

SBD-3 Dauntlesses of VB-3 and VS-3 and TBF-1 Avengers of VT-8 from *Saratoga* sank *Ryūjō* and damaged seaplane carrier *Chitose*. A Dauntless of VMSB-232 damaged light cruiser *Jintsū* north of Malaita Island, and planes from ashore sank armed merchant cruiser *Kinryu Maru* and destroyer *Mitsuki*, and damaged destroyer *Uzuki*. *Enterprise* fought off Japanese torpedo bombers but enemy

405443

A PBY-5A Catalina of VP-61 hunts for Japanese over the Aleutians near Adak, Alaska, in March 1943.

dive bombers made three direct bomb hits and four near misses that killed 74 men and wounded 95. Her crew controlled the fires and *Enterprise* made for Pearl Harbor, Hawaiian Islands. The Japanese lost fewer than 90 aircraft compared to U.S. casualties of 20 planes.

28 AUGUST • Marine and Navy SBD Dauntlesses from Henderson Field on Guadalcanal in the Solomon Islands defeated a Japanese attempt to land reinforcements from destroyers onto the island, sinking destroyer *Asagiri* and damaging *Amagiri*, *Shirakumo*, and *Yugiri*.

30 AUGUST • The Americans landed on Adak, Alaska, and established an advanced seaplane anchorage there based upon seaplane tender *Teal* (AVP 5). The operation placed Allied forces within 250 miles of Japanese-occupied Kiska and in a position to monitor enemy shipping lanes there and to Attu in the Aleutians. Japanese submarine *RO-61* torpedoed seaplane tender *Casco* (AVP 12) as she supported the landings from Nazan Bay. *Casco* was beached and subsequently salved.

31 AUGUST • Japanese submarine *I-26* torpedoed *Saratoga* (CV 3) about 260 miles southeast of Guadalcanal in the Solomon Islands, forcing the carrier to retire for repairs.

1 SEPTEMBER • Naval Air Forces, Pacific, Rear Adm. Aubrey W. Fitch commanding, was established for the administrative control of all air and air service units under Commander in Chief Pacific Fleet. This move replaced Commander Carriers, Pacific, and Commander Patrol Wings, Pacific. The establishment of the subordinate commands Fleet Air West Coast, Fleet Air Seattle, Wash., and Fleet Air Alameda, Calif., occurred simultaneously.

6 SEPTEMBER • The first Naval Air Transport Service flight to Argentia, Newfoundland, marked the beginning of air transport expansion along the eastern seaboard of North America. During September, the flights extended briefly to Iceland and reached southward to the Panama Canal Zone and to Rio de Janeiro, Brazil.

7 SEPTEMBER • VR-2, based at NAS Alameda, Calif., established a detachment at Pearl Harbor, Territory of Hawaii, and initiated a survey flight to the South Pacific preliminary to establishing routes between San Francisco, Calif., and Brisbane, Australia.

15 SEPTEMBER • Japanese submarine *I-19* attacked Task Force 18, Rear Adm. Leigh Noyes commanding, south of San Cristobal Island while the force covered a reinforcement convoy from Espíritu Santo, New Hebrides (Vanuatu), bound for Guadalcanal, Solomons. Two of the torpedoes struck *Wasp* (CV 7) in her starboard side near aviation gasoline tanks and magazines, and her commanding officer, Capt. Forrest P. Sherman, ordered the ship abandoned. Destroyer *Lansdowne* (DD 486) scuttled *Wasp*. Battleship *North Carolina* (BB 55) and destroyer *O'Brien* (DD 415) also received damage but the battleship subsequently completed repairs at Pearl Harbor, Hawaiian Islands. On 19 October, *O'Brien* sank northwest of Tutuila, Samoa while en route to the United States for repairs. Naval aviator Sherman survived to become the 12th Chief of Naval Operations.

16 SEPTEMBER • Patrol Wing 12, Capt. William G. Tomlinson commanding, was established at NAS Key West, Fla., from where it conducted operations within the Gulf Sea Frontier.

19 SEPTEMBER • Commander, Patrol Wing 1 departed NAS Kaneohe Bay, Hawaiian Islands, for the South Pacific to direct the operations of patrol squadrons already in the area. The headquarters was initially established at Nouméa, New Caledonia, and subsequently at Espíritu Santo, New Hebrides (Vanuatu), and on Guadalcanal and Munda in the Solomons.

1 OCTOBER • Airship Patrol Group 3, Capt. Scott E. Peck commanding, was established at NAS Moffett Field, Calif., to serve as the administrative command for airship squadrons operating on the West Coast.

1 OCTOBER • Three functional training commands—Air Technical Training, Air Primary Training, and Air Intermediate Training—were established with their headquarters initially at Chicago, Ill., Kansas City, Mo., and NAS Pensacola, Fla., respectively.

5 OCTOBER • Planes from *Hornet* (CV 8) attacked Japanese staging areas at Buin-Tonolei and Faisi on Bougainville in the Solomon Islands to disrupt enemy reinforcements from reaching Guadalcanal.

11 OCTOBER • Japanese transports proceeded down New Georgia Sound amid the Solomon Islands to disembark reinforcing elements of the 2nd Division for Japanese troops on Guadalcanal. A surface force, Rear Adm. Goto Aritomo commanding, was to cover their movement by shelling Henderson Field. During the ensuing Battle of Cape Esperance, Task Group 64.2, Rear Adm. Norman Scott commanding, maneuvered into a blocking position against Goto. The Japanese landed their reinforcements, but the following morning planes struck the retiring enemy ships. An SBD-3 Dauntless of VS-71 sank Japanese destroyer *Natsugumo* off Savo Island, and a TBF-1 Avenger of VT-8, SBD-3s of VS-3 and -71 and VMSB-141, and F4F-4 Wildcats of VMF-121, -212, and -224 damaged destroyer *Murakumo* off New Georgia. Destroyer *Shirayuki* scuttled *Murakumo*.

12 OCTOBER • The establishment of Naval Air Centers Hampton Roads, Va.; San Diego, Calif.; Seattle, Wash.; and Hawaiian Islands, and Naval Air Training Centers Pensacola, Fla., and Corpus Christi, Texas, consolidated under single commands various naval aviation facilities that had become operational in the vicinity of the large air stations.

14 OCTOBER • SBD-3 Dauntlesses of VS-3 flying from Guadalcanal, Solomon Islands, attacked the six ships of a Japanese convoy escorted by eight destroyers steaming toward Guadalcanal between Santa Isabel and Florida Islands, but failed to inflict damage. Overnight a Japanese force, Vice Adm. Mikawa Gunichi commanding, bombarded Henderson Field on Guadalcanal to cover the movement of six destroyers and 11 transports to Tassafaronga. Planes from Henderson Field including SBD-3s of VB-6 and VMSB-141, F4F-4 Wildcats of VF-5, a PBY Catalina that operated as the personal "flag" plane of Commanding General 1st Marine Aircraft Wing, and USAAF Boeing B-17s and Bell P-39/P-400 Airacobras attacked the Japanese ships off Tassafaronga. Transport *Azumasan Maru* and cargo ship *Kyushu Maru* were run aground and fires destroyed both ships. The strikes also sank *Sasago Maru* and damaged destroyer *Samidare*. Japanese planes from carrier *Zuikaku* eluded the Wildcats and sank destroyer *Meredith* (DD 434) off San Cristobal.

15 OCTOBER • Patrol Wing 14, Capt. William M. McDade commanding, was established at San Diego, Calif. The wing operated within the Western Sea Frontier to form, establish, and equip patrol squadrons.

16 OCTOBER • Task Force 17, Rear Adm. George D. Murray commanding, including *Hornet* (CV 8), struck Japanese troops on Guadalcanal and a seaplane base at Rekata Bay, Santa Isabel, in the Solomon Islands.

16 OCTOBER • Nine Japanese dive bombers damaged seaplane tender *McFarland* (AVD 14) as she unloaded cargo and evacuated wounded off Lunga Roads on Guadalcanal, Solomon Islands. The tender shot down one of the attackers, but the Japanese also hit a gasoline barge moored alongside her. The crew cut the blazing vessel loose, and *McFarland* was towed to Florida Island for temporary repairs before she moved for additional work.

17 OCTOBER • Inshore patrol squadrons (VS) were transferred to patrol wings for administrative control. This facilitated the operations of squadrons engaged in coastal antisubmarine reconnaissance and convoy duty within the sea frontiers.

18 OCTOBER • Vice Adm. William F. Halsey Jr. relieved Vice Adm. Robert L. Ghormley as Commander South Pacific Area and South Pacific Force on board auxiliary *Argonne* (AG 31) at Nouméa, New Caledonia.

19 OCTOBER • BUAER reported the initial installation and deployment of the ASB-3 airborne search radar. The Naval Research Laboratory developed the radar for carrier-based aircraft and had installed the system in five TBF-1 Avengers and five SBD-3 Dauntlesses at NASs New York and San Pedro, Calif., respectively. One plane of each type was assigned to Air Group 11 on board *Saratoga* (CV 3) and the others were shipped to Pearl Harbor, Hawaii. The remaining sets of the initial contract for 25 were used for spare parts and training.

21 OCTOBER • Eight men including World War I ace Capt. Edward V. Rickenbacker, USAAC (Ret.), crashed in a B-17D Flying Fortress, Serial 40-3089, in the Central Pacific as a result of a navigational error while Rickenbacker toured Allied forces in the Pacific. At one point, Sgt. Alexander Kaczmarczyk, USAAF, died and the castaways buried him at sea. On 12 November, Lt. j.g. F. E. Woodward and ARM2 L. H. Boutte flying a Vought OS2U-3 Kingfisher of VS 1 Detachment 14, spotted a life raft containing the pilot of the Flying Fortress, Capt. William T. Cherry Jr., USAAF. A patrol torpedo boat rescued him. The next day, Lt. William F. Eadie and Boutte crewed the same Kingfisher and spotted the raft carrying Rickenbacker; Capt. Hans C. Adamson, USAAF; and Pvt. John F. Bartek, USAAF; off Nukufetau in the Ellice Islands (Tuvalu). Eadie landed the Kingfisher, rescued the three men, and taxied 40 miles to the nearest land. The Navy later rescued the other three survivors.

22 OCTOBER • An amendment to a design study contract authorized Westinghouse Electric and Manufacturing Co. to construct two 19A axial-flow turbojet powerplants. The move initiated the fabrication of the first jet engine of wholly U.S. design.

25 OCTOBER • Japanese destroyers *Akatsuki*, *Ikazuchi*, and *Shiratsuyu* sank tug *Seminole* (AT 65) and district patrol craft *YP-284* off Guadalcanal in the Solomon Islands, and damaged minesweeper *Zane* (DMS 14) in Sealark Channel. Marine shore batteries and F4F-4 Wildcats of VMF-121 damaged *Akatsuki* off Lunga Point and damaged *Ikazuchi* while USAAF Bell P-39 Airacobras damaged destroyers *Akizuki* and *Samidare*. An SBD-3 Dauntless of VS-71 and USAAF aircraft damaged Japanese light cruiser *Yura* off Santa Isabel. Destroyers *Harusame* and *Yudachi* scuttled *Yura*.

26 OCTOBER • The Battle of the Santa Cruz Islands began. Task Forces 16 and 17, Rear Adms. Thomas C. Kinkaid and George D. Murray commanding, including *Enterprise* (CV 6) and *Hornet* (CV 8), respectively, fought Japanese forces, Vice Adm. Nagumo Chūichi commanding, including carriers *Shōkaku* and *Zuikaku* and light carriers *Junyō* and *Zuihō* that supported an overland thrust on Guadalcanal, Solomon Islands. *Hornet* launched SBD-3 Dauntlesses of VB-8 and VS-8 that damaged *Shōkaku* and destroyer *Terutsuki*, and TBF-1 Avengers of VT 6 that damaged heavy cruiser *Chikuma*. Dauntlesses of VS-10 from *Enterprise* damaged *Zuihō*. Planes from *Shōkaku* and *Junyō* twice damaged *Enterprise*, killing 44 men and wounding 75. Aircraft from *Shōkaku*, *Zuikaku*, and *Junyō* left *Hornet* ablaze from a total of three torpedoes, four bombs, and two crashing Aichi D3A1 Type 99 carrier bombers. Destroyers *Anderson* (DD 411) and *Mustin* (DD 413) attempted to scuttle *Hornet*, but the following day Japanese destroyers *Akigumo* and *Makigumo* sank the carrier. The Japanese lost 99 planes and the Americans 80. The Japanese attained a tactical naval victory, but Marines and soldiers repulsed the enemy's land offensive on Guadalcanal, thus conferring a strategic victory to the Allies.

28 OCTOBER • The procurement of an expendable radio sonobuoy for use in antisubmarine warfare began when Commander in Chief U.S. Fleet directed the Bureau of Ships to procure 1,000 sonobuoys and 100 associated receivers.

31 OCTOBER • Air Transport Squadrons Pacific was established over the Naval Air Transport Service squadrons based in the Pacific and those on the West Coast that flew the routes from the mainland United States to the Hawaiian Islands.

1 NOVEMBER • The War Department designated Japanese aircraft with human names to provide a uniform identification system, initially with fighter types receiving male names and all others female. The 16 major frontline naval types identified to date: Aichi D3A1 Type 99 carrier bomber "Val," Aichi E13A1 Type 0 reconnaissance floatplane "Jake," Kawanishi E7K2 Type 94 reconnaissance floatplane "Alf," Kawanishi H6K4 Type 97 flying boat "Mavis," Kawanishi H8K2 Type 2 flying boat "Emily," Mitsubishi A5M4 Type 96 carrier fighter "Claude," Mitsubishi A6M Type 0 carrier fighter "Zeke," Mitsubishi F1M2 Type 0 observation floatplane "Pete," Mitsubishi G3M3 Type 96 land attack plane "Nell," Mitsubishi G4M1 Type 1 attack plane "Betty," Nakajima A6M2-N Type 2 fighter seaplane "Rufe," Nakajima B5N2 Type 97 carrier attack plane "Kate," Nakajima B6N1 carrier attack plane "Jill," Nakajima E8N2 Type 95 reconnaissance floatplane "Dave," Yokosuka D4Y1 Type 2 carrier bomber "Judy," and Yokosuka E14Y1 Type 0 small reconnaissance seaplane "Glen." The Allies adopted additional names for succeeding Japanese aircraft.

1 NOVEMBER • Patrol wings were redesignated fleet air wings. To permit the organization of patrol aviation on the task force principle, the practice of assigning a standard number of squadrons to each of the wings shifted to provide for the assignment of all types of aircraft required by the wings to perform their missions.

1 NOVEMBER • Airship Patrol Group 1 was redesignated Fleet Airship Group 1 at NAS Lakehurst, N.J.

2 NOVEMBER • NAS Patuxent River, Md., was established to serve as a facility for testing experimental airplanes and equipment, and as a Naval Air Transport Service base. The station eventually assumed the role of the Navy's principal flight testing and of the Naval Test Pilot School in place of NAS Anacostia, D.C.

2 NOVEMBER • Fleet Air Wing 6, Capt. Douglass P. Johnson commanding, was established for multi-engine aircraft training at NAS Seattle, Wash.

8 NOVEMBER • Task Group 34.2, Rear Adm. Ernest D. McWhorter commanding, including *Ranger* (CV 4), *Suwannee* (AVG 27), *Sangamon* (AVG 26), and *Santee* (ACV 29), covered landings near Casablanca and Fedala in Morocco during Operation Torch, the Allied invasion of North Africa.

The French *2ème Escadre Légère* (2nd Light Squadron), Contre-Amiral Raymond Gervais de Lafonde commanding, attempted to disrupt the landings off Casablanca. Naval spotting planes reported the French sortie and naval gunfire and bombing and strafing attacks including F4F-4 Wildcats from VF-9 and -41 and SBD-3 Dauntlesses from VS-41 from *Ranger* overwhelmed the French. Air attacks sank four submarines and damaged light cruiser *Primaguet*, three destroyers, and one submarine. Wildcats from VF-41 fought French Dewoitine D.520s and Curtiss Hawk 75As of *Groupes de Chasse* I/5 and II/5. Planes spotted the fall of shot for ships against coastal emplacements. Battleship *Massachusetts* (BB 59) and bombing and strafing runs by naval aircraft including Wildcats from VF-41 damaged French battleship *Jean Bart*.

The next day, 14 French light tanks counterattacked along the road to Rabat. Gunfire from light cruiser *Savannah* (CL 42) and aerial runs defeated the armored thrust. The invaders then repulsed a second armored counterattack. On 10 November, scout planes from *Savannah* bombed and strafed French light tanks. *Chenango* (ACV 28) accompanied the assault forces and launched 78 USAAF Curtiss P-40 Warhawks to operate from Port Lyautey. Through 11 November and the Vichy French capitulation, 172 carrier aircraft flew 1,078 combat sorties. Forty-four planes were lost but most of their crewmembers survived. These aircraft claimed the destruction of 20 of the estimated 168 French planes deployed to Morocco.

12 NOVEMBER • The Naval Battle of Guadalcanal began when Japanese land attack planes assaulted ships of Task Force 67 in Lunga Roads at Guadalcanal in the Solomon Islands. During a savage nocturnal action, U.S. ships repulsed the Japanese from an intended bombardment of Guadalcanal's Henderson Field. The next morning, Task Force 16, Rear Adm. Thomas C. Kinkaid commanding, including *Enterprise* (CV 6)—the last operational fleet carrier in the Pacific and still completing repairs—launched aerial attacks at the retiring Japanese. TBF-1 Avengers of VT-8 from *Enterprise* and of VMSB-131 and SBD-3 Dauntlesses of VMSB-142 from Henderson sank Japanese battleship *Hiei*. Planes also damaged two destroyers.

On 14 November, the failed Japanese bombardment prompted the postponement of landings, and SBD-3s of VMSB-132 sank heavy cruiser *Kinugasa*. Planes damaged heavy cruisers *Chōkai* and *Maya*, light cruisers *Isuzu* and *Tenryu*, and a destroyer. Dauntlesses of VS-10 and VMSB-130 and -141 and Avengers of VT-10 from Henderson Field sank seven transports/cargo ships and damaged a cargo ship. Overnight, the Americans repelled a Japanese force off the island. The following afternoon, Dauntlesses from VS-10 and VMSB-132 and Avengers of VT-10, together with Marine and Army coastal guns and destroyer *Meade* (DD 602), sank four Japanese transports/cargo ships off northern Guadalcanal. The United States suffered the greater loss of warships during this series of engagements, but the Japanese withdrew and the battle marked their final attempt to dispatch large naval forces into the waters around Guadalcanal.

13 NOVEMBER • PBY-5 Catalinas of VP-73 arrived at Craw Field at Port Lyautey, Morocco, from Iceland via Bally Kelly, Ireland, and Lyncham, England. Seaplane tender *Barnegat* (AVP 10) supported the squadron during antisubmarine operations over the western Mediterranean and the Strait of Gibraltar and its approaches. During these patrols, the Catalinas encountered Spanish Fiat CR.32s over the Canary Islands and German Focke-Wulf Fw 200C Condors near Gibraltar. In addition, a detachment operated from Ben Sergao Field near Agadir. VP-92 arrived at Les Cazes at Port Lyautey via Cuba, Brazil, Ascension Island, and West Africa.

13 NOVEMBER • Two PBY-5As of VP-92 spotted a submarine on the surface that refused to answer recognition signals about 700 miles off Casablanca, Morocco. Because of the communications error, pilot Lt. H. S. Blake and the crew of his Catalina sank Vichy French boat *Le Conquerant* without sighting survivors.

16 NOVEMBER • Marine Night Fighter Squadron (VMF[N])-531, Lt. Col. Frank H. Schwable, USMC, commanding, was established at MCAS Cherry Point, N.C. This first naval aviation night fighter squadron trained initially with SNJ Texans and SB2A4 Buccaneers, and then received twin-engine PV-1 Venturas equipped with British Mark IV type radar.

23 NOVEMBER • The VS-173 full-scale model of the "Flying Flapjack" fighter with an almost circular wing made its first flight at the Vought-Sikorsky plant, Stratford, Conn. A subsequent military version of this aircraft designated XF5U-1 never flew.

1 DECEMBER • Fleet Air Wing 15, Capt. George A. Seitz commanding, was established at Norfolk, Va. to conduct operations within the Moroccan Sea Frontier.

1 DECEMBER • Fleet Airship Wing 30, Capt. George H. Mills commanding, was established at NAS Lakehurst, N.J. The wing administered Atlantic Fleet airship groups and their squadrons.

1 DECEMBER • Airship Patrol Group 3 was redesignated Fleet Airship Wing 31 at NAS Moffett Field, Calif.

15 DECEMBER • As a result of the matte-black paint schemes of the PBY-5A Catalinas of VP-12 and the night-time bombing operations conducted by the squadron from Nandi in the Fiji Islands around Guadalcanal in the Solomon Islands, VP-12 became known as a "Black Cat" squadron. Other squadrons that subsequently received the appellation included VP-11, -51, and -91.

26 DECEMBER • The Chief of Naval Operations approved the merger of the Service Force Aviation Repair Unit and Advanced Cruiser Aircraft Training Unit, which had been established in October 1941 and June 1942, respectively, to form a scout observation service unit (SOSU) to maintain battleship and cruiser aircraft and indoctrinate pilots in their specific operations. This SOSU was established on 1 January 1943 as the first of three created during World War II.

27 DECEMBER • *Santee* (ACV 29), with Air Group 29 embarked, sailed from NOB Norfolk, Va. *Santee* became the first of 11 auxiliary aircraft carriers to wage free-roving hunter-killer antisubmarine and antiraider operations in the South Atlantic.

31 DECEMBER • The chief of BUAER noted to the Naval Research Laboratory the urgent need for airborne radar that obviated the slower peacetime methods of procurement and fleet introduction, and requested the continuance of the provision of people capable of assisting the fleet in the operation and maintenance of radar equipment until the assembly of a specially trained group. Within a few months, this team evolved into the Airborne Coordination Group that provided trained civilian electronics specialists to the fleet throughout World War II and post-war.

31 DECEMBER • *Essex* (CV 9), Capt. Donald B. Duncan commanding, was commissioned at Norfolk, Va. She was the first of 17 ships of her class commissioned during World War II.

31 DECEMBER • The Japanese decided to evacuate Guadalcanal, Solomon Islands.

1943

1 JANUARY • Naval Reserve aviation bases (NRAB) engaged in primary flight training were redesignated naval air stations (NAS) without a change of mission. There were two exceptions. On 7 July 1943, NRAB Anacostia, D.C., was abolished, and on 1 September 1943, Squantum, Mass., was redesignated as a naval air station.

1 JANUARY • Air Force, Atlantic Fleet, was established, Rear Adm. Alva D. Bernhard commanding. The command provided administrative, material, and logistic services for Atlantic Fleet aviation in place of the separate commands Fleet Air Wings, Atlantic, and Carriers, Atlantic, which were abolished. The same order established Fleet Air, Quonset, R.I., as a subordinate command.

1 JANUARY • The Navy recorded its first emergency use of ground-controlled approach (GCA) equipment when a half hour before the scheduled arrival of a flight of PBYs, a snowstorm closed the field at NAS Quonset Point, R.I. The GCA crew located the incoming Catalinas on their search radar and, using the control tower as a relay station, "talked" one of the planes into position for a landing. This recovery occurred nine days after the first successful experimental demonstration of GCA.

5 JANUARY • Ships of Task Force 67 bombarded Japanese positions in Munda on New Georgia, Solomon Islands. Japanese planes counterattacked, and in the first combat use of a proximity-fuzed projectile, light cruiser *Helena* (CL 50) destroyed a Japanese dive bomber with the second salvo from her 5-inch guns off the south coast of Guadalcanal.

7 JANUARY • The opening of flight preparatory schools in 20 colleges and universities across the United States implemented a change in the pilot training program. Under the new program, students began their training at these schools with three months of academic work fundamental to ground school subjects, then proceeded to War Training Service courses conducted by the Civil Aeronautics Administration at universities for two months' training in ground subjects and elementary flight under civilian instructors, then to the pre-flight schools for three months of physical conditioning, and finally to Navy flight training beginning at one of the primary training bases.

7 JANUARY • The development of the first naval aircraft to be equipped with a turbojet engine began with the issuance of a letter of intent for engineering, development, and tooling for two fighters to McDonnell Aircraft Corporation. The agreements later specified two Westinghouse 19-B turbojet engines and the aircraft received the designation XFD-1, which became the prototypes for the FH-1 Phantom.

8 JANUARY • *Ranger* (CV 4) sailed from NOB Norfolk, Va., to west African waters with 75 embarked Curtiss P-40Es of the USAAF 325th Fighter Group. On 19 January, she launched the Warhawks from a position off Accra, Gold Coast (Ghana), for shipment to the North African Theater, and then returned to Norfolk.

10 JANUARY • Fleet Air Wing 15 headquarters was transferred from Norfolk, Va., to Port Lyautey, French Morocco, to direct patrol plane operations in the Mediterranean and Strait of Gibraltar area.

12 JANUARY • The chief of Naval Air Operational Training directed the marking of aircraft operating from stations under his command for identification purposes with letters and numerals in three groups separated by dashes. The first group provided a letter identification of the station, the second a letter identifying the unit type, and the third the number of the aircraft in the unit. The order also provided for the addition of a number to the station letter during the operations of more than one unit on board the station. Thus J2-F-22 identified a plane from NAS Jacksonville, Fla., OTU No. 2 Fighter Training Unit, aircraft No. 22.

14 JANUARY • *Independence* (CVL 22) was commissioned at Philadelphia, Pa., Capt. George R. Fairlamb Jr. commanding. She was the first of nine light carriers of her class constructed on the hulls of *Cleveland* (CL 55)-class light cruisers.

15 JANUARY • Head of the Flight Statistics Desk of the Bureau of Aeronautics, Capt. Spencer H. Warner, introduced Grampaw Pettibone in the *BUAER News Letter*. Artist Lt. Robert Osborn drew the cartoon character as a safety feature to help reduce pilot-error accidents. After Osborn's discharge from the Navy, he contributed Pettibone to *Naval Aviation News* magazine.

41221

A carrier's landing signal officer guides an F4U Corsair to land.

17 JANUARY • After tests conducted by six experienced pilots flying F4U-1 Corsairs at NAS San Diego, Calif., VF-12 commanding officer Cmdr. Joseph C. Clifton reported that antiblackout suits had raised pilot tolerance to accelerations encountered in gunnery runs and other maneuvers by three to four Gs.

24 JANUARY • Ships of Task Force 67 shelled Japanese ammunition and fuel dumps on Kolombangara, Solomon Islands. Later that day, aircraft operating from Guadalcanal's Henderson Field bombed the targets.

28 JANUARY • *Barnegat* (AVP 10)-class seaplane tender *Absecon* (AVP 23), Cmdr. Robert S. Purvis commanding, was commissioned at Puget Sound Navy Yard at Bremerton, Wash. *Absecon* had undergone the unique fitting of a catapult and two cranes to facilitate training in catapult launches and sled net recoveries. Her embarked aviation unit consisted initially of one SO3C-1 Seamew and two OS2U-3 Kingfishers. The ship completed 3,733 catapult launches during World War II, and also operated as a mobile target for torpedo planes training from NASs Ft. Lauderdale and Miami, Fla.

31 JANUARY • 1st Lt. Jefferson J. DeBlanc, USMC, of VMF-112 piloted an F4F-4 Wildcat as part of an escort for SBD Dauntlesses and TBF-1 Avengers that bombed Japanese ships in Vella Gulf in the Solomons. The Japanese intercepted the Marines, but DeBlanc shot down two Mitsubishi A6M Type 0 carrier fighters and three floatplanes over Kolombangara Island. His efforts disrupted the Japanese attacks, but the aviator bailed out from his damaged Wildcat over the enemy-held island. A coastwatcher on Kolombangara rescued DeBlanc and SSgt. James A. Feliton, USMC, who had also parachuted. Thirteen days later a J2F-5 Duck returned both men. DeBlanc received the Medal of Honor.

1 FEBRUARY • VB-127, Lt. Cmdr. William K. Gentner commanding, was established at NAS Deland, Fla., equipped with PV-1 Venturas. Although it was not the first Navy landplane patrol squadron, it was the first to receive the VB designation.

1 FEBRUARY • A new specification prescribing the color and marking of naval aircraft became effective. The basic camouflage color scheme for use on fleet aircraft was a pattern of four colors ranging from semigloss Sea Blue on surfaces viewed from above with intermediary blues to nonspecular Insignia White on surfaces viewed from below. It also involved complex countershading paint application. The terms "basic non-camouflage" and "maximum visibility" were introduced for the color schemes described in April 1942 for use on intermediate and primary trainers.

1 FEBRUARY • The revision of regulations governing the display of the national star insignia on aircraft removed those markings from the upper right and lower left wing surfaces.

9 FEBRUARY • Organized Japanese resistance ended on Guadalcanal in the Solomon Islands after the evacuation of their main forces. In addition to the desperately waged carrier battles of the campaign, Allied aircraft operating from ashore had directly supported the hard-pressed soldiers and Marines, and Navy patrol squadrons had flown search, rescue, and offensive missions from sheltered coves and harbors.

11 FEBRUARY • The Navy issued a contract for the XFR-1 to Ryan Aeronautical Corp. This fighter incorporated a conventional reciprocating engine for use in normal operations and a turbojet for use as a booster during takeoffs and maximum performance flight. The development and production were to be handled on a crash basis to equip escort carrier squadrons at the earliest possible date, but design and production problems prevented the plane from entering battle.

11 FEBRUARY • An SON-1 Seagull of VCS-9, embarked on board light cruiser *Helena* (CL 50), operated in a rare coordinated attack with destroyer *Fletcher* (DD 445) to sink Japanese submarine *I-18* in the Coral Sea.

12 FEBRUARY • Vought F4U-1s flew their first combat mission when 12 Corsairs of VMF-124, Maj. William E. Gise, USMC, commanding, based on Guadalcanal escorted a PB2Y-2 Coronado to Vella Lavella in the Solomon Islands to rescue downed pilots. Two days later, the first combat action for Corsairs occurred when the squadron encountered Mitsubishi A6M Type 0 carrier fighters while escorting VP-51 PB4Y-1 Liberators on a daylight strike in the Kahili area of Bougainville. The Japanese downed 10 aircraft, including two Corsairs, while losing three Zeros.

13 FEBRUARY • The reorganization of the Naval Air Transport Service took place and the Navy directed the establishment of wings for the Atlantic and West Coast squadrons.

14 FEBRUARY • *Ranger* (CV 4) sailed from NOB Norfolk, Va., to west African waters with 75 embarked USAAF Curtiss P-40Ls. On 24 February, she launched the Warhawks from a position off Accra, Gold Coast (Ghana), for shipment to the North African Theater. The ship returned to Hampton Roads, Va.

15 FEBRUARY • Commander in Chief, U.S. Fleet assigned the responsibility for the seagoing development of helicopters and their operation in convoys to the Coast Guard, and directed testing to determine their value when operating from merchant ships to fight submarines.

16 FEBRUARY • Fleet Air Wing 16, Capt. Rossmore D. Lyon commanding, was established at NAS Norfolk, Va.

17 FEBRUARY • Airship K-17 of ZP-51 initiated lighter-than-air operations over the Caribbean from Edinburgh Field, Trinidad.

19 FEBRUARY • A letter of intent was issued for two XP2V-1 patrol planes to Vega Airplane Co. The action initiated the development of the Lockheed Neptune.

21 FEBRUARY • Marines and soldiers made unopposed landings in the Russell Islands during Operation Cleanslate—the inaugural movement of Allied forces through the central Solomon Islands. Navy, Marine, and USAAF planes from Aircraft, South Pacific, and Aircraft, Solomons, Central Pacific Forces, including those operating from *Saratoga* (CV 3) and Henderson Field, Guadalcanal, covered the landings. The Allies leapfrogged across the islands and established bases and airfields to support their advance against the Japanese stronghold at Rabaul, New Britain. The Japanese failure to defeat the counteroffensive in the air and by sea enabled the Allies to reduce or bypass enemy garrisons piecemeal.

24 FEBRUARY • The Naval Photographic Science Laboratory was established at NAS Anacostia, D.C. The Bureau of Aeronautics oversaw the laboratory to provide photographic services to the Navy, and to develop equipment and techniques suitable for fleet use.

1 MARCH • Air Transport Squadrons, West Coast, was established at NAAS Oakland, Calif. The command controlled all Naval Air Transport Service squadrons operating west of the Mississippi River, except those that operated from the mainland to Honolulu, Hawaiian Islands.

1 MARCH • A revision of the squadron designation system changed inshore patrol squadrons to scouting squadrons (VS), escort fighting squadrons (VGF) to fighting squadrons (VF), escort scouting squadrons (VGS) to composite squadrons (VC), and patrol squadrons (VP) operating land type planes to bombing squadrons (VB). The revision also redesignated carrier scouting squadrons (VS) as VB and VC, and as a result, the types of squadrons on board *Essex* (CV 9)-class carriers fell to three. In spite of this change, the aircraft complement of their air groups remained at the previous level of 21 fighters, 36 scout bombers, and 18 torpedo bombers.

1 MARCH • Fleet Airship Group 2, Capt. Walter E. Zimmerman commanding, was established at NAS Richmond, Fla. The group oversaw lighter-than-air operations in the Gulf Sea Frontier.

4 MARCH • Secretary of the Navy William F. Knox authorized changes to the characteristics of *Essex* (CV 9)-class carriers, including the installation of a combat information center and fighter director station, additional antiaircraft batteries, and a second flight deck catapult in lieu of one athwartships on the hangar deck.

4 MARCH • Damage to U.S. carriers in early 1943 reduced the number available in the South Pacific, and the British responded to a request for reinforcements by dispatching their carrier *Victorious* (38). On this date, she reached Pearl Harbor, Hawaiian Islands. The ship embarked Martlet IVs (Grumman F4F-4Bs) of 882, 896, and 898 Squadrons, and Tarpon Is (Grumman TBF-1 Avengers) of 832 Squadron. On 8 May, she sailed for Nouméa, New Caledonia, and into the summer operated with Task Group 36.3, including *Saratoga* (CV 3), in the Solomon Islands. At one point, some of the Tarpons embarked briefly on board *Saratoga* in a rare instance during World War II of British planes operating from a U.S. carrier.

5 MARCH • *Bogue* (ACV 9), with VC-9 embarked, joined Task Group 24.4 at Argentia, Newfoundland, to begin the escort of convoys to mid-ocean and return. *Santee* (ACV 29) previously operated on hunter-killer duty, but *Bogue* became the center of the first of the hunter-killer groups assigned to convoy escort. Through 14 March the ship supported convoy HX-228.

15 MARCH • The headquarters of Fleet Air Wing 4 shifted westward on the Aleutian chain from Kodiak to Adak, Alaska.

15 MARCH • The Navy initiated a system of numbering fleets with those in the Pacific receiving odd numbers and those in the Atlantic even numbers.

20 MARCH • Maj. John W. Sapp, USMC, of VMTB-143, led 42 Navy and Marine TBF-1 Avengers on a night flight from Guadalcanal's Henderson Field in the Solomon Islands, to mine Kahili Harbor, Bougainville. A coordinated attack on the Kahili airfield by USAAF heavy bombers contributed to the success of this first aerial mining mission in the South Pacific.

23 MARCH • The Training Task Force Command was established with its headquarters at NAS Clinton, Okla. The command formed, outfitted, and trained special units for the operational employment of assault drone aircraft.

29 MARCH • Testing of forward firing rocket projectiles from naval aircraft concluded with evaluation of an SB2A-4 Buccaneer at the Naval Proving Ground, Dahlgren, Va.

29 MARCH • Air Transport Squadrons, Atlantic, was established at NAS Norfolk, Va. The command supervised and directed the operations of Naval Air Transport Service squadrons based on the Atlantic seaboard.

30 MARCH • TBF-1 Avengers laid mines near Buin, Bougainville, in the Solomon Islands. On 17 April, Japanese transport *Shinnan Maru* blundered into one of the mines and sank.

1 APRIL • Aircraft Antisubmarine Development Detachment, Cmdr. Aurelius B. Vosseller commanding, was established at NAS Quonset Point, R.I., to develop tactical training programs and techniques to make use of newly developed countermeasures equipment.

1 APRIL • Night Fighting Squadron (VF[N]) 75, Cmdr. William J. Widhelm commanding, was established at NAS Quonset Point, R.I., as the first Navy night fighter squadron.

4 APRIL • The Naval Aircraft Factory, Philadelphia, Pa., reported that during tests of an automatic flying device for use on towed gliders, a Taylorcraft LNT-1 had been towed automatically without assistance from the safety pilot.

9 APRIL • The Navy reestablished the rank of commodore.

14 APRIL • Fleet Air Wing 16 was transferred from NAS Norfolk, Va., to Natal, Brazil, to direct patrol plane antisubmarine operations within the Fourth Fleet in the South Atlantic.

16 APRIL • The Navy changed the color of the working uniform to slate grey. The change proved unpopular among officers and, on 15 October 1946, the service reinstated khakis.

21 APRIL • Capt. Frederick M. Trapnell made the first jet flight by a U.S. naval aviator in the Bell XP-59A Airacomet at Muroc, Calif.

468849

Aviation ordnancemen mount 4.5-inch high-velocity rockets onto a plane.

MAY • Lt. j.g. Richard M. Nixon, USNR, reported to Commander, Naval Air Forces Pacific as officer in charge of the South Pacific Combat Air Transport Command at Guadalcanal, Solomon Islands. Nixon had completed naval aviation indoctrination training at NAS Quonset Point, R.I. While in the South Pacific, he served in the development and maintenance of the aerial supply routes, and afterward on the Green Islands and in Fleet Air Wing 8. On 1 June 1966, Cmdr. Nixon retired from the Naval Reserve, and he subsequently became the 37th president of the United States.

3 MAY • VR-1 extended the area of its operations with a flight from NAS Norfolk, Va., via Reykjavik, Iceland, to Prestwick, Scotland. The event completed the first R5D-1 Skymaster operation of the Naval Air Transport Service.

4 MAY • Fleet Air Wing 4 commenced regular aerial patrols from Amchitka in the Aleutian Islands that extended the search coverage beyond Attu toward the Kurile Islands.

4 MAY • To expedite the evaluation of helicopters in antisubmarine operations, Commander in Chief, U.S. Fleet directed the formation of a joint board with representatives of the Commander in Chief, U.S. Fleet, the Bureau of Aeronautics, the Coast Guard, and the British Admiralty and Royal Air Force. The resulting Combined Board for the Evaluation of the Ship-Based Helicopter in Antisubmarine Warfare later underwent expansion to include representatives of the USAAF, the War Shipping Administration, and the National Advisory Committee for Aeronautics.

41693

A PV-1 Ventura hunts for enemy submarines, c. 1943.

7 MAY • Navy representatives witnessed landing trials of the XR-4 helicopter on board merchant tanker *Bunker Hill* in Long Island Sound. Col. R. F. Gregory, USAAF, made 15 flights, and in some of these, he landed on the water before returning to the platform on the ship's deck. The Maritime Commission sponsored the demonstration.

8 MAY • Navy and Marine aircraft sank destroyers *Oyashio* and *Kagero*, respectively, after mines damaged both warships off Rendova in the Solomons. Meanwhile, destroyer *Kuroshio* struck a mine laid the previous day and sank in the Blackett Strait, and planes damaged destroyer *Michisio* in the strait.

8 MAY • *Sable* (IX 81) was commissioned at Buffalo, N.Y, Capt. William A. Schoech commanding.

11 MAY • Task Forces 16 and 51 supported landings of the Army's 7th Division on Attu Island, Alaska. Navy and Marine aircraft flew close air support missions from *Nassau* (ACV 16), marking the first use of this type of direct air support from an escort carrier of amphibious operations. Planes from Fleet Air Wing 4 also took part—PV-1 Venturas from VB-136, PBY-5A Catalinas of VP-43 and -62, and PBY-5s from VP-45 flew from Adak, and Venturas from VB-135 and PBY-5As of VP-61 operated from Amchitka. The seizure of Attu was the debut of a support air commander afloat on board battleship *Pennsylvania* (BB 38), whose team consisted of three officers and a radioman led by experienced Aleutian pilot Col. W. O. Eareckson, USA. Despite extensive naval gunfire and air support the soldiers suffered disproportionately high casualties dislodging the tenacious Japanese defenders.

14 MAY • Lt. P. A. Bodinet of VP-84 piloted a PBY-5A Catalina that sank the German *U-640* using a Mk 24 airborne acoustic homing torpedo dubbed "Fido" off Iceland, east of Cape Farewell, Greenland.

15 MAY • The Naval Airship Training Command was established at Lakehurst, N.J. The command administered and directed lighter-than-air training programs at the naval air centers at Lakehurst and NAS Moffett Field, Calif., and directed Lakehurst's Experimental and Flight Test Department.

15 MAY • OS2U-3 and OS2N-1 Kingfishers of VS-62 and Cuban submarine chaser *SC-13* sank the German *U-176* northeast of Havana, Cuba.

18 MAY • The cancellation of the program for the use of gliders as transports for Marine combat troops returned the Navy's glider development to an experimental basis.

20 MAY • The Navy established the Tenth Fleet with its headquarters in Washington, D.C., to direct antisubmarine warfare efforts in the Atlantic.

One of four PB4Y-1 Liberator bombers of VB-107 out of Ascension Island drops Mk 47 depth bombs on *U-848* during the submarine's sinking on 5 November 1943.

22 MAY • During a running battle to protect convoy ON-184 in the North Atlantic, TBF-1 Avengers of VC-9, embarked on board *Bogue* (ACV 9), sank *U-569* to score the first U-boat sinking in World War II by U.S. auxiliary aircraft carriers on hunter-killer patrols. The Germans maintained that the crew scuttled their boat. Avengers also damaged *U-305*. *Bogue* claimed the destruction of 13 U-boats by her planes and escorts during the Battle of the Atlantic.

24 MAY • Special Project Unit Cast was organized at Squantum, Mass., to provide (under Bureau of Aeronautics direction) the services required to flight test electronic equipment under development at the Radiation and Radio Research Laboratories.

5 JUNE • TBF-1s of VC-9, embarked on board *Bogue* (ACV 9), damaged German submarines *U-228*, *U-603*, and *U-641* in the mid-Atlantic. The next day, Avengers from the ship sank *U-217* off the Canary Islands. On 12 June, *Bogue* and her Avengers sank *U-118* near those islands.

7 JUNE • The establishment of NAF Attu within a week of the capture of the island from the Japanese brought Fleet Air Wing 4 bases to the tip of the Aleutian chain, nearly 1,000 miles from the Alaskan mainland and 750 miles from Japanese territory in the Kurile Islands.

7 JUNE • Commander in Chief, U.S. Fleet established a project for the airborne testing by Commander Fleet Air, West Coast of high velocity, "forward shooting" rockets. These had nearly double the velocity of those that had been tested earlier at the Dahlgren, Va., Naval Proving Ground. A rocket section led by Dr. C. C. Lauritsen developed the rockets at the California Institute of Technology under National Defense Research Committee auspices and with Navy support. This test project was established in part on the basis of reports of the effectiveness in service of a similar British rocket. On 14 July, the first airborne firing from a TBF-1 Avenger of a British rocket was followed on 20 August by launching of the CalTech round. The favorable results of these evaluations led to the equipping of operational squadrons with forward firing rockets by the end of the year.

10 JUNE • Lt. Cmdr. Frank A. Erickson, USCG, proposed the development of helicopters for antisubmarine warfare, "not as a killer craft but as the eyes and ears of the convoy escorts." To this end he recommended their equipping with radar and dunking sonar.

15 JUNE • President Franklin D. Roosevelt approved a ceiling of 31,447 planes for the Navy.

17 JUNE • *Monterey* (CVL 26), Capt. Lester T. Hundt commanding, was commissioned at New York Shipbuilding Corp., Camden, N.J. The ship's company included assistant navigator Lt. Gerald R. Ford Jr., USNR. On 28 June 1963, Lt. Cmdr. Ford was discharged from the Naval Reserve, and afterward became the 38th president of the United States.

20 JUNE • Lt. E. W. Wood of VP-84 piloted a PBY-5A Catalina that sank German submarine *U-388* and damaged *U-420* in Icelandic waters. The battle marked the second combat use of Mk 24 Fido acoustic torpedoes.

20 JUNE • African American Ens. Oscar Holmes was designated a naval aviator. Navy officials apparently were unaware of Holmes' race and he thus became the first documented man of color to receive Navy wings. Holmes had attained experience as a civilian pilot and received the designation after completion of an instructor's course, rather than the entire Navy flight syllabus.

21 JUNE • Navy, Marine, and USAAF aircraft supported the move of the 4th Marine Raider Battalion into Segi of the New Georgia Group in the Solomon Islands.

28 JUNE • A change in the design of the national star insignia added white rectangles on the left and right sides of the blue circular field to form a horizontal bar, and a red border stripe around the entire design. The substitution of Insignia Blue for the red followed in September.

29 JUNE • NAS Patuxent River, Md., began functioning as an aircraft test organization with the arrival of the flight test unit from NAS Anacostia, D.C.

29 JUNE • Elements of VP-101 arrived at Brisbane from Perth, Australia, thereby extending the patrol coverage of Fleet Air Wing 10 to the east coast of Australia and marking the beginning of a northward advance of patrol operations toward the Papuan Peninsula, New Guinea.

30 JUNE • Land-based Navy, Marine, and USAAF aircraft of Task Force 33, Vice Adm. Aubrey W. Fitch commanding, supported Operation Toenails—U.S. landings on Rendova and other islands in the New Georgia area of the Solomon Islands, including Kiriwini, Onaivisi, Wickham Anchorage, and Woodlark. Rear Adm. Marc A. Mitscher held tactical command of the planes, which operated primarily from airfields on Guadalcanal and the Russell Islands. The forward echelon of the 2d Marine Aircraft Wing of Headquarters, New Georgia Air Force provided the principal intrinsic air support ashore. Fierce fighting occurred offshore when the Japanese repeatedly attacked the landing forces from the air.

2 JULY • Land-based Navy, Marine, and USAAF aircraft of Task Force 33, Vice Adm. Aubrey W. Fitch commanding, supported soldiers of the 43rd Division and Marines who stormed Viru and Zanana, Solomon Islands. A flight of Japanese Mitsubishi G4M1 Type 1 attack planes escorted by A6M Type 0 carrier fighters disrupted the landings. This is variously attributed to Japanese interception of Allied radio traffic that revealed retiring fighter cover, or the temporary maintenance of the only operating radar set on Rendova. The Bettys and Zeros killed 59 men and wounded 77. The ensuing recriminations between the Army and Navy led to enhanced combat air patrols over the beachhead that protected the landings from continual Japanese aerial counterattacks. Three days later, Allied troops landed at Rice Anchorage.

5 JULY • The first Westinghouse 19A turbojet engine developed for the Navy completed its 100-hour endurance test.

6 JULY • Commanding officer and pilot Lt. Cmdr. Bruce A. Van Voorhis of VB-102 made a daring solitary low-level attack in a PB4Y-1 Liberator against Japanese installations on Greenwich Island (Kapingamarangi). After a flight of almost 700 miles, Van Voorhis made six bombing runs on a radio station and several strafing passes against three Mitsubishi F1M2 Type 0 observation floatplanes (Petes) of the 902d *Kōkūtai* (Air Group) and vessels in the lagoon. The squadron reported that Van Voorhis flew "too low and too slow" on the last run, and that a bomb blast caught the Liberator and the bomber crashed in the lagoon. The Japanese, however, claimed that their floatplanes downed the Liberator. Van

Voorhis received the Medal of Honor, copilot Lt. j.g. Herschel A. Oehlert Jr. was awarded the Navy Cross, and each of the other crewmembers received the Distinguished Flying Cross, all posthumously.

6 JULY • The Army, Navy, and Coast Guard carried out a demonstration of helicopter operations on board Army transport *James Parker* (AP 46) while she sailed from New York City to Virginia. Two YR-4B (HNS-1) Hoverflys landed on a platform fitted to the ship that measured 60 feet long by 50 feet wide forward, tapering aft to 40 feet in width. Through 7 July, the pilots completed 98 landings and takeoffs in winds ranging from 5 to 25 knots, and while the ship pitched up to 6½ degrees.

8 JULY • *Casablanca* (ACV 55), Capt. Steven W. Callaway commanding, was commissioned at Astoria, Ore., as the first of her class and the first auxiliary aircraft carrier designed and built as such.

10 JULY • Light cruisers *Philadelphia* (CL 41) and *Savannah* (CL 42) operated with gunfire support ships during Operation Husky—the Allied invasion of Sicily. *Philadelphia* and *Savannah* launched their SOC-3 and -3A and SON-1 Seagulls to spot the fall of shot. German Messerschmitt Bf 109s shot down three of *Savannah*'s four scout planes. The pilot of one, Lt. C. A. Anderson, was killed, but ARM Edward J. True landed the riddled plane and escaped before it sank. The next day, Allied naval gunfire destroyed 13 Axis tanks and continued support over the succeeding days. On 13 July, the Army's 1st Division thanked *Savannah* for "crushing three infantry attacks and silencing four artillery batteries."

12 JULY • Light cruisers *Birmingham* (CL 62) and *Brooklyn* (CL 40) commenced coverage from off Porto Empédocle of the left flank of the advance of American forces across Sicily. A German minefield compelled the cruisers to maneuver out to sea but their scouting planes spotted the fall of 6-inch supporting fire for more than a week, afterward augmented by additional Allied ships, including light cruiser *Philadelphia* (CL 41).

13 JULY • F4F-4 Wildcats and TBF-1 Avengers of VC-13, embarked on board *Core* (ACV 13), began a month of successful assaults on U-boats during two of the carrier's patrols. Pilot Lt. Robert P. Williams, USNR, and aircrewmen ARM1 Morris C. Grinstead and AMM2 Melvin H. Paden sank surfaced *U-487* with depth charges from their Avenger about 720 miles south-southwest of Fayal, Azores. The U-boat shot down Lt. j.g. Earl H. Steiger, USNR, during a strafing run in a Wildcat, BuNo 12112, killing him. Three days later, Avengers from *Core* (which was redesignated CVE-13 the previous day) destroyed *U-67* in the mid-Atlantic, and on 24 August sank *U-84* and *U-185* at two different locations southwest of the Azores.

14 JULY • The Secretary of the Navy issued a General Order forming the Naval Air Material Center, consisting of the separate commands of the Naval Aircraft Factory, the Naval Aircraft Modification Unit, the Naval Air Experimental Station, and the Naval Auxiliary Air Station. This action became effective on 20 July and consolidated in distinct activities the production, modification, experimental, and air station facilities of the former Naval Aircraft Factory organization at Philadelphia, Pa.

15 JULY • The establishment of new designations for carriers limited the previous broadly applied CV symbol to *Saratoga* (CV 3), *Ranger* (CV 4), *Enterprise* (CV 6), and to *Essex* (CV 9)-class carriers, and added CVB (Aircraft Carrier, Large) for the 45,000-ton *Midway* (CVB 41)-class under construction and CVL (Aircraft Carrier, Small) for the nine 10,000-ton *Independence* (CVL 22)-class ships built on the hulls of *Cleveland* (CL 55)-class light cruisers. The same directive reclassified escort carriers as warships and changed their symbol from ACV to CVE.

15 JULY • The Navy modified its airship organization. Fleet Airship Wings 30 and 31 were redesignated Fleet Airships, Atlantic, and Pacific, respectively. Airship patrol groups became airship wings, airship patrol squadrons were redesignated blimp squadrons, and the addition of two more wings and the establishment of blimp headquarters squadrons within each wing was authorized.

17 JULY • SBD Dauntlesses from VB-11 and VMSB-132 and TBF-1 Avengers from VT-11 and -21, escorted by F4U-1s, including Corsairs, from VMF-122, -211, and -221, along with USAAF Consolidated B-24 Liberators escorted by Bell P-39 Airacobras and Curtiss P-40 Warhawks, and Royal New Zealand Air Force Curtiss Kittyhawks of No. 14 Squadron,

301754

Two ships of Task Group 38.2, *Intrepid* (CV 11) and *Independence* (CVL 22) (left and right, respectively) are seen from *Enterprise* (CV 6) around the time of the Battle of Leyte Gulf, October 1944. The two types formed the basis for the fast carrier task forces at sea.

attacked Japanese ships at Buin, Bougainville, in the Solomon Islands into the following day. In the face of heavy fighter opposition, the attacks sank destroyer *Hatsuyuki* and damaged destroyers *Hatsukaze* and *Yūnagi*, and auxiliary minesweeper *W. 15*.

18 JULY • Lt. N. G. Grills of ZP-21 piloted airship K-74 on a patrol off southeastern Florida from NAS Richmond, Fla. The airship's radar detected a contact at a range of eight miles and ten minutes later the blimp discovered surfaced *U-134* off the port bow. K-74 fired a .50-caliber machine gun and unsuccessfully attempted to drop depth bombs. The U-boat's deck gun and machine gun fire hit the engine and the airship bag, K-74's controls failed to respond, and it fell tail first. The wreck remained afloat until 19 July but then sank, the only U.S. airship lost to enemy action in World War II. One man died from a shark attack before a J4F-2 Widgeon from ZP-21 directed destroyer *Dahlgren* (DD 187) to the area to rescue Grills and the other eight survivors. Despite damage to her ballast and diving tanks, *U-134* escaped, but the following month British bombers sank her in the Bay of Biscay.

19 JULY • The Naval Aircraft Factory, Philadelphia, Pa., received authorization to develop the Gorgon aerial ram or air-to-air missile powered by a turbojet engine and equipped with radio controls and a homing device. The Gorgon program later underwent expansion embracing turbojet, ramjet, pulsejet, and rocket power; straight wing, swept wing, and canard (tail first) air frames; and visual, television, heat-homing, and three types of radar guidance for use as air-to-air, air-to-surface, and surface-to-surface guided missiles, and as target drones.

22 JULY • The Vice Chief of Naval Operations approved the removal of arresting gear and related equipment for landing over the bow of aircraft carriers because experience had failed to demonstrate its operational value.

23 JULY • The first of 15 VP-63 PBY-5s reached Pembroke Dock, England. Their arrival marked the initial U.S. Navy squadron operations from the United Kingdom during World War II. The Catalinas supported the British in antisubmarine patrols over the Bay of Biscay.

2 AUGUST • Fleet Air Wing 4, Capt. Walter E. Zimmerman commanding, was established at Maceio, Brazil, and Fleet Air Wing 5, Cmdr. John D. Reppy commanding, was established at Edinburgh Field, Trinidad, to conduct antisubmarine and convoy patrols in the South Atlantic and the southern approaches to the Caribbean.

4 AUGUST • The chief of Naval Air Intermediate Training directed the establishment of aviation safety boards at each training center under his command.

5 AUGUST • Commander in Chief, U.S. Fleet Adm. Ernest J. King directed the use of fleet air wing commanders in the subordinate commands of sea frontiers, and suggested their assignment as deputy chiefs of staff for air.

9 AUGUST • Allied aircraft, including planes from *Ranger* (CV 4), covered the arrival of British liner *Queen Mary* at Halifax, Nova Scotia. The ship had embarked British Prime Minister Winston S. Churchill for his participation in the conference at Québec, Canada, codenamed Quadrant, with President Franklin D. Roosevelt and key Allied leaders.

15 AUGUST • The arrival of Aircraft Experimental and Development Squadron (later Tactical Test) from NAS Anacostia, D.C., to NAS Patuxent River, Md., completed the transfer of the Navy's aircraft test activities.

15 AUGUST • The landing of Army and Canadian troops on Kiska in the Aleutian Islands marked the first use in the Pacific of air liaison parties with forces ashore. The Japanese had deserted the island but the landing provided the opportunity to prove the soundness of the principle and demonstrated the operational application of rapid and reliable voice communications between frontline commanders and the support air control unit afloat.

15 AUGUST • Navy, Marine, and USAAF aircraft supported landings on Vella Lavella that bypassed Japanese garrisons on Kolombangara in the Solomon Islands. The initial combat air patrol over the beaches included F4U-1 Corsairs of VMF-123 and -124 operating from Munda. The Japanese counterattacked vigorously during more than 100 sorties, but continual air cover over the landings and bombing raids against the enemy fields at Ballale, Buin, and Kahili secured the success of the operation. After 2d Lt. Kenneth A. Walsh, USMC, piloting a Corsair of VMF-124 shot down a Mitsubishi A6M Type 0 carrier fighter and two Aichi D3A1 Type 99 carrier bombers, he returned to Munda in a plane so battered that it was stricken. Fifteen days later, Walsh repeated his exploit by downing four Japanese aircraft near Kahili. He later received the Medal of Honor.

18 AUGUST • To provide naval aviation authority commensurate with its World War II responsibility, the Secretary of the Navy established the Office of the Deputy Chief of Naval Operations (Air) and charged it with "the preparation, readiness and logistic support of the naval aeronautic operating forces." By other orders issued the same day, five divisions were transferred from the Bureau of Aeronautics to form the nucleus of the new office. Vice Adm. John S. McCain assumed command as the first DCNO (Air).

21 AUGUST • The headquarters of Fleet Air Wing 7 was established at Plymouth, England. It directed patrol plane operations against German submarines in the Bay of Biscay, the English Channel, and the southwest approaches to England.

27 AUGUST • Navy, Marine, and USAAF aircraft supported landings of the Army's 172nd Regimental Combat Team on Arundel Island, Solomon Islands.

27 AUGUST • F4F-4 Wildcats and TBF-1 Avengers from VC-1, embarked on board *Card* (CVE 11), sank German submarine *U-847* in the mid-Atlantic. *U-508* escaped during a separate battle.

An F6F Hellcat laden with rockets and a droppable fuel tank launches from *Hancock* (CV 19).

29 AUGUST • The formation of combat units for the employment of assault drone aircraft began within the Training Task Force Command with the establishment of the first of three special task air groups. The component squadrons were designated VK and began to establish on 23 October.

30 AUGUST • Task Force 15, Rear Adm. Charles A. Pownall commanding, including *Essex* (CV 9), *Yorktown* (CV 10), and *Independence* (CVL 22), launched nine strike groups in a day-long attack on Japanese installations on Marcus Island in the prototype fast carrier strike. TBF-1 Avengers from *Independence* sank three small Japanese vessels. This second raid against Marcus marked the first attack by *Essex*- and *Independence*-class carriers and the combat debut of the F6F-3 Hellcat.

1 SEPTEMBER • The Navy assumed full responsibility for airborne antisubmarine warfare by U.S. forces in the Atlantic.

1 SEPTEMBER • Task Group 11.2, Rear Adm. Arthur W. Radford commanding, including *Belleau Wood* (CVL 24) and *Princeton* (CVL 23), and Navy patrol bombers from Canton Island, furnished day and night air cover for the landing of occupation forces on Baker Island, east of the Gilbert Islands.

9 SEPTEMBER • Operation Avalanche—an assault by the Anglo-American troops of the U.S. Fifth Army on the Gulf of Salerno, Italy—began. Allied naval gunfire proved instrumental in halting German counterattacks. SOC-3 and SON-1 Seagulls from VCS-8, embarked on board light cruisers *Philadelphia* (CL 41) and *Savannah* (CL 42), spotted the fall of shot from the cruisers' 6-inch guns. A Seagull operating from *Philadelphia* discovered 35 German *panzers* (tanks) concealed in a thicket adjacent to Red Beach. Salvoes from the cruiser knocked out seven tanks before the survivors dashed to the rear. *Savannah* silenced a railway battery and broke up an enemy armored thrust. The cruisers covered the landings until 11 September, when German Dornier Do 217E-5s damaged both ships with FX 1400 radio-controlled glide bombs. *Philadelphia* suffered minor damage and continued the battle, but *Savannah* turned for repairs at Malta.

15 SEPTEMBER • Fleet Air Wing 17, Commodore Thomas S. Combs commanding, was established for operations in the Southwest Pacific Area from Brisbane, Australia.

15 SEPTEMBER • VFP-1 was established at NAS Norfolk, Va. Through the remainder of the year, Free French sailors under U.S. Navy control manned the patrol squadron with varying numbers of PBM-3S Mariners and PBY-5A Catalinas.

18 SEPTEMBER • Task Force 15, Rear Adm. Charles A. Pownall commanding, attacked Japanese-occupied Abemama, Makin, and Tarawa Atolls in the Gilbert Islands.

A K-class airship protects a convoy of merchant ships from German submarines in the Atlantic.

18 SEPTEMBER • Fleet Air Wing 5 at NAS Norfolk, Va., was assigned a primary mission of training. Fleet Air Wing 9 assumed responsibility for all patrol plane operations within the Eastern Sea Frontier.

19 SEPTEMBER • *Ranger* (CV 4) anchored in Scapa Flow, Orkney Islands. The ship had provided air cover over British battlecruiser *Renown* while she returned Prime Minister Winston S. Churchill from the Quadrant conference, a series of strategy meetings, with President Franklin D. Roosevelt and Allied leaders at Québec, Canada.

27 SEPTEMBER • Naval airship operations over the South Atlantic began with the arrival of blimp K-84 of ZP-41 at Fortaleza, Brazil.

30 SEPTEMBER • An advance detachment of VB-107 PB4Y-1 Liberators joined USAAF planes flying antisubmarine barrier patrols and sweeps from Ascension Island over the South Atlantic.

1 OCTOBER • Air Force, Atlantic Fleet, was reorganized and Fleet Air, Norfolk, and Fleet Airships, Atlantic, were established as additional subordinate commands.

1 OCTOBER • The increase of the authorized complement of fighters in *Essex* (CV 9)-class carrier air groups raised the number of planes normally embarked on board to 36 fighters, 36 bombers, and 18 torpedo bombers. The authorized complement for CVL groups was established as 12 fighters, 9 bombers, and 9 torpedo bombers, revised the following month to 24 fighters and 9 torpedo bombers, and remained at that level through the end of World War II.

The first of the Navy's PB4Y Liberator bombers came from the U.S. Army Air Forces and included the Army's serial number. This B-24D, 41-23827, was the second to join the Navy and became BuNo 31937.

4 OCTOBER • In September, British X-craft midget submarines had temporarily immobilized German battleship *Tirpitz*. *Ranger* (CV 4) carried out the only U.S. carrier operation in Northern European waters during World War II in Operation Leader—a raid against German forces in Norway made possible by the removal of the threat posed by *Tirpitz*. On this date, *Ranger* launched a strike against German ships at Bodø and a second raid along the coast from Alter Fjord to Kunna Head. F4F-4 Wildcats of VF-4, TBF-1 Avengers of VT-4, and SBD-5 Dauntlesses of VB-4 sank German steamers *Kaguir*, *La Plata*, and *Rabat*, transport *Skramstad*, and Norwegian steamer *Vaagan*, and damaged two tankers, three steamers, and a ferry. Antiaircraft fire downed two Dauntlesses of VB-4 and an Avenger, and damaged several aircraft. Wildcats shot down two German planes that approached the task force—a Junkers Ju 88D-1 of *Fernaufklarungs Gruppe* (Long Range Reconnaissance Group) 22, and a Heinkel He 115B of *Küstenflieger Gruppe* (Coastal Patrol Group) 406. A Wildcat crashed upon landing, but British destroyer *Scourge* recovered the pilot. The *Ranger* air group, CVG-4, later requested additional training and newer aircraft.

4 OCTOBER • F4F-4 Wildcats and TBF-1C Avengers from VC-9, embarked on board *Card* (CVE 11), discovered German *U-264*, *U-422*, and *U-455* while they rendezvoused with *Milchkühe* (milk cow) refueling boat *U-460* north of the Azores, and sank *U-422* and *U-460*. This action allowed convoy UGS-19 to pass through the vicinity unmolested by the enemy.

5 OCTOBER • Coast Guard Patrol Squadron 6, Cmdr. D. B. MacDiarmid, USCG, commanding, was established at Argentia, Newfoundland. The Coast Guardsmen assumed rescue duties that had been performed by naval planes operating from Greenland and Labrador.

5 OCTOBER • Task Force 14, Rear Adm. Alfred E. Montgomery commanding, including *Essex* (CV 9), *Yorktown* (CV 10), *Lexington* (CV 16), *Independence* (CVL 22), *Belleau Wood* (CVL 24), and *Cowpens* (CVL 25), attacked Japanese installations during the second carrier raid on Wake Island. In the course of the two-day battle, the ships launched six strike groups totaling 738 combat sorties and lost 12 planes shot down and 14 from accidents. The raiders tested ship handling techniques for a multicarrier force devised by the staff of Rear Adm. Frederick C. Sherman on the basis of experience gained in the South Pacific. The lessons learned from operating the carriers as a single group of six, as two groups of three, and as three groups of two provided the basis for some of the tactics that afterward characterized carrier task force operations. The island's Japanese commander, Rear Adm. Sakaibara Shigematsu, feared the strikes portended a landing and ordered the execution of the remaining 98 U.S. civilians held captive on the island.

6 OCTOBER • The Naval Airship Training Command at NAS Lakehurst, N.J., was redesignated the Naval Airship Training and Experimental Command.

12 OCTOBER • The Bureau of Ordnance established a production program for 3,000 Pelican guided missiles at a delivery rate of 300 per month.

16 OCTOBER • The Navy accepted its first helicopter, a YR-4B (HNS-1) Hoverfly, following a one-hour acceptance test flight by Lt. Cmdr. Frank A. Erickson, USCG, at Bridgeport, Conn.

18 OCTOBER • *Cowpens* (CVL 25) and destroyer *Abbot* (DD 629) collided during maneuvers in Hawaiian waters. *Abbot* required three months of repairs at the Pearl Harbor Navy Yard.

19 OCTOBER • An Allied force, including *Ranger* (CV 4), covered the transport of Norwegian troops to Spitzbergen, Svarlbard Archipelago, to reestablish bases destroyed by the Germans during Operation *Zitronella*—a raid on 8 September 1943 on the islands by battleships *Tirpitz* and *Scharnhorst*. The Allies also embarked the survivors of the original garrison.

27 OCTOBER • Navy, Marine, USAAF, and New Zealand aircraft from the South Pacific Air Force supported landings of the 8th New Zealand Brigade Group on Mono and Stirling Islands in the Treasury Island Group of the Solomon Islands, together with a divisionary landing by the 2d Marine Parachute Battalion on the west coast of Choiseul Island.

31 OCTOBER • Lt. Hugh D. O'Neil of VF(N)-75 piloted an F4U-2 Corsair from Munda, New Georgia, and destroyed a Japanese Mitsubishi G4M1 Type 1 Betty during a night attack off Vella Lavella. O'Neil thus scored the first kill by a radar-equipped night fighter of the Pacific Fleet. Maj. Thomas E. Hicks, USMC, and TSgt. Gleason, USMC, of VMF(N)-531 provided ground-based fighter direction.

31 OCTOBER • Airship K-94 caught fire while en route from NS Guantánamo Bay, Cuba, to San Juan, P.R., and crashed 35 miles north of Cape Borinquen, P.R. Its eight-man crew was reported missing.

1 NOVEMBER • Task Force 31 landed the I Marine Amphibious Corps at Cape Torokina, Bougainville, in the Solomon Islands. Task Force 38, Rear Adm. Frederick C. Sherman commanding, including *Saratoga* (CV 3) and *Princeton* (CVL 23), launched preliminary strikes against Japanese airfields and installations in the Buka-Bonis area. SBD Dauntlesses and TBF-1 Avengers of VC-38, VMSB-144, and VMTB-143, -232, and -233, covered by F4U-1 Corsairs of VF-17 and VMF-215 and -221, bombed and strafed the Japanese defenders five minutes before the Marines landed. A combat air patrol averaging 38 fighters rotated over the beaches and disrupted major Japanese aerial counterattacks.

1 NOVEMBER • A detachment of VB-145 PV-1 Venturas began operations from Fernando Noronha Island, extending the area of Fleet Air Wing 16 antisubmarine patrols over the South Atlantic toward Ascension Island.

2 NOVEMBER • During the nighttime Battle of Empress Augusta Bay, surface Task Force 39 intercepted and turned back a Japanese force en route to attack transports off Bougainville in the Solomon Islands. Japanese planes attacked the task force during its retirement after dawn but the preliminary air strikes against enemy airfields in the Buka-Bonis area the previous day prevented a decisive counterattack.

5 NOVEMBER • Task Force 38, Rear Adm. Frederick C. Sherman commanding, launched an aerial attack on the Japanese fortress of Rabaul on New Britain. Planes from *Saratoga* (CV 3) and *Princeton* (CVL 23) damaged heavy cruisers *Atago*, *Chikuma*, *Maya*, *Mogami*, and *Takao*; light cruisers *Agano* and *Noshiro*; and destroyers *Amagiri* and *Fujinami* of the Second Japanese Fleet, Rear Adm. Takagi Takeo commanding.

8 NOVEMBER • The Chief of Naval Operations directed the establishment of aviation safety boards in the Intermediate Training Command similar to those in the Primary and Operational Training Commands.

8 NOVEMBER • Naval Ordnance Test Station, Inyokern, Calif., was established for the research, development, and testing of weapons, and to provide primary training in their use. The facility initially supported the California Institute of Technology, which developed and tested rockets, propellants, and launchers through the Office of Scientific Research and Development.

11 NOVEMBER • Task Groups 50.3, Rear Adm. Alfred E. Montgomery commanding, including *Saratoga* (CV 3) and *Princeton* (CVL 23), and 50.4, Rear Adm. Frederick C. Sherman commanding, including *Essex* (CV 9), *Bunker Hill* (CV 17), and *Independence* (CVL 22), launched the second strike on the Japanese fortress of Rabaul, New Britain. Planes sank destroyer *Suzunami*, and damaged light cruisers *Agano* and *Yūbari*, and destroyers *Naganami*, *Urakaze*, and *Wakatsuki*. This attack witnessed the introduction to combat of SB2C-1 Helldivers, embarked with VB-17 on board

An SB2C Helldiver lands on board a carrier while flight deck crewmen race to free the bomber to clear the deck for an approaching plane, c. 1945.

Bunker Hill. Lt. j.g. Eugene A. Valencia, USNR, of VF-9, embarked on board *Essex*, flew an F6F-3 Hellcat and shot down a Japanese Mitsubishi A6M Type 0 carrier fighter over Rabaul. Valencia scored 23 confirmed victories during World War II and his decorations include the Distinguished Flying Cross.

13 NOVEMBER • Navy and USAAF planes of Task Force 57, Rear Adm. John H. Hoover commanding, conducted long-range night bombing attacks through 19 November from islands of the Ellice, Phoenix, and Samoan groups and on Baker Island against Japanese bases in the Gilbert and Marshall Islands as a preliminary to the invasion of the Gilberts.

18 NOVEMBER • Task Force 50, Rear Adm. Charles A. Pownall commanding, began a two-day air attack on the Japanese during Operation Galvanic—the occupation of the Gilbert Islands. Task Group 50.4, Rear Adm. Frederick C. Sherman commanding, attacked Nauru in support. *Saratoga* (CV 3), *Enterprise* (CV 6), *Essex* (CV 9), *Yorktown* (CV 10), *Lexington* (CV 16), *Bunker Hill* (CV 17), *Independence* (CVL 22), *Princeton* (CVL 23), *Belleau Wood* (CVL 24), *Cowpens* (CVL 25), and *Monterey* (CVL 26) comprised the main force. Eight escort carriers covered the approach of assault shipping and supported the V Amphibious Corps against bitter resistance on Tarawa, and the landings on Abemama and Makin Atolls. On 20 November, a Japanese aerial torpedo damaged *Independence*.

Through 24 November, planes flew 2,278 close support, combat air patrol, and antisubmarine sorties. On 24 November, Japanese submarine *I-175* escaped after torpedoing and sinking *Liscome Bay* (CVE 56) 20 miles southwest of Butaritari Island, killing 645 men; 272 survived. On 25 November, F6F-3 Hellcats of VF-1 from *Barnes* (CVE 20) and *Nassau* (CVE 16) landed on the airstrip at Tarawa as the first planes of the garrison air force. Once the Marines secured the islands, one carrier group remained in the area for an additional week as a protective measure.

Galvanic included the first attempts at night interception from carriers. Air Group Commander Lt. Cmdr. Edward H. O'Hare led two F6F-3s and one radar-equipped TBF-1 of VT-6 from *Enterprise* for the purpose. The fighters flew wing on the Avenger and after being vectored to the vicinity of enemy aircraft by the *Enterprise* fighter director, relied on the Avenger's radar to close to visual range. The Hellcats failed to intercept on the first occasion but two days later disrupted an enemy attack during the first air battle of its type.

27 NOVEMBER • VR-8 received the first Martin XPB2M-1R Mars flying boat at NAS Patuxent River, Md.

29 NOVEMBER • TBF-1C Avengers of VC-9, embarked on board *Bogue* (CVE 9) during the ship's eighth and most successful patrol, sank German submarine *U-86* about 385 miles east of Terceira, Azores. *U-238* and *U-764* escaped. The following day, *Bogue*'s Avengers damaged *U-238* east of the Azores, on 12 December damaged *U-172* south-southwest of the Canary Islands despite the escape of *U-219*, the next day took part in sinking *U-172* 660 miles west-southwest of the Canary Islands, and on 21 December, sank *U-850* some 530 miles southwest of Fayal in the Azores.

Sailors haul torpedoes, each weighing more than a ton, toward a waiting SB2C Helldiver during strike preparations on *Hornet* (CV 12), c. fall 1944.

30 NOVEMBER • Lt. Cmdr. W. E. Coney piloted the Martin Mars from NAS Patuxent River, Md., during the first operational assignment of the aircraft. The plane delivered 13,000 pounds of cargo during a nonstop flight of 4,375 miles in 28 hours 25 minutes to Natal, Brazil.

30 NOVEMBER • The Navy authorized a department of aviation medicine and physiological research at the Naval Air Material Center to study physiological factors related to the design of high-speed and high-altitude aircraft.

1 DECEMBER • Aircraft, Central Pacific, Rear Adm. John H. Hoover commanding, was established under Commander, Central Pacific for the operational control of defense forces and shore-based air forces in the area.

1 DECEMBER • The Naval Air Ferry Command was established as a wing of the Naval Air Transport Service. The command assumed the functions previously performed by aircraft delivery units in ferrying new planes from contractor plants and modification centers to embarkation points for ultimate delivery to the fleet.

4 DECEMBER • Two groups of Task Force 50, Rear Adm. Charles A. Pownall commanding, including *Enterprise* (CV 6), *Essex* (CV 9), *Yorktown* (CV 10), *Lexington* (CV 16), *Belleau Wood* (CVL 24), and *Cowpens* (CVL 25), bombed the Japanese at Kwajalein and Wotje Atolls in the Marshall Islands at the close of Operation Galvanic—the occupation of the Gilbert Islands. About 50 Japanese fighters intercepted the attackers and heavy antiaircraft fire at 8,500 feet obliged

1061487

Marine ace Maj. Gregory Boyington briefs his pilots on an upcoming mission at VMF-214's base on Espíritu Santo.

1061902

An HNS-1 Hoverfly, BuNo 39040—the Navy's first helicopter type—from Coast Guard Air Station Brooklyn, N.Y., demonstrates its search and rescue capabilities in Jamaica Bay on 25 August 1944.

the U.S. planes to drop to 5,000 feet, and in combination with the garrison's determined achievement at camouflage reduced the effectiveness of the raid. The Americans lost five planes and claimed the destruction of 55 enemy aircraft, cargo ship *Tateyama Maru*, auxiliary submarine chaser *No. 7 Takunan Maru*, guardboat *No. 5 Mikuni Maru*, and collier *Asakaze Maru*, and damaged light cruisers *Isuzu* and *Nagara*, a stores ship, an auxiliary vessel, and three transports. During the U.S. retirement, a gale delayed escape beyond the range of Japanese shore-based bombers, and the next night, retaliatory strikes damaged three ships, including an aerial torpedo that struck *Lexington* and killed nine men and wounded 35.

8 DECEMBER • A striking force, Rear Adm. Willis A. Lee commanding, including *Bunker Hill* (CV 17) and *Monterey* (CVL 26), attacked Japanese installations on Nauru to the west of the Gilberts. The Japanese deployed few aircraft on the island and the raiders achieved meager results, claiming the destruction of at least eight planes while losing four. OS2U-3 and OS2N-1 Kingfishers from VO-6 and -9, embarked on board battleships *North Carolina* (BB 55), *Washington* (BB 56), *South Dakota* (BB 57), and *Alabama* (BB 60), strafed and photographed the area around the barracks when the ships ceased fire.

15 DECEMBER • VOF-1, Lt. Cmdr. William F. Bringle commanding, was established at NAS Atlantic City, N.J., as the first of three observation fighter squadrons raised during World War II.

17 DECEMBER • Commander Aircraft, Solomons, dispatched a fighter sweep of Navy, Marine, and New Zealand planes led by Maj. Gregory Boyington, USMC, against the Japanese naval fortress at Rabaul on New Britain. Boyington subsequently received the Medal of Honor and credit for shooting down 26 Japanese aircraft during the war. Intensive follow-up attacks through February 1944 assisted in the establishment of Allied bases that encircled the stronghold. The Allies bypassed the Japanese garrison at Rabaul but continually subjected the fortress to aerial attacks. On 9 August 1945, Marine PBJ-1 Mitchells launched the final strike.

18 DECEMBER • On the basis of his belief that experimentation had indicated the practicability of ship-based helicopters, the Chief of Naval Operations separated pilot training from test and development functions in the helicopter program. He directed that, effective on 1 January 1944, the Coast Guard was to conduct a helicopter pilot training program under the direction of the Deputy CNO (Air) at CGAS Floyd Bennett Field, N.Y. Lt. Cmdr. Frank A. Erickson, USCG, subsequently attained the designation of Coast Guard Helicopter Pilot No. 1 and oversaw the training of a total of 125 helicopter pilots during the war, including 96 Coast Guardsmen, 12 sailors, two soldiers, 11 members of the Royal Air Force, and four civilians.

20 DECEMBER • The Naval Air Training Command, under the Chief of Naval Operations, was established to coordinate and direct all naval aviation training in the activities of the Primary, Intermediate, and Operational Training Commands at NAS Pensacola, Fla.

20 DECEMBER • Two VP-43 PBY-5A Catalinas flew the first Navy photoreconnaissance and bombing mission from Attu, Aleutians, over the Japanese-held Kuriles.

20 DECEMBER • Cmdr. Frank A. Erickson, USCG, reported to the Bureau of Aeronautics concerning experiments with a helicopter used as an airborne ambulance at CGAS Floyd Bennett Field, N.Y. An HNS-1 Hoverfly made flights carrying, in addition to its normal crew of a pilot and a mechanic, a weight of 200 pounds in a stretcher suspended approximately four feet beneath the float landing gear. Early the following year, a Hoverfly made landings at the steps of the dispensary with a stretcher attached to the side of the helicopter's fuselage.

35197

Marine ace Capt. Joseph J. Foss, USMC, recounts one of his victories to his pilots.

25 DECEMBER • Task Group 50.2, Rear Adm. Frederick C. Sherman commanding, including *Bunker Hill* (CV 17) and *Monterey* (CVL 26), attacked Japanese shipping at Kavieng on New Ireland as a covering operation for landings the following day by Marines in the Borgen Bay area of New Britain. Planes sank Japanese transport *Tenryu Maru*, and damaged minesweepers *W.21* and *W.22* and transport (ex-armed merchant cruiser) *Kiyozumi Maru*.

27 DECEMBER • From 24 September to 6 November, the Navy gradually relieved the Army of antisubmarine patrols over British waters. During this period, VB-103, -105, and -110 participated in British Operation Stonewall—the interception of Axis blockade runners. On this date, the Germans attempted to rendezvous with blockade runner *Alsterufer*, but a British Royal Air Force Liberator sank the ship. The next day, a VB-105 PB4Y-1 flying from a British station at Dunkeswell, England, sighted German destroyers *Z23*, *Z24*, *Z27*, *Z32*, and *Z37*, and torpedo boats *T22*, *T23*, *T24*, *T25*, *T26*, and *T27* in the Bay of Biscay. Six of the 15 U.S. Liberators dispatched—one from VB-103 and five from VB-105—found and attacked the Germans. A Liberator shot down a Focke-Wulf Fw 200C Condor, but flak downed one U.S. bomber and the crew spent several months interned in

Spain. These planes directed British light cruisers *Enterprise* and *Glasgow* to the scene and they sank *Z27*, *T25*, and *T26*. The British subsequently transferred the station and, on 23 March 1944, it was redesignated NAF Dunkeswell.

31 DECEMBER • Fleet Air Wing 17 departed Australia to set up its headquarters at Samarai on the tip of the Papuan Peninsula, New Guinea.

1944

1 JANUARY • Task Group 37.2, Rear Adm. Frederick C. Sherman commanding, attacked a Japanese convoy off Kavieng, New Ireland. Planes from *Bunker Hill* (CV 17) and *Monterey* (CVL 26) damaged light cruiser *Noshiro*.

1 JANUARY • Lt. M. G. Taylor of VB-107 piloting Aircraft No. 107-B-9, a PB4Y-1 Liberator, sighted and tracked German blockade runner *Weserland*, 595 miles south-southwest of Ascension Island. The ship, disguised as British freighter *Glenbank*, was smuggling a load of crude rubber from Japanese waters. *Weserland* opened fire and knocked out the bomber's number three engine and wounded AOM2 Robert E. MacGregor. The plane returned to Ascension Island. The following day, pilot Lt. Robert T. Johnson attacked in Aircraft No. 107-B-12, BuNo 32065.The blockade runner returned fire and damaged the aircraft, which ditched en route to Ascension and was lost with all its crew. Destroyer *Somers* (DD 381) sank *Weserland* just after midnight. Five Germans died in these battles but *Somers* rescued 134 survivors.

3 JANUARY • During the early morning, a series of internal explosions sank destroyer *Turner* (DD 648) while she lay anchored off Ambrose Light, N.J., killing 15 officers and 123 enlisted men. Pilot Cmdr. Frank A. Erickson, USCG, and copilot Ens. Walter C. Bolton took off in an HNS-1 from CGAS Floyd Bennett Field, N.Y., and flew to Battery Park on Manhattan Island to pick up an emergency delivery of two cases of 40 units of blood plasma. With the supplies lashed to the floats of the Hoverfly, it continued to Sandy Hook, N.J., where responders administered the plasma to the survivors. Erickson and Bolton accomplished this first recorded helicopter lifesaving operation through snow squalls, sleet, and winds reaching 20 to 25 knots that grounded all other aircraft.

704377

Enterprise (CV 6), which experiences almost continuous action during World War II, carries a splinter camouflage scheme, c. mid-1944.

4 JANUARY • An accidental gasoline fire damaged *Tripoli* (CVE 64) at Naval Repair Base, San Diego, Calif.

4 JANUARY • Light cruiser *Omaha* (CL 4) and destroyer *Jouett* (DD 396) intercepted German blockade runner *Rio Grande* about 55 miles northeast of the coast of Brazil. Gunfire and scuttling charges sank the smuggler. The following day, Lt. Stanley V. Brown of VP-203 piloted a PBM-3S that sighted German blockade runner *Burgenland*. The Mariner crew summoned *Omaha* and *Jouett*, but gunfire and scuttling charges sank *Burgenland*. Through 8 January, light cruiser *Marblehead* (CL 12) rescued 72 survivors from *Rio Grande*, and destroyers *Winslow* (DD 359) and *Davis* (DD 395) recovered 56 men from *Burgenland*.

7 JANUARY • *Belleau Wood* (CVL 24) and destroyer *Dunlap* (DD 384) collided and both ships sustained minor damage during exercises off Oahu in the Hawaiian Islands.

11 JANUARY • Two TBF-1Cs of VC-58, embarked on board *Block Island* (CVE 21), during an attack against German submarine *U-758,* made the first U.S. use of forward-firing rockets. The Avengers damaged the boat and compelled her return to German-occupied St. Nazaire, France.

16 JANUARY • Lt. j.g. Stewart R. Graham, USCG, made a 30-minute flight in an R-4B (HNS-1) Hoverfly from a 60- by 80-foot flight deck fitted to British freighter *Daghestan* while en route from New York City to Liverpool, England. Graham made his flight in spite of 20-knot winds and the ship rolling 10 to 20 degrees. The harsh weather during the mid-winter North Atlantic crossing permitted only two additional flights. The sponsoring Combined Board for Evaluation of the Ship-based Helicopter in Antisubmarine Warfare decided that the marginal performance of the underpowered helicopters precluded their operations from ships in convoy, and recommended their confinement to coastal waters until the availability of models with improved performance.

18 JANUARY • PBY-5As of VP-63, operating from NAS Port Lyautey—established on 12 January—in Morocco began two-plane barrier patrols of the Strait of Gibraltar and its approaches with magnetic anomaly detection gear. The Catalinas typically flew at an altitude of 55 feet from dawn to dusk. Antiaircraft batteries in Spanish Morocco frequently shot at the patrolling planes whenever they flew close to the three-mile limit but, until the end of the war, their patrols effectively closed the strait to the transit of U-boats during daylight hours.

22 JANUARY • Operation Shingle—landings by the Anglo-American troops of the U.S. VI Corps at Anzio and Nettuno to outflank German defensive positions across the Italian peninsula—began. The Allies failed to advance inland decisively, and their inaction enabled the German forces in the area to counterattack vigorously to deter further landings in Italy and France. Allied planes proved unable to prevent *Luftwaffe* (German air force) raids on the beachhead or on the ships offshore, but air power and naval gunfire support proved essential in the efforts to hold the perimeter. SOC-1, -3, and SON-1 Seagulls of VCS-8, embarked on board light cruisers *Brooklyn* (CL 40) and *Philadelphia* (CL 41), directed the fall of the cruisers' 6-inch shot at times. By May, the Allies broke out of the beachhead, linked up with troops that pierced German defensive lines inland, and on 4 June liberated Rome.

25 JANUARY • A fire damaged *Sangamon* (CVE 26) after a barrier crash by a TBM-1C Avenger of VC-37 while the ship sailed en route to the Marshall Islands. The crew contained the conflagration within eight minutes but seven men died, two of the 15 who jumped overboard to escape the flames were lost, and seven were injured. *Sangamon* made temporary repairs at sea and took part in the fighting at the Marshalls.

29 JANUARY • Task Force 58, Rear Adm. Marc A. Mitscher commanding, including *Saratoga* (CV 3), *Enterprise* (CV 6), *Essex* (CV 9), *Yorktown* (CV 10), *Intrepid* (CV 11), *Bunker Hill* (CV 17), *Princeton* (CVL 23), *Belleau Wood* (CVL 24), *Cowpens* (CVL 25), *Monterey* (CVL 26), *Langley* (CVL 27), and *Cabot* (CVL 28), attacked the Japanese garrisons of Kwajalein, Maloelap, and Wotje during Operation Flintlock—the occupation of the Marshall Islands. Land-based planes of Task Force 57, Rear Adm. John H. Hoover commanding, also supported the landings.

These raids destroyed the Japanese air strength on the islands. Aircraft from eight escort carriers flew cover and antisubmarine patrols, and scout planes assisted naval bombardments. On 31 January, Marines and soldiers landed on islands at Kwajalein and Majuro. Into the first three days of February, planes from Task Group 58.3, Rear Adm. Frederick C. Sherman commanding, bombed Japanese aircraft and airfields at Engebi Island at Eniwetok Atoll. Through 7 February, Task Group 58.4, Rear Adm. Samuel P. Ginder commanding, supplemented Sherman. On 1 February, additional landings occurred on Kwajalein, Namur, and Roi.

Commander Task Force 51 Rear Adm. Richmond K. Turner led the joint expeditionary force from amphibious force command ship *Rocky Mount* (AGC 3). The increasing complexity of amphibious operations necessitated the use of command ships and the Marshalls marked their introduction to battle. *Rocky Mount* provided improved facilities for Commander Support Aircraft Capt. H. B. Sallada, who assumed control of target combat air patrol—a task previously vested in carriers. A force fighter director on Sallada's staff coordinated fighter direction.

428460

A carrier's fighter direction control team sends the planes of a combat air patrol against Japanese attackers.

30 JANUARY • PB2Y-3 Coronados of VP-13 and -102 flew more than 2,100 miles from Midway Island on a nocturnal bombing raid against the Japanese airfield and installations on Wake Island to prevent the garrison of Wake from threatening U.S. operations in the Marshall Islands. Previous raids on Wake had resulted in casualties because of poor navigation and radio silence breaks that alerted the Japanese. The strike marked the first employment of Coronados as bombers. They repeated the raids on the nights of 4, 8, and 9 February and completed 50 sorties without losing a plane. Commander Fleet Air Wing 2 Rear Adm. John D. Price considered the neutralization of Wake of such importance that he twice accompanied the bombers.

2 FEBRUARY • President Franklin D. Roosevelt approved the last of the World War II ceilings for Navy aircraft, which called for an increase to 37,735 useful planes.

3 FEBRUARY • The Deputy Chief of Naval Operations (Air) and the Chief of BUAER jointly issued Flight Safety Bulletin No. 1, which announced the intention to issue consecutive numbered bulletins concerning the safe operation of naval aircraft.

4 FEBRUARY • Blimp K-29 of ZP-31 made the first carrier landing by a nonrigid airship during a test of refueling operations on board *Altamaha* (CVE 18) off San Diego, Calif.

221248

The wreckage of at least four Japanese bombers litter the end a runway at Engebi in the Marshall Islands during an attack by U.S. carrier planes in late 1943 or early 1944.

4 FEBRUARY • Two PB4Y-1 Liberators of VMD-254 made the first photographic reconnaissance of Truk Lagoon, Caroline Islands, during a 12-hour night flight from the Solomon Islands. Cloud cover prevented complete coverage but the information acquired proved useful in planning a subsequent carrier strike on 17 February.

10 FEBRUARY • Planes from Task Group 58.4, Rear Adm. Samuel P. Ginder commanding, bombed Japanese installations on Eniwetok Atoll, Marshall Islands. The strikes continued to 12 February.

14 FEBRUARY • Forward Area, Central Pacific was established, Rear Adm. John H. Hoover commanding. He broke his flag in seaplane tender *Curtiss* (AV 4) and controlled the operations of shore-based planes and ships assigned to the Ellice, Gilbert, and Marshall Islands.

15 FEBRUARY • Lt. j.g. Nathan G. Gordon (Naval Aviator No. 11421) piloted a PBY-5 of VP-34 and defied close-range Japanese fire during three full-stall landings in the harbor of Kavieng, New Ireland, and rescued nine survivors from three downed Fifth Air Force bombers. Despite heavy swells, Gordon took off each time but received another report of a raft with survivors. The pilot swung the Catalina about and under intense fire brought six more men on board, and escaped with the 15 survivors to seaplane tender *San Pablo* (AVP 30) at

201986

A Japanese Nakajima B6N carrier attack plane is hit by a 5-inch shell from *Yorktown* (CV 10) off Kwajalein, 4 December 1943.

Wewak, New Guinea. Gordon received the Medal of Honor and each of his crewmembers the Silver Star.

17 FEBRUARY • Two fast carrier groups had operated to the west of Eniwetok and neutralized Japanese air and naval forces capable of defending the atoll. These operations permitted the second phase of the Marshall Islands campaign earlier than the planned date of 10 May during Operation Catchpole—the seizure of Eniwetok. On this date, planes from Task Groups 58.4 including *Saratoga* (CV 3), *Princeton* (CVL 23), and *Langley* (CVL 27), and 53.6 including *Sangamon* (CVE 26), *Suwannee* (CVE 27), and *Chenango* (CVE 28), supported landings on Engebi Island, and on 19 and 22 February landings on Eniwetok and Parry Islands, respectively.

17 FEBRUARY • The covering operations for the liberation of the Marshall Islands included Operation Hailstone—a strike on the Japanese naval anchorage at Truk Lagoon, Caroline Islands. During a two-day attack, Vice Adm. Raymond A. Spruance, whose forces included Task Force 58, Rear Adm. Marc A. Mitscher commanding, with *Enterprise* (CV 6), *Essex* (CV 9), *Yorktown* (CV 10), *Intrepid* (CV 11), *Bunker Hill* (CV 17), *Belleau Wood* (CVL 24), *Cowpens* (CVL 25), *Monterey* (CVL 26), and *Cabot* (CVL 28), launched 1,250 combat sorties that dropped 400 tons of bombs and torpedoes and sank 37 Japanese ships aggregating 200,000 tons and damaged installations.

The vessels sunk included light cruiser *Naka*; training cruiser *Katori*; destroyers *Fumizuki*, *Maikaze*, *Oite*, and *Tachikaze*; armed merchant cruiser *Akagi Maru*;

auxiliary submarine depot ship *Heian Maru;* submarine chasers *Ch 24* and *Ch 29;* aircraft transport *Fujikawa Maru;* transports *Aikoku Maru, Amagisan Maru, Gosei Maru, Hanakawa Maru, Hokuyo Maru, Kensho Maru, Kiyozumi Maru, Matsutani Maru, Momokawa Maru, No. 6 Unkai Maru, Reiyo Maru, Rio de Janeiro Maru, San Francisco Maru, Seiko Maru, Taihō Maru, Yamagiri Maru,* and *Zukai Maru;* fleet tankers *Fujisan Maru, Hoyo Maru, No. 3 Tonan Maru,* and *Shinkoku Maru;* water carrier *Nippo Maru;* auxiliary vessel *Yamakisan Maru;* army cargo ships *Nagano Maru* and *Yubai Maru;* merchant cargo ship *Taikichi Maru;* and motor torpedo boat *Gyoraitei No. 10.*

Twelve radar-equipped TBF-1C Avengers from VT-10, embarked on board *Enterprise,* carried out the first U.S. carrier-launched night bombing raid and scored several hits on ships in the lagoon. Night fighter detachments of F6F-3 Hellcats and F4U-2 Corsairs fitted with AIA radar from VF(N)-76 and -101 operated from five carriers and on occasion were vectored against enemy night raiders. The first night, however, a Japanese aerial torpedo struck *Intrepid,* but despite steering problems she returned for repairs to Pearl Harbor in the Hawaiian Islands.

Vice Adm. Marc A. Mitscher.

17 FEBRUARY • Navy SBD Dauntlesses and TBF Avengers bombed Japanese shipping in Keravia Bay near Rabaul, New Britain.

20 FEBRUARY • Upon completion of the strike on Truk Lagoon in the Caroline Islands, a small force, Rear Adm. John W. Reeves Jr. commanding, including *Enterprise* (CV 6) separated from the main force and launched two air strikes on Jaluit.

22 FEBRUARY • Two carrier groups of Task Force 58, Rear Adm. Marc A. Mitscher commanding, launched raids against the Japanese garrisons on Guam, Rota, Saipan, and Tinian in the Mariana Islands for the dual purpose of reducing enemy air strength and to gather photographic intelligence for the impending invasion. The attackers claimed the destruction of 67 Japanese aircraft in the air and 101 on the ground through 23 February.

24 FEBRUARY • Lts. Howard Baker and T. R. Woolley of VP-63 piloted two PBY-5A Catalinas on a magnetic anomaly detection (MAD) barrier patrol of the approaches to the Strait of Gibraltar. Their patrol marked the first operational employment of MAD gear for tracking a submerged submarine. Baker and Woolley joined Lt. P. L. Holmes of VB-127 flying a PV-1 Ventura and a British Catalina of the Royal Air Force's No. 202 Squadron in an attack on German submarine *U-761* as it attempted to slip through the strait from the Mediterranean to the Atlantic. The U.S. Catalinas damaged *U-761* with retrorockets and the Ventura depth-charged the boat. The Germans scuttled the submarine near Tangier, Morocco.

4 MARCH • The Navy reported a reduction in flight training and fixed the total outputs for 1944, 1945, and 1946 at 20,500, 15,000, and 10,000 pilots, respectively.

6 MARCH • A new specification for the color of naval aircraft went into effect. A modification of the basic camouflage scheme for use with fleet aircraft required nonspecular Sea Blue on upper fuselage surfaces, the retention of semigloss Sea Blue on airfoil surfaces visible from above, and semigloss Insignia White on surfaces visible from below. A new basic non-camouflage color scheme, all

Aluminum, applied for general use on aircraft not in combat theaters. The maximum visibility color scheme used on primary trainers became glossy Orange Yellow overall.

15 MARCH • PBJ-1 Mitchells received their baptism of fire in naval service during an attack by VMB-413 on the Japanese garrison at Rabaul, New Britain.

18 MARCH • Task Group 50.10, Rear Adm. Willis A. Lee commanding, including *Lexington* (CV 16), bombed and shelled the Japanese garrison on Mili in the Marshall Islands.

20 MARCH • Planes from two escort carriers provided cover and air spotting for a battleship and destroyer bombardment of Japanese installations on Kavieng, New Ireland, and nearby airfields in a covering action for the occupation of Emirau.

22 MARCH • A new specification for the color of fighter aircraft went into effect that directed they be painted glossy Sea Blue on all exposed surfaces.

26 MARCH • F4U-1 Corsairs of VMF-113 operating from Engebi Island at Eniwetok Atoll in the Marshall Islands escorted USAAF B-25 Mitchells on a 360-mile bombing mission against the Japanese garrison on Ponape. The Corsairs' effectively destroyed the enemy interceptors and thus ensured that Allied aircraft carried out their subsequent missions over the island unmolested.

27 MARCH • *Saratoga* (CV 3), Capt. John H. Cassady commanding, rendezvoused with ships of the British Eastern Fleet for temporary operations in the Indian Ocean approximately 1,000 miles south of Ceylon (Sri Lanka).

30 MARCH • Task Force 58, Vice Adm. Marc A. Mitscher commanding, including 11 carriers, launched a series of attacks on Japanese garrisons and vessels at Palau, Ulithi, Woleai, and Yap in the Western Caroline Islands. Planners intended these strikes to eliminate Japanese opposition to landings at Hollandia on northern New Guinea and to gather photographic intelligence for future battles. TBF-1C and TBM-1C Avengers from VT-8, -2, and -16, embarked on board *Hornet* (CV 12), *Bunker Hill* (CV 17), and *Lexington* (CV 16), respectively, sowed extensive minefields in the approaches to the Palau Islands in the first U.S. large-scale daylight tactical use of mines by carrier aircraft. These raids continued until 1 April and claimed the destruction of 157 Japanese aircraft, sank destroyer *Wakatake*, repair ship *Akashi*, aircraft transport *Goshu Maru*, and 38 other vessels, damaged four ships, and denied the harbor to the enemy for an estimated six weeks.

1 APRIL • The Coast Guard christened helicopter training platform *Mal de Mer* (sea sickness) at CGAS Brooklyn, N.Y. The 40-by-60–foot platform simulated landing conditions on board ships by rolling five to ten degrees within a period of ten seconds.

15 APRIL • The formation of air-sea rescue squadrons (VH) in the Pacific Fleet provided rescue and emergency services as necessary in the forward areas. Before this, regularly operating patrol squadrons performed rescue functions as an additional duty.

16 APRIL • Carrier Transport Squadron, Pacific, was established for administrative and operational control over escort carriers assigned to deliver planes, spare parts, and naval aviation servicemembers in direct support of Pacific Fleet operations.

18 APRIL • Photographic-equipped PB4Y-1 Liberators of VD-3 obtained coverage of Aguijan, Saipan, and Tinian in preparation for the campaign to occupy the Mariana Islands. During the 13-hour flight from Eniwetok, USAAF B-24 Liberators escorted the image-gathering planes and bombed the islands in a diversionary action. This operation marked the first mission by shore-based planes over the Marianas.

19 APRIL • The British Eastern Fleet, Adm. Sir James F. Somerville, RN, commanding, including British carrier *Illustrious* (87), and U.S. Task Group 58.5 with *Saratoga* (CV 3), struck Sabang off northern Sumatra, Netherlands East Indies (Indonesia), during Operation Cockpit. In the first operation in which the Pacific Fleet operated alongside the British in offensive action in the Indian Ocean, the Allies achieved poor results because of the limited number of Japanese ships in the area. Twenty-four F6F-3 Hellcats from VF-12, 18 SBD-5 Dauntlesses from VB-12, and 11 TBF-1C and TBM-1C Avengers of VT-12, together with 13 British Corsair IIs of Nos. 1830 and 1833 Squadrons, and 17 Fairey Barracuda IIs of Nos. 810 and 847 Squadrons,

Escort carriers turn toward their stations to support an amphibious landing against the Japanese.

sank Japanese minelayer *Hatsutaka*, transport *Kunitsu Maru*, and army transport *Haruno Maru*. Allied planes claimed the destruction of 24 Japanese planes on the ground and damaged oil storage tanks and installations. Antiaircraft fire shot down a VF-12 Hellcat but British submarine *Tactician* rescued the pilot. Japanese Mitsubishi G4M1 Type 1 bombers counterattacked the ships during their retirement, but Hellcats shot down three of the Bettys. On 17 May 1944 the Anglo-American force launched a similar strike against Soerabaja, Sumatra.

21 APRIL • Task Force 58, Vice Adm. Marc A. Mitscher commanding, supported the assault of the Army's I Corps at Aitape and Tanahmerah Bay (Operation Persecution) and at Humboldt Bay on Hollandia (Operation Reckless) on the north coast of New Guinea. On this date, five heavy and seven light carriers launched preliminary strikes on Japanese airfields around Hollandia, Sawar, and Wakde; the next day covered landings at Aitape, Tanahmerah Bay, and Humboldt Bay; and into 24 April, supported troop movements ashore. Planes from *Sangamon* (CVE 26), *Suwannee* (CVE 27), *Chenango* (CVE 28), *Santee* (CVE 29), *Coral Sea* (CVE 57), *Corregidor* (CVE 58), *Manila Bay* (CVE 61), and *Natoma Bay* (CVE 62), flew cover and antisubmarine patrols over ships of the attack group during the approach, and supported the amphibious assault at Aitape. Carrier aircraft claimed the destruction of 30 Japanese planes in the air and 103 on the ground.

23 APRIL • VR-3 operated the first regularly scheduled Naval Air Transport Service transcontinental hospital flight between Washington, D.C., and March Field, Calif.

26 APRIL • The headquarters of Fleet Air Wing 4 was established on Attu in the Aleutians of Alaska.

29 APRIL • While Task Force 58, Vice Adm. Marc A. Mitscher commanding, returned to Majuro following landings at Hollandia on New Guinea, Mitscher launched a two-day attack on Japanese installations and supply dumps at Truk Lagoon in the Caroline Islands. The previous strike on 17 February had wreaked havoc on the Japanese, but on 30 April aircraft reported a paucity of vessels in the area and sank only two ships and claimed the destruction of 145 enemy aircraft. Task Group 58.1, Rear Adm. Joseph J. Clark commanding, detached on the second day, launched planes for protective cover of a cruiser bombardment of Satawan, and on 1 May supported the bombardment of Ponape with air cover and bombing and strafing runs.

1 MAY • Aircraft, Central Pacific, was dissolved and Commander, Marshalls Sub-Area assumed its functions.

4 MAY • The eponymous board headed by Rear Adm. Arthur W. Radford submitted a report that impacted aviation planning into the immediate post-war period. The Integrated Aeronautic Program for Maintenance, Material and Supply evolved from these recommendations and involved the assignment of new planes to combat units, the return of aircraft to the United States for reconditioning and reassignment after specified combat tours, the retirement of second tour aircraft before maintenance became costly, and the support of the aeronautical organization through the use of factors and allowances for pools, pipelines, and reconditioning. Frequent appraisal by inspectors realistically maintained the program.

8 MAY • Seaplane tender *Kenneth Whiting* (AV 14) was commissioned as the first of four ships of the class at Tacoma, Wash., Cmdr. Raymond R. Lyons commanding.

8 MAY • Commander, Naval Forces, Northwest African Waters approved the assignment of an initial nine naval aviators from VCS-8 to the 111th Tactical Reconnaissance Squadron, Twelfth Air Force, for flight training and combat operations in North American P-51C Mustangs. Previous combat experience with SOC Seagulls and OS2U Kingfishers used in aerial spotting and reconnaissance missions had demonstrated the vulnerability of both types to enemy fighters and antiaircraft fire. Planners expected the higher performance of the Mustangs to result in a reduction of casualties on these missions. Eleven naval aviators eventually participated in combat operations in Mustangs in support of the fighting in Italy and the invasion of Southern France. On 2 September the Navy directed all of these men to return to their ships.

13 MAY • The abolition of the helicopter class designation VH plus a mission letter (i.e., VHO for observation and VHN for training) and establishment of helicopters as a separate type H helped distinguish between fixed- and rotary-wing heavier-than-air craft. The previous mission letters became classes O, N, and R for observation, training, and transport, respectively.

13 MAY • To meet the needs of the fleet for people trained in the use of electronic countermeasures equipment, the Chief of Naval Operations directed the establishment on 1 June by the chief of Naval Air Technical Training of the Special Projects School for Air, located initially at NAAS San Clemente Island, Calif.

15 MAY • Naval Air Transport Service planes made the first of 16 transatlantic flights through 23 May to the United Kingdom to deliver 165,000-pounds of minesweeping gear for the D-Day landings in Normandy, France.

17 MAY • BUAER authorized CGAS Floyd Bennett Field, N.Y., to collaborate in the installation of an automatic pilot in an HNS-1 helicopter with the Sperry Gyroscope Company.

17 MAY • During Operation Transom, the Allies attacked Japanese shipping and installations in the Netherlands East Indies (Indonesia) timed to coincide with Operation Straightline—landings in the Wakde-Toem area of New Guinea. Planes from the British Eastern Fleet, Adm. James F. Somerville, RN, commanding, including British carrier *Illustrious* (87) and U.S. Task Group 58.5, with *Saratoga* (CV 3), raided Soerabaja, Java. Twenty-four F6F-3 Hellcats from VF-12, 18 SBD-5 Dauntlesses from VB-12, and 12 TBF-1C and TBM-1C Avengers of VT-12, embarked on board *Saratoga*, and 16 British Corsair IIs of Nos. 1830 and 1833 Squadrons, and 18 Avenger IIs of Nos. 832 and 845 Squadrons, operating from *Illustrious*, sank Japanese transport *Shinrei Maru* and damaged six vessels and oil stores. One U.S. Avenger was shot down and the crew captured, and two British Avengers crashed on take-off but their crewmembers survived. *Saratoga* had delayed her departure for repairs at Puget Sound Navy Yard at Bremerton, Wash., to participate during her eastward passage. The next day the ship detached.

19 MAY • Planes from Task Group 58.6, Rear Adm. Alfred E. Montgomery commanding, attacked Marcus Island with a predawn fighter sweep, strafing and bombing Japanese

232195

Airships of ZP-14 from NAS South Weymouth, Mass., arrive at NAS Port Lyautey, Morocco, 1 June 1944.

installations for two consecutive days during the third raid on the island. On 23 May, Montgomery shifted from Marcus to attack Wake Island with five composite bombing, strafing, and rocket strikes during the third carrier raid on the atoll since the Japanese overran it.

29 MAY • Six days before, *Block Island* (CVE 21) had sailed from Casablanca, Morocco, to relieve *Bogue* (CVE 9) during hunter-killer operations around Madeira and the Cape Verde Islands. At 2013 on this date, three torpedoes from German submarine *U-549* struck the carrier in rapid succession northwest of the Canary Islands. *Block Island* sank by the stern. The U-boat then damaged destroyer escort *Barr* (DE 576) with an acoustic torpedo, but destroyer escorts *Ahrens* (DE 575) and *Eugene E. Elmore* (DE 686) sank the attacker.

31 MAY • Commander, Training Task Force was directed to establish on 1 June, within his command at NAS Traverse City, Mich., a detachment designated Special Weapons Test and Tactical Evaluation Unit to research special weapons and other airborne equipment.

1 JUNE • Blimps of ZP-14 assigned to antisubmarine operations around Gibraltar reached NAS Port Lyautey, Morocco, completing the first crossing of the Atlantic by nonrigid airships after lifting off from NAS South Weymouth, Mass., on 29 May. In 58 hours the blimps covered 3,145 nautical miles and—including time for stopovers at Argentia, Newfoundland, and the Azores—in 80 hours moved their area of operations across the ocean.

1 JUNE • VR-9 was formed at NAS Patuxent River, Md., and VR-12 at Honolulu, Territory of Hawaii, to function as headquarters and maintenance squadrons for their commands, Naval Air Transport Service Atlantic and Pacific, respectively.

4 JUNE • Task Group 22.3, Capt. Daniel V. Gallery commanding, a hunter-killer group including *Guadalcanal* (CVE 60), with FM-2 Wildcats and TBM-1C Avengers of VC-8 embarked, and destroyer escorts *Pillsbury* (DE 133), *Pope* (DE 134), *Flaherty* (DE 135), *Chatelain* (DE 149), and *Jenks* (DE 665) forced German submarine *U-505* to the surface 150 miles off Cape Blanco, Rio de Oro, Africa. During salvage operations, *Pillsbury* collided with *U-505*, but Lt. j.g. Albert L. David led a boarding party from *Pillsbury* that saved the submarine despite the dangers posed by scuttling charges. David later received the Medal of Honor. The U-boat is on display in Chicago, Ill.

5 JUNE • The Deputy Chief of Naval Operations (Air) reported that aviation safety boards that had been established in one large command had reduced the fatal accident rate by 47 percent during one quarter of operation. He thus directed the establishment of similar boards in other commands outside advanced combat areas, and the appointment of a flight safety officer to each squadron.

6 JUNE • Seventeen naval aviators from aviation detachments on board battleships and cruisers served in bombardment duty with VCS-7 during Operation Overlord—the Allied landings in German-occupied Normandy, France. From D-Day through 26 June, the squadron operated with the British Fleet Air Arm and Royal Air Force, flying gunfire-spotting missions in Supermarine Spitfires over the Normandy beaches.

10 JUNE • PB4Y-1s of VB-108 and -109 swept ahead of Task Force 58, Vice Adm. Marc A. Mitscher commanding, to intercept and destroy Japanese planes in the path of the carriers as they approached the Mariana Islands. The Liberators repeated the sweeps the next day. One bomber from each of the squadrons shot down a Japanese plane. Planners chose to use the Liberators as a diversion from the carriers because the Japanese routinely sighted the long-range planes in that region.

11 JUNE • Task Force 58, Vice Adm. Marc A. Mitscher commanding, including seven heavy and eight light carriers opened the campaign to occupy the Mariana Islands with a fighter sweep that destroyed one-third of the defending Japanese air force. Sixteen F6F Hellcats from each carrier and 12 from each small carrier, accompanied by a TBF Avenger or SB2C Helldiver from each task group to lead and navigate for the fighters, attained tactical surprise and assured control of the air over the islands. In bombing and strafing attacks on shore installations and shipping over the succeeding days, Mitscher's force prepared the way for the 15 June amphibious assault on Saipan. Carrier planes supported operations ashore with daily offensive missions on 15, 16, and 24 June; 3 and 4 July; and 4 and 5 August; isolated the area with attacks on airfields and shipping in the Bonin and Volcano Islands; and on 19 and 20 June successfully defended the landings against a Japanese counterattack during the Battle of the Philippine Sea.

12 JUNE • Planes from Task Group 58.4, including *Essex* (CV 9) and small carriers *Cowpens* (CVL 25) and *Langley* (CVL 27), destroyed a Japanese convoy northwest of Saipan en route from Tanapag, Saipan to Japan.

12 JUNE • Elements of Special Task Air Group (STAG 1) arrived in the Russell Islands in the South Pacific in the first deployment of a guided missile unit into a combat theater.

13 JUNE • Task Force 58, Vice Adm. Marc A. Mitscher commanding, launched additional strikes against the Japanese garrison on Saipan in the Mariana Islands. Carrier planes destroyed a convoy of five small cargo vessels and sank other ships separately. The Japanese shot down Cmdr. William I. Martin, commanding officer of VT-10 embarked on board *Enterprise* (CV 6), flying a TBM-1C Avenger over Saipan. The pilot parachuted into the sea off Red Beach Three and, prior to his rescue, observed that the Japanese had marked ranges to the reef offshore with red and white pennants. This valuable intelligence was given to the approaching amphibious forces.

15 JUNE • Carrier aircraft from Task Groups 58.1 and 58.4, Rear Adms. Joseph J. Clark and William K. Harrill commanding, respectively, bombed Japanese installations on Chichi Jima and Haha Jima in the Bonin Islands and Iwo Jima in the Volcano Islands. The following day, the planes repeated the attack on Iwo Jima. These raids disrupted the staging areas for Japanese aircraft en route to the Mariana Islands and contributed to the U.S. victory in the Battle of the Philippine Sea.

15 JUNE • American landings on Saipan in the Mariana Islands during Operation Forager penetrated the inner defensive perimeter of the Japanese Empire and thus triggered A-Go—a Japanese counterattack that led to the Battle of the Philippine Sea. Task Force 58, Vice Adm. Marc A. Mitscher commanding, included *Enterprise* (CV 6), *Essex* (CV 9), *Yorktown* (CV 10), *Hornet* (CV 12), *Lexington* (CV 16), *Bunker Hill* (CV 17), *Wasp* (CV 18), *Princeton* (CVL 23), *Belleau Wood* (CVL 24), *Cowpens* (CVL 25), *Monterey* (CVL 26), *Langley* (CVL 27), *Cabot* (CVL 28), *Bataan* (CVL 29), and *San Jacinto* (CVL 30).

The Japanese 1st Mobile Fleet, Vice Adm. Ozawa Jisaburō commanding, included *Taihō, Shōkaku, Zuikaku, Chitose, Chiyōda, Hiyō, Junyō, Ryūhō,* and *Zuihō*. The enemy intended for its shore-based planes to cripple Mitscher's air power to facilitate Ozawa's strikes, which were to refuel and rearm on Guam. Japanese fuel shortages and inadequate training bedeviled A-Go, however, and U.S. signal decryption breakthroughs enabled attacks on Japanese submarines that deprived the enemy of intelligence, raids on the Bonin and Volcano Islands disrupted Japanese aerial staging en route to the Marianas, and their main attacks passed through heavy U.S. antiaircraft fire to reach the carriers.

On 17 June, five PBM-3D Mariners of VP-16 commenced operations from seaplane tender *Ballard* (AVD 10) within range of Saipan's guns. Throughout the day Task Force 58 repelled Japanese air attacks and destroyed at least 300 planes in what Navy pilots called the "Great Marianas Turkey Shoot." Commander CVG-15, Cmdr. David S. McCampbell, flew an F6F-3 Hellcat from *Essex* and shot down at least seven Japanese planes. Submarines *Albacore* (SS 218) and *Cavalla* (SS 244) sank *Taihō* and *Shōkaku* in separate attacks, respectively, and Japanese suicide planes narrowly missed *Bunker Hill* and *Wasp*.

The following afternoon, Mitscher launched an air attack at extreme range on the retreating Japanese ships that sank *Hiyō* and two fleet oilers, and damaged *Zuikaku, Chiyōda,* and *Junyō*. That night, despite the risk of submarine attacks, Mitscher ordered his ships to show their lights to guide returning aircraft low on fuel, thus saving lives. The Japanese lost 395 carrier planes and an estimated 50 land-based aircraft from Guam. The Americans lost 130 planes and 76 pilots and aircrewmen.

258198 K-2178

Cmdr. David S. McCampbell is the Navy's highest scoring ace with 34 kills.

Planes from an initial force of 11 escort carriers covered the landings. *Manila Bay* (CVE 61) and *Natoma Bay* (CVE 62) ferried aircraft to operate from captured airfields. On 17 June OY-1 Sentinels of VMO-4 arrived ashore, followed on 22 and 24 June by USAAF Republic P-47 Thunderbolts and Northrop P-61 Black Widows, and on 12 July by F4U-2 Corsairs of VMF(N)-532. On 9 July, organized resistance ended on Saipan; on 21 July, the Americans landed on Guam, and three days later on Tinian.

24 JUNE • A TBM-1C Avenger from VC-69, embarked on board *Bogue* (CVE 9), sank Japanese submarine *I-52* about 800 miles southwest of Fayal, Azores, near 15°16'N, 39°55'W. The submarine sailed from Kure, Japan, reputedly carrying two tons of gold ingots valued at $25 million as the balance of a payment owed by the Japanese to the Germans for technical information and war materials. *I-52* rendezvoused with German submarine *U-530* for the transfer of three Germans and some radio equipment to the Japanese boat prior to continuing to Lorient, France, but

Allied intelligence had identified the meeting. The Avenger dropped sonobuoys to assist in locating and destroying the blockade runner.

24 JUNE • To reduce the pilot training program the Chief of Naval Operations promulgated plans that required the transfer of some students already in pre-flight and prior stages of training, and the retention of enough people to maintain a course in pre-flight schools expanded to 25 weeks. Early the next month, the chief of Naval Air Training instituted the program of "deselection" and voluntary withdrawal of surplus students. The resulting reductions proved responsible in August for the discontinuance of the War Training Service Program, and in September for the closure of the flight preparatory schools and the release of training stations.

24 JUNE • Aircraft from two carrier task groups, Rear Adms. Joseph J. Clark and Alfred E. Montgomery commanding, struck Japanese airfields and facilities on Iwo Jima in the Volcano Islands and Pagan Island in the Marianas.

26 JUNE • Seaplane tender *Currituck* (AV 7) was commissioned as the first of four ships of her class at Philadelphia, Pa., Capt. William A. Evans commanding.

29 JUNE • The Parachute Experimental Division was established for the research, development, and testing of parachutes and survival gear at NAS Lakehurst, N.J.

29 JUNE • The standardization of carrier air groups took place for all commands: CVBG, large carrier air group; CVG, medium carrier air group; CVLG, small carrier air group; CVEG, escort carrier air group—*Sangamon* (CVE 26) class; and VC, escort carrier air group—*Long Island* (CVE 1), *Bogue* (CVE 9), *Charger* (CVE 30), and *Casablanca* (CVE 55) classes.

30 JUNE • The Naval Aircraft Modification Unit of the Naval Air Material Center at Philadelphia, Pa., was relocated to Johnsville, Pa. This was prompted by Johnsville's facilities for intensified efforts in guided missile development and quantity modification of service aircraft.

4 JULY • Carrier-based aircraft and naval gunfire from two task groups, Rear Adms. Joseph J. Clark and Ralph E. Davison, commanding, attacked Japanese installations on Chichi Jima and Haha Jima in the Bonin Islands and Iwo Jima in the Volcano Islands.

6 JULY • As part of USAAF and British attempts to counter German *Vergeltungswaffen* (retaliation weapons) attacks by V-1 flying bombs (and subsequently V-2 rockets) against the United Kingdom, the Navy experimented with drones in Project Anvil. On this date, Special Air Unit 1 with Cmdr. James A. Smith, officer in charge, was formed under Commander, Air Force, Atlantic Fleet, for transfer to Commander Fleet Air Wing 7 in Europe to assail German V-weapon sites with PB4Y-1 Liberators converted to assault drones.

6 JULY • BUAER authorized Douglas to proceed with the design and manufacture of 15 XBT2D dive and torpedo bombers, jointly designed by both. Through subsequent development and model redesignation these became the prototypes for the AD Skyraider.

14 JULY • Joint action by the Deputy Chief of Naval Operations (Air) and the Chief of BUAER established the Flight Safety Council to plan, coordinate, and execute flight safety programs by coordinating all safety functions through a central organization.

14 JULY • PB4Y-1 Liberators of VB-109 flying from Saipan in the Mariana Islands made the first strike by shore-based planes on the Japanese garrison on Iwo Jima, Volcano Islands.

21 JULY • Task Force 53, Rear Adm. Richard L. Conolly commanding, including *Sangamon* (CVE 26), *Suwannee* (CVE 27), *Chenango* (CVE 28), *Coral Sea* (CVE 57), and *Corregidor* (CVE 58), supported Operation Stevedore—landings by the 3d Marine Division, 1st Provisional Marine Brigade, and the Army's 77th Division on Guam.

25 JULY • Task Force 58, Vice Adm. Marc A. Mitscher commanding, attacked Japanese installations and shipping in the Western Caroline Islands at Fais, Ngulu, Palau, Sorol, Ulithi, and Yap. Air strikes continued until 28 July and included photographic flights to obtain intelligence of enemy defenses. The ships then steamed north to attack the Bonin and Volcano Islands. By the time Guam was declared secured on 10 August, carrier aircraft claimed the destruction of 1,223 Japanese aircraft and the sinking of 110,000 tons of shipping. During this fighting, groups of the fast carrier force retired in turn to advanced fleet bases for brief periods of rest and replenishment, thus initiating a practice that continued during all future extended fighting.

27 JULY • The headquarters of Fleet Air Wing 17 was moved to Manus, Admiralty Islands.

29 JULY • In the first successful test of a Pelican guided missile, two of the four launched struck target ship *James Longstreet* 44 miles offshore of NAS New York, N.Y.

29 JULY • A detachment of PB4Y-1 Liberators of VB-114 from NAS Port Lyautey, Morocco, was established under British command for antisubmarine operations at Lajes, Azores Islands.

31 JULY • The Accelerated Field Service Test Unit was redesignated Service Test and established as a separate department at NAS Patuxent River, Md.

4 AUGUST • Task Group 58.1, Rear Adm. Joseph J. Clark commanding, savaged Japanese Convoy 4804 about 25 miles northwest of Muko Jima, Bonin Islands, sinking destroyer *Matsu*, landing ship *T 133*, a collier, four transports, and a cargo ship. Meanwhile, planes from Task Group 58.3, Rear Adm. Alfred E. Montgomery commanding, bombed Japanese airfields on Iwo Jima, Volcano Islands.

5 AUGUST • The Fast Carrier Task Force was reorganized into the First and Second Fast Carrier Task Forces, Pacific, Vice Adms. Marc A. Mitscher and John S. McCain commanding, respectively.

7 AUGUST • Carrier Division 11 was established, Rear Adm. Matthias B. Gardner commanding, at Pearl Harbor, Hawaiian Islands. The division consisted of *Saratoga* (CV 3) and *Ranger* (CV 4) and comprised the first U.S. carrier command specifically established for night operations.

9 AUGUST • A PB4Y-1 Liberator of VB-116 crashed on takeoff from Stickell Field, Eniwetok, Marshall Islands, and burned amid 340 planes in the carrier aircraft replacement pool area, resulting in the destruction of 106 aircraft—primarily FM Wildcats, F6F Hellcats, SB2C Helldivers, and TBM Avengers.

10 AUGUST • Naval air bases commands were established within each Naval District, the Training Command, and within Marine Corps bases. These received authorization for the military direction and administrative coordination of matters affecting the development and operational readiness of aviation facilities in their respective areas.

10 AUGUST • The operating aircraft complement of carrier air groups underwent a revision to 54 fighters, 24 bombers, and 18 torpedo planes, with the provision that four night fighters and two photographic planes were to be included among the 54 fighters.

11 AUGUST • An electric-powered rescue hoist was installed on an HNS-1 Hoverfly, BuNo 39040, at CGAS Floyd Bennett Field, N.Y. During the ensuing four-day test period, flights conducted over Jamaica Bay demonstrated the feasibility of rescuing victims from the water and of transferring people and equipment to and from underway boats. Six weeks later, the installation and successful testing of a hydraulic hoist led to the adoption of the device for service use because it overcame the basic disadvantages of the electric hoist. Also on this date Dr. M. F. Bates of the Sperry Gyroscope Company, submitted a brief report of the trial installation and flight test of a helicopter automatic pilot (cyclic pitch control) in a Hoverfly at Floyd Bennett Field.

12 AUGUST • Lt. Joseph P. Kennedy Jr., USNR, of VPB-110, temporarily assigned to Special Air Unit 1, and Lt. Wilford J. Willy participated in a mission in a PB4Y-1 Liberator, BuNo 32271, against a German V-1 flying bomb launching site in German-occupied France. The weight of the Liberator—which carried 21,170-pounds of high explosives—precluded take off by remote control, so Kennedy and Willy voluntarily made the takeoff from Winfarthing (Fersfield), England. The men remained with the drone to ensure the assumption of control by two "mother" planes—one used as insurance against potential equipment failure in the primary—and were then to bail out over England. At 1820, the Liberator suddenly exploded killing Kennedy and Willy. No cause was ever determined. The two each received the Navy Cross posthumously and destroyer *Joseph P. Kennedy Jr.* (DD 850) was named in his honor.

15 AUGUST • Allied carriers of the Naval Attack Force, Rear Adm. Sir Thomas H. Troubridge, RN, commanding, devastated columns of German troops, motor transport, and railway rolling stock during Operation Dragoon—landings by the U.S. VI and Free French II Corps in southern France. F6F-3N and F6F-5 Hellcats of VF-74, embarked on board *Kasaan Bay* (CVE 69), and F6F-5s of VOF-1 flying from *Tulagi* (CVE 72), together with British planes from escort carriers *Attacker* (D 02), *Searcher* (D 40), *Khedive* (D 62), *Pursuer* (D 73), *Hunter* (D 80), *Stalker* (D 91), and *Emperor* (D 98), flew defensive fighter cover over the shipping area, spotted naval gunfire, flew close air support missions, attacked enemy concentrations and lines of communication, and assisted Allied troops during their advance up the Rhône Valley. Hellcats from *Kasaan Bay* bombed and strafed enemy positions, vehicles, and tanks, and shot down two German planes over the invasion beaches. On *Tulagi*'s last day to support the landings, 21 August, her Hellcats shot down three German Junkers Ju 52s, and wreaked havoc with a German convoy retreating northward, snarling roads for miles around Remouline. The Allied carriers launched more than 1,500 sorties through 29 August.

20 AUGUST • Nonrigid airship K-111, Lt. Cmdr. Frederick N. Klein commanding, demonstrated the feasibility of refueling and replenishing airships from aircraft carriers during 72.5 hours of operations into 23 August with *Makassar Strait* (CVE 91) off San Diego, Calif. The airship's crew was relieved every 12 hours and her engines operated continuously. The airship remained on the flight deck for 32 minutes during one evolution.

24 AUGUST • CVLG(N)-43 was established as the first night carrier air group at Charlestown, R.I., along with its component squadrons VF(N)-43 and VT(N)-43.

24 AUGUST • Fleet Air Wing 10 moved forward from Perth, Australia, to Los Negros, Admiralty Islands, to support the advance of Southwest Pacific forces on the Philippines.

31 AUGUST • Task Group 38.4, Rear Adm. Ralph E. Davison commanding, opened the campaign for the occupation of Morotai and Palau with three days of attacks on Chichi Jima in the Bonin Islands and Iwo Jima in the Volcano Islands. Davison intended the raids to neutralize Japanese installations as a diversion in advance of the landings in the Morotai, Palau, and Philippine areas. Off Iwo Jima, F6F Hellcats from *Franklin* (CV 13) sank an auxiliary minesweeper and cargo ship.

During an attack on 2 September against a Japanese radio station on Chichi Jima, ground fire struck TBM-1C, BuNo 46214, of a division of four Avengers from VT-51, embarked on board *San Jacinto* (CVL 30). Lt. j.g. George H. W. Bush, USNR, (Naval Aviator No. C5907); Lt. j.g. William G. White, USNR; and ARM2 John L. Delaney manned the bomber. Despite the smoke and flames, Bush continued his dive and scored damaging hits before the Avenger crashed. Submarine *Finback* (SS 230) rescued the pilot after he spent four hours in the water, however, White and Delaney perished. Bush received the Distinguished Flying Cross for the attack, was discharged on 18 September 1945, and on 24 October 1955 resigned with the rank of lieutenant. He subsequently became the 41st President of the United States. *George H. W. Bush* (CVN 77) was named in his honor.

1 SEPTEMBER • The Bureau of Ordnance reported the beginning of an investigation by a group of scientists from Section T of the Office of Scientific Research and Development (OSRD) into the practicability of developing a guided jet-propelled antiaircraft weapon. The project subsequently was designated Bumblebee. In December, the scientists completed their preliminary analysis and the Chief of Naval Operations approved a developmental program. That month, the OSRD and the Applied Physics Laboratory of Johns Hopkins University completed their withdrawal from the proximity fuze program to concentrate upon the guided missile phase of the antiaircraft problem. The fuze endeavor thus fell completely within the Bureau of Ordnance.

3 SEPTEMBER • Pilot Lt. Ralph D. Spaulding Jr., of Special Air Unit 1 assigned to Fleet Air Wing 7, lifted off in a PB4Y-1 Liberator for a drone mission from Winfarthing (Fersfield), England. The raid involved the drone, two control planes, and fighters along with navigational, frequency search monitor, and photo aircraft. Spaulding set the radio control on the torpex-laden Liberator and parachuted to safety. Ens. James M. Simpson in a PV-1 Ventura controlled the Liberator's flight and attacked German U-boat pens on Heligoland Island. Simpson lost momentary view of the plane in a rain shower during the final alignment, and relying only upon the drone's television picture, aimed the plane into barracks near fuel dumps and shops on an airfield on Dune Island. The attackers lost reception just before impact when flak apparently struck the camera in the nose of the drone and thus proved unable to assess the damage.

3 SEPTEMBER • Task Group 12.5, Rear Adm. Allen E. Smith commanding, including *Monterey* (CVL 26), attacked Japanese installations on Wake Island. This was the fourth carrier raid on the atoll since the Japanese overran it.

6 SEPTEMBER • A contract was awarded to McDonnell Aircraft Corporation, for development of the LBD-1 Gargoyle radio-controlled low-wing glide bomb fitted with a rocket booster and designed for launching from carrier-based dive bombers and torpedo planes against enemy ships.

6 SEPTEMBER • The establishment of a Flight Safety Section in the Office of the Deputy Chief of Naval Operations (Air) expanded the scope of the aviation safety program. The section assumed responsibility for direction and supervision of the program.

6 SEPTEMBER • After wide-flung sweeps by Task Force 38, Vice Adm. Marc A. Mitscher commanding, the force arrived off Palau and began attacks against Japanese airfields and installations in the Western Caroline Islands. An unopposed fighter sweep disclosed extensive damage inflicted by earlier raids. *Independence* (CVL 22) commenced operations of an air group specifically trained for night work, marking the first time that a fully equipped night carrier operated with the fast carriers. Meanwhile, Task Group 38.4, Rear Adm. Ralph E. Davison commanding, launched a fighter sweep over Yap and continued the neutralization of Palau while Mitscher moved against the Philippines with strikes at airfields on Mindanão and in the Visayas.

9 SEPTEMBER • Task Force 38, Vice Adm. Marc A. Mitscher commanding, sent two days of fighter sweeps against Japanese airfields and port facilities on Mindanão, Philippines. Planes sank a transport in the Sulu Sea and two transports and a cargo ship in the Mindanão Sea, and aircraft from *Langley* (CVL 27) covered a surface group that decimated a Japanese coastal convoy off the west coast of Mindanão.

9 SEPTEMBER • Fleet Air Wing 17 moved forward to the Schouten Islands to direct patrol plane operations supporting the occupation by Southwest Pacific forces of Morotai in the Netherlands East Indies (Indonesia).

11 SEPTEMBER • The shift of the fighting in the South Pacific drove the transfer of Commander Fleet Air Wing 1 based on seaplane tender *Hamlin* (AV 15) from Espíritu Santo in the New Hebrides (Vanuatu) to Guam, to direct the operations of patrol squadrons in the Central Pacific.

11 SEPTEMBER • President Franklin D. Roosevelt and British Prime Minister Winston S. Churchill led a meeting named Octagon of the Allied combined chiefs of staff at Québec, Canada. The chiefs cancelled a planned attack on Yap, approved the advance of the date for the invasion of the Philippines from 20 December to 20 October, and the shifting of the assault from southern Mindanão to Leyte. Their decision occurred in large part because of the recommendation of Commander Third Fleet Adm. William F. Halsey Jr., who based his proposal on intelligence that indicated Japanese weakness in the central Philippines corroborated by a lack of aerial opposition—the Japanese preserved their forces to repel the landings. Ens. Thomas C. Tillar, USNR, of VF-2 from Carrier Air Group 2 embarked on board *Hornet* (CV 12), had crashed in an F6F-3 Hellcat near Apit Island off southwestern Leyte. Filipino freedom fighters rescued him and revealed to the pilot the vulnerable state of the Japanese defenses before his return via an SOC Seagull from heavy cruiser *Wichita* (CA 45). Octagon concluded on 16 September.

12 SEPTEMBER • Task Force 38, Vice Adm. Marc A. Mitscher commanding, launched strikes into 14 September against Japanese airfields and ports on Cebu, Negros, and Panay in the Visayas and Legaspi, Luzon in the Philippines, claiming the destruction of 26 enemy vessels.

12 SEPTEMBER • Task Group 38.4 and four escort carriers of Carrier Unit One, Rear Adm. William D. Sample commanding, began three days of preparatory aerial attacks for the occupation of Peleliu.

USMC 97976

A Marine F4U Corsair drops napalm against determined Japanese forces defending Peleliu in fall, 1944.

14 SEPTEMBER • Task Group 38.1, Vice Adm. John S. McCain commanding, detached from the main forces to attack Mindanão, Philippines, and to support Operation Trade Wind—landings the following day by the Army's 41st Division on Morotai, Netherlands East Indies (Indonesia).

15 SEPTEMBER • Aircraft of Task Group 38.4 and four escort carriers of Carrier Unit One, Rear Adm. William D. Sample commanding, supported Operation Stalemate II—the landing of the 1st Marine Division on Peleliu. The Japanese had prepared the main line of resistance inland from the beaches to escape naval bombardment, and three days of preliminary carrier air attacks in combination with intense naval gunfire failed to suppress the tenacious defenders. Through 18 September, the fleet carriers supported the landings and until the end of the month a total of ten escort carriers fought as Task Group 32.7, Rear Adm. Ralph A. Ofstie commanding. The Army's 81st Division later reinforced the Marines and, on 1 February 1945, the final Japanese forces surrendered. On 17 September, carriers also supported landings on Angaur, on 23 September at Ulithi, and on 28 September a shore-to-shore movement from Peleliu to Ngesebus assisted by Marine planes from Peleliu. On 24 September, VMF(N)-541 became the first squadron to arrive ashore.

18 SEPTEMBER • The Navy terminated the Pelican guided missile production program and returned the project to developmental status. Despite some success during the preceding six weeks, the decision stemmed from tactical, logistic, and technical problems.

21 SEPTEMBER • After the fighting at Morotai in the Netherlands East Indies (Indonesia), Task Group 38.1 rejoined the main body of fast carriers. The combined force launched two days of strikes on Clark and Nichols Fields on Luzon, shipping around Manila and Subic Bays and Cavite Island, and on a convoy off Luzon, followed on 24 September by additional raids on airfields, military installations, and shipping in the central Philippines. Planes sank 39 Japanese vessels including destroyer *Satsuki*.

27 SEPTEMBER • Special Task Air Group (STAG) 1 began a combat demonstration of TDR-1 assault drones from Stirling, Treasury Islands, during the first use of guided missiles in action in the Pacific. Ships had delivered the drones to the Russell Islands and they were then flown 45 miles to the Northern Solomons, stripped for pilotless flight, and armed with bombs of up to 2,000-pounds. At least one control operator in an accompanying TBM Avenger guided the pilotless aircraft by radio during attacks against heavily defended targets and directed the final assault by means of pictures received from the drones' nose-mounted television cameras. In the initial assault against Japanese antiaircraft guns emplaced in a beached freighter defending Kahili airstrip on South Bougainville in the Solomons, two of four TDR-1s struck the target ship.

30 SEPTEMBER • During September, carrier planes claimed the destruction of 893 Japanese aircraft and 67 ships totaling 224,000 tons.

1 OCTOBER • Patrol Squadrons (VP) and multi-engine bombing squadrons (VB) were redesignated patrol bombing squadrons (VPB).

2 OCTOBER • Lt. j.g. Stewart R. Graham, USCG, made the first Coast Guard demonstration of a helicopter rescue from the open sea off Manasquan Inlet, N.J. Graham, in an HNS-1 Hoverfly, hoisted aloft four men from two life rafts and lowered them safely to a 38- by 63-foot flight deck fitted to Coast Guard cutter *Governor Cobb* (WPG 181). Chief of BUAER Rear Adm. DeWitt C. Ramsey observed and expressed his approval of the demonstration.

7 OCTOBER • A new BUAER color specification went into effect, which provided seven different color schemes for aircraft depending upon their design and use. The most basic change concerned the use of overall glossy Sea Blue on carrier-based aircraft and seaplane transports, trainers, and utility planes. The basic nonspecular camouflage, semigloss Sea Blue above and nonspecular Insignia White below, was to be applied to patrol and patrol bombing types and to helicopters. The prescription regarding antisubmarine warfare identified two special camouflage schemes, Gull Gray on top and sides and Insignia White on bottom, or Insignia White all over (the selection depended upon the prevailing weather conditions and, since 19 July 1943, had been used by AirLant). Overall Aluminum was to be applied to landplane transports and trainers and landplane and amphibian utility aircraft, Orange Yellow on target-towing planes and primary trainers, and glossy Insignia Red on target drones. Provision allowed for the optional use by tactical commanders of special identification markings on combat aircraft, preferably with temporary paint.

10 OCTOBER • Task Force 38, Vice Adm. Marc A. Mitscher commanding, struck Japanese reinforcement staging areas in the opening blow of the campaign to liberate Leyte, Philippines. Aircraft from 17 carriers bombed airfields on Okinawa and other islands of the Ryūkyūs and sank 29 vessels. The following day, planes struck airfields on northern Luzon in preparation for raids on the Japanese bastion of Formosa (Taiwan). From 12 to 14 October the force then attacked ships, aerodromes, and industrial plants on Formosa and sank 22 vessels. These raids drew heavy Japanese aerial counterattacks and, on 13 October, a *kamikaze* suicide plane crashed *Franklin* (CV 13), and the next day *Hancock* (CV 19) received damage from bombs, but both ships continued. The destruction of Japanese air power on Formosa paved the way on 14 and 16 October for USAAF Boeing B-29 Superfortress raids on island aircraft plant and airfield facilities. On 14 October, the carriers launched a second raid on northern Luzon, and the next day, a sweep over the Manila area. These strikes in total destroyed an estimated 438 Japanese aircraft in the air and 366 on the ground and, in combination with other battles, effectively cleared the skies for landings on Leyte.

14 OCTOBER • The Navy directed Amphibious Forces Training Command, Pacific to form mobile air support training units to train carrier air groups and Marine squadrons in the techniques of close air support operations.

47012

Navy SB2C Helldivers from *Hancock* (CV 19) attack *Kumano* in Tablas Strait, off Mindoro Island, during the Battle of Leyte Gulf, 26 October 1944. The Japanese cruiser escaped despite three hits.

15 OCTOBER • Special Task Air Group (STAG) 1 launched four TDR-1 assault drones against Matupi Bridge near Simpson Harbor, Rabaul, New Britain. The drones took part in a coordinated attack by aircraft from Green Island including PBJ-1D Mitchells of VMB-423, F4U-1 and FG-1 Corsairs of VMF-218 and -222, and SBD-5 Dauntlesses of VMSB-244 and -341. The raid failed to hit the targets because of poor picture reception and pilot error.

17 OCTOBER • Commander Fleet Air Wing 10 arrived in Philippine waters on board seaplane tender *Currituck* (AVP 7) to direct patrol plane operations in support of landings on Leyte.

17 OCTOBER • Task Group 38.4, Rear Adm. Ralph E. Davison commanding, attacked Japanese installations at Legaspi and Clark Field, Luzon, in the Philippines.

17 OCTOBER • The Army's 6th Ranger Battalion landed on Dinagat and Suluan Islands at the entrance to Leyte Gulf to destroy Japanese installations capable of providing early warning of a U.S. attack. The Suluan garrison transmitted an alert that prompted Japanese Commander in Chief Combined Fleet Adm. Toyoda Soemu to order SHO-1—an operation to defend the Philippines. The raid thus helped to bring about the Battle of Leyte Gulf.

19 OCTOBER • Commander Fleet Air Wing 17 moved to Morotai in the Netherlands East Indies (Indonesia) to support operations against Japanese forces in the Philippines.

19 OCTOBER • President Franklin D. Roosevelt approved a plan providing for the acceptance of African American women in the women's Navy Reserves. The plan called for the immediate commissioning of a limited number of black women as administrative officers, and the subsequent enlistment of additional African American women.

20 OCTOBER • The Seventh Fleet, Vice Adm. Thomas C. Kinkaid commanding, landed four divisions of the

Sixth Army on Leyte, Philippines. Eighteen escort carriers organized in Task Units 77.4.1, 77.4.2, and 77.4.3 but known as Taffy 1, 2, and 3, respectively, supplemented the fast carriers by operations. Taffy 1 sailed southward off northern Mindanão, Taffy 2 off the entrance to Leyte Gulf, and Taffy 3 to the north off Samar. Japanese planes counterattacked the ships and a bomb damaged *Sangamon* (CVE 26) but she continued the fight.

20 OCTOBER • Special Task Air Group (STAG) 1 launched three TDR-1 assault drones against Japanese gun positions west of Ballale, Bougainville, in the Solomon Islands. One drone was lost, one made a hit with its bomb but crashed before striking a beached Japanese freighter—christened by the men involved "Kahili Maru"—equipped with antiaircraft guns off the airstrip at Kahili, and the final drone bombed and crashed the freighter.

21 OCTOBER • Task Group 38.2, Rear Adm. Gerald F. Bogan commanding, attacked Japanese ships and installations near Cebu, Masbate, Negros, and Panay in the Philippines.

21 OCTOBER • Marine Carrier Air Groups was established under Aircraft, Fleet Marine Force, Pacific, to direct the formation and training of Marine squadrons earmarked to operate from escort carriers. Plans called for the formation of six such groups, each composed of a fighter and a torpedo squadron. Four were to be assigned to ships and the remaining two to function as replacement and training groups.

23 OCTOBER • The Battle of Leyte Gulf began when Japanese Operation SHO-1 attempted to disrupt U.S. landings in the gulf. Commander Third Fleet Adm. William F. Halsey Jr. led nine fleet and eight light carriers. Commander Seventh Fleet Vice Adm. Thomas C. Kinkaid led 18 escort carriers organized in Task Units 77.4.1, 77.4.2, and 77.4.3 and known as Taffy 1, 2, and 3, respectively. Japanese fuel shortages compelled the dispersal of its fleet into the Northern (decoy), Central, and Southern Forces that converged separately on Leyte Gulf. Attrition had reduced the Northern Force's 1st Mobile Force, Vice Adm. Ozawa Jisaburō commanding, to carrier *Zuikaku* and light carriers *Chitose, Chiyōda*, and *Zuihō*. In the Sibuyan Sea, U.S. planes attacked the Central Force, Vice Adm. Kurita Takeo commanding, and sank battleship *Musashi* south of Luzon. Aircraft also attacked the Southern Force as it proceeded through the Sulu Sea, and sank destroyer *Wakaba* and damaged battleships *Fusō* and *Yamashiro*.

Commander CVG-15 Cmdr. David S. McCampbell and his wingman, Lt. j.g. Roy Rushing, flew F6F-3 Hellcats from *Essex* (CV 9), and broke up a formation of an estimated 60 Japanese aircraft, downing nine (claiming 15). McCampbell subsequently received the Medal of Honor for this and the action on 19 June. During a Japanese counterattack on Task Group 38.3, a bomb from a Yokosuka D4Y1 Type 2 Judy struck *Princeton* (CVL 23) and she was later scuttled. On 25 October, the Seventh Fleet turned back the Southern Force before daylight in the Battle of Surigao Strait.

The Central Force made a night passage through San Bernardino Strait and at daylight off Samar attacked Taffy 3, Rear Adm. Clifton A. F. Sprague commanding. Valiant rearguard efforts threw Kurita's ships into disarray and compelled his retirement despite the Japanese superiority in weight and firepower. Aircraft damaged battleships *Yamato* and *Kongō* and heavy cruisers *Chikuma, Chōkai*, and *Suzuya*. Japanese gunfire sank *Gambier Bay* (CVE 73), two destroyers and a destroyer escort; damaged *Kalinin Bay* (CVE 68), *Fanshaw Bay* (CVE 70), a destroyer and a destroyer escort; and straddled *St. Lo* (CVE 63), *White Plains* (CVE 66), and *Kitkun Bay* (CVE 71). *Kamikaze* planes sank *St. Lo* and damaged *Kalinin Bay, Kitkun Bay, Suwannee* (CVE 27), and *Santee* (CVE 29)—also torpedoed by submarine *I-56*—and missed *Sangamon* (CVE 26), *Petrof Bay* (CVE 80), and *White Plains*.

The Northern Force decoyed Halsey's Third Fleet beyond range to protect Taffy 3 but off Cape Engaño aircraft sank all four Japanese carriers, and *Chitose* with the assistance of cruiser gunfire. In addition, planes sank (some scuttled by the Japanese) heavy cruisers *Chikuma, Chōkai, Mogami*, and *Suzuya*; light cruisers *Abukuma* (by USAAF B-24 Liberators) *Kinu, Noshiro, Nowaki* (by gunfire) and *Tama* (also from submarine *Jallao* [SS 368]); and destroyers *Hatsuzuki* (by gunfire) *Hayashimo*, and *Uranami*; and damaged battleships *Yamato, Haruna*, and *Nagato*; heavy cruisers *Kumano, Myōkō*, and *Tone*; light cruiser *Yahagi*; and destroyers *Fujinami, Kiyoshimo*, and *Okinami*.

On 27 and 28 October, aircraft from the heavy carriers attacked airfields on Luzon and the Visayas, ships near Cebu on 28 October, and the next day, airfields on Luzon and vessels in Manila Bay. On 27 October, Allied aircraft from Tacloban assumed direct air support missions

238363

Kitkun Bay's (CVE 71) 5-inch gun makes a direct hit on a Japanese torpedo bomber attacking a carrier aft of her off Saipan, 18 June 1944.

700580

A Japanese suicide plane narrowly misses *Sangamon* (CVE 26) during the Battle of Leyte Gulf, 25 October 1944.

over Leyte and Samar, which two days later enabled the retirement of the escort carriers. During October, carrier aircraft claimed the destruction of 1,046 Japanese planes and warships totaling more than 300,000 tons. The Battle of Leyte Gulf effectively finished the Japanese surface fleet.

25 OCTOBER • In recognition of the difference in the functions performed, carrier aircraft service units and patrol aircraft service units operating at advanced bases were redesignated combat aircraft service units (forward), while those commands in the continental United States and Hawaiian Islands retained the original title.

26 OCTOBER • Special Task Air Group (STAG) 1 concluded a month-long demonstration of the first use of guided missiles in the Pacific with a final attack of two TDR-1 assault drones against a lighthouse on Cape St. George, New Ireland, making one hit that demolished the structure. Twenty-nine of the 46 drones expended during the demonstration reached their target areas. In addition to the success against the lighthouse; nine attacked antiaircraft guns on beached ships and achieved six direct hits and two near misses; and 18 attacked other targets in the Shortlands and Rabaul areas and made 11 hits.

29 OCTOBER • Task Group 38.2, Rear Adm. Gerald F. Bogan commanding, attacked Japanese airfields and shipping in the Manila area, Philippines. Planes damaged heavy cruiser *Nachi,* which was sunk on 5 November. *Intrepid* (CV 11) launched a strike against Clark Field on Luzon. A suicide plane damaged the ship, but *Intrepid* continued in action. The following day, three *kamikazes* attacked *Franklin* (CV 13) off Samar. The first two damaged the ship, while the third missed and crashed *Belleau Wood* (CVL 24). Both ships completed temporary repairs at Ulithi. Later, *Franklin* proceeded to Puget Sound Navy Yard at Bremerton, Wash., and *Belleau Wood* to Hunters Point, Calif.

5 NOVEMBER • Appalling weather and difficult terrain that delayed the development of airfields on Leyte, Philippines, and the requirement for continued carrier air support influenced the cancellation of a fast carrier strike on Tōkyō. Task Force 38, Vice Adm. John S. McCain commanding, began two days of carrier raids on airfields and shipping around Luzon and Mindoro. Planes from *Essex* (CV 9), *Lexington* (CV 16), and *Langley* (CVL 27) sank heavy cruiser *Nachi* and smaller vessels. Japanese retaliatory air strikes included a *kamikaze* that crashed *Lexington,* but the ship controlled the blaze and her guns shot down another suicide aircraft as it plunged toward *Ticonderoga* (CV 14). *Lexington* underwent repairs at Ulithi.

6 NOVEMBER • The recognition of the future importance of turbojet and turboprop powerplants prompted BUAER to request a study by the Naval Air Material Center of the requirements for a laboratory to develop and test such engines. This decision initiated action that consequently led to the establishment of the Naval Air Turbine Test Station, Trenton, N.J.

10 NOVEMBER • An estimated 3,000 tons of explosives on board ammunition ship *Mount Hood* (AE 11) exploded in Seeadler Harbor, Manus, Admiralty Islands. The blast damaged 36 nearby ships and landing craft including *Petrof Bay* (CVE 80) and *Saginaw Bay* (CVE 82), which suffered minor damage to their exteriors. The crew of *Saginaw Bay* helped care for the wounded.

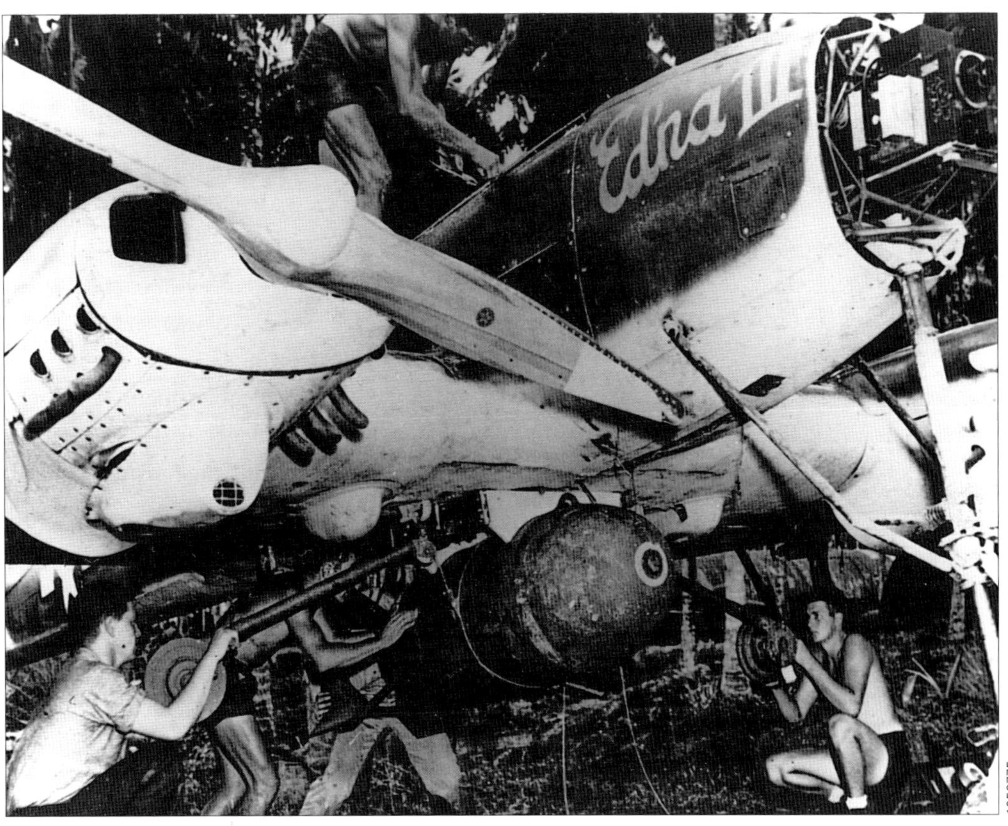

Sailors mount a 2,000-pound bomb on a TDR-1 assault drone in preparation for an attack.

11 NOVEMBER • Task Force 38, Vice Adm. John S. McCain commanding, attacked a Japanese reinforcement convoy of four transports and five destroyers in Ormoc Bay, Leyte, in the Philippines, sinking all but one destroyer. On 13 and 14 November, McCain shifted his strikes to the Manila area and central Luzon and sank light cruiser *Kiso*; destroyers *Akebono, Akishimo, Hatsuharu,* and *Okinami*; and 20 merchant and auxiliary ships. During 19 to 28 November, a group of escort carriers protected convoys from the Admiralty Islands against air and submarine attacks, and from 14 to 23 November another group protected convoys from Ulithi.

17 NOVEMBER • BUAER reported the continuation of technical studies to determine the feasibility of launching an adaptation of the USAAF JB-2 version of German V-l Buzz Bombs from escort carriers for attacks on enemy ships and shore targets. The modifications envisioned included the installation of radio controls and a radar beacon. This program subsequently developed the Loon.

23 NOVEMBER • The dissolution of Training Task Force Command enabled the relocation of its facilities, people, and equipment to other commands.

25 NOVEMBER • Task Groups 38.2 and 38.3, Rear Adms. Gerald F. Bogan and Frederick C. Sherman commanding, respectively, launched strikes against Japanese ships off central Luzon in the Philippines. In Dasol Bay, planes from *Ticonderoga* (CV 14) sank heavy cruiser *Kumano*. F6F Hellcats, SB2C Helldivers, and TBM-1C Avengers from *Essex* (CV 9), *Ticonderoga*, and *Langley* (CVL 27) attacked a convoy about 15 miles southwest of Santa Cruz off western Luzon and sank coast defense ship *Yasojima* (former Chinese light cruiser *Ping Hai*) and three landing ships. Aircraft from *Essex*, *Intrepid* (CV 11), and *Langley* sank additional vessels. Japanese suicide planes damaged *Essex, Intrepid, Hancock* (CV 19), and *Cabot* (CVL 28). A plane embarked on board *Independence* (CVL 22) accidentally crashed into the ship's island. All these ships continued in action.

27 NOVEMBER • *Commencement Bay* (CVE 105), Capt. Roscoe L. Bowman commanding, was commissioned as the first of her class built from the last U.S. escort carrier design at Tacoma, Wash.

Vice Adm. Mark A. Mitscher pins the Distinguished Flying Cross on the Navy's second highest scoring ace, Lt. Cecil E. Harris.

29 NOVEMBER • A revision of the aircraft complement of *Essex* (CV 9)–class carrier air groups to 73 fighters, 15 bombers, and 15 torpedo planes reflected the changing character of the war. Fighters consisted of two squadrons of 36 planes each plus one for the carrier air group commander.

30 NOVEMBER • The headquarters of Fleet Air Wing 10 shifted to Jinamoc Island, Philippines.

30 NOVEMBER • During November, Task Force 38 claimed the destruction of 770 Japanese planes.

1 DECEMBER • Electronics Tactical Training Unit was established at NAS Willow Grove, Pa. The unit trained people of the Airborne Coordinating Group as instructors in the operation of all newer types of airborne electronics apparatus including search, navigation, identification, and ordnance radar.

7 DECEMBER • *Chourre* (ARV 1), Capt. Andrew H. Bergeson commanding, was commissioned as the first purpose-built aviation repair ship of the Navy at Baltimore, Md.

11 DECEMBER • During the year a steady decline in U-boat attacks in the Caribbean permitted a reduction of blimp operations over the southern approaches, and Fleet Airship Wing 5 was disestablished at Trinidad.

12 DECEMBER • Three Evacuation Squadrons (VE) were established in the Pacific Fleet from air-sea rescue squadron elements already providing evacuation services.

12 DECEMBER • Six escort carriers of Task Unit 77.12.1, Rear Adm. Felix B. Stump commanding, combined with Marine shore-based aircraft to support Army landings on the southwest coast of Mindoro, Philippines. From 12 to 14 December, planes covered the passage of transports and assault shipping through the Visayas, and, from 15 to 18 December, supported the landings. On the night of D-day, seaplanes also joined with operations from Mangarin Bay. During the morning watch on 15 December, antiaircraft fire shot down two Japanese suicide planes that crashed near *Marcus Island* (CVE 77). On 14 December, Task Force 38, Vice Adm. John S. McCain commanding, including seven heavy and six light carriers, began fighter sweeps over airfields on Luzon. The planes continued with successive combat air patrols that spread an aerial blanket over the area to effectively pin down Japanese aircraft on the island, and accounted for a major share of the estimated 341 enemy aircraft destroyed.

13 DECEMBER • Escort Carrier Force, Pacific, Rear Adm. Calvin T. Durgin commanding, was established for the administrative control of all escort carriers operating in the Pacific, except those assigned to training and transport duties.

14 DECEMBER • The rank of fleet admiral was established. The next day, Adms. Ernest J. King, William D. Leahy, and Chester W. Nimitz received promotions to the rank.

16 DECEMBER • Planes from Task Force 38 sank Japanese freighter *Oryoku Maru* in Subic Bay, Philippines. Pilots attacked unaware that the ship carried at least 1,619 Allied prisoners under shipment to Japan. The men killed included Cmdr. Francis J. Bridget of Patrol Wing 10. On 27 December 1944 and 9 January 1945, the survivors endured additional attacks by U.S. planes at Takao, Formosa (Taiwan), and only 497 prisoners reached Moji, Japan.

18 DECEMBER • A typhoon roared into the Third Fleet, Adm. William F. Halsey Jr. commanding, following the refueling of some of the ships. Destroyers *Hull* (DD 350), *Monaghan* (DD 354), and *Spence* (DD 512) capsized in the

A tender hoists a PBM on board to service the Mariner.

high seas northeast of Samar, Philippines, and 21 other ships including *Cowpens* (CVL 25), *Monterey* (CVL 26), *Cabot* (CVL 28), and *San Jacinto* (CVL 30) of Task Force 38, and *Altamaha* (CVE 18), *Nehenta Bay* (CVE 74), *Cape Esperance* (CVE 88), and *Kwajalein* (CVE 98) of the replenishment group sustained damage, and 146 planes were swept or blown overboard, jettisoned, or crushed by debris or other aircraft torn lose from the carriers, battleships, and cruisers.

26 DECEMBER • A Japanese "Intrusion Force" attacked the U.S. beachhead at Mindoro, Philippines. PB4Y Liberators and PBM Mariners, together with USAAF Curtiss P-40 Warhawks, Republic P-47 Thunderbolts, Lockheed P-38 Lightnings, and North American B-25 Mitchells damaged heavy cruiser *Ashigara*; light cruiser *Oyodo*; destroyers *Asashimo*, *Kasumi*, and *Kiyoshimo*; and destroyer escorts *Kashi*, and *Kaya*. The Japanese bombarded the beachhead but motor torpedo boats intercepted the intruders. *PT-77* received damage, apparently from misidentification by U.S. planes, and *PT-223* sank *Kiyoshimo* off San Jose south of Manila.

28 DECEMBER • VMF-124 and -213 reported on board *Essex* (CV 9) at Ulithi. Their arrival marked the first Marine fighter squadrons to operate from fast carriers in combat.

30 DECEMBER • An amendment to the specification on aircraft color proscribed a color scheme for patrol and patrol bombing landplanes similar to that of carrier based airplanes—semigloss Sea Blue on top and bottom surfaces of wings and on all horizontal tail surfaces, and nonspecular Sea Blue on other tail surfaces and the fuselage.

The carriers (from front) *Wasp* (CV 18), *Yorktown* (CV 10), *Hornet* (CV 12), *Hancock* (CV 19), and *Ticonderoga* (CV 14) form a powerful centerpiece amid an array of naval power at Ulithi, 8 December 1944.

1945

1 JANUARY • Carrier Training Squadron, Pacific was established in the Pacific Fleet to provide operational control over carriers employed in training carrier air groups out of Pearl Harbor, Territory of Hawaii, and San Diego, Calif. Two carrier divisions composed the squadron.

2 JANUARY • Eighteen fighter bomber squadrons (VBF) were established within the existing carrier air groups to adjust their composition to changing combat requirements in the Pacific.

2 JANUARY • The headquarters of Fleet Air Wing 17, based on seaplane tender *Tangier* (AV 8), began to direct patrol plane support of operations in Lingayen Gulf from San Pedro Bay, Philippines.

2 JANUARY • In spite of almost continuous harsh weather during the month, the Allies invaded Lingayen Gulf on western Luzon in the Philippines. The Japanese reacted vigorously and their planes attacked the invasion forces during the transit from Leyte Gulf. Task Force 38, Vice Adm. John S. McCain commanding, including seven heavy and four light carriers, a night group of one heavy and one light carrier, and a replenishment group with one hunter-killer and seven escort carriers, concentrated on the destruction of enemy air power and air installations. On 3 January, planes bombed Japanese airfields and ships at Formosa (Taiwan). On 6 January, strikes shifted to airfields and shipping at Luzon in response to Japanese suicide attacks, and on 9 January, the Pescadores and Ryūkyū Islands, claiming the destruction of more than 100 Japanese aircraft and 40,000 tons of merchant and small warships.

During the night of 9–10 January, Task Force 38 made a high-speed run through Luzon Strait into the South China Sea. The replenishment group passed through Balintang Channel. On 12 January, the carriers launched strikes along 420 miles of the Indochina coast. Planes sank training cruiser *Kashii*, 14 small warships, 10 tankers, and

313866

Antiaircraft fire shoots down a Japanese bomber over an *Essex* (CV 9)-class carrier, 1945.

16 transports and cargo vessels totaling 126,000 tons. The raiders also sank French colonial cruiser *Lamotte-Picquet* and surveying vessel *Octant* near the Japanese ships.

The force moved northward to evade a typhoon and, on 15 January, bombed Japanese targets at Hong Kong, along the Chinese coast, Hainan, and Formosa, and the next day concentrated on Hong Kong. The Americans suffered heavy losses in the face of robust resistance, but sank 62,000 tons of shipping. Inclement weather persisted, and the attackers left the South China Sea. On 20 January, they made a nighttime run through Balintang Channel to strike Formosa, the Pescadores, and Okinawa. Japanese planes damaged *Ticonderoga* (CV 14) and *Langley* (CVL 27), but the next day aircraft raided the Ryūkyūs. During three weeks of action, the force claimed the destruction of more than 600 Japanese aircraft and 325,000 tons of shipping.

Seventeen escort carriers of Task Group 77.4, Rear Adm. Calvin T. Durgin commanding, protected the approach of the Luzon attack force to Lingayen Gulf. On 4 January, a *kamikaze* crashed *Ommaney Bay* (CVE 79) in the Northern Sulu Sea, igniting fueled aircraft on the flight deck that resulted in the deaths of 95 men and the scuttling of the escort carrier. Another *kamikaze* narrowly missed *Lunga Point* (CVE 94), and a bomb passed over seaplane tender *Half Moon* (AVP 26) but failed to explode. On 5 January, additional *kamikaze* and aerial attacks damaged *Manila Bay* (CVE 61) and *Savo Island* (CVE 78). From 7–9 January, planes conducted preliminary strikes in the assault area, on 9 January, covered the landings, and through 17 January, supported the inland advance of troops. Further aerial attacks damaged *Kitkun Bay* (CVE 71) and *Kadashan Bay* (CVE 76) on 8 January, and on 13 January, *Salamaua* (CVE 96).

6 JANUARY • The first detachment of Women Accepted for Volunteer Emergency Service (WAVES) arrived in the Territory of Hawaii. By the end of the war, 4,009 women served in the islands in the only post outside the continental United States to which the Navy permanently assigned women during World War II.

11 JANUARY • The Bureau of Ordnance assigned the first task on Project Bumblebee to the Applied Physics Laboratory. The action established the program for the development of a ram-jet powered, guided antiaircraft weapon from which the Talos, Terrier, and Tartar missiles eventually emerged.

21 JANUARY • Task Force 38, Vice Adm. John S. McCain commanding, attacked Japanese airfields and ships at Formosa (Taiwan), the Pescadores, and Sakishima Gunto and Okinawa in the Ryūkyūs. During the two-day raid, planes sank a guardboat and 22 merchantmen and fishing vessels and damaged installations. A Japanese aircraft glide-bombed *Langley* (CVL 27), and an accidental explosion of bombs carried by a TBM-1C Avenger of VT-7 damaged *Hancock* (CV 19). Two suicide planes crashed *Ticonderoga* (CV 14) and their attacks cost the ship 36 planes, 143 killed or missing, and 202 wounded including her skipper, Capt. Dixie Kiefer. *Ticonderoga* made for Ulithi for temporary repairs and then to Puget Sound Navy Yard at Bremerton, Wash. On 20 April, she completed repairs and, on 22 May, returned to Ulithi.

29 JANUARY • Planes from six escort carriers of Task Group 77.4, Rear Adm. William D. Sample commanding, covered Army landings at San Antonio near Subic Bay, Philippines; on 30 January on Grande Island at the entrance to the bay; and the following day at Nasugbu, south of the entrance to Manila Bay.

6 FEBRUARY • The Chief of Naval Operations directed the equipment of VPB-109, -123, and -124 of Fleet Air Wing 2 to employ Bat—Special Weapons Ordnance Device (SWOD) Mark 9—glide bombs in combat following a period of training at NAS Kaneohe Bay, Hawaiian Islands.

15 FEBRUARY • The disestablishment of the West Coast Wing of the Naval Air Transport Service facilitated the reassignment of its squadrons to the Pacific and Atlantic Wings.

16 FEBRUARY • Task Force 58, Vice Adm. Mark A. Mitscher commanding, including nine heavy and five light carriers and a night group of two heavy carriers launched the first carrier attack against Honshū, Japan, in preparation for Operation Detachment—landings on Iwo Jima in the Kazan Rettō (Volcano Islands) by the 4th and 5th Marine Divisions.

In addition to Navy aircraft, the carriers embarked 144 F4U-1D and FG-1 Corsairs from VMF-112, -123, -124, -213, -216, -217, -221, and -451. PB4Y-1 Liberators and PB4Y-2 Privateers and USAAF B-29 Superfortresses from the Marianas augmented carrier air patrols that swept the seas ahead of the ships to prevent their discovery. Planes bombed Japanese aircraft factories, airfields, and ships around the Tōkyō area. Heavy clouds, snow, and rain squalls impeded operations, but a momentary break in the weather enabled a major dogfight between U.S. and Japanese fighters east of the capital. On 17 February, foul weather persuaded Mitscher to cancel attacks and return to support the landings. Planes also flew neutralization strikes against the Bonin Islands.

Previous carrier raids and USAAF B-24 Liberator and Superfortress missions from the Marianas had weakened but warned the Japanese defenders, and the garrison prepared extensive defenses using the island's caves. The volcanic terrain limited the effectiveness of all but direct hits against these positions and the Marines sustained appalling casualties. On 19 February, naval aircraft that supported the landings included a flight of 24 F6F Hellcats and 24 Marine Corsairs, led by Lt. Col. William A. Millington, USMC, that attacked the Japanese in double-column approaches. The planes broke by division to port and starboard, dropped napalm on their initial runs, and made subsequent rocketing and strafing passes. On this date, 606 planes flew 765 sorties, dropped 1,558 bombs and 104 napalm tanks, and fired 2,254 rockets.

On 25 February, Mitscher returned for a second strike on Tōkyō during harsh weather, followed, on 1 March, with raids on Okinawa and the Ryūkyūs, and then retired to Ulithi, leaving in his wake the destruction of an estimated 648 Japanese aircraft and 30,000 tons of merchant shipping. Task Group 52.2, Rear Adm. Calvin T. Durgin commanding, commenced the Iwo Jima campaign with nine escort carriers, later augmented by one night heavy carrier and two additional escort carriers. From 16–18 February, Durgin dispatched preliminary air strikes against Iwo Jima, and from 19 February – 11 March, these planes supported the Marines and attacked Bonin Islands airstrips.

Planes also protected ships from Japanese submarine attacks including *kaiten* human-guided suicide torpedoes. On 26 February, FM-2 Wildcats and TBM-1C Avengers, embarked on board *Anzio* (CVE 57) and *Tulagi* (CVE 72), sank submarines *I-368* (transporting a *kaiten*) and *RO-43* in separate attacks. Aircraft of Task Group 50.5 operating from the Marianas conducted shipping reconnaissance and air-sea rescue between Japan and Iwo Jima, and offensive screens for carrier raids and expeditionary forces. From 28 February – 8 March, patrol planes of Fleet Air Wing 1 carried out similar operations from tenders anchored in the lee of Iwo Jima.

On 26 February, two OY-1 Sentinels of VMO-4 and -5 flew ashore from *Wake Island* (CVE 65), and two days later, the balance of the squadrons began to operate from airstrips while under artillery and mortar fire. On 6 March, USAAF North American P-51 Mustangs and Northrop P-61 Black Widows arrived from Saipan, followed two days later by VMTB-242. These aircraft flew day and night combat air patrols and provided all air support upon the 11 March departure of the escort carriers.

Japanese aerial counterattacks included five suicide planes and a bomber that damaged *Saratoga* (CV 3) on 21 February with a loss of 123 men killed or missing. She made for Eniwetok for temporary repairs and then to Puget Sound Navy Yard at Bremerton, Wash., and never returned to action. A *kamikaze* crashed *Bismarck Sea* (CVE 95) and triggered fires and ammunition explosions that led to the loss of the ship and 318 men. Another suicide plane damaged *Lunga Point* (CVE 94), and a bomb struck *Langley* (CVL 27). On 4 March, a crippled B-29 named *Dinah Might* made the first of more than 2,251 Superfortress emergency landings on Iwo Jima by the end of the war. The campaign included the use of altitude-determining radar on board LSTs, and a night fighter director in the organization of the air support commander. On 16 March, Iwo Jima was declared secured.

19 FEBRUARY • Commander Fleet Air Wing 1 went to sea on board seaplane tender *Hamlin* (AV 15) to direct patrol squadrons in support of the fighting on Iwo Jima, and remained in the area until the island was secure.

26 FEBRUARY • The headquarters of Fleet Air Wing 17 deployed to Clark Field on Luzon, Philippines.

3 MARCH • The Naval Air Transport Service was reorganized and established as a fleet command with its headquarters at NAAS Oakland, Calif. The service operated under the immediate direction of the Commander in Chief and Chief of Naval Operations.

3 MARCH • The Naval Air Training Command incorporated the Naval Air Technical Training Command.

6 MARCH • Ens. Jane Kendeigh became the first Navy flight nurse to serve in a combat zone when she reached Iwo Jima, Volcano Islands. The aircraft on which she arrived took Japanese mortar fire during its landing.

7 MARCH • The commanding officer of CGAS Floyd Bennett Field, N.Y., reported to BUAER the successful test of a dunking sonar suspended from an XHOS-1 helicopter.

7 MARCH • Pilot Frank N. Piasecki and copilot George N. Towson made the first flight of the tandem rotor XHRP-X transport helicopter at P-V Engineering Forum, Sharon Hill, Pa.

8 MARCH • A PBY-5A Catalina launched a rocket-powered Gorgon air-to-air missile that achieved an estimated speed of 550 mph in its first powered test flight. Lt. Cmdr. Moulton B. Taylor directed the experiment off NAS Cape May, N.J.

11 MARCH • Yokosuka P1Y Ginga (Frances) land attack planes flew from Kanoya, Japan, to attack U.S. ships at their Ulithi anchorage. One Frances crashed *Randolph* (CV 15) and killed 25 men and wounded 106. Another bomber slammed into Sorlen Island. Salvage vessel *Current* (ARS 22) sustained damage during a collision with the carrier while firefighting. *Randolph* completed repairs at the atoll.

17 MARCH • The Naval Air Transport Service received responsibility for evacuating wounded sailors and Marines.

18 MARCH • Task Force 58, Vice Adm. Marc A. Mitscher commanding, supported Operation Iceberg—the invasion of Okinawa in the Ryūkyū Islands. Through 22 March, ten heavy and six light carriers launched raids against Japanese airfields and shipping at Kyūshū and Honshū, Japan, claiming the destruction of 482 enemy aircraft by aerial attack and 46 by antiaircraft fire. Japanese planes lashed the ships and a Mitsubishi G4M1 Type 1 Betty crashed close aboard *Intrepid* (CV 11), killing two men and wounding 43. A dud bomb inflicted minor damage on *Enterprise* (CV 6) and the ship later sailed to Ulithi for repairs. Three Yokosuka D4Y1 Type 2 (Judy) dive bombers attacked *Yorktown* (CV 10) during which a bomb from the third plane damaged the ship. The next day, carrier planes attacked targets from Kure to

Kōbe and Osaka, destroyed incomplete submarine *I-205* in drydock, and damaged 14 warships.

Off Shikoku, a suicide plane and a bomber damaged *Wasp* (CV 18), killing 101 men and wounding 269, but for several days the ship continued in action before retiring for repairs. A Japanese bomber dropped two 550-pound bombs on *Franklin* (CV 13) that ignited fires and exploded ordnance and fuel among aircraft spotted on the flight deck or parked below. Despite 724 men killed or missing and 265 wounded, after brief tows, *Franklin* sailed under her own power to New York, N.Y.

On 21 March, 16 Bettys carrying MXY7 *Ohka* (Cherry Blossom) Model 11 flying bombs attacked, but fighters intercepted forcing them to prematurely release their *Ohka*s. Two days later, Task Force 58 began pre-assault strikes on Okinawa, and carrier aircraft neutralized airfields on the surrounding islands, supported ground operations, and intercepted air raids. Task Group 52.1, Rear Adm. Calvin T. Durgin commanding, including 18 escort carriers, took part in the preliminary strikes, and on 25 and 26 March, supported landings on Kerama Rettō and provided close air support. In late April, *Block Island* (CVE 106) and *Gilbert Islands* (CVE 107) arrived with MCVG-1 and -2, consisting of VMF-511 and VMTB-233, and of VMF-512 and VMTB-143, respectively, marking the combat debut of Marine air support carriers. Beginning on 3 April, OY-1 Sentinels of VMO-2, -3, -6, and -7 periodically operated ashore.

From 26 March – 20 April and from 3 – 25 May, Task Force 57, Vice Adm. Sir H. Bernard Rawlings, RN, commanding, fought south of Okinawa. At times British carriers *Formidable* (67), *Illustrious* (87), *Indefatigable* (10), *Indomitable* (92), and *Victorious* (38) launched strikes at airfields on Formosa (Taiwan) and Sakishima Gunto and intercepted air raids. The British carriers' armored flight decks enabled their survival against *kamikazes*.

On 26 March, the commander of Fleet Air Wing 1, based on seaplane tender *Hamlin* (AV 15), arrived at Kerama Rettō to direct patrol squadron operations. On 1 April, Marines and soldiers established a beachhead on western Okinawa and captured an airfield at Yontan (Yomitan), from which six days later aircraft began defensive patrols and close air support missions. On 3 April, two *kamikazes* damaged *Wake Island* (CVE 65) southeast of Okinawa, and although the crew escaped without casualties, she departed for repairs.

On 6 April, the Japanese launched the first of a series of ten mass *kamikaze* attacks, interspersed with smaller raids and named *Kikusui* (Floating Chrysanthemum) No. 1, against Allied ships operating off Okinawa. These attacks involved 1,465 aircraft through 28 May. The second of two *kamikazes* damaged *San Jacinto* (CVL 30). A U.S. fighter crashed on board *Chenango* (CVE 28) and started fires among the aircraft spotted for a strike. The carrrier left the area two days later.

The Japanese dispatched the First Diversion Attack Force, including battleship *Yamato*, across the East China Sea toward Okinawa to lure U.S. carriers from the island and to facilitate *kamikaze* attacks. Submarines *Hackleback* (SS 295) and *Threadfin* (SS 410) and a plane from *Essex* (CV 9) sighted and reported the enemy ships. Lt. James R. Young, USNR, and Lt. j.g. R. L. Simms, USNR, of VPB-21 piloted two PBM-3D Mariners that shadowed the ships and assisted in guiding aircraft toward them. On 7 April, carriers launched 386 planes that sank *Yamato*, light cruiser *Yahagi*, and destroyers *Asashimo*, *Hamakaze*, *Isokaze*, and *Kasumi*, and damaged destroyers *Fuyuzuki*, *Hatsushimo*, *Suzutsuki*, and *Yukikaze*. Antiaircraft fire downed ten U.S. planes. *Kamikazes* took advantage of the diversion and a plane crashed into *Hancock* (CV 19), but she continued the fight despite the loss of 62 men killed and 71 wounded.

On 11 April, Japanese planes damaged *Enterprise* and *Essex*. On 16 April, a *kamikaze* crashed *Intrepid*, and the next day the ship departed for repairs at San Francisco, Calif. On 17 April, Lt. Eugene A. Valencia, USNR, in his VF-9 F6F-3 Hellcat embarked on board *Yorktown* (CV 10), led a combat air patrol and shot down at least six attackers. He subsequently received the Navy Cross. On 4 May, two *kamikazes* attacked *Sangamon* (CVE 26) and the ship sailed for repairs to Norfolk, Va.

On 11 May, two *kamikazes* tentatively identified as a Mitsubishi A6M Type 0 and a Judy crashed flagship *Bunker Hill* (CV 17), which suffered 353 men killed, 43 missing, and 264 wounded. Mitscher shifted his flag to *Enterprise* and *Bunker Hill* made for repairs to Puget Sound Navy Yard, Bremerton, Wash. On 13 and 14 May, carrier aircraft attempted to blunt these counterattacks by raiding airfields on Kyūshū and Shikoku. A *kamikaze* crashed *Enterprise* on 14 May, killing 14 men and wounding 68. The next day, Mitscher shifted his flag to *Randolph* (CV 15) and *Enterprise* sailed to Puget Sound for repairs. On 6 June, a Zeke crashed *Natoma Bay* (CVE 62) and she made for San Diego, Calif.

On 27 May, a change in command from the Fifth Fleet, Adm. Raymond A. Spruance commanding, to the

A Marine F4U Corsair fires a full salvo of eight rockets at a target on Okinawa, 1945.

Third Fleet, Adm. William F. Halsey Jr. commanding, took place that adjusted all task number designations from the 50s to the 30s—the first designations are used throughout this campaign narrative. On 18 June, Japanese artillery on Okinawa killed Commander Tenth Army Lt. Gen. Simon B. Buckner Jr., USA. Pilot Maj. Gen. Roy S. Geiger, USMC, assumed temporary command of the Tenth Army until his relief on 23 June by Gen. Joseph W. Stilwell, USA.

On 21 June, the Americans declared Okinawa secured but the aerial counterattacks continued. A *kamikaze* damaged seaplane tender *Curtiss* (AV 4) and she retired for repairs. A second *kamikaze* damaged *Kenneth Whiting* (AV 14). Carrier air support—more than 40,000 combat sorties, the claimed destruction of 2,516 Japanese aircraft, 8,500 tons of bombs dropped, and 50,000 rockets fired—ensured the success of Iceberg. Marine squadrons ashore claimed the destruction of another 506 Japanese aircraft and expended 1,800 tons of bombs and 15,865 rockets. Many ships fought for long periods with *Essex* logging 79 consecutive days in battle. The fighting cost the Navy 763 aircraft and 36 ships and craft sunk and 368 damaged. At least 4,907 men on board these ships were killed or missing and 4,824 wounded.

21 MARCH • BUAER awarded a contract for 100 experimental liquid-fueled anti-*kamikaze* Lark missiles to the Ranger Engine Division of Fairchild, initiating the development of rocket-powered surface-to-air guided missiles.

27 MARCH • Ninety-four USAAF B-29 Superfortresses dropped mines provided by the Navy in Shimonoseki Strait and the waters of Suo Nada, Japan, to begin Operation Starvation—an aerial minelaying campaign to reduce the flow of merchant shipping that supplied the Japanese home islands. This operation and the six raids that followed into 12 April also supported the fighting for Okinawa, and additional minelaying runs then continued until the end of the war.

14 APRIL • The commander of Fleet Air Wing 10 arrived at Puerto Princessa, Palawan, Philippines, to direct patrol plane operations against Japanese ships in the South China Sea and along the Indochina coast.

20 APRIL • A typhoon damaged *Corregidor* (CVE 58) while she hunted Japanese submarines as part of Task Group 12.3 east of the Marianas.

A Bat radar-guided glide bomb is mounted under the wing of a PB4Y-2 Privateer. The weapon carried an internal 1,000-pound bomb.

23 APRIL • Squadron skipper Lt. Cmdr. George L. Hicks of VB-109 led PB4Y-2 Privateers that launched two Special Weapons Ordnance Device (SWOD) Mark 9 Bat glide bombs against Japanese ships in Balikpapan Harbor, Borneo, Netherlands East Indies (Indonesia). The attack marked the first combat employment of the only automatic homing bomb used by the Navy in World War II. Both devices proved defective and missed their targets. Five days later, Hicks led two Privateers in a second foray against Balikpapan. The bombers released three Bats against a large transport. Two of the bombs dove to either side of the vessel and sank two smaller freighters, while the third executed a sharp right turn to strike a large oil storage tank a quarter mile away in the Pandanseri Refinery. The squadron changed bases several times during the remainder of the war and continued to launch Bats with varying degrees of success.

1 MAY • CVBG-74 was established at NAAF Otis Field, Mass. This, the Navy's first large carrier air group, later served on board *Midway* (CVB 41).

2 MAY • Lt. August Kleisch, USCG, flying an HNS-1 Hoverfly made the first U.S. helicopter rescue when he saved 11 Canadian airmen marooned in Northern Labrador about 125 miles from Goose Bay.

4 MAY • Fleet Air Wing (FAW) 18, Rear Adm. Marshall R. Greer commanding, was established at Guam. The wing took over the operational responsibilities in the Marianas area previously held by FAW-1.

8 MAY • The Allies celebrated V-E (Victory in Europe) Day.

9 MAY • German submarine *U-249* raised the black surrender flag to a PB4Y-2 Privateer of Fleet Air Wing 7 near the Scilly Islands off Lands End, England. The incident marked the surrender of the first U-boat after the end of combat in Europe.

10 MAY • In a crash program to counter Japanese MXY7 *Ohka* (Cherry Blossom) Model 11 flying bombs, the Naval Aircraft Modification Unit received authorization to develop a ship-to-air guided missile—dubbed Little Joe—powered by a standard JATO unit.

19 MAY • The Office of Research and Inventions was established in the Office of the Secretary of the Navy to coordinate and disseminate to all bureaus full information with respect to all naval research, experimental, test, and developmental activities. The office also supervised and administered all Navy Department action relating to patents, inventions, trademarks, copyrights, and royalty payments. The directive transferred the Naval Research Laboratory and the Special Devices Division of BUAER to the newly established office.

28 MAY • The Commander, Kodiak Sector, Alaskan Sea Frontier, dispatched three PBYs from Fleet Air Wing 1 and one Catalina from NAS Kodiak via Anchorage to Fairbanks to assist in evacuating people threatened by rising floodwaters of the Yukon River. The Catalinas returned from their humanitarian mission on 31 May.

5 JUNE • Off Okinawa, a typhoon struck the Third Fleet, Adm. William F. Halsey Jr. commanding. The heavy seas damaged 36 ships including *Hornet* (CV 12), *Bennington* (CV 20), *Belleau Wood* (CVL 24), *San Jacinto* (CVL 30), *Windham Bay* (CVE 92), *Salamaua* (CVE 96), *Bougainville* (CVE 100), and *Attu* (CVE 102). Inadequate weather reporting and communications hampered the admirals' responses; however, a court of inquiry found Halsey, Vice Adm. John S. McCain, and Rear Adms. Donald B. Beary and Joseph J. Clark negligent in their implementation of precautions learned as a result of the 18 December 1944 typhoon, noting a "remarkable similarity between the situations, actions and results" of the admirals concerning the two storms.

5 JUNE • Orders resulting from the end of the war in Europe called for the disestablishment of 4 patrol wings and 23 patrol, 5 inshore patrol, and 7 composite squadrons operating in the Atlantic, and for the redeployment of 7 patrol squadrons from the Atlantic to the Pacific.

10 JUNE • Following the German surrender in Europe, Fleet Air Wing 15 departed from NAS Port Lyautey, Morocco, for NAS Norfolk, Va.

10 JUNE • During May and June, raids by PB4Y-1 Liberators, PB4Y-2 Privateers, and PBM Mariners forced Japanese ships sailing in Korean waters to operate only by night and shelter by day in small protected anchorages. On this date, PB4Y-2s of VPB-118 from Okinawa flew the first aerial minelaying mission by Privateers. The planes were to drop mines in Pusan (Busan) harbor to drive Japanese vessels into the open sea to facilitate attacks against them and to overextend Japanese minesweeping efforts. Heavy flak from enemy warships in Tsushima Strait persuaded aircrews to shift their minelaying to the coastal waters between Seigan-To and Shinchi-To. The raids continued through 1 July with varying degrees of success.

12 JUNE • The Tenth Fleet was disestablished.

13 JUNE • A ramjet engine produced power in supersonic flight in a test conducted by the Applied Physics Laboratory at Island Beach, N.J. A booster of four 5-inch high-velocity aircraft rockets launched the ramjet unit that flew a range of 11,000 yards.

15 JUNE • Fleet Airship Wing 2 was disestablished at NAS Richmond, Fla.

15 JUNE • Experimental Squadrons XVF-200 and XVJ-25 were established at NAS Brunswick, Maine. The squadrons provided flight facilities for evaluating and testing tactics, procedures, and equipment for use in special defense tasks under the direct operational control of COMINCH, particularly those concerned with defense against Japanese suicide planes.

16 JUNE • Naval Air Test Center, Patuxent River was established to be responsible for the aviation test functions formerly assigned to NAS Patuxent River, Md.

20 JUNE • Task Group 12.4, Rear Adm. Ralph E. Jennings commanding, including *Lexington* (CV 16), *Hancock* (CV 19), and *Cowpens* (CVL 25), sailed from NS Pearl Harbor, Hawaiian Islands, to Leyte, Philippines. On this date, Jennings launched five strikes against Japanese positions on Wake Island, marking the fifth carrier raid there since the Japanese overran the island.

27 JUNE • Fleet Air Wing 16 was disestablished at Recife, Brazil.

30 JUNE • Three escort carriers of Task Group 78.4, Rear Adm. William D. Sample commanding, supported landings by the Australian 7th Division at Balikpapan, Borneo, in the Netherlands East Indies (Indonesia). On 1 July, the Australians landed and, through 3 July, the carriers launched close air support missions, local combat air patrols, and strikes against Japanese installations.

10 JULY • Task Force 38, Vice Adm. John S. McCain commanding, initially composed of 14 carriers, launched a series of raids against Japanese airfields, ships, and installations from Kyūshū to Hokkaido, Japan. A replenishment group and an antisubmarine group each included escort carriers. After 16 July, Task Force 37, Vice Adm. Sir H. Bernard Rawlings, RN, commanding, including British carriers *Victorious* (38), *Formidable* (67), and *Implacable* (86) reinforced the Americans. *Indefatigable* (10) arrived eight days later.

The attack began with strikes on airfields in the Tōkyō plains area. The Japanese camouflage and dispersal of most of their aircraft reduced the aerial opposition encountered but also diminished the results obtained. On 14 and 15 July, harsh weather compelled the shift of attacks to airfields, vessels, and rail targets in northern Honshū and Hokkaido. These strikes wrought havoc with the vital shipment of coal across the Tsugaru Strait. On 17 July, the planes returned to bomb targets around Tōkyō, and night combat air patrols of planes from *Bon Homme Richard* (CV 31) protected U.S. and British ships that bombarded the industrialized Mito-Hitachi area of Honshū. The following day, the carriers launched aircraft against the naval station at Yokosuka and airfields near Tōkyō, sinking eight Japanese ships including training cruiser *Kasuga* and escort destroyer *Yaezakura*, and damaging five vessels including battleship *Nagato*. On 19 July, planes damaged battleship *Haruna* and carriers *Amagi* and *Katsuragi*.

13 JULY • Capt. Ralph S. Barnaby, commanding officer of the Johnsville Naval Aircraft Modification Unit, Pa., reported to BUAER that an LBD-1 Gargoyle air-to-surface missile completed five satisfactory runs in a series of 14 test flights including two at service weight.

14 JULY • Fleet Air Wing 12 was disestablished at NAS Key West, Fla.

14 JULY • Commander Fleet Air Wing 7 embarked on board seaplane tender *Albemarle* (AV 5) at Avonmouth, England, to transfer the wing's headquarters to NAS Norfolk, Va.

14 JULY • Commander Fleet Air Wing 1, embarked on board seaplane tender *Norton Sound* (AV 11), set up the wing's headquarters at Chimu Wan, Okinawa, and directed patrol plane operations over the East China Sea, Yellow Sea, and Japanese coastal waters from there until the end of the war.

15 JULY • Fleet Airship Wing 4 was disestablished at Recife, Brazil.

18 JULY • *Wasp* (CV 18) returned to action after repairs and overhaul by launching air strikes against Japanese targets on Wake Island, marking the sixth carrier raid there since the Japanese overran the island.

19 JULY • Fleet Air Wing 9 was disestablished at NAS New York, N.Y.

20 JULY • A rocket-propelled surface-to-air missile dubbed Little Joe made two successful flights at the Applied Physics Laboratory at Johns Hopkins University test station, Island Beach, N.J.

20 JULY • Fleet airborne electronics training units were established to train airborne early warning sailors in the theory, operation, and maintenance of their equipment.

20 JULY • The first of 16 PB-1W Flying Fortresses began training operations with the establishment of VPB-101 at NAS Willow Grove, Pa., under Project Cadillac II. Japanese suicide plane attacks convinced the Navy of the need for aircraft of adequate range and size to operate as flying combat information centers for airborne early warning

Planes of the Third Fleet savage Japanese ships at Kure during a sweep along the Inland Sea of Japan, July 1945.

and air control. The introduction of the modified bombers initiated the Navy's contribution toward what later became airborne warning and control systems (AWACS).

24 JULY • Task Force 38, Vice Adm. John S. McCain commanding, attacked Japanese airfields and shipping along the Inland Sea and northern Kyūshū, supported by USAAF long-range strikes. Carrier planes flew 1,747 sorties and sank 21 ships including battleship-carrier *Hyūga*, heavy cruiser *Tone*, training cruiser *Iwate*, and target ship *Settsu*, and damaged 17 vessels. The carriers repeated the sweep on 25, 28, and 30 July. Also, on 28 July, planes struck targets between Nagoya and northern Kyūshū. Ships sunk included battleship *Haruna*, battleship-carrier *Ise*, training ship *Izumo*, heavy cruiser *Aoba*, light cruiser *Oyodo*, escort destroyer *Nashi*, submarine *I-404*, and submarine depot ship *Komahashi*. Additional vessels sustained damage.

Task Force 32, Rear Adm. Jesse B. Oldendorf commanding, including four escort carriers, covered minesweeping operations in the East China Sea. Planes attacked vessels off the mouth of the Yangtze River but failed to locate lucrative targets. On 29 July, night combat air patrols and spotters from *Bon Homme Richard* (CV 31) supported U.S. and British ships during a two-day bombardment of Hamamatsu, Honshū.

On 1 August, the carriers sailed southward to evade a typhoon. They launched raids on 9 and 10 August against the Honshū-Hokkaido area and, on 13 August, against Tōkyō. These raids were intended to defeat enemy attempts to concentrate planes for further suicide attacks and to repel an Allied invasion. On 15 August, Commander Third Fleet Adm. William F. Halsey Jr. announced the end of the war. McCain cancelled follow-up strikes and recalled the attackers. The first raid of the day had hit Tōkyō and 15 to 20 Japanese fighters intercepted six F6Fs of VF-88, embarked on board *Yorktown* (CV 10), over an airfield at Tokurozama. The Americans claimed nine enemy planes and lost four Hellcats. The second wave approached the coastline, but heeded McCain's recall, jettisoned their ordnance and returned.

24 JULY • Marine planes flying from *Vella Gulf* (CVE 111) attacked Japanese positions on Pagan Island in the Mariana Islands, and two days later hit Rota in the same island group.

28 JULY • Fleet Air Wing 15 was disestablished at NAS Norfolk, Va.

1 AUGUST • Task Group 12.3 including *Cabot* (CVL 28) bombed and bombarded Wake Island. This was the seventh carrier raid there since the island fell to the Japanese on 23 December 1941.

4 AUGUST • Fleet Air Wing 7 was disestablished at NAS Norfolk, Va.

6 AUGUST • *Intrepid* (CV 11) sailed en route from NS Pearl Harbor, Hawaiian Islands, to Task Force 38 off Japan. On this date, she launched a strike against Japanese installations on Wake Island, marking the eighth carrier raid on the island since it fell to the Japanese.

6 AUGUST • Task Group 95.3, Rear Adm. Calvin T. Durgin commanding, including *Makin Island* (CVE 93), *Lunga Point* (CVE 94), and *Cape Gloucester* (CVE 109), covered cruisers operating in the East China Sea by launching raids on Japanese vessels in the harbor at Tinghai (Qinghai), China.

9 AUGUST • Naval aviator Cmdr. Frederick L. Ashworth participated in dropping the second atomic bomb, *Fat Man*, on the Japanese from a USAAF Boeing B-29 Superfortress named *Bockscar*. Ashworth had supervised and coordinated the field tests of the bomb. Dense smoke rising from a bombing raid two days previously shrouded the original target of Kokura and the strike diverted to the secondary target of Nagasaki on Kyūshū.

14 AUGUST • Japan accepted the terms of unconditional surrender and the Allies celebrated V-J (Victory in Japan) Day—15 August in the Western Pacific. On 27 August, ships of the Third Fleet, Adm. William F. Halsey Jr. commanding, steamed into Sagami Wan outside the entrance to Tōkyō Bay, Japan. Aircraft carriers launched reconnaissance missions over the Japanese homeland from outside the bay. On 2 September, the Japanese formally surrendered on board battleship *Missouri* (BB 63) in Tōkyō Bay. During the final carrier actions of World War II, naval aviation claimed the destruction of 1,223 Japanese aircraft, including more than 1,000 on the ground, and sank 285,000 tons of shipping.

21 AUGUST • The Asiatic Wing, Naval Air Transport Service, was established at NAS Oakland, Calif., Capt. Carl F. Luethi commanding. The service operated and maintained air transport support of establishments and units in the Western Pacific and Asiatic theaters. Early in September, the wing's headquarters was established on Samar, Philippines, and on 15 November shifted to NAB Agana, Guam.

10 SEPTEMBER • *Midway* (CVB 41), Capt. Joseph F. Bolger commanding, was commissioned as the first of the 45,000-ton class aircraft carriers at Newport News, Va.

11 SEPTEMBER • Operation Magic Carpet commenced the return of servicemembers from the war zones by ships and aircraft.

3 OCTOBER • BUAER established the Committee to Evaluate the Feasibility of Space Rocketry as an initial attempt to establish an earth satellite program. On 29 October, the committee recommended the introduction of detailed studies to determine the feasibility of an earth satellite vehicle. The proposal led BUAER to issue contracts to one university and three companies for theoretical study and preliminary design of a launch vehicle, and for determining by actual test the specific impulse of high-energy fuels including liquid hydrogen.

10 OCTOBER • The reorganization of the Office of Chief of Naval Operations included the establishment of four new deputy chiefs for personnel, administration, operations, and logistics on the same level as the existing Deputy CNO (Air). The reorganization occurred by direction of the Secretary of the Navy and in accord with an executive order, and abolished COMINCH and transferred command of the operating forces to CNO.

17 OCTOBER • The basic aircraft type designation system received the addition of the letter K for pilotless aircraft to replace the previous class designation VK. Classes A, G, and S, within the type were assigned for pilotless aircraft intended for attack against aircraft, ground targets, and ships, respectively.

27 OCTOBER • *Franklin D. Roosevelt* (CVB 42) was commissioned at New York Naval Shipyard, N.Y., Capt. Apollo Soucek commanding. The event marked the first exception to the traditional naming of fleet carriers for battles or famous ships.

1 NOVEMBER • The reorganization of the Naval Air Training Command included the assignment of its headquarters to NAS Pensacola, Fla., and the following subordinate commands: Naval Air Advanced Training, Naval Air Basic Training, Naval Air Technical Training, and the newly formed Naval Air Reserve Training. By this change, the titles Naval Air Operational Training and Naval Air Intermediate Training ceased to exist, and basic training or the reserve program absorbed the facilities of the former Naval Air Primary Training Command.

5 NOVEMBER • Ens. Jake C. West of VF-41, embarked for carrier qualifications on board *Wake Island* (CVE 65), lost power in the forward radial engine of an FR-1 Fireball shortly after take-off. The mishap compelled him to start his aft jet engine and he returned to the ship to make the first jet landing on board a carrier.

15 NOVEMBER • A Soviet fighter attacked a PBM-5 Mariner about 25 miles south of Port Arthur (Darien), Manchuria. The PBM investigating six Soviet transports and a beached seaplane in the Gulf of Chihli in the Yellow Sea escaped without damage.

29 NOVEMBER • The Special Weapons Test and Tactical Evaluation Unit was redesignated Pilotless Aircraft Unit. In December, it shifted to MCAS Mojave, Calif., receiving direction to operate detachments as necessary at NAF Point Mugu, Calif.

1 DECEMBER • Fleet Air Wing 6 was disestablished at NAS Whidbey Island, Wash.

5 DECEMBER • At 1410, Lt. Charles C. Taylor, USNR, of VTB-1 led Flight 19, consisting of five Avengers—TBM-1Cs BuNos 45714, 46325, and 73209; TBM-1E, 46094; and TBM-3, 23307—on an overwater navigation training mission from NAS Ft. Lauderdale, Fla. Within two hours Ft. Lauderdale intercepted messages between the planes that indicated the flight was lost in the vicinity of the Bahamas. At about 1800, an approximate high frequency direction-finder fix placed 23307 within a 100-mile radius of 29°15′N, 79°00′W. Lt. j.g. Walter G. Jeffrey of VPB-2 ATU-3 piloted a search PBM-5, BuNo 59225, from NAS Banana River, Fla., but the Mariner also vanished. A search-and-rescue operation to 10 December failed to recover wreckage, the 14 men from the Avengers, or the 13 of the Mariner. The mysterious losses occurred near an area subject to atmospheric variances, which later became popularly known as the "Bermuda Triangle," although the likely explanation stems from a combination of navigational errors and fuel exhaustion.

28 DECEMBER • President Harry S. Truman directed the transfer of the Coast Guard from the operational control of the Navy and its return to the jurisdiction of the Treasury Department.

CHAPTER 6

The Cold War

1946–1949

The problems of demobilization, organizational readjustment, and the tense beginning of the Cold War highlighted the years following World War II. Six years of waging the bloodiest war hitherto endured by man had exhausted the warring powers and brought the wartime alliance system to collapse. Two superpowers emerged into the ensuing void, the United States–led Western alliance and the Soviet-dominated Eastern Bloc, and their struggle for world mastery overshadowed the second half of the century.

American demobilization proceeded rapidly. Sailors and Marines placed ships and submarines into "mothballs" and aircraft into storage, even as shore stations at home and abroad deactivated. Within a year after the end of hostilities, the on-board figures for the men and women who comprised naval aviation fell to a quarter of the peak wartime strength. Only a skeleton of the force remained to carry out the new operational demands that arose.

The unsettled international situation raised familiar problems for the Navy. Fleet elements assigned to areas for the purpose of supporting occupation forces began to receive the additional yet familiar task of supporting the nation's policy in areas on opposite sides of the world. A task force built around an operational average of one to two carriers sailed into the Mediterranean, and as the years passed, the force became a fixture there. A similar force in the western Pacific provided the same tangible symbol of U.S. might and determination to support the free peoples of the world.

The organizational readjustment of naval aviation took place at several levels. At the upper echelons, problems ensued from the adjustment of a new departmental organization formed by what was, in effect, a compromise agreement. At the bureau and office level, the Navy dealt with the problems related to reducing staffs and realigning the functional elements of technical and administrative units to meet new requirements.

The fleet experienced problems of transition, partly in size, but particularly in regard to weapons and tactics developed as a result of combat experience or from technological advances. The introduction of jet aircraft posed special problems for carrier operations, and their employment renewed the dilemma that, as navies developed increased capability aircraft, they encountered the additional challenge of finding the means of taking them to sea.

These changes occurred at an ever accelerating rate. Technological and scientific advances built rapidly upon each other, and newer and greater advances superseded existing designs. New concepts included guided missiles, which had been introduced during World War II but were still in their embryonic development and, therefore, required additional efforts in all areas—from design through operational deployment. The need to complete this transition without a temporary loss of combat effectiveness increased the degree of difficulty.

A constant readjustment in planning, the continual adaptation of force organization, and the repeated revision of tactical doctrine highlighted this period. Urgency existed, largely accelerated by an appreciation of the destructive power that had been unleashed in the New Mexico desert in 1945 by the explosion of the atomic bomb. In other respects, however, the period appeared much like a repetition of the 1920s. Leaders and journalists clamored for a separate air force and for a merger of the services, which occurred by unifying them first, in 1947, under the National Military Establishment and then, in 1949, under the Department of Defense. The study of aviation and of the national air policy by a presidential commission and a congressional committee proved reminiscent of the Morrow Board and Lampert Committee of 1925. Despite infighting, the services reluctantly agreed on their respective missions and functions.

The armed forces also disputed their respective roles as they sought sufficient shares of a decreasing budget,

428458

Essex (CV 9)-class carriers mothballed at Puget Sound, Wash.

and their chiefs raised old charges of duplication. Critics of naval power renewed their declaration of navies as obsolete in the atomic era, and they shifted their derision from battleships to aircraft carriers by citing the ships' expense and vulnerabilities. Opponents claimed that the capabilities of aircraft carriers to perform atomic missions duplicated effort and that their value for conventional warfighting was too limited to warrant continued existence. Those who supported carriers retaliated with criticism of the Strategic Air Command's Convair B-36 long-range bombers as being equally vulnerable, expensive, and unable to fulfill their allotted roles in national defense.

During the height of this controversy, Secretary of Defense Louis A. Johnson canceled *United States* (CVA 58), designed to carry Navy long-range attack planes, while under construction. Secretary of the Navy John L. Sullivan resigned in protest. Journalists labeled this "The Revolt of the Admirals," even as the Air Force publicly attempted to tell the Navy how to carry out its mission and what tools the sea service needed to accomplish its tasks. Congressional hearings ended the dispute. The outbreak of the Korean War in June 1950 generated more immediate problems, but provided a greater national appreciation of the necessity for adequate military forces in an era when communist aggression endangered the survival of the free world.

1946

2 JANUARY • Fleet Air Wing 17 was disestablished in Japan.

26 JANUARY • The Naval Aviation Ordnance Test Station was established at NAAS Chincoteague, Va., under the cognizance of the Bureau of Ordnance and under the air station for administration and logistic support. The establishment order also provided for the transfer of all Bureau of Ordnance guided missile test facilities and staff from Johnsville, Pa., to perform tests and modifications as necessary to develop aviation ordnance and guided missiles at the new location.

Carrier qualification trials of jet and piston engine–propelled FR-1 Fireballs take place on board *Ranger* (CV 4), May 1945.

1 FEBRUARY • A major reorganization of the Bureau of Aeronautics aligned the technical divisions into two groups—Research Development and Engineering and Material and Services—according to function. An additional assistant chief was established over each group and the former assistant chief, and their staff divisions strengthened by the reorganization and their title of deputy and assistant chief.

1 MARCH • *Midway* (CVB 41), Rear Adm. John H. Cassady commanding, sailed from Norfolk, Va., for Operation Frostbite— weather tests. From 7 to 22 March, the task force operated in the Davis Strait, off the coast of Labrador, and above the Arctic Circle. The expedition carried out flight operations with World War II–type aircraft, newer F8F Bearcats, the combination prop-and-jet FR-1 Fireballs, and HNS-1 Hoverfly helicopters.

2 MARCH • Chief of Naval Operations Fleet Adm. Chester W. Nimitz established an aircraft storage program to stockpile up to 6,000 aircraft of operational types against future needs, together with the preparation of an additional 360 F6F-5 Hellcats for future conversion to drones.

The F8F Bearcat was designed as an interceptor.

705452

An F6F-5 Hellcat (BuNo 94409) launches a Tiny Tim rocket during testing at NAF China Lake, Calif., 6 November 1945.

402800

Submarine *Carbonero* (SS 337) launches a Loon guided missile adapted from the German V-1 rocket, 1949.

5 MARCH • Secretary of the Navy James V. Forrestal approved the conversion of two submarines into guided-missile launching vessels. The two later selected for this conversion were *Carbonero* (SS 337) and *Cusk* (SS 348).

7 MARCH • The Chief of Naval Operations directed the adoption of ground-controlled approach equipment as the standard blind landing system for the Navy.

11 MARCH • A modification of the class designation of naval aircraft eliminated the VB and VT used for bomber and torpedo aircraft, and created VA to identify aircraft with a primary mission of attacking surface targets. This change was responsible for the subsequent redesignation of BT2D and BTM aircraft as AD and AM, respectively.

12 MARCH • In a reorientation and consolidation of Navy guided-missile developments, the Chief of Naval Operations Fleet Adm. Chester W. Nimitz directed the discontinuance of the development of Glombs, Gorgon II-Cs, and Little Joes; limiting Gargoyles, Gorgon II-As, Gorgon III-As, and Doves to test and research vehicles; the continuance of Loons as launching test vehicles and possible interim weapons; the continuance of Kingfishers, Bumblebees, and Larks as high-priority missiles, and the completion of SWOD (Special Weapons Ordnance Device) Mark 9 Bats.

15 MARCH • The Bureau of Aeronautics chief formally proposed to the commanding general of the USAAF the establishment of a joint Army-Navy project to develop an earth satellite.

15 MARCH • Coast Guard aircraft scouted for ice and determined the limits of the ice field from the air during the first Coast Guard aerial patrols of the International Ice Patrol through 27 July 1946.

25 MARCH • The first twin-engine XHJD-1 helicopter, BuNo 43318, made a hovering flight. McDonnell Aircraft Corp. designed the helicopter for experimental use in a flight development program, and for tactical use in utility and air-sea rescue operations.

3 APRIL • Douglas received a contract for the design and construction of the XF3D-1 night fighter.

15 MAY • The designation of patrol squadrons reverted to their prewar status and changed back from VPB to VP.

21 MAY • Chief of Naval Operations Fleet Adm. Chester W. Nimitz outlined a program for the operational introduction of Bat missiles that called for their assignment to VP-104 in the Atlantic Fleet. He also directed the transfer to VP-104 of all PB4Y-2 Privateers already modified to operate Bats.

22 MAY • The initial operational tests of an XCF dunking sonar carried in an HO2S-1 concluded off NAS Key West, Fla. During three months of testing, Lt. Stewart R. Graham, USCG, and Ens. William H. Coffee, USCG, piloted the helicopter, and Lt. Cmdr. Roy Rather, J. J. Coop, and C. V. Scott operated the sonar. The XCF provided good sonic and supersonic listening ranges and a high degree of bearing accuracy against both conventional and snorkel-type submarines.

29 MAY • The Aeronautical Board acted upon a BUAER proposal for a joint Army-Navy earth satellite project by approving the establishment of an earth satellite subcommittee to coordinate projects already underway.

In the emergent helicopter technologies of the mid- to late-1940s, the lone XHJD-1 with its lateral twin-rotor configuration was designed to compete with tandem rotor designs.

The first production tailless F7U-1 Cutlass runs through its paces with the Naval Air Test Center, Patuxent River, Md., c. August 1950.

6 JUNE • A charter of the Secretaries of War and Navy created the Joint Research and Development Board for coordinating all research and development activities of joint interest to the two departments. Its several committees embraced aeronautics, atomic energy, electronics, geographical exploration, geophysical sciences, and guided missiles.

24 JUNE • North American Aviation, Inc. received a defense contract for the design and construction of three XAJ-1 aircraft, thereby beginning active development of a long-range carrier-based bomber capable of delivering nuclear weapons.

25 JUNE • The Navy issued a contract to Chance Vought for the development and construction of three tailless, high performance XF7U-1 carrier fighter prototypes powered by twin turbojet engines.

26 JUNE • The Aeronautical Board agreed unanimously on the adoption of the knot and the nautical mile by the USAAF and Navy as standard aeronautical units of speed and distance, and directed the specification of the use of the terms in all future procurement of air speed indicators, charts, related equipment, and future issues of applicable handbooks and technical orders.

1 JULY • Operation Crossroads began—a series of tests to determine the effects of atomic bombs on naval targets at Bikini Atoll in the Pacific. In the first—Test Able—a Boeing B-29 Superfortress dropped a Nagasaki-type bomb from 30,000 feet aimed at battleship *Nevada* (BB 36) centered amid 82 other ships of all classes anchored in the lagoon. The bomb missed its intended target, but the ensuing detonation sank five vessels outright and heavily damaged nine others.

On 25 July a shallow underwater burst, designated Test Baker, sent water nearly 6,000 feet into the air and raised the total number of vessels sunk directly or indirectly to 32. *Saratoga* (CV 3), with 19 years of active service, sank in shallow water and, on 28 August, *Independence* (CVL 22), which received severe damage and contamination that rendered her unfit for use, was decommissioned.

These tests had a broad national impact on the Navy and on naval aviation and made clear the importance of atomic weapons for control of the sea. In addition, the evaluations provided detailed data on the effects of atomic blasts and a sound technical basis for intensification of efforts to develop tactics and equipment to minimize the damage of such attacks against naval task forces.

1 JULY • The Naval Air Reserve Program was activated under the Naval Air Training Command with 21 reserve activities already in operation.

1 JULY • VX-3 was established at NAS New York, N.Y. The squadron studied and evaluated the adaptability of helicopters to naval purposes.

3 JULY • Fleet Air Wing 8 was disestablished at NAS Alameda, Calif.

11 JULY • To create clear-cut relationships for aircraft maintenance, Chief of Naval Operations Fleet Adm. Chester W. Nimitz directed the disestablishment of all carrier aircraft service units (CASU) and other maintenance units, and their replacement by fleet aircraft service squadrons (FASRON) by 1 January. According to the aircraft types serviced, FASRONs comprised three kinds of squadrons. These new organizations were designed to promote higher standards, uniformity, and efficiency in aircraft maintenance.

13 JULY • Eight specially modified aircraft—two SOC-1 and one each SOC-2 and -3 Seagulls, three PBM-5 Mariners, and an HNS-1 Hoverfly—embarked on board seaplane tender *Norton Sound* (AV 11), netlayer *Whitewood* (AN 63), cargo ships *Alcona* (AK 157) and *Beltrami* (AK 162), and Coast Guard icebreaker *Northwind* (AG 278), at Norfolk, Va. The ships sailed to operating areas north of the Arctic Circle for cold weather testing designated Project Nanook. The aircraft scouted ahead of the ships for icebergs, pack ice, and other hazards to navigation, and conducted photoreconnaissance of the coastline. On 18 September, the vessels returned to Virginia waters.

21 JULY • In the first U.S. test of the adaptability of jet aircraft to shipboard operation, Lt. Cmdr. James J. Davidson made successful landings and takeoffs (non-catapulted deck launches) in an XFD-1 Phantom on board *Franklin D. Roosevelt* (CVB 42).

1 AUGUST • An act of Congress established the Office of Naval Research to plan, foster, and encourage scientific investigation. The redesignation of the earlier Office of Research and Inventions, which had been established by secretarial order in May 1945, enabled the new office to open on 21 August.

8 AUGUST • *Franklin D. Roosevelt* (CVB 42) sailed to the Mediterranean. From 5 to 9 September, the ship called at Piraeus (Athens) as a show of support for the Greek government's efforts to stem the tide of communism in the embattled country, and launched 78 aircraft over the task force during her departure. On 30 September, President Harry S. Truman declared the permanency of the U.S. naval presence in the region, primarily to contain Soviet aggression. On 4 October, the carrier returned home.

1053757

Lt. Cmdr. James J. Davidson, in front of the second XFD-1 prototype after completion of the first carrier tests of a pure-jet aircraft on board *Franklin D. Roosevelt* (CVB 42), 21 July 1946.

13 AUGUST • Congress approved the Hale Plan, also known as the Flying Midshipmen or Aviation Midshipmen Program. This was designed to provide the Navy with qualified pilots in the post–World War II period after the loss of a large segment of experienced naval aviators to civilian life. The plan would pay for two years of college and training as naval aviators in exchange for a service obligation. Those who completed flight training and were designated naval aviators did not automatically commission at the same time, but remained as aviation midshipman and served as pilots but not commissioned officers. After a period of service in the fleet, they usually received their commissions. Early in 1950 the Naval Aviation Cadet program replaced the Flying Midshipmen program. Of the 3,000 aviation midshipmen, approximately 1,800 received designations as naval aviators including later-astronaut Neil A. Armstrong, the first man to walk on the moon. The Navy recalled many aviation midshipmen to active service during the Korean War.

14 AUGUST • Chief of Naval Operations Fleet Adm. Chester W. Nimitz standardized missile terminology within the Navy to the extent that he directed the use of the term "guided missiles" for all types developed by the sea service. He allowed past practice by authorizing the continuation of model designations, the description of missile classes, the Bureau of Ordnance term SWOD (Special Weapons Ordnance Device), and the Bureau of Aeronautics term pilotless aircraft (P/A).

15 AUGUST • The Instrument Flight Standardization Board was established under the operational control of the Deputy Chief of Naval Operations (Air), at NAS Anacostia, D.C. The board was to determine the means to improve the instrument flight proficiency of pilots.

1 SEPTEMBER • A reorganization of the Office of the Deputy Chief of Naval Operations (Air) placed its divisions into four groups entitled plans, personnel, readiness, and air logistics. The Air Planning Group was also set up on the DCNO (Air) staff to facilitate planning at the top policy level and to coordinate and direct the work of all divisions toward the same goals.

18 SEPTEMBER • A Belgian Sabena Airlines DC-4 registered OO-CBG, carrying seven crewmembers and 37 passengers en route from Brussels, Belgium, to New York, crashed during harsh weather 24 miles southwest of Gander, Newfoundland. Rescue Officer Eastern Area Capt. Richard L. Burke, USCG, organized the rescue. Lt. Cmdr. James N. Schrader, USCG, piloted a Coast Guard PBY-5A Catalina, BuNo 34008, carrying the helicopter pilots over the scene of

USCG

These crews of two Coast Guard helicopters rescued 18 survivors of a commercial airliner crash on 18 September 1946 from a remote area near Gander, Newfoundland. From left are: Lts. A. N. Fisher and Stewart R. Graham; AMMCs Oliver F. Berry, Leo Brzycki, and Cozy Eldridge; and AMM1 Merwin Westerberg.

the crash from Argentia, Newfoundland. On 20 September, a USAAF C-54 Skymaster carried an HOS-1 overnight to Gander from CGAS Brooklyn, N.Y. A second Skymaster flew an HNS-1 Hoverfly from CGAS Elizabeth City, N.C. Coast Guard helicopter crewmembers included pilots Cmdr. Frank A. Erickson, Lts. A. N. Fisher, Stewart R. Graham, August Kleisch, and Walter C. Bolton, and aircrewmen AMMCs Oliver F. Berry, Leo Brzycki, and Cozy Eldridge, and AMM1 Merwin Westerberg. These Coast Guardsmen rescued 18 survivors during 40 helicopter evacuation flights. At times, Cmdr. Larry L. David, USCG, flew an additional PBY-5A, BuNo 48314, and Lt. j.g. Charles E. MacDowell, USCG, piloted one of two PB-1Gs, BuNo 77247 (the other was 77249), that searched for survivors and dropped food and medical provisions.

29 SEPTEMBER • Cmdrs. Thomas D. Davies, Eugene P. Rankin, and Walter S. Reid, and Lt. Cmdr. Roy H. Tabeling manned the *Truculent Turtle*, a P2V-1 Neptune, BuNo 89082, during a 55 hour, 17 minute flight from Perth, Australia, to Columbus, Ohio. The plane arrived on 1 October after a journey of 11,235.6 miles, breaking the world distance record for unrefueled flight.

1 OCTOBER • The Naval Air Missile Test Center, Capt. Albert N. Perkins commanding, was established at Point Mugu, Calif., to conduct tests and evaluation of guided missiles and their components.

2 OCTOBER • The Bureau of Aeronautics recommended adoption of the designation XF9F-2 in lieu of XF9F-1,

The Truculent Turtle's record flight stood for 16 years.

thereby reflecting a decision to abandon development of the four-engine night fighter in favor of a single-engine day fighter. The decision included the substitution of a British Rolls Royce Nene engine for Westinghouse 24Cs and subsequently led to U.S. production of Nene engines.

27 OCTOBER • Airship XM-1, Lt. Harold R. Walton commanding, departed NAS Lakehurst, N.J., followed the Atlantic coast to Savannah, Ga., headed seaward to the Bahamas, then to Florida, Cuba, across the Gulf of Mexico, and, on 3 November, reached NAF Glynco, Ga. The flight of 170.3 hours set a world record for duration in self-sufficient flight for any type of aircraft.

30 OCTOBER • Under a project conducted by Naval Air Material Center Philadelphia, Pa., Lt. j.g. Adolph J. Furtek made a successful ejection from a JD-1 Invader flying at about 250 knots at 6,000 feet over NAS Lakehurst, N.J. The event marked the Navy's first live test of an ejection seat.

7 NOVEMBER • The Navy adopted a letter identification system for marking all Navy and Marine aircraft including trainers and those of the Naval Air Reserve. All carriers and wings, groups, and squadrons not assigned to carrier operations received letter assignments. Instructions further placed a wide

Cmdr. Thomas D. Davies commanded the P2V-1 *Truculent Turtle* during an unrefueled long-distance record flight of 11,235 miles from Perth, Australia, to Columbus, Ohio, 29 September to 1 October 1946.

419472

The AD-2 Skyraider was just one of seven major models and 28 versions of Douglas' attack aircraft. More than 3,000 were built over its 12-year production run, 1945–1957.

orange stripe around the fuselage, forward of the empennage, on all aircraft of the Naval Reserve. A change issued on 12 December discontinued the assignment of letters to carriers; carrier air groups and Marine squadrons operating on board escort aircraft carriers received the letter assignments instead.

8 NOVEMBER • The Office of the Deputy Chief of Naval Operations (Special Weapons) was disestablished, and its functions relating to guided missiles were reassigned to a new Assistant Chief of Naval Operations (Guided Missiles) and a Guided Missiles Division, both established under DCNO (Air).

11 NOVEMBER • Lt. Col. Marion E. Carl Jr., USMC, completed two catapult launches, four free take-offs, and five arrested landings in a jet propelled Lockheed P-80A Shooting Star on board *Franklin D. Roosevelt* (CVB 42) off the Virginia Capes. Carl made the first catapult launches on 1 November. These operations comprised part of an extensive investigation of the carrier suitability of jet aircraft that began on 29 June 1945 with the delivery of a P-80A to NAS Patuxent River, Md.

15 NOVEMBER • Sweeping changes occurred in air unit designations to correct the results of demobilization that left squadron numbers out of sequence. Carrier air groups of four types received designations according to their assigned ship: CVBG–battle carrier; CVG–attack carrier; CVLG–light carrier; and CVEG–escort carrier. The action limited carrier squadrons to fighter and attack and thus abolished the VBF, VB, and VT designations, and these squadrons received suffix letters to indicate their carrier assignments. Patrol squadrons were redesignated to show an abbreviation of their aircraft class in addition to the VP (i.e. VP-MS-1 for Patrol Squadron 1 that operated medium seaplanes). Observation squadron numbers followed the parent ship division but received the addition of the suffix letters B or C to differentiate between battleship and cruiser units. The VJ for utility became VU, VPP replaced the VD for photographic squadrons, and VPM replaced VPW for meteorological squadrons. Reserve units switched to the same system but received consecutive numbers of a higher series. The changes did not affect Marine Corps commands.

20 NOVEMBER • Lt. Cmdr. Merl W. Davenport took off in an F8F Bearcat in a distance of 115 feet from a standing start and climbed to 10,000 feet in 94 seconds at Cleveland, Ohio, to set an unofficial world record.

25 NOVEMBER • The Navy approved a report of a board headed by Rear Adm. Thomas S. Combs established to consider the steps required to adapt the Integrated

Aeronautic Maintenance, Material, and Supply Program to postwar conditions. The board's recommendations largely concerned improved program administration measures to provide for exact planning, rigid adherence to schedules and complements, the receipt of complete information from the field, and its proper evaluation. Some proposals touched on areas that were considered critical and that warranted action before their final approval.

6 DECEMBER • Capt. Victor D. Herbster (Naval Aviator No. 4) died at Naval Hospital, St. Albans, N.Y. Herbster served continuously in naval aviation from first reporting for flight training on 8 November 1911 at Annapolis, Md., until his retirement on 1 July 1936. He served again from his return to active service in August 1940 until retirement on 29 March 1946.

6 DECEMBER • VA-19A accepted delivery of the first AD-1 Skyraider for fleet service.

1947

1 JANUARY • Adm. John H. Towers (Naval Aviator No. 3) assumed the duties of the newly created post of Commander in Chief, Pacific Command.

2 JANUARY • The Navy issued a directive to display unit identification letters, which had been assigned on 15 November 1946, on both sides of the vertical fins and rudders of its aircraft, and on the upper right and lower left surfaces near the wing tips. This placement required relocation of several standard aircraft markings.

2 JANUARY • The promulgation of a new specification for aircraft color required the use of glossy Sea Blue on all shipboard and water-based aircraft and all helicopters. Landplane transports, utility aircraft, and advanced training planes retained Aluminum, and primary trainers similarly retained glossy Orange Yellow paint. Special color schemes included land camouflage (Olive Drab above and Light Gray below) for Marine observation planes, glossy Insignia Red for target drones, glossy Orange Yellow wings with glossy Sea Blue fuselages and glossy Insignia Red wing bands and rudders for target towing aircraft.

11 JANUARY • The XF2H-1 made its first flight.

14 JANUARY • A horizontal red stripe, centered on the white horizontal bar, was added to the national star insignia on all U.S. military aircraft.

15 JANUARY • Pilot Lt. James A. Cornish, USCG, and observer PhoMC Everett F. Mashburn, USCG, completed the first Coast Guard helicopter flight to the station at Little America, Antarctica. Cornish and Mashburn made the flight in an HNS-1 Hoverfly they named *Flutterbuggy* from Coast Guard cutter *Northwind* (WAG 282).

29 JANUARY • From a position 660 miles off the Antarctic continent, *Philippine Sea* (CV 47) launched the first of six R4D transport aircraft she ferried from Norfolk, Va., to Little America as part of Operation Highjump. Cmdr. William M. Hawkes piloted the first plane, which carried Rear Adm. Richard E. Byrd Jr. as a passenger. The Skytrains used JATO to takeoff, and skis attached to their landing gear facilitated ice cap operations. The event marked the first carrier takeoff for Skytrains.

2 FEBRUARY • Col. Bernard L. Smith, USMC, the second Marine aviator (Naval Aviator No. 6), died from injuries received when his car struck a train at Coral Gables, Fla. Smith served with Marine and Navy aviation elements in a variety of duties, including intelligence assignments overseas, from when he reported for flight training on 18 September 1912 at Annapolis, Md., until his resignation on 20 January 1920. From 1931 to 1937, he served as a member of the Naval Reserve, then transferred to the Marine Corps Reserve, and returned to active duty during World War II until his retirement in December 1946.

12 FEBRUARY • Submarine *Cusk* (SS 348) launched an American adaptation of the German V-1 rocket, dubbed the Loon, from off Point Mugu, Calif. The event marked the first firing of a guided missile from a U.S. submarine.

MARCH • The growing importance of maintaining strength in the Mediterranean Sea prompted the establishment of Naval Forces Eastern Atlantic and Mediterranean. On 1 June 1948, the command was redesignated the Sixth Task Fleet and, on 12 February 1950, the Sixth Fleet. The cruise of *Randolph* (CV 15)

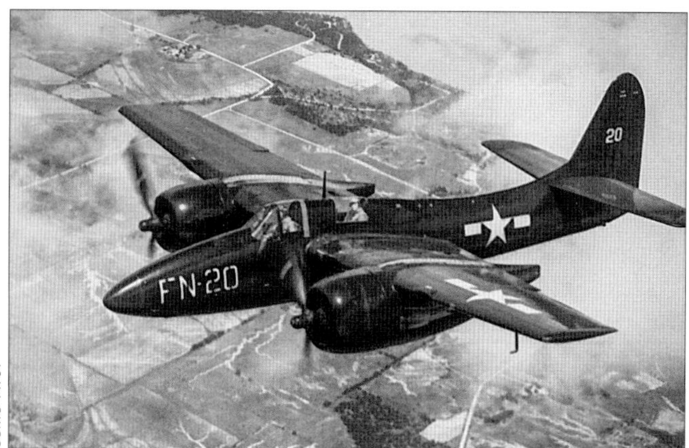

USMC 44731

This dual-seat -2N night-fighter version of the twin-engine F7F Tigercat was flown by Marines of VMF(N)-531 out of NAS Eagle Mountain Lake, Texas, in late 1945.

initiated a regular schedule of deployment of carriers to the region. She returned to the United States on 21 December.

1 MARCH • A Bureau of Aeronautics contract with P. R. Mallory & Co. initiated the development of titanium alloys for aeronautical applications. The agreement covered the study of methods of producing titanium metal and alloys and of determining their essential properties.

4 MARCH • Operation Highjump air operations in the Antarctic ended. From 24 December 1946, six PBM Mariners based on seaplane tenders operated in the open seas around the continent, and from 9 February 1947, six R4D Skytrains were based ashore at Little America. Altogether these planes logged 650 hours on photographic mapping flights that covered 150,000 square miles of the interior and 5,500 miles of coastline.

16 APRIL • On 30 January 1947, the Greeks proclaimed martial law in response to the rising threat posed by communist insurgents during the Greek Civil War. On 21 February, the British announced the reduction of their forces deployed to the eastern Mediterranean and the withdrawal of military assistance to the Greeks and Turks effective on 1 April. U.S. intervention against communist expansionism in the ensuing power vacuum included a visit on this date by *Leyte* (CV 32) to Greece as a show of support for that country's government.

30 APRIL • The Army and Navy adopted a standard system for designating guided missiles and assigning them popular names. The basic designation adopted consisted of a two-letter combination of the three letters; A (air), S (surface), and U (underwater); in which the first letter indicated the origin of the missiles and the second letter their objectives, followed by the letter M for missile. Thus, surface-to-air missiles were designated SAM. This basic designation was followed by an odd model number for Army missiles and an even number for Navy weapons. For popular names, the services agreed upon naming ASMs for birds of prey, AAMs for other winged creatures, SAMs for mythological terms, and SSMs for astronomical terms or bodies.

2 MAY • Amid ongoing Soviet pressure against the Turks and the British withdrawal from the eastern Mediterranean, U.S. ships including *Leyte* (CV 32) made a show of support for the Turkish government during a week-long visit to Istanbul.

20 MAY • Secretary of the Navy James V. Forrestal directed the relocation and redesignation of Navy Pre-Flight at NAS Ottumwa, Iowa, to Naval School, Pre-Flight, NAS Pensacola, Fla. The move was to occur from 1 June to 1 August 1947.

4 JUNE • Chief of Naval Operations Fleet Adm. Chester W. Nimitz approved new aircraft carrier characteristics for incorporation into Project 27A—a program to improve *Essex* (CV 9)-class carriers to meet new operating requirements resulting from developments in aircraft and weapons. Designers directed the principal changes toward a capability for operating aircraft of up to 40,000-pounds including the installation of two H-8 catapults, the strengthening of flight decks and the clearance of guns from these decks, an increase of elevator capacity, and the addition of special provisions for jet aircraft such as blast deflectors, increased fuel capacity, and jet fuel mixers. On 1 October 1947, *Oriskany* (CV 34) began her conversion at New York Naval Shipyard, N.Y., as the first of nine carriers scheduled for modernization under this project.

7 JUNE • Fleet Air Wing 10 was disestablished at NAB Sangley Point, Philippines.

17 JUNE • The Navy awarded a contract to the Douglas Aircraft Company for design study and engineering data for a delta wing fighter. On the basis of the technical information thus obtained, the service subsequently initiated development of the XF4D-1.

26 JUNE • The development of low-drag bombs began as the Bureau of Aeronautics authorized the design by Douglas Aircraft Company at El Segundo, Calif., of a bomb release system with clean flight characteristics at subsonic speeds. This was to overcome aircraft buffeting induced by conventional bombs when being carried externally at three-quarters the speed of sound. The basic goal was the development of an external store shape to house conventional bombs, machine guns, and rockets, and capable of adaptation for use as an external fuel tank.

30 JUNE • Fleet Air Wing 18 was disestablished at NAS Agana, Guam.

9 JULY • A Northrop P-61C Black Widow air-launched a subsonic ramjet-powered Gorgon IV (PTV-2) that made a 28-second free flight at NAMTC Point Mugu, Calif.

24 JULY • The Chief of Naval Operations initiated the adaptation of helicopters to amphibious warfare by establishing a requirement for a type capable of transporting assault troops from escort carriers, and landing them ashore with their necessary combat equipment and supplies.

26 JULY • President Harry S. Truman signed the National Security Act of 1947 into law. The measure provided the most basic reorganization of defense activities affecting the Navy Department since its creation in 1798. It established the National Security Council, Central Intelligence Agency, National Security Resources Board, and the National Military Establishment headed by the Secretary of Defense. Within the National Military Establishment, the act redesignated the War Department as the Department of the Army and established a third service, the Air Force, along with the Joint Chiefs of Staff, Research and Development Board, and Munitions Board. In addition, the act defined the Navy as "including such aviation as may be organic therein."

7 AUGUST • An act of Congress restored the Aeronautical Engineering Duty Only (AEDO) designation that had been abolished in 1940, by authorizing the assignment of qualified officers of the line including those designated EDO.

13 AUGUST • The establishment of Naval Air Development Station, Johnsville, Pa., replaced Naval Aircraft Modification Unit. The station's mission was the development of aircraft electronics, pilotless aircraft, guided missiles, and aviation armament, and research and development in the field of aviation medicine that pertained to the human centrifuge. Four appropriately named laboratories performed these functions.

704422

The D-558-1 Skystreak experimental jet was the Navy's contribution to a national program for solving high-speed flight issues. It held the world speed record until bested by the rocket-powered Bell X-1.

USMC 11986

Maj. Marion E. Carl Jr., USMC, set a world speed record in the D-558-1 on 25 August 1947.

20 AUGUST • Cmdr. Turner F. Caldwell broke the world speed record in the Douglas D-558-1 at 640.663 mph over a Muroc, Calif., three-kilometer course.

626130

F2H-4 Banshees of VF-12 fly over *Coral Sea* (CVB 43), 12 June 1951.

25 AUGUST • Maj. Marion E. Carl Jr., USMC, set a new world speed record in the D-558-1 Skystreak of 650.796 mph over the three-kilometer Muroc, Calif., course.

25 AUGUST • Tests of the Douglas Aircraft Company low-drag bomb shape began at the Southern California Cooperative Wind Tunnel at Pasadena, Calif.

6 SEPTEMBER • *Midway* (CVB 41) launched a V-2 rocket from her flight deck in the first firing of a large ballistic missile from a ship at sea. The rocket behaved abnormally after liftoff, but the launch demonstrated the feasibility of the concept.

17 SEPTEMBER • Naval aviator James V. Forrestal of World War I service took the oath of office as the first Secretary of Defense. The following day, the National Security Act of 1947 became effective, and the Departments of the Army, Navy, and Air Force became constituted as integral parts of the National Military Establishment.

30 SEPTEMBER • The Research and Development Board, which superseded the Joint Research and Development Board and dealt with research and development coordination, planning, and direction, was formally set up in the National Military Establishment. Dr. Vannevar Bush took office as its chairman. At its first meeting on 19 December, the board accepted the credentials of all of its members. One of the two Navy members was the Deputy Chief of Naval Operations (Air).

1 OCTOBER • *Coral Sea* (CVB 43), Capt. A. P. Storrs III commanding, was commissioned at Newport News, Va.

1 NOVEMBER • The Naval Parachute Unit moved from NAS Lakehurst, N.J., to NAS El Centro, Calif. Its mission was the research, development, and testing of parachutes, parachute recovery systems, and ejectable seat capsules.

21 NOVEMBER • The Grumman XF9F-2 made its first flight.

24 NOVEMBER • The first launch of a liquid-fueled RTV-N-8 Aerobee rocket for the Navy took place at White Sands Proving Ground, N.M. The rocket, designed primarily for upper atmospheric research, reached an altitude of 34.7

Tandem-rotor HRP-1s of HMX-1 lift off from Quantico, Va.

miles. The United States launched more than 1,000 Aerobees in various configurations through 1985.

28 NOVEMBER • Seaplane tender *Norton Sound* (AV 11) was assigned to the Operational Development Force for use as an experimental rocket-firing ship. The following March, the ship began the necessary alterations at Philadelphia Naval Shipyard, Pa.

1 DECEMBER • HMX-1, Col. Edward C. Dyer, USMC, commanding, was established at MCAS Quantico, Va. Its mission was development of techniques and tactics for the use of helicopters in amphibious operations.

19 DECEMBER • The New Development Board was established to review the programs of the various bureaus and offices, and to recommend the priorities of development projects to the Chief of Naval Operations. In May 1948, the Research and Development Review Board, consisting of the Chief of Naval Research and people in the Office of the CNO responsible for development, replaced the New Development Board.

19 DECEMBER • The Research and Development Board directed its committee on guided missiles to coordinate the Earth Satellite Vehicle Project, thereby taking over this function from the Aeronautical Board.

30 DECEMBER • Chairman Thomas K. Finletter of the president's Air Policy Commission submitted the commission's report *Survival in the Air Age*, based on extensive hearings over three months. The report was a broad review of the international situation in terms of the proven effectiveness of air power and its added potential for destruction with the advent of atomic weapons. It stressed the need to maintain military forces large enough to make aggression dangerous, and emphasized the urgency of building strong military aviation with its supporting industry and civil air transport, and of encouraging a progressive research and development program to maintain the existing margin of U.S. superiority.

1948

1 JANUARY • The headquarters of the Naval Air Basic Training Command shifted from NAS Corpus Christi, Texas, to NAS Pensacola, Fla., and Naval Air Training Bases, Corpus Christi, was disestablished. The establishment of the Naval Air Advanced Training Subordinate Command occurred simultaneously at Corpus Christi.

1 MARCH • Sen. Ralph O. Brewster (R-Maine), chairman of the Congressional Committee on National Aviation Policy, submitted the committee's report. The deductions of the members differed in some respects from the earlier report submitted by the president's Air Policy Commission, but generally reiterated the conclusions in regard to the effect of air power on national security, and the need for a national policy to build a strong military air force supported by a vibrant aircraft industry and civil aviation.

1053785

This FJ-1 Fury in Naval Air Test Center markings participated in carrier trials, c. 1947.

424773

An HTL-3, one of only nine built, takes off from *Valley Forge* (CV 45), parallel with an HO3S in the background, c. January 1953.

4 MARCH • The Test Pilot Training Division was established at NATC Patuxent River, Md. The division instructed experienced fleet pilots in aeronautical engineering and techniques of flight testing. Ten years later it became the Naval Test Pilot School.

10 MARCH • Pilots Cmdr. Evan P. Aurand and Lt. Cmdr. Robert M. Elder of VF-5A tested the carrier suitability of FJ-1 Furies on board *Boxer* (CV 21) off San Diego, Calif.

11 MARCH • Interservice conflict over the respective roles and missions of the services prompted Secretary of Defense James V. Forrestal to convene meetings of the Joint Chiefs at NAS Key West, Fla. These conferences resulted in limited concessions by both the Navy and the Air Force. The Navy acknowledged the primacy of the Air Force in strategic bombing, and the Air Force agreed not to hinder the construction of the world's largest carrier—a 65,000-ton, 1,090-foot long flush-deck ship without an island superstructure, designed to launch aircraft carrying atomic bombs, and subsequently named *United States* (CVA 58).

29 MARCH • The Technical Evaluation Group of the Research and Development Board noted its conclusion concerning the feasibility of the development of an earth satellite. The board recommended the delay of construction until researchers clearly established the project's utility.

30 MARCH • Secretary of the Navy John L. Sullivan approved the establishment of a Naval Air Reserve Advisory Council. This consisted of 50 Reserve aviation officers appointed from civilian life with the purpose of making available to the Navy the experience and continuing advice of reservists, who had held key positions while on active duty during World War II.

1 APRIL • HU-1, Cmdr. Maurice A. Peters commanding, was established at NAS Lakehurst, N.J., as the first helicopter squadron in the U.S. Navy.

21 APRIL • The Secretary of Defense issued a memorandum for the secretaries within his department, attaching a paper defining the functions of the armed forces and the Joint Chiefs of Staff. Based on the policy embodied in the National Security Act, this event marked the first functions paper drawn up by the services following their reorganization, and is commonly referred to as the Key West agreement.

27 APRIL • In the first carrier launchings of planes of this size and weight, pilots Cmdr. Thomas D. Davies and Lt. Cmdr. John P. Wheatley made JATO takeoffs in two P2V-2 Neptunes from *Coral Sea* (CVB 43) off Norfolk, Va.

29 APRIL • Amid fears of a communist coup in Norway, *Valley Forge* (CV 45) made a four-day visit to the capital of Oslo.

30 APRIL • The Martin XP5M-1 made its first flight.

1053754

The P5M-1 Marlin was an evolution of Martin's PBM Mariner. These are from VP-56, c. 1954.

1 MAY • Changes in aircraft marking specifications made it mandatory for carrier squadrons to use distinguishing colors on propeller spinners and across the top of vertical fins and rudders. The colors Insignia Red, Insignia White, Light Blue, Light Yellow, Light Green, and Black outlined in white marked squadrons one through six, respectively, of each carrier air group. The changes also required the painting of arresting hooks in alternate 4-inch black-and-white bands.

5 MAY • Submarine *Cusk* (SS 348) launched a Loon missile off NAMTC Point Mugu, Calif., guided it over a 46-mile course, and crashed the weapon within 100 yards of its target, Begg Rock.

5 MAY • VF-17A became the Navy's first carrier-qualified jet squadron. During three days of operations on board *Saipan* (CVL 48), all the squadron's pilots and Commander CVG-17 qualified in 16 FH-1 Phantoms with a minimum of eight takeoffs and landings each.

8 MAY • Michelson Laboratory at the Naval Ordnance Test Station, China Lake, Calif., was dedicated. This marked a major step in the transition of the station from a rocket test range to a research and development activity specially equipped to study the various aspects of rocketry and guided missiles.

400916

A Lark guided missile hurtles skyward from Point Mugu, Calif. Originally designed to combat *kamikazes*, the missile was not developed in time for World War II and never got beyond the prototype stage.

18 MAY • The Goodyear Aircraft Corporation received a contract for the design of a submarine-hunting airship with an envelope volume of 825,000 cubic feet, approximately double that of K-class airships. The proposed airship was to carry a crew of 14, extensive antisubmarine equipment, and in-flight refueling capabilities. Through subsequent contractual action initiated in September, the Navy ordered prototype ZPN-1.

25 MAY • Two support wings were established and placed under a Commander, Fleet Logistic Support Wings. They provided, subsequent to the merger of Navy and Air Force air transport commands, air logistic support services over routes of sole Navy interest as required for the internal administration and fulfillment of naval missions.

1 JUNE • The consolidation of the Naval Air Transport Service and the Air Transport Service of the Air Force's Air Transport Command formed the Military Air Transport Service as a unified element of the National Military Establishment. The service operated under the command and direction of the Air Force.

4 JUNE • To establish and maintain close relationships between the operating forces and planning agencies, arrangements were made for an air board to meet quarterly with principal members Deputy Chief of Naval Operations (Air), the chief of the Bureau of Aeronautics, ComAirLant, and ComAirPac.

4 JUNE • The Airborne Coordination Group was redesignated Naval Aviation Electronics Service Unit.

11 JUNE • The Chief of Naval Operations issued standards for training aviators as helicopter pilots and provided for the retention of their qualification of helicopter pilots previously trained by the Coast Guard or VX-3.

18 JUNE • The chief of the Bureau of Aeronautics authorized NAMTC Point Mugu, Calif., to train (on a non-interfering basis) the Air Force 1st Experimental Guided Missile Group in the operation of the Lark guided missile.

22 JUNE • Under a plan that in essence reactivated the Aviation Cadet program, men between the ages of 18 and 25 with at least two years of college became eligible for flight training. Candidates were required to serve on active duty for four years, after which they returned to inactive duty as members of the Reserve. A limited number of the cadets gained the opportunity to remain on active duty with the possibility of transferring to the regular Navy. The first of the new Aviation Cadets under the program reported for training in late August.

1053786

The radical XF5U-1 had a nearly disk-shaped wing for maneuverability and a short takeoff run.

24 JUNE • In a reaction to ongoing Allied efforts to consolidate control of their zones of occupation in divided Germany, the Soviets initiated a blockade of Berlin by cutting off all road, rail, and waterborne traffic into the German city. Despite international condemnation of their actions, the Soviets claimed that they experienced "technical difficulties" in maintaining the lines of communication into Berlin. The Allies subsequently responded with Operation Vittles—an airlift to feed and supply the troops and civilians entrapped within the city. Naval aircraft operated during the airlift, and at least one carrier battle group normally steamed in the North Atlantic.

29 JUNE • The development of TACAN –Tactical Air Navigation system– began with a Bureau of Ships contract with the Federal Telecommunications Laboratory for development of a surface beacon and airborne receiver capable of determining the direction of aircraft from surface stations. The stringent accuracy requirements originated from needs that grew out of carrier operational experience during World War II. A year later and following tests of the initial model, the company received contracts for development of equipment that also measured distances.

1 JULY • The Naval Air Transport Service was disestablished. The command had remained in existence following the establishment of the Military Air Transport Service to assist in the transfer of Navy commands to the new organization.

1 JULY • The Naval Aeronautical Rocket Laboratory was established at Lake Denmark, N.J. The laboratory provided an East Coast rocket testing facility similar in function to the Air Force Rocket Test Facility at Muroc, Calif.

3 JULY • The Chief of Naval Operations Adm. Louis E. Denfeld requested that the Bureau of Ordnance develop a 250-pound bomb on the lines of the Douglas Aircraft Company shape and a container to the same lines that could carry a number of conventional 250-pound bombs. The move initiated the ordnance aspects of low-drag bomb development.

6 JULY • VAW-1 and -2 were established in the Pacific and Atlantic Fleets, respectively, responsible for organizing and training airborne early warning (AEW) teams for carrier operations. Although AEW aircraft had operated from carriers, and land-based squadron VPW-1 was established on 1 April 1948 with a secondary mission of AEW, these wings marked the first naval commands organized specifically for the AEW mission, and the first to provide the fleet with AEW services from carriers.

20 JULY • Chief of Naval Operations Adm. Louis E. Denfeld directed the change of the standard composition of carrier air groups to comprise three fighter and two attack squadrons; thus adding an additional fighter squadron to each group. To compensate for this increase, the Navy later reduced squadron aircraft complements.

1053758

The JRM *Philippine Mars* transport, BuNo 76820, uses jet-assisted takeoff at NAS Alameda, Calif. It was one of only seven built.

22 JULY • The assembly and repair departments at Navy and Marine air stations were redesignated overhaul and repair departments.

23 JULY • The Assistant Secretary of the Navy for Air approved a plan to develop a fleet aviation center in the area of Jacksonville, Fla. The plan included reactivation of facilities at Cecil Field and Mayport to help support the air groups assigned to the center, and the relocation of the Naval Air Advanced Training Command based at NAS Jacksonville.

29 JULY • President Harry S. Truman approved the construction of *United States* (CVA 58). The Naval Appropriation Act of 1949 provided funds in a private shipyard for the ship at Newport News (Virginia) Shipbuilding and Dry Dock Company.

1 AUGUST • The dissolution of the Aeronautical Board ended more than 30 years as an interservice agency for cooperation in aviation. The National Security Act of 1947 assigned most of the board's functions to other boards.

17 AUGUST • Chief of Naval Operations Adm. Louis E. Denfeld informed the chief of the Bureau of Aeronautics of his intention to assign antisubmarine warfare as a primary mission to most patrol squadrons, and requested the institution of a vigorous program by the bureau to outfit patrol planes with the necessary equipment.

20 AUGUST • Secretary of Defense James V. Forrestal convened at the Naval War College, Newport, R.I., a second meeting of the Joint Chiefs of Staff in an effort to clarify the rationale concerning each service's national security responsibilities. Although the meeting resulted in designating the Air Force as the interim executive agent for the Armed Forces Special Weapons Project (which controlled the atomic weapons stockpile), it also provided the Navy with the authority to participate in atomic bombing.

28 AUGUST • The JRM-2 *Caroline Mars*, BuNo 76824, from VR-2 completed a record nonstop flight of 4,748 miles from Honolulu, Hawaii, to Chicago, Ill., in 24 hours, 12 minutes with 42 persons on board and carrying a 14,000-pound payload.

1 SEPTEMBER • The Navy simplified the system of group and squadron designations in effect since November 1946. The action redesignated carrier air groups as CVG without regard to their carrier assignments; changed the numbers of most squadrons to conform to the previous system (VF and VA were assigned two or three digit numbers, the first of which was the same as the parent air groups, and suffix letters were dropped); redesignated fighting squadrons as fighter squadrons; reverted patrol squadrons to the simple VP designation; redesignated VRF and VRU as VR—development, helicopter, lighter-than-air, and observation squadrons remained the same—and some VC became VAW to reflect their air warning mission, while others were redesignated VFN or VAN to reflect all-weather capabilities. These changes did not affect Marine Corps squadron designations.

5 SEPTEMBER • The JRM-2 *Caroline Mars*, BuNo 76824, from VR-2 carried a 68,282-pound cargo on a 390-mile flight from NAS Patuxent River, Md., to Cleveland, Ohio. The event marked the heaviest payload ever lifted in an aircraft to date.

9 SEPTEMBER • VC-5 was established as a result of a Navy effort to provide carriers with atomic capabilities. The squadron initially received P2V Neptunes and developed tactics and procedures to takeoff with nuclear weapons from the decks of carriers.

1 OCTOBER • Seaplane tender *Norton Sound* (AV 11) completed conversion at the Philadelphia Naval Shipyard, Pa. After a brief shakedown, she began operations as the Navy's first guided missile experimental and test ship. The ship was redesignated AVM-1 on 8 August 1951.

27 OCTOBER • VR-6 and -8 of the Military Air Transport Service received orders to move from their Pacific bases to the Allied zones in West Germany to take part in Operation Vittles—the Berlin Airlift.

1 NOVEMBER • The Naval Air Advanced Training Command shifted from NAS Jacksonville, Fla., to NAS Corpus Christi, Texas, in accordance with plans to convert the Jacksonville area into a fleet aviation center.

5 NOVEMBER • To meet the requirements of landing aircraft weighing up to 50,000-pounds at speeds as high as 105 knots, a project began for the design of Mark 7 high energy–absorption arresting gear at the Naval Aircraft Factory at Philadelphia, Pa.

9 NOVEMBER • VR-6 and -8 of the Military Air Transport Service began flying cargoes into Soviet-besieged Berlin.

17 DECEMBER • To meet the mounting requirements for transatlantic airlift in support of Operation Vittles, VR-3 switched from flying domestic routes to flying the run from Westover, Mass., to Frankfurt, Germany.

1949

23 JANUARY • *Palau* (CVE 122) completed 12 days of tests off the New England coast as part of an effort to develop carrier capabilities in conducting air operations under cold and severe weather conditions. This marked the Navy's continuing interest in cold weather evaluations first demonstrated by *Langley* (CV 1) in the same area 18 years before.

26 JANUARY • Seaplane tender *Norton Sound* (AV 11) launched her first Loon guided missile off NAMTC Point Mugu, Calif.

707741

Marines embark in HRP-1s during a vertical envelopment amphibious exercise on board *Palau* (CVE 122).

415146

Seaplane tender *Norton Sound* (AV 11) fires a Loon guided missile off Point Mugu, Calif., 26 January 1949.

27 JANUARY • Chief of Naval Operations Adm. Louis E. Denfeld authorized the conversion of all newly constructed cruisers to accommodate helicopters.

3 FEBRUARY • The Lockheed XR6O-1, which the Navy had accepted the day before at NAS Alameda, Calif., inaugurated its transcontinental service with a flight from NAS Moffett Field, Calif., to Washington, D.C. The 92-ton Constitution established a new record for the number of people carried on a transcontinental flight—18 crewmen and 78 passengers—and crossed the continent in 9 hours, 35 minutes.

25 FEBRUARY • The JRM-2 *Caroline Mars*, BuNo 76824, from VR-2 broke the world record for passenger lift by transporting 202 passengers from NAS Alameda, Calif., to San Diego, Calif. The plane carried 218 people on the return flight to break the record again the same day. These loads were in addition to its crew of four.

4 MARCH • The JRM-2 *Caroline Mars*, BuNo 76824, from VR-2, set a new record for persons carried aloft by transporting 263 passengers and a crew of six on a 2 hour, 41-minute flight from San Diego, Calif., to NAS Alameda, Calif. The passengers included officers and men of CVG-15 on a routine transfer of station.

7 MARCH • Pilot Capt. John T. Hayward of VC-5 launched in a P2V-3C Neptune from *Coral Sea* (CVB 43) off the Virginia Capes with a 10,000-pound load of dummy bombs, crossed the continent to drop the load on a West Coast target, and returned nonstop to NAS Patuxent River, Md.

24 MARCH • Pilot Lt. Stewart R. Graham, USCG, and aircrewman AM2 Robert McAuliffe, USCG, set the record for the longest unescorted helicopter flight to date when they ferried an HO3S-1G, designated Coast Guard Aircraft No. 234, from CGAS Elizabeth City, N.C., to CGAS Port Angeles, Wash. Graham and McAuliffe arrived on 3 April after a total of 57.6 hours in flight.

31 MARCH • In the highest monthly amount of the airlift to date, U.S. aircraft delivered 154,475 tons of cargo to West Berlin, East Germany. In addition, VR-8 set an airlift record to date of 155 percent efficiency for the month, and a daily utilization of 12.2 hours per squadron aircraft.

5 APRIL • The initiation of a plan to use helicopters in place of fixed-wing aircraft on board battleships and cruisers began, and VO-2 was disestablished as the last of the observation squadrons. The events marked the end of one era and the beginning of another. The changeover was to be completed by 30 June.

23 APRIL • Secretary of Defense Louis A. Johnson abruptly halted the construction of *United States* (CVA 58), just five days after her keel laying at Newport News (Virginia) Shipbuilding and Dry Dock Company. The secretary made his decision without consulting Secretary of the Navy John L. Sullivan or Chief of Naval Operations Adm. Louis E. Denfeld. Secretary Sullivan subsequently resigned in protest, and President Harry S. Truman appointed Francis P. Matthews in his place.

19 MAY • The JRM-1 *Marshall Mars* broke the record for the number of people carried on a single flight with 301 passengers and a crew of seven from NAS Alameda, Calif., to San Diego, Calif.

15 JULY • Douglas Aircraft Company test pilots completed an initial flight evaluation of the low-drag external-store shape on an XF3D-1 at Edwards AFB Calif. The aircraft carried two of the shapes, and it attained a top speed of 51 knots greater than when carrying two conventional 2,000-pound bombs and 22 knots greater than with two 150-gallon external fuel tanks.

31 JULY • VR-6 and -8's participation in the Berlin Airlift ended. During their eight months in Germany, the squadrons flew a total of 45,990 hours, carried 129,989 tons of cargo into Berlin, and established a record of payload efficiency and aircraft utilization at the hitherto unparalleled figure of better than ten hours per day per plane for the entire period.

1 AUGUST • The Seventh Task Fleet stood up as the forward-deployed U.S. naval force in the western Pacific.

1 AUGUST • The Navy established Naval Air Development Center, Johnsville, Pa., and disestablished Naval Air Development Station.

9 AUGUST • Lt. Jack L. Fruin of VF-171 made the first operational use of an ejection seat for an emergency escape in the United States. He survived ejection from an F2H-1 while the Banshee flew at more than 500 knots in the vicinity of Walterboro, S.C.

10 AUGUST • An amendment to the National Security Act of 1947 provided for an increase in the authority of the Secretary of Defense and replaced the National Military Establishment with the Department of Defense. The change further provided the continuance of the separate administration of the three military departments, and that naval aviation was to "be integrated with the naval service . . . within the Department of the Navy."

1 OCTOBER • An exchange program to indoctrinate selected Air Force, Navy, and Marine pilots in the operational and training activities of each other's service began with the exchange of 18 pilots from the services for one year. The move

A twin-jet F3D-2 Sky Knight of VF-14 overflies *Intrepid* (CV 11) during carrier qualification trials, November 1954.

407668

A dozen P2V-3 Neptunes were modified to the -3C specification for a carrier-launched nuclear bomber. To verify the ability to launch and range to get to the target, Cmdr. Frederick L. Ashworth flies from *Midway* (CVB 41) off Norfolk, Va., on a 4,800-mile route to San Diego, Calif., 5 October 1949.

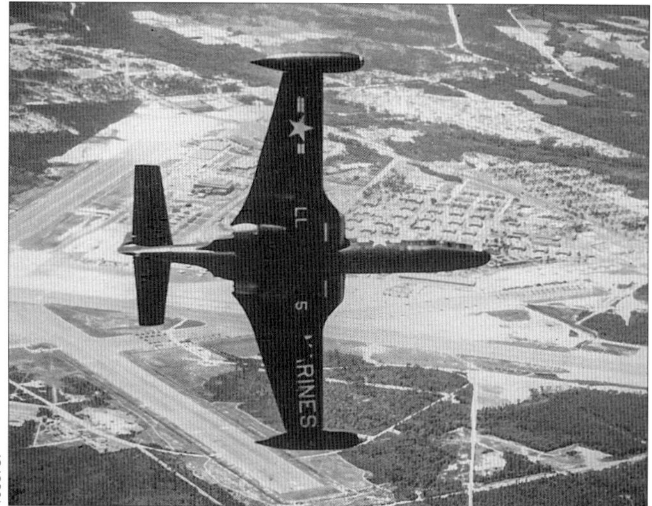

1053787

The photoreconnaissance F2H-2P Banshee had all its armament removed and replaced with cameras. This is a Marine Banshee of Headquarters Squadron 2.

accorded with an interservice agreement reached in July, which provided for the qualification of all pilots in the type of aircraft operated by the commands in which they served, and their occupation of regular pilots' billets in their new assignments.

5 OCTOBER • Pilot Cmdr. Frederick L. Ashworth took off in a P2V-3 Neptune from *Midway* (CVB 41) at sea off Norfolk, Va., flew to the Panama Canal, northward over Corpus Christi, Texas, and on to San Diego, Calif. Ashworth completed the 4,800-mile nonstop, unrefueled flight in 25 hours, 40 minutes.

5 OCTOBER • Congress opened hearings on unification and strategy. In a controversy that journalists subsequently dubbed "The Revolt of the Admirals," Adm. Arthur W. Radford spearheaded the testimony of Navy witnesses against Air Force charges of the sea service's obsolescence during the atomic age. On 17 October, despite the objections of Secretary of Defense Louis A. Johnson and Secretary of the Navy Francis P. Matthews, the Chief of Naval Operations Adm. Louis E. Denfeld supported the statements of preceding witnesses against defense policies that centered on the intercontinental bombing of enemy cities by Air Force

1053755

Patrol Squadron (VP) 21 received its first P4M-1 Mercator in June 1950.

bombers and marginalized naval aviation, as exemplified in the development of the Convair B-36. Admiral Denfeld's stand prompted his removal from office on 1 November; however, the controversy resulted in Congressional support that preserved a role for naval aviation in national deterrence.

30 OCTOBER • Lt. Giuseppe A. Rullo and M. D. Kembro of the Civil Air Patrol flew an HO3S-1 in 10 hours, 50 minutes from NAS Seattle, Wash., to NAS Alameda, Calif. Their achievement unofficially bettered the existing distance record for helicopters with a flight of 755 miles.

1 NOVEMBER • Adm. Louis E. Denfeld's controversial decision during the congressional hearings on strategic posture triggered his removal as Chief of Naval Operations, and naval aviator Adm. Forrest P. Sherman became the 12th CNO the next day.

1 DECEMBER • The consolidation of all air transport wings under a single command—the Fleet Logistic Air Wing—resulted in the dissolution of the Atlantic and Pacific Fleet Logistics Support Wings.

1053756

A landing signal officer directs an HO3S-1 landing on board *Franklin D. Roosevelt* (CVB 42).

9 DECEMBER • The reorganization of the Naval Air Reserve was completed. This placed 128 fighter, 41 attack, 25 composite, 29 patrol, 26 transport, 57 service, and 5 blimp squadrons under the command of 27 air wings established at the same number of Reserve air stations across the United States.

29 DECEMBER • Earlier in the month, the Chinese Communists had defeated the Chinese Nationalists on the mainland and driven them to Formosa (Taiwan). On this date, the Navy announced the reinforcement by *Boxer* (CV 21) to the U.S. presence in the western Pacific in an effort principally to deter Chinese Communist expansionism.

CHAPTER 7

The Korean War

1950–1953

The outbreak of the Korean War caught naval aviation in the midst of transition. The establishment of the Department of Defense in 1947 and its reorganization in 1949 required adjustments that had not been completed. Successive budgetary decreases and the prospect of further cuts had reduced the size of the service, and a reorganization of operating forces to keep within the prescribed limits had begun.

New weapons and equipment had not been fully integrated and tactical doctrine and innovative operating techniques for their employment were still under development. The introduction of jet aircraft created a composite force in which either jet or propeller-driven aircraft that differed in performance characteristics, maintenance requirements, and tactical applications equipped comparable commands.

Despite the amphibious landings at Inchon 2½ months after the North Korean invasion of South Korea, the operations of naval aviation during the Korean War diverged from the island hopping campaigns in the Pacific during World War II. The United Nations sought to confine the fighting to the Korean peninsula to avoid the specter of escalation into an atomic war, but this policy limited air operations.

The seesaw clashes on the ground during the first six months of the war demanded flexibility of force, but the air campaign developed into a predictable pattern that Commander Task Force 77 described in January 1952 as "a day-to-day routine where stamina replaces glamour and persistence is pitted against oriental perseverance." In addition, the need to sustain carrier air power for extended periods over a landmass imposed a command and logistical burden.

Carrier aircraft flew deep support missions, attacked supply lines, roamed over enemy territory for targets of opportunity, bombed bridges, interdicted highways and railroads, attacked refineries, railroad yards, and hydroelectric plants, and escorted land-based bombers on special missions. The variability of these raids challenged men trained to interdict enemy sea lines of communication and to ward off attacks by enemy naval forces. Helicopters assumed an increasingly significant role as they rescued downed aircrew, evacuated wounded, flew short-range supply missions to Marines and soldiers ashore, enhanced command-and-control options for Marines, spotted shore bombardment gunfire for ships, and scoured coastal areas for mines.

During the three years of war, Navy and Marine aircraft flew 276,000 combat sorties, dropped 177,000 tons of bombs, and expended 272,000 rockets. Their achievement reached within 7,000 sorties of the comparable World War II totals in all theaters, and surpassed the bomb tonnage by 74,000 tons and the number of rockets by 60,000. Naval and Marine aircraft completed action sorties that rose in number from less than 10 percent during World War II to more than 30 percent during the Korean War.

Outside the combat area, the fleet continuously maintained peaceful missions in the Mediterranean and eastern Atlantic, and trained on the same scale as before. Accelerated research and development nonetheless did not shift to emphasize projects that directly applied to the war effort, but continued on longer range programs aimed at progressively modernizing fleet forces and their equipment with more effective weapons.

Advances in guided missiles indicated their early operational status and the ships and submarines to employ them readied for action. The firing of research missiles such as Larks, Loons, and Vikings from shore installations and ships provided useful data and experience. Additional missiles including Regulus, Sidewinder, Sparrow, Talos, and Terrier types passed successive stages of development.

423763

A VF-191 F9F-2 rotates as the catapult bridle drops away and the Panther reaches flying speed on *Princeton* (CV 37). The squadron made two Korean War deployments flying these aircraft in 1950–1952.

The research in high-speed flight assisted by specially designed aircraft provided data that led toward advances in aircraft performance. The carrier modernization program continued and underwent revision to incorporate steam catapults and angled flight decks. Naval aviation demonstrated its continuing usefulness in war and its versatility in adapting to new combat requirements and moved forward toward new horizons.

1950

10 JANUARY • Seaplane tender *Norton Sound* (AV 11) sailed for a 19-day cruise in Alaskan waters from Port Hueneme, Calif. During the operation, the ship launched two RTV-N-8 Aerobee sounding rockets, one Lark surface-to-air guided missile, and one LTV-N-2 Loon test vehicle, evaluating an auxiliary propulsion system for the Lark under severe conditions. *Norton Sound* embarked 27 observers representing the Army, Navy, and Air Force, including eight scientists from the Aerobee upper atmosphere research program.

13 JANUARY • In the Navy's first successful automatic homing flight of a surface-to-air guided missile, a CTV-N-10 Lark was launched from NAMTC Point Mugu, Calif. The Lark passed within lethal range of its target F6F Hellcat drone and made a simulated interception at a range of 17,300 yards and an altitude of 7,400 feet.

7 FEBRUARY • In a demonstration of carrier long-range attack capabilities, pilot Cmdr. Thomas Robinson took off in a P2V-3C Neptune from *Franklin D. Roosevelt* (CVB 42) off Jacksonville, Fla., and flew over Charleston, S.C., the Bahamas, the Panama Canal, up the coast of Central America, and over Mexico, landing the next day at the Municipal Airport, San Francisco, Calif. The flight covered 5,060 miles in 25 hours, 59 minutes—the longest to date made from a carrier deck.

20 FEBRUARY • Joint exercise Operation Portrex began, which included the first peacetime maneuvers to employ airborne troops in an amphibious operation. This escalated into a combined amphibious and airborne assault on 8 March against Vieques Island, P.R. The Pentagon staged Portrex to evaluate joint service doctrine for combined operations, to service test new equipment under simulated combat conditions, and to provide training for the Caribbean Command. The exercise extended through 14 March.

10 MARCH • Secretary of Defense Louis A. Johnson announced the development under a Bureau of Aeronautics research program begun in 1946 of a lightweight titanium alloy for use in jet aircraft engines. The announcement described the alloy as being as strong as high-strength steel and only half as heavy, highly resistant to corrosion, and capable of retaining its basic properties at high temperatures.

22 MARCH • Submarine *Cusk* (SS 348) launched a Loon guided missile from a position off NAMTC Point Mugu, Calif. At the midway point of the missile's 50-mile flight, *Cusk* surrendered control to a guidance station on San Nicolas Island. This station completed the first successful operation involving the transfer of guidance by crashing the Loon 360 yards from the center of the target, Begg Rock.

1 APRIL • The Naval Air Rocket Test Station was established at Lake Denmark, N.J. The action superseded Naval Aeronautical Rocket Laboratory for the testing and evaluation of rocket engines, components and propellants, and the training of personnel to operate and service rocket engines.

8 APRIL • Soviet aircraft shot down a PB4Y-2, BuNo 59645, of VP-26 Detachment A—based at NAS Port Lyautey in French Morocco, but on patrol from Wiesbaden, West Germany—over the Baltic Sea off the coast of Liepāja, Latvia. Searchers recovered pieces of wreckage, but all ten men on board the Privateer died.

18 APRIL • The experimental model of the Convair XP5Y-1 passed its initial flight test at San Diego, Calif. Four Allison T-40 turboprop engines, each rated at 5,500 hp and turning 15-foot contra-rotating propellers, powered the 60-ton seaplane.

21 APRIL • Pilot Lt. Cmdr. Robert C. Starkey of VC-6 took off in a P2V-3C Neptune from *Coral Sea* (CVB 43) with a gross weight of 74,668-pounds—the heaviest aircraft launched from a carrier to date. In addition, pilot and VC-5 commanding officer Capt. John T. Hayward made the first heavy attack plane carrier takeoff in an AJ-1 Savage from *Coral Sea*.

A pair of AJ-1 Savages from Composite Squadron (VC) 6 cruise off the coast of Hawaii. The squadron was the second formed, in January 1950, to receive the new bombers.

3 MAY • Submarine *Cusk* (SS 348) launched a Loon guided missile. The boat submerged and tracked and controlled the flight of the missile to a range of 105 miles.

11 MAY • Seaplane tender *Norton Sound* (AV 11) launched a Viking missile from a position near Christmas Island, south of the Hawaiian Islands. The event set a new altitude record for U.S.-built single-stage rockets of 106.4 statute miles.

15 MAY • The Navy announced the completion of a new test chamber at the Ordnance Aerophysics Laboratory, Daingerfield, Texas. For the first time, full-scale ramjet engines up to 48-inches in diameter could be tested and at simulated altitudes of up to 100,000 feet.

19 JUNE • The JRM-2 *Caroline Mars*, BuNo 76824, completed a 2,609-mile flight with 144 men on board from Honolulu, Hawaii, to San Diego, Calif. The flight marked the largest passenger lift over the Pacific to date.

25 JUNE • Despite warnings from multiple intelligence sources, the North Koreans, achieving tactical surprise, invaded South Korea initiating the Korean War. The United States asked for an emergency meeting of the UN Security Council, which then adopted a resolution condemning the North Korean aggression, ordered the withdrawal of North Korean troops above the 38th parallel, and called on all members to assist the UN in the execution of the resolution. The Soviets had boycotted the council in protest of ongoing American support of the Chinese Nationalists and their absence prevented their veto of the motion.

428637

A VA-195 AD-4 Skyraider spreads its wings as it prepares to takeoff from *Princeton* (CV 37) during the Korean War.

27 JUNE • President Harry S. Truman announced that he had ordered sea and air forces in the Far East to give support and cover to the South Koreans, and directed the Seventh Fleet to take steps to prevent an invasion of Formosa (Taiwan). During a meeting later that night, the UN Security Council adopted a resolution calling upon all its members to assist the South Koreans to repel the North Korean invasion.

30 JUNE • President Harry S. Truman declared that in keeping with the UN Security Council request for support to the South Koreans to resist the communist invaders and to restore peace, he authorized the Air Force to bomb military targets in North Korea, the use of Army ground troops in action to support South Korean forces, and a naval blockade of the entire Korean coast.

3 JULY • Carrier aircraft went into action during the Korean War. *Valley Forge* (CV 45)—the only operational U.S. carrier in the western Pacific when the war began—with CVG-5 embarked and British carrier *Triumph* (R 16) operating in the Yellow Sea with Fairy Firefly FR.1s and Supermarine Seafire FR.47s of Nos. 827 and 800 Squadrons, respectively, launched strikes on North Korean airfields, supply lines, and transportation facilities in the area of Pyŏngyang. These raids marked the baptism of fire for F9F-3 Panthers and AD Skyraiders. Navy pilots also recorded their initial kills in aerial combat during the Korean War and the first by Navy jets. Lt. j.g. Leonard H. Plog and Ens. Elton W. Brown Jr. of VF-51 piloted two F9F-3s and shot down two enemy Yakovlev Yak-9P Franks over Pyŏngyang.

8 JULY • Commander in Chief Far East approved and adopted as policy an agreement of Commander Naval Forces, Far East, and Commanding General Far East Air Forces to obtain the maximum effectiveness in the employment of all air resources in the Far East Command and to ensure coordination of efforts. Under the terms of the accord, the Navy controlled the operations of its carrier aircraft whenever they flew on missions assigned to Commander, Naval Forces, Far East, and of its shore-based aircraft during naval missions. On all other sorties, the operations of carrier and shore-based naval aircraft fell under the purview of the Air Force.

The North Korean oil refinery at Wŏnsan burns following a carrier strike.

707876

Shore-based Marine aircraft operated under direct control while Navy aircraft were indirectly controlled. The selection of targets and their priority by General Headquarters Joint Service Target Analysis Group ensured coordination of the overall objectives of the air campaign.

12 JULY • Naval Air, Japan, was formed in Tōkyō to provide an interim staff to administer the expanding aviation forces in the Far East. On 9 August, the command was established as Fleet Air, Japan, Rear Adm. George R. Henderson commanding.

16 JULY • The headquarters of Fleet Air Wing 1 shifted from Guam to Naha, Okinawa, to direct patrol squadron operations over the Formosa (Taiwan) Strait.

18 JULY • After a brief respite, *Valley Forge* (CV 45) and British carrier *Triumph* (R 16) returned to action with strikes on North Korean airfields, railroads, and factories at Hamhŭng, Hungnam, Numpyong, and Wŏnsan. Their aircraft heavily damaged the oil refinery at Wŏnsan. For the remainder of the month, carrier aircraft flew interdiction strikes deep behind enemy lines and close support missions

419929

Sailors ready a heavily armed Marine Corps F4U-4B Corsair for a pre-dawn launch from *Sicily* (CVE 118) in late summer or early fall 1950.

as required, while the ships shifted entirely around the peninsula from the Sea of Japan to the Yellow Sea in operations intended to relieve the pressure on UN troops retreating toward Pusan (Busan), South Korea.

19 JULY • Ens. Donald E. Stevens of VA-55 was shot down in an AD-4 Skyraider during a strafing run in Kangmyong-ni, North Korea. He was the first naval aviator lost in action during the Korean War.

20 JULY • Fourteen squadrons of the Organized Reserve including eight carrier fighter, two carrier attack, one antisubmarine, one fleet aircraft service, and two patrol squadrons were activated for duty as a result of the Korean War.

22 JULY • *Badoeng Strait* (CVE 116), with elements of the 1st Marine Aircraft Wing embarked, arrived at Yokosuka, Japan. Four days later, *Sicily* (CVE 118) arrived at that port with a load of ammunition, and on 1 August, *Philippine Sea* (CV 47) reported to Commander Seventh Fleet at Buckner Bay, Okinawa. These arrivals marked the first carrier reinforcements to *Valley Forge* (CV 45) in Far Eastern waters and the beginning of carrier deployments to the Korean War that by the war's end totaled 11 attack, one light, and five escort carriers sent into action. Some of these carriers fought through two or three tours.

23 JULY • *Boxer* (CV 21), with a load of 145 USAF North American P-51 Mustangs and six L-5 Sentinels, 19 Navy aircraft, 1,012 passengers, and 2,000 tons of additional cargo arrived in Yokosuka, Japan. This delivery of urgently needed reinforcements for the fighting in Korea was made by breaking all existing records for a Pacific crossing in 8 days, 16 hours from NAS Alameda, Calif., to Yokosuka.

27 JULY • To meet the requirements of supporting combat forces in the Korea War, Fleet Logistic Air Wing, Pacific, was established as a unit of the Pacific Fleet and independently from the existing Fleet Logistic Air Wing.

420530

A wounded man is carried from the HO3S-1 of VMO-6, which evacuated him from the front.

3 AUGUST • HO3S-1s and OY-2 Sentinels of VMO-6 began Korean War operations in support of the 1st Provisional Marine Brigade in the vicinity of Changwon. During their first day in battle, the helicopters delivered rations and water to troops on a mountain, and evacuated men felled by the severe heat.

3 AUGUST • VMF-214, operating from *Sicily* (CVE 118) while she sailed in Tsushima Strait, began the combat operations of the 1st Marine Aircraft Wing in the Korean War with a rocket and incendiary bomb attack on North Korean troops at Chinju. *Badoeng Strait* (CVE 116), with VMF-323 embarked, joined the action three days later. Marine squadrons flew close air support from light and escort carriers that logged 12 deployments during the war.

4 AUGUST • Fleet Air Wing 6, Capt. John C. Alderman commanding (acting), was established at Tōkyō, Japan. The wing assumed operational control over all U.S. and British patrol squadrons in the Japan-Korea area.

5 AUGUST • *Valley Forge* (CV 45) and *Philippine Sea* (CV 47) began almost three years of continuous fast carrier operations with attacks on enemy lines of communication in southwestern Korea and close support missions for UN troops holding the perimeter around Pusan (Busan).

7 AUGUST • The Navy received delivery of airship ZP2K-1, subsequently redesignated ZSG-2. The modernized K-class airship was equipped with in-flight refueling equipment and attachments for picking up seawater as ballast.

7 AUGUST • An HO3S-1 equipped with a single-axis automatic pilot made the first Navy flight of a helicopter under automatic control at NAF Mustin Field, Philadelphia, Pa. The successful test confirmed the feasibility of a helicopter automatic pilot. L. S. Guarino oversaw the development of the system at the Aeronautical Instrument Laboratory, Naval Air Material Center.

14 AUGUST • At the request of the Lebanese government, *Midway* (CVB 41) and *Leyte* (CV 32) visited Beirut, and launched an aerial demonstration over the Lebanese capital.

21 AUGUST • Aircraft flying from *Valley Forge* (CV 45) and *Philippine Sea* (CV 47) indicated the escalation of the air war when they set new records for operations, completing 202 sorties in a day over the Pyŏngyang area of North Korea.

24 AUGUST • A RIM-2 Terrier surface-to-air guided missile intercepted an F6F Hellcat drone at a range of more than 11 miles from the point of launch at Naval Ordnance Test Station Inyokern, Calif.

31 AUGUST • VC-5 marked the introduction of long-range attack bombers to carrier operations with the completion of AJ-1 Savage carrier qualifications on board *Coral Sea* (CVB 43).

6 SEPTEMBER • *Leyte* (CV 32) sailed from the Atlantic Fleet and arrived in the Korean War theater on 9 October.

14 SEPTEMBER • Commander U.S. Far East Command and UN troops in Korea Gen. Douglas A. MacArthur, USA, surmised that a successful landing in the Inchon area of South Korea and the rapid seizure of the nearby airfield at Kimpo would enable the allies to liberate the South Korean capital of Seoul, turn the flank of the North Koreans, and cut their rail and road supply routes into the south. On this date, *Badoeng Strait* (CVE 116) and *Sicily* (CVE 118) launched preliminary strikes against North Korean troops around Inchon and on roads leading into Seoul.

The following day, Task Force 90, Rear Adm. James H. Doyle commanding, sailed through a narrow channel and landed the 1st Marine Division at Inchon. Aircraft and naval gunfire supported the leading Marines as they seized fortified Wolmi Island. The landing craft regrouped and incurred a delay of about 12 hours to ensure that the treacherous tide again became favorable, and the Marines followed up with an assault of the mainland.

British carrier *Triumph* (R 16) operating with the Blockade and Covering Force provided air defense for the assault forces en route, and *Boxer* (CV 21) arrived on D-day. "The Navy and the Marines," MacArthur wrote Commander Seventh Fleet Vice Adm. Arthur D. Strubble, "have never shone more brightly than this morning." Through 3 October, carrier aircraft flew close air support missions and strikes against enemy lines of communication to support the advance inland. The success of the landings changed the course of the war.

18 SEPTEMBER • Fleet Logistic Air Wing, Atlantic/Continental, replaced Fleet Logistic Air Wing, with a status parallel to that of the previously established Fleet Logistic Air Wing, Pacific.

19 SEPTEMBER • Two days after troops had fought their way inland from Inchon and captured the airfield at Kimpo, South Korea, the first elements of the 1st Marine Aircraft Wing arrived from Japan. Early the next morning, the Marine aircraft began air operations from there with strikes to support allied columns advancing on Seoul.

23 SEPTEMBER • An HO3S-1 equipped with an automatic pilot developed by the Aeronautical Instruments Laboratory was flown with three-axis automatic control at NAF Mustin Field, Philadelphia, Pa.

2 OCTOBER • The Bureau of Aeronautics authorized the establishment of Project Arowa (Applied Research: Operational Weather Analysis) at Norfolk, Va., to develop basic meteorological research data into practical weather forecasting techniques.

10 OCTOBER • Carriers moved into action off the east coast of Korea and launched strikes and sweeps from Ch'ŏngjin to Wŏnsan in preparation for amphibious landings at Wŏnsan. A heavy concentration of mines in the harbor delayed the scheduled landings and the naval attack shifted northward and inland to assist the push of UN forces. When troops landed on 26 October, the inland advance had swept past the intended objective area toward the Yalu River.

28 OCTOBER • Chief of Naval Operations Adm. Forrest P. Sherman directed the establishment by each station, air group, wing, and squadron of a permanent instrument flight board to check the instrument flying proficiency of naval aviators and naval aviation pilots, and to supervise and coordinate the instrument training of all pilots attached. He also directed the maintenance, with certain exceptions, by all Group I naval aviators of a valid instrument rating following 18 months from the date.

29 OCTOBER • The fast carrier force retired to Sasebo, Japan, because the advance of UN forces toward the Yalu River reduced the enemy-held area in Korea into which aircraft could attack.

31 OCTOBER • The National Advisory Committee for Aeronautics issued a report on tests at the Langley Aeronautical Laboratory in which a wind tunnel was used to determine the characteristics of a fully submerged,

421821

Lt. Cmdr. William T. Amen of VF-111 from *Philippine Sea* (CV 47) scored the Navy's first MiG kill, 9 November 1950.

high-speed submarine. The experiment reemphasized the interrelationships of basic naval sciences dealing with aeronautics and naval architecture.

6 NOVEMBER • United Nations forces approached the China–North Korean border along the Yalu River, and communist leaders from Moscow to Peking (Beijing) argued that the allied advance comprised part of a global U.S. conspiracy to encircle the Eastern Bloc. Chinese Premier Mao Tse-tung (Zedong) stated his expectation of American attacks across the Formosa (Taiwan) Strait, the Philippines, and French Indochina, and pledged to support the foundering North Korean regime. On 19 October, 12 Chinese divisions began to cross the Yalu from Manchuria, and several days later clashed with American and South Korean troops before deceptively withdrawing. As enemy opposition thus stiffened, the fast carriers returned on this date to attack targets in their assigned area east of the 127th meridian. Two days later the carriers received the primary mission of cutting off Chinese Communist reinforcements from Manchuria by destroying the international bridges across the Yalu River. Political considerations restricted UN aircraft from pursuing communist aircraft across the river into Chinese territory to avoid escalating the war to embroil the Soviets. These restrictions frustrated the allies and allowed enemy aircraft to escape retribution in what became a safe haven.

9 NOVEMBER • Aircraft made the initial strikes against the bridges crossing the Yalu River at Sinŭiju, North Korea. Lt. Cmdr. William T. Amen, commanding officer of VF-111, led F9F-2B Panthers that covered the strike force of F4U Corsairs and AD Skyraiders. At least five Mikoyan and Gurevich (MiG) 15 Fagots flying from the sanctuary of Antung, Manchuria, counterattacked. The battle swirled from just above ground level up to 18,000 feet, and Amen shot down a MiG-15 to make the Navy's first MiG—and jet-on-jet—kill. The Skyraiders scored three direct hits and five near misses on the bridges during the first strike, and scored four hits with 2,000-pound bombs on the railroad bridge at Manpojin. All the attackers returned despite heavy and accurate enemy ground fire.

10 NOVEMBER • The Naval Guided Missile Training Unit No. 21, under training to operate RIM-2 Terrier surface-to-air missiles, was relocated from Naval Ordnance Test Station Inyokern, Calif., to seaplane tender *Norton Sound* (AV 11), and was redesignated a fleet activity under AirPac.

14 NOVEMBER • Two days of snow-covered flight decks and heavy seas severely hampered carrier operations off Korea, which gave the Communists time to repair the Yalu River bridges. On 16 November, a reconnaissance flight of two aircraft photographed the target areas around Sinŭiju and confirmed the transfer of most of the antiaircraft guns to the Manchurian side of the river, where politics constrained the allies from attacking the flak batteries.

18 NOVEMBER • Carriers launched a strike at the bridge at Sinŭiju, North Korea, to cut the communist supply lines across the Yalu River. Twelve MiG-15 Fagots jumped the strike group of VF-54 F4U-4Bs as the Corsairs rendezvoused at 31,000 feet with their high cover F9F-2 and F9F-3 Panthers. Lt. Cmdr. William E. Lamb, VF-52 commanding officer, and Lt. Robert E. Parker flew two Panthers and downed a jet (both shared), while Ens. Frederick C. Weber of VF-31 flying another Panther shot down a second MiG-15. Meanwhile, the Corsairs attacked the antiaircraft guns with 500-pound proximity-fuzed bombs, which facilitated an attack on the bridge by the AD Skyraiders of VA-55. The planes experienced difficulties hitting the dug-in guns, intense flak riddled a pair of Skyraiders, and the raid only damaged the bridge.

27 NOVEMBER • The failure to drop the bridges over the Yalu River, enabled the Chinese Communist Ninth and Thirteenth Army Groups comprising 26 divisions, numbering 260,000 men, to launch a second offensive to close the jaws of a giant trap. "We face an entirely new war," Commander U.S. Far East Command and UN troops in Korea Gen. Douglas A. MacArthur, USA, declared.

29 NOVEMBER • Within days of their offensive, the Chinese tore gaps in the allied lines, smashing through the South Korean troops, and then attacked the exposed flanks of the U.S. soldiers and Marines especially in the rugged mountains northwest of Chosin Reservoir. Their drive sent the UN troops into a retreat through the onset of winter. The crisis required a shift of emphasis in fast carrier operations from bridge strikes to close air support, which intensified through December to cover the retreat toward east coast ports and the evacuation of the troops and civilian refugees by ships. This continued into January as the enemy advance rolled south past the 38th parallel.

30 NOVEMBER • Naval aviation flew 6,725 Korean War sorties during November; 2,728 by heavy carriers, 583 by escort carriers, 473 by naval non-carrier aircraft, and 2,941 by Marines ashore. Six aircraft were lost to enemy action and 27 operationally.

4 DECEMBER • Ens. Jesse L. Brown of VF-31—the first African American to complete the Navy's basic flight training program for pilot qualification and to be designated a naval aviator—embarked on board *Leyte* (CV 32), flew a close support mission in an F4U-4 Corsair over Hagaru-ri, North Korea. Antiaircraft fire struck the Corsair and he made an emergency landing beyond Chosin. As darkness approached and the temperature fell, his wingman, Lt. j.g. Thomas J. Hudner, deliberately crash-landed nearby and attempted to pull Brown from the burning wreck. With the buckled fuselage trapping the pilot's legs, Hudner packed snow around Brown to protect him from the flames and returned to his aircraft to radio for a rescue helicopter. An HO3S-1 flown by 1st Lt. Charles C. Ward, USMC, of VMO-6 responded, and after repeated unsuccessful attempts to free Brown, had to leave him with the onset of nightfall. Brown died and Ward rescued Hudner, who subsequently received the Medal of Honor.

6 DECEMBER • Five days after her return from Korean waters, *Valley Forge* (CV 45) sailed under emergency orders to return to the war from San Diego, Calif.

6 DECEMBER • Col. Deane C. Roberts, USMC, commanding officer of VMR-152, provided an R5D to the 1st Marine Aircraft Wing for a unique conversion into a tactical air direction center with situation maps and an extra radio.

An F4U Corsair drops napalm on Chinese communist positions while supporting Marines during the fierce fighting near the Chosin Reservoir, 6 December 1950.

6 DECEMBER • Chinese troops redoubled their attacks on retreating Marines in North Korea. Eighteen VMF-214 F4U-4B Corsairs struck the enemy with rockets and proximity-fuzed 500-pound bombs but the Chinese rallied. Cmdr. Horace H. Epes Jr., VF-33 commanding officer, led eight F4U-4s that made repeated strafing and napalm runs on the enemy. In some instances the Corsairs bombed the Chinese as close as 50 yards ahead of the Marines.

7 DECEMBER • The advance of communist forces required the evacuation of airfields in North Korea. Without an additional break in flying close air support operations, the F4U-4 Corsairs of VMF-214 flew from Yonpo and landed on board *Sicily* (CVE 118) off Hŭngnam.

9 DECEMBER • After 12 days of fighting, the Marines retreating from Chosin linked up with other UN troops at Chinhung-ni.

10 DECEMBER • Task Force 90 began to evacuate troops and refugees from Hŭngnam, North Korea. In two weeks, ships rescued 105,000 American and South Korean troops, and 91,000 civilians who had fled the pursuing Communists. The vessels also loaded 350,000 tons of supplies. Naval aircraft supplemented allied types that covered the withdrawal and delayed the onslaught of Chinese and North Korean columns. Following the evacuation of the last survivors, troops destroyed the harbor facilities with demolition charges to prevent their use by the enemy.

17 DECEMBER • *Bataan* (CVL 29), with VMF-212 embarked, joined forces in the Sea of Japan that protected the evacuation of troops and refugees from Hŭngnam and other North Korean ports. *Bataan* was pressed into service after her delivery of replacement aircraft to Japan, and her embarked F4U-4 Corsairs had been evacuated from Yonpo earlier in the month.

18 DECEMBER • VP-892 began operations from Iwakuni, Japan, as the first all-Reserve squadron to operate in the Korean War.

19 DECEMBER • President Harry S. Truman proclaimed a national emergency because of the Chinese successes in the Korean War.

22 DECEMBER • Chinese Premier Mao Tse-tung (Zedong) ordered his commanders to launch a third Korean War offensive.

31 DECEMBER • In December, naval aviation flew 6,781 Korean War sorties; 3,630 by heavy carriers, 1,470 by escort carriers, 535 by naval non-carrier aircraft, and 1,146 by Marines ashore. Enemy action claimed 16 aircraft and accidents 32 others.

1023526

AAM-N-2 Sparrow I air-to-air missiles mounted on the wing of an F3D Sky Knight of VX-4 at Naval Air Missile Test Center, Point Mugu, Calif.

1951

4 JANUARY • The Chinese Communists and North Koreans drove UN forces from the South Korean capital of Seoul.

16 JANUARY • The Navy implemented a step in a program that provided for the early service evaluation of BW-0 (subsequently redesignated RIM-2A) Terrier surface-to-air and AAM-N-2 Sparrow I air-to-air missiles, together with the development of production engineering information and the establishment of production facilities, by placing an advance order for 1,000 Sparrows with Sperry Gyroscope Company.

17 JANUARY • Commander Eighth Army Lt. Gen. Matthew B. Ridgeway, USA, ordered a counterattack against the communist forces in Korea. Naval aircraft flew close air support missions and interdicted enemy supply routes during the ensuing fighting.

29 JANUARY • Task Force 77 commenced a series of air attacks against rail and highway bridges along North Korea's east coast. The force subsequently received the additional assignment of bombing highways and lines of communication in the northeastern part of the peninsula, which occupied a major share of its attention through the end of the Korean War.

1 FEBRUARY • Heavy Attack Wing 1, Capt. Robert Goldthwaite commanding, was established at Norfolk, Va., as the first of two such units. The next day, VC-5 reported as the wing's first squadron.

5 FEBRUARY • Six AJ-1 Savages and three P2V-3C Neptunes of VC-5 departed NAS Norfolk, Va., and flew via Bermuda and the Azores to NAS Port Lyautey, French Morocco. A lack of spare parts compelled the grounding of one of the Savages at Lajes in the Azores, but the remaining five AJ-1s completed the first U.S. transatlantic flight by carrier-type aircraft three days later. Planners initially based the Savages at Port Lyautey. In the event of war, they were to load atomic bombs and fly to carriers sailing en route to the eastern

Mediterranean, and operate from them against Soviet military targets along the outer fringe of the Eastern Bloc to tear holes in the Soviet defenses to enable Air Force bombers to penetrate to strike deeper targets.

8 FEBRUARY • After a period in Japan, Marine fighter squadrons returned to the Korean War and resumed their support operations from an airfield at Pusan (Busan), South Korea.

16 FEBRUARY • United Nations forces began a naval siege of the North Korean port of Wŏnsan that continued throughout the war. The allies temporarily developed the port into a sanctuary for aircraft damaged by enemy fire that ditched in the harbor. Helicopters pulled the downed aircrew to safety and thereby saved men from death or enemy imprisonment.

6 MARCH • Naval Ordnance Test Station Inyokern, Calif., launched a ramjet-powered Talos surface-to-air missile. It operated for two minutes in the longest full-scale ramjet flight achieved to date.

29 MARCH • Carrier Air Group 101, the first all-Reserve group to deploy to Korean waters, flew its initial combat missions from *Boxer* (CV 21). Reserve squadrons composed the group called to active duty from Dallas, Texas; Glenview, Ill.; Memphis, Tenn.; and Olathe, Kans.

29 MARCH • An XSSM-N-8 Regulus test vehicle operating under airborne command took off from the lakebed, circled the field, and landed successfully at Edwards AFB, Calif.

31 MARCH • A contract issued to Convair for the XFY-1 initiated a program to develop a propeller-driven vertical takeoff fighter. Lockheed received an order three weeks later for a similar aircraft known as the XFO-1 (later redesignated XFV-1) as an alternate solution to the design problems.

2 APRIL • Two F9F-2B Panthers of VF-191, each loaded with four 250- and two 100-pound general-purpose bombs, catapulted from *Princeton* (CV 37) to attack a railroad bridge near Songjin, North Korea. Their attack marked the Navy's first recorded use of jet aircraft as bombers.

1053792

A Regulus I surface-to-surface missile uses jet-assisted takeoff rockets to boost its launch during testing.

636833

Tunny (SSG 282) launches a Regulus I surface-to-surface missile test vehicle.

5 APRIL • The Chinese Communists and North Koreans launched their fifth offensive with the aim of pushing the UN forces back from the 38th parallel and enveloping the South Korean capital of Seoul. During the following two weeks, allied aircraft flew daily close air support strikes to aid combat-engaged Marines and soldiers.

8 APRIL • Intelligence indications of a possible Chinese Communist amphibious attack on Formosa (Taiwan) compelled the temporary detachment of Task Force 77 from Korean waters to make a show of strength in the Formosa Strait. From 11 to 14 April, the ships steamed off the China

429191

F9F Panthers of VF-191 dump their reserve fuel before landing on board *Princeton* (CVA 37) following a strike over Korea.

428678

AD-4 Skyraiders destroy the Hwachon Dam with torpedoes, 1 May 1951.

coast and their aircraft flew aerial parades in international airspace off the Chinese mainland before returning to the Korean War.

1 MAY • In the first and only use of aerial torpedoes during the Korean War, carrier aircraft attacked the Hwachon Dam 50 miles northeast of Seoul, South Korea. The dam contained the waters of the Pukhan River, which ran high because of the spring thaw and thus enabled communist troops to attack the exposed flanks of allied troops. The Chinese and North Koreans emplaced antiaircraft guns along likely aerial approaches and strengthened the dam with rocks. Cmdr. Richard C. Merrick, Carrier Air Group 19 commanding officer, led a strike group from *Princeton* (CV 37) consisting of eight VA-195 AD-4 Skyraiders and three others from VC-35 Detachment 3, supported by eight VF-192 F4U-4 Corsairs and four of VF-193. The Corsairs attacked the flak batteries while the Skyraiders ran the gauntlet and dropped their torpedoes. Two of the eight torpedoes malfunctioned and missed but the remaining six weapons struck the dam and tore breaches in the flood gates, releasing millions of gallons of water. VA-195 laconically tallied the success at the bottom of a list of targets attacked as "Flood Gates: 2 Destroyed, 1 Damaged." The attack prevented communist forces from easily crossing the now flooded valleys.

1 JUNE • The 1st Marine Aircraft Wing inaugurated the policy of basing one squadron immediately in the rear of the 1st Marine Division to provide ground alert aircraft on call through the Joint Operations Center to provide close air support.

5 JUNE • Task Force 77 commenced participation in Operation Strangle—a joint offensive with the 1st Marine Aircraft Wing and the Air Force to interdict eight communist supply routes across the Korean Peninsula. These strikes continued until ongoing aerial reconnaissance missions

Korean railroad bridges fell after repeated bombing during the interdiction campaign.

revealed by 20 September that the operation failed to cut the enemy routes. Chinese and North Korean efforts to camouflage and conceal trucks, tanks, rail and boat traffic, and supply dumps and caches, and their endeavors to repair damage reduced the effectiveness of these raids.

12 JUNE • Two PB4Y-2s of VP-772 were transferred from NAS Atsugi, Japan, to Pusan (Busan), South Korea. The Privateers dropped flares to support Marine night bombing, and their success persuaded planners to continue the practice of assigning specially equipped patrol aircraft for this purpose during the subsequent months.

17 JUNE • Convair received a contract for the development of a delta wing, hydroski equipped research seaplane with fighter characteristics that subsequently became the (redesigned) XF2Y-1.

18 JUNE • Airship ZPN-1 made its first flight.

1 JULY • The Naval Air Turbine Test Station was established at Trenton, N.J. Its mission consisted of the testing and evaluation of turbojet, turboprop, ramjet, and pulsejet engines, together with their accessories and components.

3 JULY • Capt. James V. Wilkins, USMCR, of VMF-312, flew an F4U-4B as part of a four-plane armed reconnaissance mission when antiaircraft fire struck his Corsair and the plane crashed near Yon-Dong, 35 miles southwest of Wŏnsan, North Korea. Lt. j.g. John K. Koelsch of HU-1

424772

Three of eight HTL-3s transported for use in evacuating Korean War battle casualties prepare to lift off from *Valley Forge* (CV 45) off the Japanese coast in early January 1953.

1053760

Because of devastating strike damage, there is little evidence that this stranded locomotive was ever on a railway.

piloted an HO3S-1, embarked on board Japanese-manned tank landing ship *Q-007*, in an attempt to rescue Wilkins. Despite thick fog and the approach of darkness Koelsch spotted Wilkins and hovered overhead. Aircrewman AD3 George M. Neal lowered the hoist, but enemy fire shot down the helicopter. The three men evaded the communists on the ground for nine days before their capture. During their imprisonment, Koelsch inspired his fellow prisoners with his defiance of their captors, but died during captivity and posthumously received the Medal of Honor. Wilkins and Neal survived, and Neal was awarded the Navy Cross.

10 JULY • Commander Naval Forces Far East Vice Adm. C. Turner Joy led a delegation of UN military representatives for armistice discussions with communist leaders at Kaesong, Korea. The unabated fighting across the Korean Peninsula, however, compelled the repeated suspension of negotiations during the remainder of the war.

22 JULY • Chief of Naval Operations Adm. Forrest P. Sherman suffered a fatal heart attack while visiting Naples, Italy. Born on 30 October 1886 in Merrimack, N.H.,

F2H-2 Banshees of VF-172 flying from *Essex* (CV 9) seek North Korean targets.

Sherman graduated from the Naval Academy in 1917, completed flight training in 1922, and become an early proponent of naval aviation. He served through both world wars and became one of the principal authors of the National Security Act of 1947.

7 AUGUST • An experimental prototype Navy shipboard jet fighter, designated XF3H-1, completed its first flight at McDonnell Aircraft Corporation, St. Louis, Mo.

7 AUGUST • A Viking high-altitude sounding rocket developed by the Naval Research Laboratory achieved an altitude of 135.3 miles over the White Sands Proving Grounds, N. Mex.

7 AUGUST • Douglas test pilot William B. Bridgeman set an unofficial world speed record of 1,238 mph in a Navy sonic research D-558-2 Skyrocket over Edwards AFB, Calif.

8 AUGUST • Secretary of the Navy Dan A. Kimball established the classification AVM for Auxiliaries, Guided Missile Ship. The action redesignated modified seaplane tender *Norton Sound* from AV-11 to AVM-1.

15 AUGUST • Douglas test pilot William B. Bridgeman reached 79,494 feet—an unofficial world altitude record—in a Navy sonic research D-558-2 Skyrocket over Edwards AFB, Calif.

23 AUGUST • *Essex* (CV 9), the first of the postwar converted carriers to fight in the Korean War, joined Task Force 77 off the east coast of Korea and launched her aircraft into battle. During this strike, F2H-2 Banshees flown by VF-172 went into action for the first time.

25 AUGUST • F2H-2 Banshees from VF-172 and VF-51 F9F-2 Panthers, embarked on board *Essex* (CV 9) operating with Task Force 77 in the Sea of Japan, escorted Air Force

1030116

Sailors arm an F9F-3 Panther's 20mm guns.

428982

Aviation ordnancemen prepare an AD Skyraider for a raid over Korea.

Boeing B-29 Superfortresses on a high-altitude bombing mission against the Rashin railroad marshalling yards near the USSR-China border with North Korea.

7 SEPTEMBER • Guided missile ship *Norton Sound* (AVM 1) made the first RIM-2A surface-to-air missile launch, firing a Terrier that intercepted an F6F Hellcat target drone.

15 SEPTEMBER • The Department of Defense Joint Parachute Test Facility was established at NAAS El Centro, Calif. Navy and Air Force parachutists under Bureau of Aeronautics management manned the facility.

21 SEPTEMBER • By this time, Korean War fighting gradually developed into positional warfare. On this date, the fast carrier task force consequently received orders to reduce its close air support missions and to concentrate attacks on railroads as part of an interdiction program.

3 OCTOBER • HS-1, Cmdr. Joseph T. Watson Jr. commanding, was established at NAS Key West, Fla. as the first helicopter antisubmarine squadron in the Navy.

29 OCTOBER • AD Skyraiders from VF-54, embarked on board *Essex* (CV 9), raided the communist party headquarters building at Kapsan, North Korea. An intelligence report revealed the meeting to planners, and the attack killed or wounded scores of enemy officials.

6 NOVEMBER • Soviet fighters shot down a P2V-3W, BuNo 124284, of VP-6, as the Neptune flew a weather reconnaissance mission over international waters off Vladivostok, Siberia. All ten men on board were reported missing and presumed dead.

1 DECEMBER • The Naval Aviation Safety Activity was established at Norfolk, Va. This operated under the Chief of Naval Operations to promote the aviation safety program and direct a specific effort toward maintaining the highest practicable level of aviation safety throughout the fleet. In

One of the very first AD-1 Skyraiders, BuNo 09177, fires a salvo of Mighty Mouse air-to-air rockets during tests at NOTS Inyokern, Calif., 26 January 1950.

April 1955, the activity was redesignated the Naval Aviation Safety Center.

11 DECEMBER • Aircraft from Air Task Group (ATG) 1 flew their first combat mission from *Valley Forge* (CV 45) against coastal rail lines and bridges in northeastern North Korea. ATG-1 was the first such group formed following experience in the Korean War that demonstrated that the five squadrons originally comprising carrier air groups did not operate effectively in combat from *Essex* (CV 9)-class carriers. The temporary withdrawal of one squadron from each group scheduled for deployment provided the squadrons needed for the ATGs. These temporary groups did not formerly establish and operated from 1951 to early 1959 with eight in existence by 1955.

12 DECEMBER • The Kaman Aircraft Corporation K-225 made its first flight at Windsor Locks, Conn. This Navy-sponsored development of a helicopter equipped with a Boeing YB-502 turbine engine marked the first demonstration of the adaptability of gas-turbine engines to helicopters.

19 DECEMBER • *Philippine Sea* (CV 47) tested her nuclear weapons emergency assembly capabilities while at San Diego, Calif.

1952

4 JANUARY • The creation of the new classifications CAG and CLG for heavy and light cruiser guided missile ships brought about the redesignation of converted heavy cruisers *Boston* and *Canberra* from CA-69 and -70 to CAG-1 and -2, respectively.

1 FEBRUARY • Chief of Naval Operations Adm. William M. Fechteler approved a modification of the Project 27A carrier conversion program that provided an increase in the capacity of deck operating equipment. The changes included the use of more powerful arresting gear, higher performance catapults, and replacement of the number three

An F9F Panther launches from *Antietam* (CVA 36) during the operational suitability testing of the angled flight deck on 14 January 1953.

centerline elevators with a deck-edge type of greater capacity. Three *Essex* (CV 9)-class carriers that incorporated these modifications completed their conversion under Project 27C (Axial Deck) in 1954.

1 APRIL • Guided Missiles Service Unit No. 211 was formed at the Naval Mine Depot, Yorktown, Va. The first of six scheduled RIM-2 Terrier surface-to-air missile units, the command consisted of sailors trained by Guided Missiles Training Unit No. 2 at the Consolidated Vultee Aircraft Corporation, San Diego, Calif.

26 APRIL • *Wasp* (CVS 18) and destroyer minesweeper *Hobson* (DMS 26) collided as *Wasp* conducted night flying operations in the Atlantic, 700 miles west of the Azores while en route to Gibraltar. The destroyer broke in two and sank quickly. *Wasp* and destroyer minesweeper *Rodman* (DMS 21) rescued 52 survivors, but 176 men died. *Wasp* had no casualties, but a 75-foot gash in her bow required drydock work at Bayonne, N.J. In ten days, the bow of *Hornet* (CV 12)—undergoing conversion to an attack carrier at Brooklyn—was removed and floated by barge to replace *Wasp*'s shattered stem.

28 APRIL • The Navy announced the adoption of the British-developed steam catapult for use on board U.S. aircraft carriers, with the first installation scheduled for *Hancock* (CV 19). The decision followed tests conducted during the first three months of the year at the Philadelphia Naval Shipyard, Pa.; NOB Norfolk, Va.; and at sea; during which British carrier *Perseus* (A 197) had launched U.S. naval aircraft by this device.

8 MAY • The Fleet Air Gunnery Unit was established as an integral part of the operating forces of the Pacific Fleet under AirPac. Its mission was to provide air gunnery training on an individual and tactical unit basis for the Pacific Fleet.

16 MAY • Two RIM-2 surface-to-air missiles fired separately at F6F-5K target drones destroyed the Hellcats. This success culminated the Terrier developmental program, permitting the shift of emphasis to the production of the first tactical model.

26 MAY • The Navy's first, and for many years the world's largest, wind tunnel was disestablished at the Naval Gun Factory, Washington, D.C. The 8-by-8-foot wooden tunnel had been completed in 1914, and served the Navy for more than 30 years as an aerodynamic laboratory for research in aircraft design.

26 MAY • Jets and other aircraft from the Naval Air Test Center and the Atlantic Fleet demonstrated the feasibility of the angled-deck concept during three days of tests using a simulated angled deck on board *Midway* (CVB 41).

17 JUNE • The Aviation Medical Acceleration Laboratory was dedicated at the Naval Air Development Center. The laboratory featured a human centrifuge with a 110-foot arm capable of producing accelerations of up to 40 Gs, and was designed and constructed as a research tool for investigating pilot reactions to the accelerations encountered in high-speed flight at various temperatures and altitudes, and also afterward proved useful in the astronaut training program.

20 JUNE • A contract was issued for the construction of a 7-by-10 foot slotted throat transonic wind tunnel at the David Taylor Model Basin, Washington, D.C.

433345

A Marine HRS helicopter carries supplies to an isolated outpost in the Korean mountains.

23 JUNE • Air Force, Navy, and Marine aircraft virtually destroyed North Korean electric power potential with more than 1,200 sorties during two days of attacks on military targets that had been bypassed during previous raids. The main effort struck the hydroelectric plant at Suiho, 40 miles up the Yalu River from Antung, Manchuria. The raids continued the following day focused on the plants at Chosin, Fusen, and Kyosen.

1 JULY • The Naval Guided Missile School was established at the Fleet Air Defense Training Center, Dam Neck, Va. The school provided the fleet with people trained in the operation, maintenance, and control of surface- and submarine-launched guided missiles. The Naval Air Guided Missile School (Advanced) was also established at the Naval Air Technical Training Center, NAS Jacksonville, Fla., to provide technicians for air-launched guided missiles.

11 JULY • The allies gradually developed a program of mass air attack over the course of the Korean War. During one of the major coordinated air efforts of the conflict, USN, USMC, USAF, Australian, and British aircraft flew round-the-clock strikes into the following day on railroad yards and industrial facilities at the North Korean capital, Pyŏngyang.

14 JULY • The keel of *Forrestal* (CVA 59) was laid at the Newport News (Virginia) Shipbuilding and Dry Dock Company. She was the first of the 59,900-ton carriers and the name ship of her class.

1 AUGUST • The Naval Air Special Weapons Facility was established at Kirtland AFB, N. Mex. This provided for naval participation in various programs involved in the application of nuclear weapons to aircraft.

6 AUGUST • A fire swept the hangar deck of *Boxer* (CV 21), killing eight men and seriously injuring two, forcing the

An AJ-1 Savage lands on board *Lake Champlain* (CV 39).

carrier to undergo emergency repairs from 11 to 23 August at Yokosuka, Japan. *Boxer* returned to Korean waters and then, on 26 September, returned to San Francisco, Calif. The ship underwent repairs there until March 1953.

7 AUGUST • Squadron Leader John R. Gardner, RAF, on an exchange from the Royal Air Force, and airborne intercept operator SSgt. R. G. Kropp of VMF(N)-513 launched in an F3D-2 Sky Knight for a training mission from K-8 near Kunsan, South Korea. Controllers diverted them to search for aircraft showing emergency IFF and, although they failed to engage the elusive enemy, the event marked the first combat sortie of a Sky Knight. A detachment of Sky Knights from VC-4 augmented the Marine F3D-2s, and the sailors and Marines subsequently flew close escort and barrier patrols for Air Force Boeing B-29 Superfortresses during night bombing raids over North Korea.

28 AUGUST • Guided Missile Unit 90, embarked on board *Boxer* (CV 21), launched an explosive-laden F6F-5K Hellcat drone under control of two AD Skyraiders against a railroad bridge at Hŭngnam, North Korea. The attack marked the first of six such Navy drone operations.

29 AUGUST • Task Force 77 carrier air squadrons teamed with Fifth Air Force, 1st Marine Aircraft Wing, British, and South Korean aircraft for around-the-clock strikes over two days against communist supply concentrations around Pyŏngyang, North Korea.

1 SEPTEMBER • After the completion of an outfit with RIM-2 Terrier surface-to-air missiles at the Norfolk Naval Shipyard, Va., battleship *Mississippi* (AG 128) reported to Commander Operational Development Force to take part in Terrier evaluations.

1 SEPTEMBER • Vessels that participated in Operation Mainbrace, NATO's first large scale naval exercise in the North Atlantic, included battleship *Wisconsin* (BB 64), *Midway* (CVB 41), and *Franklin D. Roosevelt* (CVB 42).

1 SEPTEMBER • Carrier aircraft from Task Force 77 attacked the North Korean oil refinery at Aoji about eight miles from the Soviet border.

3 SEPTEMBER • The firing of the first fully configured AAM-N-7 Sidewinder I air-to-air missile initiated a period of developmental testing at Naval Ordnance Test Station Inyokern, Calif.

8 SEPTEMBER • The Deputy Chief of Naval Operations (Air) assumed responsibility for all phases of basic and technical training of people for air-launched missiles. The Commander Naval Air Technical Training Command administered the program. The Bureau of Naval Personnel formerly held responsibility for all individual training.

11 SEPTEMBER • After World War II, Yugoslav support of the Eastern Bloc deteriorated. On this date, *Coral Sea* (CVB 43) called at Split, Yugoslavia. The next day, Yugoslav President Josip Broz (Tito) briefly visited the ship as a demonstration of the availability and acceptability of U.S. aid to the Yugoslavs. *Coral Sea* sailed on 14 September.

15 SEPTEMBER • VX-4 was established at NAMTC Point Mugu, Calif. The squadron served within AirPac to conduct operational evaluation tests of air-launched missiles, and initially assisted with the testing of AAM-N-2 Sparrow I air-to-air missiles.

1 OCTOBER • Aircraft Carriers (CV) and Large Aircraft Carriers (CVB) were redesignated Attack Aircraft Carriers (CVA).

9 OCTOBER • Carrier aircraft struck communist troops along the front lines in the Korean Peninsula that operated beyond the range of UN artillery. Naval aviators referred to these raids as "Cherokee strikes" in recognition of the Native American ancestry of Commander Seventh Fleet Vice Adm. Joseph J. Clark.

28 OCTOBER • The XA3D-1 bomber designed to carry nuclear weapons made its first flight. Skywarriors also later served in reconnaissance, electronic warfare, and tanker configurations.

3 NOVEMBER • Guided missile ship *Norton Sound* (AVM 1) launched a Regulus assault missile from off NAMTC Point Mugu, Calif. The Regulus impacted on San Nicolas Island in the first shipboard demonstration of the system.

3 NOVEMBER • Maj. William T. Stratton Jr., USMCR, and airborne intercept operator MSgt. Hans C. Hoglind, USMC, of VMF(N)-513 manning an F3D-2 Sky Knight, shot down a North Korean Yakovlev Yak-15 by 20mm cannon fire in the vicinity of Sinŭiju, North Korea. Their victory marked the first enemy jet destroyed by U.S. airborne intercept radar–equipped night fighters.

12 NOVEMBER • The final configuration of nonrigid airship ZP3K (later ZSG-3) was flown and accepted at NAS Lakehurst, N.J. The designers intended the modernized antisubmarine adaptation of K-class airships for carrier-based operations and 30 received the modification.

18 NOVEMBER • VX-1 demonstrated the feasibility of using helicopters as aerial minesweepers in the first of a series of tests conducted with an HRP-1 off Panama City, Fla.

18 NOVEMBER • Seven Soviet MiG-15 Fagots approached ships of Task Force 77 while carriers launched strikes against North Korean targets from international waters near Vladivostok, Soviet Union. Three F9F-5 Panthers of VF-781, flying combat air patrol from *Oriskany* (CVA 34), intercepted the intruders and shot down two MiGs, damaged a third, and forced the survivors to retire.

4 DECEMBER • The Grumman XS2F-1, the prototype of the first carrier-borne aircraft designed specifically to hunt submarines, made its first flight.

16 DECEMBER • *Princeton* (CVA 37) catapulted F2H-2P Banshee control jets followed by a Regulus assault missile from the sea test range off NAMTC Point Mugu, Calif. The Banshees guided the Regulus to a transfer point on San Nicolas Island, where they handed off control to other aircraft that successfully guided the missile to its impact.

1953

12 JANUARY • Ship's skipper Capt. Samuel G. Mitchell landed in an SNJ Texan on board *Antietam* (CVA 36) in the initiation of test operations on board the Navy's first angled deck carrier. During the next four days, six aircraft models made landings, touch-and-go landings, night landings, and takeoffs in winds of varying force and direction. Angled flight decks eventually became a feature on all Navy carriers and contributed to the reduction in the number of accidents.

18 JANUARY • Chinese Communist antiaircraft guns shot down P2V-5, BuNo 127744, of VP-22 while the Neptune patrolled the Formosa (Taiwan) Strait off Swatow, China. The plane ditched in the strait, but Chinese shore batteries fired on the rescuers who had to contend with high seas. Despite fire from the island of Nan-ao Tao, a Coast Guard

687387

A P2V Neptune carries two Petrel antiship guided missiles suspended beneath its wings, April 1956.

PBM-5 rescued 11 of the 13 Neptune crewmembers, but the Mariner crashed while attempting to takeoff in 8- to 12-foot swells. Destroyer *Halsey Powell* (DD 686) rescued ten survivors while a Mariner from VP-40 that assisted took antiaircraft fire, and shore batteries targeted destroyer *Gregory* (DD 802), which held her fire and cleared the area. Eleven men died including seven from the Neptune.

9 FEBRUARY • The carriers of Task Force 77 launched two days of maximum effort strikes against Chinese and North Korean supply concentrations and transport targets from Wŏnsan on the east coast through Songjin to Ch'ŏngjin on the west coast.

13 FEBRUARY • The first full-guidance flight of an AAM-N-6 Sparrow III air-to-air missile occurred at NAMTC Point Mugu, Calif.

1 MARCH • Aircraft from Task Force 77 heavily damaged the North Korean hydroelectric plant at Chosin. Four days later, they repeated the attack and cut the penstocks and destroyed sections of the main power plant.

6 MARCH • Submarine *Tunny* (SSG 282) returned to the fleet after the completion of her refit to launch Regulus assault missiles at Mare Island Naval Shipyard, Calif.

19 MARCH • The carriers of Task Force 77 launched a heavy strike that ravaged the industrial section of Ch'ŏngjin, North Korea.

20 MARCH • ZP2N-1 (later ZPG-2) made its first flight at Akron, Ohio. The airship was the production model of the nonrigid N-class but with an envelope of 975,000 cubic feet. The designers originally intended it to conduct mid-ocean antisubmarine warfare and convoy-escort operations, thus the airship contained provisions for in-flight refueling, reprovisioning, and servicing. The Navy procured 17 of these airships in antisubmarine and airborne early warning configurations; the latter were designated ZPG-2W.

9 APRIL • The experimental delta wing XF2Y-1 jet seaplane equipped with hydroskis made its first flight at San Diego, Calif.

3 MAY • Commanding General, Far East Air Forces listed 30 major North Korean airfields that were to be rendered unserviceable in order to limit communist air action and prevent augmentation of the enemy's air strength preceding the date of a rumored armistice. Task Force 77 received the responsibility to bomb six of these fields and the naval air campaign featured periodic attacks on these targets through the end of the Korean War.

21 MAY • An AD-4 Skyraider took off with a bomb load of 10,500-pounds from NAS Dallas, Texas. Its combined weight including guns, ammunition, fuel, and pilot totaled a useful load of 14,491 pounds—3,143 pounds more than the weight of the plane.

7 JUNE • The carriers operating in Korean waters directed their major effort against the communist front lines and supporting positions to counter enemy efforts to gain ground for negotiating leverage before a cease fire. These raids continued round-the-clock through 19 June.

Maj. John F. Bolt, USMC, an ace in World War II, becomes an ace in the Korean War and the first U.S. naval aviator to claim five victories in jet aerial combat.

23 JUNE • Lt. Cmdr. George H. Whisler Jr., attached to VR-31, completed the first transcontinental round-trip solo flight between sunrise and sunset. Whisler departed NAS Norfolk, Va., in an F9F-6 Cougar, BuNo 127432, and after stops at NAS Memphis, Tenn., and Webb AFB, Texas, landed at NAS North Island, Calif. He then took off in an F3D-2 Sky Knight, BuNo 127076, from North Island, refueled at NAS Dallas, Texas, and landed at Norfolk.

One of three D-558-2 high-speed research aircraft makes an early test flight with a JATO rocket assist in October 1949. Lt. Col. Marion E. Carl Jr., USMC, later set an unofficial altitude record of 83,235 feet in the type.

25 JUNE • Task Force 77 deployed four F4U-5Ns to operate under the Fifth Air Force for an indefinite period from Kimpo, South Korea. Communist nuisance night attacks on the field by aircraft flying too slowly to be intercepted by jets prompted the Corsair deployment.

30 JUNE • Reorganization Plan No. 6 from President Dwight D. Eisenhower became effective. This included the abolishment of the Research and Development Board and three other activities of the Department of Defense whose functions shifted to the Secretary of Defense; the creation of six new assistant secretaries of Defense; and the assignment of managerial control of the Joint Chiefs of Staff to the Chairman of the Joint Chiefs.

8 JULY • The designation Anti-Submarine Support Aircraft Carrier (CVS) was established for attack carriers assigned to hunt submarines. The decision became effective one month from this date and redesignated five assigned carriers, not all operational—*Enterprise* (CVS 6), *Franklin* (CVS 13), *Bunker Hill* (CVS 17), *Leyte* (CVS 32), and *Antietam* (CVS 36).

10 JULY • The Naval Air Development Unit was established at NAS South Weymouth, Mass. The unit participated in the development and testing of equipment designed for antisubmarine warfare and air defense.

11 JULY • Maj. John F. Bolt, USMC, made his fifth and sixth MiG kills of the Korean War while operating with the 39th Fighter-Interceptor Squadron of the Fifth Air Force. He flew an F-86E Sabre named *Darling Dottie*, Serial No. 52-2852, when his second section of four aircraft turned for base because of low fuel. Bolt spotted four MiGs and despite diminishing fuel attacked, with his wingman, the enemy head-on and repeatedly engaged the MiGs. He became the first U.S. naval aviator to attain five victories in jet aerial combat and the only Marine ace of the Korean War. Bolt received the Navy Cross for this action.

15 JULY • Submarine *Tunny* (SSG 282) launched a Regulus assault missile from a position off NAMTC Point Mugu, Calif., in the first submarine firing of the missile. The missile was recovered on San Nicolas Island after the simulated attack.

16 JULY • Lt. Guy P. Bordelon Jr., temporarily deployed ashore with VC 3 Detachment D to intercept communist night harassment raids against Seoul, shot down a North Korean Polikarpov Po-2 biplane while flying an F4U-5N Corsair. This battle marked Bordelon's fifth kill and made him the Navy's only ace of the Korean War.

25 JULY • The aircraft of Task Force 77 established a record for one day of operations in the Korean War by flying 538 offensive and 62 defensive sorties.

27 JULY • On the final day of the Korean War, Task Force 77 expended its major effort against Chinese and North Korean transportation facilities and designated airfields as secondary targets. These attacks claimed the destruction or damage of 23 railroad cars, 11 railroad bridges, a railroad tunnel, nine highway bridges, and a number of buildings.

27 JULY • United Nations and communist representatives signed an armistice at Panmunjom, Korea, which ended the major fighting of the Korean War. Isolated outbreaks occurred for years, however, because of North Korean violations of the agreement.

12 AUGUST • Battleship *Mississippi* (AG 128) fired a RIM-2 surface-to-air missile in the first successful shipboard launching of a fully guided missile. The Terrier hit the approaching F6F Hellcat drone.

21 AUGUST • Lt. Col. Marion E. Carl Jr., USMC, in a D-558-2 Skyrocket, attained a new altitude record of 83,235 feet over Edwards AFB, Calif.

2 SEPTEMBER • The Navy promulgated a conversion plan for *Midway* (CVA 41)-class carriers designated Project 110. The basic changes matched those for the angled-deck versions of Project 27C but with the addition of modified C-11 steam catapults in the angled-deck areas.

11 SEPTEMBER • In the first successful interception by an AAM-N-7 air-to-air missile, a Sidewinder shot down an F6F Hellcat drone at Naval Ordnance Test Station Inyokern, Calif.

1 OCTOBER • *Hornet* (CVA 12) completed conversion as the last of nine *Essex* (CVA 9)-class carriers to be modernized under Project 27A at New York Naval Shipyard, N.Y.

3 OCTOBER • Lt. Cmdr. James F. Verdin set a new official world speed record in an F4D-1 Skyray of 752.943 mph over a three-kilometer course at Edwards AFB, Calif. The achievement marked the first time that a carrier aircraft established the record in its normal combat configuration.

16 OCTOBER • Test pilot R. O. Rahn broke the 100-kilometer closed course speed record in an F4D-1 Skyray at 728.114 mph.

30 OCTOBER • The Department of Defense adopted National Security Council Directive No. 126, which reflected President Dwight D. Eisenhower's "New Look" defense policy focused on strategic power.

19 NOVEMBER • Chief of Naval Operations Adm. Robert B. Carney endorsed the common use of the Fleet Air Gunnery Unit by the Pacific and Atlantic Fleets and the Marine Corps "as a step towards increased emphasis and standardization in the combat employment of aircraft armament."

3 DECEMBER • The Steam Catapult Facility at NAMC Philadelphia, Pa., was established with the launching of F9F Panthers and AD Skyraiders.

630092

Lt. Cmdr. James F. Verdin, here shown on board *Coral Sea* (CVA 43) in the first of two XF4D-1 Skyray prototypes during final carrier qualifications in late October 1953, had earlier in the month set a new world speed record in the second prototype.

3 DECEMBER • The first successful test of super circulation—boundary-layer control—on a high-speed aircraft took place with an F9F-4 Panther at Grumman Aircraft Corporation, Bethpage, N.Y. Bureau of Aeronautics engineer John S. Attinello received credit for developing this practical application of the aerodynamic principle.

630627

A pair of F2H-2 Banshees of VF-62 sweep past *Lake Champlain* (CV 39) en route to their North Korean targets.

Chapter 8

The New Navy

1954–1959

Despite the truce that ended large-scale fighting in the Korean War, global peace remained on unsteady footing. The two great superpowers of the United States and the Soviet Union embraced divergent ideologies that led toward repeated confrontations in the Cold War. The rivals expanded their nuclear arsenals but the specter of global thermonuclear war compelled the adversaries to wage their struggle for supremacy through proxies.

The worsening situation in the Far East and a series of crises in the Middle East gave new importance to the traditional practice of deploying naval forces to trouble spots. International maneuverings led to incidents and demands that threatened world peace, and naval forces represented the nation in critical areas. On different occasions, these forces evacuated refugees, patrolled troubled waters, provided support to menaced nations, and presented a physical symbol of freedom as a bulwark between aggressors and oppressed.

Technological and scientific advances also marked the period and naval aviation passed through tremendous changes. The effective exploitation of these advances enhanced the firepower, versatility, and mobility of naval sea and air forces. Guided missiles began to replace guns on board ships, the fleet increased capabilities to deliver nuclear weapons, aircraft speeds jumped from subsonic to supersonic, the adaptation of nuclear power to aircraft proceeded under investigation, and an increased knowledge of space affected naval operations.

Air-to-air missiles became standard equipment on interceptors and ships received air defense missiles. Planners intended fighters to intercept Soviet bombers at long ranges and high altitudes and erroneously deleted guns from the initial design of the McDonnell Aircraft Company F4H-1 Phantom II, a mistake the Navy failed to remedy. Air Force experience gained over Vietnam during the following decade led that service to fit guns to later models. The Naval Air Reserve acquired air-to-surface missiles and an interceptor missile was introduced into flight training. Polaris fleet ballistic missiles went to sea on board nuclear-powered submarines. *Forrestal* (CVA 59)-class carriers entered service and the basic carrier modernization program attained fruition. The successful application of nuclear power included the construction of nuclear-propelled carrier *Enterprise* (CVAN 65). These additions and improvements strengthened the carrier forces and enabled the operation of a new family of aircraft with high performance capabilities.

Reorganizations within the Navy Department accompanied the application of technological advances that placed greater emphasis on research. Similar adjustments set up special task groups for the progressive improvement of antisubmarine tactics, provided mobile amphibious squadrons to operate in the new tactics of vertical envelopment, and revised the Reserves to provide units trained and equipped to perform specific tasks upon mobilization. These advances in technology and improvements in weapons and equipment challenged the Navy while the sea service played its traditional role of sea control.

The space program dominated the events of the late 1950s. Soviet achievements in space generated United States investigations regarding the state of the nation's scientific advances, education, and progress in missilery. Successful orbiting of Explorer I, Vanguard, and other satellites together with tests that demonstrated the feasibility of retrieving objects from orbit prompted the launch of an astronaut training program in quest of the dream of man in space.

Cmdr. Henry J. Jackson pilots the first aircraft—an S2F-1 Tracker—to be launched by a steam catapult from an American carrier. The operational trials on board *Hancock* (CVA 19) took place on 1 June 1954.

1954

1 JANUARY • The Naval Air Weapons Systems School was established at NAS Jacksonville, Fla. The school trained cadres in the maintenance of air-launched guided missiles, aircraft armament control systems, missile external control equipment, and bomb directors.

4 JANUARY • *Leyte* (CVS 32) became the initial operational antisubmarine warfare carrier.

19 MARCH • Multiple U.S. forces in the western Pacific operated on alert because of the Battle of Dien Bien Phu between the French and the communist Viet Minh in French Indochina (Cambodia, Laos, and Vietnam). On 22 March, Task Group 70.2, including *Essex* (CVA 9), *Wasp* (CVA 18), and *Boxer* (CVA 21), began steaming to an area south of Hainan to monitor the war.

1 APRIL • Pilots Lt. Cmdr. Francis X. Brady, Lt. W. Rich, and Lt. j.g. John C. Barrow completed the first transcontinental flights in less than four hours during a 2,438-mile journey in three VF-21 F9Fs from San Diego, Calif., to NAS Floyd Bennett Field, N.Y. Brady made the crossing in 3 hours, 45 minutes, 30 seconds; Rich in 3 hours, 48 minutes; and Barrow in 3 hours, 46 minutes, 49 seconds. All were refueled in mid-air over Hutchinson, Kans. Official timers did not participate.

18 APRIL • Twenty-five F4U-7 Corsairs of VMA-324 flew from *Saipan* (CVL 48) to the *Aéronavale* (French Naval Aviation) at Tourane (Da Nang), French Indochina

(Cambodia, Laos, and Vietnam). *Saipan* then entered the harbor, unloaded spare parts and maintainers, and sailed for Manila, Philippines.

19 APRIL • A modification of model designations for airships conformed with the designations for heavier-than-air aircraft. The action included the replacement of envelope designation letters K and N by manufacturer's letters, the uniform application of standard suffix numbers and letters, and the division of the patrol class of airships into patrol and antisubmarine classes. Thus ZP2K, ZP3K, and ZP4K became ZSG-2, -3, and -4, respectively; ZP5K became ZS2G-1; ZPN-1 became ZPG-1; ZP2N-1 became ZPG-2; and ZP2N-1W became ZPG-2W.

20 MAY • In January, the leftist Guatemalan government requested arms from the Eastern Bloc in reaction to a U.S. decision to support Western opponents of the regime. On this date, the first shipment arrived and the Caribbean Sea Frontier established air and sea patrols in the Gulf of Honduras to protect Honduras from invasion and control the flow of arms to the region. On 3 June, U.S. airlifts of arms to the Hondurans began followed on 18 June by an embargo against weapons to the Guatemalans. On 29 June, a Guatemalan rightist army coup led to the overthrow of the government.

25 MAY • After a record breaking flight of 200.1 hours, Cmdr. Marion H. Eppes landed a ZPG-2 airship at NAS Key West, Fla. The voyage of more than eight days in the air began at NAS Lakehurst, N.J., ranged over the Atlantic northward to Nova Scotia, Canada, out to Bermuda and Nassau, Bahamas, and southward over the Caribbean and Gulf of Mexico. Eppes subsequently received the Distinguished Flying Cross and the 1955 Harmon International Trophy for Aeronauts.

26 MAY • The port side catapult accumulator on board *Bennington* (CVA 20) burst and released vaporized lubricating oil during flight operations off Narragansett Bay. An unidentified heat source detonated the oil spray and set off a series of secondary blasts that killed 103 men and injured 201 others. The ship proceeded under her own power to disembark the casualties at NAS Quonset Point, R.I. *Bennington* then moved for extensive repairs and rebuilding from 12 June 1954 to 19 March 1955 at New York Naval Shipyard, N.Y.

An HUP-2 Retriever of HU-2 demonstrates a pilot recovery.

The XF2Y-1 Sea Dart hydro ski fighter throws up a massive wake during early taxi trials, which began in San Diego Bay in mid-December 1952.

27 MAY • Chief of Naval Operations Adm. Robert B. Carney approved Project 125 of the carrier improvement program, which further modernized the *Essex* (CVA 9)-class carriers that completed Project 27A by changes including the installation of angled decks and enclosure of the bows to improve seaworthiness.

1 JUNE • Cmdr. Henry J. Jackson launched in an S2F-1 Tracker from *Hancock* (CVA 19) in the initial operational test of the C-11 steam catapult. The tests continued throughout the month with the ship recording a total of 254 launches by Trackers, F2H-3/4 Banshees, F3D-2 Sky Knights, F7U-3 Cutlasses, FJ-2 Furies, and AD-5 Skyraiders.

1053776

An S2F Tracker lands on board *Valley Forge* (CVS 45).

63014

The first of two XF4D-1 Skyray prototypes, BuNo 124586, lands on board *Coral Sea* (CVA 43) during final carrier qualifications in late October 1953.

15 JUNE • The Naval Air Development and Material Center, Rear Adm. Selden B. Spangler commanding, was established at Johnsville, Pa. The center coordinated and guided aeronautical research, development, and material activities in the Fourth Naval District including facilities at Johnsville and Philadelphia, Pa., and Lakehurst and Trenton, N.J.

22 JUNE • An XA4D-1 made the first flight of a Skyhawk.

22 JULY • The XZS2G-1, formerly designated XZP5K-1, made its first flight at Goodyear Aircraft Corporation, Akron, Ohio. This airship had been designed as a replacement for K-class airships and had unusual inverted "Y" control surfaces.

26 JULY • Two Chinese Communist Lavochkin La-7s attacked a pair of AD-4 Skyraiders from VF-54, embarked on board *Philippine Sea* (CVA 47). During the ensuing battle, which included five other Skyraiders and an F4U-5N Corsair, both attackers were shot down without damage to U.S. aircraft. A Chinese gunboat also fired ineffectively at the planes. The Skyraiders had been involved with other commands, including aircraft from *Hornet* (CVA 12), in the search for survivors of a British Cathay Airlines passenger plane shot down by two Chinese La-7s off Hainan on 22 June, which killed ten of the 18 people on board including six Americans.

4 SEPTEMBER • Two Soviet MiG-15 Fagots attacked a P2V-5 of VP-19 on a routine reconnaissance mission over international waters. The Neptune ditched 40 miles off the Siberian coast of the Soviet Union, and an Air Force Grumman SA-16 Albatross amphibian rescued nine of the ten-man crew.

13 OCTOBER • Helicopters operating from *Saipan* (CVL 48) off the southern coast of Haiti aided humanitarian efforts to victims of Hurricane Hazel through 19 October.

31 OCTOBER • Ens. Duane L. Varner of VF-34 completed a 1,900-mile nonstop unrefueled transcontinental flight in an F2H-2 Banshee in 3 hours, 58 minutes, from NAS Los Alamitos, Calif., to NAS Cecil Field, Fla.

2 NOVEMBER • Pilot J. F. Coleman made a successful flight in the XFY-1 delta wing experimental fighter consisting of vertical takeoff, transition to horizontal flight, and return to vertical position for landing at NAS Moffett Field, Calif. The first free vertical takeoff had been accomplished on 1 August. Coleman later received the Harmon International Trophy for 1955 for his contribution to the art of flying in testing the XFY-1.

1955

17 JANUARY • VX-6 was established for operations with Task Force 43 at NAS Patuxent River, Md. The squadron provided services for parties based ashore on Antarctica and made courier flights between that continent and New Zealand during Operation Deep Freeze—the Navy's renewed support of Antarctic research. VX-6 initially used ski-equipped planes including two R4D-5/6 Skytrains, two P2V-2 Neptunes, and two UF-1 Albatrosses to deal with the harsh conditions on the ice shelf. Two R5D-2/3 Skymasters using their conventional landing gear operated from the relatively smoother sea ice at McMurdo Sound. Additional initial aircraft comprised four UC-1 Otters and three HO4S-3s.

21 JANUARY • A one-man direct-lift rotorcraft dubbed the Flying Platform made its first flight at the Hiller Helicopters plant, Palo Alto, Calif. The flight, which occurred during ground tests, was accidental but otherwise successful.

709126

Only one of three XFY-1 experimental vertical takeoff fighter prototypes was completed and flown.

27 JANUARY • Lt. Cmdr. William J. Manby Jr. of VF-33 set an unofficial time-to-climb mark by reaching 10,000 feet from a standing start in 73.2 seconds in an FJ-3 Fury at NAS Oceana, Va.

1 FEBRUARY • Task Force 43, Capt. George J. Dufek commanding, was activated to plan Antarctic operations scheduled to begin in the fall under Operation Deep Freeze. The force's first expedition mission was the construction of facilities and airstrips and supply delivery in support of U.S. participation in the International Geophysical Year of 1957 to 1958.

1061492

The second of two F8U-2N Crusader all-weather fighter prototypes displays the type's larger radome and Y-shaped fuselage mounted pylon capable of carrying AAM-N-7 Sidewinder heat-seeking air-to-air missiles.

1 FEBRUARY • After six days of intensive training at a Spanish air base at Reus, P2V-5 Neptunes of VP-23 left Tarragona, Spain, for NAS Port Lyautey, Morocco. The event marked the first operation of U.S. forces from bases in Spain.

6 FEBRUARY • *Midway* (CVA 41) reported to Commander Task Force 77 after a voyage from the Atlantic to the Pacific around the Cape of Good Hope. The ship's arrival initiated the operation of *Midway*-class carriers in the western Pacific.

6 FEBRUARY • During January, the Chinese Communists began to bombard the Tachen Islands off the China coast. On this date, carrier aircraft covered the Seventh Fleet's evacuation of 29,000 Taiwanese garrison troops and civilian refugees from the islands through 12 February.

13 FEBRUARY • McDonnell Aircraft Company test pilot C. V. Braun set the unofficial record for time-to-climb to 10,000 feet at 71 seconds in an F3H-1N Demon.

16 FEBRUARY • The Bureau of Aeronautics issued instructions describing new aircraft color schemes for application to Marine Corps aircraft beginning on 1 July 1955, and to be applied on all currently operating aircraft within the subsequent two years. The action changed the familiar Sea Blue to nonspecular Light Gull Gray on top and glossy Insignia White below for carrier aircraft, semigloss Seaplane Gray overall for water-based aircraft and overall nonspecular Light Gull Gray for helicopters. Bare aluminum was retained for utility types and landplane transports, the latter having in addition a solar heat reflecting glossy Insignia White top. Orange Yellow remained the color for primary trainers, but a shift occurred for the advanced trainer scheme to International Orange and Insignia White. Other changes included Olive Drab above and glossy Insignia White below for land observation types, and a combination of Orange Yellow, Engine Gray, and Insignia Red for target drones and target tow aircraft.

23 FEBRUARY • Douglas test pilot R. O. Rahn reached 10,000 feet in 56 seconds in an F4D-1 Skyray. His achievement marked the fourth unofficial time-to-climb record set by Navy carrier fighters in less than a month.

24 FEBRUARY • Chief of Naval Operations Adm. Robert B. Carney directed the use of the term "angled" in lieu of "canted," "slanted," and "flamed" to describe the deck of aircraft carriers in which the landing runway was offset at an angle from the line of the keel.

One of *Hancock's* (CVA 19) bow steam catapults launches an F8U-1 Crusader of VF-154 during carrier qualifications on 25 November 1957.

1053762

24 FEBRUARY • The first high-speed seaplane R3Y-1 transport, powered by four Allison turboprop engines, arrived for service suitability evaluation and trials at NATC Patuxent River, Md. Designers intended the Tradewind for long-range over water transportation of military cargo and personnel and the aerial evacuation of wounded.

22 MARCH • An R6D-1 Liftmaster of VR-3 assigned to the Military Air Transport Service crashed and exploded on Pali Kea Peak, 15 miles northwest of Honolulu, Hawaii. The accident killed all 66 people on board, nine crewmembers and 57 passengers.

25 MARCH • An XF8U-1 Crusader exceeded the speed of sound during its first flight at Edwards AFB, Calif.

4 APRIL • The Jet Transitional Training Unit was established at NAS Olathe, Kansas. The unit provided refresher training for aviators who transferred from shore to sea duty in the rank of commander and below. It also trained pilots making the transition from propeller aircraft to jets.

22 APRIL • During a ceremony on board *Bennington* (CVA 20), Secretary of the Navy Charles S. Thomas presented medals and commendations to 178 of the crew in recognition of their heroism fighting the 26 May 1954 fire.

30 APRIL • Adm. John H. Towers (Naval Aviator No. 3) died. His career began on 26 June 1911 when he reported to the Curtiss Flying School at Hammondsport, N.Y., for flight instruction. Towers served as Chief of Bureau of Aeronautics; Commander Naval Air Forces, Pacific; Commander Second Carrier Task Force; and Commander in Chief, Pacific Fleet. He retired from active duty on 1 December 1947 while serving as chairman of the General Board.

1053800

An XP6M-1 Seamaster swept-wing jet-powered seaplane.

2 MAY • The Navy announced the Aviation Officer Candidate Program for college graduates between the ages of 19 and 26. The plan paralleled the Aviation Cadet Program insofar as flight training was concerned, but in recognition of the higher scholastic achievement of its candidates offered a commission as ensign, USNR, upon completion of the four-month preflight course.

5 MAY • Twelve P2V-5 Neptunes of VP-1 returned from the Far East by way of Asia, Europe, and North Africa to NAS Whidbey Island, Wash. Despite a tour of duty that separated the Pacific Ocean leg from the rest of the voyage, their return marked the first round-the-world flight by a Navy squadron. VP-1 had departed the continental United States on 21 April 1955. The achievement bolstered the Navy's claims to strategic airpower in the face of ongoing Air Force demands for control over all land-based airpower and of congressional calls for post–Korean War defense cutbacks.

12 MAY • A revision of naval vessel classifications included the designations Escort Helicopter Aircraft Carrier (CVHE) and Utility Aircraft Carrier (CVU). The ships were redesignated one month later.

1 JUNE • VQ-1, Lt. Cmdr. Eugene R. Hall commanding, was established at NAS Iwakuni, Japan, as the first squadron of its type. It initially flew P4M-1Q Mercators.

22 JUNE • Two Soviet MiG-15 Fagots attacked a VP-9 P2V-5 Neptune, BuNo 131515, on patrol over the Aleutian Islands from NAS Kodiak, Alaska. The Neptune crashed on St. Lawrence Island near Gambell in the Bering Sea. Four of the 11 crewmen sustained gunfire wounds, and six were injured in the crash.

1 JULY • Naval Auxiliary Air Station (NAAS) Mayport, Fla., was established. The action completed the program that began in 1948 to convert the Jacksonville area into a fleet aviation center. Mayport provided mooring facilities for carriers alongside the airstrip and thus permitted the rapid loading or unloading of special equipment and personnel and the easy movement of carrier aircraft ashore or afloat.

1 JULY • *Thetis Bay* (CVE 90) was reclassified an assault helicopter aircraft carrier (CVHA 1).

14 JULY • A swept-wing XP6M-1 seaplane powered by four Allison J-71 jet engines and incorporating a new hull design made its first flight. The Seamasters were designed for minelaying and reconnaissance tasks but were adaptable to other missions.

22 AUGUST • VX-3 began operational evaluation of the mirror landing system installed on *Bennington* (CVA 20). Squadron commanding officer, Cmdr. Robert G. Dose, made the first landing with the device in an FJ-3 Fury. Two days later, Lt. Cmdr. Harding C. MacKnight accomplished the first night landing in an F9F-8 Cougar. A favorable report from VX-3 formed the basis for a decision to procure the mirror landing system for installation on carriers and at certain shore stations.

12 SEPTEMBER • The Navy announced the fitting of all the fighters in production with in-flight refueling gear, thus establishing the technique as a standard operational procedure.

16 SEPTEMBER • Guided Missile Group 1 was established at San Diego, Calif., to provide trained detachments to operate Regulus bombardment missiles from aircraft carriers

Forrestal (CVA 59) is the lead ship of her class, and the first operational U.S. carrier designed specifically to operate jets.

and to support the employment of the weapons on board cruisers and submarines of the Pacific Fleet. Ten days later, Guided Missile Group 2 was established at Chincoteague, Va., to provide the same services in the Atlantic Fleet.

27 SEPTEMBER • The chief of Naval Research received Navy responsibilities in connection with plans to launch an earth satellite during the International Geophysical Year of 1957 to 1958. These tasks included technical management of the Department of Defense portion of the program.

1 OCTOBER • *Forrestal* (CVA 59), Capt. Roy L. Johnson commanding, was commissioned at the Norfolk Naval Shipyard, Portsmouth, Va., as the first of four ships of her class.

10 OCTOBER • Following a week of disaster relief operations in the wake of Hurricane Hilda, *Saipan* (CVL 48), with HTU-1 embarked, sailed from Tampico, Mexico. Helicopters flying from the ship rescued 5,439 people and delivered 183,017 pounds of food and medical supplies. Additional commands involved included Marines from the 2d Marine Aircraft Wing, Marine Aircraft Group 26, and VMR-153 and -252.

1006922

The seventh of nine YA4D-1 Skyhawk test aircraft, BuNo 137819, carries a Douglas NAVPAC (navigation package) during a trial flight, c. May 1956.

11 OCTOBER • The Navy announced the initial step toward monitoring surface weather in uninhabited portions of the world to provide improved weather forecasting for use in both flight and surface operations. Automatic meteorological stations developed by the Office of Naval Research and Bureau of Aeronautics were set adrift in the hurricane lanes north of Puerto Rico and provided continuous weather data on tropical storm Janet. Subsequent progress included moored automatic weather stations. In September 1960, a station provided the first alert on tropical storm Ethel; beginning in 1956, unit stations on Antarctica achieved increasing success culminating in the provision of adequate data in 1960 and, beginning in 1964, with nuclear energy power as a source for data collection and transmission.

15 OCTOBER • Lt. Gordon Gray broke the Class C world speed record for 500 kilometers at 695.163 mph in an A4D-1 Skyhawk over Muroc, Calif.

1 NOVEMBER • *Boston* (CAG 1), Capt. Charles B. Martell commanding, was commissioned at the Philadelphia Naval Shipyard, Pa., as the world's first guided-missile cruiser.

8 NOVEMBER • The Secretary of Defense established a national ballistic missile program involving joint Army-Navy development of an intermediate-range ballistic missile for shipboard and land-based operations. The decision resulted in Navy support for the Army's program to develop liquid-propellant Jupiter missiles at the Redstone Arsenal, Ala., in order to adapt the weapons for use as fleet ballistic missiles.

9 NOVEMBER • The Chief of Naval Operations informed the chief of the Bureau of Ships of his intention to equip each angled-deck carrier with mirror landing systems, and requested the procurement of equipment for 12 installations during 1956 and 1957.

14 NOVEMBER • The flagship of Commander Task Force 43, Rear Adm. George J. Dufek, sailed from Norfolk, Va., for New Zealand to rendezvous with the ships of the task force for the southward voyage to participate in Operation Deep Freeze. The force's mission was to establish bases on Antarctica for geophysical studies during the following year.

1 DECEMBER • The assignment of an element of Fleet All Weather Training Unit, Pacific with the Continental Air Defense Command began as a fighter-interceptor group under Air Force control. The element was disestablished on 2 May 1958, raised to squadron status, and designated VF(AW)-3.

4 DECEMBER • Lt. Cmdr. Charles A. Mills piloted a ZPG airship in the vicinity of NAS South Weymouth, Mass., on an experimental ice accreting flight during a project to evaluate the all-weather capabilities of airships. In spite of heavy hull and propeller icing, severe vibration, and flying ice particles, Mills directed the collection of data, returned to the field under instrument conditions, and made a ground-controlled approach landing in a manner that retained a maximum amount of ice on the ship for ground analysis. For his achievement on this and other evaluation flights, Mills received the 1956 Harmon International Trophy for Aeronauts.

20 DECEMBER • Two P2V Neptunes and two R5D Skymasters of VX-6 forged the first air link with Antarctica with a flight from Christchurch, New Zealand, to McMurdo Sound, Antarctica.

1956

3 JANUARY • ZW-1, Cmdr. John L. Mack commanding, was established at NAS Lakehurst, N.J., as the first lighter-than-air unit of its type. The squadron's initial mission was the training of personnel, evaluation of airborne early warning (AEW) equipment, and formulation of tactics in preparation for manning a station in the contiguous AEW barrier system. In February, ZW-1 began project flights into September 1956 to test and evaluate the ZPG-2W airship as an AEW vehicle, and to determine the effectiveness of its equipment for use in continental and fleet air defense.

10 JANUARY • Airborne Early Warning Wing, Pacific was established at NAS Barbers Point, Territory of Hawaii, Capt. Edward C. Renfro commanding. The wing supervised and directed aircraft flying defensive patrols protecting the United States against surprise attack.

29 FEBRUARY • Growing unrest in Jordan and dissatisfaction with British influence within the kingdom led to the dismissal of British Commander Gen. John B. Glubb of the Arab Legionnaires. The Sixth Fleet subsequently dispatched *Randolph* (CVA 15) and *Coral Sea* (CVA 43) to the eastern Mediterranean. The formation of a new Jordanian cabinet in May ended the turmoil.

7 MARCH • The assignment of F3H-2N Demons to the fleet began with the delivery of six to VF-14 at NAS Cecil Field, Fla.

12 MARCH • F7U-3M Cutlasses from VA-83 equipped with AAM-N-2 Sparrow I air-to-air missiles sailed

An F3H-2N Demon, BuNo 137010, launches an AAM-N-6 Sparrow III air-to-air missile during testing at Point Mugu Pacific Missile Range, c. 1958.

from Norfolk, Va., on board *Intrepid* (CVA 11) for the Mediterranean in the first overseas deployment of a naval squadron using air-to-air missiles. In June, VA-46 deployed equipped with AAM-N-7 Sidewinder air-to-air missiles.

12 MARCH • The Assistant Secretary of Defense for Research and Development established a titanium alloy sheet rolling program and designated the Bureau of Aeronautics as coordinator. This created an organized effort of the armed services and the titanium industry to improve the strength, uniformity, and fabricating characteristics of the alloys for use in aircraft and missiles.

20 MARCH • The Ballistic Missile Committee of the Office of the Secretary of Defense approved a Navy program to develop solid-propellant motors for use in ship-based ballistic missiles.

31 MARCH • Five A3D-1 Skywarriors ferried from NAS Patuxent River, Md., to VAH-1 at NAS Jacksonville, Fla., completed the first delivery of the type to a fleet command.

3 APRIL • The Navy announced the operational integration of Petrel air-to-surface guided missiles designed for use by patrol aircraft against shipping, with the first assigned to P2V-6M Neptunes of VP-24.

23 APRIL • The cognizance of an earth satellite launching program designated Project Vanguard within OpNav shifted to the Guided Missiles Division of Deputy Chief of Naval Operations (Air). The division received responsibility for advising the Chief of Naval Operations on general aspects

1053799

One of two A3D-1 Skywarriors, BuNo 135408, used for Naval Air Test Center carrier suitability trials in June 1956 is launched from *Forrestal* (CVA 59).

of the program, and supporting and assisting the Office of Naval Research in the resolution of problems, other than fiscal, that arose within the Navy Department and at missile test activities of other services.

25 APRIL • The Chief of Naval Operations announced the planned installation of mirror landing systems at all the principal naval air stations to improve air traffic control and reduce landing accidents.

26 APRIL • The Naval Aircraft Factory at Philadelphia, Pa., was renamed the Naval Air Engineering Facility (Ships Installations). Its revised mission included research, engineering, design, development, and limited manufacturing of devices and equipment for aircraft and guided missile launch and recovery. The redesignation ceremony occurred on 1 June.

29 MAY • The modification of the ship designation system by the use of the suffix "N" identified vessels propelled by nuclear energy.

25 JUNE • The Naval Ordnance Plant at Indianapolis, Ind., was redesignated the Naval Avionics Facility. The plant had been established early in World War II for the development and production of aviation ordnance including the Norden bombsight and was devoted to the research, development, production, and repair of aviation fire control equipment. Its redesignation completed an internal Navy realignment whereby the Bureau of Ordnance became responsible for solid propellant rocket motors and Bureau of Aeronautics for aviation fire control equipment.

27 JUNE • The first Fleet Air Gunnery Meet was held at NAAS El Centro, Calif. Six teams selected from Navy and Marine shore-based fighter squadrons, each composed of the squadron commanding officer and three pilots, competed with two firings each at 15,000 and 25,000 feet during the two-day event. The top team honors and the Earle Trophy went to VF-112 of Naval Air Forces, Pacific, and individual honors to Lt. j.g. H. N. Wellman of VF-43 from Naval Air Forces, Atlantic.

7 JULY • VW-12 and Headquarters and Maintenance Squadron 2 were established at NAS Barbers Point in the Hawaiian Islands for patrol duty along the Pacific Distant Early Warning Line of the Continental Air Defense System.

Equipment development encompasses all phases of naval aviation. An early mirror landing system aids an A3D Skywarrior as it lands on board an aircraft carrier.

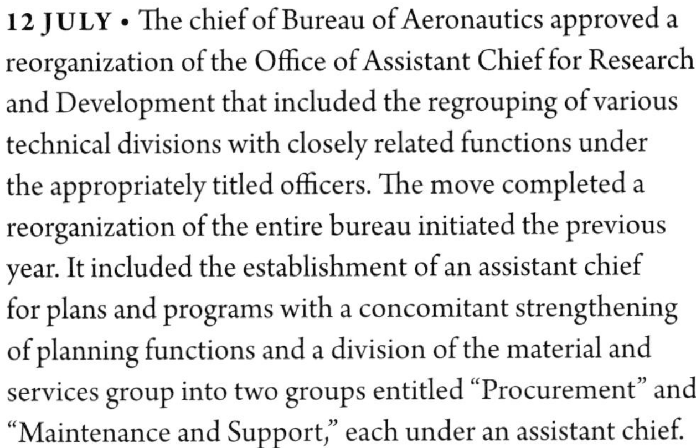

12 JULY • The chief of Bureau of Aeronautics approved a reorganization of the Office of Assistant Chief for Research and Development that included the regrouping of various technical divisions with closely related functions under the appropriately titled officers. The move completed a reorganization of the entire bureau initiated the previous year. It included the establishment of an assistant chief for plans and programs with a concomitant strengthening of planning functions and a division of the material and services group into two groups entitled "Procurement" and "Maintenance and Support," each under an assistant chief.

14 JULY • In the initial overseas deployment of a fleet command equipped with AAM-N-7 Sidewinder air-to-air missiles, the F9F-8 Cougars of VA-46, embarked on board *Randolph* (CVA 15), sailed from Norfolk, Va., for the Sixth Fleet in the Mediterranean. The following month, the deployment of Sidewinders began to the western Pacific as the FJ-3 Furies of VF-211 sailed from the West Coast on board *Bon Homme Richard* (CVA 31).

20 JULY • *Thetis Bay* (CVHA 1), Capt. Thomas W. South II commanding, was commissioned at San Francisco, Calif., as the first helicopter assault carrier. The former escort carrier (CVE 90) had been converted to operate helicopters and to accommodate 1,000 Marines to be flown ashore in the vertical envelopment tactics of amphibious assault. *Thetis Bay* was redesignated an amphibious assault ship (LPH 6) on 28 March 1959, but she never supported a combat landing in this configuration and was decommissioned on 31 March 1964.

26 JULY • The Egyptians nationalized the Suez Canal, and amid Anglo-French preparations for war to assert their claims to the canal, the Sixth Fleet subsequently deployed *Randolph* (CVA 15) and *Coral Sea* (CVA 43) to the eastern Mediterranean. The ships dispersed in mid-September following an apparent lessoning of the tensions.

31 JULY • Lt. Cmdrs. P. Harwood and Alton R. Henson and Lt. Roy R. Miears demonstrated the performance capabilities of carrier jet attack aircraft with a 3,200-mile nonstop unrefueled flight in an A3D Skywarrior from Honolulu, Hawaiian Islands, to Albuquerque, N. Mex. The trip took 5 hours, 40 minutes, at an average speed of 570 mph.

15 AUGUST • The Avionics Division, Capt. William E. Sweeney director, was established in the Bureau of Aeronautics' Research and Development Group. The merger of the electronics and armament divisions and the navigation branch of the Airborne Equipment Division formed the Avionics Division that resulted from a rapid expansion of electronics in aviation armament and air navigation, and from the closely coordinated effort required for its most effective application.

21 AUGUST • Cmdr. Robert W. Windsor Jr. captured the Thompson Trophy with a new national speed record of 1,015.428 mph in an F8U-1 over a 15-kilometer course at NOTS China Lake, Calif. This production model Crusader carried its normal armament of 20mm cannon and dummy ammunition during the record performance, making it the first operationally equipped U.S. aircraft to fly faster than 1,000 mph.

1C53795

An HUS-1 Seahorse of HMR-362 demonstrates an at-sea rescue while operating with *Thetis Bay* (CVHA 1), c. 1956.

22 AUGUST • Pilot Lt. Cmdr. Virgil Solomon completed the last scheduled passenger run for Martin Mars seaplanes after a flight from Honolulu, Hawaiian Islands, when he landed the JRM *Marianas Mars* off NAS Alameda, Calif.

22 AUGUST • The crew of a VQ-1 P4M-1Q, BuNo 124362, on a night patrol from Iwakuni, Japan, reported themselves under attack by unidentified aircraft over international waters, 32 miles off the Chinese coast near Wenchow, about 180 miles north of Formosa (Taiwan). The Mercator sent no further word and the plane and all 16 men on board disappeared. Carrier and land-based aircraft and ships searched for the aircraft and destroyer *Dennis J. Buckley* (DDR 808) recovered wreckage, empty life rafts, and the bodies of two crewmembers.

30 AUGUST • The Air Coordinating Committee approved a common military-civil short-range air navigation system called VORTAC. The system consisted of a combination of the Navy-developed tactical air navigation system (TACAN) with the Civil Aeronautic Authority's very-high frequency omni-range direction finder (VOR). The action resulted in the installation of ground beacons on civil airways that served civilian and military aircraft, each using their own specialized equipment.

1 SEPTEMBER • In the race for the North American Trophy at an event of the National Aircraft Show, four FJ-3 Furies of VF-24 took off from *Shangri-La* (CVA 38) off the Pacific coast of Mexico and flew 1,198 miles nonstop without refueling to Oklahoma City, Okla. Lt. j.g. D. K. Grosshuesch won with a time of 2 hours, 13 minutes, 38.6 seconds, at an average speed of 537.848 mph.

2 SEPTEMBER • On the second day of the National Aircraft Show, Lt. j.g. R. Carson of VF-124 captured the McDonnell Trophy with a nonstop unrefueled flight in an F3H-2N Demon from *Shangri-La* (CVA 38) at sea off San Francisco, Calif., to Oklahoma City, Okla. Carson covered 1,436 miles in 2 hours, 32 minutes, 13.45 seconds, at an average speed of 566.007 mph.

3 SEPTEMBER • Capt. John T. Blackburn, commanding officer of Heavy Attack Wing 1, and Cmdr. Charles T. Frohne launched in two A3D Skywarriors from *Shangri-La* (CVA 38) off the Oregon coast, flew across a finish line at the National Aircraft Show at Oklahoma City, Okla., and continued on without refueling to NAS Jacksonville, Fla. Blackburn received the Douglas Trophy for completing the 1,543.3-mile leg from the *Shangri-La* to Oklahoma City in 2 hours, 32 minutes, 39.7 seconds, at an average speed of

606.557 mph. This flight completed a three-day demonstration of carrier mobility in which *Shangri-La* launched jets to the same destination from widely separated points while sailing from Mexico to Oregon.

21 SEPTEMBER • Grumman test pilot Tom Attridge, flying an F11F-1 Tiger, shot himself down when he flew into 20mm projectiles he fired only seconds before while conducting test firings off eastern Long Island, N.Y.

2 OCTOBER • The Navy struck *Enterprise* (CV 6) and placed the ship for sale as scrap. The carrier was commissioned on 12 May 1938, served through World War II, and helped pioneer night combat operations. *Enterprise* received the Presidential Unit Citation and the Navy Unit Commendation. The ship was decommissioned during the demobilization period after the war and laid-up with the Reserve Fleet at Bayonne, N.J.

Cmdr. Robert W. Windsor Jr. set the world speed record of more than 1,000 mph on 21 August 1956 in this production model F8U-1 Crusader, BuNo 141345, and was awarded the Thompson Trophy.

5 OCTOBER • Cmdrs. Gerald A. Robinson and Donald Mitchie and Ens. Ronald K. Hess of VF-144 made a round-trip transcontinental flight in three F9F-8 Cougars from Miramar, Calif., to Long Island, N.Y., with fueling stops each way at Olathe, Kans. Although the flight's elapsed time of 10 hours, 49 minutes, 11 seconds, beat the existing record of 11 hours, 18 minutes, 27 seconds, the flight was not under official observation and therefore did not receive official recognition.

11 OCTOBER • An R6D-1 of VR-6 on a scheduled Military Air Transport Service flight from Lakenheath, England, to Lajes, Azores, disappeared over the Atlantic with nine crewmembers and 50 passengers on board. Ships and aircraft searched during the following 14 days and found debris from the Liftmaster, but failed to locate survivors.

16 OCTOBER • Five students received naval observer wings as the first graduates of the Navigator-Bombardier School. The course began on 26 May at NAS Corpus Christi, Texas.

29 OCTOBER • The Suez Crisis in the Middle East erupted into open warfare. All available ships and submarines of the Sixth Fleet in the Mediterranean went to sea under conditions of maximum readiness, and the Fleet received orders to evacuate U.S. citizens from the threatened area. At times, *Randolph* (CVA 15), *Antietam* (CVS 36), and *Coral Sea* (CVA 43) responded. Through 3 November, aircraft provided cover while ships and USAF transports evacuated about 2,200 people from Alexandria, Egypt; Haifa and Tel Aviv, Israel; Amman, Jordon; and Damascus, Syria. On 7 November, the United States received information of an impending Soviet deployment of six ships from the Black Sea

1011277

The supersonic F11F-1 Tiger had its origins in the subsonic F9F Panther and Cougar series of aircraft. This early prototype displays the plane's planform.

805653

The crew—(from left) AMM2 John P. Strider, Rear Adm. George J. Dufek, Lt. Cmdr. Conrad S. Shinn, Lt. John Swadener, AT2 William Cumbie, Capt. William M. Hawkes, and Capt. Douglas L. L. Cordiner—of the first plane to land at the South Pole, 31 October 1956.

to the eastern Mediterranean. The Chief of Naval Operations dispatched *Coral Sea* and *Randolph* to sail off the Egyptian coast, from where they could support the evacuation of Americans or strike against the Soviets, and sent *Franklin D. Roosevelt* (CVA 42) and *Forrestal* (CVA 59) to the vicinity of the Azores to reinforce the Sixth Fleet. Two additional carriers sailed to the western Pacific and Indian Ocean. The operations by the Sixth Fleet during subsequent weeks included the logistic support of the initial UN peacekeeping forces that arrived in the area on 15 November. On 13 December, the Sixth Fleet stood down from a 24-hour alert status.

31 OCTOBER • Commander Task Force 43 and Commander Naval Support Forces, Antarctica Rear Adm. George J. Dufek; Capt. Douglas L. L. Cordiner, commanding officer of VX-6; pilot Lt. Cmdr. Conrad S. Shinn; copilot Capt. William M. Hawkes; navigator Lt. John Swadener; crew chief AMM2 John P. Strider; and radioman AT2 William Cumbie landed in *Que Sera Sera*—an R4D-5L Skytrain, BuNo 12418—on the ice at the South Pole. The crew disembarked and at 0834 GMT became the first men to stand at the South Pole since British Capt. Robert F. Scott, RN, had accomplished the feat on 17 January 1912. The party remained at the pole for 49 minutes setting up navigational aids to assist the future delivery of materials and equipment for constructing a scientific observation station at the pole. A Navy R5D Skymaster and an Air Force C-124 Globemaster provided navigational assistance and were to drop survival gear in the event of an accident. The Naval Aviation Museum subsequently preserved *Que Sera Sera* for display at NAS Pensacola, Fla.

2 NOVEMBER • The Navy announced the award of a contract to Westinghouse Electric to design and furnish reactor components for *Enterprise* (CVAN 65).

8 NOVEMBER • Lt. Cmdrs. M. Lee Lewis and Malcolm D. Ross bettered the existing world altitude record by soaring to 76,000 feet in a Navy Stratolab balloon over the Black Hills of South Dakota. The duo received the 1957 Harmon International Trophy for Aeronauts for this record ascent, which was intended to gather meteorological, cosmic ray, and other scientific data necessary to improve safety at high altitudes.

9 NOVEMBER • Maj. Roy L. Anderson, USMC, began a three-day assault on world records in an HR2S-1 helicopter that set three new marks at Windsor Locks, Conn. On 9 November, he carried a payload of 11,050 pounds to an altitude over 12,000 feet; on 10 November, he conveyed 13,250 pounds to over 7,000 feet; and on 11 November, he set a speed record of 162.7 mph over a three-kilometer course.

29 NOVEMBER • The ZSG-4 made its initial flight as the first airship fitted with a Dacron envelope at NAS Lakehurst, N.J.

The Marines' HR2S-1 Mojave could carry 26 fully equipped troops or up to three jeeps, c. 1956.

3 DECEMBER • *Compass Island* (EAG 153) was commissioned at the New York Naval Shipyard, N.Y., Cmdr. J. A. Dare commanding, as the first ship converted to support the fleet ballistic missile program.

3 DECEMBER • *Gyatt* (DD 712), Cmdr. Charles F. Helme Jr. commanding, was recommissioned at Boston, Mass., as the first destroyer fitted with RIM-2 Terrier surface-to-air missiles.

7 DECEMBER • The Secretary of Defense directed the placement of air transport operations under a single manager service and designated the Military Air Transport Service (MATS) of the Air Force as the operating agency. This directive required the Navy to transfer to that agency all transport aircraft that it operated under MATS and all four-engine land transports of the fleet logistic air wings, except for 30 retained for fleet service and administrative airlift. The implementation of the instruction was to occur on 1 July 1957.

8 DECEMBER • The Secretary of Defense authorized the Navy to proceed with the development of the solid-propellant Polaris fleet ballistic missile as a submarine-launched weapon system, and to terminate its participation in the liquid-propellant Jupiter program.

8 DECEMBER • A Martin Viking rocket successfully launched from Cape Canaveral, Fla., during a test of launching equipment, tracking, and telemetry instruments intended for the Vanguard earth satellite.

17 DECEMBER • A WF-2 Tracer carrier early warning plane, adapted from the TF-1 design, made its first flight at the Grumman facility, Peconic River, Long Island, N.Y.

1957

1 JANUARY • The Naval Air Experimental Station, one of the four subcommands that had been grouped together on 14 July 1943 to form the Naval Air Material Center, was disestablished and consolidated within the center at Philadelphia, Pa.

659363

Converted battleship *Mississippi* (AG 128) first launched a SAM-N-7 Terrier surface-to-air missile during tests in January 1953. This is a later night launch.

3 JANUARY • The Bureau of Aeronautics ordered the retirement of the last operational PBY-6A Catalina from naval service at Naval Air Reserve Training Unit Atlanta, Ga.

10 JANUARY • The Naval Air Mine Defense Development Unit was established as a full command at Panama City, Fla. The unit had been established on 31 August 1956, under an officer in charge to develop and evaluate aviation systems, materials, and techniques for mine countermeasures.

14 JANUARY • In an evaluation of their all-weather capability, ZPG airships of ZW-1 operating in relays from NAS South Weymouth, Mass., maintained continuous radar patrols over the North Atlantic 200 miles off the New England coast through a series of fierce storms into 24 January.

15 JANUARY • *Forrestal* (CVA 59), with Carrier Air Group 1 embarked, deployed to the Mediterranean from NS Norfolk, Va. The 12 A3D-1s of VAH-1 that sailed with the ship marked the first deployment of Skywarriors with a *Forrestal*-class carrier. She returned to the United States on 22 July.

18 JANUARY • VA(AW)-35 at San Diego, Calif., received TF-1Qs, the first Navy aircraft equipped for electronic jamming.

1 FEBRUARY • Lt. Cmdr. Frank H. Austin Jr., MC, became the first Navy flight surgeon to qualify as a test pilot when he completed the Test Pilot Training Program at NATC Patuxent River, Md.

This TF-1 Trader, BuNo 136792, carrier onboard delivery transport has been converted into the aerodynamic prototype—without internal electronic systems—of the WF-2 Tracer carrier-based early warning aircraft.

4 FEBRUARY • The Chief of Naval Operations set forth a new policy for billet assignment, which provided the assignment of aviators and non-aviators alternately as either the senior or next senior officer of each important policy generating and administrative billet, and that assignment to all billets of commander-level and above were to be filled by aviators and non-aviators in the ratio of their respective numbers on board.

9 FEBRUARY • Chairman and Deputy Secretary of Defense Reuben B. Robertson Jr. issued the final report of the eponymous committee formed to study the means of shortening the time required to develop aircraft. The Robertson Committee concluded that streamlining management and administrative processes eliminated wasted motion and accomplished the development of weapon systems in less time than had been required since World War II. To this end, the services were to take specific action to correct problems. Those taken by the Navy included the establishment of managers for each weapon program within the Bureau of Aeronautics, and a long-range objectives group in the Office of Chief of Naval Operations.

21 FEBRUARY • In recognition of the increasing importance of weather information to naval operations, the Naval Aerology Branch, OP-533, received status as the Naval Weather Service Division, OP-58.

4 MARCH • Cmdr. Jack R. Hunt commanded airship ZPG-2 during a flight from NAS South Weymouth, Mass., that circled over the Atlantic Ocean toward Portugal and the African coast and landed on 15 March at NAS Key West, Fla. This set a new world record in distance and endurance by covering 9,448 statute miles and remaining airborne without refueling for 264 hours, 12 minutes. Hunt received the 1958 Harmon International Trophy for Aeronauts.

7 MARCH • A turbocatapult powered by the exhaust of six jet engines and designed primarily for use by Marine expeditionary forces, launched its first aircraft at Georgetown, Del. Test pilot Joseph Barkley took off in an AD-4NA Skyraider weighing 16,400 pounds at a speed of 90 knots in a run of 210 feet.

21 MARCH • Cmdr. Dale W. Cox Jr. broke two transcontinental speed records in an A3D-1 Skywarrior. The first occurred during a round trip of 9 hours, 31 minutes, 35.4 seconds, from Los Angeles, Calif., to New York, N.Y. The second marked an east-to-west flight completed in 5 hours, 12 minutes, 39.24 seconds.

1009749

Cmdr. Jack R. Hunt briefs the crew of airship ZPG-2 for their non-stop 11-day flight, 4 March 1957.

25 MARCH • VF-32 received the first F8U-1 Crusader delivered to a fleet unit two years after the first flight of the experimental model.

25 MARCH • African American Lt. j.g. Bobby C. Wilks, USCGR, earned his wings as Coast Guard Aviator No. 735 at NAS Corpus Christi, Texas. Wilks thus became the Coast Guard's first black pilot, and in 1959 he also qualified as Coast Guard Helicopter Pilot No. 343. The following year he transferred to the regular Coast Guard as a lieutenant, and in 1986 he retired as a captain.

5 APRIL • In the second annual Naval Air Weapons Meet, VMF-314 won the Earle Trophy for first place in air gunnery, and VA-26 took the Kane Trophy for best in the air-to-ground competition. Cmdr. Alexander Vraciu, commanding officer of VF-51 and a World War II ace, attained the best individual score of the meet.

12 APRIL • The Sperry Farragut Company of Bristol, Tenn., completed the scheduled production of AAM-N-2 Sparrow I air-to-air missiles with the delivery of the final missile on order.

13 APRIL • Aviation officer distribution functions shifted to the Bureau of Naval Personnel. The office of Deputy Chief of Naval Operations (Air) had performed these functions since its establishment in 1943.

21 APRIL • *Antietam* (CVS 36) was assigned to the chief of Naval Air Training at NAS Pensacola, Fla., to provide that command with its first angled deck carrier for use in flight training. *Antietam* operated from NS Mayport, Fla., while dredging deepened the channel into Pensacola, and physically shifted her home port in January 1959.

25 APRIL • The Sixth Fleet including *Lake Champlain* (CVA 39) and *Forrestal* (CVA 59) sailed to the eastern Mediterranean in a show of strength to support a publicized warning by President Dwight D. Eisenhower to contain a communist threat to Jordanian independence. On 27 April, Commander Sixth Fleet Vice Adm. Charles R. Brown reported to NATO the Fleet's readiness in the event of an escalation of the crisis: "For deterrent action could launch attack aircraft today and all types first light tomorrow for demonstration." The two carriers operated in those waters for a week.

30 APRIL • The Naval Aviation Medical Center was established at NAS Pensacola, Fla. The move combined under a single command the clinical, training, and research functions of the Naval School of Aviation Medicine and the Naval Hospital Pensacola.

1 MAY • A two-stage rocket consisting of the first stage of a Viking and a prototype of the Vanguard third stage launched in the second successful test of components of the Vanguard earth satellite launching vehicle from Cape Canaveral, Fla.

6 MAY • ZPG-2W made its first flight at Akron, Ohio. The early-warning airship was equipped with a large radar antenna mounted within the envelope.

17 MAY • *Badoeng Strait* (CVE 116) was decommissioned at Bremerton, Wash., as the last escort carrier in service.

23 MAY • A drone HTK-1 carrying a safety pilot operated from the fantail of frigate *Mitscher* (DL 2) in the vicinity of Narragansett Bay. These tests and other evaluations in which a piloted HUL-1 carried Mk 43 torpedoes in flights to and from *Mitscher* in February off NAS Key West, Fla., demonstrated the feasibility of assigning torpedo carrying drone helicopters to destroyers. The evaluations led to the development of the Drone Anti-Submarine Helicopter (DASH) later embodied in the QH-50C.

27 MAY • The first T2V-1 Sea Star jet trainer arrived at the Naval Air Advanced Training Command, NAS Corpus Christi, Texas.

28 MAY • In a reorganization of the Naval Air Reserve, the Chief of Naval Operations directed the disestablishment of the 73 auxiliary air units located across the country during the following six months.

JUNE • The Chinese Communists reinforced their forces opposite Formosa (Taiwan). The Seventh Fleet deployed to the region to deter an attack on the island from the mainland, and by September reached a maximum strength of three aircraft carriers operating in the area.

6 JUNE • Capt. Robert G. Dose, commanding officer of VX-3, and Lt. Cmdr. Paul Miller Jr., and Lt. Cmdrs. Charles C. McBratnie and John H. Miller completed the first nonstop carrier-to-carrier transcontinental flight in two F8U-1 Crusaders and two A3D Skywarriors, respectively, from *Bon Homme Richard* (CVA 31) at sea off San Diego, Calif., to *Saratoga* (CVA 60) steaming off the east coast of Florida. The Skywarriors accomplished the flight without aerial refueling, but the Crusaders required refueling by AJ-2 Savages of VAH-11 operating from NAS Dallas, Texas. President Dwight D. Eisenhower embarked *Saratoga* overnight and greeted the jet crews upon their arrival.

27 JUNE • Lt. Cmdr. Malcolm D. Ross and Charles B. Moore of the Arthur D. Little Company successfully completed a flight in a Stratolab balloon to investigate the interior of a thunderstorm. Ross and Moore ascended from a point close to the summit of Mount Withington near Socorro, N. Mex., into a cumulus cloud above the mountain. Their ascent marked the first of a series of flights conducted during the summer under the sponsorship of the Office of Naval Research and Bureau of Aeronautics.

30 JUNE • The release of a transosonde balloon from NAS Iwakuni, Japan, inaugurated a program to gather daily weather data by the use of such balloons over the Pacific, North America, and the Atlantic. The balloons were set to float at 30,000 feet and carried instruments that reported pressure and temperature every two hours. Each flight was planned for from five- to eight-days duration with a termination point in the Atlantic, short of the European coast.

ZPG-2 lifts off for the record-breaking voyage from NAS South Weymouth, Mass.

1 JULY • The mission of ZW-1 changed to providing all-weather airborne early warning to fleet forces and shore warning nets. The squadron worked up to the shift in tasking, and on this date, a squadron ZPG-2W airship flew its first patrol as part of the system.

15 JULY • Following the establishment of a single manager for airlift service, fleet logistic air wings were abolished, and transport squadrons not assigned to the single manager underwent redesignation to fleet tactical support squadrons and reassignment for operations directly under the control of fleet commanders.

16 JULY • Maj. John H. Glenn Jr., USMC, broke the transcontinental speed record in an F8U-1P Crusader, BuNo 144608, with a crossing in 3 hours, 22 minutes, 50.05 seconds, at an average speed of 723.517 mph from NAS Los Alamitos, Calif., to NAS Floyd Bennett Field, N.Y. Glenn's achievement marked the first upper atmosphere supersonic flight from West to East Coasts.

709847

The modified Viking 14 flew the second successful test of the Vanguard earth satellite program when it launched the Vanguard's third stage motor from Cape Canaveral, Fla., 1 May 1957.

16 JULY • Two A3Ds completed a record flight across the eastern Pacific in 4 hours, 45 minutes, from NAS Moffett Field, Calif., to Honolulu, Oahu. The Skywarriors made a routine flight to join VAH-2 at NAS Barbers Point, Hawaiian Islands.

30 JULY • The first pilotless helicopter flight occurred at Bloomfield, Conn. Kaman Aircraft designed and built the new helicopter under a joint Army-Navy contract on the basis of principles developed experimentally under a Navy contract using a modified HTK.

30 JULY • Air Force, Pacific Fleet and Air Force, Atlantic Fleet were retitled Naval Air Force, Pacific Fleet and Naval Air Force, Atlantic Fleet respectively.

12 AUGUST • Lt. Cmdr. Don Walker landed in an F3D Sky Knight using the automatic carrier landing system on board *Antietam* (CVS 36) off NAS Pensacola, Fla. Walker's "hands off" landing began the first shipboard test of the system designed to land aircraft on board during all weather conditions without help from pilots. *Antietam* completed more than 50 fully automatic landings through 20 August.

27 AUGUST • The Navy announced the obligation of all naval aviator candidates, with the exception of aviation cadets entering flight training after 1 January 1958, to serve 3 ½ years on active duty upon completion of the course instead of the two years previously required.

28 AUGUST • Royal Air Force Lt. Sydney Hughes successfully ejected from an F9F-8T Cougar while flying just above the ground at 120 mph at NAS Patuxent River, Md. The Martin-Baker Aircraft Company Ltd. of England had designed and developed the ground-level ejection seat, and Grumman Aircraft evaluated it for the U.S. Navy.

3 SEPTEMBER • The solid-propellant XKDT-1 Teal rocket-powered target drone made its first flight in a launch from an F3H Demon over NAMTC Point Mugu, Calif.

21 SEPTEMBER • German sailing ship *Pamir* sank during Hurricane Carrie in the eastern Atlantic. U.S. Navy aircraft including P2V Neptunes flying from NAS Port Lyautey, Morocco, Coast Guard cutter *Absecon* (WAVP 374, formerly seaplane tender AVP 23), USAF, and Portuguese aircraft, joined ships from 13 nations during a week-long search, but only rescued six of the 86 men on board.

28 SEPTEMBER • *Alameda County* was redesignated advanced aviation base ship (AVB 1) from tank landing ship *LST-32*. She provided fuel, spare parts, technicians, and facilities necessary to establish and operate an airstrip for patrol and carrier aircraft in locations lacking base facilities.

1 OCTOBER • The Naval Air Test Facility (Ship Installations) was established at NAS Lakehurst, N.J., Cmdr. Richard M. Tunnell commanding. The facility evaluated aircraft launching and recovery systems and supported their development.

3 OCTOBER • *Saipan* (CVL 48) was decommissioned at Bayonne, N.J., as the last of the light carriers. The ship remained in reserve status, but on 15 May 1959, was reclassified AVT 6, and on 27 August 1966, recommissioned as communications relay ship *Arlington* (AGMR 2).

11 OCTOBER • An A3D Skywarrior of VAH-4 bettered the time from the continental United States to the Hawaiian Islands with a control tower–to–control tower flight of 4 hours, 29 minutes, 55 seconds, from San Francisco, Calif., to Honolulu, Oahu.

15 OCTOBER • Chief of the Bureau of Ordnance Rear Adm. Frederick S. Withington accepted the Talos Defense Unit from the Radio Corp. of America. The land-based version of the Talos shipboard missile system was designed to launch the missiles automatically. Chief of Army Ordnance Lt. Gen. E. L. Cummings, USA, subsequently used the unit for evaluation and for potential use at Army antiaircraft installations at White Sands Proving Ground, N. Mex.

16 OCTOBER • A severe flood inundated the area around Valencia, Spain. *Lake Champlain* (CVS 39), with HMR-262 embarked, subsequently aided in locating, feeding, and rescuing thousands of victims displaced by the rising waters.

1 NOVEMBER • ZW-1 maintained an all-weather airborne early warning barrier commitment to fleet forces and shore warning nets with only two operational airships of the four normally required to be available through March 1958. Each airship operated more than 225 hours monthly during this period compared to a monthly average of approximately 110 hours during World War II.

13 NOVEMBER • A Regulus II bombardment missile with a range of 1,000 miles made its first launch with rocket boosters from Edwards AFB, Calif. Control aircraft returned the 11-ton missile to the field and landed it after a 48-minute flight.

21 NOVEMBER • The Department of Defense terminated Project Arowa (Applied Research: Operational Weather Analysis). The project attempted to develop basic meteorological research data into practical weather forecasting techniques. The people and records assigned to Arowa moved to Navy Weather Research Facility, which had been established the preceding month at Norfolk, Va.

22 NOVEMBER • VP-834 from NAS Floyd Bennett Field, N.Y., became the first Reserve squadron to launch guided missiles as a part of its regular training after completing two weeks of instruction at NAS Chincoteague, Va. The squadron fired Petrel air-to-surface missiles under the supervision of Guided Missile Unit 11.

9 DECEMBER • The cognizance of research and development programs for space vehicles was transferred from Deputy Chief of Naval Operations (Air) to Assistant Chief of Naval Operations (Research and Development), and the broadening of the responsibilities for the former Project Vanguard included all space vehicle programs prosecuted by the Office of Naval Research in the extension of, or following, Vanguard.

1958

2 JANUARY • *Princeton* (CVS 37) and destroyers *Eversole* (DD 789) and *Shelton* (DD 790) from the Seventh Fleet and seaplane tender *Duxbury Bay* (AVP 38) from the Middle East Force rescued victims of a disastrous flood in Ceylon (Sri Lanka). Twenty CH-19Es from HMRL-162 comprised the principal aviation contingent. *Princeton* left the area on 9 January.

9 JANUARY • Naval aircraft began the delivery of emergency supplies to the people of Jaluit and other islands in the Marshall Islands in the wake of devastation caused by Super Typhoon Ophelia.

3 FEBRUARY • The chief of BUAER appointed a weapons system team to accelerate the development and introduction of A2F (A-6) Intruders. The team worked under the chairmanship of the program manager and consisted of representatives from production, maintenance, and contracts divisions, and the Research and Development Group. The research and development project officer (or class desk officer) also chaired the research and development project team that included representatives of avionics, airborne equipment, and power plant divisions. This action and the assignment of systems management responsibilities to the airframe contractor marked important steps in the implementation of the management concepts recommended by the Robertson Committee.

Maj. John H. Glenn Jr., USMC, breaks the transcontinental speed record in an F8U-1P Crusader, 16 July 1957.

4 FEBRUARY • The keel of *Enterprise* (CVAN 65) was laid at Newport News Shipbuilding and Dry Dock Company, Va., as the world's first nuclear-powered aircraft carrier.

13 FEBRUARY • The creation of a selected reserve within the overall reserve organization provided fully trained and equipped people and commands for immediate deployment to specific active duty assignments during wars. The organization incorporated the entire Naval Air Reserve.

14 FEBRUARY • The operational evaluation of AAM-N-6 air-to-air missiles began when VX-4 fired the first Sparrow III.

1 MARCH • The Navy accepted and assigned an early warning WV-2E prototype with a rotodome radar antenna mounted on the fuselage for preliminary evaluation to the Naval Air Development Unit, NAS South Weymouth, Mass.

7 MARCH • *Grayback* (SSG 574), Lt. Cmdr. Hugh G. Nott commanding, was commissioned at Mare Island Navy Yard, Vallejo, Calif., as the first submarine built from the keel up with guided-missile capabilities.

10 MARCH • The Chief of Naval Operations approved a reorganization of carrier aviation to create uniform air groups, provide a more permanent group assignment to ships, and to permit a reduction of the assigned units and aircraft without also reducing combat readiness. The new organization also established permanent replacement air groups on each coast with responsibility for the indoctrination of key technicians, the tactical training of aircrew, and special programs required for the introduction of new combat aircraft models.

17 MARCH • A Vanguard rocket fired from Cape Canaveral, Fla., placed a 3 ¼-pound earth satellite into orbit in a test of the system designed for launching earth satellites for the International Geophysical Year. The Office of Naval Research supervised the design and development of the satellite. Equipped with solar-powered batteries, the satellite transmitted data for more than six years and initially was estimated to remain in orbit for up to 2,000 years.

19 MARCH • VX-4 began the operational evaluation of ASM-N-7 air-to-ground missiles with the launch of the first Bullpup.

23 MARCH • The fleet ballistic missile underwater launching apparatus off San Clemente Island, Calif., had its first practical test with the launch of a dummy Polaris missile.

2 APRIL • An important step in the development of drone antisubmarine helicopters for operations from destroyers occurred with the amendment of an existing Bureau of Aeronautics contract with Gyrodyne for the RON-1 rotocycle one-man helicopter to provide for the development, installation, and flight test of remote control equipment.

8 APRIL • Airborne firing tests of a high-performance external gun in F3H-2N Demons commenced at Naval Aviation Ordnance Test Station, Chincoteague, Va. This twin-barrel 20mm cannon underwent development for a pod installation on aircraft, making it interchangeable with other aviation ordnance.

11 APRIL • Rear Adm. John S. Thach issued the first operation order to Task Group Alpha. The group had been formed in the Atlantic Fleet to accelerate the development of antisubmarine tactics and to improve fleet antisubmarine warfare readiness.

18 APRIL • The third annual Naval Air Weapons Meet was held at NAAS El Centro, Calif. Fifteen selected squadrons participated and top honors in their class went to VF-111 in air-to-air (day), VF-213 in air-to-air (all-weather), VA-126 in air-to-ground, and VAH-5 in heavy attack events.

Galveston (CLG 3) launches a SAM-N-6 Talos long-range surface-to-air guided missile during the missile's first at-sea firing, 24 February 1959.

18 APRIL • Lt. Cmdr. George C. Watkins broke the world altitude record for the second time in three days by setting the mark at 76,939 feet in an F11F-1F Tiger at Edwards AFB, Calif.

21 APRIL • To clarify command relationships and to permit the closer integration of Navy units into the single manager airlift service, the Chief of Naval Operations directed the organization of Navy squadrons into one naval air transport wing each for the Atlantic and Pacific Fleets.

4 MAY • The practical test of an all-jet basic training program began as 14 students reported to Advanced Training Unit 206 for instruction in T2V-1 Sea Stars at NAS Pensacola, Fla.

10 MAY • Naval Missile Facility Point Arguello, Calif., was established as an activity of the National Pacific Missile Range.

11 MAY • Lt. Cmdr. Jack Neiman completed a 44-hour simulated high-altitude flight in a NAS Norfolk, Va., pressure chamber under conditions existing between 80,000 and 100,000 feet.

15 MAY • The Lebanese government informed the United States of the likelihood of their need for assistance because of the infiltration of Syrian troops. The Sixth Fleet subsequently deployed three carriers to the eastern Mediterranean. On 1 July, the Lebanese indicated the stabilization of the crisis and the ships afterward turned around.

1048502

Randolph (CVS 15) was reconfigured in 1959 for antisubmarine warfare. Throughout that year and much of the next, she and her Task Group Alpha conducted operations off the East Coast.

17 MAY • Four F3H Demons and four F8U Crusaders completed nonstop transatlantic crossings in Operation Pipeline—a practical test of the speed of delivery of carrier aircraft from the East Coast to the Sixth Fleet in the Mediterranean.

22 MAY • Maj. Edward N. LeFaivre, USMC, set five world records into the next day in an F4D-1 Skyray at NAMTC Point Mugu, Calif.—time-to-climb to 3,000; 6,000; 9,000; 12,000; and 15,000 meters with marks of 44.392, 66.095, 90.025, 111.224, and 156.233 seconds, respectively.

26 MAY • Sikorsky test pilot Jack Stultz made the initial public flight of an HSS-1N at NAS Corpus Christi, Texas. Seabats proved capable of day and night antisubmarine warfare under instrument flight conditions.

27 MAY • McDonnell Aircraft test pilot R. C. Little made the first flight of an XF4H-1 Phantom II at St. Louis, Mo.

28 MAY • *Galveston* (CLG 3), Capt. J. B. Colwell commanding, was commissioned at Philadelphia, Pa., as the first Talos surface-to-air missile equipped cruiser.

16 JUNE • The Pacific Missile Range, Point Mugu, Calif., was established. The Navy managed the site to provide range support to the Department of Defense and other government agencies in guided missiles, satellite, and space vehicle research, development, evaluation, and training. This was the third site established within the National Missile Range, and the first that facilitated the safe launching of satellites into polar orbit.

20 JUNE • The Advanced Research Projects Agency requested that the Naval Research Laboratory modify its Minitrack system under development for Project Vanguard to produce a capability for the detection, identification, and prediction of the orbits of nonradiating objects in space. In June 1959, the development of the Navy Space Surveillance System from this request first produced useful data. On 2 February 1960, the system established the existence of an unknown object in orbit later identified as the re-entry vehicle of satellite *Discoverer V*, which had been assumed lost.

26 JUNE • A VR-21 TF-1 from San Diego, Calif., made the first delivery of an aircraft engine by carrier-on-board delivery when the Trader transported a J-34 engine to *Yorktown* (CVS 10) about 300 miles at sea.

1 JULY • The Pacific extension of the continental air defense Distant Early Warning (DEW) Line began full operation.

1 JULY • Submarine Squadron 14, Capt. Norvell G. Ward commanding, was established as the first fleet ballistic missile submarine squadron under the Atlantic Fleet Submarine Force.

1 JULY • The first joint Civil Aeronautics Authority–Navy radar air traffic control center began operations at NAS Miramar, Calif.

15 JULY • Around this time, factions favoring Egyptian President Gamal A. Nasser stirred unrest in Iraq, Jordan, and Lebanon. Rebellion broke out in Lebanon, followed by the assassination of the Iraqi king and the consolidation of power in that country by the Ba'aths. The Jordanian

1042033

An A3D-2, BuNo 142652, aerial tanker refuels the third Phantom II built, the first of five YF4H-1 Phantom II, BuNo 143388, c. 1960.

and Lebanese governments requested assistance, and the United States and Great Britain launched Operation Bluebat—to restore order and to protect Americans and Britons in the area. On this date, aircraft from *Essex* (CVA 9) and *Saratoga* (CVA 60) covered landings by the Sixth Fleet of about 1,800 Marines on a beach near Beirut. Marine helicopters from *Wasp* (CVS 18) flew reconnaissance missions and evacuated the sick and injured from Beirut International Airport. A composite air strike force deployed to Turkey to sustain the northern flank of the landings. By 3 August, the dispatch of reinforcements to the area stabilized the situation. The U.S. forces withdrew by 25 October and the British by 2 November. Naval aircraft flew about 11,000 sorties during Bluebat, and a total of 82 vessels sailed with the Sixth Fleet at times during the crisis.

23 JULY • Tests conducted off the Florida coast into the next day by VW-4, Cmdr. Nicholas Brango commanding, established the feasibility of creating or destroying cloud formations by the release of carbon black into the atmosphere. Dr. Florence W. van Straten of Naval Weather Service Division, Op-58, directed the evaluations.

27 JULY • After launch the previous day, Cmdr. Malcolm D. Ross and Lt. Cmdr. M. Lee Lewis ascended in a balloon to 82,000 feet carrying a record load of 5,500-pounds and remained in the air 34 ½ hours. The flight was to test and evaluate the sealed cabin system designed to carry an externally mounted telescope for the observation of the atmosphere of Mars.

6 AUGUST • The approval of the Department of Defense Reorganization Act of 1958 provided for more direct civilian control over military operations through the offices of the Secretary of Defense, the Joint Chiefs of Staff, and the respective service secretaries; the establishment of unified or specified combatant commands; the direction of the operations of units assigned from the respective services, responsible for the accomplishment of their mission directly to the President and Secretary of Defense; the revision of the secretarial structure of the department by reducing the

1038502

Saratoga (CVA 60) sails from Augusta Bay, Sicily, during a 1958 deployment with the Sixth Fleet.

number of assistant secretaries from nine to seven, limiting the number within each service department to three, and the revocation of the statutory provision for an assistant secretary of the Navy for air. The law also maintained the separate organization of each service under its own secretary and defined the Navy Department to include naval aviation and the Marine Corps. The act became effective six months from this date.

19 AUGUST • The first successful flight of a RIM-24A surface-to-air missile occurred when a Tartar intercepted an F6F Hellcat drone at NOTS China Lake, Calif.

19 AUGUST • The XP3V-1 prototype of the Orion made its first flight.

23 AUGUST • President Dwight D. Eisenhower signed into law the creation of the Federal Aviation Agency. The action assigned the agency broad responsibilities involving the operation of airways, the regulation of military and civil air traffic, and the establishment of airports and missile and rocket sites. The measure also provided for military participation in the performance of agency functions, for military deviations from air traffic regulations in an emergency, and for appeal to the president of disagreements concerning the location of military airfields.

24 AUGUST • The Chinese Communists increased shelling of the Chinese Nationalist held Kinmen (Quemoy) and Matsu Islands in the Formosa (Taiwan) Strait. The Chief of Naval Operations directed the Seventh Fleet to support the

1039888

The A3J-1 Vigilante had a unique, but unsuccessful, bomb bay—a tunnel between the plane's twin engines from which the weapon attached to two expended fuel cans was ejected rearward. The type went on to become a successful supersonic reconnaissance aircraft.

Taiwanese. *Hancock* (CVA 19) received orders to deploy to the south of Taiwan and ready combat air patrols over the strait and air strikes to deter the communists if required. *Lexington* (CVA 16) and *Princeton* (CVS 37) sailed toward the northeast of the island. The Seventh Fleet prepared to assist the Nationalists to defend and resupply the islands, and to launch air raids against communist airfields near the Chinese coast. The Fleet operated so as to avoid clashes with the communists, however, and directed aircraft to approach no closer than 20 miles of the mainland. On 25 August, carrier aircraft received orders to fly night sweeps over the strait.

The next day, Marine Aircraft Group (MAG) 11, consisting of 20 FJ-4 Furies of VMF-323 and 16 and 20 F4D-1 Skyrays of VMF(AW)-115 and -314, respectively, received deployment orders to Taiwan. Despite delays from foul weather, the group completed the move by 9 September, supported by two TV-2 Shooting Stars and two R4D Skytrains. Planners also recommended shifting the fixed-wing aircraft of MAG-13 from Kaneohe Bay, Hawaiian Islands, to Atsugi, Japan, to restore the air defense capability of the area after the departure of MAG-11.

Additional reinforcements included the arrival of *Shangri-La* (CVA 38), *Midway* (CVA 41), and *Essex* (CVA 9) in Taiwanese waters on 30 August and 4 and 16 September, respectively. On 2 September, *Lexington*, *Princeton*, and *Shangri-La* moved south of Taiwan to evade Typhoon Grace. *Lexington* and *Princeton* returned to Taiwanese waters the following day, but repairs delayed *Shangri-La* by a day in Subic Bay, Philippines. The rotation of shore-based aerial reconnaissance patrols ensured that at least one P2V Neptune at a time covered the islands, but the carrier aerial night sweeps ceased on 7 September. The show of resolve deterred the communists, a cease-fire was signed on 6 October, and the crisis diminished by December.

25 AUGUST • Cmdr. Forrest S. Petersen was assigned to the National Advisory Committee for Aeronautics (NACA) to fly the X-15. The rocket plane program emerged from NACA's effort to research the problems associated with controlled, manned aircraft at extreme altitude and at high Mach (speed of sound) numbers—as high as 250,000 feet and as swift as 4,093 mph. Petersen's specialty was the exploration of the angle of attack envelope to obtain information on aerodynamic heating and stability and control. He completed five X-15 flights of about 40 minutes by 30 January 1962.

710498

Guided missile ship *Norton Sound* (AVM 1) fires a RIM-24 Tartar surface-to-air missile from a Mk 11 twin-arm launcher. She conducted tests on that missile and the SAM-N-7 Terrier from 1955 to 1962.

28 AUGUST • The situation in Lebanon eased and *Essex* (CVA 9) sailed from the Sixth Fleet in the Mediterranean to join the Seventh Fleet off Formosa (Taiwan) where tensions continued to flare. *Essex* transited the Suez Canal and, on 16 September, relieved *Hancock* (CVA 19) off Taiwan.

29 AUGUST • A Lockheed Electra made its first flight in the external configuration of a P3V-1. In April, the Navy selected the plane as the design most closely meeting the requirements for long-range antisubmarine warfare.

1 SEPTEMBER • The Anti-Submarine Warfare Laboratory was established at the Naval Air Development Center, Johnsville, Pa.

5 SEPTEMBER • A coordinator, missile ranges was established on the staff of Deputy Chief of Naval Operations (Air) to serve as his principal advisor on missile range matters, to determine operating requirements, and to coordinate the establishment of policies relating to missile range use.

6 SEPTEMBER • Guided missile ship *Norton Sound* (AVM 1) launched her third and final atomic tipped rocket to an altitude of about 300 miles while operating midway between the southern extremities of South America and Africa. This series of test firings included shots on 27 and 30 August conducted under the auspices of the Advanced Research Projects Agency as Project Argus. The nuclear explosions produced a visible aurora and a radiation belt around the earth that extended for almost 4,000 miles into space, lasted for several weeks, and provided significant scientific and military data.

8 SEPTEMBER • Lt. Richard H. Tabor, MC, completed a 72-hour simulated flight wearing a Goodrich lightweight full-pressure suit in a hypobaric chamber at NAS Norfolk, Va., in which he endured simulated altitude conditions up to 139,000 feet.

15 SEPTEMBER • Project officer Lt. William P. Lawrence performed an evaluation flight in an XF8U-3 Crusader at Edwards AFB, Calif. During this mission, Lawrence became the first naval aviator to fly at twice the speed of sound in a fleet-type aircraft.

16 SEPTEMBER • Submarine *Grayback* (SSG 574), off the California coast, made the first sea launch of a Regulus II bombardment missile. The missile continued under radio control inland on a simulated mission to Edwards AFB, Calif.

28 SEPTEMBER • In a preliminary test of equipment for use within International Geophysical Year solar eclipse studies, dock landing ship *Point Defiance* (LSD 31) launched a sounding rocket accelerated by a Nike missile booster from near Puka Puka Island to a height of 800,000 feet. This marked the highest altitude reached to date by ship-launched rockets.

30 SEPTEMBER • Chairman of the National Advisory Committee for Aeronautics (NACA) Gen. James H. Doolittle, USAF, issued the committee's final annual report. The forwarding letters pointed out that at the close of business that day, NACA was to cease to exist, and noted the absorption of all the committee's facilities and employees by NASA. Vice Adm. William V. Davis Jr. and Rear Adm. Wellington T. Hines comprised the final Navy members of the committee. NASA was established the next day.

30 SEPTEMBER • Commander Naval Support Force, Antarctica Rear Adm. George J. Dufek and four of his staff arrived on board a VX-6 R5D Skymaster at NAF McMurdo Sound. Their arrival marked the beginning of Operation Deep Freeze IV.

1 OCTOBER • Project Vanguard was transferred from the Navy to NASA. On 17 February 1959, NASA launched the first full-scale Vanguard earth satellite.

8 OCTOBER • FJ-4B Furies of VMA-212 and -214 completed Operation Cannonball by landing at NAS Atsugi, Japan, after a transpacific flight from MCAS Kaneohe, Hawaiian Islands. The Marines made the flight in two sections of 12 jets with layovers at Midway Island and Guam, and refueled from Air Force Boeing KB-50 tankers in the vicinity of Wake Island and from Navy AJ Savages near Iwo Jima, Volcano Islands.

10 OCTOBER • The Secretary of the Navy directed the replacement of the terms "aerology" and "aerological officer" by "meteorology" and "meteorological officer."

21 OCTOBER • To provide a highly mobile unit capable of employing Marine helicopter squadrons and troops in the fast-landing concept of vertical envelopment, the Commander in Chief Atlantic Fleet announced the formation of a new amphibious squadron consisting of *Boxer* (CVS 21) and four dock landing ships to be equipped with helicopter platforms. *Boxer* was redesignated LPH-4 on 30 January 1959.

23 OCTOBER • The fighting between Cuban revolutionaries led by Fidel R. Castro and the government troops of Gen. Fulgencio Batista threatened Americans living within Nicaro, and the State Department ordered the evacuation of U.S. nationals from the port. The next day, *Franklin D. Roosevelt* (CVA 42) provided distant air cover while transport *Kleinsmith* (APD 134) evacuated 56 Americans and three foreigners.

10 NOVEMBER • The first permanent Marine aviation detachment afloat was activated on board the *Boxer* (CVS 21) to provide supply, maintenance, and flight deck control functions necessary to support the operations of Marine helicopter squadrons.

5 DECEMBER • Experimental miscellaneous auxiliary *Observation Island* (EAG 154), Capt. Leslie M. Slack commanding, was commissioned at the Norfolk Naval Shipyard, Va. The ship's design incorporated launching, fire control, navigational, and other devices required for the fleet ballistic missile testing program.

5 DECEMBER • A Navy RIM-2 Terrier-type missile launcher fired sounding rocket Hugo from NASA's Pilotless Aircraft Research Station, Wallops Island, Va. Hugo reached a height of 86 miles and obtained the first extremely high-altitude photographs of a frontal cloud formation. The Office of Naval Research carried out Project Hugo with assistance from Bureau of Aeronautics, NASA, and the Weather Bureau, and used a camera package designed and constructed by New Mexico State University.

8 DECEMBER • F3H Demons of VF-64 flying from *Midway* (CVA 41) made the first firing of an AAM-N-6 Sparrow III air-to-air missile by a squadron deployed beyond the continental United States. Eleven days later, VF-193, embarked on board *Bon Homme Richard* (CVA 31), conducted a similar exercise. Both squadrons operated with the Seventh Fleet in the western Pacific.

12 DECEMBER • The Secretary of the Navy directed the termination of the Regulus II bombardment missile program as a measure necessary to achieve an overall balance in missile weapons systems with the available resources. The decision followed the first successful Regulus submarine launch barely three months before, but emphasized the development of Polaris submarine-launched intercontinental ballistic missiles.

16 DECEMBER • The successful firing of a Thor missile from Vandenburg AFB, Calif., inaugurated the intermediate-range ballistic missile portion of the Pacific Missile Range at Point Mugu.

19 DECEMBER • Naval Air Missile Test Center, Point Mugu, Calif., was redesignated Naval Missile Center, Point Mugu, and placed under the command of Commander, Pacific Missile Range.

25 DECEMBER • Aircraft from NAS Port Lyautey, Morocco, rescued 134 people during heavy flooding in that country.

28 DECEMBER • Nine ships of an antisubmarine group including *Yorktown* (CVS 10) turned from operations to aid people made homeless by a fire that swept through Koniya, Japan. Within 24 hours of the disaster, the ships had delivered food, medicine, clothing, blankets, and tents to victims, and sailors and Marines continued to help until the arrival of Japanese relief workers.

710394

The first prototype HSS-2 Sea King, BuNo 147137, all-weather antisubmarine helicopter made its initial flight in March 1959.

16 FEBRUARY • The Naval Air Reserve participated for the first time in a full-scale fleet exercise. Fifty-five crews from selected Reserve squadrons and 36 P2V Neptunes and S2F Trackers took part in a three-day antisubmarine defense exercise along the West Coast with the Pacific Fleet and the Royal Canadian Navy.

24 FEBRUARY • Cruiser *Galveston* (CLG 3) fired a Talos surface-to-air missile in the vicinity of Roosevelt Roads, P.R. The launch marked the missile's operational sea deployment.

1959

21 JANUARY • Tests of a new type of movable nozzle for the Polaris at Indian Head, Md., demonstrated a successful major advance in the directional control of ballistic missiles.

24 JANUARY • Maj. John P. Flynn, USMC, and Capt. Clifford D. Warfield, USMC, of Marine Aircraft Wing 2 made a nonstop unrefueled flight covering 2,082 miles in 4 hours, 25 minutes in A4D Skyhawks from El Toro, Calif., to MCAS Cherry Point, N.C.

27 JANUARY • The Naval Air Development and Material Command, Johnsville, Pa., was redesignated Naval Air Research and Development Activities Command, and its scope expanded to include aeronautical research and development activities in the Third Naval District.

5 FEBRUARY • The abolition of the office of Assistant Secretary of the Navy for Air occurred in accordance with the provisions of the Defense Reorganization Act of 1958. The Secretary of the Navy assumed the functions of the office pending an appointment to fill the newly created office of Assistant Secretary for Research and Development.

10 MARCH • The Chief of Naval Operations approved the transfer of lighter-than-air (LTA) training from the Naval Air Training Command to AIRLANT, and the end of the requirement for all LTA students to receive heavier-than-air training.

11 MARCH • Sikorsky pilot R. S. Decker made the first flight of an XHSS-2 Seabat.

13 MARCH • Aviation Cadet E. R. Clark became the first naval aviation student to solo a jet without previous experience in propeller aircraft when he flew a TT-1 Pinto.

7 APRIL • NASA announced the selection of seven prospective astronauts—including naval aviators Lt. Col. John H. Glenn Jr., USMC; Lt. Cmdrs. Walter M. Schirra Jr. and Alan B. Shepard Jr.; and Lt. Malcolm S. Carpenter—to Project Mercury, a basic program in the development of space exploration and manned orbital flight.

15 APRIL • Elements of the Naval Air Reserve took part in Exercise Slamex under the leadership of Commander, Anti-Submarine Defense Force, Atlantic. The event marked the second such participation in a full-scale fleet exercise since the organization of the Selected Reserve.

P2V Neptunes and S2F Trackers manned by 78 crews from 12 reserve stations trained round-the-clock through 22 April, logged 2,800 flight hours, and reported 75 submarine contacts while operating from Naval Air Stations Brunswick, Maine; Quonset Point, R.I.; and Lakehurst, N.J.

25 APRIL • FJ-4B Furies of VA-212, embarked on board *Lexington* (CVA 16), carried out the first deployment of ASM-N-7 Bullpup air-to-ground missiles overseas when the carrier sailed for the western Pacific from NAS Alameda, Calif. The following August, VA-34 A4D Skyhawks extended Bullpup deployments to the Mediterranean when they embarked on board *Saratoga* (CVA 60) from the East Coast for the Sixth Fleet.

26 APRIL • Helicopters of HU-2, embarked on board ice breaker *Edisto* (AG 89) while she returned from the Antarctic, completed ten days of rescue operations in the Montevideo, Uruguay, area during which they carried 277 flooding victims to safety.

28 APRIL • The office of Assistant Chief of Naval Operations (Research and Development) was disestablished and replaced by Deputy CNO (Development), Vice Adm. John T. Hayward commanding, with the authority and responsibility to execute the research, development, test, and evaluation responsibilities of the CNO.

5 MAY • The Guided Missiles Division was transferred from Deputy Chief of Naval Operations (Air) to the newly established office of DCNO (Development), and its director was designated Assistant CNO (Development).

7 MAY • The classifications of 36 escort carriers designated CVE, CVU, and CVHE were changed to cargo ship and aircraft ferry, AKV. A change of hull numbers accompanied the redesignation and marked the end of escort carriers as U.S. Navy men-of-war.

15 MAY • The classifications of four support carriers (CVS) and seven light carriers (CVL) were changed to auxiliary aircraft transport (AVT). The change removed the CVL designation from the Navy Vessels Register.

15 MAY • The establishment in the office of Chief of Naval Operations of more direct channels for technical control and program guidance over the Operational Development Force occurred to centralize and strengthen the research and development program. The revision and broadening of the mission of the force included test and evaluation, and it was thus redesignated Operational Test and Evaluation Force.

26 MAY • A concept of aircraft maintenance that assigned responsibility directly to the units having custody of the aircraft and the gradual elimination of FASRONs received approval for implementation.

27 MAY • The Naval Weather Service Division shifted from Deputy Chief of Naval Operations (Air) to DCNO (Fleet Operations and Readiness) to reflect the ever-broadening scope of the division's duties.

8 JUNE • Submarine *Barbero* (SSG 317) launched a Regulus I bombardment missile from a position about 100 miles off the Florida coast that delivered a package of U.S. Post Office mail ashore after a 22-minute flight to NS Mayport, Fla.

16 JUNE • Two North Korean MiGs attacked a VQ-1 P4M-1Q, BuNo 122209, on a routine flight over international waters about 50 miles east of the Korean demilitarized zone. Gunfire seriously wounded the tailgunner and damaged the Mercator, knocking out both starboard engines and some flight controls. The plane made an emergency landing at Miho AFB, Japan.

19 JUNE • A ZPG-3W, the first of four airships designed for use in air warning patrol and the largest nonrigid naval airship ever built, was delivered at NAS Lakehurst, N.J.

5 JULY • During mounting tension between the Chinese Communists and Nationalists, the Seventh Fleet deployed *Lexington* (CVA 16) and *Ranger* (CVA 61) to Formosan (Taiwanese) waters for six days.

11 JULY • After a lapse of 18 years, the Marine Aviation Cadet program was reinstituted when a class of 12 began preflight training at NAS Pensacola, Fla.

13 JULY • The Chief of Naval Operations approved the policy recommendations of the Connolly Board that enunciated organizational responsibilities in the CNO

710127

An FJ-4B Fury, BuNo 143494, of Air Development Squadron (VX) 4 carries a full load of five ASM-N-7 Bullpup air-to-ground missiles and their guidance pod, 16 April 1958.

office. The new policy included the Navy's use of space to accomplish naval objectives, full participation in space technology, and the assignment of a high priority to astronautics in research and development.

14 JULY • A two-stage Nike-Asp solid-propellant rocket fired from Naval Missile Facility, Point Arguello, Calif., was the first of 12 rockets designed to record radiation at altitudes of 150 miles. The event also marked the launch of the first ballistic missile from the new facility.

15 JULY • The Aviation Safety Division of Deputy Chief of Naval Operations (Air) was changed to a staff office headed by a coordinator to act as principal advisor to DCNO (Air) in all matters of air safety, and to coordinate the planning and implementation of aviation safety programs throughout the Navy.

22 JULY • Within Deputy Chief of Naval Operations (Air), the office of the Coordinator, Missile Ranges was disestablished and its functions shifted to a simultaneously established Astronautics Division. This division assisted DCNO (Air) in performing his overall task of directing the Navy astronautic program including the formulation of plans, policies, and the determination of requirements.

28 JULY • The Naval Research Laboratory issued its initial report indicating the feasibility of adapting Omega navigation to aircraft use. Researcher A. F. Thornhill of the Radio Division prepared the report, which consisted of a theoretical analysis of the problems involved in designing an airborne receiver. Thornhill described Omega as a phase comparison radio navigation technique using very-low frequency radio waves of such range that six appropriately located shore-based transmitters would provide global coverage.

30 JULY • The Navy announced the assignment of AAM-N-7 Sidewinder air-to-air missiles to Advanced Training Command units and Reserve squadrons. Program implementation began the next week when Advanced Training Unit 203 began carrying Sidewinders on its F11F-1 Tigers at NAAS Kingsville, Texas.

3 AUGUST • The first flight test of a UUM-44 Subroc antisubmarine missile took place with a launch from NOTS China Lake, Calif.

18 AUGUST • An act of Congress created the Bureau of Naval Weapons and abolished the Bureaus of Aeronautics and Ordnance upon the transfer of their functions. The bureau was established on 1 September, and on 10 September, Rear Adm. Paul D. Stroop took the oath of office as its first chief.

20 AUGUST • HUS-1s from HMRL-261, operating from *Thetis Bay* (LPH 6), completed a week of relief operations in flood-stricken Formosa (Taiwan). The Seahorses airlifted more than 1.6 million pounds of cargo and 833 passengers during 898 missions.

25 AUGUST • Lt. Cmdr. Ed Decker took off in an A3D Skywarrior at a gross weight of 84,000-pounds during suitability trials on board *Independence* (CVA 62). This was the heaviest aircraft to fly from a carrier to date.

27 AUGUST • Experimental miscellaneous auxiliary *Observation Island* (EAG 154) off Cape Canaveral, Fla., completed the first launch of a prototype Polaris A-1 fleet ballistic missile from a ship at sea.

9 SEPTEMBER • Naval aircraft and ships located and recovered an Atlas-boosted Mercury capsule in the Atlantic Ocean about 700 miles short of the predicted point of impact.

This F9F-8 Cougar, BuNo 141140, carries AAM-N-7 Sidewinder air-to-air missiles in addition to two auxiliary fuel tanks.

699330

18 SEPTEMBER • The Air Warfare Division of Deputy Chief of Naval Operations (Air) was disestablished and its functions pertaining to aviation combat readiness were transferred to DCNO (Fleet Operations and Readiness). The Aviation Plans Division was established to perform the planning requirement functions of the disestablished division.

21 SEPTEMBER • Submarine *Barbero* (SSG 317) sailed in the North Pacific on the first deterrent patrol of a submarine equipped with a Regulus I bombardment missile.

25 SEPTEMBER • The final class of lighter-than-air students also qualified in heavier-than-air completed training at NAS Glynco, Ga. Ens. John B. Hall was the last to receive the dual designation.

29 SEPTEMBER • *Kearsarge* (CVS 33) supported relief operations in the wake of a typhoon at Nagoya, Japan. This included the evacuation of almost 6,000 people, the delivery of 200,000-pounds of supplies and medicine, and more than 17,000 doses of typhoid vaccine and antibiotics administered. The ship departed on 6 October.

30 SEPTEMBER • Airship flights by reservists of Naval Air Reserve Training Unit, Lakehurst, N.J., marked the end of the airship training program after 12 years of service under the Chief of Naval Air Reserve Training.

1 OCTOBER • Lt. Cmdr. John A. Henning of VX-6 landed an R5D Skymaster at NAF McMurdo Sound, Antarctica, after a flight from Christchurch, New Zealand, with Commander, Naval Support Force Antarctica Rear Adm. David M. Tyree on board. The arrival of this first flight of the season marked the operational start of Operation Deep Freeze 60.

1 OCTOBER • Fleet Air San Diego, Calif., was established, Rear Adm. Dale Harris commanding.

2 NOVEMBER • The use of T2J-1 Buckeyes in basic training commenced with a flight at NAS Pensacola, Fla., by instructor Lt. Cmdr. Rieman A. MacDonell and student 2d Lt. David K. Mosher, USMC.

30 NOVEMBER • The Airship Training Group was disestablished at NAS Glynco, Ga. This ended lighter-than-air training in the U.S. Navy.

1 DECEMBER • The Bureaus of Aeronautics and Ordnance were abolished as Chief of the Bureau of Naval Weapons Rear Adm. Paul D. Stroop relieved Rear Adms. Robert E. Dixon and Miles H. Hubbard, the chiefs of those bureaus, respectively, and the Bureau of Naval Weapons absorbed their functions.

710604

From left, Chief of the Bureau of Naval Weapons Rear Adm. Paul D. Stroop relieves Rear Adms. Robert E. Dixon and Miles H. Hubbard, the Chiefs of the Bureaus of Aeronautics and Ordnance, respectively.

1061491

The Navy bypassed the prototype stage making this, the first service test YT2J-1 Buckeye, BuNo 144217, the first of the advanced trainers.

710526

Cmdr. Lawrence E. Flint Jr. flew the second YF4H-1 Phantom II, BuNo 142260, to a world altitude record 98,560 feet on 6 December 1959.

3 DECEMBER • Following a dam burst in the San Raphael area of France, *Essex* (CVA 9), cruiser *Boston* (CAG 1), and destroyers *Myles C. Fox* (DD 829), *Vogelgesang* (DD 862), and *Mullinnix* (DD 944), aided relief efforts.

4 DECEMBER • Teams from selected fleet squadrons completed four days of competitive gunnery, bombing, and missile firing in the championship round of the annual weapons meet at MCAAS Yuma, Ariz. VF(AW)-3 and VF-41 took the all-weather fighter titles in the F4D Skyray and F3H Demon categories, respectively. VMF-232 won the day fighter competition, VA-56 the jet light attack, VA-85 the prop light attack, and VAH-4 the heavy attack. 1st Lt. G. A. Davis, USMC, of VMF-232 was the top individual scorer in the day fighter event.

6 DECEMBER • Cmdr. Lawrence E. Flint Jr. bettered the existing world altitude record by reaching 98,560 feet in an F4H-1 Phantom II over Edwards AFB, Calif.

7 DECEMBER • *Dewey* (DLG 14), Cmdr. Elmo R. Zumwalt Jr. commanding, was commissioned at the Boston Naval Shipyard, Mass., as the first of a new class of guided-missile destroyer leaders designed to employ RIM-2 Terrier III air defense missiles.

30 DECEMBER • *George Washington* (SSBN 598) was commissioned at Groton, Conn., Cmdr. George B. Osborn commanding. She was the first of nine such nuclear-powered fleet ballistic missile submarines authorized by Congress.

1053763

Coral Sea (CVA 43), *Midway* (CVA 41), and *Hancock* (CVA 19) moor at NAS Alameda, Calif., November 1960.

1053764

Intrepid (CVA 11) and *Independence* (CVA 62) prepare at Norfolk, Va., to deploy to the Mediterranean, summer 1960.

Chapter 9

On The Brink

1960–1969

The golden anniversary of naval aviation was celebrated in 1961 along with a new stature of the fleet's air arm as an effective fighting force. One nuclear-powered and two conventionally-powered attack carriers joined the operating forces, with two additional attack carriers commissioned by the end of the decade. The Navy acquired four new amphibious assault ships and other vessels to exploit the unique capabilities of helicopters in vertical assault and replenishment. New high-performance aircraft went into operation along with the development of vertical- and short-takeoff-and-landing aircraft. Innovative types of missiles appeared and Sparrows and Sidewinders received enhanced capabilities, but the importance of blimps and flying boats faded because of the advent of new technologies.

During the Cuban Missile Crisis the Navy exerted its traditional role of sea control by imposing a naval blockade that proved instrumental in averting global thermonuclear war. The round-the-world cruise of a nuclear-powered task force and operations in the Indian Ocean carried the flag into foreign ports. Naval forces responded to crises in Africa, the Middle East, the Caribbean, and Berlin; evacuated Americans trapped by fighting, and by their presence reaffirmed the role of the service in keeping the peace. Ships and aircraft aided the stricken when hurricanes, typhoons, and earthquakes struck in widely distant points.

In Southeast Asia, the nation responded to communist aggression with retaliatory air strikes that escalated into a protracted war of limited objectives and little relevancy to U.S. national security. The aircraft of the Seventh Fleet carried the burden of the naval air war, but the requirement for sustained naval action and the support of allied troops ashore challenged logistic planners and force commanders.

The conquest of space began in earnest as manned orbital flight became a reality and culminated in the first manned lunar landing. Half the nation's astronauts possessed Navy or Marine backgrounds and naval aviators made the first American suborbital and orbital flights. Navy flight surgeons joined in the study of the physiological effects of space flight. A Navy space surveillance system helped forge the necessary links for a continuous watch on space. Satellites developed by Navy scientists expanded human knowledge of the cosmos, and a naval satellite navigation system provided an accurate means to all nations of traveling the earth's oceans. Carriers or amphibious assault ships supported orbital missions to cover emergency landings, and recovered astronauts and their spacecraft following reentry.

The Navy's support of the space program resulted in a number of organizational adjustments as well as the formation of a recovery force command. Broader and more basic changes in departmental structure occurred as a result of a series of high-level studies directed toward clarifying the lines of authority and responsibility. The abolition of the bureau system and centralization of material support under a strengthened Material Command placed under the direct control of the Chief of Naval Operations occurred, the project manager concept received new impetus, and other changes radiated outward to the operating forces and shore establishments.

1960

1 JANUARY • Electronic countermeasures squadrons were redesignated fleet air reconnaissance squadrons without a change of their VQ letter designation.

15 JANUARY • The transfer of the Naval Weather Service Division from the Office of Deputy Chief of Naval Operations (Operations & Readiness) to the staff of Vice CNO occurred, and the Office of the Naval Weather Service

1063056

Enterprise (CVAN 65) is the world's first nuclear-powered aircraft carrier.

was set up as a field activity under the management control of the CNO. The responsibilities of the new office included the management control of the integrated fleet weather central system and the technical direction of meteorological matters within shore establishments and the operating forces.

15 JANUARY • National Air and Space Administration approved the *Overall Plan for Department of Defense Support for Project Mercury Operations*. The Navy's portion, entitled *Operation Plan COMDESFLOTFOUR No. 1-60*, provided for recovery procedures covering Mercury-Redstone and Mercury-Atlas missions.

26 JANUARY • The first of two giant unmanned balloons launched from *Valley Forge* (CVS 45) south of the Virgin Islands during Project Skyhook—the recording of cosmic ray activity. The balloons were nearly 50-stories tall, had a lifting gas capacity greater than that of rigid airship *Akron* (ZRS 4), and carried 2,500-pounds including 800-pounds of film to perform the readings. The first balloon achieved an altitude of 116,000 feet and remained aloft for eight hours, while the second reached 113,000 feet during a flight of 26 ½ hours. Early warning aircraft from *Valley Forge* and ashore tracked the balloons and a destroyer recovered the instruments. The Office of Naval Research and the National Science Foundation jointly sponsored the project.

FEBRUARY • Through April, the Naval School of Aviation Medicine at NAS Pensacola, Fla., modified a standard 20-man raft to enable its placement around the base of a floating Mercury spacecraft with the impact skirt extended.

The device raised the spacecraft high enough in the water to permit egress from the side hatch.

25 FEBRUARY • An R6D-1, BuNo 131582, carrying seven crewmembers of VR-1, 19 members of the Navy Band, and a team of 12 antisubmarine warfare specialists collided with a Brazilian DC-3 of REAL Transportes Aéreos, registered PP-AXD, over Sugarloaf Mountain at Rio de Janeiro, Brazil. The accident claimed the lives of all but three of the 38 sailors on board the Liftmaster and all 26 people—four crewmembers and 22 passengers—on board the airliner.

29 FEBRUARY • The Department of Defense announced a successful demonstration by the Navy's Mine Defense Laboratory and the Air Mine Defense Development Unit of two improvements in airborne mine countermeasures at Panama City, Fla. The first consisted of air-portable minesweeping gear that enabled a helicopter to become a self-sufficient aerial minesweeper. The second concerned equipment for transferring the minesweeping-gear towline from a surface minesweeper to a helicopter, from one helicopter to another, or from a helicopter to a surface minesweeper.

1046721

Valley Forge (CVS 45) prepares to launch a Project Skyhook unmanned balloon to record cosmic ray activity, 26 January 1960.

29 FEBRUARY • An earthquake razed the area around Agadir, Morocco. Aircraft flew sailors and Marines from NAS Port Lyautey to aid the victims, and a Navy-wide effort subsequently brought food and clothing to the people from Reserve and other units from as far as Seattle, Wash.

1 MARCH • A ZPG-3W airship of ZW-1 returned to NAS Lakehurst, N.J., after 49.3 hours on station and 58 hours in the air during an Air Defense Command barrier patrol over the North Atlantic. This new record for continuous patrol more than doubled the best time logged by its smaller ZPG-2W predecessor.

18 MARCH • On the first firing test of Project Hydra, a 150-pound rocket successfully ignited underwater and launched into the air at Naval Missile Center Point Mugu, Calif. The test demonstrated the feasibility of launching rockets while floating upright in the ocean and gave promise of eliminating the cost of launching pad construction and allowing greater freedom in the choice of launching sites.

25 MARCH • *Halibut* (SSGN 587) fired a Regulus I in the first launch of a bombardment missile from a nuclear-powered submarine during training exercises off Oahu, Hawaii.

1105433

A ground antenna for navigation satellite Transit 1B.

26 MARCH • Elements of Marine Aircraft Wing 1 participating in amphibious exercise Blue Star established an operational jet airstrip on the south shore of Formosa (Taiwan) within 72 hours of landing. Expeditionary airfield matting covered the 3,400-foot strip, and the equipment included a portable mirror landing system, TACAN, fuel tank farm, and a tower control system. A4D Skyhawks operated from it with the assistance of JATO, while F4D-1 Skyrays and F8U Crusaders used afterburners to takeoff.

28 MARCH • The astronauts of Project Mercury received their first open-water egress training from a spacecraft with the Naval School of Aviation Medicine, NAS Pensacola, Fla. The men emerged from a completely restrained state in the spacecraft to a life raft in conditions of up to ten-foot swells in an average of about four minutes. The training concluded on 1 April.

1 APRIL • CVSG-53 and -59 were established at NAS North Island, Calif. Each group consisted of one HS and two VS squadrons. This marked the beginning of a reorganization of antisubmarine aviation that called for the formation of nine CVSGs, and for the assignment of an additional replacement CVSG and a patrol squadron in each fleet to perform functions paralleling those carried out by the previously established replacement carrier air groups.

13 APRIL • A Thor Able-Star missile launched the Applied Physics Laboratory–designed navigation satellite Transit 1B into orbit from Cape Canaveral, Fla. The satellite emitted a radio signal at a precise frequency that surface receiving stations used as a baseline for measurement of the signal's doppler shift to determine the station's position with high accuracy. Other experiments performed with this launch included the separation and entry into its own orbit of an uninstrumented satellite, thereby demonstrating the feasibility of launching multiple satellites from a single vehicle.

19 APRIL • The Naval Space Surveillance Facility was established at Dahlgren, Va.

1 MAY • Seventeen basic training groups of the Naval Air Training Command were redesignated training squadrons (VT) and established as separate units, each under a commanding officer.

22 MAY • An earthquake measuring an estimated 9.5 on the moment magnitude scale devastated the area around Cañete, Chile, and generated tsunamis that struck the Pacific coast of South America, the Aleutian Islands, New Zealand, Australia, the Philippines, Japan, and Hilo, Hawaii—where 61 people died. On 25 June, dock landing ship *Catamount* (LSD 17) sailed from NS San Diego, Calif., to assist victims of flooding in the area around Valparaiso. The ship disembarked and transferred landing craft to the Chilean Navy, and provided critically needed transportation in the vicinity where tidal waves had destroyed piers. *Catamount* departed on 15 July.

3 JUNE • A Marine HUS-1 Seahorse successfully completed test launchings of AGM-12 Bullpup air-to-ground missiles at NATC Patuxent River, Md.

10 JUNE • Seven HSS-1Ns of HS-4, embarked on board *Yorktown* (CVS 10), rescued 53 men from British freighter *Shun Lee* when she broke up on Pratas Reef, 500 miles northwest of Manila, Philippines. Under storm conditions in the wake of Typhoon Mary, the Seabats pulled 25 men from the wreck and 28 more from Pratas Island inside the reef.

21 JUNE • Frigate *Norfolk* (DL 1) fired an RUR-5 ASROC (Anti-Submarine ROCket) in a public demonstration from a position off Key West, Fla. The event marked the completion of a two-month technical evaluation of the weapon, which featured a rocket-powered airframe carrying a homing torpedo or depth charge.

22 JUNE • A Thor Able-Star missile launched navigation satellite Transit 2A into orbit from Cape Canaveral, Fla. Naval Research Laboratory Solar Radiation I satellite mounted pickaback also entered into orbit. Transit 2A further developed Doppler navigation techniques and confirmed the practicability of using satellites for precise geodetic surveys, provided critical measurements of the effect of the ionosphere on electromagnetic waves, and measurements of high frequency cosmic noise that had been requested by the Canadian Government. The satellite had an operating life of 2 ½ years.

1 JULY • VRC-40, Cmdr. John H. Crawford commanding, was established at NAS Norfolk, Va., as the first carrier on-board delivery squadron.

1 JULY • An experimental DSN-1 successfully demonstrated the operating capabilities of a drone helicopter designed for use in antisubmarine warfare from destroyers when it landed on board frigate *Mitscher* (DL 2) off the coast of Long Island, N.Y. A safety pilot manned the drone but remote control from ashore flew and maneuvered it around the ship and into position for a landing before the pilot took command and made the final touchdown.

1 JULY • A Pacific Missile Range Facility was established at Eniwetok, Marshall Islands, to support the operations of the Pacific Missile Range, Calif.

9 JULY • On 30 June, the Belgian Congo (Zaire) gained its independence but an army revolt led to widespread violence and the collapse of order. On this date, *Wasp* (CVS 18),

1143449

DS-1382, shown modified as the first QH-50D, was one of 373 DSN-3 (later QH-50C) drone antisubmarine helicopters built. It is carrying two Mk 44 torpedoes.

uniquely embarking a Marine company, sailed from NS Guantánamo Bay, Cuba, for the coast of Africa to evacuate Americans and support UN intervention. By the time *Wasp* departed the area in early August, the ship had also supplied some 250,000 gallons of aviation gasoline in support of the UN airlift.

18 JULY • The Navy terminated the Corvus air-to-surface missile program to permit increased emphasis on other weapon systems that offered a wider scope of employment.

20 JULY • *George Washington* (SSBN 598) launched a solid-propellant Polaris A-1 fleet ballistic missile for the first time while submerged off Cape Canaveral, Fla. The missile broke clear of the water, ignited in the air, and streaked almost 1,100 nautical miles toward its target down the Atlantic Missile Test Range. At 1239, Cmdr. James B. Osborn, commanding officer of the boat's Blue Crew, sent President Dwight D. Eisenhower a message: "Polaris—from out of the deep to target. Perfect." About two hours later, *George Washington* launched a second Polaris that also successfully struck its target.

21 JULY • The Navy announced the issuance of a contract to Douglas Aircraft Company for the development of the F6D Missileer for launching Eagle long-range air-to-air guided missiles.

1 AUGUST • Naval Air Rocket Test Station was disestablished at Lake Denmark, N.J. The Navy transferred its liquid rocket development projects to other activities

Cmdr. Leroy A. Heath (left) and Lt. Henry L. Monroe review their flight notes after breaking the altitude record for a 1,000-kilogram payload with an altitude of 91,450.8 feet in an A3J Vigilante, 13 December 1960.

including NOTS China Lake, Calif.; Naval Propellant Plant, Indian Head, Md.; and Naval Weapons Laboratory, Dahlgren, Va. The Army began the incorporation of the reassigned land into Picattinny Arsenal.

11 AUGUST • An HRS-3 operating from cargo ship *Haiti Victory* (T-AK 238) made the first recovery of a man-made object that had been in earth orbit. Satellite *Discoverer XIII* completed its 17th pass around the earth and discharged an instrumented capsule that splashed down about 330 miles northwest of Honolulu, Hawaii. Air Force planes located the capsule and directed the ship to the recovery within three hours of its landing.

2 SEPTEMBER • Capt. Holden C. Richardson, CC, (Naval Aviator No. 13) died at Bethesda, Md. Richardson became the Navy's first engineering test pilot, helped to develop the initial catapults, co-designed and supervised the construction of the NC flying boats, piloted one of the planes (NC-3) on the transatlantic attempt, and served as one of the original members of NACA.

5 SEPTEMBER • Lt. Col. Thomas H. Miller Jr., USMC, set a new world speed record for 500 kilometers at 1,216.78 mph in an F4H-1 Phantom II over a triangular course at Edwards AFB, Calif.

19 SEPTEMBER • An Argo D-8 rocket launched the NASA Nuclear Emulsion Recovery Vehicle from Naval Missile Facility Point Arguello, Calif. The instrumented capsule reached an altitude of 1,260 miles and landed 1,300 miles down range for ship recovery.

25 SEPTEMBER • Cmdr. John F. Davis averaged 1,390.21 mph for 100 kilometers in an F4H-1 Phantom II over a closed circuit course, bettering the existing world record for that distance by more than 200 mph.

20 OCTOBER • The Department of Defense announced the establishment under Navy management of an Army-Navy-Air Force program to develop the prototype of an operational vertical-takeoff-and-landing aircraft to test its suitability for air transport service.

10 NOVEMBER • The Secretary of Defense directed the placement of the Navy Space Surveillance System and the USAF Space Track System—each performing similar services over different sections of the surveillance network—under the control of the North American Air Defense Command for military functions.

15 NOVEMBER • The Polaris fleet ballistic missile weapon system became operational when submarine *George Washington* (SSBN 598) sailed with her principal armament of 16 Polaris A-1 missiles from NWS Charleston, S.C.

17 NOVEMBER • At the request of Guatemala and Nicaragua, President Dwight D. Eisenhower ordered a naval patrol of Central American waters to intercept and prevent communist-led invasion attempts of those countries from the sea. At times, *Wasp* (CVS 18) and *Shangri-La* (CVA 38) patrolled until diffused tensions prompted their recall on 7 December.

13 DECEMBER • An A3J Vigilante crewed by pilot Cmdr. Leroy A. Heath and bombardier/navigator Lt. Henry L. Monroe carried a payload of 1,000-kilograms to an attitude of 91,450.8 feet over Edwards AFB, Calif. This established a new world altitude record with payload and surpassed the existing record by more than four miles.

19 DECEMBER • A catastrophic fire erupted on the hangar deck of *Constellation* (CVA 64) during the final stages of her construction at New York Naval Shipyard, Brooklyn, N.Y. Fifty civilian workers died in the blaze and the ship sustained $75 million in damages.

19 DECEMBER • Mercury-Redstone 1A launched from Cape Canaveral, Fla. The unmanned, suborbital mission came after a failed attempt on 21 November. This mission qualified the spacecraft for space operations and the flight system for a planned primate flight. A P2V Neptune spotted the capsule during its descent toward the Atlantic and a helicopter from Marine Aircraft Group 26, embarked on board *Valley Forge* (CVS 45), recovered the spacecraft within 47 minutes of the launch.

22 DECEMBER • HSS-2 Sea Kings of HS-3 and HUP Retrievers of HU-2, embarked on board *Valley Forge* (CVS 45), rescued 27 men from oiler *Pine Ridge* when she broke-up in heavy seas about 100 miles off Cape Hatteras, N.C.

1961

1 JANUARY • By this time, North Vietnamese-supported Prince Souphanouvong and the communist Pathet Lao had seized positions on the Laotian *Plaine Des Jarres* from American-supported Prince Souvanna Phouma and his royalists. On this date, the Seventh Fleet deployed *Lexington* (CVA 16), *Bennington* (CVS 20), and *Coral Sea* (CVA 43) to the South China Sea to deter further communist gains until the situation stabilized. On 6 January the carriers received orders to turn around.

11 JANUARY • President-elect John F. Kennedy released a report from the Ad Hoc Committee on Space named to review the space and missile programs and to identify problems requiring prompt attention. The committee's conclusions included the requirement for the redefinition of the objectives of the national space program, the assignment of the National Aeronautics and Space Council as the effective agency to manage the space program, and the requirement for a single responsible agency within the defense establishment to manage the military aspects of the space program.

31 JANUARY • Mercury-Redstone 2 launched from Cape Canaveral, Fla. The suborbital mission obtained physiological and performance data during ballistic flight on the occupant, a 37-pound chimpanzee named Ham. The over acceleration of the launch vehicle coupled with the velocity of the escape rocket pushed the spacecraft to an altitude 42 miles higher and a range 125 miles farther than planned. 1st Lts. John A. Hellridger, USMC, and George F. Cox, USMC, of HMRL-262 from Marine Aircraft Group 26 manned an HUS-1 Seahorse embarked on board dock landing ship *Donner* (LSD 20), and recovered the capsule and Ham from the Atlantic. *Donner* proceeded at flank speed to disembark the chimpanzee at Grand Bahama Island, and then sailed to Cape Canaveral to offload the capsule.

1 FEBRUARY • The Space Surveillance System was established with its headquarters at Naval Weapons Laboratory, Dahlgren, Va., Capt. David G. Woosley commanding. The system had functioned as an experimental research project since 1959, but this action made it an operational command.

21 FEBRUARY • A Thor Able-Star missile launched navigation satellite Transit 3B and the piggybacked Low Frequency Transionospheric Satellite (Lofti) from Cape Canaveral, Fla. A programmer malfunction prevented their separation from the booster and each other causing them to reenter the atmosphere after only 37 days. Despite this, both functioned and Transit 3B received prototype navigational messages and reported back to provide the first complete demonstration of all features of the navigation satellite system.

21 FEBRUARY • Mercury-Atlas 2 launched from Cape Canaveral, Fla. The suborbital mission qualified the Mercury-Atlas combination in flight and evaluated the spacecraft performance under near maximum reentry loads. An HMRL-262 HUS-1 Seahorse from Marine Aircraft Group 26, embarked on board dock landing ship *Donner* (LSD 20), recovered the capsule in the Atlantic and offloaded the spacecraft at San Juan, P.R. In addition, on this date, NASA announced the selection of astronauts Lt. Col. John H. Glenn Jr., USMC; Cmdr. Alan B. Shepard Jr.; and Capt. Virgil I. Grissom, USAF; to begin special training for the first manned Mercury flight.

1069225

Kitty Hawk (CVA 63), the name ship of her class of supercarriers, is an evolution of the *Forrestal*-class ships.

6 MARCH • The Secretary of Defense established defense policies and responsibilities for the development of satellites, antisatellites, space probes, and supporting systems. The action authorized each military department "to conduct preliminary research to develop new ways of using space technology to perform its assigned function." The USAF received the responsibility for research, development, test, and engineering of Department of Defense space development programs and projects, but provisions granting exceptions made possible the Navy's development of a unique space capability.

21 MARCH • Ongoing attacks by communist Pathet Lao insurgents threatened the stability of the royalist regime in Laos, and the Seventh Fleet dispatched ships to the South China Sea to monitor the fighting. Aircraft flew reconnaissance missions over Laos into June.

10 APRIL • Cmdr. Lloyd E. Newcomer of VX-6 piloted a C-130BL Hercules carrying a double crew of 16 and a special crew of five during the emergency evacuation of Soviet exchange scientist Leonid Kuperov from Byrd Station, Antarctica, to Christchurch, New Zealand. Kuperov suffered from an acute abdominal condition. This round-trip flight from Christchurch accomplished the first aerial mission to pierce the winter isolation of the Antarctic continent.

17 APRIL • *Brigadistas* (Cuban exiles) of Brigade 2506 opposed to the regime of Fidel R. Castro sailed from British Honduras (Belize) for Bahía de Cochinos (Bay of Pigs), Cuba, during Operation Zapata—an attempt to overthrow Castro. The United States concentrated naval support for the émigrés initially within Task Group Alpha (81.8), including *Essex* (CVS 9), with Carrier Anti-Submarine Air Group 60 embarked. Aircraft from *Essex* were to fly combat air patrols over the invaders' landing craft and reconnaissance flights over Castro's forces. The force included 12 VA-34 A4D-2 Skyhawks, two S2F-1 Trackers and eight S2F-1Ss of VS-34, four AD5-W Skyraiders of VAW-12 Detachment 45, 15 HS-9 HSS-1 Seabats, one HUP-3 Retriever of HU-2 Detachment 45, and one TF-1 Trader. To accommodate the Skyhawks on board *Essex*, the S2F-1s of VS-39 temporarily operated from NAS Quonset Point, R.I.

Independence (CVA 62), with Carrier Air Group 7 embarked, sailed to host President John F. Kennedy for a scheduled naval firepower demonstration from NS Norfolk, Va. The crisis compelled the cancellation of the chief executive's visit and *Independence* made for the area south of NS Guantánamo Bay, Cuba. The United States did not intervene, however, and Castro rushed reinforcements that forced the evacuation or surrender of the *brigadistas* by 20 April. *Essex* returned to Quonset Point on 29 April. *Independence* did not reach the area in time to affect the outcome and returned on 30 April, anchoring in Hampton Roads, Va.

21 APRIL • The Office of the Pacific Missile Range Representative, Kaneohe, Hawaii, was redesignated and established as the Pacific Missile Range Facility, Hawaiian Area, to serve as the mid-Pacific headquarters for missile and satellite tracking stations located in the Hawaiian and central Pacific areas.

29 APRIL • *Kitty Hawk* (CVA 63), Capt. William F. Bringle commanding, was commissioned at Philadelphia Naval Shipyard, Pa., as the first of a class of attack carriers equipped with RIM-2 Terrier surface-to-air missiles.

4 MAY • Cmdr. Malcolm D. Ross and Lt. Cmdr. Victor A. Prather, MC, crewed a two-place open gondola Stratolab balloon from *Antietam* (CVS 36) sailing off the mouth of the Mississippi River. This, the largest balloon ever employed to date on a manned flight, attained a world record balloon altitude of 113,739.9 feet, 2 hours, 36 minutes after liftoff at a position about 136 miles south of Mobile, Ala. Prather fell from the sling of the recovery helicopter, his pressure suit filled with water, and he drowned before he could be reached. His body was never recovered.

5 MAY • Cmdr. Alan B. Shepard Jr. manned space capsule *Freedom* 7 during the flight of Mercury-Redstone 3 from Cape Canaveral, Fla. The crew of an HMRL-262 HUS-1 Seahorse from Marine Aircraft Group 26, embarked on board *Lake Champlain* (CVS 39), visually followed the descent of *Freedom* 7. The Seahorse recovered the capsule at sea at 27°13'7"N, 75°53'W, and transported the spacecraft and Shepard to the carrier. After preliminary medical and technical debriefing, a helicopter flew the astronaut to Grand Bahama Island for two days of complete debriefings. Shepard became the first American to ascend into space during this initial of two suborbital Mercury missions.

NH 69954

A Marine HUS-1 Seahorse recovers Cmdr. Alan B. Shepard Jr. after his completion of the first U.S. manned space flight, 5 May 1961.

17 MAY • Cmdr. Patrick L. Sullivan and Lt. Beverly W. Witherspoon set a new world class speed record in an HSS-2 Sea King of 192.9 mph for three kilometers at Bradley Field, Windsor Locks, Conn.

NH 69959

Cmdr. Patrick L. Sullivan (left) and Lt. Beverly W. Witherspoon flying an HSS-2 helicopter, set a world class speed record.

24 MAY • Three F4H-1 Phantom IIs competing for the Bendix Trophy bettered the existing record for transcontinental flight from Los Angeles, Calif., to New York, N.Y. The winning team of pilot Lt. Richard F. Gordon Jr. and radar intercept officer Lt. j.g. Bobbie R. Young averaged 870 mph on the 2,421.4-mile flight, and set a new record of 2 hours, 47 minutes.

24 MAY • Cmdr. Patrick L. Sullivan and Lt. Beverly W. Witherspoon set a new world class speed record in an HSS-2 Sea King with a mark of 174.9 mph over a 100-kilometer course between Milford and Westbrook, Conn.

25 MAY • President John F. Kennedy requested additional appropriations from Congress totaling $611 million for NASA and the Department of Defense to accelerate the space program. "I believe that this nation should commit itself to achieving the goal," the chief executive declared, "before this decade is out, of landing a man on the moon and returning him safely to the earth."

1 JUNE • Ships of the Second Fleet including *Intrepid* (CVA 11), *Randolph* (CVS 15), and *Shangri-La* (CVA 38), received orders to sail off the southern coast of Hispaniola when a general uprising appeared imminent after the assassination of Dominican Republic President (Gen.) Rafael Trujillo. The ships returned after the crisis passed.

21 JUNE • Secretary of the Navy John B. Connally Jr. approved plans for terminating the Navy's lighter-than-air program, disestablishing all operational units by November, putting eight of the ten remaining airships in storage, and deactivating the overhaul and repair shop at NAS Lakehurst, N.J.

29 JUNE • A Thor Able-Star missile launched navigation satellite Transit 4A from Cape Canaveral, Fla., into a nearly circular orbit at a height of about 500 miles. Greb and Injun satellites on board failed to separate from each other but otherwise operated satisfactorily. Transit 4A was the first space vehicle to be equipped with a nuclear-powered generator.

10 JULY • The distribution of the HSS-1 Seabat manual promulgated the first NATOPS (Naval Air Training and Operating Procedures Standardization) Manual. This manual prescribed the standard operating procedures and flight instructions peculiar to Seabats and complemented the more technical information contained in the HSS-1 Flight Manual—also known as the "handbook." As the system developed, the issuance of NATOPS flight manuals consolidated flight and operating instructions with the handbook information beginning with the F9F-8T Cougar manual on 15 December 1963. Further publications included the NATOPS Manual containing generalized instructions covering air operations, and other manuals dealing with such subjects as carrier operations, air refueling, instrument flight, and landing signal officer procedures.

18 JULY • An F4D-1 Skyray made the first of a series of eight unguided Sparoair II rocket launches to an altitude of 64 miles at Naval Missile Center, Point Mugu, Calif. The research rocket had been designed and built at Point Mugu by combining two Sparrow air-to-air missile rocket motors.

21 JULY • Capt. Virgil I. Grissom, USAF, piloted space capsule *Liberty Bell* 7 during the launch of Mercury-Redstone 4 from Cape Canaveral, Fla. The spacecraft

Iwo Jima (LPH 2) is the first U.S. helicopter-capable amphibious assault ship to be designed and built as such.

splashed down near 27°34'N, 75°44'W, and *Randolph* (CVS 15), with Carrier Anti-Submarine Air Group 58 embarked, accomplished the recovery. A premature ejection of the hatch cover, however, caused flooding that made capsule retrieval impossible, and it sank in 2,500 fathoms. An HUS-1 Seahorse from Marine Aircraft Group 26 rescued Grissom and delivered the astronaut to the carrier. HUP-3 Retrievers of HU-2 Detachment 1 flew plane guard and two HSS-1N Seabats of HS-7 photographed the recovery. Grissom became the second American to ascend into space during this final of two suborbital Mercury flights.

3 AUGUST • The director of Defense Research and Engineering approved revisions to the tri-service vertical takeoff and landing program, whereby the administrative responsibility for a tilting wing aircraft was transferred from the Navy to the USAF, but the three services continued to share the cost equally. The aircraft was later developed as the Ling-Temco-Vought XC-142.

18 AUGUST • NASA announced that an analysis of Project Mercury suborbital data indicated the achievement of all objectives of the initial phase of the space program, and thereby concluded planning for additional Mercury-Redstone flights.

26 AUGUST • *Iwo Jima* (LPH 2), Capt. Thomas D. Harris commanding, was commissioned at Puget Sound Naval Shipyard, Bremerton, Wash., as the first amphibious assault ship to be designed and built as such. The new ship operated a helicopter squadron and embarked Marines in the "vertical envelopment" concept of amphibious assault.

28 AUGUST • NOTS China Lake, Calif., reported on tests of Snakeye I mechanical retardation devices under development to permit low-altitude bombing with the Mk 80 family of low-drag bombs. Four designs of retarders, two made by Douglas and two by the station, had been tested in flight on the station's rocket-powered test sled or in the wind tunnel. One of the Douglas designs showed sufficient promise and resulted in the issuance of a contract to the company for a number of experimental and prototype units.

28 AUGUST • An F4H-1 Phantom II crewed by pilot Lt. Hunt Hardisty and radar intercept officer Lt. Earl H. DeEsch averaged 902.769 mph for a new low-altitude world speed record over a three-kilometer course at Holloman AFB, N. Mex.

11 SEPTEMBER • Task Force 135, Rear Adm. Frederick J. Brush commanding, including *Antietam* (CVS 36) and *Shangri-La* (CVA 38), received orders to sail to the Galveston-Freeport, Texas, area for disaster relief operations in the wake of Hurricane Carla.

114345

An aviation ordnanceman handles Snakeye bombs on board *Hancock* (CVA 19).

13 SEPTEMBER • Mercury-Atlas 4 launched from Cape Canaveral, Fla. The unmanned mission demonstrated the capabilities to fly a person in orbit and of the global Mercury tracking network. Dock landing ship *Plymouth Rock* (LSD 29) and destroyer *Decatur* (DD 936) recovered the capsule in the Atlantic after a single orbit.

1 OCTOBER • Renewed tensions over control of divided Berlin, East Germany, prompted President John F. Kennedy to activate Reserve units including five Naval Reserve patrol and 13 carrier antisubmarine squadrons.

8 OCTOBER • HUS-1 Seahorses of HMRL-362, embarked on board amphibious assault ship *Princeton* (LPH 5), plucked 84 men from U.S. merchant ship *Pioneer Muse* and Lebanese vessel *Sheik* after both ships ran aground on Kita Daita Jima in the Pacific. Attack cargo ship *Tulare* (AKA 112) directed the rescue.

16 OCTOBER • The Astronautics Operations Division Op-54 was transferred from the office of Deputy Chief of Naval Operations (Air) to Op-76 of the office of DCNO (Development) to reassign the responsibilities for the naval support of the space program's Project Mercury within OPNAV.

23 OCTOBER • Submarine *Ethan Allen* (SSBN 608) made the first underwater launch of a Polaris A-2 fleet ballistic missile. The Polaris soared 1,500 miles down the Atlantic Missile Range.

31 OCTOBER • Fleet Airship Wing One and ZP-1 and -3 were disestablished at NAS Lakehurst, N.J., as the last operating naval lighter-than-air units.

31 OCTOBER • Hurricane Hattie devastated British Honduras (Belize), killing an estimated 310 people. On 2 November, *Antietam* (CVS 36) sailed from NAS Pensacola, Fla., to render relief. HT-8 HO4S-3s and HMRL-264 HUS-1 Seahorses proved instrumental in reaching people trapped and isolated by debris, rugged country, and swamps during 207 sorties carrying more than 57 tons of food, water, and medical supplies. The helicopters also transported teams from the Naval School of Aviation Medicine and relief workers to Belize, Stann Creek, and other points. On 6 November, the ship departed but six doctors and six helicopters with 18 pilots and 25 crewmen briefly remained to continue aid at the behest of the British.

18 NOVEMBER • Dominican Republic President Joaquín Balaguer declared a state of emergency following the return to that country of Héctor and José Trujillo, brothers of assassinated President (Gen.) Rafael Trujillo. *Franklin D. Roosevelt* (CVA 42) subsequently reinforced the Caribbean Ready Amphibious Squadron off the nation's coast. The combined force launched flights of A4D Skyhawks and made amphibious feints from outside Dominican waters to emphasize U.S. resolve to prevent a reestablishment of a dictatorship there. The ships departed after the formation of a Dominican council of state on 19 December.

22 NOVEMBER • Lt. Col. Robert B. Robinson, USMC, broke the world speed record by averaging 1,606.3 mph in two runs in an YF4H-1 Phantom II over a 15/25-kilometer course at Edwards AFB, Calif.

25 NOVEMBER • *Enterprise* (CVAN 65), Capt. Vincent P. DePoix commanding, was commissioned at Newport News Shipbuilding and Dry Dock Co., Va., as the world's first nuclear-powered aircraft carrier.

In Operation Skyburner, Lt. Col. Robert B. Robinson, USMC, breaks the absolute world speed record at 1,606.342 mph in the second YF4H-1 Phantom II, BuNo 142260, 22 November 1961.

29 NOVEMBER • Mercury-Atlas 5 launched from Cape Canaveral, Fla. The suborbital mission obtained physiological and performance data during ballistic flight on the occupant, a chimpanzee named Enos. A helicopter from Marine Aircraft Group 26, embarked on board *Lake Champlain* (CVS 39), together with destroyer *Stormes* (DD 780) recovered the capsule in the Atlantic. Dock landing ship *Fort Mandan* (LSD 21) was among the vessels that supported the recovery. Also on this date, NASA selected Lt. Col. John H. Glenn Jr., USMC, as the astronaut for the first manned orbital flight and Lt. Cmdr. M. Scott Carpenter as the backup pilot.

1 DECEMBER • Capt. Bruce K. Lloyd and Cmdr. Don J. Roulstone laid claim to three new world speed records in an HSS-2 Sea King over a course along Long Island Sound between Milford and Westbrook, Conn., with performances of 182.8 mph, 179.5 mph, and 175.3 mph for 100, 500, and 1,000 kilometers, respectively.

5 DECEMBER • Cmdr. George W. Ellis surpassed the existing world record for altitude sustained in horizontal flight with a height of 66,443.8 feet in a YF4H-1 Phantom II over Edwards AFB, Calif.

NH 69961

Capt. Bruce K. Lloyd (left) and Cmdr. Don J. Roulstone break three global helicopter speed records in an HSS-2 Sea King over a course along Long Island Sound, 1 December 1961.

6 DECEMBER • Cmdr. Alan B. Shepard Jr. and Capt. Virgil I. Grissom, USAF, received new wings honoring America's first astronauts in a joint Navy–Air Force ceremony. The designs of the emblems displayed a shooting star superimposed on the traditional aviator wings of the respective services.

8 DECEMBER • The closure of the landing field at NAS Anacostia, D.C., and the termination of all approach procedures and operation of air traffic facilities ended the career of the fourth oldest air station in terms of continuous operations in the Navy.

14 DECEMBER • The completion of the installation of the Pilot Landing Aid Television (PLAT) system on *Coral Sea* (CVA 43) heralded the first carrier to have the system installed for operational use. Designers intended the system to provide a video tape of every landing for instructional purposes and the analysis of landing accidents in the promotion of safety. By early 1963, all attack carriers received PLAT and planning had begun for its installation in antisubmarine carriers and at shore stations.

29 DECEMBER • NASA issued the *Gemini Operational and Management Plan* outlining the roles and responsibilities of the Department of Defense and NASA in the Gemini space program.

30 DECEMBER • Cmdr. Patrick L. Sullivan and Capt. David A. Spurlock, USMC, bettered the existing HSS-2 Sea King three-kilometer world speed record at 199.01 mph at Windsor Locks, Conn.

1962

1 JANUARY • Three new fleet air commands were established under Commander, Naval Air Force Atlantic, one each with headquarters at Iceland, Bermuda, and in the Azores.

15 JANUARY • Through 17 January, recovery area swimmers completed training at NAS Pensacola, Fla., including jumps from a helicopter for use in the Mercury-Atlas 6 manned orbital mission.

17 JANUARY • *Enterprise* (CVAN 65) accomplished the first fleet air operations of a nuclear-powered aircraft carrier. Cmdr. George C. Talley Jr., commander of Carrier Air Group 1 from NAS Cecil Field, Fla., made an arrested landing—trap—and catapult launch in an F8U-1E of VF-62, BuNo 145375. A few minutes later, Cmdr. Joseph P. Moorer and Lt. Cmdr. Jesse J. Taylor of VF-62 landed two more Crusaders. These events marked the first of 170 catapult shots and traps over two days. On 30 October 1961, three TF-1 Traders of VR-40 took off from the ship to transport VIPs to the mainland following their observation of sea trials, but Talley's flights marked the start of *Enterprise* fleet operations.

23 JANUARY • Lt. Col. Charles E. Crew, USMC, commanding officer of VMF(AW)-451, led a flight consisting of the last of 18 F8U-2N Crusaders to complete the first transpacific mission by a Marine jet fighter squadron from MCAS El Toro, Calif., to NAS Atsugi, Japan. The Crusaders stopped at Kaneohe, Hawaii; Wake Island; and Guam; and GV-1 Hercules tankers provided aerial refueling.

NH 69960

The HSS-2 Sea King flown by Capt. Louis K. Keck, USMC (left), and Navy Lt. R. W. Crafton is the first helicopter to officially exceed 200 mph, 5 February 1962.

24 JANUARY • Two Navy F4H-1 Phantom IIs, designated F-110A by the USAF, arrived at Langley AFB, Va., for use in orientation courses prior to the assignment of Phantoms to the USAF Tactical Air Command.

26 JANUARY • To overcome deficiencies disclosed during the operations of ships equipped with surface-to-air missiles, the chief of the Bureau of Naval Weapons designated an assistant chief for surface missile systems to head a special task force and direct all aspects of surface missiles within the bureau, and to act with the Chief of Naval Personnel and the Bureau of Ships on matters involving those bureaus.

5 FEBRUARY • Navy Lt. R. W. Crafton and Capt. Louis K. Keck, USMC, flew an HSS-2 Sea King during the first officially sanctioned trial of a helicopter to exceed 200 mph. Crafton and Keck broke the 15/25-kilometer world record with a speed of 210.65 mph over a course along the Connecticut shore from Milford to New Haven.

NASA 62MA6-112

Lt. Col. John H. Glenn Jr., USMC, on board spacecraft *Friendship 7*, hurtles into space during the launch of Mercury-Atlas 6, 20 February 1962.

8 FEBRUARY • A detachment of P2V-7 Neptunes of VP-11 began ice reconnaissance flights from NAS Argentia, Newfoundland, over the Gulf of St. Lawrence to aid in evaluating satellite imagery of ice formations transmitted by Tiros 4 after the weather satellite's entry into orbit that day.

20 FEBRUARY • Lt. Col. John H. Glenn Jr., USMC, manned space capsule *Friendship 7* during the launch of Mercury-Atlas 6 from Cape Canaveral, Fla. The mission's three turns about the earth became the first U.S. manned orbital flights and accomplished the basic goals of Project Mercury—putting an astronaut into orbit, determining his ability to perform various functions during space flight, and obtaining physiological data concerning Glenn's reactions to the stresses encountered. Destroyer *Noa*

711031

During Project High Jump—(from left) Lt. Col. William C. McGraw, USMC; Cmdr. David M. Longton, Lt. Cmdr. Del W. Nordberg, and Lt. Cmdr. John W. Young—set multiple F4H-1 Phantom II time-to-climb records.

(DD 841) recovered Glenn and *Friendship* 7 about 21 minutes after splashdown about 800 miles southeast of Bermuda near 21°26'N, 68°41'W. An HUP-3 Retriever of HU-2 Detachment 36, Aircraft No. 46, delivered Glenn to *Randolph* (CVS 15), and then a VS-26 S2F-3 Tracker flew the astronaut to Grand Turk Island in the Bahamas. Additional ships that supported the flight included *Enterprise* (CVAN 65) and *Forrestal* (CVA 59) sailing in the Atlantic and *Antietam* (CVS 36) in the Pacific. On 9 March, Glenn received his astronaut wings at the Pentagon.

21 FEBRUARY • Pilot Lt. Cmdr. John W. Young and radar intercept officer Cmdr. David M. Longton established new world time-to-climb records to 3,000 and 6,000 meters with times of 34.52 and 48.78 seconds, respectively, in an F4H-1 Phantom II at NAS Brunswick, Maine.

1 MARCH • Lt. Col. William C. McGraw, USMC, established new world time-to-climb records from a standing start to 9,000 and 12,000 meters in 61.62 and 77.15 seconds, respectively, in an F4H-1 Phantom II at NAS Brunswick, Maine.

3 MARCH • Lt. Cmdr. Del W. Nordberg broke a time-to-climb record by reaching an altitude of 15,000 meters in 114.54 seconds in an F4H-1 Phantom II at NAS Brunswick, Maine.

13 MARCH • *Midway* (CVA 41) and the Caribbean Ready Amphibious Squadron established precautionary patrols in Guatemalan waters for nine days when rioting by students led to widespread disorder in that country.

13 MARCH • NASA Administrator James E. Webb recommended to President John F. Kennedy the assignment of DX priority (the highest precedence in the procurement of critical materials) to the Apollo lunar program. The president approved the recommendation on 11 April.

31 MARCH • Lt. Cmdr. F. Taylor Brown attained a new world time-to-climb record to 20,000 meters with a time of 178.5 seconds in an F4H-1 Phantom II at NAS Point Mugu, Calif.

3 APRIL • Lt. Cmdr. John W. Young broke the Phantom II's seventh world time-to-climb record by reaching 25,000 meters in 230.44 seconds in an F4H-1 at NAS Point Mugu, Calif.

5 APRIL • NASA pilot Neil A. Armstrong flew an X-15 to a speed of 2,830 miles per hour and an altitude of 179,000 feet at Edwards AFB, Calif. The naval aviator achieved the marks during a test of an automatic control system intended for incorporation in Apollo spacecraft and the Dyna-Soar rocket-boosted hypersonic glider used in the development of a manned orbital vehicle for bombing and reconnaissance. The Dyna-Soar program was subsequently cancelled. Armstrong made seven flights in X-15s from December 1960 to July 1962, attaining a maximum speed of 3,989 mph in X-15-1 and a peak altitude of 207,500 feet in X-15-3.

12 APRIL • Lt. Cmdr. Del W. Nordberg broke a time-to-climb record by reaching an altitude of 30,000 meters in 371.43 seconds in an F4H-1 Phantom II at NAS Point Mugu, Calif.

1143454

Unmodified production F4H-1 Phantom IIs set a number of time-to-climb speed records during Project High Jump.

15 APRIL • Aircraft from *Hancock* (CVA 19) provided distant cover (because of a request by the State Department to operate inconspicuously to avoid international criticism) while 24 UH-34D Seahorses of HMM-362 flew from amphibious assault ship *Princeton* (LPH 5) to Soc Trang, South Vietnam. Elements of HMM-261 assisted the landings but returned to the ship. Three OE-1 Bird Dogs of VMO-1, an R4D-8 Skytrain, and some KC-130 Hercules had already arrived. The Marines supported the Army and South Vietnamese during Operation Shufly—counterinsurgency operations against the People's Liberation Armed Forces (Viet Cong) within the Mekong Delta. The Marines subsequently recommended the installation of armor plate and machine guns on their helicopters, and the addition of new flight clothing and body armor for crewmembers. On 1 August, HMM-362 departed South Vietnam.

18 APRIL • NASA announced the acceptance of applications for additional astronauts until 1 June. The agency planned to select five to ten astronauts to augment the seven Mercury team members. The new pilots were to participate in support operations in Project Mercury and join the Mercury astronauts in piloting the two-man Gemini spacecraft. The requirements included

NH 69953

Alan B. Shepard Jr.

NASA 36911

John H. Glenn Jr.

NH 69951

M. Scott Carpenter

NASA 62MA7-24

Walter M. Schirra Jr.

experienced jet test pilots preferably engaged in flying high-performance aircraft; experimental flight test pilot status through military service, the aircraft industry, or NASA, or graduation from military test pilot schools; degree achievement in the physical or biological sciences or in engineering; U.S. citizenship under 35 years of age at the time of selection and six feet or less in height; and recommendation by their parent organizations.

30 APRIL • The Naval Air Research and Development Activities Command was disestablished, and the Bureau of Naval Weapons reassumed responsibility for the overall management and coordination of the aeronautical research and development activities in the Third and Fourth Naval Districts.

10 MAY • Up to this time, communist Pathet Lao insurgents routed Laotian royalists and advanced toward the Thai border. On this date, President John F. Kennedy dispatched ships including *Hancock* (CVA 19), *Bennington* (CVS 20), and amphibious assault ship *Valley Forge* (LPH 8) to the Gulf of Thailand, together with 3,400 Marines supported by British, Australian, and New Zealand forces, which collectively arrived between 17 and 20 May. On 17 May, HMM-261 flew from *Valley Forge* to Udorn Royal Thai AFB, Thailand, where the squadron operated until relieved by HMM-162 in late June. The North Vietnamese consequently pressured the insurgents to accept a cease-fire, and the deployments ended in July.

10 MAY • An F4H-1 Phantom II scored a direct hit with an AAM-N-6 Sparrow III air-to-air missile in a head-on attack on a Regulus II bombardment missile while both traveled at supersonic speed over the Naval Air Missile Center Point Mugu, Calif. The achievement marked the first successful head-on attack by an air-launched weapon on a surface-launched guided missile.

22 MAY • The Navy Astronautics Group, Cmdr. James C. Quillen Jr. commanding, was established as the Navy's first space satellite command at Pacific Missile Range Headquarters, Point Mugu, Calif. One of the duties of the command included the responsibility for operating the Transit Navigational System, under Navy development for the Department of Defense.

24 MAY • Lt. Cmdr. M. Scott Carpenter manned space capsule *Aurora 7* during the launch from Cape Canaveral, Fla., of Mercury-Atlas 7, the second U.S. manned orbital flight. The capsule splashed down in the Atlantic near 19°27'N, 63°59'W, miles beyond the planned impact area northeast of Puerto Rico. The overshot resulted from a yaw error during the firing of the retrograde rockets that put the capsule beyond radio and recovery vehicle range. Carpenter egressed from *Aurora 7* into a life raft on a sea of lazy swells, and waited until a P2V Neptune made visual contact a half hour later. A USAF SC-54 Skymaster dropped two pararescue men to assist the astronaut before an HSS-2 Sea King, Aircraft No. 57, of HS-3 embarked on board *Intrepid* (CVS 11), returned the astronaut to the carrier more than four hours after splashing down, and destroyer *John R. Pierce* (DD 753) retrieved the capsule. Additional ships involved included dock landing ships *Donner* (LSD 20) and *Spiegel Grove* (LSD 32). On 25 June Carpenter received his astronaut wings.

29 MAY • Vice Adm. Patrick N. L. Bellinger (Ret.), (Naval Aviator No. 8), died in Clifton Forge, Va. On 26 November 1912, Bellinger had reported for flight training to the Annapolis, Md., aviation camp and on 1 October 1947, he retired while serving on the General Board.

1 JUNE • The Materials Advisory Board of the National Research Council issued its final report on the titanium alloy sheet rolling program, thereby terminating the program as a formally organized effort. The achievements of the program during its six years of work included acquiring metallurgical and engineering data for a number of titanium alloys and familiarizing the aerospace industry with their properties and methods of fabrication. High strength, heat-treated sheet alloys developed under this program were subsequently used in aircraft including A-7 Corsair IIs, later model F-4 Phantom IIs, Lockheed SR-71A Blackbirds, and in deep submergence vehicles used in oceanographic research.

26 JUNE • The 1,500-mile-range Polaris A-2 became operational when submarine *Ethan Allen* (SSBN 608) sailed with 16 of the fleet ballistic missiles from NWS Charleston, S.C.

29 JUNE • A Polaris fleet ballistic missile carrying the new bullet-nose shape for use with A-3 missiles soared 1,400 miles down range from Cape Canaveral, Fla. On 7 August 1962, the first A-3 flight model successfully launched from the same base.

1 JULY • Fleet Air Patuxent and Naval Air Bases, Potomac River Naval Command were established, and assigned as additional duties to Commander Naval Air Test Center, Patuxent River, Md.

25 JULY • Following the defeat of Gen. Fulgencio Batista, Cuban leftists led by Fidel R. Castro harassed NS Guantánamo Bay, Cuba. In response to U.S. fears of an escalation to coincide with the celebration of the 26th of July Cuban revolutionary holiday, the Caribbean Ready Amphibious Squadron sailed for Guantánamo and aircraft flew demonstrations over the station until the termination of the alert on 27 July.

1 AUGUST • Squadrons of the Naval Air Reserve that had been called up during the Berlin Crisis on 1 October 1961 were released to inactive duty. The action reduced the strength of the naval air operating forces by 18 squadrons and 3,995 officers and men.

30 AUGUST • One of two Cuban *GC-107*–class patrol boats shot at an S-2 Tracker flying in international air space 15 nautical miles north of Cárdenas, Cuba.

31 AUGUST • The last flight of a Navy airship at NAS Lakehurst, N.J., marked the passing of an era. The flight also marked the end of a year's service by the two airships maintained in operation following the discontinuance of the lighter-than-air (LTA) program for use as airborne aerodynamics and research laboratories in the development of V/STOL aircraft and antisubmarine search systems. Cmdrs. Walter D. Ashe and Robert Shannon piloted this final flight and the passengers included LTA stalwarts Vice Adm. Charles E. Rosendahl (Ret.) and Capt. Frederick N. Klein (Ret.).

8 SEPTEMBER • Two Cuban MiG-17 Frescos overtook two S2Fs over the Caribbean, 45 miles southwest of NAS Key West, Fla. One Fresco made simulated firing runs on the Trackers, but two F4D-1 Skyrays scrambled from Key West and the MiGs disengaged.

12 SEPTEMBER • Lt. Cmdr. Donald E. Moore climbed to 29,460 feet over Floyd Bennett Field, N.Y. in a UF-2G to set a new world altitude record for amphibians carrying a 1,000-kilogram load. On the same day, Lt. Cmdr. Fred A. W. Franke Jr. piloted the Albatross to a new record for amphibians with a 2,000-kilogram load with a climb to 27,380 feet.

15 SEPTEMBER • Lt. Cmdr. Richard A. Hoffman set a new world 5,000-kilometer speed record for amphibians carrying a 1,000-kilogram load with 151.4 mph in a UF-2G Albatross on a course from Floyd Bennett Field, N.Y., to Plattsburgh, N.Y., to Dupree, S. Dak., returning to Floyd Bennett Field.

17 SEPTEMBER • At the University of Houston, Texas, NASA introduced the public to nine pilots selected to join the nation's astronaut corps: civilian test pilots and naval aviators Neil A. Armstrong and Elliott M. See Jr.; Navy Lt. Cmdrs. James A. Lovell Jr. and John W. Young; and Lt. Charles Conrad Jr.; together with Lt. Col. Frank Borman, USAF; Maj. Thomas P. Stafford, USAF; Capt. James A. McDivitt, USAF; and Capt. Edward H. White II, USAF.

NH 69950

Cmdr. Walter M. Schirra Jr. emerges from space capsule *Sigma 7* on board *Kearsarge* (CVS 33) after his six-orbit flight, 3 October 1962.

18 SEPTEMBER • A joint Army-Navy-Air Force regulation established a uniform system of designating military aircraft similar to that previously in use by the USAF. All existing aircraft received redesignations using a letter, dash, number, and letter to indicate respectively the basic mission or type of aircraft, its place in the series of that type, and its place in the series of changes in its basic design. Under the system the Crusader, formerly designated F8U-2, became the F-8C indicating the third change (C) in the eighth (8) of the fighter (F) series. A provision indicated the status of the aircraft and modifications of its basic mission by prefix letters. Thus the YF8U-1P became the YRF-8A symbolizing a prototype (Y) of the photoreconnaissance (R) modification of the F-8A.

19 SEPTEMBER • During growing tensions with the Cubans, six F-8D Crusaders deployed for defensive duties with the USAF in the North American Air Defense Command to NAS Key West, Fla.

28 SEPTEMBER • A Navy flight photographed Soviet freighter *Kasimov* en route to Cuban waters with ten crated Ilyushin Il-28s on her deck. The Soviets eventually deployed at least 42 of the Beagles, which were capable of carrying nuclear weapons, to Cuba.

1 OCTOBER • On the eve of the Cuban Missile Crisis, the Atlantic Fleet included *Essex* (CVS 9), *Wasp* (CVS 18), and *Lake Champlain* (CVS 39), in the area of Boston, Mass., and Newport, R.I.; *Intrepid* (CVS 11) off New York City, N.Y.; *Randolph* (CVS 15) at NS Norfolk, Va.; *Shangri-La* (CVA 38) at NS Mayport, Fla.; amphibious assault ships *Okinawa* (LPH 3), *Boxer* (LPH 4), and *Thetis Bay* (LPH 6) at Norfolk; and cruiser *Canberra* (CAG 2) at NS Guantánamo Bay, Cuba.

3 OCTOBER • Cmdr. Walter M. Schirra Jr. piloted space capsule *Sigma 7* during the launch of Mercury-Atlas 8 from Cape Canaveral, Fla. After six orbits, the spacecraft splashed down in the Pacific 275 miles northeast of Midway Island near 32°5'N, 174°28'W, and about 9,000 yards from primary recovery ship *Kearsarge* (CVS 33). Helicopters dropped swimmers near the capsule and *Kearsarge* hoisted *Sigma 7* and Schirra on board. Additional vessels that supported the recovery included *Lake Champlain* (CVS 39) in the Atlantic. On 16 October, Schirra received his astronaut wings.

8 OCTOBER • Lt. Col. Edwin A. Harper, USMC, of VMA-225 led a flight of 16 A-4C Skyhawks on a round-trip crossing of the Atlantic between MCAS Cherry Point, N.C., and NS Rota, Spain. The Marines flew to Bermuda and then directly to Rota. After a brief layover, the flight returned on 17 October to Cherry Point by way of Lajes, Azores, and Bermuda. Ten KC-130F Hercules of VMGR-252 refueled the Skyhawks during the operation.

8 OCTOBER • The F-4B Phantom IIs of VF-41 shifted from NAS Oceana, Va., to NAS Key West, Fla., to augment a detachment of six F-8D Crusaders for defensive duties with the USAF in the North American Air Defense Command during growing tensions with Cuba.

14 OCTOBER • During the preceding months, Soviet Premier Nikita S. Khrushchev grew concerned over the imbalance in the nuclear arsenals of the rival superpowers and launched Operation Anadyr—the infiltration into Cuba of surface-to-surface missiles capable of being fitted with nuclear warheads to expand Soviet options, and to demonstrate to the Americans their inability to halt the advance of Soviet power in proximity to the United States. Cuban leader Fidel R. Castro agreed to the plan. On this date, Maj. Richard D. Heyser, USAF, piloted CIA high-altitude reconnaissance Mission 3101 over western Cuba in a Lockheed U-2F, designated Article 342, and detected Soviet SS-4 (R-12) Sandal medium-range ballistic missile (MRBM) launchers. Navy specialists processed the film and then delivered it for evaluation to the National Photographic Interpretation Center, Washington, D.C. Additional reconnaissance missions and intelligence data revealed more MRBMs and SS-5 (R-14) Skean intermediate-range ballistic missiles. The discovery of the Soviet deception precipitated the Cuban Missile Crisis because President John F. Kennedy and his advisors considered such a threat to the United States as unacceptable.

16 OCTOBER • Chief of Naval Operations directed the conversion of some RH-46As to aerial minesweepers for use in a mine countermeasures development and training program and eventual assignment to fleet squadrons. The program later substituted RH-3As for the conversion.

17 OCTOBER • Operation Blue Moon—low-level reconnaissance flights over Cuba to help verify Soviet military deployments to that country—became operational. VFP-62 initially prepared ten photo variant RF-8A Crusaders with aerial cameras for high-speed, low-level photo missions, and placed four of the jets on a four-hour alert at NAS Cecil Field, Fla., but subsequently shifted the Crusaders to NAS Key West, Fla. The squadron maintained ten operational aircraft with seven standing by, and also deployed five detachments on board attack carriers operating in the Atlantic and Mediterranean during the Cuban Missile Crisis.

19 OCTOBER • Operational units began moving to stations in Florida to counter the threat posed by Soviet missiles and bombers in Cuba. Aircraft and squadrons there not required for air defense, reconnaissance, and antisubmarine patrols began relocating to prevent overcrowding. About 350 naval aircraft operated ashore in that region including 7 fighters, 12 bombers, and 5 maritime patrol aircraft at NS Guantánamo Bay, Cuba; 18 fighters at Homestead AFB, Fla.; 76 fighters, 57 attack, and 10 patrol aircraft at NAS Jacksonville, Fla.; 26 fighters and 5 antisubmarine planes at NAS Key West, Fla.; 12 EC-121K Constellations at McCoy AFB, Fla.; 15 patrol aircraft at NAS Roosevelt Roads, P.R.; and 11 A-5A Vigilantes of VAH-7 at NAS Sanford, Fla. By 25 October, the number of these aircraft ashore rose to 448 fighters and bombers and 67 reconnaissance and support types.

19 OCTOBER • *Enterprise* (CVAN 65) sortied in response to the Cuban Missile Crisis from NS Norfolk, Va. The emergency compelled the ship to sail with only some aircraft and the balance flew on board as she passed Cape Henry. The Atlantic Fleet provided the cover story that engineering exercises and Hurricane Ella off the southeastern coast of the U.S. imposed the rapid departure. Aircraft flew a daily average of 120 sorties from *Enterprise* during the crisis. The ship returned on 7 December.

20 OCTOBER • The Cuban Missile Crisis coincided with a routine training event designated PHIBBRIGLEX 62 (Quick Kick)—an amphibious brigade landing exercise. More than 40 ships, including *Independence* (CVA 62), *Randolph* (CVS 15), and amphibious assault ships *Okinawa* (LPH 3) and *Thetis Bay* (LPH 6), were scheduled to take part by November. On this date, the Atlantic Fleet publicly used the excuse that Hurricane Ella scattered ships to begin to reassign these forces to respond to the crisis.

20 OCTOBER • Commander in Chief Atlantic Fleet Adm. Robert L. Dennison ordered the A-5A Vigilantes of VAH-7 to transfer from *Enterprise* (CVAN 65) to NAS Sanford, Fla. Twenty-one A-4C Skyhawks of VMA-225 from MCAS Cherry Point, N.C., replaced them on board because they were more suitable for close air support. Cargo aircraft carried maintenance teams and equipment from ashore. On 5 December, these A-4Cs completed the first Marine squadron operations from a nuclear-powered carrier. In addition, *Enterprise* received orders to steam near 25°N,

75°W, and *Independence* (CVA 62) toward 23°10'N, 72°24'W. The next morning the carriers rendezvoused north of the Bahamas.

22 OCTOBER • Intelligence data that unveiled Soviet progress in Cuba and the transfer of arms via Eastern Bloc ships en route to the island prompted the Joint Chiefs to raise the U.S. defense posture from Defense Condition 5 to 3 for all forces worldwide at 1800 EDT—excluding forces in Europe that went to a precautionary stance. The Joint Chiefs of Staff issued the order prior to a televised speech by President John F. Kennedy. The president announced "unmistakable evidence" of the Soviet intrusion into Cuba and emphasized three strategic points: the imposition of a quarantine on all offensive military equipment en route to Cuba effective at 1000 EDT on 24 October; the continuation and increase of the close surveillance of Cuba; and a policy to regard any nuclear missile launched from Cuba against any nation in the Western Hemisphere as an attack by the Soviets on the United States. During the speech, submarines equipped with Polaris fleet ballistic missiles moved to their launch stations to supplement silo-launched intercontinental ballistic missiles and Strategic Air Command bombers.

23 OCTOBER • The first of three pairs of RF-8As of VFP-62 flew the initial mission of Operation Blue Moon—low-level reconnaissance flights over Cuba. Cmdr. William B. Ecker, squadron commanding officer, and Lt. C. Bruce Wilhelmy piloted two camera-equipped Crusaders during the flight from NAS Key West, Fla., over San Cristóbal. The jets completed the mission undamaged; however, Ecker received orders to personally brief at the Pentagon Chairman of the Joint Chiefs Gen. Maxwell D. Taylor, USA, Chief of Naval Operations Adm. George W. Anderson Jr., and Air Force Chief of Staff Gen. Curtis E. LeMay. Four RF-8As from VMCJ-2 together with USAF McDonnell RF-101C Voodoos and Douglas RB-66 Destroyers subsequently reinforced Blue Moon. Twelve sailors including Ecker and Wilhelmy and four Marines received the Distinguished Flying Cross. Through 15 November, aircraft of all the services made 158 low-level photo runs over Cuba.

24 OCTOBER • The blockade of Soviet offensive weapons into Cuba began. Task Force 136, Commander Second Fleet Vice Adm. Alfred G. Ward commanding, established patrol positions in a line designated Walnut to the east of Cuba beyond the known range of Soviet Ilyushin Il-28 Beagles flying from the island. Task Group 136.2, comprising at times *Essex* (CVS 9), *Randolph* (CVS 15), and *Wasp* (CVS 18), provided the principal operating forces. *Essex* operated 22 S-2D Trackers of VS-34 and -39, 14 SH-3A Sea Kings of HS-9, and one E-1B Tracer of VAW-12 Detachment 9. Eleven P-5B Marlins each of VP-45 and -49 of Task Group 81.5 patrolled to the north and east of 25°N, 65°W, and 11 P-2E Neptunes of VP-5 of Task Group 81.7 patrolled east of the quarantine line and south of 25°N. These planes proved crucial to the detection of Eastern Bloc ships and the verification of their cargoes. Commander in Chief Atlantic Fleet Adm. Robert L. Dennison later redesignated the blockade line Chestnut, moving the perimeter closer to Cuba to reduce the number of ships at sea.

24 OCTOBER • Commander NS Guantánamo Bay Rear Adm. Edward J. O'Donnell requested that Task Force 135 including *Enterprise* (CVAN 65) and *Independence* (CVA 62) alternate continuous early warning patrols over the Windward Passage and cover the U.S. enclave from a Cuban attack. *Enterprise* and *Independence* operated south of the Windward Passage between Cuba and Hispaniola and southward. Fleet Air Wing 11 and Marine Aircraft Group 26 deployed to NS Roosevelt Roads at Puerto Rico and to NS Guantánamo Bay, respectively, also supported these ships. Soviet threats against carriers sailing in Caribbean waters included four Foxtrot (Project 641)-class submarines, 3R9/10 Luna (Free Rocket Over Ground or FROG-3/5) tactical surface-to-surface rockets, FKR (*frontoviye krilatiye raketi*—frontal rocket) 1 Metors (SSC-2A Salishes), 12 P-6 Komar (Project 183-R)-class missile boats, up to 42 Ilyushin Il-28 Beagles, and MiG-21F Fishbed-Cs. Many of these were capable of being fitted with nuclear warheads.

24 OCTOBER • The P-2H Neptunes of VP-11 deployed to Argentia, Newfoundland, on 12 hours notice in response to the Cuban Missile Crisis. The squadron's planes completed 1,065 flying hours of surveillance flights through 14 November 1962.

27 OCTOBER • Senior Soviet commander in Cuba Gen. Issa A. Pliyev informed his superiors in Moscow that the SS-4 (R-12) Sandal medium-range ballistic missiles there had become operational, despite heavy rain that delayed the completion of the final site. Pliyev stated his capability to send two salvoes of 36 missiles against the United States.

27 OCTOBER • Amphibious assault ship *Boxer* (LPH 4) embarked 20 UH-34D Seahorses of HMM-263, four CH-37C Mojaves, five OH-43Ds, and nine O-1 Bird Dogs at New River, N.C. The ship deployed with an additional 16 Seahorses to reinforce HMM-261 and -264, operating from amphibious assault ships *Okinawa* (LPH 3) and *Thetis Bay* (LPH 6), respectively, and sailed for Caribbean waters in response to the Cuban Missile Crisis. Also on this date, *Iwo Jima* (LPH 2) embarked HMM-361 and a detachment of VMO-6 and sailed from the Pacific Fleet via the Panama Canal, reaching the Caribbean in two weeks.

28 OCTOBER • Soviet Premier Nikita S. Khrushchëv accepted U.S. diplomatic overtures to end the Cuban Missile Crisis. Cuban leader Fidel R. Castro initially rejected the U.S. offer but subsequently consented to the agreement.

31 OCTOBER • Geodetic satellite Anna entered orbit from Cape Canaveral, Fla. The Department of Defense developed Anna under Bureau of Naval Weapons management. The satellite contained three independent sets of instrumentation to validate measurements taken by organizations participating in the Anna worldwide geodetic research and mapping program.

31 OCTOBER • By this point during the Cuban Missile Crisis, *Enterprise* (CVAN 65) steamed in a box within 60 miles of 18°N, 80°W.

5 NOVEMBER • Two MiG-21F Fishbeds attacked the two RF-8As Crusaders of VFP-62 comprising Flight 16 flying an Operation Blue Moon low-level reconnaissance mission eight miles west of Santa Clara, Cuba. The Crusaders turned and rolled into the MiGs for a head-on approach, then hit their afterburners and escaped six miles east of their point of entry over Cuba—the MiGs pursued for five minutes. The high combat air patrol observed the action but failed to intervene in time.

5 NOVEMBER • Two Marine helicopter squadrons began a transition training program in which 500 Marine aviators qualified in fixed-wing aircraft were to be trained to operate helicopters. The need for the special program arose from the increased proportion of helicopters in the Marine Corps together with an overall shortage of pilots and the inability of the Naval Air Training Command to absorb the additional training load within the time allotted.

15 NOVEMBER • To date, naval aircraft flew 9,000 sorties during the Cuban Missile Crisis. Sixty-eight squadrons comprising 19,000 sailors participated, and each of the eight deployed carriers steamed at least 10,000 miles.

16 NOVEMBER • *Enterprise* (CVAN 65) and *Independence* (CVA 62) operated to 21 November in a rectangle formed by 18°10'N, 19°30'N, 77°W, and 80°W in response to the Cuban Missile Crisis. During this period the A-4C Skyhawks of VA-34 switched places with the Skyhawks of VA-64 from *Enterprise* onto *Independence*, and VA-64 embarked on board *Enterprise*. Helicopters lifted the balance of the men between the carriers.

16 NOVEMBER • *Saratoga* (CVA 60) began the Cuban Missile Crisis in overhaul at Norfolk Naval Shipyard, Va. On this date, she sailed 15 days ahead of schedule, and on 5 December relieved *Enterprise* (CVAN 65).

20 NOVEMBER • The Atlantic Fleet received direction to discontinue operations concerning the Cuban Missile Crisis, lift the quarantine, and return commands to normal tasks. The Soviets began to stand down their alerted forces. Through 20 December, *Enterprise* (CVAN 65) supported the defense of NS Guantánamo Bay, Cuba. A second carrier was to be ready in the Norfolk, Va., to Mayport, Fla., area against the requirement for sighting Soviet ships sailing from Cuban ports with Ilyushin Il-28 Beagles, and to support air strikes against Soviet and Cuban forces in Cuba in the event of an escalation of the crisis. By 2 December amphibious assault ships *Boxer* (LPH 4), *Okinawa* (LPH 3), and *Thetis Bay* (LPH 6) had returned to Norfolk. In addition, on 1 December *Iwo Jima* (LPH 2) sailed for the Pacific.

30 NOVEMBER • The Bureau of Naval Weapons issued a contract to Bell Aerosystems Company for the construction and flight test of two vertical takeoff and landing (VTOL) research aircraft with dual tandem-ducted propellers. The tri-service VTOL program thereby underwent expansion to include a tilting duct craft for development under Navy

An E-2A Hawkeye airborne early warning aircraft of VAW-11 operates from *Constellation* (CVA 64) in 1966.

administration in addition to the tilting wing XC-142 and the tilting engine X-19A—both administered by the USAF.

1 DECEMBER • Fleet Air Caribbean and Naval Air Bases, Tenth Naval District, were established and assigned as additional duties to Commander, Caribbean Sea Frontier.

4 DECEMBER • The landing apparatus for the Apollo spacecraft failed during the first test of the program's main parachute system at NAF El Centro, Calif. One parachute failed to inflate fully, another disreefed prematurely, and the disreefing and inflation of the third canopy incurred a delay. The system experienced repeated malfunctions during subsequent testing before its final acceptance in the mid-1960s.

11 DECEMBER • The Department of Defense established a uniform system of designating, redesignating, and naming military rockets and guided missiles with combat or combat-related missions. Each new designation consisted of a combination of eight significant letters and numbers, in sequence of listing: status prefix symbol, launch environment symbol, mission symbol, type symbol, design number, series symbol, manufacturer's [two-letter] code, and serial number.

14 DECEMBER • The Naval Air Material Center at NAS Lakehurst, N.J., was renamed the Naval Air Engineering Center.

15 DECEMBER • In response to the Cuban Missile Crisis, *Enterprise* (CVAN 65) received orders to relieve *Lexington* (CVS 16), which had just completed her conversion from an attack to an antisubmarine carrier but still embarked fighters and bombers. From 30 November, *Lexington* had stayed in the United States on call for the crisis, but because of the conclusion of the confrontation, *Enterprise* did not return to war stations before the New Year.

18 DECEMBER • A four-stage Blue Scout missile launched Navy prototype operational navigation satellite Transit 5A into a polar orbit from Naval Missile Facility Point Arguello, Calif. The satellite's radio failed after 20 hours in orbit and prevented its use for navigation purposes, but certain secondary experiments proved successful.

19 DECEMBER • Lt. Cmdr. Lee M. Ramsey piloting an E-2A Hawkeye catapulted from *Enterprise* (CVAN 65) in the first shipboard test of nose tow gear designed to replace the catapult bridle and reduce launching intervals. A few minutes later Intruder No. 8, a YA-6A, BuNo 148618, followed Ramsey.

1963

7 JANUARY • Helicopters from cruiser *Springfield* (CLG 7), NAS Port Lyautey, Morocco, and NS Rota, Spain, flew rescue and relief missions in the flooded areas of the Beth and Sebou Rivers in Morocco. Through 13 January, the aircraft delivered more than 45,000 pounds of food, medicine, and emergency supplies, and lifted 320 marooned people to safety.

21 JANUARY • Secretary of Defense Robert S. McNamara and NASA Administrator James E. Webb concluded a policy agreement defining the roles of the Department of Defense and NASA in Project Gemini. The agreement provided for the establishment of a joint Gemini Program Planning Board to plan experiments, conduct flight tests, and analyze and disseminate results.

1112651

An inert Walleye television-guided air-to-surface glide bomb with string tufts attached to its aft section is mounted on an A-6 Intruder for aerodynamic testing.

29 JANUARY • A YA-4B released a Walleye television-guided air-to-surface glide bomb that made a direct impact on its target in the first demonstration of the system's automatic homing feature at NOTS China Lake, Calif.

9 FEBRUARY • The Secretary of the Navy approved with minor modification the recommendations of his Advisory Committee on the Review of the Management of the Department of the Navy, commonly known as the Dillon Board for its chairman John H. Dillon. The approval set into motion a series of changes in the lines of authority and responsibility for implementation during the year primarily outlined in a general order issued on 1 July 1963.

22 FEBRUARY • Cmdr. William H. Everett of VX-6 piloted an LC-130F Hercules in the longest Antarctic flight to date. Everett's flight covered 3,470 miles from McMurdo Station south beyond the South Pole to the Shackleton Mountain Range, and then to the pole of inaccessibility—the point on the Antarctic continent most distant from the Southern Ocean—returning to McMurdo in a total time of 10 hours, 40 minutes.

25 FEBRUARY • The United States restarted the transmitter in the Navy-developed Solar Radiation I satellite after 22 months of silence. On 22 June 1960, a Thor Able-Star missile had launched the 42-pound satellite with Transit 2A in the first of the pickaback firings. The device provided detailed data on solar storms for eight months before magnetic drag reduced the satellite's spin to a level too low for useful scanning of the sun. The satellite was shut down on 18 April 1961.

8 MARCH • The Department of Defense and NASA announced an agreement establishing working arrangements concerning the non-military applications of the Transit navigation satellite system. NASA assumed responsibility for determining the suitability of Transit equipment for nonmilitary purposes, while the Navy retained its responsibility for overall technical direction, and for research and development as necessary.

APRIL • Communist Pathet Lao insurgents inflicted a defeat on the royalist and neutral factions within Laos. At times, the Seventh Fleet deployed *Ranger* (CVA 61) and *Ticonderoga* (CVA 14) to the area. The signature of a cease fire later in the month enabled the carriers to depart on 5 May.

1036457

With a centrifuge capable of producing accelerations up to 40g's and used for training the Mercury 7 astronauts, NADC Johnsville officially opened on 17 June 1952.

1 APRIL • To bring their title in line with their functions, replacement air groups (RAG) were redesignated combat readiness air groups (CRAG).

8 MAY • The USAF announced the addition of two squadrons of A-1Es to the 1st Air Commando Group at Hurlburt AFB, Fla. This decision followed field tests of two Skyraiders loaned by the Navy in mid-1962, and led in May 1964 to a further assessment released by the Secretary of the Air Force to deploy 75 Skyraiders to South Vietnam as replacements for B-26 Invaders and T-28 Trojans.

16 MAY • Capt. L. Gordon Cooper Jr., USAF, piloted space capsule *Faith* 7 during the launch of Mercury-Atlas 9 from Cape Canaveral, Fla. *Faith* 7 splashed down in the Pacific about 80 miles southeast of Midway Island, near 27°20'N, 176°26'W. After more than 34 hours and 22 orbits, the capsule impacted within 7,000 yards of primary recovery ship *Kearsarge* (CVS 33), which retrieved the spacecraft and the astronaut. Additional ships that supported the operation included *Wasp* (CVS 18) in the Atlantic.

12 JUNE • During testimony before the Senate Space Committee, NASA Administrator James E. Webb announced the conclusion of Project Mercury to focus resources on the Gemini and Apollo space programs.

13 JUNE • Lt. Cmdrs. Randall K. Billings and Robert S. Chew Jr., of NATC Patuxent River, Md., in an F-4A Phantom II and an F8D Crusader, respectively, made the first fully automatic carrier landings with production equipment on board *Midway* (CVA 41) off the coast of California. The pilots completed the landings "hands off" with both flight controls and throttles operated automatically by signals from the ship. The event highlighted almost ten years of research and development and followed by about six years the first such carrier landing made with test equipment.

20 JUNE • Pilot and instructor Lt. Phillip H. Flood and student Ens. Arnold J. Hupp of VT-31 marked the end of P-5s in the flight training program when they completed the last student training flight in a Marlin at NAS Corpus Christi, Texas.

29 JUNE • Fleet Air Wing 10 was established at NAS Moffett Field, Calif., Capt. John B. Honan commanding.

1 JULY • General Order No. 5 set forth new policies and principles governing the organization and administration of the Navy and directed their progressive implementation. The order redefined the principal parts of the Navy and added a Naval Military Support Establishment as a fourth part under a Chief of Naval Material, which was responsible directly to the Secretary of the Navy, and with command responsibilities over the four material bureaus and major project managers and an overall task of providing material support to the operating forces.

9 JULY • The Gemini Phase I Centrifuge Program began at the Naval Air Development Center Johnsville, Pa. The Aviation Medical Acceleration Laboratory centrifuge simulated the position of the command pilot in the Gemini spacecraft. The engineering evaluation concluded on 2 August and pilot familiarization occurred between 16 July and 17 August.

15 JULY • NASA's Manned Spacecraft Center announced it had received 271 applications for the astronaut program. Military applicants numbered 71—34 Navy, ten Marine, 26 Air Force, and one Army. Women comprised three of the 200 civilian aspirants.

1 AUGUST • VMF(AW) squadrons equipped with F-4B Phantom IIs were redesignated VMFA.

2 AUGUST • Lt. Roger Bellnap piloted an F-3B during the first of a series of five planned space probes designed to measure the ultraviolet radiation of the stars. The Demon launched a two-stage, solid-propellant Sparoair from a nearly vertical attitude at 30,000 feet over the Pacific Missile Range, and the probe reached a peak altitude of 66 miles.

23 AUGUST • Cmdr. John F. Barlow of VAH-11 piloted an A-3B Skywarrior in a joint Weather Bureau–Navy project entitled Stormfury, seeding Hurricane Beulah with silver iodide particles over a period of two days in an experiment to determine the potential of changing the energy patterns of large storms. The seedings the following day appeared to have some effect, but the indefinite results precluded firm conclusions.

6 SEPTEMBER • Five SH-3A Sea Kings of HS-9 operating from NAS Quonset Point, R.I., rescued 28 workmen from two offshore oil drilling platforms shaken by gales and heavy seas off Cape Cod, Mass.

8 SEPTEMBER • The 16 NASA astronauts selected for the manned space program began training in water and land parachute landings. The possibility of low-level aborts below 70,000 feet requiring the pilots to eject from the spacecraft drove the training. A towed 24-foot diameter parasail carried the men to altitudes up to 400 feet before the release of the towline enabled the astronauts to glide to their landings.

18 SEPTEMBER • To provide the continuing action necessary for effective management of the inactive aircraft inventory, an informal review board was established with representation from the Chief of Naval Operations, Bureau of Naval Weapons, Aviation Supply Office, and the storage facility at Litchfield Park, Arizona. The board was to review the aircraft inventory at least every six months for the purpose of recommending the retention or disposal of specific models.

18 OCTOBER • NASA announced the selection of 14 additional astronauts including five naval aviators—Lt. Cmdrs. Richard F. Gordon Jr. and Roger B. Chaffee, Lts. Alan L. Bean and Eugene A. Cernan, and Capt. Clifton C. Williams, USMC.

25 OCTOBER • After nearly two weeks of relief operations in the wake of Hurricane Flora, Navy ships began to sail from Port-au-Prince, Haiti. Four vessels, including *Lake Champlain* (CVS 39) and amphibious assault ship *Thetis*

Bay (LPH 6), aided by Navy and Marine cargo aircraft flying from East Coast stations, delivered nearly 375 tons of food, clothing, and medical supplies donated by relief agencies.

26 OCTOBER • Submarine *Andrew Jackson* (SSBN 619) completed the first underwater launch of a Polaris A-3 fleet ballistic missile from a position about 30 miles off Cape Canaveral, Fla.

30 OCTOBER • Pilot Lt. James H. Flatley III and copilot Lt. Cmdr. Walter W. Stovall of NATC Patuxent River, Md., and flight engineer AD1 Ed Brennan of VR-1 completed the first of three separate shipboard evaluations of a Marine KC-130F, BuNo 149798, on board *Forrestal* (CVA 59). At times Lockheed-Marietta test pilot Ted H. Limmer Jr. joined the crew of the Hercules. Flatley made a total of 29 touch-and-go landings and 21 full-stop landings and takeoffs on this date and 8, 21, and 22 November. He later received the Distinguished Flying Cross. The Navy concluded that C-130s could carry 25,000 pounds of cargo and people 2,500 miles and land on a carrier, but considered the large planes too risky for use in COD operations.

12 NOVEMBER • Fifteen astronauts commenced a helicopter flight familiarization program at NAS Ellyson Field, Fla., as a phase of their training for lunar landings. The Navy instituted the program at the request of NASA to simulate the operation of the Project Apollo Lunar Excursion Module. The training consisted of a series of two-week courses for two students, with the final pair completing the program on 1 April 1964.

30 NOVEMBER • Secretary of Defense Paul H. Nitze approved the use of funds effective on 1 July 1964 for the purpose of placing naval aviation observers in the same pay status as pilots.

2 DECEMBER • The Chief of Naval Material reported to the Secretary of the Navy for duty as his assistant for Naval Material Support and assumed supervision and command of the four material bureaus: Naval Weapons, Ships, Supplies and Accounts, and Yards and Docks.

6 DECEMBER • A Thor Able-Star missile launched Transit 5BN-2 into polar orbit from Vandenberg AFB, Calif. The launch marked the first operational status of a navigation satellite, providing data for use by ships and submarines.

16 DECEMBER • Phase I of the Apollo Manned Centrifuge Program began at the Navy Aerospace Medical Acceleration Laboratory, Philadelphia, Pa. The testing revealed interface problems between the couch, suit, and astronaut, and concluded on 15 January 1964.

20 DECEMBER • Carrier air groups (CVG) were redesignated carrier air wings (CVW).

21 DECEMBER • *Saratoga* (CVA 60), while moored at NS Mayport, Fla., began to receive weather pictures from weather satellite Tiros 8. This began an operational investigation of shipborne readout equipment in which *Saratoga* continued to receive test readings from Tiros 8 in port and at sea through May 1964 and, in September 1964, from experimental weather satellite Nimbus.

1964

1 JANUARY • Fleet Air Wings, Pacific, was established, Rear Adm. David J. Welsh commanding.

1 JANUARY • *Duxbury Bay* (AVP 38), *Greenwich Bay* (AVP 41), and *Valcour* (AVP 55) were transferred to Cruiser-Destroyer Force Atlantic. The employment of these last three seaplane tenders in service under Commander, Naval Air, Atlantic, had been secondary to their use as flagships for Commander, Middle East Force, for several years, but this transfer completed the phase-out of patrol seaplane operations in the Atlantic Fleet.

15 JANUARY • Fleet Air Southwest Pacific and Fleet Air Japan were disestablished.

15 JANUARY • Carrier Division 15, 17, and 19 were redesignated Anti-Submarine Warfare Group 1, 3, and 5, respectively, and transferred from Commander, Naval Air, Pacific to Commander, Anti-Submarine Warfare Force, Pacific for administrative control. The new groups' mission was the development of antisubmarine carrier group tactics, doctrine, and operating procedures including coordination with patrol aircraft operations.

17 FEBRUARY • The Office of Anti-Submarine Warfare Programs was established under Chief of Naval Operations to exercise centralized supervision and coordination of all antisubmarine warfare planning, programming, and appraising.

The P-3A Orion antisubmarine patrol plane is a derivative of the Lockheed L-188 Electra passenger airliner.

28 FEBRUARY • During combat store ship *Mars* (AFS 1) shakedown cruise off San Diego, Calif., Cmdr. Dale W. Fisher of HU-1 piloted the first helicopter to land on her deck. Discussions and testing of the concept of vertical replenishment at sea began in 1959 and certain supply ships had received helicopter platforms, but the commissioning of *Mars* provided the first genuine opportunity to incorporate helicopters into the fleet logistic support system.

9 MARCH • The David Taylor Model Basin Aerodynamics Laboratory commemorated the 50th anniversary of its establishment. The laboratory had been created at the Washington Navy Yard, D.C., but in 1944 shifted to Carderock, Md. Aerodynamics authority Capt. Walter S. Diehl (Ret.) received a citation for his contributions to the laboratory's work.

13 MARCH • Heavy attack squadrons (VAH) 3, 5, and 9 were redesignated reconnaissance attack squadrons (RVAH). In addition, VAH-1 was redesignated RVAH-1 on 1 September 1964. The decision also marked the assignment of RA-5C Vigilantes to RVAHs.

23 MARCH • Two VMO-1 OH-43Ds rescued 11 ill and injured members of a road engineering party that had escaped attacks by hostile natives in the dense jungle of the Amazon basin near Iquitos, Peru. Amphibious assault ship *Guadalcanal* (LPH 7) transferred the Marine aircraft ashore in the Panama Canal Zone, and a USAF C-130 Hercules airlifted the helicopters to Iquitos.

28 MARCH • An earthquake of such force that seismic experts identified the incident as a megathrust earthquake rocked Alaska. The quake and consequent tsunamis along the Pacific coast from Alaska to Oregon devastated Anchorage, killing at least 131 people. Within five hours, seaplane tender *Salisbury Sound* (AV 13) sailed from NAS Whidbey Island, Wash., to provide 14 days of power and heat to severely damaged NS Kodiak. Crewmembers also helped victims ashore. In addition, P-3A Orions and C-54 Skymasters deployed from NAS Moffett Field, Calif., transported emergency supplies.

19 APRIL • After an abortive rightist coup against the Laotian government, the communist Pathet Lao launched a series of raids targeting royalist outposts on the Plaine Des Jarres. *Kitty Hawk* (CVA 63) steamed to a position in the South China Sea and, on 18 May, her aircraft began to fly low-level reconnaissance missions over Laos. Three days later, the Navy also initiated a standing carrier presence at Point Yankee, later redesignated Yankee Station—the northernmost area in the Gulf of Tonkin from which carriers operated during the fighting in Southeast Asia. During 130 low-level sorties over the country through 8 June, these aircraft provided verifiable evidence of the North Vietnamese infiltration into Laos.

23 APRIL • The Chief of Naval Operations broadened the opportunities for naval aviators to qualify as helicopter pilots by extending the responsibilities for their transition training to commands outside the Flight Training Command.

1 MAY • Capt. Paul L. Ruehrmund of VX-1 completed an 18-day, 26,550-nautical-mile trans-global flight piloting a P-3A Orion to NAS Key West, Fla. On an overwater leg of the flight the aircraft dropped explosive sound devices to assist scientists from Naval Ordnance Laboratory in their study of the sea's acoustical properties as a medium for long distance sound transmission.

2 MAY • People's Liberation Armed Forces (Viet Cong) sappers detonated a mine against aircraft ferry *Card* (AKV 40) at Saigon, South Vietnam. The ship settled, but subsequently underwent salvage and repair.

7 MAY • The Chief of Naval Operations informed the chief of Naval Personnel of an agreement by which the Air Force and Coast Guard were to train Navy pilots in the techniques of operating HU-16 Albatross amphibious flying boats in search and rescue and requested its implementation.

6 JUNE • Pathet Lao machine gun and 37mm antiaircraft fire shot down Lt. Charles F. Klusmann of VFP-63 Detachment C, while he flew an RF-8A, BuNo 146823, from *Kitty Hawk* (CVA 63) during a reconnaissance mission about ten miles south near Xiengkhouang, east of the Plaine Des Jarres, Laos. Klusmann ejected, but incurred injuries and became the first naval aviator captured by the communists during the war in Southeast Asia. The enemy held him for 86 days before he escaped. On 1 September, an Air America (an "air proprietary" owned and operated by the CIA) Pilatus PC-6A Turbo Porter operating from Udorn Royal Thai AFB, Thailand, rescued him from Baum Long. Klusmann received the Distinguished Flying Cross.

24 JUNE • PHC Clara B. Johnson of VU-7 received the designation of aerial photographer, the first woman in the Navy with the right to wear the wings of an aircrewman.

26 JUNE • Lt. Robert V. Mayer of VX-6 completed a round-trip flight in an LC-130F Hercules from Christchurch, New Zealand, to McMurdo Sound, Antarctica, in the emergency evacuation of BU1 Bethel L. McMullen after the sailor's critical injury in a fall. Two of the transports carried a medical specialist team from NAS Quonset Point, R.I., and one Hercules stood by at Christchurch while the other made the flight.

29 JUNE • The issuance of a new specification for the color of naval aircraft changed the color scheme for patrol aircraft assigned to antisubmarine work to Gull Gray with Insignia White upper fuselage.

1 JULY • The Navy transferred the Pacific Missile Range facilities at Point Arguello, Calif., and on Kwajalein Atoll to USAF and Army command, respectively.

31 JULY • Nuclear Task Force 1 consisting of *Enterprise* (CVAN 65), cruiser *Long Beach* (CGN 9), and frigate *Bainbridge* (DLGN 25) began Operation Sea Orbit—a global circumnavigation by the world's first task force composed entirely of nuclear-powered ships. The goal was to test the ability of these vessels to maintain high speeds for a long voyage in all types of weather and seas without refueling or replenishing. The ships passed from the Mediterranean through the Strait of Gibraltar, sailed down the coast of West Africa, crossed the Indian Ocean and then the South Pacific, and transited up the east coast of South America. On 3 October, *Enterprise* and *Long Beach* arrived at NS Norfolk, Va., and *Bainbridge* reached Charleston, S.C. *Enterprise*—in coincidence with her hull number—completed the 30,216-nautical-mile global voyage in 65 days.

2 AUGUST • Three North Vietnamese motor torpedo boats attacked destroyer *Maddox* (DD 731) in the Gulf of Tonkin. The destroyer returned fire hitting all three. F-8E Crusaders from *Ticonderoga* (CVA 14) strafed all three, leaving one on fire and dead in the water. Commander in Chief Pacific Fleet Adm. Ulysses S. G. Sharp Jr. ordered destroyer *Turner Joy* (DD 951) to close *Maddox* but the North Vietnamese disengaged. On the night of 4 August, *Maddox* and *Turner Joy* detected apparent multiple radar contacts inbound. Despite heavy seas and a moonless and overcast night, lookouts on board *Turner Joy* believed they spotted two torpedo wakes. More recent analysis of the data and additional information now makes it clear that North Vietnamese naval forces did not attack *Maddox* and *Turner Joy* that night.

On 5 August, Operation Pierce Arrow began—retaliatory carrier strikes ordered by President Lyndon B. Johnson. *Constellation* (CVA 64) and *Ticonderoga* launched 64 sorties against vessels and facilities along the North Vietnamese coast at Bai Chay, Cua Hoi, Gianh River, and Lach Truong, and petroleum-oil-lubricants storage areas at Vinh. The attacks sank or damaged an

Enterprise (CVAN 65), cruiser *Long Beach* (CGN 9), and frigate *Bainbridge* (DLGN 25) complete the first global circumnavigation by nuclear-powered ships during Operation Sea Orbit, 1964.

estimated 25 vessels and destroyed petroleum stores and storage facilities. Antiaircraft fire shot down two *Constellation* aircraft over Hon Gai. Lt. j.g. Everett Alvarez Jr. of VA-144 was captured after ejecting from his A-4C, while Lt. j.g. R. C. Sather died in the crash of his VA-145 A-1H. These clashes led to the Joint Congressional Resolution of 7 August 1964, known as the Tonkin Gulf Resolution, approving the U.S. actions and escalating U.S. involvement in Southeast Asia.

15 AUGUST • President Lyndon B. Johnson announced the existence of a program to develop a counterinsurgency airplane. The Navy functioned as the designated Department of Defense development agency and selected North American Rockwell Corporation as the contractor for the construction of a prototype. The aircraft later was designated OV-10A Bronco.

29 AUGUST • Amphibious assault ship *Boxer* (LPH 4) and two dock landing ships arrived off the coast of Hispaniola to provide medical aid and helicopter evacuation to people in areas of Haiti and the Dominican Republic that had been damaged by Hurricane Cleo.

28 SEPTEMBER • Polaris A-3 fleet ballistic missiles became operational when submarine *Daniel Webster* (SSBN 626) sailed with a full load of the weapons from NWS Charleston, S.C.

30 SEPTEMBER • Three ski-equipped LC-130 Hercules of VX-6 flew individually from Melbourne, Australia; Christchurch, New Zealand; and Punta Arenas, Chile; to Williams Field, McMurdo Sound, Antarctica. The flight from Melbourne passed over the South Pole to drop a 50-pound sack of mail to a wintering party there and landed at Byrd Station before proceeding to McMurdo Sound. On 1 October, the arrival of Commander Naval Support Forces Antarctica Rear Adm. James R. Reedy on this flight marked the opening of Operation Deep Freeze 1965—the Navy's postwar support of Antarctic research.

1 OCTOBER • *Franklin* (AVT 8) became the first *Essex* (CV 9)-class carrier to be labeled unfit for further service and stricken from the Naval Vessel Register.

4 NOVEMBER • Typhoon Iris caused extensive flooding in South Vietnam and Typhoon Joan followed shortly thereafter.

The two storms collectively devastated the provinces of Binh Dinh, Quang Ngai, and Quang Tri, rendering an estimated one million people homeless. On 17 November, UH-34D Seahorses of HMM-162, embarked on board amphibious assault ship *Princeton* (LPH 5), supported relief efforts when they began the delivery of 1,300 tons of food and clothing to storm victims.

26 NOVEMBER • Nine helicopters of HU-2 and four from NAS Lakehurst, N.J., assisted the Coast Guard in the rescue of 17 men from Norwegian tanker *Stolt Dagali*, after a collision with Israeli liner *Shalom* cut the tanker in two off the New Jersey coast.

14 DECEMBER • The United States began Operation Barrel Roll—ground support and interdiction missions to offset tactical disadvantages on the ground in northern Laos. The theater was later divided into zones A, B, and C (from north to south), but United States and Laotian restrictions initially limited Barrel Roll strike missions to no more than four aircraft per raid, a wait of at least three days between strikes, prohibited bombing targets within two miles of the North Vietnamese border, and forbidden to fly from Thai airfields.

17 DECEMBER • Cmdr. Theodore G. Ellyson (Naval Aviator No. 1) became the first naval officer enshrined in the National Aviation Hall of Fame, Dayton, Ohio.

1965

1 JANUARY • All naval air base commands were disestablished in accordance with the provision of general orders prescribing the organization and administration of the Navy.

12 JANUARY • The Department of Defense announced the operational use of the all-weather Transit navigation satellite system since July 1964. The complete development of the system was to consist of four satellites in polar orbit to provide a ship at the equator with a navigational fix once an hour.

19 JANUARY • Unmanned space capsule Gemini 2 launched from John F. Kennedy Space Center, Fla. The suborbital mission's objectives included an evaluation of the adequacy of the reentry module's heat protection during a maximum heating-rate reentry. The capsule splashed down in the Atlantic within 23 miles of *Lake Champlain* (CVS 39), which recovered the spacecraft.

7 FEBRUARY • On 1 November 1964, communist People's Liberation Armed Forces (Viet Cong) insurgents attacked U.S. compounds at Bien Hoa near Saigon, South Vietnam, and on this date at Pleiku in the Central Highlands, followed three days later by an attack on Qui Nhon. From 7 through 9 and on 11 February, the United States carried out retaliatory Operations Flaming Dart I and II. *Hancock* (CVA 19), *Coral Sea* (CVA 43), and *Ranger* (CVA 61) launched strikes against military barracks and staging areas in the southern part of North Vietnam at Dong Hoi, Chanh Hoa, Chap Le, Vit Thu Lu, and Vu Con, and against port facilities at Dong Hoi.

8 FEBRUARY • The title and designation of naval aviation observer, 135X, was changed to naval flight officer, 132X, to be effective on 1 May.

6 MARCH • Cmdr. James R. Williford III piloted an SH-3A Sea King from *Hornet* (CVS 12) berthed at NAS North Island, Calif., and 15 hours, 51 minutes later landed on board *Franklin D. Roosevelt* (CVA 42) at sea off NS Mayport, Fla. The flight surpassed the existing distance record for helicopters by more than 700 miles.

8 MARCH • The Seventh Fleet landed about 3,500 Marines of the 9th Marine Amphibious Brigade including a helicopter squadron without opposition at Da Nang AB, South Vietnam. The Marines deployed to protect the airfield.

12 MARCH • Four enlisted men completed 24 days of living in a rotating room in a test conducted by the Naval School of Aviation Medicine, NAS Pensacola, Fla. The goals of the experiment included a determination of the spinning rate men could endure without discomfort, and checking procedures for conditioning the sailors for space flight.

23 MARCH • Gemini 3 space capsule *Molly Brown* crewed by Maj. Virgil I. Grissom, USAF, and Lt. Cmdr. John W. Young launched from John F. Kennedy Space Center, Fla. The major objectives of the mission included an evaluation of the Gemini spacecraft in manned orbital flight. The capsule splashed down in the Atlantic east of Bermuda near 22°26'N, 70°51'W within 60 nautical miles of primary recovery ship *Intrepid* (CVS 11). A Coast Guard helicopter spotted the spacecraft, and pilot Lt. Cmdr. Warren H. Winchester, copilot Lt. j.g. James R. Walker, and aircrewmen AX3 J. D. Hightower and J. A. Kerivan of HS-3 picked up Grissom and Young in SH-3A, Aircraft No. 57, and delivered them to the carrier. *Intrepid* hoisted *Molly Brown* on board and later returned the astronauts and the spacecraft to the space center.

26 MARCH • Seventh Fleet aircraft began their participation in Operation Rolling Thunder—the systematic bombing of military targets throughout North Vietnam. President Lyndon B. Johnson initially directed the goals of the campaign to convince the North Vietnamese to cease their support of communist insurgents in South Vietnam, Cambodia, and Laos; however, the bombing subsequently shifted to attacks against enemy lines of communication to reduce the flood of troops and supplies into those countries. Planners numbered the raids sequentially. On this date, *Hancock* (CVA 19) and *Coral Sea* (CVA 43) launched strikes on island and coastal radar stations in the vicinity of Vinh Son, North Vietnam.

3 APRIL • The U.S. began Steel Tiger—a program to cut communist infiltration through the south-central Laotian panhandle near the North Vietnamese border and into northern South Vietnam. The harsh mountain terrain restricted vehicles to one of several passes including Ban Karai, Ban Raving, and Mu Gia, and air strikes initially focused on closing those gateways. Road watch teams on the ground alerted aircraft to targets and discerned a pattern of enemy truck shuttles. After several incidents where aircraft bombed allied Laotian troops because of communication and identification errors, orders restricted aerial attacks to "clearly identifiable" convoys, vehicles, and troops within 200 yards of either side of roads. The Steel Tiger area of operations was later divided into zones D, E, F, and G (from north to south). Allied aircraft flew a total of 43,860 Steel Tiger sorties.

10 APRIL • The deployment of Marine fixed-wing combat aircraft to South Vietnam commenced with the arrival of VMFA-531 F-4B Phantom IIs at Da Nang AB.

A C-2 Greyhound makes a carrier onboard delivery to *Kitty Hawk* (CVA 63) in Vietnamese waters.

The AGM-45 Shrike antiradar air-to-ground missile is a development of a modified AIM-7 Sparrow. The program began in 1963.

15 APRIL • Seventh Fleet carrier aircraft supported allied troops fighting in South Vietnam with a strike against People's Liberation Armed Forces positions near Black Virgin Mountain. To carry out additional raids into the country, on 16 May 1965, the Navy established Dixie Station about 100 miles southeast of Cam Ranh Bay, South Vietnam. An average of one carrier normally operated there through 4 August 1966, when the expansion of land-based air support provided most of the required air attacks in that area. Dixie nonetheless continued to support operations across South Vietnam because the enemy did not initially develop extensive air defenses there.

A Mk 11 20mm gun pod is mounted onto an A4D-2 Skyhawk at the 1958 Naval Air Weapons Meet in El Centro, Calif., during the weapon's test phase by the Naval Aviation Ordnance Test Station in Chincoteague, Va.

Navy bombers firing AGM-12 Bullpup air-to-ground missiles knock down a span of the North Vietnamese highway bridge at Xom Ca Trang, 16 April 1965.

19 APRIL • Six Navy and two Marine Corps pilots emerged from two sealed chambers at the Aerospace Crew Equipment Laboratory, Philadelphia, Pa., after a 34-day test to learn the physical effects of prolonged stays in confined quarters with a low-pressure pure oxygen atmosphere.

24 APRIL • A revolt in the Dominican Republic threatened the safety of Americans there. Vessels that responded included amphibious assault ships *Okinawa* (LPH 3), *Boxer* (LPH 4), and *Guadalcanal* (LPH 7), and amphibious transport dock *Raleigh* (LPD 1). Into mid-June, Marines established perimeters ashore while 20 HMM-264 UH-34D Seahorses and two UH-1E Iroquois flying from *Boxer*; and 20 HMM-263 Seahorses, two VMO-1 Iroquois, and two HMM-161 CH-37C Mojaves operating from *Okinawa*; proved instrumental in evacuating more than 1,000 people.

1 MAY • Through 2 May, amphibious assault ship *Iwo Jima* (LPH 2) offloaded 77 Army helicopters, about 850 soldiers, tanker trucks, and other vehicles at Vung Tau, South Vietnam.

10 MAY • Tank landing ship *Tioga County* (LST 1158) fired a surface-to-air version of an AIM-7 Sparrow III air-to-air missile designated Seaspar in the Pacific Missile Range test area, during the first shipboard test of the weapon.

12 MAY • Amphibious assault ship *Iwo Jima* (LPH 2), with HMM-161 UH-34D Seahorses embarked, supported Marines and Seabees during the establishment of an airfield capable of accommodating jets at Chu Lai, 52 miles south of Da Nang AB, South Vietnam. *Iwo Jima* then disembarked the squadron to Hué-Phu Bai and, on 12 June, sailed for Subic Bay, Philippines.

18 MAY • Members of the Naval Air Reserve began a volunteer airlift supporting operations in South Vietnam. These sailors operated Reserve C-54 Skymasters and C-118 Liftmasters carrying personnel and urgently needed cargo to the fighting on weekend and other training flights from their home stations to the West Coast, Hawaii, and Southeast Asia. These airlifts logged more than 19,000 flight hours during the first 18 months of the operation.

1 JUNE • The arrival of the first aircraft and the departure of the first combat missions opened operations at the Marine airfield at Chu Lai, South Vietnam.

3 JUNE • Gemini IV crewed by Maj. James A. McDivitt, USAF, and Maj. Edward H. White II, USAF, launched from John F. Kennedy Space Center, Fla. The major objectives of the mission included the evaluation of the performance of spacecraft systems in a long endurance flight and the effects on the crew of prolonged exposure to the space environment. On 7 June, the capsule splashed down in the Atlantic about 450 miles east of Cape Canaveral, Fla., near 27°44'N, 74°14'W.

1047141

Independence (CVA 62), her flight deck packed with aircraft, refuels during the Vietnam War.

The landing occurred off target about 48 nautical miles of primary recovery ship *Wasp* (CVS 18). Pilot Cmdr. Clarence O. Fiske, squadron commanding officer, and Navy swimmers Lt. j.g. Martin Every, Neil G. Dow, and Everett W. Owl of HS-11 manned the SH-3A Sea King that recovered the astronauts.

10 JUNE • The Naval Air Crew Equipment Laboratory began a study of several physiological aspects of pure-oxygen environments for the space program, including a determination of the possible reversal of lung collapse and the space environment effect upon the enhancement of respiratory infections. The testing concluded on 17 June.

17 JUNE • While escorting a strike against North Vietnamese barracks at Gen Phu, two F-4Bs crewed by pilot Cmdr. Louis C. Page and radar intercept officer (RIO) Lt. John C. Smith Jr., and pilot Lt. Jack E. D. Batson Jr. and RIO Lt. Cmdr. Robert B. Doremus, of VF-21 operating from *Midway* (CVA 41), scored the first U.S. victories against MiGs during the Vietnam War. Each crew shot down one of four MiG-17 Frescoes with AIM-7 Sparrow air-to-air missiles.

17 JUNE • *Independence* (CVA 62) arrived at Subic Bay, Philippines, after a voyage from the Atlantic Fleet around the tip of Africa. *Independence* became the fifth attack carrier operating off Vietnam.

20 JUNE • Two North Vietnamese MiG-17s attacked a flight of four VA-25 A-1H Skyraiders operating from *Midway* (CVA 41) over North Vietnam. Two of the Skyraiders, piloted by Lt. Clinton B. Johnson and Lt. j.g. Charles W. Hartman III, shot down one of the Frescoes with 20mm guns. Johnson and Hartman each received the Silver Star.

23 JUNE • In an unusual mission for a seaplane tender, *Currituck* (AV 7) carried out a shore bombardment of People's Liberation Armed Forces positions in the Mekong Delta, South Vietnam.

30 JUNE • The Pacific extension of the Dew Line national early warning system ceased to operate seven years after its establishment, and Barrier Force, Pacific, and Airborne Early Warning Barrier Squadron, Pacific, went out of existence.

1 JULY • Fleet Air Wing 8, Capt. David C. Kendrick commanding, was established at NAS Moffett Field, Calif.

1 JULY • The Navy's first Oceanographic Air Survey Unit, Cmdr. Harold R. Hutchinson commanding, was established at NAS Patuxent River, Md. Its tasks included aerial ice reconnaissance in the North Atlantic and polar areas and Project Magnet, aerial operations concerned with worldwide magnetic collection and observation.

1 JULY • Helicopter utility squadrons (HU) were redesignated helicopter combat support squadrons (HC), and utility squadrons (VU) were redesignated fleet composite squadrons (VC), as more representative of their functions and composition.

14 JULY • *Yorktown* (CVS 10) sailed on a turnaround trip to deliver urgently needed materials to allied forces fighting in South Vietnam from San Diego, Calif., for Subic Bay, Philippines.

18 AUGUST • Marine aircraft and naval gunfire supported Operation Starlite—amphibious and heliborne landings by elements of the 3d, 4th, and 7th Marines against the People's Liberation Armed Forces (PLAF) on the Van Tuong Peninsula, 14 miles south of Chu Lai, South Vietnam. The assault drove the bulk of the PLAF's 1st Regiment from the area.

21 AUGUST • Gemini V, crewed by Maj. L. Gordon Cooper Jr., USAF, and Lt. Cmdr. Charles Conrad Jr., launched from John F. Kennedy Space Center, Fla. The major objectives of the mission included an evaluation of the rendezvous guidance and navigation system. On 29 August the capsule splashed down in the Atlantic at 29°47'N, 69°4'W. The impact occurred within 89 miles of primary recovery ship *Lake Champlain* (CVS 39) because of incorrect navigation coordinates transmitted to the spacecraft. Navy swimmers assisted the astronauts, a helicopter returned Cooper and Conrad to *Lake Champlain*, and the ship recovered the capsule.

26 AUGUST • The barrier air patrol over the North Atlantic ended when a VW-11 EC-121J Warning Star landed at NAS Keflavik, Iceland. This also signaled a change in which a new and advanced radar system took over from naval aircraft that had maintained vigil over the northern approaches to North America for ten years.

31 AUGUST • President Lyndon B. Johnson approved a policy on the promotion and decoration of astronauts by which each military astronaut was to receive, upon the completion of his first space flight, a one-grade promotion up to and including captain in the Navy and colonel in the USAF and Marine Corps. Gemini astronauts that completed a successful space flight were to receive the NASA Medal for Exceptional Service (or cluster).

1 SEPTEMBER • In accord with the provision of an act of Congress, the Secretary of the Navy authorized additional pay to flight deck sailors for duty performed in the hazardous environment of flight operations on the decks of attack and antisubmarine carriers.

9 SEPTEMBER • Cmdr. James B. Stockdale, commander of Carrier Air Wing 16, embarked on board *Oriskany* (CVA 34), was shot down in Old Salt 352, an A-4E Skyhawk, BuNo. 151134, by automatic weapons fire after completing a Snakeye bombing attack against a group of railroad cars south of Thanh Hoa, North Vietnam. Stockdale endured captivity until his release on 12 February 1973. The naval aviator designed a prisoner communication system and a set of rules, which gave his fellow prisoners strength and hope. Vice Adm. Stockdale (Ret.) died on 5 July 2005 of Alzheimer's disease at his home in Coronado, Calif. His decorations include the Medal of Honor, two Distinguished Flying Crosses, two Purple Hearts, and four Silver Stars.

11 SEPTEMBER • Amphibious assault ship *Boxer* (LPH 4) delivered aircraft and soldiers of the Army's 1st Cavalry Division (Airmobile) to Qui Nhon, South Vietnam, after a voyage via the Suez Canal from NS Mayport, Fla.

A CH-53A Sea Stallion of HMM-361, MAG-16, delivers a 105mm field howitzer to Marines ten miles south of Chu Lai, South Vietnam, 18 August 1965.

S54231-A

24 SEPTEMBER • A flag officer was designated Chief of Naval Operations representative and Navy deputy to the Department of Defense Manager for Manned Space Flight Support Operations because the accelerated frequency of manned space flights placed increasing demands upon Navy recovery capabilities. The assignment comprised additional duty as Commander, Manned Space Recovery Force, Atlantic, and tasking included the coordination and consolidation of operational requirements with all of the commands providing Navy resources in support of manned space flights.

14 OCTOBER • The 1,200-nautical-mile range Polaris A-1 fleet ballistic missile was retired from service when submarine *Abraham Lincoln* (SSBN 602) returned to the United States for overhaul and refitting with 2,500-nautical-mile range Polaris A-3s.

15 OCTOBER • To expand Pacific airlift capabilities, VR-22 shifted from NAS Norfolk, Va., to NAS Moffett Field, Calif.

17 OCTOBER • A VA-75 A-6A Intruder and four A-4E Skyhawks flying from *Independence* (CVA 62) knocked out a North Vietnamese surface-to-air missile site near Kep during the first successful naval air strike against air defense missiles in that country.

25 OCTOBER • The ships that supported the planned launch of Capt. Walter M. Schirra Jr. and Maj. Thomas P. Stafford, USAF, in Gemini VI included *Wasp* (CVS 18) in the Atlantic. NASA scrubbed the mission because of the catastrophic failure of the Gemini Agena 5002 target vehicle.

28 OCTOBER • The People's Liberation Armed Forces attacked the sailors and Marines at the Marble Mountain Air Facility, South Vietnam, destroying six UH-34D Seahorses and 13 UH-1E Iroquois, and damaging 26 Seahorses and four Iroquois.

2 DECEMBER • Twenty-one F-4B Phantom IIs and A-4C Skyhawks launched from *Enterprise* (CVAN 65) against People's Liberation Armed Forces installations near Bien Hoa, South Vietnam, on the first combat strikes from the ship and the first from a nuclear-powered carrier. Aircraft operating from the carrier completed 125 strike sorties and unloaded 167 tons of bombs and rockets on the enemy, and flew 131 sorties the following day.

4 DECEMBER • Gemini VII, crewed by Lt. Col. Frank Borman, USAF, and Cmdr. James A. Lovell Jr., launched from John F. Kennedy Space Center, Fla. The mission accomplished the major objectives of a demonstration of manned orbital flight and an evaluation of the effects of prolonged exposure to the space environment on the astronauts. On 18 December, the capsule splashed down in the Atlantic about 250 miles north of Grand Turk Island near 25°25'N, 70°7'W, within seven miles of primary recovery ship *Wasp* (CVS 18). The proximity to the landing point enabled HS-11 SH-3A Sea Kings to recover the astronauts and the spacecraft separately, and convey them to *Wasp* within an hour.

15 DECEMBER • Gemini VI-A crewed by Capt. Walter M. Schirra Jr. and Maj. Thomas P. Stafford, USAF, launched from John F. Kennedy Space Center, Fla. The mission accomplished the major objective of a successful rendezvous with Gemini VII. On 16 December, the capsule splashed down in the western Atlantic about 300 miles north of Puerto Rico near 23°42'N, 67°48'W, within seven miles of primary recovery ship *Wasp* (CVS 18). Schirra and Stafford remained within the capsule, and SH-3A Sea Kings of HS-11 recovered the astronauts and their spacecraft and delivered them to *Wasp*.

20 DECEMBER • The Secretary of the Navy established a director of Naval Laboratories on the staff of the assistant secretary for Research and Development, and directed the additional responsibilities of director of Laboratory Programs in the Office of Naval Material. The administrative responsibility for laboratories was subsequently transferred to this dual office while NAVAIR assumed command of test and evaluation facilities such as Naval Air Test Center, Naval Missile Center, and Naval Air Engineering Center.

1966

20 JANUARY • A contract for the production of Walleye television-guided air-to-surface glide bombs was issued to the Martin Marietta Corp.

26 FEBRUARY • Apollo-Saturn 201 lifted off via a Saturn IB rocket from John F. Kennedy Space Center, Fla. This first unmanned spacecraft of the Apollo series completed a suborbital flight and splashed down in the South Atlantic about 200 miles east of Ascension Island. A helicopter from amphibious assault ship *Boxer* (LPH 4) recovered the command module.

1 MARCH • Naval Air Transport Wing, Atlantic was disestablished.

2 MARCH • *Constellation* (CVA 64) began receiving weather data from weather satellite Essa 2. The transmission marked the second experimental shipboard installation of receivers capable of presenting a picture of major weather patterns taken from space, and the evaluation continued testing that began in 1963 on board *Saratoga* (CVA 60) with satellites Tiros 8 and Nimbus.

16 MARCH • Gemini VIII crewed by Neil A. Armstrong and Maj. David R. Scott, USAF, launched from John F. Kennedy Space Center, Fla. After only seven orbits, an attitude and maneuver system thruster malfunctioned. The astronauts regained control by using the reentry control system, but the action required the early termination of the mission, and the capsule splashed down in the western Pacific about 500 miles east of Okinawa near 25°12'N, 136°5'E. The landing occurred within seven miles of destroyer *Leonard F. Mason* (DD 852) and she recovered

K31638

A UH-2A Seasprite of HC-1 flies plane guard for *Ranger* (CVA 61) while the ship operates off Vietnam, c. 1965–1966.

the astronauts and their spacecraft. Additional vessels that supported the recovery included amphibious assault ship *Boxer* (LPH 4) in the Atlantic.

17 MARCH • The X-22A research aircraft made its first flight at Buffalo, N.Y.

31 MARCH • A flight test of a helicopter capsule escape system involving the recovery of occupants by separation of the inhabited fuselage section from the aircraft proper, demonstrated the feasibility of its use during inflight emergencies at NAF El Centro, Calif., using a modified H-25.

4 APRIL • NASA announced the selection of 19 astronauts including 11 naval aviators—John S. Bull, Ronald E. Evans, Thomas K. Mattingly II, Bruce McCandless II, Edgar D. Mitchell, and Paul J. Weitz on active duty in the Navy, and Gerald P. Carr and Jack R. Lousma on active service in the Marine Corps. The selectees also included civilians Don L. Lind, USNR, and Marine pilots Vance D. Brand and Fred W. Haise Jr.

5 APRIL • The Secretary of Defense approved a joint request from the secretaries of the Navy and Air Force for the removal of Navy air transport units from the Military Airlift Command. The disestablishment of Navy units during the first half of 1967 accomplished the withdrawal.

1111306

The first of two X-22A vertical takeoff and landing research aircraft, BuNo 151520, was removed from flight status after a hard emergency landing in August 1966.

10 APRIL • Two Navy enlisted men together with a medical officer and a civilian electronics technician acting as observers began spinning at four revolutions per minute in the Coriolis Acceleration Platform of the Naval Aerospace Medical Institute, NAS Pensacola, Fla. The event commenced a four-day test to determine the ability of humans to adapt to a new form of rotation for potential use in space stations to produce artificial gravity.

18 APRIL • The Naval Pre-Flight School was redesignated Naval Aviation Schools Command during a reorganization of Naval Air Basic Training Command schools at NAS Pensacola, Fla. In addition, six existing schools became departments of the new command—Aviation Officer Candidate, Aviation Officer Indoctrination, Flight

NH 69968

The fifth of five experimental XC-142A vertical takeoff and landing transports, SerNo 62-5925, lands on board *Bennington* (CVS 20), 18 May 1966.

Preparation, Indoctrination for Naval Academy and NROTC Midshipman, Instructor Training, and Survival Training.

1 MAY • A reorganization of the Navy Department became effective which placed material, medical, and personnel supporting organizations under the command of the Chief of Naval Operations, abolished the Naval Material Support Establishment and its component bureaus, and in their place set up the Naval Material Command composed of six functional or systems commands: Air, Electronics, Facilities Engineering, Ordnance, Ships, and Supply.

11 MAY • The commanding officer of Marine Aircraft Group 12 piloted an A-4 Skyhawk during a launch from a catapult at the expeditionary airfield at Chu Lai, South Vietnam. The event marked the first combat use of the land-based catapult, which was capable of launching fully loaded tactical aircraft from runways less than 3,000 feet long.

15 MAY • *Intrepid* (CVS 11), with Carrier Air Wing 10 embarked, arrived in Vietnamese waters to operate as an attack carrier although still classified as an antisubmarine carrier. On the first day of battle, aircraft of her air wing composed entirely of attack squadrons flew 97 combat sorties against People's Liberation Armed Forces troop concentrations and supply storage areas around Saigon, South Vietnam.

18 MAY • Lt. Roger L. Rich Jr. piloted the XC-142A tri-service vertical and/or short takeoff and landing transport during its first carrier flights on board *Bennington* (CVS 20) at sea off San Diego, Calif. Additional Navy, Marine, and Army pilots took turns at the controls of the aircraft.

3 JUNE • Gemini IX-A crewed by Lt. Col. Thomas P. Stafford, USAF, and Lt. Cmdr. Eugene A. Cernan launched from John F. Kennedy Space Center, Fla. The mission failed to accomplish the major objective of docking with the augmented target docking adapter because the target's shroud failed to separate, but Cernan spent more than an hour outside the spacecraft. On 6 June, the capsule splashed down in the western Atlantic about 345 miles east of Cape Kennedy near 27°52'N, 75°4'W, within one mile of primary recovery ship *Wasp* (CVS 18). Carrier Air Group commander Cmdr. D. A. Barksdale circled overhead in an S-2E Tracker as "Air Boss One." Six SH-3A Sea Kings from HS-11, including Aircraft No. 57, BuNo 149710, assisted the recovery, but the astronauts remained in their spacecraft and the carrier hoisted them on board. Stafford and Cernan were flown to the space center and *Wasp* returned with the capsule to Boston.

16 JUNE • *Hancock* (CVA 19) launched A-4 Skyhawks and F-8 Crusaders against an area 24 miles west of Thanh Hoa, North Vietnam. The battle marked the first carrier strike on petroleum-oil-lubricants facilities since 1964, and the beginning of what expanded into a systematic effort to destroy the North Vietnamese petroleum storage system.

1 JULY • Three North Vietnamese torpedo boats attacked frigate *Coontz* (DLG 9) and destroyer *Rogers* (DD 876) 40 miles off shore in the Gulf of Tonkin while the ships conducted search and rescue missions. Aircraft from *Hancock* (CVA 19) and *Constellation* (CVA 64) sank all three vessels with bombs, rockets, and 20mm gunfire. *Coontz* pulled 19 survivors from the water.

SH-3A Sea Kings from HS-11 hover over astronauts Lt. Col. Thomas P. Stafford, USAF, (right) and Lt. Cmdr. Eugene A. Cernan after the splashdown of Gemini IX-A, 6 June 1966.

18 JULY • Gemini X crewed by Lt. Cmdr. John W. Young and Maj. Michael Collins, USAF, launched from John F. Kennedy Space Center, Fla. The astronauts achieved the major objective during their rendezvous with the target vehicle on their fourth orbit. On 21 July, the spacecraft splashed down in the Atlantic three miles from the planned landing point about 460 miles east of Cape Kennedy, Fla., near 26°45'N, 71°57'W, within sight of the primary recovery vessel, amphibious assault ship *Guadalcanal* (LPH 7). Pilot Lt. Cmdr. Bruce S. Fleming, copilot Lt. j.g. James L. Stewart, and aircrewmen John S. Alman and Warren R. Watkins of HS-3 manned the SH-3A Sea King, BuNo 152132, Aircraft No. 63, that recovered the astronauts.

19 JULY • The Chief of Naval Operations established the LHA program to bring into being a new concept of an amphibious assault ship. The plans developed through preliminary study envisioned a large multipurpose ship with a flight deck for helicopters, a wet boat well for landing craft, the troop carrying capacity of an amphibious assault ship (LPH), and a cargo capacity nearly that of an attack cargo ship (AKA).

25 AUGUST • Apollo-Saturn 202 lifted off from John F. Kennedy Space Center, Fla. The objectives of this second unmanned spacecraft of the Apollo series included the evaluation of the heat shield during a high heat, long-duration entry simulating a lunar return. The spacecraft

NASA 66H1030

Divers recover Lt. Cmdr. John W. Young (right, in raft) and Maj. Michael Collins, USAF, after the splashdown of Gemini X, 21 July 1966.

splashed down in the Pacific about 500 miles southeast of Wake Island and 192 nautical miles from primary recovery ship *Hornet* (CVS 12) near 17°52'N, 171°52'E. *Hornet* retrieved the command module.

26 AUGUST • Cmdr. James R. Williford III, commanding officer of HS-11, made the first helicopter refueling from a ship in the Atlantic Fleet when he rendezvoused with destroyer *Charles P. Cecil* (DD 835) while piloting an SH-3A Sea King, BuNo 149718, designated Aircraft No. 64.

3 SEPTEMBER • Naval Air Test Center pilots completed a two-day open sea suitability trial of an RH-3A Sea King on board mine countermeasures ship *Ozark* (MCS 2). This trial completed the center's evaluation of the helicopters for the minesweeper role. The next year, a mine countermeasures development and training program in the Atlantic Fleet used the ship and a helicopter detachment from newly established HC-6, and a detachment from HC-7 began preparations for training and operation on board *Catskill* (MCS 1) in the Pacific.

8 SEPTEMBER • An A-3A Skywarrior carrying an AIM-54A air-to-air missile and its control system located, locked on at long range, and launched the Phoenix to score an intercept on a jet target drone over the Navy Pacific Missile Range near San Nicolas Island, Calif. A Phoenix had been launched successfully prior to this achievement, but this event marked the first full-scale test employing all functions of the missile control system.

12 SEPTEMBER • Gemini XI, manned by Lt. Cmdrs. Charles Conrad Jr. and Richard F. Gordon Jr., launched from John F. Kennedy Space Center, Fla. The astronauts attained the primary objective of the mission when they docked with the target vehicle. On 15 September, the spacecraft splashed down in the Atlantic 700 miles off Cape Kennedy

Crewmembers of amphibious assault ship *Guadalcanal* (LPH 7) salute their participation in the recovery of Gemini X.

near 24°15'N, 70°00'W, within three miles of the planned landing point. Pilot Lt. Arthur G. Doege, copilot Lt. Herman D. Rotsch, and aircrewmen Robert L. Brugh and Donald Scarborough of HS-3 manned Aircraft No. 63, an SH-3A Sea King, BuNo 152132, embarked on board amphibious assault ship *Guam* (LPH 9), that recovered the astronauts. *Guam* also retrieved the spacecraft.

16 SEPTEMBER • Helicopters operating from *Oriskany* (CVA 34) rescued the entire crew of 44 men from British merchant ship *August Moon*, when she broke up in heavy seas on Pratas Reef, 175 miles southeast of Hong Kong.

7 OCTOBER • Hurricane Inez devastated the northern tip of the Yucatán Peninsula and on 10 October made landfall near Tampico, Mexico. The U.S. Navy, Marine Corps, Air Force, and Army airlifted more than 102,000-pounds of relief supplies and evacuated 80 victims of the resulting flooding, and Navy doctors treated hundreds of additional casualties.

26 OCTOBER • *Oriskany* (CVA 34) canceled the day's strikes over North Vietnam because of inclement weather in the South China Sea. Shortly thereafter, AAs George James and James Sider accidentally ignited a Mk 24 magnesium parachute flare while stowing flares and hurled the device into a storage locker filled with 600 to 700 flares. A fire swept the hangar deck and cooked off ordnance, killing 44 men and wounding 38. *Oriskany* made to Subic Bay, Philippines, for repairs and then to San Francisco, Calif.

3 NOVEMBER • A test flight of the Air Force's Manned Orbiting Laboratory (MOL-B) was launched from John F. Kennedy Space Center, Fla., atop a Titan IIIC. The objectives of the unmanned suborbital flight included the evaluation of the performance of the heat shield during reentry. The splash down occurred in the Atlantic near 9°6'S, 14°15'W. The spacecraft landed 40 nautical miles from amphibious transport dock *La Salle* (LPD 3) that recovered the capsule.

4 NOVEMBER • Eight men were killed when a flash fire erupted in a storage compartment containing paint, oil, and hydraulic fluid four decks below the hangar deck on board *Franklin D. Roosevelt* (CVA 42) while she launched strikes from the South China Sea over North Vietnam.

8 NOVEMBER • The Chief of Naval Operations approved a reorganization of the Naval Air Reserve involving the disestablishment of all air wing staffs, establishing in the

1143453

Ships of Task Force 77 including *Oriskany* (CVA 34), center, maneuver in the Gulf of Tonkin, as viewed from the signal bridge of *Constellation* (CVA 64).

place of each an administrative unit entitled Naval Air Reserve Staff and a training unit as Naval Air Reserve Division (Fleet Air).

11 NOVEMBER • Gemini XII, manned by Capt. James A. Lovell Jr. and Maj. Edwin E. Aldrin Jr., USAF, launched from John F. Kennedy Space Center, Fla. The mission accomplished the major objective of docking with a target vehicle. On 15 November, the capsule splashed down about 600 miles east of Cape Kennedy near 24°36'4"N, 69°56'2"W, within a mile of primary recovery ship *Wasp* (CVS 18). Strong winds, rough seas, and rain plagued the recovery. Three HS-11 SH-3A Sea Kings flew the recovery mission supported by additional aircraft including a photo Sea King, eight VS-28 S-2E Trackers for contingency search, and a VAW-12 Detachment 18 E-1B Tracer. A helicopter, designated Search Three, manned by pilot Lt. Cmdr. Samuel R. Aydelotte, copilot Lt. j.g. J. E. Davis, and aircrewman AT3 Konrad Kerr, hoisted Lovell and Aldrin aloft and returned them to *Wasp*, and the carrier hoisted the spacecraft on board. On 18 November, *Wasp* returned the capsule to Boston, Mass. This operation closed the Gemini program.

1967

27 JANUARY • A fire swept through Apollo 1's Command Module 012 during a simulated launch of the first manned Apollo space flight atop its Saturn IB launch vehicle at John F. Kennedy Space Center, Fla. The blaze killed the crew, Lt. Cols. Virgil I. Grissom, USAF, and Edward H. White II, USAF, and Lt. Cmdr. Roger B. Chaffee. NASA's Apollo 204 (the mission's original designation) Review Board did not discover evidence that suggested sabotage or a single ignition

1143448

The fourth YA2F-1 Intruder, BuNo 147867, shown here, was the first fitted with the full set of advanced electronic systems which enabled later version A-6s to penetrate enemy defenses and to bomb through the clouds.

source of the fire, but determined that the most probable initiator resulted from a momentary power failure in the area of an electrical arc. On 31 January, Grissom and Chaffee were buried in the National Cemetery, Arlington, Va., and White at the Military Academy, West Point, N.Y.

26 FEBRUARY • Seven VA-35 A-6As flying from *Enterprise* (CVAN 65) participated in the first Navy aerial mining operations since World War II. Cmdr. Arthur H. Barrie, squadron commanding officer, led the Intruders through light antiaircraft fire to drop two fields of 35 Mk 50-0 and 52-2 mines overnight in the estuaries of the North Vietnamese Song Ca and Song Giang (rivers). This was to disrupt shallow draft coastal and riverine barges and sampans from slipping into otherwise inaccessible areas to supply the People's Liberation Armed Forces and Pathet Lao. F-4B Phantom IIs of VF-96 escorted the Intruders. During subsequent missions, VA-35 dropped 53 mines in 11 sorties altogether, and the following month, aircraft from *Kitty Hawk* (CVA 63) flew additional minelaying missions over the Cua Sot, Kien Giang, and Song Ma (rivers). The North Vietnamese initiated mine clearance efforts, but the missions impeded smuggling and forced its temporary suspension.

14 MARCH • A VP-17 SP-2H Neptune patrolling from NS Sangley Point, Philippines, spotted a steel-hulled North Vietnamese trawler smuggling arms to People's Liberation Armed Forces insurgents during Operation Market Time—the interdiction of enemy supplies into South Vietnam. Destroyer *Brister* (DER 327), Coast Guard cutter *Point Ellis* (WPB 82330), and patrol craft *PCF 78* intercepted the smugglers and they beached the trawler. A boarding party recovered the munitions.

1115829

An SP-2H Neptune, BuNo 150280, of VP-1 inspects a Vietnamese junk during Operation Market Time, c. 1966.

1143447

A UH-1B Iroquois of HAL-3 supports patrol boats in the Mekong Delta, 22 April 1968.

1 APRIL • The status of overhaul and repair departments at six Navy and one Marine air stations was changed to that of separate commands each titled Naval Air Rework Facility.

1 APRIL • Helicopter Attack Squadron (Light) [HAL] 3 was established at Vung Tau, South Vietnam, Lt. Cmdr. Joseph B. Howard commanding. The unit fought as the only armed UH-1 Iroquois Navy helicopter squadron during the Vietnam War, and with Light Attack Squadron (VAL) 4, comprised the only Navy air commands homeported in South Vietnam. HAL-3 uniquely provided gunship support for Navy and Army riverine operations within the Mekong Delta and pioneered tactics in support of patrol boats and shore installations. The squadron operated a mix of UH-1B/L/N and HH-1K helicopters from various bases in the delta and from specially equipped patrol craft tenders (AGP), formerly tank landing ships (LST).

12 APRIL • The Navy approved a wing insignia for aviation experimental psychologists and aviation physiologists. The new design appeared similar to flight surgeon wings except for the use of the gold oak leaf of the Medical Service Corps in place of the leaf with acorn of the Medical Corps.

24 APRIL • Aircraft from Seventh Fleet carriers launched their first strikes on North Vietnamese MiG bases with an attack on the airfield at Kep, 37 miles northeast of Hanoi. A-6 Intruders and A-4 Skyhawks from *Kitty Hawk* (CVA 63) carried out the attack and Intruders made a further raid that night. While providing cover for the bombers during the first attack, pilot Lt. Cmdr. Charles E. Southwick and radar intercept officer (RIO) Ens. James W. Laing, and pilot Lt. Hugh D. Wisely and RIO Lt. j.g. Gareth L. Anderson, manned two VF-114 F-4B Phantom IIs, and each received credit for a probable MiG-17 kill with AIM-9D/B Sidewinder air-to-air missiles.

1 MAY • *Bon Homme Richard* (CVA 31) and *Enterprise* (CVAN 65) launched a coordinated strike against more than 30 North Vietnamese MiGs at Kep, North Vietnam. The Seventh Air Force also struck MiGs at Hoa Lac. Lt. Cmdr. Marshall O. Wright of VF-211 flew an F-8E Crusader, BuNo 150923, from *Bon Homme Richard* and shot down a MiG-17F with an AIM-9D Sidewinder missile. Lt. Cmdr. Theodore R. Swartz and his wingman, Lt. John M. Waples, of VA-76 flew two A-4Cs, BuNos 148609 and 147792, respectively, from *Bon Homme Richard*, and rocketed two taxiing MiGs. One of the Frescoes exploded and the other stopped. Two additional MiG-17s attacked the two Skyhawks and Swartz shot down one with a Zuni 5-inch rocket, subsequently receiving the Silver Star. Navy and Air Force aircraft together claimed ten Frescoes at the two fields. The North Vietnamese responded by dispersing aircraft and strengthening defenses, and built dummy aircraft and antiaircraft and missile sites to entice U.S. aircraft to squander ordnance.

15 MAY • The Chief of Naval Operations directed the establishment of an aircraft intermediate maintenance department in all operating carriers except the ship operating with the Naval Air Training Command. The new organization was to assume responsibility for maintenance afloat formerly held by the air wing and air group commanders.

19 MAY • Cmdr. Charles Fritz and Capt. Alex Gillespie, USMC, piloted two A-7A Corsair IIs during a transatlantic crossing from NAS Patuxent River, Md., to Evreux, France. Their 3,327 nautical-mile flight in 7 hours, 1 minute, established an unofficial record for long-distance unrefueled flight by light attack jets.

K 58290

A crewmember reloads an M-60 machine gun on a Marine UH-1E Iroquois.

69970

An A-7 Corsair II of VA-86.

NH 69963

A Pratt & Whitney technician makes an adjustment to a TF30 turbofan engine for an A-7 Corsair II. The engine powered the Navy's A-7A, B, and Cs but was replaced by the more powerful Allison TF41 in the A-7E.

20 MAY • As tensions mounted between Arabs and Israelis, the Sixth Fleet deployed *Saratoga* (CVA 60) to the eastern Mediterranean. On 25 May, *America* (CVA 66) received orders to rendezvous with *Saratoga* north of Crete. *Intrepid* (CVS 11) operated independently within the Fleet while en route to Vietnamese waters and, on 31 May, passed through the Suez Canal southbound. These ships performed a non-combat deterrent role against Soviet naval deployments to the area during the period leading to the Six-Day War.

24 MAY • Following a ten-month deployment to the western Pacific during the last combat tour for ships of her type, seaplane tender *Currituck* (AV 7) returned to NAS North Island, Calif.

5 JUNE • The Arabs and Israelis began the Six-Day War. *Saratoga* (CVA 60) and *America* (CVA 66) maneuvered in the vicinity of Crete. On 8 June, Israeli aircraft and three motor torpedo boats attacked technical research ship *Liberty* (AGTR 5) killing 34 men and wounding 169 while she conducted communications and electronic research 13 nautical miles off the Sinai Peninsula.

The Sixth Fleet ordered *America* and *Saratoga* to respond by using "force including destruction as necessary." *America* embarked A-4Cs of VA-36, -64, and -66 and launched four of the Skyhawks to counterattack the Israelis but directed the jets to remain clear of land. The Israelis apologized and maintained that the attacks resulted from mistaken identity and the A-4s received recall orders.

America (CVA 66) tests her water washdown system for firefighting. The flush-deck nozzles can provide up to 27,000 gallons of water per minute.

Meanwhile, F-4B Phantom IIs of VF-33 and -102 flew combat air patrols over *America* and *Liberty*, and RA-5C Vigilantes of RVAH-5 completed reconnaissance missions. The following day, *Saratoga* steamed south of Cyprus as a show of force.

America aided *Liberty* and made her nearest approach to the fighting about 100 nautical miles north of Alexandria, Egypt. *America* transferred medical teams to destroyers *Davis* (DD 937) and *Massey* (DD 778), and, on 9 June, the destroyers rendezvoused with *Liberty*. Two SH-3A Sea Kings from HS-9 Detachment 66, embarked on board *America*, evacuated casualties to the carrier. *Liberty* completed temporary repairs at Valletta, Malta.

18 JUNE • An LC-130F Hercules of VX-6 completed the first scheduled winter flight to Antarctica by flying from Christchurch, New Zealand, to Williams Field seven miles from McMurdo Station. Earlier winter missions had been made to Antarctica as a result of medical emergencies.

30 JUNE • Naval Air Transport Wing, Pacific, was disestablished at NAS Moffett Field, Calif.

1 JULY • A Titan IIIC carried the Department of Defense Gravity Experiment (DODGE) satellite into orbit from John F. Kennedy Space Center, Fla. The Applied Physics Laboratory developed DODGE under the management of NAVAIR to provide a three-axis passive stabilization system for use on satellites orbiting the earth at synchronous altitudes. On 25 July, DODGE made the first full-disc color photograph of the earth from space.

1 JULY • The Office of the Naval Weather Service was redesignated the Naval Weather Service Command and its mission underwent modification to ensure the fulfillment of Navy meteorological requirements and Department of Defense requirements for oceanographic analyses and to provide technical guidance in meteorological matters. The Naval Weather Service Division, Op-09B7, was disestablished, and its functions were assigned to the new command.

1 JULY • Naval Air Propulsion Test Center was established with its headquarters at Trenton, N.J. The move resulted from the merger of the Naval Air Turbine Test Station, Trenton, and the Aeronautical Engine Laboratory, NAEC Philadelphia, Pa.

19 JULY • Air Transport Squadron 3 was disestablished as the last Navy component of the Military Airlift Command, McGuire AFB, N.J. The decision ended an interservice partnership that began on 1 June 1948 with the combination of Navy and Air Force transport squadrons to form the Military Air Transport Service.

29 JULY • A fire erupted on board *Forrestal* (CVA 59) while she launched strikes against North Vietnamese targets. Pilot Lt. Cmdr. James E. Bangert and radar intercept officer Lt. j.g. Lawrence E. McKay from VF-11 manned an F-4B Phantom II, BuNo 153061, Aircraft No. 110, that inadvertantly launched a Zuni 5-inch rocket that struck an A-4E on the port side of the ship. Some 132 men died in the ensuing fire and weapon explosions, two disappeared (missing, presumed dead), and 62 suffered injuries. Twenty-one aircraft were stricken; seven F-4Bs, 11 A-4Es, and three RA-5C Vigliantes. Investigators revealed maintenance issues but cleared Bangert and McKay, and the flight deck film became mandatory viewing for fire fighting trainees.

Ships that aided *Forrestal* included *Intrepid* (CVS 11), *Bon Homme Richard* (CVA 31), and *Oriskany* (CVA 34). Helicopters from ships and from Da Nang AB, South Vietnam, rescued men from the flames and the sea. Pilot Lt. David Clement, copilot Ens. Leonard M. Eiland Jr., and crew ADJ3 James O. James Jr. and AN Albert E. Barrows of HC-1 Detachment G, flying plane guard in a UH-2A Seasprite, saved five men from the water in the first hour.

Among those who survived the inferno was pilot Lt. Cmdr. John S. McCain III, who climbed from A-4E Skyhawk, Aircraft No. 416. On 26 October 1967, a North Vietnamese surface-to-air missile shot McCain down and he was held captive until 1973. He subsequently received the Distinguished Flying Cross, Silver Star, and Purple Heart, and became an Arizona senator and presidential candidate.

29 JULY • Vice President Hubert H. Humphrey announced the impending release of the Transit Navy Navigation Satellite System for use by merchant ships and for commercial manufacture of shipboard receivers.

15 AUGUST • Adm. James S. Russell (Ret.) convened the first meeting of the Aircraft Carrier Safety Review Panel. The panel examined the actual and potential sources of fire and explosions in aircraft carriers with the objective of minimizing their occurrence and damage, and to propose further improvements in the equipment and techniques used to fight fires and to control damage by explosions.

10 OCTOBER • Rear Adm. Albert C. Read (Ret.) (Naval Aviator No. 24) died in Miami, Fla. Read graduated from the Naval Academy Class of 1907, and contributed to the development of naval aviation from his commencement of flight training on 8 July 1915, including command of NC-4 during the first flight across the Atlantic in 1919, through his retirement on 1 September 1946.

21 OCTOBER • Lt. Cmdr. Wilmer P. Cook and Lt. j.g. Mitchell L. Watson of VA-155 each flying an A-4E Skyhawk from *Coral Sea* (CVA 43) spotted six North Vietnamese torpedo boats among a large group of fishing junks near Thanh Hoa, North Vietnam. The duo sank four of the vessels with 250- and 500-pound bombs, damaged the fifth, and compelled the sixth to escape into a river mouth.

24 OCTOBER • Cmdr. James B. Linder of Carrier Air Wing 15 led a strike group comprising aircraft from *Coral Sea* (CVA 43), *Oriskany* (CVA 34), and the USAF against the airfield at Phuc Yen, 11 miles northwest of Hanoi, North Vietnam. The following day, two additional raids concentrated on MiGs parked in revetments. The attack destroyed an estimated eight MiGs on the ground and cratered the taxiways with 500- and 750-pound bombs. Several airborne MiGs refused to engage, but the defenders fired an estimated 30 surface-to-air missiles that shot down two F-4B Phantom IIs of VF-151 manned by Cmdr. Charles R. Gillespie Jr. and Lt. j.g. Richard C. Clark, and by Lts. (j.g.) Robert F. Frishmann and Earl G. Lewis. Gillespie, Frishmann, and Lewis endured captivity until their release after the war, but Clark died.

25 OCTOBER • A Zuni 5-inch rocket ignited during a routine test in the forward assembly area on board *Coral Sea* (CVA 43) and burned nine sailors, three critically. All nine casualties were flown for treatment to Clark AFB, Philippines.

31 OCTOBER • *Currituck* (AV 7) was decommissioned as the last seaplane tender in service and transferred to the Reserve Fleet, Mare Island, Calif.

NOVEMBER • In 1966, the Navy created a project initially designated Air Launched Acoustical Reconnaissance as part of the Trail Road Interdiction Mission—better known as the "McNamara Line" after Secretary of Defense Robert S. McNamara—to monitor communist infiltration into South Vietnam, Cambodia, and Laos. In August 1966, a scientific study group proposed a broader air-supported barrier system

110794

An F-4B Phantom II of VF-143 off *Constellation* (CVA 64) fires Zuni 5-inch rockets over the South China Sea during a 1964 exercise.

and the next month the Secretary of Defense established the Defense Communications Planning Group to implement the concept. Beginning this month, 12 VO-67 OP-2E Neptunes from Nakhon Phanom AB, Thailand, flew the first naval combat missions of the project to seed suspected infiltration routes with sensors. Enemy 37mm gunfire drove the flights to 5,000 feet, and sensors dropped from the higher altitude impacted the soil and were ineffective. The Air Force absorbed the program in June 1968.

6 NOVEMBER • Pilot Cmdr. Joseph P. Smolinski and copilot Cmdr. George A. Surovik of VP-40 completed the last operational flight by seaplanes of the U.S. Navy in an SP-5B Marlin at NAS North Island, Calif.

6 NOVEMBER • Liberian freighter *Loyal Fortunes* en route from Saigon, South Vietnam, to Kaohsiung, Taiwan, ran aground and began to break up on Pratas Reef, 170 miles southeast of Hong Kong. On 7 November, two helicopters operating from *Coral Sea* (CVA 43) rescued all 37 crewmembers and the carrier returned the mariners to Hong Kong.

9 NOVEMBER • Unmanned Apollo 4 launched from John F. Kennedy Space Center, Fla. The mission accomplished the main objectives of the initial all-up test of a Saturn V launch vehicle and of the Command Module Block II heatshield. The spacecraft splashed down in the Pacific about 600 miles northwest of Hawaii and within nine miles of its target point. Heavy seas delayed the recovery of the command module, apex heatshield, and a main parachute by *Bennington* (CVS 20).

NASA 67H1536

A diver prepares the Apollo 4 space capsule for recovery by *Bennington* (CVS 20) after it splashed down 934 nautical miles northwest of Honolulu, Hawaii, on 9 November 1967.

1968

19 JANUARY • A VR-24 C-130 Hercules and helicopters from NAF Sigonella, Italy, delivered food, clothing, and medicine to aid about 40,000 people made homeless by an earthquake in the region of Montevago, Sicily.

23 JANUARY • The North Koreans seized naval intelligence vessel *Pueblo* (AGER 2) in international waters; the ship made her closest point of approach to land at 15.8 nautical miles from the island of Ung-Do. The captors took *Pueblo* into Wŏnsan. The United States alerted commands including Task Group 77.5, consisting of *Enterprise* (CVAN 65), which reached a position in the East China Sea about 550 nautical miles south of Wŏnsan near 31°17'N, 129°8'E, when Commander Seventh Fleet Vice Adm. William F. Bringle ordered her to make "best speed" to the north. Foul weather had damaged aircraft and *Enterprise* could only launch 20 bombers that would have reached the Wŏnsan area too late to affect the outcome. In addition, insufficient numbers of ready Marine Corps and Air Force aircraft existed to support the rescue.

During the succeeding days, retaliatory scenarios ranged from limited strikes against North Korean forces at Wŏnsan to aerial mining of the harbor by A-6 Intruders, a blockade of Wŏnsan or additional ports, or raids against further military targets requiring Navy, Marine, and Air Force aircraft including Boeing B-52D Stratofortresses. Reinforcements included *Yorktown* (CVS 10) and *Ranger* (CVA 61). On 27 January, six carrier squadrons of the Naval Air Reserve reported for active duty. The fighting in Vietnam required a shift in operations and, on 16 February, *Enterprise* received orders to turn around. On 1 March, *Kearsarge* (CVS 33) relieved *Yorktown*. Four days later *Coral Sea* (CVA 43) relieved *Ranger*. On 21 March, the United States ended the standing carrier presence in the area. On

A Marine UH-34D Seahorse, BuNo 150225, delivers ammunition to Marine gunners in South Vietnam. This helicopter survived the war and was stricken in 1972 at Pensacola, Fla.

NH 69965

The eighth Marine CH-53A Sea Stallion built, BuNo 151691, displays its heavy-lift capability. The type first entered service in 1966.

NAH 002810

A UH-1B Iroquois gunship of HAL-3 searches for People's Liberation Armed Forces (Viet Cong) infiltrators within the Mekong Delta, April 1968.

16 September, the Department of Defense announced the return of the six Naval Air Reserve squadrons to inactive status within the following six weeks. In early December, *Hancock* (CVA 19) sailed in the Sea of Japan just before North Korea released its captives.

28 MARCH • Secretary of the Navy Paul R. Ignatius approved the establishment of a new restricted line officer category (152x) called the aeronautical maintenance duty officer.

31 MARCH • President Lyndon B. Johnson announced the cessation of the bombing of North Vietnamese targets north of the 20th parallel on the following day as an indication of U.S. willingness to make concessions to open the way for peace talks.

4 APRIL • Apollo 6 launched from John F. Kennedy Space Center, Fla. The unmanned mission encountered mechanical and technical problems and splashed down in the mid-Pacific about 380 miles north of Hawaii and 57 miles up-range from the predicted recovery area. Despite heavy swells, amphibious assault ship *Okinawa* (LPH 3) retrieved the spacecraft. In December NASA reported that Apollo 6 was "not a success in accordance with . . . mission objectives."

5 APRIL • Astronauts Capt. James A. Lovell Jr., Stuart A. Roosa, and Charles M. Duke Jr. participated in a recovery test of Spacecraft 007 in the Gulf of Mexico through 7 April. The test crew did not encounter serious habitability problems but also did not "recommend the Apollo spacecraft for any extended sea voyages."

3 MAY • The Navy combined the Aviation and Submarine Safety Centers to form the Naval Safety Center, Norfolk, Va. The establishment of the Office of the Assistant Chief of Naval Operations (Safety) occurred at the same time.

6 MAY • Astronaut Neil A. Armstrong crashed while piloting Lunar Landing Research Vehicle No. 1 during training at Ellington AFB, Texas. Armstrong ejected after losing control of the vehicle and landed by parachute with minor injuries. A loss of attitude control caused the accident. The investigators called for improvements in the vehicle design and operating practices and more stringent control over flying programs.

22 JUNE • The keel for *Nimitz* (CVN 68) was laid at Newport News Shipbuilding and Dry Dock Company, Va.

The first Marine AV-8A, BuNo 158384, demonstrates Harrier hover capabilities while in service with VMA-513, c. 1970. This aircraft was later converted to the YAV-8C and crashed on takeoff from *Tarawa* (LHA 1) on 5 September 1980.

1 JULY • To ensure a more rapid and efficient transition to combat status in the event of mobilization, the Naval Air Reserve was reorganized into wings and squadrons known collectively as the Naval Air Reserve Force. Effective on 1 August, Commander Naval Air Reserve Training assumed additional duty as Commander, Naval Air Reserve Force.

6 JULY • VMO-2 at Da Nang received the first OV-10As to arrive in South Vietnam. The counterinsurgency warfare Broncos flew forward air control, visual reconnaissance, and helicopter escort missions.

18 JULY • *Coral Sea* (CVA 43) completed carrier suitability trials of F-4K Phantom IIs for the Royal Navy off California. On 23 and 24 July, the ship completed carrier suitability trials of the F-111B. Aircraft No. 4, BuNo 151974, carried out ten arrested and eight touch-and-go landings. *Coral Sea* reported that sailors of V-3 Division considered the results "inconsistent" with the size of the ship because F-111Bs proved large and unwieldy and difficult to move.

24 AUGUST • A change in uniform regulations provided a new breast insignia for sailors and Marines qualified as flight officers. Effective on 31 December, the new wings replaced the old naval aviation observer wings.

Maj. Jacob E. Iles, USMC, an exchange pilot with RAF Wittering, England, instructs pilots converting to AV-8A Harriers in their new vocabulary, 23 March 1971.

NASA 68H986

The Apollo 7 astronauts—(from left) Capt. Walter M. Schirra Jr., Lt. Col. Donn F. Eisele, USAF, and Maj. R. Walter Cunningham, USMCR—on board *Essex* (CVS 9) after their splashdown, 22 October 1968.

SEPTEMBER • Col. Thomas H. Miller Jr., USMC, and Lt. Col. Clarence M. Baker, USMC, generated Marine interest in the acquisition of Harrier vertical takeoff and landing jets during a flight of a Harrier in England. On 22 October 1969, NAVAIR and the British government concluded an agreement to acquire AV-8As for the Marine Corps.

11 OCTOBER • Apollo 7, crewed by Capt. Walter M. Schirra Jr., Lt. Col. Donn F. Eisele, USAF, and Maj. R. Walter Cunningham, USMCR, launched from John F. Kennedy Space Center, Fla., as the first manned Apollo flight. It accomplished all the primary mission objectives, and on 14 October, the astronauts made the first live TV broadcast from a manned U.S. spacecraft. On 22 October, it splashed down in the Atlantic about 285 miles south of Bermuda and approximately eight miles from primary recovery ship *Essex* (CVS 9). Helicopters of HS-5 operating from *Essex* returned the astronauts to the carrier.

1 NOVEMBER • In response to previous orders from President Lyndon B. Johnson, all bombing of North Vietnam ceased at 2100 Saigon time. Earlier in the day, Cmdr. Kenneth E. Enney completed the last Navy mission over the restricted area in an A-7A Corsair II from *Constellation* (CVA 64).

6 NOVEMBER • The National Park Service of the Department of the Interior designated the lighter-than-air hangar at NAS Lakehurst, N.J. a National Historic Landmark.

15 NOVEMBER • The intensification of aerial efforts to interdict communist infiltration into South Vietnam, Cambodia, and Laos following the halt of the bombing of North Vietnam included a program designated Commando Hunt. Naval aircraft flew about one-fourth of the program's raids. Commando Hunt II attacked enemy efforts to repair bombed and washed-out roads beginning with the monsoons in May 1969. Commando Hunt III alternated daytime strikes against convoys and nighttime raids on antiaircraft and surface-to-air missile sites from November 1969 to April 1970. Commando Hunts IV and V attacked trucks and transshipment points, repair shops, and supply dumps. Commando Hunts VI and VII bombed the strategic passes leading into Laos and then sowed sensors along likely smuggling routes to identify infiltrators. The campaign cratered the landscape and led to widespread deforestation but failed to halt the infiltration.

21 DECEMBER • Apollo 8, crewed by Col. Frank Borman, USAF, Capt. James A. Lovell Jr., and Maj. William A. Anders, USAF, launched from John F. Kennedy Space Center, Fla. Apollo 8 achieved all mission objectives, and the crew became the first humans to leave the earth's gravitational field and to fly around the moon. On the fourth day, the astronauts temporarily lost communications as they passed behind the moon but became the first men to view the satellite's far side. On 27 December, the spacecraft made a predawn splash down in the Pacific within three miles of primary recovery ship *Yorktown* (CVS 10). As planned, aircraft and pararescue swimmers waited until local sunrise 50 minutes later, and then helicopters of HS-4 recovered and flew the crew to *Yorktown*.

1969

1 JANUARY • Through the New Year, American aircraft had flown 183,821 tactical sorties during the war over Laos including 24,842 Navy and 10,668 Marine missions, claimed the destruction of 4,106 vehicles and 820 bridges, and cut roads almost 13,000 times.

3 JANUARY • VAL-4 was established at NAS North Island, Calif. This first Navy squadron of its type operated OV-10As and deployed to Vietnam in March, where the Broncos flew from two airfields in the Mekong Delta supporting U.S. and South Vietnamese riverine actions.

14 JANUARY • A fire erupted on board *Enterprise* (CVAN 65) while she trained off Hawaii en route to the Vietnam War. The exhaust from a No. 6 MD3A Aircraft Starter Unit overheated a Mk 32 Zuni rocket warhead on an F-4J Phantom II. The conflagration claimed 26 lives, two men were never recovered, and 371 sustained injuries. The fire destroyed 15 aircraft (eight F-4Js, six A-7B Corsair IIs, and an EKA-3B Skywarrior) and heavily damaged 14 (three F-4Js, three A-7Bs, two RA-5C Vigilantes, three EKA-3Bs, two E-2A Hawkeyes, and one UH-2C Seasprite). Frigate *Bainbridge* (DLGN 25), destroyers *Benjamin Stoddert* (DDG 22) and *Rogers* (DD 876), salvage ship *Deliver* (ARS 23), tugs *Hitchiti* (ATF 103) and *Moctobi* (ATF 105), and a Coast Guard vessel together with Navy, Coast Guard, and Air Force aircraft assisted. *Enterprise* completed repairs at Pearl Harbor Naval Shipyard and, on 11 March, continued her voyage.

27 JANUARY • Commander, Naval Air Systems Command directed the phase-out of the Naval Aviation Integrated Logistic Support (NAILS) Task Force. The force had made an in-depth study of aviation logistics with particular emphasis on spares and repair parts support management, and recommended the establishment of a NAILS Center.

3 FEBRUARY • The Naval Air Systems Command issued a contract to Grumman Corporation for the development of high-performance variable-sweep wing F-14A Tomcats to replace F-4 Phantom IIs, together with the manufacture of six experimental jets.

13 FEBRUARY • *Randolph* (CVS 15) was decommissioned and placed in the Reserve Fleet.

3 MARCH • Apollo 9 manned by James A. McDivitt, USAF, Col. David R. Scott, USAF, and civilian Russell L. Schweickart launched from John F. Kennedy Space Center, Fla. The astronauts accomplished all mission objectives, and on 13 March, the command module splashed down in the Atlantic about 180 miles east of the Bahamas. A helicopter

North Korean MiGs shoot down Deep Sea 129, an unarmed EC-121M, BuNo 135749, of VQ-1, similar to this Warning Star, killing all 31 crewmembers, 14 April 1969.

from HS-3 operating from amphibious assault ship *Guadalcanal* (LPH 7) recovered the astronauts.

14 APRIL • North Korean MiGs shot down Deep Sea 129, an unarmed VQ-1 EC-121M, BuNo 135749, while the Constellation flew a routine reconnaissance patrol from NAS Atsugi, Japan, in international airspace over the Sea of Japan near 41°12'N, 131°48'E. The attack killed all 31 crewmembers. The United States prepared contingency plans ranging from tactical air raids against North Korean military targets to aerial mining by A-6 Intruders operating from carriers, a blockade, or expanded strikes. On 16 April, the activation of Task Force 71 to protect such flights initially comprised *Enterprise* (CVAN 65) to sail in an area in the Sea of Japan designated Defender Station. Reinforcements at times included battleship *New Jersey* (BB 62), *Ranger* (CVA 61), and *Ticonderoga* (CVA 14). Negotiations gradually diffused the tension and, on 3 May, *Enterprise* turned for the East China Sea. From 25 to 27 May and on 6 June, *Kitty Hawk* (CVA 63) patrolled Defender Station.

7 MAY • Pilot Lt. Cmdr. Melvin J. Hartman, USCG, and copilot Lt. Larry Minor, USCG, in an HC-130H Hercules designated Coast Guard No. 1453, flew the first Coast Guard aircraft directly over the geographic North Pole from CGAS Kodiak, Alaska. The record was achieved during an ice reconnaissance flight along a potential route to transport oil from the North Slope of Alaska by way of the Northwest Passage.

18 MAY • Apollo 10 crewed by Maj. Thomas P. Stafford, USAF, Cmdr. Eugene A. Cernan, and Lt. Cmdr. John W. Young launched from John F. Kennedy Space Center, Fla. This first lunar orbital mission with a complete spacecraft achieved all the primary mission objectives of evaluating performance and support. On 26 May, the command module splashed down in the Pacific about three miles from amphibious assault ship *Princeton* (LPH 5). A helicopter from HS-4 carried the astronauts to the ship.

26 MAY • A major development in carrier fire prevention occurred when *Franklin D. Roosevelt* (CVA 42) put to sea from Norfolk Naval Shipyard, Va., after an 11-month overhaul that included installation of a deck-edge spray system using a new seawater-compatible, fire-fighting chemical dubbed "Light Water."

1143446

The second YOV-10A Bronco light reconnaissance aircraft flies in the nondescript Tri-Service markings. The type was flown by the Marines, Navy, and Air Force.

1 JUNE • Lt. Col. R. Lewis, USMC, and Maj. C. L. Phillips, USMC, broke a world record for point-to-point distance by a light turboprop aircraft during a 2,539.78 mile flight in an OV-10 Bronco from Stephenville, Newfoundland, to Mildenhall, England.

24 JUNE • Lt. Dean Smith and Lt. j.g. James Sherlock of VF-103 performed the first operational "hands off" arrested landing using the AN/SPN-42 Automatic Carrier Landing System in an F-4J Phantom II on board *Saratoga* (CVA 60). The AN/SPN-42 had emerged from the AN/SPN-10.

30 JUNE • *Essex* (CVS 9) was decommissioned and assigned to the Reserve Fleet.

14 JULY • Corsair II West Coast training squadron VA-122 at NAS Lemoore, Calif., received the first A-7E assigned to an operational squadron. A-7Es incorporated heads-up and map displays where vital information from flight and navigation instruments projected into the pilots' normal field of vision permitted their concentration without looking down at instruments.

16 JULY • Apollo 11, crewed by Neil A. Armstrong, Col. Edwin E. Aldrin Jr., USAF, and Lt. Col. Michael Collins, USAF, launched from John F. Kennedy Space Center, Fla. On 20 July, Armstrong and Aldrin in lunar module *Eagle* separated from command and service module *Columbia* and descended to the moon. "Houston, Tranquility Base here—the *Eagle* has landed," Armstrong reported to mission control when the lunar module touched down on the moon at 1618 EDT. At 2256 EDT, a naval aviator became the first person to walk on the moon when Armstrong stepped onto the surface. On 24 July, *Columbia* splashed down in the Pacific about 920 miles southwest of Honolulu, Hawaii, and 15 miles from primary recovery ship *Hornet* (CVS 12). Cmdr. Donald S. Jones, commanding officer of HS-4, piloted an SH-3D Sea King, BuNo 152711, designated Recovery One, that retrieved and carried the astronauts to *Hornet*. President Richard M. Nixon was on board the carrier and welcomed the astronauts through a window in their quarantine facility. The recovery force also retrieved *Columbia*. Apollo 11 achieved all the primary mission objectives.

NASA AS12497278

Apollo 12 astronaut Charles P. Conrad snaps a photograph of colleague Alan L. Bean during lunar soil collection activities on the Oceanus Procellarum in November 1969. Three of the first four men to walk on the moon, including Conrad and Bean, have flown for the Navy.

1 AUGUST • NAVAIR issued a contract to Lockheed-California Company for development of all weather carrier antisubmarine warfare S-3A Vikings to replace S-2 Trackers.

17 AUGUST • Hurricane Camille devastated the Gulf Coast with heavy rains and flooding that rendered many people homeless. The 16,500 servicemembers who supported emergency assistance in the wake of the disaster included HT-8, which evacuated more than 820 people on 20 August from Pass Christian, Miss. President Richard M. Nixon subsequently wrote HT-8 a letter praising the squadron for its services.

24 AUGUST • Icebreaker-oceanographic research vessel *Manhattan* sailed from Chester, Pa., to test the feasibility of transporting oil from the North Slope of Alaska by way of the Northwest Passage. Aircraft and vessels that supported the expedition included a Coast Guard HC-130B Hercules, Coast Guard cutters *Northwind* (WAGB 282) and *Staten Island* (WAGB 278), and Canadian icebreakers *Louis S. St-Laurent* and *John A. Macdonald*. *Northwind* and *Staten Island* each normally embarked an HH-52A Seaguard. An NC-121K Constellation, BuNo 141325, of VXN-8 named *Arctic Fox*, provided ice surveillance for *Manhattan* through the Northwest Passage as part of Project Birdseye 6-69—an Arctic ice-survey mission initiated in March 1962 to gather ice flow information for the Naval Oceanographic Office. *Manhattan* returned to New York City on 30 October.

K87381

UH-1N Iroquois approach an LC-130 to refuel from the Hercules during operations in Antarctica. The Huey was first introduced to the continent during Operation Deep Freeze 72.

31 AUGUST • Two LC-130 Hercules of VXE-6 arrived at McMurdo Sound, Antarctica, six weeks in advance of the opening of Operation Deep Freeze 70. The passengers included Commander Naval Support Force Antarctica Rear Adm. David F. Welch and seven scientists.

1 SEPTEMBER • The Naval Aviation Integrated Logistic Support Center was established to provide intensified logistics management at NAS Patuxent River, Md.

23 SEPTEMBER • A UH-2B Seasprite operating from light cruiser *Galveston* (CLG 3) rescued 15 crewmen and passengers from Greek tanker *Angel Gabriel* after she ran aground and began to break up in a storm near St. Thomas Point, Marsascal, Malta.

30 SEPTEMBER • Carrier Anti-Submarine Air Group (CVSG) 57 was disestablished. The disestablishment of Carrier Air Wing 10 followed on 28 November and CVSG-52 on 15 December.

20 OCTOBER • *Ticonderoga* (CVA 14) underwent conversion to an antisubmarine warfare aircraft carrier (CVS 14) through 28 May 1970 at Long Beach Naval Shipyard, Calif.

22 OCTOBER • NAVAIR and the British government executed a memorandum of agreement concerning the purchase of Hawker-Siddely Harriers. A subsequent letter of offer covered the procurement of 12 AV-8As for the Marines with initial delivery scheduled for January 1971.

NH 69969

A CH-46A Sea Knight, BuNo 151911, of HMM-265 lands on board *Okinawa* (LPH 3) in 1968. The medium assault transport helicopter was designed specifically for Marine Corps requirements.

5 NOVEMBER • Liberian tanker *Keo* broke in half 30 miles east of Cape May, N.J. Two C-130 Hercules, frigate *Fox* (DLG 33), destroyers *Hugh Purvis* (DD 709) and *Leary* (DD 879), and two Coast Guard cutters attempted to rescue the crew, but all 36 perished.

14 NOVEMBER • Apollo 12 manned by the all–naval aviator crew of Cmdr. Charles Conrad Jr., Cmdr. Richard F. Gordon Jr., and Lt. Cmdr. Alan L. Bean launched from John F. Kennedy Space Center, Fla. On 18 November, Conrad and Bean separated Lunar Module 6 *Intrepid* from Gordon and Command and Service Module 108 *Yankee Clipper*, and the following day *Intrepid* landed on the moon's Ocean of Storms. After 31 ½ hours on the lunar surface, the astronauts and *Intrepid* rendezvoused with the command module. On 24 November, *Yankee Clipper* splashed down in mid-Pacific within five miles of primary recovery ship *Hornet* (CVS 12). An SH-3D Sea King from HS-4 lifted the astronauts to *Hornet*. Apollo 12 achieved all mission objectives.

NH 69966

A UH-46A Sea Knight, BuNo 150966, of HC-1 makes a vertical replenishment delivery.

1 DECEMBER • Amphibious assault ship *Boxer* (LPH 4) was decommissioned.

CHAPTER 10

Defeat and Decline

1970–1979

Naval aviation began its seventh decade with the United States embroiled in the Vietnam War, but an uneasy truce resulted in disengagement from the war in 1973. Two years later, naval air power assisted in the evacuation of refugees who fled the North Vietnamese conquest of South Vietnam. During the subsequent years, naval aviation helped rescue thousands of Indochinese who set out in poor vessels to escape tyranny. Eastern Bloc naval expansion challenged Western control of the sea and Soviet cruise missiles threatened aircraft carriers. The Navy struggled to meet its commitments because of a diminishing and aging fleet that eroded through constant use, at the same time confronting declining budgets that hindered the acquisition of replacements; recruitment shortfalls and difficulties in retention; drug and alcohol abuse; and racial unrest. Americans faced recurring crises in the Middle East, and in 1979, Iranian militants captured the United States Embassy in Tehran. The decade concluded with *Midway* (CV 41) and *Kitty Hawk* (CV 63) deployed to the Indian Ocean.

The burden of naval air action in the Vietnam War fell upon the carriers and aircraft of the Seventh Fleet. To meet this responsibility, the service relied upon established weapons and material, but the war also witnessed the introduction of television-guided Walleye glide bombs designed to home automatically to their targets. Helicopters served in combat and land-based patrol aircraft scoured the South Vietnamese coastline in search of infiltrating enemy vessels during Operation Market Time. Operations Linebacker I and II waged heavy interdiction and bombing campaigns against the North Vietnamese. Aircraft carried out extensive aerial minelaying to blockade the enemy's main avenues of supply.

During his tenure, Chief of Naval Operations Adm. Elmo R. Zumwalt Jr. issued mandates, known as "Z-Grams," to change the quality of life for sailors and Marines and improved racial and gender situations in the fleet. During the 1960s and 1970s, U.S. domestic consumption of oil tripled but surplus production capacity disappeared, which made the country increasingly dependent upon foreign energy sources. In 1973, the Organization of the Petroleum Exporting Countries cut off shipments to the United States and reduced the availability of petroleum worldwide in response to President Richard M. Nixon's support of the Israelis during the Yom Kippur War. Their action only removed 10 percent of the available petroleum from the global market, but produced speculative buying by consumer countries that led to a worldwide recession. The crisis generated an acute consciousness among leaders of the position of the United States as a two-ocean nation that reemphasized the reliance upon the Navy to keep sea lanes open and commerce moving unhampered, although the American people largely failed to appreciate the shift until the 1980s.

Naval aviation nevertheless made headway in research and development. The 1970s witnessed the decommissioning of most of the remaining *Essex* (CV 9)-class carriers, the commissioning of nuclear-powered carriers *Nimitz* (CVN 68) and *Dwight D. Eisenhower* (CVN 69), and the launch of *Carl Vinson* (CVN 70). The introduction of F-14A Tomcats and AV-8A vertical and/or short takeoff and landing (V/STOL) Harriers, and the flight trials of F/A-18A Hornets took place. The addition of the Light Airborne Multipurpose System (LAMPS) combined shipboard electronics with SH-2D helicopters to confront the growing threat from submarines. The decade drew to a close with LAMPS testing in new SH-60B Seahawks, while the latest heavy-lift CH-53E Super Stallions reached readiness. Naval aviation began its eighth decade by continuing to integrate aircraft with the fleet to provide the United States with strong and flexible naval power.

NH 90350

Lt. j.g. William Belden safely ejects from A-4E Skyhawk, BuNo 150117, as it rolls into *Shangri-La*'s (CVS 38) port catwalk after suffering a brake failure following recovery, 2 July 1970. The A-4E was assigned to VA-152 of Carrier Air Wing 8.

1970

15 JANUARY • *Bennington* (CVS 20), *Valley Forge* (LPH 8), and aviation base ship *Tallahatchie County* (AVB 2) were decommissioned. The authorization for the decommissioning in 1971 of *Bon Homme Richard* (CVA 31) and *Shangri-La* (CVS 38) also occurred during 1970.

31 JANUARY • *Midway* (CVA 41) recommissioned after a four-year conversion-modernization at San Francisco Bay Naval Shipyard, Calif.

10 FEBRUARY • As part of the U.S. withdrawal from Vietnam, VMFA-542 and VMA-223 returned to MCAS El Toro, Calif. During the same month, Marine Aircraft Group 12 and VMA-211 were reassigned to Japan. In September, VMFA-122 and -314, VMA(AW)-242, Marine Aircraft Base Squadron 13, and Headquarters and Maintenance Squadron 13, returned to the United States. On 13 October, the last Marines departed from Chu Lai.

13 FEBRUARY • Amphibious assault ship *Princeton* (LPH 5) was decommissioned.

16 MARCH • The crash of an EC-121 Constellation took the lives of 23 sailors at Da Nang AB, South Vietnam.

28 MARCH • Pilot Lt. Jerome E. Beaulier and radar intercept officer Lt. j.g. Stephen J. Barkley of VF-142, embarked on board *Constellation* (CVA 64), made the first kill of a North Vietnamese MiG since the 1 November 1968 bombing halt. They shot down a MiG-21 Fishbed with an AIM-9 Sidewinder missile while escorting an unarmed Navy reconnaissance plane in an F-4J Phantom II near Thanh Hoa, North Vietnam.

Advanced aviation base ship *Tallahatchie County* (AVB 2) can beach near existing airfields and support aerial operations, such as here, at Souda Bay, Crete, in November 1968.

1 APRIL • Carrier Air Wing Reserve (CVWR) 20 and CVWR-30 were established, followed on 1 May by the establishment of Carrier Anti-Submarine Air Group Reserve (CVSGR) 70 and CVSGR-80. This move continued a program initiated in July 1968 to improve the combat readiness of the Naval Air Reserve. The reorganization placed all carrier-type squadrons in two Reserve carrier air wings and two carrier antisubmarine groups. Twelve VP and three VR squadrons joined the carrier squadrons under the control of Commander Naval Air Reserve Force.

10 APRIL • An A-4M made the first flight of the improved Skyhawk dedicated to the Marine Corps at the Douglas Aircraft Company plant, Palmdale, Calif. The aircraft included a brake parachute and an engine with 45 percent more thrust than that of the original 1954 Skyhawk design, which made the jets suitable for operations from short airfields in forward areas.

11 APRIL • Apollo 13 crewed by Capt. James A. Lovell Jr., John L. Swigert Jr., USAF, and Fred W. Haise Jr., USMCR, launched from John F. Kennedy Space Center, Fla. On 13 April, the crew reported, "Okay, Houston, we've had a problem here." A loss of oxygen and primary power in Command and Service Module 109 *Odyssey* required an immediate abort of the moon mission. On 17 April, *Odyssey* splashed down in mid-Pacific about four miles from the primary recovery vessel, amphibious assault ship *Iwo Jima* (LPH 2). An SH-3D Sea King of HS-4, Aircraft No. 407, recovered and transported the astronauts to *Iwo Jima*.

2 MAY • ALM (Antilliaanse Luchtvaart Maatschappij) Flight 980, a Douglas DC-9, crashed because of fuel exhaustion 35 miles east of St. Croix, Virgin Islands. Pilot Lt. Cmdr. James E. Rylee, copilot Lt. j.g. Donald Hartman, and aircrewmen MMC William Brazzell and MMAN Calvin Lindley of VC-8 manned an SH-3A Sea King from NS

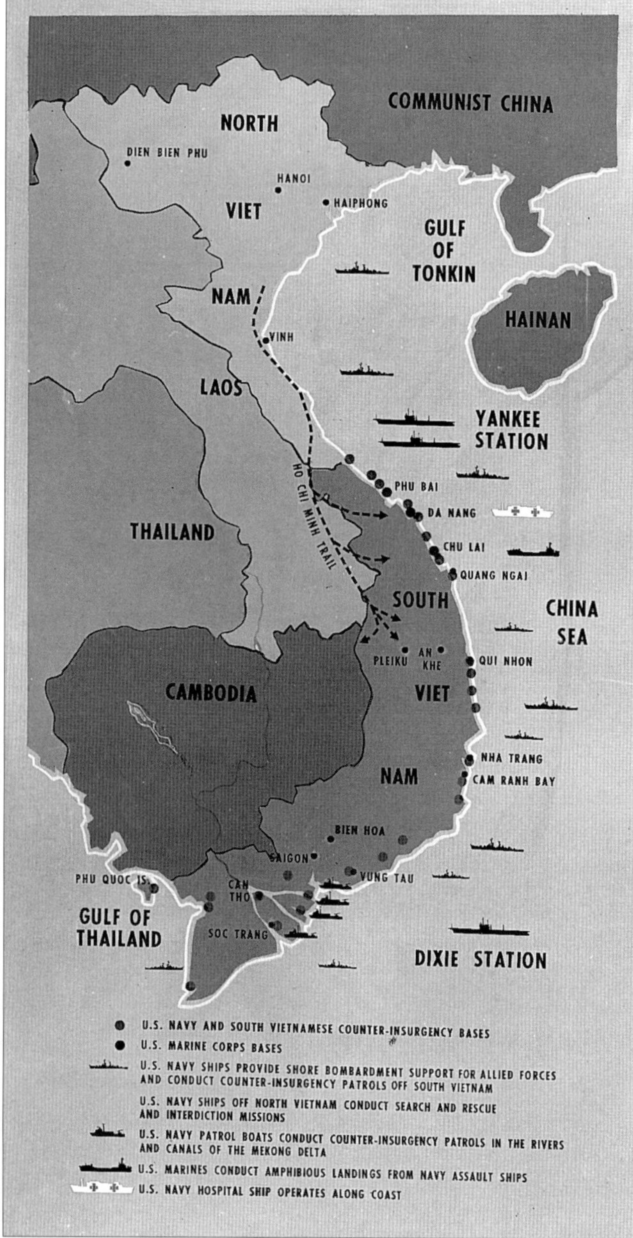

The disposition of Navy forces and bases in Southeast Asia virtually lines the coast of South Vietnam.

Roosevelt Roads, P.R., and rescued 26 of the 63 people on board. Two Coast Guard HH-52A Seaguards rescued 11 others while a Marine CH-46A Sea Knight picked up the remaining three survivors. Searchers recovered seven bodies, but failed to locate the remaining 16 victims because of harsh weather. The Sea King flew survivors to Alexander Hamilton Airport near Frederiksted, St. Croix. Rylee and Hartman received the Distinguished Flying Cross.

9 MAY • Helicopters, OV-10A Broncos, and about 30 Navy craft participated with the combined South Vietnamese/U.S. Riverine Force in strikes into the Mekong River corridor to neutralize People's Liberation Armed Forces and North Vietnamese sanctuaries in that area. These operations followed the initial series of raids by combined U.S. and South Vietnamese troops against sanctuaries in Cambodia during the first week of May.

31 MAY • An earthquake in Peru took 50,000 lives, injured 100,000 people, and rendered 800,000 homeless. Amphibious assault ship *Guam* (LPH 9), with four CH-53D Sea Stallions, ten CH-46F Sea Knights, and two UH-1E Iroquois of HMM-365 embarked, sailed from Panama and on 12 June arrived off Peru. The ship provided victims with more than 200 tons of relief supplies, and her aircraft made more than 800 mercy flights transporting medical teams into remote areas and evacuating more than 1,000 people. *Guam* departed on 21 June.

1 JUNE • Carrier Air Wings 4 and 12 were disestablished, followed on 30 June by the disestablishment of Carrier Anti-Submarine Air Group 51.

9 JUNE • Sikorsky pilot James R. Wright and copilot Col. Henry Hart, USMC, established a downtown New York, N.Y., to downtown Washington, D.C., record in a CH-53D Sea Stallion for helicopters at 156.43 mph, with an elapsed time of 1 hour, 18 minutes, 41.4 seconds. The next day they established a New York to Boston, Mass., record for helicopters of 162.72 mph, with a city-to-city time of 1 hour, 9 minutes, 23.9 seconds.

9 JUNE • Jordanian King Hussein bin Talal survived an assassination attempt. In addition, terrorists from the Popular Front for the Liberation of Palestine seized 32 hostages including 14 Americans in a hotel in Amman, Jordan. *Forrestal* (CVA 59) sailed to the eastern Mediterranean to provide air cover for a potential rescue of the hostages and evacuation of Americans endangered elsewhere within the country. The situation in Jordan calmed, but terrorists then attacked the Jordanian Embassy in Beirut, Lebanon, and the United States extended the carrier's deployment. On 15 June, the crisis abated, and two days later U.S. forces returned to normal operations.

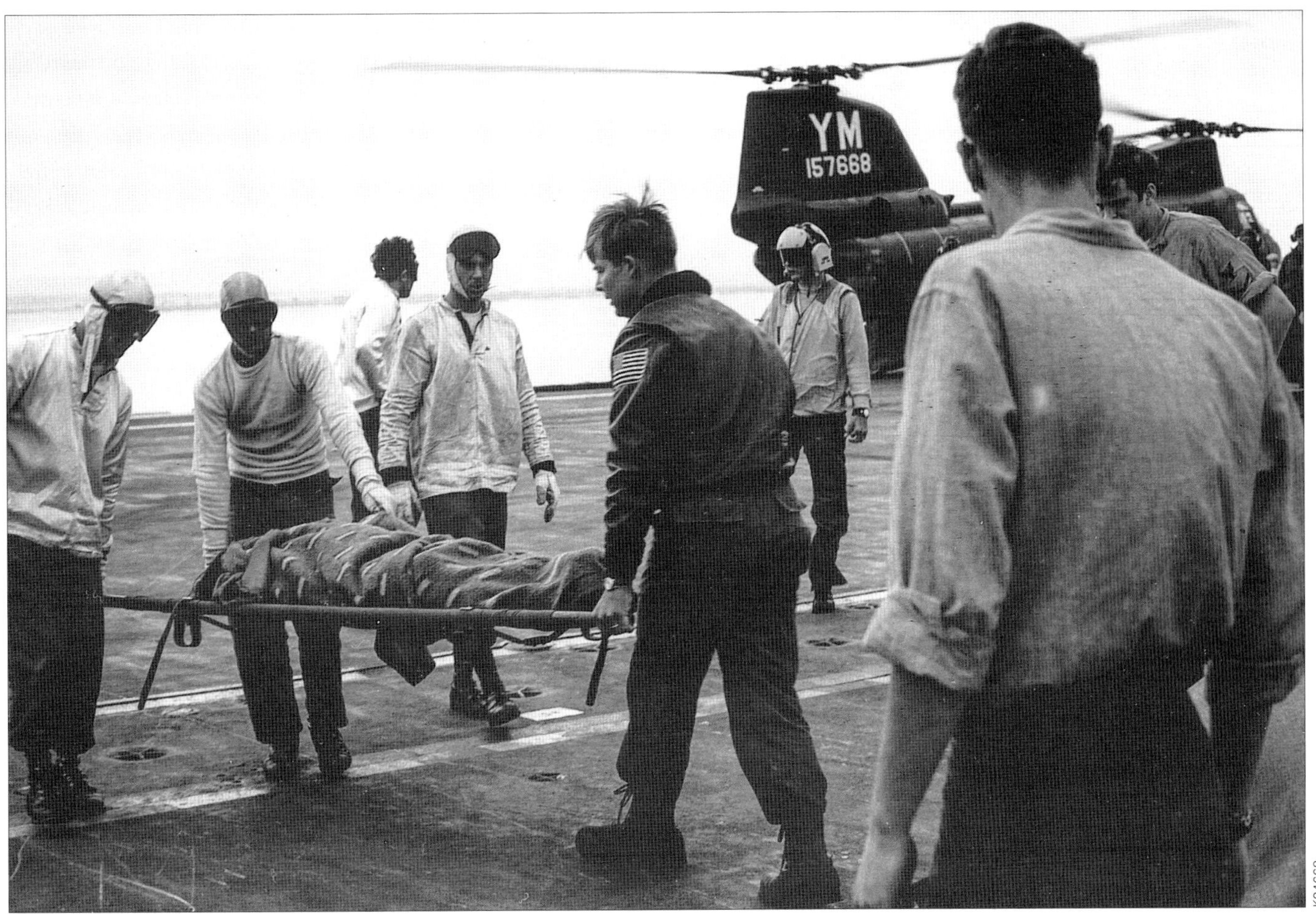

The crew of amphibious assault ship *Guam* (LPH 9) and Marines of HMM-365 assist victims of the 31 May 1970 Peruvian earthquake where more than 66,000 people died.

20 JUNE • Amphibious assault ship *Inchon* (LPH 12) was commissioned.

26 JUNE • *Hornet* (CVS 12) was decommissioned, followed the next day by the decommissioning of *Yorktown* (CVS 10).

1 JULY • NAVAIR Liaison Office, Dayton, Ohio, was disestablished. The move marked the end of an office that traced its beginning to October 1920 and the detail of an aviation officer to McCook Field to observe and report on experimental work.

17 JULY • P-3C Orions began deployed operations when VP-49 assumed patrol responsibilities at NAS Keflavik, Iceland.

15 AUGUST • The keel was laid for *Dwight D. Eisenhower* (CVN 69) at Newport News Shipbuilding and Dry Dock Company, Va.

3 SEPTEMBER • Rising tensions in the Middle East triggered an alert of the Sixth Fleet. Three days later, terrorists from the Popular Front for the Liberation of Palestine attempted to hijack four civilian airliners. The terrorists diverted two of the planes to Zarqa, Jordan, and seized and rerouted another to Cairo, Egypt, where they released the hostages and destroyed the airliner. On 8 September, the Joint Chiefs of Staff directed *Independence* (CVA 62) to a position about 100 nautical miles from the Israel-Lebanon coast. The next day, an additional hijacking brought a third aircraft to Zarqa, and on 12 September, the terrorists blew up all three (empty) airliners. On 17 September, fighting erupted between the Jordanians and terrorists, and the next day, the Syrians intervened on behalf of the Palestinians.

On 17 September, *John F. Kennedy* (CVA 67) received orders to make speed for the Mediterranean. By 22 September, *Independence* and *Saratoga* (CVA 60) steamed south of Cyprus and off the coast of Lebanon, and five

003854

An A-6A Intruder, BuNo 155668, of VA-85 drops a brace of Snakeye bombs over Vietnam. The squadron was on its single cruise with *Constellation* (CVA 64), August 1969 to May 1970.

P-3 Orions patrolled from NS Rota, Spain. *Independence* operated off the coast of Lebanon until 6 October. *Saratoga* sailed there from 17 to 25 September, and *John F. Kennedy* arrived on 24 September. Amphibious assault ship *Guam* (LPH 9), with HMM-365 embarked, reinforced these vessels from late September to 30 October. *Saratoga* departed and, on 28 September, hosted a visit by President Richard M. Nixon. The same day, Egyptian President Gamal A. Nasser died, and overnight *Saratoga* provided the president communications and intelligence support with Secretary of Defense Melvin R. Laird, Secretary of State William P. Rogers, and the joint chiefs. From 5 to 18 October, *Saratoga* returned to the eastern Mediterranean. The hijackers released their hostages, by 6 October the Sixth Fleet reduced operations to one carrier, and by July 1971 the Jordanians drove the Palestinians into Lebanon.

8 SEPTEMBER • The Department of Defense modified its basic space policy (established in March 1961) by providing for the consideration of functional responsibilities of the services in the assignment of programs for development and acquisition of space systems.

14 SEPTEMBER • Combat store ship *Niagara Falls* (AFS 3), with a UH-46A Sea Knight of HC-7 Detachment 112 embarked, rescued artist Julian Ritter and crewmembers Winifried Heiringhoff and Lauren Knox and their ketch *Galilee*, about 400 nautical miles west/northwest of Hawaii. *Niagara Falls* towed *Galilee* 150 miles to rendezvous on 16 September with Coast Guard cutter *Cape Corwin* (WPB 95326), which took the castaways and their sailboat to Oahu.

25 SEPTEMBER • An A-6A launched a Condor television-guided air-to-surface missile at a standoff distance of 56 miles from its target at NWC China Lake, Calif. The missile made a direct hit.

25 OCTOBER • Amphibious assault ship *Okinawa* (LPH 3), dock landing ship *Anchorage* (LSD 36), amphibious transport dock *Duluth* (LPD 6), and sailors and Marines from shore establishments completed four days of assistance to thousands of people following Typhoon Joan, which left 600 people dead and 80,000 without shelter across southern Luzon and Catanduanes Island, Philippines. CH-46D Sea Knights of HMM-164 lifted more than 300 tons of rice, flour, blankets, and fuel in more than 70 sorties. Naval medical teams treated more than 1,000 patients ashore.

29 OCTOBER • After the ravages of Typhoon Kate and flood waters that inundated 140 square miles of South Vietnam south of Da Nang AB, helicopters of 1st Marine Aircraft Wing performed rescue and relief operations for more than 9,000 South Vietnamese. The initial rescues began the first day when Marine Aircraft Group 16 evacuated about 900 people during floods that observers termed the most severe since 1964.

21 NOVEMBER • Aircraft flew 14 diversionary sorties from *Oriskany* (CVA 34) that included dropping flares along the North Vietnamese coast, in order to divert enemy attention from an Army–Air Force attempt to rescue U.S. prisoners from a vacated prisoner-of-war compound at Son Tây, 22 miles from Hanoi. *Oriskany* launched an additional 48 retaliatory strikes. Into 22 November, about 200 Navy and Marine aircraft from *Hancock* (CVA 19), *Oriskany*, and *Ranger* (CVA 61), together with approximately 200 Air Force aircraft also flew protective reaction air strikes—retaliation in response to enemy attacks or radar tracking—against North Vietnamese missile and antiaircraft sites south of the 19th parallel that fired on unarmed reconnaissance aircraft. President Richard M. Nixon and Assistant to the President for National Security Affairs Henry A. Kissinger thus used protective reaction raids as part of a strategy to pressure the enemy toward peace negotiations and to cover U.S. withdrawal from the war.

24 NOVEMBER • North American Rockwell test pilot Edward A. Gillespie flew a T-2C Buckeye modified with a supercritical wing configuration at Columbus, Ohio. The wing design was derived from theoretical development by Dr. Richard T. Whitcomb of NASA and promised to delay the onset of transonic shock separation, buffeting, and other aerodynamic phenomena, thus giving greater flexibility to aircraft intended for operation in the sonic speed regime.

25 NOVEMBER • The chief of Naval Material established the Navy Space Project Office with responsibility for the integration and coordination of space activities within the purview of the Naval Material Command, and responsibility for management of designated space projects.

21 DECEMBER • Grumman test pilots Robert Smyth and William Miller made the first flight of an F-14A Tomcat at Grumman's Calverton, Long Island, N.Y., plant. The aircraft's design emphasized fighter missions including air-to-air combat and fleet defense, and they became the first variable-sweep-wing fighters accepted into Navy squadron inventory.

1971

1 JANUARY • *Hancock* (CVA 19) and *Ranger* (CVA 61) continued operations with Task Force 77 from Yankee Station off Vietnam by launching interdiction missions against the Ho Chi Minh Trail in Laos, air support for allied ground forces in South Vietnam, photographic reconnaissance, combat air patrol, and electronic warfare sorties.

6 JANUARY • Maj. Gen. Homer S. Hill, USMC, accepted the first AV-8A Harrier for the Marine Corps at Dunsfold, England.

K89288

A Marine AV-8A Harrier lands on board amphibious assault ship *Guadalcanal* (LPH 7) in the Atlantic, 22 March 1971.

Apollo 14 astronauts Capt. Alan B. Shepard Jr. (left) and Maj. Stuart A. Roosa, USAF, await recovery after their splashdown in the Pacific, 9 February 1971. They, along with fellow astronaut Cmdr. Edgar D. Mitchell, and the capsule were brought on board *New Orleans* (LPH 11).

19 JANUARY • *Enterprise* (CVAN 65) completed sea trials with eight newly designed nuclear reactor cores that contained enough energy to power the ship for ten years.

22 JANUARY • Pilot Cmdr. Donald H. Lilienthal established a world record in the heavyweight turboprop class for long-distance flight in a production model P-3C Orion with a flight of 6,857 statute miles over the great circle route from NAS Atsugi, Japan, to NAS Patuxent River, Md. The 15-hour, 21-minute flight topped the Soviet Ilyushin Il-18 turboprop record of 4,761 miles set in 1967.

26 JANUARY • An AV-8A arrived to commence Board of Inspection and Survey trials for Harriers at NATC Patuxent River, Md.

27 JANUARY • Aircraft commander Cmdr. Donald H. Lilienthal established a world speed record in the heavyweight turboprop class in a P-3C Orion of 501.44 mph over a 15/25 kilometer course at NATC Patuxent River, Md.

27 JANUARY • NAVAIR directed the expedited procurement of TCW-33P VWS (ventilated wet suits) to permit their issuance to VS and VP squadrons during the winter of 1971–1972. The evaluation of 3,100 VWSs began in 1969, and enthusiastic acceptance by flight crews led to the decision to procure them for early issue rather than phased in.

29 JANUARY • EA-6B Prowlers entered service with VAQ-129 at NAS Whidbey Island, Wash. The carrier-based electronic warfare aircraft were derived from two-place A-6 Intruders and lengthened to accommodate a four-place cockpit, replacing EKA-3B Skywarriors. VAQ-129 (redesignated from VAH-10 in 1970) became the replacement training squadron when it began instructing aircrew and ground support replacement sailors for all the Navy's Prowler squadrons.

31 JANUARY • *Hancock* (CVA 19), *Ranger* (CVA 61), and *Kitty Hawk* (CVA 63) alternated on Yankee Station off Vietnam and launched a total of 3,214 sorties during January, of which 3,128 bombed in Laos. The enemy operated a seasonally high amount of road transport averaging close to 1,000 trucks per day, and A-6 Intruders and A-7 Corsair IIs proved particularly effective attacking this traffic.

31 JANUARY • Apollo 14, manned by Capt. Alan B. Shepard Jr., Cmdr. Edgar D. Mitchell, and Maj. Stuart A. Roosa, USAF, launched from John F. Kennedy Space Center, Fla. Shepard and Mitchell in Lunar Module 8 *Antares* landed on the moon. On 9 February, the trio in Command Module 110 *Kitty Hawk* splashed down in mid-Pacific, four miles from the primary recovery vessel, amphibious assault ship *New Orleans* (LPH 11). SH-3A Sea Kings of HS-6 operating from the ship recovered the astronauts.

4 FEBRUARY • Aircraft commander Cmdr. Donald H. Lilienthal set a world altitude record in horizontal flight for the heavy turboprop class in a P-3C Orion of 45,018.2 feet from NATC Patuxent River, Md.

5 FEBRUARY • Panamanian-flagged ore ship *Flamingo* lost power and drifted about 100 miles east of Sicily. Sixth Fleet destroyers attempted to take her in tow, but rough seas prevented the endeavor. *Forrestal* (CVA 59), operating in the Ionian Sea, dispatched four SH-3D Sea Kings from HS-3 through winds gusting up to 60 knots to rescue all 20 crewmembers and passengers.

5 FEBRUARY • The Navy announced the successful test firing of a Condor air-to-surface missile armed with a live warhead. An A-6 launched and guided the missile by television to score a direct hit on a target ship sailing out of sight of the Intruder.

8 FEBRUARY • Cmdr. Donald H. Lilienthal established a world altitude record for unlimited weight turboprop planes in a P-3C Orion of 46,214.5 feet, and also time-to-climb records of 3,000 meters in 2 minutes, 51.7 seconds; 6,000 meters in 5 minutes, 46.3 seconds; 9,000 meters in 10 minutes, 26.1 seconds; and 12,000 meters in 19 minutes, 42.2 seconds.

An SH-3A Sea King, BuNo 152121, of HS-6 hoists an Apollo 14 astronaut aloft from command module *Kitty Hawk* during recovery operations approximately 760 miles south of American Samoa.

17 FEBRUARY • The Weapons Systems Explosive Safety Review Board approved the service use of WMU-1/B pyrotechnic rain and snow seeding devices. These consisted of a silver iodide (catalyst) generator, and the system became the first weather modification type released for production and general use by the Navy. Later in 1971, aircraft used the device over Okinawa to enhance rainfall to help replenish the island's water reserves.

24 FEBRUARY • The Navy disclosed the deployment since June 1967 of acoubuoys—modified submarine-detecting sonobuoys—along trails in Southeast Asia to broadcast passing sounds to aircraft up to 20 miles away. The Naval Air Development Center designed the devices at Warminster, Pa.

28 FEBRUARY • Throughout February, two carriers remained on station off Vietnam as strike sorties rose to an average of 122 per day. This was the result of a 40 percent increase in enemy truck movements from the previous month that averaged more than 1,400 vehicles a day. A-7 Corsair IIs flew night all-weather minelaying missions heretofore flown exclusively by A-6 Intruders.

9 MARCH • Construction began on a joint Anglo-American naval air and radio communications station on Diego Garcia, British Indian Ocean Territory. Later in the month, Naval Mobile Construction Battalion 40 initiated the main construction effort.

10 MARCH • On Yankee Station, *Ranger* (CVA 61) and *Kitty Hawk* (CVA 63) set a record of 233 strike sorties for one day. During the ensuing six-day period, the ships scored a strike-effectiveness record that exceeded record performances by Task Force 77 during the previous three-year period.

16 MARCH • The first SH-2D LAMPS (Light Airborne Multi-Purpose System) helicopter test flight took place at the Kaman Aircraft Corporation, Bloomfield, Conn. This flight followed testing on board escort *Sims* (DE 1059) to determine deck strength for helicopter operations. Later in the month, the Navy announced the service's intention to commit 115 H-2 Seasprites to the LAMPS program.

29 MARCH • An NUH-2H Seasprite launched the first active AIM-9G Sidewinder air-to-air missile by the Weapons System Test Division of NATC Patuxent River, Md.

31 MARCH • Carriers sailing on Yankee Station launched 4,535 strike sorties in the Vietnam War during March of which 4,479 dropped bombs. These figures increased from February by 1,074 and 1,065, respectively. Aircraft flew more than 680 acoubuoy seed and interdiction missions during March with unknown results. About 75 percent of the interdiction packages, however, obtained one or more road cuts while emplacing acoubuoys.

1 APRIL • HM-12 was established at NAS Norfolk, Va., as the Navy's first helicopter squadron devoted exclusively to mine countermeasures. Squadron helicopters towed specially designed magnetic and acoustic minesweeping equipment to activate enemy mines. HM-12 flew CH-53A Sea Stallions until the deployment of RH-53D Sea Stallions built specifically for mine countermeasures.

5 APRIL • The modernization of the Naval Air Reserve continued when VA-303 received the first Reserve A-7A Corsair IIs at NAS Alameda, Calif. By the end of June, the squadron received its full complement of 12 aircraft. Less than four months later, VA-303 made the initial Reserve Corsair II deployment and marked the first extended deployment of a Reserve squadron on other than annual active duty training.

16 APRIL • A-4M Skyhawks entered squadron service with VMA-324 and -331 at MCAS Beaufort, S.C. The advanced aircraft featured a new self-contained starter, twice the 20mm ammunition load of previous Skyhawks, and 20 percent more thrust (11,200-pounds) than the latest F-variant. These M-models marked the seventh major version of the Skyhawk.

16 APRIL • VMA-513 at MCAS Beaufort, S.C., took delivery of three AV-8A Harriers, becoming the first operational U.S. high-performance vertical and/or short takeoff and landing (V/STOL) squadron.

30 APRIL • Throughout April, *Hancock* (CVA 19), *Ranger* (CVA 61), and *Kitty Hawk* (CVA 63) provided a constant two-carrier posture for Task Force 77 on Yankee Station off Vietnam with one working daylight missions and the other on a noon-to-midnight schedule. During the month, 3,648 strike sorties were flown along with an additional 12 into North Vietnam. The strikes focused on the interdiction of major Laotian entry corridors to South Vietnam.

10 MAY • *Midway* (CVA 41) relieved *Hancock* (CVA 19) off Vietnam. On 18 May, *Midway* began single-carrier operations, which had not been in effect since January when *Kitty Hawk* (CVA 63) served a solo two-week tour, on Yankee Station until the end of the month. This allowed *Kitty Hawk* and *Ranger* (CVA 61) to undergo maintenance in Japan.

21 MAY • Technical evaluation of a new fire control system with a helmet-mounted sight began at NATC Patuxent River, Md.

28 MAY • The Secretary of Defense announced measures to strengthen the Sixth Fleet by noting his intention to improve Fleet readiness by the almost continuous presence of a helicopter carrier, and by a substantial increase in the hours flown by maritime air patrols and the ship-operating days of sea patrols. The move followed an earlier announcement by the Pentagon on 24 May of the strengthening of the Sixth Fleet in response to growing Soviet naval power.

31 MAY • May strikes during the Vietnam War emphasized interdiction of Laotian entry points to South Vietnam,

Southern Laotian routes leading to Cambodia, as well as corridors throughout the South. Although weather cancellations remained at a comparatively low level, the Seventh Fleet conserved strike sorties by limiting carrier flights to 60–70 per day, resulting in a total of 2,645 sorties that delivered ordnance during the month. North Vietnamese surface-to-air missile (SAM) coverage south of 20°N continued at a high level and the increased SAM threat required additional aircraft in support of strike and reconnaissance flights. Two protective reaction strikes—retaliation in response to enemy attacks or radar tracking—occurred in North Vietnam.

28 JUNE • A proposal by the Naval Training Command Board to consolidate all naval training was approved. The board had convened under the direction of the Chief of Naval Operations on 8 February. Major recommendations included the establishment of a single training command as the chief of Naval Training with headquarters at NAS Pensacola, Fla. The chief of Naval Technical Training was established at Memphis, Tenn. The command of education and programs formerly under the chief of Naval Personnel shifted to the director of Naval Education and Training. The scheme also included the consolidation of three former air training staffs into a single staff with eight training wings to be located at major pilot training bases. Public announcement of the new single training command occurred on 21 July and became effective on 1 August.

29 JUNE • MIL-C-18263F (AS) directed the replacement of matt Light Gull Gray, Federal Standard Color No. 36440, applied to carrier aircraft with glossy Light Gull Gray, Federal Standard Color No. 16440.

30 JUNE • The southwest monsoons with attendant clouds and rain affected the operations of carriers sailing off Vietnam during June, but the realignment of the ships continued. On 5 June, *Kitty Hawk* (CVA 63) relieved *Midway* (CVA 41), and on 16 June, *Oriskany* (CVA 34) began strike operations. A total of 14 two-carrier days and 16 single-carrier days during the month resulted in a monthly strike sortie count of 2,431. The Navy's count for Fiscal Year 1971 totaled 32,230 sorties—or 172 under the annual ceiling.

7 JULY • The retirement of the last active duty Skyraider, an NA-1E (BuNo 132443), occurred at NATC Patuxent River, Md. The aircraft had participated in test programs including slow speed and ordnance release. The plane was restored and hangared at Tyler, Texas.

13 JULY • Deputy Secretary of Defense David Packard issued a new directive defining the policy for acquisition of major defense systems. He sought to return authority to the military departments, subject to approval by the Secretary of Defense at key points in the development acquisition process. The policy included an increased emphasis on the project manager (called program manager in the Department of Defense directive), the reiteration of the importance of maintaining a strong technology base, and the definition of the entire development-acquisition process as three distinct phases: program initiation, full-scale development, and production/deployment.

The new directive emphasized the importance of making accurate cost predictions and realistic schedule forecasts, and of relating the military benefits anticipated from a new technology to the cost of the technology. Prototyping as part of the advanced development effort was to reduce the magnitude of risk, and the operational suitability of a system was to be tested and evaluated before commitment to large-scale production. The policy later acquired the popular description "fly before buy."

24 JULY • Carrier Anti-Submarine Air Group Reserve 80 began antisubmarine operations from *Ticonderoga* (CVS 14). This marked the first time in U.S. Navy history that the Naval Air Reserve demonstrated the capability for immediate employment of fleet-size wings and groups, fully manned, properly equipped, and operationally ready to perform all phases of carrier operations.

26 JULY • Apollo 15 crewed by Col. David R. Scott, USAF; Lt. Col. Alfred M. Worden, USAF; and U.S. Naval Academy graduate, class of 1951, Lt. Col. James B. Irwin, USAF; launched from John F. Kennedy Space Center, Fla. On 30 July, Scott and Irwin in Lunar Module 10 *Falcon* landed on the moon. On 7 August, one of the three main parachutes of Command Module 112 *Endeavor* failed and caused a hard splashdown north of Hawaii and six miles from the primary recovery vessel, amphibious assault ship *Okinawa* (LPH 3). A helicopter carried the astronauts to the ship and *Okinawa* retrieved *Endeavor*. Apollo 15 achieved all primary mission objectives.

28 JULY • HC-7 became the second Navy helicopter squadron to receive the Presidential Unit Citation for duty during the Vietnam War. HAL-3 had previously received the award. The Navy credited HC-7 search and rescue detachments operating from ships at sea on Yankee Station with rescuing 76 aviators. During the early stages of the war, the squadron made several overland rescues in North Vietnam under intense enemy fire.

30 JULY • During July, *Oriskany* (CVA 34), *Midway* (CVA 41), and *Enterprise* (CVAN 65) served intermittently off Vietnam over a total of 22 two-carrier days and nine single-carrier days that resulted in a monthly strike sortie count of 2,001. On three different occasions, Typhoons Harriet, Kim, and Jean disrupted operations. A slight increase in strike sorties into South Vietnam occurred during the month, consisting mainly of visual strikes against enemy troop positions.

30 JULY • The Navy accepted the first operational supersonic BQM-34E Firebee II aerial target. Ryan Aeronautical Corporation developed the aircraft under contract to NAVAIR to maneuver at greater speeds and altitudes than the Firebee variants previously in use. The jet-powered, remote-controlled target system offered sub- and supersonic capabilities up to Mach 1.5.

3 AUGUST • Pilots of VMA-142, -131, and -133 began qualification landings in A-4L Skyhawks on board *Independence* (CVA 62). During a three-day period, four active duty and 20 Reserve pilots operated on board the carrier, marking the first time that Marine Aircraft Reserve squadrons qualified for carrier duty.

26 AUGUST • VAW-124 flew a carrier-based early warning E-2B nonstop across the Atlantic. The Hawkeye left NAS Norfolk, Va., and flew over Newfoundland, Canada, and Lajes, Azores, to reach *America* (CVA 66) while she sailed with the Sixth Fleet in the Mediterranean.

31 AUGUST • Dual carrier operations in the Vietnam War occurred only during the first week of August. Beginning on 16 August, *Enterprise* (CVAN 65) operated alone on station. Thus, a total of eight two-carrier days and 23 single-carrier days represented a near reversal of July's carrier mix and produced a strike sortie count for the month of 1,915.

30 SEPTEMBER • One day of two carriers operating simultaneously marked the only exception to single-carrier operations on Yankee Station throughout September in the Vietnam War. During the first four days, *Enterprise* (CVAN 65) launched raids, replaced through the middle of the month by *Oriskany* (CVA 34), and during the last four days, by *Midway* (CVA 41). The single-carrier posture combined with the low intended sortie rate produced 1,243 strike sorties during the month. On 21 September, *Oriskany* fliers participated in a joint Air Force–Navy protective reaction strike—retaliation in response to enemy attacks or radar tracking—into southern North Vietnam.

5 OCTOBER • HC-4 accepted its first SH-2D LAMPS at NAS Lakehurst, N.J. The squadron became the first command in the fleet to use the new light airborne multi-purpose system–configured Seasprites. One week later, HC-5 became the first West Coast squadron to receive the Seasprites at NAS Imperial Beach, Calif.

8 OCTOBER • C-5A Galaxys of the 437th Military Airlift Wing airlifted four CH-53 Sea Stallions and about 100 men of the Mobile Mine Countermeasure Command from NAS Norfolk, Va., and Charleston, S.C., to the Sixth Fleet at Souda Bay, Crete. The operation demonstrated a global quick reaction mine countermeasures capability. A detachment of four HM-12 CH-53As recorded the first overseas deployment of the new helicopters. The detachment began sweeping operations upon arrival, and from 2 to 7 November, the squadron participated in the first integration of airborne minesweeping operations into an amphibious assault exercise conducted from amphibious transport dock *Coronado* (LPD 11).

29 OCTOBER • HS-15 at NAS Lakehurst, N.J., was established as the first sea control ship squadron. Tactically, the unit was to protect convoys and vessels not operating with or within the protective range of carriers. The HS-15 SH-3H Sea Kings and VMA-513 AV-8A Harriers subsequently carried out tests along these lines on board amphibious assault ship *Guam* (LPH 9). The evaluations included V/STOL and helicopter compatibility, antisurface tactics, bow and cross-axial landings, night operations, and shipboard control of airborne intercepts.

31 OCTOBER • Single-carrier operations dominated Yankee Station activity off Vietnam during October except for the last day. On 10 October, *Midway* (CVA 41) completed her final line period and the next day *Enterprise* (CVAN 65) renewed her operations for the remainder of the month with *Oriskany* (CVA 34) joining the final day. Together the three carriers recorded a monthly total of 1,024 ordnance delivering strike sorties, including 30 into South Vietnam and the balance over Laos. On 20 October, the deployment of two MiGs each south of 20° N at Bai Thuong, Quan Lang, and Vinh, altered the air war in North Vietnam.

8 NOVEMBER • The first S-3A antisubmarine warfare jet was rolled out at Lockheed-California Company, Burbank, Calif. The Vikings were to replace S-2 Trackers.

17 NOVEMBER • The office of the Assistant Secretary of Defense reported the designation of the Navy as the lead service in making aircraft ready for use in Project Grass Catcher—the interception of drug smugglers. During January and February 1972, four OV-10 Broncos operated with the Bureau of Customs.

30 NOVEMBER • A team from NATC Patuxent River, Md., carried out preliminary evaluations of a prototype F-14A Tomcat at the Grumman Corporation's Calverton, N.Y., facility.

30 NOVEMBER • Carriers launched 1,766 ordnance-bearing strike sorties including 12 and nine into North and South Vietnam, respectively, and the balance into Laos. Two reconnaissance missions were flown over the airfield at Vinh, and escort aircraft on both missions expended ordnance in a protective reaction role against antiaircraft artillery sites near the field that opened fire. Aircraft also executed other protective reaction strikes during November.

2 DECEMBER • NAF Cam Ranh Bay, South Vietnam, was disestablished. Patrol squadron detachments, which had routinely rotated at NAF Cam Ranh Bay then deployed to NAS Cubi Point, Philippines. At Cam Ranh Bay, the patrol squadrons served as part of the Vietnam Air Patrol Unit under the operational control of Commander Fleet Air Wing 8 or 10. Operational tasking also originated from Commander Task Force 77 on Yankee Station or Commander Seventh Fleet. The patrol squadrons worked closely with Commander Vietnam Coastal Surveillance Force, Task Force 115. Their missions included air patrol coverage for South Vietnam along the coastline during Operation Market Time—the detection and interdiction of infiltration by North Vietnamese trawlers that smuggled men and supplies into South Vietnam. Patrol squadrons also provided aerial reconnaissance and antisubmarine patrols for ships operating in Yankee Station and other areas of the Gulf of Tonkin and the South China Sea.

2 DECEMBER • Cmdr. George W. White at NATC Patuxent River, Md., became the first Navy test pilot to fly an F-14A Tomcat. By the end of 1971, nine of the jets operated within various flight test programs. Purchase plans called for an eventual total of 313 aircraft—301 for operations and 12 for research and development.

8 DECEMBER • Amphibious Group Alpha, formed around amphibious assault ship *Tripoli* (LPH 10), received orders to move from Okinawa to the vicinity of Singapore in anticipation of a possible deployment to the Indian Ocean. This action followed indications by the head of the UN relief mission at Dacca, East Pakistan (Bangladesh), of the possible evacuation of foreign civilians as a result of the Indo-Pakistani War of 1971, which began on 3 December. On 10 December, *Enterprise* (CVAN 65) formed Task Force 74 and departed Yankee Station off Vietnam for the Indian Ocean. Two days later, the Royal Air Force evacuated Westerners from East Pakistan, thereby eliminating the requirement for an American evacuation, but on 15 December, Task Force 74 entered the Indian Ocean as a show of force. On 7 January 1972, *Enterprise* received orders to sail from the Indian Ocean, and the next morning turned for the Strait of Malacca. On 12 January, she arrived at Subic Bay, Philippines.

8 DECEMBER • Commander-in-Chief, U.S. Pacific Fleet confirmed a requirement previously enunciated by AirPac for a system of video coverage of the entire launch and recovery sequence of carrier operations.

12 DECEMBER • VX-4 reported on an extensive series of evaluations that had begun in 1969 of the visual target acquisition system—a helmet-mounted sight—in F-4 Phantom IIs. The report cited a number of shortcomings but concluded that the sight proved superior to operational equipment used by fighter pilots in air-to-air combat.

15 DECEMBER • The A-6A Intruders and KA-6D tankers of VMA(AW)-224, embarked on board *Coral Sea* (CVA 43), reached Yankee Station off Vietnam. Their arrival marked the first Marine Corps squadron to fly combat missions from a carrier into North Vietnam.

31 DECEMBER • During 1971, the helicopters of HAL-3, the only light attack helicopter squadron in the Navy, flew 34,746 hours in support of their mission to provide quick-reaction armed helicopter close air support for all naval forces and South Vietnamese forces operating in the southern part of South Vietnam. Over the course of this action, HAL-3 lost six aircraft.

31 DECEMBER • *Constellation* (CVA 64) and *Enterprise* (CVAN 65) operated on Yankee Station together during part of the month. After *Enterprise* was directed on 10 December to sail to the Indian Ocean for the possible evacuation of Americans from East Pakistan (Bangladesh) in connection with the Indo-Pakistani war, the tour of *Constellation* was extended to the end of the month. On 15 December, *Coral Sea* (CVA 43) arrived on the line. During December the carriers launched 2,462 ordnance delivery sorties.

31 DECEMBER • By the end of the month, the North Vietnamese increased the number of surface-to-air missile launches against allied aircraft, and incursions by MiGs into Laos prompted the Air Force and Navy to develop new tactics and combine efforts to suppress these threats. On 26 December, a major combined effort protective reaction strike began, ending on 30 December. Task Force 77 A-6A Intruders, led by A-7E Corsair II pathfinders, flew 423 strike sorties against targets near Dong Hoi, Quang Khe, and Vinh, North Vietnam. In addition, aircraft flying from *Constellation* introduced laser-guided bombs (LGB) to battle. The initial 16 trial LGB drops cut roads and were followed by attacks on antiaircraft artillery sites. During 1972, Air Force aircraft dropped LGBs effectively against heretofore indestructible targets such as heavy steel bridge structures built into solid rock.

1972

JANUARY • The Greek government approved in principle the concept of homeporting Commander Task Force 60 at Athens. Secretary of Defense Melvin R. Laird recommended *Independence* (CVA 62) and CVW-7 as the primary commands of the force, and the operation of a satellite airfield at the Greek station of Elefsis to supplement the existing facilities at Souda Bay, Crete.

1 JANUARY • The area of responsibility assigned to Commander-in-Chief, Pacific was shifted westward to include the Indian Ocean and the Persian Gulf. Construction continued on the U.S. naval communications, refueling, and logistical airstrip facilities on Diego Garcia, British Indian Ocean Territory, to provide communications and logistical support for U.S. forces operating in the Indian Ocean and Persian Gulf.

6 JANUARY • TraWing-5 was established at NAS Whiting Field, Fla. The new wing, the first established under the reorganization of the Naval Air Training Command, consisted of NASs Whiting and Ellyson Fields, VT-2, -3, and -6, and HT-8. It coordinated and supervised training activities that had previously been the responsibility of each of the stations and squadrons.

18 JANUARY • *Enterprise* (CVAN 65) joined *Constellation* (CVA 64) on Yankee Station off Vietnam after her brief tour in the Indian Ocean.

18 JANUARY • Amphibious assault ship *Guam* (LPH 9) began the first in a series of tests to analyze the sea control ship (SCS) concept. The SCS was to operate a smaller complement of aircraft than large carriers (CVA) and to maintain control of the sea lanes in low-threat areas of the world. They were to carry V/STOL aircraft as well as helicopters to protect underway replenishment groups, mercantile convoys, amphibious assault forces, and task groups without aircraft carriers in company.

19 JANUARY • Pilot Lt. Randall H. Cunningham and radar intercept officer (RIO) Lt. j.g. William P. Driscoll of VF-96 shot down a MiG-21 Fishbed with an AIM-9 Sidewinder missile from an F-4J Phantom II, embarked with CVW-9 on board *Constellation* (CVA 64). Their victory accounted for the Navy's 33rd MiG shoot-down in the Vietnam War since 17 June 1965, when pilot Cmdr. Louis C. Page and RIO Lt. John J. Smith Jr., of VF-21 embarked on board *Midway* (CVA 41), downed a MiG-17 Fresco with an AIM-7 Sparrow missile from an F-4B.

21 JANUARY • An S-3A Viking made the type's maiden test flight at Lockheed-California Company, Palmdale, Calif. Vikings met the Navy's requirement for aircraft capable of flying in excess of 400 knots to replace aging S-2s, and their enhanced speed, range, and sensors enabled them to search nearly three times the area covered by Trackers.

31 JANUARY • The withdrawal of U.S. ground troops from the Vietnam War and light fighting ashore ensured a low level of air operations during January, a situation that continued generally throughout the first three months of the year. During the month, only eight Navy tactical air attack sorties occurred over South Vietnam and a handful of protective reaction strikes over North Vietnam.

11 FEBRUARY • As a result of the shift from piston engine to jet aircraft, the Navy announced the closure of the Aviation Machinist's Mate Class B School on reciprocating engines at NATC Memphis, Tenn.

11 FEBRUARY • The Navy announced that the development and installation of mufflers on engine test cells had eliminated 85 percent of the audible noise in testing jet engines for A-3 Skywarriors at Naval Air Rework Facility Alameda, Calif.

29 FEBRUARY • During the month, naval air attack sorties into South Vietnam rose to 733 because of allied preemptive operations in preparation for an expected large-scale enemy offensive during Tet, which did not materialize. *Hancock* (CVA 19), *Coral Sea* (CVA 43), and *Constellation* (CVA 64) served overlapping tours on Yankee Station to assure the availability of at least two carriers on station at a time.

10 MARCH • During the period from 5 January through this date, protective reaction strikes increased. Navy and Air Force aircraft flew 90 such strikes against surface-to-air missile and antiaircraft artillery installations, compared to 108 similar raids during all of 1971.

16 MARCH • HAL-3 was disestablished.

23 MARCH • VMA-513 completed the Harrier Department of Defense sortie rate validation and demonstrated the capability of Harriers to respond rapidly and repeatedly to requests for close air support while operating from austere forward bases. During the ten-day test, the squadron flew 376 sorties with six operational AV-8As.

24 MARCH • A QF-4B target aircraft arrived for testing at the Naval Missile Center Point Mugu, Calif. The Phantom II had undergone conversion from combat configuration at Naval Air Development Center, Warminster, Pa. The aircraft fulfilled the requirement for a full-size, high-altitude, supersonic, maneuvering aerial target capable of flying at altitudes in excess of 50,000 feet and at airspeeds exceeding twice the speed of sound.

29 MARCH • The Atlantic Fleet Weapons Range used a supersonic BQM-34E for the first time during missile defense exercises with frigate *Wainwright* (DLG 28). A DP-2E Neptune launched the Firebee II from an altitude of 20,000 feet, and the target accelerated to Mach 1.52 to test the ship's ability to withstand penetrations by high-altitude, high-speed enemy aircraft.

29 MARCH • The Naval Air Technical Training Unit's Photographer's Mate Class "A" School renewed flight training as part of the course. Fleet demand for qualified aircrew drove the action after a 16-year suspension of the requirement.

30 MARCH • Naval air attack sorties over South Vietnam dropped to 113 during March. On 23 March, the United States canceled further peace negotiations in Paris, France, because of a lack of progress in the talks. On this date, the North Vietnamese launched the Nguyen Hue Campaign into South Vietnam, dubbed by journalists the "Easter Offensive." President Richard M. Nixon activated Tactical Air Command Operation Plan 100 known as Constant Guard—support for the remaining U.S. advisors in South Vietnam and the South Vietnamese forces. *Hancock* (CVA 19) and *Coral Sea* (CVA 43) sailed on Yankee Station when the offensive began, and during the month, *Kitty Hawk* (CVA 63) and *Constellation* (CVA 64) rotated through the fighting.

1 APRIL • VAL-4 departed South Vietnam. The squadron, which flew OV-10A Broncos, primarily from Binh Thuy, comprised the last Navy combat force in that country.

5 APRIL • In reaction to the North Vietnamese invasion of South Vietnam, Operation Freedom Trail involved Navy tactical air sorties against enemy military and logistic targets in the southern part of North Vietnam between 17° and 19°N. At times, aircraft also bombed special targets above the 19th parallel. The magnitude of the North Vietnamese offensive required an extended logistics network and increased resupply routes to sustain their invasion. The Americans gradually lifted many target and geographical restrictions that had been in effect since October 1968 and expanded the list of authorized targets. By the end of April the revised directives permitted attacks throughout the region below 20°25'N and special strikes above the 20th parallel.

6 APRIL • VMFA-115 F-4B and VMFA-232 F-4J Phantom IIs arrived at Da Nang AB, South Vietnam, from MCAS Iwakuni, Japan. The Marines deployed as part of the reinforcements to support the South Vietnamese, particularly around An Loc, Kontum, Pleiku, and Quang Tri. On 14 April, VMFA-212 F-4Js arrived from MCAS Kaneohe, Hawaii. Targets for Marine sorties included enemy tanks, trucks, and troops, and enabled the South Vietnamese to regroup north and west of Hué.

6 APRIL • An F-14A Tomcat arrived at NATC Patuxent River, Md., for a series of catapult launches, automatic carrier landing system checks, airspeed system calibrations, and weight and balance checks to determine the suitability of the fighters for naval operations.

7 APRIL • During the week ending this date, Navy aircraft flew 680 sorties in South Vietnam to counter North Vietnamese troop concentrations and their equipment flow, and to assist the South Vietnamese with close air support, direct air support, and interdiction missions. This week marked a five-fold increase in naval air sorties since March.

11 APRIL • A P-3 performed the first drop test of a BGM-84A Harpoon stand-off antiship missile from 20,000 feet over the Naval Missile Center Point Mugu, Calif. An AGM-84 air-to-ground version subsequently entered the fleet.

12 APRIL • The P-3C Acoustic Sensor Operator Trainer (Device 14B44) became available for training aircrew at the Fleet Aviation Specialized Operational Training Group, Pacific Detachment. The simulator duplicated the real world conditions of underwater acoustical data and the detection, classification, and localization procedures of the Orion AQA-7 Jezebel system.

14 APRIL • For the week ending this date, Navy aircraft averaged 191 sorties per day, primarily against targets to the west and north of Quang Tri, South Vietnam, a 97 percent increase over the previous week.

16 APRIL • Apollo 16, manned by Capt. John W. Young; Lt. Col. Charles M. Duke Jr., USAF; and Lt. Cmdr. Thomas K. Mattingly II; launched from John F. Kennedy Space Center, Fla. On 19 April, Young and Duke in Lunar Module 11 *Orion* landed on the moon. On 27 April, Command Module 112 *Casper* splashed down in the mid-Pacific several miles from primary recovery ship *Ticonderoga* (CVS 14). An SH-3G Sea King of HC-1, embarked on board *Ticonderoga*, retrieved the astronauts. Apollo 16 achieved all primary mission objectives of lunar and space exploration and experimentation.

16 APRIL • Aircraft from *Coral Sea* (CVA 43), *Kitty Hawk* (CVA 63), and *Constellation* (CVA 64), flew 57 sorties in the Haiphong area of North Vietnam in support of Air Force B-52 strikes on petroleum storage facilities during Operation Freedom Porch.

25 APRIL • During the final six days of April, A-4F Skyhawks of VA-55, -164, and -211 flying from *Hancock* (CVA 19) struck the North Vietnamese and People's Liberation Armed Forces around Kontum and Pleiku, South Vietnam. A-6A Intruders from VA-165 and A-7E Corsair IIs of VA-146 and -147, embarked on board *Constellation* (CVA 64), attacked the enemy around An Loc in support of South Vietnamese troops, in some cases only 40 miles outside the capital of Saigon.

28 APRIL • An F-14A Tomcat over the Naval Missile Center Point Mugu, Calif., launched an AIM-54A Phoenix air-to-air missile for the first time.

30 APRIL • The expansion of naval air operations in the Vietnam War led to a total of 4,833 Navy sorties over South

Vietnam and 1,250 sorties into North Vietnam during April. The Marines flew 537 sorties over South Vietnam. The increased effort included the deployment of four carriers. *Hancock* (CVA 19) and *Coral Sea* (CVA 43) had sailed to Yankee Station when the North Vietnamese spring offensive began. On 3 April, *Kitty Hawk* (CVA 63) arrived at Yankee Station, followed on 7 April by *Constellation* (CVA 64). Between 8 and 30 April, the Navy effort grew gradually from 240 sorties a day to a peak of more than 300, resulting in a monthly average of 270 sorties per day.

1 MAY • Improved weather conditions during the first seven days of May facilitated a daily average of 97 Navy attack sorties into North Vietnam and 168 into South Vietnam. The first week also witnessed the enemy's deployment of SA-7 Grail infrared-seeker surface-to-air missiles.

4 MAY • The Navy unveiled its first night carrier landing trainer, for A-7E Corsair IIs, at NAS Lemoore, Calif.

5 MAY • The P-3Bs of VP-9 departed NAS Moffett Field, Calif., for NAS Cubi Point, Philippines. The Orions subsequently augmented aircraft tasked with ocean surveillance patrols concerning the mining of North Vietnamese harbors and the corresponding movement of Eastern Bloc ships.

6 MAY • In the second most active Navy dogfight day of the Vietnam War, two F-4B Phantom IIs, crewed by pilot Lt. Gary L. Weigand and radar intercept officer (RIO) Lt. j.g. William Freckleton of VF-111, and pilot Lt. Cmdr. Jerry B. Houston and RIO Lt. Kevin T. Moore of VF-51, both jets embarked on board *Coral Sea* (CVA 43), each shot down a MiG-17 Fresco with an AIM-9 Sidewinder air-to-air missile. Two F-4Js manned by pilot Lt. Robert G. Hughes and RIO Lt. j.g. Adolph J. Cruz, and pilot Lt. Cmdr. Kenneth W. Pettigrew and RIO Lt. j.g. Michael J. McCabe, from VF-114 embarked on board *Kitty Hawk* (CVA 63), each shot down a MiG-21 Fishbed with a Sidewinder.

7 MAY • A tank cart defueling Apollo 16 Command Module 112 *Casper* after its return from the lunar mission exploded because of overpressurization at NAS North Island, Calif. Forty-six people suspected of inhaling of toxic fumes underwent hospitalization but examination did not reveal symptoms of inhalation.

8 MAY • For the first time in more than three weeks, U.S. air power, including 50 Navy sorties, attacked targets in the vicinity of Hanoi, North Vietnam. Naval aircraft flew another 96 sorties into southern North Vietnam between Hanoi and the Demilitarized Zone, while 99 sorties were directed against the enemy in South Vietnam.

9 MAY • Operation Pocket Money—the mining of the principal North Vietnamese ports—began. An EC-121M Constellation from Da Nang Air Base and an EKA-3B Skywarrior of VAQ-135 Detachment 3 from *Coral Sea* (CVA 43) supported the minelaying. *Kitty Hawk* (CVA 63) launched 17 diversionary ordnance delivering sorties against a railroad siding at Nam Dinh, but poor weather compelled the aircraft to divert to secondary targets at Thanh and Phu Qui.

Cmdr. Roger E. Sheets, commander of Carrier Air Wing 15, led three A-6As from VMA(AW)-224, and Cmdr. Leonard E. Guiliani led six A-7Es of VA-22 and -94 from *Coral Sea*. Each Intruder and Corsair II carried four 2,000-pound Mk 52-2 magnetic mines. Bombardier/navigator Capt. William R. Carr, USMC, flew in the lead Intruder to establish the critical attack azimuth and timed the release of the mines. The Marines dropped 12 mines in the inner channel of Haiphong Harbor and the Corsair IIs placed 24 in the port's outer channel. All the mines were set with 72-hour arming delays to permit merchant ships time for departure or a change in destination consistent with a public warning by President Richard M. Nixon. Supporting aircraft flew 150 fighter escort, bombing of surface-to-air missile sites, diversionary strike, and electronic countermeasures sorties. The raiders surprised the North Vietnamese and met minimal resistance.

These missions initiated a campaign that sowed 108 Mk 52-2s and at least 11,603 Destructor (DST) mines in 1,149 sorties from ten carriers at Cam Pha and Hon Gay, and in the river estuaries of Cap Mui Ron, Cua Sot, Dong Hoi, Quang Khe, Thanh Hoa, and Vinh, along with Cua Day and Cua Lac Giang, south of Don Son and Haiphong. On Christmas Eve, an A-7E Corsair II from *Ranger* (CVA 61) was lost on a reseeding mission to Cam Pha. On 14 January 1973, a VA-35 Intruder from *America* (CVA 66) flew the last mining mission. The Air Force also dropped 2,048 DSTs to interdict trains and trucks. Pocket Money played a significant role in bringing about a peace arrangement, because the mining hampered the enemy's ability to receive war supplies.

In the VF-96 ready room on board *Constellation* (CVA 64), Lt. Randall H. Cunningham demonstrates how he and Lt. j.g. William P. Driscoll shot down three MiG-17 fighters over North Vietnam on 10 May 1972. Damage to their F-4J Phantom II forced them to eject after their combat, but they were quickly rescued by a helicopter from *Okinawa* (LPH 3).

10 MAY • On 9 May, President Richard M. Nixon announced an air campaign against the North Vietnamese named Operation Linebacker—subsequently designated Linebacker I. This counteroffensive emerged as an outgrowth of Operation Freedom Trail and the chief executive's mining declaration during Operation Pocket Money. Its three principal objectives were the destruction of military supplies within North Vietnam, the isolation of North Vietnam from external suppliers, and stoppage of the supply flow to their troops in South Vietnam. On this date, the Navy launched the first attacks of Linebacker I during a shift from targets in southern North Vietnam to the coastal region from Haiphong north to the Chinese border. Carriers launched 173 attack sorties into North Vietnam and 62 into South Vietnam.

Navy flyers shot down eight MiGs during a day of intense air-to-air combat. Pilot Lt. Randall H. Cunningham and radar intercept officer Lt. j.g. William P. Driscoll of VF-96, embarked on board *Constellation* (CVA 64), shot down three MiG-17 Frescoes with AIM-9 Sidewinder air-to-air missiles from their F-4J Phantom II. These victories, combined with their claims of a MiG-21 on 19 January and a Fresco on 8 May, made Cunningham and Driscoll the first MiG aces of the Vietnam War.

Most of the raids consisted of armed reconnaissance flights against targets of opportunity within three main areas near Hanoi, Haiphong, and the Chinese border, and of preplanned strikes against fixed targets. During Linebacker I, the Navy contributed more than 60 percent of the total sorties into North Vietnam, with about 25 percent of them at night. A-6 Intruders and A-7 Corsair IIs comprised the principal Seventh Fleet bombers and accounted for roughly 15 and 60 percent of the naval attack sorties, respectively. The heaviest tactical air operations occurred from July to September with 12,865 naval sorties. On 22 October, the imposition of restrictions on operations above 20°N because of ongoing peace negotiations curtailed Linebacker I.

10 MAY • NAVAIR promulgated a plan for the management of advanced prototype development and demonstration of a thrust-augmented wing attack plane-fighter V/STOL aircraft. The planned establishment of a prototype development manager under the deputy commander for Plans and Programs was to be assisted by a small cadre of management and technical people located in the assistant commander for research and technology's organization and at the contractor's facility.

13 MAY • CH-46D Sea Knights and CH-53D Sea Stallions of HMM-164, embarked on board amphibious assault ship *Okinawa* (LPH 3), airlifted 1,000 members of the South Vietnamese 369th Marine Brigade from a landing zone near Hué to an area 24 miles northwest of the city behind North Vietnamese lines.

17 MAY • A-4E Skyhawks of VMA-211 and -311 arrived from Japan at the recently reactivated base at Bien Hoa, South Vietnam. The Marines concentrated air strikes against enemy troops surrounding An Loc and responded to calls from counterattacking South Vietnamese forces in adjacent areas.

18 MAY • The scope of the air war in Vietnam changed when aircraft bombed an electric power plant at Uong Bi near Haiphong, North Vietnam. This raid marked the beginning of strikes on a class of targets formerly avoided including power plants, shipyards, and a Haiphong cement plant. Over 60 of the more than 200 naval sorties into North Vietnam that day occurred in the Haiphong region, the first since 10 May.

25 MAY • Secretary of the Navy John W. Warner signed the Incidents at Sea Agreement between the United States and Soviet Union. There were 15 serious incidents of Eastern Bloc aircraft firing on U.S. Navy planes since 1945. This agreement was designed to help prevent unintentional incidents between the two navies and to reduce tension on and over the high seas.

1151760

Lt. Curt Dose explains how he and Lt. Cmdr. James McDevitt of VF-92 shot down a North Vietnamese MiG-21, 10 May 1972. Their victory was one of ten that day by *Constellation* (CVA 64) aircraft.

31 MAY • During the month, Navy aircrew flew 3,949 attack sorties into North Vietnam as compared to 1,250 during April; those into the South numbered 3,290 for May compared to 4,833 the previous month. While naval sorties into South Vietnam dropped by more than 500 from the previous month, Marine missions over South Vietnam increased from 543 in April to 1,502 during May. Targets in North Vietnam hit by naval planes increased to 2,416 in May from 719 during April. Railroads accounted for 16 percent of the targets bombed, roads and trucks 14, storage areas 13, and bridges 10 percent. During May, naval flyers shot down 16 enemy jets including 11 MiG-17 Frescoes, two MiG-19 Farmers, and three MiG-21 Fishbeds over North Vietnam. The Navy lost six aircraft including two F-4 Phantom IIs and two A-7 Corsair IIs to SA-2 surface-to-air missiles, and one F-8 Crusader and one RA-5 Vigilante to unknown causes.

Saratoga (CVA 60) joined five other carriers on Yankee Station during the month to raise carrier strength to six ships—the greatest number since the war began. The fighting reached a stalemate as air power and the regrouped South Vietnamese halted the North Vietnamese forward thrust.

20 JUNE • The A-6A Intruders of VMA(AW)-533 arrived at Nam Phong, Thailand, as a reaction to the North Vietnamese attacks in the South Vietnamese highlands. A joint Navy/Marine engineering team prepared the advance base by hacking roads and aircraft parking and storage areas from the jungle. Marine Task Force Delta, KC-130 Hercules of VMGR-152 Detachment D, CH-46 Sea Knights of H&MS-36 Detachment D, and VMFA-115 F-4B and VMFA-232 F-4J Phantom IIs arrived at the base from 23 May to 18 June.

21 JUNE • Pilot Cmdr. Samuel C. Flynn Jr. and radar intercept officer (RIO) Lt. William H. John of VF-31, embarked on board *Saratoga* (CVA 60), shot down a MiG-21 Fishbed with an AIM-9 Sidewinder air-to-air missile from an F-4J Phantom II. Their victory marked the third MiG downed by Navy pilots during June. Earlier, on 11 June, pilot Cmdr. Foster S. Teague and RIO Lt. Ralph M. Howell, and pilot Lt. Winston W. Copeland with RIO Lt. Donald R. Bouchoux, all of VF-51 embarked on board *Coral Sea* (CVA 43), shot down two MiG-17 Frescoes with Sidewinders from their F-4Bs in the Nam Dinh area of North Vietnam.

21 JUNE • The chief of Naval Material directed Commander, Naval Electronic Systems Command (ELEX) to assume the responsibility and authority for final decisions in development, acquisition, and support for equipment and capabilities that provided platform-to-platform command, control, and communications involving satellites, air, surface, and subsurface elements. The directive included a proposal to rename the ELEX to reflect this assignment and prohibited large-scale lateral movements between the systems commands.

Despite these qualifications, a dispute arose as to whether ELEX was to undertake the detailed management of most of the electronic material program or to apply control through broadly gauged decisions. The decision transferred project management offices for Space (PM-16) and Reconnaissance, Electronic Warfare, and Special Operations (REWSON PM-7) from the chief of Naval Material to Commander, ELEX (PME-107), and redesignated NAVAIR's Electronic Warfare Project Management Office as REWSON, followed by the physical merging of the two REWSON project management offices with a double hatting of the incumbents.

23 JUNE • HS-2, -15, -74, and -75 aided flood victims in the Wilkes-Barre, Scranton, and Pottstown areas of Pennsylvania. The squadrons carried out evacuation, and medical, food, and clothing supply flights.

29 JUNE • NAVAIR announced the formation of a "Buddy-Up" program whereby Reserve officers attached to NAVAIR Reserve Units were to establish a working relationship with various NAVAIR activities. Planners envisioned the program as a means for Reserve officers to identify and undertake meaningful project work for the activities.

30 JUNE • Naval aircraft flew 2,021 tactical air attack sorties into South Vietnam during June, a decrease in comparison to the figures for April and May that reflected the stalemated fighting on the ground. The Navy launched 3,844 attack sorties in June against Operation Linebacker I targets in North Vietnam. Attacks against the road transport system, water transport craft, and storage targets increased from pre-June levels. The greatest number of Navy concentrated strikes that involved ten or more attack aircraft striking a compact cluster of targets took place from April through June, and comprised 40 percent of its total attack effort.

1 JULY • A reorganization of the Naval Air Training system occurred with the disestablishment of Naval Air Advanced Training Command and the relocation of chief of Naval Air Training to NAS Corpus Christi, Texas. This was part of the Navy's effort to consolidate training under the "single base training" concept—the assignment of pilots after their completion of primary training to a specific program training in jets, propeller-driven aircraft, or helicopters. The pilots were to complete this training at one specific base before receiving their wings. The new structure/organization fell under the control of the chief of the Naval Air Training Command.

1 JULY • Tactical Electronic Warfare Wing 13 was disestablished at NAS Whidbey Island, Wash. The wing had been established to introduce EA-6B Prowlers into the fleet.

15 JULY • A three-day test demonstration of the ability of a UH-2C to fire Sparrow III air-to-air missiles configured to attack surface targets concluded at the Pacific Missile Range, Sea Test Range, Calif. The modified Seasprite carried a single missile mounted on a rail launcher, and fired a total of four Sparrow IIIs during the demonstration.

22 JULY • Typhoon Rita caused disastrous flooding that affected tens of thousands of people across the central Luzon valley between Manila and Lingayen Gulf, Philippines. Amphibious assault ship *Tripoli* (LPH 10), with HMM-165 embarked, arrived in Subic Bay to provide relief support. The Marine helicopters evacuated more than 2,000 flood victims to *Tripoli*.

31 JULY • On 24 May, the Navy began regular night operations in the Vietnam War. During June and July, night sorties constituted 30 percent of the total Navy attack effort into North Vietnam. These raids relied primarily on A-6 Intruders and A-7 Corsair IIs. The Intruders flew more night than day armed reconnaissance sorties during the summer months, and the Corsair IIs flew about as many night as day sorties. About 45 percent of the Navy armed reconnaissance effort took place at night during June and July. The total number of Navy night sorties during those months numbered 1,243 and 1,332, respectively. During the summer, an operational average of three to four carriers sailed on Yankee Station.

31 JULY • During the summer months, a dramatic change in the North Vietnamese air defense effort occurred. In April and May, the Navy air effort into the North involved intensive air-to-air combat and a large number of surface-to-air missile (SAM) launches. In contrast, during June and July, the number of Linebacker I Navy attack sorties increased, but the number of air-to-air battles and SAM firings decreased. MiG kills by Navy aircraft decreased to three in June and zero in July compared to 16 in May. After mid-June, almost all North Vietnamese aircraft sighted or engaged consisted of MiG-21 Fishbeds. Navy aerial encounters took place primarily against Fishbeds and represented a considerable change from the 11 MiG-17 Frescoes of 16 Navy kills that occurred in May.

5 AUGUST • Amphibious assault ship *New Orleans* (LPH 11) relieved *Tripoli* (LPH 10) during Typhoon Rita flood relief operations in the Philippines. HMM-165 transferred to *New Orleans* to continue support because of the Marines' knowledge of terrain and problems inherent in the operations.

6 AUGUST • A North Vietnamese surface-to-air missile shot down A-7A Corsair II, BuNo 153147, piloted by Lt. James R. Lloyd of VA-105 operating from *Saratoga* (CV 60), during a night armed reconnaissance mission about 20 miles northwest of Vinh. Pilot Lt. Harry J. Zinser, crew chief AE3 Douglas G. Ankney, and aircrewman AN Matthew Szymanski of HC-7 Detachment 110, manned an HH-3A that rescued Lloyd, supported by aircraft from *Midway* (CVA 41) and *Saratoga*. Zinser flew the Sea King inland over mountains the following day and used its searchlight to assist in locating and rescuing the downed man despite heavy ground fire. This retrieval marked the deepest penetration of a SAR helicopter into North Vietnam since 1968. Over all of 1972, the detachment completed 48 rescues including 35 under combat conditions.

17 AUGUST • The Naval Material Command and the Air Force Systems Command reached an agreement relating to Navy and Air Force responsibilities for aircraft engine production at the Pratt & Whitney Aircraft Divisions, East Hartford, Conn., and West Palm Beach, Fla. The memorandum of agreement provided the assignment of an Air Force deputy plant representative and staff to the Naval Plant Representative Office (NAVPRO) to represent the F-15 Eagle program director on F-15 matters and to advise the NAVPRO on the in-plant management of Air Force engine programs.

29 AUGUST • Vought Aeronautics test pilot John Konrad made the first flight of a modified A-7E Corsair II in a two-seat version under development by the company to demonstrate to the Air Force and Navy the advantages of the configuration for use as an advanced trainer or for such tactical duties as electronic countermeasures.

31 AUGUST • Navy aircraft flew 4,819 sorties into North Vietnam in August as the downward trend of Navy attack sorties over the South continued. A stepped-up campaign in the Mekong Delta accounted for a sharp rise in Marine Corps air activity in South Vietnam—from 8 percent of the total allied air effort during May to 43 percent during

August. In August, the Marines concentrated their air efforts in the South but contributed significantly to U.S. efforts in the North to prevent the offloading and transportation of supplies from Chinese merchant ships at Hon La and Hon Nieu. In late June, seven AH-1Js of HMA-369 operated from amphibious transport dock *Denver* (LPD 9) against water transport traffic, and in early August from *Cleveland* (LPD 7). In August, the operations of HMA-369 expanded to include night surveillance and attack, and the helicopters also served as air spotters for naval gunfire and as airborne tactical controllers.

11 SEPTEMBER • Pilot Maj. Lee T. Lassiter, USMC, and radar intercept officer Capt. John D. Cummings, USMC, in a VMFA-333 F-4J Phantom II operating from *America* (CVA 66), downed a MiG-21 Fishbed with an AIM-9 Sidewinder air-to-air missile near Phuc Yen, North Vietnam. This victory marked the only MiG kill for the Navy/Marine Corps during September, and brought the total of MiGs downed by naval aircrew since the beginning of the war to 55.

30 SEPTEMBER • The number of Navy tactical air attack sorties in the Vietnam War decreased during September from the level flown in August. Navy aircraft flew 3,934 sorties into North Vietnam, some 800 fewer that the previous month. During July and August, more than 45 percent of the Navy armed reconnaissance sorties occurred at night, but that figure dropped to 31 percent in September. There was a similar decline in sorties flown in the South—1,708. About half the Navy's tactical air sorties consisted of close and direct air support missions in South Vietnam. Marine Corps activity stayed relatively high during the month—1,296 sorties—because of increased fighting in the Mekong Delta.

1 OCTOBER • VF-1 and -2 at NAS Miramar, Calif., were established as the first two F-14A Tomcat squadrons.

8 OCTOBER • VF-124, the lone training squadron that served all Tomcat fighter squadrons of the Atlantic and Pacific Fleets, received its first F-14A.

11 OCTOBER • A series of racially motivated disturbances occurred on board *Kitty Hawk* (CVA 63) while she operated in support of Operation Linebacker I off Vietnam. Extended deployments and long line periods compounded the strain generated by the racial tension endemic throughout the armed forces. On this date, a series of incidents led to fighting between whites and blacks across a number of areas of the ship including the sick bay and hangar deck. Marines, officers, chief petty officers, and the ship's master-at-arms force helped restore order. Commanding officer Capt. Marland W. Townsend and African American executive officer Cmdr. Benjamin W. Cloud several times addressed rioters including African American sailors armed with aircraft tie-down chains. Cloud's efforts in particular helped defuse the situation, and the crowd dispersed and threw their weapons overboard. The Medical Department reported 47 injuries and, on 13 October, the ship resumed air strikes. The riot on board *Kitty Hawk* and conflicts during this period on several other ships including *Constellation* (CVA 64) caused the Navy to place more emphasis on equal opportunity and diversity.

23 OCTOBER • The United States ended all tactical air sorties into North Vietnam above the 20th parallel and brought to a close Operation Linebacker I raids as a goodwill gesture to promote the peace negotiations in Paris, France. From May through October, Navy aircraft flew a total of 23,652 attack sorties into North Vietnam, which helped stem the flow of supplies into South Vietnam.

31 OCTOBER • Navy aircraft flew 2,661 tactical sorties into North Vietnam and 2,097 into the South, along with 1,599 by Marines, during October. Air operations there followed the general pattern of the ground war. The North Vietnamese increased their small-scale attacks throughout the South in an apparent effort to gain territory before a cease-fire. The main objective of Navy and Marine tactical air sorties thus became close and direct air missions in support of allied ground troops.

22 NOVEMBER • Adm. Arthur W. Radford (Ret.) officiated at groundbreaking ceremonies for the new Naval Aviation Museum building at NAS Pensacola, Fla. The former chairman of the Joint Chiefs of Staff also served as the chairman of the Naval Aviation Museum Association, Inc.

30 NOVEMBER • Close and direct air support attacks comprised more than 75 percent of all known targets of the Navy tactical air sorties flown into South Vietnam during

October and November. The percentage of Navy sorties flown for interdiction purposes there decreased markedly during that period compared to the previous spring and summer months.

7 DECEMBER • The final manned lunar mission, Apollo 17, crewed by Capt. Eugene A. Cernan, Cmdr. Ronald E. Evans, and geologist Harrison H. Schmitt, launched from John F. Kennedy Space Center, Fla. On 11 December, Cernan and Schmitt in Lunar Module 12 *Challenger* landed on the moon. On 19 December, command module *America* splashed down in the mid-Pacific several miles from the primary recovery ship *Ticonderoga* (CVS 14). An SH-3G Sea King of HC-1 Detachment 3 recovered and returned the crew to *Ticonderoga*, the mission having achieved all the primary objectives. Naval aviation squadrons and ships performed all the recovery operations for the 11 Apollo missions, and 22 of the 33 astronauts involved in the Apollo program had Navy backgrounds.

13 DECEMBER • An SH-3G from HC-1 Detachment 5 rescued Lt. Thomas B. Scott of VFP-63 Detachment 4 when he crashed in an RF-8G Crusader, BuNo 144608, while launching from *Oriskany* (CVA 34) in the Gulf of Tonkin. Scott was the 15th pilot rescued by HC-1 detachments while operating on board Yankee Station carriers during 1972 and, over the year, the squadron rescued a total of 36 men including the 15 pilots.

17 DECEMBER • From 23 October through 17 December, the United States halted bombing above the 20th parallel in North Vietnam.

18 DECEMBER • President Richard M. Nixon attempted to force the communists into earnest peace negotiations by launching Operation Linebacker II. This intensified version of Linebacker I resumed strikes above the 20th parallel including raids against hitherto restricted areas near Hanoi and Haiphong. The Americans reseeded mine fields and carried out concentrated strikes against surface-to-air missile and antiaircraft artillery sites, army barracks, petroleum storage areas, naval and shipyard areas, and railroad and truck stations. The Navy flew 505 sorties centered on the coastal areas around Hanoi and Haiphong. Between 18 and 22 December, it conducted 119 Linebacker II strikes into North Vietnam with harsh weather limiting the number of attacks flown. On 29 December, the operation concluded when the North Vietnamese returned to the Paris, France, peace table.

23 DECEMBER • VA-56 concluded its seventh line period while deployed with Carrier Air Wing 5 on board *Midway* (CVA 41). The squadron recorded 180 days on the line, flew 5,582.9 combat hours on more than 3,000 sorties, performed 2,090 day and 781 night carrier landings, and amassed 6,301 flight hours. The squadron lost four A-7B Corsair IIs to antiaircraft artillery fire and surface-to-air missiles, with two pilots taken prisoner-of-war, one listed as missing in action, and one rescued.

25 DECEMBER • Beginning at 2400 on Christmas Eve, none of the U.S. air services flew sorties in the Vietnam War during a 24-hour holiday bombing halt. The North Vietnamese used the truce to repair damage, draw lessons, and analyze tactics. Since the beginning of Operation Linebacker II, B-52s had carried out 420 raids, with 122 on 18 December, the highest number. Task Force 77 carrier strikes and tactical aircraft from Thailand supplemented the raids, mainly to suppress missile sites and confuse North Vietnamese air defense systems. Heavy attacks resumed on 26 December with 113 B-52 raids, the next highest sortie count.

28 DECEMBER • Pilot Lt. j.g. Scott H. Davis and radar intercept officer Lt. j.g. Geoffrey H. Ulrich, in an F-4J Phantom II of VF-142 embarked on board *Enterprise* (CVAN 65), downed a MiG-21 Fishbed with an AIM-9 Sidewinder air-to-air missile. Their victory marked the 24th MiG downed by Navy/Marine aircrews during 1972.

29 DECEMBER • Heavy raids around Hanoi, which had resumed the day after the Christmas bombing halt, eased when the North Vietnamese showed indications of returning to the conference table. More than 700 sorties by B-52 Stratofortresses during the 11 heavy-bombing days strongly influenced the communist decision to resume negotiations, which led to the peace agreement and the release of U.S. POWs. American bombing and electronic warfare virtually paralyzed North Vietnamese air defenses, which failed to shoot down a single B-52 during the 160 raids flown on 28 and 29 December. Only 2 percent—15 B-52s—were lost during more than 700 Operation Linebacker II raids.

30 DECEMBER • The United States called another bombing halt in North Vietnam and the Navy ended all tactical air sorties above the 20th parallel because of the resumed peace talks.

31 DECEMBER • In summary for 1972, the Navy conducted more than 60 percent or 28,093 of the tactical air attack sorties flown into North Vietnam where the Navy and Marine Corps lost 49 aircraft. Carriers spent a total of 1,403 on-line days at Yankee Station, with an average period of slightly more than 25 days for each ship. The Navy conducted 33.9 percent of all tactical air attack sorties flown into South Vietnam, where its fixed-wing aircraft flew 23,802 tactical air attack sorties and dropped 160,763 general-purpose bombs, and Marine fixed-wing aircraft delivered 111,859 general-purpose bombs. The Navy and Marine Corps each lost five fixed-wing aircraft in the South.

1973

1 JANUARY • A major reorganization in Naval Reserve affairs began as a result of the announcement two days earlier by the Secretary of the Navy of the consolidation of the Naval Surface and Air Reserve Commands into Commander Naval Reserve Force located in New Orleans, La.

8 JANUARY • Representatives of the U.S. and Greek navies signed an accord in Athens formally granting the Sixth Fleet homeport facilities in the Athens vicinity. The arrangement provided for the stationing of one of the Sixth Fleet's two carrier task forces in the Athens area.

12 JANUARY • Pilot Lt. Victor T. Kovaleski and radar intercept officer Lt. James A. Wise of VF-161, embarked on board *Midway* (CVA 41), shot down a North Vietnamese MiG-17 Fresco with an AIM-9 Sidewinder air-to-air missile from their F-4B Phantom II. Theirs was the last victory of the war, making a total of 62 enemy aircraft shot down by Navy and Marine Corps pilots during the Vietnam War.

27 JANUARY • The Vietnam cease-fire, announced four days earlier, came into effect. *Oriskany* (CVA 34), *Ranger* (CV 61), *Enterprise* (CVAN 65), and *America* (CVA 66) sailed on Yankee Station and cancelled all combat sorties into North and South Vietnam. During the major U.S. involvement in the Vietnam War from 1961 to 1973, the Navy lost 526 fixed-wing aircraft and 13 helicopters to hostile action and the Marine Corps lost 193 fixed-wing aircraft and 270 helicopters. Operation Homecoming—the repatriation of U.S. POWs between 27 January and 1 April 1973—began and the North Vietnamese and the People's Liberation Armed Forces released 591 prisoners. Sailors numbered 145 of the POWs freed during the operation, all but one of whom served within naval aviation.

The family of Cmdr. William R. Stark joyfully greets the freed POW upon his arrival at NAS Miramar, Calif., after nearly six years in captivity.

27 JANUARY • Task Force 78 was formed to conduct Operation End Sweep—minesweeping operations in North Vietnamese waters stipulated by the Paris Peace Accords. An air mobile mine countermeasures command comprised the principal aviation strength of the force and consisted of elements of HM-12, HMH-463, and HMM-165.

On 3 February, amphibious assault ship *New Orleans* (LPH 11) and the flagship of Task Force 78 began a six-day mine countermeasures exercise at Subic Bay, Philippines, in preparation for End Sweep. Two days later, Commander, Task Force 78 and other Navy mine demolition experts met with North Vietnamese leaders in Haiphong to discuss the operation. Task Force 78 surface minesweepers swept for an anchorage in deep water off the approaches to Haiphong harbor on 6 February. The task force at this point included amphibious assault ships *Inchon* (LPH 12) and *New Orleans*.

On 27 February, a CH-53 Sea Stallion from HM-12 made two sweeps in the Haiphong shipping channel during the first U.S. airborne minesweeping of live mines. President Richard M. Nixon abruptly halted the operations and the minesweeping task force moved to sea, while the chief executive called for "clarification . . . on a most urgent basis" of North Vietnamese delays in releasing American POWs. After North Vietnamese overtures to release the prisoners, the withdrawal of U.S. troops from Vietnam and minesweeping resumed on 4 March. On 27 July, Operation End Sweep concluded and Task Force 78 was disbanded. Helicopters made 3,554 sweeping runs totaling 1,134.7 sweeping hours in 623 sorties. Three helicopters were lost in accidents. Minesweeping ships completed 208 sweeping runs over 308.8 hours.

28 JANUARY • On the first day of the Vietnam cease-fire, aircraft from *Ranger* (CV 61) and *Enterprise* (CVAN 65) flew 81 combat sorties against lines-of-communication targets in Laos. The corridor for their overflights stretched between Hué and Da Nang, South Vietnam. These sorties were flown because the Laotian government requested the assistance and the missions were not related to the Vietnam cease-fire.

1 FEBRUARY • The merger of the First Fleet and Anti-Submarine Warfare Forces, Pacific Fleet resulted in the activation of the Third Fleet at NS Pearl Harbor, Hawaii. The change took place to reduce fleet staffs and achieve economies while retaining control of operational units including 100 ships and submarines and 60,000 sailors and Marines that served a 50-million-square-mile area from the West Coast to beyond Midway Island.

6 FEBRUARY • NAVAIR established a policy stipulating the design of new avionics equipment for troubleshooting by the computerized general-purpose Versatile Avionics Shop Test (VAST) equipment with the capability to test the majority of avionics within the naval aviation inventory.

11 FEBRUARY • Aircraft from *Oriskany* (CVA 34) and *Constellation* (CVA 64) operating on Yankee Station flew strikes against targets in southern Laos. Combat sorties from carriers against Laotian targets had continued since the cease-fire in the Vietnam War, and the station's location was shifted to a position off the coast of the northern part of South Vietnam.

14 FEBRUARY • The Pentagon announced a step-up of U.S. air strikes in Laos from 280 to 380 daily sorties. On this date, aircraft from *Oriskany* (CVA 34) and *Enterprise* (CVAN 65) flew about 160 of these missions into Laos.

A helicopter tows a minesweeping sled off Haiphong, North Vietnam, during Operation End Sweep, which began in February 1973.

25 FEBRUARY • Aircraft from *Oriskany* (CVA 34) and *Ranger* (CV 61) flew combat support missions over Cambodia at the request of that country's government.

4 MARCH • *America* (CVA 66) received orders to sail from the Far East for the United States, as an initial move to reduce the number of carriers deployed off Southeast Asia from six to three by mid-June 1973.

21 MARCH • VXN-8 returned to NAS Patuxent River, Md., from a deployment to the Southern Hemisphere. The squadron completed the operation as part of Project Magnet under the direction of the Naval Oceanographic Office. Its aircraft completed two flights around the world within the hemisphere and, on 4 March, an RP-3D Orion flew over the South Pole—the first flight over the pole by that aircraft type.

29 MARCH • The Military Assistance Command, Vietnam was disbanded, and the remaining U.S. combat troops left South Vietnam. The last phase of Operation Homecoming concluded with the release of the final group of 148 American POWs.

29 MARCH • *Forrestal* (CVA 59) received orders to proceed to Tunisia at speed to assist victims of a flood in the Medjerda River Valley. The carrier led an amphibious assault ship and a destroyer from the Sixth Fleet, and appeared off Tunis at first light 13 hours after receiving orders. SH-3D Sea Kings of HS-3 flying from *Forrestal* evacuated about 200 people and airlifted four tons of relief supplies to flood victims. French, Italian, Libyan, and Tunisian teams also supported the efforts of the Sixth Fleet into 31 March.

1 APRIL • Air Anti-Submarine Wing One with VS-22, -24, -27, -30, -31, and -32, and Helicopter Anti-Submarine Wing One with HS-1, -3, -5, -7, and -11 were established. The move completed the final phase of the functional wing concept in the reorganization of the AirLant community.

13 APRIL • The Secretary of the Navy announced an agreement with the British for an eight-month joint study of an enhanced V/STOL Harrier. The plan was to determine the feasibility of the joint development of the aircraft incorporating a Rolls-Royce Pegasus 15 engine and an advanced wing.

16 APRIL • The Cruise Missile Project Office was established within NAVAIR with the responsibility to develop both tactical and strategic versions of the weapons.

30 APRIL • MGySgt Patrick J. O'Neil, USMC, who had enlisted during World War II, retired as the last Marine enlisted naval aviation pilot.

3 MAY • The Palestinian Yarmuk Brigade entered Lebanon from Syria, leading to fighting between Lebanese soldiers and the Palestinian guerrillas and the declaration of martial law. The U.S. forces in the Mediterranean including *Forrestal* (CVA 59) and *John F. Kennedy* (CV 67) were alerted for possible contingencies. By 9 May, a cease-fire agreement stabilized the situation.

8 MAY • The Navy accepted the first C-9B Skytrain IIs, military versions of the DC-9, during a ceremony at Douglas Aircraft Division, Long Beach, Calif. VR-1 and -30 received the initial squadron deliveries.

18 MAY • A four-day trial of a prototype glide slope indicator concluded on board cruiser *Truxtun* (CGN 35). The Naval Air Engineering Center developed the device as one of several steps taken to achieve an all-weather capability with LAMPS helicopters.

25 MAY • The first production RH-53D Sea Stallion specially configured for airborne mine countermeasures arrived for weapons systems trials at NATC Patuxent River, Md. The Navy preliminary evaluation and the initial phase of the Board of Inspection and Survey trials had begun at Sikorsky Aircraft Division on 15 May.

25 MAY • The all-Navy crew of Capt. Charles Conrad Jr., and Cmdrs. Joseph P. Kerwin, MC, and Paul J. Weitz in Skylab II rendezvoused with the earth-orbiting Skylab workshop. The first tasks of the astronauts included the repair of the lab's solar shield and solar array system, which were damaged during launch from John F. Kennedy Space Center, Fla. On 22 June, Skylab II splashed down in the Pacific. An SH-3G Sea King of HC-1 Detachment 1, embarked on board primary recovery ship *Ticonderoga* (CVS 14), retrieved the astronauts.

7 JUNE • The Deputy Secretary of Defense directed the Navy to produce preliminary plans for a $250-million prototype development plan for a jet fighter aircraft costing less than an F-14 Tomcat.

13 JUNE • The National Aeronautic Association presented the Robert J. Collier Trophy for 1972 jointly to the Navy's Task Force 77 and to the Seventh and Eighth Air Forces for their "demonstrated expert and precisely integrated use of advanced aerospace technology" during Operation Linebacker II against the North Vietnamese during December 1972.

30 JUNE • Fleet Air Wing 1 and 2 were redesignated Patrol Wings (PatWings) 1 and 2. The move marked the end of the use of the FAW (Fleet Air Wing) designation and the return of the PatWing designation.

28 JULY • Capt. Alan L. Bean; Maj. John R. Lousma, USMC; and civilian Dr. Owen K. Garriott launched with Skylab 3 from John F. Kennedy Space Center, Fla. Mission commander Bean set a new record for the most time in space by eclipsing that of naval aviator Capt. Charles Conrad Jr. of 49 days, 3 hours, 37 minutes, by more than 20 days, 12 hours. After a 59-day flight, Skylab 3 splashed down in the Pacific on 25 September. An SH-3G Sea King of HC-1 Detachment 4, embarked on board amphibious assault ship *New Orleans* (LPH 11), recovered the astronauts.

31 JULY • HSL-33 was established as the first squadron dedicated solely to providing LAMPS detachments for LAMPS-configured ships of the Pacific Fleet at NAS Imperial Beach, Calif.

15 AUGUST • The United States ended its combat involvement in Cambodia after six months of intensive bombing in adherence to a vote by Congress on 30 June. During February, aircraft from *Oriskany* (CVA 34) and *Ranger* (CV 61) had conducted combat sorties into Cambodia. From March 1973, aircraft from carriers operating on Yankee Station had flown air, electronic intelligence, surface, subsurface, and surveillance coordinator patrols; and training, tanker, communications relay, and reconnaissance sorties.

16 AUGUST • An F-14 demonstrated the Tomcat's quick-reaction dogfight capability when the jet shot down a maneuvering QT-33 target drone with a Sparrow III air-to-air missile from a distance of less than a mile at the Pacific Missile Range Point Mugu, Calif.

29 AUGUST • HM-12 received the first RH-53D Sea Stallions configured for minesweeping.

6 SEPTEMBER • A BQM-34E target drone equipped with a graphite-epoxy composite wing was test flown at the Point Mugu Sea Test Range, Calif. The Firebee II reached a speed of Mach 1.6 at an altitude of 40,000 feet. The Naval Air Development Center designed and fabricated the test wing at Warminster, Pa. Designers calculated that the composite saved 40 percent of the weight of metal counterparts.

7 SEPTEMBER • The Navy announced the intention to switch the F-4J Phantom IIs that the Navy Flight Demonstration Team—Blue Angels—had flown since 1969 with the slower, smaller, and less expensive A-4F Skyhawks.

1 OCTOBER • The Board of Inspection and Survey service acceptance trials of the S-3A Viking began at NATC Patuxent River, Md.

5 OCTOBER • *Midway* (CVA 41), with CVW-5 embarked, entered Yokosuka, Japan. This marked the first homeporting of a complete carrier task group in a Japanese port as a result of the of 31 August 1972 accord between the United States and Japan. The forward deployment facilitated the continuous positioning of three carriers in the Far East at a time when the economic situation demanded the reduction of carriers in the fleet.

6 OCTOBER • The Yom Kippur (or October) War began between Arabs and Israelis. On 11 October, the ships of the Sixth Fleet available to respond to the crisis included Task Force 60.1 with *Independence* (CV 62) south of Crete, Task Force 60.2 with *Franklin D. Roosevelt* (CVA 42) in the vicinity of the Strait of Bonifacio, and Task Force 61/62 with amphibious assault ship *Guadalcanal* (LPH 7). On 13 October, *John F. Kennedy* (CV 67) sailed from Edinburgh, Scotland, to a holding area 100 miles west of Gibraltar.

One SH-2D Seasprite each embarked with HSL-32 Detachment 1 on board frigate *Belknap* (DLG 26) and Detachment 3 on board escort *Edward McDonnell* (DE 1043), and an SH-2F of HSL-32 Detachment 4, embarked on board escort *W. S. Sims* (DE 1059), provided additional aerial antisubmarine capabilities. Aircraft that supported the Sixth Fleet included nine VP-10 P-3B Orions operating from NS Rota, Spain; eight VP-45 P-3Cs flying from NAS Sigonella, Sicily; and two EC-121M Constellations, four (later six) EA-3B Skywarriors, three EP-3E Aries Is, and one P-3A from VQ-2 deployed to various locations. From 19 to 24 October, the United States provided 50 A-4Ns to the Israelis via the Azores and *Franklin D. Roosevelt*. *Independence* and *John F. Kennedy* assisted Israeli-bound Skyhawk IIs that suffered malfunctions. The Skyhawk pilots returned on board USAF C-5A Galaxys to Dover AFB, Del.

The Israelis rallied and drove the Arabs back and a cease fire ended the war on 23 October. Egyptian President Anwar as-Sadat asked the Americans and Soviets to dispatch forces to enforce the truce. The United States feared Soviet intervention and shifted to Defense Condition (DEFCON)–3 alert status early the next morning. On 24 October, amphibious assault ship *Iwo Jima* (LPH 2) entered the Mediterranean, and the next day *John F. Kennedy* reinforced the Sixth Fleet. By 28 October, *Franklin D. Roosevelt*, *Independence*, *John F. Kennedy*, *Guadalcanal*, and *Iwo Jima* steamed in the Mediterranean. Negotiations defused the tensions and, on 31 October, European Command (less the Sixth Fleet) returned to DEFCON-5. The Arabs and Israelis accepted the diplomatic arrangements, and on 17 November, the Sixth Fleet stood down.

29 OCTOBER • Prompted by the Yom Kippur War and the consequent Arab oil embargo, the Defense Department announced the deployment of *Hancock* (CVA 19) from the South China Sea to the Indian Ocean. She became the first of four carriers to sail in the Indian Ocean through 1974 to focus on such areas as the Strait of Hormuz entrance to the Persian Gulf and the Bab-al-Mandeb entrance to the Red Sea.

16 NOVEMBER • Mission Commander Lt. Col. Gerald P. Carr, USMC; Lt. Col. William R. Pogue, USAF; and civilian Edward G. Gibson launched in Skylab 4 from John F. Kennedy Space Center, Fla. The goals of their scheduled 56-day open-ended space flight included the study of the Comet Kohoutek, earth resources, and the sun. On 8 February 1974, Skylab 4 splashed down in the Pacific after a record-setting 84 days in space. An SH-3G Sea King of HC-1 Detachment 4, embarked on board the primary recovery vessel, amphibious assault ship *New Orleans* (LPH 11), recovered and returned the men to the ship. This event marked the 32nd astronaut retrieval by naval aviation since the beginning of the manned space program in 1961.

21 NOVEMBER • An F-14A Tomcat fired six AIM-54A Phoenix air-to-air missiles and guided them simultaneously to six separate targets 50 miles away over the Pacific Missile Sea Test Range, Calif. The Tomcat obtained four direct hits during this first test of its full Phoenix arsenal.

1 DECEMBER • The Blue Angels became the Navy Flight Demonstration Squadron (Blue Angels) and was designated a shore activity located at NAS Pensacola, Fla.

7 DECEMBER • The launching of *Tarawa* (LHA 1) at Pascagoula, Miss., heralded the first of a new class of amphibious assault ships.

17 DECEMBER • Amphibious assault ship *Iwo Jima* (LPH 2) departed Tunisia after three days of flood relief assistance by her helicopters that included the rescue of people and deliveries of equipment and other flood-associated missions to victims.

20 DECEMBER • Lts. Jane O. McWilliams and Victoria M. Voge became the first women naval flight surgeons upon their graduation from the Naval Flight Surgeon Training Program.

20 DECEMBER • The relocation of the Naval Air Engineering Center from Philadelphia, Pa., to NAS Lakehurst, N.J., occurred, and the authority and responsibility for the air station was reassigned to the chief of Naval Material to be exercised through NAVAIR. On 8 January 1974, the air station was placed under the Naval Air Engineering Center. This concluded the basic organization arrangements involving the relocation of the center from Philadelphia's League Island to NAS Lakehurst, although the physical transfer continued into 1974. The relocation was part of the shore establishment realignment announced by the Secretary of Defense in March 1973.

31 DECEMBER • Ellyson Field, NAS Pensacola, Fla., became the Naval Education and Training Program Development Center, responsible for the administration of the Navy's enlisted advancement system including the development of examinations as well as administering and conducting courses, studies, and training programs.

1974

4 JANUARY • On board *John F. Kennedy* (CV 67), VT-4 students conducted the final flights of TF-9J Cougars.

5 JANUARY • The Naval Aerospace Institute, NAS Pensacola, Fla., announced the scheduling of periodic checks of the physical and mental status of repatriated Navy and Marine prisoners-of-war from the Vietnam War.

18 JANUARY • The Secretary of the Navy named the fourth nuclear-powered carrier *Carl Vinson* (CVN 70), in honor of the Georgia congressman's contributions to national defense during his 50 years in the House of Representatives.

20 JANUARY • VS-41 accepted the first S-3A Vikings introduced to the fleet during ceremonies at NAS North Island, Calif.

22 FEBRUARY • Lt. j.g. Barbara A. Allen became the Navy's first designated female aviator during a ceremony at NAS Corpus Christi, Texas.

161723

An F-14A of VF-1 lands on board *Enterprise* (CVAN 65) during the introduction of Tomcats to the fleet in 1974.

1 MARCH • The YCH-53E Super Stallion, a growth version of the CH-53D Sea Stallion that had been in service since 1965, made its first flight. The new helicopter had three turbine engines instead of two as fitted in Sea Stallions, carried mission loads of 16 tons compared to nine tons, used seven rotor blades in place of six, and accommodated up to 55 troops.

1 MARCH • *John F. Kennedy* (CV 67) began a year-long conversion to accommodate the new CV concept (an air wing capable of performing strike and antisubmarine operations and to operate F-14 Tomcats and S-3A Vikings) at Norfolk Naval Shipyard, Va.

2 MARCH • Two naval aircraft searched an area of 1,230 square miles southwest of the Azores for balloonist Thomas L. Gatch during his unsuccessful attempt to cross the Atlantic.

15 MARCH • *Intrepid* (CVS 11) was decommissioned and placed in the Reserve Fleet after 30 years of service. Since her commissioning on 16 August 1943, *Intrepid* had seen duty as a CV, CVA, and CVS. During World War II, aircraft flying from her flight deck claimed the destruction of 266 enemy planes in the air and 298 more on the ground, and the damage of 178 others. The ship subsequently served as the centerpiece of the nonprofit Intrepid Sea, Air & Space Museum, which opened in New York in 1982.

18 MARCH • The maiden F-14A Tomcat carrier landing was made by pilot Lt. Cmdr. Grover Giles and radar intercept officer Lt. Cmdr. Roger McFillen of VF-1 on board *Enterprise* (CVAN 65). Later that day, a pair of Tomcats also landed from NATC Patuxent River, Md. VF-1 and -2 of CVW-14 led the introduction of Tomcats to the fleet.

1151672

An RH-53D Sea Stallion of HM-12 using Mk 105 minesweeping gear sweeps the Suez Canal during Operation Nimbus Star in May 1974.

22 MARCH • Commander Task Force 65, Rear Adm. Brian McCauley, arrived with a small staff in Cairo, Egypt, to help plan the clearing of the Suez Canal of unexploded ordnance. The Americans, British, Egyptians, and French participated in this operation, Operation Nimbus Star.

2 APRIL • The last C-54Q in naval flying inventory was retired to storage. The Skymaster, BuNo 56501, had flown almost 15,000 hours and more than 2,500,000 nautical miles since its acceptance on 24 March 1945. Its last service was with the Naval Test Pilot School, NAS Patuxent River, Md.

11 APRIL • A P-3A fired the first BGM-84A Harpoon from an Orion at Naval Missile Center Point Mugu, Calif. The missile scored a direct hit on a remote-controlled SEPTAR target boat.

14 APRIL • The Navy donated *Yorktown* (CVS 10) to the National Naval Museum, Charleston, S.C. The carrier had operated with the Pacific Fleet for 25 years before her transfer to the Atlantic Fleet in 1969. She was decommissioned on 27 June 1970.

22 APRIL • A detachment of 12 RH-53D Sea Stallions from HM-12 began sweeping mines from the Suez Canal as part of Operation Nimbus Star.

20 MAY • VQ-4 received the first fleet EC-130G Hercules, BuNo 151889, later used in TACAMO (Take Charge And Move Out) IV low-frequency communication tests.

4 JUNE • NAVAIR established an aircraft survivability/vulnerability branch, which answered the need for a thoroughly coordinated Navy technical program addressing better aircraft survivability in combat.

5 JULY • Majs. John H. Pierson, USMC, and David R. Shore, USMC, flew an OV-10A Bronco 4,480 kilometers from NAS Whidbey Island, Wash., to Homestead AFB, Fla. This set a new world record for distance in a straight line by a Class C-1-F, Group II aircraft, which was sanctioned by the National Aeronautic Association.

15 JULY • Greek Cypriot factions seeking union with Greece overthrew Archbishop Makarios III on Cyprus. On 22 July, U.S. Ambassador to Cyprus Roger Davies requested the evacuation of American citizens. *America* (CVA 66) augmented the Sixth Fleet, and *Forrestal* (CV 59) provided air cover while HMM-162 CH-46F Sea Knights, embarked on board amphibious assault ship *Inchon* (LPH 12), evacuated 466 people including 384 Americans from Dhekelia to amphibious transport dock *Coronado* (LPD 11). Additional evacuation ships included amphibious transport dock *Trenton* (LPD 14) and dock landing ship *Spiegel Grove* (LSD 32). *Trenton* and British carrier *Hermes* (R 12) then proceeded to Akrotiri, Cyprus. On 24 July, they evacuated an additional 286 people including 114 Americans, using medium landing craft and Westland Sea King HAS.1/2 helicopters from No. 814 Squadron and Westland Wessex HU.5s from a detachment of No. 845 Squadron operating from *Hermes*. *Coronado* and *Trenton* disembarked the evacuees in Beirut, Lebanon. The Sixth Fleet forces were released on 2 September.

5 AUGUST • The world's largest unmanned balloon launched from Fort Churchill, Manitoba, Canada. The Office of Naval Research and NASA's Office of Space Science sponsored the flight, which used the Navy's Skyhook program facilities. The entire flight train—balloon, an 800-pound instrument package, and a parachute—lifted to an altitude of 155,000 feet. As the balloon rose, it assumed a fully inflated form of 512 feet in diameter with a volume of 50.3 million cubic feet. A DC-3 of Project Skyhook tracked the balloon during its 500-mile westerly flight.

10 AUGUST • Sikorsky's YCH-53E, designated Aircraft No. 1, flew in a hover at a gross weight of 71,700-pounds. The helicopter carried an external load of 17.8 tons and hovered at a height of 50 feet. This was the heaviest gross weight ever flown and the heaviest payload ever lifted by a helicopter in the Western world.

18 AUGUST • After major flooding in Central Luzon in the Philippines, HMM-164 CH-46D Sea Knights and CH-53D Sea Stallions, embarked on board amphibious assault ship *Tripoli* (LPH 10), and Navy and Marine helicopters operating from combat stores ship *San Jose* (AFS 7) and NAS Cubi Point, together with Air Force aircraft from Clark AFB, flew rescue missions and airlifted emergency food supplies during 244 sorties through 24 August.

28 AUGUST • The Chief of Naval Operations released a formal advanced experimental fighter aircraft (VFAX) operational requirement directing NAVAIR to solicit bids and oversee full-scale development. The VFAX concept resulted in the F/A-18 Hornet.

8 SEPTEMBER • TWA Flight No. 841, a Boeing B-707-331B, from Athens, Greece, en route from Tel Aviv, Israel, to Rome, Italy, crashed into the Ionian Sea, 50 nautical miles west of Cephalonia, Greece. All 88 people on board perished. The National Transportation Safety Board determined that the probable cause of the loss was the detonation of a bomb within the aft cargo compartment. *Independence* (CV 62) and frigate *Biddle* (DLG 34) diverted to the scene and, despite 15- to 20-foot swells, located 24 bodies. SH-3D Sea Kings of HS-5 operating from *Independence* and Greek and Italian sailors assisted boat crews from *Biddle* in the recovery of 12 of the bodies from the shark-infested water. The SAR concluded on 10 September.

10 SEPTEMBER • A boiler explosion ripped through Liberian registered tanker *Eliane* in the Atlantic. *Forrestal* (CVA 59) responded and evacuated two crewmembers.

12 SEPTEMBER • A fire erupted on board liner *Ambassador* in the Caribbean. Oiler *Tallulah* (T-AO 50) rescued 256 crewmembers from the burning ship, and aircraft from NAS Key West, Fla., and three Coast Guard cutters also supported the firefighting efforts.

14 SEPTEMBER • The SEU-3/A Lightweight Ejection Seat manufactured by Stencel Aero Engineering Co. primarily for AV-8A Harriers was approved for service use.

17 SEPTEMBER • VF-1 and -2 began the initial deployment of F-14As Tomcats while embarked on board *Enterprise* (CVAN 65), when she sailed from NAS Alameda, Calif.

17 SEPTEMBER • The prototype LAMPS Mk III H-2/SR helicopter arrived for flight certification tests at Kaman Aircraft Corporation. The aircraft received extensive design modifications to incorporate the LAMPS Mk III avionics package at Naval Air Development Center, Warminster, Pa.

2 OCTOBER • The joint logistics commanders signed an agreement making Dupont's HT-4 the standard fabric for all naval flight suits.

19 NOVEMBER • The Central Treaty Organization exercise Midlink 74 began in the Arabian Sea. *Constellation* (CVA 64) and seven U.S. ships joined British, Iranian, Pakistani, and Turkish vessels during the large-scale training problem.

2 DECEMBER • The Navy's advanced low volume ramjet (ALVRJ) successfully completed its first free flight at Pacific Missile Range Point Mugu, Calif. LTV developed the engine for use by NAVAIR in high performance missiles.

1975

3 JANUARY • The Association of Naval Aviation was founded "to stimulate and extend appreciation of Naval Aviation . . . past, present and future." The nonprofit organization was opened to officers, enlisted persons, or civilians who contributed to, or were interested in, U.S. naval aviation.

17 JANUARY • VX-1 received the first production model of an updated P-3C Orion with new avionics and software at NAS Patuxent River, Md.

18 JANUARY • After violent demonstrations on Cyprus that included disturbances outside the U.S. Embassy in Nicosia, the joint chiefs ordered the Sixth Fleet to deploy *Saratoga* (CV 60) to a position southwest of the island for possible assistance in the evacuation of Americans. On 21 January, the situation quieted and the chiefs released *Saratoga* from her contingency response.

28 JANUARY • Escort *Meyerkord* (DE 1058), with an SH-2F Seasprite from HSL-35 Detachment 4 embarked, rescued all 31 crewmembers from Panamanian-flagged freighter *Gulf Banker* when she sank in the South China Sea. *Meyerkord* returned the survivors to Subic Bay, Philippines.

28 JANUARY • The AIM-54A Phoenix air-to-air missile was approved for service use.

6 FEBRUARY • Cyclone Gervaise killed at least nine people as it cut a path of destruction across Mauritius. The island's Prime Minister Sir Seewoosagur Ramgoolan accepted U.S. offers of aid, and, on 9 February, combat support ship *Camden* (AOE 2) began disaster relief operations at the capital of Port Louis, followed on 12 February by the arrival of *Enterprise* (CVAN 65) and cruiser *Long Beach* (CGN 9). Combat store ship *Mars* (AFS 1) sent two HC-3 Detachment 104 CH-46D Sea Knights to the carrier, which enabled sailors to transport heavy loads including large sections of water pipe into inaccessible remote areas. On 15 February, *Enterprise* sailed from Mauritius.

15 FEBRUARY • The Sikorsky YCH-53E completed Navy preliminary evaluation conducted by HMX-1 and NATC Patuxent River, Md.

2 MARCH • The F-14A Tomcat and AIM-54A Phoenix air-to-air missile received approval for integrated service use.

17 MARCH • The S-3A Viking was approved for service use.

18 MARCH • NAVAIR established an assistant commander for Test and Evaluation (T & E). This came from a mid-1960s Secretary of Defense decision that stressed the need for adequate T & E data to help determine the level of development of new equipment to warrant procurement.

23 MARCH • *Hancock* (CVA 19) embarked HMH-463 at NS Pearl Harbor, Hawaii, while en route from Subic Bay, Philippines, to relieve *Enterprise* (CVAN 65) in the South China Sea. The squadron was to support the potential evacuations of Americans and others from Southeast Asia. Meanwhile, the North Vietnamese continued their southward advance and prepared to cut off the entire northern quarter of South Vietnam, 300 miles north of Saigon.

1 APRIL • Chief Aviation Pilot Eugene T. Rhoads died at Veterans Hospital, San Diego, Calif. In May 1919, Rhoads

C121073

An S-3A catapults from *Forrestal* (CVA 59) during the Viking's initial carrier suitability tests.

had served as a crewmember in the NC-4 during the first transatlantic flight.

12 APRIL • Operation Eagle Pull—the extraction of Americans and allied Cambodians from Cambodia—was activated. Marines of the 31st Marine Amphibious Unit established a perimeter from which to rescue the evacuees within the capital of Phnom Penh. Twelve HMH-462 CH-53D Sea Stallions, embarked on board amphibious assault ship *Okinawa* (LPH 3), evacuated 287 people including U.S. Ambassador John G. Dean and Cambodian President Saukhm Khoy. Upon completion of these flights, HMH-463 CH-53Ds embarked on board *Hancock* (CVA 19), retrieved the Marines.

13 APRIL • The Naval Aviation Museum, NAS Pensacola, Fla., was dedicated, and the Naval Aviation Museum Foundation, Inc. presented the building to the Navy. It replaced the small temporary museum set up in 1962. Seventy-two vintage aircraft were displayed, including the NC-4, the first airplane to fly the Atlantic Ocean.

19 APRIL • *Hancock* (CVA 19), *Midway* (CVA 41), *Coral Sea* (CVA 43), *Enterprise* (CVAN 65), and amphibious assault ship *Okinawa* (LPH 3) deployed to Vietnam for possible evacuation of Americans and allied nationals trapped by the North Vietnamese invasion of South Vietnam. The enemy pronounced the presence of these ships a brazen challenge and violation of the 1973 Paris Peace Accords. During a brief period at NAS Cubi Point, Philippines, *Enterprise* hosted CVW-21 from *Hancock*, thus making possible the use of *Hancock* as a helicopter platform for the evacuations.

29 APRIL • Navy and Marine helicopters from the Seventh Fleet and Army and South Vietnamese helicopters carried out Operation Frequent Wind—the evacuation of Americans and allied nationals from Saigon, South Vietnam. North Vietnamese and People's Liberation Armed Forces mortar and rocket fire compelled the closure of Tan Son Nhut airport. President Gerald R. Ford Jr. consequently ordered the evacuations by helicopter. Marines of the 9th Amphibious Brigade established a perimeter around the

At least nine Vietnamese Air Force UH-1 Huey helicopters packed with people frantically fleeing the communist conquest of South Vietnam approach *Midway* (CVA 41) during Operation Frequent Wind, the evacuation of Saigon, 29 April 1975.

main helicopter landing zone at Tan Son Nhut, and *Hancock* (CVA 19) launched the first evacuation helicopter from a position about 17 miles off Vung Tau.

Aircraft from *Coral Sea* (CVA 43) and *Enterprise* (CVAN 65) flew 173 sorties that covered 638 Air Force and Marine fixed-wing and about 250 CIA rotary-wing missions. Frequent Wind evacuated 395 Americans and 4,475 South Vietnamese and others from Tan Son Nhut as well as 978 Americans, including Ambassador Graham A. Martin and his family, and 1,120 South Vietnamese and allied nationals from the embassy. Helicopters recovered on board vessels including *Midway* (CVA 41) and command ship *Blue Ridge* (LCC 19), but to reduce top hamper and to make room for more aircraft, sailors heaved helicopters overboard. Aircraft from *Coral Sea, Enterprise,* and *Hancock* covered the exodus of a floating city totaling almost 80,000 people, including those who had already reached the ships, en route to the Philippines and Guam.

30 APRIL • VW-4 was disestablished as the Navy's last squadron specifically detailed for hurricane reconnaissance. VJ-2 was established on 15 November 1952 and redesignated VW-4 in 1953. The squadron made major contributions to meteorological science, oceanographic research, the National Weather Service, and the Naval Weather Service Command.

South Vietnamese Air Force Maj. Buang-Ly lands an O-1B Bird Dog carrying his wife and five children on *Midway* (CVA 41) during Operation Frequent Wind, 29 April 1975.

2 MAY • *Midway* (CVA 41) at U'Tapao, Thailand, off-loaded more than 40 Air Force helicopters used in the evacuation of South Vietnam. Crewmembers assisted in the recovery and loading there of more than 95 South Vietnamese Air Force aircraft including F-5A Tigers and A-37B Dragonflies that had been flown there during the fall of Saigon. *Midway* transported the aircraft to Guam.

2 MAY • NAVAIR announced the development of a new carrier-based fighter by the McDonnell Douglas and Northrop aircraft corporations with emphasis on improved maneuvering performance, reliability, and maintainability. The design criteria included speed in excess of Mach 1.5, a combat ceiling of more than 45,000 feet, and a radius of action greater than 400 nautical miles.

5 MAY • The first training class for a new type of physician designated aviation medical officer (AMO) commenced at the NAS Pensacola, Fla., Naval Aerospace Medical Institute. An acute shortage of flight surgeons prompted the program. The AMOs were not scheduled to undergo flight training nor assignment to duty involving flying, but instead were to augment the efforts of flight surgeons during heavy aeromedical workloads, performing flight physicals, and providing routine medical care.

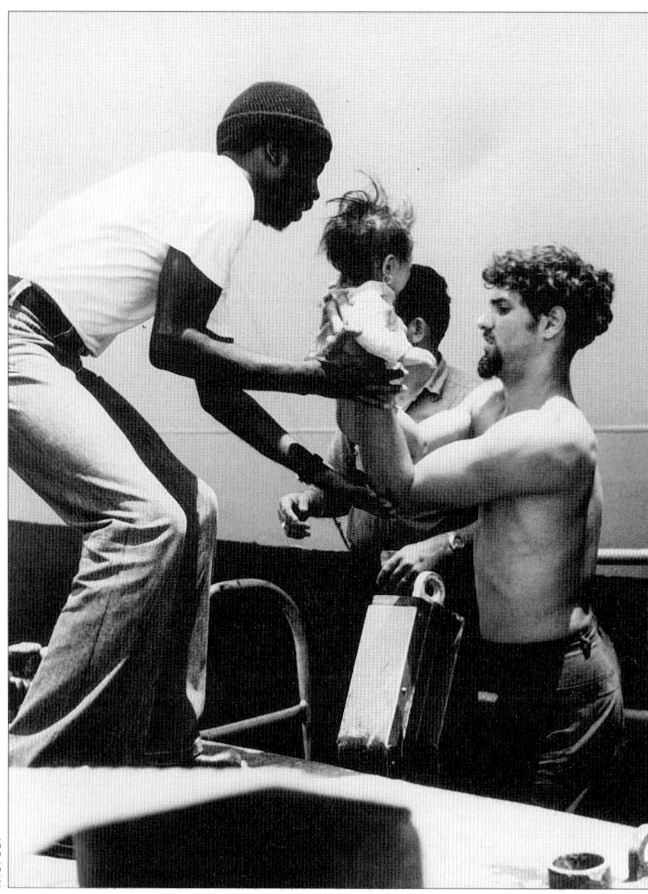

K107587

Sailors from amphibious cargo ship *Durham* (LKA 114) lend a hand with people evacuated from Saigon.

12 MAY • Soldiers from a Khmer Rouge gunboat illegally seized U.S. flagged container ship *Mayaguez* in international waters. The communists held her master, Charles T. Miller, and 39 sailors captive near the island of Koh Tang. On 15 May, *Coral Sea* (CVA 43) and Air Force aircraft operating from Thailand launched protective air strikes against Cambodian naval and air installations on the mainland. Air Force helicopters carried 288 Marines of Battalion Landing Teams 2 and 9 from U'Tapao, Thailand. They assaulted Cambodian troops on Koh Tang, and 60 Marines and sailors from escort *Harold E. Holt* (DE 1074) boarded the deserted merchantman. The Americans freed *Mayaguez* but the Khmer Rouge had already released their hostages. The battle cost the lives of 18 Marines and sailors, the wounding of 50, and the loss of three helicopters and damage to two. *Hancock* (CVA 19) received orders to support the rescue by operating as a helicopter platform with amphibious assault ship *Okinawa* (LPH 3), but neither ship participated.

1 JULY • The termination of all naval gunfire training activities at Culebra Island, P.R., occurred through a joint U.S.–Puerto Rican Commonwealth agreement. Air-to-ground weapons training at Culebra Cays would continue for a limited time because of previously scheduled activities.

1 JULY • The aircraft carrier designation CVA was replaced with CV to improve the accuracy of designations. By removing the letter A, which stood for attack, the new CV designation denoted a multipurpose air, surface, and antisubmarine role, depending on the type of aircraft carried.

23 JULY • The Department of Defense announced the conclusion of U.S. participation in mine-clearing operations in the Suez Canal. From August to October, however, aircraft and ships of the Sixth Fleet assisted the Egyptians in clearing additional mines from Damietta.

24 JULY • Astronauts Col. Thomas P. Stafford, USAF; Vance D. Brand, a former Navy pilot; and Capt. Donald K. Slayton, USAF; splashed down in their Apollo spacecraft after participating in the joint U.S.-Soviet Apollo-Soyuz space mission. Helicopters from HS-6, embarked on board amphibious assault ship *New Orleans* (LPH 11), recovered the astronauts and their spacecraft. This event marked the conclusion of the Apollo-Soyuz mission, the end of the Apollo Program, and the final planned at-sea recovery in the U.S. space program.

28 JULY • The Senate cleared the way for construction at Diego Garcia by voting to expand the U.S. support facility on the British Indian Ocean Territory. The action ended a long dispute over construction at the installation, and permitted the Navy to begin an $18.1 million expansion to include aircraft runway extension, petroleum-oil-lubricants storage areas, a pier, and additional power plant facilities.

29 JULY • The Navy created the lighter-than-air project office at the Naval Air Development Center, Warminster, Pa., to enhance expertise in lighter-than-air technology within the fleet.

1 AUGUST • A KA-3B attached to VAQ-208 completed the longest nonstop flight to date by a carrier-based tactical aircraft. The Skywarrior took off from NS Rota, Spain, and after a 13-hour flight that covered approximately 6,100 miles, landed at NAS Alameda, Calif.

2 AUGUST • The Commandant of the Marine Corps announced that the 12 Marine fighter/attack squadrons were to continue to operate only F-4 Phantom IIs until their replacement by F/A-18 Hornets, beginning in the early 1980s. The Marines had originally intended to equip four squadrons with F-14A Tomcats.

8 AUGUST • Frigate *Capodanno* (FF 1093), with an SH-2F Seasprite of HSL-32 Detachment 4 embarked, rescued all 18 crewmembers of Liberian freighter *Brilliant* when the merchantman sank 35 miles east of Sicily. *Capodanno* returned the survivors to Augusta Bay, Sicily. Additional ships involved in the rescue included destroyer *Stribling* (DD 867), frigate *Donald B. Beary* (FF 1085), and salvage ship *Hoist* (ARS 40).

14 AUGUST • The newly commissioned *Nimitz* (CVN 68) completed refresher training at NS Guantánamo Bay, Cuba, before beginning her cruise with a nuclear task force to northern European waters. The Navy's second nuclear-powered carrier was named in honor of former Chief of Naval Operations Flt. Adm. Chester W. Nimitz.

26 SEPTEMBER • The Chief of Naval Operations approved the popular name Tomahawk for the Navy's sea/surface-launched cruise missile.

3 OCTOBER • VMGR-352 took delivery of the first fleet KC-130R Hercules refueler/transport.

27 OCTOBER • As increased fighting among rival Lebanese political factions led to U.S. concerns for Americans within the country, on this date the State Department advised Americans to evacuate their dependents from Lebanon. The Sixth Fleet dispatched amphibious assault ship *Inchon* (LPH 12) as a contingency evacuation ship, supported by *John F. Kennedy* (CV 67).

1 NOVEMBER • Effective on this date, Naval Aerospace Recovery Facility was disestablished at NAF El Centro, Calif. The National Parachute Test Range at El Centro absorbed the facility's functions. The NAF was assigned to Chief of Naval Operations for command and support.

8 NOVEMBER • Aircraft and more than 100 sailors and Marines from amphibious assault ship *Inchon* (LPH 12) and amphibious transport dock *Shreveport* (LPD 12) extinguished a fire on board Spanish freighter *Cuidad de Valencia* at Palma de Mallorca, Spain.

1161470

Nimitz (CVAN 68), the second nuclear-powered carrier to be commissioned, steams in Chesapeake Bay, 28 February 1975.

22 NOVEMBER • At 2159, *John F. Kennedy* (CV 67) and guided missile cruiser *Belknap* (CG 26) collided during maneuvers, approximately 70 nautical miles east of Sicily. The carrier's firefighters controlled her fires, but heavy smoke forced the temporarily evacuation of the fire rooms and she went dead in the water. Embarked HS-11 SH-3D Sea Kings rescued survivors, and the ship diverted her other flights to NAF Sigonella. *John F. Kennedy*'s angled deck sliced into *Belknap*'s superstructure from her bridge aft as the cruiser passed beneath, and fuel from the carrier's ruptured lines ignited an inferno on board the cruiser. One man died on board *John F. Kennedy* and seven on board *Belknap*. The cruiser was later rebuilt at Philadelphia Naval Shipyard, Pa.

25 NOVEMBER • The first launch in the XJ521 program took place at Point Mugu, Calif. The XJ521 medium-range air-to-air missile resulted from British modifications to U.S. AIM-7E-2 Sparrows. An F-5A Tiger fired the missiles at QT-33 targets.

6 DECEMBER • CH-46s from NAS Whidbey Island, Wash., began search and rescue operations in areas of northwestern Washington flooded by heavy rains. The sailors evacuated 113 people during four days of this humanitarian work.

8 DECEMBER • The production prototype CH-53E Super Stallion made its first flight—about 30 minutes of low-altitude hovering and limited maneuvering—at the Sikorsky Aircraft Division's Stratford, Conn., plant.

1976

28 JANUARY • The Navy awarded a contract for an initial funding of $16 million to McDonnell Douglas Corporation to begin full-scale development of the F/A-18 Hornet.

11 FEBRUARY • The first flight of a terrain contour matching (TERCOM) guidance test vehicle using a modified Navy Firebee drone occurred. TERCOM was subsequently introduced into Tomahawk cruise missiles.

18 FEBRUARY • The night attack weapons system scored a direct hit on a moving M-48 tank during a test at NWC China Lake, Calif. The system, which consisted of a modified AGM-65 Maverick air-to-surface missile, was designed to enhance the performance of tactical and strike aircraft during night operations.

2 MARCH • Two VS-22 S-3As completed the first Atlantic crossing by Vikings when they landed on board *Saratoga* (CV 60) off the coast of Italy. The aircraft departed NAS Cecil Field, Fla., and made stops at NAS Bermuda, NAS Lajes in the Azores, and NS Rota, Spain. The flight validated rapid long-range augmentation by Vikings.

15 APRIL • Offshore drilling platform *Ocean Express* capsized and sank while moving in 15-foot seas in the Gulf of Mexico east of NAS Corpus Christi, Texas. *Lexington* (CVT 16) assisted Coast Guard rescue efforts, hoisted on board a collapsed survival capsule, and recovered the bodies of 16 victims.

6 MAY • An earthquake rocked the Tagliamento River valley northeast of Venice, Italy. Navy C-130 Hercules flew more than ten tons of relief supplies to victims of the disaster.

20 MAY • An AH-1T Sea Cobra made its first flight. The next week, a Sea Cobra flew at 120 knots indicated airspeed, and performed mild sideslips, climbs, and descents.

26 MAY • A contract for a new Navy multi-engine aircraft trainer to be designated T-44A and replace TS-2A Trackers was awarded to Beech Aircraft.

28 MAY • Following the devastation caused by Typhoon Olga across Central Luzon, Philippines, helicopters from HS-4 operating from *Ranger* (CV 61), detachments from HC-3 flying from *Camden* (AOE 2), combat store ships *Mars* (AFS 1) and *White Plains* (AFS 4), and others from NAS Cubi Point and the Air Force assisted in disaster relief efforts. The sailors and airmen evacuated more than 1,900 people, and delivered over 370,000 pounds of disaster relief supplies and 9,340 gallons of fuel.

29 MAY • Amphibious assault ship *Tarawa* (LHA 1) was commissioned at Ingalls Shipbuilding, Pascagoula, Miss.

5 JUNE • The Navy launched the first fully guided Tomahawk cruise missile over the White Sands Missile Range, N.M. An A-6 Intruder of Pacific Missile Test Center launched the missile at an altitude of 11,500 feet and it flew for 61 minutes. This was the first in a series of flights to test the weapon's capability to perform navigation, guidance updates, and low-terrain following maneuvers. It was also the first flight using a turbofan engine; previous tests used a turbojet.

6 JUNE • An A-6 Intruder successfully test fired the tactical version of a Tomahawk cruise missile using the terrain contour matching navigation system.

24 JUNE • The Navy accepted its first T-34C Mentor. The new planes were to replace aging T-34B Mentors and T-28B/C Trojans used in primary and basic flight training. They were also to be the first training command aircraft to have maintenance and supply support provided by civilian contractors.

24 JUNE • The Navy's air-launched low volume ramjet set a distance record traveling more than 100 nautical miles at sustained speeds of over 1,700 miles per hour. This was the fifth flight for the ramjet at Pacific Missile Test Center, Point Mugu, Calif.

30 JUNE • A new major caliber lightweight gun mounted in destroyer *Hull* (DD 945) successfully fired an 8-inch laser-guided projectile developed jointly by the Navy and the Marines.

Tarawa (LHA 1) is the first of a new class of five amphibious assault ships. These combined in one ship type the functions previously performed by four different types: the amphibious assault ship (LPH), amphibious transport dock (LPD), amphibious cargo ship (LKA), and dock landing ship (LSD).

An F-4J Phantom II, BuNo 153088, of VX-4 awaits the final touches on its colorful 1976 bicentennial markings. Its final scheme included a blue stripe down the fuselage side with U.S. Navy and VX-4 in gold lettering.

The radome of an E-2B Hawkeye, BuNo 149819, of VAW-116, embarked on board *Nimitz* (CVN 68), displays the "Spirit of 76" in honor of the nation's 1976 bicentennial.

An SH-3D Sea King, BuNo 154111, of HS-8 bears the squadron's celebratory markings during the nation's 200th anniversary. The American Bicentennial Committee honored HS-8 as a bicentennial command.

30 JUNE • A naval aviation tradition came to an end when the Navy struck brown shoes from the uniforms of officers and chiefs. The practice initially distinguished the brown shoes of naval aviators from the black shoes of surface officers. On 20 October 1986, however, the Navy authorized the restoration of the tradition.

1 JULY • The Navy's Sea-Air Operations Gallery within the new National Air and Space Museum of the Smithsonian Institution opened to the public. This featured depictions of naval aviation history events and contained a mock-up of an aircraft carrier hangar deck, bridge, and preflight operations room. The bridge areas included audio/visual presentations of takeoffs and landings from a carrier, and the hangar deck included Navy aircraft past and present.

9 JULY • The delivery of the first two CH-46Es extended the effectiveness and useful life of the Sea Knight program. The major addition and modifications to CH-46A, D, and Fs to E standards included T-58-GE-16 engines, an Omega-Doppler navigation system, crashworthy pilot and copilot seats, a combat crashworthy fuel system, rescue hoist, and an infrared engine exhaust suppressor.

12 JULY • On 3 July, Israeli commandoes rescued more than 100 hostages held by Palestinian terrorists at the Entebbe, Uganda, airport. Ugandan President Idi Amin lashed out at the Israelis and anyone he perceived as supporting them. On this date, *Ranger* (CV 61) of Task Group 77.7 entered the Indian Ocean from the South China Sea and made for the coast of Kenya in response to a threat of military action by Amin. A VP-17 P-3A Orion that visited the Kenyan capital of Nairobi and the visit of a Middle East Force ship to Mombassa further demonstrated U.S. friendly ties and support for Kenya during the crisis. The United States released *Ranger* from this tasking on 27 July.

An F-4J Phantom II, BuNo 155752, of VF-21 slams into the barricade on board *Ranger* (CVA 61) during Carrier Air Wing 2's Vietnam War operations between 14 October 1969 and 1 June 1970. Both crewmen were uninjured and the aircraft received minimal damage.

12 JULY • The Navy retired the last C-117 Skytrain.

27 JULY • *America* (CV 66) and other elements of Task Force 61 supported the evacuation of 160 Americans and 148 other nationals from Beirut, Lebanon. Amphibious transport dock *Coronado* (LPD 11) removed the evacuees from Lebanon and, on 29 July, arrived in Athens, Greece. *Nimitz* (CVN 68) stood ready to support the evacuations. From January through July 1976, contingency evacuation forces for the Lebanese Civil War involved at different intervals *America*, *Independence* (CV 62), *Nimitz*, and *Saratoga* (CV 60), and amphibious assault ships *Guadalcanal* (LPH 7) and *Iwo Jima* (LPH 2).

27 JULY • The Department of Defense approved the first phase of a program to develop the AV-8B Harrier II, with improved payload and range over the AV-8A.

13 AUGUST • An HU-16 Albatross, the Navy's last operational seaplane, made its final water landing in Pensacola Bay, Fla.

18 AUGUST • North Korean border guards murdered two U.S. Army officers and wounded four other officers and five South Korean soldiers during the so-called Korean Tree Incident. *Midway* (CV 41) received orders to sail from Yokosuka, Japan, and from 21 August to 8 September made a show of force in the Korea Strait.

20 AUGUST • Frigate *Ainsworth* (FF 1090) became the first ship to undergo the installation of a production version of the Harpoon command and launch missile system.

29 AUGUST • The Navy withdrew from VS-37 the last S-2 Tracker in active service. The type entered service with VS-26 in February 1954.

15 SEPTEMBER • Test flights began on the Air Combat Maneuvering Range (ACMR) under construction off the coast of Cape Hatteras, N.C. The range provided air combat training for East Coast squadrons and followed a Navy ACMR at Yuma, Ariz.

17 SEPTEMBER • NASA publicly unveiled the new space shuttle program. Twelve of the 28 astronauts in the program had Navy or Marine Corps aviation backgrounds.

29 SEPTEMBER • The ship-deployable, tactical airborne remotely-piloted vehicle (RPV) made the first automatically closed-loop recovery of an RPV into a net arresting assembly at the National Parachute Test Range, NAF El Centro, Calif.

30 SEPTEMBER • *Oriskany* (CV 34) was decommissioned as the last *Essex*-class carrier at San Francisco, Calif. The ship then entered the Mothball Fleet.

4 OCTOBER • The first overseas operational commitment for the AV-8A on a carrier began when the Harriers of VMA-231, embarked with CVW-19 on board *Franklin D. Roosevelt* (CV 42), sailed for a deployment to the Sixth Fleet in the Mediterranean.

5 NOVEMBER • The Marine Corps received an AH-1T from Bell Helicopter Textron for further testing. This version of the Sea Cobra offered an improved payload of 4,392 lbs over previous versions' 2,739 lbs.

13 NOVEMBER • Cruiser *Wainwright* (CG 28) completed the first at-sea firing tests of RIM-66 SM-2 (extended range) guided missiles. *Wainwright* used a modified Terrier fire control system to control the flight of a Standard missile, and the test capped a five-year program that demonstrated its accuracy.

1 DECEMBER • NAF China Lake, Calif., was disestablished after more than 30 years of operation as a separate facility and became part of the Naval Weapons Center.

1 DECEMBER • Naval Auxiliary Air Station Saufley Field, Fla., was disestablished.

1977

6 JANUARY • The first General Electric F404 development engine underwent testing at the company plant in Lynn, Mass.

13 JANUARY • NAS Jacksonville, Fla., announced that two AV-8A Harriers had made a bow on approach and landing on board *Franklin D. Roosevelt* (CV 42). The event marked the first time in U.S. naval history that fixed-wing aircraft made a bow-on, downwind landing on board a carrier at sea. The Harriers completed their landings and demonstrated the capabilities of V/STOL aircraft to land on board carriers without many of the conditions necessary for fixed-wing conventional aircraft.

14 JANUARY • The simultaneous operations of *Enterprise* (CVN 65) within the Seventh Fleet and *Nimitz* (CVN 68) within the Sixth Fleet marked the first all-nuclear-powered task group operations in both deployed fleets.

31 JANUARY • The Navy accepted delivery of two-seat TA-7C Corsair IIs converted from earlier models and designated combat crew and instrument trainers for replacement pilots of the light attack squadrons that flew Corsair IIs at NAS Cecil Field, Fla., and NAS Lemoore, Calif.

25 FEBRUARY • Ugandan President Idi Amin criticized the United States and directed that all Americans living in Uganda were to meet with him personally. The issue caused concern for the safety of these people, and the joint chiefs ordered *Enterprise* (CVN 65) to maintain station 300 nautical miles east of Kenya. Negotiators persuaded Amin to lift the travel restrictions on Americans, and on 3 March the chiefs released *Enterprise*.

1 MARCH • NARF and NAS Lakehurst, N.J., were disestablished. The modification of the mission of the Naval Air Engineering Center, Lakehurst, enabled the center to absorb their functions.

1 MARCH • The F/A-18 was officially named Hornet.

24 MARCH • The initial service acceptance trials for the CH-53E Super Stallion concluded at NATC Patuxent River, Md.

25 MARCH • NAVAIR announced the testing of the Aerocrane lighter-than-air craft by the Advanced Concepts Division and the Naval Air Development Center, Warminster, Md. The project represented the first government-sponsored study of lighter-than-air flight in several years.

5 APRIL • The Navy took delivery of T-44A Pegasus (King Air 90) trainers at NAS Corpus Christi, Texas.

8 APRIL • VAW-121 received the first fleet E-2C automatic radar processing system (ARPS)–equipped Hawkeye at NAS Norfolk, Va. The new aircraft was designed to improve the radar capability in its airborne early warning mission.

12 APRIL • An operational requirement was established for night vision capability in Marine Corps transport helicopters.

21 APRIL • *Franklin D. Roosevelt* (CV 42) returned to the United States from the Mediterranean after her final overseas deployment prior to decommissioning on 1 October 1977.

22 JUNE • An OV-10D Bronco equipped with a forward-looking infrared (FLIR) imaging system underwent testing and evaluation at NATC's Strike Aircraft Test Directorate, Patuxent River, Md. FLIR allowed the two-man crew to pinpoint targets obscured by dark, camouflage, dust, smoke, haze, and light fog by detecting thermal radiation they emitted compared to their surroundings. The system also proved useful for navigation, terrain avoidance and surveillance, target detection, recognition and tracking, gun laying, and as a landing aid.

13 JULY • A pilot in an F-4J Phantom II from NATC Patuxent River, Md., made the first landing using the microwave landing system (MLS) at the FAA Test Facility, Atlantic City, N.J. The system was designed to reach out electronically, catch target aircraft, and fly them to safe landings without the pilots touching the controls.

23 JULY • The National Aviation Hall of Fame, Dayton, Ohio, inducted Rear Adm. Alan B. Shepard Jr.

11 AUGUST • Marine Corps pilots flew the first of 400 CH-46E Sea Knights retrofitted with newly developed fiberglass rotor blades that were less susceptible to corrosion and fatigue damage.

26 AUGUST • The Navy unveiled the XFV-12A V/STOL research aircraft at the Rockwell International facility in Columbus, Ohio. The single-engine single-seat thrust-augmented wing prototype high-performance fighter was designed to operate from small ships.

29 AUGUST • The first production model P-3C Update II arrived for technical evaluation at NATC Patuxent River, Md. The upgraded Orions incorporated enhanced avionics and weapons systems including a turret-mounted infrared detection device to identify targets day or night, and AGM-84 Harpoon air-to-ground missiles.

1 SEPTEMBER • The Navy selected LAMPS Mk III helicopter contractors; Sikorsky Aircraft Division to build the aircraft and General Electric's Aircraft Engine Group to provide the engines.

30 SEPTEMBER • The Joint Cruise Missile Project Office was established in the Naval Material Command. The Navy and Air Force shared responsibility for developing cruise missiles. The Cruise Missile Project Office had been a NAVAIR project.

1 OCTOBER • The Naval Aviation Logistics Center became fully operational at NAS Patuxent River, Md. It was responsible for the implementation, coordination, and management of Navy-wide depot-level aviation maintenance programs.

31 OCTOBER • The Department of Defense directed a significant relocation of the essential mission of the National Parachute Test Range, El Centro, Calif. The range had been responsible for research, development, training, and evaluation (RDT&E) for parachute systems and for providing common airfield support to aviation units. The RDT&E mission shifted to NWC China Lake, Calif., while the airfield support mission remained at NAF El Centro.

14 NOVEMBER • The chief of Naval Air Training formally accepted turboprop T-34C Mentor trainers. The planes subsequently were renamed Turbomentors.

1978

7 JANUARY • A fire erupted on board Indian freighter *Jagat Padmini* 30 miles southeast of Sicily, Italy. An HS-9 SH-3H Sea King, embarked on board *Nimitz* (CVN 68), spotted the blaze and alerted rescuers. *Nimitz*, cruiser *South Carolina* (CGN 37), and destroyer *Bigelow* (DD 942) battled exploding oil drums, heavy seas, and 25- to 30-knot winds to rescue 43 crewmembers and extinguish the blaze. A Sea King struck an obstruction and crashed, but the four crewmembers survived. Italian tug *Monte Priolo* took the stricken ship in tow.

2 FEBRUARY • Submarine *Barb* (SSN 596) successfully launched a Tomahawk cruise missile that flew a fully guided land attack test flight that terminated at Edwards AFB, Calif. This was the first launch of a Tomahawk from a submarine.

9 FEBRUARY • The first satellite of the Navy Fleet Satellite Communications System was launched. The system satisfied the need for worldwide tactical command, control, and communications for the entire fleet.

27 FEBRUARY • A contract for full-scale production of the CH-53E Super Stallion was awarded to Sikorsky Aircraft.

28 FEBRUARY • The Department of Defense authorized the full-scale development of the SH-60B LAMPS Mk III Seahawk.

FEBRUARY • During the latter part of the month, ships began surveillance operations of the Somali invasion of the Ogaden region of Ethiopia. The invasion quickly collapsed and *Kitty Hawk* (CV 63) received orders to a holding point north of Singapore until 23 March.

17 MARCH • NASA selected four two-man crews for early flights of the space shuttle. The first scheduled orbital test included Navy Capt. John W. Young as commander and Cmdr. Robert L. Crippen as pilot, while Col. Joe H. Engle, USAF, and Cmdr. Richard H. Truly comprised the backup crew. The first group of two-man crews also included Lt. Col. John R. Lousma, USMC.

10 APRIL • The first TA-7C Corsair II attack trainer arrived for Board of Inspection and Survey trials at NATC Patuxent River, Md.

14 APRIL • The first of 12 C-2A Greyhounds rolled off the service life extension program (SLEP) line at NARF North Island, Calif. SLEP added seven to ten years of service to the carrier-on-board-delivery planes.

9 JUNE • Commander NWC Rear Adm. William L. Harris accepted the Daedalian Weapons Systems Award in San Antonio, Texas. The Order of Daedalians, a national fraternity of military pilots, selected NWC and NAVAIR as co-winners in recognition of the success of the commands in working as a team on the Sidewinder family of heat-seeking guided missiles.

JULY • During growing unrest in Afghanistan, *Enterprise* (CVN 65) operated until 31 July in the vicinity of Diego Garcia, British Indian Ocean Territory.

8 JULY • The Naval Air Test and Evaluation Museum opened its doors to the public at NAS Patuxent River, Md.

21 JULY • The final flight of the service acceptance trials for the AH-1T Sea Cobra took place at NATC Patuxent River, Md.

22 JULY • Capt. Holden C. Richardson, CC (Naval Aviator No. 13), was inducted into the National Aviation Hall of Fame, Dayton, Ohio. He was the first naval aviation engineering officer so honored.

25 JULY • Through the following day, a mock-up of an SH-60B Seahawk underwent shipboard compatibility trials on board frigate *Oliver Hazard Perry* (FFG 7). On 2 and 3 August, evaluators carried out additional similar trials with destroyer *Arthur W. Radford* (DD 968).

3 AUGUST • NAVAIR announced that testing of a vertical-seeking ejection seat took place during the summer at NWC China Lake, Calif. While carrying a dummy crewmember, the seat was fired downward from a suspended test module. The seat traveled less than 45 feet before reversing direction and traveling upward, and then parachuted safely to the ground. These tests demonstrated the capabilities of vertical-seeking seats to safely eject while upside down within 50 feet of the surface, and thus increase the safety envelope of ejection seats.

14 SEPTEMBER • A 60-hour technical test of CH-53Es undertaken to determine if changes made since the initial trials had altered the performance of the Super Stallions ended successfully.

15 SEPTEMBER • A test bed P-3C for the Update III program arrived at Naval Air Development Center, Warminster, Pa. The Orion featured an advanced signal processor developed by IBM, which provided a four-fold improvement in isolating sounds of submerged targets from ocean background noise.

9 NOVEMBER • An AV-8B Harrier II flew for the first time at McDonnell Douglas Corporation, St. Louis, Mo.

18 NOVEMBER • An F/A-18A Hornet flew for the first time at McDonnell Douglas Corporation, St. Louis, Mo.

18 DECEMBER • Commander NAVAIR established the undergraduate Jet Pilot Training System Project. This was designed to provide naval aviation with an integrated intermediate and advanced jet training program consisting of aircraft, simulators, academics, and training management.

27 DECEMBER • The United States directed *Constellation* (CV 64) to the vicinity of Singapore in response to the Iranian hostage crisis and because of vital U.S. interests in the Persian Gulf area. On 2 January 1979, President James E. Carter Jr. ordered the ship to remain in the South China Sea. On 16 January, the crisis temporarily abated when Iranian Shah Mohammad R. Pahlavi departed for exile. The ongoing situation nonetheless prompted the State Department to order the evacuation on 30 January of all U.S. government dependents and nonessential Americans from the country. On 28 January, *Constellation* was released from her tasking, and on 18 and 21 February, the British evacuated many Westerners from Iran.

1979

2 JANUARY • A Soviet Aeroflot Ilyushin Il-14FKM Crate crashed near Molodezhnaya, Antarctica, killing four of the seven crewmembers. An LC-130 Hercules of VXE-6 rescued the survivors.

16 JANUARY • The first F/A-18 Hornet arrived for evaluation trials at NATC Patuxent River, Md. Testing was to include in-flight refueling, land-based catapult launchings and arrested landings, speed tests, and at-sea carrier takeoffs and landings on board *America* (CV 66).

25 JANUARY • The Navy's YAV-8B Harrier II prototype arrived to test its aerodynamic improvements at NATC Patuxent River, Md.

9 FEBRUARY • Secretary of the Navy W. Graham Claytor Jr. announced the decision to name the helicopter portion of the Navy's SH-60B LAMPS Mk III program as the Seahawk. The name honored the Curtiss F7C and SC-1 Seahawks.

14 FEBRUARY • Submarine *Guitarro* (SSN 665) launched a Tomahawk missile from off the California coast. This successful evaluation was part of a planned series of three submarine launches and flight tests of Tomahawks conducted in February and June that demonstrated the over-the-horizon capability of the missiles to carry out simulated searches of, and attacks on, target ships at sea.

22 FEBRUARY • The Chinese invaded Vietnam in retaliation for the Vietnamese invasion of China's ally Kampuchea (Cambodia). On 25 February, *Constellation* (CV 64) entered the South China Sea to monitor the crisis and increased Soviet naval deployments to the region.

27 FEBRUARY • The Navy took delivery of the last A-4—an A-4M assigned to VMA-331—from McDonnell Douglas Corporation. The delivery ended a continuous Skyhawk production run of 2,960 aircraft over 26 years.

7 MARCH • The United States directed *Constellation* (CV 64) from the South China Sea to the Gulf of Aden to monitor fighting between North and South Yemen. Tankers carrying oil to the United States and its allies passed through the gulf. An aircraft carrier operated in the area until 6 June.

A P-3A Orion, BuNo 152170, of VP-17 patrols over a Soviet *Boris Chilikin*–class replenishment oiler in the Sea of Japan, c. 1976.

11 MARCH • A P-3B Orion from NATC Patuxent River, Md., flew the first transoceanic flight guided by the space-based NavStar radio navigation system on a six-hour mission from NAS Barbers Point, Hawaii, to NAS Moffett Field, Calif. The NavStar system comprised 24 satellites in earth orbit providing radio navigational information.

20 MARCH • The last variant of the P-2 Neptune rolled off the production line during ceremonies in Japan. This concluded a manufacturing run of 34 years.

26 MARCH • An AV-8A at NATC Patuxent River, Md., tested a ski jump ramp developed by the British to reduce Harrier takeoff distance. The 130-foot-long ramp with a 12 degree inclination reduced the total takeoff distance for Harriers from 930 to 230 feet.

16 APRIL • *Midway* (CV 41) relieved *Constellation* (CV 64) as the Indian Ocean contingency carrier. Ongoing crises involving Iran and Yemen prompted the carrier deployments.

21 APRIL • The Navy's supersonic tactical missile test vehicle made its first flight at the Pacific Missile Test Center.

Naval officers examine one of two Northrop YF-17 lightweight fighters, c. 1974–1975, most likely 72-1570, the second aircraft, which was painted in Navy colors. The design served as the basis for the later F/A-18 Hornet.

Vought developed this advanced integral rocket/ramjet test vehicle, which the designers intended as a major step toward development of a new generation of high performance, air-to-surface tactical standoff missiles.

NAH 002785

With his sole possessions clasped in his teeth, a Vietnamese refugee climbs netting to combat store ship *White Plains* (AFS 4). He and 28 other Vietnamese boat people were found floating in a 35-foot wooden boat in the South China Sea, 30 July 1979.

23 APRIL • Vice Adm. Forrest S. Petersen transferred ownership of the sole remaining Kawanishi H8K2 flying boat to the Japanese Museum of Maritime Science during a ceremony at NAS Norfolk, Va. The Navy brought the Emily to the United States late in 1945 to undergo tests at Patuxent River, Md. After test completion, the plane was stored at Norfolk and outlasted all its sister aircraft. In July 1979, the museum transported the Emily to Tokyo.

30 APRIL • Lt. Rodney M. Davis of HM-12 set a transcontinental long-distance, non-stop flight record by piloting an RH-53D, Aircraft No. 430, from NAS Norfolk, Va., to San Diego, Calif. Davis flew the Sea Stallion 2,077 nautical miles in 18.5 hours, refueling in the air from an Air National Guard HC-130 Hercules.

5 MAY • After pirates repeatedly attacked a vessel packed with Vietnamese refugees in the South China Sea, on this date *Robert E. Peary* (FF 1073) rescued the 442 survivors adrift about 400 miles south of Thailand. Three days later, the frigate transferred the refugees to amphibious assault ship *Tarawa* (LHA 1). On 12 May, *Tarawa* put the people ashore in Thailand.

22 MAY • The first of two AV-8Cs arrived for service acceptance trials at NATC Patuxent River, Md. Improvements in these Harriers included a new UHF radio, a chaff and flare dispensing system, lift improvement devices, a radar warning system, and secure voice equipment.

30 MAY • The United States released *Midway* (CV 41) from contingency operations in the Arabian Sea and the ship sailed for the Pacific.

12 JUNE • The Deputy Secretary of Defense approved the mission element need statement for the Jet Pilot Training System Project. The system facilitated the provision of undergraduate pilot training for student naval aviators and transition students of the Navy and Marine Corps.

20 JUNE • Lt. Donna L. Spruill of VRC-40 became the first female naval aviator to carrier qualify in a fixed-wing aircraft. Spruill and copilot and squadron commanding officer, Cmdr. Jerry L. Wright, made ten landings and three catapult launches in a C-1A Trader on board *Independence* (CV 62) in the Atlantic.

1 JULY • The deactivation of the Army's Executive Flight Detachment left HMX-1 as the single source of helicopter support for the White House.

17 JULY • Amphibious assault ship *Saipan* (LHA 2) operated off the coast of Nicaragua for possible evacuation of Americans because of the turmoil surrounding the fall of that government to the Marxist Sandinistas.

18 JULY • A P-3C Orion of VP-23 fired an AGM-84 Harpoon air-to-ground missile. VP-23 was the first operational fleet patrol squadron to receive, fire, and make an operational deployment with Harpoons. On 17 August, the announcement of the entry of Harpoons into operational service as air-launched weapons occurred during a ceremony at NAS Brunswick, Maine.

19 JULY • President James E. Carter Jr. announced that he had instructed the Seventh Fleet to aid Vietnamese refugees, dubbed "boat people" by the media, and assist them to safety. Aircraft and ships of the Seventh Fleet thus stepped up patrolling, assistance, and rescue efforts.

1175289

Vietnamese refugees displaying an SOS sign from their fragile craft signal the crew of a VP-22 P-3B Orion in the Western Pacific, August 1979.

21 JULY • The National Aviation Hall of Fame in Dayton, Ohio, inducted Neil A. Armstrong. He served as a Navy pilot during the Korean War and later, as commander of the Apollo 11 mission, became the first man to step on the moon.

24 JULY • The Bell XV-15 successfully transitioned in flight from helicopter- to fixed-wing mode. The joint Navy/Army/NASA XV-15 flight test program evaluated the tilt-rotor concept.

27 JULY • A turbojet-powered Northrop BQM-74C aerial target successfully completed its first flight over the Pacific Missile Test Center, Point Mugu, Calif. The 33-minute flight also marked the first airborne launch of the type from an A-6 Intruder.

30 AUGUST • The first prototype of an SH-60B Seahawk was unveiled at the Sikorsky Aircraft Division, Stratford, Conn.

30 AUGUST • A CH-53D Sea Stallion of VR-24 lifted a 12-foot bronze statue of the Madonna and Child to the top of Mt. Tiberius on Capri, Italy. Lightning had destroyed the original statue and the replacement proved too large for overland transportation.

15 SEPTEMBER • The first naval UC-12B Huron arrived for preliminary evaluation tests at NATC Patuxent River, Md.

18 SEPTEMBER • The circulation control rotor made its first flight using the airframe and propulsion system from an HH-2D helicopter. The Navy's advanced rotor system project was to improve performance, reduce maintenance requirements, and reduce vibration levels over extant rotor systems.

28 SEPTEMBER • RVAH-7 was disestablished as the last RA-5C Vigilante squadron. The Navy planned to use some of the Vigilantes as drones.

1 OCTOBER • AV-8A shipboard trials began on board amphibious assault ship *Saipan* (LHA 2). The testing consisted of 33 flights involving short and vertical takeoffs, and vertical landings by the Harriers through 8 October.

2 OCTOBER • In the wake of reports concerning a possible build-up of Soviet troops in Cuba, the joint chiefs ordered the establishment of a Caribbean contingency task force. On 11 October, amphibious assault ship *Nassau* (LHA 4) and other amphibious ships made for NS Guantánamo Bay, Cuba. President James E. Carter Jr. ordered the ships to make a show of force in response to maneuvers by Soviet troops on the island. On 17 October, 1,800 Marines landed in Guantánamo Bay as a demonstration of naval power in the wake of the Soviet refusal to withdraw their combat brigade.

Later in the month, *Forrestal* (CV 59) transited close to Cuba in conjunction with the U.S. policy of an increased presence in the Caribbean.

14 OCTOBER • A-6E target recognition attack multisensor-equipped all-weather Intruders began fleet operations at NAS Oceana, Va.

26 OCTOBER • South Korean President Park C. Lee was assassinated. On 28 October, *Kitty Hawk* (CV 63) received orders to operate in the East China Sea off Cheju Do in the Korean Strait. Aircraft from the ship completed flight operations within the detection envelope of North Korean early warning radars to demonstrate U.S. support of the South Koreans. *Kitty Hawk* left the area on 5 November.

30 OCTOBER • An F/A-18 made the first landing of a Hornet at sea on board *America* (CV 66). The plane completed 32 catapult and arrested landings during five days of sea trials.

4 NOVEMBER • A mob of revolutionaries seized 66 Americans including one naval aviator and 14 Marines at the U.S. Embassy and the Iranian Foreign Ministry in Tehran, Iran. Their demands included the return to Iran from the United States of deposed Shah Mohammad R. Pahlavi.

18 NOVEMBER • *Midway* (CV 41), which had been operating in the Indian Ocean, arrived in the northern Arabian Sea in connection with the ongoing hostage crisis in Iran.

20 NOVEMBER • The last RA-5C in the Navy departed on its final flight from NAS Key West, Fla. The mission completed the phase-out of the entire reconnaissance inventory of 156 Vigilantes.

21 NOVEMBER • The United States directed *Kitty Hawk* (CV 63) to sail to the Indian Ocean to join *Midway* (CV 41) in the northern Arabian Sea in response to the Iranian hostage crisis. On 3 December, *Kitty Hawk* arrived, marking the first time since World War II that the United States had deployed two carriers in the Indian Ocean in response to a crisis situation. *Kitty Hawk* recorded continual Soviet surveillance by Antonov An-12 Cubs flying from Aden, Yemen, supplemented at three-day intervals by Il-38 Mays. On 21 and 22 January 1980, Soviet spy trawler *No. 477* conducted what *Kitty Hawk* reported as "provocative maneuvers close aboard." *Kitty Hawk* left the area on 24 January.

12 DECEMBER • The development program for SH-60B LAMPS Mk IIIs reached a milestone when one of the Seahawks completed its first flight at Sikorsky's West Palm Beach, Fla., test facility.

17 DECEMBER • The first two-seat F/A-18B Hornet arrived for armament and stores separation testing at NATC Patuxent River, Md. During 1979, the center conducted 416 F/A-18 flights for a total of 555 hours testing. On 12 December, it completed a successful live firing of an AIM-9 Sidewinder air-to-air missile from a Hornet.

21 DECEMBER • The Department of Defense announced the deployment of *Nimitz* (CVN 68) from the Sixth Fleet in the Mediterranean to the Indian Ocean to relieve *Kitty Hawk* (CV 63).

24 DECEMBER • The Soviets airlifted 5,000 airborne troops into Kabul, Afghanistan. The United States protested the move, which the Soviets claimed had been conducted at the request of the Afghan government. On 27 December, a Soviet-backed coup installed a new regime in the country. The Soviet invasion reinforced the U.S. decision to maintain two carriers in the region, and *Kitty Hawk* (CV 63) and *Midway* (CV 41) extended their contingency operations in the northern Arabian Sea.

31 DECEMBER • Ships and aircraft of the Seventh Fleet continued their patrols and rescue assistance efforts connected with the Vietnamese boat people. During the final six months of 1979, Navy ships rescued more than 800 Vietnamese refugees, and P-3 Orions directed merchant vessels to the rescue of more than 1,000 others.

CHAPTER 11

The 600-Ship Navy

1980–1989

A build-up of naval aviation, the rise of global acts of terrorism, and the U.S. response to global crises characterized the eighth decade of naval aviation. As the decade began, aircraft carriers sailed ready to project U.S. power against extremists who held Americans hostage in Tehrān, Iran. These ships had increasingly deployed to the Indian Ocean during the latter part of the 1970s, and strengthened the trend into the 1980s as a result of ongoing and growing problems in the Middle East, East Africa, and Asia.

Eastern Bloc naval expansion threatened Western control of the sea, and the United States countered by developing a maritime strategy that focused on the three pillars of deterrence, forward defense, and alliance solidarity. To accomplish this plan, the Navy developed a maritime component in which carriers were to thrust toward strategic points encircling the Eastern Bloc and contain the Soviet fleet to enable U.S. warships to patrol the open oceans and reinforce allies.

Naval aviation experienced resurgence in strength and capabilities through building programs and new technology research. A number of naval aircraft joined the fleet, including F/A-18 Hornets, SH-60B LAMPS (Light Airborne Multi-Purpose System) Mk III Seahawks and their derivatives, MH-53E Sea Dragons, and AV-8B Harrier IIs. The rollout of fixed-wing, tilt-rotor V-22 Ospreys capable of vertical takeoff and landing (VTOL) and high-speed horizontal flight introduced new aircraft concepts.

Missile development kept pace with aircraft progress. New introductions included AGM-88 High-speed Anti-Radiation Missiles (HARM), AGM-114 Hellfire precision strike air-to-ground missiles, and R/UGM-109 Tomahawk Land Attack Missiles (TLAM, originally known as cruise missiles) capable of attacking ships and targets ashore. The platforms for these missiles also kept pace. Additional *Nimitz* (CVN 68)-class nuclear-powered aircraft carriers and *Wasp* (LHD 1)-class multipurpose amphibious assault ships were commissioned, and Congress authorized more of these ships for construction. Naval aviation celebrated its 75th anniversary in 1986, and throughout the year the Navy lauded the men and women who had contributed to the force.

Involvement in confrontations during the decade began with the Iranian hostage crisis from 1979 to 1981. Clashes with the Libyans demonstrated naval aviation's air-to-air and strike capabilities, and Operation Urgent Fury reestablished democracy on the Caribbean island of Grenada. Operations in and around Lebanon kept naval aviation occupied during the mid-1980s, and responding to terrorist crimes and hijackings around the Mediterranean basin became an ongoing requirement for most of the decade.

The Persian Gulf War between Iran and Iraq escalated and the fleet became involved in short but fierce battles in that area. Escorting reflagged oil tankers and monitoring the fighting kept naval aviation on the line in the region from the mid-1980s. As the decade ended, Saddam Hussein invaded Kuwait and the UN imposed an economic blockade on Iraq to force its withdrawal.

In 1982 the Navy began working with U.S. Customs and the Coast Guard to curb the influx of drugs into the United States, and E-2C Hawkeyes became permanent participants in the detection of drug smuggling aircraft. Other activities included continued involvement in the manned space program and assistance during natural disasters. As the 1980s ended, the détente between the Americans and Soviets continued. During these years, naval aviation demonstrated diverse capabilities.

KN 29933

CNO Adm. Thomas B. Hayward delivers remarks at the launching of *Carl Vinson* (CVN 70), 15 March 1980. The third *Nimitz*-class carrier was named after the long serving Georgia congressman.

1980

1 JANUARY • VP-23 deployed from Keflavik, Iceland, to Diego Garcia, British Indian Ocean Territory. The squadron made its first operational flight from the atoll within ten days of its receipt of orders.

2 JANUARY • A detachment of P-3B Orions from VP-10 deployed to NS Rota, Spain, flew photoreconnaissance missions to locate areas damaged by an earthquake that struck the Azores the previous day, killing 50 people and injuring about 500 others.

4 JANUARY • *Nimitz* (CVN 68) rendezvoused with her nuclear-powered escort ships in the Mediterranean and made for the Indian Ocean via the Cape of Good Hope to relieve *Kitty Hawk* (CV 63) during contingency operations in the Indian Ocean. The departure of *Nimitz* left *Forrestal* (CV 59) as the only U.S. carrier operating in the Mediterranean.

4 JANUARY • The test flight of the first TA-7C Corsair II assigned to the Pacific Missile Test Center occurred at Point Mugu, Calif.

7 JANUARY • Reconnaissance Attack Wing One was disestablished. The wing had consisted of nine fleet squadrons, one training squadron, and a support command that provided tactical reconnaissance for deployed carriers. The phase out coincided with the disestablishment of the last RVAH squadron on 28 September 1979, in preparation for the final retirement from the fleet of all RA-5C Vigilantes on 20 November 1979.

22 JANUARY • *Nimitz* (CVN 68) rendezvoused with *Midway* (CV 41) and *Kitty Hawk* (CV 63) in the Arabian Sea.

5 FEBRUARY • *Coral Sea* (CV 43) relieved *Midway* (CV 41) in the Arabian Sea.

29 FEBRUARY • VMO-1 at New River, N.C., began flying OV-10D Broncos equipped with forward looking infrared and laser rangefinder designator systems.

1 MARCH • The Navy confirmed that Chief of Naval Operations Adm. Thomas B. Hayward had proposed to Secretary of Defense Harold Brown a plan to reactivate *Oriskany* (CV 34) and several other mothballed ships, to help fulfill the Navy's missions in the Indian Ocean and other areas.

6 MARCH • Amphibious assault ship *Nassau* (LHA 4) began a month-long cruise to the Caribbean to demonstrate U.S. capabilities to defend the Panama Canal in accordance with the 1979 Panama treaty.

16 APRIL • *Dwight D. Eisenhower* (CVN 69) sailed from the East Coast to relieve *Nimitz* (CVN 68) in the Indian Ocean. Two days later, *Constellation* (CV 64) departed Subic Bay, Philippines, to relieve *Coral Sea* (CV 43) in the Indian Ocean.

24 APRIL • The United States launched Operation Blue Light (Eagle Claw) to rescue the 53 Americans held hostage by Iranian militants in Tehrān, Iran. Eight RH-53D Sea Stallions lifted off from *Nimitz* (CVN 68) in the Arabian Sea to rendezvous with Special Forces troops and with six USAF C-130 Hercules flying from al Masirah Island, Oman. A *haboob*—a huge dust cloud—forced helicopters No. 2 and 5 to land short of their objective, and mechanical problems compelled No. 6 to put down at a secret refueling site within Iran designated Desert One. Planning called for a minimum of six operational helicopters to rescue the hostages, and with only five capable of continuing, commanders aborted the mission. During the withdrawal of a helicopter, it collided with a Hercules when they repositioned to refuel, killing eight men. The remaining Hercules evacuated the survivors.

25 APRIL • A P-3B of VP-4 deployed to NAS Cubi Point, Philippines, spotted a vessel carrying Vietnamese refugees 300 miles northeast of Ho Chi Minh City (Saigon), Vietnam. The Orion directed oiler *Sealift Antarctic* (T-AOT 176) to the rescue of 59 people.

30 APRIL • *Constellation* (CV 64) relieved *Coral Sea* (CV 43) in the Indian Ocean.

30 APRIL • President James E. Carter Jr. ordered the Navy to divert ships scheduled for exercise Solid Shield 80 in the Atlantic and Caribbean to assist the Coast Guard in the rescue of Cuban refugees, who fled their country en masse in dangerously overcrowded boats through the Florida Strait for the United States. Amphibious assault ship *Saipan* (LHA 2), and amphibious transport docks *Ponce* (LPD 15) and *Shreveport* (LPD 12) led a combination of amphibious vessels and minesweepers that supported the Coast Guard, and P-3 Orions flew patrols primarily from NAS Key West, Fla. Eleven Navy ships ultimately took part in what became known as the Mariel boatlift. On 8 July, the Navy terminated its support. More than 125,000 Cuban refugees fled to the United States by 12 June, when the tempo of Solid Shield 80 diminished.

8 MAY • Following a voyage from the United States via the Cape of Good Hope, *Dwight D. Eisenhower* (CVN 69) relieved *Nimitz* (CVN 68) in the Arabian Sea.

27 MAY • *Coral Sea* (CV 43) was diverted to operate south of Cheju-do in the Korea Strait in response to South Korean civil unrest. *Midway* (CV 41) relieved *Coral Sea* on 30 May.

28 MAY • The Naval Academy Class of 1980 graduated the first group of students to include women—55 of the 770 graduates.

3 JUNE • A Marine A-4M launched the first AGM-65E Maverick air-to-ground missile from a Skyhawk during tests at Eglin AFB, Fla. Hughes Aircraft Company had developed the laser-guided version of the Maverick with a heavier warhead for use by the Marines in close air support.

6 JUNE • Ens. Brenda E. Robinson, USNR, became the first African American female naval aviator at NAS Corpus Christi, Texas. Robinson was the 59th woman to enter naval flight training and the 42nd to earn her wings. On 23 March 1979, she graduated from Aviation Officer Candidate School, NAS Pensacola, Fla. Robinson later flew C-1A Traders of VRC-40 at NAS Norfolk, Va.

10 JUNE • A P-3 Orion discovered a vessel carrying 28 Vietnamese in the South China Sea and directed U.S. merchant ship *Point Margo* to the area to rescue the refugees.

23 JUNE • The Navy granted approval for service use for two advanced sonobuoys, the AN/SSQ-2 Directional Command Active Sonobuoy System and the AN/SSQ-77 Vertical Line Array DIFAR, which represented the first major improvements in the sonobuoy field since the introduction of the AN/SSQ-53 DIFAR in 1968.

15 JULY • A P-3 flying from NAS Cubi Point, Philippines, spotted a vessel carrying 43 Vietnamese refugees adrift in the South China Sea about 115 miles northwest of Lingayen Gulf. The Orion directed cruiser *Joseph Strauss* (DDG 16) to the area to rescue the refugees, and the cruiser disembarked the survivors at Subic Bay.

18 JULY • NASA astronaut Charles Conrad Jr. became the 12th naval aviator enshrined at the National Aviation Hall of Fame, Dayton, Ohio.

30 JULY • The Navy announced that SEAPAC, developed by Vought Corporation, had seawater-activated switches that automatically released a parachute harness when a pilot entered the water.

31 JULY • A T-2C Buckeye launched successfully from a 3-degree angle ski jump at NATC Patuxent River, Md. The launch was the first of feasibility demonstrations to evaluate the use of ramps for takeoffs by conventional aircraft.

31 JULY • A limited duty officer aviator program for second class, first class, and chief petty officers, pay grades E-5 through E-7, was established with the first 35 enlisted sailors selected and scheduled to report in April 1981 to NAS Pensacola, Fla. After completion of aviation officer indoctrination, primary flight, and maritime (propeller) training, the new officers served an initial three-year tour as primary flight instructors. The major objectives of the program included the improvement of use and retention of aviators, provision of further upward mobility for enlisted personnel, improvement of the flight instructor program, and provision for replacement of aviators in selected shipboard billets.

31 JULY • The number of refugees fleeing Southeast Asia rose during this period, and in July, VP-1 P-3C Orions spotted nine vessels and directed rescuers to assist. On 15 August, a tenth vessel was spotted and British tanker *Staffordshire* was directed to the rescue of the 205 refugees on board. From 20 May to 10 November, VP-1 participated in the rescue of more than 4,000 people.

17 AUGUST • *Midway* (CV 41) relieved *Constellation* (CV 64) and supported *Dwight D. Eisenhower* (CVN 69) as both carriers performed contingency operations in the Arabian Sea.

21 AUGUST • Soviet *Echo I*–class nuclear-powered submarine *K-122* suffered a fire that killed at least nine sailors, about 85 miles east of Okinawa. During the subsequent three days, P-3C Orions from VP-26 flew around the clock surveillance of the boat as she made for Soviet waters.

22 AUGUST • A VP-1 P-3B Orion and a VP-26 P-3C guided oiler *Passumpsic* (T-AO 107) to the rescue of 28 Vietnamese refugees in the South China Sea.

8 SEPTEMBER • Four Navy ships and three patrol boats received orders to assist the Coast Guard in a patrol to blockade Cuban refugee boats from reaching the United States.

22 SEPTEMBER • Iraq invaded Iran. *Dwight D. Eisenhower* (CVN 69) and *Midway* (CV 41) continued their contingency operations in the north Arabian Sea.

30 SEPTEMBER • *Saratoga* (CV 60) became the initial carrier to undergo the Aircraft Carrier Service Life Extension Program (CV SLEP).

1 OCTOBER • The Office of Anti-Submarine Warfare and Ocean Surveillance Programs was redesignated Office of Naval Warfare.

4 OCTOBER • An engine room fire erupted on board Dutch cruise ship *Prinsendam* and the crew abandoned ship in the Gulf of Alaska, 120 miles south of Yakutat, Alaska. A Coast Guard HH-3F Pelikan and an HC-130B Hercules from CGASs Kodiak and Sitka; Coast Guard cutters *Boutwell* (WHEC 719), *Mellon* (WHEC 717), and *Woodrush* (WLB 407); Air Force aircraft flying from Elmendorf AFB; and Canadian Coast Guardsmen—a total of 13 U.S. and Canadian aircraft—along with three merchantmen responded. Tanker *Williamsburg* took 175 people on board from lifeboats via the Pelikan. The next morning, *Boutwell* spotted a flare from a lifeboat containing the final 20 passengers and two Air Force technicians, completing the rescue of all 519 crewmembers and passengers.

6 OCTOBER • Command ship *Blue Ridge* (LCC 19), and her embarked SH-3A Sea King of HC-1 Detachment 6, rescued 91 Vietnamese refugees in the western Pacific.

12 OCTOBER • Ships of the Amphibious Force, Sixth Fleet, including amphibious assault ship *Guadalcanal* (LPH 7), assisted the victims of a massive earthquake that devastated Al Asnam, Algeria.

6 NOVEMBER • *Ranger* (CV 61) relieved *Midway* (CV 41) in the northern Arabian Sea.

8 NOVEMBER • Frigate *Francis Hammond* (FF 1067), and her embarked SH-2F Seasprite, rescued 85 Vietnamese refugees in the South China Sea, 200 miles southeast of Vietnam.

11 NOVEMBER • For the first time, a LAMPS SH-60B Seahawk worked with the recovery assist, securing and traversing system (RAST) on board an underway ship. Frigate *McInerney* (FFG 8) conducted the shipboard aspect of the exercise, which included primarily electronic communications and not an actual landing, from the Bath Iron Works yard, Maine.

13 NOVEMBER • VFA-125 at NAS Lemoore, Calif., was established as the first squadron to train sailors and Marines to fly and maintain F/A-18 Hornets.

22 NOVEMBER • Aircraft carrier suitability tests of the Tomahawk II medium range air-to-surface missile concluded successfully.

25 NOVEMBER • RH-53D Sea Stallions from VR-24, together with Army and Air Force elements, began disaster relief assistance to victims of an earthquake that killed more than 3,000 people on 23 November at Avellino, Italy. Commander Fleet Air Mediterranean directed the U.S. military support efforts.

8 DECEMBER • *Independence* (CV 62) relieved *Dwight D. Eisenhower* (CVN 69), which had been involved in Iranian contingency operations since 8 May. Cruisers *South Carolina* (CGN 37) and *Virginia* (CGN 38) also departed after their operations with *Dwight D. Eisenhower*.

22 DECEMBER • *Dwight D. Eisenhower* (CVN 69) returned to NS Norfolk, Va., after a 251-day deployment, including an underway period of 152 continuous days.

1981

1 JANUARY • The Naval Aviation Museum announced the first group of selectees for the newly inaugurated Naval Aviation Hall of Honor, NAS Pensacola, Fla. On 10 July 1980, the Chief of Naval Operations approved 12 men for the honor: Adm. John H. Towers; Vice Adm. Patrick N. L. Bellinger; Rear Adms. Richard E. Byrd Jr., William A. Moffett, and Albert C. Read; Capt. Holden C. Richardson, CC; Lt. Col. Alfred A. Cunningham, USMC; Cmdr. Theodore G. Ellyson; Lt. Cmdr. Godfrey de C. Chevalier; Machinist Warrant Officer Floyd Bennett; and civilians Glenn H. Curtiss and Eugene B. Ely.

6 JANUARY • The LAMPS Mk III antisubmarine warfare system went to sea for the first time. An SH-60B Seahawk landed on board *McInerney* (FFG 8) by using recovery assist, securing and traversing system (RAST) gear as the frigate sailed off the northeastern coast of Florida. Designers intended RAST to recover helicopters in seas with ship movements of up to 28-degree rolls, 5 degrees of pitch, and heaves of 15 feet per second.

10 JANUARY • Aircraft from NS Guantánamo Bay, Cuba, and NS Roosevelt Roads, P.R., responded to a request by the Jamaican government for assistance to fight a fuel oil storage tank fire in the Montego Bay area. The aircraft transported firefighters, equipment, and water.

14 JANUARY • Ens. Brenda E. Robinson, USNR, of VRC-40 became the first African American female naval aviator to be carrier qualified, when she trapped in a C-1A Trader on board *America* (CV 66) in the Atlantic.

15 JANUARY • Submerged submarine *Guitarro* (SSN 665) launched a BGM-109 Tomahawk cruise missile from off the California coast. The missile struck its target at a range of more than 100 miles. The Navy repeated the test six days later with the same results. In a third test conducted on 20 March, a missile hit its target at a range of more than 200 miles. These trials demonstrated the Tomahawk's capability to search for, locate, and attack targets at sea.

20 JANUARY • Iranian students and militants released 52 Americans who had been held hostage since the seizure of the United States Embassy in Tehrān on 4 November 1979. Twelve of the hostages served as active duty members of the Navy and Marine Corps including naval flight officer Cmdr. Don A. Sharer, a naval advisor at the time of the embassy takeover. Sharer became the senior leader of the naval hostages.

31 JANUARY • The era of enlisted naval aviators came to a close when the last enlisted pilot, ACCM Robert K. Jones, retired after 38 years of service. Enlisted pilots had performed their duties for more than 61 years as naval aviators on combat missions, as transport pilots, and instructors. The enlisted naval aviator program had ended in 1947.

The last U.S. Navy enlisted pilot, ACCM Robert K. Jones (right) conducts a pre-flight of a US-2B Tracker. Jones retired 31 January 1981 with more than 11,000 flight hours and qualification in over 25 different aircraft.

FEBRUARY • Despite the conclusion of the Iranian hostage crisis, the strategic importance of the region influenced the U.S. decision to maintain two carriers deployed to the Indian Ocean.

5 FEBRUARY • John F. Lehman Jr., a Reserve naval flight officer, took office as the Secretary of the Navy.

19 FEBRUARY • VFA-125 became the first squadron to receive the F/A-18A for fleet operations. Hornets had undergone extensive operational tests and evaluations at Patuxent River, Md., and additional testing by VX-4 at Point Mugu, Calif. VFA-125 trained technicians and pilots for future Hornet squadrons.

8 MARCH • A P-3 Orion and a Coast Guard HC-130H Hercules rescued 11 survivors from Israeli merchant ship *Masada* when she sank in a gale 96 miles southeast of Bermuda. *Forrestal* (CV 59), destroyer *Edson* (DD 945), and frigates *Miller* (FF 1091) and *Paul* (FF 1080) assisted.

10 MARCH • During Merlion exercises with the Singaporeans, an A-6E Intruder from VA-115, embarked on board *Midway* (CV 41), sighted a downed Gulf Oil Co. helicopter and three life rafts afloat in the South China Sea, 27 miles northeast of Singapore. *Midway* dispatched an SH-3G Sea King manned by pilot Lt. Cmdr. Ludwig K. Tande, copilot Lt. j.g. Lawrence D. Mizak, and, at times, aircrewmen AM1 D. C. Piper, AE2 R. N. Dains, AM2 W. Reynolds, AM3 M. A. Velazquez, and AMAN M. J. Sanguigni of HC1 Detachment 2, that rescued all 17 people on board the downed helicopter. Sailors also plucked the chartered helicopter from the water to *Midway*'s flight deck. Two days later *Midway* returned the survivors to Singapore.

An F/A-18A Hornet undergoes climatic testing at the Air Force's 3246th Test Wing at the McKinley Climatic Laboratory, Eglin AFB, Fla. The tests, begun in March 1981, evaluated the aircraft's ability to withstand wide temperature ranges and climatic conditions.

23 MARCH • F/A-18As began testing by the Air Force's 3246th Test Wing at the McKinley Climatic Laboratory, Eglin AFB, Fla. The tests evaluated the ability of Hornet airframes to withstand wide ranges of temperatures and climatic conditions.

12 APRIL • Space shuttle mission STS-1, orbiter *Columbia*, launched from John F. Kennedy Space Center, Fla., crewed by naval aviators Capt. John W. Young, USN (Ret.), and Capt. Robert L. Crippen. After 36 orbits, *Columbia* touched down on 14 April at Edwards AFB, Calif. On 19 May, President Ronald W. Reagan presented medals to Young and Crippen at the White House. Young received the Space Medal of Honor, the seventh person so honored, and the fifth of Navy or Marine Corps recipients.

13 APRIL • AV-8A Harriers deployed as a group with an LHA for the first time when Marine Aircraft Group 32, composed of VMA-231 and -542, sailed to the Mediterranean on board amphibious assault ship *Nassau* (LHA 4).

15 APRIL • Adm. John S. Thach, one of the Navy's early fighter tacticians, died. The commanding officer of VF-3 when World War II began, Thatch developed a two-plane fighter tactic, which proved to be effective against highly maneuverable Japanese Mitsubishi A6M Zero fighters. American pilots quickly adopted the innovation, which became known as the "Thach Weave."

3 MAY • Following Israeli reprisals against Syrian surface-to-air missile batteries in southern Lebanon, *Forrestal* (CV 59) received orders to sail to the eastern Mediterranean. The ship steamed for 53 consecutive days.

The all-Navy crew of John W. Young and Robert L. Crippen lands space shuttle *Columbia* at Edwards AFB Calif., after its two-day maiden space voyage, 14 April 1981.

4 MAY • *America* (CV 66) transited the Suez Canal as the first U.S. carrier to travel through the channel since *Intrepid* (CVS 11) had navigated the waterway on 1 June 1967.

20 MAY • TACGRU 1 and its subordinate commands TACRONS 11 and 12 were established. These three commands performed functions relating to tactical control of aircraft in support of amphibious operations.

26 MAY • Pilot Capt. Elwood M. Armstrong Jr., USMC, along with 1st Lt. Lawrence D. Cragun and 1st Lt. Steve E. White, USMC, of VMAQ-2 Detachment Y, crashed in an EA-6B Prowler, BuNo 159910, on board *Nimitz* (CVN 68) off eastern Florida. In addition to the three Marines, AB3 Robert W. Iser, F3 Dennis R. Driscoll, AAs Thomas E. Barnhart and Frank J. Swider Jr., and ARs Peter R. Iannetti and Jackie L. Gothard from the ship's company, together with AO3 Lewis J. McLaurin of VF-41, ANs Alberto Colon and Arthuro Hinojosa Jr. of VF-84, and AN Patrick D. Louis and AEAN Ronald L. Wildermuth of VF-41, died. The tragedy also injured 48 sailors and Marines. On 30 May, *Nimitz* returned to operations at sea after two days of repairs at Norfolk, Va.

26 MAY • *Independence* (CV 62) left contingency operations in the eastern Mediterranean after passing through the Suez Canal from the Indian Ocean in response to a Middle East crisis.

1 JUNE • Patrol Wing 10 was established at NAS Moffett Field, Calif. The operational wing was to serve as the link between patrol squadrons and Commander Patrol Wings Pacific. The action marked the third use of the Patrol Wing 10 designation. It had originally been established in December 1940, disestablished in June 1947, reestablished in June 1963, and disestablished in 1973.

A Marine AV-8A Harrier vertical/short takeoff and landing attack plane hovers over amphibious assault ship *Tarawa* (LHA 1).

15 JUNE • The Navy Flight Demonstration Squadron (Blue Angels) celebrated its 35th anniversary. Since its establishment in 1946, the squadron had flown F6F-5 Hellcats, F8F-1 Bearcats, F9F-2 and -5 Panthers, F9F-6 and -8 Cougars, F11F-1 Tigers, F-4J Phantom IIs, and A-4F Skyhawks.

16 JUNE • The first fleet operational CH-53E arrived at Marine Aircraft Group 26 for assignment to HMH-464. E-version modifications included the addition of a third engine, a larger main rotor system, and changes to the tail rotors, which allowed the Super Stallions to carry three times the payload of their predecessor RH-53D Sea Stallions. The CH-53E could transport cargoes of more than 16 tons or ferry 55 fully equipped Marines.

29 JUNE • Secretary of Defense Caspar W. Weinberger approved full production of the F/A-18 Hornet.

1 JULY • VS-0294 was established at NAS North Island, Calif. The Reserve command's mission was to train and qualify pilots, naval flight officers, aircrewmen, and technicians to augment fleet carrier antisubmarine squadrons. The squadron, with the exception of maintainers, was to train on simulators or realistic mockups of S-3A Vikings to reduce the cost of using operational aircraft.

7 JULY • A strike by the Professional Air Traffic Controllers Organization led President Ronald W. Reagan to assign 116 Navy and Marine air traffic controllers to man civilian airport towers across the nation. Some servicemembers continued their tasks through the summer.

8 JULY • A newly modified Learjet 24 arrived for use as part of the Naval Test Pilot School's fleet of flying teaching aids at NAS Patuxent River, Md.

The CH-53E Super Stallion is the largest and heaviest U.S. military helicopter. Designed specifically for the Marines, the first one flew in 1974.

9 JULY • During ceremonies at NAS Pensacola, Fla., American and West German representatives—including the chief of Naval Air Training and the Deputy Commander-in-Chief German Fleet—marked the 25th anniversary of the program established in 1956 for training German naval pilots, flight officers, and flight surgeons at U.S. naval aviation facilities.

16 JULY • An S-3A of Carrier Air Wing 11, embarked on board *America* (CV 66), spotted burning merchant ship *Irene Sincerity* about 180 miles southwest of Karachi, Pakistan. The Viking directed *California* (CGN 36) to the rescue of its 39 crewmembers.

23 JULY • VMFA-312 received a camouflaged F-4S sporting a new paint scheme tested by NAVAIR. The new camouflage consisted of a scientifically designed, countershaded gray tactical paint scheme to help Phantom IIs escape visual detection.

19 AUGUST • Cmdr. Henry M. Kleeman and Lt. David J. Venlet and Lts. Lawrence M. Muczynski and James Anderson of VF-41 manned two F-14As that shot down two Libyan Sukhoi Su-22 Fitter-Js with AIM-9L Sidewinder air-to-air missiles over international waters. The Tomcats flew a reconnaissance mission for a missile-firing exercise during freedom of navigation operations from *Nimitz* (CVN 68), sailing with *Forrestal* (CV 59), when the Libyans opened fire.

18 SEPTEMBER • The first night flight of a conventional AGM-109L Medium Range Air-to-Surface Missile (MRASM) occurred over White Sands Missile Range, N.M. A Navy A-6 equipped with the weapon took off from the Pacific Missile Test Center, Point Mugu, Calif., and flew to White Sands. The Intruder used the Tomahawk's terrain contour matching updates for guidance. Once inside the range, the jet launched the missile, which flew a complex night land attack mission.

20 SEPTEMBER • During Typhoon Clara, Philippine frigate *Datu Kalantiaw* (PF 76) ran aground while at anchor near Clayan Island, 340 miles north of Manila. The next day, helicopters from NAS Cubi Point assisted ammunition ship *Mount Hood* (AE 29) in the rescue of 18 survivors and the recovery of 40 bodies.

5 OCTOBER • An A-7E Corsair II from the Pacific Missile Test Center Point Mugu, Calif., fired an AGM-88A High-speed Anti-Radiation Missile against destroyer *Savage* (DER 368) during the first live warhead launch of one of the missiles.

14 OCTOBER • The dedication of the Naval Aviation Hall of Honor and enshrinement of the first 12 selectees took place at the Naval Aviation Museum, NAS Pensacola, Fla.

21 OCTOBER • With enhanced security measures, *America* (CV 66) transited the Suez Canal northbound in the wake of the assassination of Egyptian President Anwar As-Sadat.

28 OCTOBER • Walter K. Hinton, the last surviving participant in the historic NC-4 flight of May 1919, died.

31 OCTOBER • The Navy announced the name for carrier CVN-71 as *Theodore Roosevelt* and her keel was laid at Newport News Shipbuilding and Dry Dock Company, Va. Secretary of Defense Caspar W. Weinberger delivered the address.

5 NOVEMBER • An AV-8B flew for the first time. The U.S.-developed Harrier IIs with British Aerospace participation as advanced versions of the Hawker-Siddeley AV-8A Harriers in Marine service. The AV-8B design provided twice the performance of their predecessors and, with more than 25 percent of their structural weight composed of carbon epoxy composite material, they offered twice the payload and combat radius.

7 NOVEMBER • VMAQ-4 was established at NAS Whidbey Island, Wash., as the first Marine Reserve squadron to fly EA-6A Intruders.

12 NOVEMBER • Space shuttle *Columbia* on mission STS-2 launched from John F. Kennedy Space Center, Fla. On 14 November, it returned to Edwards AFB, Calif. The two astronauts, Capt. Richard H. Truly, who had been designated a naval aviator in October 1960, and Col. Joe H. Engle, USAF, became the first men to fly into and return from space in a previously used spacecraft.

13 NOVEMBER • Secretary of the Navy John F. Lehman Jr. announced the forthcoming retirement of Director of the Division of Naval Reactors Adm. Hyman G. Rickover. The Navy had recognized Rickover for his tireless efforts to develop nuclear-powered ships including carriers and submarines by awarding him honorary wings on 21 July 1970.

17 NOVEMBER • Destroyer *Fletcher* (DD 992) fired the first Harpoon Block 1B missile from a ship. The air-launched version of Harpoons had made their initial carrier deployment in October 1981 with VA-65 on board *Constellation* (CV 64).

2 DECEMBER • Capt. Cecil E. Harris, (Ret.), died. The Navy's second-highest scoring ace during World War II, he had received credit for downing 24 enemy aircraft.

1982

8 JANUARY • An F/A-18 made a Hornet's first fully automatic landing on a simulated carrier deck at NATC Patuxent River, Md.

28 JANUARY • CY Douglas L. McGowan Jr. and AW1 Michael A. Gray inaugurated the Limited Duty Officer Aviator Program, which enabled enlisted sailors to receive flight training and commissions. McGowan and Gray were the first noncommissioned officers to complete flight training since the end of the NAVCAD program in 1968.

3 FEBRUARY • *John F. Kennedy* (CV 67) transited the Suez Canal from the Mediterranean Sea to the Red Sea, en route to the Indian Ocean for an extended deployment. She was the largest carrier to pass through the canal to date.

13 FEBRUARY • VF-84 returned from the Mediterranean on board *Nimitz* (CVN 68) to NS Norfolk, Va. The squadron completed the first operational deployment of the tactical air reconnaissance system fitted on F-14 Tomcats for low- to medium-altitude photoreconnaissance missions.

5 MARCH • The Navy assumed command of the government plant representative office at McDonnell Douglas Corporation's facilities, St. Louis, Mo. The Navy thereby replaced the Air Force plant representative office, which had been responsible for contract administration there for the previous 11 years.

16 MARCH • Vice President George H. W. Bush announced that the Navy was to work actively with customs officials and the Coast Guard to curb the influx of illicit narcotics into the United States. E-2C Hawkeyes subsequently began ongoing participation in the detection of drug smugglers.

18 APRIL • The Navy celebrated the 40th anniversary of the Doolittle raid on the Japanese home islands during World War II. On 14 April, four rebuilt North American B-25 Mitchells had flown over Washington, D.C., and Gen. James H. Doolittle, USAF (Ret.), greeted the pilots when they landed.

2 JUNE • An AV-8B made the first Harrier II flight of its Navy preliminary evaluation.

7 JUNE • The Navy began receiving advanced Block 1B versions of the Harpoon missile, which had been in service since 1977. These had improved radar-guidance systems and were capable of flying at lower altitudes than the initial versions.

One of four AV-8B full-scale development Harrier IIs is used for heavy load tests c. 1983 prior to the first flight of a production model. The test craft first flew in November 1981.

24 JUNE • Lebanon had collapsed into civil war among Muslims, Christians, and Jews. On this date, *Dwight D. Eisenhower* (CVN 69), dock landing ship *Hermitage* (LSD 34), and amphibious transport dock *Nashville* (LPD 13), began the extended evacuation of U.S. Embassy staff and civilians from Beirut. The forces involved included HC-4 CH-53E Sea Stallions, which carried more than 1,200 people and 380,000-pounds of cargo to ships offshore. Meanwhile, a multinational peacekeeping force including U.S. Marines worked to maintain an uneasy truce among Lebanon's warring factions.

25 JUNE • The history of the Navy's C-121 Constellations—whose previous designations included PO, R7O, R7V, and WV—ended after 33 years when the last Warning Star retired from active service with VAQ-33.

25 JUNE • The Lebanese crisis prompted reinforced deployments as *Forrestal* (CV 59) and *Independence* (CV 62) rendezvoused with *John F. Kennedy* (CV 67) and *Dwight D. Eisenhower* (CVN 69) in the Mediterranean Sea. After steaming together in the eastern Mediterranean for several days, *Forrestal* and *Independence* relieved *Dwight D. Eisenhower* and *John F. Kennedy*, enabling those ships to sail home to NS Norfolk, Va.

30 JUNE • VFP-63 was disestablished as the last active duty photographic squadron. This also brought to a close the era of active duty F-8 Crusader squadrons in the Navy. The only F-8

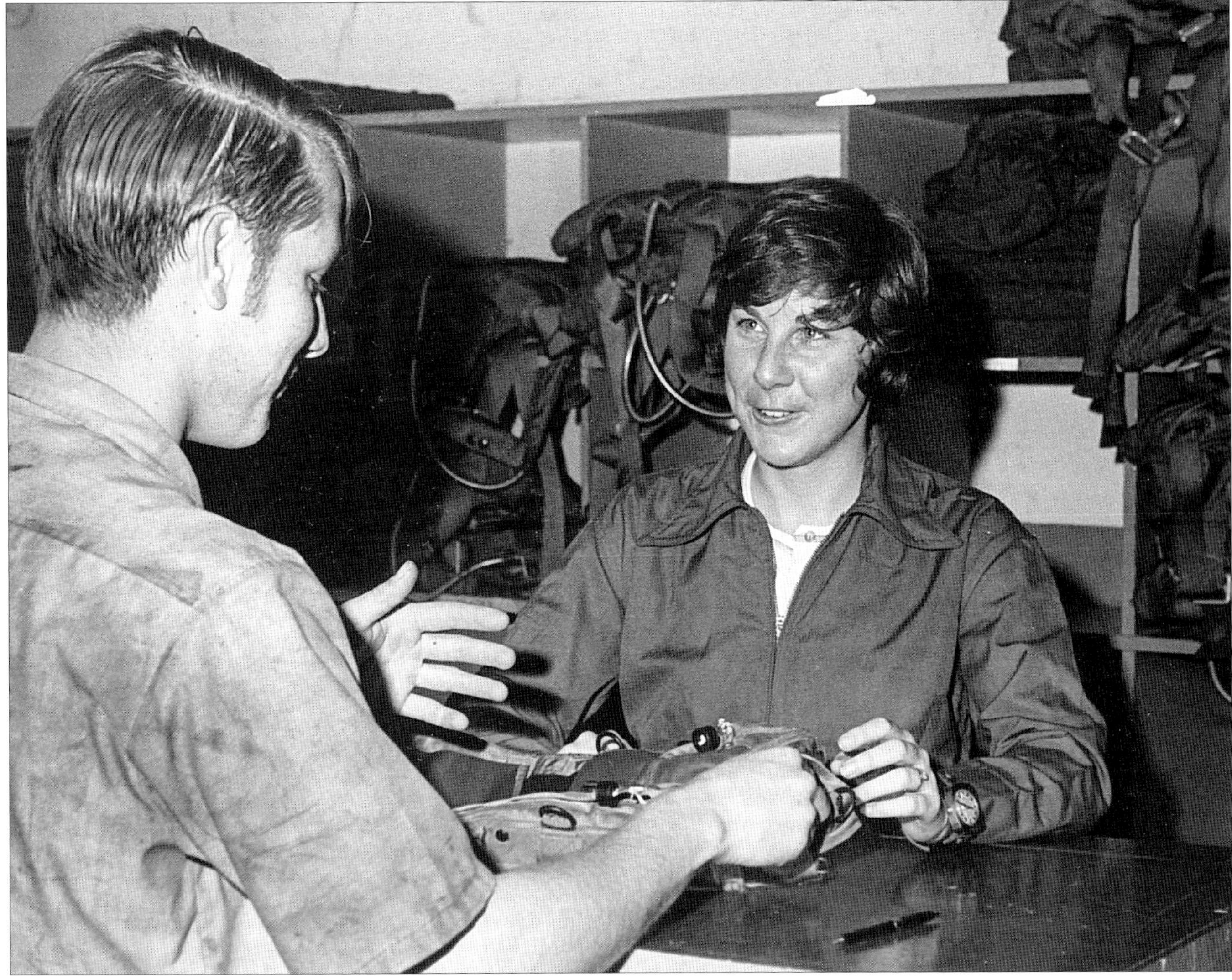

Lt. j.g. Barbara A. Allen, the first woman to be designated as a naval aviator, receives part of her equipment at NAS Corpus Christi, Texas, May 1974.

and photographic squadrons still in existence, VFP-206 and -306, defaulted to Reserve squadrons at NAF Washington, D.C.

30 JUNE • Chief of Naval Operations Adm. Thomas B. Hayward, the Navy's number one aviator, retired. A graduate of the U.S. Naval Academy in 1947, Hayward had been designated a naval aviator on 26 July 1950, and became the 21st Chief of Naval Operations on 1 July 1978.

7 JULY • Walter Wagner became NAVAIR's first civilian project manager when he relieved Capt. John E. Hock Jr. as project manager for the E-2/C-2 airborne tactical data system.

13 JULY • Instructor Lt. Cmdr. Barbara A. Rainey and student Ens. Donald B. Knowlton of VT-3 crashed in a T-34C Turbomentor while avoiding another aircraft during touch-and-go landings at NAS Whiting Field, Fla., killing both crewmembers. On 22 February 1974, Rainey (then Allen) had become the first woman to be designated a naval aviator.

30 JULY • Ens. Jannine Weiss became the first enlisted woman to receive her wings and to receive a commission under the new Limited Duty Officer Aviator Program.

31 JULY • GMU-41 was disestablished as the last guided missile unit after 29 years of service. It had been established on 11 May 1953, with a varied mission of providing missile training and technical support to ships and squadrons and supporting commands that tested and evaluated missiles and associated equipment in the fleet environment.

2 AUGUST • Navy test pilot Lt. Cmdr. John Ball and Bell Helicopter Textron test pilot Dorman Cannon flew the first at-sea shipboard landings and takeoffs of the Bell XV-15 on board amphibious assault ship *Tripoli* (LPH 10). The experimental vertical lift tilt-rotor aircraft had a conventional fixed wing, with engines and rotors mounted on the wingtips capable of swiveling to provide either vertical or horizontal flight.

5 AUGUST • The Naval Air Test Center successfully completed evaluations on the first aircraft tire made entirely of guayule natural rubber. The Goodyear tire was mounted on the right main landing gear of an F-4J Phantom II and underwent a series of maximum gross weight—56,000 pounds—takeoffs and landings.

8 AUGUST • The Chief of Naval Operations established the first naval plant representative office outside the United States in Melbourne, Australia. The office was to administer U.S. contracts with Australian companies involved in building F/A-18 Hornets for the Royal Australian Air Force.

14 SEPTEMBER • A bomb killed Lebanon's Christian President Bashir Gemayel, and on 22 September, his Phalangist followers retaliated by killing Muslim Palestinian refugees at camps at Sabra and Shatila, Lebanon. From 27 September through 21 January 1983, an average of two carriers at a time sailed in the eastern Mediterranean to support Marines deployed ashore during the crisis.

24 SEPTEMBER • The Navy awarded a pre-full-scale development contract for the fixed-wing experimental training aircraft training system (VTXTS) to McDonnell Douglas, which was teamed with British Aerospace and Sperry. The program was designed around the British Aerospace Hawk, with appropriate simulators, academics, training management system, and support equipment.

30 SEPTEMBER • NAVAIR acted as executive agent for a tri-service program that signed a $400,000 contract with the Gila River Apache Native American community at Sacaton, Ariz., to research, develop, and establish a prototype guayule rubber industry in the United States. The program was intended to reduce U.S. dependence on imported natural rubber. Potential military applications for guayule rubber included aircraft tires, jet engine mounts, hydrophone arrays, truck tires, tank treads, submarine acoustic tiles, and medical supplies.

1 OCTOBER • AVCM Billy C. Sanders assumed the duties of Master Chief Petty Officer of the Navy. Sanders became the second man with an aviation background that filled the billet following its establishment on 1 March 1967—CM Thomas S. Crow had been the first.

1 OCTOBER • Helicopter Tactical Wing 1 was established at NAS Norfolk, Va., Capt. John W. Osberg commanding. The wing consisted of HC-6 and -16, and HM-12, -14, and -16, and assumed responsibility for the administrative and operational activities of these helicopter squadrons with regard to training, material support, and overall readiness.

7 OCTOBER • ARAPAHO—a research and development project to demonstrate the feasibility of equipping merchant ships with emergency aviation support in wartime, and of operating antisubmarine helicopters and other combatant aircraft—at-sea testing concluded when 18,000-ton container ship *Export Leader* returned to Norfolk International Terminal, Va. The ship had been configured with a portable modular aviation facility and logged 178 day and 45 night helicopter landings.

16 OCTOBER • *Saratoga* (CV 60) completed the final phase of SLEP (service life extension program) when she conducted her first sea trials since entering the shipyard as the initial carrier to undergo the program.

28 OCTOBER • Naval aviation celebrated the 30th anniversary of the first flight of the A-3 Skywarrior. The versatile aircraft had served in the fleet since 1956 in heavy attack, radar bomber training, electronics reconnaissance, tanker, electronics jamming, photoreconnaissance, dedicated electronics jamming, airborne weapons testing, and VIP transport roles.

11 NOVEMBER • Astronauts Vance D. Brand, Robert F. Overmyer, Joe P. Allen, and William B. Lenoir manned space shuttle *Columbia* during the launch of mission STS-5 from John F. Kennedy Space Center, Fla. Brand and Overmyer were former Navy and Marine Corps aviators, respectively, and Lenoir and Allen were civilians. This was the first operational flight of *Columbia* and the first time four astronauts crewed a mission. Previous flights carried only two astronauts.

3 DECEMBER • *Nimitz* (CVN 68) and cruisers *Mississippi* (CGN 40) and *Arkansas* (CGN 41) assisted the sinking Greek cargo vessel *Andalusia*. A P-3C from VP-49 vectored *Mississippi* to *Andalusia* where the cruiser rescued all 19 crewmembers. Two Sea Kings of HS-9 from *Nimitz*—an SH-3H with pilot Lt. Michael G. Mulcahy, copilot Lt. j.g. Randall K. Ewald, and aircrewmen AW2 Robert S. Chronister and AWAN Henry J. Miller; and an SH-3G with pilot Lt. Cmdr. David B. Small Jr., copilot Lt. Cmdr. Larry W. Zimmer, and aircrewmen AW2 Richard M. Lane and AWAN Allen L. Estel—transferred survivors from *Mississippi* to the carrier.

15 DECEMBER • *Naval Aviation News* celebrated its 65th year of publication as the Navy's oldest periodical in continuous print and one of the oldest aviation magazines in the country. It began as a weekly bulletin published by the Office of Chief of Naval Operations.

1983

1 JANUARY • From this date to 26 June 1989, aircraft and ships of the Pacific Fleet rescued a total of 1,380 Vietnamese refugees in the western Pacific.

7 JANUARY • The first F/A-18s—excluding those in operational training squadrons—entered operational service and replaced F-4s in VMFA-314. This transition marked the beginning of the replacement of Phantom IIs and A-7 Corsair IIs with Hornets.

21 JANUARY • HSL-41 was established, Cmdr. Michael B. O'Connor Jr. commanding. Equipped with SH-60Bs as the LAMPS Mk III fleet readiness squadron, HSL-41 trained aircrew and maintainers for Seahawk fleet squadrons.

11 MARCH • The first fleet CH-53E Super Stallion arrived at HM-12.

21 MARCH • An all-female flight crew from VRC-30 consisting of pilot Lt. Elizabeth M. Toedt, copilot Lt. j.g. Cheryl A. Martin, and aircrewmen AMM3 Gina Greterman and AMMAN Robin Banks conducted an operational mission in a C-1A Trader that concluded with an arrested landing on board *Ranger* (CV 61).

25 MARCH • Fighter attack squadrons were redesignated strike fighter squadrons during their transition to F/A-18 Hornets. The VFA designation was retained.

1 APRIL • Naval Air Reserve Units (NARUs) were redesignated Naval Air Reserve (NAR) Alameda, Calif.; Jacksonville, Fla.; Memphis, Tenn.; Norfolk, Va.; North Island, Calif.; Point Mugu, Calif.; and Whidbey Island, Wash.

7 APRIL • Reserve squadrons VF-201 and -202 participated in National Week '83 exercises with the Sixth Fleet. Their F-4N Phantom IIs deployed from NAS Dallas, Texas, to NAS Sigonella, Sicily, via NAS Oceana, Va.; Gander, Newfoundland; Lajes, Azores; and NS Rota, Spain.

1 MAY • RVAW-110 and -120 were redesignated VAW-110 and -120, respectively. Responsible for training sailors in early warning services for future assignment to fleet units, VAW-110 was based at Norfolk, Va., and VAW-120 at NAS Miramar, Calif.

2 MAY • Naval aviator Lt. Leslie E. Provow of VRC-40 became the first woman to be designated a landing signal officer.

6 MAY • HC-4 was established at NAS Sigonella, Sicily. The squadron operated CH-53E Super Stallions and provided vertical on-board delivery for the Sixth Fleet.

23 MAY • An S-3A Viking made the first launch of an EX-50 advanced lightweight torpedo at NATC Patuxent River, Md.

10 JUNE • Lt. Colleen Nevius became the first female naval aviator to graduate from the Naval Test Pilot School, NAS Patuxent River, Md., and be designated a Navy test pilot.

23 JUNE • A British-built airship, Skyship 500, arrived for test and evaluation at NATC Patuxent River, Md. Navy and Coast Guard officials had considered the airship for possible maritime patrol, search and rescue, and geo-survey missions.

1 JULY • Civilian technician Dr. Angelo J. DiMascio was appointed to the newly established position of deputy commander, bringing a new alignment to NAVAIR headquarters.

In 1983, Lt. Colleen Nevius becomes the first female naval aviator to graduate from the Naval Test Pilot School and be designated a Navy test pilot. She began her naval aviation career in 1977 and retired as a captain.

6 JULY • A Marine CH-53E flew coast-to-coast in a 15-hour flight from Patuxent River, Md., to MCAS Tustin, Calif. Marine KC-130s refueled the Super Stallion four times.

18 JULY • U.S. concerns over the threat posed by expansion of the leftist Sandinista National Liberation Front in Nicaragua led to the diversion of *Ranger* (CV 61) from her intended deployment to the Indian Ocean to the vicinity of Central America through 12 August. On 16 August, *Coral Sea* (CV 43) arrived in the area, followed ten days later by battleship *New Jersey* (BB 62). In mid-September, these vessels departed the region.

20 JULY • Through 28 July, P-3 Orions directed merchant ships to the rescue of 80 Vietnamese refugees in the western Pacific, while cruiser *Sterett* (CG 31) and destroyer *Callaghan* (DDG 994) rescued 262 and 284 others, respectively.

23 JULY • The National Aviation Hall of Fame in Dayton, Ohio, enshrined the Navy's only World War I ace, David S. Ingalls. He was honored for his service during that war, in the Naval Air Transport Service during World War II, and for his postwar role in commercial aviation.

1 AUGUST • A Marine OV-10A landed on board the flight deck of amphibious assault ship *Nassau* (LHA 4). The event marked the first time that a Bronco landed on an LHA, and the recovery opened up the possibility of a future role for OV-10As in amphibious operations.

1 AUGUST • Following Libyan aggression against Chad, aircraft from *Dwight D. Eisenhower* (CVN 69) operated over the Gulf of Sidra. In addition, the Navy delayed the departure of *Coral Sea* (CV 43) from the Mediterranean because of uncertainty over the situation.

25 AUGUST • The Navy accepted a production prototype of the P3-C Update III. The Orion was flown for test and evaluation by VX-1 to NATC Patuxent River, Md. Planners anticipated that it would be twice as effective in submarine detection as the Update II because of the increased effectiveness of its acoustic processing system owing to state-of-the-art computer integration equipment, an improved infrared detection system, Harpoon air-to-surface missile capabilities, and its ability to carry a variety of other weapons.

26 AUGUST • In reaction to increased terrorist attacks against Marines deployed as peacekeepers in Lebanon, the Navy dispatched *Dwight D. Eisenhower* (CVN 69) to render assistance. Those trapped within the devastated city could see the ship as she arrived off Beirut, bringing respite to the Marines and civilians ashore. During the following days, *Dwight D. Eisenhower* aircraft flew 39 reconnaissance missions over Lebanon to identify frequently shifting artillery batteries that fired sporadically at peacekeepers.

29 AUGUST • The first flight of a production model AV-8B Harrier II was made at the McDonnell Douglas plant, St. Louis, Mo.

30 AUGUST • Space shuttle *Challenger* launched on mission STS-8 from John F. Kennedy Space Center, Fla., and returned on 5 September to Edwards AFB, Calif. One of the crewmembers, Lt. Cmdr. Dale A. Gardner, served in naval aviation and became the first naval flight officer in space.

31 AUGUST • A Soviet Sukhoi Su-15 Flagon shot down Korean Air Lines 007, a Boeing 747-230B, west of Sakhalin Island, killing all 269 crewmembers and passengers, including 61 Americans, when the airliner allegedly strayed into Soviet air space. Despite acrimonious allegations between the rival superpowers and repeated Soviet interference with the searchers, P-3C Orions of VP-40 deployed to northern Japan searched for survivors, while the Air Force maintained operational control of the search and rescue.

1 SEPTEMBER • An MH-53E Sea Dragon production prototype made its first flight. The MH version of the CH-53E heavylift helicopter was developed to meet the Navy's needs for airborne mine countermeasures missions that provided tow tension capabilities, longer on-station times, and new digital automatic flight control systems. The Sea Dragons would also augment vertical on-board delivery requirements.

20 SEPTEMBER • An A-7E Corsair II launched the Navy's first AGM-65F IR Maverick air-to-ground missile. The weapon was designed to enhance antiship capabilities and made a direct hit on a destroyer target in its first use.

26 SEPTEMBER • The first takeoffs of F/A-18 Hornets from a ski-jump ramp occurred at NAS Patuxent River, Md. The tests were part of an evaluation of conventional jet aircraft, employing an upward curved ramp to shorten takeoff rolls.

28 SEPTEMBER • HSL-41 received its first production SH-60B Seahawk.

1 OCTOBER • A reorganization of Commander Naval Reserve Force (formerly Chief of Naval Reserve) included a change in which Commander Naval Air Reserve Force reported to Commander Naval Reserve Force instead of to the Chief of Naval Operations. The restructuring was intended to improve command and control of the Reserves and enhance readiness.

1 OCTOBER • The Naval Space Command was established, former astronaut Capt. Richard H. Truly commanding. The new authority consolidated the Navy's space-related activities under one organization, including the Naval Space Surveillance System, Naval Astronautics Group, and activities supporting the Fleet Satellite Communications System.

3 OCTOBER • Ens. Don E. Slone received his wings as a naval flight officer, becoming the first former enlisted man to complete the Enlisted Commissioning Program and the Aviation Officer Candidate School.

4 OCTOBER • *Dwight D. Eisenhower* (CVN 69) received authorization to leave Lebanese waters.

9 OCTOBER • Assassins detonated a bomb amid a South Korean delegation led by President Chun D. Hwan as they prepared to visit the Martyr's Mausoleum, Rangoon, Burma, killing 21 and injuring 48 others. The president escaped, but the bombing caused widespread geopolitical repercussions, and *Carl Vinson* (CVN 70) delayed her departure from Korean waters off Pusan (Busan) to perform contingency operations as a demonstration of U.S. support for the South Korean regime.

10 OCTOBER • After an 18 September Iranian threat to block oil exports from the Persian Gulf, *Ranger* (CV 61) had been diverted from Australian port calls and, on this date, arrived in the northern Arabian Sea. *Ranger* fulfilled 122 days of extended tasking in that area as a result of a gap in power projection because of multiple crises.

23 OCTOBER • A suicide bomber identified with the Free Islamic Revolutionary Movement, a group affiliated with Hizballah, drove a truck packed with explosives into a barracks at Beirut International Airport, and detonated its cargo killing 241 servicemembers, mostly Marines from the 1st Battalion, 8th Marines, 24th Marine Amphibious Unit. A second bomber drove a vehicle into the nearby French barracks and killed 56 French paratroopers. On 26 October, *Dwight D. Eisenhower* (CVN 69) sailed from Naples, Italy, for the eastern Mediterranean. At various times during the following weeks, *Independence* (CV 62) and *John F. Kennedy* (CV 67) rendezvoused with *Dwight D. Eisenhower* for operations off Lebanon. *Independence* had originally been scheduled to relieve *Dwight D. Eisenhower* but responded initially to the onset of Operation Urgent Fury in Grenada.

25 OCTOBER • The United States began Operation Urgent Fury—an invasion of Grenada to reestablish democracy on the embattled Caribbean island. Maurice Bishop, the island's leader, was killed in a power struggle, and Cubans had infiltrated the ensuing power vacuum, arming Marxist

Lieutenant Robert O. Goodman of VA-85, shot down over Beirut, Lebanon, on 4 December 1983, speaks to journalists after his release from Syrian captivity a month later.

rebels. Aircraft from Carrier Air Wing 6 embarked on board *Independence* (CV 62) and amphibious assault ships *Guam* (LPH 9) and *Saipan* (LHA 2) supported the U.S. landings, and a number of shore-based squadrons flew surveillance and support missions.

1 NOVEMBER • A fire broke out in the engine room of *Ranger* (CV 61) as she operated in the Arabian Sea, killing 6 men and injuring 35.

23 NOVEMBER • A modified CH-46 Sea Knight lifted off for its first flight from Boeing Vertol's ramp at Philadelphia, Pa. The helicopter had been fitted with improvements that, when incorporated in all Navy and Marine Sea Knights, would extend their service lives through the end of the century.

3 DECEMBER • The Syrians fired at two F-14A Tomcats of VF-31, embarked on board *John F. Kennedy* (CV 67), while they flew a reconnaissance mission for peacekeepers over Lebanon. The next day, after additional reconnaissance flights to identify Syrian positions, 16 aircraft from *Independence* (CV 62) and 10 from *John F. Kennedy* bombed artillery and air defense sites east of Beirut despite what VA-85 described as "heavy opposition." A surface-to-air missile shot down Cmdr. Edward K. Andrews of VA-15, embarked on board *Independence*, in an A-7E Corsair II, but he survived. The Syrians also downed Lts. Mark A. Lange and Robert O. Goodman of VA-85, embarked on board *John F. Kennedy*, in an A-6E Intruder, BuNo 152915. Lange died, and the Syrians captured Goodman and took him to Damascus. These actions marked the first Navy fixed-wing aircraft lost to hostile fire since the Vietnam War.

27 DECEMBER • The Secretary of the Navy announced the assignment of the name *Wasp* to LHD-1. *Wasp* was the first of a class of multipurpose amphibious assault ships designed to deploy and land elements of a Marine air and ground task force during an assault, by employing aircraft, air cushion and conventional landing craft, and amphibious vehicles.

1984

4 JANUARY • Lt. Robert O. Goodman of VA-85 was returned to the United States after a month of captivity as a POW in Syria. His A-6E Intruder had been one of the two jets shot down by the Syrians on 4 December 1983, while participating in a retaliatory strike into Lebanon.

10 JANUARY • HC-1 received its first two CH-53Es, becoming the only Navy West Coast squadron to fly Super Stallions. The squadron also continued to operate SH-3G Sea Kings.

12 JANUARY • VMAT-203 received its first AV-8B Harrier II at MCAS Cherry Point, N.C.

Capt. Bruce McCandless II becomes the first person to walk untethered in space, as an astronaut of space shuttle *Challenger*, February 1984. His father and grandfather were Medal of Honor recipients.

3 FEBRUARY • Space shuttle *Challenger* launched from John F. Kennedy Space Center, Fla., on mission STS-41B, and on 11 February, landed back at the center—a first for any shuttle. It flew with a crew of five that included naval aviators: its commander, Vance D. Brand, had been a Marine Corps flier for five years, and two Navy officers, Capt. Bruce McCandless II and Cmdr. Robert L. Gibson, also comprised the crew.

13 FEBRUARY • Ens. Michael L. Gierhart of VT-27 made the last instructional flight of a T-28 Trojan, ending the 31-year career of the aircraft as a naval aviator trainer.

12 MARCH • A Beech Aircraft AQM-37 variant target drone attained a speed of Mach 4.2 (2,775 mph) at an altitude of 102,000 feet over the Pacific Missile Test Center Point Mugu, Calif.

The display of the last T-28B Trojan in the Training Command, BuNo 137796, at NAS Anacostia marks the end of an era. Now a memorial near the main gate, it was retired in March 1984.

13 MARCH • In late January, Secretary of Defense Caspar W. Weinberger had authorized an increase in operations off Central America from 1 February to 31 July to demonstrate U.S. support for El Salvadoran elections, and to deter expansion of the leftist Sandinista National Liberation Front in Nicaragua. On this date, *America* (CV 66) sailed for several weeks of operations in those waters.

14 MARCH • The last T-28 Trojan in the Training Command, BuNo 137796 of VT-27, departed for display at NAS Anacostia, D.C.

20 MARCH • Lt. Catherine H. Osman piloted an HH-46A Sea Knight on board *Iowa* (BB 61), making her the first female pilot to land a helicopter on a battleship.

21 MARCH • While *Kitty Hawk* (CV 63) conducted night operations during Exercise Team Spirit 84-1, she collided with a Soviet Victor I–class sub, tentatively identified as *K-314* (610), in the Sea of Japan, 150 miles east of Pohang, South Korea. The submarine broached the surface ahead of the carrier and failed to display navigation lights. Two SH-3H Sea Kings of HS-2 inspected the unlit submarine through AN/PVS-5A night vision goggles and with sonobuoys without noting serious damage. *Kitty Hawk* sustained minor damage and attempted by flashing light to contact Soviet task force flagship cruiser *Petropavlovsk*, but she did not respond. The Soviet boat received damage that required her to be taken under tow to Vladivostok, Soviet Union.

26 APRIL • The Navy received the first EA-6B Improved Capability (ICAP) II Prowler, BuNo 161776. The service intended to upgrade 15 Expanded Capability (EXCAP) models already serving witht the fleet.

28 APRIL • The first master augmentation unit (MAU) was established at NAS Brunswick, Maine. Similar in composition to a Reserve VP squadron, MAUs trained reservists in the same type of aircraft operated by active duty patrol squadrons, so Reserve crews could rapidly augment those squadrons in emergencies. Squadron augment units, MAU predecessors, were scheduled to consolidate into the MAUs when they established.

8 MAY • During the 73rd annual Aviation Ball, Deputy Chief of Naval Operations (Air Warfare) Vice Adm. Robert F. Schoultz presented the first aviation supply wings to Vice Adm. Eugene A. Grinstead Jr., SC; Rear Adm. Andrew A. Giordano, SC (Ret.); and Commodore John H. Ruehlin, SC, commanding officer Aviation Supply Office, Philadelphia, Pa. The establishment of a naval aviation supply officer program and the authorization of a breast insignia for qualifying officers had been planned since 1982.

2 JULY • Reserve Carrier Air Wing (CVWR) 20 concluded its first deployment at sea since 1978, after a week on board *Dwight D. Eisenhower* (CVN 69). This also marked the first time in four years that CVWR-20 had operated as a complete wing as well as the first deployment of A-7E Corsair IIs with a Reserve squadron, VA-203.

21 JULY • The National Aviation Hall of Fame in Dayton, Ohio, enshrined four individuals including World War II Marine ace Joseph J. Foss. From 9 October 1942 to 25 January 1943 Foss downed 26 Japanese aircraft.

25 JULY • ComPatWingsPac Commodore Oakley E. Osborn accepted the first P-3C Update III from Lockheed at NAS Moffett Field, Calif. VP-31 was to train aviators in the operation of the updated Orions beginning with VP-40, the first fleet operational squadron scheduled to receive the planes.

3 AUGUST • The United States began Operation Intense Look—minesweeping the Gulf of Suez—after a series of mysterious underwater explosions struck 19 ships there and, on 31 July, Islamic terrorists linked to Iran claimed to have lain 190 mines in the gulf and Bab el-Mandeb. Egypt requested international assistance. On 6 August, four RH-53D Sea Stallions of HM-14 embarked on board amphibious transport dock *Shreveport* (LPD 12) for deployment to the Gulf of Suez. Other aircraft from the squadron's detachment and a Super Stallion of HM-12 later augmented the deployment. On 17 August, HM-14 began 22 consecutive days of minehunting operations. The British, French, Italians, and Soviets also participated.

13 SEPTEMBER • A newly configured S-3B made its first flight at Lockheed facilities in Palmdale, Calif. The latest version of the Viking featured improved avionics and weapons systems, including AGM-84 Harpoon air-to-ground missiles.

20 SEPTEMBER • Terrorists detonated a truck bomb at the U.S. Embassy Annex at Awkar near Beirut, Lebanon, killing 20 people including two U.S. servicemembers, and wounding more than 75. Amphibious transport dock *Shreveport* (LPD 12), destroyer *Semmes* (DDG 18), and frigate *John L. Hall* (FFG 32) sailed to the eastern Mediterranean to render assistance. Four RH-53D Sea Stallions of HM-14, embarked on board *Shreveport*, and a CH-53E Super Stallion flew logistical, medical, and embassy staff evacuation missions.

26 SEPTEMBER • The XV-15 tiltrotor aircraft demonstrator completed two weeks of concept tests at NATC, Patuxent River, Md.

2 OCTOBER • The Navy signed a contract to initiate full-scale development of the T-45TS Goshawk jet flight training system by McDonnell Douglas. The system's aircraft—T-45—were to replace the T-2C Buckeye and TA-4J Skyhawk used by the Chief of Naval Air Training in the intermediate and advanced phases of jet flight training.

12 OCTOBER • VF-301's acceptance of its first F-14 marked the introduction of Tomcats into the Naval Air Reserve Force as part of the service's total force defense concept.

28 NOVEMBER • Four months after McDonnell Douglas had announced that it would bear the costs of modifications to correct a fatigue-related problem in the tail area of F/A-18s, Hornet deliveries resumed.

30 NOVEMBER • U.S. Navy chartered oceanographic research ship *Seaward Explorer* broke down and drifted into Cuban waters en route from Haiti to Miami, Fla. The Cubans denied Coast Guard cutter *Reliance* (WMEC 615) permission to enter Cuban territorial waters to tow *Seaward Explorer*, but a Cuban patrol boat would tow her to international waters. A fire erupted on board the research ship that released the towing hawser, which fouled the patrol boat's propellers. *Reliance* rushed in, put out the fire, and towed *Seaward Explorer* to Miami. *Nimitz* (CVN 68) received an emergency sortie notice while at Charlotte Amalie, St. Thomas, U.S.V.I., but the situation was concluded before her arrival.

8 DECEMBER • VA-105 returned from a six-month deployment to MCAS Iwakuni, Japan. The squadron's assignment to MAG-12 in the 1st Marine Aircraft Wing initiated the Navy's participation in the Marine Corps Unit Deployment Program, and marked the first time that a Navy squadron had served under Marine operational control since World War II.

28 DECEMBER • During the relocation of the field camp of scientific field team S-079, a VXE-6 LC-130 Hercules crashed in the vicinity of Nimrod Glacier, Antarctica, stranding survivors in a crevasse on Starshot Glacier. Within 16 hours, another squadron Hercules rescued the victims under extreme environmental conditions. Sailors later repaired the crashed LC-130 and, on 12 January, flew the plane from the site.

31 DECEMBER • Under a five-year agreement with Cessna Aircraft Company that encompassed a total training concept, the first T-47A for naval flight officer navigation training arrived at the Naval Air Training Command.

1985

7 JANUARY • The Navy selected the F-16N as aggressor surrogate to simulate Soviet tactical aircraft during air-to-air combat training. The purchase of an initial 14 Fighting Falcons from General Dynamics included support material and services.

24 JANUARY • Lt. Cmdr. John Parker of VA-83 piloted an A-7E Corsair II at NWC China Lake, Calif., during the first successful fleet operational squadron firing of an AGM-88A High-speed Anti-Radiation Missile.

30 JANUARY • The AV-8B Harrier II began operational service with VMA-331 at MCAS Cherry Point, N.C.

21 FEBRUARY • F/A-18A Hornets and SH-60B LAMPS helicopters deployed overseas for the first time, with Battle Group Delta headed by *Constellation* (CV 64), to the Seventh Fleet in the western Pacific and Indian Ocean. The Hornets replaced A-7E Corsair IIs operated by VFA-25 and -113 of Carrier Air Wing 14, making *Constellation* the first carrier to have F/A-18s assigned to her air wing. The Seahawks deployed on board frigate *Crommelin* (FFG 37).

1 MARCH • The undergraduate naval flight officer (NFO) training system upgrade began with the first class training in Cessna T-47A Citations at NAS Pensacola, Fla.

6 MARCH • NAVAIR and United Technologies' Sikorsky Aircraft signed a contract for full-scale development and production options for a carrier-borne version of the SH-60B Seahawk. Designated SH-60F, the variant was to replace the SH-3H Sea King for protection from enemy submarines within a carrier battle group's perimeter.

7 MARCH • After terrorist threats against the U.S Embassy in Beirut, Lebanon, *Dwight D. Eisenhower* (CVN 69) sortied from Palma de Mallorca, Spain, and made for the eastern Mediterranean. Helicopters subsequently evacuated personnel from Beirut to Cyprus.

29 MARCH • The Navy awarded a contract to McDonnell Douglas for development of F/A-18 night attack capabilities. About 750 Hornets were to receive navigational forward-looking infrared pods, television-like heads-up displays, and night-vision goggles for pilots.

1 APRIL • VP-68 completed its move from NAS Patuxent River, Md., to NAF Washington, D.C. (at Andrews AFB). Relocation of the Reserve squadron, which operated P-3B Orions, made room for the JVX test program at Patuxent River and also helped balance base loading at Washington. Planners scheduled the V-22 Osprey—formerly JVX—for testing at the Naval Air Test Center starting in 1988.

12 APRIL • VAQ-133 returned the last fleet EA-6B Expanded Capability (EXCAP) Prowler, BuNo 159585, for Improved Capability (ICAP) II modification at Grumman Aircraft Corp., Long Island, N.Y. VAQ-133 had begun transitioning to ICAP II Prowlers in January 1985.

26 APRIL • David S. Ingalls (Naval Aviator No. 85), the Navy's only World War I ace, died at his home in Chagrin Falls, Ohio, following a stroke. A member of the First Yale Unit before being ordered to the British Royal Flying Corps, he

Twenty-two F-16N Fighting Falcons—modified Air Force F-16s—delivered between 1987 and 1988, were used by Navy adversary squadrons, but all had been retired by 1995.

An F/A-18A of VFA-113 prepares to launch from *Constellation* (CV 64) during the first deployment of Hornets, with CVW-14 to the western Pacific and Indian Oceans, 21 February to 24 August 1985.

served with the Royal Air Force's No. 213 Squadron, located in Berguess, France. Ingalls shot down four enemy planes and one balloon. He later served as Assistant Secretary of the Navy for Aeronautics during the Hoover administration.

30 MAY • The keel was laid for amphibious assault ship *Wasp* (LHD 1) at Ingalls Shipbuilding, Pascagoula, Miss.

14 JUNE • Two Lebanese Shi'a Muslim gunmen hijacked Trans World Airlines Flight 847 from Athens, Greece, and flew the airliner to Beirut, Lebanon. The terrorists murdered SW2 Robert D. Stethem of Navy Underwater Construction Team 1 and held 37 other Americans hostage. *Nimitz* (CVN 68) cancelled a visit to Livorno, Italy, and steamed at flank speed to the eastern Mediterranean, where she conducted contingency operations off the Lebanese coast. On 30 June, the hijackers released the last of the hostages, and on 1 August, after 68 consecutive days at sea, *Nimitz* departed for Egyptian waters.

19 JUNE • The Navy announced the selection of Goshawk as the popular name for T-45A trainers, a part of the T-45 training system (formerly VTXTS) scheduled to replace the T-2C Buckeye and TA-4J Skyhawk operated by the Training Command. Curtiss Aircraft had previously applied the name Goshawk to its F11C-2 and BF2C-1 beginning in 1933.

19 JUNE • A modified C-2A with more powerful engines than those of fleet Greyhounds arrived for three months of flight testing at NATC Patuxent River, Md.

8 JULY • VAW-120—traditionally an E-2C Hawkeye training squadron—received its first upgraded C-2A Greyhounds for the training of replacement sailors. The plane's initial operational capability was achieved on time, after the delivery in October of five Greyhounds to VR-24 at NAS Sigonella, Sicily.

An F/A-18A Hornet, BuNo 161705, fires an AIM-120 Advanced Medium-Range Air-to-Air Missile over the Pacific Missile Test Center, Point Mugu, Calif. The missile entered fleet service in 1993.

15 JULY • The Pacific Missile Test Center successfully demonstrated the maintainability phase of AIM-120 Advanced Medium Range Air-to-Air Missiles (AMRAAMs) at Point Mugu, Calif. The evaluation for the Navy and Air Force was under the auspices of the Air Force Systems Command, Joint Systems Program Office at Eglin AFB, Fla. The demonstration, repeated several times a day through 17 July, proved it possible to load four AMRAAMs onto the wings of F/A-18 Hornets in less than 15 minutes. The unloading procedures, designed not to exceed four minutes, were completed in an average of two minutes.

29 AUGUST • The Secretary of the Navy announced the decision to homeport *Nimitz* (CVN 68) at Everett, Wash., which was envisioned as a base for up to 15 vessels.

2 SEPTEMBER • Reserve squadron HSL-84 completed a deployment of two detachments on board Reserve frigates, marking the first time that a Reserve LAMPS detachment remained embarked. While at sea for two weeks beginning on 16 August, Detachment 1 assigned to frigate *Grey* (FF 1054), and Detachment 2 on board *Lang* (FF 1060), operated as part of a five-ship all-Reserve squadron.

3 OCTOBER • Space shuttle *Atlantis* launched on its maiden voyage, mission STS-51J, from John F. Kennedy Space Center, Fla., and on 7 October landed at Edwards AFB, Calif. The crew included naval flight officer Col. David C. Hilmers, USMC (Ret.), during this second shuttle mission dedicated to Department of Defense tasking.

7 OCTOBER • Palestinian terrorists hijacked Italian cruise ship *Achille Lauro*. They alternately threatened and negotiated with Western diplomats and journalists, but subsequently murdered U.S. citizen Leon Klinghoffer. On 10 October, four of the terrorists attempted to escape on board an Egypt Air Boeing 737 airliner, but four of seven F-14As of VF-74 and -103 launched from *Saratoga* (CV 60) intercepted the aircraft

The prototype S-3B Viking, BuNo 159742, and full scale engineering flight test aircraft, undergoes testing at NATC Patuxent River, Md. It made its first flight on 13 September 1984.

over international waters and directed it to NAS Sigonella, Sicily. KA-6D tankers refueled the Tomcats. Other aircraft that assisted in the interception included E2-C Hawkeyes of VAW-125, EA-6B Prowlers, and an Air Force KC-135 Stratotanker.

13 OCTOBER • *Coral Sea* (CV 43), Capt. Robert H. Ferguson commanding, returned to the Mediterranean for her first Sixth Fleet deployment since 1957. This cruise marked the first deployment of Hornets to the Mediterranean, with VFA-131 and -132.

15 OCTOBER • Research ship *Norton Sound* (AVM 1) fired an RGM/UGM-109B Tomahawk antiship missile from the Pacific Missile Test Center's Sea Test Range off the California coast. The test successfully demonstrated the missile's vertical launch system, as well as its ability to search for, find, and strike a target at sea.

19 OCTOBER • VFA-303, the first Reserve squadron to transition to the F/A-18, received its initial Hornet during ceremonies at NAS Lemoore, Calif. Delivery of the eight jets ended two years of preparation at NAS Alameda, Calif., where the squadron had homeported until its move to Lemoore in 1983 for Hornet training. On 31 October, Lt. Bram B. Arnold of VFA-303 landed on board *Ranger* (CV 61) to become the first Reserve pilot to land a Hornet on board a carrier.

28 OCTOBER • The first prototype model S-3B Viking arrived for developmental test and evaluation at NATC Patuxent River, Md. The operational capability upgraded B configurations included state-of-the-art avionics, a new acoustic processor, electronic support measures system, target imaging radar, AGM-84 Harpoon air-to-ground missiles, and an electronic countermeasures system to counter the threat of sophisticated Soviet submarines, and to enhance the Vikings' multi-mission capabilities.

31 OCTOBER • Chief of Naval Operations Adm. James D. Watkins ordered cuts in deployment schedules to eliminate excessive at-sea periods for ships and aircraft squadrons. The decision was intended to enhance efficient use of the expanded Navy and, at the same time, allow crews more time at home with their families. He announced major turnaround ratios of 2:1 or better, assuring sailors that battle groups would spend a maximum of six months at sea.

9 NOVEMBER • A detachment from VP-66 operating from NS Roosevelt Roads, P.R., participated through 17 November in Operation Hat Trick II—a coordinated operation with the Coast Guard involving general area surveillance and location of vessels suspected of illegal drug trafficking.

23 NOVEMBER • Three Palestinian terrorists of the Abu Nidal Organization hijacked Egypt Air Flight 648, a Boeing 737-266, en route from Athens, Greece, to Cairo, Egypt, and flew it to Malta. *Coral Sea* (CV 43) sailed to the area for contingency purposes. On 25 November, Egyptian commandoes stormed the jet, and 60 of the 98 people on board perished in addition to the terrorists. *Coral Sea* subsequently departed.

13 DECEMBER • VC-10 was tasked to fly cover for a U.S. warship exercising rights of navigation in international waters off the southern coast of Cuba. The squadron's regular mission included air service for Atlantic Fleet ships and aircraft and air defense of Guantánamo Bay, Cuba.

DN-ST-85-08601

The Navy and Marines leased 25 Israeli F-21A Kfirs for adversarial training from 1985 to 1989.

1986

8 JANUARY • Capt. Frederick L. Lewis relieved Capt. Daniel L. Rainey Jr., as Commander Carrier Air Wing (CVW) 8 at NAS Oceana, Va. CVW-8 became the first to incorporate the wing commander/deputy commander concept (Super CAG), which provided an improved focus on power projection and enhanced tactical development and strike planning. The system restructured the chain of command and made wing commanders directly responsible to battle group commanders ashore and afloat, and additionally to carrier commanding officers when embarked. As part of the restructuring, CVW-8 was redesignated a major sea command and reported to Commander Carrier Group 8 and additionally to commanding officer *Nimitz* (CVN 68) when embarked.

13 JANUARY • After 20 years and 300,000 hours of service within the naval flight officer program, the T-39 Sabreliner ended its utility as a Navy training aircraft when VT-86 retired its last T-39D, BuNo 150983, at NAS Pensacola, Fla. This aircraft and five of the eight remaining Sabreliners were sent to Davis Monthan AFB, Ariz. The last two were scheduled for use as VIP transports at other Navy and Marine air stations.

15 JANUARY • VA-27 became the first recipient of the Grampaw Pettibone Trophy during a ceremony at the Officer's Club, Washington Navy Yard, D.C. Commanding officer Cmdr. Joseph P. Sciabarra of the NAS Lemoore, California-based squadron, accepted the award from Secretary of the Navy John F. Lehman Jr. Paul Warner, son of the originator of Grampaw Pettibone, had commissioned the trophy for an annual award to the individual or organization that contributed the most toward aviation safety awareness through written communications.

22 JANUARY • Vice President George H. W. Bush was the key participant at the inaugural marking the year-long observance of the 75th anniversary of naval aviation held at the National Air and Space Museum, Washington, D.C. Secretary of Defense Caspar W. Weinberger and Secretary of the Navy John F. Lehman Jr. also attended.

Aviation ordnancemen roll Rockeye cluster bombs across the flight deck of *Coral Sea* (CV 43) for use against Libyan targets in the spring of 1986.

A Libyan *Nanuchka II*–class corvette burns after a hit by an AGM-84 Harpoon air-to-ground missile fired by an A-6E Intruder of VA-85, 24 March 1986.

28 JANUARY • At 1138, space shuttle *Challenger* launched from John F. Kennedy Space Center, Fla., on mission STS-51L. Its payload included NASA Tracking and Data Relay Satellite B and the Spartan 203 satellite. A solid rocket booster seal failed allowing burning gasses to cut into the shuttle's external liquid fuel/oxidizer tank that, 73 seconds after launch, triggered a massive explosion. *Challenger* was destroyed and all seven astronauts on board died: Lt. Col. Francis R. Scobee, USAF, shuttle commander; pilot naval aviator Cmdr. Michael J. Smith; mission specialists Lt. Col. Ellison S. Onizuka, USAF; Judith A. Resnik; Ronald E. McNair; and payload specialists Capt. Gregory B. Jarvis, USAF; and S. Christa McAuliffe. Smith had graduated from the Naval Academy.

20 FEBRUARY • Rear Adm. Richard H. Truly was appointed the associate administrator of space flight within NASA. Truly had led the Naval Space Command since its establishment in 1983.

10 MARCH • *America* (CV 66) deployed to the Mediterranean. When she returned on 10 September, her voyage marked the first time that a carrier spent not longer than six months overseas as part of an initiative to reduce deployments. *John F. Kennedy* (CV 67) later relieved *America*.

18 MARCH • VMFT-401 was established at MCAS Yuma, Ariz., as the second squadron equipped with F-21A Kfirs and the first assigned to the Marine Corps. The squadron provided adversary training support to the Fleet Marine Force and other commands. In March 1985, VF-43 at NAS Oceana, Va., had been the first Navy squadron to receive the Israeli-built fighters.

24 MARCH • After Libyan strongman Col. Muammar al-Qadhafi announced a "line of death" that stretched across the Gulf of Sidra at 32°30'N, the United States initiated a series of freedom of navigation exercises in the gulf below the line. On this date, Operation Attain Document III (Prairie Fire) began—an armed response to Libyan-sponsored acts of terrorism. Into the following day, Commander Sixth Fleet Vice Adm. Frank B. Kelso II deployed elements of Task Force 60 including *Coral Sea* (CV 43), *Saratoga* (CV 60), and *America* (CV 66), with upward of 250 aircraft and 26 ships and submarines across the line and triggered Libyan action.

The F-4S Phantom IIs of VF-151 cross the eastern Pacific from *Midway* (CVA 41) toward NAS North Island, Calif., during the retirement of the last Phantoms in the fleet, from VF-151 and -161, 24 March 1986.

Libyan SA-2 Guideline and -5 Gammon surface-to-air missiles at Surt fired ineffectively at the Americans. A-6E Intruders of VA-34 and -85 sank La Combattante II G–class missile boat *Waheed* with two AGM-84 Harpoon air-to-ground missiles and Mk 20 Rockeye cluster bombs, marking the first operational use of Harpoons in combat. Additional strikes from VA-85 damaged Nanuchka II–class corvette *Ean Mara* with a Harpoon and Rockeyes, and compelled her to return to Benghazi. Two Intruders of VA-55 attacked but missed a second Nanuchka II–class corvette with Rockeyes, and an Intruder from VA-85 sank it with a Harpoon. Aircraft also damaged a corvette. VAQ-137 co-authored a plan to attack an SA-5 battery at Surt. EA-6B Prowlers flying from the carriers executed the plan using principally electronic warfare capabilities, and VA-81 A-7E Corsair IIs acted as decoys for VA-83 Corsair IIs that knocked out the battery with AGM-88 High-speed Anti-Radiation Missile. P-3C Orions of VP-56 hunted for Libyan submarines, and amphibious assault ship *Guadalcanal* (LPH 7) acted as the primary casualty receiving/treatment ship. Naval aircraft completed 1,546 sorties, 375 of them south of the line.

25 MARCH • Lts. Alan S. Colegrove and Gregory Blankenship of VF-151 made the final carrier launch of a fleet Phantom II in an F-4S, BuNo 153879, from *Midway* (CV 41) in the East China Sea.

28 MARCH • VFA-106, the Atlantic Fleet Hornet readiness squadron, graduated its first class of replacement pilots. Nine of the ten graduates then served with VFA-137.

DN-SN-86-03931

An A-6E Intruder, BuNo 155712, of VA-55 returns to *Coral Sea* (CV 43) after a mission over Libya, 29 January 1986. Intruders from VA-34 off *America* (CV 66) joined the fight.

29 MARCH • Lt. Cmdr. Donnie L. Cochran, the first African American member of the Flight Demonstration Squadron, completed his initial performance during the team's air show at Luke AFB, Ariz. Cochran had been selected in September 1985 for the Blue Angels number three position.

14 APRIL • After additional terrorist attacks sponsored by Libyan dictator Col. Muammar al-Qadhafi, the United States launched Operation El Dorado Canyon—attacks against Libyan military targets. Overnight into 15 April, U.S. aircraft struck three target areas near Tripoli: a frogman school at Murat Sidi Bilal, a military zone at Tripoli International Airport, and a command and control building at Bab al-Azziziyyah barracks. Jets also bombed the al-Jamahiriyyah barracks and Benina Airfield, both near Benghazi.

F/A-18A Hornets from *Coral Sea* (CV 43) and A-7E Corsair IIs from *America* (CV 66) suppressed Libyan radars electronically and with AGM-88 High-speed Anti-Radiation Missiles and AGM-45 Shrike air-to-ground missiles. F-14A Tomcats from *America* and Hornets from *Coral Sea* flew fighter support, and A-6E Intruders from VA-34 and -55 conducted low-level bombing. Eighteen USAF F-111F Aardvarks of the 48th Tactical Fighter Wing and four EF-111A Ravens of the 20th Tactical Fighter Wing flew a round trip of nearly 6,000 miles from England because of French and Spanish air restrictions.

The attacks struck at least three Ilyushin Il-76 Candids, 14 MiG-23 Floggers, one Fokker F-27 Friendship transport, and two Mil Mi-8 Hip helicopters on the ground, and killed 37 Libyans and wounded 93 more, including some civilians. One bomb also hit the French Embassy. The Libyans shot down one Aardvark killing both crewmembers. Qadhafi ineffectually launched two SS-1 Scud-B surface-to-surface missiles at a Coast Guard long-range navigation station on the island of Lampedusa.

DN-SC-87-03198

A restored PBY-6A Catalina—registered N4NC—takes part in the 75th anniversary of naval aviation with a reenactment flight of the 1919 NC-4 crossing of the Atlantic, May 1986. The aircraft's color scheme is reminiscent of that of the original NC-4 and carries its silhouette on the fin and rudder.

28 APRIL • *Enterprise* (CVN 65) became the first nuclear-powered carrier to pass through the Suez Canal when she steamed from the Red Sea to relieve *Coral Sea* (CV 43) in the Mediterranean.

2 MAY • A Navy board determined the feasibility of blimps for active duty, and later presented recommendations to the Secretary of the Navy for funding. Studies had been completed earlier in 1985 concerning the usefulness of Navy airships to provide airborne early warning capabilities for non-carrier battle groups, with the secondary missions of antisubmarine warfare and search and rescue.

2 MAY • The Navy initiated a contract for co-developers of joint services V-22 Ospreys with Bell Helicopter Textron, Fort Worth, Texas, and Boeing-Vertol Co. Philadelphia, Pa.

5 MAY • Secretary of the Navy John F. Lehman Jr. designated 1986 as the Diamond Anniversary of naval aviation. The planning for the celebration during this year included the recognition of significant historical naval aviation achievements.

5 MAY • As one of the naval aviation 75th anniversary commemorative events, two privately owned PBY Catalinas, one painted with NC-4 colors, made a reenactment flight of the NC-4's 1919 transatlantic crossing. The flight originated from NAS Pensacola, Fla., and followed the original route from NAS Rockaway Beach, N.Y., to Lisbon, Portugal.

27 MAY • After testing with UH-1N Iroquois, SH-3H Sea Kings, SH-60B Seahawks, and TH-57 Sea Rangers, the Navy approved helicopter landing trainer *IX-514* for use by student naval aviators. The craft provided a platform to qualify student helicopter pilots on board a ship before they joined the fleet.

The helicopter landing trainer, *IX-514*, begins operations in April 1986. The former Army yard freight utility craft, *YFU-79*, provided an FFG-7–size landing deck and relieved *Lexington* (AVT 16) of rotary-wing training responsibilities.

1 JUNE • Medium Attack Weapons School Pacific (MAWSPAC), previously composed of sailors from VA-128, was designated as a separate shore command. Fifteen days later, Cmdr. Richard P. Dodd became the first commanding officer of the combat readiness training school at NAS Whidbey Island, Wash. The school operated under the operational and administrative control of Commander Medium Attack Tactical Electronic Warfare Wing Pacific Fleet.

6 JUNE • The first naval aviation cadet in 17 years began active duty when Sean D. Farrar was sworn in by his father, Deputy Commander Navy Recruiting Command Capt. Bobby C. Farrar. The program, which allowed people to enter aviation officer candidate school and eventually flight training without a college degree, had been suspended in 1969.

28 JUNE • As a tribute to the 75th anniversary of naval aviation and Glenn H. Curtiss, a week of festivities began at Hammondsport, N.Y. Events included a reenactment of the Navy's first flight of the A-1, and a permanently mounted scale model of the aircraft, which was unveiled on the shore of Keuka Lake on 29 June.

1 JULY • The Helistat, a Piasecki Aircraft Company lighter-than-air craft flight demonstrator designed for use by the Forestry Service, crashed during flight tests at NAEC Lakehurst, N.J. The aircraft was a composite of fuselages, engines, and main rotors of four SH-34J Seahorses attached to a ZPG-2 airship envelope.

1 JULY • Secretary of the Navy John F. Lehman Jr. approved a formal naval airship development program.

5 AUGUST • Cmdr. William F. Headridge, Lt. Cmdr. Kenneth P. Parks, and Lts. Robert E. Smith and Michael J. Quinlan of VAQ-131 performed the first fleet launch of an AGM-88A High-speed Anti-Radiation Missile from an EA-6B Prowler at NWC China Lake, Calif.

18 AUGUST • A modified F/A-18 fired an AIM-120 AMRAAM (Advanced Medium-Range Air-to Air Missile) that shot down a QF-86 target flying at low altitude in a high-clutter radar environment. The Hornet flew 890 feet above sea level over the Pacific at Mach .49, and the drone at Mach .68 was 625 feet above the water.

19 AUGUST • *Carl Vinson* (CVN 70), with Carrier Air Wing 15 embarked exercised in the Bering Sea, making her the first carrier since World War II to operate in that part of the world. On 5 February 1987, *Carl Vinson* returned to NAS Alameda, Calif.

19 AUGUST • Tests of the close-in approach indicator (CAI) Mod 2, an optical system for landing operations by AV-8B Harrier IIs on board LHAs, began on board amphibious assault ship *Belleau Wood* (LHA 3). The tests ran through 29 August, and again from 6 to 23 October.

1 SEPTEMBER • The initiation of the *Coral Sea* concept—approved by the Secretary of the Navy to provide *Coral Sea* (CV 43) and *Midway* (CV 41) with two squadrons of eight A-6E Intruders each—commenced with VA-65's assignment from Carrier Air Wing (CVW) 7 to CVW-13 on board *Coral Sea*.

5 SEPTEMBER • At Karachi, Pakistan, four Abu Nidal terrorists hijacked Pam Am Flight 73, a Boeing 747-121, en route from Bombay (Mumbai), India, to New York City.

An AV-8B Harrier II demonstrates the type's unique abilities by operating from a road within a heavily wooded area.

Some of the flight crew escaped and the hijackers demanded the release of Palestinian terrorists. *Forrestal* (CV 59) sortied from Naples, Italy, and made for the Tyrrhenian Sea. Pakistani commandoes stormed the airliner and 22 people died in addition to the hijackers and another 150 sustained injuries. *Forrestal* then returned to her original operations.

29 SEPTEMBER • Grumman test pilot Joe Burke completed the maiden flight of an F-14A Plus during engine compatibility and flutter tests. He flew the Tomcat to Mach 1.1 at 25,000 feet and a maximum altitude of 35,000 feet. The improved Tomcat's new F110-GE-400 turbofan engines provided approximately 35 percent more thrust than the TF30s in fleet use.

1 OCTOBER • VRF-31 was disestablished at NAS Norfolk, Va., as the Navy's last aircraft ferry squadron. It had been established as VRF-1 and was redesignated in 1957. In 1972, it became the fleet's only ferry squadron with the disestablishment of VRF-32 on the West Coast.

17 OCTOBER • On board *America* (CV 66), Lt. Cmdr. Barry D. Gabler of VFP-206, the Navy's last photoreconnaissance squadron, made the final catapult takeoff and carrier landing of an F-8 Crusader.

20 OCTOBER • ALNAV message 202001Z Oct authorized naval aviation sailors and Marines to wear brown shoes and khaki socks with summer khaki uniforms, effective 1 April 1987. A part of naval aviators' uniforms since 1913, brown shoes had been removed from the uniform regulation on 1 July 1976.

3 NOVEMBER • A VR-57 C-9B Skytrain II flew into Quingdao, China, becoming the first naval aircraft to do so since the Chinese closed the port to the United States in 1949. The flight preceded by two days the visit of three naval ships. Cmdr. A. W. Boyce led the Reserve squadron, which was based at NAS North Island, Calif.

31 DECEMBER • A fire engulfed the Dupont Plaza Hotel and Casino, San Juan, P.R., killing an estimated 98 people and injuring at least 140. Three SH-3G Sea Kings of VC-8 launched on short notice and saved 75 persons stranded on the hotel roof in twilight and darkness, and rescued 24 more when the fire reignited after dusk.

1987

5 JANUARY • The first extended deployment for AV-8B Harrier IIs began when VMA-331 deployed on board *Belleau Wood* (LHA 3) for a six-month western Pacific cruise.

6 JANUARY • Reserve Carrier Air Wings 77 and 78 loaned E-2C Hawkeyes to the Customs Service and Coast Guard to bolster their drug enforcement efforts.

12 JANUARY • The airfield at MCAS Camp Pendleton, Calif., was designated Munn Field in honor of Lt. Gen. John C. Munn, a former assistant commandant of the Marine Corps and the first Marine aviator to command Camp Pendleton.

29 JANUARY • *John F. Kennedy* (CV 67) anchored for a four-day visit off Malaga, Spain. Growing tension concerning hostages held by terrorists in Lebanon compelled the Sixth Fleet to cut the carrier's visit short and to dispatch her on a high-speed transit to the eastern Mediterranean. On 2 February, the ship arrived off Lebanon, beginning intermittent dual operations with *Nimitz* (CVN 68). On 17 February, *John F. Kennedy* left the area.

13 FEBRUARY • Ens. Kamin A. Bell of HT-8 at NAS Whiting Field, Fla., became the Navy's first female African American helicopter pilot.

19 FEBRUARY • The Navy's E-6A prototype flew for the first time. The Hermes, a militarized version of Boeing's 707-320B, was scheduled to replace the EC-130Q TACAMO in VQ-3 with the Pacific Fleet and VQ-4 with the Atlantic Fleet. These aircraft provided airborne communications links between ballistic missile subs and national command authorities. Flight testing of the new aircraft began on 1 June.

18 MARCH • VF-301 took part in an AIM-54A air-to-air missile launch at the Pacific Missile Test Range Point Mugu, Calif. This marked the first time that a Reserve squadron had used a Phoenix.

19 MARCH • An SH-60F carrier inner zone helicopter made its first flight.

29 MARCH • VFP-206 was disestablished at NAF Washington, D.C., as the Navy's last light photographic

The first E-6A Hermes, BuNo 162782, enters flight testing at Boeing Field in Seattle, Wash. in 1988. The type, later renamed Mercury, entered Navy service in August 1989.

squadron. The action signaled the end of F-8 Crusaders in naval aviation. Some VFP-206 RF-8Gs went into storage at Davis-Monthan AFB, Ariz., one was transferred to the National Air and Space Museum, and the final two provided test support for NAVAIR.

30 MARCH • The Navy conducted the first flight of a BQM-126A target drone at Pacific Missile Test Center Point Mugu, Calif. Designed as lower cost, state-of-the-art replacement targets, the BQM-126As could fly from sea level up to 40,000 feet.

31 MARCH • As part of a reorganization for centralized support of fleet aviation maintenance approved by the Under Secretary of the Navy, NARFs were redesignated naval aviation depots (NADEP), the Naval Aviation Logistics Center became the Naval Aviation Depot Operations Center, and the Aircraft Intermediate Maintenance Support Office assumed the new title Naval Aviation Maintenance Office.

1 APRIL • HM-12 became the first fleet squadron to receive an MH-53E Sea Dragon.

6 APRIL • The Navy received the first of 26 F-16N Fighting Falcon aggressor jets.

25 APRIL • The Navy Flight Demonstration Squadron held its first air show using F/A-18 Hornets.

17 MAY • An Iraqi Dassault F.1EQ-5-200 Mirage fired two AM.39 Exocet air-to-ground missiles into frigate *Stark* (FFG 31) near 26°47'N, 51°55'E, killing 36 sailors plus one missing, and wounding 21. The Iraqis claimed that the attack resulted from mistaken identity. Vessels that aided *Stark* included command ship—former amphibious transport dock—*La Salle* (AGF 3), destroyers *Coontz* (DDG 40), *Conyngham* (DDG 17), and *Waddell* (DDG 24), and frigate *Reid* (FFG 30). An SH-3G Sea King of HC-2 Detachment 2 flew flight surgeon Lt. Cmdr. Terry A. Miller and supplies

A C-20G Gulfstream IV, BuNo 165094, assigned to VR-48 flies from Naval Air Facility, Andrews Air Force Base, Washington, D.C.

to the stricken ship from NSA Bahrain, and then searched unsuccessfully for survivors in the water. *Conyngham* towed *Stark* to Bahrain.

18 MAY • Oscar 13—a satellite designed to function as part of the Navy's Transit Satellite Navigation System—became the oldest active U.S. satellite when it celebrated its 20th year of service.

22 MAY • Marine Corps Aviation celebrated its 75th anniversary. On 22 May 1912, 1st Lt. Alfred A. Cunningham, USMC, had reported for "duty in connection with aviation" to an aviation camp at Annapolis, Md.

JUNE • NASA selected Lt. Cmdr. Bruce E. Melnick, USCG, as the first Coast Guard astronaut. He subsequently completed two space shuttle flights.

5 JUNE • The Navy awarded a contract to Westinghouse Airship Industries to build a prototype airship as an airborne early warning and communications platform. The Navy had terminated its lighter-than-air program in 1961 and ceased operation of its last airship the next year.

22 JUNE • Fleet Logistics Support Wing Detachment, NAF Washington, D.C., received its first C-20D Gulfstream IV.

26 JUNE • A night attack equipped AV-8B Harrier II conducted its maiden flight at the McDonnell Douglas St. Louis, Mo., facility. Operational tests and evaluation of the aircraft continued later that summer. The upgrade greatly expanded the operational envelope of Harrier IIs by using state-of-the-art navigation equipment and night-vision devices.

30 JUNE • The Navy received its first SH-60F carrier inner zone helicopter. Operational tests and evaluation of the aircraft began in December.

30 JUNE • A VX-5 A-6E conducted the first successful firing of an AGM-88A High-speed Anti-Radiation Missile from an Intruder. This marked the first in a series of missile launches planned to test the A-6E System Weapons Integration Program configuration. This also allowed Intruders to carry AGM-65 Maverick and AGM-84 Harpoon air-to-ground missiles, which increased the stockpile of standoff weapons for carrier air wings.

The RQ-2A Pioneer remotely piloted vehicle is based on the Israeli-designed Mastiff drone. The American version served with both the Navy and Marines.

6 JULY • SH-2F Seasprites and SH-60B Seahawks deployed for special Middle East Force duties were modified with additional defensive equipment such as M-60 machine guns, special countermeasures, and infrared electronic devices.

10 JULY • The Navy awarded a contract to Boeing to upgrade a P-3 Orion to an Update IV version, which was to include an advanced avionics suite to address the problems that newer, quieter submarines posed.

14 JULY • VAQ-131 on board *Ranger* (CV 61) began the first Pacific Fleet deployment of EA-6B Prowlers equipped with AGM-88 High-speed Anti-Radiation Missiles.

15 JULY • Commander Naval Air Force Pacific Fleet initiated extensive modifications to LAMPS Mk I and Mk III helicopters to increase their survivability and surface surveillance capabilities during Persian Gulf operations.

25 JULY • The National Aviation Hall of Fame, Dayton, Ohio, enshrined naval aviator Adm. Thomas H. Moorer.

27 JULY • For some time, the Iranians had laid mines that imperiled international shipping in the Persian Gulf. To combat this, on this date, HM-14 received tasking for rapid deployment to the region and three days later departed with eight RH-53D Sea Stallions. Eight USAF Lockheed C-5A Galaxies and two Lockheed C-141A Starlifters from Travis AFB, Calif., carried some men and gear to Diego Garcia, British Indian Ocean Territory. The sailors reassembled and embarked on board amphibious assault ship *Guadalcanal* (LPH 7), which had sailed with the 24th Marine Amphibious Unit. HM-14 conducted minesweeping and hunting operations in the Persian Gulf until six minesweepers relieved the squadron.

1 AUGUST • To counter the emerging threat that lasers presented, the Pacific Fleet began to distribute laser eye protection devices to its aviation commands.

1 AUGUST • Commander Naval Air Force Atlantic Fleet began support of an average of five to seven LAMPS helicopter detachments operating on convoy duty in the Persian Gulf.

10 AUGUST • The first of four new P-3 Orion weapons systems trainers (2F140) arrived at NAS Moffett Field, Calif. These provided state-of-the-art capabilities for antisubmarine warfare crew training.

The Marine's AH-1-4BW Supercobra begins testing its new four-bladed rotor with VX-5 in January 1989. Originally an AH-1T Sea Cobra that became the prototype AH-1W, BuNo 161022 later also became the prototype AH-1Z.

21 AUGUST • Commander Naval Air Force Pacific Fleet Vice Adm. James E. Service retired, relinquishing his Gray Eagle title to Commanding General Marine Corps Development and Education Command Lt. Gen. Frank E. Petersen at Quantico, Va. Petersen, the first African American aviator in the Marine Corps, had been designated a naval aviator in October 1952. He was the first African American to receive the Gray Eagle.

10 SEPTEMBER • VC-6 Detachment 1, Lt. Cmdr. Wayne T. Moore officer in charge, deployed on board *Iowa* (BB 61) with an RQ-2A Pioneer RPV (remotely piloted vehicle). This began battleship-operated RPVs (later redesignated unmanned aerial vehicle or UAV) that provided independent reconnaissance and naval gunfire support capabilities. During operations ranging from the area off Puerto Rico to the Norwegian Sea, Mediterranean, north Arabian Sea, and Persian Gulf, the Pioneer identified ships, enhanced threat assessments, and greatly reduced the number of rounds that the battleship required to destroy simulated targets. In 1987, the Pioneer made 54 flights, continuing operations into the New Year. On 10 March 1988, *Iowa* returned to NS Norfolk, Va.

19 SEPTEMBER • *Wasp* (LHD 1) was christened.

21 SEPTEMBER • The Navy received its first F/A-18C. The upgraded Hornets included AIM-120 AMRAAM (advanced medium-range air-to-air missiles) and infrared imaging AGM-65 Maverick air-to-ground missiles.

29 SEPTEMBER • *Coral Sea* (CV 43) sailed for a Mediterranean cruise while operating under a new plan called the *Coral Sea* concept. The two attack squadrons on board relied on a shared maintenance concept to streamline the process.

30 SEPTEMBER • *Nassau* (LHA 4) sailed from NS Norfolk, Va. The AV-8Bs from VMA-231 embarked on board the amphibious assault ship, thus beginning the deployment of the first Harrier IIs to the Mediterranean.

8 OCTOBER • HMLA-169 became the first Marine squadron to deploy operationally with the AH-1W when the squadron sailed to the Persian Gulf on board amphibious assault ship *Okinawa* (LPH 3). Super Cobras employed AGM-114 Hellfire air-to-ground and BGM-71 tube-launched, optically tracked, wire command-link (TOW)

The 558th F-14 Tomcat—and the first purpose-built F-14B—BuNo 162910, awaits delivery to the Navy at Grumman's Calverton, N.Y. flight test facility in November 1987. The B-models, originally designated F-14A (Plus), received much needed uprated engines.

anti-tank missiles, AIM-9 Sidewinder air-to-air missiles, and new heads-up displays and bigger engines to increase their ground support capabilities.

16 OCTOBER • The Iranians launched a Chinese HY-2G Silkworm (CSS-C-2 Sea Eagle-2) surface-to-surface missile from the al-Fāw Peninsula that damaged reflagged Kuwaiti tanker *Sea Isle City* (renamed from *Umm al Maradex*). Two days later, the Americans began Operation Nimble Archer—retaliation against the Iranian-occupied Rashadat rig, 120 miles east of Bahrain. Gunners on the rig had previously shot at U.S. aircraft. Navy and Marine helicopters supported destroyers *Kidd* (DDG 993), *Hoel* (DDG 13), *John Young* (DD 973), and *Leftwich* (DD 984), when they blasted the platform with gunfire, and as SEALs then searched the rig. The flames started by the bombardment prevented the special operations forces from boarding the complex, but the Iranians abandoned a third nearby rig, which SEALs boarded and searched.

18 OCTOBER • Battleship *Iowa* (BB 61) recovered an RQ-2A Pioneer remotely piloted vehicle from VC-6 Detachment 1 at night for the first time.

30 OCTOBER • The Navy established the designation C-28A for the Cessna 404 (Titan Ambassador) eight- to ten-passenger, twin-engine planes.

16 NOVEMBER • The service accepted the first production F-14A (Plus) Tomcat.

5 DECEMBER • VP-62 became the first Reserve squadron to transition to P-3C Update III Orions. At times during 1987, the Naval Air Reserve Force consisted of 52 operational squadrons comprising more than 400 aircraft.

7 DECEMBER • The Naval Test Pilot School at NAS Patuxent River, Md., received the first of three HH-65A Dolphins on loan from the Coast Guard.

10 DECEMBER • The Navy established the X-31A designation and applied it to the enhanced fighter maneuverability (EFM) technology demonstrator aircraft. The EFM was not planned for production, but to provide significant improvements in fighter aircraft agility during close-in aerial combat, as well as in transonic and supersonic engagements, and in ground-attack applications.

12 DECEMBER • Iranian speedboats sank Cypriot tanker *Pivot* in the Persian Gulf. Destroyer *Chandler* (DDG 996), with an SH-2F Seasprite of HSL-33 Detachment 5 embarked, rescued 11 people from the tanker.

15 DECEMBER • The YEZ-2A designation was established and assigned to the Navy's operational development model airship. The vehicle was to be an organic asset of surface action groups to serve as a fuel-efficient, long-endurance airborne platform for area surveillance and communications, command, and control.

17 DECEMBER • The first fleet S3A Vikings retro-fitted to S-3B configuration entered service with VS-27 at NAS Cecil Field, Fla.

21 DECEMBER • Changes to the Office of Chief of Naval Operations, required by the Goldwater-Nichols Department of Defense Reorganization Act of 1986, resulted in redesignation of the Deputy Chief of Naval Operations (Air Warfare) as Assistant Chief of Naval Operations (Air Warfare). On 18 August 1943 this organization had been established as Deputy Chief of Naval Operations (Air), and on 15 July 1971 was modified to Deputy Chief of Naval Operations (Air Warfare).

21 DECEMBER • The Secretary of the Navy announced the approval of the opening of aircrew assignments to women for the Navy's two shore-based fleet air reconnaissance squadrons flying EP-3 Orions.

25 DECEMBER • An Iranian speedboat attacked South Korean tanker *Hyundai No. 7* with rocket-propelled grenades near Abū Mūsá, 20 miles southwest of Sharjar. Pilot Lt. Neil W. T. Hogg, copilot Lt. Gregory P. Curth, and aircrewmen AW2 Charles Crissman and AWAN Robert Bauch of HSL-44 Detachment 3, manned an SH-60B operating from frigate *Elrod* (FFG 55), and rescued and flew 11 of the 20 crewmembers to British frigate *Scylla* (F 71). A Westland Lynx HAS.3 from *Scylla* recovered the remaining nine.

1988

11 JANUARY • Col. Gregory Boyington, the top Marine ace of World War II and Medal of Honor recipient, died at age 75. Boyington received credit for destroying 28 Japanese aircraft. On 3 January 1944, he was shot down over Rabaul, and held as a POW for the next 20 months.

17 MARCH • *Vanguard I*—built by the Naval Research Laboratory—the world's longest orbiting man-made satellite and the first to be solar powered, marked its 30th anniversary in space. The satellite had provided information on air density, temperatures, and micrometeorite impact during the nearly seven years its radio transmitter functioned.

11 APRIL • VF-101 at NAS Oceana, Va., accepted the first F-14A (Plus) Tomcat assigned to an operational squadron.

14 APRIL • An Iranian mine damaged frigate *Samuel B. Roberts* (FFG 58) in the Persian Gulf. The vessels that assisted included amphibious transport dock *Trenton* (LPD 14). On 18 April, the United States launched Operation Praying Mantis—retaliation against the Iranian-occupied Rakhsh, Salman (Sassan), and Sīrrī-D (Nassr) oil platforms.

From the north Arabian Sea, *Enterprise* (CVN 65) launched VAW-117 E-2C Hawkeyes that provided airborne early warning, and VAQ-135 EA-6B Prowlers that jammed Iranian radar and fire control systems. P-3C Orions of VP-46 flying from NSA Bahrain took part, and naval aircraft and frigate *Gary* (FFG 51) protected Mobile Sea Bases *Hercules* and *Wimbrown VII*. Four AH-1T Sea Cobras, two UH-1N Iroquois, and two CH-46E Sea Knights of Contingency Marine Air-Ground Task Force 2-88 supported the assaults.

The first service test T-45A Goshawk trainer, BuNo 162787, the Navy version of the British Aerospace Hawk, is delivered in 1988.

Five Iranian F-4s attempted to intercept a Hawkeye, but four F-14A Tomcats drove them off. The Americans attacked an orbiting Hercules that Iranians had modified to provide targeting data to their Chinese HY-2G Silkworm surface-to-surface missiles, but the plane escaped. Cruiser *Wainwright* (CG 28) and frigates *Bagley* (FF 1069) and *Simpson* (FFG 56) sank missile boat *Joshan* (P 225).

Wainwright fired a Standard SM-2ER surface-to-air missile that damaged an Iranian Phantom II. The Iranian *Sepah-e Pasdaran-e Enqelab-e Islami* (Islamic Revolutionary Guard Corps) dispatched at least seven RL-120-2A Boghammar gunboats from Abū Mūsá against the Mubarak oil field southeast of the United Arab Emirates, damaging an oil rig, British tanker *York Marine*, and U.S.-flagged supply ship *Willi Tide*. Two A-6E Intruders of VA-95 sank one of the Boghammars, and the survivors beached two of the boats on Abū Mūsá. An Intruder damaged Iranian frigate *Sahand* (F 74), and a second Intruder, six A-7E Corsair IIs of VA-22 and -94, and destroyer *Joseph Strauss* (DDG 16) sank *Sahand*. An Intruder disabled frigate *Sabalan* (F 73) with a 500-pound Mk 82 laser-guided bomb.

An AH-1T, manned by pilot Capt. Kenneth W. Hill, USMC, and copilot Capt. Stephen C. Leslie, USMC, of HMLA-167, crashed from undetermined causes. Both

Col. Gregory Boyington is the top Marine ace of World War II. He died in 1988 at the age of 75.

The Americans retaliate against these platforms in Iranian territorial waters, which were used by Iran as bases during attacks on Persian Gulf shipping, during Operation Praying Mantis, 18 April 1988.

Marines posthumously received the Distinguished Flying Cross. Cmdr. Arthur N. Langston, Lt. Cmdrs. James H. Engler and Joseph E. Nortz, and Lt. Robert P. Papadakis of VA-95 also received the Distinguished Flying Cross.

16 APRIL • The maiden flight of a T-45A Goshawk took place at Douglas Aircraft Company, Long Beach, Calif.

6 MAY • A night attack prototype F/A-18D made its first flight at McDonnell Douglas, St. Louis, Mo. Equipped with a new forward looking infrared sensor, the two-seat Hornets were designed to help pilots and naval flight officers navigate and assist in locating, identifying, and attacking ground targets at night.

16 MAY • A production model E-6A Hermes communications aircraft arrived for extensive electromagnetic testing at NATC Patuxent River, Md.

23 MAY • The V-22 Osprey debuted during rollout ceremonies at Bell Helicopter's Arlington, Texas, facility.

14 JUNE • Cmdr. John T. Meister and Lt. Cmdr. Richard D. Jaskot of VA-75, flew the latest Intruder variant, an A-6E SWIP (System Weapons Integration Program), when they launched an AGM-88 High-speed Anti-Radiation Missile (HARM) and struck a target ship, becoming the first fleet A-6E to do so. Upgrades to the Intruders included the ability to launch HARM, AGM-65 Maverick, and AGM-84 Harpoon air-to-ground missiles.

14 JUNE • During coordinated fleet operations with the Second Fleet, Reserve squadron VP-62 fired the first AGM-84 Harpoon air-to-ground missile from a P-3C Update III Orion and hit its target. The squadron had been selected earlier as the first Reserve patrol squadron to receive the Orions as part of the horizontal integration program at NAS Jacksonville, Fla.

The first V-22 Osprey, BuNo 163911, makes its maiden flight, 19 March 1989. It was a decade before the first production model was delivered to the Marines on 25 May 1999.

2 JULY • As the United States pressed freedom of navigation rights within the Strait of Hormuz and the Persian Gulf, an Iranian RL-120-2A Boghammar and two Boston Whaler–type armed speedboats fired three rockets at Danish tanker *Karama Maersk*, 20 nautical miles southwest of Abū Mūsá. Frigate *Elmer B. Montgomery* (FF 1082) fired an illumination round and the Iranians fled. The next morning, *Forrestal* (CV 59) sailed into the Gulf of Oman and launched a VAW-122 E-2C Hawkeye, escorted by F-14A Tomcats of VF-11 and -31. Tomcats also flew photoreconnaissance missions over Iranian coastal and island defense sites. *Elmer B. Montgomery* detected up to 13 Iranian speedboats that approached a Pakistani merchantman. Cruiser *Vincennes* (CG 49) dispatched an HSL-43 SH-60B, designated Oceanlord 25, to investigate the vessels. The Americans also monitored an orbiting Iranian P-3F Orion, and a *Hengam*-class tank landing ship that acted as a mother ship for speedboats. The speedboats fired at—but missed—Oceanlord 25, and the Seahawk returned to *Vincennes*. Four speedboats exchanged fire with *Vincennes*, and in error, the cruiser fired two Standard SM-2 Block II surface-to-air missiles that shot down Iran Air Flight 655, a civilian Airbus A300B2-203, en route from Bandar-e Abbās to Dubai, killing all 290 people on board. *Vincennes* sank two speedboats and possibly damaged a third.

Two to three Iranian F-4D/E Phantom IIs operating from Bandar-e Abbās attempted to lock onto *Vincennes*, but U.S. electronic jamming compelled their retirement. A Soviet Ilyushin Il-38 May observed these operations during a flight from Aden, Yemen.

13 JULY • The Carrier Airborne Early Warning Weapons School was established as a separate command on the same principles as Top Gun and Strike University with emphasis placed on E-2C Hawkeye aircrew warfare training.

22 JULY • VA-304 took delivery of a KA-6D, marking the introduction of Intruders to the Naval Air Reserve. By September 1988, the squadron had three KA-6Ds and two A-6Es.

2 AUGUST • Using installed halon firefighting equipment, *Constellation* (CV 64) successfully fought a severe fire in her main engineering space. This action marked the first use of the system by a carrier in fighting a fire.

5 AUGUST • Dwaine L. Lyon received his wings and was commissioned an ensign, becoming the first NAVCAD to complete the jet strike training pipeline since the reinstitution of the program in 1986. Begun in 1935, it had become an important source of naval aviators until it ended 30 years later. Under the revived NAVCAD, aviation cadets with a minimum of two years of college or its equivalent could undergo flight training as noncommissioned officers.

17 AUGUST • The HH-60H Seahawk made its maiden flight at Sikorsky Aircraft, Stratford, Conn. Derived from the SH-60F, the new variant's primary mission was strike rescue, with secondary tasks involving special warfare missions. The HH-60Hs were the first new aircraft purchased for and operated exclusively by the Naval Air Reserve.

25 AUGUST • A NASA-designed Scout rocket launched two Navy navigation satellites from Vandenberg AFB, Calif. The event marked the culmination of the planned launch program for the Transit system, also known as the Navy Navigation Satellite System, which had begun in 1962. The Navy relied on Transit for precise position information anywhere on the earth and in all weather conditions. The two satellites were launched piggyback style using the Stacked Oscars on the Scout system.

13 SEPTEMBER • *Midway* (CV 41) and *Nimitz* (CVN 68) sailed at times through 2 October off the Korean Peninsula to provide security during the Games of the XXIV Olympiad at Seoul, South Korea.

29 SEPTEMBER • Space shuttle *Discovery* on mission STS-26 launched from John F. Kennedy Space Center, Fla. On 3 October, it returned to Edwards AFB, Calif. Naval aviators Capt. Frederick H. Hauck and Col. David C. Hilmers, USMC, former naval aviator John M. Lounge, and Col. Richard O. Covey, USAF, and George D. Nelson comprised the crew. Their principal payload included NASA Tracking and Data Relay Satellite 3, which was propelled into orbit after being deployed from *Discovery*. Vice President George H. W. Bush greeted the astronauts upon their return.

30 SEPTEMBER • The Navy's last operational reciprocating-engine aircraft, a C-1A, BuNo 146048, retired from active service and was transferred to the Naval Aviation Museum, NAS Pensacola, Fla. The Trader had provided carrier onboard delivery support from the station for *Lexington* (AVT 16).

1 OCTOBER • HAL-5 was redesignated HCS-5 at NAS Point Mugu, Calif. Established on 1 March 1977 at Point Mugu, the Reserve squadron, commanded by Cmdr. Robert W. Womble, had fulfilled a primary mission of combat search and rescue (strike rescue) and special warfare support. The squadron operated eight HH-1K helicopters that year, which were later replaced with HH-60H Seahawks. On 31 December 2006, HCS-5 was deactivated at NAS North Island, Calif.

3 OCTOBER • The aircraft designation A-12A, denoting a new carrier-based attack aircraft with a two-man crew, was established.

14 OCTOBER • The Navy selected Lockheed Aeronautical Systems Co. to develop a replacement aircraft for P-3C Orions. The new plane—initially designated LRAACA (long-range, air antisubmarine warfare–capable aircraft) and later redesignated P-7A—was to possess new fuel-efficient, modern-technology turboprop engines to boost range and efficiency, increased payload capacity, and improved avionics suites. The program was cancelled on 20 July 1990.

3 NOVEMBER • The Navy's initial AGM-84E Standoff Land Attack Missile (SLAM) was rolled out at McDonnell Douglas' St. Charles, Mo., facility. The weapons were derived from AGM-84 Harpoons for deployment from carrier-based aircraft to allow them to attack land targets and ships from ranges in excess of 60 nautical miles.

10 NOVEMBER • Ens. Joy D. Warner became the first woman to earn her wings through the newly reinstated NAVCAD program. Warner had joined the program in June 1987 and completed her basic flight training with HT-8.

29 NOVEMBER • The Navy transferred a F-4S, BuNo 157307, to the Smithsonian's National Air and Space Museum after its arrival at Dulles International Airport, Va. This jet had seen action in Vietnam and was a MiG killer. On 21 June 1972, pilot Cmdr. Samuel C. Flynn Jr. and radar intercept officer Lt. William H. John of VF-31, flying from *Saratoga* (CV 60), shot down a MiG-21 Fishbed. The museum planned to display the Phantom II in a future Vietnam War exhibit.

31 DECEMBER • The Aviation Officer Continuation Pay program concluded. On 1 January 1989, a new program—Aviation Continuation Pay (ACP)—began, and applied only to pilots and naval flight officers below pay grade O-5. The ACP payment reached up to $12,000 for each year of contracts if officers agreed to remain on active duty to complete 14 years of continuous service.

1989

4 JANUARY • Two F-14As crewed by pilot Cmdr. Joseph B. Connelly and radar intercept officer (RIO) Cmdr. Leo F. Enwright Jr., and pilot Lt. Herman C. Cook III and RIO Lt. Cmdr. Steven P. Collins of VF-32, embarked with Carrier Air Wing 3 on board *John F. Kennedy* (CV 67), shot down two Libyan MiG-23s. The carrier sailed in routine training exercises off the northeastern tip of the Libyan coast when the two Floggers launched from a field at Al Bumbah and approached the carrier. After repeated attempts to intercept the aggressive Libyans peacefully, the Tomcats fired AIM-7 Sparrow and AIM-9 Sidewinder air-to-air missiles, downing the MiGs over international waters in the central Mediterranean north of Tobruk, Libya.

20 JANUARY • George H. W. Bush (Naval Aviator No. C5907) was inaugurated as the 41st President of the United States.

23 FEBRUARY • The Navy's Mid-InfraRed Advanced Chemical Laser/SeaLite Beam Director (an experimental high-energy laser system) destroyed an MQM-8G Vandal supersonic missile during a test at White Sands Missile Range, N.M. This marked the first time that a high-energy laser system had successfully engaged and destroyed a Vandal flying low and fast in a cruise missile profile.

19 MARCH • A V-22 made its first flight at Bell Helicopter Textron's Flight Research Center, Arlington, Texas. In Phase 1 of the flight tests, the Osprey reached a maximum speed of 20 knots and an altitude of 30 feet during a 15-minute flight in the helicopter mode.

31 MARCH • VP-62 completed transition to the P-3C Update III, marking the first time that a Reserve patrol squadron had received the latest state-of-the-art Orions.

3 APRIL • An A-6E modified with a new composite wing made its first flight at Wichita, Kans. Manufactured by Boeing from graphite/epoxy composite materials, the new wing proved stronger than the Intruder's original metal structure.

16 APRIL • VS-30 became the first fleet S-3 Viking squadron to fire an AGM-84 Harpoon air-to-ground missile when a detachment participated in exercise North Star '89 on board *America* (CV 66). The launch resulted in a direct hit on the target.

19 APRIL • While operating in the Caribbean, *Coral Sea* (CV 43) responded to a call for assistance from *Iowa* (BB 61) after an explosion in the battleship's number two gun turret killed 47 crewmembers. The explosive ordnance disposal team from *Coral Sea* removed volatile powder charges from the ship's 16-inch guns and flooded powder magazines. *Coral Sea* also dispatched a surgical team and medical supplies, and SH-3G Sea Kings of VC-8 performed medical evacuations and logistical support to *Iowa*.

15 MAY • H. Lawrence Garrett III was sworn in as the Secretary of the Navy. Garrett was commissioned as a naval aviation cadet in 1964, and had served as a naval flight officer with VP-50 during the Vietnam War.

22 JUNE • HS-10 accepted the Navy's first SH-60F carrier inner zone helicopter at NAS North Island, Calif. In October, HS-10 became the Navy's only SH-60F Seahawk fleet readiness squadron when it transferred all SH-3 Sea King training to HC-1 and HS-1.

24 JUNE • The initial development freeflight test of an AGM-84E Standoff Land Attack Missile (SLAM) resulted in a direct hit on a simulated surface-to-air missile communication site at San Nicholas Island, Pacific Missile Test Center Range, Calif. An A-6E System Weapons Integration Program Intruder launched the missile, and an F/A-18 Hornet using the Walleye data link for man-in-the-loop control guided the SLAM during its flight.

1 JULY • Associate Administrator for Space Flight, Office of Space Flight, NASA Rear Adm. Richard H. Truly retired from the Navy and was confirmed by Congress as the administrator of NASA. A naval aviator, Truly had been selected as an astronaut in 1965, and received credit for bringing the United States back into an active space program after the space shuttle *Challenger* accident.

1 JULY • The Naval Aviation Museum at NAS Pensacola, Fla., changed its name to the National Museum of Naval Aviation.

8 JULY • HCS-5 accepted its first HH-60H Seahawk strike rescue and special warfare operations helicopters at NAS Point Mugu, Calif.

22 JULY • The National Aviation Hall of Fame in Dayton, Ohio, enshrined Adm. Marc A. Mitscher (Naval Aviator No. 33). In 1919, Mitscher commanded flying boat NC-1 during the first airborne transatlantic crossing, and nine years later in a Vought UO-1, made the first takeoff and landing on board *Saratoga* (CV 3). His service during World War II included the commissioning and command of *Hornet* (CV 8), and command of Patrol Wing 2; Fleet Air, Noumea; and elements of the USAAF, Navy, Marine Corps, and Royal New Zealand Air Force contingents. Of particular significance was his command of Task Force 58, the fast carrier task force, during 1944 and 1945.

1 AUGUST • Arab terrorists in Beirut hanged Lt. Col. William R. Higgins, USMC, a member of the UN peacekeeping forces in Lebanon, and threatened to murder additional hostages they held. *America* (CV 66) departed early from a visit to Singapore and made for the Arabian Sea, and *Coral Sea* (CV 43) steamed from Alexandria, Egypt, to the eastern Mediterranean as a show of force. *Midway* (CV 41) had originally been scheduled to participate in Pacific Exercise–89, but sailed to fill a carrier commitment in the Indian Ocean, where she operated until mid-October.

3 AUGUST • An A-6E Intruder from VA-145 spotted 37 Vietnamese refugees adrift in a barge in heavy seas and monsoon rains in the South China Sea. Eight people had drifted in the barge for ten days, and 29 other refugees from a sinking boat had clambered on board. SH-3H Sea Kings from HS-14, deployed on board *Ranger* (CV 61), assisted in their rescue from the derelict boat's final position 80 miles from NAS Cubi Point, Philippines.

3 AUGUST • VQ-3 took delivery of two E-6As at Seattle, Wash. The arrival of the new strategic communications Hermes aircraft marked the entry into the fleet of the newest generation of TACAMO aircraft.

6 SEPTEMBER • Cruiser *Bunker Hill* (CG 52), with an SH-60B Seahawk of HSL-45 Detachment 7A embarked, rescued 49 Vietnamese refugees in an overcrowded boat 130 nautical miles northeast of Singapore. *Bunker Hill* sank the derelict vessel with gunfire to prevent a navigational hazard, and the following day transferred the people to ammunition ship *Kilauea* (T-AE 26) for transportation to a resettlement center.

7 SEPTEMBER • An NS-3A modified as the aerodynamic prototype of an ES-3A Shadow made its first flight. Sixteen ES-3As eventually replaced EA-3B Skywarriors in fleet air reconnaissance squadrons.

12 SEPTEMBER • The Coast Guard retired its last HH-52A. Sea Guard helicopters had served more than 26 years as the Coast Guard's primary short-range, search and rescue aircraft, and were replaced by Aerospatiale HH-65A Dolphins.

14 SEPTEMBER • The first HH-60J medium-range, search and rescue helicopters were rolled out in Stratford, Conn. The Jayhawks replaced HH-3Fs in Coast Guard service.

14 SEPTEMBER • A V-22 made its first flight in full airplane mode. The Osprey was airborne for about one hour over Bell Helicopter Textron's Arlington, Texas, facility.

14 SEPTEMBER • The Aircrew Common Ejection Seat successfully completed a 600-knot dual ejection from an F-14D Tomcat test sled at China Lake, Calif.

17 SEPTEMBER • *Enterprise* (CVN 65) deployed from NAS Alameda, Calif., for World Cruise 89–90. On 16 March 1990, the ship concluded her global circumnavigation at NS Norfolk, Va.

17 SEPTEMBER • Responding to the destruction caused in the Caribbean by Hurricane Hugo, a number of Navy and Marine Corps squadrons under the direction of Commander Fleet Air Caribbean, including HC-2 Detachment 6, VC-8, and VP-93, flew needed supplies to Puerto Rico and evacuated seriously injured people to hospitals. Commands that responded included eight CH-53E Super Stallions, two KC-130s, and dock landing ships *Gunston Hall* (LSD 44), *Pensacola* (LSD 38), and *Whidbey Island* (LSD 41).

22 SEPTEMBER • VMFT-401 transferred its last F-21A Kfir, marking the retirement from U.S. naval aviation of these Israeli-built fighters that had been used as aggressor aircraft.

30 SEPTEMBER • VAK-208 was disestablished as the last Navy squadron dedicated solely to aerial refueling. Assigned to Reserve Carrier Air Wing 20, the squadron had provided aerial refueling and pathfinder support since its establishment in July 1970 as VAQ-208. On 1 October 1979, it had been redesignated VAK-208. VA-304 and -205, transitioning to A-6E and KA-6Ds, assumed Reserve carrier air wing aerial refueling responsibilities.

1 OCTOBER • Reserve squadron HAL-4, the last naval gunship squadron, was redesignated HCS-4, with an added mission of strike rescue.

3 OCTOBER • Through 5 October, frigates *Wadsworth* (FFG 9), *Duncan* (FFG 10), *Lewis B. Puller* (FFG 23), and *Mahlon S. Tisdale* (FFG 27), withdrew from an exercise in the North Pacific and rescued 20 crewmembers from stricken South Korean merchantman *Pan Dynasty* south of Attu, Aleutians.

17 OCTOBER • An earthquake measuring 7.1 on the Richter scale devastated northern California killing 62 people. HM-15 Detachment 3, HC-1, and HC-11 Detachment 3 conducted lifts of food, water, and relief materials to the heavily damaged areas from ammunition ship *Flint* (AE 32) and fast combat support ship *Kansas City* (AOE 3). Amphibious assault ship *Peleliu* (LHA 5) provided food and shelter to 300 homeless earthquake victims.

29 OCTOBER • A developmental prototype of the advanced capability version of the EA-6B Prowler made its first flight.

29 OCTOBER • Student aviator Ens. Steven E. Pontell of VT-19 crashed in a T-2C Buckeye onto the flight deck of *Lexington* (AVT 16) during carrier qualifications in the Gulf of Mexico. The accident killed Pontell, ABM3s Timmy L. Garroutte and Burnett Kilgore Jr., and AN Lisa L. Mayo of the ship's company, together with contractor Byron G. Courvelle, and injured 15 people.

30 OCTOBER • An F/A-18A Hornet operating from *Midway* (CV 41) accidentally dropped a 500-pound bomb on cruiser *Reeves* (CG 24), which wounded five sailors during a night bombing exercise 32 miles south of Diego Garcia, British Indian Ocean Territory.

1 NOVEMBER • NAS Pensacola, Fla., became the last Chief of Naval Air Training command to fully convert to the use of civilian contractors for aircraft maintenance. Sailors in maintenance ratings had normally performed this work, but planners considered that civilians would be more cost-effective.

3 NOVEMBER • The Navy approved the designation VH-60N for the version of Seahawks to be used as executive transports by HMX-1.

6 NOVEMBER • VX-1 set a naval aviation record for flying the longest nonstop, air-refueled flight in an E-6A TACAMO

A Marine F/A-18 Hornet, BuNo 161248, displays an early maximum payload. In addition to four Mk 83 1,000-pound bombs, it carries two AIM-9L Sidewinder missiles, three 315-gallon fuel tanks, an ASQ-173 Laser Spot Tracker on its starboard fuselage station, and an AAS-38 forward looking infrared pod on its port.

aircraft, refueling twice in flight from Air Force Boeing KC-10A Extenders operating from March AFB, Calif.

1 DECEMBER • *Enterprise* (CVN 65) rendezvoused with *Midway* (CV 41) for Operation Classic Resolve—support of Philippine President Corazon Aquino against an attempted Philippine military coup and the potential evacuation of Americans trapped by the fighting. *Enterprise*, *Midway*, and Marine forces operated off Luzon's west coast. The carriers launched E-2C Hawkeyes to provide continuous radar coverage of the Manila Bay area, and to support Air Force F-4 Phantom IIs flying from Clark AFB to deter Filipino aircraft from taking off and attacking Manila and its environs. After the situation was stabilized, *Midway* returned to Yokosuka, Japan, and *Enterprise* continued her deployment to the Indian Ocean.

2 DECEMBER • VAQ-309 became the first Reserve squadron to operate EA-6Bs when it received Prowlers at NAS Whidbey Island, Wash.

Chapter 12

From the Sea

1990–1999

The collapse of the Eastern Bloc and changes in the world order defined the 1990s, a decade also characterized by the containment of localized fighting and a revised naval strategy. As the 15 January 1991 UN deadline for the Iraqis to withdraw their troops from Kuwait approached, U.S. aircraft carriers advanced to their stations near the Persian Gulf.

The following night (17 January in the Middle East), nine ships sailing in the gulf and in the Mediterranean and Red Seas fired BGM-109 Tomahawk cruise missiles at Iraqi military and political targets, and a massive armada of allied aircraft struck a variety of targets. Later that same night, President George H. W. Bush announced to the American people the beginning of the liberation of Kuwait. The attacks devastated the Iraqis so thoroughly that the principal fighting on the ground ended in barely 100 hours, and on 27 February, President Bush declared the liberation of Kuwait.

Following the Persian Gulf War, UN economic sanctions against Iraq remained in effect. During the rest of the decade, naval aviation patrolled Iraqi airspace and supported UN-imposed sanctions as well as limiting the Iraqi threat to minorities within the county and to their neighbors across the Middle East. In October 1994, after the deployment of Iraqi troops to the Kuwaiti border, President William J. Clinton dispatched *George Washington* (CVN 73) to the Red Sea to protect Kuwait. The Iraqis withdrew and announced recognition of Kuwait's sovereignty. The next year, aircraft from *Independence* (CV 62), *Constellation* (CV 64), and *Theodore Roosevelt* (CVN 71) patrolled the Iraqi no-fly zone during Operation Southern Watch.

The Soviets had cooperated with the United States during the Persian Gulf War, but their *glasnost* (openness) and *perestroika* (restructuring) brought about changes and unrest among their diverse peoples that culminated in the collapse of the Eastern Bloc. The fall of the communists left the United States as the world's only superpower, but the new global order presented regional and transnational rather than world threats as challenges shifted from the historical aberration of political conflicts back to wars of tribes and faith. In response, the Navy developed a new strategy promulgated in a white paper entitled "... From the Sea," which emphasized littoral warfare (along coastlines) and maneuver from the sea.

The new global situation also called for the largest draw-down for the fleet since World War II, and many naval aviation squadrons were consequently disestablished, reorganized, or consolidated. The Defense Base Closure and Realignment Commission had begun the shutdown of multiple shore facilities, and the Navy ended 42 years of modern support of Antarctic research.

The break up of the composite Yugoslav state into constituent republics presented the first major challenge to the new strategy. Aircraft carriers kept watch over the situation from the Adriatic Sea and supported Operation Provide Promise, the UN relief effort, and Operation Deny Flight, which monitored the air space over Bosnia-Herzegovina to prevent the warring parties from using their air strength. At times, *Saratoga* (CV 60), *America* (CV 66), and *Dwight D. Eisenhower* (CVN 69) supported both operations. On 30 August 1995, aircraft from *Theodore Roosevelt* (CVN 71) carried out early morning strikes that began Operation Deliberate Force—action against Serbian military targets in Bosnia-Herzegovina.

The Dayton Accords, which the Bosnian Federation and the Bosnian Serbs signed in Paris in December 1995, brought a temporary lull to the Balkan fighting. Operation Joint Endeavor enforced the military aspects of these accords by providing a stable environment in which civil action could proceed, which in turn enabled Deny Flight to end. Four years later, Serbian President Slobodan Milosevic's "cleansing" of ethnic Albanians from Kosovo compelled NATO to launch Operation Allied Force to counter his crimes.

Dwight D. Eisenhower (CVN 69) with Carrier Air Wing 7 embarked, the first carrier to conduct sustained operations in the Red Sea in response to Iraq's invasion of Kuwait, passes through the Suez Canal on 8 August 1990.

The changes in the global balance had also enabled Muslim extremists to rise to power. In the early 1980s, Saudi émigré terrorist Osama bin Laden and others had developed al-Qaeda (The Base, or the International Front for Fighting Jews and Crusaders) to support the war in Afghanistan against the Soviets. They subsequently refocused their hatred against the United States and its allies after the expulsion of the Marxist regime from that country. One of their primary goals was to drive U.S. armed forces, which they perceived as representing America's "infidel" policies (and which the terrorists deemed inconsistent with al-Qaeda's Islamic extremism) from Saudi Arabia and its neighboring countries.

The decade also marked a first for women when, in April 1993, Secretary of Defense Leslie Aspin dropped most of the restrictions that prohibited women from engaging in aerial and naval combat. Later in the year, Congress supported the secretary's decision to allow women in combat by repealing the Combat Exclusion Law. In October 1994, *Dwight D. Eisenhower* became the first carrier to deploy with women permanently assigned on board.

The last production F-14D Tomcats and A-6E Intruders entered the fleet, and F/A-18E/F Super Hornets, E-6A Mercurys, SH-60F Seahawks, T-45A/C Goshawks, AGM-65E laser-guided Maverick air-to-surface missiles, AGM-84H SLAM-ER (Standoff Land Attack Missile–Expanded Response), AGM-154A JSOW (Joint Standoff Weapon), and RIM-116A RAM (Rolling Airframe Missile) systems were prepared for their integration into operations. Meanwhile, the Navy and the Marine Corps phased-out McDonnell Douglas F-4 Phantom IIs. During the 1990s, naval aviation continued to adjust to changing world events, the development of new technologies, and of new strategies in order to serve the Republic.

1990

25 JANUARY • A helicopter from amphibious assault ship *Guadalcanal* (LPH 7) rescued three fishermen after their boat sank three miles off Cape Henry, Va.

25 JANUARY • An SH-60B Seahawk of HSL-45 Detachment 10 and SH-2F Seasprites of HSL-33 Detachment 3 and -35 Detachment 1, embarked on board cruiser *Lake Champlain* (CG 57), frigates *Lockwood* (FF 1064) and *Stein* (FF 1065), and tanker *Navasota* (T-AO 106), rescued 19 crewmembers from Chinese merchant vessel *Huazhu* when she sank 40 miles off northern Luzon, Philippines.

21 MARCH • Kaman Aerospace Corporation introduced the SH-2G Seasprite at the company's Bloomfield, Conn., production facility. The upgraded version of the SH-2F had been part of LAMPS Mk I, and their improvements included a sonobuoy data processing system, changes in the tactical navigation system, more powerful engines, composite rotor blades, an infrared target detection system, and several countermeasures systems.

27 MARCH • HS-2 at NAS North Island, Calif., became the first squadron to receive SH-60F Seahawks for operational deployment with the fleet.

17 APRIL • Lockheed Aeronautical Systems Company delivered the last P-3C, BuNo 163295, to the Navy at Palmdale, Calif. The delivery marked the 548th Orion accepted into naval inventory since August 1962.

18 MAY • NAVAIR established the model designation BQM-145A for the medium-range unmanned aerial vehicles—programmable reconnaissance drones that could be launched from the ground and tactical aircraft.

18 MAY • Night attack F/A-18Ds, the first two-seat Hornets designated to fly tactical as opposed to training missions, began service at MCAS El Toro, Calif. They replaced A-6 Intruders as the Marines' day/night bombers.

3 JUNE • Three days after President George H. W. Bush's orders to an amphibious task force, amphibious assault ship *Saipan* (LHA 2), amphibious transport dock *Ponce* (LPD 15), and tank landing ship *Sumter* (LST 1181) began their watch off Liberia. The ships were to assist evacuations of U.S. citizens threatened by an uprising there.

Cmdr. Rosemary B. Mariner becomes the first woman to command an operational naval aviation squadron, 12 July 1990. She led VAQ-34 during Operation Desert Storm and retired as a captain in 1997 after 24 years of service.

24 JUNE • Navy submersible *Sea Cliff* (DSV 4) located the wreckage of rigid airship *Macon* (ZRS 5) and her four F9C-2 Sparrowhawks off the coast of Point Sur, Calif. *Macon* had crashed on 12 February 1935.

26 JUNE • Cruiser *Lake Champlain* (CG 57), operating within the Pacific Missile Test Center's sea test range off California, made the first ship launch of an AGM-84 Standoff Land Attack Missile from a Harpoon canister. A LAMPS Mk III helicopter controlled the launch and down-linked video images to the ship's command information center via the helicopter's Walleye data link pod.

12 JULY • Cmdr. Rosemary B. Mariner relieved Cmdr. Charles H. Smith as commanding officer of VAQ-34, becoming the first woman to command an operational aviation squadron.

16 JULY • An earthquake rocked Manila and devastated much of the northern portion of Luzon, Philippines. Helicopters assigned to Marine Aircraft Group Task Force 4-90 and HMM-164 hauled food, water, and medical supplies to victims. CH-46E Sea Knights, CH-53D Sea Stallions, and CH-53E Super Stallions flew as transports, while UH-1N Iroquois, AH-1W Super Cobras, and OV-10 Broncos searched for survivors. SH-3G Sea Kings and Super Stallions from VC-5 at NAS Cubi Point also flew resupply and medical missions.

20 JULY • Citing default, the Navy terminated a contract with Lockheed Aeronautical Systems for the P-7A, formerly designated Long-Range Air Anti-Submarine Warfare Capable Aircraft.

31 JULY • HC-9 was disestablished, concluding the operations of the Navy's only combat search and rescue helicopter squadron. Its mission then passed to two Reserve special operations squadrons—HCS-5 at Point Mugu, Calif., and HCS-4 at NAS Norfolk, Va.

2 AUGUST • Iraq invaded Kuwait. *Independence* (CV 62) sailed in the Indian Ocean, *Dwight D. Eisenhower* (CVN 69) steamed in the Mediterranean Sea, and eight Middle East Force ships operated in the Persian Gulf. *Independence* was directed to proceed to the northern Arabian Sea to support what subsequently became Operation Desert Shield, a UN sanctioned economic blockade of Iraq by a coalition that eventually comprised 29 nations.

2 AUGUST • A VA-145 A-6E Intruder, embarked on board *Ranger* (CV 61), spotted a barge carrying Vietnamese refugees adrift in heavy seas and torrential rains 60 miles from NAS Cubi Point, Philippines. Over the next two days, an HS-14 SH-3H Sea King and a motor whaleboat from the carrier rescued 39 people.

5 AUGUST • *Independence* (CV 62) arrived on station in the Gulf of Oman.

5 AUGUST • The State Department authorized Operation Sharp Edge—the evacuation of people caught in the Liberian civil war. Amphibious assault ship *Saipan* (LHA 2) and other ships sailed to the area, and helicopters flew Marines from the 22d Marine Expeditionary Unit (MEU) to the U.S. Embassy compound in Monrovia. The MEU's air combat element included HMM-261 CH-46E Sea Knights, HMH-362 CH-53D Sea Stallions, HMLA-167 UH-1N Iroquois and AH-1T Sea Cobras, and VMA-223 AV-8B Harrier IIs. On 28 November, the opposing Liberian factions signed a cease-fire, and two days later the limited evacuation of noncombatants from Monrovia concluded after the American evacuation of 2,609 people including 330 U.S. citizens. Sharp Edge concluded on 9 January 1991.

7 AUGUST • *Saratoga* (CV 60) sailed for a scheduled deployment to the eastern Mediterranean.

7 AUGUST • *Dwight D. Eisenhower* (CVN 69) transited the Suez Canal, and the next day entered the Red Sea. The ship formed the basis of the Red Sea Battle Group to defend Saudi Arabia in the event that Iraqi dictator Saddam Hussein continued his aggression beyond Kuwait. A comprehensive strike plan provided battlefield air interdiction and close air support that was designed to stop Iraqi armored forces. *Dwight D. Eisenhower* and *Independence* (CV 62) carried more than 130 aircraft into potential action against Iraqi forces in Kuwait and southern Iraq, and protected airfields on the Arabian Peninsula that lay close to vital sea routes.

7 AUGUST • An EP-3E Aries II, an electronic warfare version of the P-3C, arrived to begin four months of extensive performance testing at NAS Patuxent River, Md.

15 AUGUST • *John F. Kennedy* (CV 67) deployed from NS Norfolk, Va. The ship sailed as a potential relief for *Dwight D. Eisenhower* (CVN 69) or for additional tasking to be determined by the Middle East situation.

16 AUGUST • Iraqi smuggling compelled the UN to begin multinational maritime interception operations (MIO) to enforce UN Security Council resolutions that had been imposed after the invasion of Kuwait. Resolution 661 prohibited the export of cargo that originated in Iraq, while Resolution 665 called upon the coalition to verify compliance, including the food-for-oil agreement that permitted Iraq to sell limited amounts of oil to pay for food and medicine. The coalition consistently refined MIOs to contain brazen efforts by Iraqi criminals and on occasion, terrorists, who used lucrative drug trafficking that specialized in heroin and methamphetamines to finance terrorism.

Allied ships and aircraft began to track and intercept ships that entered or left Iraqi and Iraq-occupied Kuwaiti ports.

22 AUGUST • *Saratoga* (CV 60) sailed through the Suez Canal to relieve *Dwight D. Eisenhower* (CVN 69) in the Red Sea.

28 AUGUST • Lack of space on board amphibious ships sailing en route to the Persian Gulf forced VMO-2 when deploying for the Persian Gulf War to ferry six of their OV-10 Broncos east across the United State from MCAS Camp Pendleton, Calif.

30 AUGUST • *John F. Kennedy* (CV 67) transited the Strait of Gibraltar into the Mediterranean Sea.

3 SEPTEMBER • *Dwight D. Eisenhower* (CVN 69) transited the Strait of Gibraltar en route to the United States.

6 SEPTEMBER • Amphibious assault ship *Nassau* (LHA 4) passed through the Suez Canal into the Red Sea.

7 SEPTEMBER • Amphibious assault ships *Guam* (LPH 9) and *Iwo Jima* (LPH 2) transited the Suez Canal into the Red Sea.

14 SEPTEMBER • Amphibious assault ship *Nassau* (LHA 4) arrived in the Gulf of Oman, and *John F. Kennedy* (CV 67) transited the Suez Canal into the Red Sea.

16 SEPTEMBER • Amphibious assault ships *Guam* (LPH 9) and *Iwo Jima* (LPH 2) arrived in the Gulf of Oman.

1 OCTOBER • *Independence* (CV 62) transited the Strait of Hormuz en route to the Persian Gulf. The next day, she conducted flight operations there, becoming the first carrier to do so since *Constellation* (CV 64) in 1974. On 4 October, *Independence* (CV 62) sailed from the gulf.

8 OCTOBER • Two Marine UH-1N Iroquois disappeared with eight men during routine night training operations from amphibious assault ship *Okinawa* (LPH 3) in the Gulf of Oman.

28 OCTOBER • Marines from amphibious transport dock *Ogden* (LPD 5) boarded Iraqi vessel *Amuriyah*, which was bound for Iraq through the Persian Gulf. The Iraqis had refused to halt despite a summons from U.S. and Australian ships. The allied vessels fired shots across her bow and aircraft from *Independence* (CV 62) buzzed low in warning passes. The Marine boarding party found no banned cargo, and the craft was allowed to proceed.

1 NOVEMBER • *Midway* (CV 41) relieved *Independence* (CV 62) in the north Arabian Sea.

2 NOVEMBER • Three Iraqi aircraft briefly penetrated Saudi airspace near the northern gulf combat air patrol. The incident tested coalition vigilance just a day before Central Command and the Saudis began a scheduled air defense exercise.

8 NOVEMBER • President George H. W. Bush announced a decision to double the number of carrier battle groups deployed in support of Operation Desert Shield. By 15 January 1991, *Ranger* (CV 61), *America* (CV 66), and *Theodore Roosevelt* (CVN 71) were to join *Midway* (CV 41), *Saratoga* (CV 60), and *John F. Kennedy* (CV 67).

15 NOVEMBER • U.S. and Saudi forces began Operation Imminent Thunder—an eight-day combined amphibious landing exercise in northeastern Saudi Arabia involving about 1,000 U.S. Marines, 16 ships, and more than 1,100 aircraft. Aircraft from *Midway* (CV 41), which had entered the gulf from the north Arabian Sea, and Marine aircraft flew close air support.

16 NOVEMBER • The Navy accepted F-14D Tomcats for fleet service at NAS Miramar, Calif.

29 NOVEMBER • The UN approved Security Council Resolution 678 authorizing the use of military force unless Iraq vacated Kuwait by 15 January 1991.

8 DECEMBER • *Ranger* (CV 61) sailed on an unscheduled deployment for Operation Desert Shield from San Diego, Calif.

20 DECEMBER • *Independence* (CV 62) returned to NAS North Island, Calif., from her deployment to the Persian Gulf.

21 DECEMBER • Israeli ferry *al-Tovia* (70290) capsized 200 yards astern of *Saratoga* (CV 60) while transporting 102 men back to the carrier after liberty at Haifa. Israeli military and police officers in boats and helicopters pulled victims from the water, and helicopters flew injured men to two hospitals in Haifa. Twenty U.S. sailors died, and an additional crew member disappeared and was presumed drowned.

28 DECEMBER • *America* (CV 66) and *Theodore Roosevelt* (CVN 71) deployed in support of Operation Desert Shield from NS Norfolk, Va. Five OV-10A Broncos and one OV-10D from VMO-1 also embarked on board *America*, and six squadron OV-10Ds sailed with *Theodore Roosevelt*. The Marines subsequently joined Marine Aircraft Group 13 (Forward) at King Abdul Aziz Naval Base, Saudi Arabia.

1991

1 JANUARY • HC-4 relocated its detachment from Jeddah, Saudi Arabia, to Hurghada, Egypt. The detachment constructed an airhead operating site within 48 hours, and began to transport passengers, cargo, and mail to carrier battle groups and amphibious forces steaming in the Red Sea during Operation Desert Shield.

2 JANUARY • CH-53E Super Stallions from amphibious assault ship *Guam* (LPH 9) helped insert Marines into the United States Embassy compound in Mogadishu, Somalia, during Operation Eastern Exit. The operation rescued U.S. Ambassador James K. Bishop, the Soviet ambassador, and other foreign nationals caught in the midst of the Somali civil war.

6 JANUARY • *Saratoga* (CV 60) transited the Suez Canal into the Red Sea to participate in Operation Desert Shield.

7 JANUARY • Secretary of Defense Richard B. Cheney canceled the A-12A Avenger carrier-based aircraft program. He cited the inability of the principal contractors, General Dynamics and McDonnell Douglas, to design, develop, fabricate, assemble, and test Avengers within the contract schedule, and to deliver aircraft that met contract requirements. The action marked the largest Pentagon weapons contract cancellation to date.

8 JANUARY • Six VMO-1 OV-10Ds launched to NS Rota, Spain, from *Theodore Roosevelt* (CVN 71) without the aid of the ship's catapults. The carrier then passed through the Strait of Gibraltar into the Mediterranean Sea. Two Marine KC-130s then flew the Broncos (three in each Hercules) through Palma de Mallorca, Spain; NAS Sigonella, Sicily; Souda, Crete; Cairo, Egypt; Jeddah, Saudi Arabia; and, on 17 January, to King Abdul Aziz Naval Base, Saudi Arabia.

9 JANUARY • *America* (CV 66) sailed through the Strait of Gibraltar into the Mediterranean Sea.

12 JANUARY • Congress voted 52 to 47 in the Senate, and 251 to 183 in the House, on a joint resolution that gave President George H. W. Bush the support he sought for military action against Iraq.

12 JANUARY • *Ranger* (CV 61) arrived in the north Arabian Sea to participate in Operation Desert Shield.

12 JANUARY • Amphibious Group Three, with the 5th Marine Expeditionary Brigade embarked, arrived in the Arabian Sea. Eighteen vessels, including amphibious assault ships *New Orleans* (LPH 11), *Okinawa* (LPH 3), *Tarawa* (LHA 1), and *Tripoli* (LPH 10), later joined the 13 ships of Amphibious Group Three to comprise the largest amphibious task force that the United States had committed to battle since the Korean War.

12 JANUARY • *Midway* (CV 41) reentered the Persian Gulf and participated in Operation Desert Shield.

14 JANUARY • *Theodore Roosevelt* (CVN 71) passed through the Suez Canal into the Red Sea.

15 JANUARY • *America* (CV 66) transited the Suez Canal into the Red Sea.

15 JANUARY • *Ranger* (CV 61) transited the Strait of Hormuz into the Persian Gulf.

16 JANUARY • *Theodore Roosevelt* (CVN 71) transited Bab el-Mandeb from the Red Sea to the Gulf of Aden.

16 JANUARY • At 1650 (EST), a squadron of fighter-bombers took off from a field in central Saudi Arabia and struck targets in Iraq and Kuwait just before 1900 (EST; it was the night of 17 January in the Middle East). Six carrier battle groups, two battleships, and a 31-ship amphibious task force sailed in the Red and Arabian Seas and Persian Gulf. The Navy had more than 100 ships and submarines in the area, and 75,000 sailors afloat and ashore, while more than 67,000 Marines ashore comprised a Marine expeditionary force with another nearly 18,000 Marines embarked on board naval vessels.

16 JANUARY • President George H. W. Bush addressed the nation and announced the commencement of Operation Desert Storm—the liberation of Kuwait.

17 JANUARY • At 0130, nine ships in the Mediterranean, Persian Gulf, and Red Sea fired the first of 122 BGM-109 cruise missiles at Iraqi targets. This marked the first combat launch of the Tomahawk. Meanwhile, *Saratoga* (CV 60), *America* (CV 66), and *John F. Kennedy* (CV 67) sailing in the Red Sea; *Midway* (CV 41) and *Ranger* (CV 61) in the Persian Gulf; and *Theodore Roosevelt* (CVN 71) en route to the gulf; launched 228 combat sorties.

17 JANUARY • At 0130, an (apparent) Iraqi surface-to-air missile shot down Lt. Cmdr. Michael S. Speicher in an F/A-18C Hornet, BuNo 163484, of VFA-81 embarked on board *Saratoga* (CV 60), during a night strike over Iraq. Speicher thus became the first American casualty of the Persian Gulf War. Additional information subsequently suggested his possible survival, and on 11 January 2001, Secretary of the Navy Richard J. Danzig changed the pilot's status from killed in action/body not recovered to missing in action. On 11 October 2002, Secretary of the Navy Gordon R. England issued a memorandum that further changed the pilot's status to missing/captured. In July 2009, Iraqi Bedouins directed a recovery team from Multi-National Force–West to a crash site in the desert 62 miles west of Ramadi in Anbar province. The team recovered remains later confirmed as those of Speicher.

17 JANUARY • At 0215, the Iraqis began to fire an estimated eight Scud-B (R-17E) surface-to-surface missiles at Haifa and Tel Aviv, Israel. Saddam Hussein's ploy threatened to drag the Israelis into the war, which would have enraged Arabs and unraveled the coalition. The Pentagon announced that allied forces had destroyed stationary Scud sites in Iraq, but pilots started to seek out elusive mobile sites in what they termed

A VF-32 F-14A Tomcat and an A-6E Intruder assigned to CVW-3, deployed with *John F. Kennedy* (CV 67) in support of Operation Desert Shield, cruise at low level over the Saudi desert, 25 October 1990.

"The Great Scud Hunt." The United States also prepared to dispatch additional Army PAC-3 Patriot (Phased Array Tracking Intercept of Target) antimissile batteries to help the Israelis defend against the Scuds.

17 JANUARY • Lt. Cmdr. Mark I. Fox and Lt. Nicolas Mongillo of VFA-81 flying F/A-18Cs, embarked on board *Saratoga* (CV 60), each shot down an Iraqi MiG-21 Fishbed with AIM-7 Sparrow and AIM-9M Sidewinder air-to-air missiles. After these first Hornet aerial victories, the two completed bombing runs against a hangar, fuel stores, and a control station as they maneuvered to avoid antiaircraft fire and hand-held surface-to-air missiles.

18 JANUARY • The Navy mounted its first carrier-launched aerial minelaying operation since the Vietnam War to isolate Iraqi vessels operating in the Persian Gulf from facilities at Basra, an important southern Iraq port and crossroads, and nearby Umm Qasr and az-Zubayr; and to prevent enemy

A P-3C Orion of VP-4 patrols over the Arabian Desert during Operation Desert Storm.

boats at those ports from entering the gulf. Four A-6Es supported by 14 aircraft from *Ranger* (CV 61) dropped 42 Mk 36 Destructor mines at the mouth of the Az-Zubayr River. As the Intruders made their low-level runs, the Iraqis shot down one flown by Lts. Charles J. Turner and William T. Costen of VA-155. Initial reports indicated that these men were missing, but the Pentagon later announced their status as prisoners of war. Commander Naval Forces Central Command Vice Adm. Stanley R. Arthur cancelled further aerial minelaying because of this loss and the large number of Iraqi mines in the gulf.

18 JANUARY • Naval aircraft bombed Iraqi installations near Umm Qasr, and airfields at al-Jaber and Ash Shuaybah, Kuwait. By the end of the day, they had flown 1,100 combat sorties and ships and submarines launched 216 BGM-109 Tomahawk cruise missiles against 17 Iraqi military leadership, electric, and oil targets.

18 JANUARY • VA-35 A-6E crews, embarked on board *Saratoga* (CV 60), used night vision goggles in battle for the first time in the squadron's history during their initial strikes against the Iraqis. Four Intruders bombed H-3 airfield, but antiaircraft fire shot down Lts. Jeffrey N. Zaun and Robert Wetzel of VA-35 in an A-6E, BuNo 161668, ten nautical miles south-southwest of the field. The Iraqis captured and beat the men, paraded Zaun before TV cameras, and did not repatriate the prisoners until 4 March. An Iraqi Roland surface-to-air missile struck A-6E, BuNo 158539, manned by Lts. Mark F. Eddy and John A. Snevely Jr., during the same strike and forced it to divert to Al Jouf, Saudi Arabia.

18 JANUARY • An Iraqi infrared surface-to-air missile shot down Lt. Col. Clifford M. Acree, USMC, and CWO4 Guy L. Hunter, USMC, of VMO-2 in an OV-10A Bronco, about 14 miles northeast of Mishab, Kuwait. Both Marines were captured.

18 JANUARY • SH-60B Seahawks from HSL-44 Detachment 8, embarked on board frigate *Nicholas* (FFG 47), provided air targeting while *Nicholas*, Kuwaiti patrol boats *al-Sanbouk* (P 4050) and *Istiqlal* (P 5702), two Army Bell OH-58D Kiowas, and a British Lynx HAS.3 from destroyer *Cardiff* (D 108) neutralized Iraqi garrisons on nine oil platforms in the ad-Dorra oil field. AGM-114 Hellfire air-to-surface missiles proved especially effective against the Iraqi sandbag and plywood shelters. The attack killed five Iraqis, and 23 survivors surrendered in this first combined helicopter, missile, and surface-ship gun engagement. It was also the first capture of Iraqi prisoners during the Persian Gulf War.

19 JANUARY • *Theodore Roosevelt* (CVN 71) transited the Strait of Hormuz into the Persian Gulf.

19 JANUARY • A-6E Intruders and A-7E Corsair IIs, flying from *Saratoga* (CV 60) and *John F. Kennedy* (CV 67), made the first combat launches of AGM-84E SLAM (Standoff Land Attack Missile).

20 JANUARY • Iraqi TV broadcast what it claimed as interviews with three downed U.S. and four Allied airmen including Lt. Col. Clifford M. Acree, USMC, and CWO4 Guy L. Hunter, USMC, of VMO-2, and Lt. Jeffrey N. Zaun of VA-35. The State Department called the Iraqi charge d'affaires in Washington to protest that the broadcast ran contrary to the Third Geneva Convention governing the treatment of prisoners of war, and to demand that any prisoners be granted immediate access to representatives of the International Committee of the Red Cross. The footage shocked Americans during a broadcast on U.S. TV the next day. The Iraqis also announced that they had used prisoners as human shields to deter attacks.

20 JANUARY • A Grumman A-6E Intruder and an Air Force Fairchild Republic A-10 Thunderbolt destroyed an Iraqi artillery battery.

20 JANUARY • By this point, allied air and missile attacks had eviscerated the Iraqi command, control, communications, and intelligence network, and had torn apart Saddam Hussein's integrated air defense system.

21 JANUARY • President George H. W. Bush signed an executive order that designated the Arabian Peninsula areas, that airspace, and the adjacent waters as a combat zone.

21 JANUARY • Poor weather hampered coalition air operations throughout late January, which forced the Joint Force Air Component Commander to cancel or divert many aerial sorties.

21 JANUARY • A surface-to-air missile, tentatively identified as a modified SA-2 Guideline, shot down over Iraq an F-14B Tomcat of VF-103, embarked on board *Saratoga* (CV 60). Special operations crew recovered pilot Lt. Devon Jones the next day, but radar intercept officer Lt. Lawrence R. Slade was captured.

21 JANUARY • *Theodore Roosevelt* (CVN 71) arrived on station in the Persian Gulf.

23 JANUARY • A-6Es disabled an *al-Qadisiya*-class Iraqi tanker that had been collecting and reporting intelligence data. The Intruders also attacked and sank a Zhuk-class patrol boat and an SR.N6 Mk 6C Winchester–class hovercraft that the tanker had refueled.

24 JANUARY • A-6Es attacked and destroyed an Iraqi *Spasilac*-class minelayer and a Zhuk-class patrol boat. Another enemy minesweeper hit an Iraqi mine while attempting to evade the aerial attacks. Intruders and F/A-18 Hornets also attacked the Iraqi Umm Qasr naval station.

24 JANUARY • A patrol aircraft spotted an Iraqi minesweeper moored at Qaruh Island between the oilfield at ad-Dorra and the Kuwaiti coast. Two VA-65 A-6E Intruders from *Theodore Roosevelt* (CVN 71) then discovered and disabled the *Yevgenya*-class minesweeper. Destroyer *Leftwich* (DD 984) and frigates *Curts* (FFG 38) and *Nicholas* (FFG 47) patrolling a nearby minefield turned toward the action. An SH-60B LAMPS Mk III, operating from *Curts*, sank a floating mine about 1,000 yards off the ship's starboard bow with machine gun fire. The Seahawk detected Iraqi patrol boat *P4027*, which while attempting to evade the ensuing air attacks, struck a drifting Iraqi mine and sank. Two Army helicopters from the 4th Squadron, 17th Cavalry, embarked on board *Curts*, covered the Seahawk and the frigate during the apprehension of 11 Iraqi prisoners and the recovery of two bodies.

24 JANUARY • Up to five Iraqi aircraft flew from an airfield at al-Kut southeast of Baghdad for the Kuwaiti coast. Two Dassault-Breguet F-1 Mirages continued southeast along the boundary between Air Force and Navy radar coverage and penetrated into the screen surrounding ships in the Persian Gulf. An Air Force Boeing E-3A Sentry AWACS failed to notify cruisers *Bunker Hill* (CG 52), *Mobile Bay* (CG 53), and *Worden* (CG 18) by normal procedures and informed them by voice. F/A-18A Hornets operating from *Midway* (CV 41) and *Theodore Roosevelt* (CVN 71) attempted unsuccessfully to intercept the intruders. The Sentry vectored four Saudi McDonnell Douglas F-15 Eagles, and Capt. Ayedh al-Shamrani shot down both Mirages with AIM-9 Sidewinder air-to-air missiles. The Iraqis had reached a point 60 nautical miles from *Mobile Bay* and within range to launch Aérospatiale AM.39 Exocet air-to-surface missiles at the cruiser. Communications and radar errors and inexperience led to a nearly calamitous encounter.

24 JANUARY • The allies reclaimed the first Kuwaiti territory, the island of Jazirat Qurah.

24 JANUARY • The Iraqis began to set fire to many of the oil refineries and wells in their possession. Flames and smoke plumes posed challenging navigational hazards to low-flying aircraft. In addition, the Iraqis dumped oil into the gulf from their Sea Island crude oil tanker loading terminal off the Kuwaiti coast, from five tankers at Mina' al Ahmadi, Kuwait, and from storage tanks ashore through an underwater pipeline. The ensuing spill grew to be at least 20 miles long, 3 miles wide, and several feet deep in what the Department of Defense branded "an act of environmental terrorism."

28 JANUARY • The Iraqis downed Capt. Michael C. Berryman, USMC, in a VMA-311 AV-8B. His section had been unable to locate their target because of inclement weather and turned to strike an Iraqi Luna FROG (free rocket over ground) tactical surface-to-surface rocket, when an enemy surface-to-air missile hit the Harrier II. The Iraqis captured the Marine but did not acknowledge the fact.

29 JANUARY • A-6Es attacked Iraqi ships in the Bubiyan Channel at Umm Qasr Naval Base and in Kuwait harbor in what aircrew termed the "Bubiyan Turkey Shoot." Cdrs. Richard K. Noble and Richard J. Cassara of VA-145 in an Intruder embarked on board *Ranger* (CV 61), discovered off al-Fāw (al-Fāo) Peninsula four Iraqi missile boats that had been captured from the Kuwaitis, tentatively identified as an FPB 57, two TNC 45s, and an Osa II. An E-2C Hawkeye controlled the Intruder and its wingman from VA-155 as they attacked with 500-pound laser-guided bombs. Canadians Maj. David W. Kendall and Capt. Stephen P. Hill flew two CF-18s that strafed the Osa, which escaped. The next morning, many of the remaining Iraqi vessels attempted to flee, and during 21 engagements over the following 13 hours, allied aircraft sank or damaged 7 enemy missile boats, 3 amphibious ships, a minesweeper, and 9 additional vessels between Bubiyan Island and the marshlands of the Shatt al Arab (the confluence of the Tigris and Euphrates Rivers). American sailors rescued 20 Iraqi survivors. One missile boat and an amphibious ship reached Iran, but were seized by the Iranians.

29 JANUARY • Iraqi tanks and troops thrust across the Kuwait border into Saudi Arabia, but coalition forces stopped these attacks during a series of engagements. Marines at R'as al-Khafji, Saudi Arabia, directed air and artillery strikes and, overnight, allied aircraft also struck enemy concentrations in Kuwait. All 18 F/A-18C Hornets of VFA-81 and -83, embarked on board *Saratoga* (CV 60), dropped 100 Mk 83 1,000-pound bombs. Marine AH-1 Cobras also attacked and by daybreak on 31 January the combined firepower had broken the Iraqis. These battles distracted enemy attention away from their vulnerable desert flanks where the main allied attacks subsequently fell.

1 FEBRUARY • VAW-123 coordinated aircraft on the first of 11 patrols to locate and destroy Scud-B (R-17E) surface-to-surface missiles through 7 February. On 3 February, *America* (CV 66) confirmed the destruction of two Scud-related vehicles.

2 FEBRUARY • Iraqi antiaircraft fire shot down Lt. Cmdr. Barry T. Cooke and Lt. Patrick K. Connor in a VA-36 A-6E Intruder, BuNo 155632, embarked on board *Theodore Roosevelt* (CVN 71), near Jazīrat Faylakā (Island). Both were killed in action; Cooke's body was not recovered.

2 FEBRUARY • An E-2C Hawkeye, BuNo 158638, of VAW-125, damaged a KA-6D of VA-35 and an F-14A+ Tomcat during a taxiing accident on board *Saratoga* (CV 60). Two sailors suffered minor injuries and the ship later disembarked the damaged tanker at Jeddah, Saudi Arabia.

3 FEBRUARY • Battleship *Missouri* (BB 63) supported Marines fighting in Kuwait with her 16-inch guns. Crewmembers launched the battleship's embarked RQ-2A Pioneer remotely piloted vehicle with the assistance of a rocket-powered booster, and recovered the aircraft by using a net strung between two cables on the fantail. The vehicle transmitted images to shipboard TV monitors that enabled gun directors to "walk" rounds onto their targets. At one point, sailors watched images as a truck delivered food to Iraqi soldiers dug into camouflaged positions near R'as al-Khafji, and after its departure, *Missouri* shelled the site.

5 FEBRUARY • Lt. Robert J. Dwyer of VFA-87 was killed when his F/A-18A Hornet, BuNo 163096, operating from *Theodore Roosevelt* (CVN 71), crashed while returning from a combat mission over Iraq.

6 FEBRUARY • Cmdr. Ronald D. McElraft and Lt. Donald S. Broce of VF-1 in an F-14A Tomcat, embarked on board *Ranger* (CV 61), downed an Iraqi Mi-8 Hip with an AIM-9M Sidewinder air-to-air missile.

6 FEBRUARY • Battleship *Wisconsin* (BB 64) temporarily relieved *Missouri* (BB 63) on the gunline near the Kuwaiti border to enable *Missouri* to rearm. *Wisconsin* often used an RQ-2A Pioneer remotely piloted vehicle equipped with infrared and daylight TV cameras that relayed signals to the battleship to help direct gunfire missions. A Marine OV-10 Bronco called in the first mission against an Iraqi artillery battery in southern Kuwait, and *Wisconsin* knocked it out with 11 16-inch rounds.

7 FEBRUARY • A-6E Intruders attacked and heavily damaged two Iraqi patrol boats in the northern Persian Gulf near al-Fāw (al-Fāo) Peninsula.

8 FEBRUARY • A-6E Intruders attacked and neutralized Iraqi training frigate *Ibn Marjid* (507) at Cor al Zubayr, because she was colocated with a TNC 45–class patrol boat capable of firing surface-to-surface variants of Exocet missiles.

S-3B Vikings of VS-29 from *Abraham Lincoln* (CVN 72) fly over burning Kuwaiti oil fields, c. 1991.

9 FEBRUARY • After two attacks against Iraqi troops, an F/A-18D Hornet forward air controller marked enemy soldiers dug into a revetment as new targets. An AV-8B, flown by Capt. Russell A. C. Sanborn, USMC, of VMA-231, made a run on the Iraqi troops, but an enemy surface-to-air missile shot down the Harrier II and Sanborn was captured.

14 FEBRUARY • *America* (CV 66) transited the Strait of Hormuz en route to the Persian Gulf. The next day, after her sail of almost 2,000 miles around the Arabian Peninsula, she became the first carrier during the Persian Gulf War to conduct strikes from both sides of the peninsula.

15 FEBRUARY • Marines from HMLA-369 launched their first AGM-114 Hellfire air-to-surface missile in battle using the Night Eagle laser system.

18 FEBRUARY • An Iraqi mine damaged the forward section of amphibious assault ship *Tripoli* (LPH 10), the flagship of minesweeping clearance operations in the northern gulf. Crewmembers contained the flooding and the ship continued fighting for five days before sailing to a drydock at Bahrain for a month of repairs. Four men sustained injuries. A Manta mine detonated beneath the stern on the port side of cruiser *Princeton* (CG 59), but the crew saved the ship. Battleship *Missouri* (BB 63) turned away from the minefield barely 3,000 yards before she entered the danger zone. MH-53Es swept limited channels through Iraqi minefields, the Sea Dragons moved more rapidly than ships and accordingly covered more water.

20 FEBRUARY • The S-3Bs of VS-32, embarked on board *America* (CV 66), became the first Vikings to bomb and destroy an enemy vessel when they sank an Iraqi gunboat.

20 FEBRUARY • By this point in the fighting, AV-8B Harrier IIs of VMA-331 had flown 243 sorties along the Iraqi borders and throughout Kuwait.

23 FEBRUARY • Six carriers concentrated their power against the Iraqi forces: *Midway* (CV 41), *Ranger* (CV 61), *America* (CV 66), and *Theodore Roosevelt* (CVN 71) sailed in the Persian Gulf; while *Saratoga* (CV 60) and *John F. Kennedy* (CV 67) operated in the Red Sea.

23 FEBRUARY • Aircraft from *America* (CV 66) destroyed an Iraqi Silkworm battery after the unsuccessful launch of a surface-to-surface missile at battleship *Missouri* (BB 63).

23 FEBRUARY • The Iraqis shot down and killed Capt. James N. Wilbourn II, USMC, in a VMA-542 AV-8B, during a night bombing run on Iraqi troops.

23 FEBRUARY • The search-and-rescue team from NAS Lemoore, Calif., saved a 19-year-old man who had been missing for five days when they found him at the 6,000-foot level in rugged terrain at the southern edge of Sequoia National Park. The Tulare County Sheriff's Department had requested the team's assistance.

24 FEBRUARY • Operation Desert Sabre—the ground offensive against Iraq—began.

24 FEBRUARY • While the allies continued to experience difficulties directing fixed-wing aircraft through the smoke from burning oil wells, Capt. Randall W. Hammond, USMC, led a division of four AH-1 Cobras on a long-range raid that penetrated Iraqi defenses north of Objective Ice Tray near Ali Al Salem Airfield, Kuwait. OV-10 Broncos coordinated the Cobras and laser-designated a column of Iraqi T-72 main battle tanks. The Cobras knocked out many vehicles with BGM-71 TOW (tube-launched, optically tracked, wire-command-link) antitank missiles and eight AGM-114 Hellfire air-to-surface missiles. Capt. Steven R. Rudder, USMC, led the second section and raked the surviving Iraqis with 2.75-inch rockets and 20mm rounds.

24 FEBRUARY • Iraqi troops emerged from the smoke and early morning fog to counterattack Marines of Task Force Papa Bear. An OV-10 Bronco directed Capt. Randall W. Hammond, USMC, and a division of four AH-1 Cobras that had refueled at a forward arming and refueling point, onto the advancing Iraqis. The Marines left burning tanks and armored vehicles from 2.75-inch rockets, 16 AGM-114 Hellfire air-to-surface missiles, and 20mm fire. The Cobras rearmed, refueled, and returned, but the enemy capitulated.

24 FEBRUARY • Marine Aircraft Group 16 helicopters lifted Marines of Task Force X-Ray toward positions to protect the flank of the 1st Marine Division as it advanced inland. High winds blew a massive cloud of dust into the path of approaching aircraft as the lead AH-1Ws and Zs escorted four following waves of 10 to 12 CH-46 Sea Knights and CH-53 Super Stallions each. Heavy Iraqi fire over the landing zone forced some Cobras and Vipers into the path of the inbound transports. Despite the confusion and near misses, no aircraft were lost. The mission diverted and some helicopters returned to Saudi fields at Lonesome Dove AB near Al Khanjar and to Kibrit, while others low on fuel landed in the desert.

25 FEBRUARY • An Iraqi hand-held surface-to-air missile shot down Capt. John S. Walsh, USMC, in a VMA-542 AV-8B Harrier II, near Al Jaber Airfield, Kuwait. Walsh ejected between the opposing forces, but advancing Marines rescued and transferred him to an HMLA-369 UH-1N Iroquois, which returned him to Lonesome Dove AB, Saudi Arabia.

25 FEBRUARY • An Iraqi infrared surface-to-air missile shot down Maj. Joseph J. Small III, USMC, and Capt. David M. Spellacy, USMC, of VMO-1 in an OV-10A Bronco during a forward air control mission. Spellacy died and Small was captured.

26 FEBRUARY • Commander Seventh Fleet/Naval Forces Central Command Vice Adm. Stanley R. Arthur ordered amphibious diversions at Būbiyān and Faylakā Islands to delay the retreat of routed Iraqi troops from Kuwait City. Marine helicopters flew from amphibious assault ships *Iwo Jima* (LPH 2), *Guam* (LPH 9), and *Nassau* (LHA 4), rendezvoused with A-6E Intruders and EA-6B Prowlers, and collectively strafed and bombed Iraqi troops dug in on the islands. In the interim, most of the retreating enemy fled toward Basra along a highway in hundreds of military and civilian vehicles. The Iraqis moved through kill boxes assigned to Carrier Air Wing 2, embarked on board *Ranger* (CV 61). Aircraft dropped aerial mines to partially block their escape creating what journalists dubbed the "Highway of Death." Some panicked and drove off the road into the desert only to become mired in the sand, but most

An F-14A Tomcat of VF-114 off Abraham Lincoln (CVN 72) patrols over Kuwait City with Kuwait Towers as a prominent landmark, c. 1991.

dismounted and fled there on foot. Air strikes killed several hundred of them and destroyed an estimated 1,400 tanks, armored vehicles, jeeps, cars, buses, and tractor-trailers.

27 FEBRUARY • F/A-18A/C Hornets and A-6E Intruders operating from *Ranger* (CV 61), *America* (CV 66), and *Theodore Roosevelt* (CVN 71) flew more than 600 combat missions against Iraqi troops, primarily to disrupt an orderly retreat from the advancing coalition forces.

27 FEBRUARY • At 2100 EST, President George H. W. Bush declared that the allies had liberated Kuwait, ending the Persian Gulf War. At midnight EST, all U.S. and coalition forces were to suspend further offensive combat operations.

27 FEBRUARY • The RQ-2A Pioneer remotely piloted vehicle flying from battleship *Wisconsin* (BB 64) detected two boats purportedly filled with Iraqi secret policemen who attempted to flee from Faylakā Island. Controllers directed bombers on a strike that sank the boats.

27 FEBRUARY • Two or more Iraqi surface-to-air missiles shot down and killed Capt. Reginald C. Underwood, USMC, in a VMA-331 AV-8B, while he led a section of four Harrier IIs from amphibious assault ship *Nassau* (LHA 4) against Iraqi troops along the northern highway from Kuwait City.

27 FEBRUARY • The RQ-2A Pioneer remotely piloted vehicle from battleship *Wisconsin* (BB 64) spotted Iraqi stragglers on Faylakā Island. Battleship *Missouri* (BB 63) had previously bombarded the island, and when the Pioneer flew over at low level with its recognizable noisy engine, the Iraqis anticipated that they were about to receive additional 16-inch gunfire. Forty men then surrendered to the Pioneer as it flew over their position.

3 MARCH • Loudspeaker equipped CH-46 Sea Knights rounded up surrendering Iraqi troops on Faylakā Island. Helicopters ferried the prisoners to amphibious transport dock *Ogden* (LPD 5) for further transport to Saudi prisoner of war camps.

3 MARCH • The Iraqis agreed to a ceasefire during deliberations at Safwan Airfield, Iraq.

4 MARCH • The Iraqis released POWs including eight naval aviators: Lt. Col. Clifford M. Acree, USMC; Capt. Michael C. Berryman, USMC; CWO4 Guy L. Hunter, USMC; Capt. Russell A. C. Sanborn, USMC; Lt. Lawrence R. Slade; Maj. Joseph J. Small III, USMC; Lt. Robert Wetzel; and Lt. Jeffrey N. Zaun. Their captors turned the prisoners over to U.S. officials through the International Committee of the Red Cross near the Jordanian Ruwayshid border station. The men were flown to hospital ship *Mercy* (T-AH 19) moored at Bahrain, and five days later, a Boeing 737, designated Freedom Zero-One, flew them to the United States.

4 MARCH • *America* (CV 66) departed the Persian Gulf and returned to the Red Sea. The ship had launched 3,008 combat sorties during the war.

6 MARCH • Amphibious assault ship *New Orleans* (LPH 11), with HM-14 embarked, led minesweeping activities with four minecountermeasures ships.

6 MARCH • "Aggression is defeated," President George H. W. Bush reported to a joint session of Congress. "The war is over."

8 MARCH • Lt. Kathleen P. Owens of VRC-40 became the last pilot to land on board *Lexington* (AVT 16), following a Navy decision to decommission the ship. Owens thus became the first female pilot to attain that distinction on a carrier. *Lexington* also had become the first carrier with female crewmembers. The C-2A Greyhound flight crew included Lt. Paul Villagomez, AM1 Donnie E. Kicklighter, and AD2 Mark F. Pemrick.

11 MARCH • *Midway* (CV 41) and *Saratoga* (CV 60) departed the Persian Gulf for their homeports—*Midway* to Yokosuka, Japan, and *Saratoga* via the Suez Canal to NS Mayport, Fla.

12 MARCH • *John F. Kennedy* (CV 67) transited the Suez Canal into the Mediterranean.

13 MARCH • By executive order, President George H. W. Bush established the Southwest Asia Service Medal for award to veterans who had served in the Persian Gulf area during the war.

16 MARCH • *America* (CV 66) visited Hurghada, Egypt, for five days. The visit marked her first port call of the deployment after 78 consecutive days at sea.

28 MARCH • *John F. Kennedy* (CV 67) and *Saratoga* (CV 60) arrived at their homeports of NS Norfolk, Va., and NS Mayport, Fla., respectively. They were the first carriers involved in the Persian Gulf War to return to the United States.

29 MARCH • *Kitty Hawk* (CV 63), her flight deck modified to accommodate F/A-18 Hornets, sailed for sea trials from the Philadelphia Naval Shipyard, Pa. This marked the first time that the ship had moved under her own power since commencing a service life extension program overhaul 3 ½ years before.

1 APRIL • *Theodore Roosevelt* (CVN 71) transited Bab-al-Mandeb and began three weeks of operations in the Red Sea.

3 APRIL • *America* (CV 66) transited the Suez Canal into the Mediterranean.

6 APRIL • The Iraqis accepted UN terms for a formal ceasefire.

6 APRIL • HC-4 detachments deployed from NAS Sigonella, Sicily and Hurghada, Egypt for Diyarbakir, Turkey. Two days later, they flew Secretary of State James A. Baker III, and his party of 60 along the Turkish and Iraqi border to a remote Kurdish refugee camp. In March, the Kurds rose

A-7E Corsair IIs of VA-72 return home from *John F. Kennedy* (CV 67) after their service during Operation Desert Storm. The return of VA-46 along with VA-72 marks the final operational deployment of Corsair IIs.

against Saddam Hussein, but the Iraqis recaptured the main towns and cities of Kurdistan. The Turk refusal to allow refugees entry left many Kurds stranded in the mountains during bitterly cold weather. The coalition initiated Operation Provide Comfort to aid the refugees.

8 APRIL • *America* (CV 66) transited the Strait of Gibraltar into the Atlantic.

9 APRIL • HC-4 returned to Incirlik, Turkey, to become the primary and first heavy lift helicopter combat logistics support asset for Operation Provide Comfort to aid Kurdish refugees.

9 APRIL • The UN Security Council approved Resolution 689 establishing a UN-Iraq-Kuwait Observer Mission to monitor Resolution 687 (the cease-fire). The Persian Gulf War ended at 1000 EDT two days later when the council issued Resolution 687.

15 APRIL • NAVAIR established the HH-1N designation for many of the H-1 Iroquois helicopters. The redesignation was to be completed by 30 September.

17 APRIL • *Midway* (CV 41) returned from the Persian Gulf War to Yokosuka, Japan.

17 APRIL • Secretary of Defense Richard B. Cheney signed an order directing military commanders to begin implementing the president's plan, announced the previous day at a press conference, which called for the establishment of several encampments in northern Iraq. United States,

A TA-4J Skyhawk of VC-5 departs NAS Cubi Point, Philippines, during the eruption of Mount Pinatubo, June 1991.

British, French, and Turkish service members had been delivering relief supplies to the refugees. The Sixth Fleet's 24th Marine Expeditionary Unit commenced operations 17 hours after the arrival of the Marines at the Silopi, Iraq, humanitarian service support base. A similar forward base was also established at Diyarbakir, Turkey.

18 APRIL • *America* (CV 66) returned from the Persian Gulf War to NS Norfolk, Va.

19 APRIL • *Theodore Roosevelt* (CVN 71) transited the Suez Canal and joined vessels including amphibious assault ship *Guadalcanal* (LPH 7) operating off the Syrian and Turkish coasts in an area northeast of Cyprus. These vessels supported the 7,000 American troops of Combined Joint Task Force Provide Comfort that helped Kurdish refugees displaced by Iraqi attacks after the Persian Gulf War. During the following days, aircraft flew 820 air cover, tactical photographic reconnaissance, and close air support sorties from *Theodore Roosevelt*. VF-84 F-14A Tomcats provided more than 6,000 aerial photographs to allied troops in northern Iraq, with VS-24 S-3B Vikings delivering them using an innovative system of sonobuoy drops. The images identified Iraqi troop emplacements, armored concentrations, early warning sites, and command posts, in addition to providing valuable assistance in locating widely scattered groups of Kurds fleeing from Iraqi atrocities.

1 MAY • The Navy redesignated F-14A Tomcats that had undergone the A+/A(Plus) conversion as F-14Bs.

12 MAY • Amphibious assault ship *Tarawa* (LHA 1) and seven ships of an amphibious assault group arrived off Bangladesh for Operation Sea Angel—large-scale relief efforts in the wake of a cyclone that devastated the country on 30 April. CH-46 Sea Knights, CH-53 Super Stallions, UH-1N Iroquois, and AH-1T Sea Cobras carried food and medical supplies to victims, and rescued people isolated by flood waters.

15 MAY • An ES-3A made the first flight of a Shadow at Lockheed's Palmdale, Calif., plant.

22 MAY • The House Armed Services Committee voted to allow women to fly combat missions in Air Force, Navy, and Marine Corps aircraft. The measure was included in an amendment to the 1992 defense budget.

23 MAY • Commander Naval Forces Middle East declared the Kuwaiti port of Ash-Shuwaikh free of ordnance and Iraqi mines. The action made the facility the fifth and final operation in a series of port clearing missions by Allied forces.

30 MAY • *Forrestal* (CV 59) deployed from NS Mayport, Fla., to relieve *Theodore Roosevelt* (CVN 71) in the eastern Mediterranean.

3 JUNE • An LC-130 from VXE-6 at NAS Point Mugu, Calif., completed the first mid-winter medical evacuation from Antarctica since 1966, flying a member of New Zealand's Division of Science and Industrial Research from McMurdo Station.

12 JUNE • Mount Pinatubo on Luzon in the Philippines erupted. Typhoon Yunya added to the devastation when it slammed inland with fierce winds and rain. The eruption and typhoon killed more than 300 people and displaced more than 300,000. *Midway* (CV 41), *Abraham Lincoln* (CVN 72), and ships from Amphibious Readiness Group Alpha led by amphibious assault ship *Peleliu* (LHA 5) participated in Operation Fiery Vigil—the evacuation of victims. *Abraham Lincoln* transported 4,323 people including Navy and Air Force dependents from Subic Bay, NAS Cubi Point, and Clark AB to Cebu City, Cebu, for further evacuation to Guam and the continental United States. Additional squadrons that assisted humanitarian efforts through 27 June included VFA-94, VC-5, and HSL-47.

14 JUNE • *Forrestal* (CV 59) relieved *Theodore Roosevelt* (CVN 71) in the eastern Mediterranean, which enabled the latter to pass westward through the Strait of Gibraltar two days later.

18 JUNE • Amphibious assault ship *Tripoli* (LPH 10) turned over her duties as flagship for Commander, Mine Countermeasures Group, to cruiser *Texas* (CGN 39). The group had located and destroyed nearly 1,200 mines in the Persian Gulf.

23 JUNE • Amphibious assault ship *Tripoli* (LPH 10) transited the Strait of Hormuz en route to San Diego, Calif.

28 JUNE • *Theodore Roosevelt* (CVN 71) returned to NS Norfolk, Va., the last carrier involved in the Persian Gulf War to return to her homeport.

10 JULY • The president approved a list of military base closures proposed by the Defense Base Closure and Realignment Commission. This included NAS Moffett Field, Calif.; NAS Chase Field, Texas; and MCAS Tustin, Calif.

13 JULY • *Nimitz* (CVN 68) turned over operations in the Persian Gulf to *Abraham Lincoln* (CVN 72) and then transited the Strait of Hormuz.

29 JULY • Grumman delivered the last scheduled production EA-6B Prowler to the Navy during ceremonies at its Calverton, N.Y. plant.

30 JULY • After 40 months of repairs and new equipment, *Kitty Hawk* (CV 63) left her berth at the Philadelphia Naval Shipyard, Pa., as the fourth carrier overhauled at that yard under the Service Life Extension Program.

31 JULY • The Senate voted overwhelmingly to overturn a 43-year-old law that had barred women from flying warplanes in combat. The new measure, which was an amendment to the military budget bill for the 1992 fiscal year, permitted—but did not require—the armed forces to allow women to fly combat missions.

19 AUGUST • The Naval Air Reserve celebrated its 75th anniversary.

27 AUGUST • A ceremony marked the introduction of SH-60F Seahawks into operational service with the Atlantic Fleet at NAS Jacksonville, Fla. HS-3 became the first East Coast squadron to trade SH-3H Sea Kings for the new helicopters.

27 AUGUST • The last U.S. Navy participants of the Persian Gulf War arrived home including amphibious assault ship *New Orleans* (LPH 11), with HMM-268 embarked.

6 SEPTEMBER • The first naval flight of an X-31A took place at Patuxent River, Md. The Advanced Research Projects Agency had developed the thrust-vectoring technology aircraft.

7 SEPTEMBER • After the banquet of the annual Tailhook Association convention at the Las Vegas Nevada Hilton, groups of naval aviators gathered overnight for private parties across the hotel. Women caught in the bacchanal proceedings accused conventioneers of misconduct ranging from verbal to physical/sexual abuse. The scandal rocked the fleet as widespread media attention generated a panel to investigate the allegations, from which the Navy initiated an "intense campaign" to increase awareness throughout the fleet, including new policies to address sexual misconduct and harassment.

27 SEPTEMBER • The Navy retired A-3s from active duty during ceremonies hosted by VAQ-33 at NAS Key West, Fla. The attendees included Ed Heinemann, who had designed the Skywarrior. The EA-3Bs of VQ-2 became the last operational "Whales."

27 SEPTEMBER • In a televised address, President George H. W. Bush announced that the United States would unilaterally reduce nuclear arms including the withdrawal of all tactical nuclear weapons from Navy ships. The order's provisions identified the withdrawal of Navy air-deliverable nuclear weapons from aircraft carriers and land-based naval aircraft such as patrol planes, and the storage or destruction of the weapons.

1 OCTOBER • NWC China Lake, Calif.; NADC Warminster, Pa.; and Naval Ordnance Missile Test Station, White Sands, N.M.; were transferred into NAVAIR. The action was in preparation for the consolidation of all naval air activities under the Naval Air Warfare Center as an activity of NAVAIR.

18 OCTOBER • An F/A-18 Hornet successfully launched an improved version of an AGM-84 SLAM (Standoff Land Attack Missile) at White Sands Missile Range, N.M.

20 OCTOBER • A fire broke out on a hillside above California State Highway 24 near the entrance to Caldecott Tunnel, and spread from the crest of the Oakland–Berkley Hills. Naval aviation commands at NAS Alameda, NAS Moffett Field, and NS Treasure Island assisted firefighters. HS-85 provided airlift support with SH-3 Sea Kings and reservists were put on alert.

8 NOVEMBER • *Lexington* (AVT 16) was decommissioned at NAS Pensacola, Fla. She had been commissioned on 17 February 1943, and subsequently served as a training carrier assigned to the Naval Air Training Command at Pensacola.

12 NOVEMBER • A ceremony at NAS Corpus Christi, Texas, marked the establishment in September of the Naval Air Training Maintenance Support Activity, Capt. David R. Timmons commanding. The establishment culminated a trend of more than 15 years toward maintaining training aircraft with contract civilians in place of service members.

4 DECEMBER • A T-45A landed on board *John F. Kennedy* (CV 67) in the Atlantic to make the type's first carrier landing.

1992

1 JANUARY • Naval Air Warfare Center (NAWC) was established, Commander NAVAIR Rear Adm. George H. Strohsahl Jr. commanding. The center was to consist of aircraft (AD) and weapons (WD) divisions.

2 JANUARY • The Naval Air Warfare Center Aircraft Division—NAWC (AD)—was established at NAS Patuxent River, Md., Rear Adm. George H. Strohsahl Jr. commanding (acting). Under the realignment, NAS Patuxent River reported to Commander NAWC (AD). The division assumed the responsibility for aircraft, engines, avionics, and aircraft support, and absorbed the activities of Naval Air Development Center, Warminster, Pa.; Naval Air Engineering Center, Lakehurst, N.J.; Naval Air Propulsion Center, Trenton, N.J.; Naval Avionics Center, Indianapolis, Ind.; and Naval Air Test Center, Patuxent River, Md. Planners intended to consolidate Warminster at Patuxent River.

2 JANUARY • The Flight Test and Engineering Group (FTEG) was established within the Naval Air Warfare Center Aircraft Division, Capt. Robert Parkinson, director. The disestablishment of NATC Patuxent River, Md., occurred simultaneously, and the previous NATC directorates became directorates under FTEG.

9 JANUARY • The Department of Defense announced the acceptance of a Saudi offer to award its Kuwait Liberation Medal to members of the U.S. armed forces who had directly participated in Operation Desert Storm. King Fahd bin Abdul Aziz of Saudi Arabia had established the award to honor the coalition troops that liberated Kuwait during the Persian Gulf War.

13 JANUARY • In a memorandum, Secretary of the Navy Henry L. Garrett III directed the integration of VMFAs and VMAQs into Navy carrier air wings, in order to reduce the requirements for F-14 Tomcats, F/A-18 Hornets, and EA-6B Prowlers. Marine tactical squadrons had historically operated from time to time as part of air wings, but the fleet had not institutionalized the concept in any permanent form.

18 JANUARY • VMFA-112, the last operational squadron to fly F-4s, held a retirement ceremony for its final Phantom II at NAS Dallas, Texas. On 10 January, Col. John Brennan,

USMC, made the squadron's last operational flight of the aircraft. The first flight of a Navy F-4B (F4H-1) had occurred on 27 May 1958.

19 JANUARY • The Naval Aviation History Office commemorated its 50th anniversary by preparing to move its archives to the Washington Navy Yard, D.C.

21 JANUARY • The Naval Air Warfare Center Weapons Division—NAWC (WD)—was established at Point Mugu, Calif., Rear Adm. William E. Newman commanding. Headquartered at Point Mugu and China Lake with a facility at White Sands, N.M., it assumed responsibility for aircraft weapons and weapons systems, simulators, and targets. NAWC (WD) absorbed the activities of Pacific Missile Test Center Point Mugu, Calif.; NWC China Lake, Calif.; Naval Weapons Evaluation Facility, Albuquerque, N.M.; and Naval Ordnance Missile Test Station, White Sands, N.M.

21 JANUARY • NAS Point Mugu, Calif., was disestablished, and NAWS Point Mugu took its place.

22 JANUARY • NAWS China Lake, Calif., was established at the site of the former Naval Weapons Center.

23 JANUARY • The first production Navy T-45A Goshawk rolled out at McDonnell Aircraft, St. Louis, Mo.

31 JANUARY • The Navy took delivery of the last production A-6E from Grumman, closing out more than 31 years of Intruder production. The aircraft was scheduled for delivery to VA-145 at NAS Whidbey Island, Wash.

4 FEBRUARY • Assistant Secretary of Defense (Public Affairs) Louis A. Williams announced to the press Navy plans to attain a goal of 12 active aircraft carriers.

5 FEBRUARY • *Forrestal* (CV 59) was redesignated a training carrier at her new homeport of NAS Pensacola, Fla. The action dropped the Navy's total of active carriers to 14 plus *Forrestal*, which was scheduled to relieve *Lexington* (AVT 16).

6 FEBRUARY • HSL-37 held a ceremony at NAS Barbers Point, Hawaii, to mark the beginning of its transition from SH-2F Seasprites to SH-60B Seahawks.

11 FEBRUARY • VA-34 became the first fleet squadron equipped with A-6E Intruders to fire an AGM-65E laser-guided Maverick air-to-surface missile, during an exercise in the Persian Gulf.

14 FEBRUARY • VMFA(AW)-225 accepted its first fleet two-seat F/A-18D Hornet, the first aircraft capable of operating the advanced tactical air reconnaissance pod system, at MCAS El Toro, Calif.

24 FEBRUARY • McDonnell Douglas and British Aerospace reached an exclusive partnership agreement, pending U.S. government approval, to work together to develop and produce advanced short takeoff/vertical landing strike fighter aircraft.

4 MARCH • The Navy stood up Naval Air Warfare Center Aircraft Division Patuxent River, Md., Rear Adm. (sel.) Barton D. Strong commanding.

4 MARCH • VAW-113 at NAS North Island, Calif., became the first fleet squadron to accept delivery of an E-2C Group II Hawkeye equipped with APS-145 radar.

10 MARCH • The Department of Defense announced a plan to withdraw from the Philippine Naval Facility, Subic Bay, Luzon. Major milestones in the plan included the closure of Department of Defense dependents schools in June, transfer of the majority of dependents through the summer, relocation of VRC-50 to Andersen AFB, Guam, in August, disestablishment of the Ship Repair Facility in September, and the formal turnover of the facility in December.

21 MARCH • *Independence* (CV 62) sailed from Subic Bay, Philippines, the last carrier scheduled to call at the base before its closure.

31 MARCH • NASA announced the selection of Lt. Cmdr. Wendy B. Lawrence among the agency's new astronauts. Lawrence became the first female line officer and naval aviator astronaut.

1 APRIL • The Fleet Electronic Warfare Support Group (FEWSG) merged with the Fleet Deception Group Atlantic to form the Fleet Practical Readiness Group. The new command, based at Naval Amphibious Base, Little Creek, Va., assumed operational control of FEWSG's electronic aggressor squadrons VAQ-33, -34, and -35.

This E-6A Mercury, BuNo 163918, is one of 16 of the strategic communications relay aircraft type. The Navy subsequently upgraded all of these jets to E-6B standard.

1 APRIL • The Chief of Naval Operations directed the retirement of the remaining A-7 Corsair IIs in active inventory by 1 April. The service subsequently partially reversed the decision in order to retain 11 TA-7Cs and three EA-7Ls with NAWC as chase aircraft for various activities, including the BGM-109 Tomahawk missile program.

8 APRIL • McDonnell Douglas delivered the 6,000th production AGM-84 Harpoon air-to-surface missile to the Navy during a ceremony at the company's St. Charles, Mo., manufacturing facility.

13 APRIL • Volcanic activity from Mount Etna pushed a lava flow toward the town of Zafferana, Sicily. The Italian authorities requested assistance, and two CH-53Es of HMM-226, embarked on board amphibious assault ship *Inchon* (LPH 12), augmented by another Super Stallion of HC-4 flying from NAS Sigonella, placed 8,000-pound concrete blocks in the path of the lava. The plan, developed by geologists, succeeded and forced open another lava vent further down the mountain and away from the town. Italian troops supplemented these measures with explosives to divert lava streams. The relief operations continued until 25 April.

1 MAY • The first class of flight instructors from VT-21, assigned to train the next generation of naval aviators in T-45As, began their own training in Goshawks.

1 MAY • Strategic Communications Wing 1 was established at Tinker AFB, Okla. The wing reported operationally to the Strategic Command and administratively to CINCPAC via AirPac. The wing's mission was command and control of fleet ballistic missile submarines, and the coordination of all Take Charge and Move Out (TACAMO) operations and liaison with the host, Tinker. Its role later expanded to include the manning, training, and equipping of the Navy squadrons responsible for command and control communications with the nuclear triad. The Navy's two TACAMO squadrons, VQ-3 and -4, later relocated to Tinker.

7 MAY • A Take Charge and Move Out EC-130 began the final deployment of the modified Hercules with VQ-4 from NAS Patuxent River, Md. The squadron had begun to transition from EC-130Qs to E-6A Mercury strategic communications relay aircraft, which used Boeing 707-320 airframes.

This V-22 Osprey test aircraft, BuNo 163914, was the fourth built. It crashed during a demonstration flight near MCAS Quantico, Va., 20 July 1992, killing seven.

22 MAY • VQ-5 took delivery of its first ES-3A at NAS Agana, Guam, marking the operational service entry of the electronic reconnaissance version of the Vikings.

31 MAY • Aircraft of VS-21 attached to *Independence* (CV 62) assisted the rescue of 19 crewmen from sinking Panamanian cargo ship *Great Eagle*, 580 nautical miles off the coast of Diego Garcia, British Indian Ocean Territory.

27 JUNE • VT-21 became operational as the first squadron to instruct trainees on T-45A Goshawks.

1 JULY • Helicopter Sea Control Wing 3 was redesignated Helicopter Anti-Submarine Light Wing 1, at the same time absorbing Helicopter Sea Control Wing 1. The action placed all Atlantic Fleet HSLs under a single wing.

10 JULY • The Navy received the last production F-14D, marking the end of 22 years of Tomcat production.

20 JULY • The fourth prototype V-22A crashed into the Potomac River on approach to MCAF Quantico, Va., killing three Marines and four Boeing employees. The Navy and

With rotated wing, engine pods, and folding rotor blades, the MV-22A Osprey makes a compact package for shipboard storage.

the Marine Corps grounded the remaining three prototype Ospreys pending the results of the mishap investigation. Investigators blamed the accident on mechanical failure caused by a flash fire, engine failure, and a failed drive shaft.

22 JULY • In a Pentagon press conference, Acting Secretary of the Navy Sean O'Keefe and Chief of Naval Operations Adm. Frank B. Kelso II announced a sweeping reorganization of OPNAV staff. The plan, developed by Adm. Kelso, aligned the staff with the Joint Staff, effective 1 January 1993. This included the merger of the assistant chiefs of Naval Operations for Submarine Warfare (OP-02), Surface Warfare (OP-03), Air Warfare (OP-05), and Naval Warfare (OP-07) into one staff under DCNO for Resources, Warfare Requirements and Assessment (code N8). Director, Air Warfare (N88), became the new designation assigned to Air Warfare (OP-05).

24 JULY • *Saratoga* (CV 60) and amphibious assault ship *Iwo Jima* (LPH 2) carried out sustained operations in the Adriatic Sea because of fighting in Bosnia-Herzegovina, Yugoslavia.

5 AUGUST • The Pentagon revealed that it would ask contractors to develop a less expensive version of the V-22 Osprey.

10 AUGUST • The OPNAV staff commenced the administrative conversion to N-codes.

12 AUGUST • CINCPAC Adm. Robert J. Kelly announced the formation of six carrier battle groups for service within the Pacific Fleet.

22 AUGUST • Hurricane Andrew ravaged the Bahamas, Florida, and Louisiana, killing at least 65 people and leveling Homestead AFB, Fla. Naval aviation commands and ships with supplies and repair capabilities responded to the crisis during the succeeding days.

23 AUGUST • Following the Persian Gulf War, the UN had established two no-fly zones over Iraq. In April 1991, it authorized the northern zone to protect the Kurds from the Iraqis. Air Force aircraft predominated during the patrols over the north during these flights, designated Operation Northern Watch, mainly from Incirlik AB near Adana, Turkey. Meanwhile, the Iraqis lashed out at Shi'as and the Madan (Marsh Arabs) in southern Iraq. *Independence* (CV 62) entered the Persian Gulf prepared to enforce the southern no-fly zone established by the UN below the 32nd parallel. The coalition later extended the zone to the 33rd parallel to grant pilots more tactical options and further limit the Iraqis. Carriers usually launched patrols over the south during what became Operation Southern Watch, and in time the two zones covered half of Iraq.

26 AUGUST • President George H. W. Bush announced the commencement within 24 hours of allied aerial surveillance over southern Iraq, which included the provision to shoot down Iraqi aircraft that flew south of the 32nd parallel. The patrols began the next day that included 20 aircraft of Carrier Air Wing 5, embarked on board *Independence* (CV 62), together with AV-8B Harrier IIs of VMA-211 operating from amphibious assault ship *Tarawa* (LHA 1). *Saratoga* (CV 60) and amphibious assault ship *Iwo Jima* (LPH 2) also participated.

28 AUGUST • Typhoon Omar devastated Guam. Elements of Joint Task Force Marianas including HC-5, VQ-1 and -5, VRC-50, VR-59, and NAS Agana, coordinated the relief efforts.

3 SEPTEMBER • An unidentified faction fired a surface-to-air missile that shot down an Italian Air Force Aeritalia G.222 over (former) Yugoslavia. Two CH-53E Super Stallions and two AH-1J Sea Cobras operating from amphibious assault ship *Iwo Jima* (LPH 2), sailing in the Adriatic in support of UN Bosnian relief efforts, aided in the search for survivors and wreckage. The helicopters drew ground fire but escaped undamaged.

4 SEPTEMBER • Cmdr. Linda V. Hutton assumed command of VRC-40, becoming the first woman to command an Atlantic Fleet aviation squadron.

11 SEPTEMBER • Hurricane Iniki devastated more than 75 percent of Kauai, Hawaii. Although the storm slightly damaged the island's Barking Sands Pacific Missile Range Facility, it served as a hub of relief flight operations. Volunteers from NAS Barbers Point and tenant commands assisted victims, and amphibious assault ship *Belleau Wood* (LHA 3) sailed to Kauai with troops and relief supplies. Additional commands that responded included HSL-37 and VP-1.

11 SEPTEMBER • The plight of famine-wracked Somalians was made worse when marauding gangs blocked distribution of humanitarian supplies. The UN consequently began Operation Provide Relief—the air delivery of food from Mombassa, Kenya, to Kenyan and Somali sites. On this date, President George H. W. Bush dispatched amphibious assault ship *Tarawa* (LHA 1) and amphibious transport docks *Fort Fisher* (LPD 40) and *Ogden* (LPD 5) to the area. On 17 September, *Tarawa* arrived off Somalia to provide command and control for Air Force flight operations at Mogadishu and for possible search and rescue missions. The ship's embarked AV-8B Harrier IIs of VMA-221, AH-1W Super Cobras and UH-1N Iroquois of HMLA-367, CH-46E Sea Knights of HMM-161, and CH-53E Super Stallions of HMH-466, protected the insertion of UN relief teams and Pakistani security troops into Mogadishu. *Tarawa* departed on 29 September.

14 SEPTEMBER • *Forrestal* (CV 59) arrived from NAS Pensacola, Fla., at Philadelphia Naval Shipyard, Pa., to begin a 14-month, $157 million conversion to a training carrier. In early 1993, the Navy decided instead to mothball *Forrestal* at Philadelphia, leaving the fleet without a dedicated training carrier.

16 SEPTEMBER • *Ranger* (CV 61) arrived in the Persian Gulf to support Operation Southern Watch patrols over the Iraqi no-fly zone.

28 SEPTEMBER • Secretary of the Navy Sean O'Keefe, Chief of Naval Operations Adm. Frank B. Kelso II, and Commandant of the Marine Corps Gen. Carl E. Mundy Jr. signed ". . . From the Sea," a Navy/Marine Corps strategy

Amphibious assault ship *Tripoli* (LPH 10) provides humanitarian relief to refugees at Mogadishu, Somalia, during her deployment to support Operation Restore Hope, 3 December 1992–2 February 1993.

developed in response to the shift from global to regional threats against U.S. national security. The plan emphasized littoral warfare and maneuver from the sea.

30 SEPTEMBER • AirLant's four functional wings—Helicopter Wings, Atlantic; Patrol Wings, Atlantic; Strike Fighter Wings, Atlantic; and Tactical Wings, Atlantic—were disestablished in a sweeping change that eliminated an entire echelon of command in the administrative structure of East Coast naval aviation.

30 SEPTEMBER • The United States turned the station at Subic Bay over to the Philippines.

7 OCTOBER • *John F. Kennedy* (CV 67) deployed to the Mediterranean to relieve *Saratoga* (CV 60) during ongoing tensions resulting from the civil war in Yugoslavia, and the confrontation with Iraq.

15 OCTOBER • HS-14 became the first U.S. squadron to land aircraft on the deck of a Russian warship, when an SH-3H Sea King set down onto *Udaloy*-class destroyer *Admiral Vinogradov* (DDG 554) during joint exercises in the Persian Gulf.

22 OCTOBER • The Department of Defense announced the award of a contract to the Bell-Boeing Joint Program Office for the modification and test of a V-22 derivative, a scaled-down version of the Osprey tilt-rotor.

24 OCTOBER • The Atlantic Fleet was reorganized into six carrier battle groups. Previous plans had called for forming groups for specific workups and deployments.

30 OCTOBER • NAS Cubi Point, Philippines, was disestablished.

3 NOVEMBER • The Presidential Commission on the Assignment of Women in the Armed Forces recommended against allowing women to fly in combat, but for allowing them to serve in some combat ships.

7 NOVEMBER • In support of Operation Provide Promise—UN efforts to supply Bosnia-Herzegovina with humanitarian supplies—amphibious assault ship *Guam* (LPH 9), with HMM-261 embarked, relieved amphibious assault ship *Iwo Jima* (LPH 2), with HMM-365 on board, in the Adriatic.

14 NOVEMBER • The RIM-116A RAM (Rolling Airframe Missile), a lightweight quick-reaction fire-and-forget system designed to counter antiship missiles attacking in waves or streams, was installed on board amphibious assault ship *Peleliu* (LHA 5).

14 NOVEMBER • The Navy transferred *Lexington* (AVT 16) to the city of Corpus Christi, Texas, for use as a memorial/museum ship.

7 DECEMBER • The Navy and McDonnell Douglas Aerospace finalized the $3.715 billion development contract for F/A-18E/Fs. The cost-plus incentive contract covered 7 ½ years of engineering and support activities, including the manufacturing and testing of seven flight test Super Hornets and three ground test airframes.

7 DECEMBER • After her diversion from the Persian Gulf, *Ranger* (CV 61) reached Somali waters to support Operation Restore Hope—UN directed humanitarian aid for the Somalis.

9 DECEMBER • Operation Restore Hope—UN directed humanitarian aid for the Somalis—began. HMM-164, reinforced from amphibious assault ship *Tripoli* (LPH 10), provided the initial Marine helicopter support to the UN peacekeepers.

16 DECEMBER • *Kitty Hawk* (CV 63) deployed five air traffic controllers to cruiser *Leahy* (CG 53) to establish approach control services in support of Operation Restore Hope at Mogadishu, Somalia. An E-2C Hawkeye of VAW-114 picked up approaching aircraft, tracked their flights, and issued advisories from 200 miles out. When the flights reached to within a range of 50 miles, *Leahy* took over and led them to within visual range of the airport ten miles away.

Marines embark CH-46E Sea Knights of HMM-164 on board amphibious assault ship *Tripoli* (LPH 10) during the early stages of Operation Restore Hope, 3 December 1992–2 February 1993.

An SH-60B Seahawk flies past dock landing ship *Rushmore* (LSD 47) en route to amphibious assault ship *Tripoli* (LPH 10), during operations off Somalia in late 1992 or early 1993.

19 DECEMBER • *Kitty Hawk* (CV 63) relieved *Ranger* (CV 61) off Somalia in support of Operation Restore Hope.

27 DECEMBER • In December, Iraqi dictator Saddam Hussein had surreptitiously deployed antiaircraft missile batteries south of the 32nd parallel in violation of the cease-fire accords, warning the coalition that they would shoot down aircraft. On this date, an Air Force F-16D Fighting Falcon shot down an Iraqi MiG-25 with an AIM-120 AMRAAM (Advanced Medium Range Air-to-Air Missile) when the Foxbat violated the southern no-fly zone. *Kitty Hawk* (CV 63) left Somalia and by the New Year had dispatched 51 F-14A Tomcat and F/A-18A Hornet combat air patrol sorties to enforce the Operation Southern Watch no-fly zone.

1993

1 JANUARY • In a reorganization of the OPNAV staff, the position of ACNO (Air Warfare)/(OP-05), held by Rear Adm. Riley D. Mixon, became Director, Air Warfare (N88) and reported to DCNO (Resources, Warfare Requirements and Assessment)/(N8). The N88 billet dropped from a three-star flag officer to a two-star.

13 JANUARY • On 6 January, President George H. W. Bush issued an ultimatum to Iraqi leader Saddam Hussein to remove missiles from the southern no-fly zone within 48 hours. Iraq responded by looting four Silkworm surface-to-surface missiles from a portion of Umm Qasr that they had ceded to the Kuwaitis. On this date, Cmdr. Kevin J. Thomas of VFA-97 led a coalition night strike of 35 aircraft from *Kitty Hawk* (CV 63) joined by 75 additional Air Force, British, and French aircraft against four Iraqi air defense command and control centers, and two concentrations of SA-3 Goa surface-to-air missiles.

17 JANUARY • Iraqi antiaircraft guns and surface-to-air missiles fired at allied aircraft, and enemy fighters darted back and forth across the 36th parallel in an attempt to draw coalition aircraft toward heavier concentrations of air defenses deployed just below the boundary. Meanwhile, cruiser *Cowpens* (CG 63) and destroyers *Hewitt* (DD 966) and *Stump* (DD 978) steaming in the Persian Gulf, and destroyer *Caron* (DD 970) in the Red Sea, launched 42 BGM-109 Tomahawk cruise missiles at the Zaafaraniyah Fabrication Facility, a plant near Baghdad that intelligence analysts suspected of making nuclear weapons parts. At least 30 missiles struck the target area, and Air Force F-15E Strike Eagles bombed the Tallil Station Air Operations Center.

18 JANUARY • *Kitty Hawk* (CV 63) launched F-14A Tomcats, F/A-18A Hornets, and E-2C Hawkeyes from the Persian Gulf to support an Air Force strike against military targets in northern Iraq, in response to Iraqi violations of the UN-imposed no-fly zone. The ship aborted an additional planned strike of 29 aircraft against mobile surface-to-air missiles in southern Iraq when the Iraqis moved the batteries. Meanwhile, *John F. Kennedy* (CV 67) headed to the eastern Mediterranean.

17 FEBRUARY • The Aircraft Carrier Memorial, a ten-foot black obelisk honoring those who have served on board U.S. carriers, was dedicated at the North Embarcadero, San Diego, Calif.

25 FEBRUARY • *John F. Kennedy* (CV 67) entered the Adriatic in support of Operation Provide Promise—UN efforts to supply those displaced by the fighting in Bosnia-Herzegovina with food and supplies.

4 MARCH • *Constellation* (CV 64) departed Philadelphia Naval Shipyard, Pa., as the fifth and final carrier to complete the Service Life Extension Program.

23 MARCH • Amphibious assault ship *Wasp* (LHD 1) arrived off Somalia to support Operation Restore Hope. Her embarked helicopters and AV-8B Harrier IIs of HMM-263 flew sorties in support of Marines deployed ashore.

31 MARCH • Two EP-3E Aries IIs of VQ-2 supported humanitarian air drops over eastern Bosnia-Herzegovina during Operation Provide Promise—UN efforts to supply those displaced by the fighting in Bosnia-Herzegovina with food and supplies.

1 APRIL • Sea Strike Wing 1 was redesignated Sea Control Wing Atlantic, and Air Anti-Submarine Squadrons were redesignated Sea Control Squadrons—but retained the short "VS" designator. The name change reflected the broader and all-encompassing VS mission of these commands, particularly in light of the increased multi-mission versatility of S-3B Vikings.

12 APRIL • NATO and the UN began Operation Deny Flight—the enforcement of a no-fly zone over Bosnia-Herzegovina. Twelve F/A-18 Hornets temporarily shifted from *Theodore Roosevelt* (CVN 71) to NATO operational control. At one point, 26 Navy EA-6B Prowlers operating from Aviano AB Italy provided the primary allied electronic warfare aircraft to suppress enemy air defenses. Marines and sailors of the Mediterranean Amphibious Ready Group provided search and rescue and tactical recovery of aircraft and personnel duties from amphibious assault ship *Saipan* (LHA 2).

Sailors prepare a shipboard variant of the Army's RQ-5 Hunter for launch during testing on board amphibious assault ship *Essex* (LHD 2) in December 1993. Although the tests were positive and encouraging, the Navy did not purchase the RQ-5.

14 APRIL • Former President George H. W. Bush, his wife Barbara, two of their sons, and former Secretary of State James A. Baker III, arrived in Kuwait to participate in ceremonies commemorating the allied victory in the Persian Gulf War. The Kuwaitis arrested and charged 17 men with an attempt to assassinate the president and Kuwaiti Emir (Sheikh) al-Ahmed al-Jaber al-Sabah with a car bomb. On 29 April, the CIA reported that the bomb bore evidence of Iraqi origins. The plot heightened tensions in the region that resulted in additional coalition operations including patrols by naval aircraft.

22 APRIL • An EA-6B Prowler from VAQ-209 fired the first successful over-the-horizon AGM-88 HARM (High-speed Anti-Radiation Missile) using targeting data from a satellite delivered directly to the cockpit. A P-3B Orion of VP-60 assisted.

26 APRIL • VC-6 Detachment 2 carried out the first launch of an unmanned aerial vehicle from an amphibious vessel by operating an RQ-2A Pioneer on board amphibious transport dock *Denver* (LPD 9).

28 APRIL • Secretary of Defense Leslie Aspin lifted the ban on combat flights for women and opened up additional ships to female sailors. He further stated his intention to forward a draft proposal to Congress to remove the last legislative barrier to the assignment of women to combat vessels. Chief of Naval Operations Adm. Frank B. Kelso II concurred. On 30 November, President William J. Clinton signed legislation that lifted the ban on women serving on board combat ships.

29 APRIL • After the decision by Secretary of Defense Leslie Aspin to expand combat roles for women, Chief of Naval Operations Adm. Frank B. Kelso II opened six enlisted naval aviation ratings to women: aviation antisubmarine warfare operator (AW), electronic warfare technician (EW), fire controlman (FC), gas turbine technician (GS), gas turbine technician–electrical (GSE), and gas turbine technician–mechanical (GSM).

5 MAY • Commander, Helicopter Anti-Submarine Light Wing, Pacific Fleet, was established at NAS North Island, Calif., Capt. John R. Brown commanding.

6 MAY • Naval Reservist Lt. Cmdr. Kathryn P. Hire was selected for assignment to VP-62, thus becoming the Navy's first woman to be eligible to compete for assignments in aircraft engaged in combat missions.

7 MAY • Chief of Naval Personnel Vice Adm. Ronald J. Zlatoper outlined the Navy's plan to open new opportunities for women during the seventh annual Naval Aviation Symposium at NAS Pensacola, Fla. VAQ-130 became the first squadron expected to receive women. He also revealed the impending assignment of women to Carrier Air Wing (CVW) 3, embarked on board *Dwight D. Eisenhower* (CVN 69), and CVW-11 on board *Abraham Lincoln* (CVN 72).

1 JUNE • Commander, Strike Fighter Wing, Pacific, shifted from a flag-level functional wing to a type wing as part of the ongoing reorganization of wings in the Pacific Fleet.

8 JUNE • Patrol Wing 2 was disestablished after 56 years of service.

11 JUNE • A groundbreaking ceremony took place for the Aircraft Technology Laboratory at NAS Patuxent River, Md.

26 JUNE • Cruiser *Chancellorsville* (CG 62) launched nine BGM-109 Tomahawk cruise missiles from the northern Persian Gulf, and destroyer *Peterson* (DD 969) fired 14 more missiles from the Red Sea, in a coordinated night attack against the Iraqi intelligence service headquarters building in Baghdad. At least 13 missiles struck the compound. During a press conference, Chairman of the Joint Chiefs of Staff Gen. Colin L. Powell, USA, described the attack as a "proportionate" response to the Iraqi assassination plot against former President George H. W. Bush, his wife Barbara, two of their sons, and former Secretary of State James A. Baker III, during their visit to Kuwait on 14 April. The United States subsequently dispatched *Theodore Roosevelt* (CVN 71) and destroyer *Arleigh Burke* (DDG 51) to reinforce allied forces in the Red Sea.

14 JULY • Secretary of Defense Leslie Aspin approved an order directing U.S. aircraft to join NATO's planned air support to UN protection forces in Bosnia-Herzegovina. *Theodore Roosevelt* (CVN 71) thus entered the Mediterranean to participate in Operation Deny Flight—the enforcement of a no-fly zone over Bosnia-Herzegovina.

17 AUGUST • An EA-6B Prowler of VAQ-209 at NAS Point Mugu, Calif., conducted the first successful over-the-horizon AGM-88 HARM (High-speed Anti-Radiation Missile) and AGM-84 Harpoon air-to-surface missile war-at-sea strike using targeting data from space-based sensors delivered directly to the cockpit. A P-3B Orion of VP-60 assisted.

1 SEPTEMBER • President William J. Clinton unveiled a revised plan to cut the armed forces based on a doctrine developed by President George H. W. Bush that prepared the United States to fight two simultaneous major regional wars and one low-intensity war. The plan called for 11 carrier battle groups, with a 12th carrier to serve as a Reserve and training ship. The original plan called for 12 battle groups.

3 SEPTEMBER • AIM-120 AMRAAM (Advanced Medium Range Air-to-Air Missile) achieved initial operating capability for the Navy with Carrier Air Wing 11 on board *Abraham Lincoln* (CVN 72).

9 SEPTEMBER • The creation of the fleet's largest aviation squadron occurred during the merger of VP-30 at NAS Jacksonville, Fla., with VP-31 at NAS Moffett Field, Calif. The consolidation resulted from downsizing, and enabled the Navy to train all P-3 Orion crews at Jacksonville.

11 SEPTEMBER • *Forrestal* (CV 59) was decommissioned at Philadelphia Naval Shipyard, Pa.

1 OCTOBER • The NAVCAD program was disestablished. It had begun during World War II as the V-5 program, and had subsequently been redesignated V-12. It was disestablished in 1966, but later reinstated in 1986 to help train more pilots for the planned 600-ship fleet.

1 OCTOBER • The Atlantic Command became responsible for the joint training and deployment of all continental U.S.-based forces. The action merged the Atlantic Fleet, Marine Forces Atlantic, Army Forces Command, and USAF Air Combat Command into a single combat command. The Atlantic Command was to support all U.S. involvement in UN peacekeeping operations, plan for the land defense of the homeland, and respond to natural disasters within the United States.

1 OCTOBER • The Naval Training Systems Center, Orlando, Fla., was redesignated Naval Air Warfare Center, Training Systems Division, although without a change of mission.

1 OCTOBER • The first phase of a new joint primary training program began when five Air Force aviators reported to NAS Whiting Field, Pensacola, Fla. Meanwhile, Navy, Marine Corps, and Coast Guard flight instructors reported for training to Randolph AFB, Texas.

3 OCTOBER • Overnight, the Army's Task Force Ranger became embroiled in a battle against Somali clansmen in Mogadishu, Somalia. The Somalis killed 18 Americans and wounded 84, and claimed losses of 312 dead and 814 wounded. On 5 October, the Navy ordered *Abraham Lincoln* (CVN 72) to make for Somali waters to aid the allied troops. On 8 October, the carrier passed through the Strait of Hormuz, and on 12 October, arrived off the Horn of Africa to participate in Operation Restore Hope. Three days later, the ship disembarked Marines of her detachment in Somalia to reinforce international peacekeepers. The Marines remained ashore until 22 October while carrying out this unique operation from an aircraft carrier. *Abraham Lincoln* departed on 3 November.

15 OCTOBER • Secretary of the Navy John H. Dalton announced the consolidation at the Naval Aviation Schools Command, NAS Pensacola, Fla., of Aviation Officer Candidate School and Officer Candidate School as a cost-saving initiative.

17 OCTOBER • Amphibious assault ships *Guadalcanal* (LPH 7) and *New Orleans* (LPH 11) arrived off Somalia.

29 OCTOBER • *America* (CV 66) transited the Suez Canal southbound, and subsequently relieved *Abraham Lincoln* (CVN 72) off the coast of Somalia.

16 NOVEMBER • The aviation antisubmarine warfare operator rating changed to aviation warfare systems operator to reflect the broadened scope of responsibilities. The existing rating badge and abbreviation "AW" remained the same.

24 NOVEMBER • The X-31A international test program announced the first supersonic flights of its enhanced fighter maneuverability demonstrator when Aircraft No. 1 flew nine sorties, achieving Mach 1.08 at an altitude of 37,500 feet.

30 NOVEMBER • President William J. Clinton signed legislation that lifted the ban on women serving on board combat ships.

1 DECEMBER • Secretary of the Navy John H. Dalton announced the first assignment of women to combat ships to begin by June 1994, pending notification of Congress as required by the fiscal year 1994 Defense Authorization Bill. *Dwight D. Eisenhower* (CVN 69) and *Abraham Lincoln* (CVN 72) were scheduled to be the first carriers to embark women, followed by *John C. Stennis* (CVN 74) at the end of 1994.

9 DECEMBER • A V-22 Osprey returned to NAWC (AD) Patuxent River, Md., from facilities in Wilmington, Del., to begin full engineering manufacturing development testing. The new program ushered in an integrated team concept of testing and evaluation.

1994

1 JANUARY • The Navy began to train aviators in the T-45 Training System at NAS Kingsville, Texas, which included T-45A Goshawks that replaced aging T-2 Buckeyes and TA-4 Skyhawks.

18 JANUARY • In a press briefing held at the Pentagon, Chief of Naval Operations Adm. Frank B. Kelso II

Army and Navy helicopters pack the flight deck of *Dwight D. Eisenhower* (CVN 69) as she steams to Haitian waters, September 1994. During Operation Uphold Democracy she transported about 1,800 soldiers of the Army's XVIII Airborne Corps.

emphasized that the naval forces of the future would deploy smaller numbers of ships, aircraft, and personnel but operate at enhanced capability because of new technologies and prudent cost-cutting measures.

1 FEBRUARY • *Saratoga* (CV 60) took station in the Adriatic Sea. During this deployment the carrier's joint task group participated in various U.S., NATO, and UN missions throughout the Mediterranean, Black, and Red Seas including combat air patrol, and command, control, and surveillance aircraft for Operations Deny Flight and Provide Promise—to enforce the no-fly zone over Bosnia-Herzegovina and UN efforts to provide humanitarian assistance to the victims of the fighting there, respectively.

18 FEBRUARY • Ens. Alta J. DeRoo became the first female naval aviator to receive her wings in the Grumman E-2 Hawkeye community during a ceremony at Norfolk, Va.

21 FEBRUARY • Lt. Shannon L. Workman of VAQ-130, embarked on board *Dwight D. Eisenhower* (CVN 69), became the first female combat pilot to successfully pass fleet carrier qualifications. She was slated as one of four female aviators to deploy to *Dwight D. Eisenhower* in October.

3 MARCH • Amphibious assault ship *Peleliu* (LHA 5) joined amphibious assault ship *Inchon* (LPH 12) off the coast of Somalia to support the withdrawal of U.S. troops from that country.

3 MARCH • The A-6 Composite Rewing Program at NAD Norfolk, Va., ended when the last A-6E Intruder completed its new wing upgrade. The program, which began in 1990, replaced an aircraft's original metal wing with a composite structure as it reached the end of its fatigue life.

7 MARCH • The Navy ordered the first 63 women of the ship's crew to report to *Dwight D. Eisenhower* (CVN 69).

19 MARCH • An experimental T-45A Goshawk equipped with the digital Cockpit 21 made its inaugural flight at McDonnell Douglas, St. Louis, Mo.

24 MARCH • Troopship *Empire State* (T-AP 1001) sailed from Modgadishu as the last American military transport ship to depart Somalia. Amphibious assault ship *Peleliu* (LHA 5) sailed off the coast to cover the evacuation and support UN operations.

31 MARCH • The Department of Defense assigned the name Peregrine to the BQM-145A medium-range unmanned aerial vehicle.

1 APRIL • The first operational flight of the airborne multisensor pod system took place at NAWCWD Point Mugu, Calif.

29 APRIL • Short-range, inertially guided AGM-119B Penguin Mk 2 Mod 7 air-to-surface missiles reached initial operational capability with the Navy. On 25 June, an SH-60B Seahawk of HSL-51 Detachment 6, embarked on board destroyer *Hewitt* (DD 966), made the first fleet launch of a Penguin at the Pacific Missile Range Facility off Hawaii during exercise RIMPAC '94.

2 MAY • Two F-14B Tomcats of VF-103, embarked on board *Saratoga* (CV 60), dropped three GBU-16 laser-guided bombs that scored direct hits at Capo Frasca Target Complex, Sardinia. The action marked the first time that Tomcats dropped Paveway IIs.

5 MAY • The House Armed Services Committee approved $3.65 billion for CVN-76 and advance procurement for the large-deck amphibious ship LHD-7 as part of the $263.3 billion defense budget for 1995.

Army UH-60 Black Hawks lift off from the flight deck of *Dwight D. Eisenhower* (CVN 69) off the coast of Haiti during Operation Uphold Democracy, September 1994.

16 MAY • Seventeen Russian pilots tested nine two-seat F/A-18s at NAS Patuxent River, Md., accompanied by U.S. Navy pilots in the back seats.

5 JUNE • President William J. and First Lady Hillary R. Clinton led an entourage of the nation's leaders on board *George Washington* (CVN 73) during the commemoration of the 50th anniversary of D-Day. *George Washington* sailed off the coast of Portsmouth, England, and then crossed the English Channel toward the Omaha and Utah invasion beaches of Normandy, France.

28 JUNE • A P-3C, ordered by South Korea, rolled out of the assembly hangar at Lockheed Aeronautical Systems Company, Marietta, Ga. The event marked the return to production of the maritime patrol Orions.

1 JULY • A ceremony marked the closing of NAS Moffett Field, Calif.

1 JULY • The schedule for the Joint Primary Aircraft Training System (JPATS) flight evaluation was established at Wright-Patterson AFB, Ohio. From 24 July through 8 October, inspectors evaluated various aircraft. The JPATS eventually replaced T-34C Turbomentors and Air Force T-37B Tweets with a common training system.

6 JULY • Amphibious assault ship *Inchon* (LPH 12) sailed from Norfolk, Va., in response to a crisis in Haiti. After the Haitian Army's overthrow of President Jean-Bertrand Aristide in September 1991, a succession of governments led to sectarian violence, and in May 1994 the Haitian Army imposed Supreme Court Justice Emile Jonassaint as the

Former *Saratoga* (CV 60) under tow to Philadelphia, Pa., from Naval Station Mayport, Fla., where she was decommissioned on 20 August 1994.

provisional president. The UN authorized force to restore order and the United States initiated Operations Support Democracy and Uphold/Restore Democracy—Uphold Democracy for a peaceful entry into Haiti, and Restore Democracy in the event of resistance.

7 JULY • The name White Hawk was established for the VH-60N, whose primary mission was to provide executive transport in support of the president and his staff.

31 JULY • Lt. Kara S. Hultgreen of VF-213 made her first qualifying landing in an F-14A on board *Constellation* (CV 64) southwest of San Diego, Calif. She thus became the first fully qualified female Tomcat pilot, and Lt. j.g. Carey Dunai became the second woman to reach the milestone with her qualifying trap in another Tomcat moments later.

17 AUGUST • Amphibious assault ship *Inchon* (LPH 12) returned to Norfolk, Va., following her relief by amphibious assault ship *Wasp* (LHD 1) off Haiti.

31 AUGUST • Five Navy MH-53E Sea Dragons arrived at MCAS Tustin, Calif., during the consolidation of helicopter training for sailors and Marines. With the disestablishment of HM-12, the Navy's H-53 fleet readiness squadron, HMT-302, had assumed the training responsibility.

12 SEPTEMBER • The ongoing crisis in Haiti prompted a response by a multinational force that included *America* (CV 66) and *Dwight D. Eisenhower* (CVN 69). About 1,800 soldiers of the Army's XVIII Airborne Corps embarked on board *Dwight D. Eisenhower*. Most of the carrier's fixed-wing aircraft remained ashore to make room for, at times,

HC-2, HCS-4, and HS-7 operated with dozens of Army helicopters—a total of 51 Navy and Army aircraft. In addition, *Dwight D. Eisenhower's* Marines provided a security force for search and rescue. The Haitians agreed to allow the Americans to land peacefully, and on 31 March 1995, the United States transferred peacekeeping functions to international forces. The crisis marked the first operational deployment of Army helicopters on board a carrier in lieu of most of an air wing.

30 SEPTEMBER • The aircraft model designation TC-18F was established for two Boeing B-707-382Bs, which had been modified to include cockpit avionics and a universal air refueling receptacle for dry contacts only. The naval training support unit at Tinker AFB Okla., used these aircraft to train pilots of VQ-3 and -4 for Take Charge and Move Out missions with E-6A Mercury aircraft.

1 OCTOBER • NAS Fort Worth, Texas, was established as a joint reserve force base. The station was to be home for Navy and Marine squadrons formerly based at two stations after the closure of NAS Dallas, Texas, and the discontinuance of air operations at NAS Memphis, Tenn.

1 OCTOBER • Commander, Patrol Wings, Atlantic Fleet was established at Norfolk, Va., Rear Adm. Michael D. Haskins commanding.

5 OCTOBER • The first aviator class to use the T-45 Training System graduated from VT-21 at NAS Kingsville, Texas.

6 OCTOBER • Intelligence analysts identified the apparent preparations of five Iraqi divisions to invade Kuwait, and the United States launched Operation Vigilant Warrior to protect the Kuwaitis. The next day, President William J. Clinton dispatched *George Washington* (CVN 73) from the Adriatic to the Red Sea, which she reached on 10 October. In addition, amphibious assault ship *Tripoli* (LPH 10) and 2,000 Marines of the 15th Marine Expeditionary Unit moved to the northern Persian Gulf. These moves convinced Saddam Hussein to withdraw his mobile troops from the Kuwaiti border.

6 OCTOBER • President William J. Clinton visited *Dwight D. Eisenhower* (CVN 69). The ship provided national-level command and control for the chief executive during his visit.

An F-14 Tomcat of VF-143, deployed on board *Dwight D. Eisenhower* (CVN 69), flies over a destroyed Iraqi radar site, c. 2000.

Cmdr. Donnie Cochran is the first African American commanding officer of the Navy's Flight Demonstration Squadron (Blue Angels). He took command on 15 November 1994.

20 OCTOBER • *Dwight D. Eisenhower* (CVN 69) deployed to the Mediterranean and Persian Gulf as the first carrier with women permanently assigned. More than 400 women served on board at times during the cruise. The ship returned on 13 April 1995.

The creator of Grampaw Pettibone, Dilbert the Pilot, and Spoiler the Mechanic is artist Robert C. Osborn. His drawings of Gramps appeared in *Naval Aviation News* for 51 years.

25 OCTOBER • Pilot Lt. Kara S. Hultgreen and radar intercept officer Lt. Matthew P. Klemish of VF-213 crashed in F-14A Tomcat, BuNo 160390, while attempting to land on board *Abraham Lincoln* (CVN 72) off San Diego. Hultgreen thus became the first naval female combat pilot to die in an aircraft accident. Klemish ejected and survived with minor injuries.

15 NOVEMBER • Cmdr. Donnie Cochran became the first African American commanding officer of the Navy's Flight Demonstration Squadron (Blue Angels). He had previously commanded VF-11 at NAS Miramar, Calif., and flown with the Blue Angels from 1985 to 1988.

6 DECEMBER • The "Spirit of Naval Aviation," a monument dedicated to the Navy, Marine Corps, and Coast Guard aviation personnel who had earned their wings, was unveiled at the National Air and Space Museum, Washington, D.C. The National Museum of Naval Aviation subsequently displayed the monument at NAS Pensacola, Fla.

8 DECEMBER • NASA announced the selection of five naval aviators among 19 new astronaut candidates for the space shuttle pilot instruction program: Cmdr. Jeffery S. Ashby of VFA-94; Cmdr. Dominic L. Gorie of VFA-106; Lt. Cmdr. Scott D. Altman of VF-31; Lt. Cmdr. Joe F. Edwards Jr. of the Joint Staff; and Lt. Susan L. Still of VF-101. Still's appointment marked the first female naval aviator selected for the program. In addition, Naval Reservist Lt. Cmdr. Kathryn P. Hire was chosen for training as a mission specialist.

20 DECEMBER • Robert C. Osborn died at the age of 90 at his home in Salisbury, Conn. For more than 51 years he had drawn the cartoon "Grampaw Pettibone" in *Naval Aviation News*. During World War II, Osborn created the "Dilbert the Pilot" and "Spoiler the Mechanic" posters and the "Sense" pamphlets, which were disseminated throughout the fleet.

1995

17 JANUARY • T-45A Goshawks and their associated training system elements completed a successful Department of Defense Milestone III review. The approval enabled prime contractor McDonnell Douglas to continue to produce 12 Goshawks per year for a total order of 174 aircraft by 2003.

2 FEBRUARY • Secretary of the Navy John H. Dalton announced that President William J. Clinton had approved his recommendation to name the two *Nimitz* (CVN 68)-class carriers under construction as *Harry S. Truman* (CVN 75) and *Ronald Reagan* (CVN 76).

14 FEBRUARY • A groundbreaking ceremony occurred for the Naval Air Technical Training Center at Chevalier Field, NAS Pensacola, Fla.

17 FEBRUARY • A groundbreaking ceremony took place at NAS Patuxent River, Md., for a facility to house NAVAIR headquarters, which was to be relocated from Arlington, Va.

28 FEBRUARY • More than 1,800 sailors and Marines from amphibious assault ship *Belleau Wood* (LHA 3) and amphibious transport dock *Ogden* (LPD 5), supported by 350 Italian Marines, landed and established a rear-guard security perimeter at Mogadishu, Somalia, to support Operation United Shield—the withdrawal of UN forces from Somalia.

Harry S. Truman (CVN 75), laid down on 29 November 1993, is under construction at Newport News, Va. She was commissioned on 25 July 1998.

Marines and SEALs clashed with Somali clansmen during the withdrawal. Amphibious assault ship *Essex* (LHD 2) also took part in the evacuations, which concluded on 2 March.

1 MARCH • Amphibious assault ship *Inchon* (LPH 12) was redesignated a mine countermeasures ship (MCS 12).

2 MARCH • Space shuttle *Endeavour* launched from John F. Kennedy Space Center, Fla., on mission STS-67. Naval aviator Cmdr. Stephen S. Oswald, USNR, commanded the mission, and Lt. Cmdr. Wendy B. Lawrence, the first female Naval Academy graduate astronaut, also became the first female naval aviator in space when she launched as a crewmember. On 18 March, *Endeavour* touched down at Edwards AFB, Calif.

6 MARCH • The first Air Force F-117A Nighthawk stealth fighter engine was delivered for depot-level repair at NAD Jacksonville, Fla.

14 MARCH • Naval aviator and astronaut Capt. Michael A. Baker was assigned as NASA Manager of Operational Activities at the Gagarin Cosmonaut Training Center, Star City, Russia. The assignment coincided with the launching of naval aviator Capt. Norman E. Thagard, USMC, and two cosmonauts on board a Soyuz TM-12 spacecraft for Mir-18, a three-month stay on board Russian orbital research station *Mir*. On 7 July, Thagard returned with space shuttle *Atlantis*, on mission STS-71, to John F. Kennedy Space Center, Fla.

Lt. Cmdr. Wendy B. Lawrence is the first female U.S. Naval Academy graduate astronaut, and on 2 March 1995 became the first female naval aviator in space.

10 APRIL • VA-196 accepted the last rewinged A-6E, BuNo 159579, at NAS Whidbey Island, Wash. From June 1989, NAD Alameda, Calif., had rewinged 23 Intruders.

3 MAY • AW3 Carly R. Harris of VS-22 became the first aircrew-qualified female warfare systems operator in the S-3 Viking community.

20 MAY • *Theodore Roosevelt* (CVN 71) transited the Suez Canal and made for the Adriatic Sea to participate in Operation Deny Flight. The ship reached the Adriatic six days later.

1 JUNE • The Department of Defense unveiled the low-observable Tier III Minus unmanned aerial vehicle, known as DarkStar, designed for the reconnaissance of highly defended areas, in a ceremony at Lockheed's Skunk Works, Palmdale, Calif.

2 JUNE • A Serbian SA-6 surface-to-air missile shot down Capt. Scott F. O'Grady, USAF, of the 555th Fighter Squadron, in an F-16C Fighting Falcon over Banja Luka, Bosnia-Herzegovina. On 8 June, the allies established voice contact with O'Grady and orchestrated a search-and-rescue involving 40 NATO aircraft including VF-41 F-14A Tomcats and F/A-18C Hornets of VFA-15 and -87 and VMFA-312, embarked on board *Theodore Roosevelt* (CVN 71); two EA-6B Prowlers of VAQ-141 and -209 operating from Aviano AB, Italy; and four AV-8 Harrier IIs, two AH-1W Super Cobras, and two CH-53E Super Stallions of a tactical recovery of aircraft and personnel force from amphibious assault ship *Kearsarge* (LHD 3). Despite fire from Serbian antiaircraft guns and several surface-to-air missiles, the Super Stallions rescued O'Grady.

27 JUNE • Space shuttle *Atlantis*, on mission STS-71, launched from John F. Kennedy Space Center, Fla. Naval aviator Capt. Robert L. Gibson commanded *Atlantis* on this first shuttle mission to Russian orbital research station *Mir*, and the first joint docking mission between the Americans and Russians since the Apollo-Soyuz test project flight in 1975. Capt. Norman E. Thagard, USMC, on board *Mir*, returned on the shuttle when it landed at the space center on 7 July.

30 JUNE • Thirty-six-year-old *Independence* (CV 62), Capt. David P. Polatty III commanding, became the oldest ship in the active fleet. On 1 July, Polatty received the "Don't Tread on Me" Navy jack during a ceremony. The flag had been transferred from ammunition ship *Mauna Kea* (AE 22) after her decommissioning.

1 JULY • The Fifth Fleet was established at NSA Bahrain, Vice Adm. John S. Redd commanding.

14 JULY • An F-14D Tomcat of NAWC (AD) Patuxent River, Md., flew for the first time using a new digital flight control system designed to protect aviators against unrecoverable flat spins and carrier landing mishaps.

19 AUGUST • The winter fly-in to McMurdo Station, Antarctica, began when LC-130 Hercules of VXE-6 delivered supplies and support personnel. The teams were to construct an ice runway in preparation for the 1995–1996 season during the 40th year of Operation Deep Freeze.

Former President George H. W. Bush, a naval aviator during World War II, visits *George Washington* (CVN 73) during the 50th anniversary of V-J—Victory in Japan—Day, August 1995.

30 AUGUST • *Theodore Roosevelt* (CVN 71) launched the initial NATO strikes against the Serbs in Bosnia-Herzegovina that began Operation Deliberate Force—aerial attacks to reduce Serbian military capabilities to threaten safe areas, UN peacekeepers, and humanitarian aid workers. Targets included enemy field forces and heavy weapons, command and control facilities, direct and essential military support facilities, supporting infrastructure, and lines of communication in the southeast of the country. The strike consisted of two waves of four F-14A Tomcats of VF-41; 31 F/A-18C Hornets of VFA-15 and -87 and VMFA-312; and two EA-6Bs; supported by other Prowlers from Aviano AB Italy. During the second wave, the ship also launched an S-3B Viking of VS-24 and an ES-3A Shadow. Five echelons of allied strikes followed the naval aircraft with attacks on targets in and around Sarajevo. Through 4 September, aircraft flew 492 sorties from *Theodore Roosevelt*.

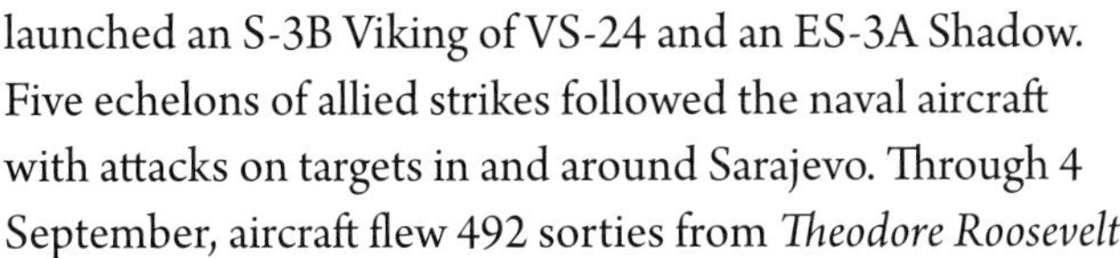

9 SEPTEMBER • *America* (CV 66) conducted strike and flight operations in the Adriatic Sea in support of Operation Deliberate Force. The ship continued her strikes through 30 September.

1 OCTOBER • VAW-77 was established at NAS Atlanta, Ga. The squadron worked in tandem with the Coast Guard and federal law enforcement agencies to combine and coordinate counter narcotics operations.

1 OCTOBER • The Naval Aviation Supply Office was disestablished at Philadelphia, Pa., and Naval Inventory Control Point, Philadelphia/Mechanicsburg, Pa., was established in its place. The new command took over both the functions of the supply office and the Ships Parts Control Center at Mechanicsburg, which also was disestablished.

12 NOVEMBER • Space shuttle *Atlantis*, on mission STS-74, launched from John F. Kennedy Space Center, Fla. Naval aviator Col. Kenneth D. Cameron, USMC, commanded this second shuttle flight to dock with Russian orbital research station *Mir*. *Atlantis* returned to the center on 20 November.

29 NOVEMBER • F/A-18E1, the first Super Hornet, made its first flight at Lambert International Airport near St. Louis, Mo.

11 DECEMBER • *America* (CV 66) arrived in the Adriatic Sea to begin Operation Joint Endeavor—a venture under NATO leadership to oversee the military aspects of the implementation of peace in Bosnia-Herzegovina. On 18 December, amphibious assault ship *Wasp* (LHD 1) rendezvoused with *America* and also began Joint Endeavor participation.

The first F/A-18E Super Hornet, designated E1, takes off on its maiden flight at St. Louis, Mo., 29 November 1995.

14 DECEMBER • The Bosnian Federation and the Bosnian Serbs signed the final Dayton Accords concerning Bosnia-Herzegovina, in Paris, France.

21 DECEMBER • NATO commemorated the end of Operation Deny Flight, the enforcement of a no-fly zone over Bosnia-Herzegovina, at Dal Molin Airport, Vincenza, Italy.

1996

4 JANUARY • Lt. Jean L. O'Brien of VP-16 became the first woman to earn the designation of patrol squadron tactical coordinator in a P-3C Orion.

7 JANUARY • An HH-60 Seahawk embarked on board *America* (CV 66), piloted by squadron commanding officer Cmdr. Robert L. Wilde, with copilot Lt. Craig M. Davis, and aircrewmen AW1 Rob Betts and AW3 Brett Shopsin of HS-11, transported Commander Sixth Fleet Vice Adm. Donald L. Pilling to *Admiral Kuznetsov* (Project 1143.5). HS-11 thus became the Navy's first squadron to land on board a Russian aircraft carrier.

10 JANUARY • The roll out of the first production F-14A/B to complete the major upgrade program to provide Tomcats with a multimission capability took place at NAD Norfolk, Va.

11 JANUARY • Space shuttle *Endeavour*, on mission STS-72, launched from John F. Kennedy Space Center, Fla. The crew included naval aviators Cmdr. Winston E. Scott and Lt. Cmdr. Brent W. Jett Jr. *Endeavour* returned to the center on 20 January.

18 JANUARY • Lts. Dane L. Dobbs and James F. Skarbek of VF-101 made the first F-14B Tomcat arrested landing on board *John C. Stennis* (CVN 74).

N1601-BS-10/95-004

Before commissioning, *John C. Stennis* (CVN 74) leaves the James River and heads to sea for builders trials off the Virginia Capes, 23 October 1995.

24 JANUARY • NAWC (WD) Point Mugu, Calif., conducted flight performance testing of the ADM-141C Improved TALD (tactical air launch decoy), which was designed to deceive enemy radar and interception aircraft in hostile environments.

5 FEBRUARY • The Carrier Airborne Early Warning Weapons School completed its move from NAS Miramar, Calif., to NAS Fallon, Nev., and began training a class for the E-2C Hawkeye community.

15 FEBRUARY • McDonnell Douglas delivered the first of seven F/A-18E/F Super Hornets to NAWC (AD) Patuxent River, Md., to begin a three-year flight test program to prepare the type for duty on aircraft carriers.

20 FEBRUARY • HSL-44 became the initial East Coast LAMPS Mk III squadron to fire an AGM-119B Penguin air-to-surface missile. Pilot Lt. Cmdr. John W. Funk, copilot Lt. Richard Davis, and aircrewmen AWC Todd Sitler and AW2 Matthew Polzin of Detachment 5 flew an SH-60B Seahawk, while embarked on board destroyer *Briscoe* (DD 977).

1 MARCH • VPU-1, which had been established on 1 July 1982, became a full command after 13 years as an independent detachment with an officer in charge. Cmdr. Walter Kreitler became the initial commanding officer when he relieved Lt. Cmdr. Jack Scorby.

21 MARCH • Cmdrs. Edward Baden and Edward Arcand, Lt. Cmdrs. Claude Nelson and Mike Lamb, Lt. Garry Vagt, AW1s Jack Peebles and Joe Taylor, AT1 Randy Osborne, AD1 Roger Pullman, AW2 Sam Rabideau, AO2 Ron Clarke, and AE2 Chris George of VP-69 manned a P-3C and assisted in the rescue of 17 people from fishing vessel *Toku*, disabled and adrift 450 nautical miles south of Guam. The Orion dropped supplies and directed merchant vessel *Microtrader* to pick up the victims and take *Toku* under tow.

E-2C Hawkeyes are the eyes of the fleet. The airborne early warning and command and control aircraft were first deployed in 1964.

29 MARCH • The Tier III Minus DarkStar high-altitude long-endurance unmanned aerial vehicle successfully completed its first flight at the USAF Test Flight Center, Edwards AFB, Calif.

29 MARCH • Cmdr. Nora Tyson became the first female naval flight officer to assume duties as executive officer of an operational squadron, VQ-4.

29 MARCH • Lt. Col. Marcelyn A. Adkins, USAF, became the first Air Force officer to serve as executive officer of VT-10, after the squadron's assumption of responsibility for basic navigation training for the Air Force, Navy, and Marine Corps.

4 APRIL • VF-2 began the F-14 homeport shifts resulting from the Defense Base Closure and Realignment Commission when it arrived from NAS Miramar, Calif., at NAS Oceana, Va. The consolidation of Tomcat squadrons was scheduled for completion by January 1997 with the additional transfer of VF-11, -31, -101, -211, and -213.

12 APRIL • McDonnell Douglas project test pilot Fred Madenwald completed the first supersonic F/A-18E Super Hornet flight tests at NAS Patuxent River, Md.

29 APRIL • VAW-123 became the initial East Coast squadron to deploy with E-2C Hawkeye Group 2 aircraft.

1 MAY • The first T-1A Jayhawks arrived at NAS Pensacola, Fla., for use in naval flight officer and Air Force navigator training conducted by VT-4 and -10. This heralded the first step in creating the Joint Navigator/Naval Flight Officer Training Program, which eventually trained all such applicants for the Air Force, Navy, and Marine Corps.

6 MAY • AE3 Michelle Rehak sailed with HSL-42 Detachment 7 on board destroyer *Hayler* (DD 997),

National Museum of Naval Aviation 1996.253.6851

An A-6E Intruder, BuNo 160423, from VA-34 assigned to CVW-7 launches an AGM-65 Maverick air-to-ground missile near Naval Air Station Fallon, Nev., in late 1993.

marking the first deployment of a female LAMPS aircraft maintenance technician on board a surface combatant.

14 MAY • The Navy selected Hughes Technical Services to assume operation of NAWCAD Indianapolis, Ind. Hughes began to control daily operations in 1997 during the first privatization of a naval facility.

20 MAY • Helicopters flew Marines of the 22d Marine Expeditionary Unit from amphibious assault ship *Guam* (LPH 9) to Bangui, Central African Republic, to evacuate Americans and to safeguard the U.S. Embassy during a crisis there.

30 MAY • The Navy approved the Cockpit 21 concept to replace analog displays in T-45A Goshawks with digital displays similar to those in carrier-based jets, in an effort to make training more effective for student aviators.

4 JUNE • Japanese destroyer *Yūgiri* (DD 153) inadvertently shot down Lt. Cmdr. William E. Royster and Lt. Keith A. Douglas in an A-6E, BuNo 155704, with her Phalanx Close-In Weapons System. The Intruder towed a gunnery target while operating from *Independence* (CV 62) during exercise RIMPAC '96. Royster and Douglas ejected and *Yūgiri* recovered both men.

6 JUNE • Helicopter Landing Trainer *IX-514* achieved her 50,000th landing since beginning operation in 1986. An MH-60G Pave Hawk of the Air Force 55th Special Operations Squadron landed on board while the vessel operated near NAS Pensacola, Fla.

7 JUNE • VMU-1, the first Marine unmanned aerial vehicle squadron, deployed to Bosnia-Herzegovina. The Marines provided real-time imagery for reconnaissance, surveillance, and target acquisition in support of Operation Joint Endeavor.

13 JUNE • Vice Adm. Donald D. Engen, a World War II naval aviator who had received the Navy Cross for his service during the Battle of Leyte Gulf, was named as the director of the Smithsonian's National Air and Space Museum in Washington, D.C.

14 JUNE • The F-14B LANTIRN (low altitude navigation/targeting infrared for night) system, which gave Tomcats the ability to drop laser-guided bombs, was introduced to the fleet at NAS Oceana, Va. LANTIRN-equipped F-14Bs first deployed operationally with VF-103 on board *Enterprise* (CVN 65) on 28 June 1996.

15 JUNE • The Navy's Flight Demonstration Squadron (Blue Angels) celebrated its 50th anniversary on the date of the squadron's first organized performance in 1946.

21 JUNE • Cmdr. David J. Cheslak relieved Lt. Col. Carl K. Hergesell, USAF, as commanding officer of the 562nd Flying Training Squadron, and became the first naval flight officer to command an Air Force squadron.

28 JUNE • A-6E Intruders deployed for the last time on a carrier, with VA-75 on board *Enterprise* (CVN 65).

30 JUNE • Capt. David S. McCampbell, the Navy's top-ranking ace in World War II credited with 34 aerial victories and a Medal of Honor recipient, died at the age of 86.

1 JULY • Under a joint program in which EA-6B Prowlers replaced General Dynamics EF-111A Ravens as the Air Force's primary electronic countermeasures aircraft, the initial Air Force Prowler crew, Lt. Col. Ronald Rivard, and Capts. David Shintaku and Richard Armstrong of VAQ-129, carrier qualified in an EA-6B on board *Constellation* (CV 64).

10 JULY • HMLA-167 and -169 at MCAS Cherry Point, N.C., conducted the first fleet firings of two types of weapons: BGM-71E TOW (tube-launched, optically tracked, wire-command-link) antitank and AGM-114K Hellfire II air-to-surface missiles.

11 JULY • NSAWC stood up at NAS Fallon, Nev., Rear Adm. Bernard J. Smith commanding. The center focused on tactics development and assessment, training for fleet-experienced aviators, joint operations, and training and standardization of training within aviation communities.

5 AUGUST • Naval aviator Adm. Jay L. Johnson, who had flown F-8 Crusaders during the Vietnam War, was sworn in by Secretary of the Navy John H. Dalton as the 26th Chief of Naval Operations.

16 AUGUST • NASA selected Cmdr. Wendy B. Lawrence, the first female naval aviator in space, to train for shuttle mission STS-86, which involved extended stays on board Russian orbital research station *Mir*.

16 AUGUST • 1st Lt. Jeanne Buchanan, USMC, became the first female naval flight officer in the Marine Corps.

3 SEPTEMBER • Operation Desert Strike began—retaliation against the 31 August dispatch by Saddam Hussein of 40,000 Iraqi Republican Guardsmen and regulars against Irbil, a Patriotic Union of Kurdistan town 48 miles east of Mosul. Desert Strike attacked Iraqi fixed surface-to-air missile sites and air defense command and control facilities in southern Iraq. Cruiser *Shiloh* (CG 67) and destroyer *Laboon* (DDG 58) fired 14 of 27 BGM-109 Tomahawk TLAMs (Tomahawk–Land Attack Missile) launched in the first wave. Four F-14D Tomcats of VF-11, embarked on board *Carl Vinson* (CVN 70), escorted two Air Force B-52H Stratofortresses that staged through Guam and launched 13 AGM-86C CALCMs (Conventional Air-Launched Cruise Missile). The next day, destroyers *Hewitt* (DD 966), *Laboon*, and *Russell* (DDG 59), and submarine *Jefferson City* (SSN 759) fired 17 more TLAMs. A P-3C Orion of VP-1 operated in the area forward deployed through NAF Diego Garcia, British Indian Ocean Territory. In addition, *Enterprise* (CVN 65) received notification of deployment to the north Arabian Sea a month ahead of schedule.

3 SEPTEMBER • *George Washington* (CVN 73) became the first carrier to undergo more frequent maintenance periods under the Planned Incremental Maintenance Availability program. This aimed to save money by performing maintenance on a regular basis, thus allowing carriers to return to the fleet after shorter but more intensive overhaul periods.

12 SEPTEMBER • *Enterprise* (CVN 65) received orders to support Operation Desert Strike—retributive attacks against

Crewmembers of *Constellation* (CV 64)—Go Navy—and *Kitty Hawk* (CV 63)—Beat Army—spell out their sentiments, 18 October 1995. Unfortunately, Army won 14–13.

Iraq for crimes against the Kurds. *Enterprise* sprinted from the Adriatic Sea and, on 19 September, arrived in the Red Sea.

12 SEPTEMBER • Lt. Todd White of NAWC (AD) Patuxent River, Md., piloted a P-3C at Point Mugu, Calif., during the first guided launch of an AGM-84E SLAM (Standoff Land Attack Missile) from an Orion.

13 SEPTEMBER • Cmdr. Ruth A. Forrest became the Navy's first female Aircraft Intermediate Maintenance Department officer on a carrier when she reported to *John F. Kennedy* (CV 67).

20 SEPTEMBER • The Senate Armed Services Committee modified the Tailhook reporting requirements for officers nominated for promotion. It continued the requirement of Tailhook certification for officers potentially implicated by a post-Tailhook investigation, but it did not require further certification for subsequent nominations. The revision did not address the issue of officers not on active duty as of September 1991, and also allowed the personnel subject to Tailhook certification—but not yet nominated—to review all information held by the Navy relating to their activities at Tailhook, allowing them to submit information on their behalf.

NOVEMBER • The Improved Fresnel Lens Optical Landing System completed shore-based technical evaluation at NAS Patuxent River, Md. The system was consequently installed on board *George Washington* (CVN 73).

9 DECEMBER • AH-1Ws of HMLA-269, deployed with the 26th Marine Expeditionary Unit, became the first Super Cobras to do so with a night targeting system that allowed the helicopters to operate in all battlefield conditions.

1997

During 1997, *Independence* (CV 62) received the first flight simulator installed on board a carrier. The Carrier-Based Weapons Systems Trainer, designed by Boeing, enabled F/A-18 Hornet pilots to perform training and operating procedures standardization checks, review emergency procedures, and simulate various types of flight operations with different weapons.

18 JANUARY • Lt. Francis D. Morley made the first F/A-18F arrested landing, in the first two-seat Super Hornet, designated F1, on board *John C. Stennis* (CVN 74) during the ship's sea trials.

28 FEBRUARY • 1st Lt. Kerri L. Schubert, USMC, completed her naval flight officer (NFO) training and became the first female Marine NFO chosen to fly an F/A-18D Hornet.

1 MARCH • The operational testing and evaluation of the Improved Fresnel Lens Optical Landing System began when an F/A-18 Hornet from NAWC (AD) Patuxent River, Md., trapped on board *George Washington* (CVN 73).

15 MARCH • The first V-22 Osprey built to production standards arrived for testing and evaluation at NAWC (AD) Patuxent River, Md.

18 MARCH • Lt. Carl P. Chebi of Naval Weapons Test Squadron, China Lake, in an F/A-18C Hornet, made the first test firing of an AGM-84H SLAM-ER (Standoff Land Attack Missile–Expanded Response).

10 APRIL • VF-213 arrived at NAS Oceana, Va. The move marked the final F-14 Tomcat squadron transfer from NAS Miramar, Calif., mandated by the Defense Base Closure and Realignment Commission.

11 APRIL • Capt. Jane S. O'Dea retired. O'Dea had been one of an initial group of six women who trained as naval aviators, receiving her wings in April 1974.

21 APRIL • Lts. Michael J. Angelopoulos, Timothy R. Worthy, and Jamie Marek, and AW2 Brent Hudson of VS-22, made the first S-3B Viking launch of an AGM-65F Maverick infrared air-to-surface missile.

29 MAY • During Operation Noble Obelisk, Marine CH-53E Super Stallions flying from amphibious assault ship *Kearsarge* (LHD 3) evacuated people from Sierra Leone, West Africa, because of instability generated by a coup in that country.

2 JUNE • The Navy and Air Force at Randolph AFB, Texas, unveiled the Joint Primary Aircraft Training System aircraft, the T-6A Texan II designed to replace Navy T-34C Turbomentors and Air Force T-37 Tweets.

8 JUNE • A Northrop Grumman crew flew an EA-6B Block 89A upgrade validation aircraft during its first flight. The Navy intended to upgrade all Prowlers to the Improved Capability II Block 89A configurations.

9 JUNE • NADEP Cherry Point, N.C., completed the first conversion of an F-4S Phantom II, BuNo 155524, to a QF-4S drone to provide fighter-sized targets for weapon system testing and evaluation. The depot also delivered to HMM-162 the first CH-46E Sea Knight, BuNo 157697, to undergo a full-scale airframe change.

18 JUNE • The Rotary Wing Aircraft Test Squadron at NAS Patuxent River, Md., assisted a Sea, Air and Land (SEAL) team in testing a cargo hook restraint system, which allowed SEALs to attach their assault raft to the bottom of an HH-60H Seahawk for faster deployment, instead of occupying space in the cabin area.

8 AUGUST • Capt. Rosemary B. Mariner, the last of the original group of female naval aviators, retired after 24

An older EA-6B Expanded Capability Prowler, BuNo 159586, leads a newer Improved Capability II version, BuNo 162934. Both are from VAQ-132, CVW-17, operating from NAS Whidbey Island, Wash., 1993.

years of service. Mariner's accomplishments included the first female naval aviator to fly tactical jet aircraft—A-4E Skyhawks and A-7E Corsair IIs—and to command an operational squadron, VAQ-34.

22 AUGUST • The Navy received the first of 17 T-39N Sabreliners as part of a $42.5 million acquisition for use in undergraduate naval flight officer training. The Navy owned the jets, but Boeing North American provided all the pilot services, maintenance, and ground support.

1 SEPTEMBER • *Nimitz* (CVN 68) completed a global circumnavigation when she shifted her homeport from Puget Sound Naval Shipyard, Bremerton, Wash., to Newport News, Va. The sail marked the first operational deployment of the AGM-154A JSOW (Joint Standoff Weapon).

11 DECEMBER • Researchers from the Science Applications International Corporation flew the manned version of the Vigilante, designed as an optionally piloted or unmanned aerial vehicle, under consideration to perform tactical reconnaissance from destroyers and cruisers.

15 DECEMBER • A T-45C Goshawk modernized with the Cockpit 21 system entered service with TraWing 1 at NAS Meridian, Miss.

The Navy's SH-60B Seahawk is a sea-adapted version of the Army's UH-60 Black Hawk. The first production versions flew in February 1983.

1998

18 JANUARY • Iraq's unwillingness to cooperate with UN weapons inspectors and other issues prompted Central Command to launch Operation Desert Thunder I—a large-scale deployment to the Middle East that included the planned continual availability of two aircraft carriers. On this date, *Nimitz* (CVN 68), *George Washington* (CVN 73), and British carrier *Invincible* (R 05) operated in the region along with a total of more than 50 additional allied ships and submarines, including amphibious assault ship *Guam* (LPH 9). A resurgence of tensions later in the year led to additional deployments as part of Operation Desert Thunder II.

19 JANUARY • Magnum 447, an SH-60B Seahawk manned by Lts. Paul A. Puopolo and Dabney R. Kern, and AW2 Ron Williams of HSL-44 Detachment 4, made the first fleet firing of an AGM-114 Hellfire air-to-surface missile.

3 FEBRUARY • Capts. Richard J. Ashby, USMC; Joseph P. Schweitzer, USMC; William J. Rancy II, USMC; and Chandler P. Seagraves, USMC; of VMAQ-2 from MCAS Cherry Point, N.C., severed the cable of a ski gondola near Cavalese, Italy, while on a low-level training mission in an EA-6B Prowler, BuNo. 163045. The accident killed all 20 people in the gondola. The crew was uninjured and the plane made an emergency landing at Aviano Air Base.

8 FEBRUARY • *Independence* (CV 62) relieved *Nimitz* (CVN 68) in the Persian Gulf during Operation Desert Thunder I—a large-scale deployment to the Middle East to pressure the Iraqis and bolster the UN's negotiating position.

20 FEBRUARY • The Navy ended 42 years of modern support of Antarctic research and Operation Deep Freeze with the disestablishment of Naval Support Unit Antarctica. The service transferred the mission to the 109th Mobility Air Wing, New York Air National Guard, but provided limited flight support to the program throughout the 1998–1999 research season.

20 FEBRUARY • Judge Robert Hodges Jr. of the U.S. Court of Federal Claims ruled concerning the Navy's decision to cancel the A-12A Avenger. Hodges ruled that the Navy was liable for $1.8 billion because the government, not the contractors, had canceled the program. The Navy appealed the decision.

3 MARCH • British carrier *Illustrious* (R 06) replaced *Invincible* (R 05) in the Persian Gulf while operating with *George Washington* (CVN 73) and *Independence* (CV 62) during Operation Desert Thunder I.

3 MARCH • Maj. Bill Wainwright, USMC, and Capt. William Witzig, USMC, made the first night flight of a V-22 while using night vision goggles during Osprey testing and evaluation at NAS Patuxent River, Md.

5 MARCH • NAWC (AD) Patuxent River, Md., coordinated the first test flight of a Teledyne Ryan Aeronautical RQ-4A Global Hawk unmanned aerial vehicle at Edwards AFB, Calif.

5 MARCH • Pilot Lt. Cmdr. Jeffrey M. Bocchicchio, copilot Lt. Jason A. Burns, and AW2 Ferninand Hollis of HSL-44 Detachment 1, in an SH-60B Seahawk operating from destroyer *Scott* (DDG 995) 110 miles east of Honduras, assisted in the capture of a 35-foot boat, four suspected narcotics smugglers, and 57 bales of cocaine weighing more than 3,000 pounds.

12 MARCH • *John C. Stennis* (CVN 74) relieved *George Washington* (CVN 73) in the Persian Gulf during Operation Desert Thunder I.

12 MARCH • The Aircraft Intermediate Maintenance Division rolled out the first of nine OPT II Pioneer Plus unmanned aerial vehicles at NAS Patuxent River, Md.

14 MARCH • Capt. Duncan H. Read (Naval Aviator No. 145), who had served during both world wars and was one of four naval aviator brothers, died at the age of 101.

25 MARCH • Two SH-60Bs of HSL-40 from NS Mayport, Fla., successfully rescued six utility workers stranded on a 670-foot-high burning smoke stack at the Palatka Seminole Electric Plant, Palatka, Fla. Lts. Andrew I. Krasny and Mark T. Murray, AW1 Andy Zawolik, and AW2 Heath Rominger in Airwolf 407, and Lts. Billy Carter and Dana R. Gordon, and AW2s Eric Kazmerchak and Scott West in Airwolf 403 made the rescue.

30 MARCH • The Chief of Naval Operations approved the redesignation of all VAQs from tactical electronic warfare squadrons to electronic attack squadrons. The action reflected a shift toward joint doctrine in the suppression of enemy air defenses, and in joint Navy/Air Force expeditionary squadrons.

3 APRIL • *George Washington* (CVN 73) returned from a six-month deployment to the Mediterranean and Persian Gulf and disembarked the 26 Marines of her security detachment, ending an era of a Marine Corps security presence on board carriers.

8 APRIL • Boeing delivered the first production AGM-84H SLAM-ER (Standoff Land Attack Missile–Expanded Response) to the Navy.

11 APRIL • The first flight of a Hawkeye 2000 occurred at Northrop Grumman, St. Augustine, Fla. The fifth generation of the E-2C airborne early warning command and control aircraft integrated improvements to the mission computer, advanced control indicator set workstations, satellite communications, and an advanced equipment cooling system.

18 MAY • The Navy announced the relocation of all East Coast F/A-18 Hornet squadrons from NAS Cecil Field, Fla. Nine fleet squadrons and the fleet readiness squadron subsequently shifted to NAS Oceana, Va., and two fleet squadrons relocated to MCAS Beaufort, S.C. The plans called for the squadrons to have completed their moves by October 1999.

19 MAY • A search team headed by Dr. Robert D. Ballard operating from deep submergence support ship *Laney Chouest* located *Yorktown* (CV 5), which had been sunk by the Japanese during the Battle of Midway on 7 June 1942, on the bottom of the Pacific Ocean at 16,650 feet.

26 MAY • Secretary of the Navy John H. Dalton approved the transfer of *Hornet* (CV 12) to the Aircraft Carrier *Hornet* Foundation. The organization restored the ship, and on 17 October 1998 opened the *Hornet* Memorial Museum to the public at former NAS Alameda, Calif.

2 JUNE • Deputy Assistant Secretary of the Navy (Installation and Facilities) Duncan Holaday signed a record of decision to move VAW-112, -113, -116, and -117 from MCAS Miramar to NAWS Point Mugu, Calif.

6 JUNE • Two C-130 Hercules from the 11th Marine Expeditionary Unit evacuated 172 Americans and third-country nationals from Asmara, Eritrea, to Amman, Jordan, because of a border dispute that led to fighting between the Eritreans and Ethiopians.

15 JUNE • The first production T-6A Texan II made its maiden flight at Raytheon, Wichita, Kans.

17 JUNE • An SH-60F Seahawk of HS-3 conducted air searches and provided aerial reconnaissance to assist firefighters battling fires near Jacksonville, Fla.

26 JUNE • World War II ace Maj. Gen. Marion E. Carl Jr., USMC, was shot and killed during a burglary at his home in Roseburg, Oreg.

29 JUNE • A Tier III Minus DarkStar high-altitude long-endurance unmanned aerial vehicle flew for the first time since the initial vehicle crashed on 22 April 1996. The mishap prompted the redesign of the landing gear and flight control software.

3 JULY • An MH-53E Sea Dragon of HC-4 from NAS Sigonella, Sicily, helped combat a series of wildfires by providing water to firefighters battling the blazes.

8 JULY • The Navy and Air Force accepted the AGM-154A JSOW (Joint Standoff Weapon) as ready for operational service at NAS JRB Fort Worth, Texas.

8 JULY • Lt. Cmdr. Thomas A. Kennedy, Lts. James B. Smelley and Mike Zaner, Lt. j.g. Thomas F. Foster Jr., AW1 Bill Trippett, and AW2 Brian Mowry of HSL-44 Detachment 5, in an SH-60B Seahawk embarked on board frigate *John L. Hall* (FFG 32), assisted in the recovery of more than 2,000 pounds of cocaine from two boats near Panama.

8 JULY • The Naval Air Warfare Center Training Systems Division accepted the UH-1N Iroquois weapon system trainer for training Marine pilots, at Orlando, Fla.

18 JULY • *Independence* (CV 62) turned over duties as the permanently forward-deployed aircraft carrier to *Kitty Hawk* (CV 63) while at NS Pearl Harbor, Hawaii.

20 JULY • The Navy inaugurated FlashJet, a less expensive and more environmentally friendly method to remove paint from T-45 Goshawks via pulsed light energy and dry ice pellets, at NAS Kingsville, Texas.

22 JULY • Rear Adm. Alan B. Shepard Jr. died at the age of 74 after a lengthy battle with leukemia. Shepard had been one of the original seven Mercury astronauts and, on 5 May 1961, became the first American in space during his flight on board *Freedom 7*. On 31 January 1971, Shepard returned to space on board *Apollo 14*, becoming the fifth man to walk on the moon.

7 AUGUST • Al-Qaeda terrorists detonated truck bombs at the U.S. Embassies at Nairobi, Kenya, and Dar es Salaam, Tanzania, killing at least 301 people including 12 Americans, and injuring an estimated 5,000 victims.

13 AUGUST • General Electric delivered the first two F414 production engines for the F/A-18E/F Super Hornet program.

This EP-3E Aries II, BuNo 149668, is a modified P-3A Orion, which was delivered on 31 July 1962. It was converted in 1970 and transferred to VQ-2 on 30 July 1971 and provided intelligence, surveillance, and reconnaissance until retired in 1995.

20 AUGUST • Operation Infinite Reach (Resolute Response) began—two simultaneous retaliatory raids in response to the twin al-Qaeda attacks on the embassies in East Africa on 7 August. Cruisers *Cowpens* (CG 63) and *Shiloh* (CG 67), destroyers *Elliot* (DD 967) and *Milius* (DDG 69), and submarine *Columbia* (SSN 771) of the *Abraham Lincoln* (CVN 72) Carrier Battle Group sailing in the north Arabian Sea fired 73 BGM-109 TLAMs (Tomahawk Land Attack Missiles) at the Zhawar Kili al-Badr terrorist training and support complex, 30 miles southwest of Khowst, Afghanistan. Destroyers *Briscoe* (DD 977) and *Hayler* (DD 997) steaming in the Red Sea launched six TLAMs against the al-Shifa pharmaceutical plant near Khartoum, Sudan. Intelligence analysts suspected the plant of having ties to terrorist leader Osama bin Laden and of manufacturing precursor chemicals for the deadly VX series of nerve gas. The Sudanese and critics claimed that the plant did not produce VX. Vessels involved in these battles included amphibious assault ship *Essex* (LHD 2), dock landing ship *Anchorage* (LSD 36), and amphibious transport dock *Duluth* (LPD 6), with the 15th Marine Expeditionary Unit embarked. Forward-deployed VQ-1 EP-3E Aries IIs and VP-9 P-3C Orions operated as part of Task Force 57. The attacks killed at least 11 terrorists. *Abraham Lincoln* evaluated the "pivotal" role of her command, control, communications, computers, and information suite in the two simultaneous operations on two separate continents, and in the dissemination of the initial battle damage assessment.

20 AUGUST • The reconfigurable flight controls of an F/A-18E/F Super Hornet were demonstrated at NAS Patuxent River, Md. The control system replaced the mechanical backup of earlier Hornets, greatly enhancing aircraft safety and the pilot's ability to recover control of the aircraft.

25 SEPTEMBER • E-6B Mercury Take Charge and Move Out aircraft operating from Tinker AFB, Okla., took over the flying command post mission from the Air Force following the retirement of the last EC-135 Looking Glass aircraft.

1 OCTOBER • VFA-122 at NAS Lemoore, Calif., was established as the first F/A-18E/F Super Hornet fleet readiness squadron.

19 OCTOBER • HSL-46 Detachment 9 participated in its first successful drug interdiction mission during a deployment on board cruiser *Ticonderoga* (CG 47). The detachment recovered about four metric tons of cocaine with a street value of $50 million.

20 OCTOBER • VXE-6 departed for its final tour of duty in Antarctica to provide aerial and logistical support for the Antarctic program.

1 NOVEMBER • P-3Cs began flying daily surveillance missions over Kosovo in support of NATO enforcement operations. The Orions' onboard surveillance equipment provided allied commanders with real-time video and radar images of the fighting on the ground.

2 DECEMBER • NAWS Point Mugu, Calif., was redesignated NAS Point Mugu.

3 DECEMBER • Lt. Cmdr. William C. Hamilton fired two AGM-88 HARMs (High-speed Anti-Radiation Missile) from F/A-18F, BuNo 165170, in the first full-system live-fire test of the Super Hornet program with forward-firing ordnance.

16 DECEMBER • The coalition launched Operation Desert Fox against the Iraqis.

1999

5 JANUARY • In a dogfight over Iraq, Navy and Air Force aircraft unsuccessfully fired six air-to-air missiles against Iraqi MiG-25 Foxbats that violated the no-fly zone.

14 JANUARY • An engineering and manufacturing development MV-22, designated Osprey No. 10, began initial sea trials on board amphibious assault ship *Saipan* (LHA 2) and dock landing ship *Tortuga* (LSD 46). The trials extended through 8 February.

25 JANUARY • F/A-18C Hornets of VFA-22 and -94, embarked on board *Carl Vinson* (CVN 70), made the first operational launch of the AGM-154A JSOW (Joint Standoff Weapon) in action against Iraqi military targets during Operation Southern Watch.

27 JANUARY • The United States promulgated new rules of engagement that allowed allied aircraft patrolling the no-fly zones to target a wider range of Iraqi air defense systems and supporting installations, in order to reduce their overall capabilities against the aerial patrols.

24 FEBRUARY • Three LC-130R Hercules of VXE-6 returned to NAS Point Mugu, Calif., after a four-month deployment to Antarctica during Operation Deep Freeze 1998 to 1999. This marked the end of VXE-6's support of the Antarctic program.

3 MARCH • The F/A-18F completed its second round of sea trials on board *Harry S. Truman* (CVN 75) during the ship's sea trials off the Virginia Capes through 14 March. Capt. Robert O. Wirt Jr.; Lt. Cmdrs. Timothy H. Baker, Robert L. Floyd, and Michael M. Wallace; Maj. Matt Shihadeh, USMC; and Lts. Alan D. Armstrong, Erik O. Etz, and Klas W. Ohman flew the first two dual-seat Super Hornets.

10 MARCH • VC-6 Detachment A completed a four-week RQ-2A Pioneer unmanned aerial vehicle deployment in support of the counternarcotics Operation Alliance to NAF El Centro, Calif. Over 32 sorties, the detachment used a forward-looking infrared-sensor equipped Pioneer to apprehend 438 suspected drug traffickers/illegal aliens, together with narcotics valued at $8.9 million.

18 MARCH • NADEP Jacksonville, Fla., completed the modification of 32 P-3C Orions designed to enhance the fleet's ability to seek out drug runners from standoff ranges. The Counter Drug Upgrade modifications included the replacement of the air search radar by the same APG-66 multimode radar used in many General Dynamics F-16 Fighting Falcons. The modification of the first Orion, BuNo 157311, had begun on 15 September 1995, and the final plane, BuNo 161014, completed the upgrade on this date.

USN 990412-N-CQ140-004

An F-14D Tomcat launches from the port catapult of *Theodore Roosevelt* (CVN 71) during Operation Allied Force, 12 April 1999.

24 MARCH • After diplomatic efforts to counter what Serbian President Slobodan Milosevic termed "cleansing" of ethnic Albanians from Kosovo collapsed, on this date, NATO began Operation Allied Force—an air campaign to reduce the ability of the Serbs to sustain their operations. Naval aviation contributed land-based EA-6B Prowlers and EP-3E Aries IIs and F/A-18D Hornets. Allied aircraft dropped Joint Direct Attack Munitions (JDAMs) operationally for the first time. Additional aircraft involved included five Antisurface Warfare Improvement Program–modified P-3C Orions of VP-5 equipped with synthetic aperture radar and AGM-84E SLAM (Standoff Land Attack Missiles), and RQ-1A Predator camera-carrying unmanned aerial vehicles.

24 MARCH • VS-31 bid farewell to the last aviation warfare systems operator–rated crewmen during their removal from S-3 Viking mission requirements and transfer to other aircraft.

26 MARCH • The Navy released plans to select 12 limited duty officers and chief warrant officers as naval flight officers (NFO). One new NFO was scheduled to be assigned to each patrol squadron, with periodic selection boards held to determine replacements as needed.

27 MARCH • A surface-to-air missile shot down an Air Force Lockheed F-117A Nighthawk on a night mission over Kosovo. VAQ-134 assisted with the rescue of the pilot, neutralizing Yugoslav air defenses by jamming and firing AGM-88 HARMs (High-speed Anti-Radiation Missile).

3 APRIL • *Theodore Roosevelt* (CVN 71) arrived in the Mediterranean to support Operation Allied Force. Aircraft flew a total of 4,270 sorties of all types from the carrier during the operation, and destroyed or damaged 447 tactical and 88 fixed military targets.

USN 990414-N-6240R-513

After a strike into Kosovo, an AV-8B Harrier II of HMM-266 returns to amphibious assault ship *Nassau* (LHA 4), 14 April 1999.

11 APRIL • MH-53E Sea Dragons and H-46 Sea Knights of HM-14 and -15, embarked on board mine countermeasures ship *Inchon* (MCS 12), delivered 6,000-pounds of relief supplies to refugees in Kukes, Albania. These flights began the Navy's contribution to NATO Operation Shining Hope—humanitarian assistance to people displaced by the fighting in Kosovo.

13 APRIL • Lts. Christopher D. Marrs, Michael W. Reinmuth, and Douglas W. Carpenter, and Lt. j.g. Dirk J. Hart of VS-31, successfully guided an AGM-84 SLAM (Standoff Land Attack Missile) from an S-3B Viking for the first time. Lt. Kevin Healey of VFA-131 piloted the F/A-18 Hornet that launched the missile at San Nicolas Island, Calif.

1 MAY • Five P-3C Orions of VP-40 operating out of Kadena, Okinawa, rescued 18 survivors from a Filipino ship that broke apart during Tropical Storm Leo in the South China Sea.

12 MAY • "The Today Show" made the first live television broadcast from an aircraft carrier underway on board *Theodore Roosevelt* (CVN 71) in the Mediterranean.

27 MAY • F/A-18E/F Super Hornets entered their six-month operational evaluation with VX-9 at NAWS China Lake, Calif.

27 MAY • Aircraft No. 11, the first of 360 low-rate initial production MV-22 Ospreys planned for the Marine Corps, arrived at the MV-22 Multi-Service Operational Test Team, MCAF Quantico, Va.

1 JUNE • A ceremony celebrated the ground breaking for a $2.1 million hangar to house VC-6 Detachment A at Webster Field Annex, NAS Patuxent River, Md. This was the Navy's first RQ-2A Pioneer unmanned aerial vehicle hangar.

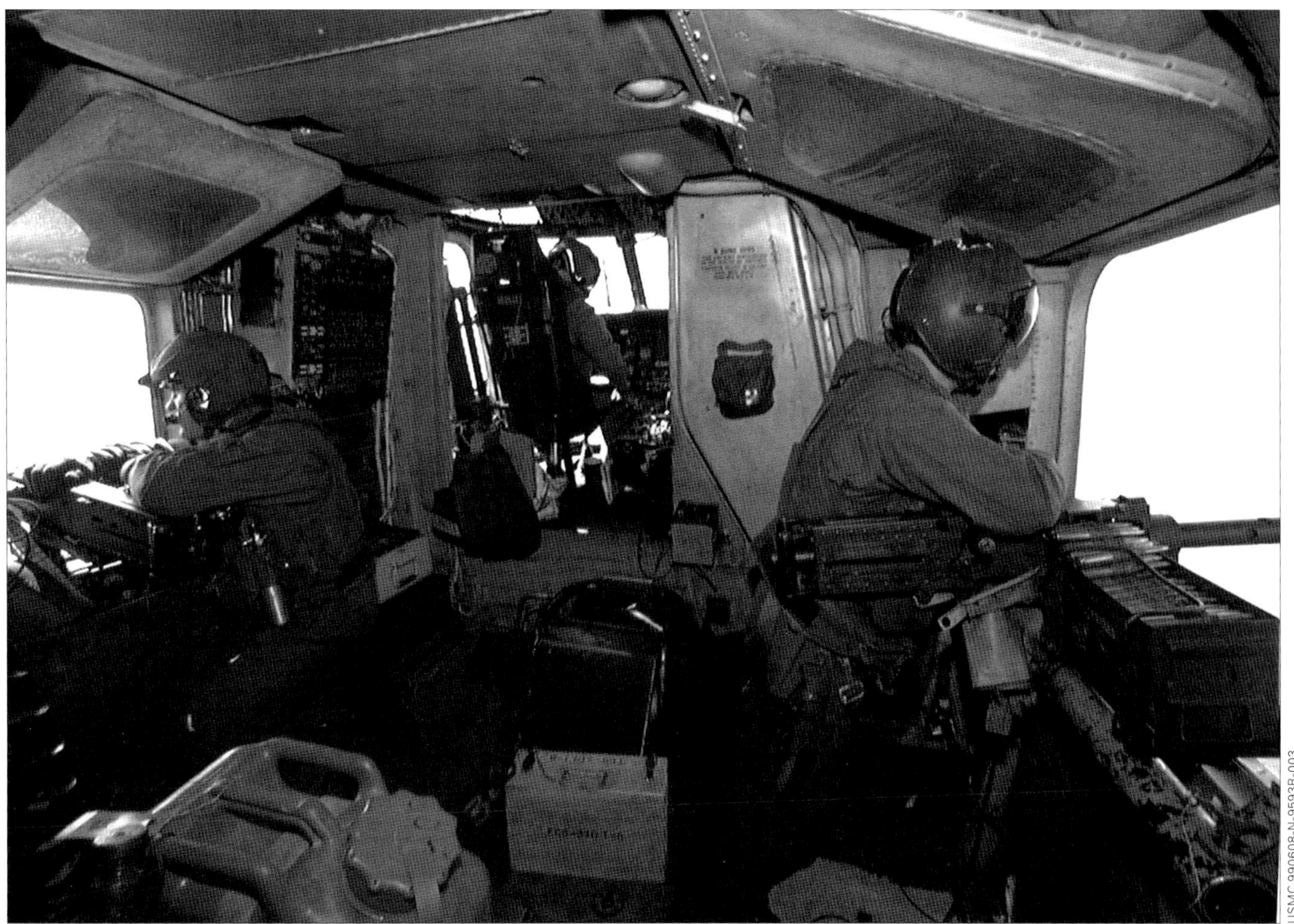

USMC 990608-N-9593R-003

Marine Sgts. Todd Abbott and Andrew McInally man their .50-caliber machine guns on board a CH-53D Sea Stallion while transporting Marines of the 26th Marine Expeditionary Unit to Skopje, Macedonia, 8 June 1999.

30 JUNE • An F/A-18D made the first guided launch of an AIM-9X air-to-air missile from a Hornet at NAWS China Lake, Calif. The Sidewinder successfully intercepted a QF-4 drone.

5 AUGUST • The first fully upgraded SH-60R Seahawk rolled out at Lockheed Martin, Owego, N.Y. The Navy planned a total of 250 SH-60Rs for upgrades through 2012.

10 AUGUST • The Navy retired the last two ES-3A Shadows during the deactivation of VQ-6 at NAS Jacksonville, Fla. The retrofitting of 16 Shadows from S-3B Vikings had provided battle group commanders with state-of-the-art organic reconnaissance, but the upgrade cost proved prohibitive. Shore-based EA-6B Prowlers and EP-3E Aries IIs subsequently performed the specialized tasking.

11 AUGUST • Secretary of the Navy Richard J. Danzig announced the assignment of a team to observe the 1999 Tailhook convention to evaluate the possibility of reestablishing the Navy's connection with the organization.

19 AUGUST • Amphibious assault ship *Kearsarge* (LHD 3) crossed the Mediterranean to Turkey in response to a 17 August 7.4-magnitude earthquake that devastated the region, killing more than 24,000 people. On 23 August, helicopters from *Kearsarge* began to ferry aid to the victims, and on 12 September the ship left the area.

2 SEPTEMBER • In the Caribbean, a P-3C Orion of VP-26 assisted Coast Guardsmen with the seizure of a vessel smuggling 2,000-pounds of cocaine.

15 SEPTEMBER • Hurricane Floyd forced the evacuation of 80 Navy ships and dozens of aircraft from between Mayport, Fla., and Norfolk, Va. Two HH-60H Seahawks of HS-11 rescued eight crewmembers when heavy seas swamped tugboat *Gulf Majesty* and her tow, a container barge, 300 miles off Florida. In another incident, HS-11 rescued another mariner.

1 OCTOBER • NavAdmin 271/99 established career enlisted flyer incentive pay, and also increased the selective reenlistment bonus. Simultaneously, the service offered aviation continuation pay program for Fiscal Year 1999 to pilots who had reached or surpassed their minimum service requirement.

7 OCTOBER • As tensions caused by rival independence movements in East Timor erupted into warfare, the UN launched Operation Stabilise—a multinational peacekeeping effort. On this date, amphibious assault ship *Belleau Wood* (LHA 3) arrived in the area to participate. On 26 October, amphibious assault ship *Peleliu* (LHA 5) relieved *Belleau Wood*, and on 26 November *Peleliu* left the region.

31 OCTOBER • Egypt Air Flight 900, a Boeing 767-300ER, crashed 60 miles east of Nantucket Island, Mass., killing all 217 on board. Navy commands that assisted in the search for victims and wreckage included three MH-53E Sea Dragons operating from amphibious transport dock *Austin* (LPD 4).

17 NOVEMBER • The first seven training and evaluation F/A-18E/Fs arrived at Super Hornet fleet readiness squadron VFA-122, NAS Lemoore, Calif. A total of 92 aircraft were scheduled for delivery to the squadron's parent strike fighter wing by 2004.

22 NOVEMBER • The Navy and Coast Guard participated in the first successful shipboard landing of a CL-327 Guardian vertical takeoff and landing unmanned aerial vehicle (UAV) on board Coast Guard Cutter *Thetis* (WMEC 910) off Key West, Fla. Sailors simultaneously tested the UAV common automatic recovery system for fleet compatibility.

24 NOVEMBER • Lt. Cmdr. Gregory C. Huffman piloted the first ATFLIR (advanced targeting forward looking infrared)-equipped F/A-18D Hornet at NAWS China Lake, Calif. The system featured improved target acquisition at greater standoff ranges.

3 DECEMBER • Local opposition drove the Puerto Rican government to ask the Navy to abandon its live-fire exercises on Vieques Island. The government rejected the Navy's proposal to end the exercises in five years, which undermined fleet readiness and compelled *Dwight D. Eisenhower* (CVN 69) and amphibious assault ship *Wasp* (LHD 1) to disrupt their training schedules.

17 DECEMBER • Civilians from Seaward Services, Inc., replaced the Navy crew of helicopter landing trainer *IX-514* at NAS Pensacola, Fla.

Chapter 13

Dawn of the Twenty-first Century

2000–2010

Naval aviation entered the third millennium responding to crises around the world while developing the weapons to project American power. Sailors and Marines deployed to challenge dictators who sought weapons of mass destruction, rescued victims of natural disasters, and turned up the heat in the war on drugs. On 11 September 2001, terrorists owing allegiance to al-Qaeda attacked the United States aided and abetted by the Islamic fundamentalist Taliban who ruled most of Afghanistan. The refusal of the Taliban to extradite them left the United States no alternative but to demonstrate globally that harboring terrorists carried a steep price. During the months after the attacks on 9/11, the Americans and their allies overcame fierce opposition and appalling weather and terrain and liberated the country, and then protected the Afghan people during the reconstruction after decades of war.

The coalition also met repeated Iraqi violations of cease-fire accords and presumed attempts to develop weapons of mass destruction with continued vigilance. Years of embargoes and bombardment to deprive Hussein of weapons of mass destruction had disrupted the illicit program, and the transition to a stable government collapsed from an insurgency fueled by internecine religious and tribal strife. Al-Qaeda terrorists and Muslim militants infiltrated the void produced by the ensuing chaos. In 2003, these clashes culminated in the liberation of Iraq from the tyranny of Saddam Hussein and his Ba'ath supporters. Sailors and Marines provided air support and spearheaded ground assaults. Naval aviation carried out missions over dynamic and fluid battlefields in Afghanistan and Iraq. Aircrew supported rapidly developing operations when the need for time-sensitive strikes led to the reception of target assignments while already airborne.

The fleet tackled global security missions with aerial surveillance and sea control sorties to ensure the uninterrupted flow of oil, provided intelligence and situational awareness to theater commanders, participated in maritime interceptions, evacuated casualties from battlefields and the high seas, and hunted for drug smugglers to reduce the flow of contraband onto America's streets. Space shuttle missions launched with predominately Navy crews, and the Coast Guard celebrated its 217th birthday by announcing its rescue of more than a million lives since its inception.

Naval aviation organizational and operational methods evolved to reflect changing missions. The redesignation and restructuring of carrier battle groups as carrier strike groups occurred, and the groups fell under numbered fleet commanders for operational and administrative control. Under the "six-plus-two" concept of the Fleet Response Plan of the Sea Power 21 strategy, the Navy projected power by deploying six such groups in less than 30 days for contingency operations, with two more groups to follow within three months for rotation or reinforcement. New ships wore the names of pioneers of naval aviation and U.S. history including carriers *Ronald Reagan* (CVN 76), *George H. W. Bush* (CVN 77), and *Gerald R. Ford* (CVN 78), destroyer *Stockdale* (DDG 106), and auxiliary dry cargo ships *Wally Schirra* (T-AKE 8) and *Washington Chambers* (T-AKE 11).

Additional fighter squadrons became strike-fighter squadrons during the transition from F-14 Tomcats to F/A-18 Hornets and Super Hornets. Sea control squadrons dropped from the roster as submarine hunting missions shifted to helicopters, and wings and squadrons underwent reorganization to reflect the transition from five helicopter models to two. Aircraft that took flight or hurtled through testing toward introduction included the F/A-18E/F Super Hornet, F-35A/B/C Lightning II, EA-18G Growler, E-2D Advanced Hawkeye, P-8A Poseidon, C-40A Clipper, KC-130J Super Hercules, MV-22 Osprey, MH-60R/S Seahawk, AH-1Z Viper, UH-1Y Venom, and VH-71A presidential helicopter.

Naval aviation also integrated unmanned aerial systems such as RQ-4A/B Global Hawks, RQ-8A Fire Scouts, and ScanEagles into operations and added deadly weapons including the AIM-9X Sidewinder short-range air-to-air missile, AGM-84K SLAM-ER (Standoff Land Attack Missile–Expanded Response), JASSM (Joint Air-to-Surface Standoff Missile), JDAM (Joint Direct Attack Munition), and Laser-JDAM. The speed and lethality of naval aviation proved crucial to the defense of the free world.

2000

10 JANUARY • Marines from the 2d Reconnaissance Battalion of the II Marine Expeditionary Force became the first to deploy from an MV-22B Osprey in a parachute free fall from 10,000 feet at Fort A. P. Hill, Va.

19 JANUARY • The Navy announced the restoration of ties to the Tailhook Association after a lengthy review that included a visit by a team led by Secretary of the Navy Richard J. Danzig to the organization's August 1999 convention in Reno, Nev. The Navy had suspended the relationship on 29 October 1991.

26 JANUARY • Cruiser *Lake Erie* (CG 70) fired a Standard SM-3 surface-to-air missile that completed an Aegis Light Exo-Atmospheric Projectile intercept at the Pacific Missile Range Facility at Kauai, Hawaii.

27 JANUARY • The first production CH-60S Seahawk made its initial flight at Sikorsky Aircraft Corp. Stratford, Conn. Sikorsky and Lockheed Martin of Owego, N.Y., had signed a $3 billion contract to provide 237 CH-60Ss through 2007, with ten of the aircraft listed for delivery in 2000. The helicopters were an amalgam of Army Black Hawks and Navy Seahawks to replace CH-46 Sea Knights in the cargo utility role, MH-53 Sea Dragons in antimine warfare, and HH-60s in combat search and rescue. Navy scheduling directed fleet helicopter readiness squadron HC-3 to introduce the aircraft to the fleet at NAS North Island, Calif.

28 JANUARY • HSL-46 Detachment 10 completed a counternarcotics deployment on board frigate *Robert G. Bradley* (FFG 49) in the Caribbean and eastern Pacific with their return to NS Mayport, Fla. From the beginning of its cruise on 24 August 1999, the detachment proved instrumental in the interdiction and seizure of 204 kilos of cocaine and more than a ton of marijuana, as well as search and rescue and medical evacuation missions.

31 JANUARY • A McDonnell Douglas MD-83 airliner, Alaska Airlines Flight 261, crashed into the Pacific north of Anacapa Island, Calif., killing all 88 people on board. An NP-3D Orion from NAWC Point Mugu, Calif., two HH-60H Seahawks from HCS-5 from NAWS Point Mugu, and Coast Guard helicopters and an HC-130H Hercules responded. *Abraham Lincoln* (CVN 72) supported rescue crews, and Navy mapping with underwater side scanning sonar and video enabled the searchers to recover pieces of wreckage. Reinforcements included amphibious transport dock *Cleveland* (LPD 7), destroyer *Fife* (DD 991), and frigate *Jarrett* (FFG 33), with HH-60 and SH-60 Seahawks embarked, and an S-3B Viking from NAS North Island, Calif.

31 JANUARY • After three years of studies, the Navy announced the revision of carrier homeports on the West Coast. In early 2002, *Nimitz* (CVN 68) was to join *John C. Stennis* (CVN 74)—already stationed there—followed in 2005 by *Ronald Reagan* (CVN 76) at NAS North Island, Calif. The announcement stipulated that *Abraham Lincoln* (CVN 72) remain at Bremerton, Wash. The need to replace *Constellation* (CV 64) after her retirement in 2003, and forward-deployed *Kitty Hawk* (CV 63) in Japanese waters in 2008, prompted the moves.

7 FEBRUARY • The Pentagon released a report that characterized the 78 days of bombing of Operation Allied Force as an effective air campaign that helped end Serbian atrocities in Kosovo.

USN 010912-N-1407C-001

Smoke rises from the stricken remains of the World Trade Center as *George Washington* (CVN 73) arrives to defend New York the day following the terrorist attacks of 11 September 2001.

8 FEBRUARY • The Military Sealift Command (MSC) announced a $31.2 million contract with Geo-Seis Helicopters, Inc. of Fort Collins, Colo., for two SA-330J Pumas to replace Navy helicopters normally assigned to MSC combat store ships for vertical replenishment and ship-to-shore services. Plans called for the rotation of the Pumas among three such ships during deployments to the Mediterranean. On this date, a Puma performed its first replenishment with combat store ship *Sirius* (T-AFS 8) off the Italian coast.

10 FEBRUARY • The Secretary of the Navy approved the merger of the AK (aviation storekeeper) and SK (storekeeper) ratings during ongoing efforts to balance sea-shore rotation, with a completion date of 1 January 2003.

15 FEBRUARY • The operational evaluation of F/A-18E/Fs concluded and the Super Hornet was recommended for introduction into the fleet. During six months of tests, VX-9 completed 1,233 flight hours in more than 850 sorties, and dropped more than 400,000-pounds of ordnance at NAWC China Lake, Calif.

1 MARCH • Secretary of Defense William S. Cohen approved the merger of the AMS (aviation structural mechanic structures) and AMH (aviation structural mechanic hydraulic mechanic) ratings. Conversion to the AM (aviation structural mechanic) rating became automatic and sailors retained the insignia.

13 MARCH • The Navy celebrated the opening of the first permanent hangar designed and built specifically for unmanned aerial vehicles at the Webster Field annex, NAS Patuxent River, Md. The $2.4 million project proved crucial to VC-6 Detachment A because the sailors had hitherto operated and maintained RQ-2A Pioneers at the mercy of the elements.

16 MARCH • Commander Operational Test and Evaluation Force issued a final report that declared the operational suitability and effectiveness of the AGM-84K SLAM-ER (Standoff Land Attack Missile–Expanded Response).

18 MARCH • Twenty-two F/A-18C Hornets of VFA-82 and -86 were reassigned to MCAS Beaufort, S.C., in preparation for the disestablishment of NAS Cecil Field, Fla.

20 MARCH • "The Spirit of Space" exhibit dedicated to Rear Adm. Alan B. Shepard Jr. was unveiled at the National Museum of Naval Aviation, NAS Pensacola, Fla. The centerpiece of the exhibit is a bronze statue of the astronaut sculpted by Capt. Robert Rasmussen.

24 MARCH • The Department of Defense issued the Laser Master Plan, which included a statement concerning the potential of laser technology to undermine U.S. air power by targeting aircrew vision with ground-based lasers.

27 MARCH • Cmdr. Ronald E. Weisbrook and Lt. Cmdr. Daryl J. Martis of the Naval Strike Aircraft Test Squadron made the first release of a GBU-31 (v) 2/B JDAM (Joint Direct Attack Munition) from an F-14D Tomcat during testing at NAS Patuxent River, Md.

28 MARCH • An Omega Air Boeing 707-321B arrived to begin conversion into the first modern commercial aerial refueling tanker for the fleet at NAS Patuxent River, Md.

31 MARCH • Lt. Cmdr. Terry S. Barrett of the Naval Weapons Test Squadron completed the fourth guided launch of an AIM-9X short-range air-to-air missile from an F/A-18C Hornet at NAWC China Lake, Calif. The Sidewinder intercepted a QF-4 Phantom II target during the first evaluation in a dogfight scenario involving defensive infrared countermeasure flares, and the first using the joint helmet-mounted cueing system.

4 APRIL • The Navy approved the name Clipper for C-40A transports converted from Boeing 737-700Cs. The Clipper was intended to replace the C-9 Skytrain, with six of the aircraft earmarked for reservists by 2001—four at Fort Worth, Texas, and two at NAS Jacksonville, Fla. The aircraft carried up to 121 passengers, eight pallets, or a combination thereof. The Navy later added a seventh Clipper.

6 APRIL • F/A-18C Hornets flying from *John C. Stennis* (CVN 74) struck Iraqi air defense targets in the southern no-fly zone in response to antiaircraft fire.

14 APRIL • A C-40A Clipper made its initial flight at Renton Municipal Airport, Wash.

26 APRIL • The Navy announced the development of an advanced neural network technique to increase the detail in satellite images. The technique used the human eye as a model to reveal the composition of information contained in a pixel, and was under consideration for F/A-18 Hornets to assist pilots in passive surveillance.

28 APRIL • The program to upgrade F/A-18A Hornets to F/A-18C capabilities began with the arrival of the first F/A-18A from VFA-203 at Atlanta, Ga., to Naval Weapons Test Squadron, NAWC China Lake, Calif.

11 MAY • The first of two proof-of-concept SH-60Rs—a remanufacture of SH-60B/Fs and HH-60Hs with modified airframes and avionics—arrived for developmental and contractor testing at NAS Patuxent River, Md. Plans called for 243 Seahawk antisubmarine warfare and ship surveillance and targeting conversions from 2000 to 2010.

12 MAY • The Naval Museum of Armament and Technology was established at NAWC China Lake, Calif.

15 MAY • The first production CH-60S arrived to begin developmental testing at NAS Patuxent River, Md.

17 MAY • Lt. Cmdr. Kevin Mannix of VFA-25 became the first pilot to fly and perform carrier qualifications following corrective laser eye surgery, when he landed an F/A-18C Hornet on board *Abraham Lincoln* (CVN 72).

25 MAY • Pilot Lt. Cmdr. John M. Hunt, copilot Lt. j.g. Jeremy P. Niles, and aircrewman AW3 Paul Amado of HSL-49 Detachment 2, manned an SH-60 Seahawk embarked on board cruiser *Valley Forge* (CG 50) during a counternarcotics operation in the eastern Pacific and helped to rescue 12 castaways adrift in their vessel.

1 JUNE • The Navy announced the introduction of a six-ounce passive and continuous emergency distress signaling pocket rescue unit designated SEE/RESCUE that did not require batteries, chemicals, or electronics. During testing, search and rescue teams visually identified the device from an altitude of up to 3,000 feet and more than a mile away.

16 JUNE • Images from an Advanced Tactical Airborne Reconnaissance System (ATARS)–equipped F/A-18D Hornet were data-linked to the Marine Corps Tactical Exploitation Group during evaluations at NAWC China Lake, Calif.

29 JUNE • Naval Force Aircraft Test Squadron began testing an eight-bladed propeller for E-2C Hawkeyes and C-2A Greyhounds at NAS Patuxent River, Md.

29 JUNE • The Navy announced that the AGM-84K SLAM-ER (Standoff Land Attack Missile–Expanded Response) was available for duty with the fleet.

5 JULY • The Chief of Naval Operations (CNO) established the office of Assistant CNO for Missile Defense on his immediate staff with the responsibility for theater ballistic and cruise missile defense.

12 JULY • The Navy announced the increase of the 2000 Aviation Career Continuation Pay program to improve retention. This gave naval aviators potential earnings of up to $245,000 in bonuses through 25 years of aviation service.

16 JULY • F/A-18Fs made their worldwide debut when two of the Super Hornets from VFA-122 flew nonstop from NAS Patuxent River, Md., to the international air show at Farnborough, England.

24 JULY • The P-3C Block Modernization Upgrade Program Development Test Integration Facility opened at NAS Patuxent River, Md.

26 JULY • Amphibious assault ships *Belleau Wood* (LHA 3) and *Essex* (LHD 2) swapped commands in Sasebo, Japan. This enabled crewmembers of forward-deployed ships to switch ships rather than impacting families by moving them to new homeports. The move marked the largest swap to date and required six weeks to complete.

21 AUGUST • NAS Fallon, Nev., commanding officer Capt. David A. Rogers replaced (retired) Capt. Lonny McClung as president of the Tailhook Association. Rogers was the first active duty president of the association since 1991 and initiated the restoration of the association's ties with active duty naval aviators.

23 AUGUST • Two SH-60F Seahawks from HS-15, embarked on board *George Washington* (CVN 73), directed rescuers to the scene of the crash of Gulf Air Flight 072, an Airbus A320, in the Persian Gulf. All 143 passengers and crew died in the crash.

24 AUGUST • The initial test flight of an Improved Tactical Air Launched Decoy took place at NAWC China Lake, Calif. Israeli Military Industries developed the decoy designed to more accurately imitate manned aircraft.

25 AUGUST • The final F/A-18D Hornet rolled off the production line. It was delivered to VMFA(AW)-121 at MCAS Miramar, Calif.

9 SEPTEMBER • The introduction of the C-40A Clipper to Naval Reservists occurred at Boeing Field, Seattle, Wash.

14 SEPTEMBER • Lt. Robert L. Dinunzio of VP-45 piloted a P-3C Orion that directed destroyer *Briscoe* (DD 977) to the rescue of 12 Moroccan castaways adrift in the Mediterranean Sea.

27 SEPTEMBER • The testing of the cooperative engagement capability (CEC) system against drone-simulated threats concluded off Wallops Island, Va. Commands that participated included *Dwight D. Eisenhower* (CVN 69) and amphibious assault ship *Wasp* (LHD 1). The Navy intended the system, designed to defend the fleet at greater ranges against advanced threats such as cruise missiles, to enable the development of a single integrated air picture. Plans included an initial operational capability for 2004 and the eventual allocation of about 160 systems.

1 OCTOBER • Under a realignment in the office of the Chief of Naval Operations, the Director, Air Warfare Division (N88) was redesignated N78.

12 OCTOBER • Two al-Qaeda terrorists in an inflatable Zodiac-type speedboat detonated a bomb alongside destroyer *Cole* (DDG 67) while the ship refueled in Aden, Yemen, killing 17 sailors and wounding 42 others. Damage control efforts saved *Cole*. Vessels that responded included amphibious assault ship *Tarawa* (LHA 1), dock landing ship *Anchorage* (LSD 36), amphibious transport dock *Duluth* (LPD 6), destroyer *Donald Cook* (DDG 75), frigate *Hawes* (FFG 53), and tug *Catawba* (T-ATF 168), along with British frigates *Cumberland* (F 85) and *Marlborough* (F 233).

13 OCTOBER • The Navy declared the MV-22B operationally effective and fit for land-based operations. Plans included additional testing of the Osprey's blade-fold wing stow system to measure its shipboard suitability.

30 OCTOBER • Harry S. Gann died at the age of 75. Gann joined Douglas Aircraft in 1954 and helped design aircraft control systems for the A-3 Skywarrior, A-4 Skyhawk, and F4D-1 Skyray. A founder of the American Aviation Historical Society, he retired in 1992. His awards include the designation of Honorary Marine Aviator in 1975, Honorary Blue Angel in 1979, and Honorary Naval Aviator No. 24 in 1997.

8 NOVEMBER • Capt. John B. Hollyer and Lt. Kevin M. Quarderer completed the first flight of a T-34C Turbomentor with the addition of wing pylons for external stores at NAS Patuxent River, Md.

8 NOVEMBER • The MV-22B was declared suitable for shipboard operations. The announcement followed a successful demonstration on 31 October of the aircraft's blade-fold wing stow system during sea trials on board amphibious assault ship *Bataan* (LHD 5).

17 NOVEMBER • A CH-60S Seahawk at Sikorsky Aircraft Corp. Stratford, Conn., received an experimental coat of three-shade matt Haze Gray paint specifically designed to reduce air pollution through the elimination of volatile organic compounds. The project was considered for possible Navy-wide adoption.

7 DECEMBER • An AH-1Z Viper flew for the first time at Bell Helicopter Textron, Arlington, Texas.

7 DECEMBER • Cmdr. Jeffrey R. Penfield piloted the first fleet F/A-18E Super Hornet, BuNo 165781, to VFA-115 at NAS Lemoore, Calif.

20 DECEMBER • Amphibious assault ship *Nassau* (LHA 4) rescued 29 people adrift in a boat in the Mediterranean Sea.

29 DECEMBER • *Abraham Lincoln* (CVN 72) launched the final flights of her deployment supporting Operation Southern Watch over Iraq, and then turned for Australian waters.

30 DECEMBER • An SH-60B Seahawk from HSL-42 Detachment 8, embarked on board cruiser *San Jacinto* (CG 56), participated in the rescue of 11 Yemenis adrift in a boat 60 miles off the coast of Yemen.

2001

1 JANUARY • Aircraft operating from *Harry S. Truman* (CVN 75) during her maiden deployment struck an Iraqi radar system with precision-guided munitions during Operation Southern Watch.

11 JANUARY • The Navy changed the status of Lt. Cmdr. Michael S. Speicher of VFA-81 from killed in action/body not recovered to missing in action. Speicher had been shot down over Iraq on 17 January 1991.

20 JANUARY • Naval aviator Donald H. Rumsfeld was sworn in as the 21st Secretary of Defense.

25 JANUARY • Flight tests concluded on the AQS-22 dipping sonar for the SH-60R Seahawk.

5 FEBRUARY • During a maritime interception operation surge in the Persian Gulf to enforce Iraqi compliance with UN sanctions, an HS-7 Seahawk operating from *Harry S. Truman* (CVN 75) proved instrumental in halting the smuggling of 2,300 metric tons of Iraqi oil worth $460,000 by vessels *Al Salam* and *Mustafa*. The surge concluded on 11 February.

6 FEBRUARY • NAVAIR redesignated the CH-60S Seahawk as MH-60S to reflect the diverse primary missions of armed helicopter, organic airborne mine countermeasures, and vertical replenishment.

15 FEBRUARY • After an earthquake that devastated Mumbai, India, cruiser *Cowpens* (CG 63), with HSL-51 Detachment 2 embarked, delivered more than $80,000 worth of disaster relief supplies to victims in the area.

16 FEBRUARY • Since Operation Desert Fox in 1998, the Iraqis had launched more than 60 surface-to-air missiles and fired antiaircraft guns more than 1,000 times at coalition aircraft. Initially, Iraqi gunners learned to briefly radiate their radars, then shut down and run to escape allied AGM-88 HARMs (High-speed Anti-Radiation Missiles). Iraqi dictator Saddam Hussein later linked the air defense network with fiber optic cabling so that radars from around Baghdad—outside the no-fly zones—could radiate and send targeting data to remote antiaircraft sites.

The Americans and British, therefore, attacked military targets with the largest strikes since Desert Fox. F/A-18Cs from VFA-37 and -105 and VMFA-312, and EA-6B Prowlers from VAQ-130, embarked on board *Harry S. Truman* (CVN 75), and Air Force F-15E Strike Eagles and British GR.1 Tornados, struck five Iraqi radar, and command, control, and communication nodes outside Baghdad with a variety of ordnance including Hornet-launched AGM-154A JSOW (Joint Standoff Weapons).

7 MARCH • The Navy announced the adaptation of blendable borescope technology—developed by Pratt & Whitney for repairing commercial jet engines—to service AV-8B engines without removing them from the aircraft.

24 MARCH • The Shared Reconnaissance Pod Program began testing on board F/A-18E E2 at NAWC China Lake, Calif. The pod, carried on the jet's centerline, was intended to provide high- and medium-altitude tactical reconnaissance capabilities.

28 MARCH • The Navy agreed to allow sailors in the AD (aviation machinist's mate) and AM (aviation structural mechanic) ratings to apply skills learned in "A" School toward an associate's degree in aviation maintenance technology.

1 APRIL • A Chinese Jianjiji J-8 collided with EP-3E, BuNo 156511, piloted by Lt. Shane J. Osborn of VQ-1, while the Aries II flew a routine surveillance mission in international airspace over the South China Sea. The impact disabled the plane, but Osborn recovered and executed an emergency landing at a Chinese station at Lingshui, Hainan Island. For 15 days the Chinese disregarded U.S. protests and detained the 24 crewmembers before allowing their return to NAS Whidbey Island, Wash. On 5 July, the disassembled pieces of the Aries II arrived on board a Russian Antonov An-124 transport at Dobbins ARB, Marietta, Ga.

1 APRIL • HSL-60 at NS Mayport, Fla., was established as the first Naval Reserve LAMPS Mk III squadron. Its six SH-60B Seahawks were to support Reserve frigates by eliminating the gap between the total of 82 active duty LAMPS detachments and the 88 required. On this date, the deactivation of HSL-94 also occurred.

3 APRIL • The Navy ordered 24 T-6A Texan IIs and technical support from Raytheon Company, Wichita, Kans. The $148 million order comprised part of the Joint Primary Aircraft Training System with the Air Force.

19 APRIL • An NP2000 E-2C, equipped with digitally controlled all-composite eight-bladed propeller systems, completed its first flight at NAS Patuxent River, Md.

21 APRIL • The initial Naval Reserve C-40A Clipper arrived at NAS JRB Fort Worth, Texas.

23 APRIL • A Naval Strike Aircraft Test Squadron F/A-18A Hornet made the first fully automated landing at sea using the global positioning system on board *Theodore Roosevelt* (CVN 71) off Norfolk, Va.

25 MAY • SH-60R Seahawks were redesignated MH-60Rs to reflect their diverse primary missions of undersea warfare, antisurface warfare, and naval surface fire support.

29 MAY • Naval aviation artist Robert G. Smith died at his home in California. In 1936, Smith began his career as an engineer with Northrop Aircraft. In 1994, the Naval Aviation Museum Foundation acknowledged his excellence in naval aviation art by naming him the first recipient of the R. G. Smith Award, which it had named in his honor.

25 JUNE • VFA-115 became the first operational squadron to complete the transition to F/A-18E/F Super Hornets when it received a safe-for-flight certification at NAS Lemoore, Calif.

30 JUNE • The deactivation of HSL-84 at NAS North Island, Calif., marked the passing of the Navy's LAMPS Mk I program.

30 JUNE • Amphibious assault ship *Iwo Jima* (LHD 7) was commissioned.

9 JULY • An E-2C Hawkeye equipped with a Surveillance Infrared Search and Track sensor detected and tracked a theater ballistic missile launched from White Sands Missile Range, N.M.

31 JULY • The Pentagon announced an increase in Iraqi violations after a 19 July surface-to-air missile (SAM) launch against an E-2C Hawkeye flying inside Kuwaiti airspace. During the preceding year, there had been 221 provocations against coalition aircraft in Operation Southern Watch, but in 2001 there were 370 to date. During 2000, some 145 violations occurred in Operation Northern Watch and since January 2001 another 62. To date in 2001, the coalition had struck Iraqi antiaircraft and SAM batteries 19 times in the south and 7 in the north.

1 AUGUST • VS-24 S-3Bs from *Enterprise* (CVN 65) began to fly missions over Iraq in support of Operation Southern Watch. Equipped with the surveillance system upgrade synthetic aperture radar, Viking crewmembers coupled the system with a tactical common data link that facilitated the tracking and identification of multiple targets, and provided coordinates for RQ-1A Predators from ranges of more than 50 miles.

3 AUGUST • Coast Guard HH-60J Jayhawks and HH-65A Dolphins supported three cutters in the rescue of 22 survivors from a Cuban migrant vessel that on 2 August capsized southeast of NAS Key West, Fla. During the two-day search and rescue mission, the helicopters flew 26 sorties covering more than 1,000 square miles.

5 AUGUST • A team of ten specialists began a 30-day excavation on the slope of Mutnovsky volcano in Kamchatka, Russia. On 11 August 2000, investigators tentatively identified the area as the crash site of a PV-1 and its crew of seven men. On 25 March 1944, the Ventura had failed to return to Attu in the Aleutians from a five-plane reconnaissance and bombing mission against a Japanese garrison in the Kuriles.

10 AUGUST • About 20 coalition strike aircraft comprising F/A-18C Hornets from VFA-15 and -87 and F-14B Tomcats from VF-14 and -41, embarked on board *Enterprise* (CVN 65), Air Force F-16 Fighting Falcons, and British GR.1 Tornados, attacked communication, radar, and missile sites near Baghdad, Iraq.

21 AUGUST • The Pentagon authorized aviation career continuation pay, a sea- and performance-based incentive designed to enhance the retention of experienced naval aviation officers. Eligibility requirements included officers designated as naval aviators or active duty naval flight officers at or below O-6 pay grade, qualified to perform operational flying duty, and having less than 24 years aviation service.

29 AUGUST • The first guided BLU-109 2,000-pound JDAM (Joint Direct Attack Munition) launch from an F/A-18E Super Hornet occurred at NAWC China Lake, Calif.

29 AUGUST • The Joint Unmanned Aerial Vehicle (UAV) in Time Sensitive Operations project of the Joint Test and Evaluation Program Office was established at NAS Fallon, Nev. A Navy director led the temporary joint Department of Defense organization to address commonality in UAV operations and training.

31 AUGUST • The Marines accepted the delivery of the first three production KC-130Js and a Cessna UC-35D Encore. On 7 September, the first of the Super Hercules arrived at VMGRT-253, MCAS Cherry Point, N.C. The Super Hercules, scheduled to replace all 79 Marine KC-130F/R/Ts, had digitally controlled cockpits and six propellers per engine rather than four. The Marines had requested seven aircraft during 2001 for VMGRT-253 after testing at NAS Patuxent River, Md. The Encore marked the third of seven jets planned to replace CT-39 Sabreliners and was assigned to MCAS Miramar, Calif. Over the next six months, two more followed, one to MCAS Futenma, Okinawa, and one to Marine Reserve NAF Washington, D.C. Two of the initial UC-35C Ultras had been assigned to Marine Reserve NAS New Orleans, La.

10 SEPTEMBER • On the eve of the 9/11 terrorist attacks, the Navy comprised 375,618 active and 170,168 Reserve sailors, and 4,108 operational aircraft and 317 ships and submarines—44,638 sailors and 91 vessels were deployed. Carriers deployed or underway (all separately) consisted of *Enterprise* (CVN 65) and *Carl Vinson* (CVN 70) in the Indian Ocean, *Constellation* (CV 64) and *John C. Stennis* (CVN 74) in the Pacific, and *Kitty Hawk* (CV 63) forward deployed to Japan. Amphibious ready groups deployed included *Boxer* (LHD 4), with the 11th Marine Expeditionary Unit (MEU) embarked, in the Pacific; *Essex* (LHD 2) forward deployed to Japan; *Kearsarge* (LHD 3), 24th MEU, Marmaris, Turkey; and *Peleliu* (LHA 5), 15th MEU, Darwin, Australia.

11 SEPTEMBER • Al-Qaeda terrorists hijacked four airliners, crashing two into the twin World Trade Center towers in New York City, one about 80 miles southeast of Pittsburgh, Pa., and a Boeing 757, American Airlines Flight 77, into the Pentagon. There, the impact thrust the aircraft into the reinforced building and severely damaged the newly opened Navy Command Center. The Pentagon attack killed 189 people, all 64 on board the flight including Naval Reservist and pilot Capt. Charles F. Burlingame III, and injured 125 in the building including 33 sailors and nine Navy civilians. The terrorists killed an estimated 2,977 people in all four 9/11 attacks.

The Department of Defense declared Force Protection Condition Delta—the highest alert. *George Washington* (CVN 73) sailed from Norfolk, Va., to protect New York City. The carrier responded to tasking from NORAD, and supported hospital ship *Comfort* (AH 20) during relief efforts. *John F. Kennedy* (CV 67) and *John C. Stennis* (CVN 74) positioned themselves to defend the East and West Coasts, respectively, while across the globe many aircraft ashore sortied. Coast Guardsmen began to escort Navy ships during their departures or arrivals at ports. Commander Fifth Fleet Vice Adm. Charles W. Moore Jr. oversaw an emergency meeting at NSA Bahrain, and directed some of the nearby aircraft and vessels toward the north Arabian Sea. *Enterprise* (CVN 65) sailing en route to South African waters turned around and raced northward. *Carl Vinson* (CVN 70) rounded India to relieve *Enterprise* but made speed to rendezvous with her and became the first carrier on station in international waters off Pakistan.

14 SEPTEMBER • President George W. Bush declared a national emergency because of the 9/11 terrorist attacks, authorizing the mobilization of up to 50,000 Reservists and National Guardsmen. The initial participation included 13,000 Air Force, 10,000 Army, 7,500 Marine, 3,000 Navy, and 2,000 Coast Guard servicemembers.

19 SEPTEMBER • The induction of the first AH-1W Super Cobra occurred at NADEP Cherry Point, N.C. The move formed a part of the integrated maintenance concept to produce a shorter maintenance turnaround time.

19 SEPTEMBER • *Theodore Roosevelt* (CVN 71) deployed from NS Norfolk, Va. HS-11 HH-60H Seahawks escorted the ship to sea.

24 SEPTEMBER • The Navy accepted delivery to VFA-115 of the first full-rate production F/A-18F Super Hornet, BuNo 165875. To date, the delivery of 67 Super Hornets had occurred including 12 to VFA-115 and 34 to VFA-122.

24 SEPTEMBER • Secretary of Defense Donald H. Rumsfeld delegated his stop-loss authority to the heads of military departments, which allowed the services to retain individuals on active duty beyond their date of separation. In 1990, President George H. W. Bush had originally delegated stop-loss authority to Secretary of Defense Richard B. Cheney during Operation Desert Shield, although leaders had not implemented it since Operation Allied Force in 1999. The decision affected approximately 10,500 sailors in 11 critical specialties.

25 SEPTEMBER • Secretary of Defense Donald H. Rumsfeld announced the designation of America's war on terrorism outside the United States as Operation Enduring Freedom. Activities to sustain homeland defense and civil support received the designation Operation Noble Eagle.

30 SEPTEMBER • While *Theodore Roosevelt* (CVN 71) sailed en route to the Arabian Sea she hoisted aloft a national flag that New York City firefighters George Johnson and Dan McWilliams of Ladder 157 and Billy Eisengrein of Rescue 2 had raised over Ground Zero. On 23 September, New York Governor George E. Pataki and the city's Mayor Rudolph W. Guiliani had signed the flag. The flag was flown to *Theodore Roosevelt,* where sailors then transferred the colors to other vessels. On 26 March 2002, the carrier returned the flag to the firefighters.

USN 011005-N-2669G-005

An F-14A Tomcat of VF-41 and two F/A-18C Hornets cruise in formation as another Hornet refuels from an Air Force KC-10A Extender of the 763d Expeditionary Air Refueling Squadron, 5 October 2001. The Navy aircraft were operating from *Enterprise* (CVN 65).

1 OCTOBER • *Kitty Hawk* (CV 63) sailed from Yokosuka, Japan, for the Indian Ocean. "I needed a steel lily pad—a Forward Operating Base—just off the coast of Pakistan, and I needed it soon," CentCom commander Gen. Tommy R. Franks, USA, afterward explained. On 27 September, *Kitty Hawk* had received notification of deployment to serve uniquely as an afloat forward staging base for special operators, and in ten days she completed carrier qualifications and sea trials that normally take 2½ weeks. To accommodate and support the special operators, the *Kitty Hawk* Carrier Battle Group reconfigured from an average of 8,000 sailors, ten ships, and 72 aircraft to deploy with 4,000 sailors, three ships, and 15 aircraft—eight F/A-18C Hornets, three S-3B Vikings, two C-2A Greyhounds, and two SH-60B Seahawks.

2 OCTOBER • Commandant of the Coast Guard Adm. James M. Loy, USCG, announced that during 2001 maritime interdictions seized an all-time record amount of cocaine.

2 OCTOBER • NATO Secretary-General Lord George Robertson announced that investigators had provided "clear and compelling" evidence of the guilt of Osama bin Laden behind the terrorist attacks on 9/11. The next day, NATO implemented Article 5 of the charter, under which an attack on a signatory was "an attack on all."

4 OCTOBER • In preparation for the air campaign against Afghanistan, HS-3 and -6 were designated the Navy's combat search and rescue alert package for the northern Arabian Sea. The Navy received the initial responsibility for all combat search and rescues in Pakistan south of latitude 28° north, and all overwater search and rescues.

4 OCTOBER • P-3C Orions executed intelligence, surveillance, and reconnaissance flights over Afghanistan, and F/A-18C Hornets from VFA-15 flew combat air patrols over Pakistan. The enormous distances necessitated the eventual establishment of forward operating bases and forward arming and refueling points ashore in Pakistan including Pasni on the coast, Shamsi about 90 miles inland from Pasni, and Jacobabad and Dalbandin in the interior.

6 OCTOBER • Aircraft and ships of NATO Standing Naval Force, Mediterranean, began patrols in the eastern Mediterranean in support of the war on terrorism.

7 OCTOBER • *Enterprise* (CVN 65) and *Carl Vinson* (CVN 70) spearheaded the first coalition strikes against al-Qaeda terrorists and the Taliban in Afghanistan.

7 OCTOBER • While *Kitty Hawk* (CV 63), destroyer *Curtis Wilbur* (DDG 54), and frigate *Gary* (FFG 51) passed through the Strait of Malacca en route to the Indian Ocean, they rescued five Indonesian fishermen from their sinking 40-foot fishing vessel.

8 OCTOBER • The Office of Homeland Security was established to develop and coordinate a national strategy to protect the United States from terrorists. Naval aviation early warning and intelligence aircraft subsequently received tasking for integration into the plan.

USN 011007-N-1523C-001

Cruiser *Philippine Sea* (CG 58) launches a BGM-109 Tomahawk Land Attack Missile against al-Qaeda and Taliban extremists in Afghanistan during the opening strikes of Operation Enduring Freedom, 7 October 2001.

12 OCTOBER • *Kitty Hawk* (CV 63), after a ten-day voyage of almost 6,000 miles to the Arabian Sea, embarked Task Force Sword at al Masirah Island off Oman. Sword was a composite Army command of more than 600 soldiers including men of Special Forces Operational Detachment Delta, and the 2nd Battalion, 160th Special Operations Aviation Regiment. It initially comprised about 20 helicopters including Boeing MH-47D and E Chinooks, Sikorsky MH-60K and L Black Hawks, and Hughes Little Birds—either AH-6Js, MH-6Js, or M500s or a combination thereof. Four days later, *Kitty Hawk* commenced operations in her unique configuration. During the cruise, aircraft from Carrier Air Wing 5 flew more than 600 missions including 100 combat sorties.

14 OCTOBER • As the war in Afghanistan entered its second week, Air Force AC-130U Spooky gunships worked with naval aircraft for the first time in the fighting during

011017-N-6187M-006

A pilot and radar intercept officer brief a plane captain on the performance of their F-14A Tomcat after a mission from *Enterprise* (CVN 65) over Afghanistan, 17 October 2001.

attacks against a Taliban stronghold near Kandahar. About 15 naval strike aircraft, eight to ten Air Force bombers, and British and U.S. naval-launched BGM-109 T-LAM (Tomahawk Land Attack Missiles) attacked seven target areas—two near Kandahar, one near the crucial crossroads of Mazār-e-Sharīf, and two around the capital of Kabul that collectively consisted of training facilities, surface-to-air missile storage sites, garrisons, and troop staging areas. The Taliban acknowledged damage at Kabul to the military academy and an artillery garrison. The allies also hit a terrorist training camp near Jalālābād. VF-14 maximized forward air control flexibility by configuring five F-14B Tomcats to carry four GBU-12 laser-guided bombs each, and configured the remainder for two GBU-16s.

16 OCTOBER • Joint Staff Deputy Director of Operations for Current Readiness and Capabilities Adm. John D. Stufflebeem announced the use of engagement zone doctrine in Afghanistan because of the reduction of enemy air defenses. This concept allowed the adoption of "flex targeting" as aircraft bombed a target, refueled in the air, and then hit another target.

17 OCTOBER • Shortly after midnight, *Theodore Roosevelt* (CVN 71) launched her first strikes into Afghanistan in Operation Enduring Freedom. Almost 40,000 allied servicemembers and nearly 50 ships and submarines operated in the northern Arabian Sea. *Theodore Roosevelt* made a concession to *Carl Vinson* (CVN 70) and shifted her schedule 12 hours to accommodate night operations, which allowed the carriers to maintain pressure on the enemy around the clock. Reveille changed to 1800 and taps to 1000.

USN 011031-N-3405L-007

Two 500-pound GBU-12 laser-guided bombs (left) and an AIM-9 Sidewinder air-to-air missile are visible on the wing of a VFA-94 F/A-18C Hornet flying from *Carl Vinson* (CVN 70) over Afghanistan, 31 October 2001.

18 OCTOBER • F/A-18C Hornets from VMFA-251, embarked on board *Theodore Roosevelt* (CVN 71), made the first Marine air strikes in Operation Enduring Freedom against Taliban infrastructure in Afghanistan.

19 OCTOBER • The first American ground offensive of the war on terrorism began near Kandahar, Afghanistan, when helicopters lifted solders of the Army's Task Force Sword from *Kitty Hawk* (CV 63). Many of the troops then switched to four Lockheed Martin MC-130E/H Combat Talons and raided the compound of Taliban leader Mullah Muhammad A. Umar. The soldiers also struck an unpaved desert airstrip used by terrorist Osama bin Laden at Dolangi near Bibi Tera, 80 miles southwest of the city. Task Force 57 aircraft that supported the raid included aircraft improvement program–equipped P-3C Orions.

An Army Sikorsky MH-60K crashed during a night approach to an airfield in Pakistan, killing two soldiers and injuring five. Marines from the 15th Marine Expeditionary Unit launched four CH-53E Super Stallions from amphibious assault ship *Peleliu* (LHA 5) to retrieve the Black Hawk. Supporting aircraft included one P-3C Orion, four VMA-331 AV-8B Harrier IIs, and a KC-130 Hercules. Super Stallion pilot Capt. Jay M. Holtermann, USMC, of HMM-163 led the mission. The force landed at the scene and rigged slings to enable a Super Stallion to retrieve the helicopter, but the weight of the Black Hawk compelled the Super Stallion to jettison fuel and stop at a forward arming and refueling point (FARP). Militants shot at the Marines who returned fire and Holtermann ordered an abort. On 24 October, four AH-1W Super Cobras circled overhead when the Marines returned to the FARP and recovered the Black Hawk.

19 OCTOBER • Developmental testing of Block II AGM-84 Harpoon air-to-ground missiles concluded at NAWC Point Mugu, Calif.

21 OCTOBER • As the war in Afghanistan entered its third week, approximately 80 strike aircraft, including about 60 carrier-based, struck 11 target areas including airfields, radar, tanks, vehicles, and military training facilities.

22 OCTOBER • The Navy, at Northrop Grumman, St. Augustine, Fla., received the first of 21 new production E-2C Hawkeyes featuring the cooperative engagement capability system, advanced control workstations, and an integrated satellite communications system.

25 OCTOBER • The Taliban and al-Qaeda defiantly clung to their positions around the besieged city of Mazār-e-Sharīf. A forward air controller passed control of an air strike to Maj. Brantley Bond, USMC, of VMFA-251, who flew an F/A-18C Hornet from *Theodore Roosevelt* (CVN 71). Bond knocked out at least four antiaircraft guns and dropped a 500-pound bomb in front of a Taliban tank. The attack flushed additional enemy troops, tanks, and armored personnel carriers from cover, and Bond repeatedly attacked them. He guided other aircraft using his forward-looking infrared system to target enemy vehicles with laser illumination. The survivors attempted to flee in their vehicles and on foot, but the jets accounted for the destruction of 15 armored vehicles. Bond subsequently received the Distinguished Flying Cross.

1 NOVEMBER • Secretary of Defense Donald H. Rumsfeld announced that as of the 25th day of combat operations of Operation Enduring Freedom, coalition aircraft had flown more than 2,000 sorties and delivered more than one million humanitarian rations to Afghan refugees.

1 NOVEMBER • Task Force 58 activated by combining the 15th and 26th Marine Expeditionary Units (MEU). Each MEU included a detachment of six AV-8B Harrier IIs from VMA-331 and -223, respectively. The two KC-130 Hercules normally allotted to each unit proved insufficient and the task force received six of the planes—two from VMGR-252 and four from VMGR-352.

2 NOVEMBER • Two Air Force Sikorsky MH-53J Pave Low IIIs of the 20th Special Operations Squadron attempted a night medical evacuation of a soldier in northern Afghanistan. One crashed during a whiteout at an altitude of about 10,000 feet in Pakistan, and the other recovered the crew, four of whom had been injured. Amphibious assault ship *Peleliu* (LHA 5) prepared to launch an HMM-163 CH-53E Super Stallion and two AH-1W Super Cobra escorts to retrieve the downed helicopter. Instead of risking the recovery forces, however, two VF-102 F-14B Tomcats, embarked on board *Theodore Roosevelt* (CVN 71), destroyed it with two GBU-16 bombs.

2 NOVEMBER • OpNavNote 3111 formally completed the disestablishment of the Navy's last active duty adversary squadron, VFA-127, which had occurred on 31 March 1996 at NAS Fallon, Nev.

3 NOVEMBER • Three AV-8Bs from the 15th Marine Expeditionary Unit, embarked on board amphibious assault ship *Peleliu* (LHA 5), flew the first Harrier II strikes in the war on terrorism against targets in southern Afghanistan with Mk 82 500-pound bombs.

8 NOVEMBER • Almost all of the 78 coalition strike sorties flown into Afghanistan—about 60 naval aircraft, seven to ten bombers, and the remainder land-based tactical jets—attacked targets near Mazār-e-Sharīf and north of Kabul. F-14 Tomcats and F/A-18C Hornets dropped precision-guided munitions on enemy positions, which aided Islamic State of Afghanistan (Northern Alliance) troops opposed to the Taliban in their siege of the city. One raid killed a Taliban leader and an estimated 85 Islamic militants.

9 NOVEMBER • Air strikes forced terrorists and the Taliban from their positions around Mazār-e-Sharīf and Kabul, Afghanistan, to flee or melt into the civilian population. Some 400 to 500 holdouts barricaded themselves in the three-story Sultan Razia Girls School, Mazār-e-Sharīf. They confidently prepared for a siege because of their proximity to the Blue Mosque, a sacred shrine that houses the remains of Ali, the fourth Caliph of Islam and a cousin and son-in-law to the prophet Muhammad. Afghan warlord Abdul R. Dostum led the Islamic State of Afghanistan (Northern Alliance) forces opposed to the Taliban and requested a raid. Aircraft dropped four bombs directly into the building that enabled allied warriors to capture the school, and with it, the city.

USAF 011107-F-5795G-014

An F/A-18C Hornet prepares to refuel from an Air Force KC-10A Extender during an Operation Enduring Freedom mission, 7 November 2001.

This unhinged the Taliban front in the north, gave the coalition its first large airfield in the country, and opened an overland supply route through Uzbekistan.

10 NOVEMBER • Aircraft bombed al-Qaeda terrorists and the Taliban as they retreated from the northern battlefields of Afghanistan. An E-2C Hawkeye directed a VF-102 F-14B Tomcat to attack a column moving eastward from the city. The Tomcat blasted the lead truck that blocked the remaining vehicles into a narrow mountain defile. Cmdr. Roy J. Kelley, VF-102 commanding officer, flew another Tomcat and led the destruction of vehicles packed with enemy troops in the ensuing traffic jam that stretched for almost ten miles.

14 NOVEMBER • At 0640 near Ghazni, about 50 miles southwest of Kabul, Afghanistan, naval aircraft helped cover three U.S. special operations helicopters during the rescue of eight Christian relief workers including Americans Dayna Curry and Heather Mercer of Shelter Now held hostage by the Taliban.

15 NOVEMBER • Lt. Andrew P. Hayes, piloting a VF-102 F-14B Tomcat, with his radar intercept officer spotted several bivouacs of Taliban armored vehicles in Afghanistan two miles from Army Special Forces. Despite antiaircraft and small arms fire, the fliers dropped three laser-guided bombs that hit two moving tanks and a revetted armored vehicle, and guided three GBU-12 bombs released by their wingman that destroyed two revetted tanks and a fuel truck. Secondary explosions forced more than 50 Taliban troops to flee their positions. Over the next six hours, Hayes guided 12 coalition aircraft until low fuel forced his disengagement. Aircraft dropped 20 laser-guided and 16 general-purpose bombs that resulted in the destruction of 33 vehicles including 27 armored. Hayes received the Distinguished Flying Cross.

15 NOVEMBER • An EA-18 airborne electronic attack concept aircraft—an F/A-18F Super Hornet carrying three ALQ-99 jamming pods—completed initial demonstration flights at Boeing Company, St. Louis, Mo.

16 NOVEMBER • The first of two prototype Improved Capability (ICAP) III EA-6B Prowlers logged its first flight at Northrop Grumman, St. Augustine, Fla.

18 NOVEMBER • Destroyer *Peterson* (DD 969) intercepted and diverted suspected smuggler *Samra* to a holding anchorage during maritime interception operations in the northern Persian Gulf. A boarding party discovered 1,700 metric tons of Iraqi oil, but the weather deteriorated with heavy winds and seas. *Samra* sank and EN1 Vincent Parker, ET3 Benjamin Johnson, and four smugglers died. A LAMPS Mk III helicopter from HSL-44 Detachment 4 embarked on board *Peterson*, an SH-60B Seahawk of HSL-42 Detachment 2 from cruiser *Leyte Gulf* (CG 55), two rigid hull inflatable boats from the cruiser, and frigates *Ingraham* (FFG 61) and Australian *Sydney* (FFG 03) rescued six Americans and ten smugglers.

19 NOVEMBER • An Air Force RQ-4A Global Hawk made the first wartime flight of one of the unmanned aerial vehicles over Afghanistan. The Navy subsequently adopted Global Hawks as part of the Broad Area Maritime Surveillance program.

22 NOVEMBER • Overnight, four VMA-223 AV-8Bs, embarked on board amphibious assault ship *Bataan* (LHD 5), flew the first sorties of the 26th Marine Expeditionary Unit into Afghanistan. Just before dawn, the Harrier IIs destroyed an al-Qaeda convoy with laser-guided bombs.

25 NOVEMBER • Operation Swift Freedom began—the liberation of southern Afghanistan in the area of Kandahar. Six HMM-163 CH-53E Super Stallions launched from amphibious assault ship *Peleliu* (LHA 5) carrying Marines of the 15th Marine Expeditionary Unit. AH-1W Super Cobras covered the insertion at lower altitudes, and F-14B Tomcats of VF-102 and F/A-18C Hornets flew top cover from *Theodore Roosevelt* (CVN 71). The Marines rendezvoused with KC-130 Hercules tankers to refuel en route. Four hours later they reached a desert airstrip, secured by SEALs, at Dolangi southwest of Kandahar and more than 300 miles from their ships. Within an hour, a Hercules landed with additional equipment and supplies. The Marines designated their position Forward Operating Base (FOB) Rhino, which journalists called Camp Rhino. By the next morning, 519 Marines and sailors had landed and developed a perimeter. They later established an additional forward arming and refueling point and an unmanned aerial vehicle base nearby.

25 NOVEMBER • More than 300 coalition prisoners rebelled at the fortress of Qala-e-Jhangi, six miles west of Mazār-e-Sharīf, Afghanistan. They killed CIA agent and former Marine Johnny M. Spann, stormed the armory, and seized most of the citadel. F/A-18C Hornets dropped seven Joint Direct Attack Munitions on the fortress and two Air Force AC-130H Spectres raked the compound with 40mm and 105mm rounds that touched off a hidden munitions dump. Three days later the holdouts surrendered.

26 NOVEMBER • A Joint Surveillance Target Attack Radar System–equipped E-8 detected a column of about 15 Taliban vehicles including several armored personnel carriers probing the northwest perimeter of Forward Operating Base Rhino at Dolangi southwest of Kandahar, Afghanistan. F-14B Tomcats of VF-102 from *Theodore Roosevelt* (CVN 71) broke up the attack and two Marine AH-1W Super Cobras routed the survivors.

28 NOVEMBER • Concerned about the escape of terrorists from Afghanistan via ships, the coalition developed leadership interception operations to catch suspicious vessels sailing off the Iranian and Pakistani coasts. Beginning on this date through 8 December, cruiser *Princeton* (CG 59) conducted some of the first of these operations near Gwadar off southwestern Pakistan. Aircraft from *Theodore Roosevelt* (CVN 71) searched for smugglers, and ships from her group participated in patrols and interceptions.

30 NOVEMBER • The Battle of Tora Bora began when naval reconnaissance aircraft spotted Taliban troops fleeing toward Tora Bora, a summit that rises from the Spin Ghar Mountains about 35 miles southwest of Jalālābād, Afghanistan. Al-Qaeda terrorist Osama bin Laden had lavished gifts among the local Suleiman Khel tribesmen who thus sheltered the fugitive and his followers.

1 DECEMBER • Amphibious assault ship *Bonhomme Richard* (LHD 6), with the 13th Marine Expeditionary Unit embarked, deployed six weeks ahead of schedule for Operation Enduring Freedom.

An SH-60F Seahawk leaves the deck of motor vessel *Kota Sejarah* after dropping off SEALs and Marines during a search for al-Qaeda terrorists in the Arabian Sea, 6 December 2001.

1 DECEMBER • VF-14 and -41 were redesignated VFA-14 and -41, respectively. Both squadrons began to transition from F-14B Tomcats to F/A-18E/F Super Hornets and to relocate from NAS Oceana, Va., to NAS Lemoore, Calif.

4 DECEMBER • An F/A-18C/D Hornet launched a unitary warhead variant of an AGM-154C during the first free-flight tests of a joint standoff weapon at NAWC China Lake, Calif.

5 DECEMBER • Marine and Navy aircraft flew close cover for lines-of-communication interdiction missions along Route 1 between Lashkar Gah and Kandahar, Afghanistan, to cut off the escape of the Taliban and al-Qaeda terrorists fleeing from the battles in the north of the country.

5 DECEMBER • An SH-60F and two HH-60H Seahawks from HS-11, two of the helicopters detached from *Theodore Roosevelt* (CVN 71) and one from ashore, and additional sailors from HS-6, carried out a visit, board, search, and seizure of container ship *Kota Sejarah*, suspected of smuggling contraband and terrorists, in the Arabian Sea. The Seahawks intercepted the ship and flew armed cover as they guided SEALs in two boats who boarded and stopped the ship and mustered her 22 crewmembers. HS-11 deployed 71 additional Marines, explosive ordnance disposal sailors, and SEALs via fastrope for security and search, supported by a leadership interception operation detachment from amphibious transport dock *Shreveport* (LPD 12). Through 7 December, inspectors detained *Kota Sejarah*, but later released the ship. This marked the first noncompliant boarding in leadership interception operations. Into the New Year, HS-11 joined Task Force Cutlass for additional similar and maritime interception operations.

USN 011225-N-6119T-001

An S-3B Viking of VS-32 returns to *Theodore Roosevelt* (CVN 71) after a mission over Afghanistan, 25 December 2001.

6 DECEMBER • A P-3C Orion orbiting overhead confirmed a Taliban and al-Qaeda probe against Forward Operating Base Rhino at Dolangi southwest of Kandahar, Afghanistan. The Marines fired 81mm mortars and the Taliban disengaged. Later that evening, a convoy of seven vehicles attempted to slip past the Marines but an Orion spotted the infiltrators as they dismounted to advance. F/A-18C Hornets and F-14 Tomcats disrupted the attack by dropping six 500-pound and two 1,000-pound laser-guided bombs. A UH-1N Iroquois, BuNo 160440, crashed while taking off and all on board escaped, but a fire destroyed the helicopter.

7 DECEMBER • The Marine Corps accepted the first AN/AAQ-28 Litening II targeting pod, which was designed to enable AV-8B Harrier IIs to autonomously deliver precision-guided munitions.

7 DECEMBER • Aircraft and ships of NATO's Task Force Endeavour began their first deployment in the eastern Mediterranean to track shipping capable of smuggling to terrorists.

11 DECEMBER • The induction of the last of 74 Marine day-attack AV-8Bs for modification into night-attack Harrier II Plus configurations occurred at NADEP Cherry Point, N.C. The aircraft were expected to return to fleet service in September 2003.

12 DECEMBER • An Air Force B-1B Lancer of the 20th Bomb Wing lost power to an engine while outbound from a night strike over Afghanistan, crashing about 30 miles north of Diego Garcia, British Indian Ocean Territory. Lt. William Pennington of VP-4 piloted a P-3C Orion that supported SAR mission commander Maj. Brandon Nugent, USAF, in an Air Force KC-10A Extender. The aircraft located the Lancer and alerted destroyer *Russell* (DDG 59). Despite shallow shoal water that prevented the vessel from closing the wreck, she lowered two rigid hull inflatable boats that recovered all four survivors. Ships subsequently retrieved the bomber.

13 DECEMBER • A combined antiarmor team from the 26th Marine Expeditionary Unit, designated Task Force Sledgehammer, advanced to the Kandahar airport in Afghanistan, linking up en route with Army special operators. AV-8B Harrier IIs and AH-1W Cobras supported by additional coalition aircraft provided close air support. CH-53E Super Stallions flew in reinforcements that enabled the Marines to establish a forward operating base.

16 DECEMBER • *John C. Stennis* (CVN 74) relieved *Carl Vinson* (CVN 70) in the Arabian Sea and launched her first strikes in Operation Enduring Freedom.

17 DECEMBER • The coalition claimed victory at Tora Bora, Afghanistan. F/A-18C Hornets bombarded escape routes as Taliban and their al-Qaeda allies straggled across the Pakistani border. From 25 November, allied aircraft had dropped more than 1,600 bombs including precision Joint Direct Attack Munitions on the enemy around the cave complex. Terrorist leader Osama bin Laden was not found.

18 DECEMBER • French Task Force 473 rendezvoused with U.S. Task Force 50 about 50 miles off the Pakistani coast. The combined group comprised four carriers—*Theodore Roosevelt* (CVN 71), *John C. Stennis* (CVN 74), French *Charles de Gaulle* (R 91), and Italian *Guiseppe Garibaldi* (C 551). On this date, almost 100 coalition vessels operated across the Indian Ocean.

24 DECEMBER • The 15th Marine Expeditionary Unit began to withdraw from Forward Operating Base Rhino, Afghanistan.

2002

3 JANUARY • Coalition aircraft including four F/A-18C Hornets, four Air Force B-1B Lancers, and an AC-130 Spectre gunship struck the terrorist training and support complex at Zhawar Kili al-Badr, 30 miles southwest of Khowst, Afghanistan. The United States had attacked the facility on 20 August 1998 in retaliation for the terrorist attacks against U.S. Embassies in East Africa. During this battle, coalition aircraft leveled the facility's buildings, sealed all known caves, and knocked out antiaircraft artillery and tracked military vehicles. The battle concluded on 14 January.

USN 011228-N-2383B-509

An AH-1W Super Cobra covers Marines on a LAV-25 light armored vehicle as they begin a patrol at Kandahar, Afghanistan, 28 December 2001.

8 JANUARY • HSL-46 Detachment 3, embarked on board destroyer *Hayler* (DD 997), conducted the year's first maritime interception operation in the Mediterranean Sea when an SH-60B Seahawk intercepted merchant vessel *Rasha J*. During 2002, five detachments from HSL-46 deployed to the Fifth and Sixth Fleets collectively conducted more than 500 interceptions and queried over 700 merchant vessels.

USN 080424-N-4658L-139

An MH-60R Seahawk of HSM-71 fires an AGM-114 Hellfire air-to-ground missile during testing off San Diego, 24 April 2008.

13 JANUARY • Two HH-60H Seahawks of HS-11 and one from HS-8, operating from amphibious transport dock *Shreveport* (LPD 12), and reinforced by additional sailors from destroyer *Elliot* (DD 967), provided sniper and AGM-114B Hellfire air-to-ground missile coverage for SEALs during a night boarding of suspected smuggling vessel *al Obeid* in the north Arabian Sea.

28 JANUARY • Soldiers of the Army's 101st Air Assault Division began to relieve the 26th Marine Expeditionary Unit in Afghanistan.

3 FEBRUARY • Naval Forces Central Command established Combined Task Force 150 to deny terrorists unimpeded use of the seas by countering illicit movements of them, weapons, and drugs. The multinational command's theater of operations included an area that stretched from the Red Sea across the Gulf of Aden, Horn of Africa, Somalia Basin, Arabian Sea, Gulf of Oman, and Strait of Hormuz.

5 FEBRUARY • Task Force 58 redeployed to Bahrain followed three weeks later by its disestablishment, as the amphibious command structure in Southwest Asia began to return to the pre-9/11 organization.

8 FEBRUARY • The Navy unveiled an MH-60S Seahawk during a ceremony with fleet readiness squadron HC-3 at NAS North Island, Calif.

10 FEBRUARY • Naval aircraft supported a Coast Guard law enforcement detachment in the seizure of 12.65 tons of cocaine from smugglers on board Colombian-flagged fishing vessel *Paulo*, 300 miles south of the Galapagos Islands.

14 FEBRUARY • Reserve CH-53E Super Stallion squadron HMH-772 was activated for one year at NAS JRB Willow Grove, Pa. The squadron provided heavy lift capability for the 24th Marine Expeditionary Unit via HMM-263 at MCAS New River, N.C.

4 MARCH • Pilot Cmdr. Don Burns, copilot Lt. Cmdr. Eric Humphreys, and aircrewmen AW1 Jim Peters and AD1 Shawn Robertson flew the maiden flight of HSL-60 at NS Mayport, Fla.

4 MARCH • Operation Anaconda began—a coalition thrust to trap al-Qaeda terrorists and Taliban in the Shah-e-Kot valley of southeastern Afghanistan. At times during the first several days, *Theodore Roosevelt* (CVN 71) and *John C. Stennis* (CVN 74) supported allied troops with Joint Direct Attack Munitions and BLU-118 thermobaric bombs. This was the first combat deployment of the class of fuel-rich compositions that generated high sustained blast pressures for use against tunnels and underground facilities. Within the first 24 hours, Navy, Marine Corps, and Air Force aircraft dropped 177 GBU-31 JDAMs and GBU-12 laser-guided 500-pound bombs. P-3C Orions flew intelligence, surveillance, and reconnaissance missions. Five AH-1Ws and three CH-53E Super Stallions of HMM-165 from the 13th Marine Expeditionary Unit flew from amphibious assault ship *Bonhomme Richard* (LHD 6) to operate out of Bagram Air Base. The Marines later established a forward arming and refueling point that enabled the Super Cobras to fight at extended ranges. The fighting raged through 18 March.

6 MARCH • *John F. Kennedy* (CV 67) relieved *Theodore Roosevelt* (CVN 71) in the northern Arabian Sea.

11 MARCH • From 9/11 to this date, the Navy deployed six carrier battle groups, four amphibious ready groups, and about 60,000 active and 13,000 Reserve sailors and Marines to the Indian Ocean area.

12 MARCH • Commanding officer Cmdr. John C. Aquilino and Lt. Cmdr. Kevin J. Protzman of VF-11 made the first combat strike with a Mk 84 2,000-pound JDAM (GBU-31) from an F-14B Tomcat during Operation Anaconda in Afghanistan.

27 MARCH • *Theodore Roosevelt* (CVN 71) returned from deployment. Aircraft embarked from Carrier Air Wing 1 had flown more than 10,000 sorties and dropped over 1.7 million pounds of ordnance.

31 MARCH • In Guam, HC-5 received the first three MH-60S Seahawks to be delivered to an operational squadron.

4 APRIL • The first fully remanufactured SH-60B to MH-60R standards completed its first flight at Owego, N.Y. During 2001, the Navy had decided to shift the program from remanufacturing existing H-60 airframes to producing new aircraft and planned a total of 243 MH-60Rs.

15 APRIL • Six F/A-18D Hornets from VMFA(AW)-121 arrived in Kyrgyzstan to initiate the first naval aviation fighter operations from that country. The Marines integrated into the Air Force's 376th Air Expeditionary Wing during strikes over Afghanistan.

15 APRIL • NATO's Standing Naval Forces Atlantic returned to the eastern Mediterranean Sea for a second deployment as Task Force Endeavour to support Operation Enduring Freedom.

1 MAY • Test squadrons without alphanumeric designations were redesignated air test and evaluation squadrons in keeping with fleet standards—HX-21, and VX-20, -23, -30, and -31.

3 MAY • The Department of Defense announced the certification of six acquisition projects including a program to remanufacture 280 H-1 replacements for AH-1 Cobras and UH-1 Hueys.

3 MAY • HX-21 received the second test AH-1Z Viper to arrive at NAS Patuxent River, Md.

10 MAY • Two Coast Guard HH-60J Jayhawks and an HU-25 Guardian supported cutter *Harriet Lane* (WMEC 903) in the rescue of 71 Haitian migrants from an overloaded 35-foot vessel that capsized six miles west of Great Inagua, Bahamas. The Coast Guard also recovered the bodies of 14 migrants who perished. An HC-130H Hercules and patrol boat *Nantucket* (WPB 1316) carried additional medical personnel and supplies to the area.

13 MAY • Through 16 May, testing of the integration of the Cooperative Engagement Capability (CEC) system with E-2C Hawkeye 2000 weapon systems occurred at NAS Patuxent River, Md.

19 MAY • An RQ-8A Fire Scout Vertical Takeoff and Landing Tactical Unmanned Aerial Vehicle (VTUAV) began its flight test program at NAWS China Lake, Calif. The Navy intended Fire Scouts to provide situational awareness and precision targeting, and to be fully autonomous with little required operator intervention. The design of littoral combat ships included the provision to operate Fire Scouts.

31 MAY • Bell Helicopter Textron, Inc. selected the Thales TopOwl Avionics helmet-mounted display for Marine H-1s, with 180 AH-1Z Vipers and 100 UH-1Y Venoms receiving the system.

31 MAY • Central Command activated Combined Joint Task Force 180 to assume control of allied operations in Afghanistan.

17 JUNE • An S-3B Viking from VS-31, embarked on board *John F. Kennedy* (CV 67), and an SH-60B from HSL-42 Detachment 7, embarked on board cruiser *Vicksburg* (CG 69), encountered 20-foot seas during the rescue of all 16 crewmembers from merchant vessel *al Murtada*, adrift off Oman.

18 JUNE • The Americans and British exchanged diplomatic notes terminating their World War II agreement on leased bases in Bermuda. The United States had sought additional Atlantic bases to protect shipping from German submarines and famously traded 50 obsolete destroyers for the rights. After the war, NAF Bermuda continued to support naval aviation operations against Soviet submarines until its disestablishment on 1 September 1995.

24 JUNE • The Navy accepted the first engineering and development version of the Shared Reconnaissance Pod.

23 JULY • Two SH-60B Seahawks of HSL-48 Detachment 7 began a six-month deployment to the Mediterranean Sea and the Persian Gulf on board frigate *Kauffman* (FFG 59), which sailed with *George Washington* (CVN 73). The detachment conducted multiple maritime interception operations during the cruise including one that involved 60 flight hours tracking a merchant vessel, leading to the capture of 15 suspected al-Qaeda terrorists by Italian authorities.

24 JULY • *Abraham Lincoln* (CVN 72) deployed to the western Pacific, Indian Ocean, and Persian Gulf. Twelve F/A-18E Super Hornets of VFA-115 and two MH-60S Seahawks of HC-5 embarked during the first operational deployment of these two aircraft types. The ship also put to sea with 1,000-pound Joint Direct Attack Munitions for use with F/A-18Es. During the first few days of the cruise, pilot Lt. Corey L. Pritchard of VFA-115 accomplished the initial deployed Super Hornet landing on board the carrier.

30 JULY • The Navy released a draft environmental impact statement for public comment on the introduction of F/A-18E/Fs to the East Coast. The statement affected ten fleet squadrons (130 Super Hornets) and one fleet readiness squadron (32 aircraft). The preferred alternatives comprised either the fleet readiness and six fleet squadrons at NAS Oceana, Va., and four squadrons at MCAS Cherry Point, N.C.; or the fleet readiness and eight squadrons at Oceana, and two squadrons at Cherry Point. In addition, planners proposed an outlying landing field in either Craven or Washington counties, N.C.

6 AUGUST • The first rescue using a TRI-SAR harness occurred when a UH-3H Sea King from NAS Patuxent River, Md., rescued a man stranded on a mud flat.

16 AUGUST • An RQ-8A Fire Scout Vertical Takeoff and Landing Tactical Unmanned Aerial Vehicle completed its first in-flight sensor payload demonstration at NAWS China Lake, Calif.

26 AUGUST • Maj. Pat Mohr, USMC, of HX-21, and Bell Helicopter test pilot Herb Moran, flew the first AH-1Z Viper with an integrated all-digital cockpit on its maiden flight at NAS Patuxent River, Md.

6 SEPTEMBER • The Center for Aviation Technical Training was activated at NATTC Pensacola, Fla. The center defined all curriculum and educational tools, and developed technical training solutions and professional development programs for all aviation sailors and Marines and for nondesignated airmen.

11 OCTOBER • Secretary of the Navy Gordon R. England issued a memorandum concerning the first American casualty of the Persian Gulf War, Capt. Michael S. Speicher, that changed his status to missing/captured. Under international law, the action entitled Speicher to treatment as a prisoner of war.

29 OCTOBER • Commander Central Command Gen. Tommy R. Franks, USA, announced the impending deployment of 700 to 800 Marines to Djibouti as part of Combined Joint Task Force–Horn of Africa.

5 NOVEMBER • The Navy announced the relocation of the Aviation Maintenance Officer School the next month from NAS Pensacola, Fla., to operate as part of Naval Air Maintenance Training Group Detachment Milton at NAS Whiting Field, Fla.

6 NOVEMBER • Lts. John E. Turner and Eric C. Doyle of VFA-115 flew the first F/A-18E Super Hornet combat live-fire action. During a mission from *Abraham Lincoln* (CVN 72), they dropped four GBU-31 Mk 84 2,000-pound Joint Direct Attack Munitions against an Iraqi command and control facility near Tallil and against two surface-to-air missile systems near Al-Kut, both sites located southeast of Baghdad.

13 NOVEMBER • Two CH-46D Sea Knights from HC-6 Detachment 6 augmented about 400 Marines of Headquarters Combined Joint Task Force–Horn of Africa during a deployment on board command ship *Mount Whitney* (LCC 20) from Morehead City, N.C., to a former French Foreign Legion base at Camp Lemonier, Djibouti. On 10 December, *Mount Whitney* arrived off the Horn of Africa, and two days later Central Command transferred authority for that region to the task force. On 27 December, an Air Force Sikorsky MH-53 Pave Low performed landing qualification trials on board the command ship, which on 13 June 2003, returned to Norfolk, Va.

23 NOVEMBER • Space shuttle *Endeavour*, on mission STS-113, launched from John F. Kennedy Space Center, Fla. During this mission to the International Space Station, naval aviator crewmembers included Capts. James D. Wetherbee and Michael E. Lopez-Alegria, and Cmdr. John B. Herrington—the first Native American in space. *Endeavour* returned to the center on 7 December.

4 DECEMBER • *Abraham Lincoln* (CVN 72) launched her last Operation Southern Watch mission of the deployment. VFA-115 had flown a total of 214 F/A-18E Super Hornet combat sorties.

8 DECEMBER • Super Typhoon Pongsana devastated Guam. Naval aircraft spearheaded relief efforts that included the airlift of more than $4 million worth of supplies.

31 DECEMBER • During 2002, the Iraqis fired at coalition aircraft about 500 times.

2003

1 JANUARY • The merger of the AK (aviation storekeeper) and SK (storekeeper) ratings into SK became effective for enlisted pay grades E1 to E6, with E7 and above eligible for the exams over succeeding months.

16 JANUARY • HC-5 Detachment 6, forward deployed to Japan on board *Essex* (LHD 2), made the first deployment of MH-60S Seahawks with an amphibious assault ship. The detachment returned to the United States on 30 January.

16 JANUARY • Space shuttle *Columbia*, on mission STS-107, launched from John F. Kennedy Space Center, Fla. At about 0900 on 1 February, the shuttle broke apart during reentry over Texas killing all seven crewmembers including naval aviation veterans Capts. David M. Brown and Laurel B. S. Clark and Cmdr. William C. McCool. Investigators concluded that a thermal protection system breach on the left wing leading edge allowed superheated air to penetrate during reentry and progressively melt the wing's aluminum structure, which weakened it until aerodynamic forces caused its failure and loss of control.

26 JANUARY • HSL-45 Detachment 6 relieved HSL-37 Detachment 2 on board destroyer *Fletcher* (DD 992) during the first Sea Swap experiment at Perth, Australia. An Air Force Lockheed C-5 Galaxy returned part of the original detachment and its helicopters to Hawaii. The Navy intended the program to maintain the deployment of ships in forward areas by swapping crews and air detachments.

USN 030320-N-9593M-039

An F/A-18C Hornet of VFA-113 launches from *Abraham Lincoln* (CVN 72) in the Arabian Gulf during Operation Iraqi Freedom, 20 March 2003.

28 JANUARY • An SH-60 Seahawk from HSL-48 Detachment 2, embarked on board frigate *John L. Hall* (FFG 32), coordinated with maritime patrol aircraft and Coast Guard cutter *Diligence* (WMEC 616) to intercept a 40-foot go-fast vessel in the Caribbean Sea. The four smugglers scuttled their boat when captured, but the combined Navy–Coast Guard team recovered 4,265 pounds of cocaine with an estimated street value of $130 million.

4 FEBRUARY • The last E-6A Mercury, BuNo 164409, departed Tinker AFB, Okla., to undergo E-6B modifications to enable it to communicate with strategic defense forces.

12 FEBRUARY • The Marines began their first operational assessment through 27 March of AH-1Z Viper and UH-1Y Venom upgrades.

1 MARCH • The first F-14D equipped with a Joint Direct Attack Munition deployed. In February, a NAVAIR team had modified all forward-deployed Tomcats.

13 MARCH • The crew of an SH-60B Seahawk of HSL-51, deployed with frigate *Gary* (FFG 51), assisted in the rescue of all eight Iraqi fishermen from dhow *Kaptain Muhamadat* when she lost steerage and propulsion in heavy seas and capsized 20 miles south of the Iranian coast.

19 MARCH • The coalition launched Operation Iraqi Freedom. From June 2002 to this date, allied aircraft had struck nearly 400 Iraqi military targets. During the first 19 days of March, the pace of operations increased and aircraft flew 4,000 strike and support sorties against Iraqi radar, antiaircraft guns, and fiber-optic links to suppress enemy air defenses in preparation for the invasion of Iraq.

An F/A-18C Hornet of VFA-105 launches from *Harry S. Truman* (CVN 75) in the Mediterranean, 20 March 2003.

22 MARCH • Despite intense fire from numerous Iraqi guns and surface-to-air missiles, VFA-113 led a strike that used Joint Direct Attack Munitions to destroy the Iraqi Ba'ath Party headquarters comprising 12 targets in four cities.

22 MARCH • *Theodore Roosevelt* (CVN 71) launched her first strikes of Operation Iraqi Freedom. The raid struck Iraqi command and control and infrastructure targets including a palace complex used by Saddam Hussein as military facilities, and one of the primary Iraqi AM broadcasting stations used to direct troops. During the first several days of the fighting, aircraft suppressed Iraqi air defenses and destroyed an *Ansar al-Islam*—Supporters of Islam, a radical Kurdish Islamic group—terrorist camp near the Iranian border. E-2C Hawkeyes proved especially useful in enabling pilots to link-up with special operators on the ground despite harsh weather that interfered with radio and satellite communications.

23 MARCH • A *turab*—dust storm—blew fine ochre dust and sand that coated exposed skin and gear across the southern half of Iraq and most of Kuwait. Four VMFA-323 F/A-18C Hornets launched a strike from *Constellation* (CV 64) against Special Republican Guard barracks and presidential security buildings near Saddam International Airport and each hit their targets with three 2,000-pound Joint Direct Attack Munitions. The raid directly contributed to the subsequent capture of the airport and the advance on Baghdad.

23 MARCH • The Iraqis ambushed 33 soldiers of the Army's 507th Maintenance Company in An Nasiriyah, killing 11 Americans and capturing seven more including

USN 030323-N-5319A-005

A British Royal Navy Westland Lynx HMA.8 flies plane guard for an MH-53E of HM-14, embarked on board amphibious transport dock *Ponce* (LPD 15), while the Sea Dragon pulls a Mk 105 mine countermeasures magnetic sled near the mouth of the Khawar Abd Allah (river) in Iraq, 23 March 2003.

Pfc. Jessica D. Lynch, USA. On 1 April, Marines from Task Force Charlie staged a diversionary attack while CH-46E Sea Knights from HMM-165, embarked on board amphibious assault ship *Boxer* (LHD 4), CH-53E Super Stallions, SEALs, and soldiers of Task Force 20 rescued Lynch from Saddam Hospital in the town.

24 MARCH • Commander Task Force 50 Rear Adm. John M. Kelly announced that aircraft had flown about 550 sorties against the Iraqis from *Kitty Hawk* (CV 63), *Constellation* (CV 64), and *Abraham Lincoln* (CVN 72). The long ranges required the configuration of four VFA-115 F/A-18E Super Hornets as tankers.

24 MARCH • Aircraft of Carrier Air Wing 3 struck Iraqi SA-2 and Roland surface-to-air missile sites in the Kirkuk area with AGM-88 High speed Anti-Radiation Missiles.

25 MARCH • Two VFA-151 F/A-18C Hornets and a VS-38 S-3B Viking destroyed Saddam Hussein's presidential yacht *Al Mansur*, Osa I–class missile boat *P-205*, and training ship *Ibn Khaldoum* (A 507) on the Tigris River near Basra. This was done after receiving a short order tasking for the time-sensitive strike. A Hornet laser-designated one of the targets, while the Viking struck it with an AGM-65E Maverick air-to-ground missile during the first instance of a Viking combat overland strike.

26 MARCH • A *turab*—dust storm—blanketed *Abraham Lincoln* (CVN 72) during flight operations. The carrier shifted almost 30 miles in a vain attempt to outrun the storm but the tempest wreaked havoc with operations. Commander Central Command Gen. Tommy R. Franks, USA, learned that the storm had immobilized Iraqi troops preparing to counterattack U.S. forces, and thus directed repeated strikes into 27 March by naval aircraft and Air Force bombers that

USN 030324-N-1512S-024

CH-53E Super Stallion pilot Maj. Richard Focht, USMC, prepares his flight gear on board amphibious assault ship *Kearsarge* (LHD 3) before flying a combat resupply mission into Iraq, 24 March 2003.

decisively broke up enemy troop concentrations. During one battle, the Iraqi *Medina* Republican Guard Tank Division took advantage of inclement weather to attack the Army's V Corps. F/A-18C Hornets of VFA-113 persevered through heavy overcast and, at one point with no visibility, bombed the Iraqis to a standstill.

26 MARCH • Coalition aircraft struck nine Iraqi surface-to-surface missiles and their launchers in Baghdad with precision guided munitions. The Iraqis had hidden the weapons within a residential area barely 300 feet from civilian homes.

26 MARCH • Some 954 paratroopers of the Army's 173rd Airborne Brigade seized an airfield near Bashur in northern Iraq. During the following days, aircraft from *Theodore Roosevelt* (CVN 71) supported the soldiers against Iraqi counterattacks.

27 MARCH • While flying a jamming mission, a VAQ-131 EA-6B Prowler received a request to assist three aircraft strikes against Iraqi surface-to-air missile (SAM) sites. Despite antiaircraft fire, the Prowler coordinated with the strike aircraft and knocked out the SAMs with AGM-88 High-speed Anti-Radiation Missiles.

27 MARCH • The Navy ordered a seventh C-40A Clipper to improve transportation capabilities.

28 MARCH • Naval and other coalition aircraft attacked nine enemy meeting places northeast of Basra, Iraq, killing an estimated 200 Ba'ath party officials and paramilitary chiefs.

28 MARCH • Naval aircraft helped Marines defeat a ferocious attack by Iraqi irregulars supported by armored personnel carriers, rockets, and antiaircraft artillery at An

USN 030415-N-4142G-106

An F-14D Tomcat of VF-2 makes a hard landing while returning to *Constellation* (CV 64) from a mission into Iraq, 15 April 2003.

Nasiriyah. Additional strikes supported allied troops locked in firefights with Iraqi troops and *Fedayeen Saddam* (Saddam's Martyrs) in the Rutbah and Samawah areas. Other air assaults used 1,000-pound bombs to destroy Republican Guard missile sites and fuel depots around Baghdad.

28 MARCH • Two F/A-18 Hornets knocked out three Iraqi Al Samoud surface-to-surface missile launchers approximately 25 miles northwest of Basra.

30 MARCH • Lt. Cmdrs. Hal Schmitt and Jason H. Norris of VFA-14 piloted two F/A-18Es, and Lt. Cmdrs. Brian M. Garrison and Mark W. Weisgerber and Lts. Thomas R. Poulter and Tom Brodine of VFA-41 manned two F/A-18Fs during a temporary 1,700 mile shift from *Nimitz* (CVN 68) to *Abraham Lincoln* (CVN 72). The transfer was to provide *Abraham Lincoln* with an improved mix of fighter-tanker capabilities, and raised the number of Super Hornets embarked on board that ship to 16. On 6 April, the four Super Hornets returned to *Nimitz* after her arrival in the Persian Gulf.

31 MARCH • Iraqi troops advanced upon paratroopers of the Army's 173rd Airborne Brigade in northern Iraq. Aircraft from *Theodore Roosevelt* (CVN 71) flew nearly 50 sorties that stopped the attack by bombing artillery installations, a barracks, and a surface-to-air missile site.

2 APRIL • Allied aircraft used 40 Joint Direct Attack Munitions to destroy a heavily secured Iraqi storage facility used by the regime's Special Security Organization in Baghdad's Al Karkh district.

2 APRIL • The Navy took delivery of the first low-rate initial production Shared Reconnaissance Pod system at Raytheon Technical Services Co., Indianapolis, Ind.

3 APRIL • F/A-18Fs embarked on board *Abraham Lincoln* (CVN 72) made the first operational flight of the Super Hornet Fast Tactical Imagery photoreconnaissance module during a strike over Iraq.

Amphibious assault ship *Tarawa* (LHA 1) leads an impressive display of naval power in the northern Persian Gulf—(from left) *Bonhomme Richard* (LHD 6), *Kearsarge* (LHD 3), *Bataan* (LHD 5), *Saipan* (LHA 2), and *Boxer* (LHD 4)—on 20 April 2003.

5 APRIL • The allies won the Battle of Debecka Pass, Iraq. Army Special Forces and Kurdish *Peshmerga* militiamen aided by Navy bombing guided by Air Force combat controllers captured and held the gap, but Iraqi troops and armored vehicles contained their advance. An F/A-18 Hornet from *Theodore Roosevelt* (CVN 71) knocked out a Ba'ath command group with a 750-pound bomb and the Iraqis subsequently fled, leaving eight tanks and 16 armored personnel carriers burning. Two VF-213 F-14Ds flying from *Theodore Roosevelt* attacked a group of Iraqi tanks firing from the south. One of the Tomcats accidentally bombed a group of *Peshmerga* gathered around a disabled T-55 Iraqi main battle tank, killing 17 Kurds and injuring another 45 including its commander, Wajih Barzani.

11 APRIL • The Navy designated the Mediterranean east of 30°E longitude as a zone for eligibility for Imminent Danger Pay or Combat Zone Tax Relief benefits. This move fell short of reaching all veterans who had served in the conflict because it failed to identify those who had participated from 19 March. On 18 February 2004, Navy officials thus announced the retroactive eligibility of veterans of Operation Iraqi Freedom for the benefits during that initial 24-day period. The decision principally impacted Task Force 61, Carrier Air Wings 3 and 8, *Harry S. Truman* (CVN 75), and *Theodore Roosevelt* (CVN 71).

20 APRIL • Twenty-six ships of Task Force 51, including amphibious assault ships *Tarawa* (LHA 1), *Saipan* (LHA 2), *Kearsarge* (LHD 3), *Boxer* (LHD 4), *Bataan* (LHD 5), and *Bonhomme Richard* (LHD 6), sailed in the northern Persian Gulf.

30 APRIL • VC-8's last TA-4J Skyhawk departed NS Roosevelt Roads, P.R., for display at the Glenn Martin Museum, Baltimore, Md.

1 MAY • President George W. Bush arrived on board *Abraham Lincoln* (CVN 72) in a VS-35 S-3B Viking, BuNo 159387, crewed by squadron executive officer Cmdr. John

This F-14D Tomcat of VF-2 on board *Constellation* (CV 64) displays its record of 60 bomb drops during Operation Iraqi Freedom, 29 May 2003.

P. Lussier and Lt. Ryan M. Phillips, and accompanied by a Secret Service agent. At one point during the 30-mile flight from NAS North Island, Calif., Lussier turned control of the aircraft, called Navy 1, over to the president. The Viking later was sent for display at the National Museum of Naval Aviation, NAS Pensacola, Fla.

12 JUNE • Amphibious assault ship *Kearsarge* (LHD 3) diverted to Liberian waters for Operation Shining Express—the potential evacuation of Americans stranded by fighting in that country. On 19 June, the ship left the region.

22 JUNE • During a training exercise at Godoria Range near Djibouti, one of two Boeing B-52H Stratofortresses accidentally dropped nine M-117 bombs on Combined Joint Task Force–Horn of Africa troops, killing Capt. Seth R. Michaud, USMC, of HMH-461, wounding nine other Americans, and destroying two squadron CH-53E Super Stallions.

24 JUNE • A P-3C Orion, an MH-60 from *Concord* (T-AFS 5), and British landing ship *Sir Tristram* (L 3505) rescued all 27 crew members of Egyptian-flagged cargo vessel *Green Glory* in the Arabian Sea, about 350 miles off the coast of Oman. Sailors hoisted the last survivor aloft just as the ship sank amid heavy seas after it caught fire the previous evening.

30 JUNE • The initial naval flight officer class of four Navy, one Marine, and one Air Force students to train in T-6A Texan IIs commenced with VT-10 at NAS Pensacola, Fla.

1 JULY • VF-2 was redesignated VFA-2 as the first squadron to transition from F-14D Tomcats to F/A-18F Super Hornets and relocated from NAS Oceana, Va., to NAS Lemoore, Calif.

10 JULY • A site survey team consisting of F/A-18 Hornet and Air Force F-15E Strike Eagle and F-16 Fighting Falcon pilots and technicians evaluated the feasibility of deploying their aircraft at Djibouti.

17 JULY • VT-9's E-2/C-2 standardization officer, Lt. Charles B. Bassel, performed the last arrested landing of a T-2C Buckeye during carrier qualifications on board *Harry S. Truman* (CVN 75).

30 JULY • An F/A-18 Hornet carried out the first flight of an integrated APG-79 Active Electronically Scanned Radar at China Lake, Calif.

5 AUGUST • The first student naval flight officer training flight in a T-6A Texan II occurred with VT-10 at NAS Pensacola, Fla.

14 AUGUST • United Nations humanitarian relief workers required protection during their distribution of aid to victims of the fighting in Liberia, and on this date, nine helicopters of the 26th Marine Expeditionary Unit flew from amphibious assault ship *Iwo Jima* (LHD 7) and transported 200 Marines, together with SEALs and explosive ordnance disposal specialists, to Roberts International Airport, Monrovia.

25 AUGUST • The Marines announced their deployment of the Ramp Mounted Weapon System on board CH-53Es of HMH-461 at Djibouti. The system includes a Fabrique Nationale M3M .50-caliber machine gun.

28 AUGUST • VMX-22 was activated as an MV-22 Osprey operational test and evaluation squadron at MCAS New River, N.C.

3 SEPTEMBER • Expeditionary Strike Group (ESG) 1 deployed from NS Pearl Harbor, Hawaii, to the Indian Ocean, Persian Gulf, and the Horn of Africa, as the first fully formed such group, with amphibious assault ship *Peleliu* (LHA 5) as its principle ship. ESG development provided flexible responses for global power projection. It returned on 9 March 2004.

10 SEPTEMBER • The Navy announced the record of decision concerning the basing of F/A-18E/F Super Hornets. Eight squadrons comprising 96 aircraft and one fleet readiness squadron of 24 jets were to be stationed at NAS Oceana, Va., two squadrons of 24 Super Hornets at MCAS Cherry Point, N.C., and construction of an outlying landing field in Washington County, N.C.

18 SEPTEMBER • Hurricane Isabel had already devastated much of the Gulf and East Coasts of the United States, and on this date threatened Hampton Roads, Va. *Theodore Roosevelt* (CVN 71) turned from an emergency sortie into the wake of the hurricane to make for NS Norfolk, Va. Upon arrival, crewmembers assisted storm victims along the Virginia and North Carolina coasts. Isabel also damaged historic naval aircraft preserved at the National Museum of Naval Aviation, NAS Pensacola, Fla., and at the Battleship *Alabama* (BB 60) Memorial, Mobile, Ala.

24 SEPTEMBER • Forward-deployed VF-154 relocated from NAF Atsugi, Japan, to NAS Lemoore, Calif., in preparation for its redesignation on 1 October to VFA-154 and transition from F-14A Tomcats to F/A-18F Super Hornets.

30 SEPTEMBER • VMA-231 at MCAS Cherry Point, N.C., received the Marine Corps' last remanufactured AV-8B Harrier II, BuNo 166288.

9 OCTOBER • A UH-1Y Venom made its first flight as a fully configured and functional H-1 upgrade at NAS Patuxent River, Md.

31 OCTOBER • The Naval Service Training Command was established at NS Great Lakes, Ill. The move aligned all enlisted and officer training accessions programs, which averaged more than 50,000 trainees annually. The naval aviation commands impacted included Officer Candidate School, Limited Duty Officer and Warrant Officer School, Direct Commissioned Officer School, and Officer Training Command.

13 NOVEMBER • The first four F/A-18F Super Hornets permanently forward deployed arrived at VFA-102, NAF Atsugi, Japan.

21 NOVEMBER • A UH-1Y Venom completed testing at MCB Quantico, Va., of the Special Warfare Kit.

22 NOVEMBER • On board *John F. Kennedy* (CV 67), pilot Lt. Cmdr. Thomas M. Santomauro completed the first carrier landing of an upgraded eight-bladed propeller equipped E-2C Hawkeye.

24 NOVEMBER • The Marines received their final CH-53E Super Stallion, BuNo 165243, at HMH-461, MCAS New River, N.C.

NAVAIR

Developed by the Navy and Marines to replace the EA-6B Prowler, a Marine EA-18G Growler of VX-23 cruises near Patuxent River, Md., during testing in August 2006.

5 DECEMBER • HSL-49 Detachment 4 departed to participate in the second sea swap during the relief of HSL-45 Detachment 6 on board destroyer *Fletcher* (DD 992).

15 DECEMBER • Through 20 December, allied forces seized three dhows and 33 drug smugglers who supported al-Qaeda terrorists. On 15 December, destroyer *Decatur* (DDG 73) intercepted a dhow and detained her 12 crewmen after the discovery of 54 bags of hashish valued at almost $10 million. Three days later, a New Zealand P-3K Orion located two suspicious dhows and worked with Australian, British, and U.S. aircraft to track the boats across the north Arabian Sea. On 20 December, cruiser *Philippine Sea* (CG 58) backed by a British Royal Air Force Aerospace MR.2 Nimrod intercepted the dhows and seized 21 smugglers, 150-pounds of methamphetamines, and 35- and 50-pound bags of heroin. Analysts used video footage taken by a VP-47 P-3C to verify the smugglers' activities.

17 DECEMBER • An RQ-8A completed the 100th Fire Scout flight at Webster Field, NAS Patuxent River, Md.

18 DECEMBER • The EA-18G received Milestone B approval to proceed into system design and development. The contract covering 2005 to 2009 included a total of 56 aircraft.

2004

6 JANUARY • The E-2 Integrated Test Team announced the completion of flight testing of an eight-bladed NP2000 propeller at NAS Patuxent River, Md.

9 JANUARY • Frigate *McClusky* (FFG 41) and her embarked helicopter from HSL-43 Detachment 6 rescued 169 migrants on board Ecuadorian vessels *The Andrea* and *San Luis* when the ships foundered in the eastern Pacific.

10 JANUARY • Ex-*Midway* (CV 41) arrived to serve as a naval museum and event facility at Broadway Pier, San Diego, Calif.

12 JANUARY • Frigate *Samuel B. Roberts* (FFG 58) and Coast Guard Law Enforcement Detachment 403 intercepted a suspicious vessel tracked by the frigate's embarked helicopter from HSL-44 Detachment 7 and seized eight drug traffickers and more than 7,000 pounds of cocaine.

14 JANUARY • Amphibious assault ship *Boxer* (LHD 4), with aircraft and Marines from I Marine Expeditionary Force embarked, deployed in support of Operation Iraqi Freedom. *Boxer* arrived in the Persian Gulf on 20 February and returned on 29 April.

19 JANUARY • Amphibious assault ship *Bataan* (LHD 5), with Marines of II Marine Expeditionary Force embarked, deployed in support of Operation Iraqi Freedom. *Bataan* returned on 31 March.

23 JANUARY • The Navy announced the signing of an almost $570 million, second multi-year procurement contract with Northrop Grumman Corp. for E-2C Hawkeye 2000s.

5 FEBRUARY • Boeing Integrated Defense Systems announced the completion of the integration of AGM-84K SLAM-ER (Standoff Land Attack Missile–Expanded Response) into P-3C Orions.

10 FEBRUARY • The Officer Training Command consisting of Officer Candidate School, Limited Duty Officer/Warrant Officer School, and the Direct Commissioned Officer School celebrated its establishment at NAS Pensacola, Fla.

17 FEBRUARY • Expeditionary Strike Group (ESG) 2 including amphibious assault ship *Wasp* (LHD 1), with the 22d Marine Expeditionary Unit embarked, began the first deployment of an East Coast–based ESG. Some of the Marines, including elements of the 2d Marine Aircraft

Wing, later deployed near Kandahar, Afghanistan and fought in Operation Mountain Storm—a preemptive campaign against an anticipated spring offensive by the Taliban. ESG-2 returned on 18 September.

19 FEBRUARY • The Airframe and Powerplant Program was established at CNATT Pensacola, Fla. The program gave Navy aviation technicians the opportunity to earn the Federal Aviation Administration's airframe and powerplant license.

MARCH • During the month, Muslim militants increased their infiltration into Iraq along a route that ran principally across the Syrian mountains and down the Tigris and Euphrates Rivers into Fallujah and Ramadi, west of Baghdad. Navy and Marine aircraft struck these insurgents during Operation Vigilant Resolve. On 9 April, the coalition suspended the operation to allow negotiations, but Fallujah remained an extremist stronghold.

11 MARCH • VX-20 accepted its first T-6A Texan II for testing at NAS Patuxent River, Md.

21 MARCH • Frigate *Stephen W. Groves* (FFG 29) and her embarked SH-60B Seahawk from HSL-42 Detachment 10 rescued 103 Ecuadorian migrants from their unseaworthy 40-foot fishing boat in the eastern Pacific.

22 MARCH • Greek-flagged tanker *Everton* and Korean-flagged fishing vessel *Chun Ying* collided off the Omani coast, igniting a fire on board the tanker. Cruiser *Yorktown* (CG 48) and her embarked SH-60B Seahawk from HSL-42 Detachment 2 assisted in the multinational search and rescue of 24 of the 25 crewmembers on board *Everton*.

2 APRIL • An Improved Capability (ICAP) III EA-6B Prowler began operational evaluation with VX-9 at NAWS China Lake, Calif.

5 APRIL • The Navy announced the transfer scheduled for June 2005 of *Oriskany* (CV 34) to the state of Florida for use as an artificial reef. The decision marked the first disposal of a carrier in this manner.

7 APRIL • The V-22 Osprey program manager announced the decision to use the MV-22 designation instead of HV-22.

8 APRIL • The Fleet Anti-Submarine Warfare Command was established to integrate advanced submarine hunting networks at San Diego, Calif.

29 APRIL • Commander Operational Testing and Evaluation Marine Corps recommended the full fleet introduction of the KC-130J Super Hercules for operational use.

6 MAY • Cmdr. Stewart R. Graham, USCG, (Coast Guard Aviator No. 114 and Helicopter Pilot No. 2) was inducted into the Hall of Honor at the National Museum of Naval Aviation, NAS Pensacola, Fla. Graham pioneered helicopter development during World War II.

15 MAY • The Department of Defense authorized AIM-9X Sidewinder air-to-air missiles for full-rate production.

17 MAY • A UH-1Y Venom fired weapons for the first time during a test flight at Fort A.P. Hill, Va.

27 MAY • *Ronald Reagan* (CVN 76), with elements of six squadrons from Carrier Air Wing 11 embarked, sailed from NS Norfolk, Va., rounded Cape Horn, and on 23 July reached her new homeport of NAS North Island, Calif. The guests who greeted the arrival of the ship included former First Lady Nancy D. Reagan.

JUNE • During Summer Pulse 04, the Navy tested changes to operational methods that resulted from the Fleet Response Plan. At times, *Kitty Hawk* (CV 63), *Enterprise* (CVN 65), *John F. Kennedy* (CV 67), *George Washington* (CVN 73), *John C. Stennis* (CVN 74), *Harry S. Truman* (CVN 75), and *Ronald Reagan* (CVN 76) deployed in five theaters. The operations of these ships extended into September during scheduled deployments, surge operations, and joint and international exercises.

21 JUNE • The V-22 Osprey Integrated Test Team successfully completed the fifth at-sea tests of the aircraft's shipboard suitability on board amphibious assault ship *Iwo Jima* (LHD 7) off the coast of Maryland. The tests resulted in expanded operational wind envelopes and cleared the use of more shipboard spots than previous tests. The evaluations concluded on 29 June.

24 JUNE • A ceremony commemorated the last overhaul of an F-14 at NADEP Jacksonville, Fla. The depot had received the responsibility to rework and repair Tomcats in 1994.

5 JULY • *George Washington* (CVN 73) returned from the Persian Gulf after more than four months of supporting Operation Iraqi Freedom. Her aircraft had flown strikes into Iraq and participated in maritime interception operations that led to the boarding of more than 200 vessels.

15 JULY • Pilot Lt. j.g. Scott Timmester and radar intercept officer Lt. Cmdr. Mark W. Tankersley of VF-213 made the last firing of an AIM-54C Phoenix long-range air-to-air missile. The Navy continued to phase the weapons from inventory by 30 September. On 17 September 1974, VF-1 and -2 had first deployed with Phoenixes on board *Enterprise* (CVN 65). More than 4,566 had been built.

20 JULY • Aircraft embarked on board *John F. Kennedy* (CV 67) in the Persian Gulf struck insurgents threatening Multi-National Corps–Iraq. A VF-103 F-14B Tomcat dropped GBU-12 guided bombs and an F/A-18C Hornet dropped GBU-32s on enemy positions.

23 JULY • The last NF-14D, BuNo 163416, made its final flight with VX-30 at Naval Base Ventura County, Calif. The event marked the conclusion of research, development, test, and evaluation flight operations with Tomcats.

13 AUGUST • The Naval Aerospace Medicine Institute named its Aerospace Medicine Academic Center in honor of naval aviation members Capts. David M. Brown and Laurel B. S. Clark, who died on 1 February 2003 when space shuttle *Columbia* broke apart during reentry.

28 AUGUST • Frigate *Curts* (FFG 38) and her embarked SH-60B Seahawk from HSL-45 Detachment 6 rescued 106 Ecuadorian migrants from foundering smuggling vessel *El Poder de Dios*, 300 miles east of Ecuador.

30 AUGUST • The 200th F/A-18 Super Hornet, a two-seat F model, arrived at VX-9, NAWS China Lake, Calif.

SEPTEMBER • During the middle of the month, Hurricane Ivan devastated the area from Louisiana to Florida, and caused more than $100 million in damage at NAS Pensacola, Fla., including 34 display aircraft on the flight line of the National Museum of Naval Aviation. It also forced 3,300 students at NATTC to resume classes in temporary classrooms on 27 September. The Navy issued a stop movement order to all people with orders to stations in the region that remained in effect until early December.

7 SEPTEMBER • Commander Operational Test and Evaluation Force issued the final report on the assessment of EP-3E Aries II Sensor System Improvement Program upgrades, which found them operationally effective and suitable for introduction to VQ-1 and -2.

9 SEPTEMBER • A P-3C from VP-16 spotted a suspected go-fast vessel in the Pacific Ocean and alerted Coast Guard cutter *Jarvis* (WHEC 725). The cutter's HH-65A Dolphin and the Orion observed the smugglers throw contraband overboard, and despite the escape of the boat, *Jarvis* recovered bales of cocaine valued at more than $40 million.

9 SEPTEMBER • Expeditionary Strike Group (ESG) 3 conducted a flag-staff crossdeck in the Persian Gulf from amphibious assault ship *Belleau Wood* (LHA 3) to *Essex* (LHD 2). The *Essex* ESG was activated the following day.

17 SEPTEMBER • After surveillance by P-3C Orions from VP-16 and -65, frigate *Curts* (FFG 38), with an embarked SH-60B Seahawk from HSL-45 Detachment 6 and a Coast Guard law enforcement detachment intercepted fishing vessel *Lina Maria* and seized 14 tons of cocaine southwest of the Galapagos Islands.

23 SEPTEMBER • A P-3C Orion from VP-16 vectored frigate *Crommelin* (FFG 37), with an embarked SH-60 Seahawk from HSL-37 Detachment 3 and a Coast Guard law enforcement detachment, to the seizure of smuggling vessel *San Jose* and 13 tons of cocaine west of the Galapagos Islands.

1 OCTOBER • The Navy transferred operation of the Naval Space Surveillance System—used to track satellites and debris orbiting the earth—to the Air Force at Naval Network and Space Operations Command, Dahlgren, Va.

2 OCTOBER • Two joint interceptions involving a Navy P-3C Orion and Coast Guard cutter *Gallatin* (WHEC 721) seized nearly 8,000 pounds of cocaine and eight smugglers from two go-fast vessels in Columbian waters; the second interception occurred on 8 October. In both instances, *Gallatin*'s embarked MH-68A Mako of Helicopter Interdiction Tactical Squadron 10 disabled the boats with gunfire when the smugglers attempted to escape and jettison their contraband.

6 OCTOBER • The first of two RQ-4A Global Hawks allocated for the Navy's Global Hawk Maritime Demonstration Program made its initial flight from Northrop Grumman Corp., Palmdale, Calif., to Edwards AFB, Calif.

22 OCTOBER • The production line for EA-18Gs was activated at Boeing Company, St. Louis, Mo.

28 OCTOBER • A prototype Multi-Mission Maritime Aircraft, subsequently named Poseidon, began low-speed wind tunnel testing, which concluded on 5 November at Boeing Company, St. Louis, Mo. The aircraft, based on Boeing's commercial 737, was designed to operate at up to 41,000 feet with a storage capacity of 120 sonobuoys, 50 percent greater than that of the P-3C. Initial operating capability was scheduled for 2013, and it was to be fully operational by 2019. The Navy intended to purchase up to 108 aircraft to replace Orions.

USN 050125-N-9079D-056

An SH-60B Seahawk of HSL-47 lands on board *Abraham Lincoln* (CVN 72) in the Indian Ocean in January 2005 during Operation Unified Assistance, a humanitarian relief effort in the wake of a tsunami that devastated South East Asia, 26 December 2004.

6 NOVEMBER • The coalition launched Operation Phantom Fury (later renamed Al Fajr, Dawn) to drive insurgents from Fallujah, Iraq. In late October and early November, allied aircraft attacked positions in the city, and on this date, the 3d Marine Aircraft Wing bombed seven separate Iraqi weapons caches in eight hours. On 8 November, soldiers and Marines entered ferocious house-to-house fighting in northern Fallujah. The low cloud ceiling compelled fixed-wing aircraft to fly at lower altitudes and required greater involvement by helicopters. Because insurgents fought from mosques and hospitals, precision-guided munitions proved vital to their defeat while sparing civilians. Al Fajr marked the combat debut of GBU-38 500-pound Joint Direct Attack Munitions when F/A-18C Hornets of VFA-34, embarked on board *John F. Kennedy* (CV 67), dropped two of the weapons. The battle continued into December.

12 NOVEMBER • The V-22 Integrated Test Team conducted shipboard suitability testing on board amphibious assault ship *Wasp* (LHD 1) off the mid-Atlantic coast. The testing, which concluded on 23 November, primarily consisted of interaction between two Ospreys during flight operations.

USN 050124-N-0168J-001

Marine Cpl. Tyler Samms and FC3 Bethany A. Deadman (foreground) deployed with amphibious assault ship *Essex* (LHD 2), pass bags of rice for victims of a tsunami at an airfield at Sabang, Indonesia, 24 January 2005.

16 NOVEMBER • Raytheon Missile Systems unveiled the AGM-154C Joint Standoff Weapon to the Navy at Tucson, Ariz.

27 NOVEMBER • A VP-9 P-3C Orion proved instrumental in a multinational search and rescue of eight United Arab Emirates fishermen when their dhow sank off the Bahrain coast.

1 DECEMBER • Lockheed Martin announced receipt of a $15.6 million contract to integrate Armed Helicopter Mission Kits for MH-60S Seahawks as part of the Navy's armed helicopter program.

2 DECEMBER • A yola carrying 94 Dominican migrants capsized off the northern coast of Puerto Rico. A Coast Guard HU-25 Guardian spotted the distressed vessel and alerted search and rescue forces including three HH-65A Dolphins from CGAS Borinquen, P.R., cutters *Chincoteague* (WPB 1320) and *Key Largo* (WPB 1324), the Border Patrol, and Immigration and Customs Enforcement. Into the next day, these teams rescued 85 survivors and recovered the bodies of nine migrants.

4 DECEMBER • Two E-2Cs of VAW-126 deployed from *Harry S. Truman* (CVN 75) in the Persian Gulf to Kandahar AB, Afghanistan, to provide airborne command and control for the inauguration of President Hamid Karzai. The Hawkeyes returned to the ship on 13 December.

14 DECEMBER • Commander Operational Test and Evaluation Force announced the completion of the operational testing of AGM-154C Joint Standoff Weapons, and their operational effectiveness and suitability for fleet deployment.

26 DECEMBER • A magnitude 9.0 earthquake struck off the west coast of Sumatra, Indonesia, triggering a tsunami across the Indian Ocean littoral that killed more than 230,000 people. Combined Support Force 536 coordinated Operation Unified Assistance—multinational relief efforts. United States naval forces often reached disaster zones before aid agencies, and aircraft delivered supplies and emergency responders to otherwise inaccessible inland areas. On 1 January 2005, four SH-60B Seahawks from HSL-47 and some SH-60Fs and HH-60Hs of HS-2, embarked on board *Abraham Lincoln* (CVN 72), began to ferry supplies from collection points in Sumatra. Reinforcements at times included amphibious assault ships *Essex* (LHD 2) and *Bonhomme Richard* (LHD 6); P-3C Orions of VP-4 and -8; VRC-30; HC-11; four MH-53E Sea Dragons from HM-15 Detachment 2; six CH-46E Sea Knights from Okinawa; two MH-60Ss from HC-5, embarked on board combat store ship *Niagara Falls* (T-AFS 3); VMGR-352; and a USCG HC-130H Hercules. Despite earthquake aftershocks, these aircraft flew 1,747 missions, transported 3,043 passengers, and delivered 5.92 million pounds of supplies to people in Indonesia, Sri Lanka, and Thailand. On 3 February, *Abraham Lincoln* departed Indonesian waters, and 11 days later the force ceased relief operations.

2005

27 JANUARY • The EA-18G completed wind tunnel testing. Engineers had validated the F/A-18F Super Hornet airframe for the electronic attack mission during 1,412 hours of testing at Boeing Company and NASA facilities.

30 JANUARY • Aircraft from *Harry S. Truman* (CVN 75) provided on-call close air support in 32 sorties during the Iraqi national elections.

FEBRUARY • In September 2004, Hurricane Jeanne had devastated Haiti, killing more than 2,000 people and leaving 300,000 homeless. The annual Southern Command exercise Operation New Horizons focused on relief efforts there, and at times through June, amphibious assault ships *Saipan* (LHA 2) and *Nassau* (LHA 4), HC-6, HSC-28, HM-14, and VR-55 took part.

10 FEBRUARY • The Marine Corps announced the passage of the second operational evaluation of the KC-130J at NAWC China Lake, Calif., and MCASs Cherry Point, N.C., and Yuma, Ariz. On 13 February, VMGR-252 began the first Super Hercules deployment during the relief of VMGR-452 in Iraq.

14 MARCH • The Navy announced the designation of the Advanced Hawkeye as E-2D. Designers intended the plane's more powerful radar to elevate it from an airborne early warning platform to a battle management command and control system. Construction began in early April, with plans to procure 75 aircraft and initial operational capability in 2011.

15 MARCH • The first Improved Capability (ICAP) III EA-6B Prowler arrived at VAQ-139 at Northrop Grumman facilities, St. Augustine, Fla.

20 MARCH • *Carl Vinson* (CVN 70) relieved *Harry S. Truman* (CVN 75) in the Persian Gulf. A detachment comprising half the SH-60F and HH-60Hs of HS-8 deployed from *Carl Vinson* to Camp Arifjan, Kuwait. The Seahawks patrolled southeastern Iraq and flew maritime security operations over the northern Persian Gulf, and returned to the carrier on 29 June.

28 MARCH • VMX-22 began the operational evaluation of the MV-22 Osprey.

30 MARCH • The Multi-Mission Maritime Aircraft received the designation P-8A.

18 APRIL • A Joint Common Missile (JCM) completed initial F/A-18E/F Super Hornet integration wind tunnel testing at NASA Ames Research Center, San Jose, Calif., and Boeing Company, Philadelphia, Pa. Super Hornets were intended to carry up to 12 JCMs.

29 APRIL • A multinational force including cruiser *Normandy* (CG 60) and her embarked SH-60 Seahawk of HSL-42 Detachment 1, coastal patrol ships *Firebolt* (PC 10) and *Typhoon* (PC 5), and German frigate *Karlsruhe* (F 212), rescued 89 people from a dhow that capsized in the Gulf of Aden off the Somali coast.

29 APRIL • President George W. Bush signed a memorandum for the Secretary of Defense approving the redesignation of the Naval Reserve to the Navy Reserve.

7 MAY • UH-1Y Venoms and AH-1Z Vipers made their first shipboard landings during testing on board amphibious assault ship *Bataan* (LHD 5) off the Virginia Capes. Over six days, the two H-1 upgrade aircraft, Y-2 and Z-3, completed 127 and 140 landings and 13.4 and 14.5 flight hours, respectively.

9 MAY • The MH-60R Seahawk entered operational evaluation.

11 MAY • *Carl Vinson* (CVN 70) coordinated the rescue of all 27 sailors from Panamanian-flagged merchantman *Olympias* off Iran in the Persian Gulf. An engine room fire had engulfed the ship, and the carrier directed destroyer *Mustin* (DDG 89) and her embarked SH-60B Seahawk of HSL-45 Detachment 5 to the vessel's aid.

12 MAY • Capt. Eugene A. Cernan received NASA's first Ambassador of Exploration Award, which recognizes the sacrifices and dedication of the Mercury, Gemini, and Apollo astronauts. Naval aviator Cernan flew three times in space and twice to the moon, and was the second American to walk in space.

14 MAY • *America* (CV 66) was sunk off the East Coast as a live-fire test and evaluation and weapons effects platform for the CVN-21 program.

25 MAY • Ships that surged under the Fleet Response Plan for three months to the European and Central Command areas of responsibility included amphibious assault ship *Saipan* (LHA 2) from NS Norfolk, Va.

1 JUNE • The Naval Test Parachute Team was disestablished at NAWC China Lake, Calif.

18 JUNE • VMX-22 completed the operational evaluation of the MV-22 Osprey.

21 JUNE • An MH-60S Seahawk of HSC-28 Detachment 2, embarked on board amphibious assault ship *Kearsarge* (LHD 3), provided food and fuel to the nine people on board an Iranian fishing dhow adrift and taking on water in the Persian Gulf. The Iranians refused further assistance.

22 JUNE • Australian S70A-9 Black Hawks of the 5th Aviation Regiment completed more than 1,200 takeoffs and landings in ten days of operations on board amphibious assault ship *Boxer* (LHD 4) during Exercise Talisman Sabre.

22 JUNE • Instructor Lt. Carl J. Wells of VT-4 and student Ens. Luis Diez flew the last T-34C Turbomentor training flight of Training Wing 6 at NAS Pensacola, Fla.

24 JUNE • Lt. j.g. Jeanine MacIntosh, USCG, became the first African American female aviator in the Coast Guard at NAS Corpus Christi, Texas. MacIntosh subsequently flew an HC-130H Hercules from CGAS Barbers Point, Hawaii.

30 JUNE • *Carl Vinson* (CVN 70) turned for home from supporting Operation Iraqi Freedom and maritime surveillance operations in the Persian Gulf. Aircraft from Carrier Air Wing 9 had logged more than 6,500 sorties during these battles.

7 JULY • The next-generation presidential helicopter received the mission design series designator VH-71A.

22 JULY • An RQ-8B Fire Scout unmanned aerial vehicle test fired two Hydra 2.75-inch unguided rockets at Yuma Proving Grounds, Ariz.

28 JULY • The first production MH-60R Seahawk made its initial flight at Sikorsky Aircraft Corporation, Stratford, Conn.

4 AUGUST • Two F/A-18F Super Hornets under construction were moved from Boeing's St. Louis, Mo., assembly line to a separate hangar for conversion to EA-18Gs.

19 AUGUST • Terrorists of the al-Qaeda–linked Abdullah Azzam Brigades fired three Katyusha-type rockets at amphibious assault ship *Kearsarge* (LHD 3) and dock landing ship *Ashland* (LSD 48) in Al Aqabah, Jordan. The rockets missed the ships moored for the two-week Infinite Moonlight exercise with the Jordanians, but killed one Jordanian sentry and wounded another. The ships left the port but operated in the area until 25 August.

Search and rescue swimmer AWC Scott Pierce of HS-75 looks out from an SH-60 Seahawk at New Orleans streets flooded by Hurricane Katrina, 7 September 2005.

29 AUGUST • Hurricane Katrina made landfall along the coast of the Gulf of Mexico. A catastrophic storm surge inundated the levees along the Mississippi River and the rising waters flooded 80 percent of New Orleans, La. Six E-2C Hawkeyes from VAW-77, -121, and -126 monitored airspace and directed rescue aircraft. On 30 August, amphibious assault ship *Bataan* (LHD 5) arrived and augmented two embarked MH-60S Seahawks of HSC-28 with four MH-53E Sea Stallions from HM-15. Meanwhile, amphibious assault ship *Iwo Jima* (LHD 7) moored at New Orleans and became a hub for helicopters as Headquarters, Joint Task Force Katrina. On 1 September, *Harry S. Truman* (CVN 75) arrived with elements of 13 helicopter squadrons embarked. Additional naval aviation reinforcements included MH-60s of HSL-43, -47, and -49, and HC-11, two CH-46E Sea Knights and six CH-53E Super Stallions from six Marine squadrons at MCAS New River, N.C., four Super Stallions from HMH-772, and VR-57 and -58. Seventy-six Coast Guard and Coast Guard Auxiliary aircraft rescued 12,535 people during 1,817 sorties. Altogether, more than 5,000 Coast Guardsmen saved 33,545 lives. More than 70 fixed wing aircraft and 350 helicopters from all the services responded.

SEPTEMBER • Hurricane Rita struck the Texas coast, and the Navy evacuated all naval installations in that state including NASs Corpus Christi and Kingsville.

1 SEPTEMBER • During the Navy's transformation of forces in Europe, VQ-2 changed homeports from NS Rota, Spain, to NAS Whidbey Island, Wash. Five days later, HC-4 shifted from NAS Sigonella, Sicily, to NS Norfolk, Va.

USN 050910-N-2383B-537

Amphibious assault ship *Iwo Jima* (LHD 7) is moored at New Orleans and serves as a hub for helicopters flying relief missions in the aftermath of Hurricane Katrina, 10 September 2005.

14 SEPTEMBER • HC-2 Detachment 2 passed the mission of combat logistics in the Naval Forces Central Command area of responsibility to HSC-26 Detachment 1. The change concluded 27 years of an HC-2 detachment at Bahrain.

17 SEPTEMBER • While *Theodore Roosevelt* (CVN 71) visited Palma de Mallorca, Spain, two VAQ-141 EA-6B Prowlers detached for three weeks to Al Asad, west of Baghdad, Iraq. On 24 September, the Prowlers flew the first of 37 combat sorties in support of VMAQ-1.

28 SEPTEMBER • The Defense Acquisition Board cleared the MV-22 Osprey for full-rate production.

30 SEPTEMBER • Sea Control Wing, Pacific Fleet, was deactivated at NAS North Island, Calif. Sea Control Wing, Atlantic Fleet, assumed the administrative duties for the remaining Pacific VS squadrons.

OCTOBER • Hurricane Wilma ravaged southern Florida and forced the evacuation of NAS Key West. Amphibious assault ship *Wasp* (LHD 1) supported relief efforts in the area.

8 OCTOBER • A 7.6 magnitude earthquake near the Indo-Pakistani border killed more than 73,000 people and rendered nearly three million homeless. Commander *Tarawa* (LHA 1) Expeditionary Strike Group Rear Adm. Michael A. LeFever coordinated the operations of the Disaster Assistance Center at Islamabad, Pakistan. Through 13 February, two HM-15 MH-53E Sea Dragons, two HSC-26 MH-60S Seahawks, a VQ-2 EP-3E Aries II detachment, a VR-56 C-9B Skytrain, a VR-64 C-130T Hercules, and Army, Air Force, and allied aircraft flew more than 4,000 missions, delivered over 11,000 tons of supplies, and transported more than 18,000 people.

USCG

HH-65As from Coast Guard Air Station New Orleans fly over that city in the early 1990s. A decade later, three Coast Guard Dolphins rescued more than 300 residents in 85 sorties in the wake of Hurricane Katrina.

12 OCTOBER • The Air Force Headquarters Materiel Command at Wright-Patterson AFB, Ohio, confirmed the name Growler for the EA-18G.

31 OCTOBER • A Navy and Boeing Company team began a five-day preliminary design review of the P-8A in Seattle, Wash.

4 NOVEMBER • The coalition began Operation al Hajip Elfulathi (Steel Curtain)—an offensive to prevent cells of al-Qaeda terrorists from crossing the Syrian border into Iraq. Aircraft from *Theodore Roosevelt* (CVN 71) flew reconnaissance and close air support missions with VF-31 and -213 F-14D Tomcats and VFA-15 and -87 F/A-18C Hornets bombing the enemy at Husaybah, Karabilah, and Ubaydi. Her aircraft flew more than 400 sorties through 17 November.

11 NOVEMBER • AV-8Bs of VMA-214 carried out the first Harrier II launches from a ship at sea while carrying Joint Direct Attack Munitions during operations on board amphibious assault ship *Peleliu* (LHA 5) off Camp Pendleton, Calif.

28 NOVEMBER • A Global Hawk Maritime Demonstrator participated in the first exercise of the system in Trident Warrior '05 off southern California. During the 12-day exercise, the RQ-4A transmitted data to participants on the East Coast including Commander Second Fleet, amphibious assault ship *Iwo Jima* (LHD 7), and command ship *Mount Whitney* (LCC 20).

LATE NOVEMBER • *Theodore Roosevelt* (CVN 71) visited Jebel Ali, and five F/A-18C Hornets of VFA-15 and -87 flew ashore to Al Asad, Iraq. The detachment combined with Marine and Air Force elements, flying an average of eight sorties a day.

USAF 050607-F-WZ253-002

The maiden flight of the second of two Navy RQ-4A Global Hawks was made 7 June 2005. The pair are used in the Broad Area Maritime Surveillance–Demonstrator program to refine tactics, techniques, and procedures for large persistent unmanned aerial vehicles in the maritime environment.

2 DECEMBER • The Navy announced the selection of *George Washington* (CVN 73) to relieve *Kitty Hawk* (CV 63) in 2008 as the forward-deployed carrier at FSA Yokosuka, Japan.

5 DECEMBER • HSL-41 at NAS North Island, Calif., became the first fleet squadron to receive the MH-60R Seahawk.

8 DECEMBER • The Marine Corps accepted the first production Block B MV-22 Osprey at Amarillo, Texas.

11 DECEMBER • An F-14D of VF-213, embarked on board *Theodore Roosevelt* (CVN 71), conducted the first mission of a Tomcat equipped with the Remotely Operated Video Enhanced Receiver system, which allowed a forward ground controller near Baghdad, Iraq, to see real-time images acquired by the Tomcat's sensors.

19 DECEMBER • During flight tests at NAS Patuxent River, Md., an E-2C fitted with a refueling probe connected to a KC-130 tanker to test the Hawkeye's inflight refueling capabilities.

22 DECEMBER • Cruiser *Gettysburg* (CG 64), with her embarked SH-60B Seahawk of HSL-46 Detachment 5 and a Coast Guard law enforcement detachment, intercepted a vessel carrying more than 11 tons of cocaine in the eastern Pacific.

2006

4 JANUARY • *Ronald Reagan* (CVN 76) made her maiden deployment to the western Pacific, Indian Ocean, and Persian Gulf. The cruise also marked the first deployment of Improved Capability (ICAP) III EA-6B Prowlers of VAQ-139, and F/A-18C Hornets and F/A-18E Super Hornets of VFA-22, -25, -113, and -115 equipped with the Remotely Operated Video Enhanced Receiver system.

16 JANUARY • Into the next day, two RQ-8A Fire Scout Vertical Takeoff and Landing Tactical Unmanned Air Vehicles (VTUAV) made nine autonomous landings on board amphibious transport dock *Nashville* (LPD 13) in the sea range off NAS Patuxent River, Md. These operations marked the first time that a major defense autonomous VTUAV had landed on board a fleet ship.

25 JANUARY • The Navy announced the opening for applications from 30 sailors in pay grades E-5 to E-7 for a trial Flying Chief Warrant Officer Program for possible fleet-wide introduction. The program allowed enlisted sailors the opportunity to become aviators in patrol squadrons, helicopter sea combat squadrons, and light helicopter antisubmarine squadrons.

1 FEBRUARY • The P-8A entered the critical design phase.

3 FEBRUARY • A fire erupted on board Egyptian ferry *al Salam Boccaccio 98* and she sank in the Red Sea, 50 miles off the coast of Egypt. High winds and a sandstorm impeded rescue efforts, but the infrared capabilities of a VP-47 P-3C Orion proved instrumental in the rescue of the 380 survivors of the estimated 96 crewmembers and 1,193 passengers.

8 FEBRUARY • Pilots Capt. William G. Sizemore II, of VF-213 and Lt. Bill Frank of VF-31 flew the last two F-14D Tomcat combat missions from *Theodore Roosevelt* (CVN 71). On 13 April, Sizemore's jet, BuNo 161159, arrived for historic preservation at the National Museum of Naval Aviation, NAS Pensacola, Fla.

15 FEBRUARY • Expeditionary Strike Group 3 including amphibious assault ship *Peleliu* (LHA 5) deployed from NS San Diego, Calif., to the western Pacific, Indian Ocean, and Persian Gulf. On 9 July the group returned from operations with the Fifth Fleet.

17 FEBRUARY • Joint Task Force Balikatan 2006, including Expeditionary Strike Group 7 and amphibious assault ship *Essex* (LHD 2), operated with U.S. and Filipino authorities to assist victims of a mudslide on southern Leyte, Philippines. Marine KC-130 Hercules, CH-46E Sea Knights, CH-53E Super Stallions, and UH-1N Iroquois, Army UH-60 Black Hawks, and Air Force C-130 Hercules and C-17A Globemaster IIIs searched for survivors, delivered relief supplies to victims, and provided immediate, life-sustaining support. On 14 March, *Essex* returned to Sasebo, Japan.

3 MARCH • VMM-263 at MCAS New River, N.C., was activated as the first operational MV-22B Osprey squadron.

21 MARCH • The Marine Corps accepted delivery of the final UC-35D Citation Encore, BuNo 166767, at Cessna Aircraft Company, Wichita, Kans.

22 MARCH • The Navy announced the redesignation of Navy Reserve Centers as Navy Operational Support Centers to more accurately describe the integrated role these held in operations.

23 MARCH • The Chief of Naval Air Training began to realign under NAVAIR as part of an effort to create greater efficiency and synchronization while increasing aviation warfighting readiness.

30 MARCH • Lt. Cmdr. William R. McCombs and Lt. Matthew E. Doyle of VX-23 flew an F/A-18F configured as an EA-18G at NAS Patuxent River, Md. The unique Super Hornet included ALQ-218(V)2 electronic warfare tactical receiver pods from an Improved Capability (ICAP) III EA-6B Prowler suite fitted onto the wingtips to contribute to the evaluation of flying qualities, loads, and flutter testing before accepting the initial two preproduction Growlers.

31 MARCH • The Navy approved the MH-60R Seahawk for full-rate production. In December 2005, West Coast Seahawk fleet readiness squadron HSM-41 had received the first four MH-60Rs.

U.S. Navy via Boeing

The first P-8A Poseidon test aircraft, BuNo 167951, (left) is escorted by NP-3C Orion, BuNo 158204, of VX-20 to its landing at Naval Air Station Patuxent River, Md., on 10 April 2010.

4 APRIL • Cruiser *Gettysburg* (CG 64), with an SH-60B Seahawk of HSL-46 Detachment 5 and a Coast Guard law enforcement detachment embarked, returned from a six-month counter-narcotics deployment to the western Caribbean and eastern Pacific. Working with other agencies and P-3C Orions, these teams had seized seven vessels, 40 smugglers, and 750 bales totaling more than 28 metric tons of cocaine and heroin valued at $1.95 billion.

12 APRIL • A 5.3-pound, 25-inch long Spike tactical precision-guided missile impacted a target during testing at NAWC China Lake, Calif. Spike was designed to arm unmanned aerial vehicles to attack bunkers, small boats, and armored vehicles without inflicting collateral damage on civilians.

27 APRIL • The Navy disestablished the F-14 Tomcat program during a ceremony at NAS Patuxent River, Md. Grumman had received its initial contract for the aircraft on 3 February 1969, the plane made its first flight on 21 December 1970, and on 14 January 1973, the first squadron F-14As arrived at VF-1. From 17 September 1974 to 20 May 1975, VF-1 and -2 completed the first Tomcat deployment with Carrier Air Wing 14 on board *Enterprise* (CVN 65) to the western Pacific and Indian Oceans. Through 10 July 1992, the Navy accepted 679 Tomcats.

2 MAY • An AH-1W Super Cobra fired two AGM-114N thermobaric Hellfire air-to-ground missiles 30 minutes apart at land test ranges in southern California. The tests evaluated modified flight control software that allowed the Hellfires to fly flatter trajectories and hit targets at a near zero angle for better penetration of buildings and caves, and thus minimize casualties.

2 MAY • *Enterprise* (CVN 65) deployed to the Mediterranean, Indian Ocean, Persian Gulf, and western Pacific through 18 November 2006. She operated with four fleets—the Second, Fifth, Sixth, and Seventh—and in two linked but distinct wars in Afghanistan and Iraq.

17 MAY • The Navy sank *Oriskany* (CV 34) as an artificial reef approximately 24 miles off the coast of NAS Pensacola, Fla.

24 MAY • The Department of Defense Office of Inspector General issued a Defense Base Closure and Realignment Commission (BRAC) notification of the failure of the Commonwealth of Virginia and municipal governments of Virginia Beach and Chesapeake, Va., to meet all requirements of the 2005 BRAC law regarding NAS Oceana, Va. The decision enabled the state of Florida to attempt to meet these requirements and allow the potential realignment of the F/A-18 strike fighter wing, aviation operations, and support schools from Oceana to NAS Cecil Field. The notice granted Florida through the end of the year to meet the requirements.

6 JUNE • Amphibious assault ship *Iwo Jima* (LHD 7) deployed from NS Norfolk, Va., for the Mediterranean Sea, Indian Ocean, and Persian Gulf.

26 JUNE • Lockheed EP-3Es upgraded to Spiral 1 of the Joint Airborne Signals Intelligence Architecture Modernization Configuration completed operational evaluation. Three days later the Navy approved an $18 million full-rate production contract for six of the improved Aries IIs.

29 JUNE • HMM-464 accepted the first restored war reserve CH-53E, BuNo 161542, at MCAS New River, N.C. This was one of three Super Stallions retrieved in August 2005 from the Aerospace Maintenance and Regeneration Center at Davis-Monthan AFB, Ariz., and delivered for refurbishment to NADEP Cherry Point, N.C.

3 JULY • During a week-long Rim of the Pacific multinational exercise, VX-20 sailors augmented by the Air Force 452nd Flight Test Squadron flew an RQ-4 Global Hawk Maritime Demonstrator. During four maritime surveillance missions from Edwards AFB, Calif., to Hawaii, the Global Hawks demonstrated their ability to identify targets in coastal or littoral environments as well as in wide-area maritime search and tracking.

7 JULY • Air Force Chief of Staff Gen. T. Michael Moseley, USAF, announced the name of the F-35 Joint Strike Fighter as Lightning II at Lockheed Martin, Fort Worth, Texas. The Department of Defense intended Lightning IIs to replace AV-8B Harrier IIs, Fairchild Republic A-10A Thunderbolt IIs, General Dynamics F-16 Fighting Falcons, and F/A-18 Hornets.

16 JULY • After Hezbollah terrorists attacked Israeli settlements with rockets, the Israelis began Operation Change of Direction to drive the terrorists from Israel's northern border. On this date, amphibious assault ship *Iwo Jima* (LHD 7), amphibious transport dock *Nashville* (LPD 13), and dock landing ship *Whidbey Island* (LSD 41), with the 24th Marine Expeditionary Unit embarked, received orders to transit from the Red Sea and operate as part of Task Force 59 for what became Operation Strengthen Hope—the evacuation of Americans from Lebanon. On 23 August, European Command directed Joint Task Force Lebanon to assume the mission performed by Task Force 59, Air Force MC-130P Combat Shadows and MH-53M Pave Lows, and Army CH-47 Chinooks. Naval aviator Vice Adm. John D. Stufflebeem took command of the force from command ship *Mount Whitney* (LCC 20). On 25 August, amphibious assault ship *Wasp* (LHD 1), with HM-14 Detachment 1 embarked, deployed to the area from NS Norfolk, Va. Amphibious transport dock *Trenton* (LPD 14) also participated in the force that evacuated nearly 15,000 Americans and provided humanitarian assistance to victims of the fighting.

28 JULY • Pilot Lt. Blake C. Coleman and radar intercept officer Lt. Cmdr. David P. Lauderbaugh of VF-31 made the final operational carrier launch of an F-14 Tomcat, in BuNo 163147, from *Theodore Roosevelt* (CVN 71).

29 JULY • Two MV-22B Ospreys of VMX-22 completed the tiltrotor's first transatlantic flights by flying from North Carolina to England and back.

3 AUGUST • Chief of Naval Operations Adm. Michael G. Mullen accepted EA-18G Growlers into naval service at the Boeing Company, St. Louis, Mo.

USN 061215-N-8053S-228

The first F-35A Lightning II takes off for its maiden flight at Joint Reserve Base Fort Worth, Texas, 15 December 2006.

5 AUGUST • Frigate *Stephen W. Groves* (FFG 29), with HSL-46 Detachment 8 and Coast Guard Law Enforcement Detachment 105 embarked, intercepted a small boat and recovered a metric ton of cocaine in the eastern Pacific. About two tons of cocaine sank with the boat after the drug traffickers set it afire.

15 AUGUST • The EA-18G Growler made its first flight at Lambert International Airport, St. Louis, Mo.

25 AUGUST • Helicopter Landing Trainer *IX-514* logged her 100,000th accident-free landing when a TH-57 Ranger of HT-8 touched down on board in Pensacola Bay, Fla.

18 SEPTEMBER • The Marine Corps accepted the first KC-130T aerial refueler. After several months of flight testing, the Hercules returned to VMGR-234 at NAS JRB Fort Worth, Texas.

19 SEPTEMBER • Amphibious assault ship *Saipan* (LHA 2), with elements of HM-15 on board, successfully completed the first integration of an LHA-class ship in minesweeping operations with an MH-53E Sea Dragon and the Mk 105 magnetic minesweeping system during an exercise in the Persian Gulf.

22 SEPTEMBER • VX-23 received its first EA-18G Growler developmental test aircraft for flight testing at NAS Patuxent River, Md.

22 SEPTEMBER • After 36 years of service, the Navy retired the F-14 Tomcat in a final flight ceremony at NAS Oceana, Va. On 4 October, an F-14D of VF-31, BuNo 164603, completed the last Tomcat flight from Oceana to Republic Airport, Farmingdale, N.Y. The jet spent just over a year on display at the American Airpower Museum at the airport, and was then assigned for display at Northrop Grumman, Bethpage, N.Y.

2 OCTOBER • VR-54 relieved VR-55 as the Navy's C-130 detachment operating from NSA Bahrain. The detachment continued to operate a single Hercules with two rotational crews.

31 OCTOBER • The Atlantic Fleet and Fleet Forces Command transitioned into Fleet Forces Command, naval aviator Adm. John B. Nathman commanding, during a ceremony on board *Theodore Roosevelt* (CVN 71) at NS Norfolk, Va. In May, Chief of Naval Operations Adm. Michael G. Mullen had disestablished Commander, Fleet Forces Command, and Commander, Atlantic Fleet, and redesignated them as Commander, Fleet Forces Command.

3 NOVEMBER • NAS Keflavik, Iceland, was disestablished, marking the conclusion of 45 years of Navy control. In 1941, Marines and sailors had deployed to Iceland to replace British troops and to stave off possible German landings. After World War II, patrol squadrons flew intelligence and surveillance missions on a rotational basis from Keflavik over the North Atlantic. On 1 July 1961, the Navy assumed command of the station from the Air Force. Keflavik held its disestablishment ceremony on 8 September 2006.

3 NOVEMBER • NAVAIR announced the planned installation in 2007 of the Advanced Recovery Control system on board *Ronald Reagan* (CVN 76). This replaced mechanical arresting systems and controls with state-of-the-art digital control technology.

30 NOVEMBER • A ceremony marked the delivery of the final upgraded E-6B Mercury at NAS Cecil Field, Fla.

1 DECEMBER • The first group of Aviator Chief Warrant Officers, consisting of ten pilots and four naval flight officers, received their bars as part of the Flying Chief Warrant Officer Program.

15 DECEMBER • The first flight of an F-35A Lightning II took place at Lockheed Martin, Fort Worth, Texas.

20 DECEMBER • An MQ-8B Fire Scout completed its first series of flights at Webster Field Annex, NAS Patuxent River, Md.

2007

7 JANUARY • During fighting between Ethiopians and Muslim extremists in Somalia, an Air Force AC-130 gunship attacked al-Qaeda terrorists at a Somali fishing village near Ras Kamboni on the Kenyan border. The next day, the Fifth Fleet moved *Dwight D. Eisenhower* (CVN 69) to join dock landing ship *Ashland* (LSD 48) and other ships as they searched vessels for terrorists who attempted to escape from Somalia.

16 JANUARY • The Navy named the first of the CVN-21–class aircraft carriers *Gerald R. Ford* (CVN 78). Designers intended the new ships to replace the *Enterprise* (CVN 65) and *Nimitz* (CVN 68)-classes. *Gerald R. Ford* would raise aircraft sortie capacity by 25 percent, generate three times more electricity than the older ships, and included an improved fully integrated warfare system.

26 JANUARY • The Department of Defense acting inspector general notified the president and Congress that the state of Florida had not met the Defense Base Closure and Realignment Commission criteria for the move of the Navy's East Coast master jet base from NAS Oceana, Va., to NAS Cecil Field, Fla.

29 JANUARY • The Department of Defense announced the identification of the remains of a Navy pilot lost during the Vietnam War. On 25 June 1965, Cmdr. Peter Mongilardi Jr. launched in an A-4C, BuNo 149574, from *Coral Sea* (CVA 43) on an armed reconnaissance mission over North Vietnam's Thanh Hoa province. Mongilardi's wingman lost visual and radio contact with the Skyhawk amid enemy ground fire and a rainstorm.

30 JANUARY • VX-21 at NAS Patuxent River, Md., announced that MH-60Ss had fired AGM-114 Hellfire air-to-ground missiles for the first-time. The squadron also completed developmental testing of armed helicopter mission kits that doubled the Seahawks' weapons capability from four to eight missiles.

31 JANUARY • NAVAIR awarded Raytheon Company, Tucson, Ariz., a firm fixed-price contract worth more than $100 million for the third full-rate production of 376 AGM-154C Joint Standoff Weapons and associated equipment.

5 FEBRUARY • President George W. Bush delivered his fiscal 2008 defense budget request and 2007 emergency supplemental request of $484 billion to Congress. Procurement requests for the Navy totaled $39 billion with $14 billion for shipbuilding including *Gerald R. Ford* (CVN 78), and $13 billion for aircraft procurement including 24 F/A-18E/F Super Hornets, 18 EA-18G Growlers, and six F-35 Lightning IIs.

6 FEBRUARY • NAVAIR awarded a $16 million contract to Northrop Grumman Corporation, San Diego, Calif., for two additional MQ-8B Fire Scouts.

6 FEBRUARY • President George W. Bush announced the creation of Africa Command. The unified command highlighted the region's growing strategic importance and held responsibility for the entire continent with the exception of Egypt and its adjacent islands, which fell under the cognizance of Central Command. Africa Command was activated on 1 October 2008.

8 FEBRUARY • The 54-aircraft fleet of MV-22 Ospreys was grounded through 27 February for evaluation after a computer chip malfunction in subzero temperatures.

1 MARCH • The first Block 20 RQ-4A and the 17th Global Hawk built, designated AF-8, completed its maiden flight from Northrop Grumman Corp. Palmdale, Calif.

6 MARCH • HSC-85 held a retirement ceremony for the Navy's last H-3 at Coronado, Calif. The squadron had flown Sea Kings for 37 years for search and rescue missions, as well as to launch and recover mobile antisubmarine warfare targets and torpedoes.

9 MARCH • Sikorsky Aircraft Corporation of Stratford, Conn., announced the delivery of the 100th MH-60S Seahawk to the Navy.

16 MARCH • The Boeing Company, St. Louis, Mo., delivered the 200th T-45C to the Navy. More than 3,000 Navy and Marine pilots had undergone training on Goshawks at NAS Meridian, Miss., and NAS Kingsville, Texas. Navy procurement plans called for at least 23 additional aircraft.

21 MARCH • AH-1W Super Cobra pilot Maj. William D. Chesarek Jr., USMC, received the British Distinguished Flying Cross from Queen Elizabeth II at Buckingham Palace, England. In 2006, Chesarek was an exchange pilot with the Royal Navy's 847 Naval Air Squadron in Iraq. During a battle near Al Amarah on 10 and 11 June 2006, he flew a Lynx AH.7, providing communications relay support to British troops, and airlifted a wounded soldier to safety.

30 MARCH • The Navy announced the change of homeports for *Carl Vinson* (CVN 70) in early 2010 from Norfolk, Va., to San Diego, Calif. The 2006 Quadrennial Defense Review prompted the move because of the strategic reassessment for the presence of six of the 11 carrier strike groups in the Pacific. *Carl Vinson* joined *Nimitz* (CVN 68) and *Ronald Reagan* (CVN 76) already berthed at NAS North Island.

31 MARCH • The first KC-130J Super Hercules in the Pacific arrived to serve as a maintenance trainer with VMGRT-152 at MCAS Futenma, Okinawa.

9 APRIL • The initial EA-18G Growler arrived for testing at NAS Whidbey Island, Wash.

19 APRIL • Frigate *Rodney M. Davis* (FFG 60) and her embarked Coast Guard law enforcement detachment intercepted fishing vessel *Mariana de Jesus* in the eastern Pacific. The arrival of a maritime patrol aircraft overhead had panicked the ship's master and crew and they had abandoned the vessel and the 31 migrants on board. *Rodney M. Davis* assisted and transferred the migrants to the El Salvadoran Navy. Four days later, the frigate and Costa Rican Coast Guard vessel *Juan Rafael Mora* intercepted fishing vessel *Kuerubin* and 61 Chinese migrants en route from Ecuador to Guatemala. The smugglers also abandoned the migrants after a maritime patrol aircraft flew over, and the frigate transferred the people to *Juan Rafael Mora*.

20 APRIL • EA-18G Growlers completed the first phase of test and evaluation.

26 APRIL • HSL-45 Detachment 4 deployed to the eastern Pacific with frigate *McClusky* (FFG 41) during the first Navy deployment of the Airborne Use of Force doctrine against drug traffickers. Coast Guard helicopters had hitherto employed the doctrine, which involved using snipers equipped with .50-caliber rifles capable of disabling fire. At one point, *McClusky* and embarked Coast Guard Law Enforcement Detachments 101 and 103 confiscated 12 tons of cocaine with an estimated value of $306 million. HSL-45 Detachment 4 returned to NAS North Island, Calif., on 22 October 2007.

30 APRIL • Northrop Grumman unveiled its first System Design and Development E-2D Advanced Hawkeye.

3 MAY • Retired Capt. Walter M. Schirra Jr., one of the original seven Mercury astronauts, died at the age of 84.

3 MAY • The Broad Area Maritime Surveillance Unmanned Aircraft System source selection process formally began. Based on the RQ-4B Global Hawk, the system was designed to conduct maritime surveillance, collect enemy order-of-battle information, provide battle damage assessment, port surveillance, and communications relay.

5 MAY • The U. S. Court of Federal Claims upheld the Secretary of Defense's 1991 termination of the A-12A Avenger contract for default by McDonnell Douglas and General Dynamics. Unless the ruling was overruled on appeal, the action required the companies to repay the government $2.6 billion.

11 MAY • The BLU-126/B Low Collateral Damage Bomb was cleared for deployment by NAVAIR. The precision strike weapon is externally identical to the 500-pound BLU-111, but contains less explosives to reduce fragmentation patterns and blast radii.

15 MAY • The Navy christened auxiliary dry cargo ship *Richard E. Byrd* (T-AKE 4) at General Dynamics National Steel and Shipbuilding Company, San Diego, Calif. The ship honored early aviation pioneer Rear Adm. Richard E. Byrd Jr.

18 MAY • VFA-213 became the first Navy fleet squadron to fly an F/A-18F Super Hornet retrofitted with an aft cockpit Joint Helmet-Mounted Cueing System.

23 MAY • *Nimitz* (CVN 68), *John C. Stennis* (CVN 74), and amphibious assault ship *Bonhomme Richard* (LHD 6) led seven other ships through the Strait of Hormuz into the Persian Gulf for an exercise to demonstrate U.S. resolve. The exercise concluded on 6 June.

25 MAY • HT-28 was activated as a third advanced helicopter training command at NAS Whiting Field, Fla.

29 MAY • Boeing Integrated Defense Systems, St. Louis, Mo., completed developmental flight testing of its Integrated GPS Anti-Jam System for Joint Direct Attack Munitions (JDAMs), at NAWC China Lake, Calif. The system maintained JDAM precision under different mission and GPS jamming situations.

30 MAY • The Department of Defense announced the identification of the remains of a serviceman missing in action from the Vietnam War. On 14 December 1966, Lt. Michael T. Newell of VF-194 launched in an F-8E Crusader, BuNo 149148, from *Ticonderoga* (CVA 14) during a raid on a vehicle depot at Van Dien, North Vietnam. A surface-to-air missile burst near Newell, and his wingman did not see a parachute or hear an emergency beacon signal.

31 MAY • The Department of Defense announced that MQ-8B Fire Scouts had reached Milestone C, signifying the start of the low-rate initial production phase.

4 JUNE • VMGR-152 received its first KC-130J Super Hercules at MCAS Futenma, Okinawa.

8 JUNE • Space shuttle *Atlantis* launched from John F. Kennedy Space Center, Fla., on mission STS-117. Naval aviator Col. Frederick W. Sturckow, USMC, commanded the mission to the International Space Station. On 22 June, *Atlantis* returned to Edwards AFB Calif.

10 JUNE • Training Wing 2 celebrated the 500,000th training hour in T-45 Goshawks at NAS Kingsville, Texas.

13 JUNE • The MV-22 achieved initial operational capability and became ready for expeditionary operations with the Osprey's first combat squadron, VMM-263.

14 JUNE • An RQ-4A completed the 1,000th Global Hawk flight.

15 JUNE • NAVAIR announced the completion of the critical design review of the P-8A, a necessary step before production of the first test Poseidons.

NAVAIR

A Marine Corps MV-22B Osprey demonstrates its capabilities in extreme brownout conditions during testing in 2007 at the Army Yuma Proving Ground, Ariz.

25 JUNE • The Assistant Secretary of the Navy for Research, Development, and Acquisition authorized full-rate production of Block II F/A-18E/F Super Hornets and EA-18G Growlers equipped with the AESA aircraft radar system.

1 JULY • About 55 candidates of Officer Candidate School class 20-07 began to check in as the final class of candidates to train at NAS Pensacola, Fla. As part of the Defense Base Closure and Realignment Commission process, Officer Training Command Pensacola started to transition to Newport, R.I.

3 JULY • Maj. Rich Marigliano, USMC, AgustaWestland test pilot Dick Trueman, and flight engineers Clive Bowditch and Richard Parkes completed the maiden flight of VH-71A test aircraft TV-2, for the presidential helicopter at AgustaWestland's test facility, Yeovil, England.

10 JULY • A Marine MV-22B landed on a foreign ship for the first time when an Osprey embarked on board British carrier *Illustrious* (R 06), in preparation for exercise Bold Step off the East Coast. Two days later, detachments from VMA-223, -513, and -542 embarked the British ship, and at times, 14 AV-8B Harrier IIs operated from her. Thirty ships and submarines from five countries—including *Dwight D. Eisenhower* (CVN 69), *Theodore Roosevelt* (CVN 71), *Illustrious*, amphibious assault ships *Wasp* (LHD 1) and *Bataan* (LHD 5), dock landing ship *Oak Hill* (LSD 51), and amphibious transport dock *Shreveport* (LPD 12)—participated in the exercise, which concluded on 28 July.

23 JULY • Naval aircraft and ships including Coast Guard cutters *Diligence* (WMEC 616), *Dolphin* (WPB 87354), and *Knight Island* (WPB 1348), buoy tender *Elm* (WLB 204), and an HH-65A Dolphin from CGAS Miami, Fla., assisted in the interception of 94 Cuban migrants between the Bahamas and Florida in six events. Officials detained some, but repatriated most of the migrants to Cuba.

27 JULY • Two F/A-18D Hornets from VMFA(AW)-121 destroyed an Iraqi insurgent van and a sedan with an AGM-65E Maverick air-to-ground missile and a GBU-51/B laser-guided bomb with the BLU-126/B low-collateral damage explosive, respectively. The action marked the first time that naval aircraft had dropped the BLU-126/B in battle. On 12 August, naval aircraft made a second similar attack against Iraqi insurgents.

3 AUGUST • Lt. Drew Ballinger, Northrop Grumman test pilot Tom Boutin, and flight test weapon system operator Zyad Hajo completed the first flight of an E-2D Advanced Hawkeye test aircraft at St. Augustine, Fla.

3 AUGUST • The Navy awarded Northrop Grumman Corporation a six-year, $635.8 million contract to conduct the first at-sea launches and recoveries of X-47B Unmanned Combat Air System aircraft. The program was intended to validate the capabilities of autonomous, low-observable aerial vehicles, and planned two initial vehicles, with the first to fly in late 2009 and in 2013 to undertake carrier flight operations.

4 AUGUST • During a ceremony in Grand Haven, Mich., to commemorate the Coast Guard's 217th birthday, the service announced that it had saved an estimated 1,109,310 lives since 7 August 1789 when the first Congress federalized existing lighthouses built by the colonies.

8 AUGUST • Space shuttle *Endeavour* launched from John F. Kennedy Space Center, Fla., on mission STS-118. During this 22nd shuttle flight to the International Space Station, crewmembers Cmdr. Scott J. Kelly, Col. Charles O. Hobaugh, USMC, and Col. Benjamin A. Drew Jr., USAF—who had completed naval test pilot school—had naval aviation experience. *Endeavour* returned to earth on 21 August.

14 AUGUST • Amphibious assault ship *Wasp* (LHD 1) deployed to the Indian Ocean and Persian Gulf with ten MV-22Bs from VMM-263 embarked during the first combat deployment of Ospreys. The Ospreys flew to Al Aqabah, Jordan, and then to Al Asad Air Base, Iraq. The MV-22Bs hauled troops and equipment between forward operating bases, and on 6 December landed Marines and Iraqi troops on a raid near Lake Tharthar, about 150 miles north of Baghdad. *Wasp* returned to Norfolk, Va., on 20 December.

SEPTEMBER • The Navy accepted its 3,000th AGM-154 Joint Standoff Weapon (JSOW) from Raytheon Co., Tucson, Ariz. Naval and Air Force aircraft had dropped more than 400 JSOWs in battle.

SEPTEMBER • A KC-130T from VMGR-234 flew a Navy RQ-8B Fire Scout from Northrop Grumman's Unmanned Systems Center, Moss Point, Miss., for flight testing at NAS Patuxent River, Md. This was the first such flight in a Marine Hercules.

4 SEPTEMBER • Hurricane Felix devastated northeastern Nicaragua. U.S.-led international relief forces, including amphibious assault ship *Wasp* (LHD 1) and frigate *Samuel B. Roberts* (FFG 58), played a major role. Prior to continuing eastward to the Indian Ocean and Persian Gulf, *Wasp* airlifted more than 125,000-pounds of relief supplies and evacuated 34 people. Joint Task Force Bravo coordinated efforts by the two SH-60B Seahawks from HSL-48 Detachment 7 embarked on board *Samuel B. Roberts*, and Army, Navy, and Marine helicopters including MH-53E Sea Dragons, MH-47 Chinooks, and UH-60 Black Hawks that flew dozens of missions into an airfield at Puerto Cabezas. An Air Force C-130 from Homestead Air Reserve Base, Fla., and a Marine Hercules arrived later with additional supplies. Relief efforts continued to 18 September.

24 SEPTEMBER • The Boeing Company delivered the first production EA-18G, constructor number G-1, to the Navy at St. Louis, Mo. The Growler consequently joined the flight test program at NAS Patuxent River, Md.

26 SEPTEMBER • Destroyer *James E. Williams* (DDG 95), with an SH-60B from HSL-44 Detachment 9 embarked, assisted Tanzanian-flagged passenger ferry *Spice Islander I* off the Somali coast. With no fuel on board and little food and water while en route without passengers from Oman to Tanzania, the ferry was adrift in pirate-infested waters. The Seahawk directed destroyer *Stout* (DDG 55) to the scene, which took the ferry in tow and provided the mariners with food, water, and fuel to continue their voyage.

30 SEPTEMBER • Jazirat at Ta'ir (Bird Mountain), a volcano about 70 miles off the Yemen coast, erupted and collapsed part of the island, destroying a Yemeni coast guard station. A NATO convoy of six ships sailing toward the Suez Canal—including destroyer *Bainbridge* (DDG 96) and allied frigates Canadian *Toronto* (FFH 333), Danish *Olfert Fischer* (F 355), Dutch *Evertsen* (F 805), and Portuguese *Álvares Cabral* (F 331)—diverted and rescued two survivors and recovered four bodies through 1 October.

5 OCTOBER • The Departments of Defense and Veterans Affairs named the Federal Health Care Facility at NS Great Lakes, Ill., in honor of astronaut and naval aviator James A. Lovell Jr.

9 OCTOBER • The Boeing Co. delivered the first factory-installed, dual-cockpit F/A-18F Super Hornet Joint Helmet-Mounted Cueing System to VX-9 at NAWC China Lake, Calif.

22 OCTOBER • Santa Ana winds drove 23 wild fires across 12 southern Californian counties. Marines evacuated more than 40 aircraft from MCAS Miramar, and all the armed forces aided civilian firefighters. Commander Maritime Strike Wing Pacific established the Helicopter Coordination Center at NAS North Island. The center coordinated aircraft including a VP-46 P-3C Orion, MH-60S Seahawks from HSC-3 and -85, SH-60Fs from HS-4 and -6, HSL-45 SH-60Bs, Marine CH-46E Sea Knights and CH-53E Super Stallions from Camp Pendleton and Miramar, and a UH-1N Iroquois from NAS Fallon, Nev. Other facilities including NAS North Island accommodated evacuees. Ships involved in firefighting included *Ronald Reagan* (CVN 76), amphibious assault ships *Boxer* (LHD 4), *Peleliu* (LHA 5), and Pre-Commissioning Unit *Makin Island* (LHD 8), and amphibious transport dock *Cleveland* (LPD 7). Firefighters contained the blazes by 3 November.

23 OCTOBER • Space shuttle *Discovery* launched from John F. Kennedy Space Center, Fla., on mission STS-120.

The pilot of this 120th shuttle flight and the 23rd to the International Space Station was U.S. Naval Academy graduate and former F/A-18 Hornet pilot Col. George D. Zamka, USMC. *Discovery* returned to earth on 7 November.

25 OCTOBER • An RQ-2 flew the final Pioneer unmanned aerial vehicle (UAV) operational training flight at NAS Whiting Field's outlying Choctaw Field, Navarre, Fla. Planners intended Shadow 200 unmanned aerial systems to replace Pioneers, and on 7 August 2008, Training Wing 6 UAV Detachment deactivated to allow the Army to oversee Shadow training at Fort Huachuca, Ariz. Beginning with VC-6 Detachment 1's deployment on board battleship *Iowa* (BB 61) on 10 September 1987, Pioneers had flown more than 50,000 flight hours of which nearly half—23,000—were during Operation Iraqi Freedom.

31 OCTOBER • A groundbreaking ceremony heralded the opening of the Growler Support Center at NAS Whidbey Island, Wash. The facility accommodated 24 consultants to aid the transition from EA-6B Prowlers to EA-18G Growlers.

NOVEMBER • An Air Force C-17A Globemaster III delivered VH-71A test aircraft TV-2 from AgustaWestland in the United Kingdom for testing at NAS Patuxent River, Md. TV-5 followed in December.

NOVEMBER • The Navy announced the completion at General Atomics, Rancho Bernardo, Calif., of the final critical design review of the Electromagnetic Aircraft Launch System intended to equip *Gerald R. Ford* (CVN 78)–class carriers.

5 NOVEMBER • Amphibious assault ship *Tarawa* (LHA 1), with Marines of the 11th Marine Expeditionary Unit embarked, sailed on her 14th and final deployment from San Diego, Calif. The ship supported Operations Enduring and Iraqi Freedom, visited four continents, and provided humanitarian relief to people in Bangladesh and Djibouti. *Tarawa* returned on 3 June 2008, and was decommissioned after 32 years of service on 31 March 2009.

17 NOVEMBER • Destroyer *Oscar Austin* (DDG 79) of the *Harry S. Truman* (CVN 75) Carrier Strike Group completed intelligence, surveillance, and reconnaissance testing of a ScanEagle long-endurance fully autonomous unmanned aerial vehicle while en route to the Middle East. ScanEagles had previously completed at-sea testing principally on board amphibious and high-speed ships.

22 NOVEMBER • Medal of Honor recipient Col. Jefferson J. DeBlanc, USMC (Ret.), died in Lafayette, La. The fighter pilot and ace received the award for his actions against the Japanese off Kolombangara Island in the Solomons Group during World War II.

27 NOVEMBER • Lt. Gen. Thomas H. Miller Jr., USMC (Ret.), died in Arlington, Va. Miller served in World War II, impacted naval aviation's early transition into the jet age, and in 1968 flew an AV-8A Harrier with Lt. Col. Clarence M. Baker, USMC, in the United Kingdom.

2 DECEMBER • AW1 Robert Antonucci and AD1 John Fuller of HSL-43, and AW2 John Barile of HSL-45, were commissioned through the Flying Chief Warrant Officer Program at NAS North Island, Calif.

11 DECEMBER • The Navy marked the production of the first P-8A Poseidon at Spirit AeroSystems, Wichita, Kan.

12 DECEMBER • The Army and Navy signed a five-year, multi-service $11.6 billion contract for the delivery of 537 UH-60M Black Hawk, HH-60M, and MH-60R/S Seahawk helicopters, with options for an additional 263 aircraft, spares, and kits from Sikorsky Aircraft Corporation, Stratford, Conn.

13 DECEMBER • The Navy inaugurated an unmanned aerial systems (UAS) airstrip at Armitage Field, NAWC China Lake, Calif. Two Cobra unmanned systems used to test future UAS capabilities flew missions from the 2,200-by-50-foot asphalt strip.

15 DECEMBER • Amphibious transport dock *Mesa Verde* (LPD 19) was commissioned at Panama City, Fla. She was the first man-of-war so named and honored Mesa Verde National Park, Colo.

20 DECEMBER • CWO2s Dale Courtney and Adam Rittierodt of VP-30, who received their wings as naval flight officers (NFO), were two of the initial applicants of the Flying Chief Warrant Officer Program at NAS Jacksonville,

Fla. German Lts. 2d Grade Christian Hegemann and Patrick Leisner also received NFO wings.

2008

3 JANUARY • While *Abraham Lincoln* (CVN 72) conducted JTFEX 03-08 off southern California, the U.S. District Court for the Central District of California ordered further limitations on mid-frequency sonar use because of its potential effect upon sea creatures. The Navy announced that the restrictions "created a significant and unreasonable risk" that impacted sonar training. President George W. Bush noted that, with the provisions of the Coastal Zone Management Act of 27 October 1972, continuing the exercise concerned "the paramount interests of the United States." On 16 January, Secretary of the Navy Donald C. Winter signed a decision of memorandum agreeing to alternative arrangements that included 29 voluntary adaptive management measures.

5 JANUARY • An irrigation canal ruptured and water inundated several hundred houses in Fernley, Nev. Lt. Brent Hardgrave led two HH-1N Iroquois from NAS Fallon, about 30 miles away, that rescued 18 people, and Coast Guard HC-130Hs delivered food and water to victims.

22 JANUARY • An HSM-71 MH-60R completed the Seahawk variant's first at-sea operations through 25 January while embarked on board destroyer *Preble* (DDG 88) off California.

25 JANUARY • The Navy announced requirements for the Active Duty Flying Chief Warrant Officer Pilot Program in NavAdmin 020/08. Among them, sailors were required to receive commissions by their 27th birthdays, possess associate or higher degrees, and maintain physical fitness for aviation duties.

11 FEBRUARY • Sailors consigned the ashes of nine Navy veterans including astronaut Capt. Walter M. Schirra Jr. to the Pacific during a ceremony on board *Ronald Reagan* (CVN 76).

22 FEBRUARY • HS-7, embarked on board *Harry S. Truman* (CVN 75), and auxiliary dry cargo ship *Sacagawea* (T-AKE 2) rescued ten Iraqis from sinking Korean-flagged tanker *Nadi* in the Persian Gulf. The next day, HS-7 transferred the rescued mariners to British dock landing ship *Cardigan Bay* (L 3009) for their return to the Iraqi Navy.

27 FEBRUARY • The third helicopter built for the VH-71A Presidential Helicopter Replacement Program, TV-3, made its initial flight at Yeovil, England.

1 MARCH • Amphibious transport dock *New York* (LPD 21) was christened at Northrop Grumman Shipbuilding, New Orleans, La. The ship's name honored the state, city, and victims of 9/11. Her hull contained 7½ tons of steel salvaged from the wreckage of the World Trade Center.

3 MARCH • Secretary of the Navy Donald C. Winter announced the name of the eighth *Lewis and Clark*–class auxiliary dry cargo ship as *Wally Schirra* (T-AKE 8) in honor of astronaut and naval aviator Capt. Walter M. Schirra Jr.

13 MARCH • Director Navy Staff Vice Adm. John D. Stufflebeem announced the change of homeports for *Kitty Hawk* (CV 63) from Yokosuka, Japan, to Bremerton, Wash., effective 31 January 2009 in preparation for her decommissioning.

23 MARCH • Fishing vessel *Alaska Ranger* sank during a storm in the Bering Sea, about 125 miles west of Dutch Harbor, Alaska. Aircraft and ships that responded included a Coast Guard HH-60J Jayhawk, cutter *Munro* (WHEC 724) and her embarked HH-65A Dolphin, two HH-130H Hercules from Elmendorf AFB, and fishing vessel *Alaska Warrior*, which collectively rescued 42 of the 47 crewmembers.

7 APRIL • *George Washington* (CVN 73), with Carrier Air Wing 17 embarked, sailed from NS Norfolk, Va., to relieve *Kitty Hawk* (CV 63) at Yokosuka, Japan.

22 APRIL • The Navy awarded Northrop Grumman Corp. a system development and demonstration contract for Broad Area Maritime Surveillance unmanned aerial systems. The $1.16 billion cost-plus-award-fee contract was to develop a persistent maritime intelligence, surveillance, and reconnaissance data collection and dissemination capability using RQ-4B Global Hawks.

24 APRIL • Chief of Naval Operations Adm. Gary Roughead announced the reestablishment of the Fourth Fleet, Rear Adm. Joseph D. Kernan commanding, at NS Mayport, Fla. This was to address the increasing role of maritime forces in the Naval Forces Southern Command area of operations, the Caribbean, and Central and South America.

28 APRIL • The Navy announced the deletion of AGM-119B Penguin air-to-ground missiles from inventory.

2 MAY • Cyclone Nargis caused widespread flooding along the Irrawaddy Delta and coast of Myanmar (Burma). International ships that rushed to the area as part of Joint Task Force Caring Response included amphibious assault ship *Essex* (LHD 2), amphibious transport dock *Juneau* (LPD 10), and dock landing ship *Harpers Ferry* (LSD 49), with the 31st Marine Expeditionary Unit embarked. The U.S. ships left some of their aircraft behind in Thailand and on 13 May arrived off Myanmar. The country's ruling junta rejected aid offers and, on 5 June, Commander Pacific Command Adm. Timothy J. Keating directed the ships to leave. The next day, two Marine C-130 Hercules flew 70 UN relief tents from Medan, Indonesia, to Thailand, from where aid workers shipped the tents and other vital supplies to the cyclone victims.

10 MAY • The Navy christened destroyer *Stockdale* (DDG 106) at Bath Iron Works, Maine. The ship honored Vice Adm. James B. Stockdale (Ret.), the highest ranking naval prisoner held by the North Vietnamese and a recipient of the Medal of Honor.

13 MAY • The EA-18G Growler Support Center opened at NAS Whidbey Island, Wash.

22 MAY • A fire erupted on board *George Washington* (CVN 73) while conducting an underway replenishment with frigate *Crommelin* (FFG 37) in the Pacific. The ships performed an emergency breakaway and sailors fought the blaze for 12 hours during which 38 *George Washington* crewmembers received treatment for injuries. The fire apparently resulted from the ignition of improperly stowed refrigerant compressor oil and delayed *George Washington* en route to relieve *Kitty Hawk* (CV 63) in Japan. In August, *George Washington* relieved *Kitty Hawk* at NAS North Island, Calif.

11 JUNE • BAE Systems, Inc. test pilot Graham Tomlinson flew an F-35B for the first flight of the short takeoff/vertical landing Lightning II at Lockheed Martin, Fort Worth, Texas.

20 JUNE • The Department of Defense announced the identification of the remains of a pilot missing in action from the Vietnam War and his return for interment. On 4 August 1967, Lt. j.g. Ralph C. Bisz of VA-163 launched in an A-4E, BuNo 150052, from *Oriskany* (CVA 34) to bomb a North Vietnamese petroleum depot near Haiphong. An enemy surface-to-air missile shot down the Skyhawk near Hai Duong in Hai Hung province.

23 JUNE • The U.S. Supreme Court agreed to review a preliminary injunction that restricted the Navy's ability to train realistically with sonar in Californian waters.

25 JUNE • *Ronald Reagan* (CVN 76) supported relief efforts to victims of Typhoon Fengshen on Panay, Philippines. HS-4 HH-60H and SH-60F Seahawks flying from the carrier; and SH-60Bs from HSL-43 embarked on board destroyer *Howard* (DDG 83), HSL-37 deployed with frigate *Thach* (FFG 43), and HSL-49 embarked on board cruiser *Chancellorsville* (CG 62); delivered food and water to people in the area. Two VRC-30 C-2A Greyhounds flew rice and water from the carrier to Santa Barbara Airport, Iloilo. *Ronald Reagan* departed from the Sulu Sea on 3 July.

27 JUNE • Secretary of the Navy Donald C. Winter announced the name *America* for the lead ship (LHA 6) and class of amphibious assault ships, the fourth vessel in the fleet to honor the name.

12 JULY • VMU-3, Lt. Col. James W. Frey, USMC, commanding, was activated at Lance Cpl. Torrey L. Gray Field, Marine Corps Air Ground Combat Center, Twentynine Palms, Calif. The squadron flew reconnaissance missions, assisted in deployments and training, and rotated with VMU-1 and -2 at MCAS Cherry Point, N.C. The Marines also announced their receipt of RQ-7B unmanned aerial vehicles that used the Shadow 200 system.

14 JULY • The Navy announced the award of a $48 million contract for six aircraft from Hawker Beechcraft Corporation, Wichita, Kan., to replace Marine UC-12 Huron twin-engine utility aircraft.

17 JULY • The Navy acknowledged the award of a $232 million system development and demonstration contract for the Joint Precision Approach and Landing System (JPALS) from Raytheon Company, Fullerton, Calif. Plans called for JPALS to integrate into naval landing systems, and for F/A-18E/F Super Hornets, EA-18G Growlers, and MH-60R/S Seahawks to be the lead aircraft during evaluations.

23 JULY • Lt. Jeff Millar of VX-9 and Lt. Elizabeth Somerville of VX-31 completed the first EA-18G Growler live fire of an AIM-120 Advanced Medium Range Air-To-Air Missile against a BQM-74E target drone at NAWCWD China Lake, Calif.

31 JULY • EA-18G Growlers completed sea trials through 5 August on board *Dwight D. Eisenhower* (CVN 69) in the Atlantic.

4 AUGUST • The Department of Defense announced the identification of the remains of a sailor missing in action from the Vietnam War and his return for interment. On 8 October 1963, HM3 Manuel R. Denton was one of six men killed on board a UH-34D Seahorse shot down by ground fire during a search and rescue mission over Quang Nam province, South Vietnam. Searchers recovered four men, but failed to locate Denton and LCpl. Luther E. Ritchey Jr., USMC.

7 AUGUST • VC-6, which had operated BQM-74E aerial target drones and RQ-2A Pioneer unmanned aerial vehicles, was deactivated at NS Norfolk, Va. This enabled the Army to oversee Shadow 200 UAS training to replace Pioneers at Fort Huachuca, Ariz.

7 AUGUST • Operation Assured Delivery began—humanitarian assistance to victims of the fighting between the Russians, Georgians, and South Ossetians in the Caucasus. From 13 August to 10 September, Navy C-9B Skytrain, C-40A Clipper, and C-130 Hercules, and Air Force C-17A Globemaster IIIs flew 1,145 short tons of supplies from Ramstein AFB, Germany to Tbilisi, Georgia. Command ship *Mount Whitney* (LCC 20), destroyer *McFaul* (DDG 74), and Coast Guard cutter *Dallas* (WHEC 716) also provided aid via Bat'umi and Poti.

8 AUGUST • Deputy Commandant for Marine Aviation Lt. Gen. George J. Trautman III, USMC, announced that UH-1Y Venoms had achieved their initial operating capability.

11 AUGUST • The crew of Pre-Commissioning Unit *George H. W. Bush* (CVN 77) began to move on board the ship at Northrop Grumman shipyard, Newport News, Va.

15 AUGUST • The High Speed Anti-Radiation Demonstration project displayed the maturity of an integral rocket-ramjet propulsion system at White Sands Missile Range, N.M. The objectives included a flight test of a near tactically configured vehicle.

16 AUGUST • A fire broke out in a cargo hangar at Tocumen International Airport in Panama during Southern Command exercise Fuerzas Aliadas Panamax 2008. Deputy maritime patrol aircraft commander Cmdr. Sam Sorgen for Commander Task Force 805, and his operations officer, Cmdr. Douglas Rosado, discovered the blaze and together with Air Force, Columbian, and Panamanian servicemembers saved up to eight aircraft from destruction.

22 AUGUST • The Navy celebrated the end of the North American T-2 program and its 3.4 million hours flight time with a sundown ceremony and fly-by at the Mustin Beach Officer's Club, NAS Pensacola, Fla. VT-86 made the final Buckeye training flights.

26 AUGUST • Hurricane Gustav made landfall on the southwestern peninsula of Haiti. The tempest swept across the Caribbean and on 1 September struck Cocodrie, La. VR-53 flew rescue workers and equipment to the Gulf Coast.

28 AUGUST • The Navy and Air Force signed a memorandum of agreement to streamline their joint acquisition processes regarding RQ-4 Global Hawks, and to pursue common objectives concerning the development and introduction of the unmanned aerial vehicles.

SEPTEMBER • VAQ-133 deployed to Bagram AB, Afghanistan. The squadron returned on 21 March 2009.

3 SEPTEMBER • The Electromagnetic Aircraft Launch System reached the 10,000 High Cycle Testing, Phase 1 milestone, at General Atomics, Tupelo, Miss.

8 SEPTEMBER • Naval aviator Nathan G. Gordon, 92, died at University of Arkansas for Medical Sciences, Little Rock, Ark. Gordon had received the Medal of Honor for his actions at Kavieng Harbor in the Bismarck Sea during World War II.

10 SEPTEMBER • The Navy awarded a $5.1 billion contract for the detail design and construction of *Gerald R. Ford* (CVN 78) to Northrop Grumman Shipbuilding, Newport News, Va.

13 SEPTEMBER • Frigate *McInerney* (FFG 8), with Coast Guard Law Enforcement Detachment 404 embarked, and a VP-26 P-3C Orion collaborated in the seizure of a 59-foot semi-submersible vessel smuggling an estimated $107 million worth of cocaine, about 350 miles east of Guatemala. The smugglers attempted to escape and jettison the drugs, but boarders captured the vessel before the submersible was scuttled.

25 SEPTEMBER • *George Washington* (CVN 73), which had been delayed by her 22 May fire, arrived as the forward-deployed carrier at Yokosuka, Japan.

29 SEPTEMBER • The Navy announced the impending completion of a six-year program to purchase and refurbish 44 retired Swiss Air Force F-5E Freedom Fighters to replace F-5E Tiger IIs in the dedicated adversary role as F-5Ns. The process averaged five months per jet, and on 29 April 2009, the Navy accepted the final refurbished aircraft at St. Augustine, Fla.

30 SEPTEMBER • The Navy accepted destroyer *Stockdale* (DDG 106), named in honor of Medal of Honor recipient Vice Adm. James B. Stockdale, at Bath Iron Works, Maine.

30 SEPTEMBER • The Navy approved the AGM-88E Advanced Anti-Radiation Guided Missile for service.

1 OCTOBER • Africa Command was activated.

1 OCTOBER • The Naval Air Pacific Repair Activity was redesignated Fleet Readiness Center Western Pacific at NAF Atsugi, Japan. It provided ready-for-tasking aircraft and aviation support equipment to naval forces permanently sited in or deployed to Pacific and Central Commands.

1 OCTOBER • Fleet Aviation Specialized Operational Training Group, Atlantic Fleet, Detachment Jacksonville (Fla.) was disestablished, and merged with the Center for Naval Aviation Technical Training Unit, also at Jacksonville.

6 OCTOBER • The Navy announced a contract for EADS North America to provide five UH-72A Lakotas for use in helicopter pilot training at the Naval Test Pilot School, NAS Patuxent River, Md.

6 OCTOBER • United States Forces–Afghanistan was activated, Gen. David D. McKiernan, USA, commanding, with responsibility for all commands deployed to Afghanistan.

7 OCTOBER • HMM-163 of the 13th Marine Expeditionary Unit engaged in sea testing through 16 October of a UH-1Y Venom during an integration exercise on board amphibious assault ship *Boxer* (LHD 4).

28 OCTOBER • E-2D Advanced Hawkeyes completed their initial operational assessment at Northrop Grumman, St. Augustine, Fla. Over a period of four weeks, a team from VX-1 at NAS Patuxent River, Md., and the Carrier Airborne Early Warning Weapons School at NAS Fallon, Nev., made ten test flights.

4 NOVEMBER • The Navy certified F/A-18E/Fs to fly at altitudes between 29,000 and 41,000 feet. This affected all Super Hornets produced from Lot 22 and beyond, approximately 340 aircraft.

7 NOVEMBER • NAVAIR announced the delivery of Laser Joint Direct Attack Munition (LJDAM) kits to the fleet. These consisted of laser sensors installed onto 500-pound bomb bodies with JDAM guidance kits, and provided a laser guidance mode to F/A-18A–D Hornets, F/A-18E/F Super Hornets, AV-8B Harrier IIs, and certain USAF aircraft.

7 NOVEMBER • Fleet Readiness Center Southeast announced the completion of repairs on the first of 39 P-3C

Orions grounded in December 2007 for structural fatigue concerns on a portion of their lower outer wings.

12 NOVEMBER • The United States Supreme Court ruled for the Navy on the challenge to the service's use of sonar for 14 antisubmarine warfare combat certification training exercises off southern California. The Navy agreed to train while applying mitigating measures set forth by a National Defense Exception and imposed by the President's Council on Environmental Quality. In December, the Navy entered into an agreement to resolve the lawsuit with several plaintiffs, which included directing $14.75 million in research funds during the following three years to marine mammal topics of "mutual interest" to the parties concerned.

14 NOVEMBER • Space shuttle *Endeavour* launched from John F. Kennedy Space Center, Fla., on mission STS-126. During this 27th mission to the International Space Station, naval aviator Capt. Christopher J. Ferguson commanded the shuttle, which landed at Edwards AFB, Calif., on 30 November.

17 NOVEMBER • The Navy announced its "preferred alternative" to homeport a nuclear-powered carrier at NS Mayport, Fla. The service had assessed 13 options because of the decommissioning of *John F. Kennedy* (CV 67) on 23 March 2007.

21 NOVEMBER • The Navy held a dedication ceremony at NAS Whidbey Island, Wash., to welcome the first EA-18G Growler, BuNo 166858—the fourth production aircraft—accepted for the fleet. The Navy had received six Growlers: EA-1 and -2 as engineering and development models used to support developmental testing; and production aircraft G-1, -2, and -3 used for developmental and operational testing.

2 DECEMBER • Secretary of the Navy Donald C. Winter announced the names of four *Lewis and Clark*–class auxiliary dry cargo ships, two of which honored pioneers in naval aviation. *Washington Chambers* (T-AKE 11) was named for Capt. Washington I. Chambers, who had arranged for aviator Eugene B. Ely to fly a plane from *Birmingham* (Cruiser No. 2) on 14 November 1911. *William McLean* (T-AKE 12) honored William B. McLean, who had helped conceive and develop the AIM-9 Sidewinder air-to-air missile while serving as a physicist for the Navy. These were the first ships named for the men.

NAWCWD

A Laser Joint Direct Attack Munition destroys a target during testing at the China Lake Naval Weapons Station, Calif. in August 2008.

2 DECEMBER • Frigate *Samuel B. Roberts* (FFG 58), with HSL-60 Detachment 2 and Coast Guard Law Enforcement Detachment 402 embarked, recovered 41 bales of cocaine that smugglers on board a go-fast vessel jettisoned during an interception in the eastern Pacific.

5 DECEMBER • Frigate *Rodney M. Davis* (FFG 60), with HSL-43 Detachment 2 and Coast Guard Law Enforcement Detachment 106 embarked, intercepted a fishing vessel and her crew of nine smugglers in the eastern Pacific carrying over four metric tons of cocaine valued at more than $90 million.

2009

2 JANUARY • The Navy announced the decision to base P-8A Poseidons. One fleet replacement squadron would be located at NAS Jacksonville, Fla.; four squadrons at NAS Whidbey Island, Wash.; and three squadrons at MCB Hawaii, Kaneohe Bay. Periodic detachments were also to operate from NAS North Island, Calif.

5 JANUARY • The Coast Guard and Lockheed Martin exercised contract options valued at $13.25 million to install mission systems including belly-mounted surface search radar on board two long-range surveillance HC-130J Hercules.

8 JANUARY • Combined Task Force (CTF) 151 was established to conduct counterpiracy operations at Al Manama, Bahrain. In August 2008, the Maritime Security Patrol Area had been created in the Gulf of Aden to support international efforts to fight piracy, but the task force's charter focused the command's objectives on maritime security operations (MSO) in the Gulf of Aden, Gulf of Oman, Arabian Sea, Red Sea, and Indian Ocean. Some CTF-150 members operated within legal restrictions, and the establishment of CTF-151 enabled those nations to pursue MSO while other members transported pirates to justice.

9 JANUARY • Three UH-1Ys of the 13th Marine Expeditionary Unit made the initial deployment of Venoms on board amphibious assault ship *Boxer* (LHD 4) from NS San Diego, Calif., to the western Pacific, Indian Ocean, and Arabian Sea. The ship returned on 1 August.

9 JANUARY • The first pilot production VH-71A Presidential Helicopter, PP-3, arrived to begin the integration and final processing at Lockheed Martin, Owego, N.Y. The aircraft made its maiden flight on 13 January.

10 JANUARY • *George H. W. Bush* (CVN 77) was commissioned at NS Norfolk, Va. From 13 to 16 February, the ship conducted and completed builder's sea trials and, from 7 to 10 April, her acceptance sea trials off the Virginia Capes.

13 JANUARY • HSM-71 began the deployment of the first operational squadron equipped with MH-60R Seahawks when *John C. Stennis* (CVN 74) sailed from NB Kitsap, Bremerton, Wash., to the western Pacific, Indian Ocean, and Arabian Sea. The ship returned on 10 July.

14 JANUARY • The Navy signed the formal record of decision to homeport a single nuclear-powered aircraft carrier at NS Mayport, Fla. The Navy had assessed 13 alternatives including a "no action" option.

21 JANUARY • The Navy signed the formal record of decision to continue the current level of training on the Southern California Range Complex. This included an evaluation of the effects of sonar upon marine life. Two days later, the service announced its signature of a record of decision concerning the Atlantic Fleet Active Sonar Training Environmental Impact Statement/Overseas Environmental Impact Statement. Based on the study and the effectiveness of the measures in place, the Navy selected the "no action" alternative to continue the protections in place.

24 JANUARY • Amphibious transport dock *Green Bay* (LPD 20) was commissioned at Long Beach, Calif.

31 JANUARY • During the deactivation of Sea Control Wing Atlantic and VS-22, the Navy also retired the last ten active S-3B Vikings from fleet service at NAS Jacksonville, Fla.

23 FEBRUARY • The Airborne Strategic Command, Control, and Communications program office accepted the first modified E-6B Mercury Block 1 at L-3 Integrated Systems Group, Waco, Texas.

25 FEBRUARY • The second F-35B Lightning II, BF-2, made its first flight at Fort Worth, Texas. Together with a conventional takeoff and landing F-35A and the first F-35B, BF-1, Lightning IIs had logged a total of 84 flights.

8 MARCH • The Navy launched and christened auxiliary dry cargo ship *Wally Schirra* (T-AKE 8) at General Dynamics–National Steel and Shipbuilding Co., San Diego, Calif.

10 MARCH • The Navy changed the status of Capt. Michael S. Speicher in the Persian Gulf War from "missing/captured" to "missing in action."

15 MARCH • Space shuttle *Discovery* launched from John F. Kennedy Space Center, Fla., on mission STS-119. During the flight to the International Space Station, the crewmembers included naval aviators Capt. John L. Phillips, USNR (Ret.), and Cmdr. Dominic A. Antonelli. The shuttle returned to the center on 28 March.

18 MARCH • Lockheed Martin announced the Navy's certification of the terminal phase capability of the Aegis Ballistic Missile Defense System. The system has the capability to defeat short-range ballistic missiles during the terminal stage of flight and, by 2010, had been installed in 18 ships.

19 MARCH • Maj. Joseph T. Bachmann, USMC, at Lockheed Martin, Fort Worth, Texas, made the first flight by a Marine in an F-35A Lightning II—AA-1.

20 MARCH • Amphibious transport dock *New Orleans* (LPD 18) and submarine *Hartford* (SSN 768) collided in the Strait of Hormuz. *New Orleans* did not report casualties but 15 sailors on board the submarine received minor injuries. The LPD underwent repairs in a Bahrain drydock and returned to sea on 12 May. *Hartford* returned to the United States for repair.

20 MARCH • Amphibious assault ship *Boxer* (LHD 4) coordinated the capture of six pirates in the Gulf of Aden. Philippine-flagged motor vessel *Bison Express* sent a distress call as she was being pursued by the suspects in a skiff. An SH-60B from HSL-46, embarked on board cruiser *Gettysburg* (CG 64), spotted the pirates throwing objects overboard, and a visit, board, search, and seizure team from the cruiser seized the suspects, who were taken for questioning to *Boxer* as the afloat staging base for Combined Task Force 151.

29 MARCH • Seven pirates in a skiff attacked German oiler *Spessart* (A 1442) in the Gulf of Aden. Three task forces representing seven nations including amphibious assault ship *Boxer* (LHD 4), an SH-60B from Spanish frigate *Victoria* (F 82), and a Spanish P-3M pursued the suspects. An AH-1W Super Cobra and a UH-1Y Venom operating from *Boxer* delayed the escape of the pirates until a German boarding team from Greek frigate *Psara* (F 454) took them into custody for transfer to German frigate *Rheinland-Pfalz* (F 209).

A still frame from a video taken by a P-3C Orion shows the pirate-held U.S.-flagged container ship *Maersk Alabama* in the Indian Ocean, 9 April 2009.

31 MARCH • Amphibious assault ship *Tarawa* (LHA 1) was decommissioned at San Diego, Calif.

8 APRIL • Pirates captured U.S.-flagged motor vessel *Maersk Alabama* and her 22 crewmembers, 300 miles from the Somali coast. The crew recaptured their ship along with one of the pirates, but the three surviving pirates held the vessel's skipper, Capt. Richard Phillips, hostage on a lifeboat. On 12 April, SEAL snipers on board destroyer *Bainbridge* (DDG 96) killed the pirates and rescued Phillips. Amphibious assault ship *Boxer* (LHD 4) participated in the rescue, and a ScanEagle unmanned aircraft system provided timely intelligence. In early November 2009, four pirates in a skiff attempted to board *Maersk Alabama* again, but the crew fought off the attackers.

16 APRIL • The Navy accepted the delivery of amphibious assault ship *Makin Island* (LHD 8) at Northrop Grumman Shipbuilding, Gulf Coast, Pascagoula, Miss.

18 APRIL • Destroyer *Stockdale* (DDG 106) was commissioned at Port Hueneme, Calif.

21 APRIL • Frigate *Rodney M. Davis* (FFG 60) returned to NS Everett, Wash. from a counternarcotics deployment in the eastern Pacific. During her sail, the ship and her embarked SH-60B of HSL-43 Detachment 2 intercepted and seized six tons of cocaine and 160 pounds of marijuana, and disrupted shipments of 18 tons of cocaine and three tons of marijuana.

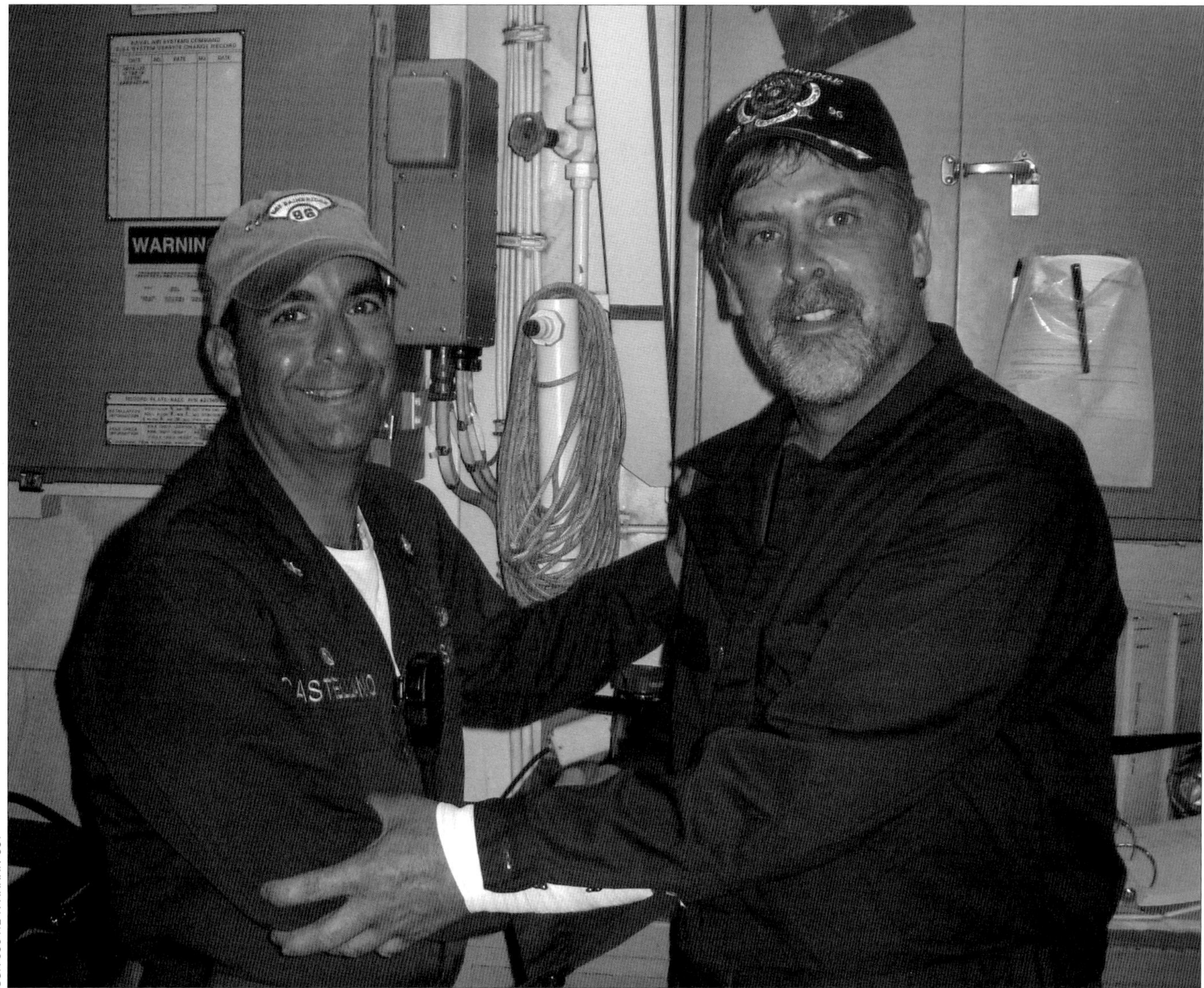

USN 090412-N-XXXXN-001

Capt. Richard Phillips (right) of U.S.-flagged container ship *Maersk Alabama* poses with Cmdr. Frank Castellano, commanding officer of destroyer *Bainbridge* (DDG 96), after his rescue from pirates, 12 April 2009.

25 APRIL • The initial P-8A Poseidon flight test aircraft, T1, completed its first flight near Seattle, Wash.

11 MAY • Space shuttle *Atlantis* launched from John F. Kennedy Space Center, Fla., on mission STS-125. During this final flight to the Hubble Space Telescope, the crewmembers included naval aviators retired Capts. Scott D. Altman and Gregory C. Johnson. On 24 May, *Atlantis* touched down at Edwards AFB, Calif.

13 MAY • Combined Task Force 151 defeated a pirate attack in the Gulf of Aden. Cruiser *Gettysburg* (CG 64) and South Korean destroyer *Munmu the Great* (DDH 976) responded to a distress call from Egyptian-flagged motor vessel *Amira* when pirates attacked her, 75 nautical miles south of Al Mukalla, Yemen. An SH-60B from HSL-46 Detachment 9, embarked on board *Gettysburg*, located a dhow suspected of serving as a mother ship for pirates. A visit, board, search, and seizure team and Coast Guard Law Enforcement Detachment 409 from the cruiser discovered a variety of weapons on board and detained her 17 crewmembers.

15 MAY • The under secretary of defense for acquisition, technology and logistics issued a stop work order for Increments I and IV of the VH-71A Presidential Helicopter contract to Lockheed Martin Systems Integration, Owego,

N.Y. On 1 June, the Navy issued a letter of termination to the company for Increments I and II, affecting all activities associated with the helicopter's systems design and demonstration requirements, excepting those technologies undergoing development and evaluation that presented potential benefit to other programs.

23 MAY • An SH-60B of HSL-45 Detachment 4, embarked on board cruiser *Lake Champlain* (CG 57), spotted a skiff in distress in the Gulf of Aden. The Seahawk directed the ship to the area, which rescued 52 people who had been adrift in the vessel for nearly a week.

26 MAY • An SH-60B of HSL-46 Detachment 9, embarked on board cruiser *Gettysburg* (CG 64), responded to Yemeni motor vessel *Alaseb* adrift in the Gulf of Aden. The Seahawk guided the cruiser to the area, which towed the boat and her 11 passengers to a rendezvous with the Yemeni Coast Guard for repairs.

JUNE • CWO2 Michael S. Adams Jr. reported to HSC-22 on board amphibious assault ship *Bataan* (LHD 5) as the first helicopter pilot to complete his training in the Flying Chief Warrant Officer program and the first to deploy.

1 JUNE • Air France Flight 447 crashed into the Atlantic Ocean during a flight from Rio de Janeiro, Brazil, to Paris, France, killing all 228 people on board—12 crewmembers and 216 passengers. A P-3C Orion of VP-5 subsequently assisted in the search for survivors from Augusto Severo Airfield at Natal, Brazil. The Navy concluded its support of rescue operations on 13 July.

2 JUNE • The U.S. Circuit Court of Appeals for the Federal Circuit affirmed the 5 May 2007 decision by U.S. Court of Federal Claims Judge Robert B. Hodges Jr. sustaining the government's default termination of the A-12A Avenger contract.

11 JUNE • The E-2D Advanced Hawkeye program reached Milestone C and received approval to begin low-rate initial production.

19 JUNE • 1st Lt. Michael Brown, USMC, at NAS Whiting Field, Fla., became the 30,000th naval helicopter pilot.

25 JUNE • An MV-22B from VMM-263 of the 22d Marine Expeditionary Unit, embarked on board amphibious assault ship *Bataan* (LHD 5) in the Red Sea, conducted the first ship-to-shore emergency medical evacuation by an Osprey.

2 JULY • The Navy declared the AGM-84K Standoff Land Attack Missile–Expanded Response operationally effective against land-based moving targets after an operational evaluation.

7 JULY • A P-3C Orion and a British warship from Combined Task Force 150 coordinated the seizure of 10 tons of narcotics with an estimated value of $70 million from a dhow in the Gulf of Aden, about 150 miles southeast of Salalah, Oman.

10 JULY • Amphibious assault ship *Makin Island* (LHD 8) sailed from Pascagoula, Miss., around South America to her commissioning. During the voyage, she inaugurated flight operations with Army CH-47 Chinooks attached to Joint Task Force Bravo, CH-46E Sea Knights, and CH-53E Super Stallions, and Coast Guard HH-60J Jayhawks and HH-65A Dolphins. She arrived at NS San Diego, Calif., on 14 September.

15 JULY • Space shuttle *Endeavour* launched from John F. Kennedy Space Center, Fla., on mission STS-127. During this 29th mission to the International Space Station, the crewmembers included naval aviator Col. Douglas G. Hurley, USMC. The shuttle returned to the center on 31 July.

28 JULY • Chief of Naval Operations Adm. Gary Roughead participated in the introduction of the F-35C Lightning II at Lockheed Martin, Fort Worth, Texas.

29 JULY • The Department of Defense announced that the initial operational test and evaluation of EA-18Gs found them operationally effective, operationally suitable, and recommended them for introduction to the fleet.

30 JULY • Chief of Naval Operations Adm. Gary Roughead delivered remarks during the roll-out of the P-8A Poseidon at Boeing Co., Renton, Wash.

AUGUST • The AGM-84K Standoff Land Attack Missile–Expanded Response achieved two milestones: its 100th launch (from an F/A-18C Hornet) and the first launch from an F-16 Fighting Falcon. Both events occurred at NAWS China Lake, Calif.

1 AUGUST • Consolidated Maintenance Organization 10 was disestablished at NAS Whidbey Island, Wash. This final such command in service had maintained P-3C Orions for four patrol squadrons and EP-3E Aries IIs for two fleet air reconnaissance squadrons, but the projection of a virtually all-sailor maintenance force for P-8A Poseidons drove the decision to revert to organic patrol community maintainers.

2 AUGUST • The Armed Forces Institute of Pathology positively identified the remains of Capt. Michael S. Speicher. Bedouins had directed a recovery team from Multi-National Force–West to two sites in the Iraqi desert about 62 miles west of Ramadi. On 17 January 1991, an (apparent) Iraqi surface-to-air missile shot down Speicher's Hornet and he became the first American casualty of the Persian Gulf War.

5 AUGUST • EA-18Gs from VAQ-129 and -132 completed the first Growler at-sea landings on board *Harry S. Truman* (CVN 75).

7 AUGUST • Typhoon Morakot struck central and southern Taiwan, triggering severe flooding and mudslides that claimed hundreds of lives. HSC-25 Detachment 6 helped move food, water, and medical supplies from sea to shore to assist Taiwanese relief efforts.

18 AUGUST • Frigate *Carr* (FFG 52), with an SH-60B Seahawk from HSL-42 Detachment 8 and Coast Guard Law Enforcement Detachment 409 embarked, intercepted a go-fast vessel and her three smugglers in the Caribbean, seizing 46 bales—more than one ton—of cocaine with an estimated value of $22 million.

21 AUGUST • The Navy accepted the delivery of amphibious transport dock *New York* (LPD 21) at Northrop Grumman Shipbuilding, Avondale, La.

27 AUGUST • The arrival of the first two T-6B Texan IIs began the turnover from T-34C Turbomentors for primary flight training at NAS Whiting Field, Fla.

28 AUGUST • Space shuttle *Discovery* launched from John F. Kennedy Space Center, Fla., on mission STS-128. During this 30th mission to the International Space Station, the crew included Col. Patrick G. Forrester, USA (Ret.), who had graduated from the Naval Test Pilot School, and naval aviator Col. Frederick W. Sturckow, USMC. On 11 September, *Discovery* landed at Edwards AFB, Calif.

1 SEPTEMBER • The Navy accepted the delivery of auxiliary dry cargo ship *Wally Schirra* (T-AKE 8) at General Dynamics–National Steel and Shipbuilding Company, San Diego, Calif.

17 SEPTEMBER • Super Typhoon Choi-Wan struck Alamagan and Agrihan, about 146 nautical miles north of Saipan, Marianas Islands. Two MH-60S Seahawks from HSC-25 Detachment 1, embarked on board auxiliary dry cargo ship *Alan B. Shepard* (T-AKE 3), delivered relief supplies.

21 SEPTEMBER • The Navy accepted the final production E-2C Hawkeye 2000—A-205—at Northrop Grumman, St. Augustine, Fla.

22 SEPTEMBER • EA-18G Growlers attained their initial operational capability.

25 SEPTEMBER • Tropical Storm Ketsana (known as Ondoy in the Philippines) struck central Luzon, Philippines, killing more than 250 people and rendering tens of thousands homeless. On 27 and 28 September, U.S. and Filipino servicemembers rescued 52 people from rising floodwaters in the capital. On 4 October, dock landing ships *Tortuga* (LSD 46) and *Harpers Ferry* (LSD 49), with elements of the 31st Marine Expeditionary Unit embarked, arrived to assist Joint Special Operations Task Force–Philippines in providing humanitarian relief.

28 SEPTEMBER • The Navy announced the completion of two steps in the introduction of the Electromagnetic Aircraft Launch System. The first phase of Highly Accelerated Life Testing gauged the launch motor's ability to operate in simulated at-sea conditions. The second phase System Functional Demonstration replicated full-scale launching capabilities.

29 SEPTEMBER • The Boeing Company concluded a 42-month risk reduction program for GBU-40 Small Diameter Bombs when an F-15E Strike Eagle dropped one of the weapons at Eglin AFB, Fla. Previous test flights had occurred in May and August 2007.

29 SEPTEMBER • An 8.3 magnitude earthquake struck 125 miles south of Apia on American Samoa, generating a tsunami that inundated the eastern coast of Samoa and parts of Tonga killing more than 160 people. The next day, frigate *Ingraham* (FFG 61), with an embarked SH-60B Seahawk, arrived and helped members of the Federal Emergency Management Agency and Army National Guardsmen, who had been flown to the area by Air Force C-17A Globemaster IIIs. A Coast Guard HC-130H flew aerial surveillance missions.

30 SEPTEMBER • An earthquake measuring 7.6 on the Richter scale rocked western Sumatra, Indonesia, killing more than 750 people and triggering landslides that wiped-out villages and blocked roads. On 9 October, amphibious transport dock *Denver* (LPD 9), with Marines of the 31st Marine Expeditionary Unit embarked, and destroyer *McCampbell* (DDG 85), arrived to support international relief efforts. Three HMM-265 CH-53E Super Stallions from *Denver*, and two HSL-51 Detachment 5 SH-60B Seahawks from *McCampbell*, delivered essential relief supplies and teams to people in remote areas isolated by the landslides. Additional aircraft, including two SA-330J Pumas from auxiliary dry cargo ship *Richard E. Byrd* (T-AKE 4), reinforced these operations. The Navy concluded its humanitarian assistance on 16 October.

1 OCTOBER • A Broad Area Maritime Surveillance Demonstrator (BAMS-D) returned from the first eight-month deployment to Central Command of the RQ-4B–based system. The Global Hawk flew more than 60 sorties that supplied Commander Task Force 57 with maritime intelligence and surveillance. A second BAMS-D deployed prior to the return of the first.

1 OCTOBER • Carrier Strike Group 1 was established at San Diego, Calif.

2 OCTOBER • Electronic Attack Wing Pacific Fleet declared the first operational EA-18G Growler-equipped squadron, VAQ-132 at NAS Whidbey Island, Wash., "safe for flight operations."

2 OCTOBER • Typhoon Parma (known as Pepeng in the Philippines) struck Luzon. Dock landing ships *Tortuga* (LSD 46) and *Harpers Ferry* (LSD 49), with elements of the 31st Marine Expeditionary Unit embarked, responded. Aircraft that provided airlift support to more than 1,400 people included ten CH-46E Sea Knights operating from the two ships with U.S. and Filipino servicemembers.

4 OCTOBER • Amphibious assault ship *Wasp* (LHD 1) deployed to the Fourth Fleet from NS Norfolk, Va. The ship served as a forward operating base with the Security Cooperation Marine Air-Ground Task Force, Joint Interagency Task Force–South, Drug Enforcement Administration, and Coast Guard Law Enforcement Detachment 405 during counternarcotics operations. *Wasp* returned from this first deployment of its kind to that fleet on 22 December.

5 OCTOBER • Two MQ-8B Fire Scouts, BuNos 167791 and 167792, made the first deployment of the unmanned aerial vehicles (UAV) during a counternarcotics cruise to the Caribbean with HSL-42 Detachment 7 on board frigate *McInerney* (FFG 8) from NS Mayport, Fla. *McInerney* made the first interception of drug smugglers using Fire Scouts on 3 April 2010. The UAVs flew 24 counternarcotics and systems evaluation flights. The ship returned on 15 April.

7 OCTOBER • Frigate *Hawes* (FFG 53), with HSL-48 Detachment 10 embarked, returned to NS Norfolk, Va., from a counternarcotics deployment to the Caribbean and western Atlantic. The ship's operations resulted in the seizure of 200 barrels of cocaine.

15 OCTOBER • Lt. Roger Stanton, accompanied by Boeing pilot Doug Benjamin, completed the first flight by a Navy pilot of a P-8A Poseidon in test aircraft T1 over Puget Sound, Wash. The mission initiated a 36-month formal naval flight test program by VX-1 and -20 and the Boeing Company to evaluate Poseidons T1, T2, and T3.

15 OCTOBER • Cruiser *Anzio* (CG 68), with an SH-60B from HSL-48 Detachment 7 embarked, seized approximately four tons of hashish with an estimated street

USN 090508-N-2821G-146

An MQ-8B Fire Scout hovers over the flight deck of frigate *McInerney* (FFG 8) while the ship sails in the Atlantic, 8 May 2009.

value of $28 million from a skiff in the Gulf of Aden, about 170 miles southwest of Salalah, Oman.

19 OCTOBER • Frigate *Jarrett* (FFG 33) returned to NS San Diego, Calif., from a counternarcotics deployment to the eastern Pacific. The ship's operations resulted in the seizure or disruption of the smuggling of more than nine tons of narcotics with an estimated value of $266 million.

20 OCTOBER • The Navy accepted the delivery of its final T-45C, the 221st Goshawk delivered, at Boeing Company, St. Louis, Mo.

NOVEMBER • The first of five UH-72A Lakotas, BuNo 168245, arrived for use in helicopter pilot training at the Naval Test Pilot School, NAS Patuxent River, Md. The fifth Lakota arrived in January 2010.

6 NOVEMBER • Ten MV-22Bs from VMM-263 of the 22d Marine Expeditionary Unit launched from amphibious assault ship *Bataan* (LHD 5) to Camp Bastion, Afghanistan. The aircraft made the first deployment of Ospreys into that country in three waves, making the 510 nautical-mile flight in just over two hours to VMM-261 of the 2d Marine Expeditionary Brigade.

7 NOVEMBER • Amphibious transport dock *New York* (LPD 21) was commissioned at New York City, N.Y.

12 NOVEMBER • The Navy opened the Electromagnetic Aircraft Launch System armature at the system functional demonstration site, Joint Base McGuire–Fort Dix–Lakehurst, N.J.

14 NOVEMBER • Lockheed Martin test pilot David Nelson made the inaugural flight of the first optimized F-35A Lightning II, aircraft AF-1, at Fort Worth, Texas.

15 NOVEMBER • Lockheed Martin test pilot Jon Beesley flew the first F-35B, BF-1, from Fort Worth, Texas, via Dobbins AFB, Ga., to NAS Patuxent River, Md. The ferry flight initiated a series of Lightning II arrivals for testing at Patuxent River.

16 NOVEMBER • Space shuttle *Atlantis* launched from John F. Kennedy Space Center, Fla., on mission STS-129. This 31st flight to the International Space Station marked the final crew rotation mission to the facility, and the crew included naval aviators Col. Charles O. Hobaugh, USMC; Lt. Col. Randolph J. Bresnik, USMC; and Navy Capts. Michael J. Foreman (Ret.) and Barry E. Wilmore. *Atlantis* returned to the center on 27 November.

20 NOVEMBER • The Navy released a draft environmental impact statement concerning the military build-up on Guam and the Northern Marianas Islands. The proposed actions included the construction of a deep-draft wharf and shoreside infrastructure improvements to support a transient nuclear-powered carrier at Apra, Guam, and the expansion of aviation facilities ashore for Marines transferred from Okinawa. The service released the final statement on 29 July 2010.

23 NOVEMBER • The Department of Defense approved EA-18Gs for full-rate production, and authorized the procurement and construction of 54 Growlers remaining in the program of record.

24 NOVEMBER • Amphibious assault ship *Makin Island* (LHD 8) was commissioned as the eighth and final vessel of the *Wasp* (LHD 1) class at NAS North Island, Calif.

11 DECEMBER • The retirement of the last operational Navy UH-3H, BuNo 154121, took place at NAS Patuxent River, Md. HMX-1 then used the Sea King as a trainer.

2010

7 JANUARY • BAE Systems, Inc. test pilot Graham Tomlinson engaged the short takeoff/vertical landing propulsion system of an F-35B Lightning II for the first time during a flight at NAS Patuxent River, Md.

12 JANUARY • A magnitude 7.3 earthquake devastated Port-au-Prince, Haiti, killing an estimated 230,000 people. The United States initiated Operation Unified Response—humanitarian aid to victims. At the operation's peak, 23 Navy ships participated including *Carl Vinson* (CVN 70) with Carrier Air Wing 17 embarked; amphibious assault ships *Bataan* (LHD 5) and *Nassau* (LHA 4); dock landing ships *Ashland* (LSD 48), *Carter Hall* (LSD 50), *Fort McHenry* (LSD 43), and *Gunston Hall* (LSD 44); amphibious transport dock *Mesa Verde* (LPD 19), with the 22d and 24th Marine Expeditionary Units embarked; and 10 Coast Guard ships.

A total of 264 U.S. fixed-wing aircraft took part including C-2A Greyhounds of VRC-40; C-40A Clippers; C-130 Hercules; E-2C Hawkeyes of VAW-125; and P-3C Orions of VP-26 and -62; along with 57 helicopters and tiltrotor aircraft including USCG HH-60J Jayhawks; MH-53E Sea Dragons of HM-14 and -15; SH-60B Seahawks of HSL-46 and -60; MH-60Ss of HSC-9, -22, -26, and -28; MV-22B Ospreys of VMM-162; and Marine CH-46E Sea Knights and UH-1N Iroquois. The Air Force diverted an RQ-4A en route to Afghanistan and operated the Global Hawk on several reconnaissance missions over Haiti from NAS Patuxent River, Md. Airlifters of all the services and international aid agencies staged through NAS Jacksonville, Fla. *Carl Vinson* departed on 1 February, and by 24 March these vessels largely sailed from Haitian waters, although relief efforts continued into the summer.

18 JANUARY • Amphibious transport dock *Mesa Verde* (LPD 19) sailed on her maiden deployment to the Caribbean, Mediterranean, Indian Ocean, and Persian Gulf from NS Norfolk, Va.

20 JANUARY • A P-3C Orion and a Coast Guard HC-130H Hercules located a Chinese fishing vessel in distress about 575 miles from Guam, and directed a merchantman to aid the mariners.

USN 130514-N-UZ648-298

Assigned to VX-23, the second of two X-47B Unmanned Combat Air System demonstrators, BuNo 168064, flies by *George H. W. Bush* (CVN 77), 14 May 2013. Two months later, this test vehicle made the first arrested carrier landing at sea by an unmanned aircraft.

25 JANUARY • Ethiopian Airlines Flight 409 crashed in the Mediterranean Sea while en route from Beirut, Lebanon, to Addis Ababa, Ethiopia, killing all 90 people on board. Aircraft and vessels of the Sixth Fleet that assisted in the search and rescue included a P-3C Orion, destroyer *Ramage* (DDG 61), and salvage ship *Grapple* (T-ARS 53).

26 JANUARY • The Navy announced adjustments to the Aviation Career Continuation Pay program to provide selected bonuses as an incentive to eligible pilots and naval flight officers through department head, sea duty, and command billets. The changes contained within NAVADMINs 031/10 and 032/10 included the reduction of long-term annual, at-sea, and command bonuses.

27 JANUARY • *George H. W. Bush* (CVN 77), through 29 January, completed sea trials off the Virginia Capes.

29 JANUARY • The Tenth Fleet, Vice Adm. Bernard J. McCullough III commanding, and the Fleet Cyber Command were reestablished and established, respectively, at Ft. George G. Meade, Md.

1 FEBRUARY • Secretary of Defense Robert M. Gates delivered the 2010 Ballistic Missile Defense Review to Congress. From March 2009 through January 2010, the department conducted this first such review, and its recommendations included the further development of ship-based RIM-161B Standard SM-3 Block 1A Interceptor Missiles.

1 FEBRUARY • The Direct Attack Moving Target Capability program achieved Milestone C. The system facilitated strikes by F/A-18 Hornets, F/A-18E/F Super Hornets, and AV-8B Harrier IIs with Joint Direct Attack Munitions against maneuvering targets.

7 FEBRUARY • The Navy, through 10 February, evaluated the integration of shipboard systems with X-47B Unmanned Combat Air Systems during flight deck certifications with *Abraham Lincoln* (CVN 72) and Carrier Air Wing 2 off southern California.

8 FEBRUARY • Space shuttle *Endeavour* launched from John F. Kennedy Space Center, Fla., on mission STS-130. During this 32d mission to the International Space Station, naval aviation crewmembers comprised Col. George D. Zamka, USMC, and Capt. Kathryn P. Hire. *Endeavour* returned to the center on 21 February.

16 FEBRUARY • Littoral combat ship *Freedom* (LCS 1) began the vessel's maiden deployment to the Caribbean and eastern Pacific via the Panama Canal from NS Mayport, Fla. An MH-60S Seahawk of HSC-22 Detachment 2 and a Coast Guard Law Enforcement detachment embarked. On 22 February, *Freedom* made the ship's first drug seizure when she disrupted a go-fast vessel and recovered more than a quarter ton of cocaine. During the voyage, the ship made four drug interceptions seizing more than 5¼ tons of cocaine and 13 smugglers. On 23 April, she reached her new homeport of NS San Diego, Calif.

24 FEBRUARY • Chief of Naval Operations Adm. Gary Roughead presented his Fiscal Year 2011 Posture Statement to Congress, which included the intention to reduce Navy unit deployed squadrons from 12 to 10 aircraft each to match a corresponding decrease in Marine expeditionary squadrons.

25 FEBRUARY • NAVAIR celebrated the completion of one million operational flight hours by Block I AIM-9X Sidewinder air-to-air missiles at Raytheon Missile Systems, Tucson, Ariz.

2 MARCH • Boeing Company, St. Louis, Mo., was awarded an $11.4 million Navy contract to supply Laser Joint Direct Attack Munitions for the fleet's Direct Attack Moving Target Capability program. The initial contract called for the delivery of 23 munition kits for testing and evaluation, and expected follow-on options totaling 11,000 more.

4 MARCH • An F/A-18F Super Hornet performed the first captive carriage test of an AGM-154C-1 Joint Standoff Weapon at NAWCWD China Lake, Calif.

10 MARCH • Neil A. Armstrong received honorary naval astronaut wings during a ceremony on board *Dwight D. Eisenhower* (CVN 69).

18 MARCH • BAE Systems, Inc. test pilot Graham Tomlinson completed the first vertical landing of an F-35B Lightning II at NAS Patuxent River, Md.

18 MARCH • NAVAIR's Common Aviation Support Equipment program office awarded Lockheed Martin, Orlando, Fla., an $83.3 million five-year development contract to design, fabricate, and test the Electronic Consolidated Automated Support System.

26 MARCH • The North Koreans torpedoed and sank South Korean corvette *Cheonan* (PCC 772) in the Yellow Sea. Allied ships that responded to the crisis included dock landing ship *Harpers Ferry* (LSD 49), and MH-60S Seahawks of HSC-25 Detachment 6 operating from the LSD assisted South Korean salvage efforts. The detachment returned to Guam on 3 June.

31 MARCH • Lockheed Martin, Orlando, Fla., announced the successful completion of a wide range of tests on the multi-mode seeker for Joint Air-to-Ground Missiles.

31 MARCH • President Barack Obama, at Joint Base Andrews, Md., announced his administration's plans on energy security including the Navy's biofuel program. The service's critical protocols to certify alternative fuels included an experimental 50/50 biofuel blend for F/A-18E/F Super Hornets, the intended use of biofuels in all aircraft by 2016, and alternative energy sources to power half of all shore aviation establishments by 2020.

1 APRIL • Eleven pirates in three skiffs attacked Sierra Leone–flagged tanker *Evita*, 310 miles northwest of the Seychelles. A Swedish maritime patrol aircraft responded to the tanker's distress call and located the boats, after which an SH-60B Seahawk from *Farragut* (DDG 99) directed the destroyer to intercept the pirates.

1 APRIL • Pirates fired on *Nicholas* (FFG 47) west of the Seychelles. The frigate and her embarked SH-60B Seahawk sank their skiff, captured the mother ship, and five pirates from the two vessels.

3 APRIL • An MQ-8B of HSL-42 Detachment 7, embarked on board frigate *McInerney* (FFG 8), proved crucial in the interception of a go-fast vessel smuggling drugs in the eastern Pacific. The Fire Scout filmed the smugglers' activities after which the frigate seized the boat and 132 pounds of cocaine, and compelled the traffickers to jettison an estimated 440 pounds of the illicit cargo. This was the first Fire Scout operation to combat drug smugglers.

5 APRIL • Space shuttle *Discovery* launched from John F. Kennedy Space Center, Fla., on mission STS-131. During this 33rd mission to the International Space Station, naval aviator Capt. Alan G. Poindexter was the spacecraft's commander. It returned to the center on 20 April.

7 APRIL • Test pilot David Nelson flew F-35B BF-4 at Fort Worth, Texas, during the first flight of a mission systems–equipped Lightning II.

7 APRIL • Littoral combat ship *Freedom* (LCS 1) completed her first integrated at-sea operations with *Carl Vinson* (CVN 70) off southern California.

8 APRIL • The initial proof-of-principle flight test of an AGM-114R Hellfire II air-to-ground missile with a live warhead occurred at Eglin AFB, Fla.

9 APRIL • A groundbreaking ceremony heralded the opening of the P-8A Poseidon Multi-Mission Maritime Aircraft Integrated Training Center at NAS Jacksonville, Fla.

10 APRIL • T1, the first P-8A Poseidon test aircraft, BuNo 167951, arrived for evaluations at NAS Patuxent River, Md.

10 APRIL • Six pirates on board a skiff attacked dock landing ship *Ashland* (LSD 48) in the Gulf of Aden. *Ashland* sank the boat and captured the pirates.

12 APRIL • Lockheed Martin delivered the 1,000th production AGM-158 Joint Air-to-Surface Standoff Missile (JASSM) to the USAF. The Navy intended JASSMs to be compatible with F/A-18E/F Super Hornets, F-35B/C Lightning IIs, and P-3C Orions.

17 APRIL • Destroyer *William P. Lawrence* (DDG 110) was commissioned in honor of Vice Adm. William P. Lawrence at Northrop Grumman Shipbuilding, Pascagoula, Miss. On 28 June 1967, pilot and squadron commanding officer Cmdr. Lawrence and radar intercept officer Lt. j.g. James W. Bailey of VF-143 launched in an F-4B, BuNo 152242, from *Constellation* (CVA 64) to bomb North Vietnamese petroleum and transshipment facilities at Nam Dinh. Antiaircraft fire shot down the Phantom II and both men endured captivity until 1973. Lawrence's decorations include the Silver Star, Distinguished Flying Cross, and Purple Heart.

19 APRIL • Fleet Readiness Center East at MCAS Cherry Point, N.C., accepted the first two MQ-8B Fire Scouts to perform maintenance on them in conjunction with a corrosion assessment.

19 APRIL • Training Wing 5 initiated ground school training for the T-6B Texan II flight training syllabus at NAS Whiting Field, Fla., with 14 students.

20 APRIL • An accident on board British Petroleum/Transocean drilling rig *Deepwater Horizon* led to a catastrophic oil spill in the Gulf of Mexico. Emergency responders subsequently established five staging areas along the Gulf coast including NAS Pensacola, Fla. Sailors, Marines, Coast Guardsmen, and civilian aid workers set out oil containment booms at the naval air station and along areas of the Alabama and Florida coastlines, and NAS Pensacola trained two-week classes of 50 students each to clean beaches.

23 APRIL • Ground was broken for the construction of the Weapons Dynamic Research, Development, Test, and Evaluation Center at NAWCWD China Lake, Calif., to test weapon systems. This marked the center's tenth and final Defense Base Closure and Realignment Commission 2005 construction project.

5 MAY • Joint Air-to-Ground Missiles successfully completed 200 hours of F/A-18E/F Super Hornet wind tunnel testing at NASA's Ames Research Center, Moffett Field, Calif.

5 MAY • Submarine *Cheyenne* (SSN 773) successfully fired a BGM-109 Block IV-E Tomahawk Land Attack Missile from off the southern California coast into China Lake Test Range, Calif.

7 MAY • Fleet Readiness Center East at MCAS Cherry Point, N.C., completed rework on the last retired CH-53E, BuNo 161181, and delivered the Super Stallion to HMT-302. From August 2005, the center reworked two CH-53Ds and eight CH-53Es from the Aerospace Maintenance and Regeneration Group at Davis-Monthan AFB, Ariz.

7 MAY • Amphibious transport dock *San Diego* (LPD 22) was launched at Northrop Grumman Shipbuilding, Pascagoula, Miss.

14 MAY • Space shuttle *Atlantis* launched from John F. Kennedy Space Center, Fla., on mission STS-132. During this 34th mission to the International Space Station, naval aviators Capt. Kenneth Ham and Cmdr. Dominic A. Antonelli served respectively as spacecraft commander and pilot. *Atlantis* returned to the space center on 26 May.

14 MAY • The Undersecretary of Defense for Acquisition, Technology, and Logistics certified to Congress that the proposed F/A-18 multi-year procurement met statutory requirements for 124 F/A-18E/F Super Hornets and EA-18G Growlers into Fiscal Year 2013. The action supported the Navy's intention to acquire the remaining program of record of 515 Super Hornets and 114 Growlers.

18 MAY • Instructor Capt. Michael Perkins, USMC, and student Ens. Christopher D. Farkas of VT-3 at NAS Whiting Field, Fla., completed the first naval student flight in a T-6B Texan II.

26 MAY • Cruiser *San Jacinto* (CG 56), with her embarked SH-60B Seahawk of HSL-42, designated Proud Warrior 433, and a Coast Guard law enforcement detachment, rescued five Yemeni mariners and their dhow *Al Jawat* from 13 pirates, 68 miles southeast of Ras Fartak, Yemen. *San Jacinto* apprehended the suspects and transferred them to the Yemeni Navy. On 31 May and 1 June, the cruiser disrupted nine more pirates in a skiff from attacking merchant vessel *Avenue Beauty*, about 90 miles north of Somalia. Proud Warrior 433 aircrewmen AW2 Casey Halliwell tracked the pirates with radar, and AW2 Corey Whittle fired warning shots across the skiff's bow and compelled the pirates to surrender.

27 MAY • Two eruptions of Pacaya volcano followed by the impact of Tropical Storm Agatha caused widespread devastation in Guatemala. On 31 May, frigate *Underwood* (FFG 36) and her embarked SH-60B of HSL-60 arrived off the coast and began humanitarian assistance flights. Into early June, the Seahawk and four other U.S. helicopters flew more than 40 sorties to deliver supplies to victims. On 5 October, *Underwood* completed her counternarcotics deployment after four interceptions that resulted in the seizure of 4.3 metric tons of cocaine valued at $301.7 million.

28 MAY • NAVAIR announced the readiness of the first AH-1Z Viper full-motion cockpit simulator to train pilots at Camp Pendleton, Calif.

5 JUNE • Destroyer *Spruance* (DDG 111) was christened in honor of Adm. Raymond A. Spruance at Bath Iron Works, Bath, Maine.

6 JUNE • Test pilot Jeff Knowles completed the first flight of an F-35C Lightning II, CF-1, at NAS JRB Fort Worth, Texas.

8 JUNE • The transfer of the last P-3C Orion of VP-26 completed the transition of patrol squadrons from NAS Brunswick, Maine, to NAS Jacksonville, Fla.

8 JUNE • The E-6B Airborne Strategic Command, Control, and Communications program completed a Milestone C review that enabled Mercury Block I aircraft to enter the production and deployment phase.

12 JUNE • Amphibious transport dock *San Diego* (LPD 22) was christened at Northrop Grumman Shipbuilding, Pascagoula, Miss.

USMC 100821-M-3497D-378

An MH-53E Sea Dragon of HM-15 Detachment 2 evacuates flood victims from Khyber-Pakhtunkhwa Province, Pakistan, 21 August 2010.

18 JUNE • Commercial vessel *Sea Adventure II* ran aground near South Coronado Island, Mexico. A Coast Guard MH-60T Jayhawk and cutter *Edisto* (WPB 1313), harbor police, and civilian mariners rescued all 26 people on board. After temporary repairs, *Sea Adventure II* reached San Diego, Calif.

2 JULY • Pakistani fishing vessel *Al An Wari* sank in the Gulf of Aden. On 5 July, a P-3C Orion of VP-16 forward deployed to Djibouti spotted 16 survivors in a life raft about 144 miles west of Socotra Island, and directed an SH-60B from frigate *Elrod* (FFG 55) to the area. The Seahawk rescued 12 of the mariners and the frigate saved the remaining four men.

8 JULY • Navy-manned MZ-3A Advanced Airship Flying Laboratory arrived at Lake Front Airport, New Orleans, La. The Coast Guard requested the assistance of the airship, which was a modified American Blimp Corporation A-170 blimp, to detect spreading oil and wildlife threatened by the accident on board the British Petroleum/Transocean drilling rig *Deepwater Horizon* in the Gulf of Mexico on 20 April.

22 JULY • The Army and Navy authenticated the keel of joint high-speed vessel *Spearhead* (JHSV 1) at Austal USA Shipyard, Mobile, Ala. The vessel was intended for fast intra-theater transportation of troops and equipment, and was equipped with a small flight deck to support air vehicle launches and recoveries.

28 JULY • Heavy rains into the first week of August caused flooding in Pakistan that killed an estimated 1,600 people and rendered hundreds of thousands homeless. On 9 August, amphibious assault ship *Peleliu* (LHA 5), dock landing ship *Pearl Harbor* (LSD 52), and amphibious transport dock *Dubuque* (LPD 8) arrived off Karachi, Pakistan. At times, 15 CH-46E Sea Knights of HMM-165 and CH-53E Super Stallions of HMH-465 from the 15th Marine Expeditionary Unit (MEU), augmented by HSC-23

MH-60S Seahawks and three HM-15 Detachment 2 MH-53E Sea Dragons, contributed to the evacuation of more than 10,000 people and delivery of 1.9 million pounds of relief supplies. Some of these helicopters operated from Pakistani airfields at Chaklala, Ghazi, and Pano Aqil, and two SA-330J Pumas flew from auxiliary dry cargo ship *Lewis and Clark* (T-AKE 1). Meanwhile, VMA-311 AV-8B Harrier IIs carried out close air support missions from *Peleliu* for coalition troops fighting Islamic extremists in Afghanistan. On 16 September, amphibious assault ship *Kearsarge* (LHD 3), dock landing ship *Carter Hall* (LSD 50), and amphibious transport dock *Ponce* (LPD 15), with MV-22B Ospreys of VMM-266 and helicopters from the 26th MEU embarked, arrived to participate. Air Force cargo aircraft and ten Army CH-47 Chinooks and eight UH-60 Black Hawks also provided humanitarian assistance. *Peleliu* departed on 31 October. *Harry S. Truman* (CVN 75) subsequently arrived, and on 15 November, four Super Stallions of the 26th MEU refueled on board.

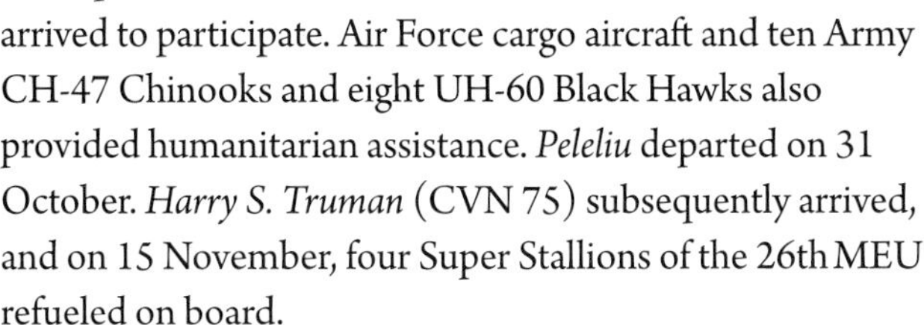

The devastation of heavy flooding in Pano Aquil, Pakistan, is apparent to crewmembers of an HMM-165 CH-46E Sea Knight.

USMC 100904-M-3497D-266

29 JULY • Chief of Naval Operations Adm. Gary Roughead accepted the E-2D to the fleet with the delivery of the first Advanced Hawkeye to VAW-120 at Norfolk, Va.

11 AUGUST • P-8A reached Milestone C and the Defense Acquisition Board approved the commencement of low-rate Poseidon production.

18 AUGUST • An F/A-18C Hornet of VFA-37, embarked on board *Harry S. Truman* (CVN 75) in the north Arabian Sea, spotted a vessel on fire about 50 miles from the carrier. Two SH-60F Seahawks of HS-7 rescued eight Iranian mariners from the boat.

26 AUGUST • The Naval Air Training Command celebrated one million T-45 Goshawk flight hours at NAS Cecil Field, Fla.

SEPTEMBER • GAU-21 .50-caliber weapon systems deployed for the first time with the UH-1Y Venoms of HMLA-169 from Camp Pendleton, Calif.

7 SEPTEMBER • NAVAIR redesignated the Broad Area Maritime Surveillance unmanned aircraft system, based on the RQ-4B Global Hawk, as MQ-4C.

8 SEPTEMBER • Pirates seized Antigua-Barbuda–flagged merchant vessel *Magellan Star* in the Gulf of Aden. The next day, Marines from the 15th Marine Expeditionary Unit, embarked on board amphibious transport dock *Dubuque* (LPD 8) and covered by helicopters and assisted by cruiser *Princeton* (CG 59) and Turkish frigate *Gökçeada* (F 494), boarded *Magellan Star*, rescuing all 11 crewmembers and capturing nine pirates.

11 SEPTEMBER • Auxiliary dry cargo ship *Washington Chambers* (T-AKE 11) was christened and launched at General Dynamics National Steel and Shipbuilding Company, San Diego, Calif. The ship was delivered to the fleet on 23 February 2011.

20 SEPTEMBER • The Department of Defense released the Record of Decision concerning the Guam and Commonwealth of Northern Mariana Islands Military Relocation Final Environmental Impact Statement. The

USN 100909-N-5133N-135

A UH-1N Iroquois covers Marines during the boarding and seizure of motor vessel *Magellan Star* in the Gulf of Aden, 9 September 2010.

Navy deferred for the near term the selection of a location for the construction of a transient carrier berth at Apra. The Marines determined the only reasonable site for their air operations was Andersen AFB, North Ramp.

24 SEPTEMBER • The In-Service Engineering Facility, designed for the inspection, maintenance, and packaging of bombs and missiles, opened at NAWCWD China Lake, Calif.

27 SEPTEMBER • The Defense POW/Missing Personnel Office announced the identification and return of the remains of Lt. Francis B. McIntyre and ARM2 William L. Russell of VC-24. On 10 November 1943, they launched in an SBD-5, BuNo 35931, on a bombing and strafing raid from Munda Airfield, New Georgia. Witnesses last saw the Dauntless flying through an explosion on Buka Island, Papua New Guinea.

28 SEPTEMBER • NAVAIR announced the purchase of 124 F/A-18E/F Super Hornets and EA-18G Growlers based on a multi-year procurement contract through 2014.

6 OCTOBER • The Naval Medical Research Unit Dayton was activated at Wright Patterson AFB, Ohio. The action completed the merger of the Naval Aerospace Medical Research and the Naval Medicine Environmental Health Effects Laboratories.

8 OCTOBER • The Dr. William B. McLean Laboratory, designed for engineering, logistics, modeling, and simulation, opened at NAWCWD China Lake, Calif. This

USN 101106-N-0000X-098 (courtesy of Lockheed Martin)

The first F-35C Lightning II carrier variant arrives at NAS Patuxent River, Md., 6 November 2010.

laboratory was the largest planned Defense Base Closure and Realignment Commission 2005 construction project at the center.

13 OCTOBER • NAVAIR announced the completion of the Barking Sands Underwater Range Expansion refurbishment off Kauai, Hawaii. The program enhanced antisubmarine warfare training through increased acoustics and frequency bandwidth.

13 OCTOBER • The Navy successfully tested the AN/DVS-1 Coastal Battlefield Reconnaissance Analysis Block I system with an MQ-8B Fire Scout at Yuma Proving Ground, Ariz. The system was designed to detect minefields and obstacles prior to amphibious assaults.

15 OCTOBER • The Navy accepted the first 11 production AGM-154C-1 Joint Standoff Weapons at McAlester Army Ammunition Plant, McAlester, Okla.

15 OCTOBER • One of three test P-8As completed several sonobuoy launches in the Atlantic Test Range. These were the first sonobuoy drops by Poseidons since they began testing at NAS Patuxent River, Md.

5 NOVEMBER • Hurricane Tomas struck western Haiti. On 6 November, helicopters operating from amphibious assault ship *Iwo Jima* (LHD 7) began damage assessment flights in support of international relief teams. *Iwo Jima* departed on 9 November.

5 NOVEMBER • Fleet Weather Center San Diego was established at NAS North Island, Calif. This completed the relocation of Naval Aviation Forecasting Detachment San Diego, Strike Group Oceanography Team San Diego, and Naval Maritime Forecast Center to the command.

6 NOVEMBER • Test pilot David Nelson flew CF-1, the first F-35C Lightning II, for testing to NAS Patuxent River, Md.

8 NOVEMBER • A fire erupted in the aft engine room of Carnival cruise ship *Carnival Splendor* and she lost power 150 nautical miles southwest of San Diego, Calif. The next day, C-2A Greyhounds of VRC-30 transported supplies from NAS North Island, Calif., to *Ronald Reagan* (CVN 76), and HH-60H and SH-60F Seahawks of HS-4 then delivered the provisions to the stricken ship. A Coast Guard HC-130H Hercules, an HH-65C Dolphin, MH-60T Jayhawks, and cutters *Aspen* (WLB 208), *Edisto* (WPB 1313), *Morgenthau* (WHEC 722), and *Petrel* (WPB 87350) also participated. Tugs towed the cruise ship to San Diego.

10 NOVEMBER • Two F-35Bs completed the first formation flight of Lightning IIs at NAS Patuxent River, Md.

12 NOVEMBER • Two EA-18G Growlers began validation training at NSAWC Fallon, Nev.

18 NOVEMBER • An F-35 completed the 500th test flight of a Lightning II.

18 NOVEMBER • An MH-60S Seahawk of HX-21 flew powered by an experimental 50/50 biofuel blend at NAS Patuxent River, Md.

28 NOVEMBER • NAVAIR approved AH-1Z Vipers for full-rate production.

2 DECEMBER • NAVAIR announced the award of two fixed-price contracts valued at $29.9 million and $45.8 million, respectively, for the Cargo Resupply Unmanned Aerial System to Boeing/Frontier Systems and Lockheed Martin. These originated from an urgent need to reduce the exposure of Marines to enemy improvised explosive devices in Afghanistan and Iraq.

6 DECEMBER • Frigate *Doyle* (FFG 39) and her embarked Coast Guard Law Enforcement detachment intercepted smuggling vessel *Rio Tuira* in the eastern Pacific about 180 miles from Panama and seized 22 bales of cocaine with an estimated street value of $15.4 million.

9 DECEMBER • The F-35 Lightning II program achieved its 2010 goal of 394 test flights.

10 DECEMBER • NAVSEA announced the successful completion of the first phase of shipboard mine countermeasure mission package testing for littoral combat ship *Independence* (LCS 2) with a reconfigured MH-60S Seahawk.

18 DECEMBER • Lt. Daniel Radocaj of VX-23 made the first launch of the Electromagnetic Aircraft Launch System in an F/A-18E Super Hornet at Joint Base McGuire–Fort Dix–Lakehurst, N.J.

Index

The nature of this volume as a chronology allows for the creation of an index, albeit unusual, that is more precise and quicker for the reader to use. Rather than indicating a page, this index directs the reader to a specific area on the page by citing a date.

The entries give the year, month, and date in this format: 1948Nov12.

The citation is found by first looking at the running heads at the top of each page, which indicate the year covered. The specific date is then found chronologically within the section. In some instances only a year and month are given. There are specific entries for such citations, which appear before the first day of the indicated month.

To further aid the researcher the index has been broken into six major subject groups: Aircraft by Designation, Aircraft by Name, Missiles and Rockets, Ships, U.S. Military Units, and Individuals. Topics that do not naturally fall under those headings are listed in the General index.

Contents

Aircraft by Designation

Aircraft by Name

Missiles and Rockets

Ships

Naval/Military Ships by Country

Australia
Canberra (RAN cruiser), 1942Aug09
Sydney (FFG 03), 2001Nov18

Canada
John A. Macdonald, 1969Aug24
Louis S. St-Laurent, 1969Aug24
Saguenay, 1939Oct16
Toronto (FFH 333), 2007Sep30

Costa Rica
Juan Rafael Mora, 2007Apr19

Cuba
GC-107 class, 1962Aug30
SC-13, 1943May15

Denmark
Olfert Fischer (F 355), 2007Sep30

France
Ardente, 1918Apr22
Charles de Gaulle (R 91), 2001Dec18
Jean Bart, 1942Nov08
Lamotte-Picquet, 1945Jan02
Le Conquerant, 1942Nov13
Leger, 1918Oct22
Octant, 1945Jan02
Primaguet, 1942Nov08

Germany
Admiral Graf Spee, 1939Oct16
Alsterufer (blockade runner), 1943Dec27
Bismarck, 1941May19
Burgenland (blockade runner), 1944Jan04
Emmy Friedrich (tanker), 1939Oct16
Frankfurt, 1921Jun21
G-102, 1921Jun21
Karlsruhe (F 212), 2005Apr29
Milchkühe, 1943Oct04
Odenwald (blockade runner), 1941Nov04
Ostfriesland, 1921Jun21
Prinz Eugen, 1941May19
Rheinland-Pfalz (F 209), 2009Mar29
Rio Grande (blockade runner), 1944Jan04
Scharnhorst, 1943Oct19
Spessart (A 1442), 2009Mar29
T22, 1943Dec27
T23, 1943Dec27
T24, 1943Dec27
T25, 1943Dec27
T26, 1943Dec27
T27, 1943Dec27
Tirpitz, 1943Oct04, Oct19
U-66, 1942Jan13
U-67, 1942Feb16; 1943Jul13
U-84, 1943Jul13
U-86, 1943Nov29
U-117, 1921Jun21
U-118, 1943Jun05
U-123, 1942Jan13
U-125, 1942Jan13
U-129, 1942Feb16
U-134, 1943Jul18
U-156 (WWI), 1918Jul19
U-156 (WWII), 1942Feb16
U-161, 1942Feb16
U-166, 1942Aug01
U-172, 1943Nov29
U-176, 1943May15
U-185, 1943Jul13
U-217, 1943Jun05
U-219, 1943Nov29
U-228, 1943Jun05
U-238, 1943Nov29
U-249, 1945May09
U-264, 1943Oct04
U-305, 1943May22
U-388, 1943Jun20
U-420, 1943Jun20
U-422, 1943Oct04

Civilian Ships/Vessels

U. S. Military Units

Individuals

General Index